BRITISH WRITERS

BRITISH WRITERS

GEORGE STADE

CAROL HOWARD

Editors

SUPPLEMENT IV

CHARLES SCRIBNER'S SONS

MACMILLAN LIBRARY REFERENCE
SIMON & SCHUSTER MACMILLAN
NEW YORK

SIMON & SCHUSTER AND PRENTICE HALL INTERNATIONAL
LONDON MEXICO CITY NEW DELHI SINGAPORE SYDNEY TORONTO

Charles Scribner's Sons
An imprint of Simon & Schuster Macmillan
1633 Broadway
New York, New York 10019

Library of Congress Cataloging-in-Publication Data

British writers: Supplement IV / George Stade and Carol Howard, editors.
        p.   cm.
Includes bibliographical references and cumulative index.
ISBN 0-684-19593-3 (alk. paper: full set).—ISBN 0-684-80496-4 (alk. paper)
1. English literature—History and criticism.   2. English literature—Bio-bibliography.
3. Authors, English—Biography.   I. Stade, George.   II. Howard, Carol, 1963–
PR85.B688 Suppl. 4
820.9—dc20
[B]   95-38155
                                                                                                  CIP

1 3 5 7 9 11 13 15 17 19   20 18 16 14 12 10 8 6 4 2

Printed in the United States of America

The paper used in this publication meets the requirements of ANSI/NISO Z39.48-1992
(Permanence of Paper).

Acknowledgments

Acknowledgment is gratefully made to those publishers and
individuals who permitted the use of the following materials in copyright:

MARTIN AMIS   Excerpt from *London Fields* by Martin Amis. Copyright © 1990 by Martin Amis. Reprinted by permission of Harmony Books, a division of Crown Publishing, Inc. Excerpt from *Money* by Martin Amis. Copyright © 1984 by Martin Amis. Used by permission of Viking Penguin, a division of Penguin Books USA Inc.

JOHN BERGER   Excerpt from *Ways of Seeing* by John Berger. Copyright © 1972 by Penguin Books Ltd. Used by permission of Viking Penguin, a division of Penguin Books USA Inc.

THOM GUNN   Excerpts from *Collected Poems* by Thom Gunn, Farrar, Straus & Giroux, 1994. Excerpts from *Positives* by Thom Gunn, Faber, 1966; University of Chicago Press, 1967.

IAN McEWAN   Excerpt from *Black Dogs* by Ian McEwan, Nan A. Talese/Doubleday, 1992.

PAUL MULDOON   Excerpts from *Mules* by Paul Muldoon, Wake Forest University Press, 1977. Excerpts from *Why Brownlee Left* by Paul Muldoon, Wake Forest University Press, 1981. Excerpts from *Meeting the British* by Paul Muldoon, Wake Forest University Press, 1987. Excerpts from *Quoof* by Paul Muldoon, University of North Carolina Press, 1983. Excerpts from *Selected Poems* by Paul Muldoon, Ecco Press, 1986. Excerpt from *Madoc* by Paul Muldoon, Farrar, Straus & Giroux, 1991. Excerpts from *Annals of Chile* and *New Weather* by Paul Muldoon, Faber & Faber, 1994.

CHRISTINA STEAD   Excerpt from *Cotters' England* by Christina Stead, Angus & Robertson, 1989. Excerpt from *For Love Alone* by Christiana Stead, Harvest/Harcourt Brace Jovanovich, 1979.

D. M. THOMAS   Excerpt from "Weddings" by D. M. Thomas, in *Selected Poems*, Viking Press, 1983. Excerpts from *The Puberty Tree* by D. M. Thomas, Bloodaxe Books, 1992. Translation by D. M. Thomas of Anna Akhmatova, "The Pillow" and "The Sentence," in *The Way of All the Earth*, Ohio State University Press, 1979. Translation by D. M. Thomas of Aleksandr Pushkin, "To Olga Masson," in *The Bronze Horseman: Selected Poems of Alexander Pushkin*. Viking Press, 1982.

Editorial and Production Staff

Contents

Introduction

The twenty-six articles in *British Writers, Supplement IV* survey writers who for one reason or another are not represented in either the initial seven volumes of *British Writers* (1979–1984) or in supplements I (1987), II (1992), or III (1996). In Supplement IV, as distinct from its predecessors, all but a couple of the writers came of age following World War II; they are not only moderns, but contemporaries, their careers still evolving.

From its inception, *British Writers* was designed as a companion to the ongoing *American Writers* (1974–). These two sets were followed by *Ancient Writers: Greece and Rome* (2 vols., 1982), by *European Writers* (14 vols., 1983–1991) and its three-volume redaction, *European Writers* (1992), by *Latin American Writers* (3 vols., 1989), and by *African Writers* (2 vols., 1996). These volumes constitute, so far, the Scribner World Literature series. And they are allied to works such as *Science Fiction Writers* (1982), *Supernatural Fiction Writers* (2 vols., 1985), *William Shakespeare: His World, His Work, His Influence* (3 vols., 1985), *Writers for Children* (1988), *The Books of the Bible* (1989), *Modern American Women Writers* (1991), *African-American Writers* (1991), and *American Nature Writers* (2 vols., 1996).

Each article in *British Writers Supplement IV* is devoted to a single writer; each is between twelve and fifteen thousand words long. Each article presents an account of the writer's works, life, and relations to his or her time, place, and literary context. But from article to article the emphasis varies, just as from writer to writer the relative interest of the life, the reading, the situation varies. Whatever the relative emphasis, the works come first; other matters are taken up to the extent that they form or inform the works.

In style and scope, the articles are expressly written for that mythical but inspiring figure, the general reader, rather than for the specialist. They are written, that is, for high school, college, and graduate students, as well as for their teachers; for librarians and editors; for reviewers, scholars, and critics; for literary browsers; for anyone who wants to repair an erosion or gap in his or her reservoir of knowledge. The article that can at once inform the general reader and stimulate the specialist will have achieved its goal.

Above all, and in consultation with librarians, the editors asked themselves whether a writer under consideration for inclusion was someone that English-speaking readers were likely to look up—upon publication of Supplement IV or twenty years later. The editors therefore took into account a shift in reader interest and critical activity and classroom attention that has not yet worked itself out. That shift, which is often thought of as a process of decanonization, includes a weakening of the distinction between popular literature and the other kind, whatever we call it. Thus in earlier supplements there were articles on such "popular" writers as Agatha Christie, John le Carré, Bram Stoker, H. Rider Haggard, Dorothy L. Sayers, and Daphne du Maurier; and thus, in Supplement IV, there are articles on Eric Ambler and P. D. James.

In accordance with a practice that evolved early in the series, not all the writers represented in Supplement IV are "British" in one or another restricted sense of the word. Salman Rushdie, for example, was born in Bombay; Christina Stead and Thomas Keneally are Australian-born; Paul Muldoon is very much an Irishman. But their relation to British literary culture was continuous and formative, if sometimes adversarial; their work shows up most vividly for what it is against the background of that British literary culture it enlarges or contests. In any case, the editors felt that readers would want to look up Keneally and Muldoon, for example, but could not do so elsewhere in articles like the ones that make up this volume. This last justification, however, could apply to all the articles in this volume: they are all about writers who are well worth looking up.

GEORGE STADE

Chronology

1901–1910   Reign of King Edward VII

1901   William McKinley assassinated; Theodore Roosevelt succeeds to the presidency

First transatlantic wireless telegraph signal transmitted

Chekhov's *Three Sisters*

Freud's *Psychopathology of Everyday Life*

Rudyard Kipling's *Kim*

Thomas Mann's *Buddenbrooks*

Potter's *The Tale of Peter Rabbit*

Shaw's *Captain Brassbound's Conversion*

August Strindberg's *The Dance of Death*

1902   Barrie's *The Admirable Crichton*

Arnold Bennett's *Anna of the Five Towns*

Cézanne's *Le Lac D'Annecy*

Conrad's *Heart of Darkness*

Henry James's *The Wings of the Dove*

William James's *The Varieties of Religious Experience*

Kipling's *Just So Stories*

Maugham's *Mrs. Cradock*

Christina Stead born

Stevie Smith born

Times Literary Supplement begins publishing

1903   At its London congress the Russian Social Democratic Party divides into Mensheviks, led by Plekhanov, and Bolsheviks, led by Lenin

The treaty of Panama places the Canal Zone in U.S. hands for a nominal rent

Motor cars regulated in Britain to a 20-mile-per-hour limit

The Wright brothers make a successful flight in the United States

Burlington magazine founded

Samuel Butler's *The Way of All Flesh* published posthumously

Cyril Connolly born

George Gissing's *The Private Papers of Henry Ryecroft*

Thomas Hardy's *The Dynasts*

Henry James's *The Ambassadors*

Alan Paton born

Shaw's *Man and Superman*

Synge's *Riders to the Sea* produced in Dublin

Yeats's *In the Seven Woods* and *On Baile's Strand*

1904   Roosevelt elected president of the United States

Russo-Japanese war (1904–1905)

Construction of the Panama Canal begins

The ultraviolet lamp invented

The engineering firm of Rolls Royce founded

Barrie's *Peter Pan* first performed

Cecil Day Lewis born

Chekhov's *The Cherry Orchard*

Conrad's *Nostromo*

Henry James's *The Golden Bowl*

Kipling's *Traffics and Discoveries*

Georges Rouault's *Head of a Tragic Clown*

G. M. Trevelyan's *England Under the Stuarts*

Puccini's *Madame Butterfly*

First Shaw-Granville Barker season at the Royal Court Theatre

The Abbey Theatre founded in Dublin

1905   Russian sailors on the battleship *Potemkin* mutiny

After riots and a general strike the czar concedes demands by the Duma for legislative powers, a wider franchise, and civil liberties

Albert Einstein publishes his first theory of relativity

The Austin Motor Company founded

Bennett's *Tales of the Five Towns*

Claude Debussy's *La Mer*

E. M. Forster's *Where Angels Fear to Tread*

Henry Green born

Richard Strauss's *Salome*

xiii

H. G. Wells's *Kipps*
Oscar Wilde's *De Profundis*

1906   Liberals win a landslide victory in the British general election
The Trades Disputes Act legitimizes peaceful picketing in Britain
Captain Dreyfus rehabilitated in France
J. J. Thomson begins research on gamma rays
The U.S. Pure Food and Drug Act passed
Churchill's *Lord Randolph Churchill*
William Empson born
Galsworthy's *The Man of Property*
Kipling's *Puck of Pook's Hill*
Shaw's *The Doctor's Dilemma*
Yeats's *Poems 1899-1905*

1907   Exhibition of cubist paintings in Paris
Henry Adams' *The Education of Henry Adams*
Henri Bergson's *Creative Evolution*
Conrad's *The Secret Agent*
Daphne du Maurier born
Forster's *The Longest Journey*
Christopher Fry born
André Gide's *La Porte étroite*
Shaw's *John Bull's Other Island* and *Major Barbara*
Synge's *The Playboy of the Western World*
Trevelyan's *Garibaldi's Defence of the Roman Republic*

1908   Herbert Asquith becomes prime minister
David Lloyd George becomes chancellor of the exchequer
William Howard Taft elected president of the United States
The Young Turks seize power in Istanbul
Henry Ford's Model T car produced
Bennett's *The Old Wives' Tale*
Pierre Bonnard's *Nude Against the Light*
Georges Braque's *House at L'Estaque*
Chesterton's *The Man Who Was Thursday*
Jacob Epstein's *Figures* erected in London
Forster's *A Room with a View*
Anatole France's *L'Ile des Pingouins*
Henri Matisse's *Bonheur de Vivre*
Elgar's First Symphony
Ford Madox Ford founds the *English Review*

1909   The Young Turks depose Sultan Abdul Hamid
The Anglo-Persian Oil Company formed
Louis Bleriot crosses the English Channel from France by monoplane
Admiral Robert Peary reaches the North Pole
Freud lectures at Clark University (Worcester, Mass.) on psychoanalysis
Serge Diaghilev's Ballets Russes opens in Paris
Galsworthy's *Strife*
Hardy's *Time's Laughingstocks*
Eric Ambler born
Malcolm Lowry born
Claude Monet's *Water Lilies*
Stephen Spender born
Trevelyan's *Garibaldi and the Thousand*
Wells's *Tono-Bungay* first published (book form, 1909)

1910–1936   **Reign of King George V**

1910   The Liberals win the British general election
Marie Curie's *Treatise on Radiography*
Arthur Evans excavates Knossos
Edouard Manet and the first post-impressionist exhibition in London
Filippo Marinetti publishes "Manifesto of the Futurist Painters"
Norman Angell's *The Great Illusion*
Bennett's *Clayhanger*
Forster's *Howards End*
Galsworthy's *Justice* and *The Silver Box*
Kipling's *Rewards and Fairies*
Rimsky-Korsakov's *Le Coq d'or*
Stravinsky's *The Firebird*
Vaughan Williams' *A Sea Symphony*
Wells's *The History of Mr. Polly*
Wells's *The New Machiavelli* first published (in book form, 1911)

1911   Lloyd George introduces National Health Insurance Bill
Suffragette riots in Whitehall
Roald Amundsen reaches the South Pole
Bennett's *The Card*
Chagall's *Self Portrait with Seven Fingers*
Conrad's *Under Western Eyes*
D. H. Lawrence's *The White Peacock*
Katherine Mansfield's *In a German Pension*
Edward Marsh edits *Georgian Poetry*
Moore's *Hail and Farewell* (1911–1914)
Flann O'Brien born
Strauss's *Der Rosenkavalier*
Stravinsky's *Petrouchka*

CHRONOLOGY

Trevelyan's *Garibaldi and the Making of Italy*

Wells's *The New Machiavelli*

Mahler's *Das Lied von der Erde*

1912 Woodrow Wilson elected president of the United States

SS *Titanic* sinks on its maiden voyage

Five million Americans go to the movies daily; London has four hundred movie theaters

Second post-impressionist exhibition in London

Bennett's and Edward Knoblock's *Milestones*

Constantin Brancusi's *Maiastra*

Wassily Kandinsky's *Black Lines*

D. H. Lawrence's *The Trespasser*

1913 Second Balkan War begins

Henry Ford pioneers factory assembly technique through conveyor belts

Epstein's *Tomb of Oscar Wilde*

New York Armory Show introduces modern art to the world

Alain Fournier's *Le Grand Meaulnes*

Freud's *Totem and Tabu*

D. H. Lawrence's *Sons and Lovers*

Mann's *Death in Venice*

Proust's *Du Côté de chez Swann* (first volume of *À la recherche du temps perdu*, 1913–1922)

Barbara Pym born

Ravel's *Daphnis and Chloé*

1914 The Panama Canal opens (formal dedication on 12 July 1920)

Irish Home Rule Bill passed in the House of Commons

Archduke Franz Ferdinand assassinated at Sarajevo

World War I begins

Battles of the Marne, Masurian Lakes, and Falkland Islands

Joyce's *Dubliners*

Shaw's *Pygmalion* and *Androcles and the Lion*

Yeats's *Responsibilities*

Wyndham Lewis publishes *Blast* magazine and *The Vorticist Manifesto*

1915 The Dardanelles campaign begins

Britain and Germany begin naval and submarine blockades

The *Lusitania* is sunk

Hugo Junkers manufactures the first fighter aircraft

Poison gas used for the first time

First Zeppelin raid in London

Brooke's *1914: Five Sonnets*

Norman Douglas' *Old Calabria*

D. W. Griffith's *The Birth of a Nation*

Gustav Holst's *The Planets*

D. H. Lawrence's *The Rainbow*

Wyndham Lewis's *The Crowd*

Maugham's *Of Human Bondage*

Pablo Picasso's *Harlequin*

Sibelius' Fifth Symphony

1916 Evacuation of Gallipoli and the Dardanelles

Battles of the Somme, Jutland, and Verdun

Britain introduces conscription

The Easter Rebellion in Dublin

Asquith resigns and David Lloyd George becomes prime minister

The Sykes-Picot agreement on the partition of Turkey

First military tanks used

Wilson reelected president of the United States

Henri Barbusse's *Le Feu*

Griffith's *Intolerance*

Roald Dahl born

Joyce's *Portrait of the Artist as a Young Man*

Jung's *Psychology of the Unconscious*

Moore's *The Brook Kerith*

Edith Sitwell edits *Wheels* (1916–1921)

Wells's *Mr. Britling Sees It Through*

1917 United States enters World War I

Czar Nicholas II abdicates

The Balfour Declaration on a Jewish national home in Palestine

The Bolshevik Revolution

Georges Clemenceau elected prime minister of France

Lenin appointed chief commissar; Trotsky appointed minister of foreign affairs

Conrad's *The Shadow-Line*

Douglas' *South Wind*

Eliot's *Prufrock and Other Observations*

Modigliani's *Nude with Necklace*

Sassoon's *The Old Huntsman*

Prokofiev's *Classical Symphony*

Yeats's *The Wild Swans at Coole*

1918 Wilson puts forward Fourteen Points for World Peace

Central Powers and Russia sign the Treaty of Brest-Litovsk

Execution of Czar Nicholas II and his family

Kaiser Wilhelm II abdicates

The Armistice signed

Women granted the vote at age thirty in Britain

Rupert Brooke's *Collected Poems*

Gerard Manley Hopkins' *Poems*

Joyce's *Exiles*

Lewis's *Tarr*

Sassoon's *Counter-Attack*

Oswald Spengler's *The Decline of the West*

Strachey's *Eminent Victorians*

Béla Bartók's *Bluebeard's Castle*

Charlie Chaplin's *Shoulder Arms*

1919 The Versailles Peace Treaty signed

J. W. Alcock and A. W. Brown make first transatlantic flight

Ross Smith flies from London to Australia

National Socialist party founded in Germany

Benito Mussolini founds the Fascist party in Italy

Sinn Fein Congress adopts declaration of independence in Dublin

Eamon De Valera elected president of Sinn Fein party

Communist Third International founded

Lady Astor elected first woman Member of Parliament

Prohibition in the United States

John Maynard Keynes's *The Economic Consequences of the Peace*

Eliot's *Poems*

Maugham's *The Moon and Sixpence*

Shaw's *Heartbreak House*

The Bauhaus school of design, building, and crafts founded by Walter Gropius

Amedeo Modigliani's *Self-Portrait*

1920 The League of Nations established

Warren G. Harding elected president of the United States

Senate votes against joining the League and rejects the Treaty of Versailles

The Nineteenth Amendment gives women the right to vote

White Russian forces of Denikin and Kolchak defeated by the Bolsheviks

P. D. James born

Karel Čapek's *R.U.R.*

Galsworthy's *In Chancery* and *The Skin Game*

Sinclair Lewis' *Main Street*

Katherine Mansfield's *Bliss*

Matisse's *Odalisques* (1920–1925)

Ezra Pound's *Hugh Selwyn Mauberly*

Paul Valéry's *Le Cimetière Marin*

Yeats's *Michael Robartes and the Dancer*

1921 Britain signs peace with Ireland

First medium-wave radio broadcast in the United States

The British Broadcasting Corporation founded

Braque's *Still Life with Guitar*

Chaplin's *The Kid*

Aldous Huxley's *Crome Yellow*

Paul Klee's *The Fish*

D. H. Lawrence's *Women in Love*

John McTaggart's *The Nature of Existence* (vol. 1)

Moore's *Héloïse and Abélard*

Eugene O'Neill's *The Emperor Jones*

Luigi Pirandello's *Six Characters in Search of an Author*

Shaw's *Back to Methuselah*

Strachey's *Queen Victoria*

1922 Lloyd George's Coalition government succeeded by Bonar Law's Conservative government

Benito Mussolini marches on Rome and forms a government

William Cosgrave elected president of the Irish Free State

The BBC begins broadcasting in London

Lord Carnarvon and Howard Carter discover Tutankhamen's tomb

The PEN club founded in London

The *Criterion* founded with T. S. Eliot as editor

Kingsley Amis born

Eliot's *The Waste Land*

A. E. Housman's *Last Poems*

Joyce's *Ulysses*

D. H. Lawrence's *Aaron's Rod* and *England, My England*

Sinclair Lewis's *Babbitt*

O'Neill's *Anna Christie*

Pirandello's *Henry IV*

Edith Sitwell's *Façade*

Virginia Woolf's *Jacob's Room*

Yeats's *The Trembling of the Veil*

1923 The Union of Soviet Socialist Republics established

French and Belgian troops occupy the Ruhr in consequence of Germany's failure to pay reparations

Mustafa Kemal (Ataturk) proclaims Turkey a republic and is elected president

Warren G. Harding dies; Calvin Coolidge becomes president

Stanley Baldwin succeeds Bonar Law as prime minister

Adolf Hitler's attempted coup in Munich fails

Time magazine begins publishing

E. N. da C. Andrade's *The Structure of the Atom*

Brendan Behan born

Christine Brooke-Rose born

Bennett's *Riceyman Steps*

Churchill's *The World Crisis* (1923–1927)

J. E. Flecker's *Hassan* produced

Nadine Gordimer born

Paul Klee's *Magic Theatre*

Lawrence's *Kangaroo*

Rainer Maria Rilke's *Duino Elegies* and *Sonnets to Orpheus*

Sibelius' *Sixth Symphony*

Picasso's *Seated Woman*

William Walton's *Façade*

1924 Ramsay MacDonald forms first Labour government, loses general election, and is succeeded by Stanley Baldwin

Calvin Coolidge elected president of the United States

Noël Coward's *The Vortex*

Forster's *A Passage to India*

Mann's *The Magic Mountain*

Shaw's *St. Joan*

1925 Reza Khan becomes shah of Iran

First surrealist exhibition held in Paris

Alban Berg's *Wozzeck*

Chaplin's *The Gold Rush*

John Dos Passos' *Manhattan Transfer*

Theodore Dreiser's *An American Tragedy*

Sergei Eisenstein's *Battleship Potemkin*

F. Scott Fitzgerald's *The Great Gatsby*

André Gide's *Les Faux Monnayeurs*

Hardy's *Human Shows and Far Phantasies*

Huxley's *Those Barren Leaves*

Kafka's *The Trial*

O'Casey's *Juno and the Paycock*

Virginia Woolf's *Mrs. Dalloway* and *The Common Reader*

Brancusi's *Bird in Space*

Shostakovich's *First Symphony*

Sibelius' *Tapiola*

1926 Ford's *A Man Could Stand Up*

Gide's *Si le grain ne meurt*

Hemingway's *The Sun also Rises*

Kafka's *The Castle*

D. H. Lawrence's *The Plumed Serpent*

T. E. Lawrence's *Seven Pillars of Wisdom* privately circulated

Maugham's *The Casuarina Tree*

O'Casey's *The Plough and the Stars*

Puccini's *Turandot*

John Berger born

1927 General Chiang Kai-shek becomes prime minister in China

Trotsky expelled by the Communist party as a deviationist; Stalin becomes leader of the party and dictator of the Soviet Union

Charles Lindbergh flies from New York to Paris

J. W. Dunne's *An Experiment with Time*

Freud's *Autobiography* translated into English

Albert Giacometti's *Observing Head*

Ernest Hemingway's *Men Without Women*

Fritz Lang's *Metropolis*

Wyndham Lewis' *Time and Western Man*

F. W. Murnau's *Sunrise*

Proust's *Le Temps retrouvé* posthumously published

Stravinsky's *Oedipus Rex*

Virginia Woolf's *To the Lighthouse*

1928 The Kellogg-Briand Pact, outlawing war and providing for peaceful settlement of disputes, signed in Paris by sixty-two nations, including the Soviet Union

Herbert Hoover elected president of the United States

Women's suffrage granted at age twenty-one in Britain

Alexander Fleming discovers penicillin

Anita Brookner born

CHRONOLOGY

William Trevor born
Bertolt Brecht and Kurt Weill's *The Three-Penny Opera*
Eisenstein's *October*
Huxley's *Point Counter Point*
Christopher Isherwood's *All the Conspirators*
D. H. Lawrence's *Lady Chatterley's Lover*
Wyndham Lewis' *The Childermass*
Matisse's *Seated Odalisque*
Munch's *Girl on a Sofa*
Shaw's *Intelligent Woman's Guide to Socialism*
Virginia Woolf's *Orlando*
Yeats's *The Tower*

1929 The Labour party wins British general election
Trotsky expelled from the Soviet Union
Museum of Modern Art opens in New York
Collapse of U.S. stock exchange begins world economic crisis
Thom Gunn born
Robert Bridges's *The Testament of Beauty*
William Faulkner's *The Sound and the Fury*
Robert Graves's *Goodbye to All That*
Hemingway's *A Farewell to Arms*
Ernst Junger's *The Storm of Steel*
Hugo von Hoffmansthal's *Poems*
Henry Moore's *Reclining Figure*
J. B. Priestley's *The Good Companions*
Erich Maria Remarque's *All Quiet on the Western Front*
Shaw's *The Applecart*
R. C. Sheriff's *Journey's End*
Edith Sitwell's *Gold Coast Customs*
Thomas Wolfe's *Look Homeward, Angel*
Virginia Woolf's *A Room of One's Own*
Yeats's *The Winding Stair*
Second surrealist manifesto; Salvador Dali joins the surrealists
Epstein's *Night and Day*
Mondrian's *Composition with Yellow Blue*

1930 Allied occupation of the Rhineland ends
Mohandas Gandhi opens civil disobedience campaign in India
The *Daily Worker*, journal of the British Communist party, begins publishing
J. W. Reppe makes artificial fabrics from an acetylene base

John Arden born
Auden's *Poems*
Coward's *Private Lives*
Eliot's *Ash Wednesday*
Wyndham Lewis's *The Apes of God*
Maugham's *Cakes and Ale*
Ezra Pound's *XXX Cantos*
Evelyn Waugh's *Vile Bodies*

1931 The failure of the Credit Anstalt in Austria starts a financial collapse in Central Europe
Britain abandons the gold standard; the pound falls by twenty-five percent
Mutiny in the Royal Navy at Invergordon over pay cuts
Ramsay MacDonald resigns, splits the Cabinet, and is expelled by the Labour party; in the general election the National Government wins by a majority of five hundred seats
The Statute of Westminster defines dominion status
Ninette de Valois founds the Vic-Wells Ballet (eventually the Royal Ballet)
Coward's *Cavalcade*
Dali's The *Persistence of Memory*
John le Carré born
Fay Weldon born
O'Neill's *Mourning Becomes Electra*
Anthony Powell's *Afternoon Men*
Antoine de Saint-Exupéry's *Vol de nuit*
Walton's *Belshazzar's Feast*
Virginia Woolf's *The Waves*

1932 Franklin D. Roosevelt elected president of the United States
Paul von Hindenburg elected president of Germany; Franz von Papen elected chancellor
Sir Oswald Mosley founds British Union of Fascists
The BBC takes over development of television from J. L. Baird's company
Basic English of 850 words designed as a prospective international language
The Folger Library opens in Washington, D.C.
The Shakespeare Memorial Theatre opens in Stratford-upon-Avon
Faulkner's *Light in August*
Huxley's *Brave New World*

F. R. Leavis' *New Bearings in English Poetry*
Boris Pasternak's *Second Birth*
Ravel's *Concerto for Left Hand*
Rouault's *Christ Mocked by Soldiers*
Waugh's *Black Mischief*
Yeats's *Words for Music Perhaps*

1933 Roosevelt inaugurates the New Deal
Hitler becomes chancellor of Germany
The Reichstag set on fire
Hitler suspends civil liberties and freedom of the press; German trade unions suppressed
George Balanchine and Lincoln Kirstein found the School of American Ballet
Lowry's *Ultramarine*
André Malraux's *La Condition humaine*
Orwell's *Down and Out in Paris and London*
Gertrude Stein's *The Autobiography of Alice B. Toklas*

1934 The League Disarmament Conference ends in failure
The Soviet Union admitted to the League
Hitler becomes Führer
Civil war in Austria; Engelbert Dollfuss assassinated in attempted Nazi coup
Frédéric Joliot and Irene Joliot-Curie discover artificial (induced) radioactivity
Einstein's *My Philosophy*
Fitzgerald's *Tender Is the Night*
Graves's *I, Claudius* and *Claudius the God*
Toynbee's *A Study of History* begins publication (1934–1954)
Waugh's *A Handful of Dust*

1935 Grigori Zinoviev and other Soviet leaders convicted of treason
Stanley Baldwin becomes prime minister in National Government; National Government wins general election in Britain
Italy invades Abyssinia
Germany repudiates disarmament clauses of Treaty of Versailles
Germany reintroduces compulsory military service and outlaws the Jews
Robert Watson-Watt builds first practical radar equipment
Thomas Keneally born
David Lodge born
D. M. Thomas born
Karl Jaspers' *Suffering and Existence*

Ivy Compton-Burnett's *A House and Its Head*
Eliot's *Murder in the Cathedral*
Barbara Hepworth's *Three Forms*
George Gershwin's *Porgy and Bess*
Greene's *England Made Me*
Isherwood's *Mr. Norris Changes Trains*
Malraux's *Le Temps du mépris*
Yeats's *Dramatis Personae*
Klee's *Child Consecrated to Suffering*
Benedict Nicholson's *White Relief*

1936 Edward VII accedes to the throne in January; abdicates in December

1936–1952   Reign of George VI
1936 German troops occupy the Rhineland
Ninety-nine percent of German electorate vote for Nazi candidates
The Popular Front wins general election in France; Léon Blum becomes prime minister
Roosevelt reelected president of the United States
The Popular Front wins general election in Spain
Spanish Civil War begins
Italian troops occupy Addis Ababa; Abyssinia annexed by Italy
BBC begins television service from Alexandra Palace
A. S. Byatt born
Auden's *Look, Stranger!*
Auden and Isherwood's *The Ascent of F-6*
A. J. Ayer's *Language, Truth and Logic*
Chaplin's *Modern Times*
Greene's *A Gun for Sale*
Huxley's *Eyeless in Gaza*
Keynes's *General Theory of Employment*
F. R. Leavis' *Revaluation*
Mondrian's *Composition in Red and Blue*
Dylan Thomas' *Twenty-five Poems*
Wells's *The Shape of Things to Come* filmed

1937 Trial of Karl Radek and other Soviet leaders
Neville Chamberlain succeeds Stanley Baldwin as prime minister
China and Japan at war
Frank Whittle designs jet engine
Picasso's *Guernica*
Shostakovich's Fifth Symphony
Magritte's *La Reproduction interdite*

Hemingway's *To Have and Have Not*
Malraux's *L'Espoir*
Orwell's *The Road to Wigan Pier*
Priestley's *Time and the Conways*
Virginia Woolf's *The Years*

1938 Trial of Nikolai Bukharin and other Soviet political leaders
Austria occupied by German troops and declared part of the Reich
Hitler states his determination to annex Sudetenland from Czechoslovakia
Britain, France, Germany, and Italy sign the Munich agreement
German troops occupy Sudetenland
Caryl Churchill born
Edward Hulton founds *Picture Post*
Cyril Connolly's *Enemies of Promise*
du Maurier's *Rebecca*
Faulkner's *The Unvanquished*
Graham Greene's *Brighton Rock*
Hindemith's *Mathis der Maler*
Jean Renoir's *La Grande Illusion*
Jean-Paul Sartre's *La Nausée*
Yeats's *New Poems*
Anthony Asquith's *Pygmalion* and Walt Disney's *Snow White*

1939 German troops occupy Bohemia and Moravia; Czechoslovakia incorporated into Third Reich
Madrid surrenders to General Franco; the Spanish Civil War ends
Italy invades Albania
Spain joins Germany, Italy, and Japan in anti-Comintern Pact
Britain and France pledge support to Poland, Romania, and Greece
The Soviet Union proposes defensive alliance with Britain; British military mission visits Moscow
The Soviet Union and Germany sign non-aggression treaty, secretly providing for partition of Poland between them
Germany invades Poland; Britain, France, and Germany at war
The Soviet Union invades Finland
New York World's Fair opens
Eliot's *The Family Reunion*
Margaret Drabble born
Seamus Heaney born
Isherwood's *Good-bye to Berlin*
Joyce's *Finnegans Wake* (1922–1939)

MacNeice's *Autumn Journal*
Powell's *What's Become of Waring?*

1940 Churchill becomes prime minister
Italy declares war on France, Britain, and Greece
General de Gaulle founds Free French Movement
The Battle of Britain and the bombing of London
Roosevelt reelected president of the United States for third term
Betjeman's *Old Lights for New Chancels*
Angela Carter born
Bruce Chatwin born
Chaplin's *The Great Dictator*
Disney's *Fantasia*
Greene's *The Power and the Glory*
Hemingway's *For Whom the Bell Tolls*
C. P. Snow's *Strangers and Brothers* (retitled *George Passant* in 1970, when entire sequence of ten novels, published 1940–1970, was entitled *Strangers and Brothers*)

1941 German forces occupy Yugoslavia, Greece, and Crete, and invade the Soviet Union
Lend-Lease agreement between the United States and Britain
President Roosevelt and Winston Churchill sign the Atlantic Charter
Japanese forces attack Pearl Harbor; United States declares war on Japan, Germany, Italy; Britain on Japan
Auden's *New Year Letter*
James Burnham's *The Managerial Revolution*
F. Scott Fitzgerald's *The Last Tycoon*
Huxley's *Grey Eminence*
Shostakovich's *Seventh Symphony*
Tippett's *A Child of Our Time*
Orson Welles's *Citizen Kane*
Virginia Woolf's *Between the Acts*

1942 Japanese forces capture Singapore, Hong Kong, Bataan, Manila
German forces capture Tobruk
U.S. fleet defeats the Japanese in the Coral Sea, captures Guadalcanal
Battle of El Alamein
Allied forces land in French North Africa
Atom first split at University of Chicago
William Beveridge's *Social Insurance and Allied Services*
Albert Camus's *L'Étranger*

CHRONOLOGY

Joyce Cary's *To Be a Pilgrim*
Edith Sitwell's *Street Songs*
Waugh's *Put Out More Flags*

1943 German forces surrender at Stalingrad
German and Italian forces surrender in North Africa
Italy surrenders to Allies and declares war on Germany
Cairo conference between Roosevelt, Churchill, Chiang Kai-shek
Teheran conference between Roosevelt, Churchill, Stalin
Pat Barker born
Eliot's *Four Quartets*
Henry Moore's *Madonna and Child*
Sartre's *Les Mouches*
Vaughan Williams' *Fifth Symphony*

1944 Allied forces land in Normandy and southern France
Allied forces enter Rome
Attempted assassination of Hitler fails
Liberation of Paris
U.S. forces land in Philippines
German offensive in the Ardennes halted
Roosevelt reelected president of the United States for fourth term
Education Act passed in Britain
Pay-as-You-Earn income tax introduced
Beveridge's *Full Employment in a Free Society*
Cary's *The Horse's Mouth*
Huxley's *Time Must Have a Stop*
Maugham's *The Razor's Edge*
Sartre's *Huis Clos*
Edith Sitwell's *Green Song and Other Poems*
Graham Sutherland's *Christ on the Cross*
Trevelyan's *English Social History*

1945 British and Indian forces open offensive in Burma
Yalta conference between Roosevelt, Churchill, Stalin
Mussolini executed by Italian partisans
Roosevelt dies; Harry S. Truman becomes president
Hitler commits suicide; German forces surrender
The Potsdam Peace Conference
The United Nations Charter ratified in San Francisco
The Labour Party wins British General Election

Atomic bombs dropped on Hiroshima and Nagasaki
Surrender of Japanese forces ends World War II
Trial of Nazi war criminals opens at Nuremberg
All-India Congress demands British withdrawal from India
De Gaulle elected president of French Provisional Government; resigns the next year
Betjeman's *New Bats in Old Belfries*
Britten's *Peter Grimes*
Orwell's *Animal Farm*
Russell's *History of Western Philosophy*
Sartre's *The Age of Reason*
Edith Sitwell's *The Song of the Cold*
Waugh's *Brideshead Revisited*

1946 Bills to nationalize railways, coal mines, and the Bank of England passed in Britain
Nuremberg Trials concluded
United Nations General Assembly meets in New York as its permanent headquarters
The Arab Council inaugurated in Britain
Julian Barnes born
Frederick Ashton's *Symphonic Variations*
Britten's *The Rape of Lucretia*
David Lean's *Great Expectations*
O'Neill's *The Iceman Cometh*
Roberto Rosselini's *Paisà*
Dylan Thomas' *Deaths and Entrances*

1947 President Truman announces program of aid to Greece and Turkey and outlines the "Truman Doctrine"
Independence of India proclaimed; partition between India and Pakistan, and communal strife between Hindus and Moslems follows
General Marshall calls for a European recovery program
First supersonic air flight
Britain's first atomic pile at Harwell comes into operation
Edinburgh festival established
Discovery of the Dead Sea Scrolls in Palestine
Princess Elizabeth marries Philip Mountbatten, duke of Edinburgh
David Hare born

CHRONOLOGY

Salman Rushdie born
Auden's *Age of Anxiety*
Camus's *La Peste*
Chaplin's *Monsieur Verdoux*
Lowry's *Under the Volcano*
Priestley's *An Inspector Calls*
Edith Sitwell's *The Shadow of Cain*
Waugh's *Scott-King's Modern Europe*

1948 Gandhi assassinated
Czech Communist Party seizes power
Pan-European movement (1948–1958) begins with the formation of the permanent Organization for European Economic Cooperation (OEEC)
Berlin airlift begins as the Soviet Union halts road and rail traffic to the city
British mandate in Palestine ends; Israeli provisional government formed
Yugoslavia expelled from Soviet bloc
Columbia Records introduces the long-playing record
Truman elected president of the United States for second term

Ian McEwan born
Greene's *The Heart of the Matter*
Huxley's *Ape and Essence*
Leavis' *The Great Tradition*
Pound's *Cantos*
Priestley's *The Linden Tree*
Waugh's *The Loved One*

1949 North Atlantic Treaty Organization established with headquarters in Brussels
Berlin blockade lifted
German Federal Republic recognized; capital established at Bonn
Konrad Adenauer becomes German chancellor
Mao Tse-tung becomes chairman of the People's Republic of China following Communist victory over the Nationalists

Martin Amis born
Simone de Beauvoir's *The Second Sex*
Cary's *A Fearful Joy*
Arthur Miller's *Death of a Salesman*
Orwell's *Nineteen Eighty-four*

1950 Korean War breaks out
Nobel Prize for literature awarded to Bertrand Russell
R. H. S. Crossman's *The God That Failed*

T. S. Eliot's *The Cocktail Party*
Fry's *Venus Observed*
Doris Lessing's *The Grass Is Singing*
C. S. Lewis' *The Chronicles of Narnia* (1950–1956)
Wyndham Lewis' *Rude Assignment*
George Orwell's *Shooting an Elephant*
Carol Reed's *The Third Man*
Dylan Thomas' *Twenty-six Poems*

1951 Guy Burgess and Donald Maclean defect from Britain to the Soviet Union
The Conservative party under Winston Churchill wins British general election
The Festival of Britain celebrates both the centenary of the Crystal Palace Exhibition and British postwar recovery
Electric power is produced by atomic energy at Arcon, Idaho

Paul Muldoon born
W. H. Auden's *Nones*
Samuel Beckett's *Molloy* and *Malone Dies*
Benjamin Britten's *Billy Budd*
Greene's *The End of the Affair*
Akira Kurosawa's *Rashomon*
Wyndham Lewis' *Rotting Hill*
Anthony Powell's *A Question of Upbringing* (first volume of *A Dance to the Music of Time*, 1951–1975)
J. D. Salinger's *The Catcher in the Rye*
C. P. Snow's *The Masters*
Igor Stravinsky's *The Rake's Progress*

1952 Reign of Elizabeth II
At Eniwetok Atoll the United States detonates the first hydrogen bomb
The European Coal and Steel Community comes into being
Radiocarbon dating introduced to archaeology
Michael Ventris deciphers Linear B script
Dwight D. Eisenhower elected president of the United States
Beckett's *Waiting for Godot*
Charles Chaplin's *Limelight*
Ernest Hemingway's *The Old Man and the Sea*
Arthur Koestler's *Arrow in the Blue*
F. R. Leavis' *The Common Pursuit*
Lessing's *Martha Quest* (first volume of *The Children of Violence*, 1952-1965)
C. S. Lewis' *Mere Christianity*

Thomas' *Collected Poems*

Evelyn Waugh's *Men at Arms* (first volume of *Sword of Honour*, 1952-1961)

Angus Wilson's *Hemlock and After*

1953 Constitution for a European political community drafted

Julius and Ethel Rosenberg executed for passing U.S. secrets to the Soviet Union

Cease-fire declared in Korea

Edmund Hillary and his Sherpa guide, Tenzing Norkay, scale Mt. Everest

Nobel Prize for literature awarded to Winston Churchill

General Mohammed Naguib proclaims Egypt a republic

Beckett's *Watt*

Joyce Cary's *Except the Lord*

Robert Graves's *Poems 1953*

1954 First atomic submarine, *Nautilus,* is launched by the United States

Dien Bien Phu captured by the Vietminh

Geneva Conference ends French dominion over Indochina

U.S. Supreme Court declares racial segregation in schools unconstitutional

Nasser becomes president of Egypt

Nobel Prize for literature awarded to Ernest Hemingway

Kazuo Ishiguro born

Kingsley Amis' *Lucky Jim*

John Betjeman's *A Few Late Chrysanthemums*

William Golding's *Lord of the Flies*

Christopher Isherwood's *The World in the Evening*

Koestler's *The Invisible Writing*

Iris Murdoch's *Under the Net*

C. P. Snow's *The New Men*

Thomas' *Under Milk Wood* published posthumously

1955 Warsaw Pact signed

West Germany enters NATO as Allied occupation ends

The Conservative party under Anthony Eden wins British general election

Cary's *Not Honour More*

Greene's *The Quiet American*

Philip Larkin's *The Less Deceived*

F. R. Leavis' *D. H. Lawrence, Novelist*

Vladimir Nabokov's *Lolita*

Patrick White's *The Tree of Man*

1956 Nasser's nationalization of the Suez Canal leads to Israeli, British, and French armed intervention

Uprising in Hungary suppressed by Soviet troops

Khrushchev denounces Stalin at Twentieth Communist Party Congress

Eisenhower reelected president of the United States

Anthony Burgess' *Time for a Tiger*

Golding's *Pincher Martin*

Murdoch's *Flight from the Enchanter*

John Osborne's *Look Back in Anger*

Snow's *Homecomings*

Edmund Wilson's *Anglo-Saxon Attitudes*

1957 The Soviet Union launches the first artificial earth satellite, *Sputnik I*

Eden succeeded by Harold Macmillan

Suez Canal reopened

Eisenhower Doctrine formulated

Parliament receives the Wolfenden Report on Homosexuality and Prostitution

Nobel Prize for literature awarded to Albert Camus

Beckett's *Endgame* and *All That Fall*

Lawrence Durrell's *Justine* (first volume of *The Alexandria Quartet*, 1957–1960)

Ted Hughes's *The Hawk in the Rain*

Murdoch's *The Sandcastle*

V. S. Naipaul's *The Mystic Masseur*

Eugene O'Neill's *Long Day's Journey into Night*

Osborne's *The Entertainer*

Muriel Spark's *The Comforters*

White's *Voss*

1958 European Economic Community established

Khrushchev succeeds Bulganin as Soviet premier

Charles de Gaulle becomes head of France's newly constituted Fifth Republic

The United Arab Republic formed by Egypt and Syria

The United States sends troops into Lebanon

First U.S. satellite, *Explorer 1,* launched

Nobel Prize for literature awarded to Boris Pasternak

CHRONOLOGY

Lyndon Johnson elected president of the United States

The Labour party under Harold Wilson wins British general election

Nobel Prize for literature awarded to Jean-Paul Sartre

Saul Bellow's *Herzog*

Burgess' *Nothing Like the Sun*

Golding's *The Spire*

Isherwood's *A Single Man*

Stanley Kubrick's *Dr. Strangelove*

Larkin's *The Whitsun Weddings*

Naipaul's *An Area of Darkness*

Peter Shaffer's *The Royal Hunt of the Sun*

Snow's *Corridors of Power*

1965   The first U.S. combat forces land in Vietnam

The U.S. spacecraft Mariner transmits photographs of Mars

British Petroleum Company finds oil in the North Sea

War breaks out between India and Pakistan

Rhodesia declares its independence

Ontario power failure blacks out the Canadian and U.S. east coasts

Nobel Prize for literature awarded to Mikhail Sholokhov

Robert Lowell's *For the Union Dead*

Norman Mailer's *An American Dream*

Osborne's *Inadmissible Evidence*

Pinter's *The Homecoming*

Spark's *The Mandelbaum Gate*

1966   The Labour party under Harold Wilson wins British general election

The Archbishop of Canterbury visits Pope Paul VI

Florence, Italy, severely damaged by floods

Paris exhibition celebrates Picasso's eighty-fifth birthday

Fowles's *The Magus*

Greene's *The Comedians*

Osborne's *A Patriot for Me*

Paul Scott's *The Jewel in the Crown* (first volume of *The Raj Quartet*, 1966–1975)

White's *The Solid Mandala*

1967   Thurgood Marshall becomes first black U.S. Supreme Court justice

Six-Day War pits Israel against Egypt and Syria

Biafra's secession from Nigeria leads to civil war

Francis Chichester completes solo circumnavigation of the globe

Dr. Christiaan Barnard performs first heart transplant operation, in South Africa

China explodes its first hydrogen bomb

Golding's *The Pyramid*

Hughes's *Wodwo*

Isherwood's *A Meeting by the River*

Naipaul's *The Mimic Men*

Tom Stoppard's *Rosencrantz and Guildenstern Are Dead*

Orson Welles's *Chimes at Midnight*

Angus Wilson's *No Laughing Matter*

1968   Violent student protests erupt in France and West Germany

Warsaw Pact troops occupy Czechoslovakia

Violence in Northern Ireland causes Britain to send in troops

Tet offensive by Communist forces launched against South Vietnam's cities

Theater censorship ended in Britain

Robert Kennedy and Martin Luther King, Jr., assassinated

Richard M. Nixon elected president of the United States

Booker Prize for fiction established

Durrell's *Tunc*

Graves's *Poems 1965–1968*

Osborne's *The Hotel in Amsterdam*

Snow's *The Sleep of Reason*

Solzhenitsyn's *The First Circle* and *Cancer Ward*

Spark's *The Public Image*

1969   Humans set foot on the moon for the first time when astronauts descend to its surface in a landing vehicle from the U.S. spacecraft *Apollo 11*

The Soviet unmanned spacecraft *Venus V* lands on Venus

Capital punishment abolished in Britain

Colonel Muammar Qaddafi seizes power in Libya

Solzhenitsyn expelled from the Soviet Union

Nobel Prize for literature awarded to Samuel Beckett

Carter's *The Magic Toyshop*

Fowles's *The French Lieutenant's Woman*

CHRONOLOGY

Storey's *The Contractor*

1970   Civil war in Nigeria ends with Biafra's
        surrender
        U.S. planes bomb Cambodia
        The Conservative party under Edward
        Heath wins British general election
        Nobel Prize for literature awarded to
        Aleksandr Solzhenitsyn
        Durrell's *Nunquam*
        Hughes's *Crow*
        F. R. Leavis and Q. D. Leavis' *Dickens the
        Novelist*
        Snow's *Last Things*
        Spark's *The Driver's Seat*

1971   Communist China given Nationalist Chi-
        na's UN seat
        Decimal currency introduced to Britain
        Indira Gandhi becomes India's prime
        minister
        Nobel Prize for literature awarded to
        Heinrich Böll
        Bond's *The Pope's Wedding*
        Naipaul's *In a Free State*
        Pinter's *Old Times*
        Spark's *Not to Disturb*

1972   The civil strife of "Bloody Sunday" causes
        Northern Ireland to come under the di-
        rect rule of Westminster
        Nixon becomes the first U.S. president to
        visit Moscow and Beijing
        The Watergate break-in precipitates scan-
        dal in the United States
        Eleven Israeli athletes killed by terrorists
        at Munich Olympics
        Nixon reelected president of the United
        States
        Bond's *Lear*
        Snow's *The Malcontents*
        Stoppard's *Jumpers*

1973   Britain, Ireland, and Denmark enter Eu-
        ropean Economic Community
        Egypt and Syria attack Israel in the Yom
        Kippur War
        Energy crisis in Britain reduces produc-
        tion to a three-day week
        Nobel Prize for literature awarded to
        Patrick White
        Bond's *The Sea*
        Greene's *The Honorary Consul*
        Lessing's *The Summer Before the Dark*
        Murdoch's *The Black Prince*

Shaffer's *Equus*
White's *The Eye of the Storm*

1974   Miners strike in Britain
        Greece's military junta overthrown
        Emperor Haile Selassie of Ethiopia de-
        posed
        President Makarios of Cyprus replaced
        by military coup
        Nixon resigns as U.S. president and is
        succeeded by Gerald R. Ford
        Betjeman's *A Nip in the Air*
        Bond's *Bingo*
        Durrell's *Monsieur* (first volume of *The
        Avignon Quintet*, 1974–1985)
        Larkin's *The High Windows*
        Solzhenitsyn's *The Gulag Archipelago*
        Spark's *The Abbess of Crewe*

1975   The U.S. *Apollo* and Soviet *Soyuz* space-
        crafts rendezvous in space
        The Helsinki Accords on human rights
        signed
        U.S. forces leave Vietnam
        King Juan Carlos succeeds Franco as
        Spain's head of state
        Nobel Prize for literature awarded to Eu-
        genio Montale

1976   New U.S. copyright law goes into effect
        Israeli commandos free hostages from hi-
        jacked plane at Entebbe, Uganda
        British and French SST Concordes make
        first regularly scheduled commercial
        flights
        The United States celebrates its bicenten-
        nial
        Jimmy Carter elected president of the
        United States
        Byron and Shelley manuscripts discov-
        ered in Barclay's Bank, Pall Mall
        Hughes's *Seasons' Songs*
        Koestler's *The Thirteenth Tribe*
        Scott's *Staying On*
        Spark's *The Take-over*
        White's *A Fringe of Leaves*

1977   Silver jubilee of Queen Elizabeth II cele-
        brated
        Egyptian president Anwar el-Sadat visits
        Israel
        "Gang of Four" expelled from Chinese
        Communist party
        First woman ordained in the U.S. Episco-
        pal church

xxvi

After twenty-nine years in power, Israel's Labour party is defeated by the Likud party

Fowles's *Daniel Martin*

Hughes's *Gaudete*

1978 Treaty between Israel and Egypt negotiated at Camp David

Pope John Paul I dies a month after his coronation and is succeeded by Karol Cardinal Wojtyla, who takes the name John Paul II

Former Italian premier Aldo Moro murdered by left-wing terrorists

Nobel Prize for literature awarded to Isaac Bashevis Singer

Greene's *The Human Factor*

Hughes's *Cave Birds*

Murdoch's *The Sea, The Sea*

1979 The United States and China establish diplomatic relations

Ayatollah Khomeini takes power in Iran and his supporters hold U.S. embassy staff hostage in Teheran

Rhodesia becomes Zimbabwe

Earl Mountbatten assassinated

The Soviet Union invades Afghanistan

The Conservative party under Margaret Thatcher wins British general election

Nobel Prize for literature awarded to Odysseus Elytis

Golding's *Darkness Visible*

Hughes's *Moortown*

Lessing's *Shikasta* (first volume of *Canopus in Argos, Archives*)

Naipaul's *A Bend in the River*

Spark's *Territorial Rights*

White's *The Twyborn Affair*

1980 Iran-Iraq war begins

Strikes in Gdansk give rise to the Solidarity movement

Mt. St. Helen's erupts in Washington State

British steelworkers strike for the first time since 1926

More than fifty nations boycott Moscow Olympics

Ronald Reagan elected president of the United States

Burgess's *Earthly Powers*

Golding's *Rites of Passage*

Shaffer's *Amadeus*

Storey's *A Prodigal Child*

Angus Wilson's *Setting the World on Fire*

1981 Greece admitted to the European Economic Community

Iran hostage crisis ends with release of U.S. embassy staff

Twelve Labour MPs and nine peers found British Social Democratic party

Socialist party under François Mitterand wins French general election

Rupert Murdoch buys *The Times* of London

Turkish gunman wounds Pope John Paul II in assassination attempt

U.S. gunman wounds President Reagan in assassination attempt

President Sadat of Egypt assassinated

Nobel Prize for literature awarded to Elias Canetti

Spark's *Loitering with Intent*

1982 Britain drives Argentina's invasion force out of the Falkland Islands

U.S. space shuttle makes first successful trip

Yuri Andropov becomes general secretary of the Central Committee of the Soviet Communist party

Israel invades Lebanon

First artificial heart implanted at Salt Lake City hospital

Bellow's *The Dean's December*

Greene's *Monsignor Quixote*

1983 South Korean airliner with 269 aboard shot down after straying into Soviet airspace

U.S. forces invade Grenada following left-wing coup

Widespread protests erupt over placement of nuclear missiles in Europe

The £1 coin comes into circulation in Britain

Australia wins the America's Cup

Nobel Prize for literature awarded to William Golding

Hughes's *River*

Murdoch's *The Philosopher's Pupil*

1984 Konstantin Chernenko becomes general secretary of the Central Committee of the Soviet Communist party

Prime Minister Indira Gandhi of India assassinated by Sikh bodyguards

Reagan reelected president of the United States

Toxic gas leak at Bhopal, India, plant kills 2,000

British miners go on strike

Irish Republican Army attempts to kill Prime Minister Thatcher with bomb detonated at a Brighton hotel

World Court holds against U.S. mining of Nicaraguan harbors

Golding's *The Paper Men*

Lessing's *The Diary of Jane Somers*

Spark's *The Only Problem*

1985   United States deploys cruise missiles in Europe

Mikhail Gorbachev becomes general secretary of the Soviet Communist party following death of Konstantin Chernenko

Riots break out in Handsworth district (Birmingham) and Brixton

Republic of Ireland gains consultative role in Northern Ireland

State of emergency is declared in South Africa

Nobel Prize for literature awarded to Claude Simon

A. N. Wilson's *Gentlemen in England*

Lessing's *The Good Terrorist*

Murdoch's *The Good Apprentice*

Fowles's *A Maggot*

1986   U.S. space shuttle *Challenger* explodes

United States attacks Libya

Atomic power plant at Chernobyl destroyed in accident

Corazon Aquino becomes president of the Philippines

Giotto spacecraft encounters Comet Halley

Nobel Prize for literature awarded to Wole Soyinka

Final volume of *Oxford English Dictionary* supplement published

Amis's *The Old Devils*

Ishiguro's *An Artist of the Floating World*

A. N. Wilson's *Love Unknown*

Powell's *The Fisher King*

1987   Gorbachev begins reform of Communist party of the Soviet Union

Stock market collapses

Iran-contra affair reveals that Reagan administration used money from arms sales to Iran to fund Nicaraguan rebels

Palestinian uprising begins in Israeli-occupied territories

Nobel Prize for literature awarded to Joseph Brodsky

Golding's *Close Quarters*

Burgess's *Little Wilson and Big God*

Drabble's *The Radiant Way*

1988   Soviet Union begins withdrawing troops from Afghanistan

Iranian airliner shot down by U.S. Navy over Persian Gulf

War between Iran and Iraq ends

George Bush elected president of the United States

Pan American flight 103 destroyed over Lockerbie, Scotland

Nobel Prize for literature awarded to Naguib Mafouz

Greene's *The Captain and the Enemy*

Amis's *Difficulties with Girls*

Rushdie's *Satanic Verses*

1989   Ayatollah Khomeini pronounces death sentence on Salman Rushdie; Great Britain and Iran sever diplomatic relations

F. W. de Klerk becomes president of South Africa

Chinese government crushes student demonstration in Tiananmen Square

Communist regimes are weakened or abolished in Poland, Czechoslovakia, Hungary, East Germany, and Romania

Lithuania nullifies its inclusion in Soviet Union

Nobel Prize for literature awarded to José Cela

Second edition of *Oxford English Dictionary* published

Drabble's *A Natural Curiosity*

Murdoch's *The Message to the Planet*

Amis's *London Fields*

Ishiguro's *The Remains of the Day*

1990   Communist monopoly ends in Bulgaria

Riots break out against community charge in England

First women ordained priests in Church of England

Civil war breaks out in Yugoslavia; Croatia and Slovenia declare independence

Bush and Gorbachev sign START agreement to reduce nuclear-weapons arsenals

President Jean-Baptiste Aristide overthrown by military in Haiti

Boris Yeltsin elected president of Russia

Dissolution of the Soviet Union

Nobel Prize for literature awarded to Nadine Gordimer

1992   U.N. Conference on Environment and Development (the "Earth Summit") meets in Rio de Janeiro

Prince and Princess of Wales separate

War in Bosnia-Herzegovina intensifies

Bill Clinton elected president of the United States in three-way race with Bush and independent candidate H. Ross Perot

Nobel Prize for literature awarded to Derek Walcott

1993   Czechoslovakia divides into the Czech Republic and Slovakia;

playwright Vaclav Havel elected president of the Czech Republic

Britain ratifies Treaty on European Union (the "Maastricht Treaty")

U.S. troops provide humanitarian aid amid famine in Somalia

United States, Canada, and Mexico sign North American Free Trade Agreement

Nobel Prize for literature awarded to Toni Morrison

1994   Nelson Mandela elected president in South Africa's first post-apartheid election

Jean-Baptiste Aristide restored to presidency of Haiti

Clinton health care reforms rejected by Congress

Civil war in Rwanda

Republicans win control of both houses of Congress for first time in forty years

Prime Minister Albert Reynolds of Ireland meets with Gerry Adams, president of Sinn Fein

Nobel Prize for literature awarded to Kenzaburo Öe

Amis's *You Can't Do Both*

Naipaul's *A Way in the World*

1995   Britain and Irish Republican Army engage in diplomatic talks

Barings Bank forced into bankruptcy as a result of a maverick bond trader's losses

United States restores full diplomatic relations with Vietnam

NATO initiates air strikes in Bosnia

Death of Stephen Spender

Israeli Prime Minister Yitzhak Rabin assassinated

Nobel Prize for literature awarded to Seamus Heaney

1996   IRA breaks cease-fire; Sein Fein representatives barred from

Northern Ireland peace talks

Prince and Princess of Wales divorce

Cease-fire agreement in Chechnia; Russian forces begin to withdraw

Boris Yeltsin reelected president of Russia

Bill Clinton reelected president of the United States

Nobel Prize for literature awarded to Wislawa Szymborska

1997   Labour party under Tony Blair wins British general election

Bertie Ahern becomes prime minister of Ireland

Britain cedes Hong Kong to People's Republic of China

NATO expands to include Czech Republic, Hungary, and Poland

List of Contributors

RONALD J. AMBROSETTI. Associate Dean of the Faculty, State University of New York College at Fredonia. Coeditor of two anthologies, *Continuities in Popular Culture* and *Popular Culture and Curricula*. Has also published numerous articles in the areas of American literature, folklore, and popular culture. **Eric Ambler**

SVEN BIRKERTS. Author of four books of essays, *An Artificial Wilderness: Essays on Twentieth-century Literature; The Electric Life: Essays on Modern Poetry; American Energies: Essays on Fiction;* and *The Gutenberg Elegies: The Fate of Reading in an Electronic Age.* Has also edited *Tolstoy's Dictaphone: Technology and the Muse.* **Julian Barnes**

TIMOTHY BRENNAN. Associate Professor of English and Comparative Literature, State University of New York at Stony Brook. Books include *Salman Rushdie and the Third World: Myths of the Nation* and *At Home in the World: Cosmopolitanism Now,* as well as an anthology on the black cultures of modern Britain and another entitled *Narratives of Colonial Resistance.* Coeditor of the "Cultural Margins" series at Cambridge University Press. **Salman Rushdie**

GABRIEL BROWNSTEIN. Professor of English, Barnard College and Parsons School of Design. Also regularly writes reviews and criticism. **Kazuo Ishiguro**

KATRIN R. BURLIN. Associate Professor of English, Bryn Mawr College. Publications include "'The Pen of the Contriver': The Four Fictions of *Northanger Abbey,*" in *Jane Austen: Bicentenary Essays;* "'Pictures of Perfection' at Pemberley: Art in *Pride and Prejudice,*" in *Jane Austen: New Perspectives;* "Games," in *The Jane Austen Companion;* and "'Women Writers at the Crossroads': The Hercules Topos in the Novels of Mary Brunton, Maria Edgeworth, and Jane Austen," in *Fetter'd or Free?* **P. D. James**

SHARON CARSON. Associate Professor of English, Kent State University, Stark Campus. Author of essays on women in literature, in sports, and in war. **Pat Barker**

ANGUÏS R. B. COCHRAN. Preceptor, Literature Humanities, Department of English and Comparative Literature, Columbia University. **Ian McEwan**

JOSEPH DONAHUE. Assistant Professor of English, Stevens Institute of Technology. Writer of three books of poetry: *Before Creation, Monitions of the Approach,* and *World Well Broken.* Coeditor of *Primary Trouble: An Anthology of Contemporary American Poetry.* **Paul Muldoon**

LAURA ENGEL. Doctoral candidate, Columbia University. Dissertation examines the memoirs of eighteenth-century British actresses. Other areas of study include the eighteenth-century novel, British portraiture, and contemporary drama. Teaches courses in theater, women's studies, and European literature at the Spence School in New York City. **A. S. Byatt**

DAVID HAWKES. Assistant Professor, Department of English, Lehigh University. His most recent book is *Ideology,* published by Routledge in 1996. **Martin Amis**

ANGELYN HAYS. Poet, playwright, journalist. Writing a screenplay adaptation of *Beowulf.* **Bruce Chatwin**

URSULA K. HEISE. Assistant Professor of English and Comparative Literature, Columbia University. She has published articles on Renaissance theater and various contemporary authors, as well as *Chronoschisms: Time, Narrative, and Postmodernism,* a book on postmodern studies published by Cambridge in 1997. **Jeanette Winterson**

DANELL JONES.   Writer and Critic. Author of essays on modernism, Virginia Woolf, and World War I. Has received several distinctions for her writing, most recently a Jovanovich Imaginative Writing Award from the University of Colorado at Boulder. Currently at work on a narrative title *Ultima Thule: The Dust Bowl Psalms.* **Thomas Keneally**

BENJAMIN LA FARGE.   Professor of Literature, Bard College. **William Trevor**

JONATHAN LEVIN.   Associate Professor of English, Columbia University. Teaches courses in nineteenth- and twentieth-century American literature. Author of *Life in the Transitions: Emerson, Pragmatism, and American Literary Modernism.* Associate Editor of *Raritan Review.* **Thom Gunn**

LISA HERMINE MAKMAN.   Doctoral candidate, Department of English and Comparative Literature, Columbia University. Preceptor in Literature and the Humanities, Columbia University. **Roald Dahl**

A. MICHAEL MATIN.   Teaches courses in literature and writing at Columbia University. Currently at work on a book on the late Victorian and Edwardian invasion narrative. **David Lodge**

GITA MAY.   Professor of French and Romance Philology, Columbia University. Has published extensively on French Enlightenment, eighteenth-century aesthetics, the post-revolutionary era, and women in literature, history, and art. Author of *Diderot et Baudelaire, critiques d'art; Stendahl and the Age of Napoleon;* and *Madame Roland and the Age of Revolution.* Publications also include articles on Denis Diderot (in *European Writers: The Age of Reason and the Enlightenment*), Elisabeth Vigée Le Brun, Julie de Lespinasse, Madame Roland, George Sand (in *European Writers: The Romantic Century*), Germaine de Staël, and Rebecca West (in *British Writers Supplement III*). Coeditor of *Diderot Studies III,* contributing editor of Diderot's *Oeuvres complètes,* and general editor of the series "The Age of Revolution and Romanticism." **Anita Brookner**

TYRUS H. MILLER.   Assistant Professor of Comparative Literature and English, Yale University. Author of essays on Walter Benjamin, John Cage, Ezra Pound, William Empson, Samuel Beckett, Andrea Zanzotto, Michel Leiris, Georges Bataille, and Cecil Day Lewis. **Christine Brooke-Rose**

MARGARET E. MITCHELL.   Doctoral student at the University of Connecticut. Has worked extensively with modern British literature, Victorian literature and culture, and eighteenth-century literature and culture. Her current research focuses on the connection between economics and the construction of gender ideologies in the nineteenth century. **Fay Weldon**

BRIDGET ORR.   Assistant Professor, Fordham University. Has also taught at the University of Auckland, New Zealand, and at the University of Iowa. Specializes in Restoration and eighteenth-century literature and has also published extensively on post-colonial Pacific literature and culture. **Margaret Drabble**

SUSANA POWELL.   Assistant Professor of Speech, Communications, and Theatre Arts, Borough of Manhattan Community College, City University of New York; Visiting Professor, Columbia University. Regular contributor to *The Shakespeare Bulletin.* Her current research focuses on *Shakespeare's Demonic Women* and ACTorvism. **David Hare**

MINNIE SINGH.   Assistant Professor of English, University of Pittsburgh. **John Berger**

VICTORIA D. SULLIVAN.   Professor of English, Saint Peter's College; Assistant Professor, City College of New York; Lecturer, Columbia University. Has coedited *Plays by and About Women* and has published essays on Shakespeare, Saul Bellow, Doris Lessing, Zelda Fitzgerald, among others. Has had four Equity Showcase productions of her plays. **Caryl Churchill**

RACHEL WETZSTEON.   Instructor of literature and writing, Columbia University and the Ninety-Second Street Y Poetry Center. Her first book of poetry, *The Other Stars,* was selected for the 1993 National Poetry Series and was published by Penguin Books in 1994. Her next poetry collection, *Home and Away* is forthcoming from Penguin in 1998. **D. M. Thomas**

LOUISE YELIN.   Associate Professor, Literature, Purchase College, State University of New York. Writings include the forthcoming *From the Margins of Empire: Christina Stead, Doris Lessing, Nadine Gordimer* and essays on Christina Stead, Nadine Gordimer, Charles Dickens, and feminist criticism in selected scholarly journals. **Christina Stead**

BRITISH WRITERS

ERIC AMBLER

(1909–   )

Ronald J. Ambrosetti

AN ENCOMPASSING CRITIQUE of Eric Ambler's writing must investigate his key role in shaping what is increasingly referred to as modern global culture. Popular culture and, in particular, popular literature took a peculiar turn in the proletarian 1930s. Owing either to the dire necessities forced by a global economic depression or to the tantalizing vision of collectivist hope and aspiration, Anglo-American culture voraciously digested the intellectual legacies of Karl Marx and Charles Darwin in the nineteenth century. The ingestion of these ideas by an eager reading audience in the decade leading up to World War II marked the beginning of mass culture, including film and radio, and a more complex popular literature that surpassed the old, familiar pulp genres of dime novels and broadside-style detective sensationals. For the first paperback edition of Ambler's first novel, *The Dark Frontier* (1936), published in 1991, Ambler wrote in a new introduction: "At the time my literary tastes were those of any other guilt-ridden young man who had rejected all orthodox religious texts in favour of the teachings of C. G. Jung, G. I. Gurdjieff, and Osvald Spengler. The novels of Dostoyevski and the plays of Ibsen were my bedside books" (p. xvi). As with Joseph Conrad's *Secret Agent*, Ambler created a higher quality of style and complexity in the popular tradition of novels of intrigue and espionage. Ambler was the first, in a long and ongoing line of literary craftspersons, to reveal the soul of the spy as the corrosive and vitiated soul of the twentieth century. Over the shoulders of the spy novelist loom the baleful figures of Franz Kafka, Fyodor Dostoyevsky and Carl Jung, whose works often explore the existentialist themes of despair and isolation. Ambler's novels are the forerunner of the thriller genre and many of the "psychological intrigue" novels and tales of the past fifty years.

EARLY LIFE

IN 1989, at the time of his eightieth birthday and after more than fifty years as a published writer, Eric Ambler wrote a new introduction to the first American paperback edition of *The Dark Frontier*. Once again, however, readers came to discover that the venerable Ambler, like one of his fugitive and reluctant "wrong man" heroes (innocent bystanders caught through mistaken identity and drawn into the melee), had slipped the noose by covering only half of his life. The curious historians of literary intrigue should have known better; after all, Ambler was the autobiographer who published *Here Lies: An Autobiography* in 1985 but had effectively covered the years only up to 1953. Surely Ambler, by simply ignoring the last thirty years of his life, was reminding mystery buffs of Raymond Chandler's famous quip that the ideal mystery is the narrative one would read if the end were missing.

The span and the composition of Ambler's literary output mirror the protean nature of his dilettante-as-hero. In his nearly sixty years as a writer he has produced both the durability and resourceful genius that sustain the agent provocateur in the field, along with an uncanny knack to foresee and link global events to his literature of international intrigue, politics, and espionage. Ambler's eighteen novels, written from 1936 to 1981, defy any single classification; his literary career has been punctuated by long spells of military service and film screenwriting; yet there was a purposeful and seemingly predestined incursion into the profession of writing thrillers. In an interview with Joel Hopkins, published in the *Journal of Popular Culture* in 1975, Ambler revealed his then-conscious effort at transforming the old right-wing, brownshirted, garden variety of secret service adventure thriller. When

1

asked by Hopkins about what led up to Ambler's flurry of literary activity between 1937 and 1940, during which he wrote five novels, Ambler responded:

What happened was simply having failed at playwriting, having failed as a songwriter, failed as an engineer, I looked around for something I could change and decided it was the thriller–spy story. I would do something different. The detective story genre had been worked over and worked over, but no one had looked at the thriller. It was still a dirty word. So I decided to intellectualize it, insofar as I was able. . . . I changed the genre and couldn't write the books fast enough.

(p. 286)

London at the time of Eric Ambler's birth, on 28 June 1909, was somnolently basking in the last rays of the setting sun of the staid Victorian order. Not far from where he was born a gargantuan ocean liner was being built as the pride and symbol of the far-flung power of British rule. By the time he became the accomplished novelist and screenwriter he was nearly fifty years later, in 1958, he was chosen to write the film script of the doomed voyage of the *Titanic, A Night to Remember,* when the lost luxury liner had already been lying in its Atlantic grave for many decades. And Ambler himself was by then known as the internationally famous writer who had predicted a brave new world of fearsome technological might and dark treachery—a world that prospered in violence and the spread of empires, all without the presence of the formerly ubiquitous Union Jack and the cumbersome gilt-framed sea power of the Edwardian *Titanic.*

The son of Alfred Percy (Alf) and Amy Madelin Andrews, Ambler was born into a family of vaudeville entertainers. His father had been reared in Salford, Lancashire, but the family had finally settled in Lee, in southeast London. Grandpa Andrews was a cabinetmaker in Tottenham. Married in 1906, Ambler's parents were stagestruck and performed in troupes for "concert parties"; they billed themselves as "Reg and Amy Ambrose." As a teenager, Eric was keen to join his parents' troupe, called "The Whatnots," but they wished for him a more respectable and substantial career than show business. Instead of the music hall, the venue for young Ambler's early education was the nearby academic secondary school, Colfe's Grammar School, which he entered in 1917. Ambler was so good in science

that at age fifteen he scored 100 percent in chemistry and physics for the university examination at the University of London, and he was awarded one of only four prestigious scholarships. He chose to study engineering, but even from the beginning there was evidence of his irrepressible literary talent.

The engineering student found the curriculum easy, and like most students in that situation saw the burden of guilt as a truant even easier to cope with. Ambler preferred to spend his study time at the library of the Institute of Electrical Engineers, but as he later revealed in *Here Lies:* "The Institute was on the Thames Embankment only a few minutes walk from the Law Courts. Soon I was spending whole mornings in the public galleries of the King's Bench Division or the Criminal Division of the Court of Appeal" (pp. 64–65). Ambler soon found himself forsaking the scientific journals for the "foxed thirty-year-old copy of Winwood Reade's *Martyrdom of Man.* This was the book that Sherlock Holmes had casually recommended to Watson during their early days in Baker Street, and it was because of that recommendation that I had first been drawn to it" (p. 66). During his engineering studies, distracted but richly inspired by the excursions to the law courts and the reading in the theoretical underpinnings of the British tale of detection, Ambler remained fascinated with the stage. Theater was the central beacon of his vocation (or avocation) to the arts. He attended plays incessantly and took to writing down certain scenes that seemed to work particularly well. He applied (unsuccessfully) for work as a stage electrician; he haunted the tea shops and pubs frequented by stagehands and assistant stage managers. Diversion piled on diversion, and at the suggestion of a friend, Ambler enlisted in the London Rifle Brigade regiment of the Territorials (akin to the American Army National Guard) in late 1925. This connection to the British military establishment turned out to be important in 1940 at the outbreak of World War II; Ambler eventually found himself in the inner circle of the military escort for Winston Churchill (he once corrected the Prime Minister's incorrect knowledge of a film cast) and eventually in the company of the American film director John Huston.

In 1927, the inevitable finally happened. Ambler left his engineering studies to take advantage of an apprentice engineer's job with the Ponders End

(London) works of the Edison Swan Electric Company. In *Here Lies*, he explained that the Great Depression was already looming, and many engineering graduates were out of work. Transferred in 1928 to Lydbrook, in the scenic valley of the River Wye, Ambler supervised for a time the manufacture of colliery cable—the cable works itself was near the Waterloo, the deepest pit (mine) in England. In that summer at Lydbrook, Ambler wrote the first two chapters of a biographical novel about his father. The work was never completed, but for Ambler the active practice of daily writing began when he was appointed to full membership of the publicity department staff. After this turning point, he never again plied his engineering trade, except as the technically astute writer of spy stories.

From 1929 to 1930, Ambler frequented the library shelves that contained the "contemporary realities" that were not to be denied:

The librarian of the Public Library at Addiscombe . . . would let me have six books at a time. . . . It was on his shelves that I found Jung's *Psychology of the Unconscious* and *Collected Papers*. Jung led me to Nietzsche and *The Birth of Tragedy*. In the same part of the library I found my way to Spengler.

(*Here Lies*, p. 92)

Such tomes are strange primers for music-hall laughter. In the early thirties, Ambler went to work for the copy department of a London advertising agency. Ambler found the atmosphere of the ad agency to be bristling with literary ambition. At the same time, Dorothy L. Sayers was working at a rival London agency, Benson's, and turning out high-quality detective stories. Literary quality and ambition were not the only conditions that energized the working environment of these big ad agencies, for the Great Depression had begun, and many of the copywriters in the burgeoning business of public relations had also been to Oxford and Cambridge and thus were staunch exponents of socialist ideologies. Ambler's politics of this period (1930–1936) has received a good deal of attention. In *Mortal Consequences*, Julian Symons stated: "In the six novels he wrote before the outbreak of World War II, Eric Ambler . . . infused warmth and political color into the spy story by using it to express a Left Wing point of view" (p. 238). Likewise, in a long chapter in his *Sleuths, Inc.*, Hugh Eames described the socioeconomic milieu of Britain in

the early thirties: "London seethed with new social solutions, and Eric Ambler was engaged."

With a steady income as a copywriter in the early thirties, Ambler was able to afford to travel, and his journeys fed later writings. Gavin Lambert chronicled Ambler's meanderings through the Mediterranean, the fabled sea that beckoned the maturing writer from the time of his early education in the classics; he gravitated toward the Balkans and the Middle East, following the Orient Express route to Belgrade, Athens, and Istanbul. He reconnoitered Beirut and Cairo, and in Tangier he met a blowsy, motherly Central European refugee who ran a beach café and turned out to be a spy. When Ambler set out to write a novel in 1935, he focused his sights on a specific form of fiction. The advance on *The Dark Frontier* was thirty pounds from Hodder and Stoughton; Ambler's career as adventure-thriller-spy novelist was launched with its publication in 1936.

The rest of Eric Ambler's life is that which has attracted the most interest and yet oddly shrinks in proportion and known detail to his first twenty-five years. Like one of his "displaced person" protagonists (amnesiac and/or multiple persona), Ambler (according to the received opinions of his traditional critics) is the flash-in-the-pan, best-selling novelist who moved to Paris in 1937, wrote six blockbuster thriller novels, and then disappeared into the British army in 1940. In actuality, throughout the intervening years Ambler was a prolific writer of film scripts. Between 1946 (the year of his discharge from the British army) and 1958 (the year of his move to California), Ambler worked for the British film company, J. Arthur Rank's Cineguild. His screenplays include *The October Man* (1947), *The Passionate Friends* (1948), *Highly Dangerous* (1951), *The Magic Box* (1951), *The Card* (1952), *Rough Shoot* (1952), *Campbell's Kingdom* (1957), *The Cruel Sea* (1952), *The Purple Plain* (1954), *Lease of Life* (1954), *Windom's Way* (1957), *Nightrunners of Bengal* (1955), *Body Below* (1955), *Yangtse Incident* (1957), *A Night to Remember* (1958), *The Night-Comers* (1957), *The Guns of Navarone* (1961), *Blind Date* (1959), and *The Wreck of the Mary Deare* (1959).

In addition to the film work, between 1952 and 1957, Ambler covered notorious cases in the courts and current events (including the infamous disappearance of the spy Kim Philby) for the British print media. He traveled widely and slowly but certainly gravitated back to the domain of the adventure–spy–international intrigue thriller. On his return to novel writing, Ambler stated in *Here Lies:*

I had not written a book for ten years and in the army had lost the habit of a concentrated and solitary writing routine. The process of its recovery was slow. Besides, during those ten years the internal world which had so readily produced the early books had been extensively modified and had to be re-explored.

(p. 226)

Despite this modest disclaimer, Ambler during this period also not only wrote and published three novels that reintroduced him to the popular postwar reading audience—*Judgment on Deltchev* (1951), *The Schirmer Inheritance* (1953), and *State of Siege* (1956)—but also, under the pseudonym of Eliot Reed, collaborated with the Australian writer Charles Roda on the publication of five books in England and America. In the late fifties, as Ambler began moving away from film writing and production, he relocated to America and took up a brief period of enchantment with television. In 1958, Ambler divorced Louise Crombie, whom he had married in 1939, and married Joan Harrison. He stayed in America for approximately a decade, living in Bel Air (until a catastrophic brushfire destroyed his and his wife's home and belongings in 1961) and Los Angeles.

In 1961, after traveling again to Turkey, Greece, and the Middle East, Ambler began the manuscript for *The Light of Day.* The first three chapters were destroyed in the Bel Air brushfire; but Ambler rewrote the entire novel, which was published in 1962 and was successfully filmed in 1964 as *Topkapi.* Throughout the sixties, Ambler continued to write novel-length fiction and edited two anthologies of favorite detective and spy stories. His introduction to *To Catch a Spy* (1964) is a first-rate analysis of his and others' work in this rapidly developing genre of popular literature. About 1972, Eric Ambler was "rediscovered" by both the expanded popular reading audience and the critics of a genre that had become securely established in mass culture through the popularity of the character of James Bond. Ambler may be viewed as having written through three distinct phases: first, the celebrated prewar flurry of the sensationally popular and famous six novels; the second beginning

with *Judgment on Deltchev* followed by *The Schirmer Inheritance,* and rounded out with *State of Siege.* The critics have found the hallmarks of the immediate postwar period to be the diminution of his customary adventure and violence but with the intellectually attractive addition of the elements of refined character development, social and political verisimilitude, and a moral subtlety. Gone are the monodimensional ideologues from the collectivist thirties; in their place are ambivalent characters with the morally murky perspectives more closely akin to the quixotic purism of John Le Carré and Graham Greene or the black humorist vision of Anthony Burgess. To be sure, these are the trademarks of the genre in mature transition, and Ambler came out of "retirement," like the best of that heroic ilk, to push the peculiar genre to its limits. In this critical view, the third period of Ambler's work comprises his oeuvre from 1972 to about 1977, the time of his "rediscovery." This recrudescence of the Ambler formula is highlighted by the return of Charles Latimer (from his high-water mark, *Dimitrios*) in *The Intercom Conspiracy* (1969).

DARK CROSSINGS AND EARLY SUCCESS

THE origins of the spy novel in the Ambler formula owe several distinct notions and themes to the work of Carl Jung—a writer and thinker who attracted Ambler's attention from his youthful days of truancy. Ambler himself provides the essential clue in the epilogue to the first novel insofar as he reveals the historical and clinical background in the early work of Jung: "Such cases of dual personality do occur. C. G. Jung in his *Collected Papers on Analytical Psychology* describes the case of a young German girl who was subject to periods of amnesia, or loss of memory, during which she exhibited a completely different personality" (p. xvi). That volume of papers by Jung, published in 1917, is an extraordinary series of psychological investigations into the "pathology of so-called occult phenomena." Jung defines "rare states of consciousness" as mental twilight zones that include the conditions related to "narcolepsy, lethargy, *automatisme ambulatoire,* periodic amnesia, double consciousness, somnambulism, pathological dreamy states, pathological lying, etc." He proceeds to depict these conditions as being nearly indistinguishable from the so-called neuroses and says that they can be separated from each other only with great difficulty. In the same volume Jung then makes the curious comment about the landmark conditions known as the neuroses: "Recently the view has even been maintained that there is no clean-cut *frontier* [italics added] between epilepsy and hysteria" (pp. 1–2). Ambler, it seems, appropriated this metaphor of the dark regions of the mind for his amnesiac/dual personality hero of *The Dark Frontier*, Professor Henry Barstow. In the first section of the novel titled "The Man Who Changes His Mind," Ambler renders the musings of Barstow, as a prelude to events on the morning of his amnesia attack, in the very language of the Jungian idealized self conflicted by strange and dark fantasies:

His day-dreaming had always been of statesmanship behind the scenes with himself as the presiding genius, of secret treaties and *rapprochements,* of curtain intrigue conducted to the strains of Mozart, Gluck and Strauss, with Talleyrand and Metternich hovering in the background. Queer, too, how dreams of that sort stayed with you. One half of your brain became an inspired reasoning machine, while the other wandered over dark frontiers into strange countries where adventure, romance and sudden death lay in wait for the traveller.

(pp. 1–2)

The dark frontiers of Ambler's successors—Le Carré and Len Deighton—have always been the dangerous back alleys of love and betrayal in East Berlin (and central London); ironically, Ambler had first trudged through a similar landscape ridged by the deep recesses of the modern psyche, in the wake of the early clinicians, preceded only by Joseph Conrad.

The years immediately preceding the incursion of Ambler into the field of the literary thriller witnessed the publication of a flurry of books and pamphlets in London on the subjects of amnesia, dual personality, and parapsychology. The impetus for this sudden and massive public interest in Western Europe in these subjects was the intellectual residue of World War I. Not only did the cases of shell shock and battle fatigue attract the informed medical interests of the burgeoning school of clinicians (in the line of succession of Jean-Martin Charcot, Sigmund Freud, and Jung), but the displacement of populations effected by the war also brought an influx of Middle Eastern and Eastern European religious and philosophical teachings to the West. One notable emigrant who influenced Ambler was the Armenian-born mystic, Georges Ivanovitch Gurdjieff. In 1925 the Parisian habitués, European (mostly British) intellectuals and artists who frequented the Grand Hotel de la Paix, were in attendance on Gurdjieff, who for years afterward engaged the attention of an international group of aficionados of Eastern mysticism. In London, shrill condemnation of Gurdjieff was issued by literati D. H. Lawrence and Wyndham Lewis in the 1920s; however, the response on the part of the London intelligentsia hardly impeded his widely received books in the early thirties.

THE DARK FRONTIER

The Dark Frontier begins with a prefatory "Statement of Professor H. J. Barstow, F.R.S., Physicist, of Imperial College, University of London." This section is rendered in the language of a legal deposition, but the point of view is markedly reminiscent of the monograph *I Lost My Memory, The Case As the Patient Saw It,* circulated in London in 1932. Like the anonymous narrator of the earlier document, Professor Barstow gives indisputable evidence, collected by the police and medical authorities, that indicates a period of time in his life of which he has no recollection. For Barstow, five weeks in late spring of the previous year are a complete blank. Also like the amnesiac patient of the earlier memoir, Barstow writes movingly of the strange sensation of reading about oneself as a distant character in an unknown text. In Barstow's case, the narrative is further enhanced with foreign travel and international intrigue.

At the start of his adventure Barstow, for all of his brilliance as a scientist, is nevertheless innocent of, and unaware of, the complex depths of both frontiers that he is about to cross. Barstow is the Newtonian man, *capax rationis,* who personifies the eighteenth-century vision of the orderliness of Nature; he is about to be thrust into the twentieth-century nightmare of total loss of control over the natural world and become subject to its latent disorder and destructiveness. Ambler deftly constructs the juxtaposition of seventeenth-century Newtonian fixity with the twentieth-century relativity of Einstein. The Newtonian Barstow is unprepared for the dark terrains of Einsteinian relativity and Jungian irrationality:

Professor Barstow did everything methodically, whether it was applying the laws of electrodynamics to a case of electronic aberration or combing his Blue Persian cat. His very appearance spelt order. His lectures before the Royal Society were noted and respected for their dispassionate reviews of fact and their cautious admissions of theory.... The truth of the matter is, perhaps, that he distrusted his imagination because it told him things he did not wish to believe.

(pp. 7–8)

After an automobile accident in which he suffers a head injury, and vacillating between his two identities as academic scientist and secret agent, Barstow/Carruthers discovers that the tiny Balkan country of Ixania (Ambler's fictional name for Albania or Bulgaria) has developed the world's first atomic bomb. A vindictive scientific genius in the employ of the impulsive nation has successfully exploded the prototype of the nuclear device, and an unscrupulous arms manufacturer is ready to duplicate and sell the bomb. Barstow realizes that only he has the technological sophistication to destroy the bomb before it falls into the wrong hands. He leaves straightaway for Ixania and for two weeks leads the double life of an *agent provocateur* in the twilight zone of the unconscious mind and apocalyptic science. By the end of the novel, Ambler has shown the transformation of this man, who no longer trusts any orderly accounting of events and has only theories and speculation on which to base a quest for the reality of his own identity and actions.

The transformation of Barstow's innocence provides further insight into a claim that Ambler has made about the nature of his first novel since the time of its publication. Ambler has steadfastly avowed that *The Dark Frontier* was a parody. The critics have always assumed that the parody was aimed at the old Edwardian secret service pulp fare; it was, but Ambler achieved more. In his introduction to the paperback edition, Ambler furnishes a more relevant statement to the real target of his obloquy—Britain's prime minister Stanley Baldwin and his smug Edwardian innocence. In *The Dark Frontier*, while Baldwin and Britain sleep, Barstow awakes from the numbing consciousness of innocence to a call to action from the collective unconscious. Barstow's awakening reflects the un-

mistakable influence of Jungian sources on Ambler's writing. On the moonlit night when Barstow wrecks his car and wakes to his amnesiac and heroic five weeks as a secret agent, his first and sudden realization is that he must save the world from nuclear proliferation. "Suddenly he spoke. He seemed to be repeating a lesson learnt by heart [he had a little earlier been reading a spy thriller]. 'And so,' he said slowly, 'we are to save civilization. . . . I leave for Zovgorod tonight' " (p. 34).

Ambler thus found his way via Jung to Arthur Schopenhauer and Friedrich Nietzsche (philosophers who wrote about the existentialist alienation and isolation of human beings), as he combined the elements of amnesia and the dark frontier of the collective unconscious and transformed them into the inflated, but beneficent will to power of the agent Carruthers. But what would happen, as Jung asks, if the will to power should prove pathological? Ambler provides the other half of the diptych in the person of the scientist Jacob Kassen of Ixania. In the spiritually deformed figure of Professor Kassen, Ambler delivers the hellish half of the collective unconscious—the demonic will to power that might lead to the dissolution of both inner and outer worlds, including society.

Simon Groom, the unsavory arms merchant from Cator and Bliss, is the purveyor of the Nietzschean philosophical connection. Groom is the satin-smooth voice of seduction; he approaches Barstow with the rationalist and positivist justification for war. As the first exponent of Nietzschean principles in the Ambler canon, Groom articulates the consummate value of the will to power in a new world order (or disorder) and the universal basis of that value within the collective unconscious. The force of modernism is contained in Groom's character—whether in terms of biology or psychology, the lessons of Darwin, Freud, and Jung corroborate the valorization of power (and the will to power) as enunciated by Nietzsche in the latter half of the nineteenth century. The conquest of nature is the key to power in the future; whether Kassen is the sport of evolution or the product of the psyche, he is the superman who represents all of modern knowledge about nature and human nature. In *The Dark Frontier*, Groom, the first of Ambler's apocalyptic soothsayers, appears as the mythical Prometheus of many guises—the modern agent of chaos and destruction, all in the name of progress and positivism. Groom delivers the modernist message that the disarray of the old order must be reshuffled according to new laws and principles (the Promethean fire of the atom is suggested by Groom). Barstow the physicist unwittingly becomes the prime witness to the unlevering (or exploding) of the mechanical world order of Newton by the atomic power of Einsteinian and Nietzschean relativism. In addition, Barstow accompanies Jung to the outposts of psychology and consciousness; the sum effect of this experience is the harrowing glimpse into disorder and the dark periphery of the twentieth century.

The case of Ixania, the fictitious country that attempts to develop an atomic bomb in 1935, is also a thinly veiled parody of the powder keg that was the Balkan states in the thirties. The turbulent events in Bulgaria between the world wars are mirrored in the factional strife of Ixania. If the verisimilitude, along with its concomitant parody, was lost on the first generation of critics, the book found an eager reading audience and one very important ally in America. In 1936, as Ambler was rewriting the last chapters of his second novel, *Background to Danger,* his agent at Curtis Brown informed him that Alfred A. Knopf, the famous American publisher, was in London and wanted to meet with him. Knopf had read *The Dark Frontier* and was interested in publishing Ambler's forthcoming novels in the United States. The relationship between Knopf and Ambler remained friendly through the years, and Ambler was secured an international audience from that time forward.

BACKGROUND TO DANGER

IN *The Spy Story,* John Cawelti and Bruce Rosenberg cite an elaborate set of parallel devices and events in *Background to Danger* (1937) and John Buchan's *Thirty-Nine Steps.* While one might agree substantially with their assertion that Ambler's second novel owes much to Buchan's book, one must ultimately recognize and accept their concession that "none of this accumulation of similarities" proves that Ambler based his novel on Buchan's work (p. 105). In fact, Ambler developed in this novel a pattern with roots in his own first novel, namely, the use of a journalist (who becomes the protagonist this time) and an uncanny forecasting of geopolitical events (this time it is about oil, long before Middle Eastern cartels and Arab embargoes). Cawelti and Rosenberg are on target when they cite Ambler's perpetuation of an original theme: the condemnation of war as big business and the product of international greed and capitalism. Ambler's schooling in socialism, by his own avowal, had only been from the party speaker in Hyde Park on Sundays and his studied reading of George Gissing, a late-nineteenth-century British writer of proletarian novels, and his *New Grub Street. Background to Danger* begins not in the back streets of some Balkan labyrinth but in the central business district of London, where a very important meeting of the Pan-Eurasian Petroleum Company's board of directors is convening. Ambler is still very much the astute student of engineering and science as he invades the corporate boardroom with the dirty business of espionage and bribery. The "background to this danger" is the engineer's knowledge of the supply and technological disposition of raw materials. The novel is prefaced by a brief but essential excerpt from the World Petroleum Institute. As an engineering apprentice in Britain's mining industry, Ambler had learned of the crucial relationship between raw materials and national security.

Ambler was the first popular writer to decry capitalism, or any other ostensible ideology, in his progressive movement toward his classic ironic vision, heralded in this first articulation of the spy's enterprise as "dirty work." This dirty work is the coin of big business, and the two sides of that currency involve the distinctions between appearances and realities: international business and industrial espionage. Ambler's invective against international capitalism is not as significant in the light thrown on the hypocrisy of the so-called legitimate workings of business and geopolitics as it is in the more subtle and dim beam of attention that he casts on the other end of such dealings. His instincts are to seek out dingy barrooms and smoke-filled offices near the waterfront or the *souk;* his deep intuitions are to investigate the "psycho-neuroses and violence" in the dead-end alleys of some grimy Balkan maze or Middle Eastern hill town. Ambler's hazardous foray into the low end of big business dealings is microcosmic in its stumbling into the dark netherworlds of the murky moral landscape of the individual who actually does the dirty work. Throughout his career, Ambler has been fascinated by the titanic events wrought by the hapless isolate or the vindictive psychopath—but the result is the same, history can be, and is, changed frequently by the minuscule or the accidental.

This central theme of political disaffection, rooted in Gissing's undercurrent skepticism, was enormously attractive to Ambler. His own ambivalence about science and learning, sustained by his lifelong opposition to elitism in all forms, most likely found an early sponsor and model in Gissing and his proletarian sympathies. Despite Ambler's relentless assault on international capitalism in *Background to Danger,* he never fully became affiliated with the Socialist Party because of his loathing of its "academic" language and atmosphere of privilege. The literary sources of his so-called "left-wing politics" exerted much more influence than any formal party association.

EPITAPH FOR A SPY

THE third of Ambler's novels opens with Josef Vadassy's arrival at the French Riviera resort Hôtel de la Réserve in St. Gatien. Vadassy is a teacher of languages at the end of his summer vacation, and he is due back in Paris in a few days. Vadassy is also a man without a country; his personal history as a Hungarian working in Paris without valid papers is a reflection of the Eastern European turmoil in the years between the wars. To read Ambler in the 1990s is to remember the violent and perpetually shifting hegemonies of the Balkans before the relative calm of the nearly fifty-year *pax Russiana* after World War II. To observe the atrocities of the former Yugoslavia in the 1990s is to appreciate Ambler's lessons of the immediacy and proximity of danger and violence.

As Ambler has noted in *Here Lies, Epitaph for a Spy* was not picked up for American publication by Knopf in 1938. When the novel was finally published by Knopf in 1952, Ambler wrote a footnote in which he makes this famous statement: "In most human beings ideas of spying and being spied upon touch the fantasy system at deep and sensitive levels of the mind" (p. 200). Even some thirteen years after the writing of the novel, Ambler's use of Jungian notions and language shows his most abiding response to a prewar narrative of a "civilization hastening to destruction." Both individuals and whole societies were struggling to save themselves from "the primeval ooze that welled from its own subconscious being." Ambler's wrong-man protagonists are the unwitting witnesses—the spies—who maintain the reserve of rational consciousness against the onslaught of the unconscious elements. The Hôtel de la Réserve is one of the last Victorian houses of crime and detection, but the lizards and the shadowy world of ambiguity and design suggest the level of the overwhelming danger of that invasive "primeval ooze"—the violence of the reptilian and the spasmodic threatens the reserve of reason with extinction.

CAUSE FOR ALARM

ERIC Ambler's fourth novel also heralds the imminent conflagration of world war and is his most explicit in naming the Axis powers—Germany and Italy—as the insidious incendiaries. Into this dangerous liaison steps the British engineer, Nicholas Marlow, who inadvertently becomes the object of recruitment by both sides. Of Marlow's predicament, Gavin Lambert has stated: "Like all of Ambler's best work this novel is about a rite of passage" (p. 109). Marlow's passage includes two dark crossings: the first is the initiation into the moral questions of conducting big business at the international level (the first half of the novel); the second is the arduous night journey across the mountains into Yugoslavia (the second half). In both passages Marlow loses an innocence that seems irretrievable when he returns home to an England somnolently reposing in an economic depression and a "phony war."

Like Barstow the physicist, Marlow finds that his scientific training in the observable physical data of the universe's appearances gives him precious little preparation for the discovery of the hidden realities of human nature. In this regard, Ambler provides the reader once again with a Jungian clue early in the novel. The hint is also supplied to Marlow by the crafty General Johann Vagas, but the foreshadowing in the language of analytical psychology is lost on the trained engineer. Vagas, who first comes to visit Marlow wearing makeup with a touch of the grotesque, instructs Marlow in the area of appearances versus reality:

It is, I think, impossible to know any man. His thoughts, his own secret emotions, the way his mind works upon the things he sees—those things are the man. All that the outsider sees is the shell, the mask—you understand? Only some-times do we see a man and then . . . it is through the eyes of an artist.

(p. 34)

In the final analysis, *Cause for Alarm* (1938) posits the central ideological opposition of the historical period in the juxtaposition of General Vagas (the Nietzschean and, by extension, the Nazi) and Russian General Zaleshoff (the Communist). Vagas' unswerving allegiance is to Germany, and his most articulate beliefs are intellectually indebted to Nietzsche's *The Birth of Tragedy*. When Vagas invites Marlow out to an evening at the ballet at Milan's La Scala, he delivers one of the novel's finest and most frightening speeches:

The ballet interests me enormously. It is, I believe, the final expression of a disintegrating society. The idea of the dance, you know, and the preparation for death have been inseparable since the human animal first crept through the primaeval forest. Ballet is merely a new rationalisation of society's instinctive movement towards self-destruction. A dance of death for the Gadarene swine. It has always been so. . . . If I never read a newspaper, Mr. Marlow, one evening at the ballet would tell me that once again society is preparing for death.

(p. 75)

This Dionysiac message of the necessary destruction of the Apollonian world of beautiful appearances by the strenuous and violent forces of inevitable annihilation comes with a trenchant clarity from Nietzsche—reformulated here without a trace of sarcasm in the balconies of the Hellenic La Scala.

A COFFIN FOR DIMITRIOS

A Coffin for Dimitrios (1939) was a pivotal novel for both Ambler and the genre of the popular thriller. From the chrysalis of the Victorian crime novel emerges, by virtue of its own immanent and transcendent strengths, the novel of espionage and international intrigue. The subjects are crime and the main character's "experiment in detection." But in the very act of applying the techniques of deductive reasoning and the science of investigation, the putative detective discovers the limits of the process. The methodical investigator reaches the outer boundaries of his art and science, and in this swift discovery of the defeat of detection lies the even more menacing delimitation of reason itself. One of Ambler's great achievements in *Dimitrios* is the adumbration of the presence of new forces and powers that stump and mystify the traditional human intellect and its rational faculties. He has chronicled the end of that Victorian and Edwardian social construction found in the detective novel of manners. By the end of *Dimitrios,* even the providentially survived detective/writer longs for that evanescent world; he dreams of a return to the ideal crime scene—an English country village where there are garden parties at the vicarage and the obligatory clink of teacups. It is a place that he knows no longer exists. A salient feature of *Dimitrios* is the narrative style and technique—it is a multivalent and multifaceted series of third-party narratives. This structure looks ahead to the narrative techniques of Le Carré, who constructs a legendary and secret world about the spies who investigate spies. Le Carré and certainly Ambler have blazed the trail, have created a kind of spy novel in which the ultimate spy is the reader—the assemblage of information and narrative available to the reader alone must give the final meanings to the tale.

A Coffin for Dimitrios precipitates a powerful crescendo of suspense when Charles Latimer, an English professor of political economy and well-known author of detective stories, becomes engrossed in the search for the true identity of one "Dimitrios." Latimer learns of the existence of Dimitrios by chance. At a party in Istanbul, Latimer is introduced to Colonel Haki. Unknown to Latimer, Colonel Haki is the head of the Turkish secret police—a soldier of fortune turned intelligence chief. Haki's intentions are benign, for he has admired Latimer's detective stories and proposes to give him a plot gratis. So far the shadow of W. Somerset Maugham's sinister Colonel R and the reluctant enlistment of the British agent Ashenden hangs heavy in the air. In 1927, the spy genre reached another important milestone when W. Somerset Maugham decided to fictionalize, in print, his memories of his World War I service as an agent of the British Intelligence Department. In *Ashenden, or, The British Agent*, Maugham unwittingly shaped the main formulaic pattern of the genuine tale of espionage and thus directed the course the genre was to take for the next sixty-five years.

Maugham's profound influence lies precisely in the formula he created in *Ashenden*, which was followed closely by Eric Ambler and Graham Greene through the 1940s. But the world of Ambler is replete with chance and the dispassionate timing of the blind gods. Colonel Haki's intentions really are innocent, but while he and Latimer are discussing academic murder in mystery novels, Haki is informed of the discovery of the corpse of Dimitrios the Greek. It is this chance discovery, revealed at a time when Latimer happens to be in Colonel Haki's office, that sends Latimer on an odyssey across Europe toward a confrontation with death.

The opposition of art and reality is sustained throughout the novel, and Latimer's close brush with death is born from his momentary movement from the aseptic and tidy ideology of academic murder in fiction to the unruly, chaotic real world of smoky bistros where actual murder and assassination are plotted. In short, Latimer progresses from observer to participant and finds that the neat ground rules in the detective's process of deduction are ineffectual in the face of brutal reality.

A philosophy of history is always as important in Ambler's novels as the social context in which the novel is written—one complements the other. *A Coffin for Dimitrios* was written on the eve of World War II. Ambler's particular philosophy of history reflects his readings of Nietzsche and Oswald Spengler, along with the opinion that Europe (and Western civilization) had reached a stage of decadence in necessitating, ineluctably, self-destruction. The articulation of this philosophy of history is usually reserved for Ambler's villains, although a residual ambiguity always seems to infect the surviving protagonists insofar as they are left to ponder the nature of civilization and its shadowy discontents. One of the minor ironies of this novel consists in the fact that Latimer, aside from writing detective fiction, is a lecturer in political economy at a minor English university (the quintessential nexus of vicarage and garden); yet when he moves from his secure sphere of observation to take up the role of participant in actual melodrama, he learns a lesson in both politics and economics. Or, more precisely, he learns that it is in the realms of politics and economics where Good and Evil meet:

Dimitrios was not evil. He was logical and consistent; as logical and consistent in the European jungle as the poi-

son gas called Lewisite and the shattered bodies of children killed in the bombardment of an open town. The logic of Michael Angelo's *David,* Beethoven's quartets and Einstein's physics had been replaced by that of the *Stock Exchange Year Book* and Hitler's *Mein Kampf.*

(pp. 174–175)

In the course of the nineteenth century, new scientific and positivistic systems offered more appealing and more practical explanations for the haphazard facts of the universe. Meanwhile, in popular polemic, theories of evolution and psychotherapy routed the belief that God's intervention and order were the mainsprings of history. Ambler's judgment on Europe in 1939 is quite unmistakable.

After an international pursuit, Latimer comes face to face with the real Dimitrios and the threat of death. And Latimer also returns to his original point of departure: the art of detective fiction. The conclusion of the novel neatly implies that the antinomy between art and reality might never be resolved. In the outer world of experience, Latimer sees brutality and selfishness produce assassination, poison gas, and bombardment—all under the sacrosanct aegis of nationalism and capitalism. Politics and economics—the new theologies—reign supreme, and Dimitrios the Greek is in his own logical way the incarnate paradigm of the age. Latimer therefore returns to the inner world of art, in particular, detective fiction. The detective story is but an extension of Michelangelo's *David* and Beethoven's quartets—it is the construct emanating from a new harmony of the sphere. It is a world of limited systems, made up of deductively ordered arrays of facts. The novel of detection is an enclosed world congenial to the refugee from the environment of armed hostility and imminent cosmic chaos.

Latimer's academic pursuits become a deadly real-life drama of the pursuer becoming the pursued. He discovers random violence. The act of detection is transformed from the Newtonian and Holmesian world of physics into the Jungian sphere of psychology. Thus Latimer explains away the biological mask of Dimitrios as the "features of bone structure and tissue," which are something quite different from the psychological mask—that "statement of his habitual emotional attitude" (p. 188). The Jungian mask is the conduit for Latimer's experiment in detection. And, in his essay on "Anima and Animus," Jung states, "To the degree that the world invites the individual to identify with the mask, he is delivered over to influences from within" (p. 205). This is the invisible system of relations to the unconscious. The collective unconscious is the dark underworld to which Latimer's experiment leads; like visitors to the mythical underworld of ancient epic, he finds a hellish vision of the past, present, and future. This glimpse of Dimitrios as the "other self" is the epiphany of Latimer's "experiment in detection." Much like the classic conundrum of the oedipal search for the patricidal killer, the detective who collides with the unconscious and the instinctive must himself become the quarry. Jung labels this collision as the "identification with the shadow," and herein lies the origins of the obsession with the shadow of Dimitrios that Latimer bumps into, quite by accident. Latimer is greeted by the shade (or shadow) of Dimitrios in the Istanbul "house of death." Latimer's recoil at the end of the novel represents his profound shock at the moment of recognition in that silent greeting: it is the greeting between old and kindred spirits.

But, at the moment of recoil at the end of the novel, Latimer has more important things to think about—he has that novel that must be finished:

He needed, and badly, a motive, a neat method of committing a murder and an entertaining crew of suspects. Yes, the suspects must certainly be entertaining. His last book had been a trifle heavy. He must inject a little more humour into this one. As for the motive, money was always, of course, the soundest basis. A pity that Wills and life insurance were so outmoded. Supposing a man murdered an old lady so that his wife should have a private income. It might be worth thinking about. The scene? Well, there was always plenty of fun to be got out of an English country village, wasn't there? The time? Summer; with cricket matches on the village green, garden parties at the vicarage, the clink of tea-cups and the sweet smell of grass on a July evening. That was the sort of thing people liked to hear about. It was the sort of thing that he himself would like to hear about.

(p. 214)

Latimer retreats completely to the inner cosmos of order, sweetness, and light. But as he peers from the train window, the train runs into a tunnel. The writer's retreat is an escape of ambiguous efficacy. Which is the twentieth-century man, the child of history, Dimitrios or Latimer?

JOURNEY INTO FEAR

IF Ambler's solution to the dilemma of whether the man of thought or the man of action shapes the progression of history is too obliquely stated in *A Coffin for Dimitrios*, the next novel, *Journey into Fear* (1940), makes that answer more explicit. Perhaps Ambler's most critically underrated novel, it focuses on the Jungian "blond beast" of Nazi Germany and makes full use of the Spenglerian philosophy of history—the idea of the decline of the West, which is to say, the belief that the golden age of European civilization was exhausted. In some ways, this last of the six prewar novels is a sequel to *A Coffin for Dimitrios*; it is the chaotic and lawless arena of conflict bequeathed by the eternal return of Dionysus as Dimitrios.

The plot of *Journey into Fear* develops when a British ballistics engineer is dispatched to Turkey to provide the technical data to convert British armaments for Turkish naval vessels. On the night before he is to return to England, a lone gunman attempts to murder him in his Istanbul hotel. It is late 1940, and Allied forces *must* arm the Turkish vessels before the imminent German spring offensive. Colonel Haki enters the scene, and convinces Graham, the engineer, that the safest route back to England is on an Italian steamer—and not on the Orient Express (shades of Graham Greene). What follows is the "journey into fear." The Englishman Graham is a devotee of detective stories and one of the top ballistics engineers in the world, but the lessons he learns from his journey into fear come from the pages of Darwin, Jung, James Frazer, and Spengler. Like his predecessor Latimer, Graham comes to find that the deductive processes of the detective and the mathematician are based on systems of harmony and order, nowhere to be found in the grim, grimy game of international espionage and the instinctive drive of self-preservation.

As in his previous novels, the thematic core of the work resides in the philosophy of history. In *Journey into Fear*, the thread of the novel and its philosophy of history are a hybrid form of the social and cultural Darwinism of Frazer and Spengler, ironically expounded by the chief German agent, who is disguised as a German archaeologist. Writing during the "phony war" of late 1939 and early 1940, Ambler seems to indicate that it is the German nation that has learned the principal Nietzschean lesson of history: might makes right, especially in a transitional epoch. The very same portal to destruction that Graham entered is the one that now awaits Europe, and indeed all Western countries, apparently on a collision course with doom. Once again, the background is Europe headed for self-destruction, and history is the cosmic working out of the death and resurrection ritual. Because of her power and will to exercise that power, Ambler warns, through the pronunciations of the German agent, that Germany may be the new phoenix rising from the ashes of Europe's destruction. The German "archaeologist" Haller preaches to the Englishman on the subject of historical destiny. His first little lecture derives from Frazer's *Golden Bough* and comparative science—the logic of the growth of Western civilization and religions warns of the twilight of the European gods.

Journey into Fear is a fictional analogue of the historiography of Spengler. If the stentorian tones of Spengler are somewhat muted in the evolution of Western religions in Haller's first speech, the influence of the Spenglerian method is irrefutable. Haller unabashedly echoes Spengler's grand design when he says, "I helped in the search for a logic of history" (p. 75). Spengler himself asks in his introduction to *The Decline of the West* (1918): "Is there a logic of history? Is it possible to find in life itself . . . a series of stages which must be traversed . . . in an ordered and obligatory sequence? For everything organic the notions of birth, death, youth, age, lifetime, are fundamentals. . . . In short, is all history founded upon general biographic archetypes?" (p. 3).

Like his prototype and fellow physicist Barstow, Graham is Ambler's portrait of the modern and reasonable person who discovers the frightening but inevitable by bumping into the Jungian shadow of the unconscious. The shadow intrudes suddenly in the form of Petre Banat. Banat is the German agent who bungles the assassination of Graham in the early pages of the novel. But it is the shadow of Banat who will figure significantly in Ambler's deep design for this novel's ideological undercarriage. And it is precisely in these terms that Ambler describes the homicidal agent, for Banat, like Dimitrios, is the Dionysiac emissary from the dark unconscious. Together, Banat and Haller present to Graham a startling and harrowing glimpse of the modern mind and its ineluctable course in Nazi Germany. The latter, a political and ideological monstrosity, concretized the cleft between man's conscious and instinctual natures. In the modern world the inevitable lag of psychic evolution could not keep abreast of intellectual and scientific developments; the unconscious is left behind and because of instinct seeks its self-preservation. With his visionary descriptions of atomic energy and of political power, Ambler mapped out the horrifying world of the late thirties.

A Coffin for Dimitrios and *Journey into Fear* represent Ambler's remarkably trenchant and prescient analysis of the events in Europe from 1935 to 1945. In many ways, the novels are the fictional cognates of Jung's essays covering the Weimar Republic and the rise of Hitler going back to 1918. From a more narrow perspective, Nazi Germany is the Jungian shadow that lurks at the edges of all six of Ambler's pre–World War II novels; it is the nexus of all of Ambler's studied readings of the interwoven threads of Nietzsche, Jung, and Spengler. Of these three major influences on Ambler, only Jung was alive at the outbreak of the war. Between 1936 and 1947, Jung wrote a number of essays that dealt with the German catastrophe and its implications for the study of the modern mind. Amazingly, much of Jung's formal analysis parallels Ambler's fictional representations in their ironically and psychologically sharp etchings of a world rushing to its own destruction.

For the perspicacious Ambler, the actual war and its experiences took a long time to filter into his postwar literary consciousness—ironically, Ambler never wrote a war novel. In the late forties and early fifties, when he finally returned to lengthy fiction, the old routine did not come back easily. The imaginary landscape to which Ambler returned is a close parallel of the nameless Balkan country of his novice novel and becomes the starting point of the second stage of his literary career.

JUDGMENT ON DELTCHEV

IN the aftermath of World War II, Ambler found the turmoil of conflicting ideologies spilling over into England from a Europe fractured by contesting political and economic forces. He decided to make his literary debut after the war in the form of a foray into this welter of ideologies. *Judgment on Deltchev* reveals the many-headed monster of totalitarianism, the awful survivor of the slaying of the "blond beast" of fascism. In a return to Ixania (actually the novel portrays a nameless Balkan state) in *Judgment on Deltchev,* Ambler retains the narrative device of a visiting journalist; he discovers that the technological terror is not a nuclear bomb but the instrument of modern propaganda. The visiting journalist is a well-known British playwright who is asked by an American newspaper publisher to cover a trial in the Balkan state. The Ixania revisited in *Judgment on Deltchev* retains Ambler's earlier spiritual landscape with the accretion of an Orwellian atmosphere of surveillance and oppressive technology.

Whereas Peter Lewis, in *Eric Ambler,* has made an excellent argument that Albania was Ambler's real-life model, an equally persuasive case could be made for Bulgaria. In either case, Lewis is absolutely correct in stating that the imaginary trial of Yordan Deltchev is representative of what happened in most Eastern European countries liberated by the Soviet army after the occupation of Nazi forces during the war. Premonitions of Le Carré are present in Ambler's depiction of historical background as the forces of the Cold War gather greedily in the midst of the wreckage of ideologies and ideals. The ideological jungle into which the British playwright-cum-journalist Foster steps is both dangerous and violent. After World War II, socialist regimes were hunting for and trying nationalists or Nazi sympathizers. Having been commissioned by the American press to cover one such trial, Foster is prepared for a travesty of justice and is preeminently qualified to portray the proceedings as part Stalinist ritual and part theater. And he is not disappointed. But he is not prepared for the complexity of the truth, especially when the nugget of truth masquerades as part of the falsehood of the political theater of propaganda.

Like his forerunner Latimer in *A Coffin for Dimitrios,* Foster finds that every path in this maze of Balkan intrigue leads necessarily to center stage. And the actors are never quite what they seem, even in simple matters such as innocence and guilt. In the ambiguous words of Petlarov, Deltchev's former legal clerk and secretary, when he too advises caution before judgment on the part of Foster: "The lie stands most securely on a pinpoint of truth" (p. 43). Foster begins to realize that he is getting dangerously close to stepping onto a stage of ambiguous shadows. Foster's mind wanders to a long quotation from Plato's *Crito,* in which the

integrity of Socrates humiliates the posturing judges of ancient Greece. Foster then recognizes the scale of political theater enacted before him: "This, I thought suddenly, was more than just the crooked trial of a politician by his more powerful opponents. Here, epitomized, was the eternal conflict between the dignity of mankind and the brutish stupidity of the swamp" (p. 55).

From this point onward in the novel, Ambler reaches his stride as a prose stylist. The twisted convolutions (it is a complex plot) of political intrigue are matched by Ambler's intricate and subtle sentence structures. Gone are the stereotypic cartoonish characters and the sometime wooden dialogue of the earliest novels; Ambler creates character through a denouement of each person's increasingly complex inner world. *Judgment on Deltchev* delivers a "judgment" for nearly every major character. These are essential plays on the title word "judgment," for Ambler extends the meaning of the term far beyond the legalistic definition within the courtroom. Ambler's highly developed manipulation of character and theme are interwoven within a leitmotif of appearance versus reality.

THE SCHIRMER INHERITANCE

PUBLISHED two years after *Judgment on Deltchev, The Schirmer Inheritance* continues to explore the aftermath of World War II and also contains an integral element of political and ideological intrigue in the Balkans. Like its predecessor, *The Schirmer Inheritance* takes up the convoluted theme of the collapse of idealism after the betrayal of collective aspirations by political leaders. Ambler, more than a decade before Le Carré, invents a character that anticipates the gentle spy-hunter Smiley, and creates a splendid and powerful drama of the last illusion held after all other beliefs and ideologies fail—the need for love and family. In his eighth novel, Ambler forged the alloys of political disillusionment and the Jungian process of individuation that became the central themes and forms of the genre for the next forty years. In Ambler's distinct footsteps come the variations on these themes in the work of Le Carré, Deighton, Burgess, and even Greene. The spies, or the clandestine agents of some cause, who desperately desire the "attainable felicities of wife and hearth," to borrow Herman Melville's phrase, in their coming in from the cold of ideology and betrayal, find the eloquent forerunner in this Ambler novel.

In *The Schirmer Inheritance*, a Philadelphia-based corporate lawyer, George Carey, is assigned an old case of intestacy and travels back through a Mediterranean odyssey that finds human motivations that overshadow self-preservation and greed. The fledgling attorney comes from a prominent Delaware family "that looked like an illustration for an advertisement of an expensive make of car" (p. 15). Carey graduates from Princeton just in time for World War II. After a stint as a bomber pilot in Europe, he attends Harvard Law School and graduates cum laude. Thus, when he joins the firm of Lavater, Powell, and Sistrom, one of the most important firms on the East Coast, he has justifiably high expectations of dealing with landmark cases and important public figures. When the news arrives on his desk that he is assigned to the Schneider Johnson case, it comes as a disagreeable disappointment. The case of an intestate fortune, with all of the makings of missing heirs coming out of the woodwork, dates to 1938, more than twelve years earlier. A three-million-dollar estate left by a soft-drink tycoon is at issue; Pennsylvania law decrees that any proven blood-relative could be entitled to a share in the estate. In 1939, even the Nazis in Germany were producing fake relatives (the search for bona fide relations had led to Germany in 1938). By 1950, the Commonwealth of Pennsylvania wants to know whether any living heir can be found. George Carey inherits the case with eight thousand claimants—a legacy of complex and daunting dimensions.

Carey is dispatched to Germany by the senior partners to pick up the trail abandoned there at the outbreak of World War II. After hiring an interpreter, Maria Kolin, in Paris, he follows the trail of the Schneider/Schirmer family with the help of the old prewar parish vicar assigned to a hospital in Stuttgart. Father Weichs narrates a riveting tale that in turn leads to other informants and their narratives. This referential system of third-party narratives hearkens back to Dimitrios and Deltchev, a technique that might properly be called the "absentee protagonist." Le Carré came to imitate this invention in his novels of intrigue and detection. This technique usually culminates in a crescendo with the absent party's powerful entrance into the

novel—the device contributes to both the matter and form of suspense.

After Father Weichs comes the petulant Frau Gresser. The belligerent Frau contributes the final and vital missing piece of information—she had personally known the last scion of the Schneider family, a sergeant in the German Nazi *Fallschirmjäger* (paratrooper) corps during World War II. The name of the missing paratrooper is Sergeant Franz Schirmer. One hundred and forty years after his great-great-great-grandfather had disappeared in Poland, Sergeant Franz Schirmer was presumed dead, and missing in action in Macedonia during the Nazi retreat from Greece. His death—that of the last heir of the Schirmer inheritance—was never confirmed by the German or Greek authorities.

The trail of the Nazi paratrooper leads from Stuttgart to Bonn, where the German army records are held. From Bonn, Carey and Miss Kolin travel to Cologne and Geneva. After nearly two weeks of investigation, they ascertain that Sergeant Schirmer had been born in 1917 and joined the Hitler *Jugend* at age eighteen. From the Hitler Youth movement, Franz Schirmer had entered the army and moved from the combat engineers to the airborne training unit, the *Fallschirmjäger*. In Italy, in 1943, while working as a parachutist instructor, he had fractured a hip. After months of unsuccessful rehabilitation and physical therapy, the young sergeant was declared unfit for combat duty. He was then posted to the occupation forces in Greece, in the Salonika area. While leading a convoy of German supply trucks, Sergeant Schirmer's lead vehicle was mined and ambushed by a militant band of Macedonian nationalist guerrillas. The ambush killed nearly all, and the sergeant went missing and was believed killed. The Macedonian freedom fighters, related to the Internal Macedonian Revolutionary Organization (IMRO) of *Judgment on Deltchev*, were not in a position to shelter and feed prisoners for very long. Schirmer's death was considered a foregone conclusion by the German army.

The senior partners in Philadelphia send Carey into Greece, where he picks up the trail in Salonika. Colonel Chrysantos (a latter-day version of Haki) is the Greek senior intelligence officer in the Salonika area. The Colonel arranges for Carey to interview a former guerrilla leader, Phenganos, now imprisoned in Salonika. The prisoner refuses Carey's cigarettes and then delivers a short sermon meant to ease Carey's conscience. Carey will remember later the example of this wretched prisoner who refuses to concede one iota. Mysteriously, Phengaros seems to communicate encouragement to Carey, although he can say nothing because of the code of silence and honor that he follows.

A final search of the hill towns near the scene of the ambush in 1944 leads nowhere for Carey; he is on the brink of quitting when he opens the door to his hotel room, only to find a gunman with a British accent. The gunman, a British soldier of fortune, asks whether Carey wishes to meet the former Nazi paratrooper. The last seventy-five pages of the novel introduce Carey and Miss Kolin to the subterranean world of freedom fighters who have sloughed off the fatuous husk of causes and ideals. Carey, like Latimer, learns of the life after death of political naïveté. Sergeant Schirmer is the leader of a former revolutionary band of Greek and Macedonian *andartes* (guerrilla freedom fighters) who have learned that robbing banks yields a better subsistence than the violent overthrow of a repressive government that merely springs back up under the leadership of the former revolutionaries. Schirmer is the Dionysian trickster living an idyll of the returned hero in the hills and groves of arcadian Greece and Macedonia. In his present happy circumstances, the sergeant has to think about a return to the land of the living, even if the inheritance is ostensibly lucrative.

The Schirmer Inheritance is a bildungsroman in terms of Carey and Schirmer. For each the tortuous trail of the Schirmer family legacy leads to self-knowledge and an understanding of the deep connections to the past. Just as Carey is found by the ex-Nazi paratrooper, in a typical Ambler reversal of the story of hunter and hunted, something of Carey's own family history and inheritance is also illuminated. Carey's pursuit of the Schirmer inheritance and the concomitant quest for self knowledge are symmetrically arranged by Ambler's adroit manipulation of his favorite Jungian themes: the descent to the underworld in the company of one's own shadow and the return of the Dionysian trickster. The real legacy of the Schirmer inheritance is the genius for survival—in the land of the dead Carey discovers the legacy of the gift of life. In the bowels of this underworld no demonic figure reigns—Carey finds the modern incarnation of the trickster.

What is the nature of the transformation and self-knowledge induced by the pursuit of the Schirmer inheritance? As Le Carré later succeeds in showing in similar novels, the answer is always fairly simple. After the convolutions of political ideology and dangerous intrigue, the therapeutic and restorative element is usually found in a simple (but complex) human emotion. Sometimes it is love, sometimes revenge. But for both George Carey and Franz Schirmer it is the lesson of consanguinity—the value of the blood and its relations that bind the individual to a family both immanent and transcendent. The connection of the blood to the past is the Schirmer inheritance. At the novel's resolution, when confronted with the fact that he is the sole heir to a fortune in America, Schirmer surprisingly tells Carey that he needs time to think about it—he asks for twenty-four hours. He tells Carey and Kolin to return to his mountain hideout on the next night and impresses upon Carey the importance of bringing the family papers and photographs—the contents of the deed box. Schirmer has already, as events unfold, made his decision.

The plans for the following evening are wrecked when Miss Kolin is caught by Schirmer's men in an abortive attempt to bring in the Greek authorities. Part of her miscalculation lies in the fact that the hideout is in Yugoslav territory, across the invisible frontier. Schirmer and his merry crew of fellow tricksters dwell in untouchable Macedonia, beyond the reach of the princes who had betrayed them after the revolution. Renegade soldier of misfortune Schirmer runs from his outlaw life to family responsibilities; George Carey runs in the opposite direction; he is the dutiful son and lawyer who can laugh at the absurdities of financial legacies and legal justice. Having penetrated the underworld, he can only laugh at the joke of existence and its implicit absurdities.

The Jungian trickster and the sacred clown—Schirmer and his sidekick, the funny, but lethal Arthur—are the residents of the last circle in Hell. In his illuminating essay "The Trickster and the Sacred Clown, Revealing the Logic of the Unspeakable," Thomas Belmonte has described the Jungian processes of individuation and *enantiodromia* ("running backward to opposites") through the encounter with the negations of death and the trickster:

The Greek trickster, Hermes, was the patron of herdsmen, thieves, graves and heralds. He was the god of boundaries and of those engaged in the risky business of crossing them. Like Charlie Chaplin's tramp, perpetually hopping from the wrong to the right side of the tracks (until claimed by infinity), the trickster-clown gives us a fleeting glimpse of the process of creation as order and chaos in alternation. In the clown's laboratory of far-from-equilibrium states, structure is renewable only if it is able to make contact with its negative.

(p. 52)

The Apollonian Carey confronts his Dionysian shadow in the shapes of the trickster and clown far up in the hills of mythical Macedonia. Carey encounters a supposedly nonexistent band of Bible-quoting, bank-robbing pranksters in a land that equally does not exist. In this fantastic setting, Carey and Schirmer exchange their positions; they run to opposites in radial transformation in several sets of opposites, to include freedom versus structure, orphanhood versus family belonging, communal versus individual identity. The resultant tableau is one of harmony and equilibrium. By gaining his freedom, Carey has the last laugh of the novel, and he shares it with all the other freedom fighters in the Schirmer inheritance. Only princes and other fools indulge in the fatuous fantasy of exterminating the Other. The gift of laughter is the Schirmer inheritance.

FACING EAST

THE long encounter with the East—both Near and Far—is the taproot that gives depth and sustenance to the next brace of books by Ambler. Ironically, as Ambler was preparing to move to California (the ultimate Golden West) in the late fifties, his intellectual gaze turned in the other direction upon the source of his perennial themes of the "Other" and "danger"—the underlying origins of his intellectual fascinations and literary imagination moved beyond the Balkans and riveted upon the East. This cluster of novels includes *State of Siege* (published in England as *The Night-Comers*), *Passage of Arms* (1959), *The Light of Day, Dirty Story* (1967), and *The Levanter* (1972). Two other novels—*A Kind of Anger* (1964), and *The Intercom Conspiracy*—were also written in this time frame, but the oriental grouping forms a cohesive exploration of a new direction for Ambler. A more circumspect opinion might actually be that the direction and issues are similar to

his early work, but in his quest for ultimate origins of historical and political issues in the Western mind, he comes full circle to the East and that murky median where East meets West—his old favorite symbol of Istanbul.

In the very image and symbol of Istanbul—a city that is literally split by the line between East and West—Ambler confronts the complex mythography of orientalism. Ambler's previous work had always taken the Western European (writer or engineer or journalist) into the heart of the mystical maze of the Orient and then exposed him to the labyrinthine power of the Dionysian (Latimer first glimpses the death mask of Dimitrios in the Istanbul morgue). This pattern persists for a time in this group of writings, and then that lineage of protagonists gives way to a new kind of Ambler character—the hero who inherits the legacies of both East and West. In *The Light of Day*, and in that figurative literary dawn or birth of a new Ambler character, Arthur Abdel Simpson makes his debut (he returns in *Dirty Story*) as a character who is half British and half Egyptian. His story takes place in a city similarly divided. Before Ambler focuses in *The Light of Day* on the hemispherical and bicameral consciousness of Arthur Simpson and the Istanbul metaphor of the (literally) "Middle" East, the first two novels of this series place the setting of Ambler's orientalism in the Far East (Southeast Asia) outposts of Indonesia and Malaysia. Before centering on the Istanbul cleavage of geographical and geopolitical orientalism, Ambler must first explore the periphery. Both literally and figuratively, in the Ambler canon all roads lead to the modern colossus of dual existence and identity—the West's ultimate confrontation with its Asian origins on the shores of the bicontinental Bosphorus.

THE LIGHT OF DAY

LIKE its main character, *The Light of Day* was born of a curiously double identity. The original manuscript, along with all research materials, burned in a house fire when Ambler was living in Bel Air, California. Ambler, with great patience and fortitude, rewrote the entire novel. In many ways, *The Light of Day* is the cornerstone of Ambler's discovery and construction of his second great theme (after the Jungian depth psychology) of orientalism and the Asian sources of the Dionysian eternal return. Ambler's coup in the examination of orientalism explores the legacies of colonial exploitation. Long before the last decade of the twentieth century explored, for example, the 500-year legacy of Columbus and the multifarious experience of "the Columbian exchange," Ambler was examining the effects of imperialism and colonization in the locales he knew best—just to the east of the Balkans, where one can find the dawn of Western civilization and the philosophical light of day. In the twilight of the Levantine dawn, Apollo—the light of day and of early civilization—drags forth the chariot of the gods from the dark Orphic and Dionysian mysteries. Nietzsche's "twilight of the idols" issues from that same dark frontier. In this half light and half darkness, Arthur Abdel Simpson issues forth from both Eastern and Western origins as the "mongrel" avatar of a Dionysian spirit that outlasts and outwits the postcolonial suppressor.

The main plot of *The Light of Day* is the exquisitely planned looting of the Turkish royal treasury, principally its legacy of jewels (hence, its natural resources commingled with a national history), by British and German gang members. Symbolically speaking, the looting of Asia by the old European powers is continued, right down to the involuntary enslavement of Simpson, the progeny of the unequal union of the hegemonic West and the exploited East. In a final note of profound irony at the conclusion of the novel, the theme of imperial European reprise is brought to completion when the thieves escape from the Istanbul airport in an air flight to Rome—the Eternal City and the seat of the ancient Roman Empire, one of the first of the Western powers to colonize the East. In his development of this theme of orientalism, Ambler is following the rich traditions of Rudyard Kipling and George Orwell. Like Kipling and Orwell, Ambler was sensitized to the inevitable cycles of history and political powers, and, like his predecessors, Ambler also understood the veneer of civilization, especially its thinness and fragility when imposed from the top of a hierarchy. In the East, the veneer of Western civilization is neither civil nor ever totally distinct from the West in its confrontation with orientalism.

Much of this analysis of Ambler's canon has adopted the perspective that Ambler, through the appropriation of the Jungian apparatus of depth psychology, was working toward an evaluation of the Apollonian culture and comportment of the West. Aided by his readings of Nietzsche and Spengler, Ambler found a powerful undercurrent of textual meanings in the modern confrontation of the isolated self that "bumps into the Shadow"—the unconscious and mysterious (and Eastern) sources of the unrecognized self. Ambler, as we have seen, worked through several versions of the Dionysian spirit and its eternal return in various characters (and villains) in that early work. In his oriental novels, Ambler moves to the symbolic formulation that "the light of the European day" derives from the radiant dawn of the oriental daybreak—and it is the dawn of both civilization and consciousness. His literary critique of the smug superiority of the West is founded on his own recognition of Orwell's suggestion in *Down and Out in Paris and London* that the intellectual and moral honesty of taking historical inquiry into the authentic Dionsyian sources involved a long journey to the East. Ambler went one step farther by tapping back into the underpinnings of the collective unconscious.

FRUITION AND FINALE

At the same time that Ambler was finishing *A Kind of Anger*, he edited an anthology of spy stories, *To Catch a Spy* (1964), for which he wrote an introduction. In that introductory essay, Ambler makes an interesting observation that perhaps escaped even his own considered reflection: "Spying is lonely and often depressing work. The spy's friendships can only be warily professional. His appetites and weaknesses, even the small ones, must be rigidly self-controlled. He must be capable of living for long periods under exceptional nervous strain" (p. 5). The corrosive despair and the monumental alienation of the latter half of the twentieth century have surely found an articulation in the literary milieux of espionage created by Ambler, Greene, and Le Carré. The lonely and dangerous gauntlets run by their introspective and doubt-ridden spies are the same corridors of deceit recognized in a quotidian world beset by global and personal angst. In a landmark study entitled "The White Negro," Norman Mailer rendered the defining properties of the postatomic neurosis epitomized in the absolute freedom of the psychopath. Mailer accurately foresaw the culture of liberation that emerged in the sixties because of the intensely personal and, at the same time, universal threat of annihilation. Mailer also described the despair and the alienation that would accompany the breakout into liberated modes of existence. Ambler recognized the same conditions. Having read Nietzsche, Jung, and Spengler, he knew well the risks attendant on the return of Dionysus and the sometimes psychopathic trickster.

The two final novels in this set represent, in similar and different ways, Ambler's final treatment of this most continuous of his themes and subjects. Piet Maas of *A Kind of Anger* and Theodore Carter of *The Intercom Conspiracy* are kindred spirits to the trickster character; both novels, although not Ambler's last, represent the fruition and finale of Ambler's long encounter with the Nietzschean and oriental principle of eternal return and transformation.

A KIND OF ANGER

A Kind of Anger combines two of Ambler's most powerful and recurrent narrative and thematic devices: the journalist who turns from observer into participant and the transformation of the hero in an awakening to the dangerous and quickening Dionysiac consciousness. The story opens in New York on a late Friday night in February 1963. In the upper-management offices of the weekly news magazine, *World Reporter*, the editor in chief, Mr. Cust, is preparing for his weekly ritual of making a harassing call to one of his unfortunate bureau chiefs. On this particular evening, Cust calls his bureau chief in Paris, Sy Logan and informs the Paris bureau of a hot lead on a Swiss murder case from the month before. An Iraqi exile, a former military man living in Zurich, is mysteriously murdered, and the only known witness, a woman in a bikini, has disappeared. The Swiss authorities have hit a dead end, and every magazine and newspaper in western Europe is trying to find leads on the so-called "bikini murder." Mr. Cust has a tip from the U.S. Treasury Department and he is calling to charge his Paris bureau with a long-shot mission. Logan tries to fend off the assignment, but Cust wants to give the job to Piet Maas, the "Dutch psycho" who will accept any assignment regardless of risk. Because of Maas's checkered past and because

he once made a big mistake for the newsmagazine, Cust harbors a deep resentment. Logan suspects that Cust is really setting Maas up for an assignment that will inevitably fail.

The homicide has taken place in Zurich at the sumptuous residence of an Iraqi colonel in exile from the revolutionary Baghdad government. Colonel Ahmed Fathir Arbil had, nearly four years earlier, been in attendance at a Geneva conference when his government was shaken by an army revolt. At that time Arbil asked the Swiss authorities for political asylum and set up residence in Zurich. While he worked as an army intelligence chief, Colonel Arbil was known as a sympathizer of the Kurdish nationalist movement. Cust tells Logan that at the time Lucia Bernardi, the "bikini woman," met Arbil in St. Moritz, she was working a confidence swindle on rich old men with a male partner named Patrick Chase, whose real name is Phillip Sanger. According to Cust, Sanger can be found in Nice. Maas's job is to locate Sanger and determine whether he is involved in the hiding of Miss Bernardi.

Piet Maas eventually finds Lucia Bernardi. But by the time he locates her, his quest is for more than a simple newsmagazine story. Maas admits to himself, on the way to his first meeting with her, "I had become interested in the mystery of Lucia Bernardi. I wanted to know what lay behind it, and I wanted to hear the truth from her own lips" (p. 71).

Maas gets part of the story from Lucia, but his editor in Paris wants to run the larger story, which includes the role of Sanger and his wife, Adèle. Maas refuses, and when the editor threatens him, he hangs up the phone and decides to cut and run. When he goes to Sanger to warn him of the magazine's intention to print the whole story, Maas ends up throwing in with the Sangers and once again speaks to Lucia. Through the course of several conversations with Lucia, Maas begins to discover the truthful recesses of her story. Her account of Arbil's murder was accurate, but she omitted the fact that she had been able to take out of the house his briefcase full of secret papers. Arbil had anticipated his demise; the briefcase and its contents were to be Lucia's equity and insurance policy. The secret papers would command a monumental selling price from either the Italian oil concessionaires in Iraq or from the Iraqi government. Lucia had no defense for dealing with those agents, but she finds a bodyguard in Maas.

But being bodyguard to a beautiful and treacherous woman is not enough for Piet Maas; he transforms completely in the Dionysian tradition of the trickster. He proposes a deal to Lucia: "You have something to sell—a suitcase full of records, perhaps. But first you have to let the prospective buyers know that it is for sale. At the same time you have to be very careful not to let them know too much, or they might try to take it without paying" (p. 130). Maas presents himself as her new business partner—and Lucia bursts out laughing. After the laughter subsides, their illegal partnership is effected, and soon another pact—that of the flesh—is consummated between the two fugitives from a nicer world.

As that outer and more refined world begins to get the picture of Maas's defection from the newsmagazine and his possible alliance with the missing "bikini woman," the news reports characterize Maas as an "unpredictable screwball." In the meantime, the "screwball" excels in the most dangerous game of selling national secrets to foreign powers. Maas exercises a natural talent for the big-time scam; he is trickster par excellence. Like Franz Schirmer, Maria Kolin, and Michael Howell (*The Levanter*), Maas had dwelled temporarily in the land of the dead; at the wondrous moment of his rebirth into a full life of the senses, he returns from death with the gifts of prophecy, vision, and wholeness. The title plays on this transformation from death to life.

When Sanger and his wife join Maas and Lucia Bernardi at the conclusion of the scam and the novel (actually, the Sangers join in, for a fee, the successful finale of extorting from all sides), Sanger confides in Maas as the four partners-in-crime glow in their triumph. Maas tries to protest and explain the transformation by the change of circumstances. But Sanger is too keen an observer of human nature:

"Oh no," he said when he could speak again. "Oh no, that's not the answer. I thought I knew what made you tick. 'A new kind of anger,' I said. How wrong I was! Your kind of anger is as old as the hills. You've just bottled it up all these years—just like the man who becomes a policeman instead of a crook. Or is that sublimation? It doesn't matter. The point is that you have a taste for larceny. It agrees with you. Therapy!" He started to giggle. "Instead of giving you all those shock treatments, you know what they should have done? They should have sent you out to rob a bank!"

(pp. 232–233)

Piet Maas is the apotheosis of the Apollonian hero who transmogrifies into the opposite—the Ambler character who enacts the Nietzschean drama of the "destruction of the old self and the rebirth of the Dionysiac." He is the culmination of a long line of Ambler protagonists who epitomize the Nietzschean (and later Jungian) conflict between the rational and irrational forces that determine the human and social makeup of an age.

Slowly and gradually, Ambler's articulation of his main characters, through the course of his novels, evolves into Piet Maas in *A Kind of Anger*. Some of the early characters discover their "opposite selves" in amnesia and other altered states of consciousness; others merely witness and approximate the wondrous transformation inherent in Jungian *enantiodromia*, the process of "running contrariwise" or the larger Nietzschean notion that "sooner or later everything runs into its opposite." Latimer descends into the underworld of shadows in the Istanbul morgue and bumps into the shadow of his unconscious. Carey descends into the asphyxiating cellar of legal tomes and finds a resurrection on the third month of a quest that ends on an obscure acadian mountaintop grove in Macedonia.

Ambler pays homage to both Jung and Frazer in a curiously bucolic sense at the end of *A Kind of Anger*—a scene reminiscent of the resolution of the arcadian and prelapsarian union of Franz Schirmer and Maria Kolin. When Maas and Lucia go to a house in Cagnes to retrieve the suitcase full of national secrets "for sale"—they must approach the house, which is under surveillance, from a back garden. The garden is presented as an olive grove in an arcadian setting. Maas and Lucia enter an ancient and mythical world on their way to the fabulous mysteries and fortunes that await:

It was all very quiet there, but the olive grove possessed a special stillness of its own. The trees were old, and the light breeze did not move their thick, twisted limbs. Only the leaves moved, fluttering softly. Once, as we walked up, the black shape of a goat stirred, and the chain that tethered it made a clicking noise. Then, the bulk of the cistern loomed ahead and there was a sound of trickling water. A moment or two later, we had found the path.

(p. 218)

This pastoral portrait conveys the connubial criminals into the mythic space of Eden. It is the combined age-old idyll of the escape to the primeval garden and the wedding in the woods. The two orphans of a ruthless and Apollonian world have retreated back into the Dionysiac sanctuary—outside time, place, and the law. Fiendishly capable, the two orphans are self-sufficient and find their only family in their true blood relations to the Sangers and each other. But, of course, they do have other blood—somewhat to the east, in the imaginary frontier of Macedonia, are their first cousins, Franz and Maria, from the family known as trickster. The fortuitous human pairings, emergent from the common themes between *The Schirmer Inheritance* and *A Kind of Anger*, allow the two couples to inhabit the dark/bright, amoral frontier, suspended between good and evil, fixed between childhood and the inevitable: death.

THE INTERCOM CONSPIRACY

AFTER a lapse of exactly thirty years, Charles Latimer reappeared in *The Intercom Conspiracy*. This novel attains an innovative style of narrative, suspense, characterization; it even surpasses the former novels in Ambler's experimentation with a Conradian point of view. But gone is the undercurrent philosophy of history. In this case the ironic perspective is the Cold War reality of two superpowers who must seek a *rapprochement* in maintaining a balance of power (even if it means conspiring together to maintain a balance of terror). *The Intercom Conspiracy* is, however, not straight Cold War plot. The spark of Ambler's old ingenuity becomes evident when Latimer stumbles on the successful extortion of both the United States *and* Russia by a pair of NATO intelligence chiefs. The superpowers are eager to stop the leakage of information by paying a handsome ransom and thereby preserve the equilibrium of power and access to intelligence. Ambler's revelation of this plan comes through the eyes of the innocent victim (not Latimer this time), and the whole method of discovery is still presented in terms of deductive detection. The novel is typical Cold War in its general structure, but Ambler's own unique details have resurfaced along with his basic detective-novel approach. The "trapped innocent" enters the Cold War. But *The Intercom Conspiracy* depicts the final

utter failure of the detective hero in the modern era of Cold War espionage. Latimer is no match for the two traitorous NATO confederates; he is liquidated and silenced forever. The modern, corporate "organization" is both hero and villain in the Cold War setting of bloc versus bloc. There is really nothing heroic in Brand and Jost's plot to blackmail the superpowers. Jost and Brand came to power in the early fifties and established themselves in the NATO intelligence community during the bitter Cold War years of that decade. They could accept the necessity for the alliance to which their countries were committed. They could accept with resignation the knowledge that their countries meant no more to NATO than Romania or Bulgaria meant to the Warsaw Pact and that they were pygmies involved in a struggle between giants. What they could not do was change their ways of thinking about giants. They had known the German giant, so omnipotent in his day, and had helped to bring him down. Now, they were able to observe and appraise from peculiar vantage points the American and Russian giants. The appraisals they made were not flattering. What impressed them most about these giants, they ultimately decided, was not their strength, still less the loud and threatening noises they made, but their inherent clumsiness. The bureaucratic spies are successful because of their cognizance of organizational weaknesses. Their guarded daring is always protected by transactions through Swiss banks and telegrams—the personal confrontation of heroic encounter is totally absent.

Latimer's failure and death ultimately pose the ethical dilemma of the observer of history—one either observes at the Apollonian distance or incurs a fatal set of consequences by active participation. For Ambler, the choice is basic, yet as old as the Platonic dialogues and as awe-inspiring as Hamlet's soliloquy: Is history the product of an inescapable process of events, or is there a morality of action that demands the participation of the individual in the flux of society? Perhaps the solution lies in the very birth of the spy novel: it shows a complex world where the logician can no longer solve the riddle of the sphinx. But there is the eternal rub: Was Oedipus the logical detective or the political man of action? Either way, the result was self-destruction. This is the crucial dilemma of Eric Ambler's novels. Latimer's return and demise betray the failure of the Apollonian interventionist—

the logician, last in a long line of Amblerian engineers, journalists, and technicians. On the other hand, there is the alternate Ambler protagonist, the "progeny" of survivors—the tricksters who slough off the Apollonian shell and emerge in a Dionysiac rebirth and transformation in an ebullient and amoral mode of pure existence.

CONCLUSION

THE assessment of Eric Ambler's achievement as a popular writer of spy novels and the fiction of international intrigue must necessarily transcend all such parochial labels. Ambler set out consciously to transform these genres of popular literature, but to read his canon is to perceive that the mutations wrought may not have necessarily been the effects initially intended. One distinctly senses that Ambler himself entered into a process much like that represented in his best novels, a recurrent motif of radical metamorphosis and rebirth, which drew the Newtonian electrical engineer into a dramatic and unexpected realm of relativity and chaos. In short, Ambler became a purveyor of modernism, and the conveyance of popular pulp fiction happened to be a vehicle much beset and berated by the critics of "received art" and acceptable tastes. Slowly, however, Ambler's critics turned into his supporters.

From the perspective of this critique, the critics of the past have done little service to Ambler's reputation by emphasizing the earliest novels so consistently. In paying close attention to those six prewar novels and at the same time overemphasizing the eleven-year hiatus after the war, the critics have shone a narrow and false light of intensity on a small part of a literary career spanning sixty years and eighteen novels. With the exception of *The Mask of Dimitrios*, those celebrated first six novels are generally inferior in narrative style and structure to the much more versatile and polysemous novels later. *Judgment on Deltchev* and *The Schirmer Inheritance* are crafted by a writer who takes the time to develop character and detail of narrative. These two novels show us an Eric Ambler who did indeed read Nietzsche and Jung, but they reflect a subtle and considered incorporation of those intellectual influences without the doctrinaire intrusiveness of the prewar novels.

The marvelous transformation of Ambler in his art entails the method and material of his fiction itself. Like one of his "wrong man" protagonists, Ambler is the stilted and stuffy writer of detective/spy novels in the period from 1936 to 1941; in 1951, and certainly by 1953, Ambler is a more complex thinker and writer, exploring with ironic perspectives the terrain of Orwell and Conrad, stylistic light-years beyond Somerset Maugham and Graham Greene, who had paced the course in the previous generation. Like many of his own fictional creations, somewhat trapped and artless, Ambler learns the tricks of the trade. The literary trickster delves into the unconscious of his art and devices and emerges as the artist of the mutable and the metamorphic spy. But the spy is principally the etymologic agent of "espionage"—to espy is to witness, and to witness is to know. Ambler takes the figure of the spy—the homeless stranger and distant witness—into the depths of the unconscious and there espies the shadow; to witness the Other within is to know the modern self.

Ambler's stateless and alienated protagonists capture for a popular literary audience the twentieth-century obsession with metaphysical homelessness. One of his definitive contributions to the genres of popular and suspense fiction was the interpenetration of the consciousness of the popular reading audience and the Freudian and Jungian explorations of the modern mind and its "scientific" structures. In some ways, perhaps, the theorists of the dynamics of a modern popular culture might even argue that the immediate and sustained (never fully intended) popular interest in the arcane and academic investigations into modern depth psychology—the newly discovered "altered states of consciousness" with their explanation of human motivation—influentially shaped the course and constituents of Anglo-American popular culture. And, of course, that this modern science should arise at the same time that the twentieth-century enigma—Nazi Germany in all of its cultured and brutal glory—reared up before the Western world, was either pure happenstance or incontrovertible proof of Jungian synchronicity. Ambler's use of Nazi Germany as the horrendous and at the same time ebullient outbreak of the modern Dionysiac spirit was a literary and psychological coup of brilliant proportions. He read clearly the interior contours of the Western world.

In Ambler's critique of the Western bias toward the East, that bifurcated psyche of the modern human being came to be illustrated in his portraitures of the so-called mongrel—his theme of miscegenation and the disenfranchised progeny of those relationships recurs throughout the five oriental novels, in "the double-heritaged hero." Ambler's sympathetic depiction of these doubly endowed characters strikes the first blow in a popular genre traditionally etched by a deep and abiding ethnocentrism. In many ways, his novels belong to another popular genre—travel writing—which has been insightfully described by Paul Fussell's study *Abroad: British Literary Traveling Between the Wars.* Fussell claims that the 1920s and 1930s were the final age of literary traveling, when the independent traveler, almost always the bearer of empirical design, became an endangered species. This traveler, an unmistakable envoy of empire, was nearly always European or North American, of the middle or upper class, and a white man. This figure grew disillusioned in the search of adventure, discovery, knowledge, redemption—all of which were abstracted from utopian idylls and converted into the molding of a better character to return to the dystopian domains of civilization.

Ambler's explorations of the new dimensions of the "spy novel" and the literature of international intrigue, particularly in his innovative materials and methods of the novels of the 1950s, blazed the trail for the accomplished works of John le Carré, which were reflective of Ambler's great themes of the Unconscious Other and the universality of the conflicted human mind. Le Carré's *Looking Glass War* becomes the central metaphor of the gaze of the distant and alienated observer and the nature of that gaze that would articulate the Other as forever alien. But Ambler and Le Carré turn those transformative and appropriative "Western eyes" into an apprehension of the sameness of the observer and the other. Ambler's coup as a writer was to take a genre that marginalized and distanced the "others" of the colonized lands of the British empire and transform that literature into a looking glass that examined the self and found the alter ego. Within the profound depths of the alter ego, Eric Ambler rejuvenated an effete and stilted genre of popular literature that celebrated the dark fron-

tiers of the universal unconscious and the bright mirror of the universality of the human capacity for regeneration and harmony.

SELECTED BIBLIOGRAPHY

I. NOVELS. *The Dark Frontier* (London, 1936); *Uncommon Danger* (London, 1937), repr. as *Background to Danger* (New York, 1937); *Epitaph for a Spy* (London, 1938; rev. New York, 1951); *Cause for Alarm* (London, 1938; New York, 1939); *The Mask of Dimitrios* (London, 1939), repr. as *A Coffin for Dimitrios* (New York, 1939); *Journey into Fear* (London and New York, 1940); *Judgment on Deltchev* (London and New York, 1951); *The Schirmer Inheritance* (London and New York, 1953); *The Night-Comers* (London, 1956), repr. as *State of Siege* (New York, 1956); *Passage of Arms* (London, 1959; New York, 1960); *The Light of Day* (London, 1962; New York, 1963), repr. as *Topkaki* (New York, 1964); *A Kind of Anger* (London and New York, 1964); *Dirty Story: A Further Account of the Life and Adventures of Arthur Abdel Simpson* (London and New York, 1967); *The Intercom Conspiracy* (New York, 1969; London, 1970), repr. as *A Quiet Conspiracy* (Glasgow, 1989); *The Levanter* (London and New York, 1972); *Doctor Frigo* (London and New York, 1974); *Send No More Roses* (London, 1977), repr. as *The Siege of the Villa Lipp* (New York, 1977); *The Care of Time* (London and New York, 1981).

II. THE "ELIOT REED" NOVELS (written with Charles Rodda). *Skytip* (New York, 1950; London, 1951); *Tender to Changer* (New York, 1950), repr. as *Tender to Moonlight* (London, 1952); *The Maras Affair* (New York and London, 1953); *Charter to Danger* (London, 1954); *Passport to Panic* (London, 1958).

III. SHORT STORIES. "The Army of the Shadows," in *The Queen's Book of the Red Cross* (London, 1939), repr. in Vincent Starrett, ed., *World's Great Spy Stories* (Cleveland, Ohio, 1944); "Belgrade 1926," in Eric Ambler, ed., *To Catch a Spy: An Anthology of Favourite Spy Stories* (London, 1964: New York, 1965); "The Blood Bargain," in George Hardinge, ed., *Winter's Crimes*, vol. 2 (London, 1970), repr. in Ellery Queen, ed., *Ellery Queen's Windows of Mystery* (New York, 1980), George Hardinge, ed., *The Best of Winter's Crimes* (London, 1986) and *The Mammoth Book of Modern Crime Stories* (London, 1987).

See also "The Intrusions of Dr. Czissar," which comprise six tales: "The Case of the Pinchbeck Locket," in *The Sketch [London]* (3 July 1940), repr. in *Ellery Queen's Mystery Magazine* (November 1945); "The Case of the Emerald Sky," in *The Sketch* (10 July 1940), repr. in *Ellery Queen's Mystery Magazine* (March 1945), Ellery Queen, ed., *To the Queen's Taste* (Boston, 1946), and Bill Pronzini,

Barry H. Malzberg, and Marty H. Greenberg, *The Arbor House Treasury of Mystery and Suspense* (New York, 1981); "The Case of the Cycling Chauffeur," in *The Sketch* (7 July 1940), repr. as "A Bird in the Tree," in *Ellery Queen's Mystery Magazine* (May 1947); "The Case of the Overheated Service Flat," in *The Sketch* (24 July 1940), repr. as "Case of the Overheated Flat," in *Ellery Queen's Mystery Magazine* (April 1948); "The Case of the Drunken Socrates," in *The Sketch* (31 July 1940), repr. as "Case of the Landlady's Brother," in *Ellery Queen's Mystery Magazine* (February 1949); and "The Case of the Gentleman Poet," *The Sketch*, 7 August 1940, repr. as "Case of the Gentleman Poet," *Ellery Queen's Mystery Magazine*, September 1947; *Waiting for Orders: The Complete Short Stories of Eric Ambler* (New York, 1991).

IV. SCREENPLAYS. *The Way Ahead*, with Peter Ustinov (1944); *United States* (1945); *The October Man* (1947); *The Passionate Friends*, from the novel by H. G. Wells (1948); *The Clouded Yellow* (1950); *Highly Dangerous* (1951); *The Magic Box*, from a biography of W. Friese-Greene (1951); *Campbell's Kingdom* (1957); *The Card*, from the novel by Arnold Bennett (1952); *Gigolo and Gigolette*, from a short story by W. Somerset Maugham (1952); *Rough Shoot*, from the novel by Geoffrey Household (1952); *The Cruel Sea*, from the novel by Nicholas Monsarrat (1952); *The Purple Plain*, from a novel by H. E. Bates (1954); *Lease of Life*, from a story by Patrick Jenjins (1954); *Windom's Way* (1957); *Body Below* (1955); *Nightrunners of Bengal* (1955); *The Yangtse Incident* (1957); *The Guns of Navarone* (1961); *The Night-Comers* (1957); *A Night to Remember*, from the book by Walter Lord (1958); *Blind Date* (1959); *The Eye of Truth* (1958); *The Wreck of the Mary Deare*, from the novel by Hammond Innes (1959); *Mutiny on the Bounty*, uncredited, with others (1962); *Love Hate Love* (1970).

V. UNCOLLECTED ESSAYS. "The Novelist and Films," in Michael Gilbert, ed., *Crime and Good Company: Essays on Criminals and Crime-Writing* (Boston, 1959); "Introduction," in Sir Arthur Conan Doyle's *The Adventures of Sherlock Holmes* (London, 1974); "A Better Sort of Rubbish: An Inquiry into the State of the Thriller," in *The Times Saturday Review* (30 November 1974); "The End of the Affair," in *New Statesman* (13 January 1978); "Voyages—and Shipwrecks," in H. R. Keating, ed., *Whodunit? A Guide to Crime, Suspense, and Spy Fiction* (London and New York, 1982).

VI. OTHER WORKS. *The Ability to Kill and Other Pieces* (London, 1963), repr. as *The Ability to Kill: True Tales of Bloody Murder* (New York and London, 1987); Eric Ambler, ed., *To Catch a Spy: An Anthology of Favourite Spy Stories* (London and New York, 1964); *Here Lies: An Autobiography* (London, 1985; New York, 1986); Karen Marie Linville, "The Film Adaptations of the Detective and Spy Novels of Dashiell Hammett, Raymond Chandler, and Eric Ambler," unpublished M.A. thesis, UCLA Theatre Arts (1974).

The Eric Ambler Archive is located in the Special Collections Department of the Mugar Memorial Library at Boston University.

VII. INTERVIEWS. Joel Hopkins, "An Interview with Eric Ambler," in *Journal of Popular Culture* 9, no. 2 (fall 1975); Herbert Mitgang, "Interview: The Thrilling Eric Ambler," in *New York Times Book Review* (13 September 1981); David Taylor, "Passing Through: Eric Ambler Talks to David Taylor," in *Punch* (6 September 1972).

VIII. CRITICAL STUDIES. General: Alfred Hitchcock, Introduction to *Intrigue: The Great Spy Novels of Eric Ambler* (New York, 1943); "Return to the Balkans," in *Time* (19 March 1951); Graham Greene, "The Sense of Apprehension," in *The Month* (July 1951); J. D. Scott, "New Novels," in *New Statesman and Nation* (25 August 1951); Seymour Krim, "Suspense," in *Commonweal* (1 August 1953); William Hogan, "Eric Ambler Covers a Coup in the Indies," in *San Francisco Chronicle* (1 October 1956).

Lenore Glen Offord, "Melodrama in Sumatra in the Ambler Manner," in *San Francisco Chronicle* (27 March 1960); Phoebe Adams, "This Trade of Gunrunning," in *Atlantic Monthly* (April 1960); Howard Haycraft, ed., *Five Spy Novels* (Garden City, N.Y., 1962); "Mystery and Crime," in *New Yorker* (2 March 1963); Stanley Kauffmann, "Simple Simenon," in *New Republic* (9 December 1967).

Jacques Barzun and Wendell Hertig Taylor, *A Catalogue of Crime* (New York, 1971); Charles Elliot, "Ambling On," in *Time* (26 June 1972); Paxton Davis, "The World We Live In: The Novels of Eric Ambler," in *Hollins Critic* 8, no. 1 (February 1971); Julian Symons, *Mortal Consequences: A History, From the Detective Story to the Crime Novel* (New York, 1972); James Clive, "Prisoners of Clarity Series 2: Eric Ambler," in *New Review* 1, no. 6 (September 1974); Malcolm Oram, "Eric Ambler," in *Publishers Weekly* (9 September 1974); Peter S. Prescott, "I Spy," in *Newsweek* (14 October 1974); Roy Fuller, "Warts and All," *Times Literary Supplement* (22 November 1974); Mark Armory, "The Ambler Way," in *Sunday Times Magazine* (5 January 1975); Gavin Lambert, *The Dangerous Edge* (London, 1975; New York, 1976); Ronald Ambrosetti, "The World of Eric Ambler: From Detective to Spy," in Larry N. Landrum, Pat Browne, and Ray B. Brown, eds., *Dimensions of Detective Fiction* (Bowling Green, Ohio, 1976); Chris Steinbrunner and Otto Penzler, eds., *Encyclopedia of Mystery and Detection* (New York, 1976); James Fenton, "The Ambler Memorandum," in *Vogue* (UK; July 1977); Robert Emmett Ginna, "Bio: Outside His Window, Within His Heart, Eric Ambler Finds the Stuff of Great Spy Novels," in *People* (6 June 1977); Paul Gray, "Capital Gains," in *Time* (6 June 1977); Hugh Eames, *Sleuths, Inc.* (Philadelphia, 1978).

Michael Demarest, "Forever Ambler," in *Time* (14 September 1981); Michael Gilbert, "The Professionals and the Predatory Pikes," in *Times Literary Supplement* (5 June 1981); LeRoy L. Panek, *The Special Branch: The British Spy*

Story, 1890–1980 (Bowling Green, Ohio, 1981); Karl Heinz Wegmann, "Filmographic Eric Ambler," in *Filmkritik* 26, no. 12 (December 1982); John M. Reilly, ed., *Twentieth-Century Crime and Mystery Writers,* 2d ed. (New York, 1985); Tim Heald, "Chilled Vintage Old Ambler," in *London Times* (13 June 1985); Bernard Bergonzi, *The Myth of Modernism and Twentieth-Century Literature* (New York, 1986); Dorothy Salisbury Davis, "Some of the Truth," in Robin Winks, ed., *Colloquium on Crime: Eleven Renowned Mystery Writers Discuss Their Work* (New York, 1986); Tony Hillerman, "Mystery, Country Boys, and the Big Reservation," in Robin Winks, ed., *Colloquium on Crime: Eleven Renowned Mystery Writers Discuss Their Work* (New York, 1986); John G. Cawelti and Bruce Rosenberg, "At a Crossroads: Eric Ambler and Graham Greene," in *The Spy Story* (Chicago, 1987); David Lehman, "Epitaph for a Spymaster," in *Partisan Review* (spring 1987); John Bayley, "Madly Excited," in *London Review of Books* (1 June 1989); Peter Lewis, *Eric Ambler* (New York, 1990); James Moore, *Gurdjieff* (Rockport, Mass., 1991).

Relevant studies of psychology, philosophy, and civilization: Carl Gustav Jung, *Collected Papers on Analytical Psychology* (New York, 1917); Carl Gustav Jung, *Two Essays on Analytical Psychology* (New York, 1953); Sir James George Frazer, *The New Golden Bough,* ed. by Theodor Gaster (New York, 1959); Ira Progoff, *The Death and Rebirth of Psychology* (New York, 1964); Warren F. Otto, *Dionysus: Myth and Cult* (Bloomington, Ind. 1965); Crane Brinton, *Nietzsche* (New York, 1965); Carl Gustav Jung, *Symbols of Transformation* (Princeton, 1967); Joseph Campbell, *The Portable Jung* (New York, 1971); Volodymyr Walter Odajnyk, *Jung and Politics: The Political and Social Ideas of C. G. Jung* (New York, 1976); Edward Said, *Orientalism* (New York, 1978); Paul Fussell, *Abroad: British Literary Traveling Between the Wars* (New York, 1980); Oswald Spengler, *The Decline of the West,* abridged edition prepared by Charles Francis Atkinson, with an introduction by H. Stuart Hughes (New York, 1991).

Reviews in the *New York Times Book Review*: Isaac Anderson, "A Spy Story" (29 January 1939); William Du Bois, "Journey into Terror" (18 March 1951); Joseph Wood Krutch, "Mr. Ambler's Spies" (16 March 1952); C. Day Lewis, "With a Flair for Creating Alarm" (26 July 1953); Anthony Boucher, "Trouble in Sunda" (23 September 1956); James M. Cain, "Color of the East" (6 March 1960); George Grella, "Who's for Treachery" (8 October 1967); Allen J. Hubin, "The Intercom Conspiracy" (21 September 1969); Julian Symons, "Subtleties of Power" (13 September 1981); John Russell, "Summer Reading: Art" (31 May 1987).

Other book reviews: *New York Herald Tribune Book Review* (15 April 1951); "Confidential Agents," *Times Literary Supplement* (20 July 1956).

MARTIN AMIS

(1949–   )

David Hawkes

WHEN MARTIN AMIS was born on 25 August 1949 in Oxford, his father, Kingsley Amis, was an unknown assistant lecturer at a provincial university in Wales. Amis senior and his first wife, Hilary Bardwell, had recently moved to South Wales, where the twenty-seven-year-old Kingsley had taken up an appointment in the English department at Swansea University. This relative obscurity of the Amis family did not last long. In 1954 Kingsley Amis published his first novel, *Lucky Jim*, a resounding though controversial success that firmly established him as an important presence on the British literary scene. From an early age, then, Martin Amis was the son of a well-known novelist whose fame continued to flourish throughout the younger Amis' own career. Kingsley and Martin Amis are virtually unique as a father and son who were successful and popular novelists during the same twenty-year period (until Kingsley's death in 1995).

LIFE AND INFLUENCES

MARTIN Amis was the second son of Kingsley Amis. Martin's childhood was peripatetic; he attended fourteen different schools in Britain, Spain, and (in 1959–1960) the United States, where his father taught at Princeton University. His parents divorced when he was sixteen, and his father married the novelist Elizabeth Jane Howard. They separated in 1980, and Kingsley moved into a private apartment in the house where Martin's mother lived, now happily remarried. All parties were content with this arrangement, though late in life, when Kingsley was asked whether he ever wished he was still married to his first wife, he answered, "Only *all the time.*"

After attending various preparatory courses in London and Brighton, Martin Amis passed the Oxford entrance exam in 1967. Like many British eighteen-year-olds, Amis took a year off between school and university; unlike many of them, he did not hitchhike through Europe or backpack across the Andes, but worked in his stepuncle's record shop in Rickmansworth. In 1969 he arrived at Exeter College, Oxford University, to read English, feeling, according to his later account, alienated and diffident. Considering himself "originally a child of the lower middle-classes" (*My Oxford*, 1986, p. 204), he had little in common with the patrician aesthetes and athletes who predominated at the university, or with the northern chemists and plebeian nerds who provided the only alternative milieu. At first he felt that "I had no friends, no friends whatever" (p. 207), but later he fell in with a fashionable, London-oriented set, many of whom would remain friends and literary rivals for decades. His socializing was, however, interspersed with bouts of monastic devotion to study, eventually resulting in a formal first, the highest possible grade, the fourth highest in his class.

Amis graduated from Oxford in 1971 and, following very brief stints at an art gallery and an advertising agency, took a job as editorial assistant at the *Times Literary Supplement*, where he became fiction and poetry editor in 1974. The *TLS* was a venerable institution, donnish, stuffy, and conservative; Amis later recalled that "the average age of our readers was something like ninety-three" (*TLS*, 17 January 1992). The atmosphere, under the genial editorship of Arthur Crook, was amateurish and chaotic. In the same issue of the *TLS* Amis recalled an early incident that captured this mood:

Almost my first assignment was a new and expensive edition of Coleridge's verse with a long introduction by William Empson. I read the book, then sold it, then reviewed it. I was enthusiastic, but I did object to Empson's excision of the prose gloss to "The Ancient Mariner"; perhaps, I said ("or so this reviewer feels"), the prose gloss should have been included in an appendix. Empson replied the next week. His opening point was that the prose gloss to "The Ancient Mariner" *was* included in an appendix. Even that Arthur forgave.

(p. 18)

At the age of twenty-three Amis published *The Rachel Papers* (1973), a brilliant first novel that won the Somerset Maugham Award. The *TLS* reviewer correctly called it "a book that will put Martin Amis on the map" (18 November 1973), and from then on Amis was, like his father, a famous novelist, consolidating his reputation with *Dead Babies* (1975) and *Success* (1978). In 1977 he became literary editor of the *New Statesman,* which was then still a left-wing journal posing as the conscience of James Callaghan's Labour government. During Amis' tenure, the review section was erudite and amusing, with frequent contributions from Amis' friends and contemporaries, such as Julian Barnes. With the publication of *Other People: A Mystery Story* (1981), Amis had become a full-time writer, dividing his time between fiction and occasional journalism for the *Observer.* He was also firmly established—together with Barnes, Salman Rushdie, and Ian McEwan—as one of the leading novelistic voices of the younger generation.

With *Money: A Suicide Note* (1984), Amis made a clear breakthrough. The book is epic in scale, radically innovative in form and style, and hugely ambitious in its thematic concerns and philosophical implications. Most important, *Money* was perceived as defining a particular epoch; it seemed to many reviewers—and the impression is confirmed in hindsight—to capture and encapsulate the zeitgeist of the 1980s. Following the publication of *Money,* and especially after the equally triumphant *London Fields* (1989), Amis was regularly described as the most important British novelist of the late twentieth century.

Support for this claim was provided by the lurid interest of the British media in Amis' personal affairs between 1994 and 1996. In 1985 he had married an American, Antonia Phillips, and the couple had two sons. In 1994 they separated, and he began an affair with a younger woman. This won Amis some impertinent disapprobation, as did the news that he had fired his longtime agent, the wife of his old literary friend Julian Barnes. Worse yet, it

seemed that the new agent had secured Amis an advance of a half million pounds for his novel *The Information* (1995). This was an unprecedented sum for a serious novelist in Britain, and it evoked howls of envy and reproach from the less fortunate. To cap it all, it was revealed that Amis planned to spend a large portion of the money on his teeth. Finally, in 1996 it was announced that during a brief affair in the 1970s Amis had sired an illegitimate daughter, aged twenty and a student at Oxford, who for two decades had been unaware of her genetic father's identity.

The attention paid to these incidents by the popular press (AMIS AND THE BOOK BABE, screamed a typical headline) may have been prurient, but it was also significant. It had been a long time since a writer as avant-garde, difficult, and challenging as Amis was sufficiently well known for his romantic and business adventures to provide fodder for the tabloids. Amis was a member of an endangered species once thought extinct: he was a genuinely popular writer who made no compromises with or concessions to accessibility. In true postmodern style, his work evades the distinction between highbrow art and mass culture. His oeuvre seems likely to become a major influence on future generations of British novelists, and clear echoes of his style and preoccupations may be found in the work of younger writers such as Will Self and Irvine Welsh.

There are three obvious influences on Amis' own work: Vladimir Nabokov, Saul Bellow, and Kingsley Amis. Nabokov, a Russian émigré who settled in the United States in 1940, composed much of his work in English, which was his second language. As a result, he displays an idiosyncratic vocabulary replete with neologisms, parodic brand names, and unexpected but felicitous usages. Amis' choice of words is just as exuberantly eccentric: he often tries to distance the reader from everyday surroundings, to make his audience perceive the world anew by describing it from an alien perspective similar to the "Martian" style made fashionable in the 1980s by poets like Craig Raine. Many of Amis' favorite themes are also drawn from Nabokov, such as the literary jealousy and competition of Nabokov's *Pale Fire* (1962) and the harrowing depiction of male sexuality in *Lolita* (1958). Nabokov's narrators are often unreliable, obsessive, possibly insane, and the authorial voice makes frequent appearances in his novels. The reader's attention is constantly being drawn to the fact that this is a work of fiction; strange editors, annotators, and commentators keep popping up between the reader and the text. These techniques have come to define literary postmodernism and, like Nabokov, Amis puts them to exemplary use.

The Canadian-born American writer Saul Bellow is an even more pervasive presence in Amis' work. Like Nabokov, Bellow invents narrators who constantly undermine their own credibility, and he confuses the matter further by apparently using them as mouthpieces for his own philosophical speculations. He also shares Nabokov's interest in literary rivalry and his habit of constructing his plots around the conflict between a pair of contradictory yet complementary characters; the relationship in *Humboldt's Gift* (1975) between Humboldt and Citrine, for example, parallels the one between Shade and Kinbote in *Pale Fire*, and Amis uses the same technique in works like *Success, London Fields,* and *The Information.*

Bellow's fiction entails minute explorations of individual consciousnesses. Although the narrators of Bellow's books are complex, intellectual, and sensitive people, there is something peculiar about them: they are not trustworthy; their voices seem to shift and change; they become the vehicles for what seem to be authorial interpolations on the meaning of life. Clearly, while figures such as Citrine and Herzog are finely drawn and intricately detailed, they are not credible or consistent "characters" in the realist tradition. In fact, Bellow's work suggests that the coherent, unified personality represented by the realist novel does not accurately reflect the state of the human mind in the postmodern era.

Amis shares Bellow's preoccupation with the condition of the character. He often remarks on the historical decline in the social and ethical status of literary protagonists. The main actors in fictional texts, Amis notes, have experienced a steady decline throughout the history of Western literature, from gods and heroes, noblemen and the high bourgeois to the ordinary, flawed folk of the modern novel. A modernist writer like James Joyce drew attention to this development when he rewrote Homer, substituting the humble concerns of an ordinary Dubliner for the epic adventures of Odysseus. Characters like John Updike's Harry ("Rabbit") Angstrom are often reprehensible, ignorant, and unreflective. More critical and less

sympathetic than Joyce, Updike uses his major character as a way of studying what is wrong with the contemporary psyche. Amis' own fiction takes this process a stage further. His leading actors have sunk below the level of everyday people and become grotesques, gargoyles, caricatured personifications of the maladies afflicting the postmodern mind.

Amis has been quoted as saying that the difference between him and Bellow is that while Bellow really believes in the soul, "it's a rather weaker belief in my case. Not . . . a belief, but a kind of inkling, or suspicion" (Alexander, p. 584). This difference is reflected in the way Amis treats his characters. We learn a great deal about the thought processes of John Self and Keith Talent—we often see the world from their perspective—but they lack the stable core personality, the integral identity, that would enable us to say they had a "soul." However, while they may not be "characters" in the traditional sense, they are certainly recognizable figures drawn from real-life Britain in the 1980s. The disturbing thing about Amis' characters is that they are extremely lifelike without being fully human.

The influence of Kingsley Amis on his son's work is simultaneously more obvious and more oblique. *The Rachel Papers* is a response to and an updating of *Lucky Jim;* both works feature a youthful literary smart aleck deriding and defeating his elders and social superiors. Amis senior, however, soon wearied of the role of Angry Young Man to which his rebellious first novel had consigned him, and by early middle age he, along with friends like the poet Philip Larkin, had settled into the irascible, Blimpish persona of the "Little Englander." There is a photograph in Kingsley Amis' *Memoirs* (1991) of the author doing his "Evelyn Waugh face": a triple-chinned, pop-eyed grimace of startled disgust. In a sense, Amis senior spent the rest of his life doing his Evelyn Waugh face, bemoaning the foibles of modernity in a semiparodic vein of chauvinistic, boozy, cantankerous exasperation. This Waughian voice finds its way into the younger Amis' prose as well; Charles Highway's deadpan aside, in *The Rachel Papers,* to the effect that "a high proportion of the children were obviously insane" (p. 61) is quintessential Waugh. But Martin Amis also retains more of the Angry Young Man's outlook than Kingsley, and his work is consequently more multivocal and less didactic than his father's reactionary grousings.

EARLY WORK: THE RACHEL PAPERS, DEAD BABIES, *AND* SUCCESS

ASKED whether it had been difficult for him to develop as a novelist with a famous writer for a father, Martin Amis replied, "It wasn't tough. It was nice—it increased your confidence. It meant that your first novel *would* be published, out of mercenary curiosity if nothing else" (*New Yorker*, 6 March 1995, p. 106). It also meant, of course, that Martin's first novel would suffer comparisons to Kingsley's. The younger Amis was clever enough not to make the obvious response of writing in a completely different mode from that of his father. Rather, he produced a modernized version of *Lucky Jim*. He has said of his father, "I've always thought that if our birth-dates were transposed then he would have written something like my novels, and I would have written something like his" (Alexander, p. 589). In fact, Amis *did* write something like his father's first novel, but it was written under different conditions. Charles Highway, the arrogant, cynical, witty narrator of *The Rachel Papers* is Jim Dixon transposed from the 1950s to the 1970s.

Another way of putting this would be to say that while Jim Dixon is a realistic character, Charles Highway is a postmodern character who lives through literary texts—both the ones he reads in order to find out how to act in real life and those he writes as records and analyses of his real life. The "Rachel Papers" are one such set of notes and files. In fact, Highway has no "real" life at all; he experiences the world on an entirely textual basis. This is how he discusses his relationship with his family:

It's strange; although my father is probably the most fully documented character in my files, he doesn't merit a note-pad to himself, let alone a folder. Mother, of course, has her own portfolio, and my brothers and sisters each have the usual quarto booklet (excepting the rather inconsequential Samantha, who only gets a 3p. Smith's memorandum). Why nothing for my father? Is this a way of getting back at him?

(p. 12)

In what will become a typical Amis maneuver, the reader is invited to draw an analogy between the character in the novel and its author. Is Amis having an Oedipal joke here?

When *The Rachel Papers* was published, Amis was a clever young man, just down from Oxford, with literary aspirations. His novel paints a portrait of a clever young man with literary aspirations about to go up to Oxford. As in *Lucky Jim*, such plot as there is involves the seduction of a young woman, but *The Rachel Papers* is primarily an analysis of Charles Highway's adolescent character, written in the tradition of Goethe's *The Sorrows of Young Werther* or Salinger's *The Catcher in the Rye*. With such a book there is an inevitable temptation to identify the writer with his creation; Kingsley Amis was so annoyed that people identified him with Jim Dixon that he became Evelyn Waugh instead. The egregious Charles Highway is dangerously similar to what the average reader knows about Martin Amis, and many readers have formed permanent antipathies toward Amis on that basis. A sensitive audience, however, will notice the way in which Highway is subtly but deliberately differentiated from his creator. For example, he puts a great deal of emphasis on his own artificiality, constantly reminding us that he is playing a series of roles, acting out scenes from the books he reads. At times this knowledge seems to develop into an awareness that he is a character in a narrative written by someone else. Here is Highway plotting his first date with Rachel:

What persona would I wear? On the two occasions I had seen her since last August I underwent several complete identity-reorganizations, settling finally somewhere between the pained, laconic, inscrutable type and the knowing, garrulous, cynical, laugh a minute, yet something demonic about him, something nihilistic, muted death-wish type. Revamp these, or start again?

Why couldn't Rachel be a little more specific about the type of person *she* was? Goodness knew, if she were a hippie I'd talk to her about her drug experiences, the zodiac, tarot cards. If she were left-wing I'd look miserable, hate Greece, and eat baked beans straight from the tin. If she were the sporty type I'd play her at . . . chess and backgammon and things. No, don't tell me she's the very girl to show me what egotistical folly it is to compartmentalize people in this sad way; don't tell me she's going to sort me out, take me on, supply the *cognitio* and comic resolution. I couldn't bear it.

(p. 42–43)

So Highway progresses from being a self-conscious manipulator of his own persona to intimating that even his "true" personality is a literary construction. He ultimately tires of Rachel when it is revealed that she, too, has built up a fictional image for herself, inventing stories about a glamorous Parisian father who fought in the Spanish Civil War. Highway's reaction is revealing: "Come on, she must be mad, mustn't she. I lied and fantasized and deceived; my existence, too, was a prismatic web of mendacity—but for me it was far more—what?—far more ludic, literary, answering an intellectual rather than an emotional need. Yes, that was the difference" (p. 207).

When she is no longer a character in one of his stories, or when she invents a character for herself, she loses his attention. Highway can only perceive the world through his writing and his reading: he first greets Rachel with a quote from Alfred Tennyson; to facilitate seduction, he leaves Jane Austen's *Persuasion* on the bed and discusses William Blake; to delay orgasm, he mentally recites the poetry of T. S. Eliot. Other characters are similarly defined by their relation to literature. For instance, when George Eliot's *Daniel Deronda* is mentioned, Highway's boorish, proletarian brother-in-law remarks, "I've seen that. BBC 2." Rachel is writing a paper on it in school, and Highway falsely denies having read it. The only significant rebuke Charles receives comes from the tutor who interviews him at Oxford: "Literature has a life of its own, you know. You can't just use it . . . ruthlessly, for your own ends" (p. 215). But he can—and he does—right up until the end. When Rachel reproaches him for the "horrible" letter he has written to tell her their affair is over, he replies, "The content or the style?" He does not reform, remaining resolute in his determination to manipulate his personality as circumstances dictate: "I will not be placed at the mercy of my spontaneous self" (p. 180). There is more curiosity than contrition in his musing on the novel's last page: "I wonder what sort of person I can be" (p. 223).

Amis' other books attempt to answer that question. That is to say, they investigate the question of what has happened to the human personality in the late twentieth century. His second novel, *Dead Babies*, was published in 1975, but it is set in the mid 1980s. His purpose was to extrapolate from the tendencies he saw among his contemporaries and push them to their logical conclusion in order to form a moral judgment about his society. The epigraph from Menippus makes this clear: "And so even when [the satirist] presents a vision of the future, his business is not prophecy; just as his subject is not tomorrow . . . it is today." The target of Amis'

satire here is the hedonistic, self-indulgence of his generation. *Dead Babies* is a moralistic, even puritanical, book worthy of Kingsley Amis at his most Waughian; in fact, Amis senior takes much the same line toward the youth of the 1960s and 1970s in books like *Girl, 20* (1971) and *Jake's Thing* (1978). The gusto and relish with which the younger Amis describes decadence and dissolution, however, gives a certain ambivalence to the portrayal; the audience is made to feel that this report on youth culture comes from the inside.

The plot concerns a group of students at London University who share a large rectory house outside the city and spend their time taking drugs and having casual sex. Visiting them for the weekend is a group of Americans, led by the countercultural guru Marvell Buzhardt, author of *The Mind Lab*. Shortly after arriving, he summarizes the thesis of his book as follows:

For some time now it's been clear to all the genuine people studying this thing that the brain is a mechanical unit and that its aberrations aren't down to environmental, psychological contexts but to purely *chemical* reactions—that's all, nothing more. This idea has had a lot of trouble getting through because people won't let go of the belief that *no* part of us is divine. . . . The only mysterious thing about the brain is its complexity. Nothing cerebral about it, man, just one mother of a terminal of chemicals and nerve ends, and science can keep up with it now. So: why not apply this positively? . . . why not do with your brain what you do with your body? *Fuck* all this dead babies about love, understanding, compassion—*use* drugs to kind of . . . cushion the consciousness, guide it, protect it, stimulate it. . . . We have chemical authority over the psyche—so let's use it, and have a *good* time.

(pp. 43–44)

Buzhardt exploits his theories to rationalize self-indulgence, but what he says is hardly more extreme than much respectable mainstream psychology. In fact, he is describing the death of the soul; he is arguing that the human spirit cannot survive in our age of enlightenment. The philosopher Theodor Adorno has analyzed this phenomenon in works such as *Dialectic of the Enlightenment* (1947), in which he connects the death of the spirit to the rise of a postmodern hyperreality in which "real life has become indistinguishable from the movies" (p. 126). Amis' work makes this point repeatedly; as he stated in an interview with Victoria Alexander, "People feel they are in some soap.

That is the mild delusion that most people are suffering from" (p. 586). He seems to acknowledge the philosophical heritage of this idea in the name of one of the characters in *Dead Babies:* "He called himself Adorno, after the German Marxist philosopher whose death had brought so much despondence to the commune in the summer of 1972, when Andy was just a boy. *Andy Adorno*—it was the most exquisite name he had ever heard" (p. 179).

In Amis' later work, the demise of the soul will figure alongside the death of love and the degradation of art as the characteristic developments of the postmodern era. These themes are prefigured in *Dead Babies*, being introduced by means of pornography, another perennial Amis theme, which is avidly consumed by the book's characters. As Buzhardt tells them, "In the seventies. That's what they achieved. They separated emotion and sex" (p. 122). The aristocratic Englishman Quentin Villiers disagrees, claiming that he and his wife, Celia, are in love, that they married for that reason. Buzhardt dismisses the notion: " 'Forget it. The iconography of desire's too pervasive now. The minute you're . . . fucking Celia here and you start to think about something else—some model or screen actress that's on every billboard and magazine you look at'—he snapped his fingers—'you'll know that's true' " (p. 123).

Amis has often been accused of a lack of sympathy for or interest in his female characters, and it is true that the leading women in this book, Celia and Diana, are wan and almost indistinguishable. There is also the American Roxeanne, a one-dimensional parody of pornographic fantasy. It would be an obtuse reader, however, who failed to detect the irony behind Amis' treatment of women. It is through the misogyny of their male characters—in Amis' work the narrator and even the author are also characters—that his novels (like Nabokov's *Lolita*) endorse the most radical feminist indictments of male sexuality. Here, for example, are Keith Whitehead's thoughts on being introduced to a prostitute:

To little Keith's narrow blue eyes she was something of a disappointment. The tales he had heard about her were, by and large, dehumanizing in tendency. Lucy was a thing that fucked people for money, that would wank you off for a favor, that removed its clothes if you asked it to. But here she was—to all appearances spectacularly human. . . . No, Lucy was palpably the holder of views, the entertainer of thoughts, the proprietress of some individuality.

(pp. 73–74)

The figure who is so affronted by Lucy's humanity is, by the standards of naturalism, barely human himself. Whereas *The Rachel Papers* is generally realistic in mode, *Dead Babies* presents a world peopled by excessive, exaggerated parodies of human beings. Most memorably, there is Keith, an immensely fat and ugly midget whose main function is to be routinely tormented by the rest of the household. Amis is brutally frank in his depiction of Keith's predicament: in a world that values only good looks, sensual pleasure, and money, Keith simply has no role except that of victim. At one stage he loses his sanity and is treated by a psychoanalyst who fulminates about trauma, blocks, and phobias. Keith interrupts him:

It's quite straightforward. No one likes me—actually most people dislike me instinctively, including my family—I'm not much good at my work, I've never had a girlfriend or a friend of any kind, I've got very little imagination, nothing makes me laugh, I'm fat, poor, bald, I've got a horrible spotty face, constipation, B.O. [body odor], bad breath, no prick and I'm one inch tall. That's why I'm mad now. Fair enough?

(pp. 133–134)

The doctor, like the reader, can only agree, and throughout the novel Keith suffers one humiliating torture after another. Occasionally the authorial voice seems to creep into the narrative, half-apologizing, half-gloating over Keith's deformity and misfortune: "Well, we're sorry about it Keith, of course, but we're afraid that you simply *had* to be that way. Nothing personal, please understand—merely to serve the designs of this particular fiction" (pp. 146–147).

Amis describes (and perspicuously predicts) the degeneration of the 1960s counterculture, with its ethos of peace and fellowship, into a merciless, loveless environment of egotism and hedonism. Toward the end of the book, the community is threatened by a vicious practical joker who leaves notes to his victims signed "Johnny." After he has caused most of the residents of the house to kill themselves or each other, it is revealed that "Johnny" is actually Quentin—the one character who had defended love and compassion. His advocacy of these old-fashioned virtues turns out to have been a cruel trick to deflect suspicion. More explicitly than *The Rachel Papers*, *Dead Babies* gives vent to an unremittingly dark and pessimistic vision of the contemporary personality.

Amis' next novel, *Success*, is no less grim in its morality, but it is more inventive in its form. This book represents Amis' first sustained experiment with multiple narrators and his earliest study of the relations between two complementary antagonists. Gregory Riding and Terence Service are foster brothers; the working-class Terence was adopted by the aristocratic, philanthropic Ridings after his father brutally murdered his little sister. In the novel the pair, in their early twenties, are sharing a flat in the West London area that would become the locale of many Amis novels. Gregory is handsome, rich, popular, sexually active, and employed in an undemanding job at an art gallery. Terence is ugly, poor, lonely, sex-starved, and works in a wretched and undefined sales capacity. The book recounts a year in their lives, with each character giving us separate and conflicting accounts of events each month.

Both narrators address the reader directly, wondering about their status as characters, appealing for our sympathy, and denigrating the credibility of the other. Terence says of Gregory: "What am I doing here? My job, I think, is to make *you* hate him also" (p. 12), while Gregory urges us to "have a laugh at Terence's expense. . . . That's what we're here for, after all—to have some fun with him" (p. 22). The reader quickly understands that their identities are interdependent: Gregory's success gains its luster from, and is made possible by, Terence's failure. At first Gregory seems the more perceptive about this situation: "*Terence* thinks—he doesn't actually dare say it—that my life is in some sense a gloating parody of the huff-and-puff of his own quotidian dreads. . . ." (p. 48). As the plot unfolds, however, we notice that Gregory's descriptions are becoming less and less plausible. His stories begin to conflict with Terence's, and the reader is forced to decide whose story to believe.

Here is Gregory's account of a childhood incident during which Terence had been caught stealing:

We undertook a search of the house and quickly cornered Public Enemy Number One in the north attics, where he had crawled beneath the chassis of a warped bed. I was the first to discover him and raise the cry. His explosive confession and bawled apologies soon had us all in stitches.

(p. 96)

And here is Terence's account of the same event:

Gregory was alone when he found me. I waited for him to rally the others with a whoop, but instead he paused, crouched at the side of the bedstead, and slowly edged beneath it towards me. His face was as wet with tears as my own. "Come down, Terry," he said. "We're not cross any more. It's all over now."

(p. 88)

Terence is more credible because his account makes Gregory seem human, while in Gregory's own version he casts himself as a monster of conceit and snobbery. We gradually learn that this is a persona Gregory has constructed, one that is proving increasingly difficult to maintain. We find out that he is, in fact, underpaid and overworked at his job, that his sexual prowess is waning, and that he harbors an incestuous passion for his sister, Ursula, who is becoming schizophrenic. Terence notes the decline in his foster brother's fortunes with satisfaction, giving thanks to what seems to be authorial providence: "I don't think I need to do anything about him after all. Something else is doing it for me. I think things are being taken care of quite nicely" (p. 174).

As Gregory declines, Terence prospers. He does so, however, by means of a pronounced moral degeneration; at the nadir of his fortunes, he vows that "from now on, boy, am I going to be nasty." He saves his job and earns cash bonuses by informing on his fellow employees; he seduces the vulnerable and ill Ursula, who commits suicide when he rejects her; and he beats up a vagrant in a parking lot outside a pub. He finally sleeps with a woman on whom he had a crush during the first half of the novel, reflecting: "It was okay—with myself in sparkling form, both athletic and pitiless—but nothing special" (p. 223). With a consternation that recalls the end of Orwell's *Animal Farm*, we realize that the positions have merely been reversed: Terence has turned into Gregory.

At this early stage in his career, then, Amis had already outlined a vision of a world ruthlessly divided into winners and losers, successes and failures. The fortunate display no pity or empathy for the unlucky, who by virtue of their social, sexual,

31

and financial failures appear to be less than human. As Terence puts it while down on his luck, "*I'm one of the people whom people like you see in the streets and think, 'Sometimes I wouldn't mind being like him—no joys, no pains, no soul to vex you.' But I have got a soul . . .*" (p. 64). But the sufferers of Amis' world are no nicer or more ethical than the others: Terence kicks tramps, and Keith Whitehead victimizes his elderly neighbors. It seems that empathy, art, and love are fast disappearing from the human personality, to be replaced by avarice, envy, and lust. Amis has an almost medieval sense of sin functioning as an active force in the postmodern world, and in most of his books there is a demonic tempter and destroyer—such as the diabolical "Johnny" in *Dead Babies*—who gives an overtly satanic flavor to Amis' understanding of evil.

The righteous indignation that drives these three books has been missed by many readers and reviewers, who notice only the hip, flippant tone and the trendy allusions to youth and popular culture. All three were published before Amis was thirty; their major characters are all around twenty. Amis is writing about a specific generation in a particular place and time, namely, London in the 1970s. The themes he explored in his early work reached fruition in the 1980s, when Amis was in his thirties. In many ways that decade saw the fulfillment of the dire prognostications Amis had made in the 1970s. The government of Margaret Thatcher (1979–1990) transformed British society, committing it to free-market capitalism and glorifying individualism, materialism, and acquisitiveness. Amis was perfectly positioned to analyze these developments, and their implications for the human condition are the central preoccupation of his mature fiction.

MATURE WORK: MONEY, LONDON FIELDS, *AND*
THE INFORMATION

Money (1984) is by any measure an astonishing book. Its stylistic virtuosity enhances its philosophical profundity; it combines highbrow allusion and postmodern technique with an acute ear for the demotic and the vernacular. Here Amis finally identifies the culprit behind the aberrations dissected in his early work: the power of money has distorted all

human identity and perverted all human relationships. If Amis had called his book *Capital,* his diagnosis might have seemed to be a conventional socialist critique of Thatcher's Britain and Reagan's America. But Amis deals in more universal human predicaments than the narrowly topical. As he stated in an interview with John Haffenden:

I have strong moral views, and they are very much directed at things like money and acquisition. I think money is the central deformity in life, as Saul Bellow says, it's one of the evils that has cheerfully survived identification as an evil. Money doesn't mind if we say it's evil, it goes from strength to strength. It's a fiction, a tacit conspiracy that we all go along with. My hatred for it does look as though I'm underwriting a certain asceticism, but it isn't really that way: I don't offer alternatives to what I deplore.

(pp. 13–14)

Certainly Amis has never been an overtly political writer. His revulsion toward money does not spring from the injustices of capitalism but from a concern over what money does to the human consciousness. In the same interview he opines that "you can't start thinking clearly until you've got over money" (p. 14). Money, says Amis, is a "fiction" that has become the stuff of reality. It is the ultimate fixture of the postmodern world, transforming image into reality and reality into a mere image; this hyperreality deforms and degrades the spirit of everyone who comes into contact with it.

The arena within which Amis explores the effects of money on our consciousness is the mind of John Self, the novel's narrator and antihero. Self represents the self in its postmodern form; as he puts it, "I am addicted to the twentieth century" (p. 89). The ultimate consumer, Self is addicted to alcohol (which adds a new dimension to the device of the unreliable narrator in the sense that he often cannot remember what has happened); pornography and prostitutes; cigarettes and fast food; video games and gambling; and brawling with men and beating up women. He earns his living making advertisements for alcohol, cigarettes, fast food, violent movies, and pornographic magazines. Throughout the novel he shuttles between London and New York while working on a new project, a feature film variously entitled *Good Money* and *Bad Money.* Amis recounts Self's depraved misadventures in both cities in intimate and gruesome detail. Despite the fact that Self never actually says anything interesting or intelligent, his thought processes, which form the text of *Money,* are sophisticated and insightful. The reader suspects that Self is not always speaking in his own voice, that the author is surreptitiously adding his own marginal gloss to Self's musings. Take, for example, the following passage where Self notes the changes the 1980s have wrought on Ladbroke Grove, the raffish district of West London where Amis and most of his protagonists live:

This area is going up in the world. There used to be a third-generation Italian restaurant across the road: it had linen tablecloths and rumpy, strict, black-clad waitresses. It's now a Burger Den. There is already a Burger Hutch on the street. There is a Burger Shack, too, and a Burger Bower. Fast food equals fast money. I know: I helped. Perhaps there is money-room for several more. . . . There used to be a bookshop here, with the merchandise ranked in alphabetical order and subject sections. No longer. The place didn't have what it took: market forces. . . . There used to be a music shop (flutes, guitars, scores). This has become a souvenir hypermarket. There used to be an auction room: now a video club. A kosher delicatessen—a massage parlour. You get the idea? My way is coming up in the world.

(p. 71)

Self merges into Amis and Amis speaks through Self. The disintegration of a stable personality that this narrative technique reveals is itself a consequence of the dominance of money. There is a sense, it seems, in which people living in an unrestricted market economy cease to be fully human. Here is Self, toward the end of the book, in a New York restaurant:

The waitresses in this dark place had been obliged to squeeze themselves into wench outfits—bibs, stockings, all *that* again. Market research had no doubt established that this was the most common male fetish. They also said *enjoy your meal* and *have a nice day* and *you're welcome* the whole time. People think that's a natural American foible, a natural winsomeness. Don't they *understand*? Its just company policy. They're trained to say it. They're programmed. It's all money. God I can't wait to leave this moneyworld.

(p. 335)

Self can't escape from money, however, and the strong implication of the novel is that nobody else can either. The only transcendence available to Self is in the form of cheap thrills and fleshly pleasures;

Money contains some of the most unflinching, appalling accounts of drunkenness and pornography in twentieth-century literature. Self's girlfriend, Selina (who owes a great deal to Renata in Bellow's *Humboldt's Gift*) is a gold digger who fosters and indulges his pornographic lust, the better to extract money from him. His separation from the world of art and culture is ironically emphasized: he grew up in a gloomy pub called the Shakespeare and recalls a visit to Stratford to make "a TV-ad for a new kind of flash-friable pork-and-egg bap or roll or hero called a Hamlette" (p. 70). He is unable to comprehend the message contained in the handful of works on his shelf: *Treasure Island, The Usurers, Timon of Athens, Our Mutual Friend, Silas Marner,* "The Pardoner's Tale," and *Success.* The astute reader will recognize that these books are all morality tales about the evil of money—and that *Success* is by none other than Martin Amis. But Self is not an intellectual; he can read and write, but complex cultural issues are beyond him. In several touching moments, Self achieves a degree of self-awareness about himself. He is, he admits, a great success financially:

But my life is also my private culture. . . . And I mean *look* at my private culture. Look at the state of it. It really isn't very nice in here. And that is why I long to burst out of the world of money and into—into what? Into the world of thought and fascination. How do I get there? Tell me, please. I'll never make it by myself. I just don't know the way.

(p. 118)

Two characters in the novel help Self to understand the world beyond money. One is Martina Twain, a glamorous American who encourages him to read books (and whose last name takes on added significance for the reader who recalls that "Mark Twain" is a famous literary pseudonym meaning "two fathoms deep"). They begin with Orwell's *Animal Farm*—whose achievement is marred for Self because of his failure to realize that it is an allegory—and proceed to *Nineteen Eighty-Four,* which reveals to Self the significance of his hotel room number (101). They attend a performance of Verdi's *Otello,* where Self is self-righteously censorious of Desdemona's sluttish infidelity. Martina also gives him books on Marx, Freud, Einstein, Hitler—"And I thought *I* was aggressive" (p. 275)—and a volume on capitalism entitled *Money.* This latter work causes Self some consternation, provoking one of his frequent direct addresses to the reader: "Sometimes *Money* gives me an odd feeling, a worried feeling. . . . I get the sense that everything is ulterior. And you're in on it too, aren't you" (pp. 263–264).

Self almost comes to understand that he is a character in a novel. He is aided in this by the appearance of a writer called Martin Amis. Amis lives near Self and hangs out in the same pub, where Self initially attempts to pick fights with him. When the script for *Good Money* turns out to be a dud, however, Self is forced to turn to Amis for assistance, and the writer obligingly provides him with a workable rewrite. The two characters establish a prickly friendship, in the course of which Self is given several warnings about his situation. In one of their earliest conversations, Amis begins to ask Self about his fee:

He brooded. "What exactly are we looking at here?"
"Uh?"
"*Money.* I'm in the book. Call me when you know."
(p. 218)

But Self never knows; he lacks the cultural sophistication to pick up on Amis' warnings. At a subsequent meeting Amis essays a conversation with Self about the novelist's art:

"The distance between author and narrator corresponds to the degree to which the author finds the narrator wicked, deluded, pitiful or ridiculous. I'm sorry, am I boring you?"
"—Uh?"
"This distance is partly determined by convention. In the epic or heroic frame, the author gives the protagonist everything he has, and more. The hero is a god or has godlike powers or virtues. In the tragic . . . Are you all right?"
"Uh?" I repeated . . .
. . . "The further down the scale he is, the more liberties you can take with him. You can do what the hell you like to him, really. This creates an appetite for punishment. The author is not free of sadistic impulses. . . ."
(p. 229)

Amis has said much the same in interviews, and we cannot help feeling that this is the creator of Keith Whitehead and Terence Service speaking in his own voice. Biographical details match: the real Martin Amis and his fictional counterpart both live in Ladbroke Grove, are short of stature, roll their own cigarettes, and so on. At one point Self asks him, "Your dad, he's a writer too, isn't he? Bet that made it easier." "Oh, sure," replies Amis, "It's just like taking over the family pub" (p. 86). But it is John Self who grew up in a family pub, and his relationship with his father forms one of the novel's subplots. Self senior is a nasty and avaricious lout—Self wonders, "Why do I bother with my father?" (p. 170)—who at one point sends John a bill for his childhood and eventually pays someone to have him beaten up. It is eventually revealed that Self is actually the illegitimate son of the pub bouncer, Fat Vince. Revelations in the media about the real-life Amis' unknowing illegitimate daughter give an extra autobiographical twist to Self's reaction: "Should you ever find yourself in a paternity or maternity mix-up, should you ever have a child who isn't really his or isn't really hers, tell the kid. Tell the kid soon. Do it" (p. 362).

All sorts of jokes are being played here—on the author, on the characters, on the reader. But all this postmodern self-referentiality has a serious purpose. Amis is indicating that money (like *Money*) destroys all authenticity, all reference points, all integral identity. When the free market is allowed to operate without impediment (as it was during the period in which *Money* was written and set), market forces will obliterate everything that is good in the world; love, the soul, and art will be replaced by pornography, egotism, and television. On the rare occasions when topical events impinge on Self's consciousness, he reacts as though they were part of a soap opera; he worries about Danuta Walesa's new baby, he weeps at the wedding of Prince Charles. The implication is that if authentic culture is obliterated by capitalism, it will be replaced by what the Martin Amis character calls "yob art." The novel's most perspicacious observations about postmodernism are put into the mouth of the loutish Self: "Television is working on us. Film is. We're not sure how yet. We wait, and count the symptoms. There's a realism problem, we all know that. TV is real! some people think. And where does that leave reality? Everyone must have, everyone demands their vivid personalities, their personal soap opera, street theatre, everyone *must have* some art in their lives . . ." (p. 332).

If such energies are denied proper expression, they become perverted and destructive. Self's stepmother is pathetically proud of her "artistic" poses in a porn magazine. The plot of the entire novel turns out to have been an extended hoax orchestrated by Self's American "moneyman" for no better reason than aesthetic pleasure. The Martin Amis character explains all this to Self during the novel's last major scene, in which he precipitates Self's final collapse by beating him in an epic struggle at chess. At the end of the book, Self has lost all his money and is so poor that he is mistaken for a beggar on the street. It is a testament to the novel's searing indictment of materialism that the reader understands that Self's financial ruin provides the only basis for any possible spiritual salvation.

In the deregulated, free-market period of the 1980s, the effect of money on the personality was a potent and enduring theme, and Amis explored it further in *London Fields* (1989). This book features Amis' most memorable character, a cockney petty criminal named Keith Talent. Like John Self, Keith is incapable of distinguishing between reality and representation—the result, once again, of his lack of real culture: "TV came at Keith like it came at everybody else; and he had nothing whatever to keep it out. He couldn't grade or filter it. So he thought TV was real" (p. 55). Talent's interior monologues and conversations are among Amis' most richly comic inventions; he speaks in a blend of superbly observed cockney pub argot ("yeah cheers," "innit," "as such," "im feory") and the tabloid jargon of the mass media. At one point the normally monosyllabic Talent is asked about a football match he has recently attended, to which he replies:

During the first half the Hammers probed down the left flank. Revelling in the space, the speed of Sylvester Drayon was always going to pose problems for the home side's number two. With scant minutes remaining before the half-time whistle, the black winger cut in on the left back and delivered a searching cross, converted by Lee Fredge, the East London striker, with inch-perfect precision. . . .

(p. 91)

The narrator's reaction provides the key to Keith's character: "At first I thought he just memorized sections of the tabloid sports pages. Absolutely wrong. Remember—he is modern, modern. . . . When Keith goes to a football match, that misery of stringer's clichés *is what he actually sees*" (pp. 97–98).

Keith is engaged in a series of abusive relationships with deranged and deluded women, and he

is obsessed with pornography—"He wanted it on *when he was asleep*. He wanted it on *when he wasn't there*" (p. 295). Further, he is enthusiastic though unsuccessful in his career as petty criminal or "cheat," and—the quirk that provides much of the book's narrative momentum—a remarkably proficient player of darts. (In the 1980s the unlikely sport of darts became hugely popular in Britain, with big money at stake and many matches televised.) Keith's skill at this sport energizes him as he plays his way toward the big final match of a darts competition. The only book Keith has ever read is *Darts: Master the Discipline*, which, in addition to being a how-to guide, attempts to rewrite history through the medium of darts:

Those Pilgrim Fathers are said to have thrown darts while sailing to America in 1620 on the so-called Mayflower.

1620! thought Keith.

Christ knows how they managed it as they only had a small boat as they were tossed about on the "Atlantic" ocean. King Arthur was also said to have played a form of darts.

"Heritage," Keith murmured.

(p. 313)

As he progresses through the tournament's stages, Keith, inspired by a dream of the televised final match, becomes more and more single-minded in his pursuit of darting excellence. Amis includes an exquisite parody of the language of sports reporting as Keith constantly rehearses television interviews in his head and listens to tape recordings of famous darts matches. Keith is obsessed, consumed by darts—"A darts brain, that's what he had: darts nerve, darts sinew. A darts heart. A darts soul" (p. 312)—and the competitive, individualistic ethos of the sport empties him of those qualities that have traditionally been thought to define humanity. As Keith writes in his diary: "Remember you are a machine. Delivering the dart the same way every time. . . . Clear ideas from your head. You don't want nothing in your fucking head" (p. 316).

In many ways, then, Keith is an even more plebeian and grotesque version of John Self. Unlike the transatlantic, jet-setting Self, however, Keith is a strictly local character, and *London Fields* is a lovingly intimate depiction of Amis' multiethnic, bohemian neighborhood. Most of the action takes place in the Black Cross, a seedy and disorderly pub that might seem farfetched to anyone who has never had a beer on Portobello Road. The pub provides the setting in which Keith encounters the novel's other main characters: Guy Clinch, a dim and effete aristocrat; Nicola Six, a beautiful and sinister man-eater who is Amis' most effective female protagonist and effectively becomes the "author" of the book, manipulating Keith and Guy into a mutually destructive struggle (a recurring theme in Amis' novels) for her affections; and Samson Young, a terminally ill Jewish American novelist who is—or seems to be—the book's narrator.

At the beginning of the novel we are told that Nicola Six suspects she is going to be murdered, that she knows when and where it will happen, and that Keith will be the murderer. Samson Young decides to use Nicola's premonition as the plot for his novel, and the two of them begin to construct and act out an elaborate narrative, using the unwitting Guy and Keith as their "characters." Their ruse involves convincing Guy that Keith is not the lout he seems to be, and to this end Nicola videotapes him in a heavily scripted discussion of Keats's poem "Bright Star." Keith reads his lines convincingly enough, and Nicola is able to edit out his tabloid-inspired references to "the plucky little . . . talented Romantic" (p. 356). After the charade is over, however, we hear Keith's true ruminations, which return us to the mode of "yob art":

John Keats, thought Keith, as he drove away. Top wordsmith and big in pharmaceuticals. Books: one way to make a fast quid. Breakfast by the pool. Wife in good nick. "Really, dahling, I got to stop writing them Hollywood scripts and get down to serious writing." Fucking great study full of leather. Snooker! Jesus. Lady Muck with the schoolmarm skirt round her waist. Wasn't bad. No. In the end I thoroughly enjoyed it. Showed Guy. But an awful lot of old balls. Keith wondered, parenthetically, if Keats had ever played a form of darts.

(pp. 356–357)

Guy is fooled by Nicola's ruse, however, and so, eventually, is Keith. She pretends to be enamored of them both, thus ruining Guy's marriage and ensuring Keith's darting downfall. Her life, we are told, has consisted of a series of such machinations—she lives to deceive and destroy the male of the species. Nicola Six is Amis' cleverest response to the perceived inauthenticity of his female characters, and once again he evades criticism by

endorsing the claims of his detractors. Devastatingly beautiful and provocatively dressed, Nicola Six is, as she announces, "a male fantasy," and there is a sense in which this is necessarily true of any woman in a patriarchal society. But Nicola turns men's objectifying fantasies against them in order to undermine and destroy:

Nicola was amazed—Nicola was consternated—by how few women really *understood* about underwear. It *was* a scandal. If the effortless enslavement of men was the idea, or one of the ideas (and who had a better idea?), why halve your chances by something as trivial as a poor shopping decision? . . . To ephemeral flatmates and sexual wallflowers at houseparties and to other underequipped rivals Nicola had sometimes carelessly slipped the underwear knowledge. It took about ten seconds. Six months later the ones who got it right would be living in their own mews houses in Pimlico and looking fifteen years younger. But mostly they got it wrong. . . . Perhaps women couldn't believe how simple men really were—how it could all be decided in five minutes at the hosiery store. . . . Men were so *simple.* But what did that do to the thoughts of women, to the thoughts of women like Nicola Six?

(pp. 70–71)

The answer is that it makes her despise them. The two men she destroys form another of Amis' mirror images, and the tools Nicola uses to ensure their dooms are correspondingly varied. She shows pornographic videos of herself to the carnal Keith; to the sentimental Guy she pretends to be a lovesick virgin. Thus, she exploits the patriarchal madonna/whore dichotomy with casual ease and to devastating effect.

The destruction wrought by Nicola is connected throughout to a matter with which Amis became increasingly concerned during the 1980s, namely, nuclear holocaust. A political "crisis" of some kind is developing as the plot of *London Fields* unfolds. Although we are sure of its severity, we are never certain of its nature; in the world Amis depicts, reality and fantasy have become indistinguishable. It is impossible to get any news of the "crisis"; Keith's tabloid occasionally features headlines such as RED NYET or TOWELHEAD DEADLOCK among the pinups, but no details are given. Even the more sophisticated papers read by Samson Young bury the serious news under human-interest stories about the health of the president's wife or reports on the condition of YURI IN KIEV and VIKTOR IN MINSK. The pseudoindividualism of postmodernity blinds the book's characters to their impending doom. *London Fields* is Amis' most compelling indictment of the false consciousness that pervades all social classes in the late twentieth century. The mass media, consumerism, money, and pornography have made it impossible to see the world as it really is. At one point Keith and Nicola watch sparrows frolicking in a puddle ("birds" is London vernacular for "girls"):

> Keith grinned fondly.
> "It's like birds playing in a pool."
> "*Like* birds playing in a pool, Keith?"
> "You know. Girls. Playing in a swimming-pool."
> "Ah, yes." Nicola thought of the kind of video Keith might occasionally get his hands on. The white villa, the baby blue of a Marbellan swimming-pool, the handful of English slags, "playing" . . .
>
> (p. 128)

To the degree that they are excluded from literacy, art, and culture, Amis' characters exist in an artificial, pornographic hyperreality in which, to quote Adorno again, "real life has become indistinguishable from the movies." Keith sees not the sparrows but porno stars. In *London Fields* the dangers of such a condition are made abundantly clear: with the exception of Nicola (who welcomes disaster), the characters are blind and helpless as they lurch toward catastrophe. At the end of the novel it is revealed that Nicola has fooled Samson as well. The murderer turns out to be not Keith but Guy, thus ruining the plot of the novel Samson has been writing. To take revenge, Samson persuades Guy to let him kill Nicola instead. Having done so, he laments the death of art, which can now be added to the death of love, something Nicola has been proclaiming throughout. The author/narrator has been duped by one of his own characters: "She outwrote me. Her story worked. And mine didn't. . . . Nicola destroyed my book. . . . She knew I wouldn't find it worth saving, this wicked thing, this wicked book I tried to write, plagiarized from real life" (pp. 466–467).

London Fields may be plagiarized from Samson Young's real life, but Young is himself a character in a rather unrealistic (or hyperrealistic) novel. Amis' novel *The Information* (1995) largely refrains from the convoluted self-referentiality characteristic of the incompetent, drunk, and dying narrators of *Money* and *London Fields*, although it is no less disturbing in its implications. It relates the friendship and rivalry of two novelists who, like Terence and Gregory of *Success*, were born one day apart. Richard Tull, once a promising young writer, has seen his career wane and die after a series of convoluted, overly complex, and unpublishable failures. After a slow start, Gwyn Barry has recently achieved phenomenal success with *Amelior*, a cloying, politically correct utopian fantasy (this character gives a nod to another Welsh literary pseudo-intellectual—Alun in Kingsley Amis' 1986 novel, *The Old Devils*). Barry's triumph, which has nothing to do with his book's artistic value but is due solely to the poor taste of the reading public, infuriates the disappointed Tull, who decides that he must take a horrible revenge on his self-satisfied friend.

The Information takes the observations on the postmodern condition of *Money* and *London Fields* and applies them to a specifically literary milieu; Tull and Barry are members of a higher class and possess a greater intelligence than Self and Talent. But the elimination of class distinctions is part of postmodernism's effect; for example, the middle-class Richard and Gwyn are able to attend a working-class pool hall in safety, something that would have been inconceivable twenty years earlier: "In those days the Englishmen all had names like Cooper and Baker and Weaver, and they beat you up. Now they all had names like Shop and Shirt and Car, and you could go anywhere you liked" (p. 40). The English class system has changed, along with the postmodern shift from a production-based economy (symbolized by trade-oriented names like "Weaver") to a consumer society (in which people are called "Shop"). Traditional distinctions have been eliminated in the maelstrom of the market; analogous developments have taken place within the field of literature. *The Information* is full of digressions and asides on the condition of art in the postmodern world. Richard Tull writes difficult, intellectual fiction for which there is no market; he hates Gwyn Barry for successfully pandering to the tastes of the masses: "Essentially Richard was a marooned modernist. If prompted, Gwyn Barry would probably agree with Herman Melville: that the art lay in pleasing the readers. Modernism was a brief divagation into difficulty; but Richard was still out there, in difficulty. He didn't want to please the readers. He wanted to stretch them until they twanged" (p. 125).

Gwyn, in contrast, is delighted to tailor himself and his fiction to the demands of the market. He is a master of publicity and promotion; the marketing of his work determines its content. In one interview he absentmindedly compares writing to carpentry; when asked if he actually does carpentry, he is compelled to answer in the affirmative. Worried lest his imposture be discovered, Gwyn buys a workbench and lathe and really does take up carpentry; his image thus determines his reality. He appears in rock videos, mouths fashionable antiracist and nonsexist platitudes, and constantly composes his own biography in his head. Watching Gwyn pose for a photographer, Richard considers the effect of such immersion in the mass media:

What *happened* inside the much-photographed face—what happened to the head within? The Yanomano or the Ukuki were surely onto something. One shot wouldn't do it, but the constant snatch of the camera's mouth—it would take your reality, in the end. Yes, probably, the more you were photographed, the thinner it went for your inner life. Being photographed was dead time for the soul.

(p. 12)

Richard, in contrast to Gwyn, resists the pressure to market himself. He rejects his agent's suggestion that he might be salable as a "young fogey"—"You wear a bow tie and a waistcoat. Would you smoke a pipe?" (p. 94)—and he is completely out of his element in an American radio interview with Dub Traynor. At a loss in a world where ordinary conversation and advertisement blend seamlessly, Richard keeps trying to reply to Traynor's commercial "messages" ("Do you like great musicals?" "No"). Traynor's first direct question to him is: "What's your novel trying to say?"

Richard thought for a moment. The contemporary idea seemed to be that the first thing you did, as a communicator, was come up with some kind of slogan, and either you put it on a coffee mug or a T-shirt or a bumper sticker—or else you wrote a novel about it. Even Dub clearly thought you did it this way round. And now that writers spent as much time telling everyone what they were doing as they spent actually doing it, then they would start doing it that way round too, eventually.

(pp. 252–253)

This view of the novel is shared by the deranged pair of readers who form Richard's only audience.

As Darko, a mysterious Serb, puts it in one fan letter, "First, you get the topic. Next you package it. Then, comes the hipe [*sic*]" (p. 34). Thus art is degraded by commerce and the mass media. Gwyn Barry's success exploits this degradation, and this lends a righteous veneer to Richard's envy of his friend. Right from the start, however, we are aware that Tull will be as impotent in his revenge as he is in bed. His outrage at Gwyn's popularity is really a protest against the zeitgeist. As usual in Amis' works, the death of art is linked to the decline of the individual self, which is presented as universal and unavoidable:

Even when he was in familiar company (his immediate family, for instance) it sometimes seemed to Richard that those gathered in the room were not quite authentic selves—that they had gone away and then come back not quite right, half remade or reborn by some blasphemous, backhanded and above all inexpensive process. In a circus, in a funhouse. All flaky and carny. Not quite themselves. Himself very much included.

(p. 18)

Because his own work remains resolutely inaccessible, Richard is forced to make ends meet by working as an editor at a vanity press. There he encounters the direst effects of the decline of art. Evaluating the manuscripts he reads, he muses: "It wasn't bad literature. It was anti-literature. Propaganda, aimed at the self" (p. 54). The pressures and tendencies against which Richard struggles pervade the entire culture. As a "marooned modernist," Richard has been unable to adapt to the new circumstances and gain the knack, illustrated so effortlessly in Amis' own work, of mixing the popular and the recondite in postmodern pastiche. As Amis puts it, "He was a modern. But he wasn't a postmodern" (p. 238). At one point Richard pays a visit to one of Gwyn's young fans intending either to blackmail Gwyn or infect him with HIV:

Belladonna wore a printed body-stocking which bodied forth—the body: the naked female body. Unlike the nipples, which were pink and rubbery, the kind of nipples a plumber might need a bag of in his kit, the pubic triangle, Richard judged, was quite tastefully rendered: an economic delta of dark brushstrokes. She was definitely younger than him. He was a modernist. She was the thing that came next.

(pp. 152–153)

In Belladonna's postmodern sensibility, artifice and reality are indistinguishable. The distinction between high and low art is untenable. The demands of the market become the only criteria for evaluating human endeavor. According to those criteria, Gwyn's books are far better than Richard's even though they are aesthetically inferior. This is what maddens Richard Tull, driving him to increasingly desperate measures, including hiring thugs to beat up his friend and eventually rewriting Gwyn's entire novel in a crazed attempt to slap him with a plagiarism charge. All Richard's schemes predictably misfire, although his embittered snipings provide Amis with the chance to satirize many contemporary literary pieties. Here, for instance, Richard mocks Gwyn's politically correct habit of following neuter antecedents with feminine pronouns:

> "Guess what. We had an intruder last night."
> "Really? Did she take anything?"
> "We're not really sure."
> "How did she get in? Was she armed, do you know?"
> (p. 175)

Such petty jibes are the only successes Richard achieves, despite the blundering assistance of Amis' typical array of West London lowlife. *The Information* is as pessimistic about the future of art as *London Fields* is about love or *Money* is about the soul. The thematic and stylistic unity of these three works, together with their common location in Ladbroke Grove (the sinister Black Cross pub reappears at the end of *The Information,* as do the names of several local characters) has prompted some readers to think of them as a trilogy. They certainly represent a sustained and profound meditation on the postmodern condition, which they investigate with a thoroughness and accuracy unmatched by any contemporary British writer.

EXPERIMENTAL WORK: OTHER PEOPLE, EINSTEIN'S MONSTERS, *AND* TIME'S ARROW

AT various points in his career Amis tried—with varying degrees of success—to expand his thematic register and experiment with his narrative technique. *Other People* (1981) is often described as a "Martian" novel since it attempts to portray the world as though seen by a visitor from outer space. The rationale for this device is that the novel recounts the experience of total amnesia. Mary Lamb wakes up one day in London, homeless and alone, without any idea as to who she is. She encounters a succession of desperate and dissolute figures, giving Amis the opportunity to portray London as a Hades of poverty and despair, before her fortunes improve under the tutelage of John Prince, an enigmatic detective. It emerges that the gentle, innocent Mary is in fact Amy Hide, a beautiful, malicious young woman who was believed murdered. Prince functions as a surrogate narrator, trying to revive Mary's memory by guiding her around the sordid and vice-ridden environment Amy frequented. The precise nature of Amy's character and the reasons for her presumed demise, however, are never made sufficiently clear and the novel's plot is too mysterious and its style too elliptical to be fully satisfying.

The reader of *Other People* will be aided by Amis' explanation, as stated in an interview with John Haffenden, that "the novel is the girl's death, and her death is a sort of witty parody of her life" (p. 17). There is a clue to this situation in the book's title, which alludes to the famous phrase in Jean-Paul Sartre's play *Huis clos* (1945; *No Exit*): "Hell is other people." It seems that we are to understand the life of Mary Lamb as the life after death—the hell—of Amy Hide. The shadowy Prince is thus revealed as a Lucifer figure, the Prince of Darkness. Once we have grasped this, the novel makes a good deal more sense: Through her innocence, Mary Lamb causes the same kind of distress and disaster that Amy Hide brought about out of malice. We are now in a position to appreciate the significance of such passages as the one in which Mary/Amy is told: "You're already dead—can't you see? Life is hell, life is murder, but then death is very lifelike" (p. 222). But the action and characters of *Other People* are not substantial enough to support such an ambitious theme. The novel is remarkable chiefly for its anticipations of Amis' later work (for example, Amy Hide is clearly a prototype for Nicola Six). The morality that Amis brings to bear on postmodernity is prefigured here in schematic and skeletal form:

> These are the Seven Deadly Sins: Avarice, Envy, Pride, Gluttony, Lust, Anger, Sloth.
> These are the seven deadly sins: venality, paranoia, insecurity, excess, carnality, contempt, boredom.
> (p. 195)

In the twentieth century, the vices of traditional morality have changed their names but not their essential natures. The shift to lowercase, however, indicates that they have ceased to be recognized as "sins." The postmodern world has lost its sense of sin—in *Money*, John Self wonders, "What is this state, seeing the difference between good and bad and choosing bad" (p. 29)—and it is this sense that Amis tries to reawaken through his fiction.

In *Einstein's Monsters* (1987), Amis focuses on the cosmic sinfulness of nuclear weapons. This book is unique for two reasons: it is Amis' only overtly political work, and it is his only collection of short stories. In the introduction, entitled "Thinkability," Amis connects the potential for nuclear destruction with the nature of postmodern experience. By threatening to end human life, he observes, nuclear weapons jeopardize not only the present and the future but also the past. If the human race is annihilated, all the achievements and struggles of human history will have been meaningless. As a result, "something seems to have gone wrong with time—with modern time; the past and the future, equally threatened, equally cheapened, now huddle in the present" (p. 22). It is perhaps in reaction to the possible obliteration of the species that Amis has chosen to believe in an imperishable soul. As he told Victoria Alexander during an interview, "If we're to believe in perfectibility or even improvement, then we need to be able to think of the human soul as an imperishable image of our potential and our battered innocence" (p. 584). An ambitious novelist, Amis necessarily has written for posterity. If the human race faces physical annihilation—as the prevalence of nuclear weapons strongly suggests—the only posterity available would be spiritual. The existence of nuclear weapons thus impels Amis toward a belief in the soul. However, he is too skeptical and materialistic to embrace this position wholeheartedly. As a result, through various means these stories express the fervent hope that a nuclear catastrophe will not occur, even though they do not fully pursue the philosophical implications of its possibility.

The first story, "Bujak and the Strong Force," presents a semiallegorical injunction to disarm. A tough Polish war veteran resists the temptation to kill the men who have murdered his family; reconciliation, he reasons, has to start somewhere. "Insight at Flame Lake" and "The Time Disease" are explorations in altered perspective, after the manner of *Other People*, though set in the shadow of the mushroom cloud. "The Immortals" is narrated by a man who believes he has lived forever; this conviction is ultimately revealed to be a universal fantasy of humanity's postholocaust detritus.

"The Little Puppy That Could" is completely different from any of Amis' other works and is also the most successful piece in the collection. Told in the simple, repetitive style of children's stories, this strangely affecting tale concerns the love that blossoms in the midst of a nuclear wasteland between a young girl and a small, mutant creature that thinks of itself as a "puppy." She nurtures and protects the animal, sheltering it from the scorn and hatred of the townsfolk, whose wretched settlement is threatened by a Grendel-like monster to which they are compelled to offer repeated sacrifices. One day the girl is picked as the monster's next meal, but she is saved by the self-sacrificing heroism of her little friend. Amis clearly runs a serious risk of sentimentality here. Incredibly, however, he avoids mawkishness through the quiet, matter-of-fact tone in which he recounts the events. The story is moving without being cloying, and it is a testament to Amis' skill that he is able to achieve this effect while writing in a medium that does not really suit him.

For Martin Amis is above all a novelist. The short story seems too constricting a mode for his effervescent diction; his sprawling, gargantuan characters need fuller development than they receive in twenty or thirty pages. In his next experiment in formal innovation, the novella *Time's Arrow; or, The Nature of the Offence* (1991), Amis allowed himself more room to maneuver. This remarkable book is a bildungsroman in reverse: it tells the story of a man's life backward. The narrator wakes up and finds himself surrounded by doctors, feels awful at first but gradually becomes stronger and more active, pities babies because they are approaching death, and so on. Amis brilliantly sustains this technique throughout the book, never flinching from even the smallest details. Eating, for example, involves taking food from the garbage, regurgitating it onto the plate, placing it in cans and packets, returning these to the supermarket, and receiving money for your pains. *Time's Arrow* could only have been written so successfully in the video age; Amis has clearly spent a great deal of time with his finger on the rewind button of his remote control. His method can often be hilariously funny: love affairs always seem to begin with a furious argument; the main protagonist takes candy from children and steals from the collection plate at church; his professional career is a series of humiliating demotions; and, with consistent though still surprising logic, all sustenance springs magically from the toilet.

Amis did not invent this mode of storytelling; one obvious influence is Philip K. Dick's *Counter-Clock World* (1966). In *Time's Arrow,* however, events are narrated by a second consciousness that inhabits but is not identical with the mind of the book's hero, Tod Friendly. This narrative voice acts as an observer of Tod's actions; its relation to him parallels that of a narrator to a character but also, as soon becomes increasingly clear, that of the soul to the mind. It seems, then, that *Time's Arrow* is the story of a man's life narrated in reverse by his soul. The narrative voice senses that something is amiss with Tod's mind, that he is ill at ease, that an unpleasant secret lurks in his past—which in this book is his future. At first it assumes that this unspecified guilt must have to do with his job as a doctor. The narrator is appalled to see Tod take healthy patients and inflict horrific injuries on them before sending them away to be dumped on the streets. He cannot understand why Tod isn't stopped. No one, after all, can pretend to be ignorant of the atrocities Tod commits; his victims leave the hospital with ambulance sirens blaring and lights flashing. Before arriving at the hospital, children send Dr. Friendly charming thank-you letters; the narrator grimly reflects that "they won't be so grateful when we're through" (p. 86). What, he wonders, would it take to make Tod desist from his evil practices: "If I died, would he stop? If I am his soul, and there were soul-loss or soul-death, would that stop him? Or would it make him even freer?" (p. 96).

As the story unfolds backward, we follow Tod Friendly through prior incarnations as "John Young" in New York, and then back across the Atlantic to Portugal, where, in 1948, he lives as "Hamilton de Souza." Eventually he changes his name again, this time to "Odilo Unverdorben" (*unverdorben* means "unspoiled" in German) and makes his way in great haste to Auschwitz, where he goes to work as a camp doctor under the auspices of "Uncle Pepi"—Josef Mengele. The narrator is delighted that his host is now doing good, constructive work, curing people instead of injuring them. Better yet, it transpires that Unverdorben is playing his part in a remarkable, godlike project: the creation of an entire race of people, the Jews. His soul remarks testily on the lack of gratitude he receives for this work, but it is pleased to note the amazing success of the project, followed by the gradual integration of the Jews into German society (after the initial resentment of many Gentiles has subsided). After the Bolsheviks are humiliatingly defeated and driven out of Germany at the end of the war, the narrator encounters many of the people Unverdorben had created unconcernedly going about their business and leading normal lives. This provides some consolation as he ages into childhood; he comes to think of these happily assimilated Jews as his "children."

To write a comedy—even a black comedy—about the Holocaust is clearly a dangerous undertaking. Amis brings it off with aplomb and without causing offense. The hideous irony of the book is that while Doctor Friendly is healing people in America, the backward-moving narrator believes that he is inflicting the wounds he actually cures. While Doctor Unverdorben is assisting Doctor Mengele in his heinous experiments, the narrative voice applauds his skill in restoring people back to health and giving them the gift of life. By this means Amis brings home the evil paradox of the death-camp doctors. The disgusting inversion of medical ethics whereby Mengele and his cohorts used their medical knowledge to inflict pain and death is revealed in its full insanity. The reader experiences events at Auschwitz from a distanced, "Martian" perspective. The effect is one of salutary shock; the unnatural feeling of moving backward in time conveys the monstrous unnaturalness of the events described.

As with *Einstein's Monsters,* however, the final impression left by *Time's Arrow* is that Amis has made a highly creditable attempt at an impossible task. Perhaps the issues raised and the emotions stirred by nuclear or Nazi holocaust are too implacably profound to be satisfactorily treated in short works of fiction. The cynical, satirical point of view from which Amis usually surveys the world is unsuited to the sentiments demanded by the cosmic tragedies of the twentieth century. Amis is at his best when he considers the more local manifestations of barbarism and turpitude, and he has no equal when it comes to depicting the heinous instincts that impel a Keith Talent or a John Self. His experimental fiction would be considered an un-equivocal triumph for a less proficient writer, but it seems flimsy and slight when set against the compendious epics of Amis' longer works.

CRITICISM

IN addition to his steady output of fiction, Martin Amis also produced a polished and impressive corpus of journalism. His articles, reviews, interviews, and profiles dating from the 1980s mostly appeared in the *Observer;* in the 1990s he became a regular contributor to the *New Yorker.* He has published a journalistic monograph, *Invasion of the Space Invaders* (1982), and two collections of previously published pieces, *The Moronic Inferno* (1986) and *Visiting Mrs. Nabokov and Other Excursions* (1993). All are remarkable for the extent to which they reflect and anticipate the themes treated in the novels. *Invasion of the Space Invaders,* for example, is an attempt to exploit the early 1980s fad for video games: it is of coffee table size and contains glossy photographs, a user's guide to the latest games, and an introduction by Steven Spielberg. But it also offers a fluent, intellectual analysis of its subject, which gives a practical valence to the issues raised in Amis' fiction: "It would seem that many of us have vacant or dormant areas in our minds, empty spaces waiting for invasion. This is the area whose expansion leads to quirkiness, eccentricity, madness. It used to be the Devil who invaded these spaces in the common mind. Now, for obvious reasons, it is the Martians, the Space Invaders, who seek entry" (p. 43).

Only a writer as young, trendy, and postmodern as Amis was in the 1980s could have gotten away with saying that video games were the invention of the devil. If his father had said such a thing, it would have been mocked and dismissed as the quintessence of crustiness. There is no doubt, however, that Amis meant what he said. Throughout the book he connects Space Invaders to his novels' perennial concern with addiction, which he takes to be the defining experience of postmodernity: "What we are dealing with here is a global addiction. . . . Anyone who has ever tangled with a drink or drugs problem will know how the interior monologue goes. . . . The obsession/addiction factor is central to the games' success: you might even say that video-dependence is actually programmed into the computer" (pp. 14, 16, 19). Since the book's intended audience is aficionados of such games, Amis' moralism here is daring and subversive—all the more so since the author is clearly addicted to the games himself. When, in his other work, Amis describes the vices of lust, envy, and concupiscence, his writing avoids the appearance of diatribe by virtue of the fact that the author appears to be familiar with the sins he discusses. Here Amis exploits the addict's love-hate relationship with his vice to produce a subtle, nuanced, and very knowledgeable study of a symptomatic social phenomenon.

The Moronic Inferno derives its title from Wyndham Lewis by way of Saul Bellow's description of Chicago in *Humboldt's Gift.* The book is subtitled *And Other Visits to America.* In an attempt to impose a unity on the various pieces, Amis notes that they are all somehow concerned with the United States. The effect of the title is rather unfortunate, however, seeming to pander to the puerile British anti-Americanism that Amis has always loudly and publically despised. In *Einstein's Monsters,* he brilliantly skewers the historian E. P. Thompson, leader of the British Campaign for Nuclear Disarmament, for his ahistorical prejudice against the United States; in *The Information,* Richard Tull is mocked for his pride at never having been to the States; and in the introduction to *The Moronic Inferno,* Amis notes his many connections to the United States, even claiming that "I feel fractionally American myself" (p. ix).

Certainly the essays contained in this volume evince a respect and an affection for the United States that contradict the book's title. There are (largely favorable) reviews of and interviews with many of the most important American writers: Saul Bellow, Gore Vidal, Philip Roth, Truman Capote, Kurt Vonnegut, Gloria Steinem, Diana Trilling, William Burroughs, Norman Mailer, John Updike, and Joan Didion. Refreshingly, Amis displays an equal familiarity with the figures from popular culture he studies: Elvis Presley, Steven Spielberg, Hugh Hefner. Many of the pieces betray key aspects of Amis' own thinking. In a frankly adulatory piece on Bellow, for instance, Amis remarks, " 'I don't know what the world's coming to' may not sound like much of a topic-sentence when you hear it at the bus stop—yet this is Bellow's subject. Actually it is the central subject, and always has been" (p. 8). Whatever the truth of the final generalization, there is no doubt that it has always been Amis' central subject. A similar self-referentiality occurs in an interview with Brian De Palma, originally published in 1984, the same year as *Money*: "The illogicality, the reality-blurring, the media-borne cretinisation of modern life is indeed a great theme" (p. 88). Writing about Updike's character Rabbit in 1983, Amis anticipates his own treatment of Self and Talent:

This is what the unexamined life would be like: venality, fear, and the violence born of knowing no better. Rabbits are the victims of whatever set of values gets to them first. They are the people whom you see every day and dismiss as junior aspirants, junior sufferers, unvexed by soul. But the Rabbit . . . does have his inner life, his private culture, and Updike dissects it with tingling fascination.

(p. 157)

In passages like this it might appear that Amis is more preoccupied with himself than with his ostensible subject. Rather, he sees the common ground between his own opinions and those of the figures he analyzes. The effect is intriguing for a student of Amis' work: it establishes the relevance, topicality, and centrality of his concerns for the postmodern condition. Here, for example, Amis discusses the politics of the New Evangelist movement:

Nor is their critique of American society contemptible in itself. One of [Jerry] Falwell's TV specials is called *America, You're Too Young to Die*. It shows leathery gay necking in Times Square, sex-aid emporia, child pornography, aborted foetuses in soiled hospital trays. A predictably alarmist collage, certainly. But some of us who have been born only once find plenty that is cheerless here, and fail to buy the "humanist package" entire.

(p. 118)

Certainly Amis' work exhibits a puritanism like Falwell's. When, however, he declares that "to dismiss the beliefs of the Evangelicals is to dismiss the intimate thoughts of ordinary people" (p. 118), we may detect a certain disingenuousness. Amis' fiction does not merely "dismiss the intimate thoughts of ordinary people"; it ridicules, excoriates, and burlesques these thoughts with unremitting, merciless brilliance. When he holds his satirical fire, as in his discussion of the Evangelicals, the reader

must assume that it is because his subject has struck a chord within him.

Visiting Mrs. Nabokov is in many ways a companion volume to *The Moronic Inferno*. As in the earlier collection, most of the pieces date from the first half of the 1980s, but they generally deal with topics on the European side of the Atlantic. The writers discussed here include Graham Greene, J. G. Ballard, V. S. Naipaul, Salman Rushdie, Anthony Burgess, Philip Larkin, and V. S. Pritchett. The title piece parallels Amis' earlier praise of Bellow, being a tribute to the widow and the memory of Amis' other literary idol, Vladimir Nabokov. The essays on popular culture are just as clever as, if somewhat less enthusiastic than, those in the earlier book. A dismissive 1976 review of the Rolling Stones provides an interesting foretaste of the disillusion Amis experienced when Madonna refused to grant him an interview. In the introduction, he explains why this failure did not deter him from writing and publishing his article: "The great postmodern celebrities are a part of their publicity machines, and that is all you are ever going to get to write about: their publicity machines" (p. viii). The theme of postmodernism draws Amis back to America, which he seems to regard as a testing ground for tendencies that are not yet fully developed in Europe. Here he comments on the 1988 Republican convention:

Reagan's is a style-setting administration, and there has been trickle-down. Nowadays, when Chris Evert gets a regular boyfriend, the first thing she does is make an ad about it. On *The Dating Game* the dude will report that his new friend is "open" and "communicative"—"and I admire those skills." Who is the role model of the nascent media-coaching industry? Forces are working on the American self. Thirty-five-year-olds have spent half their adult lives in the Reagan era. This has gone on long enough.

(p. 100)

As Amis' work makes clear, the forces behind the postmodern disintegration of the self are no longer—if they ever were—a specifically American phenomenon. His novels form a protracted, bitter, satirical protest against this disintegration, this soul-destroying tendency of contemporary life. Unfortunately (to borrow a phrase from Nabokov, one of Amis' literary heroes) they increasingly read like laughter in the dark.

MARTIN AMIS

SELECTED BIBLIOGRAPHY

I. NOVELS. *The Rachel Papers* (London, 1973; New York, 1974); *Dead Babies* (London, 1975; New York, 1976); *Success* (London, 1978; New York, 1992); *Other People: A Mystery Story* (London, 1981; New York, 1981); *Money: A Suicide Note* (London, 1984; New York, 1985); *London Fields* (London and New York, 1989); *Time's Arrow; or, The Nature of the Offence* (London and New York, 1991); *The Information* (London and New York, 1995).

II. COLLECTIONS OF CRITICAL WORKS. *Invasion of the Space Invaders* (London and Millbrae, Calif., 1982); *The Moronic Inferno and Other Visits to America* (London, 1986; New York, 1987); *Visiting Mrs. Nabokov and Other Excursions* (London, 1993; New York, 1994).

III. AUTOBIOGRAPHICAL WORK. "My Oxford," in *My Oxford*, rev. ed., ed. Ann Thwaite (London, 1986).

IV. COLLECTION OF STORIES. *Einstein's Monsters* (London and New York, 1987); *Two Stories:* Denton's Death *and* Let Me Count the Times (Marlborough, Eng., 1994).

V. INTERVIEWS. "Martin Amis," in *Novelists in Interview,* ed. John Haffenden (London, 1985); Victoria N. Alexander, "Martin Amis: Between the Influences of Bellow and Nabokov," in *Antioch Review* 52 (fall 1994).

VI. CRITICAL STUDIES. Karl Miller, *Doubles: Studies in Literary History* (London, 1985); James Diedrick, *Understanding Martin Amis* (Columbia, S.C., 1995); Jonathan Wilson, "A Very English Story," in *New Yorker* (6 March 1995); Brian Finney, "Narrative and Narrated Homicides in Martin Amis's *Other People* and *London Fields,*" in *Critique* 37 (fall 1995).

PAT BARKER

(1943–)

Sharon Carson

WINNER OF THE prestigious Booker Prize for *The Ghost Road* (1995), the final novel in her World War I trilogy, Pat Barker had already been hailed as a writer of remarkable vision for the first book in the trilogy, *Regeneration* (1991). That brilliant antiwar novel won critical acclaim on both sides of the Atlantic and was nominated by the *New York Times Book Review* as one of the four best novels of 1991— the only novel by a British writer to be so distinguished. *The Eye in the Door* (1993), the second book in the trilogy, won the Guardian Fiction Prize and was described by the *Sunday Telegraph* as "extending the boundaries not only of the antiwar novel but of fiction generally."

But Barker has not always written about scenes and characters so momentous as those of the Great War; it was only with these that she claimed international attention. In fact, Barker's first three novels, *Union Street* (1982), which was later made into a film, *Stanley and Iris* (1990), starring Jane Fonda and Robert De Niro, *Blow Your House Down* (1984), and *The Century's Daughter* (1986; retitled *Liza's England* in 1996), concentrate on the lives of characters of little consequence, British working-class women, characters for whom she feels there is no literary tradition, and her fourth, *The Man Who Wasn't There* (1989), focuses on a fatherless working-class adolescent boy. Barker herself came from this class; in *Union Street* she evokes the desperation and poverty of the slum community of her childhood.

Pat Barker's interest in history and politics is a major wellspring for her fiction; she is an avid and thorough researcher, and her works are replete with overt and sometimes covert clues leading directly to historic texts. But Barker is interested not so much in re-creating history as in retrieving the unrecorded and in giving voice to persons silenced in the rush of passing events. Hers is an exemplary voice in fiction, a fiction that creates, in Roland Barthes' terms, "a multidimensional space" within the text, free from the "author-gods" of the past.

"Gritty," "unremitting," "chilling," "down to earth," "spare"—the adjectives used to describe it do not prepare the reader for Barker's work. Typed as a working-class writer, a realist, and a feminist, Pat Barker escapes all these definitions, as her fiction fits neatly into no classification. Her innovative point of view (which she calls the "compound eye"), the chorus of multiple voices and voice-overs, her attention to "silence" and the "silencing" of her characters, her emphasis on alternative readings of historic events and persons, and her inclusion of dreams and fantasies in the daylight space of her narratives make her a writer who provokes our assumptions about speech and silence, class and gender, and history and fiction. By 1996 Barker had published seven novels, and was considered the prophet of a commanding new literary vision, one that is deeply aware of human contradictions, contradictions often lost in the narrative structure of fiction and in the high gloss of history.

LIFE

BARKER was born Patricia Margaret Drake in Thornaby-on-Tees near the Northeast industrial town of Middlesbrough on 8 May 1943. Her father was a pilot in the Royal Air Force who did not survive World War II. She spent her early life on a chicken farm with her mother, her grandmother, and her grandfather. Her grandfather, who had been bayoneted by a German soldier during his service in World War I, still had a deep scar on his stomach to prove it. Her grandfather's scar and her absent father made early and lasting impressions on the young Pat about the consequences of war.

When she was seven, her mother, Moira, married and moved out, leaving Pat behind with her grandparents. Soon after, her grandparents began running a fish-and-chips shop, and it was here that Pat, while helping serve customers, began to hear the authentic Teesside vernacular which energizes the dialogue of her early fiction.

Barker was an avid reader while she was growing up, borrowing prodigiously from the local library, and she decided at age eleven to become a writer. She attended a strict local girls' grammar school, and later majored in international history at the London School of Economics and Political Science. After graduating in 1965, she taught A-level history, politics, and English in vocational classes for civil servants. In 1969 she was teaching in Middlesbrough when she met her future husband, David Barker, a professor of zoology at the University of Durham. He encouraged her in her writing, and in fact rescued the discarded manuscript of her first novel from the trash. She has since dedicated five of her novels to him. Through David Barker, she was introduced to the work of the English physiologist W. H. R. Rivers and his study of protopathic and epicritic nerve regeneration. Her fascination with Rivers inspired her to make him the pivotal character in her World War I trilogy.

Pat Barker began writing fiction seriously in her thirties while she was raising her son and her daughter. But it was in 1979, when she attended her first creative writing course at the Arvon Foundation, in the Lumb Bank, in Yorkshire, that she met the writer Angela Carter, who was teaching the course. Barker showed Carter a section of what was to become her first novel, *Union Street*. It was Angela Carter, Barker claims, who gave her "permission to write." Her earlier attempts at writing had been modeled on the "refined and sensitive" novels of the middle class, and had collected nothing but rejection slips. Carter encouraged her to stick to what she knew: the lives of working-class women in the postindustrial northeast of England.

Thus Barker places such women center stage in her first three novels, *Union Street, Blow Your House Down,* and *The Century's Daughter,* but with her fourth, and shortest, novel, she centers the action in the mind of a twelve-year-old boy, Colin Harper; in *The Man Who Wasn't There,* we begin to see a gender shift in her areas of concentration. Not surprisingly, it is a shift that questions the predictable stereotypes of male and female. The adolescent protagonist of *The Man Who Wasn't There* is "there" all right, but ambivalent about being a man.

Barker's fifth novel, *Regeneration,* begins to explore the gender codes decreed in the social and political mandates of war and affirms the feminist thesis that "the personal is political." As one critic puts it, she humanizes the experience of men by thinking of it in terms of the experience of women. Like W. H. R. Rivers, the central character of her trilogy, Barker has an ingenious capacity to associate differences and similarities, and to demonstrate that often it is the differences that are similar. In *The Eye in the Door* and *The Ghost Road,* she expands on these similarities, to suggest that the psychic vulnerabilities of men are the same as those of women. While her fiction measures likeness, it simultaneously celebrates difference and implies that diversity is impossible so long as sexual codes are enforced. Enforced differences between the sexes become the mandates of stereotype, denying human beings the freedom to evolve beyond gender imperatives. Barker's work suggests that gender stereotypes are ritually dramatized not only in domestic abuse and prostitution but also in scapegoating and war and that coercive violence is no less political in personal relations than in public ones. At the same time that these gender codes promote aggression against women and other men, they simultaneously deny men the expression of their compassionate and nurturing sides, further dehumanizing them. Barker's work contains, she says, "a lot of brutality but very little cruelty. Looking straight at the world is your duty as a writer. If you can't you shouldn't introduce the material, or you leave the reader in more of a mess than they began in" (quoted in Spufford, p. 3).

UNION STREET

Union Street, Pat Barker claims, from her 1995 perspective as Great Britain's Booker Prize winner, typed her as "Northern, feminist, and working-class," and as she looks back on her earlier fiction, she is startled that it is "so uncompromising, so unrelieved" (quoted in Rodd, 1995, p. 28). Nevertheless, in spite of Barker's judgments about her early work, in this first novel she creates the innovative technique she calls the compound eye, a point of view integral to her fiction, and one she develops even more intricately in her later work. Barker is an inquisitive narrator, not content with a single voice or point of view, and her compound eye animates the multifaceted qualities of her characters by eliciting their personalities from within their own points of view and by qualifying those points of view through the inner narrations of others.

Barker produces this effect in *Union Street* by dividing the novel into seven chapters and narrating each from the point of view of a different female character, all of whom live in Union Street. The characters range in age from eleven-year-old Kelly Brown to Alice Bell, who is well past seventy. Barker's omniscient narration shifts back and forth among the characters as they observe, converse, judge, condemn, condone, and recall their impressions of themselves and each other. As Lyn Pykett notes, the reader receives realistic impressions and observations combined with "a stream of consciousness or dream-narrative technique" that periodically abandons realism and makes one character able "to remember the experience of another character as if it were her own" (p. 72). Immersed in a narrative hall of mirrors, Barker's readers watch her characters reflect, refract, remember, and even dream one another into existence.

Not only does Barker's compound eye allow us to see her characters distinctly, but her use of language also allows us to hear them. Barker claims that when she begins to write, her head is "full of voices," and *Union Street* is an echo chamber of voices, all of them interconnecting to convey a communality of expression. "These women," Barker claims, are "highly articulate, but their problem is that nobody is listening to them." Perhaps that is because it has taken Barker to finally make the chorus accessible. On one level these voices constitute a barrage of dialectal conversations, rich with such working-class, streetwise expressions as "filthy sod," "barmy bugger," "bloody cow," and "on the hump." On another level, we hear the characters' inner narrations about themselves and one another, and on a third level we hear Pat Barker's omniscient observations on the characters as she makes note of their behavior, physical traits, and attitudes. Peter Hitchcock defines this technique as Barker's "double-voiced" discourse, as she shifts in and out of the language of the sign community (the shared arena of discourse) that is the focus of the story (p. 62).

Barker's complex discourse constitutes the dynamic flip side of the isolated single narrators of much traditional fiction. But Pat Barker is inventing more than just a new technique—she is inventing a new tradition: a literature of working-class women. Her technique in *Union Street* is in part her response to the paradox of these women in cultural discourse, and to their historic absence. Barker recognizes that none of us is an isolated subject, but that we create ourselves and each other from moment to moment in a web of complex intersubjective relations. Her illuminating narrative stance and her ingenious voicing demonstrate the intersubjectivity of our multiple selves and the difficulty of defining a "subject" or an "object" in any interaction, much less the traditional "male subject" and "female object" of dominant systems of meaning. To Barker, gender is a cultural construct, and she defines even class through sexual difference, identifying working-class women as the "working class within the working class" (Fairweather, p. 21).

Barker's work suggests that middle-class writers have forgotten their working-class neighbors, and male working-class writers like Alan Sillitoe, John Braine, Stan Barstow, and David Storey have forgotten their wives—who have been "silenced" in the struggle. This unrecorded history of working-class women is the "silenced" story Barker so eloquently speaks; and since memories fade, and oral histories finally depend on them, she is retrieving their history in her narratives, for, as the Chinese proverb says, "the strongest memory is weaker than the palest ink."

Even though Barker's silenced story presupposes that power is disproportionately conferred by gender, her novels are not feminist tracts that "blame the oppressor." Barker has an acutely modern and educated intelligence and is impatient with simple solutions. Her readers find that her warmest sympathies lie with the oppressed, but she compels us to question the causes of oppression. Her fiction assumes that gender, poverty, race, youth, and age can bring about domination and "silencing" by the family, accepted social codes, and the law. However, she emphasizes that the dominated internalize those oppressive attitudes, and will, in turn, often subject and silence themselves; men and women are not only produced through social relations, but they also actively form them.

Typically the characters in *Union Street* endure the circumstances of their lives with stoic acceptance and with a kind of ironic detachment that

Barker has called "trench humor," generated in reaction to a hostile environment. Set in a slum neighborhood in an unnamed city in England's postindustrial Northeast, *Union Street* is reminiscent of Teesside. It survives on the edge of demolition in a town full of rubble from other demolished streets. It is the winter of 1973, during the coal miners' strike, and the lack of fuel further complicates the lives of these women, who already subsist on the verge of starvation. Their poverty is further compounded by domestic abuse, dead-end jobs, disease, pregnancy, and childbirth. Here Barker pictures life at the bottom of the bottom, where a person's only choices are to go on the dole and to grub for survival.

Too often at the bottom of the bottom are the children. In the opening chapter of *Union Street*, little Kelly Brown wakes up in a dingy bed under a broken window, while her mother entertains Arthur, a stranger to Kelly, in the adjoining bedroom. As Kelly struggles downstairs to start a fire in the frigid grate, we tune in to Barker's many voices: Kelly observes her mother "sucking up" to Arthur, using her "posh" or "middle-class" voice—pretending to be what she is not, in an attempt to impress Arthur, while at the same time she harasses Kelly for carrying on and "stirring the shit" (p. 7). Meanwhile, Kelly deeply needs her mother's attention and even wears her mother's sweaters to get close to her: "They were warmer, somehow, and she liked the smell" (p. 4). Barker emphasizes that Kelly's lack of nourishing food and warm clothing is less important than her need for attention and affection. In Barker's world, one form of deprivation often leads to another, and Kelly is a pitiable example. Kelly begs money from Arthur to go to a fair and on the way is followed by a stranger Barker calls The Man. Later, the Hall of Mirrors and the Ghost Train do not prepare Kelly for what is to come: The Man forces her into an alley and rapes her. Kelly at first fears death, but The Man is so repulsive she is overcome by disgust. He succeeds in "forcing her hand . . . around the smelly purple toadstool" before he lies on top of her, his breath reeking of "peppermint and decay" (p. 29).

Barker underscores the pathos of Kelly's conflicting emotions; though The Man is repugnant, Kelly is so needy she seeks his affection as the only person who has shown her any attention. When she later maneuvers him into a fish-and-chips bar,

she tries to make him look at her: "She needed him. He was all she had," but his eyes only "skittered about like ants in a disturbed nest" (p. 32). The Man begins to cry, Kelly's anger, fear, and neediness turn into contempt, and she runs from the bar.

With traditional point of view that is less enriched with the inner narrations of multiple characters, we would be tempted to blame Mrs. Brown for Kelly's plight. But Barker switches us into Mrs. Brown's consciousness the morning after Kelly tells her about the rape. Mrs. Brown thinks about her daughter waking up with the memory of it:

Was she lying awake, staring at the ceiling? Mrs. Brown didn't know and was afraid to go upstairs and find out. The sight of her daughter's misery would bring her own gushing to the surface again, and it had taken most of the night for her to get it under control. . . . She . . . heard herself start to whimper. The whimpering frightened her. . . . For she thought of herself as a hard, tough, realistic woman, able to cope with most things.

(p. 35)

Earlier we were sorry for Kelly; now we are sorry for Mrs. Brown. We learn that Kelly is difficult to raise, as Mrs. Brown thinks: "You'd need eyes in your arse to keep track of her" (p. 35). In her misery, Mrs. Brown goes up the street to talk with Iris King, who takes her into her living room, "resting one massive freckled arm on the other woman's thin shoulders, for she was a woman who needed to touch people" (p. 36). Barker's omniscient voice tells us that Iris "was a formidable sight with her bare arms and massive breasts" (p. 36). While Iris sympathizes with Mrs. Brown—"They should flog 'em. . . . It's no good mucking around with probation and all that"—Iris's inner narration tells us a different story about her opinion of Mrs. Brown: "Her bairn! Where had she been when it happened?" (p. 38). And when Iris goes into the kitchen to make tea, Mrs. Brown looks "uneasily around the fanatically clean and tidy living room" and wonders "what on earth had possessed her to come" (p. 38). Thus, during one tragic incident and its aftermath, Barker's presentation of the dialogue and inner narration of her characters combined with her own omniscient observations reveal Kelly's attitudes about herself, her mother, Arthur, and The Man; Mrs. Brown's attitudes about herself, Kelly, The Man, Arthur (we learn she can barely tolerate him though her need for him is great), and

PAT BARKER

Iris King; and Iris King's opinions of herself, Mrs. Brown, Kelly, and The Man.

Barker moves this way through the successive *Union Street* chapters, letting us into the lives of Joanne Wilson, Lisa Goddard, Muriel Scaife, Iris King, Blonde Dinah, and Alice Bell. And in the midst of a disturbing commentary on codependency and the pathology of abuse, she injects her ironic humor and warm human sympathy, discloses the complexities of human cravings and desires, and proves that sometimes even the downside has an upside. Joanne Wilson, who is really in love with Joss, whom she can't even consider marrying because he is a midget—"She could just imagine the jokes. Step-ladders. Everybody the same size in bed. All that" (p. 70)—is pregnant by her "upwardly-mobile" boyfriend who half despises her, and they are finally forced to marry. Pregnant Lisa Goddard has two little boys and an unemployed husband who drinks every night and comes home to beat her; yet she perpetuates the beatings by defending him, because he has "nobody else" to beat. But when her unwanted baby girl is born, she is mysteriously overjoyed to have a daughter. Muriel Scaife's husband dies of lung cancer, abusing himself through smoke and drink, and abusing Muriel with his self-abuse; yet overcome by her deep love for him she tries to drag him from the coffin.

These women are not only abused by their family and by their social relations, but they sometimes internalize the abusive attitudes and use them against each other. For example, Elaine Watson, a bakery worker, continually harasses Bertha, an African-American woman hired to work on the assemby line with her. Finally Bertha grows tired of the abuse and beats Elaine with her fists. Barker's remarks here are clues to her analysis of gender and violence in her later fiction. The other factory women have no sympathy for Elaine's behavior, but they can't condone Bertha's either: "Many of the women were horrified by it. Men fought, sometimes man and wife fought, but violence between women was unthinkable" (p. 84); thus Bertha becomes doubly ostracized by retaliating.

But in Barker's world women are not always victims, just as men are not always aggressors. She claims she consciously avoids making her male characters "card-board, cut-out baddies, as in so much feminist fiction" (quoted in Fairweather, p. 21). In the "Blonde Dinah" chapter for instance,

we meet George Harrison, a pathetic victim of age and economics. Retired after forty years at the factory, George finds he has been displaced at home. His wife, Gladys, hates having him in the house, and he feels alienated from her and his children: "At times he envied her, she seemed so secure, with her children and grandchildren around her" (p. 222). George faithfully gives Gladys his pension money, leaving little for himself. Since he can't afford to drink with his old mates from work, he goes to the park in good weather and the library reading room in bad. But in the library, Barker pictures "the real derelicts," the men at the bottom of the bottom: "They were dirty. They picked their noses. . . . They made noises. They made smells. They were afraid" (p. 223).

In his walks along the river George meets the prostitute Blonde Dinah, who has also worked for forty years. At first put off, George begins to feel sorry for her because she was "no age to be hawking it round the pubs" (p. 225). In Dinah, he recognizes himself. Old, idle, and feeling useless, George and Dinah form a bond in their one night of sex: "It produced a sort of intimacy, a feeling of being conspirators" (p. 229), and we find ourselves hoping that George has found a friend. But George leaves Dinah the next morning, puzzling over a disturbing problem: Dinah and Gladys look alike in their sleep, and he knows there are only two kinds of women, "the decent ones and the rest" (p. 230). They ought to look different, George feels, so that you could tell them apart! Thus Barker subtly adds the dimension of class defined by gender, as "decent" George indicts Dinah as being one of "the rest." George thinks that Dinah is "indecent" for selling her body and in a class beneath him, while he maintains the illusion that he is "decent" even though he has purchased her favors. He conveniently forgets that Dinah's profession would soon become obsolete if there were no demand for it from people like him.

Perhaps the most pathetic of Barker's characters in *Union Street* is Alice Bell, whose story closes the book. Alice has come to the end of her life in poverty. As a little girl more than seventy years earlier, she had often witnessed "the final rejection"—the funerals of paupers, with children following the coffins, jeering and throwing stones. Alice's only treasures are her independence and her self-respect. So she saves for her funeral from her meager pension by skimping on food and fuel and spends most of her final years in bed to keep warm. The reader is first introduced to Alice in the book's opening chapter, when Kelly meets her sitting on a park bench at nightfall and asks if anybody will be expecting her at home. Alice tells her "not a living soul" and that they're trying to put her in a nursing home. Kelly tries to reason with her that in a home she would get her meals and be warm. In Alice's response, Barker sums up the pathos of these characters, who spend their lives struggling for the lowest level of subsistence: "Is not the life more than meat and the body than raiment?" (p. 67).

Kelly and Alice are Barker's sorry picture of youth and age in *Union Street,* the one enduring rape and the other starvation. At opposite ends of life, they face in the same direction, and as the subtle strain of stoicism emerges in the girl, it hardens in the crone. Alice exercises her independence by resisting the home, sits on the park bench until she freezes to death, and remains independent till the end.

Union Street is characterized by this stoic acceptance of deprivation, sometimes with a streak of trench humor, in a pattern that foreshadows Barker's second novel. The theme of endurance in the face of grim reality is played out compellingly in her World War I trilogy, but never more graphically than in her second novel.

BLOW YOUR HOUSE DOWN

THE epigraph of Barker's *Blow Your House Down* is from Nietzsche's *Beyond Good and Evil:* "Whoever fights monsters should see to it that in the process he does not become a monster. And when you look long into an abyss the abyss also looks into you." But it is Barker who triumphs in *Blow Your House Down,* revealing the monster in all its grotesque dimensions, a malevolent presence in the house of the mind, a house which she does "blow down." For *Blow Your House Down* is a two-way mirror that compels us to question some of our deepest assumptions about sex, class, and the origin of evil.

Like the women of *Union Street,* the characters of *Blow Your House Down* are British working-class women struggling through the depression of the coal-miners' strike; faced with starvation, some of them turn to prostitution. But three of these women are stalked not just by poverty, but by a serial killer referred to as the Ripper, who murders, then mutilates and defiles the bodies of his victims.

Barker's Ripper is a thinly disguised version of the Yorkshire Ripper, Peter Sutcliffe, who between July 1975 and January 1982 terrorized cities in northern England, killing thirteen women and wounding seven. He became known as one of the most vicious mass murderers of all time. Although a small number of Sutcliffe's victims were prostitutes, most were simply working-class.

Because the police in the Peter Sutcliffe case insisted that the killer must be a kind of Jack the Ripper reborn, they thought prostitution was the key link to his crimes and they failed to investigate the real status of his victims. In fact, Barker remarked in an interview that the police reaction to the Yorkshire Ripper killings was a commentary on class: "Nobody paid any attention to the Ripper killings until a middle-class girl was killed" (quoted in Perry, p. 50). The unforgivable fact that middle-class women in the United Kingdom in the 1970s and 1980s were more likely to receive police protection than working-class women became startlingly apparent in this case, and so did the tendency of the authorities to identify working-class women with prostitutes and to regard both groups as somehow not worth the effort of protecting. And because of that attitude, Peter Sutcliffe, more demonic even than his Whitechapel prototototype, stayed at large for more than five years, murdering and mutilating women with a hammer, a hacksaw blade, a knife, and a sharpened Phillips screwdriver.

A starkly nightmarish novel, *Blow Your House Down* answers the question that thousands of police failed to ask in the Yorkshire Ripper case: What kinds of women were Sutcliffe's victims? Barker's female characters are vivid portrayals of the types of working-class women who could have been the Yorkshire Ripper's targets. And although Barker emphasizes that poverty as well as gender puts these women at risk as victims of violence, she underscores some of the factors in their lives that are the negative effects more of their gender than of their class. For instance, these characters receive inequitable treatment and pay in the workplace, they are discriminated against by social welfare agents, and they are frequently left responsible for the total financial and emotional welfare of their children. Such circumstances make it more likely that they will live in poverty simply because they are women. In Barker's world, to be both poor and female is to be in double jeopardy.

The unjust social and economic circumstances creating poverty for these women conspire to invite violence, and Barker's Ripper is the vehicle for that conspiracy. Like Sutcliffe's historical prototype, whose identity was never discovered, Barker's anonymous killer is the perfect decoy for her questions about society's culpability. Ingeniously, she focuses not on the killer, but on the scene surrounding the killer, and on the mystification and eroticization of violence by the spectators—so that the killings become not only physical acts of violence by the Ripper, but also psychic acts of brutality further perpetrated on the victims by onlookers, neighbors, policemen, even the self-satisfied readers of the newspapers. To illustrate the dynamics of this psychic conspiracy, Barker chooses her killer even more carefully than the killer chooses his victims, for he is not just a killer but a sex killer. Such a personage gives Barker the opportunity to reveal the social exploitation which makes a spectacle of the victims and that fetishizes their sex. By focusing on the spectators rather than the killer, Barker displaces the origin of the violence, and in another strategic plot maneuver, cinematizes the garish details surrounding gender: a male victim is only a victim, but a female victim is often a spectacle. A spectacle can be conjectured about, poked, prodded, and pried into, and as one critic notes, we can question what it is that made her "ask for it." While the male victim is pitied, the female victim is often blamed. Thus voyeurism becomes central to the plot, and as readers we are drawn pruriently into the crime. In Barker's subtle dialectic, the culpability of onlookers and speculators—and thus even the reader—is at issue.

Barker divides *Blow Your House Down* into four sections, each told from the perspective of a different woman, Brenda, Kath Robson, Jean Jordan, and Maggie Walker. In the first section we are introduced to Brenda, whose husband has left her with three children and deeply in debt. When she applies for child support, the service agents tell her that because she is married she is ineligible; Brenda can receive no assistance simply because she *has* a husband. The implication is that marriage is a class system and the man pays the wife—somewhat as he would a prostitute—for sex and to feed "her" children. Angered by the hypocrisy of the agents,

Brenda concludes that if she is just a married harlot, she "might just as well be standing on a street corner in bloody Northgate—at least it'd be honest" (p. 30).

Dismissed by the social service agents, Brenda applies for a job at the notorious chicken factory nearby and discovers that it too has a class system. The higher-paying jobs, killing the chickens, are reserved for the working-class men, who have "families to support." Brenda takes a job, for far less money, gutting the birds. Worn out with fighting inequities, as she walks home at night Brenda notices the women who are walking their rounds, and who "must take home in a night more than she had left at the end of a week" (p. 40). Barker emphasizes that these women are earning more money simply because they are *not* respectable wives and mothers. Only a few weeks later, Brenda loses her job and is driven to the streets to survive.

On the streets Brenda meets Kath Robson, who teaches her the trade. Brenda learns to "switch off," to take a detached attitude toward peddling her body. Four years pass, Kath is arrested by the police, and social services takes her children and puts them into foster care. We already know that Kath is now ripe as a victim, and Barker doesn't disappoint us. Kath is soon picked up by a trick who just happens to be the killer: "He'd been waiting a long time, waiting for the moment when it *felt right*" (p. 57). It may "feel right" to him because Kath is already so visibly and hopelessly dispossessed that she has turned to drink and carelessness in her grief. Kath's love for her children was the primary reason she worked the streets to begin with. As in *Union Street*, one form of dispossession often leads to another, and as Kath unwittingly leads the killer to a street of boarded-up houses, Barker tells us, with a touch of gruesome irony, that he carries with him "little purple, violet-scented sweets," because his breath is bad and he plans to "be close."

Barker switches from character to character, picking up speed until she moves in for the kill. Kath's murder is a spectacle both graphic and pornographic, from which we as readers cannot disengage. Much like popular "slice-and-dice" cinema, the novel drags us into the horror and deliberately focuses our attention on the serial killer's ritual: he hits Kath on the jaw with a hammer; he drags Kath onto a mattress; he slices Kath open with a knife; he stuffs her with bedding feathers. As the killer distances himself from the grisly scene, we are brought up close. Like a moving camera, Barker focuses in on the body, and we are left alone with Kath after the killer's departure as onlookers at the scene of the crime.

Later, Brenda learns of Kath's death from a newspaper account; the trick she is with comments that "he's got another" with an air of satisfaction (p. 70), and we are again drawn into the duplicity, the multiplicity, of the deed. It is a deed easily attributed to a serial killer, but Barker implies that society's response to the crime makes it complicit. She probes even deeper into communal culpability back at the morgue, where like a chicken in the factory, Kath's corpse is laid out as a carcass and sadistically "poked, prodded, measured, photographed," and then "gutted, filleted and parcelled up again" (p. 71).

Part 2 introduces the group of women who work the streets. As they gather in Beattie Miller's flat, Beattie circulates a photo of her former friend, Irene Waddell, who was the Ripper's first victim, and they debate about the danger of continuing work. The police are in the neighborhood, but are only taking license plate numbers and are using the women as bait. Incredibly, the women rationalize their lack of police protection, having internalized the attitudes that endanger them.

At the end of part 2, when Jean Jordan's lesbian lover, Carol, is found dead and mutilated, another victim of the Ripper, we know that part 3 will be the story of Jean's revenge. And Barker gets her own revenge by naming Jean Jordan after one of Sutcliffe's actual victims, found murdered in Manchester with a marked five-pound note in her purse that led to Sutcliffe's conviction. But Barker's Jean Jordan is anything but a victim, and because Barker puts us into her mind using an unnerving first-person narration, we begin to grasp Jean's logic. The only character who hooks because she "likes the life," Jean is hardened against her own destruction and has an appetite for retribution.

Through Jean Jordan we are once again made conscious of Kath Robson. A photographic enlargement of Kath's face has been plastered on a billboard above the viaduct where she was picked up by the Ripper. Jean now deliberately works the viaduct, expecting the killer to return, and she carries on a dialogue with Kath's billboard face. But Jean too is unsettled by Kath's cardboard eyes, which stare accusingly. The eyes hang eerily above the scene of Kath's demise, and like Barker's compound eye, they search the psychic landscape as if seeking the killer's identity. Jean concludes from her conversations with Carol that he is the trick whose breath stinks of decay and violets, and later when she meets up with him, she is carrying in her purse not a five-pound note but a knife. The man gets closer, the odor of violets becomes intense, and Jean stabs him in the neck.

Jean wants to believe she has killed the Ripper, but she and we are left wondering if she has gotten the right man. As if to validate our doubt, Barker moves immediately into the final section, that of Maggie Walker, a "decent married woman" who, because of her husband's income, can afford "respectable" work in the chicken factory. However, we soon find her respectability does not exempt her from violence. One Friday night Maggie goes to the pub with her friends. As she walks home afterward, she is assaulted, hit on the head from behind.

It is Brenda who comes to Maggie's assistance in the alley. Brenda summons the police and has Maggie taken to the hospital. It is clear that Barker enjoys the irony of the "decent" woman as the victim and the prostitute as her savior. Brenda tells Maggie that "it was only what anybody would've done" (p. 154).

But in the end it is only Brenda who has the humanity to help Maggie. We learn that others heard her scream and walked the other way, but "this woman, clattering down Blind Lane in her high heels, had put him off the kill" (p. 154). And ultimately, it is the "respectable" people who do more damage to Maggie than the assailant. The police and the neighbors suspect she has "asked for it," and they speculate, interrogate, insinuate, and treat Maggie as if her assault is nothing more than a drama for them to enjoy. Maggie's realization of the emotional damage being done to her comes after she talks with her proper neighbor Mrs. Bulmer, who implies that Bill, Maggie's husband, was her assailant. Mrs. Bulmer is evil, Maggie concludes, and "you couldn't put evil into a single, recognizable shape" (p. 156).

As *Blow Your House Down* ends, we are not certain either of the killer's identity or if he has been stopped. Barker seems to want us to see the killer as an unidentifiable and ubiquitous evil force rather than as an actual person. And though Jean Jordan is capable of murdering the Ripper, she could never kill all the Mrs. Bulmers in the world.

But by the end of the novel, Barker has rounded up the usual suspects. In this case, the police unintentionally aid and abet the killer, keeping him at large for over five years; the decent neighbors promote the killer's cause by enjoying the spectacle of his victims; inequitable laws and discriminatory hiring practices against women perpetuate the killer by creating a social subclass jeopardized by violence; the prostitutes themselves encourage the killer by submitting to a system that does them in; and as readers recoiling from the spectacle of Barker's text, we are accessories after the fact, left holding the book in our hands. So that finally, Barker's killer becomes the demon we all face in the mirror—and the abyss looks into us.

Finally, the situation of these women is not improved, because they never overcome the forces that put them on the street to start with. They merely cope, and in so doing participate in their own oppression. Barker comments on the futility of this behavior when she says that the friendships of women in *Blow Your House Down* merely "support . . . the status quo," but do not change the situation, much as men's friendships did not change their appalling circumstances in the trenches in World War I (Perry, p. 51). The crisscrossing patterns of gender and poverty in *Blow Your House Down* invite violence, and Barker indicts the cruel and coercive threads forcing the weave. They are threads she reworks even more intricately into the backdrop of her third novel.

THE CENTURY'S DAUGHTER

Eighty-four-year-old Liza Jarrett, the central character of *The Century's Daughter*, like the last of a dying species, is the "sole remaining inhabitant of a street scheduled for demolition" (p. 1, 1986 ed.). Called Barker's "sociological" novel, *The Century's Daughter* chronicles England's twentieth century and its progression through two world wars to modern postindustrial decline. The story of Liza Jarrett's life is Barker's barometer to measure the century's afflictions, from the irrevocable losses of war to the unraveling of family ties and the gradual dissolution of community.

Born in 1900 at the precise moment the century turned, Liza has lived at number twenty-nine Walker Street since 1922 and cannot be coaxed into moving into the Parkhouse development for the elderly. Stephen is a young, homosexual community worker trying to get her to leave her now-condemned house, but Liza is intent upon staying where she is. Barker combines Liza's retrospective past and Stephen's troubled present to form the fulcrum of the plot: Liza teaches Stephen the meaning of her past, and Stephen learns from Liza the meaning of his future. In the process, Liza and Stephen, decades apart in age, become intimately linked in a powerful bond of human connection.

The links Barker creates between Liza and Stephen are amplified by the historic and social forces that propel them together. Liza's impoverished past, the deaths of almost everyone she loves, and the gradually disintegrating landscape around her are reflected in Stephen's isolation as a young homosexual in an unsympathetic world. Yet ancient Liza is still a well of vitality, and on Stephen's first visit, she attempts to explain herself by showing him her greatest treasure, an old metal box. On the lid of the box is a mysterious painting of women dancing in a ring. Behind this ring of women are two other figures even more enigmatic: one is draped in a long robe, revealing neither age nor sex, and "exchanging [a] mysterious gift" (p. 21) with the other figure, a young man. Stephen tries to see what the cowled figure holds, but cannot because "the box-lid was so filmed with dirt" (p. 7). As Lyn Pykett notes, Barker creates the box as Liza's matrilineal legacy, passed down from her grandmother to her mother to Liza (p. 73), but the box takes on an even more intriguing signficance in the narrative and reappears at the end of the novel to reveal its secret. From the box Liza takes a tattered news clipping proving her birth as "the century's daughter," and shows it to Stephen, telling how her father long ago took it and her around to the pubs and showed her off to his friends: "Me Dad treasured that bit of paper, and then after he died it come to me" (p. 6). Liza's love for her father is still alive in her voice and it is apparent she wants to stay in her house because she cherishes those who once lived there; the house is her place in time where they once were. Like the house, her metal box is the symbolic space for that history, a memory-box, containing mementos, photos, and clippings, and by retelling her story many times, Liza has strung the contents of the box together like beads, to salvage from her past a story that is uniquely hers. We are privy to that history through

Liza's memory, as Liza bears witness to the community memory of working-class women Barker's work records. Liza may be modeled on Barker's own grandmother, who Barker says was a storyteller; by listening to her grandmother's memories, Barker "came to know my great-grandmother and even her mother as real people, even though their lives had left apparently no trace" (quoted in Fairweather, p. 22). Liza, too, is destined to leave apparently no trace, for her house is now decrepit and sits among other decrepit houses, hangouts for glue sniffers, hoodlums, and drunks. It is to be demolished, and the land, like Liza, will be covered over with "new developments."

Stephen, on the other hand, has been cut from his moorings and is trying to fix his life into a place. He has lived nowhere in particular and belongs nowhere. The alienated Stephen personifies the transience and detachment of the century at its close; living in a world drained of stable social relations and symbolic bonds, he tells Liza he has already "given up trying to make sense" (p. 20) of his life. The modern landscape he inhabits is cheapened beyond repair with the billboards of progress dedicated to "spend, spend, spend" (p. 218). Lonely, and seeking connections, he has for years come back from the university to his parents' house by train to search: "slipping back . . . not merely into his own past, but into the country's past" (p. 35). Stephen arrives at his parents' house a stranger. His father, near death from cancer, has never been able to relate to him; they are "like a pair of electric plugs that wouldn't fit into each other" (p. 40).

Barker makes Stephen's disconnection from his father a central dilemma in his life. As a homosexual he does not conform to his father's idea of who he "should be." His father passes nothing of himself on to his son, and Stephen is unlikely to have children himself. Thus Stephen, like Liza, is also a "sole remaining inhabitant," cut off both from his past and from his future. Although Stephen's father has been the faithful family breadwinner, turning "the same bloody crank handle" for "thirty bloody years" (p. 40), he has ended up on the dole. Consumed by the very machine he worked, he is now past use.

Stephen also feels useless; there is no "community" at the community house in which he works, and he becomes increasingly detached from the angry young men he tries to help. Most of them are undereducated, unemployed, and frustrated to the point of violence. Barker paints a poignant picture of what they, as the century's sons, have become:

Dole-queue wallahs built like their steel-making and ship-building fathers, resembling them in this, if in nothing else. . . . Tight jeans, boots, skinhead crops . . . tattoos on their arms. Girls' names, a rose, a dragon, a heart with "Mam" underneath: all this on boys who, staggering home tonight, full of northern macho and Newcastle Brown would strike terror into anybody who crossed their path.

(p. 71)

Born late into a century gone awry, their family attachments are replaced with tattoos, names that have become shibboleths of exchange in a system that values only cash. Their only "community" is in getting drunk and violent together on Newcastle Brown.

Barker questions how these "dole-queue wallahs" got that way and why England has consigned its young to the trash with its old. In a flashback, she takes us to the community of Liza's childhood and the Great War, when Liza's brother Edward enlists and is killed at the front. Liza's grief-stricken mother attends spiritualist meetings to hear Frank Wright, a young wounded veteran, whose injured throat is a channel for the voices of the dead. The voices are those of his battalion killed in the war. Since Wright grew up in Liza's neighborhood, Edward's voice is among them, one of the many voices the mothers strain to hear as they lean forward together to grieve. The mothers have lost all they have, their life's work and their families. The work of the war has destroyed the work of the family, and the sons they have "labored" to produce have been exterminated in whole battalions.

Liza is a young woman when she begins grieving her brother Edward, but will be an old woman before she stops. She marries Frank Wright, they have two children, Tom and Eileen; when the postwar economy slows, Frank loses his job. They go on the dole and move into a smaller house where Liza still resides. Liza has moved only four blocks from her first home, but must now gain acceptance in the new neighborhood on Walker Street. As Liza explains to Stephen, "We had a way of life, a way of treating people" (p. 218). You didn't just talk about loving your neighbor, "because you knew if you didn't you wouldn't survive and neither would she" (pp. 218–219). Liza adapts, but Frank, already brutalized by the war, is further demoralized by the postwar economy. When he loses his job he loses his self-esteem and finally leaves his family to seek work.

When Frank leaves, Liza begins gathering coal in the winter to sell for food. Among the coal gatherers is Ben, who like Frank is a war "survivor." Ben tells stories about his time in France in a burial party that picked up pieces of bodies to assemble for burial. Like Humpty-Dumpty, the bodies can never be pieced back together again, and in one incident Ben announces to his sergeant that one of the corpses "got three heads and one of them's a Jerry" (p. 160). Barker's image of the corpse with three heads is much like the dismembered corpse of community that is dissolving in the absence of fathers and sons. Ben and Liza are Barker's metaphorical burial party, picking up debris in a society burned out, searching for fuel to reignite the connections of the past.

Bit by bit through a series of flashbacks, as Barker interweaves Liza's past with Stephen and Liza's present, we learn that Frank Wright turns up after five years of looking for work and dies shortly afterward. Stephen's father, after "thirty bloody years" at the factory, dies on the dole, feeling useless, while family ties and community bonds are submerged in a rising materialism. As Liza says later to Stephen: "That's where it went wrong you know. It was all *money*. You'd've thought we had nowt else to offer. But we *did*" (p. 218).

With the resurrection of war comes the burial of the dead, and when Liza's son Tom is killed in World War II, Liza has three names chiseled on a single gravestone: her brother Edward's, her husband Frank's, and her son Tom's. Because Edward and Tom were lost at the front, only the body of Frank is in the grave, but the graveyard becomes her only place to commune with all three. It "had come to have for her the slight unreality of a place visited frequently in dreams. She saw . . . how the roots of the elms reached down like a net to catch and hold the gleaming dead" (p. 201).

Though everything seems taken away from her by time and by war, Liza stays connected through her memories and her daughter Eileen. When Eileen gives birth to a daughter, Liza ponders the irreducible bonds of childbirth that are the "links in a chain of women stretching back through the centuries, into the wombs of women whose names

they didn't know" (p. 211). Though the "links in a chain of women" may promote solidarity, they cannot be forged without men, and without fathers, brothers, and sons, they are bonds without soul. The loss of the "century's sons" in two world wars changes the century's landscape. Barker emphasizes the depth of the loss by juxtaposing the birth of Liza's granddaughter with a scene in which Liza leaves her house for the first time in years to visit Stephen. Ironically, Stephen's apartment is in the house of the once-wealthy Wynyards, former owners of the steelworks where Liza's father worked, and the house in which her mother was a maid. The Wynyards are long gone through war, alcohol, and disease, and the house is partitioned off into shabby "postindustrial" apartments. The wealth of the war didn't save the Wynyards either. Liza and Stephen pass the scene of the old factory where the chimneys, kilns, and furnaces have long been shut up, and Liza realizes how much has been lost to time: "vanished communities, scattered families, extinguished fires" (p. 216).

Like Liza's house and the landscape around her, Liza too is "scheduled for demolition." Near the end of the novel, the community house hoodlums break in to rob her, and stumbling upon the metal box, they litter its contents to the floor. In a fury over finding no money, they strike Liza down and leave in a panic. Liza, barely alive, gathers the scattered contents of the box and puts them back inside. When she wraps a quilt around her, the reader cannot help but make the connection between her and the cowled figure on the box. She hears in her mind the music of her childhood, led by her childhood friend, Lena Lowe, as they danced and sang songs in the street at night before they came in to bed. Finally tempted in her dream by the image of her mother in a doorway telling her to come inside, Liza dies a death of homecoming.

Stephen, too, dreams that night of the dancing figures on Liza's box. He reaches out in the dream to the cowled figure who offers him the box itself and realizes the figure's hands are his father's—"Somehow, in the labyrinth of the dream, his father and Liza were one" (p. 272). We suspect the cowled figure is offering Stephen a space in which to record the narratives of his past.

Stephen never sees the metal box again, and we are left with him to wonder about the identity of the "mysterious gift." But Barker's riddle of history is much like that of the sphinx; perhaps she is telling us that history does not have to be a nightmare, as James Joyce believed, from which we are trying to awake. Barker's cowled figure may be offering us the book in our hands—a gift of recorded memories retrieved from the past to heal and redeem our souls for the future, and to remind us that as men and women we create our meanings, and we can change them.

THE MAN WHO WASN'T THERE

The Man Who Wasn't There is a short novel whose twelve-year-old protagonist, Colin Harper, is ambivalent about his sexual identity. Because the point of view is third-person limited omniscient (the reader knows Colin's thoughts but *only* his), the reader is let in on Colin's confusion, and is entertained, amused, and at times even disturbed by his quest to sort himself out. *The Man Who Wasn't There* takes place over three days' time—the sections are labeled "Thursday," "Friday," and "Saturday." Colin Harper has been reared by his mother; he knows nothing about his father except that he had something to do with World War II. A point of embarrassment for him is his birth certificate, which is the "shorter version" (no father listed). His mother will tell him nothing, and Colin suspects she doesn't know who his father was. Thus Colin's father's identity and the war become inextricably linked in his mind: "For Colin, the mystery of his father's identity was bound up with the war, the war he'd been born into, but couldn't remember" (p. 32).

Colin's birth certificate sets his birth date as 5 March 1943, which dates the plot at 1955. He lives in an unnamed town littered with rubble and constant reminders of World War II; the railings of the low walls along the street were "pulled up in the last war to make Spitfires, [and] had never been replaced" (p. 9). There is much about Colin's life and the lives of others in the town that has "never been replaced" since the war. Colin lives alone with his mother, Viv; he spends his days drifting from place to place while his mother works: school, the beach, the Odeon Theatre, and the amusement arcade.

While Colin meanders through his shabby environment, he constantly imagines another, more intriguing world. In the narrative, Barker integrates Colin's fantasies with his daily life. His inner narration is in italics, playing in his mind like a film while he goes through the motions of his day.

Deprived of a family life, Colin creates a surrogate extended family, all members of the French Resistance. Their names and personalities bear a humorous and sometimes pathetic resemblance to those around him. Colin himself is Gaston, a twelve-year-old British agent "parachuted into France because of his superb command of the French language" (p. 48). His mother, Viv, and her friend Pauline are Vivienne and Paulette, waitresses at a French bar the Resistance group frequents. The group is continually pursued by the Gestapo chief Von Strohm, who is in search of a "mysterious code book," and who keeps making random identity checks to find it. Von Strohm is the fantasy version of both Sawdon and Sedgewick, Colin's headmasters at school. They randomly harass Colin about his absent father, his waitress mother, his chronic lateness, his lack of a tie—all outward manifestations of Colin's conscious and subconscious concerns about his identity and authenticity.

Colin can identify his absent father only with the cinema, for all that Colin knows about the war he has learned at the movies. Colin's father takes on a series of imagined identities in these films, as Colin tries to assimilate the images played out on the screen. (Barker remarked in an interview that the "fifties war films . . . in England portrayed a false image of people who lived through the war" [Perry, p. 57]). Yet questions of courage and fear and masculinity become part of Colin's daily dialogue with himself as he watches war films. In the midst of one of these films, Colin feels the fear of the parachutist on the screen as he stands at the top of a high tower terrified to jump as "beads of sweat gathered on his upper lip" (p. 31), and he questions whether real people are not in fact far different from their cinematic counterparts.

On the way home from the cinema one night, Colin and his friend Ross see a person standing across the street window-shopping. The person is dressed like a woman, but Ross, insisting it is a man, tells Colin to go ask the person the time. Colin does so and receives a startling revelation as he looks into the face of a man dressed as a woman. The face is heavily made up: a "shiny cupid's bow had been painted over a thin mouth." But as Colin stares, "the lips opened, and a deep, baritone voice said, 'Piss off, sonny'" (p. 34).

This character is Bernie Walters, who keeps the sweetshop. Not surprisingly, Bernie soon appears in livid color in Colin's French Resistance fantasies as Bernard, a man in drag, who saunters into the bar heavily made up and alone. A "master of disguise," Bernard furtively slides a thin package inside Gaston's shirt, "the plans." Bernard is apprehended by Von Strohm and a squad of German soldiers, but Gaston knows that Bernard will "never talk." The reader sees the irony in a "mysterious code book" being planted on Colin. For Colin's concerns about secret codes are besieged more by his hormones than by German soldiers. Bernard becomes another of Colin's fantasy alter egos to help him cope with his sexual ambivalence. Like Stephen in *The Century's Daughter*, Colin wonders whether he fits the gender prescription. No role model has been set for Colin; thus he lacks "the plans" for his adult identity. Left to create himself, he keeps watch over who he is becoming in the mirror, sometimes feeling "almost as if another face was pushing its way to the surface, somebody else's face, and he didn't know whose" (p. 92).

Barker questions how much control Colin finally has over his fate, scripted as he is by the gender codes he is destined to play like roles from the bad B movies he watches. More powerful even than his genetics, these roles can distort, cripple, or even kill him. Colin's father's destiny as male, for example, sent him to die in the war, and Colin's mother, Vivian, as female, is condemned to squeeze into a bunny costume and serve men.

The direction Barker's fiction begins to take in *The Man Who Wasn't There* is developed extensively in her fifth novel, *Regeneration*, the first part of her World War I trilogy, where she questions how masculine and feminine roles promote war. The trilogy is Barker's testament to the power of these codes to warp, damage, and exterminate human potential, as they do to millions of young men sent to the slaughter in the Great War.

REGENERATION

IN *Regeneration* Barker expands her interlocking themes of domination and violence and acquiescence and silence as overtly political acts encoded in gender and brutally ritualized in the Great War. Her World War I trilogy, *Regeneration*, *The Eye in the Door*, and *The Ghost Road*, are novels crafted from an intriguing blend of fact and fiction. Among the several historic characters, the central narrator of the trilogy is William H. R. Rivers (1864–1922), a renowned neurologist and social anthropologist and a captain in the Royal Army Medical Corps. It is July 1917 when *Regeneration* opens. Rivers is on duty at the Craiglockhart War Hospital near Edinburgh, Scotland, a hospital famous for treating soldiers suffering mental breakdowns, or shell shock, from their war experiences. Here he meets and cares for two of the most famous poets in World War I's literary history, Siegfried Sassoon (1886–1967) and Wilfred Owen (1893–1918). Both poets are protagonists in the trilogy, and so is Billy Prior, Barker's fascinating, fictional, "temporary gentleman."

"I never thought for a second that feminism is only about women," Barker commented when asked about the novel *Regeneration* (Perry, p. 51) and indeed, she speaks of her trilogy as "very much a female view of war" (Spufford, p. 3). Barker's writing is all of a piece, and her portrayal of the physical and psychic violence against women in *Union Street* and in *Blow Your House Down* are paradigms for her vision of the brutality wrought in the lives and minds of the inmates of Craiglockhart. A place Sassoon later referred to as "Dottyville" (Showalter, p. 61), Craiglockhart is the waste yard for the pitiful remnants of the trenches, soldiers mutilated in body and mind, bereft of limbs and sense. The war that produced such phrases as "gas mask" and "basket case" also produced "shell shock," a euphemistic term created to describe the epidemic of male hysteria that accompanied the carnage of the Great War. Paul Fussell says in *The Great War and Modern Memory* (1975) that the war was the catastrophe in modern history "that domesticates the fantastic and normalizes the unspeakable" (p. 74), and the shell-shock epidemic that overtook eighty thousand British soldiers is their unwitting response to a horror that could not be expressed, and that was, in fact, "unspeakable" to many of its victims, made mute by emotional agony. But in May 1917, Siegfried Sassoon, by now a war hero, spoke for them by publicly protesting the war in his famous pacifist denunciation, "A Soldier's Declaration," in which he claimed that the war was "being deliberately prolonged by those who have the power to end it" (quoted in *Regeneration*, p. 3). Since the military authorities found it impolitic to prosecute a war hero for treason, Sassoon was persuaded by his friend, the poet and writer Robert Graves (1895–1985), to go before a medical board, which conveniently decided he was suffering a mental breakdown and placed him in Craiglockhart under Rivers' care.

Barker focuses the plot of *Regeneration* around the three and a half month friendship between the fifty-three-year-old Rivers and the young poet Sassoon, and on Rivers' attempts to "cure" him of his pacifism and discharge him back to the front. During this time Sassoon meets the emerging poet Wilfred Owen, also hospitalized there, and encourages him to pursue his writing; in fact, Owen drafts "Anthem for Doomed Youth" while at Craiglockhart.

But just as Sassoon changes Owen, he also changes Rivers, because the regeneration of the title takes place in the mind and heart of the doctor rather than in his patient. Rivers finally realizes the nature of the neurosis he is treating and knows that he is "curing" his patients only to send them back to face the same suicidal conditions that caused their trauma. Barker emphasizes Rivers' recognition of the underlying gender codes that create his patients' neuroses: the illness is not in his patients, Rivers concludes, but in the violent codes of the society he supports.

Rivers, finding that the active pilots of the RAF break down less severely than the passive pilots of observation balloons, who suffer the highest incidence of breakdown, concludes that it is not sudden shock that creates neurosis, but prolonged strain, immobility, and helplessness—the conditions in the trenches. The final irony of the war is that men are traumatized not by mobilization, but by immobilization: "They'd been *mobilized* into holes in the ground so constricted they could hardly move . . . crouching in a dugout, waiting to be killed" (p. 107). Although shell-shock symptoms included a vast array of physical and emotional disorders and typically differed between soldiers and officers, some common symptoms were paralysis, lameness, blindness, deafness, mutism, vomiting, fatigue, insomnia, and dizziness, all disorders brought on by inactivity and powerlessness, symptoms indicative today of post-traumatic stress disorder. Passivity and helplessness also produced such deep gender anxiety that many feared being "feminized"; many were, in fact, made impotent.

The fear of being "feminized" clarifies the connection between the wartime neuroses of men and the peacetime neuroses of women. Rivers realizes that because of their more restricted and defenseless lives, women were suffering from shell shock long before the war. He was poignantly aware of the epidemic of female hysteria in Victorian England, because it affected his beloved sister, Katherine, who as a child had been his intellectual and emotional equal, but was now confined to her bed as a neurasthenic. In an ironic reversal, Rivers understands men because their experience is like that of women, and he is Barker's psychic barometer to measure gender correlatives and to question the social organization of sexual differences. Perhaps we would understand history better, Barker quietly implies, if we used a different gender to interpret it.

In contrast to the immobilized men at the front, the women without men on the home front experience unprecedented mobility. They work in munitions factories, make a "man's wage," and are empowered with energy, financial freedom, and independence. One such fictional character is Sarah Lumb, who becomes romantically involved with Billy Prior, Rivers' former Craiglockhart patient. Sarah makes detonators in a munitions factory and is one of the thousands of female munitions-workers called "canaries," whose skin and hair have turned a sickly yellow from the fumes of the chemicals. With their husbands at the front, many of these women are also free for the first time in their lives from domestic abuse. Lizzie, Sarah's friend and fellow munitions-worker, has been beaten by her husband for years. In a passage which eerily echoes the pub scene in T. S. Eliot's *The Waste Land*, Sarah asks Lizzie if she wants her husband back from the war, and Lizzie replies: "I do not. . . . Do you know what happened on August 4th 1914? . . . *Peace broke out*" (p. 110).

Typical of the women on the home front, Lizzie becomes more audible in wartime. In contrast, the men at the front are deliberately "silenced." Barker intensifies her theme of silencing the voices of resistance by bringing into the narrative a second neurologist, the historical Dr. Lewis Yealland, who works to silence even the protests of the silent. Barker models her episode of Yealland's "therapy" session on case histories found in his book *Hysterical Disorders of Warfare* (1918). Rivers visits Yealland and witnesses one of his sessions with a mute patient named Callan. He watches as Yealland administers shock therapy to Callan. He straps Callan into a chair, applies a pad electrode to his lumbar spine, a long pharyngeal electrode to his throat, inserts a tongue depressor, and turns on the voltage. Callan is thrown back with such force that the leads are ripped out of the battery. Yealland continues the treatment and threatens him: "You must speak, but I shall not listen to anything you have to say" (p. 231). Callan begins sobbing as words are ripped from his throat—whereupon Yealland pronounces the terrified Callan "cured" and ready to go back to war.

Rivers, horrified by the inhumanity of the episode, has a nightmare linking Yealland's treatment of Callan with oral rape. In Rivers' dream, he sees the electrode as a horse's bit (p. 328)—both the horse's bit and the electrode are used to "silence" the wearer—and concludes that he and Yealland are both in the same business. The business of the military is to turn medicine into a horse's bit, an instrument of control, and even Yealland and Rivers are being used to perpetuate war like everyone else: "Each of them fitted young men back into the role of warrior, a role they had—however unconsciously—rejected" (p. 238). Rivers sees parallels between the electrode used on Callan, the horse's bit in his dream, the bit used on the scold's bridle to silence recalcitrant women in the Middle Ages, and the bit used to silence American slaves in "the land of the free" (p. 238). Callan's silence had been his most powerful protest; ironically, when Callan speaks, Rivers feels he is "witnessing the *silencing* of a human being" (p. 238).

Although Rivers' own belief in the war is finally undermined, he is also imprisoned in the cycle, and when he discharges Sassoon back to France on 26 November 1917, it is with deep misgivings about his culture and its goals: "A society that devours it own young deserves no automatic or unquestioning allegiance" (p. 249). As Barker says, "in the end, Rivers is silenced, too" (Perry, p. 55).

The system silences Rivers, but Barker gives him voice in his patient Billy Prior, cured of his mutism by Rivers' therapy. Barker says that Prior is Rivers' alter ego, as there are parts of Rivers' personality she could not bring out in any other way than through Prior (see Perry, p. 52). Whereas Rivers is compassion personified, Billy Prior, Barker says humorously, was "constructed to get up Rivers' nose" (quoted in Spufford, p. 3). Prior emerges from his silence not only to provoke Rivers, but

also to charge the plot with a touchy, nervy, sometimes nasty and spiteful tension, making him a character we wouldn't want to live with, but an engrossing character to read about. Although Prior regains his voice in *Regeneration*, he begins making peace with his demons by escaping into amnesia, or "hysterical fugue," and as the trilogy progresses he has additional periods of blackout. This is particularly risky given Prior's new assignment in military intelligence, in the sequel to *Regeneration*, *The Eye in the Door*.

THE EYE IN THE DOOR

BARKER intensifies the "silencing" of *Regeneration* by magnifying the dimension of surveillance in its sequel, *The Eye in the Door*. Eyes are everywhere in *The Eye in the Door*; the populace of England lives in an environment calculated to induce exposure and is caught up in making others visible. The fear of being "feminized" at the front spreads to the home front, and in a hysterical attempt to project power, the citizens seek scapegoats. The hypermasculinized gender codes mandated in the trenches are now compulsory at home, and anyone who deviates is judged subversive.

Set in 1918, when the war is going badly for the Allies, the narrative focuses on a national hysteria that breaks out in Great Britain, one that produces witch-hunts for scapegoats: homosexuals, pacifists, and feminists. These groups are allegedly vulnerable to blackmail and coercion by the Germans. Billy Prior emerges from his minor role as Rivers' neurasthenic patient in *Regeneration* to become the central character in *The Eye in the Door*; traumatized in the trenches, he now faces war as an ethical dilemma. Prior is sexually intimate with Sarah Lumb in *Regeneration*, but in the first chapter of *The Eye in the Door*, he picks up fellow officer Charles Manning in Hyde Park for a homosexual encounter. Furthermore, he has been assigned home duty in London at the Ministry of Munitions Intelligence Unit. Thus Barker establishes Prior as ambivalent on all fronts: of working-class origins, he is only a "temporary gentleman"; as a former shell shock victim, he is unclear about his patriotic loyalties; and as a bisexual he defies the distinctions of sexual difference.

Early in the narrative, Charles Manning, Prior's

homosexual partner, receives a newspaper cutting about the "Cult of the Clitoris," a libelous article that appears in April 1918 in MP Pemberton Billing's sleazy newspaper, the *Vigilante.* It implies that subscribers to Oscar Wilde's private performance of *Salomé* are part of "the 47,000" who are alleged homosexuals and lesbians in the black book of "a certain German Prince" and are ostensibly targets for blackmail. As one character, Major Lode, puts it, the country has been brought to its knees by "an unholy alliance of socialists, sodomites and shop stewards" (p. 48).

Manning is sent the clipping anonymously; this is ominous, for it suggests he is being watched. Thus Barker sets the scene for the class and gender antagonisms underlying the hysteria. Because war depends on "masculine" codes of behavior, all homosexuals, all pacifists, and all feminists, who fail to support the war by failing to support the hypermasculinized codes, are suspect. In war, all must fall in to support the dominant political order. Men must be potent, aggressive, and violent toward the enemy. Women must support that violence and encourage men to exterminate other men. The distinction and enforcement of sexual difference takes on a distorted moral significance. Any deviation suggests treason, and traitors are watched, imprisoned if necessary.

One such traitor is Beattie Roper, a former suffragette in Aylesburg Prison doing a ten-year sentence. Billy Prior's assignment in intelligence demands that he spy on her, and since she cared for Prior as a child, his loyalties are divided. It is rumored that Beattie conspired to poison Lloyd George with a curare-tipped blowdart. Beattie Roper's story, Pat Barker tells us in her author's notes (p. 278), is based upon that of the historical Alice Wheeldon, and the "'poison plot' of 1917." Wheeldon was convicted on unsupported evidence and sentenced to ten years' hard labor.

Barker reinforces her surveillance theme in the imagery of her settings and pictures Prior as going to Aylesburg to spy on the already exposed. Aylesburg Prison is a scene at once reminiscent of Michel's Foucault's prison Panopticon and of No Man's Land; Prior finds himself standing in "what felt like a pit" surrounded by "high walls . . . ringed with three tiers of iron landings, studded by iron doors" (p. 29); in the center is a "wardress who, simply by looking up, could observe every door" (p. 29). Prisoners are the objects of humiliating

scrutiny. It is "No Man's Land seen through a periscope" (p. 30), thinks Prior, where millions of men are watched and forced to perform according to code.

Barker creates a psychic mindscape that is visually oppressive. A particularly disturbing image is the "eye in the door" of Beattie Roper's cell, an elaborately painted peephole made to look like a large human eye. The effect is nightmarish, and this particular eye is not a fiction: "That eye actually existed in Aylesburg Prison," Barker comments: "Imagine the sadism of it" (quoted in Rodd, 1993, p. 29).

A recurring theme in the novel, the "eye" becomes part of Prior's chronic nightmares. In the trenches a year earlier Prior had found the eyeball of his friend Powers lying in the palm of his hand shortly after Powers was blown to bits by an artillery shell. The image of the eye also serves to link Prior with Rivers, who claims that his mind's eye was put out as a child, so he lacks a visual memory of some earlier events. Prior and Rivers are Barker's contradictory doubles, and because her characters often dream alike, Prior's nightmares may be those that Rivers has but cannot recall. Just as Prior says what Rivers will not, he sees what Rivers cannot, and Rivers and Prior in tandem reverberate Barker's echoing themes of silenced speech and sighted blindness.

Prior's visit to Beattie Roper in Aylesburg is a cover for his search for his closest childhood friend, Patrick MacDowell, a socialist, pacifist, and deserter sought by Intelligence. Prior is entrusted to find him and to turn him in, but the idea of betraying his once best friend does not sit well with his conscience. His search for MacDowell sends him back to his old neighborhood and to a demoralizing homecoming. He is haunted in the streets of his past by the black-edged cards in the windows bearing the names of dead men, names to which he can put faces, and in a scene foreshadowing *The Ghost Road,* Prior feels the streets are "full of ghosts, grey, famished, unappeasable ghosts" (p. 97).

At home Prior begins having blackouts, symptoms of "hysterical fugue," wherein hours pass that he cannot recall. He fears that his sadistic impulses emerge during these blackouts and that he functions as his own "malignant double." Rivers warns him about filling in the gaps with monsters, but like some medieval mapmaker, Prior persists. His condition intensifies on his return to London and like Rivers, he is finally unsure where he belongs in the war: with the government or with the scapegoats. Working in Intelligence is doubly dangerous for Prior, because Lionel Spragge, a former intelligence officer who indicted Beattie Roper on fabricated evidence, hates Prior and wants to indict him as well. After several blackouts Prior discovers he has made mysterious appointments with Spragge which he subconsciously tries to keep when he is conscious, and that he has told Spragge about his friend MacDowell's whereabouts. When MacDowell is later imprisoned, Prior is guilt-stricken.

Ambivalent Billy Prior is the personification of the human contradictions implied in Barker's theme and addressed in the epigraph from Robert Louis Stevenson's *The Strange Case of Dr. Jekyll and Mr. Hyde* concerning "the thorough and primitive duality of man." Like her technique in *Blow Your House Down*, Barker focuses her lens on the unexpected, on the trauma surrounding the action, and on the subterranean forces that spur it on. Her memoirs of war do not analyze the battles, but the struggles and contradictions in the minds of its participants. If the war develops a life of its own, as Prior later contends in *The Ghost Road*, the "thorough and primitive duality of man" and woman is more its cause than the few yards of ground to be gained in the trenches. Like the centrifugal force of the plot in *Blow Your House Down*, Barker moves in on the eye of this storm in the final volume of her trilogy.

THE GHOST ROAD

IF *Regeneration* is the nerves and *The Eye in the Door* is the flesh, then *The Ghost Road* is the bones of Barker's human offering for peace. Readers of the first two books know that by 1918 millions of men have died in France; England is in a state of mass hysteria and has resorted to witch-hunts to seek out "conchies" (conscientious objectors), sodomites, and suffragettes, and the hospitals in Europe are overrun with an epidemic of shell-shock victims unprecedented in medical history. The two intertwining narratives of *The Ghost Road* alternate principally between Billy Prior's diaries from the front and Rivers' memories of his experiences in Melanesia eight years earlier. And in classic Barker style, the plot becomes an echo chamber of voices, images, and experiences, flowing together in dreamlike sequence toward a final resolution.

W. H. R. Rivers now practices at a hospital in London, and Billy Prior, Rivers' former Craiglockhart patient, having served a stint in military intelligence in London is now preparing for his fourth tour of duty at the front with another former Craiglockhart inmate, Wilfred Owen. Early in the narrative, Rivers contracts Spanish flu, and alternating in and out of consciousness, he permits his "newly opened mind's eye" (p. 117) to voyage back to the time he spent in the South Pacific on the Melanesian isle of Eddystone, where he conducted anthropological research among a community of former headhunters. It is nearing the end of the war, and by now Rivers is profoundly disturbed with his role of sending "cured" young men back to the front to die. He ponders the parallels between their dilemma and that of the Eddystone community. Like the "colonized" Melanesians, the destiny of British soldiers is at an impasse.

One of Rivers' recurring dreams about Eddystone concerns the *tomate patu*, or "stone ghosts"— pieces of rock "erected as memorials to men who died and whose bodies could not be brought home" (p. 207), parallel totems of the thousands of headstones erupting like teeth from the soil of France. Images of Eddystone are the indelible ink of Rivers' unconscious, and the profound cross-cultural connections he makes with the Melanesian witch doctor Njiru become the major dream source from which he ponders the war. The enigmatic Njiru becomes Rivers' "primitive" counterpart, as Rivers discovers that the headhunters and the English are not far removed from each other. Like Billy Prior in *The Eye in the Door*, who emerges from his fugue states wondering which side of the war he is on, Pat Barker implies that Rivers awakens from his dreams not knowing whether he is a witch doctor in a country of neurologists or a neurologist in a country of witch doctors.

In Eddystone, Rivers visits Pa Na Gundu, where seven houses heaped with the skulls of dead warriors are cleaned and attended by Nareti, a blind mortuary priest. British colonial laws imposed on Melanesian culture no longer permit head-hunting, but the skull houses remain sacred, tributes to the continuity of the indigenes' culture and their rituals of birth and death. Yet only eight years later in "civilized" Europe, the very country that imposes the law against head-hunting litters the battlefields of France with the skulls and bodies of dead warriors—bones not kept sacred in skull houses, but left to rot.

Rivers is fascinated by the Melanesian "spirit ghosts" central to the headhunters' rituals. Even though Njiru "knows Ave," he is not always communicative, "one moment clamming up completely, even ordering the other people to withhold information, and yet at other times easily the best informant on the island" (p. 234). Rivers is somewhat intimidated by him, but at last asks Njiru about the most feared evil spirit of all, Ave, whom Njiru describes as "both one spirit and many spirits," who kills "all people 'long house," and is "the destroyer of peoples" (p. 268). (The " 'long house" is the all-inclusive community of humankind.) With his long mouth filled with blood, Ave is the incarnation of greed, and destroys not only single nations, but also entire cultures. Ironically, the spirit of Ave is at work in Melanesia at that very moment—a strong imperialist nation, Great Britain, has redefined the culture of Melanesia in terms of its own greed, and has imposed control over its value system to subject and silence it. Rivers recognizes the paradox of England's imperialistic stance and his own position as an emissary of English science studying a culture whose "view of *his* society was neither more nor less valid than his of theirs" (p. 119).

While Rivers is drawing these conclusions, his other counterpart, Prior, prepares to return to France. But lest her readers think her long on tragedy and short on comic relief, Barker first takes us with Prior to visit Beale Street and the resourceful Ada Lumb, mother of Prior's fiancée, Sarah. Ada is an earthy, independent woman with "a sense of humour . . . and an eye for male flesh" (p. 67). She strongly disapproves of granting the vote to women over thirty because "it had pleased Almighty God . . . to create the one sex visibly and unmistakably superior to the other" (p. 67). Once we get to know Ada, it is clear she is referring to the female sex. A paragon of mock gentility, Ada rears her two daughters single-handedly by running a successful "lock-up" shop featuring secondhand clothes and a motley assemblage of patent medicines "designed to procure abortion or cure clap" (p. 65), the profits from which allow her to keep house in a tawdry facsimile of gentility.

But in part two Prior must leave Ada's house, Sarah's arms, and Rivers' misgivings to return to France. We learn of Prior's experiences at the front through his diary entries beginning 29 August 1918 and ending 3 November 1918. His journal consoles him because he says ironically that "first-person narrators can't die" (p. 115). The poisonous landscape of the front is saturated with "stinking mud, stagnant water . . . rotting men, dead horses, gas" (p. 240). The heavy rain and churning mud create a demonic terrain: an eighteen-inch quagmire that makes movement almost impossible, but still won't hide the men. A permanent feeling of wrongness settles at the nape of Prior's neck—exposure, he says, is the word, because now they are out in the open all the time. In the trenches they had hidden like rats, but now they are not only immobile, they are exposed. Barker's images of visibility in *The Eye in the Door* now become images of immobilized exposure, and the British troops are pictured as so many wooden ducks in a row.

In the intertwining narratives of the plot, Prior's musings at the front parallel those of Rivers, and as was Rivers among the Eddystone headhunters, Prior too is surrounded by ghosts. Even the living have entered the state of *mate*, a Melanesian term for those meant to be dead: "the state of which death is the appropriate and therefore the desirable outcome" (p. 264). Prior ponders the future of his charges, young recruits, most of whom will certainly die: "Ghosts everywhere. Even the living were only ghosts in the making" (p. 46).

Prior's friend Potts argues that the war is to feather the nests of profiteers and safeguard access to Mesopotamian oil wells, not to protect Belgian neutrality and the rights of small nations. But Prior replies that Potts's "conspiracy theory" is optimistic, simply because it implies the war is being fought for a reason, when in fact it is much worse: "It's become a self-perpetuating system. Nobody benefits. Nobody's in control. Nobody knows how to stop" (p. 144). The war, Barker implies, has taken on a life of its own. Now out of control, it exists beyond all cultural constraint and is Njiru's evil spirit Ave, who kills "all people 'long house"— a featureless absurdity orchestrated by a faceless Nobodaddy (William Blake's expression for chaos). Like the primitive rituals of the Melanesian headhunters, it is the barbaric rite of one savage country crushing another.

As Barker's trilogy and the war move inexorably toward their close at the battle of the Sambre Canal, we as readers suspect what must be coming. And when Barker's compound eye switches from Prior's first-person diary entries to omniscient narration, we know. First-person narrators do die. In fact, Billy Prior is already dying when he watches Wilfred Owen get hit by machine-gun fire; "his body lifted off the ground by bullets, describing a slow arc in the air as it fell" (p. 273). The slow arc Owen's body describes becomes part of the vortex of Barker's plot. She has circled into the eye of the storm and in the center is the perfect calm of an indelible image. It is the image of Rivers in Eddystone, standing beside Njiru, holding in his hand a sacred human skull and thinking: "This blown eggshell had contained the only product of the forces of evolution capable of understanding its own origins" (p. 238). The image resonates with a central scene in Shakespeare's *Hamlet*, when Hamlet holds a skull aloft and declares, "Alas, poor Yorick! I knew him. . . ." But four hundred years later, Pat Barker answers Hamlet's cry with a question that echoes back through the centuries: We knew you, Yorick, but did we ever understand you? And as a species not exempt from extinction, we must ask this question. For Barker has shown us that violence is the tragedy that turns human culture inside out and against itself.

Barker's triumphant trilogy is her own plainspoken counterattack on war and her provocative challenge to us all to understand its causes. The twentieth century spawned two world wars and the Holocaust, but "history," Barker claims, "has no shame, history lays it on with a trowel" (quoted in Young, p. 28).

SELECTED BIBLIOGRAPHY

I. NOVELS. *Union Street* (London, 1982; New York, 1983); *Blow Your House Down* (London and New York, 1984); *The Century's Daughter* (London and New York, 1986; retitled *Liza's England* [London, 1996]); *The Man Who Wasn't There* (London, 1989; New York, 1990); *Regeneration* (London and New York, 1991); *The Eye in the Door* (London, 1993; New York, 1994); *The Ghost Road* (London and New York, 1995).

II. INTERVIEWS AND CRITICAL STUDIES. Eileen Fairweather, "The Voices of Women," in *New Statesman and Nation* (14 May 1982); Elaine Showalter, "Rivers and Sassoon: The Inscription of Male Gender Anxieties," in *Behind the Lines: Gender and the Two World Wars* (New Haven, Conn., 1987); Lyn Pykett, "The Century's Daughters: Recent Women's Fiction and History," in *Critical Quarterly* 29 (autumn 1987); Peter Hitchcock, "Radical Writing," in his *Dialogics of the Oppressed* (Minneapolis, 1993); Donna Perry, *Backtalk: Women Writers Speak Out: Interviews by Donna Perry* (New Brunswick, N.J., 1993); Candice Rodd, "A Stomach for War," in *Independent on Sunday* (12 September 1993); Candice Rodd, "Spirits in Waiting," in *Independent on Sunday* (10 September 1995); Philip Young, "A Voice from the Front Line," in *Journal* (11 September 1995); Francis Spufford, "Exploding Old Myths," in *Guardian* (9 November 1995).

JULIAN BARNES

(1946–)

Sven Birkerts

JULIAN BARNES ONCE remarked—or, better, proclaimed—that "in order to write, you have to convince yourself that it's a new departure not only for you but for the entire history of the novel" (quoted in Stout, p. 68). This is a young man's take-on-all-comers kind of statement, and one that Barnes may have regretted making as soon as the reporter packed up her notebook and left; it tells us, however, that the writer not only harbors a great ambition but also sustains a commitment to literary seriousness that is uncommon at the end of the twentieth century.

Few writers even think in terms of history and departures from it—these are modernist, not postmodernist, preoccupations. Which brings us to a paradox: How is it that the author of two defiantly postmodern novels—*Flaubert's Parrot* (1984) and *A History of the World in 10½ Chapters* (1989)—can still strike the reader as essentially a modernist? The answer, perhaps, is that Barnes is a writer determined to have it all ways; that he has adopted a coolly cerebral modernist stance that is flexible enough to accommodate some postmodern dalliance, but never in a way that would be binding. The postmodernist stance all but condemns a writer to ironic distance. Barnes, a consummate ironist, nonetheless reserves the right to get serious without the telltale arching of the brow.

Barnes's claim about the novelist's mission may strike some as being grandiose, but one could argue that in spirit at least he has made good on it. That is, of all the inventive and prolific writers in his approximate generation (including Martin Amis, Graham Swift, Salman Rushdie, and Ian McEwan), Barnes seems the most deeply pledged to the ideal of incessant transformation, moving in a mere decade and a half from a fairly conventional coming-of-age novel, *Metroland* (1980), to the bold collagism of *Flaubert's Parrot*, to the vast word-cycle of *A History of the World in 10½ Chapters,* to the historicopolitical investigation of *The Porcupine* (1992). Alongside these bolder departures, Barnes was also producing his quieter, but no less singular, books—the novels *Before She Met Me* (1982), *Staring at the Sun* (1986), *Talking It Over* (1991), the nonfiction prose of *Letters from London* (1995), and the story collection *Cross Channel* (1996). Although he is prolific, Barnes gives no signs of being hurried. The prose is ever calm and manicured, and even when Barnes modulates into freer idioms, whether the wordplay of *A History of the World in 10½ Chapters* or the saltier expressions of, say, *Talking It Over,* we always feel that we are in the hands of a meticulous artificer.

The question may be fairly asked whether Barnes has not spread himself over a wide area at some sacrifice of depth and penetration. The novels are seen to say this and that without gathering the central momentum that makes a writer's oeuvre truly commanding. And it is true—one can set down a Barnes novel and feel that issues and situations have been cunningly worked up but that certain deeper truths and implications remain undisturbed. Another critic, however, might counter in several ways. First, by suggesting that various though the works are, they *do* mount a recursive exploration of certain themes—faith and faithlessness in human relations, for example, or the subjective constructedness and inevitable relativeness of all truths. Second, by proposing that while Barnes has run through a gamut of experimental possibilities in his writing, the later works, especially the stories in *Cross Channel,* show greater density and greater concern for the specific characters that he has created.

65

EARLY LIFE AND FIRST NOVEL

JULIAN Barnes was born in Leicester, England, on 19 January 1946. His parents, Albert and Kaye, were teachers in French, a fact which may in some way account for the prominence of France and things French in many of his writings. Barnes's family moved to a London suburb when the boy was ten, and Julian won a scholarship to a private boys' school in the city. Barnes has given a few hints about his upbringing in interviews. As one profile expressed it, his parents "raised their two sons in a typically English spirit of sound middle-class caution, stability and routine.... Times-reading agnostics, they were moderate in their politics but fanatical about gardening.... Julian and his elder brother, Jonathan (now a philosophy don), were the first of their family to attend Oxbridge" (Stout, p. 72).

At Oxford, Barnes moved from languages (he had studied French and Russian intensively at City of London School) to psychology and philosophy. Neither of these disciplines gratified sufficiently, and after graduation Barnes found himself adrift. He ended up working as a lexicographer on a supplement to the *Oxford English Dictionary*. When he became disenchanted with the incessant pursuit of usages and variations, he thought he might read for the bar. En route to a possible career in contract law, Barnes was again derailed, now by reviewing books for the *Times Literary Supplement*, the *New Statesman*, and other publications. By the age of thirty he had become a full-time book and television critic. And then, in 1980, he published his first novel under his own name, *Metroland*.

Well paced, smartly written, and wearing its J. D. Salinger qualities lightly, *Metroland* tells the coming-of-age story of Chris Lloyd and his friend Toni. The novel begins in 1963. The boys are in their waning teen years, living in the eponymous Metroland, a suburban outcropping of London, and they are seasoning their rebellion with a defiantly French bohemianism. Barnes has great fun skewering the pretensions of these two mates:

Toni and I were strolling along Oxford Street, trying to look like *flâneurs*. This wasn't as easy as it might sound. For a start, you usually needed a *quai* or, at the very least, a *boulevard*; and, however much we might be able to imitate the aimlessness of the *flânerie* itself, we always felt that we hadn't quite mastered what happened at each end of the stroll.

(p. 17)[1]

Like many first novels, *Metroland* is less interesting in itself than for what it reveals about its young author. In Barnes's case, it is safe to assume—at least to a point—that we are reading cunningly remastered self-portraiture, if not autobiography. Chris, who has been given Barnes's own birth year, casts a cold eye on the idiosyncrasies of his parents. "On my right," he observes, "my father had *The Times* folded back at the stock-exchange prices and was murmuring his way down them. ... From time to time he would toss my mother a dutiful question about the garden" (p. 40).

Part 2 of the novel jumps forward to 1968. We find Chris living in Paris on a research grant. "I installed my few possessions, greased up to the concierge, Mme Huet, in her den of houseplants and diarrhoeic cats ... registered at the Bibliothèque Nationale (which wasn't too conveniently close) and began to fancy myself, at long last, as an autonomous being" (p. 85).

While in Paris Chris meets Annick, loses his virginity, and, in letters to Toni, tries to gloss over his sense of betraying the old friendship by growing up. As Chris philosophizes to himself: "The enemies who had given us common cause were no longer there; our adult enthusiasms were bound to be less congruent than our adolescent hates" (p. 97).

Nearing the end of his stay in Paris, Chris meets a group of young fellow Brits and falls in love with one of their number, Marion. Parting with Annick, he ends a chapter of his sentimental education. A look back over the shoulder compresses the whole adventure: "Ask me what I did in 1968 and I'll tell you: worked on my thesis ... fell in love, had my heart chipped; improved my French; wrote a lapidary volume, issued in a handwritten edition of one; did some drawing; made some friends; met my wife" (p. 128).

And indeed, when we reconnect with Chris in part 3, it is 1977 and he is married to Marion, settled, and in essential conflict with his old friend

[1]Except where noted, page references to Barnes's books are made to the paperback editions published by Vintage Books (Random House).

Toni, who now as writer-critic still espouses the old antiauthoritarian line. But now Chris is threatened, feels judged. Pay lip service as he may to those old ideals, he is safely grown into what he warned himself against. He has moved, though, from the abrasive sarcasm of youth to the roomier ironies of young middle-age—roomy, that is, in that they can accommodate all manner of private regrets: "On Saturday afternoon, as I track the lawn mower carefully across our sloping stretch of grass, rev, slow, brake, turn and rev again, making sure to overlap the previous stripe, don't think I can't still quote you Mallarmé" (p. 174).

Metroland ends with a final image of the domesticated rebel awake in the small hours of the night. He is staring out the kitchen window at the street lamp: "The lamp snaps off, and I am left with a lozenge-shaped blue-green after-image. I continue to stare; it diminishes, and then, in its turn, and in its quieter way, snaps off" (p. 176).

Though *Metroland* is in many ways a young man's book, its attitudes and energies familiar from other such books, it does allow us to catch glimpses of what will become some of Barnes's signature themes. The friendship-become-opposition of Chris and Toni will surface in various guises in *Before She Met Me* and *Talking It Over,* both of which use the betrayal of one friend by another as part of their core premise. This first novel also deploys the England-France opposition, which turns up, to greater and lesser degree, in *Before She Met Me* and *Flaubert's Parrot,* and becomes a full-blown preoccupation in *Cross Channel.*

The novel is, further, very much a *written* work, the product of a stylist with a strong pull toward Nabokovian artifice. Significantly, though, Barnes is not a thoroughgoing artificer. Rather, his writing is governed by a kind of ticktock pattern, with the more crafted books alternating with the less adorned presentations. Thus, *Metroland, Flaubert's Parrot, Staring at the Sun,* and *A History of the World in 10½ Chapters* are counterbalanced by *Before She Met Me, Talking It Over,* and *The Porcupine,* all of which rally to a more realist banner. The reader must at least question whether Barnes is not in some fundamental way a writer divided against himself. We think not only of the symbolic opposition between the dutiful Chris and the renegade Toni, but also of the aesthetic divergence from work to work; if that were not enough, there is the fact that in addition to writing literary works under his own name, Barnes has written a number of genre mysteries under the name of Dan Kavanagh. But then, such surmises are as dubious in their ultimate merit as they are intriguing to ponder.

BEFORE SHE MET ME *AND* FLAUBERT'S PARROT

BARNES'S second literary novel, *Before She Met Me,* was published in 1982. A slight work, it rides more on conceptual cleverness and deftness of execution than upon any greater substance. The plot conceit is simple, and probable only if you grant the all-consuming force of passion, in this case expressed as sexual jealousy. Graham Hendrick is sent by his former wife to a movie that his present wife, Ann, acted in (before she met him). In the movie, Ann plays the part of an adulteress, and with the iron-clad logic of the insecure, Graham not only conceives the idea that she had a lurid sexual past, but also begins to wonder if she might not be deceiving him in the present. Graham confides his fears to his friend Jack—the man who originally introduced him to Ann—and who had once, we learn, been involved with her. No matter what advice Jack offers—that Graham should try "wanking" (masturbating), for example—the obsession with finding out the truth about his wife keeps growing stronger. Graham continues to seek out revival movie houses that show films Ann acted in, and before long he experiences a breakdown. From there it is but a short step to a paranoid's retribution scheme, and Graham's leads finally to his stabbing Jack and then killing himself. All because his ex-wife suggested he see a certain movie—how well she must have read his soul!

Barnes tries to give this somewhat improbable narrative a thematic grounding. His epigraph, from an article by Paul D. MacLean in the *Journal of Nervous and Mental Diseases,* reads:

Man finds himself in the predicament that nature has endowed him essentially with three brains which, despite great differences in structure, must function together and communicate with one another. The oldest of these brains is basically reptilian. The second has been inherited from the lower mammals, and the third is a late mammalian development, which . . . has made man peculiarly man. Speaking allegorically of these brains within a brain, we might imagine that when the psychiatrist bids the patient to lie on the couch, he is asking him to stretch out alongside a horse and a crocodile.

Barnes takes this notion up at strategic moments of his story, as here, when Graham has gone to Jack for advice, and Jack, who has been reading a work of Arthur Koestler's (Barnes befriended Koestler late in that writer's life), explains why no rational solution to his problem can possibly work. Jack tells him that "the old brainbox isn't at all like we imagine. We all believe it's a big deal, our brain. We all think it's the shit-hot part of us—I mean, it stands to reason, doesn't it, that's why we aren't monkeys or foreigners. . . . Trouble is, there are a couple of other layers, different colours or something, don't quote me" (p. 78). And then later, again, Graham finds himself musing: "What was the latest theory which Jack—Jack of all people—had explained to him? That there were two or three different layers of the brain constantly at war with one another. This was only a different way of saying that your guts fucked you up, wasn't it?" (p. 169).

The problem with *Before She Met Me* is that Barnes relies too much on his theory and not enough upon the deeper psychology of disintegration. The reader is asked to make an enormous leap, from the engaging and relatively humorous recounting of Graham's growing obsession to the suddenly serious business of his breakdown. His attack on Jack and his suicide do not grow naturally from the character we have been tracking; both incidents feel macabre and distended, not unlike a simple shadow that magnifies and then breaks along wall and ceiling.

Before She Met Me is important to Barnes's oeuvre mainly because it introduces what will become a consistent theme in the work—that of appearances and their underlying realities and, secondarily, of the inevitable failure of congruence among competing worldviews. Graham's vision of things is not Jack's and it is not Ann's. Must one vision be the truth and the others deceptions, or is reality the ever shifting construct of differently constituted individuals? Graham is, in a sense, driven as much by epistemology as he is by jealousy. This theme resurfaces in *Flaubert's Parrot, Talking It Over,* and *The Porcupine.*

If *Before She Met Me* is fanciful in its narrative conception, the writing is quite straightforward, with Barnes striving for a fairly conventional immediacy. The opening sentence sets the stylistic pace for the rest of the novel: "The first time Graham Hendrick watched his wife commit adultery he didn't mind at all" (p. 11). How different is the beginning of the work that may well be Barnes's most beguiling to date, *Flaubert's Parrot:*

Six North Africans were playing *boules* beneath Flaubert's statue. Clean cracks sounded over the grumble of jammed traffic. With a final, ironic caress from the fingertips, a brown hand dispatched a silver globe. It landed, hopped heavily, and curved in a slow scatter of hard dust. The thrower remained a stylish, temporary statue: knees not quite unbent, and the right hand ecstatically spread.

(p. 11)

Taking the magus of the mot juste as his subject and stylistic conscience, Barnes essays in this short novel a tour de force of literary collagism. The narrative, which works less as a plot, more as a force field in which Barnes situates his various perspectives, is rudimentary. Geoffrey Braithwaite, a widower and retired doctor, indulges his scholarly obsession with Gustave Flaubert. Only gradually, and very obliquely, does he realize that his story may be a kind of echo to that of Flaubert's *Madame Bovary* (1857), a tale that stands to the textual one as the posed *boules* player stands to the statue beside him. Braithwaite's deceased wife, Ellen, whom he loved a great deal, apparently had affairs; she may also have, like Emma Bovary, taken her own life. Part of Barnes's great accomplishment here is to keep these strands of Braithwaite's and Ellen's past the merest suggestions and to give the Flaubert obsession free rein.

In an important set of passages late in the book, the convergence of experience and scholarly motivation is suggested. As Braithwaite writes:

I loved Ellen, and I wanted to know the worst. . . . Ellen never returned this caress. She was fond of me—she would automatically agree, as if the matter weren't worth discussing, that she loved me—but she unquestioningly believed the best about me. That's the difference. She didn't ever search for that sliding panel which opens the secret chamber of the heart, the chamber where memory and corpses are kept. . . . That's the real distinction between people: not between those who have secrets and those who don't, but between those who want to know everything and those who don't. This search is a sign of love, I maintain.

(pp. 126–127)

Braithwaite goes on: "It's similar with books. . . . If you love a writer, if you depend upon the drip-feed of his intelligence, if you want to pursue him and find him—despite edicts to the contrary—then it's impossible to know too much. You seek the vice as well" (p. 127).

So, in seeking the true Flaubert, Braithwaite is, in essence, seeking the secrets of the sensibility that perhaps understood the heart of a deceiving woman. He is looking for the wound at the heart of his marriage, of his life.

But Braithwaite is in a very fundamental way divided against himself. Proclamations about his search for Ellen's secret chamber notwithstanding, he is a monumentally repressed character. His scholarship—which he thinks of as his search—is also his primary defense. Barnes's most brilliant stroke was in allowing the man's rigid and defended and obsessive sensibility to determine the structure of the book. *Flaubert's Parrot* is a collage because the fragmentation of some imagined unity—the true picture of Gustave Flaubert—represents the narrator's psyche.

The structure does double duty, however, for it allows Barnes to assemble a delightful and utterly idiosyncratic catalogue of Flaubertiana. The most unexpected—indeed, at times *satirically* unexpected—vantages are proposed. Chapter 8, for instance, is entitled "The Train-spotter's Guide to Flaubert"; it filters the whole of Flaubert's career through the highly selective mesh of his connection with railway trains. Other vantages include an official chronology, a chapter called "Louise Colet's Version," and a bestiary chapter which assesses the writer's relation to various forms of creature life. We are never far from spirited wordplay:

Exactly what species of bear was Flaubear? We can track his spoor through the Letters. At first he is just an unspecified *ours,* a bear (1841). He's still unspecified—though owner of a den—in 1843, in January 1845, and in May 1845 (by now he boasts a triple layer of fur). In June 1845 he wants to buy a painting of a bear for his room and entitle it "Portrait of Gustave Flaubert"—"to indicate my moral disposition and my social temperament."

So far we (and he too, perhaps) have been imagining a dark animal: an American brown bear, a Russian black bear, a reddish bear from Savoy. But in September 1845 Gustave firmly announces himself to be "a white bear."

(p. 52)

One of the many less overt fascinations of *Flaubert's Parrot* is that it applies a postmodern methodology—a fragmented study of biographical indeterminacy—to a decisively protomodern figure. That is, Flaubert labored with documented agonies to perfect a freestanding masterpiece (*Madame Bovary*), and for that became one of the presiding gods of the modernist enterprise, influencing Samuel Beckett, James Joyce, and countless others. That his centripetal presence should be run through Barnes's centrifuge is aesthetically dissonant in the extreme. Barnes manages the task mainly because he has such an unflinching command of irony. Braithwaite's narrative tone, the weary civilized inflections, serves his obsessive mania in a way Flaubert would have understood, perhaps finally even approved of.

As in *Before She Met Me,* Barnes in this novella explores the fragile constructedness of our understandings. It seems that the closer Braithwaite comes to his idol's actual world, the more he penetrates the real details—details of the sort that finally make up a life—the less certain things become. He is thrown into great confusion by the realization that the Master kept changing his description of Emma Bovary's eyes. But more upsetting still is the mystery of the eponymous parrot. Everywhere Braithwaite goes he finds yet another stuffed bird billed as the authentic model for the bird in Flaubert's celebrated story, "Un Coeur Simple" (1877; "A Simple Heart"). And when the novel ends, for all the insight our narrator has accumulated about Flaubert's life and work—and, obliquely, his own situation—he must concede that life will not gratify him with unambiguous answers. Taken to a back room where three of fifty original stuffed Amazonian parrots remain, he relents:

They gazed at me like three quizzical, sharp-eyed, dandruff-ridden, dishonourable old men. They did look—I had to admit it—a little cranky. I stared at them for a minute or so, and then dodged away.

Perhaps it was one of them.

(p. 190)

That the book's final sentence should begin with the adverb "perhaps" speaks volumes.

Flaubert's Parrot was published at just the right moment—its preoccupations were those of the intellectual culture at large. Relativism and textual instability were, of course, front-burner topics; fragmented presentation still had a whiff of the avant-garde about it; and the biographer/biographee—or scholar/subject—relationship carried a certain charge. That the volume was slim and wittily ironic could only favor its reception.

Looking past the charm and celebrity of the novel, one registers a distinct bleakness of outlook. *Flaubert's Parrot* is very much a late-culture offering, its pleasures built upon sad recognitions—about the failure of human connections, the insufficiency of art, and, on a formal level, about the collapse of sensible explanatory narratives. The distance that Braithwaite keeps from the emotional immediacies of life—intellectual obsession is finally a "cool" rather than "hot" engagement—comes to stand in for a larger sort of impotence. This most literate novel is also, in a sense, a damning of the literary vocation. Flaubert, the idol of all who would live by the word, is reduced in good measure to the musty artifacts and half-cocked missionaries he has left in his wake. One of the blurbs on the back of the paperback edition calls *Flaubert's Parrot* an "anti-novel," a term which may have more resonances than the reviewer intended. The book can be seen as being *anti* the very understandings and assumptions about character and art that make the novel possible.

STARING AT THE SUN *AND* A HISTORY OF THE WORLD IN 10½ CHAPTERS

IN 1986, Barnes published his fourth novel, *Staring at the Sun,* and once again ventured such a departure from the preceding work that one could be forgiven for supposing that the author's career path grew, not from organic imperatives, but from a determination to simply veer away from the last path pursued. Where *Flaubert's Parrot* is arch and contrived, a mandarin tour de force, *Staring at the Sun* opts for a fairly straightforward presentation of a woman, Jean Sargeant, who begins her days simply enough in the early twentieth century and lives on into the beginning of the new millennium. Her life gradually gathers into extraordinariness—a quality that it owes, at least in part, to the extraordinariness of the times themselves.

Barnes here enjoys manipulating the tension between the stolid commonsensical side of his character and the presence of the marvelous, which she is also alert to. The novel is framed, at the start and finish, by what might be called visionary glimpses. In the first chapter, a roomer in Jean's childhood home tells her the story of how he got the name "Sun-Up Prosser." He had been out on a flying mission and had, from a certain high altitude, seen the sun rise. But then:

I must have lost half my height, down to eight or nine. And then, guess what? I'd descended so quickly, you see, that it all happened all over again: this bloody great orange sun started popping up from under the horizon. Couldn't believe my eyes. All over again. Like running a film back and having another look at it.

(p. 28)

The imagery of flight and, no less important, its detached perspectives govern this most curious novel. Barnes's "aerial" premise would seem to be to present the passage of a century—more—through the medium of the life of a middle-class woman. The close-up scenes are rendered with a conspicuous lack of affect, possibly to encourage the distancing. Here, for example, the author portrays Jean's short-lived involvement in a sexual relationship with her son's girlfriend, Rachel: "Twice more they tried, if try was the word: Jean lay turned away on her side, wearing a borrowed nightdress, holding her breath. She wanted to want to—but the actual achievement of wanting seemed inaccessible. When it seemed that Rachel was asleep, Jean relaxed; she was also struck by how well she then slept" (p. 128).

Barnes's point here is not to shock, but rather to suggest that in her utterly matter-of-fact way Jean is an explorer, what the writer Robert Musil called a "possibilitarian"—one who researches the options of life with an experimental interest. If this scene seems distanced, though, we need only look at the extraordinary telescoping of decades that Barnes indulges in later in the novel:

Jean had often wondered what it would be like to grow old. When she had been in her fifties, and still feeling in her thirties, she heard a talk on the radio by a gerontologist. "Put cotton wool in your ears," he had said, "and pebbles in your shoes." . . .

At sixty she had still felt like a young woman; at eighty she felt like a middle-aged woman who had something a bit wrong with her; at nearly a hundred she no longer bothered to think whether or not she felt younger than she was—there didn't seem any point.

(p. 141)

Jean is presented throughout in just this way. We know her as she is refracted to us through the author's omniscience, as he reports on her patient efforts to fathom herself.

The novel ends many decades after Jean's first conversation with Sun-Up Prosser, with Jean, like Sun-Up Prosser himself, in an airplane, only instead of seeing the sun rise twice, she gets to see its second setting. Barnes has hit upon a wonderful figure, a kind of double illusion that yet partakes of resonance. Not only does the sun not rise or set twice, it does not, finally, rise or set at all. Yet the human determination to see against the facts—to keep the earth at the center of the picture—is decisive for our experience here below. Barnes seems to suggest that even after the passing of nearly a hundred years in this most remarkable era of science and technology, we are refusing to be dethroned—indeed, we are insisting on our dose of wonder:

After several minutes the pilot flattened out and began a second southward run. Jean turned away . . . and looked out the window. . . . The sun's descent seemed quicker this time, a smooth slipping away. The earth did not greedily chase it, but lay flatly back with its mouth open. The big orange sun settled on the horizon, yielded a quarter of its volume to the accepting earth, then a half, then three-quarters, and then, easily, without argument, the final quarter. For some minutes a glow continued from beneath the horizon, and Jean did, at last, smile towards this postmortal phosphorescence. Then the aeroplane turned away, and they began to lose height.

(pp. 196–197)

We think, perhaps, of the final passage of Barnes's *Metroland*, which similarly depicts a loss of light, a glow, and then a more final turn away. There is no question that we are in the hands of a clever and coordinated stylist. Unfortunately, *Staring at the Sun* does not bring Jean Sargeant persuasively to life—her myriad encounters and conflicts and accommodations feel like paper events. The woman has emerged from her creator's brain. She is thought forth, but in no sense is she full-blooded. And while the beauties of some of Barnes's set pieces—not least his fabulous sunrises and sunsets—stay with the reader, their ostensible pretext, Jean Sargeant, does not.

Barnes's next novel, *A History of the World in 10½ Chapters*, is often cited by critics as his most ambitious achievement. And if the measure of ambition is seen as being how much heterogenous material can be brought together between a set of covers, then these critics are right. For here is a "novel" that wants to be all things: epic in scope, mythic in reference, comic in execution, tragic in implication, and compendious in realization. Barnes has selected diverse images and thematic elements and around these has conjured a set of narratives that could not possibly be more different from one another. The ten and a half chapters (the "½" is really a "parenthesis," an essay on marital love) tell as many different stories; they are linked mainly by a recurrence of boats and aquatic settings. Thus, the first tale is a reimagining of the biblical tale of Noah's ark; the fourth is a narrative of a woman adrift in the South Pacific in the days after a nuclear holocaust; the fifth attempts to tell the story behind Théodore Géricault's famous painting *The Raft of the Medusa* (1818–1819); and so on.

A charitable response to *A History of the World* would be to say that it recalls Giovanni Boccaccio, or Italo Calvino's *If on a Winter's Night a Traveller* (1979), or John Barth's modern Arabian Nights fantasias. But the sprawl of disconnected episodes and reflections lacks the frame support of those works. Boccaccio had the plague in the background, Calvino his playful assumption about the function of suspense in reading, and Barth generally pits his storytelling divagations against a prevailing contemporary situation. But Barnes gives his reader precious little. An author who imagines that recurring appearances of a woodworm or a deathwatch beetle—or one of a dozen other peripheral elements—are sufficient linkage in the construction of a novel is like a dinner host who assumes that a few bowls of mixed nuts will carry his guests through the long cocktail hour.

This is not to say that there is not abundant cleverness or that there are not many moments of stylistic triumph. The "Shipwreck" chapter, which tells the story behind the Géricault painting, is at once precise and attuned to indeterminacies and the pitfalls of relativism. It stands, both in conception and execution, with the very best of Barnes's work. Here, for example, the author reflects upon a few specific ways in which the painting differs from the documentation given by two survivors of the actual wreck:

The ignorant eye yields, with a certain testy reluctance, to the informed eye. Let's check "Scene of Shipwreck" [Géricault's original catalog title] against Savigny and Corréard's narrative. It's clear at once that Géricault hasn't painted the hailing that led to the final rescue: that happened differently, with the brig suddenly close upon the raft and everyone rejoicing. No, this is the first sighting, when the *Argus* appeared on the horizon for a tantalizing half hour. Comparing paint with print, we notice at once that Géricault has not represented the survivor up the mast holding straightened-out barrel-hoops with handkerchiefs attached to them. He has opted instead for a man being held up on top of a barrel and waving a large cloth. We pause over this change, then acknowledge its advantage: reality offered him a monkey-up-a-stick image; art suggested a solider focus and an extra vertical.

(pp. 130–131)

The reader encounters a chatty pedantry of tone, not unlike the tone adopted from time to time by Braithwaite in *Flaubert's Parrot*. This is Barnes's favored idiom—precise, knowing, verging on irony. Indeed, reading the Géricault chapter we wonder at times whether the whole business is not a send-up. But if it is, then we have to ask, to what end?

While we read *A History of the World in 10½ Chapters*, watching Barnes move from one sort of pastiche to another, this same question of purpose keeps rearing up. The Géricault prose is at least arresting in terms of its perspectives and detail, but much of the rest of the book is in a very different idiom—a kind of faux comic writing that is finally neither comic nor particularly expressive. Barnes's account of Noah and his animals—the base narrative—suffers in the extreme from this ill-judged presentation:

I gather that one of your early Hebrew legends asserts that Noah discovered the principle of intoxication by watching a goat get drunk on fermented grapes. What a brazen attempt to shift responsibility onto the animals; and all, sadly, part of a pattern. The Fall was the serpent's fault, the honest raven was a slacker and a glutton, the goat turned Noah into an alkie. Listen: you can take it from me that Noah didn't need any cloven-footed knowledge to help crack the secret of the vine.

(p. 29)

Barnes goes on in this vein at great length, pushing willfully in the face of his greatest writerly gifts—his elegant concision and linguistic brio. The quip about Noah turning into an "alkie" is neither funny nor interesting, and there are too many other such lapses in these pages.

A History of the World in 10½ Chapters is finally a book without a significant point. Barnes is clearly playing a variation on the postmodern collagism he used so effectively in *Flaubert's Parrot*. But where that novel had a binding energy at its core—a repressed psyche in extremis—this novel has no agenda except possibly that of showing what a literate and thoughtful stylist can do with a cooked-up premise and a bag full of archetypal tales.

TALKING IT OVER

IF *A History of the World in 10½ Chapters* is the most centrifugal of Barnes's novels, then *Talking It Over* is one of his most formally balanced and restrained. Taking as its epigraph a pungently paradoxical saying—"He lies like an eye-witness"—Barnes directs the full beam of his attention upon the romantic/sexual triangle that so clearly compels his narrative imagination. This terse, sophisticated work uses the voices of its three principals—Stuart, Oliver, and Gillian—to tell what is hardly a new tale in the repertoire. Stuart and Oliver are friends. Stuart, the shy and bumbling businessman, meets and marries Gillian. Oliver, smooth and impetuous, falls in love with Gillian at the wedding and promptly begins to lay siege. It is giving nothing away to reveal that he finally succeeds in winning her—indeed, marrying her himself—but that no one finds lasting happiness from the shift of the arrangement.

Talking It Over rides on the verve of its three voices and on the comic possibilities of the staple psychological premise, which is, in effect, that Stuart not only cedes Gillian to Oliver, but that he acquires the emotional power and simplicity of the devastated, while Oliver, initially blessed with a kind of dark complexity and purpose, fades into fearful ineptitude.

At first it is Oliver who captures the reader. His amatory scheming powers the narrative. Studying Gillian at the wedding, for instance, he is very much the poet:

She was all pale green and chestnut, with an emerald blaze at her throat; I roamed her face, from the bursting curve of her forehead to the plum-dent of her chin; her cheeks, so often pallid, were brushed with the pink of a Tiepolo dawn, though whether the brush was external and garaged in her handbag or internal and wielded by ecstasy, I was unable or unwilling to guess; her mouth was besieged by a half-smile which seemed to last and last; her eyes were her lustrous dowry. I *roamed* her face, do you hear?

(p. 62)

This is obsessive aestheticism à la Nabokov, and Barnes sustains it without apparent exertion. To get a sense of Barnes's comfortable range, one need only compare Oliver's words with a passage in the voice of his former friend and now-embittered rival, Stuart:

People find me more interesting now I've got more money. I don't know if I am—I'm probably not—but they find me so. That's a consolation. I like buying things and owning things and throwing them away if I don't like them. I bought a toaster the other day and after a week I didn't like the way it looked so I chucked it out.

(p. 233)

And Gillian? Plausible as she is as the object of Stuart's and Oliver's devotions, she does not possess the distinctness of presence the men do. Almost out of structural necessity, she is engagingly neutral—which is to say alert, observant, and articulate, but somehow lacking the tormented will of either Stuart or Oliver. There is a detachment, a sobriety, in Gillian's tone:

The only bit of the village which attracts visitors is the medieval frieze on the west end of the church. It runs all the way along the outside wall, doing a curve over the door in the middle. There are about thirty-six carved stone heads, alternating in design. Half of them are angels' heads, the other half skulls with a neat pair of crossed bones beneath. Paradise, hell, paradise, hell, paradise, hell, they go. Or perhaps it's resurrection and death, resurrection and death, resurrection and death, clatter, clatter like the railway that passes. Except that we don't believe in hell and resurrection any more.

(p. 243)

Like so many of Barnes's other works, *Talking It Over* is a study in the limitations of private subjectivity and in the invariably different construction placed on all situations by the various participants—hence the epigraph. By rotating the basic narrative steadily through three very different fields of consciousness, Barnes ensures that we find no absolute purchase. Every plausible interpretation, it seems, is undermined by the next speaker's version of things.

Where Barnes reveals his higher artistic sensibility is in the details. Not content merely to work through the premises of relativism, he unfolds subtler glimpses along the way. A case in point would be Oliver's speculation on Gillian's profession, which is the cleaning and restoring of old paintings:

And I've discovered this really tasty metaphor. Fashions in the universe of picture restoration—I speak from recent but devoted authority—tend to change. One moment it's out with the Brillo pad and scour, scour, scour. Another moment it's retouch with a decorator's brush, load every rift with pigment, and so on. . . . This means (you don't mind if I simplify matters a tad?) that the restorer should at all times do only what she knows may be undoable later by others. She must appreciate that her certainties are only temporary, her finalities provisional. . . . What does the restorer do first? She uses an *isolating varnish* to ensure that the paint she applies can be removed without trouble at some later date. . . . This is what we understand by *reversibility*.

(p. 126)

As this passage shows, Barnes has the novelist's gift of not merely presenting a character, but of inhabiting him. Oliver's perspective, his sense of things, is captured at the level of his language. These are his words, his terms; this is how he thinks. And by achieving this re-creation with three different characters—all first-person—Barnes ensures that the reader will experience the dramatic complications at more than just the intellectual level.

It is not hard to see how Oliver's discovered "metaphor" connects with certain of Braithwaite's preoccupations in *Flaubert's Parrot* or the discussion of Géricault's painting in *A History of the World*. Nor is it out of place, finally, to connect this admittedly concrete imagining with the overarching interrogation carried out in Barnes's next novel, *The Porcupine*. Here, too, reversibility is at issue.

Only now it is not the aesthetic rendition of events but their historical interpretation in the light of changing ideologies.

THE PORCUPINE *AND* LETTERS FROM LONDON

The Porcupine is, in a way, Barnes's updating of Arthur Koestler's novel about the Moscow show trials, *Darkness at Noon* (1940). The confinements, the interrogations, the anguished soul-searching are all there. It is a novel so bereft of setting that the reader begins to believe that the material world has fallen away and left nothing but voices, ideologies, ancient rancors, and here and there the glimmers of political idealism. Peter Solinsky, the son of a party intellectual in an unnamed Eastern European country, is appointed to prosecute the former president, Stoyo Petkanov. His mandate is to scapegoat the former leader, to put on trial the excesses and failures of the old regime.

As the novel begins, Solinsky is cocky with the supposition that history is now on his side. But he does not expect the psychological wiliness of the old leader, who knows the realities of politics well enough to know that there is no ultimately defensible moral high ground and that past events can support any construction placed upon them. Petkanov does not deliver himself over—indeed, he can be said to outfox his younger opponent at every turn. In such a way, moreover, the reader is led to root for the supposedly discredited version of things.

Barnes's twist, then, is to undermine Solinsky morally even as he is trying to do the same for Petkanov. Solinsky's bright-boy zealousness quickly crumbles, and in its place is disclosed an emasculated lack of center. Here, in a crucial scene, Solinsky's wife, Maria, tells him that her feelings for him have changed:

"... I can't love you any more, and after today I doubt that I can even respect you." Peter did not respond, did not even turn to see her face. "Still, others will respect you more and, who knows, perhaps others will love you ..."

"The man was a tyrant, a murderer, a thief, a liar, an embezzler, a moral pervert, the worst criminal in our nation's history. Everyone knows it. My God, even you are beginning to suspect it."

"If that's the case," she replied, "it shouldn't have

been difficult to prove without whoring for television and inventing fake evidence."

(p. 112)

The charge that can be leveled against *The Porcupine* is that Barnes is too facile about playing against expectation: having established that evil is more complex and interesting than well-intentioned righteousness, he should have reversed the reverse. That he did not do so is, of course, to suggest that the new order has its own besetting flaws—relativism, shallow expediency, and a kind of unearned moral smugness—but in the scenario as presented, there is no deeper sense of context, and no deeper condemnation of the genuine evils perpetrated by Petkanov's regime.

After *The Porcupine*, Barnes published *Letters from London*, a collection of journalistic essays written over several years for the *New Yorker*. These are mainly topical, interpreting English politics for American readers, reflecting on political-cultural issues, like the *fatwa* against Barnes's close friend Salman Rushdie. In his preface, Barnes recognizes a certain temper to the times he has been commenting upon, asking:

Was there, in the first half of the nineties, a tiredness and repetition to public life, a sense of things unraveling? It seemed to be the case. And if so, there are pleasures as well as despondencies to be had: Flaubert said that his favorite historical periods were those which were ending, because this meant that something new was being born.

(p. xi)

That "something new" could be, for Barnes and many of his contemporaries, the return to power of the Labour Party in the person of Tony Blair. But his final sentences in the last essay of the collection, "Left, Right, Left, Right: The Arrival of Tony Blair," certainly caution against any excessive optimism: "He may very well be the British Prime Minister as the century turns. But millenarians would be premature in renting space on mountaintops" (p. 311).

Barnes is a superb practitioner of thoughtful, opinionated, and irony-leavened journalism. Indeed, while his sardonic humor leaks through here and there in the novels, particularly the marital shooting matches, the free-ranging topical article offers a swifter and more diverse procession of targets. Here is a coolly acute reflection on a photograph of Margaret Thatcher's first cabinet:

Twenty-four men, plus one central woman, lined up beneath the dewdrop chandelier, Axminster at their feet, Gainsborough behind them. Twenty-four men trying, variously, to exude gravitas, to look youthfully dynamic, to dissemble serious surprise at being there in the first place. Ten of the two dozen are faced with the first real problem of political office: what to do with your hands when sitting in the front row of an official photograph. Folding your arms, like Keith Joseph, looks a defensive, prim, keep-off gesture. Clasping your hands over your capacious stomach, like Lord Hailsham, looks the boast of a gourmandizer. Grasping the left wrist with the right hand and allowing the left hand to dangle on the thigh, like Lord Carrington, seems indecisive, semiwet.

(p. 41)

What strikes the American reader about Barnes's essays is his supple use of irony—for irony has many modes and inflections—and the effect, both immediate and cumulative, of a civilized voice speaking out on matters of presumed public interest. There is no real counterpart in American journalism. Barnes's incisive and wide-ranging prose—his critical precision and his humor—is a much-needed reminder of what intellectual registers one loses by living in a mass culture.

CROSS CHANNEL

BETWEEN his many novels and his highly visible reportage, Barnes has established himself as a writer of international stature—too elusive and publicly clever to be seen as a pundit, but certainly to be heeded both as artist and opinion maker. Never one for public display—he does not hunt real or metaphorical lions—Barnes seems to follow Flaubert's advice, living like a bourgeois the better to vent himself in his work.

In the late 1990s the author lived in a house in North London with his wife and literary agent, Patricia Kavanagh. He moved in literary circles, counting writers Ian McEwan, Kazuo Ishiguro, and Salman Rushdie as close friends. (A long-standing friendship with Martin Amis was, reportedly, ruptured when Amis left Kavanagh for another agent.) Barnes and his wife gardened and entertained with notorious style. Barnes followed various sports with uncharacteristically unbuttoned enthusiasm.

But these details tell us little about a most enigmatic man. The writer Mira Stout, in a 1992 profile

of Barnes, quotes Martin Amis as saying: "There has always been an inscrutability about him, even to his best friends. The rest of us are a bunch of cheerful blabbermouths compared to him. He was always more discreet, more grown up. . . . He takes longer to get to know than most people, but he sort of looms up on you as a friend" (p. 72). And then, of course, he writes—writes prodigiously.

In 1996, Barnes published his first collection of stories, *Cross Channel*, and if we are searching for tendencies and directions, this book might represent the author's movement from more stylish to more substantial approaches to subject matter. Barnes has taken the complex oppositions of England and France as his subtle linking element, with each story in some way refracting their historical destiny as neighbors. The stories range over several centuries and are presented not chronologically but in thematic sequences. Thus, the collection opens with "Interference," a tale about a self-exiled English composer living in the French countryside at the beginning of the twentieth century, and ends with the formerly futuristic "Tunnel," in which an elderly writer travels via tunnel-train from England to Paris and uses the occasion to sift through the memories of a long lifetime. The large-scale sense of a rupture healed can be found in myriad local forms throughout the book, as can the theme of memory as a process of reconciliation.

At the center of *Cross Channel* are two powerfully realized stories about the persistence of the past in the present. "Melon" shows how a single event—a nonevent, in fact—can become the axis of association and longing in a life, while "Evermore" tells the tale of a woman who makes an annual pilgrimage to her brother's grave at Cabaret Rouge, France. This latter story, in particular, seems unafraid of its emotional charge and marks a change of presentation for Barnes, who until *Cross Channel* had always raised the decorated screen of articulate irony. The story ends with a powerful passage, a moment of elegiac anticipation that irradiates the collection. The woman, Miss Moss, imagines the day when her mourning ritual will cease. She then finds that

even as she pronounced herself an antique, her memories seemed to sharpen. If this happened to the individual, could it not also happen on a national scale? Might there not be, at some point in the first decades of the twenty-first century, one final moment, lit by evening sun, before the whole thing was handed over to the archivists? Might there not be a great looking back down the mown grass of the decades, might not a gap in the trees discover the curving ranks of slender headstones, white tablets holding up to the eye their bright names and terrifying dates, their harps and springboks, maple leaves and ferns, their Christian crosses and their Stars of David? Then, in the space of a wet blink, the gap in the trees would close and the mown grass disappear, a violet indigo cloud would cover the sun, and history, gross history, daily history, would forget. Is this how it would be?

(p. 111, 1996 ed.)

The passage resonates in "Tunnel," in which the gathering force of memory is again unleashed upon the sprawl of history—personal and collective.

As *Metroland*, Barnes's first literary novel, featured in Chris Lloyd a protagonist just his age, "Tunnel" has as its protagonist a writer likewise born in 1946. Now, of course, he is projectively aged. But he has not lost his fierce edge, and he still finds in France, and in things French a counterpoint sensibility, one he seems to require. As Barnes now explains:

As for sentimentality, that was sometimes the charge against him for his view of the French. If accused, he would always plead guilty, claiming in mitigation that this is what countries are for. It was unhealthy to be idealistic about your own country, since the least clarity of vision led swiftly to disenchantment. Other countries therefore existed to supply the idealism: they were a version of pastoral.

(p. 207, 1996 ed.)

After seven novels, a book of essays, and a collection of stories, Barnes appeared strong enough to relinquish some of his irony and stylistic consciousness and to follow the threads he has laid out in dazzling abundance.

SELECTED BIBLIOGRAPHY

I. NOVELS. *Metroland* (London and New York, 1980); *Before She Met Me* (London, 1982; New York, 1986); *Flaubert's Parrot* (London, 1984; New York, 1985); *Staring at the Sun* (London, 1986; New York, 1987); *A History of the World in 10½ Chapters* (London and New York, 1989); *Talking It Over* (London and New York, 1991); *The Porcupine* (London and New York, 1992).

Crime novels under the name Dan Kavanagh. *Duffy* (London and New York, 1980); *Fiddle City* (London and New York, 1981); *Putting the Boot In* (London and New York, 1985); *Going to the Dogs* (London and New York, 1987).

II. SHORT STORIES. *Cross Channel: Stories* (London and New York, 1996).

III. ESSAYS. *Letters from London* (London and New York, 1995).

IV. CRITICAL STUDIES. Tom Paulin, "National Myths," in *Encounter* (June 1980); David Coward, "The Rare Creature's Human Sounds," in *Times Literary Supplement* (London) (5 October 1984); Wendy Lesser, "Bloated and Shrunken Worlds," in *Hudson Review* (autumn 1985); Terrence Rafferty, "Watching the Detectives," in *Nation* (6–13 July 1985); Richard Locke, "Flood of Forms," in *New Republic* (4 December 1989); Mira Stout, "Chameleon Novelist," in *New York Times Magazine* (22 November 1992); Michael Scammel, "Trial and Error," in *New Republic* (4 and 11 January 1993); Ian Buruma, Review of *Letters from London* in *New York Review of Books* (21 March 1996); James Wood, Review of *Cross Channel,* in *New Republic* (24 June 1996).

JOHN BERGER

(1926–   )

Minnie Singh

JOHN BERGER IS a committed Marxist who is also a confessed romantic, a tireless popularizer but also a bold innovator, an ardent demystifier who believes deeply in mystery. These nominal tensions, always apparent in his writing, have been exaggerated by Berger's reception. His career was born out of, and largely coincided with, the Cold War; and because his work militates against the typically narrow ideological certitudes of the period, he has been repudiated by the Left almost as often as he has been reviled by the Right.

Berger's work includes numerous books and essays on art, eight works of fiction, poetry, philosophical investigations, and, in collaboration, photomontage narratives, plays, translations, and film and television scripts. Its unusual variety, spanning a number of genres and media, raises questions about his intellectual niche among British writers. At first glance Berger does not belong to a strictly literary tradition: his inspirations and subjects come from other areas, chiefly from the history of European art—especially painting—and from Marxist thought. Although the early fiction sometimes recalls Joyce and the later fiction has invited comparison with Hardy and Lawrence, Berger seems essentially eccentric to English literary history because his imagination was shaped not by literature but by pictures and ideas. Yet he can and should be placed in an important tradition of English writing: the robust continuity of oppositional cultural criticism, which for the last two centuries has absorbed the imaginative energies of both the Right (Edmund Burke, Thomas Carlyle, Matthew Arnold, John Ruskin, T. S. Eliot) and the Left (early Wordsworth, William Cobbett, William Morris, and occasionally George Orwell). The "creative" writing grows directly out of, and is continuous with, the polemic: the fiction is likely to illustrate, execute, or further a passionately held idea or belief.

It is the organizing centrality of the moral judgment that affords the reader a reasonably sure grasp of the work as a whole. Berger's work is striking for its strong internal consistencies and its concentrated unity of intention. Everything he has ever written is motivated by the conviction that writing is at the very least an ethical act and often an activist medium, a belief that itself stems from an insistently materialist view of history. (Writing can be an intervention only if one accepts the premise that men make their own history.) The frequent shifts in genre and subject matter notwithstanding, his chosen themes remain constant: the commodification of human labor in capitalist society; the evils of private property and money; alienation; the destruction of community; and, above all, the possibilities for resistance and the moral necessity of a nonutopian vision of social justice. These thematic interests are realized through a common method: inhabiting the consciousness of another. For Berger, empathy is necessarily the imaginative manifestation of solidarity.

The career, too, has a distinct trajectory. On the one hand, Berger has sought a means of representation compatible with, and adequate to, his political purpose—hence the experimentation, the restless change of medium—even while his precise vision of this purpose has changed and developed. On the other hand, Berger's search has been for a geographic and cultural constituency, an experiential base that might function as an aesthetic proving ground. In the terms suggested by his 1969 translation of Aimé Césaire's *Cahier d'un retour au pays natal* (*Return to My Native Land*) Berger's writing enacts his wish to find and celebrates his relation to his "unique people."

JOHN BERGER

LIFE AND CAREER

BERGER'S autobiographical comments are sparse, but even the bare facts of his life hold an extraordinary dramatic interest. Many of its elements have been mythologized: the idealism, seen by some as humorless; the love of risk, emblematized in his passion for motorbikes; a capacity to generate controversy by instinctively putting his critical finger on troubled cultural hot spots; and a certain flair for the heroic gesture. No armchair intellectual, Berger has played many roles: painter, art critic, novelist, cultural theorist, anthropologist, agricultural laborer. His role changes are never undertaken simply in search of subjects to write about. As Sven Birkerts (1991) astutely observes,

With Berger . . . while the writing is central to the life, it is not the center. The real focus . . . is upon the hidden momentum of the destiny. . . . [T]he life is not . . . passively regarded as the source of literary materials, as a kind of past tense, but is and remains the active laboratory for the discovery and testing of meanings. That is, the writer is an individual living in accord with a particular—and perhaps romantic—assumption. That the whole of the life is the chosen life, and that as such it will finally comprise a shape, or narrative, that *means.*

(p. 149)

The shape of Berger's life is inseparable from the life work: he has sought alternative ways of being as well as of seeing and has assumed these categories to be indivisible.

Berger is especially reticent about his early life. He was born in Stoke Newington, London, on 5 November 1926. His father was an accountant; his mother, the parent to whom he seems to have been closer, always wanted her son to be a writer, as she revealed to him when he was in his thirties. (Berger has written about this disclosure in a 1986 essay about his mother's death, adding that it was not books that fostered his literary interests—there were few books in his parents' house—but rather his mother's habitual secretiveness that led him to seek out and decipher secrets; the formulation is telling and suggests much about Berger's understanding of a writer's work.) The parents had class ambitions and sent the young John to boarding school, which he found brutal. At the age of sixteen he ran away from Saint Joseph's, Oxford, a minor Anglo-Irish public school, to study art at the Central and Chelsea schools of art in London.

Drafted in 1944, he declined the commission his public-school background was thought to merit, joined the Oxford and Buckinghamshire Infantry, and was stationed in Ireland for two years.

After his military service, Berger returned to London to continue his studies (with the help of an army grant) at the Chelsea School of Art. He began to paint seriously and to teach art. He was involved in organizing and speaking on behalf of the British Communist party but has denied that he was ever a card-carrying member. In 1952 he became the art critic for the *New Statesman,* to which he contributed a semimonthly column more or less regularly for the next ten years. Meanwhile, he had stopped painting; as he explained in 1988, "I gave up painting not because I thought I had no talent, but because painting pictures in the early '50s seemed a not direct enough way to try to stop the world's self-annihilation by nuclear war. The printed word was a little more effective" (*A Painter of Our Time,* 1989, p. 198).

It is necessary to acknowledge the larger political and cultural background against which Berger began his career. The landslide electoral victory of the British Labour party at war's end in 1945 (when Berger was eighteen) seemed to herald the arrival of a socialist democracy. But the welfare state it created was quickly co-opted by the long period of Conservative rule that began in 1951. The 1950s marked the Labour party's growing retreat from its socialist agenda, a movement to the Right that was exaggerated by the Cold War: in mainstream politics, socialism had come to be negatively associated with Stalinism. Although Britain experienced no real equivalent of the U.S. McCarthyist scourge, in the prevailing Cold War climate anything suggesting communism was regarded with suspicion. Culturally, Britain was then dominated by a politically conformist establishment, against which various short-lived dissenting voices arose—the angry young men with whom the period has come to be identified, and whose anger, as many observers have noted, had no political source or focus. The trend in all the arts favored an increased distancing from political life; the mood was one of cynicism and disillusionment. The antifascist fervor that had propelled the careers of the 1930s generation had soured into rhetorical anti-Communist rancor by the 1950s. It was in this difficult milieu that a handful of leftist writers—Kenneth Tynan, Lindsay Anderson, Doris Lessing, and, of course, John Berger (already a political anarchist in school, and by the end of his teens an orthodox Marxist)—began their careers.

Berger's first novel, *A Painter of Our Time,* came out in 1958 and was so controversial that after a few months it was recalled by the publisher, Secker and Warburg. The story of an expatriate Hungarian artist, the novel presents an uncompromising position concerning the social responsibility of art. Far more inflammatory, however, is its overtly political ending, in which the protagonist flees London during the "Hungarian crisis" of 1956, apparently to join the revolutionary Hungarian Communists under János Kádár—an event that the narrator unequivocally views as an act of hope. *A Painter of Our Time* gained Berger an instant notoriety, as did his outspoken articles for the *New Statesman.* In 1960 some of these were collected and reprinted under the provocative title *Permanent Red: Essays in Seeing* (published in the United States rather more cautiously as *Toward Reality*). Increasingly an uncomfortable outsider in Cold War Britain, Berger became correspondingly more strident in his attacks on English "philistinism"—an Arnoldian term that Berger inflects with a rather different brand of politics than Matthew Arnold's. In 1962 he left England—and professional journalism—for good to live as a creative writer, first in Paris and later in Geneva. His next two novels, *The Foot of Clive* (1962) and *Corker's Freedom* (1964) are both probing criticisms of English culture.

Berger admired the politically committed philosophers Jean-Paul Sartre and Maurice Merleau-Ponty and was drawn to French intellectual life for the possibilities it promised for organized political action. For him, as for so many others, these hopes were dashed in 1968 by the massive containment of a national revolutionary coalition of workers and intellectuals. In 1973 Berger wrote with eloquent reserve about the events of that watershed year: "When I look around at my friends—and particularly at those who were (or still are) politically conscious—I see how the long-term direction of their lives was altered or deflected at that moment just as it might have been by a private event: the onset of an illness, an unexpected recovery, a bankruptcy" (*About Looking,* 1980, p. 127). In his own case, the demonstrated bankruptcy of the Western European revolutionary apparatus subtly altered the direction of his inquiry. Berger's political vision survived intact—perhaps even gained in clarity—but revolution irrevocably receded beyond its horizon, henceforth to be located only in the past, in some other place, in the imagination, and as an end increasingly displaced from political to aesthetic practice.

His formally and stylistically ambitious novel *G.* (1972), begun before but completed after 1968, places revolutionary hope firmly in Europe's past and ambiguously identifies it with sexual energy. The novel was awarded the James Tate Black Memorial Prize, the *Guardian* fiction prize, and Britain's prestigious Booker Prize. In his acceptance speech for the latter award, Berger characteristically denounced the source of the prize money, the Booker McConnell Corporation's sugar plantations. He donated half his winnings to the Black Panthers, a London-based West Indian revolutionary group; the other half he planned to devote to a study of the eleven million migrant workers of Europe.

Berger's art-critical interests came to be fully integrated with his social criticism in a series of works published in the late 1960s and early 1970s: *The Success and Failure of Picasso* (1965); the important essay "The Moment of Cubism" (1969); *Art and Revolution: Ernst Neizvestny and the Role of the Artist in the U.S.S.R.* (1969); and the work for which he remains best known, *Ways of Seeing* (1972). Based on the BBC television series of the same name (which Berger narrated), *Ways of Seeing* quickly became a staple in media and art-history courses and sold over a million copies in twenty-five years. Berger increasingly exploited visual media: he collaborated on three screenplays with the Swiss filmmaker Alain Tanner. Of these, *Jonah Who Will Be 25 in the Year 2000* (1976), which traces the intersecting lives of eight marginal characters of the generation of 1968, in 1975 Geneva, was awarded the New York Film Critics prize in 1976 and has become something of a cult classic. Berger also collaborated with the Swiss photographer Jean Mohr on several experimental photomontage narratives. It was in the course of his work with Mohr on their documentation of migrant labor—which resulted in *A Seventh Man: Migrant Workers in Europe* (1975)—that Berger decided to learn at first hand about the peasant communities from which his subjects came. In 1974 he moved (ostensibly for a few months) to the mountain village of Quincy in the Giffre river valley of the French Haute-Savoie, where he remained.

Berger's reverse migration from the city to the country was announced at the height of his European fame as a metropolitan "critic-hero" (Sven Birkert's term). It shocked many and has routinely been interpreted as a gesture of throwaway romanticism, a regressive retreat to pastoralism. In fact, the move to rural life quickened rather than abated Berger's lifelong social concerns, which were now explored in the arena of a moribund social formation: peasant life. Berger has memorably recorded the ways of his peasant neighbors and friends in the quasi-ethnographic trilogy *Into Their Labours* (1979–1990), positioning himself partly as community storyteller, partly as anthropologist. Berger's work on *Into Their Labours* and the later writing was supported by the Transnational Institute, a left-wing think tank based in Amsterdam.

He himself lives permanently in Quincy with his second wife, Beverly, and their son, Yves. He rents a house from a neighbor, whom he pays partly by helping with farmwork, and writes when all the other chores are done. He has continued to be prolific: his essays have appeared in the *Village Voice, Harper's, Granta,* the *New Yorker,* as well as other magazines, and have periodically been collected and published in book form. Another novel, *To the Wedding,* which takes as its subject the threat of AIDS in a pan-European setting, came out in 1995. (In a familiar Bergeresque gesture, royalties from the book were donated to the Harlem United Community AIDS Center in New York City.)

EARRY ESSAYS

BERGER'S art-critical columns, written for the *New Statesman* between 1952 and 1962, are intended to restore history to art history. Following the example of his acknowledged mentor, the Marxist art historian Frederick Antal (famous for his voluminous study *Florentine Painting and Its Social Background,* first published in English in 1949), Berger's object is to fight two regnant orthodoxies: abstraction in art and formalism in art criticism, both tending to detach art from the experience of its production and reception. Berger was, of course, writing under rigorous journalistic constraints that enjoined economy of expression and precluded the development or elaboration of a theoretical apparatus. But his aims were always clear. He insisted that art is not eternal and timeless, as the formalists claim, but exists in history. "Only if we recognize the mortality of art shall we cease to stand in such superstitious awe of it; only then shall we consider art expendable and so have the courage to risk using it for our own immediate, urgent, only important purposes" (*Toward Reality,* p. 152).

What, then, are these urgent purposes? In 1958 Berger announced: "It is our century, which is preeminently the century of men throughout the world claiming the right of equality, it is our own history that makes it inevitable that we can make sense of art only if we judge it by the criterion of whether or not it helps men to claim their social rights" (p. 9). Yet the social content of art is not to be found in its approximation to propaganda but in its ability to "increase our awareness of our own potentiality" (p. 7)—not, that is to say, in its power to make us act in a particular way but in its power, through the artist's way of viewing his subject, to promise "the possibility of an increase, an improvement" (p. 7). These declarations suggest a complex dialectical relation between the work, trammeled as it is in its own history, and the viewer, whose task is to understand its promise for his own quite different history.

Much of Berger's early polemic is directed against the excesses of abstraction (abstract art was still a hotly contested area in 1950s aesthetic debates):

No student of twentieth-century European culture can reasonably deny that certain abstract artists have contributed to the development of painting, sculpture, and architecture. The division now is between those artists who have a sense of responsibility and those who have not; or, to put it another way, between those artists whose view of life can sustain a minimum faith in the value of human exchange and those whom alienation has made pathological.

(pp. 35–36)

In the abstract "non-art" shown at the 1958 Venice Biennale Berger saw passively reflected "the fears, the cynicism, the human alienations that are accompanying the death throes of imperialism" (p. 37). He attacked the "subjective chaos" of paintings in the London galleries (p. 41), lamented the breakdown of artistic tradition, which leaves art students floundering, criticized Paul Klee for his abdication of intention, and denounced Jackson Pollock for his willed isolation and his acceptance of decadence.

Harsh as Berger was to many of his contemporaries, there was also a fundamental generosity in his valuations: he was as quick to praise talent as he was to censure what he considered (as in the case of Pollock) its waste.

Many of Berger's critical judgments during this period took their terms from the work of György Lukács (1885–1971), the foremost Marxist aesthetician of his day. Lukács unfashionably championed realism over modernism (he unabashedly preferred Mann to Kafka), arguing that bourgeois or critical realism portrays the social totality, with all its contradictions, through the use of typical characters. Modernism, on the other hand, participates in the reified and fragmented character of human life under capitalism. Lukács espoused a socialist realism that would inherit bourgeois realism's critical project and its aesthetic understanding (through "types") of social and historical reality. Berger finely adapted Lukács' perceptions: he extended their applicability from literature to the visual arts, preserved the emphasis on an examination of totality through types, and even echoed Lukács' disparagement of "naturalism" (which, unlike critical realism, is content simply to record surface appearances), but ultimately eschewed Lukács' vehement antimodernism.

In fact, some of Berger's most affectionate portraits are of twentieth-century masters, the first generation of modernists for whom abstraction was not yet a fashionable habit, emptied of social content: Juan Gris, Fernand Léger, Pablo Picasso, Henri Matisse, Raoul Dufy, Oskar Kokoschka. About Matisse's "haute bourgeoise" imagination and taste, Berger suggestively has written:

It was Matisse's narrowness (I can think of no modern artist with less interest in either history or psychology) that saved him from the negative and destructive attitudes of the class-life to which his art belonged. It was his narrowness that allowed him to enjoy this milieu without being corrupted by it or becoming critical of it. He retained throughout his whole career something of Veronese's naive sense of wonder that life could be so rich and luxurious.

(p. 134)

This passage accurately conveys Berger's characteristic methods: the class analysis sensitively articulated with an imaginative understanding of the artist's intention, in a rhetorical style that has been compared to George Orwell's technique of first asserting and then arguing within that assertion (Raymond Williams' formulation about Orwell is applied to Berger in Geoff Dyer's *Ways of Telling: The Work of John Berger*, p. 11).

Berger's tenure at the *New Statesman* was essentially an apprenticeship. In a number of ways it formed the conceptual groundwork for his later writing. First, the internationalism of the art world early established for Berger a broad intellectual arena of which England, far from being the center, was only a provincial outpost. His artistic and political interests were to become increasingly European and eventually global. Second, the inflation of the post–World War II art market vividly demonstrated the commodification of art by capitalism and thus provided a major premise of Berger's revolutionary socialism. Berger would come to argue that as long as art was property (a proposition he qualified in *Ways of Seeing*), artistic innovation could never be a political intervention, as it would inevitably be co-opted by the ruling class. It is important to note that Berger's constant agitation for the abolition of private property takes its force from the value he attributes to artistic work. In his preface to the 1979 reissue of *Permanent Red*, Berger wrote that "property must be destroyed before imagination can develop any further."

Berger's training in art criticism had another significant consequence for his later writing. His critique of representation emerged from, and remained grounded in, his study of the visual arts. "Seeing" remained for him the most acute artistic and critical act: the artist sees his subject in order to realize it artistically, just as the viewer/critic must see the work through the "screen of clichés" that obscures it. Vision is, of course, an endlessly rich metaphorical field; and Berger cultivated it for both his aesthetics and his epistemology. Looking carefully and seeing well become not only the determinants of an authentic artistic vision but also the only guarantors of truthful meaning.

A PAINTER OF OUR TIME

BERGER'S only novel about art draws on and contributes to what may have been the crucial debate of the first half of the twentieth century, namely, the vexed question of the relation of politics and aesthetics which engaged the great Marxist theorists Theodor Adorno, Bertolt Brecht, Walter Benjamin, and Georg Lukács, not to mention the machinations (around a socialist-realist ideal) of Stalin and Andrei Zhdanov. Curiously, the novel does not seem dated, perhaps because the debate has never been satisfactorily resolved. In the repressive political atmosphere of the 1950s, the question was still vital and politically interesting. One persuasive way in which a revolutionary Marxist could explain the disappointments of Soviet communism (Berger had been pro-Soviet until 1956) was by pointing to Stalinism's failure to mobilize the revolutionary potential of art and to sketch an alternative, mutually sustaining relation of the aesthetic to the political.

Berger's novel consists of a layering of two first-person narratives, the diary maintained for three years by János Lavin, a Hungarian émigré painter living in London, and the interpolated comments of John, his English friend and admirer, an art critic who finds and publishes the diary after János has fled London under mysterious circumstances. Utilizing a framing device borrowed from the mystery genre, the novel opens with the scene of John's discovery of the diary in János' empty flat, where John is puzzling over the motives for János' sudden disappearance. "János" is, of course, the Hungarian cognate of "John": both narrators share Berger's name and may usefully be regarded as components of an authorial self split between the foreign and the domestic, the artist and the critic, and—most important, for the novel—between the public and the private. János' narrative unmistakably furnishes the grand moral principles of the novel: his diary entries record his agonized struggle with a political conscience that finally dictates his departure from England on the very eve of his long-delayed artistic success. John, on the other hand, is a rather sorry figure who wistfully covets János' friendship but is barely mentioned in his diary. In his desire for intimacy with János, John resembles János' upper-class English wife, Diana, who had been attracted by the glamour of János' foreignness but who finally has no experience or emotion in common with him. János' potently tragic isolation is achieved at the expense of the two well-meaning but naive English characters, John being feminized by his structural likeness to Diana.

János' real intimacy is reserved for his imaginary conversations with László, the friend of his Hun-garian youth, a poet-turned-Communist administrator who comes to personify János' guilt in the novel. László had remained in Hungary, while János, who shared László's commitment to revolutionary socialism, had lived in Berlin and in 1938 sought refuge from the Nazis in London; for obvious reasons the two had not remained in touch. (János explains that he had fled West rather than East—to the Soviet Union—because he wanted to live in a country where socialism still had to be fought for, a conviction that is quickly dispelled by his experience of England's political desolation.) The dramatic interest of the novel is propelled by János' casual discovery while reading a newspaper that László, now a high-ranking official, has been arrested as a traitor, tried, and will eventually be executed. László's impending trial sets the scene for János' relentless self-interrogations: to János, László's accusors implicitly condemn him—János—whose guilt is far greater, for he has deserted his country and reneged on his party. When László's name is finally cleared, it is as if János, too, has been exonerated and is free to return to Hungary to finally resume a public role. László's martyrdom symbolically liberates János from the prison of his own alienation.

János is cripplingly alone in his struggles with the specter of László. The diary is his only confidant. To it he bequeaths not only the burden of his private drama but also his increasingly tortured speculations on the role of the artist under capitalism and socialism. These meditations continue and extend the insights of Berger's contemporaneous journalistic pieces: János' diary serves as a more capacious vehicle for Berger's art criticism. At first János' comments are aphoristically brief. In their compression they often tend toward the slogan, perhaps a residual effect of Berger's habituation to newspaper style (although the declarative shorthand is entirely convincing in a diary entry): "Art can turn corners so much more rapidly than Policy. Use it as a ferret, not as a four for pulling the State Coach" (*A Painter of Our Time*, 1989, pp. 76–77). "Do not demand a Socialist Art. . . . Demand Socialist propaganda when it is needed and encourage art. Then artists will suddenly realize that they have created Socialist works, while only thinking about the truth" (p. 147).

The key distinction between art and propaganda becomes the basis for János' schematic development of the artist's social role:

There are three ways in which an artist can fight for what he believes:
(1) With a gun or stone. . . .
(2) By putting his skill at the service of the immediate propagandists—by producing cartoons, emblems, posters, slogans.
(3) By producing works entirely on his own volition. By working under circumstances in which neither the enemy police nor the enemy troops nor his own edit.prop. prompt his actions, but in which the no-less-strong force he works under is his own inner tension.

(p. 142)

János disparages neither the militant nor the propagandist, according a special place to the independent artist. "Every modern attempt to create a work of art is based on the desire (usually undeclared) to increase the value of the experience that gave rise to the work. In the nineteenth and twentieth centuries such an increase in *value* must inevitably be counted in terms of human pleasure, truth or justice" (p. 143). The artist who works under the force of his own inner tension becomes, in this view, a militant for human pleasure, truth, or justice. Yet the ending of the novel purposely destabilizes the categorical distinctions among militant, propagandist, and artist: when János, the successful artist, returns to Hungary, we are not told whether he fights with gun or stone, cartoon or poster; indeed, John's final comments about János' return to Hungary make irrelevant the means of János' resistance.

János' own art functions as the crucible in which his theories of art and life are tested. Facetiously dismissed by a London gallery owner as belonging to the school of Desperate Optimism, the Léger-like paintings monumentalize figures and moments from modern life—the Lido, swimmers, athletes, welders—resembling the kind of artwork Berger had himself produced in the early 1950s, Lukácsian realism in the visual arts. János explains why his paintings must be large:

If you want to paint a personal possession—and we can possess a cornfield, an apple, the face of a friend, a city skyline—then you must not over-enlarge it, for it will become vulgar, like all possessions that are made to appear more imposing than they are. But if you want to paint a legend that expresses a way of life that you cannot possess but only contribute to, then you must paint it large so that it remains impersonal, unpossessable.

(pp. 123–124)

This social intelligence governs not only the scale but every artistic choice János makes, be it design, color, or thickness of line. The paintings are, of course, unfashionable and unpopular; galleries consistently reject them in favor of inane abstractions or ornamental arrangements produced out of no apparent intention. János' isolation is exacerbated by his divorce from a receptive public and his financial dependence on his wife's meager earnings as a librarian. The artist who preaches and attempts to practice a necessary relation to society is cruelly alienated from society. Only through the intercession of a famous friend does János finally get an exhibition of his own. He becomes an overnight success, but by then it is too late for him to be integrated into the English art scene, for he has recognized that his pressing allegiances are to more public struggles.

England and the English are the easy target of the novel's formidable social criticism. In his 1988 afterword to *A Painter of Our Time*, Berger wrote about those aspects of English culture he found inimical and from which he sought solace among his émigré artist friends: "Pain is, by English definition, undignified. This is the starting-point of all English philistinism. The European refugees and I (I in my relative naivety!) believed otherwise. Our complicity, our opposition, grew from the assumption that pain is at the source of human imagination" (p. 198). English complacency is impervious to artistic innovation, and in *A Painter of Our Time* the inclemency of English weather and England's lack of light are made to stand for a more general emotional and cultural coldness. England also serves as the emblem of a capitalist state. János muses on the squalor of capitalist consciousness as revealed by a joke on the back of a book of matches: "Time: the stuff between pay days" (p. 85). But the novel's final indictment of capitalism's impoverished relation to art is made indirectly, through John's descriptive accounts of the galleries' slavish devotion to the current fashion and, most crushingly, through its representation of Sir Gerald Banks, the avaricious art collector.

Sir Gerald's last name effectively spells out the dubious source of his vast disposable income, which he lavishes on the acquisition of art treasures from every period, to be displayed and shown off in his country mansion. An especially powerful scene early in the novel (recounted by John) pits János' ferocious rage against Sir Gerald's oily aestheti-

83

cism; appropriately, at the end of the novel Sir Gerald has turned his covetous attention to János' own paintings. The portrait of Sir Gerald is Berger's embryonic version of the criticism he was later to develop fully in *Ways of Seeing,* namely, the commodification of art according to a system of private ownership.

A Painter of Our Time clearly determined the direction of Berger's fictional engagement. Many first novels are autobigraphical; not only does Berger's not tell his own story but it also performs a remarkable act of identification with a character whose history and culture were quite remote from his own. At the time of its composition, Berger had never been to Hungary, yet he writes convincingly and movingly in János' voice of the latter's youth in Budapest. In the afterword that Berger wrote thirty years after the novel was first published, he tells of a Hungarian historian in Budapest who read a smuggled copy of the novel, assumed that it was a true account, and wrote to him to ask where János' paintings might be found. The lesson Berger drew from this incident was to prove instructive for his later fictional practice:

It confirmed to me that if you listened well enough, lent yourself enough to somebody else whose experience was totally different from your own, you could nevertheless speak for them and do so authentically. All storytellers knew this, of course, until the middle of our century. But then it began to be said—with increasing dogmatism—that nobody has the right to write about anything they themselves have not lived. Fictional autobiography became the golden rule of the day.... I have never accepted this golden rule.

(pp. 197–198)

On many counts *A Painter of Our Time* is an impressive work. It appropriates elements of the mystery novel to animate and humanize an abstract political debate, thus redirecting toward the public realm the modernist novel's customary focus on private consciousness. It formulates, and compels our consent to, its vision of a juster society. It unsentimentally dramatizes the loneliness of the modern artist (the novel's suggestive and allusive subtitle is "A Portrait of the Artist as Émigré"). Its greatest achievement, however, is surely the character of János; although loosely based on Hungarian émigrés of Berger's acquaintance, he is ultimately the product of Berger's extraordinary feat of empathy.

THE FOOT OF CLIVE, CORKER'S FREEDOM, *AND* G.

BERGER'S second and third novels also derive from acts of imaginative identification. Both amplify the criticism of English culture begun in the earlier work, but they differ in tone and scope. Although they were not intended as a diptych, *The Foot of Clive* and *Corker's Freedom* constitute an extended and schematic diagnostic account of the ills of late capitalist England. Both works are generally acknowledged to be seriously flawed, and *The Foot of Clive* is considered to be Berger's least successful novel. They owe their failure partly to overschematization, partly to an experimental style that has not been fully realized, and perhaps partly to a blind spot in Berger's vision. He is so intent to scrutinize the problems that he neglects to hint at a solution; or, to put the matter in the terms of his Marxist critics, Berger fails to actualize the second part of the dialectic, the possibility of resistance.

The Foot of Clive is set entirely in the male ward of a London hospital—obviously treated as a venue in which a sociological cross-section can be examined under laboratory conditions. The ward is named "Clive" after the eighteenth-century British general and founder of the empire of British India; its counterpart across the hall is "Pitt"—a reference, one assumes, to William Pitt the Younger, who as a statesman promulgated important imperial legislation (Pitt's India Act of 1784) and went on to become an expansionist prime minister at the turn of the eighteenth century. Clearly the names are allegorical gestures, an indictment of postimperial England, an intention that is not well served by the novel's circumscribed setting and limited cast of characters. Not much happens externally in *The Foot of Clive.* The routinized life of the six patients at the foot of the ward, whose ages and class positions vary widely, is rudely disrupted by the arrival in the ward of Jack House, a terminally injured bank robber and murderer. The presence in their midst of a supposedly bona fide criminal jolts each of the six men into an examination of his own social responsibility, a psychological encounter that is played out—not quite convincingly—through a dramatic dialogue in an almost cinematic extended fantasy sequence.

The Foot of Clive aims to expose English political hypocrisy and psychological repression, specifically targeting English masculinity. The only emotionally aware character in the novel is Pepino Baldino, an Italian shopkeeper whose vocal expressiveness is literally incomprehensible to the Englishmen. Two scenes frame the emotional core of the novel. In the first, the sixteen-year-old upper-middle-class Robin Garton is embarrassed—even humiliated—to see Pepino weep over his amputated arm and for lack of news of his wife and newborn child. In the parallel scene with which the novel ends, just before the men are discharged, Robin, too, unabashedly weeps with Pepino. Their communion of tears not only marks a new moment of intersubjectivity but also heavily endorses the feminized foreign at the expense of the English masculine.

Like *The Foot of Clive, Corker's Freedom* develops its social critique from a metonymic situation: a day in the life of William Corker, the sixty-three-year-old proprietor of a London employment agency. By bringing together people of different social strata, the agency serves exactly the same highly artificial function as the hospital ward of the earlier novel. Here the dessicated and genteel Corker lords it over his hopeful clients while fearfully plotting to escape the censorious domestic clutches of his maiden sister and fantasizing about setting himself up in a permissive bachelor establishment of his own. In the climax to an eventful day, Corker delivers a slide lecture to a local church society about his vacation in Vienna—as the employment agency is being burgled by one of Corker's clients. Corker is suspected of the crime, loses the agency, and ends up as a Hyde Park soapbox orator, preaching to passersby about an imaginary European union. The farcical ending emphasizes the irony of the novel's title: for such as Corker there can be no liberation, only a travesty of freedom in terms of escape (tourism) or craziness (utopian politics).

Corker, seen mostly from the increasingly disaffected and cynical point of view of his office boy, Alec, is an overwhelmingly comic figure, but one senses that Berger is always trying to nudge him in a different, noncomic direction that the character is not equipped to assume. Long explanatory introspections are devoted to Corker's memories of his childhood, and too much is made of his symbolic exile from the world of his mother. Berger has insisted that his intention in *Corker's Freedom* was to demonstrate the crippling gap between reality and fantasy in capitalist society. Stylistically this intention is best carried out through Berger's use of captions to register Corker's alienation: "WHAT CORKER THOUGHT" is juxtaposed with "WHAT CORKER SAID" (quite different from what he thought) and "WHAT CORKER MADE BELIEVE" (nothing at all like what he thought or said). But even this stylistic conceit breaks down after countless repetitions of the same formula. Finally, Corker is just not psychologically interesting enough for one to care very much what he thinks, let alone what he fantasizes.

The Foot of Clive and *Corker's Freedom* measure the limits—and the limitations—of the novel as social critique. Their experimental techniques—the imaginary interrogations at the center of *The Foot of Clive* and the typographically innovative representation of Corker's split consciousness—seem to be imposed from without rather mechanically; the characters often appear as tortured and not quite credible animations of abstract ideas. In *G.*, his most celebrated novelistic achievement, Berger magnificently backs out of this creative dead end. *G.* occupies a pivotal place in Berger's career as a creative writer. It enacts a shift from the England of the first three novels to a new European setting (a shift that is internalized within the novel, for *G.*'s English childhood is followed by a European career); more important, it abandons the critique-based projects of the 1960s in favor of a new exploration of alternative aesthetic possibilities.

In a rather different context Berger himself tracked the political force behind this movement. His 1973 essay "About Two Colmars" tells of his two professional visits, in 1963 and 1973, to Matthias Grünewald's Isenheim Altar in Colmar. In his first assessment Berger read the scenes of plague depicted on the altarpiece as a record of medieval misery; on his second visit the panels surrounding the altarpiece, in their luminous representation of the saints, instead offered a vision of hope in the midst of misery. Berger explained these markedly different interpretations in terms of his changed historical understanding after 1968: "In a period of revolutionary expectation, I saw a work of art which had survived as evidence of the past's despair; in a period which has to be endured, I see the same work miraculously offering a narrow pass across despair" (*About Looking*, p. 133). The insight is as relevant to Berger's own writing: *The Foot of Clive* and *Corker's Freedom*, written in a period of "revolutionary expectation," disclose capitalism's despair; *G.*, written during and after revolutionary failure, hopefully recalls the revolutionary possibilities of the past.

G. resists summary: it is both encyclopedic and elliptical. Ostensibly it is the turn-of-the-century life story of the eponymous character, the illegitimate son of an Italian businessman and an Anglo-American heiress. *G.*'s name implicitly connects him to his namesake, a marginal Jacobin, in Victor Hugo's novel *Les Misérables,* but Berger's stated interest is in a "*G.*" from a rather different revolutionary period: the Italian nationalist Giuseppe Garibaldi (1807–1882). (*G.*'s uptight English schoolfellows jeeringly call him "Garibaldi.") The Garibaldi connection signals Berger's interest in Italian insurrectionary history. The novel's key moments involve two failed uprisings—the workers' revolution in Milan in 1898 and multilateral nationalist agitation in Trieste in 1915—bridged by a revolutionary event from a different historical register: Chávez' pioneering flight across the Alps in 1910.

Born in revolutionary times, G. himself hardly seems a revolutionary. His affinity is to another subversive figure, albeit from European literary history: the sexual adventurer Don Juan. Indeed, in wholesale fashion the novel transfers revolutionary authenticity from politics to sex. As the intrusive narrator remarks in one of his many asides, "In a static hierarchic world sexual desire is reinforced by a longing for an alternative certainty: with her I am free" (p. 110). *G.* romanticizes the sexual act, even absolutizes it; only sexual union can provide the glimpse of an unknown potential. Driven by explosive sexual energies, in moments of political unrest G. seeks liberating erotic encounters with women of many nationalities and classes. The narrator comments about G.'s role as a messenger of possibility: "The stranger who desires you and convinces you that it is truly you in all your particularity whom he desires, brings a message from all that you might be, to you as you actually are" (p. 133).

Berger is here literally addressing a generalized female reader. For the novel's politics of sex and gender, men are the enemy class. In a powerful interior monologue, G. scathingly denounces bourgeois men, whose control of global resources is linked to their possession of women. Throughout the novel a tense cluster of associations connects imperialist hegemony (the Boer War, colonial exploitation of Africa) to the oppression of women. In a central discursive note entitled "A Situation of Women," the narrator speculates about the "social presence" of women:

A woman's presence was the result of herself being split into two, and of her energy being inturned. A woman was always accompanied—except when quite alone—by her own image of herself. Whilst she was walking across a room or whilst she was weeping at the death of her father, she could not avoid envisaging herself walking or weeping. From earliest childhood she had been taught and persuaded to survey herself continually. And so she came to consider the surveyor and the surveyed within her as the two constituent yet always distinct elements of her identity as a woman.

(p. 149)

This analysis bears a striking resemblance to other formulations of the psychic violence of political oppression—notably to W. E. B. Du Bois' understanding of the "double consciousness" of the American Negro in his book *The Souls of Black Folk* (1903). Berger's radical innovation is contained in his phrase "to survey," which means "to regard" as well as "to measure (property)" and also hints at "to keep under surveillance"—all of which senses (not surprisingly, drawn from Berger's long interest in the figurative matrix of vision and seeing) are apposite to men's control of women.

G. is a sexual revolutionary because he subverts the property-based economy of gender and promises to deliver women from the prison of double consciousness. (The novel is dedicated to Anya Bostock, Berger's first wife and longtime literary collaborator, and "her sisters in Women's Liberation.") But Berger proposes an even more urgent relation between sex and revolution: they both explode time. The narrator examines the temporal content of the sexual act:

Sexual desire . . . is subjectively fixed to two points in time: our beginning and our end. When analysed, sexual desire has components which are violently nostalgic and lead us as far back as the experience of birth itself: other components are the result of an ineradicable appetite for the unknown, the furthest away, the ultimate of life—which can finally only be found in its negation—death. At the moment of orgasm these two points in time, our beginning and our end, may seem to fuse into one. When this happens everything that lies between them, that is to say our whole life, becomes instantaneous. It is thus that I explain the protagonist of my book to myself.

(p. 142)

Berger's sense of the collapsibility of time relies heavily on the work of Walter Benjamin (1892–1940), the German philosopher and literary critic whose fragmentary writings have shaped postwar Marxist cultural theory. In his posthumously published "Theses on the Philosophy of History," Benjamin maintains that time is neither "homogeneous" nor "empty"—as Berger recalled in a glowing 1970 appreciation of Benjamin (*The Look of Things*, 1972, p. 89). Benjamin instead advances the concept of "Messianic time," in which the flow or continuum of history is arrested at a revolutionary moment, the time of the present. Benjamin's aphoristic, quasi-theological speculations are the intellectual wellspring of *G*. In the latter Berger redirects his theoretical affiliations from Lukács, the guiding spirit of the first three novels, to Benjamin. (A touchstone for this change is Bertolt Brecht, about whom Lukács was critical and Benjamin admiring; Berger translated Brecht's *Poems on the Theatre* in collaboration with Anya Bostock in 1961.)

G. is a meditation on revolutionary time, but it is also a daring experiment in the organization of narrative. All narratives are temporal events, unfolding in time. *G*. challenges the tyranny of time as an ordering mechanism. In the course of an important digression on method, the narrator confesses:

Whatever I perceive or imagine amazes me by its particularity. . . . I am deeply struck by the uniqueness of each event. From this arises my difficulty as a writer—perhaps the magnificent impossibility of my being a writer. How am I to convey such uniqueness? The obvious way is to establish uniqueness through development. . . . In this way the uniqueness of an event can be explained by its causes and effects. But I have little sense of unfolding time. The relations which I perceive between things . . . tend to form in my mind a complex synchronic pattern. I see fields where others see chapters. And so I am forced to use another method to try to place and define events. A method which searches for co-ordinates extensively in space, rather than consequentially in time. I write in the spirit of a geometrician.

(pp. 136–37)

This disarming account of narrative contingency masks what is most iconoclastic about Berger's ex-periment, for *G*. shatters the linear, temporal structure of the bildungsroman, the novel of development, and reconfigures its shards in a constellation of static tableaux. There is no aggregation of causality in *G*.; events are arranged in a radial network of relations (metaphor or simile, as the narrator explains) rather than the temporal concatenation we expect from novels (the forward-thrusting chain of cause and effect).

G.'s rejection of developmental causality should also be read in the context of Berger's contemporaneous interest in cubism, first explored in his 1965 monograph on Picasso. According to Berger, cubism in its early phase (1907–1914) overturned received pictorial conventions not simply by incorporating novel materials and subject matter but by inventing a new pictorial language by which to represent the unprecedented character of modernity. The innovation of cubism amounted to a rejection of perspective, which had governed pictorial representation since the Renaissance; cubism replaced the bird's-eye view to which painting had customarily adhered with an assemblage of disjunct vantage points. What cubism, according to his own argument, did to the convention of perspective, Berger is now attempting to do to the convention of development. *G*. is a form of literary cubism applied not to space but to time.

In its discursive expansiveness *G*. resembles Joyce's *Ulysses*, which also cannibalizes other texts, but it is limited not just to reportage, poetry, and slogans but also to musical scores and Berger's own stylized drawings. *G*. might be thought of as modernist in that it is concerned not so much with events but with the means by which the narrative consciousness makes sense of them. But Berger is an antimodernist (or postmodernist, as has sometimes been claimed) in his animadversion to Freud. *G*. is curiously recalcitrant toward psychoanalytic grids, perhaps because the story Freud tells is yet another developmental narrative. Berger locates the sources of meaning not in the unconscious but in history; meaning itself resides in the consciousness of the artistic act. The character G., like the aviator Chavez with whom the novel attempts to connect him, stands for both the revolutionary and the artist. *G*. is the post-1968 counterpart of the revolutionary artist János Lavin in Berger's first novel. Unlike János, G. works in no particular medium or material and suffers no excruciating crisis of political conscience. His revolutionary politics simply lie in the power of his consciousness to link private act with public event and personal with collective desire.

WAYS OF SEEING

WIDELY recognized as the most influential art-critical project of the postwar period, *Ways of Seeing* is the only one of Berger's works to have achieved canonical status. Indeed, the book is so exclusively identified with Berger's trademark debunking style and politics that most readers neglect its origins in a collective endeavor with Sven Blomberg, Chris Fox, Michael Dibb, and Richard Hollis. Artistic collaboration is never a mere matter of the pooling of expertise. In Berger's case, collaboration has especially complex motivations and comes loaded with weighty aesthetic and political intentions. Aesthetically, collaboration questions the received theory of the solitary genius that Berger is anxious to criticize. As a political gesture, collaboration exercises and renews a faith in the potency of collective labor and action. It should also be noted that many of Berger's collaborations of the early 1970s were experimental, mixed-media endeavors: they attempted to reconcile the verbal with the visual and, more ambitiously, to patch together a revolutionary and liberating aesthetic practice.

Ways of Seeing marks the culmination of Berger's long engagement with critique. Berger's art criticism in the decade following his regular columns for the *New Statesman* focused on the twin studies *The Success and Failure of Picasso* and *Art and Revolution*, which offer a compound analysis of the place of the artist in capitalist and socialist society, respectively. They are both highly specific case studies of individual artists, particularly of the artistic career; as such they demand to be read alongside Berger's earlier fictional reconstruction of an imagined career in *A Painter of Our Time*. The refugee János Lavin marks one possible relation of the artist to society; other positions are now provided by Picasso, the willed exile, and Neizvestny, the internal dissident. But even as the two works reiterate the concerns of Berger's early writing about art, they also point in new directions. Their joint project is to recuperate the artistic energies of modernism for a renewed vision of political inter-

vention. The Picasso project is critique, the Neizvestny near-eulogy; in *Ways of Seeing* Berger returns to critique.

Of the seven chapters (three using only images without text) that make up *Ways of Seeing,* the first openly declares its debt to the exemplary work of Walter Benjamin, who in a 1936 essay had examined the impact on art of the then new techniques of mechanical reproduction. Benjamin is always present in Berger's more direct and colloquial formulation of the problem: "The uniqueness of the original [painting] now [since photography] lies in it being *the original of a reproduction. . . .* It is defined as an object whose value depends upon its rarity" (p. 21). Berger here articulates Benjamin's key philosophical interests in aura ("uniqueness" as Berger puts it), in modernity as epistemologically disruptive, and in cultural value as historically determined. Other rhetorical echoes can also be heard in the language of *Ways of Seeing.* (Thus, a parenthetical remark that the "world-as-it-is is more than pure objective fact, it includes consciousness" evokes the phenomenology of Maurice Merleau-Ponty, another formative influence.) They supply an inclusive authority for the book's combatively oppositional strategies.

Chapter 1 is devoted to demystifying the "bogus religiosity" (p. 23) that surrounds art; "mystification" Berger trenchantly glosses as "the process of explaining away what might otherwise be evident" (pp. 15–16). Pointedly aimed at exposing the complicity between the property-owning ruling class and the authenticating expertise of the art-historical establishment, chapter 1 reiterates the political polemic in Berger's early art criticism while also hinting at an alternative relation to, and use of, the image:

What the modern means of reproduction have done is to destroy the authority of art and to remove it—or, rather, to remove its images which they reproduce—from any preserve. For the first time ever, images of art have become ephemeral, ubiquitous, insubstantial, available, valueless, free. They surround us in the same way as a language surrounds us. They have entered the mainstream of life over which they no longer, in themselves, have power. . . .

If the new language of images were used differently, it would, through its use, confer a new kind of power. Within it we could begin to define our experiences more precisely in areas where words are inadequate.

(pp. 32–33)

The essay itself does not propose exactly what this alternative use would be, except in a passing recommendation of the bulletin boards on which people assemble collections of images from various sources, giving them a personal meaning: Berger rather cryptically comments that "logically these boards should replace museums" (p. 30). (Later, in essays on photography and through his own experiments in photomontage, Berger was to suggest the revolutionary possibilities for this "new language of images."

The most controversial section of *Ways of Seeing* is chapter 3, which examines the position of the female nude in the history of oil painting and, more generally, in Western culture. The essay opens with an analysis of gender distinctions adapted from "A Situation of Women" in *G.* (Berger often recycles his own work.) From this generalized polemic Berger proceeds to argue that nudity must be distinguished from nakedness: "To be naked is to be without disguise. . . . Nudity is a form of dress" (p. 54). Berger analyzes the frontal address of the female nude:

In the average European oil painting of the nude the principal protagonist is never painted. He is the spectator in front of the picture and he is presumed to be a man. Everything is addressed to him. Everything must appear to be the result of his being there. It is for him that the figures have assumed their nudity. But he, by definition, is a stranger—with his clothes still on.

(p. 54)

This demystification becomes the basis of an understanding of what Berger calls the "spectator-owner" to whom, as he suggests in chapter 5, oil painting makes lushly visible and tangible the availability of the world—material possessions as well as women—as property.

Chapter 3's radical critique of gender in the oil painting is somewhat diffused by the closing section of the chapter, in which Berger discusses "a few exceptional nudes" of "loved women"—Rembrandt's *Danae*, Rubens' *Hélène Fourment in a Fur Coat*—proposing that in these paintings "the painter's personal vision of the particular women he is painting is so strong that it makes no allowance for the spectator" (p. 57). Feminist art historians have rightly challenged what amounts to a mystification here of both sexual passion and

artistic production. By exalting the union of the artist-lover with his female subject, Berger is claiming for these works an exemption from the processes of men's historical domination of women: he is attempting to rescue these exceptional works from history.

In chapter 5 Berger expands this theory of exceptionality:

Art history has totally failed to come to terms with the problem of the relationship between the outstanding work and the average work in the European tradition. The notion of Genius is not in itself an adequate answer. Consequently the confusion remains on the walls of the galleries. Third-rate works surround an outstanding work without any recognition—let alone explanation—of what fundamentally differentiates them.

(p. 88)

But Berger is himself hard-pressed to find an answer that is more adequate than mere genius:

Hack work is not the result of either clumsiness or provincialism; it is the result of the market making more insistent demands than the art. . . . [I]t is in this contradiction between art and market that the explanations must be sought for what amounts to the contrast, the antagonism existing between the exceptional work and the average.

(p. 88)

"Art" here becomes an inarticulate substitute for the romantic "Genius": both transcend history and economics. Berger himself admitted in a 1978 essay that "the immense theoretical weakness of my own book [*Ways of Seeing*] is that I do not make clear what relation exists between what I call 'the exception' (the genius) and the normative tradition" (*The White Bird*, p. 199).

The theoretically fragmentary character of *Ways of Seeing* is least evident in its superb closing chapter, which persuasively establishes a continuity between the language of publicity and the language of oil painting. But where oil painting addresses the "spectator-owner," publicity (what we would call advertising) addresses the "spectator-buyer." Berger is at his most brilliantly insightful in his analysis of the appeal of the publicity image: "Publicity is never a celebration of pleasure-in-itself. Publicity is always about the future buyer. It offers him an image of himself made glamorous by the product or opportunity it is trying to sell. The image then makes him envious of himself as he might be. . . . The happiness of being envied is glamour" (p. 132). Berger's theorization of the split consciousness produced by consumer culture—the working self envying the consuming self—looks back to Corker's daydreaming alienation in Berger's third novel, but the new reading is sharpened by a politicized understanding of "glamour" as "a modern invention" (p. 146):

Glamour cannot exist without personal social envy being a common and widespread emotion. The industrial society which has moved towards democracy and then stopped half way is the ideal society for generating such an emotion. The pursuit of individual happiness has been acknowledged as a universal right. Yet the existing social conditions make the individual feel powerless. He lives in the contradiction between what he is and what he might be.

(p. 148)

Throughout *Ways of Seeing* Berger sees visual culture—oil painting as well as publicity—as a system or structure. His interest is always in the total weight of the tradition and its relation to political and social structures, but his analyses never lose sight of the human lives and labor that constitute these structures; nor does he reduce the aesthetic structure to a reflection of the political or social structure. In his own writing one senses the constant presence of a flexible, idiosyncratic mind. Influential as *Ways of Seeing* has been—it is almost solely responsible for inaugurating a now-institutionalized left-wing academic concern with the political effects of visual media—Berger's critical methods pointedly diverge from one of the most commonly practiced forms of Marxist aesthetic criticism, namely, ideological analysis.

Berger is especially hostile to the antihumanist, antiempiricist philosophy of Louis Althusser (1918–1990), the French Marxist whose reinterpretation of Marx generated a large academic following. In an important 1979 review of Nicos Hadjinicolaou's *Art History and Class Consciousness*, Berger expostulates against Hadjinicolaou's reliance on the deterministic Althusserian notion of ideology, whereby all institutions and artifacts have built into them a distorted sense of reality that serves the interests of power: "[A]ccording to such a theory of ideology . . . we are, in some ways, like blind

men who have to learn to allow for and overcome our blindness, but to whom sight itself, whilst class societies continue, cannot be accorded" (*The White Bird,* p. 198). Berger's own critical practice in refusing to be blind (elsewhere he had written that "the only excuse for criticism is that it allows us to see more clearly") rejects the pseudoscientism of the Althusserians:

The culture of capitalism has reduced paintings, as it reduces everything which is alive, to market commodities, and to an advertisement for other commodities. The new reductionism of revolutionary theory . . . is in danger of doing something similar. What one uses as an advertisement (for a prestige, a way of life and the commodities that go with it), the other sees as only a visual ideology of a class. Both eliminate art as a potential model of freedom, which is how artists and the masses have always treated art when it spoke to their needs.

(p. 203)

Despite its theoretical inconsistencies, *Ways of Seeing* draws its articulate political passion from the force of Berger's own fervent belief in art.

INTO THEIR LABOURS

IN two essays on the paintings of Millet, Berger had boldly claimed that the great artist of peasant labor, himself of peasant extraction, lacked the visual language to represent his subjects working the land: the conventions of oil painting, as Berger analyzed them, permitted land to be represented only as a backdrop for the spectator-owner, as property, not as the site of labor. Berger's narratives of peasant life are undertaken, with the authority of his own cohabitation with his subjects, as a corrective to oil painting's representation of peasants. That is to say, Berger offers not only a new method but also a new medium, a medium that is not wholly reducible to what we think of as narrative fiction.

Berger's theoretical rationale for *Into Their Labours* is elaborately recorded, both in his "Historical Afterword" (sometimes published as an introduction) to *Pig Earth* (1979), the first volume of the trilogy, and in a 1978 essay entitled "The Storyteller." At the end of the polemical afterword, he firmly announces his "solidarity with the so-called 'backward' " for whom the trilogy is written. The temporal signification of the disparaging term "backward" spurs Berger to inquire into the teleology of progress, which he argues is the organizing principle of both bourgeois and Marxist theories of history. It is not only oil painting that has neglected peasants; generally excluded from "the culture of progress" (both bourgeois and Marxist), peasants constitute a "culture of survival":

Modern history begins—at different moments in different places—with the principle of progress as both the aim and motor of history. This principle was born with the bourgeoisie as an ascendant class, and has been taken over by all modern theories of revolution. The twentieth-century struggle between capitalism and socialism is, at an ideological level, a fight about the content of progress. . . .

Cultures of progress envisage future expansion. They are forward-looking because the future offers ever larger hopes. At their most heroic these hopes dwarf Death (*La Rivoluzione o la Morte!*). At their most trivial they ignore it (consumerism). . . .

A culture of survival envisages the future as a sequence of repeated acts for survival. Each act pushes a thread through the eye of a needle and the thread is tradition. No overall increase is envisaged.

(*Pig Earth*, 1992, pp. xviii–xix)

Survival, repetition, and tradition become the key tropes in Berger's representation of the peasant culture of survival.

If the afterword lays out the political urgency of Berger's project, then his essay "The Storyteller" proposes its intention in compelling narrative terms. Berger's title for this essay harks back to Walter Benjamin's frankly nostalgic 1936 piece of the same name. For Benjamin a critical distinction can be made between the novel, produced and consumed in solitude, and the fast-disappearing tale, which springs from a lived relation to a community. The former registers a modern, urban, and alienated experience; the latter records a premodern experience of connection to a craft, a place, and a community. In Benjamin's understanding, two distinct kinds of consciousness are represented by these narrative modes, signified by two related German terms, both of which are generally translated as "experience": *Erlebnis,* having to do with the episodic and discontinuous experience of city life; and *Erfahrung,* the practical wisdom gained by a traveler or craftsman over a long period of time, which then becomes the continuing basis for his experience of communal life. The *Erfahrung* embodied in the tale

is clearly preferred by Benjamin to the *Erlebnis* found in the novel: the tale is to be valued because it carries the traces of a residual and rapidly vanishing form of experience.

As a practicing storyteller, Berger compounds and qualifies Benjamin's analysis of *Erfahrung:*

To approach experience, however, is not like approaching a house. Experience is indivisible and continuous, at least within a single lifetime and perhaps over many lifetimes. I never have the impression that my experience is entirely my own, and it often seems to me that it preceded me. In any case experience folds upon itself, refers backwards and forwards to itself through the referents of hope and fear; and, by the use of metaphor which is at the origin of language, it is continually comparing like with unlike, what is small with what is large, what is near with what is distant. And so the act of approaching a given moment of experience involves both scrutiny (closeness) and the capacity to connect (distance). The movement of writing resembles that of a shuttlecock: repeatedly it approaches and withdraws, closes in and takes its distance. Unlike a shuttlecock, however, it is not fixed to a static frame.

(*The White Bird*, pp. 14–15)

The analogy of the shuttlecock (recalling Benjamin's connection of *Erfahrung* with craft) permits Berger the writer to occupy a range of shifting positions in relation to his subjects, even as his elaboration of "experience" blurs the boundary between his own subjectivity and the subjectivity of others.

In practice this potential erasure of categorical distinctions proves tricky and often problematic. Readers of Berger's trilogy will wonder where, exactly, the narrative intelligence is located. Even the title is a tease: as the epigraph discloses, the phrase "into their labors" comes from an enigmatic parable in John 4. Christ admonishes his skeptical disciples that the harvest is at hand and exhorts them to reap what others have sown: "I sent ye to reap that for which ye did not labour; others have laboured, and ye are entered into their labours." Berger's title literalizes the figurative economic terms of the Christian parable, implicating in the labor of peasants all of Berger's (nonpeasant) readers. But in borrowing Christ's omniscient words it also raises important questions about the narrative position and didactic authority Berger is claiming.

To complicate matters, when Berger is writing about writing for peasants, he sometimes tends to position himself simply as a witness:

The life of a village, as distinct from its physical and geographical attributes, is the sum of all the social and personal relationships existing within it, plus the social and economic relations—usually oppressive—which link the village to the rest of the world. . . . What distinguishes the village is that it is also *a living portrait of itself*: a communal portrait, in that everybody is portrayed and everybody portrays; and this is only possible if everybody knows everybody. . . . A village's portrait of itself is constructed, not out of stone, but out of words, spoken and remembered: out of opinions, stories, eyewitness reports, legends, comments and hearsay. And it is a continuous portrait; work on it never stops. . . .

Without such a portrait . . . the village would have been forced to doubt its own existence. Every story and every comment on the story which is a proof that the story has been *witnessed* contributes to the portrait, and confirms the existence of the village.

(*The White Bird*, p. 16)

Is Berger participating in this communal project of portraiture (if so, who is portraying him?) or is he giving witness to a prior act of village storytelling?

Pig Earth (1979), the first volume in the trilogy, plays with what Jeff Blaustone has deftly called "polymorphous point-of-view." The opening dedication names a catalogue of Berger's peasant friends as teachers and, implicitly, collaborators, but the first story, "A Question of Place," moves sharply from this localized specificity to a stylized scene from peasant life viewed emphatically from the outside: the slaughter of a cow by characters identified only as "the peasant," "the father," "the mother," and "the son." The universalizing nominations, together with the obvious attempt broadly to sketch the rhythms of rural labor, signal Berger's interest in the pastoral. Notoriously the most conservative of literary forms, it nostalgically mixes idyll with elegy. Berger's version preserves the elegy but repudiates the idyll: it is oppositional or counterpastoral. In "A Question of Place" this intention is conveyed by a relentless numerical exactitude. The sides of meat weigh "two hundred and fifty-seven kilograms"; they will sell at "nine francs a kilo" (p. 6). Animal life and peasant labor are quantified and commodified in the very moment that seems intended to represent their timeless universality.

The other stories trace particular peasant histories, always locating them against the encroachments of what Berger evocatively calls "the metaphysic of capitalism," for which "the word

credit, instead of referring to a past achievement, refers only to a future expectation" (p. xxvi). In "The Value of Money" the dour and irascible Marcel explains why he, unlike others in the village, has planted new apple trees:

My sons won't work on the farm. They want to have free week-ends and holidays and fixed hours. . . . They have gone to earn money, and are mad about it. Michel has gone to work in a factory. Edouard has gone into commerce. . . . I believe they are mistaken. Selling things all day, or working forty-five hours a week in a factory is no life for a man—jobs like that lead to ignorance. It is unlikely that they will ever work this farm. The farm will end with Nicole and me. Why work with such effort and care for something which is doomed? And to that I reply: Working is a way of preserving the knowledge my sons are losing. I dig the holes, wait for the tender moon and plant out these saplings to give an example to my sons if they are interested, and, if not, to show my father and his father that the knowledge they handed down has not yet been abandoned. Without that knowledge, I am nothing.

(pp. 66–67)

In the story's climax, Marcel is fined for producing more than the statutory twenty liters of eau-de-vie from these apples: "It means I'm going to have to pay, pay money for my own produce" (p. 83). Marcel avenges this injustice by kidnapping the inspectors who have leveled the fine and holding them prisoner in a storage shed. The bewildered and frightened officials misinterpret Marcel's motives and offer him a ransom, declaring that they have more experience than he of "the value of money" (p. 90). Marcel angrily declines their money and concludes that "you can only take revenge on those who are your own. Those two up there belong to another time. They are our prisoners and yet no revenge is possible. They would never know what we were avenging" (p. 91). He releases the officials and is tried and imprisoned for his misdeeds. The story starkly proposes that the value of money swallows up and eradicates all other values. Those who speak the language of money become deaf and impervious to older and (the story insists) more authentic symbolic systems.

"The Three Lives of Lucie Cabrol," the volume's long, novella-like closing story, powerfully conveys the devastating effect of a modern capitalist economy on premodern peasant communities. Lucie Cabrol ("the Cocadrille") is a diminutive peasant woman whose physical deformity and strange, secretive ways make her an outsider in the village. The story is told by Jean, Lucie's contemporary and onetime lover, who had moved away from the village in his youth and returned to it in old age; much of his narrative is simply a critical frame for the Cocadrille's own account. Unmarried and ousted from her family's land, the Cocadrille develops two spheres of economic action: she forages in the high-altitude wilderness for wild berries, herbs, and flowers, which she then sells in a city across the frontier; and she smuggles back contraband items, like American cigarettes, to her side of the border. The Cocadrille's dual entrepreneurship amounts both to a commodification of communal property (the wilderness from which she scavenges) and to an illicit trade in luxury items. From these activities she amasses a vast amount of money, which she hoards in the remote mountaintop cottage where she lives alone. At the end of the climactic second section of the tripartite story, the Cocadrille is murdered for this money, evidently by an avaricious neighbor, although the culprit is never identified. "There were fewer than a hundred people at her funeral; her death was a kind of disgrace for the village," the narrator concludes somberly. "She had been killed for her fortune and only somebody from the village was likely to have known about it" (p. 152).

In this story, as in "The Value of Money," the colonizing force of money is shown to be fiercely inimical to peasant traditions. Money violently disrupts community and turns neighbors into criminals. In "The Three Lives of Lucie Cabrol" money is viewed not just as a foreign language but as another country: the international border between money and the peasant is perilously traversed. But the story does not end with this sharp indictment, for Berger inserts as a coda a sort of magic realist epithalamion; the still living Jean is to wed the already dead but finally lovable Cocadrille, while, in a joyful affirmation of communal labor, the men of the village construct a magnificent chalet for the uncanny matrimonial union. (Berger had confessed, around the time of *Pig Earth*, that his favorite living author was Gabriel García Márquez, and the story distinctly bears the imprimatur of the Latin American magic realists.) The story—and the book—ends with an act of hope, a testament of faith in the tenacity of peasant customs.

The prose narratives in *Pig Earth* are interspersed with passages of incantatory verse, from the closing stanza of one of which ("Ladle") the volume's title is taken:

> Ladle
> pour the sky steaming
> with the carrot sun
> the stars of salt
> and the grease of the pig earth
> pour the sky steaming
> ladle
> pour soup for our days
> pour sleep for the night
> pour years for my children.
> (pp. 15–16)

In yoking together transcendent cosmos and daily need, the poem poignantly celebrates the peasants' cyclic understanding of time and defines their community in two mutually sustaining ways: through a shared attachment to work ("our days") and through generational continuity ("my children").

If *Pig Earth* is largely about the erosion of this community, *Once in Europa* (1987), the second volume of *Into Their Labors*, takes its cue from the tenderly fantastic ending of the preceding volume. The five narratives in the volume are all love stories. The romantic passion they celebrate staves off the violent disruptions caused by an ever-invasive modernity. Thus, in the title story the middle-aged narrator Odile finds security and peace with her childhood beau years after her lover, the father of her child, died in a factory explosion. Community in these stories has dwindled to a partnership of two; continuity means not the passing on of an inherited way of life on ancestral land but the propagation of family, often in an urban setting. Sometimes romantic desire fails to achieve any union, as in "Boris Is Buying Horses," the story of a villager's unrequited and suicidal passion for a calculating, city-bred housewife. Here unsatisfied romantic longing defines the emotionally unbridgeable gap between village and city.

Lilac and Flag: An Old Wives' Tale of a City (1990), the trilogy's closing volume, dramatically shifts the narrative arena from the village to the city. More unified and more densely novelistic than the earlier volumes, *Lilac and Flag* is both love story and postmodern epic. The book appropriates the voice of an all-seeing village woman to tell the story of Zsuzsa and Sucus (who refer to themselves by the emblematic names "Lilac" and "Flag," respectively), the children of migrant workers in the invented European city of Troy, an uneasy conglomeration of shantytowns, construction sites, luxurious hotels, and pleasure districts. The Homeric allusion announces a grand conflict: the innocent Zsuzsa and Sucus, armed only with native insouciance and a consuming passion for each other, fearlessly take on the forces of modernity, represented in the story by a relentlessly commodifying capitalist economy and a seemingly pitiless police force headed by the unhappy Inspector Hector. After many adventures involving lawlessness, the young lovers are hunted as criminals; the narrative reaches its culmination with the revelation that Sucus' father came from the same village as did Hector. Hector and Sucus accidentally shoot and kill each other, and in his Lucie Cabrol-like life-after-death experience Sucus journeys back to the ancestral village, where he waits eternally to be reunited with the lost Zsuzsa.

Berger's remarks in his 1984 compendium of philosophical meditations, *And Our Faces, My Heart, Brief as Photos,* elaborate on the political intention of *Lilac and Flag.* In an extended speculation on home and homelessness, Berger argues against the received meanings of "home," as property to be safeguarded or (national) land to be defended, both of which senses have served the interest of the ruling class. Berger instead proposes an ontological meaning of "home" as the center of the universe. Home is where two lines meet, a vertical or temporal line connecting the living with their dead ancestors, and a horizontal or spatial line representing the traffic of the world. Global diaspora has shattered this sense of home:

After the migrant leaves home, he never finds another place where the two life lines cross. The vertical line exists no more; there is no longer any local continuity between him and the dead, the dead now simply disappear; and the gods have become inaccessible. The vertical line has been twisted into the individual biographical circle which leads nowhere but only encloses. As for the horizontal lines, because there are no longer any fixed points as bearings, they are elided into a plain of pure distance, across which everything is swept.

(pp. 65–66)

Since the beginning of the nineteenth century, Berger suggests, only two things can grow on this "site of loss" to offer an alternative shelter. One is passionate romantic love: "Romantic love, in the modern sense, is a love uniting or hoping to unite two displaced persons" (p. 66). (In an image that recalls Aristophanes in Plato's *Symposium,* Berger muses on love as the rejoining of two fragmentary parts that had once formed a whole.) The other possibility is solidarity. "The one hope of recreating a center now is to make it the entire earth. Only worldwide solidarity can transcend modern homelessness" (p. 67). Read in the light of these formulations, *Lilac and Flag* becomes an exploration of the emotional content of homelessness, but of the two antidotes that Berger offers against homelessness, Zsuzsa and Sucus seem able to grasp only romantic love, not solidarity. Thus, the revolutionary slogan first spoken by Murat, the Turk, Sucus' socialist fellow worker—"If not now, when? If not here, where?" (p. 60)—is uttered by the lovers at the end of the book simply as a passionate mating cry.

Indeed, *Lilac and Flag* has been strongly criticized for what is perceived as its utopian retreat from history. Fred Pfeil, Berger's most persistent leftist American interlocutor, decries Berger's wistful fantasy of a return to authentic origins, scathingly terming it "Heideggerian" (with all the opprobrium that term carries based on the German philosopher's documented complicity in national socialism). Pfeil notes that in *Into Their Labours* all the characters who represent revolutionary socialism are wounded or maimed: the young Saint-Just in "The Three Lives of Lucie Cabrol," a Resistance fighter and now a fugitive, whose injured leg the Cocadrille tends and whose eventual execution by the Nazis causes her final estrangement from her family; Michel in "Once in Europa," who has lost his leg in the war; and Murat, who is paralyzed as a result of a construction-site injury. Pfeil reads these figures as a wry comment on the exhausted possibilities of revolutionary action. He also complains about Berger's new essentialization of gender categories. Unlike *G.,* whose subversive account of sexual politics was intended to expose men's domination of women, *Lilac and Flag* affirms traditional gender roles, celebrating sex as primal and women as "rivers of pain and relief" (p. 30).

These cavils notwithstanding, the trilogy is remarkable for the high seriousness with which it treats its subjects. With the possible exceptions of some of the works of Leo Tolstoy, Thomas Hardy, and D. H. Lawrence, twentieth-century European literary history has produced little that equals Berger's scrupulous and compassionate representations of rural life, and *Lilac and Flag* remains unique for its empathy for the urban poor. Elsewhere in *And Our Faces, My Heart, Brief as Photos*, Berger writes about his admiration for the painter Caravaggio: "He was the first painter of life as experienced by the popolaccio, the people of the backstreets, les sans-culottes, the lumpenproletariat, the lower orders, those of the lower depths, the underworld. There is no word in any traditional European language which does not either denigrate or patronize the urban poor it is naming" (Vintage ed., p. 79). *Lilac and Flag* does not denigrate or patronize; nor is it at all voyeuristic or prurient. Instead, it unsentimentally dignifies the scattered, fragmented lives of its romantically heroic protagonists. (Fittingly, the cover illustrations for the Vintage edition of the trilogy reproduce details from Caravaggio's *Supper at Emmaus*.)

The final achievement of *Into Their Labours* must be measured in formal terms and in relation to earlier events in Berger's literary career. In an interview about the end of his collaboration with the filmmaker Alain Tanner, Berger discussed his growing uneasiness with modernist forms:

Alain, I think, was more interested in making films of a looser structure, films which, in a certain sense, were more experimental in their narrative, whereas I, because of my experience in writing stories not for the cinema, had come to a different position. Several years previously, you see, I had written the novel *G.*, which is an experimental work in terms of its narrative. But after *G.*, the next major fiction work I wrote, *Pig Earth*, was about peasants, and in writing this I found it necessary to return to a much more traditional form of narrative. Therefore, when this moment arrived after *Jonah* [Berger's final collaboration with Tanner], my current thinking about narrative was tighter and more traditional, just the opposite of Alain's.

(Dyer, p. 164)

Berger's critical terms are perhaps misleadingly schematic ("looser" is made synonymous with "experimental," "tighter" with "traditional"), but it is clear that in his view *G.* had exhausted the possibilities of the modernist novel. Yet despite Berger's self-deprecating comment, *Into Their Labours* should not be dismissed simply as "traditional": it invents a new, hybrid genre, a compound of ethnography, oral history, and fiction, realized through a seamless fusion of traditional realism and magic realism. The latter, as literary critics have observed, is the narrative form that springs from, and attempts

to record, a postmodern cultural hybridity that is too bizarre to be represented by mere realism. Berger's radical innovation, then, is to have devised an aesthetic form that bears the weight of his political interest in the great global hybrid of ever-expanding city and rapidly disappearing country.

CONCLUSION

IF Berger's work continues to be undervalued, if not neglected or denounced, in post–Cold War intellectual circles, it may be because his political energies are exorbitant in the eyes of the institutional arbiters of intellectual value. The academy is the place where such valuations are authoritatively made; not only has Berger never sought an academic credential or affiliation, but he has also traveled, both in his thinking and in his lived experience, a long way from the ivory tower. His contributions to Marxist aesthetic theory, although significant and manifold, are seldom acknowledged, because academic Marxism has come to define itself as antihumanist. By fluidly moving from critique to alternative practice, Berger suggests theoretical possibilities that are considered dubious precisely because they are read as humanist. As Bruce Robbins has pointed out, this is an interpretative fate that Berger shares with other Marxist humanists, notably E. P. Thompson and Raymond Williams, both of whom, to a greater or lesser degree, also eschewed the specialized vocabulary of academic writing in order to address a wider audience.

In the 1950s, Stephen Spender once angrily dismissed Berger as a foghorn in a fog, in response to which Berger reasonably asked what could be more useful in the English climate. For all our cultural discomfort with prophetic zeal, we should see Berger, if not quite as a foghorn, then as a sort of latter-day prophet, alternately warning and praising, exhorting and exalting. In his life, as in his work, Berger has been drawn to, and driven by, the determining issues of modernity. In their most insistent intellectual manifestation, these problems involve the question of representation, primarily of the latter's relation to power; in experiential terms they appear most powerfully as migration, displacement, and deracination. Berger's achievement is exemplary in his instinctive sympathy with these issues and the unswerving integrity with which he has allowed them to shape his choices.

SELECTED BIBLIOGRAPHY

I. FICTION. *A Painter of Our Time* (London, 1958; New York, 1959, 1989); *The Foot of Clive* (London, 1962); *Corker's Freedom* (London, 1964; New York, 1993, 1995); *G.* (London, 1972; New York, 1972, 1991); *Into Their Labours: A Trilogy* (New York, 1992), contains *Pig Earth* (London, 1979; New York, 1980), *Once in Europa* (New York, 1987; Cambridge, 1989), and *Lilac and Flag: An Old Wives' Tale of a City* (New York, 1990; Cambridge, 1991); *To the Wedding* (New York, 1995, 1996).

II. PLAYS. *Jonas qui aura 25 ans en l'an 2000*, with Alain Tanner (Lausanne, 1978; trans. as *Jonah Who Will Be 25 in the Year 2000*, by Michael Palmer, Berkeley, Calif., 1983); *A Question of Geography*, with Nella Bielski (London, 1987); *Les Trois Chaleurs* (produced Paris, 1985); *Boris*, trans. into Welsh by Rhiannon Ifans (produced Cardiff, 1985); *Goya's Last Portrait: The Painter Played Today*, with Nella Bielski (London, 1989).

III. SCREENPLAYS. *La Salamandre*, with Alain Tanner, 1971; *Le Milieu du monde*, with Alain Tanner, 1974; *Jonah Who Will Be 25 in the Year 2000*, with Alain Tanner, 1976; *Play Me Something*, with Timothy Neat, 1989.

IV. TRANSLATIONS. *Poems on the Theatre* (with Anya Bostock), by Bertolt Brecht (London, 1961; published as *The Great Art of Living Together: Poems on the Theatre*, Bingley, Yorkshire, Eng., 1972); *Helene Weigel, Actress* (with Anya Bostock), by Bertolt Brecht (Leipzig, 1961); *Return to My Native Land* (with Anya Bostock), by Aimé Césaire (London, 1969); *Oranges for the Son of Asher Levy* (with Lisa Appignanesi), by Nella Bielski (London, 1982); *After Arkadia: "The Wickerwork Tram" and "The Barber's Head"* (with Jonathan Steffen), by Nella Bielski (London, 1991).

V. OTHER WORKS. *Marcel Frishman*, with George Bresson (Oxford, 1958); *Permanent Red: Essays in Seeing* (London, 1960, 1979; published as *Toward Reality*, New York, 1962); *The Success and Failure of Picasso* (London, 1965, 1992; New York, 1980, 1989); *A Fortunate Man; The Story of a Country Doctor*, with photographs by Jean Mohr (London and New York, 1967); *Art and Revolution: Ernst Neizvestny and the Role of the Artist in the U.S.S.R.* (London and New York, 1969, 1993); *The Moment of Cubism and Other Essays* (London and New York, 1969); *The Look of Things*, ed. Nikos Stangos (London, 1972; New York, 1974); *Ways of Seeing* (London, 1972; New York, 1973); *A Seventh Man: Migrant Workers in Europe*, with photographs by Jean Mohr (London and New York, 1975); *About Looking* (London and New York, 1980); *Another Way of Telling*, with photographs by Jean Mohr (London and New York, 1982); *And Our Faces, My Heart, Brief as Photos* (London and New York, 1984); *The White Bird: Writings by John Berger*, ed. Lloyd Spencer (London, 1985; published as *The Sense of Sight*, New York, 1986, 1993).

VI. CRITICAL STUDIES. Peter Fuller, *Seeing Berger: A Revaluation of Ways of Seeing* (London, 1980; rev. ed. *Seeing Through Berger*, London, 1988); Joseph H. McMahon, "Marxist Fictions: The Novels of John Berger," in *Contemporary Literature* 23 (spring 1982); Bruce Robbins, "Feeling Global: Experience and John Berger," in *boundary 2*, vol. 11 (fall/winter 1982–1983); Kiernan Ryan, "Socialist Fiction and the Education of Desire: Mervyn Jones, Raymond Williams and John Berger," in H. Gustav Klaus, ed., *The Socialist Novel in Britain: Towards the Recovery of a Tradition* (Brighton, Eng., and New York, 1982); Harvey J. Kaye, "Historical Consciousness and Storytelling: John Berger's Fiction," in *Mosaic* 16 (fall 1983); A. R. Bras, "A Sense of the Future: The Work of John Berger," in *Critique* 25 (spring 1984); Raymond A. Mazurek, "Totalization and Contemporary Realism: John Berger's Recent Fiction," in *Critique* 25 (spring 1984); Geoff Dyer, *Ways of Telling: The Work of John Berger* (London, 1986); Michael W. Messmer, "Apostle to the Techno/Peasants: Word and Image in the Work of John Berger," in *Works and Days* 6 (spring/fall 1988); Russel Banks, "A Few Thoughts on John Berger," in *Pequod*, no. 32 (1991); Sven Birkerts, "John Berger: A Notion," in *Pequod*, no. 32 (1991); Wendy Lesser, "Tribute," in *Pequod*, no. 32 (1991); Robin Lippincott, "One Big Canvas: The Work of John Berger," in *Literary Review* 35 (fall 1991); Jeff Blaustone, "Ethnography as Art: Polymorphous Point of View in John Berger's *Pig Earth*," in *Arkansas Quarterly* 2 (October 1993); Nikos Papastergiadis, *Modernity as Exile: The Stranger in John Berger's Writing* (Manchester, Eng., and New York, 1993).

CHRISTINE BROOKE-ROSE

(1923–)

Tyrus Miller

WOMEN WRITERS WHO are not "safely dead, who at any one living moment are trying to 'look in new ways' or 'reread' and therefore rewrite their world, are rarely treated on the same level of seriousness as their male counterparts," Christine Brooke-Rose writes in her essay "Illiterations." "They can get published, they can even get good reviews. But they will be more easily forgotten between books and mysteriously absent from general situation surveys or critical books about contemporary literature" (*Stories, Theories and Things*, 1991, p. 261). In the novel, *Textermination* (1991), Brooke-Rose's fictive woman-author Mira Enketei peruses the ponderous "world-list" of characters who have fallen short of the canon and hence are doomed to an unread limbo of nonexistence. "What they don't realise, these numskulls," Mira muses, "is that it functions like an Index, in the ecclesiastical sense you know, an Index of Forbidden Works. Forbidden by time and neglect, because unavailable to the general public" (p. 104). These two passages treat a single problem from two positions—that of the author and that of characters—and present it in two idioms—one critical, the other fictional. Both passages, however, are permeated by Brooke-Rose's awareness, as critic and fabulist, that writing is only one side of that tenuous whole known as literature. The other side belongs to reading, for writing has no life if it is not animated by readers. Neither authors, whose identity is defined by their writing, nor characters, whose very existence rests in their being written, stand a chance of enduring within "literature" if they are not read.

Considerable danger lies in this question of reading, as Brooke-Rose is aware. For reading—or at least a certain historically defined way of reading—it seems, is in eclipse, having faded in the bright glare of the video screen and the silvery glint of the CD-ROM. Who reads anymore? What? How? What does it mean, "to read," anyway? Brooke-Rose has taken the cultural terrain circumscribed by these simple questions as the basic setting of her fictional works and as the fundamental context of her critical essays. Her novels, with their erudite references to a vast range of literary texts, with their extreme self-consciousness of their own status as things "to be read," are deeply engaged with the problem of the meaning of reading today. They persist in posing a paradoxical question, in the guise of addressing ex-readers, to those readers who remain. "Why do you no longer read?"—her works ask an allegorical phalanx of Readers-No-Longer, who will never, alas, perceive the question addressed to them. Even professional readers often fail to read, Brooke-Rose complains. In a critical essay in *A Rhetoric of the Unreal: Studies in Narrative and Structure, Especially of the Fantastic* (1981), she catalogues with ruthless fidelity her fellow critics' wildly varying and tendentious paraphrases of Henry James's novella *The Turn of the Screw*.

Reading, however, is not only necessary to carry to completion the author's leading gambit. It also precedes the act of writing, and accompanies it at every stage. For the author, before ever putting pen to page, is a reader too. Brooke-Rose, as an author with a tremendous command of the world of books and a penetrating analyst of other authors' writings, is indeed a better reader than most. The author-reader plays a constant and key role in her works. Her novels, accordingly, speak not only to ex-readers but also to hungry verbivores: those who, like her, devour words with gusto. Her books challenge those who still read to continue to read, to learn to read better, and to reflect on what in that beleaguered practice might help resist the creeping onset of global-village idiocy. Brooke-Rose's novels hestitate before the void that yawns beyond the end of reading, and they peer long and hard into it, making their report. Her critical writings, in contrast, seem to emanate from a different place, as

97

if that dark abyss were somehow not so close after all. For they speak in the confident tones of the true believer, of an author profoundly convinced, against all evidence, of the continued value of reading. The Anglo-Gallic scholar and woman novelist enters the room, shuffling her notes before her small but attentive crowd; she opens the first of a tall stack of her favorite books and commences to show her audience how reading gets done.

LIFE

CHRISTINE BROOKE-ROSE was born on 16 January 1923, in Geneva, Switzerland. Her mother, Evelyn Blanche Brooke, was Swiss of American descent, while her father, Alfred Northbrook Rose, was a rakish Englishman who abandoned the family early in her childhood. If the autobiographical matter of her early novel *The Dear Deceit* (1960) and her reluctantly autobiographical meditation *Remake* (1996) serve as evidence, her father was a monk as a young man and was defrocked and briefly imprisoned for the theft of books. He was then involved in some unsuccessful businesses and investment schemes. After her father returned to England to take up with his nurse, Brooke-Rose, her mother, and her siblings went to live with grandparents in Brussels. Brooke-Rose grew up in a bilingual household, acquiring French and English, and experienced the multilingual life of Switzerland and the Low Countries. She learned German with relatives in Germany, by that time under Nazi rule. In 1936, she went to an English school and remained in England during World War II.

As she describes in *Remake,* both childhood and later life were marked by abrupt moves and accompanying forays into new languages, some of which she had already learned and subsequently forgotten. This geographical and linguistic mutability left an intricate pattern of palimpsest-like traces in her memory that are reflected in the complex web of tongues and signs in such novels as *Between* (1968) and *Thru* (1975):

Once upon a time there is a little girl born in France, of an English father and a Swiss mother born of an American father and an Anglo-Swiss mother. The English father lives in London, the American-Swiss mother in Geneva, with the now Swiss grandpère and the Anglo-Swiss grandmère. . . .

Back to London, back to Geneva, back to London, back to Brussels, back to back. Forgetting French, forgetting English, relearning French, relearning English, learning Flemish, learning German, forgetting Flemish, relearning English not really forgotten. Etc.

(*Remake,* p. 10)

This linguistic experience had more immediate effects on her life as well. After living and working in Liverpool, where she was when the war broke out, she enlisted in the Women's Auxiliary Air Force and was assigned to a unit that intercepted, decoded, translated, and analyzed enemy messages, sending them on to the military authorities. Her war work was life changing, awakening both her intellectual ambitions and her senses to the adult, urbane environment of London. She married a man connected to her unit, but the marriage did not survive the routine of peacetime; her divorce was later a source of personal tribulation for Brooke-Rose, who had strong inclinations toward Roman Catholicism.

Following the war and a stint in occupied Germany, Brooke-Rose took advantage of the state scholarships offered to young servicemen and servicewomen after the war and began study at Oxford. From 1946 to 1949, she attended Somerville College, where she studied English and philology. In 1954, she was awarded a doctorate in medieval French and English literature from University College, London, for a thesis on metaphor in Old French and Middle English poetry. This work, in turn, laid the methodological groundwork for her first major critical study, *A Grammar of Metaphor* (1958).

Shortly after the end of the war, while preparing for an entrance exam to Oxford in the reading room of the British library, she met her future husband, the Polish poet and novelist, Jerzy Pietrkiewicz. In his autobiography, *In the Scales of Fate* (1993), Pietrkiewicz describes their first, rather comical encounter: "A very young woman in an Air Force uniform—she looked smart in it—found a seat near me and kept glancing at the spines of my books. This disturbed me, so I reciprocated and tried to see what her titles were" (p. 207). This bibliographic flirtation became in time a full-fledged romance, in which poetry, study, and love were deeply intermingled; in 1948, the two poet-scholars married.

Finding the doors of professional academia once again closed to women after the brief moment of opportunity after the war, Brooke-Rose worked as a literary journalist in London from 1956 until 1968. She published a book of poetry, *Gold: A Poem,* in 1955, and, needing money when her husband became seriously ill, she began writing novels, publishing *The Languages of Love* in 1957, *The Sycamore Tree* the following year, *The Dear Deceit* in 1960, and *The Middlemen: A Satire* a year later. Her own near-fatal illness in 1962–1963, for which she was hospitalized for months, represented a crucial turning point in her career. Whereas her first four novels had been relatively conventional formally and stylistically, the novel she wrote following her illness, *Out* (1964), inaugurated the series of innovative novels that constitute her mature corpus. Brooke-Rose has described her growing interest at this time in the work of Nathalie Sarraute and Alain Robbe-Grillet, as well as in the novelistic writings of Samuel Beckett. She also found her own reading interests shifting from "novels, good or bad, about love-affairs, class-distinctions and one-upmanships, or portraits of society on any scale from parochial to professional" to scientific literature (Brooke-Rose, quoted in Friedman, *Utterly Other Discourse,* p. 11). Her new taste for "experimental" literature and her fascination with the "poetry" of technical discourse would leave a permanent mark on her later fiction. Following *Out,* she published two other novels that deepened her engagement with radical textual forms: *Such* (1966) and *Between.*

The year 1968 brought another major turning point in Brooke-Rose's life and career. Her marriage to Pietrkiewicz, which had been going downhill for some time, finally reached a breaking point. The end of this long-standing and intellectually crucial relationship coincided with an exciting new opportunity for Brooke-Rose: an academic career in France. Brooke-Rose was invited by Hélène Cixous to join the faculty of the Université de Paris VIII at Vincennes, which was founded in the wake of the May–June 1968 revolts in France and widely considered a bastion of political and theoretical radicalism. She started teaching in 1968 and stayed on until her retirement in 1988. After retiring, Brooke-Rose lived in Provence.

The last chapter of *Remake* includes an anecdote that encapsulates the atmosphere of the new university and exhibits Brooke-Rose's capacity to flourish in it. Of her autobiographical character Tess, Brooke-Rose recounts: "Tess enjoys teaching, a wholly new experience, if unsettling at first, with strikes and demos and invasions of classes. Dégueulasse, says an early student that first term, at something Tess has said. Say that in English, Tess replies with cool sangfroid, remember? And then writes SHIT on the board, and the other students laugh. A dirty trick but silencing" (p. 167).

Brooke-Rose absorbed the heady theoretical and literary atmosphere in France, drawing into her works of fiction and criticism the radical textual semiotics of the *Tel Quel* writers and critics, the innovative psychoanalytic theories of Jacques Lacan and his followers, and the technical discourse of structuralist narratology. Her academic production during this period includes her guide to the work of her poetic mentor, *A ZBC of Ezra Pound* (1971); her more technical study of Pound, *A Structural Analysis of Pound's Usura Canto* (1976); a collection of related essays on fantastic elements in nineteenth- and twentieth-century fiction, *A Rhetoric of the Unreal* (1981); and many of the essays included in *Stories, Theories and Things.* As her reputation as a theorist and novelist grew, she was invited as a visiting professor to the State University of New York at Buffalo, New York University, the Hebrew University of Jerusalem, and Brandeis University in Waltham, Massachusetts.

Her first novel of the 1970s, *Thru,* reveals the impact of Brooke-Rose's new intellectual and literary context. Its difficult, largely nonnarrative form, its extensive use of technical concepts and jargon, and its "concrete" typographical elements scared off her publisher and aroused puzzlement, when not ire and dismissal, in reviewers. As Brooke-Rose recounts in her essay "Stories, Theories and Things," "It was . . . a novel about the theory of the novel, that is, a narrative about narrativity, a fiction about fictionality, a text about intertextuality and . . . it took four summers to get 'right.' . . . The external harm this book did to her reputation as incomprehensible and pretentious was lasting and profound" (*Stories, Theories and Things,* p. 8). While this essay tells the story in a witty way, Brooke-Rose's consternation must have been real enough. Her later novels back down somewhat from the multi-semiotic, dissipative textuality of *Thru,* but in each, Brooke-Rose reveals her highly developed self-consciousness about writing and theory, playfully spinning out new complexes of form, idea, and theme. These later works include: *Amalgamemnon*

(1984), *Xorandor* (1986), *Verbivore* (1990), and *Textermination.*

POETRY, EARLY NOVELS, SHORT STORIES

BROOKE-ROSE'S first published work, *Gold,* is a poetic dream-vision written in the alliterative meter and form of the Middle English poem *Pearl.* While adopting this medieval allegorical mode, however, Brooke-Rose's poem treats contemporary subject matter: the deportation of Poles to Russian gulags during the Soviet occupation of Poland. She derived her historical material from an anonymous 1946 work on the deportations, *The Dark Side of the Moon,* to which T. S. Eliot had contributed a preface. Brooke-Rose comments in her introductory note to *Gold* that its allegorical form seemed to her "the only way of visualizing a scene barely imaginable in the West" (p. 3). In her use of alliterative metrical form, she had not only medieval precedents but also the more recent examples of Ezra Pound, who had used Anglo-Saxon meter in "The Seafarer" and in some *Cantos,* and W. H. Auden, who had published his alliterative eclogue *The Age of Anxiety* in 1947. Auden's poem also treated contemporary historical concerns through the estranging lens of an obsolete poetic mode.

Brooke-Rose's poem consists of fifty twelve-line stanzas, each of which begins with a thematically important word or phrase, such as: gold, tin, Kolyma, the Soviet East, the moon. These words are subject to transformation from stanza to stanza: for example, "tin" in stanza 5 yields "tingling," "tintinnabula," "tinted," and "tinder" in successive stanzas. These changes dramatize in the very language of the poem its allegorical theme of alchemical transformation, the communists' attempt to distill the "gold" of their social utopia out of the base metal of human bodies. The word "gold" itself functions on four allegorical levels in the poem: literally, it refers to the gold extracted by the prisoners from Siberian mines; allegorically, it designates the communist utopian ideal of a "new man"; morally, it suggests the potential for ideals to become pretexts for brutality and violence; and anagogically or mystically, it refers to the salvational image of the "marigold," the Lady of Light who appears at the end to intercede for "the living dead." As Brooke-Rose suggests in her introduction, her poem echoes the elegiac overtones of *Pearl,* but her elegy is paradoxically "for many million souls, still half-alive" (p. 3).

Brooke-Rose turned to writing novels as a way of distracting herself from worries over her husband's health. Brooke-Rose's witty but learned manner, her reference to specialized academic knowledge within enjoyable plots, and her exploration of Roman Catholic themes led reviewers and critics to compare these early novels to contemporaneous works by Iris Murdoch and Muriel Spark. Brooke-Rose's early novels are largely conventional in form and realist in style. Yet in retrospect, their urbanity and focus on intellectual literary characters also seem to anticipate some aspects of her more self-consciously experimental later fiction.

Her first novel, *The Languages of Love* (1957), is a witty account of the trials in love of two women, the protagonist and medievalist, Julia Grampion, and her friend, the fashionable journalist Georgina Raymond. Having just earned her doctorate but finding no immediate prospects in the university, Julia is torn in her career choices: Should she hold out for an academic post or follow the advice of several friends and become a journalist, popular critic, or lady-novelist? These career choices are burdened with personal choices as well. For Julia loves Paul Brodrick, a researcher in African languages, but cannot marry him. Because of her brief, failed wartime marriage and his firm Roman Catholic faith, the relationship is deadlocked. She wants to forget her past "error" and persuade Paul to buck the Church, but he will not; both are troubled by the prospect of living in sin, though their desire for one another remains strong. Paul represents for Julia a moral and intellectual integrity that she later misses, yet the solidity of his values leads to the devastating impasse in their relationship. Partly out of exasperation, partly out of a dawning sexual desire, Julia accepts the advances of one of her examiners, the young, married professor Bernard Reeves. Despite his vulgarity and failure to acknowledge her interests and needs, she finds herself increasingly drawn into this new relationship. As she juggles her love relationships, she also moves between types of writing: from reviewing for popular magazines to contributing to Bernard's sellable collection of essays on adultery in the Middle Ages to revising her doctoral thesis, a scholarly study of medieval poetry and courtly love. Through paralleling the literary and sexual plots,

Brooke-Rose explores the ambiguity implicit in her title. For not only does Julia discover the different registers and voices in which love may "speak" to a woman, from the gasps and moans of the purely sexual to the silent plenitude of the purely spiritual, she also comes to understand the different ways in which love can make its way into language, from its commercial prostitution in throwaway journalism to its sanctification by the poetry of agape, or love.

Whereas Julia's predicament provides Brooke-Rose with the thematic core of her novel, Georgina Raymond's situation provides drama and exotic interest. Georgina is passionately involved with an African man, Hussein Abdillahi, who is in England to provide Paul Brodrick with linguistic data for his research into the Sanurian language. Throughout the novel, Hussein provides humor and lyricism by perceiving the everyday world of the British through very foreign eyes and reciting the colorful proverbs and poetry of his native language. Georgina has recently returned from Tokyo, where she has learned the sparse style of decoration and the habit of wearing kimonos, and Hussein is charmed by the beautiful, frank blond in Japanese clothes. While their love for one another is nearly overwhelming, they express their passion sexually only when crisis approaches: the day is drawing near when Hussein must return to his country. At the last minute, he does not take his ship home and arrives with a camel he has bought as a gift of love for Georgina. Yet in the end, he cannot stay. Threatened by missives and cryptic threats from his father, Hussein accepts his fate, leaves Georgina, and boards the ship back to Sanuri.

At first glance, Brooke-Rose's novel is rich with plot and characters arranged in satirical tableaux of intellectual and literary circles: the university, the publication party, the journalistic caste. Through Julia's medievalizing mind-set, however, Brooke-Rose suggests that the events of the novel may also be read allegorically, as a spiritual progress or an allegorical dream vision. This allegorical dimension touches especially on the temptations, sexual and literary, to which Julia falls prey and finds its fulfillment in her richer understanding of Paul's Roman Catholicism at the end of the book. In this allegorical dimension, Brooke-Rose attempts to redeem the often silly character of Hussein, with his camels and gnomic utterances. Briefly reunited with Paul on the docks at Hussein's departure,

Julia takes inspiration from Hussein's acceptance of loss. Hussein sends Georgina a "dove of peace" and tells Julia to "pray to her guardian angel" (p. 210). She learns that Paul will follow Hussein to Sanuri shortly, and Paul and Julia kiss goodbye. She suggests that the summer has been, not a nightmare, but an "allegorical dream-vision," and he agrees, adding, "With Hussein as the moral meaning" (p. 212).

Julia spells out that moral meaning in her last meeting with Bernard. Through Paul, Hussein, and Georgina, she says, she has discovered what it means to annihilate self-love for a greater love. She has resolved not to marry and to become a Roman Catholic. She also has come to terms with her vocation. She accepts an academic post, where, as a medieval philologist, she will occupy herself with "the bare bones of language." For, as she recognizes, her calling is appropriate to her new understanding of herself and her limitations: "[S]elfish people can't be truly creative, either in art or in living. They can only be interpreters, making their mistakes and scoring their successes as pianists, actors, minor artists, journalists, critics, scholars" (p. 239). Yet implicitly, her humility before the facts of language may become the path to a higher love, the annihilation of the self in a "*philo-logy*," a love of the word as such.

After the relative success of her first novel, Brooke-Rose's second attempt, *The Sycamore Tree*, veered into the improbable and sentimental. The book reviewer and literary failure Howard Cutting sues the bright, successful novelist Gael Jackson for slander, on the basis of a coincidental similarity between an episode in Jackson's new novel, *The Sycamore Tree*, and Cutting's private life. The scene from the novel implies that a disturbing call at a dinner party was from Cutting's wife's lover. Cutting wins his suit, despite its erroneous premises, and the novel's publication is suppressed. At the trial, however, Cutting is smitten by Jackson's vivacious and lovely wife, Nina. Though deeply in love with her husband, she eventually succumbs—rather inexplicably—to the mediocre and vulgar Cutting. The contrivance of the plot does not end here, however, because the phone call actually *was* from the wife's lover, Zoltan, a Hungarian student and refugee from the communist regime in his homeland. He is writing a book on a poet who disappeared in Siberia after World War II. On a chance meeting with Gael Jackson in a church, however, he reveals that he is not actually a student, but the missing poet himself. In a final twist, he goes mad under the strain of his split identity and the danger of being found out by communist agents and in a tragic turn of events shoots Nina Jackson. Having delivered herself of a message of Roman Catholic hope to her children and of encouragement to her husband to rewrite *The Sycamore Tree,* Nina dies with words of love for Gael on her lips.

Brooke-Rose's satire of the literary world is broad, but unlike the screwball-academic "changing places" plots that David Lodge would later so successfully manage, her attempts at humor fall flat beneath unconvincing situations and characters. There is some hint of her later metafictional self-consciousness, since Gael Jackson's suppressed novel is called *The Sycamore Tree.* The novel the reader has in hand, one might surmise, is the rewrite Gael promised Nina on her deathbed, his memorial tribute to his wife, who indeed dies from the fatal effects of the first version of the book. These metafictional implications, however, are peripheral to the main lines of the novel. They frame the main narrative cleverly but never substantially call into doubt Brooke-Rose's general appeal to the conventions of realism.

Where the book has greater success, however, is in one of its moral and historical themes. As convoluted and melodramatic as the subplot involving the Hungarian poet ends up, it nevertheless affords Brooke-Rose a stage on which to present a serious issue: the attitude of Western intellectuals to Eastern European communism, an issue with strong topical force following the Hungarian uprising of 1956 and its brutal suppression by the Russian army. Through her exiled student-poet, she effectively exposes the complicity of intellectuals and literati in lending legitimacy to the Stalinist regime through their attendance of conferences and congresses carefully staged by the government for publicity purposes. Knowing nothing of the languages of these countries and totally reliant on official "translators" for communicating, such visitors nevertheless returned with an aura of knowing what was "really going on" there, and of being in the right, since they had "spoken their minds" to the leaders and "made frank criticisms." This steady current of Western opinion, of course, never reached the people of these countries. Instead, they saw pictures of famous writers, thinkers, and politicians shaking hands with hated

officials. Brooke-Rose's relationship with a Polish poet, no doubt, added a measure of bile to her depiction of such choreographed visits.

With her third novel, *The Dear Deceit,* Brooke-Rose made a substantial leap forward in her mastery of narrative structure and style. While not radically breaking with realism, she used a sophisticated range of stylistic and narrational devices, thus enriching her novel's engagement with the problem of memory. The novel concerns the efforts of a young man, Philip Hayley, to discover the truth about his dead father, Alfred Northbrook Hayley. The father has abandoned the family and gone to live with his mistress, and Philip has grown attached to his mother, who harbors deep resentments toward the father. When, at an advanced age, his mother enters a convent, Philip begins to investigate the past, delving into his father's letters and other writings. Early in the novel, the father's death is rendered in a vivid interior monologue. From this point on, each chapter takes Philip—along with the reader and the father character—further into the past, in a chainlike, regressing narrative. Each chapter adds to the complex portrait of the father, at once a braggart, scoundrel, and pathetic, aging child-man.

The characters and situations in *The Dear Deceit* are closely entangled with Brooke-Rose's own life and family, as her autobiographical text *Remake* suggests. Philip seems a composite of her own wartime past and aspects of her first husband, while Philip's father and mother have striking similarities to Brooke-Rose's parents. Nevertheless, like *Remake,* her novel treats this autobiographical material with resistance and self-conscious doubt. Philip, the narrator, explores the limits of a person's ability to know the past, especially when that knowledge is mediated by written texts. Implicitly, too, the reader of Brooke-Rose's novel, with its distorted and elliptical incorporation of autobiographical data, comes up against analogous obstacles to knowledge. Facts from a life only lead to other facts, but not to a total portrait. The essential motivations and meaning of the life remain enigmatic.

Philip has sought in his father's story moral guidance for his own action, by negative example. He has hoped to make his life a redress of his father's wrongs, a compensation for the sins of the immediate past. But he is left at the end with the enigma of a weak, fallible, idiosyncratic man, sinful but not dramatically evil. The father's moral failure is singular and circumstantial, not exemplary. Despite his attempt to allegorize his father's story, and hence his own as its spiritual opposite, Philip must continue to bear the burden of moral choice. The closing words are spoken by a sister in the convent where his mother has become mother superior. This friendly sister advises Philip that his father's legacy is not one of hereditary guilt, but of lack of faith. "Of course, you know, one can always refuse a legacy, or give it away," she adds. "You should make an offering of it, Philip, boy, make an offering of your lack of faith" (p. 319). As in *The Languages of Love,* Brooke-Rose finds novelistic resolution to the intractable problems of her characters in a paradoxical Roman Catholicism. Philip must come to see that his spiritual and personal predicament will become clear only when he examines his own life and can never be resolved by paying penance for another's sins in the past.

Brooke-Rose's next novel, *The Middlemen,* takes as its satirical target the increasingly important social stratum of mediators between products and their consumers. These middlemen include advertisers, public relations people, literary agents, journalists, lawyers, book reviewers, and literary critics. The main plot of the book is provided by a pair of twins, the psychoanalyst Serena and her difficult, neurotic, fashionable, and flighty sister, Stella. Stella's life is marked by an obsessive pattern of taking a job abroad and later abandoning it for reasons ranging from personal conflicts with her employers to revolutions and natural disasters in the latest country of her choice. Stella then returns to London with the request to stay with Serena and her husband, who have learned from experience to turn Stella down. Stella then returns to London, where she drops in on Serena and her husband, every time driving them half-insane with her criticisms, social gaffes, and general intensity. As the novel opens, Stella has once again returned from abroad, and Serena and her husband turn down her request to stay with them. But this "question of the flat" that Stella repeatedly poses sets in motion a key subplot: Serena's search for a new house, which is constantly foiled by new inanities and exacerbated by the foibles of middlemen. Eventually Serena can take no more of her sister and employs a stratagem to earn herself some peace: she contrives a quarrel that results in a break with her sister. Profoundly strained by the house hunt and the struggles with Stella, Serena goes off with her husband on a vacation to a Greek volcanic island. The sight of lava, however, triggers a nervous breakdown in Serena, undoing that essence of her character underscored by her name. Just as she begins to come out of her mental turmoil, an unexpected volcanic eruption buries the whole tourist community in hot magma. The novel ends with Stella aboard another plane for another exotic location, dismissing a moment of regret and curiosity about her estrangement from her sister, unaware of Serena's unfortunate death by fire.

The Middlemen is not, generally speaking, a well-crafted or richly imagined work. It plays with metafictional techniques, such as reintroducing peripheral characters like Howard Cutting from *The Sycamore Tree* and Philip Hayley from *The Dear Deceit,* yet the overall narrative design remains unaffected by them. These devices function more as clever flourishes than as any interrogation of literariness or fictionality. If anything, they suggest Brooke-Rose's growing boredom with the mode of writing she had adopted and, in the course of three fairly successful novels, mastered. The sudden disaster that ends the book might be seen as a gesture of throwing up her hands in frustration with her characters and their goings-on. In killing them off with so little preparation or motivation, she seems to reject outright the conflict-resolution model of storytelling.

In her collection of stories *Go When You See the Green Man Walking* (1970), Brooke-Rose moves tentatively in the direction of her later style. This collection includes minimalist character sketches like "They All Go to the Mountains Now" and "Queenie Fat and Thin," clever satirical fables like "The Troglodyte," and relatively simple allegories like "The Chinese Button" and "George and the Seraph." But some stories test out more sophisticated techniques of subjective narration, strongly distanced description, and metafictional play. The title story, for example, is almost plotless, being largely a present-tense description of a foreign city as seen by a woman from her hotel-room balcony and later from the street as she walks around. The title refers to the pedestrian traffic light that signals it is safe to cross the street. The story is strongly marked by an alternating rhythm of stopping and starting, as the woman is confronted in succession by the green man and the red man, "rectangular legs apart" (p. 187). "Red Rubber Gloves" is another experiment in detached description, akin to the estrangement techniques and cool violence of the *nouveau romancier* Alain Robbe-Grillet. In Brooke-Rose's story, an event of horror, the cutting up and disposal of either an aborted fetus or a murdered newborn, is told with utter matter-of-factness from the partially blocked perspective of a narrator looking in from an apartment opposite. More momentous than the murder itself is its banal reduction to a metonymy: the red rubber gloves that have appeared throughout the story, and that are the part Brooke-Rose uses to symbolize the whole horrible event, disappear at the end, replaced with a pair of yellow rubber gloves.

The richest of these stories is "The Foot," which has as its narrator the phantom limb of a model, who has had her leg amputated after an automobile accident. The phantom foot, felt by the woman as an excruciating pain below the stump of her severed leg, asserts itself anthropomorphically in sadistic eroticism—it feels the pleasure of existing insofar as "he" can make his "beloved" suffer. Brooke-Rose leaves in question the ultimate status of this narrator, suggesting that his autonomy flickers in and out with the changes in the woman's psychic and physical state. When her stump is palpated by the doctor, for example, the real pain she feels tends to disturb the phantom foot's sense of existence, threatening to obliterate him. At times, this phantom narrator appears to be a retrospective literary invention of the woman, who with her injury has turned from modeling to writing. The woman's dialogue, for example, repeats phrases used earlier by the narrator-foot, suggesting that he is dependent upon her, even in his apparent separateness and power over her. Both foot and woman function alternately as character and narrator, and the relation between these terms is one of a continually reversible chain. It is suggested, for example, that the foot-narrator creates a story about the foot-character and the woman-character, who, in the course of the narration, the foot-narrator decides to tell her story and becomes a woman-narrator. Yet the phantom foot seems a psychic or literary projection of the woman's mind; and she begins to write about the same experiences we have read earlier in the voice of the foot-narrator. It is thus equally plausible to turn the narrator-character, woman-foot relation the other way around. In this view, the woman-narrator, who remains hidden, invents a story about a woman and a foot, which in the course of the story functions as her surrogate. The structure loops back on itself, with no definite point of departure or exit. In fact, though the story begins with the foot-narrator's assertion that "the victim to be haunted is female," these are also the very words the woman writes in her notebook three pages from the story's end, as she begins to write. The narrator-foot, then, tells of his own "origin" as narrator. Where does the story start? At the beginning of the text's narration or at the "beginning" narrated *in* the text, indeed, in its last few pages? The paradox implied in this question parallels the uncanny fictional-real, absent-present status of the phantom limb itself. Unfortunately, in this otherwise masterful story, Brooke-Rose cannot resist making explicit the analogy between amputation and castration. Yet despite this heavy-handedness she effectively connects "lack" and narration in a thought-provoking way. The phantom limb that tells stories is an unsettling image of the persistent force of loss, and it suggests that the impulse to write fiction may emerge, ultimately, out of an absence, out of a melancholy endurance of grief and psychic pain.

THE BREAK WITH REALISM

THE FOUR NOVELS that follow *The Middlemen*—*Out, Such, Between,* and *Thru*—reveal a radical shift in Brooke-Rose's literary orientation. While her satirical focus and use of specialized knowledge are deepened in these novels, the new forms and narrational techniques she explores allow a more dramatic handling of her social, psychological, and theological concerns. These novels are less direct in their commentary on such issues, which were treated in the earlier novels either in the dialogue of characters or in significant turns of events in realistically rendered plots. Instead, they tend to enact the themes at the level of narration itself. Thus, for example, in these novels the danger of personal disintegration is not represented through a character's move toward mental breakdown, as is the case with Nina's deathbed delirium in *The Sycamore Tree* and Serena's nervous collapse in *The Middlemen.* Rather, the later narrators are already fractured or dispersed, and the difficulties they suffer in putting together a coherent story dramatize the outcome and implications of their psychic state. A central image in *Out,* for instance, is "the displacement from cause to effect" (p. 119), so that the narrator has a great deal of trouble putting events in order. But this displacement, taken more generally, also describes the shift in the narrative center of gravity of Brooke-Rose's own work, from the causal chains of realist storytelling to the effects of events that have already taken place and that may be only partly reconstructed.

A technique common to all four novels is the creation of interference between two or more perspectives, discourses, or narrations. These interferences cause unexpected points of opacity, insistent repetitions and fixations, knots and nets occasioned by the conflict of incompatible literary or linguistic elements. In *Out,* this interference is above all temporal: as the narrator's radiation sickness grows progressively worse, a process whose pace is remarked at various points in the book, his ability to hold his narrative to a consistent time flow erodes. In *Such,* Brooke-Rose presents psychological and interpersonal dynamics in the language of astrophysics, thus stretching the boundaries of her central character between earthly and cosmic dimensions. *Between* explores the interferences of multiple languages and geographical spaces through a focus on international conferences, travel, and translation. *Thru,* examines the dynamics of fiction-making itself. By causing different elements of fiction writing, from character to narration to typography, to conflict with one another, Brooke-Rose captures a freeze-frame image of a fiction coming together and falling apart at the same time.

Out is set in an unspecified future time, following, apparently, a major nuclear accident or war. The radiation has affected the races differently, for the "colorless," as whites are called in the book, are subject to cancerous sickness, while other races are resistant to radiation illness. This biological difference has led to profound social effects as well. A great "displacement" has occurred, as class and even geographical boundaries have been restructured to reflect the new superiority of Africans and Asians. Although officially the society is "color-blind," the colorless are subject to an apartheid-like system of caste discrimination, encampment housing, employment restrictions and controls, mass unemployment, and individual prejudice, while all positions of power are occupied by the previously "inferior" races. As far as one can tell from its

fragmentary form, *Out* is narrated by a sick white worker, perhaps once a professor and now an odd-jobs man. He seems to be in the terminal stages of his illness, unable to leave his hut, and his mind moves incoherently through memories, imagined scenes, and minimal descriptions of his present state. The shattered, repetitive form of his story suggests a profound disintegration of the mind, at times approaching schizophrenia or delirium.

Thematically, *Out* is a biting satire of liberal ideologies of racial equality in the context of persistent discrimination and bigotry. It uses the classic satirical technique of symbolic inversion, the world turned upside down, to dump whites to the bottom of the racial hierarchy. In this way, Brooke-Rose compels her largely Anglo-American readership to empathize imaginatively with victims of overt racism, while at the same time exposing the abuse of language implicit in the familiar pieties mouthed by her fictive ruling class. It is worth recalling, too, the historical context in which the book was written: the Civil Rights movement was in full swing in the United States; the struggles in South Africa against apartheid were on the rise, while anticolonialization efforts and Pan-African sentiments were sweeping Africa; and the Algerian war for independence was reaching its peak of intensity. In 1961, Frantz Fanon had published *Les Damnés de la terre (The Wretched of the Earth),* in which he discussed the profound ties between colonial wars and mental illness in the colonizing soldiers and police, while Jean-Paul Sartre declared in his preface to that volume that France should take care not to become the name for a nervous disease. The same problems that occupied Fanon—the centrality of the racial and colonial questions, the manifestations of racism in everyday life, the interpenetration of racism and mental illness—lie at the core of Brooke-Rose's book. As the somber tone and unrelentingly grim humor of *Out* suggest, however, Brooke-Rose was skeptical about whether a new world was really in birth for the wretched of the earth. Her satire cuts two ways: while its primary target is European racism, it also alludes to the disheartening conduct of the native elites that replaced the colonial rulers. The world in an inverted glass, she suggests, still shows the same brutish face.

The effectiveness of a satire depends on the specific reference of the text to its context. *Out's* relation to its context is ambiguous and skeptical, an interference pattern that arrests the easy consumption of ideologies and beliefs, forcing readers to reflect on the duplicity of stock phrases. Another frame of reference for the story, however, distinct from the satiric dimension, is constituted by the narrator and his relation to the story he tells. Here the interferences lend the book a greater pathos and complexity than its satire alone could. The narrator's sick, immobilized body interferes with his ability to tell about his previous movements, work, and sexual encounters; his vitiated ability to remember the past and his inability to distinguish that memory from its present enactment in storytelling affect the shape of the story itself; the confining space of the room in which he tells his story seems to contaminate the wider story space in which he moves as a character in his narrative. In one particularly striking passage, the narrator recalls a scene that takes place in the Labor Exchange, in which he watches a fly resting on a picture on the wall as he calls to mind the words of a letter he has written to a prospective employer whose head gardener has treated him badly; a fly is also one of the few things the narrator describes about his own room, which suggests it may only be in the story as an afterimage of the scene of narration. It is all told in the present tense, as if photograph and person, memory and invention, past and present, narration and description, fact and hypothesis were only faintly distinguishable and of equal status to the dying narrator:

> The sound in the air . . . is mottled with human voices. It is all the more astonishing in view of the fact that your head gardener seems to be, to all appearances, himself an ex-Ukayan. The only possible explanation I can think of is all the more astonishing in view of the fact that the wall is dirty green and peeling. The portrait of the Governor on the far wall beyond the strong back heads of the employment clerks at their grilled partitions, the portrait of the Governor with his vain Asswati face, the fly sits like a wart on the corner of the Governor's stalwart lips. The fly is reflected in the glass, like two warts. Unless perhaps it is a different fly, there being one fly inside the glass and one outside.

(*Out*, in *Omnibus*, pp. 44–45)[1]

Throughout the book, instruments of measurement are named, forming a kind of leitmotiv of the narrator's presence while underscoring the absence of any objectively determinable status for the events that occur in his ramblings. Usually these instruments appear in a hypothetical sentence, further emphasizing the lack of clear standard of temporal or ontological measure in the story: "A microscope might perhaps reveal animal ecstasy" (p. 11); "A telescope might perhaps reveal a planet off course" (p. 18); "An oscillograph might reveal curious fluctuations" (p. 24); "A tape-recorder might perhaps reveal this to be the phrase that came and went" (p. 32); and so on, with teinoscope, bronchoscope, electroencephalograph, seismograph, and numerous other scientific instruments. As in Samuel Beckett's postwar trilogy, *Molloy, Malone Dies,* and *The Unnamable,* the loss of measure both provides the impulse for the narrator to tell his story and dooms it in advance to failure. All the absent measures in *Out*—of scale, of affect, of oscillation, of deviation, of transition—seem to relate to the narrator's primary condition, his inability to know himself and hence justify his status as narrator. Returning to the racial problematic that forms the satirical premise of the book, Brooke-Rose's white narrator reflects a crisis in the self-understanding of the European male in a global society that no longer allows him to assume that he is the standard and measure of everything. Yet Brooke-Rose's conclusion is pessimistic: her narrator's attempts at recapturing his identity through storytelling are in no way redemptive. Rather than offering a model of how one comes to accept and survive difference, her narrator remains caught in the solipsism of his sickness.

Such, published two years after *Out,* reverses the narrator's relation to death. The narrator-protagonist, a psychiatrist who works among astrophysicists at a research institute, dies and, already laid out in a coffin, returns to life two days later. While dead, he exists in a transformed state in another cosmos, composed of himself, a "girl-spy" who is his female alter ego, and five moons or planets who are their "children." In this world, he is named Someone, the woman is named Something, and the celestial children have the names of Louis Armstrong blues: Dippermouth, Gut Bucket, Potato Head, Tin Roof, and Really. Gradually, Someone begins to emerge from this death-world and coalesces into his previous self, the psychiatrist Larry, with his wife, friends, colleagues, and rivals. Yet especially in the first days after his return from the dead, he is prone to shift unexpectedly back into his cosmic

---

[1] All page citations for *Out, Such, Between,* and *Thru,* refer to *The Christine Brooke-Rose Omnibus: Out, Such, Between, Thru.*

persona or to speak of the other world as if people share his knowledge and experience. He has also been granted a new and disillusioning insight into the motives and thoughts of those around him, whom he now understands as if human subjectivity were reducible to the logic of mechanics and physics. His eyes have become like dish-telescopes, inordinately sensitive to the faint currents of human motivation. What he had once conceived professionally in depth-psychological terms, he can now only see in the light of astrophysical concepts. Despite his attempts to reconnect with his former work and personal life, Larry's psyche has been permanently altered by his experience of death and rebirth. His friends and wife find him increasingly bizarre, and their concern and chipper advice begin to dwindle; eventually, his wife abandons him. In his renewed isolation, he begins to revisit the death-cosmos. The book ends ambiguously, but one possible reading is that he dies a second time or, what would amount to the same thing, dies to the world by regressing into his mad hallucinatory universe of death.

Brooke-Rose simultaneously uses two formal devices in *Such*. The first is its peculiar narrative structure. The general narrative trajectory is, as in *The Dear Deceit*, a receding one. As Larry says at one point, "I seem to live backwards, or rather, part of me, my eyes and ears, as if their atoms consisted of anti-matter" (*Such*, in *Omnibus*, p. 300). Unlike the earlier novel, however, *Such* does not recede into the past, but into the future away from the death-state: from the cosmic condition of being that Larry has experienced in his coffin, back into his ordinary earthly life. The novel begins at maximum visionary intensity with little to orient the reader or to indicate what is happening to whom: "The five moons unless planets perhaps hang about anxiously as the stairs creak out of the grave. The planets move in their orbits and the orbits surround me like meridians in slight ellipses" (p. 203). This cosmic description yields to dialogue between the celestial characters, which in turn increasingly lapses into everyday speech, characters, and situations. Yet Larry's recovery is traversed by oscillation between the two states. One might conceive of the novel's narrative line as akin to a plucked string, its maximum oscillation coming at the beginning and its intensity gradually diminishing and converging on a state of rest, represented perhaps by a second death at the end.

The other formal device is Brooke-Rose's often humorous blurring of diction. Especially important is her overlaying of the language of physics and psychology: "The permutations of desires start grinding round his inner automation at the slow speed of unhealing time, rejecting in each cycle the one decoying premiss in two parts *a* and *b* with the basement of his life feeding in again the same two blocking items" (p. 301). Larry's progressive estrangement suggests that he fuses such incompatible idioms as a symptom of the psychic disturbance he suffered in his death experience. For the reader, however, "Larry" and his psychological condition only emerge gradually. In the first section of the book, at least, one could just as easily say that it is not the character who explains the aberrant use of language, but the strange hybrid language that reveals crucial qualities of the character. The language *is* the character, who has no existence apart from that imputed by a particular image of language, in this case a distorted and duplicitous one.

Closely related to her hybrid dictions is Brooke-Rose's use of pronouns and adverbs as proper names: Someone, Something, Really. This naming of characters allows her to move humorously between their apotheosis as celestial beings and their reduction to linguistic functions in the ordinary world, in a kind of science-fiction version of Abbott and Costello's famous comedy routine "Who's on first?":

—Why did you tell them nothing, Someone?
—I didn't. I told them . . . Something.

. . .

—I dreamt I died, and came back to life and could read people.
Good people.
—Really?
—Yes. No. Not Really.

(pp. 229–230)

In ordinary usage, such words are dependent on context for their meaning. They mark the positions of speakers, listeners, or objects of speech (I, you, she, they, and so on) or point to something. In *Such*, on the contrary, they are the hinges around which changes from one context—the cosmic—and another—the everyday world—are effected. The mere appearance of "someone" as a proper name signals that the visionary scene has reappeared. Moreover, implicit in Brooke-Rose's play with these words is a view of myth akin to Friedrich Nietzsche's insight that as long as we have grammar we will not be finished with God. Through Larry's thanatological visions, Brooke-Rose projects abstract grammatical markers into a pseudo-heaven of celestial Ideas. Indeed, it is precisely because these words are without fixed meaning that they can become the perfect vehicles of myth. For myth is not primarily a set of contents (tricksters, gods, and the like), but rather a system of categories, a way of perceiving relations between things. Like a positional term in language, a mythic figure has meaning only in particular contexts and changes or even vanishes as the context changes. Brooke-Rose's hero Larry suffers from just this dependence of myth on context, for he discovers that the mythic world he has invented in his death-state has no meaning for people in the ordinary world. They either misunderstand him or worry that he has gone mad.

Between was begun in 1964 but not completed until three years later. Brooke-Rose had started the novel using a male protagonist, as in *Out* and *Such;* it was not until she rethought her narrative with a female protagonist that it fell into place. *Between* also represents a departure from the preceding two novels in that Brooke-Rose abandoned the science-fiction or futuristic premises of those books and developed an idiosyncratic, but basically realistic situation: the repeated airplane flights, hotel-room stays, conference work, and personal encounters of a simultaneous translator. Even more than in the previous books, plot is extremely minimal. The book is more a cluster of repeated, slightly varied episodes and fragmentary conversations than a story line. One peculiarity of the book is Brooke-Rose's conscious use of an arbitrary restraint: she eliminated any use of the verb "to be." Replacing it is a concept of being in motion, marked by the copula-like preposition "Be-tween" that gives the novel its title. Accordingly, more central to the book's construction than identifiable narrative events or agents is a restless movement of "translation," the patterned conjunction of two or more idioms, discourses, or national languages at a point where they converge.

The story, such as it is, develops out of Brooke-Rose's elaboration of a central metaphor: the fornication of languages. Languages cross, clash, and intermingle in the narrative, reflecting her characters' swift movement through linguistic and geographical space: "In fondo a sinistra the men in the café sit transfixed by the flickering local variation in the presentation of opposite viewpoints on every aspect of an instant world through faceless men who have no doubt acquired faces for them as their arch-priests of actualitá that zooms flashcuts explodes to OMO! Da oggi con Perboral! Lava ancora più bianco! Gut-gut. Più bianco than what?" (*Between,* in *Omnibus,* pp. 418–419). The narrator slides across languages, as well as from discourse to meta-discourse ("Più bianco than what?"—More white than what?), in mimesis of the inner speech of a woman immersed in a veritable bath of words.

In other instances, Brooke-Rose repeats the same idea with linguistic variations. These iterated phrases usually refer to the anonymous, featureless spaces of transportation and lodging. While sometimes they simply suggest a frictionless passage across national and linguistic borders, the richest instances in the book underscore details from everyday life that encapsulate gender differences:

Higienska vreća za binde (Ulošci za dame). Molimo Vas ne bacajte ih u W.C. Sobarica će ih ukloniti zajedno sa vrećom. Sac pour bandes hygiéniques. Prière de ne pas jeter dans le W.C. La femme de chambre les enlèvera. Bag for sanitary pads. Please do not throw into W.C. The chambermaid will remove them. Hygienebeutel für Damenbinden. Bitte nicht ins Klosett werfen for one day the man will come and bring you out of this or that zone with a tremendous force and the intensity of a love lost or never gained . . .

(p. 415)

Collocating a series of phrases read off a hotel bathroom door and eschewing direct commentary, this passage effectively suggests a complex set of observations about language, society, and gender. Across the European continent and in each European language, it implies, the demands of "feminine hygiene" have generated a specialized product and an accompanying vocabulary. Just as menstruation once held the force of a mythical taboo, now, in contemporary Europe, it retains a trace of the implication of "pollution," which must be avoided through special measures. The "woman's curse" cuts across ideological lines, for it seems no less of a problem for communist Yugoslavia ("Higienska vreća za binde") than for capitalist Britain ("Bag for sanitary pads") or France ("Sac pour bandes hygiéniques"). Even hygienic removal of the remnants of this pollution is fraught with danger, for the "bandes hygiéniques" might clog the toilet, unleashing a filthy torrent of urine and excrement onto the sanitized WC floor. The soiled pads cannot be disposed of by ordinary means but must be removed by another woman, whose specially designated task this is. Finally, this removal of the unsanitary reminders of women's physiological specificity segues directly into romantic fantasy, with the passionate man carrying away the lonely woman who menstruates disconsolately in some foreign hotel, saving her at last from her joyless life of work, travel, and solitude. Through such scenes in *Between*, Brooke-Rose takes up the intertwining of gender difference and language in concrete situations. While she engages in little explicit feminist commentary, these passages nonetheless suggest Brooke-Rose's inflection of the issue of women's writing. Far from being excluded from discourse, she implies, women have been obsessively included, written and overwritten, and most often by men. The problem that faces the woman writer is how to relate to this plethora of language about women, how to negotiate a conscious position in its midst, how to detect and resist its truisms and hidden dogmas.

Thru, published in 1975 after a long hiatus and difficulties with publishers and typesetters, represents an extreme in Brooke-Rose's experimental writing. It is a relentlessly self-deconstructing novel, in which no character is allowed to retain its illusory anthropomorphism as a "fictional person." In an interview with David Hayman and Keith Cohen contemporaneous with the writing of *Thru*, Brooke-Rose carefully distinguished between her self-conscious aim in this novel and the aim of metafiction. Her novel, she claims, unlike metafiction, is not about the process of writing; it is about the fictionality of fiction itself. In other words, she is not interested in asserting the virtuoso role of the author, but rather the inescapably textual and intertextual nature of her characters and events. Not even authorship offers a place outside the text, since she includes characters who claim to be the authors of the text but repeatedly turn out to be fictional inventions of still other characters. At points, she implies that a creative writing class is writing, collectively or in parallel assignments, the texts that we are reading. The class engages ostentatiously in meta-discourse, commentary about the plausibility of characters or the felicity of expression in given passages, thus further implying its

existence above the level of the anecdotes and episodes that appear. But in turn, the creative writing class, including its commentaries and critical discussions, is shown to be a fictional invention of other characters. Brooke-Rose flattens to a single dimension the metaphorical hierarchy that relates different types of diction and address as a set of narrative planes, rising from character to observing character to explicit narrator to implicit narrator to implied author to real author. Through playful reversals, transgressive leaps across registers, intermingling dictions, and willful alterations of structure, she reveals how images of voice, person, and point of view emerge out of specific and highly contingent practices of language.

Thru is also singular in Brooke-Rose's corpus for its ambitious, if humorous, attempt to incorporate critical discourse and concepts into a work of fiction. Not only are diverse aspects of fiction reduced to the same level and allowed to interfere with one another, but fictional and theoretical discourses are also treated as equivalents, adding a further complexity to the interference patterns that result from the mélange. Thus, for example, Brooke-Rose engages in typographical play, spelling out crisscrossed, ideogramic phrases of indeterminate meaning:

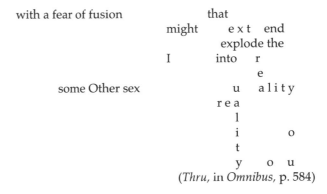

(*Thru*, in *Omnibus*, p. 584)

In this passage, Brooke-Rose dramatizes a theoretical discussion about sexual difference, which is centered on the danger that the sexual Other poses for the isolated, individual ego. In the play of letters within the horizontal and vertical dimensions of the page, Brooke-Rose creates a textual emblem of a new relation to an Other. Where the single "I" yields to a plural "you," and where the "you" itself is not closed up, another reality and another sexuality become possible.

Theoretical notions, typographically enacted on

the page, in turn become generative kernels for new narrative episodes, spun out in the prose passages that follow. This narrative embodiment of theoretical notions is the precise corollary of Brooke-Rose's translation of characters and events back into pedagogical demonstrations of narrative structure, intertextual allusion, and metaphor. At the end of the novel, theorists, characters, source authors, figures of popular culture, and abstractions all receive grades, marked on a register by a Greek letter, as they would be on a European university transcript. In Brooke-Rose's fictional roster, however, the grades are assigned not for academic performance, but for the named figure's "degree of presence" in her text. George Bataille, Karl Marx, the mistress of the moment, the Student Body, and Thanatos lead the class with A+ grades; Snoopy gets an A; musicians Joan Baez and John Cage earn a respectable A–; the radical French theorists Julia Kristeva, Roland Barthes, and Gilles Deleuze weigh in with a B+, while the philosopher Jacques Derrida earns a merely adequate B.

LATER FICTION: THE INTERCOM QUARTET

FOR NINE YEARS following the publication of *Thru*, Brooke-Rose published no novels, although this period was fruitful for her critical writing and teaching. Her intensive engagement with theory and her growing awareness of the constructed nature of fiction—that self-reflexive impulse that so powerfully characterizes *Thru*—seem to have been key factors in the long pause. As she remarks in "Stories, Theories and Things," largely a meditation on her own development as a writer, "The intensity of super-consciousness guides my pen and also paralyses it. Theory has released an immense hidden strength in me, but it has also made writing more and more difficult, because more and more demanding" (p. 13). When she returned to writing novels in the late 1970s after a long gathering of forces, her work revealed previously untapped powers. Between 1984 and 1991, she brought out a remarkable quartet of interlinked novels often referred to as "The Intercom Quartet": *Amalgamemnon, Xorander, Verbivore,* and *Textermination.*

Amalgamemnon overlays the situation of a soon-to-be "redundant" humanities professor, Mira Enketei ("inside the whale"), with that of the clas-

sical prophetess-in-vain Cassandra. Brooke-Rose engages the issue of prophecy at the level of grammar by not using the present tense in the book; every sentence is cast as a projection of something that might transpire sooner or later. She weaves together her contemporary projections and prophecies with extensive borrowings from Herodotus, playing off the protohistorical status of the ancient text with the free-floating, post-historical situation of her own; the mythical geography of Herodotus' ancient world passes unmediatedly into the global flux of postmodern space. Similarly, counterpointing references to the Iranian situation of the early 1980s, the revolutionary upheavals following the overthrow of the Shah, are events and personages from ancient Persia.

The biblical reference to the Book of Jonah implied by the female protagonist's name provides a further layer of intertextuality. Jonah's story, like Cassandra's, reveals the limits of the role of prophet. The Book of Jonah, in fact, is severely satirical in tone. After his self-serving psalm from the fish's belly, Jonah is vomited out and dispatched by God to the people of Nineveh to warn them of God's anger at their iniquities. But when the people of Nineveh are penitent and God tempers his justice with mercy, Jonah becomes petulant and complains to God that he should have made good on his word to raze the city. The book ends with his getting a solid dressing-down by God, which puts a seal on this story of ineffectual prophecy and ethnic intolerance. These ancient problems resonate across the ages within the postmodern cosmos of Mira, giving ironic purchase to her future-tense, hypothetical narration. The allusion is further thickened by the implicit reference to George Orwell's essay "Inside the Whale," which somewhat unwittingly suggests the special status of the woman experimental writer in a politically riven world. Orwell derives his title from Henry Miller's description of Anaïs Nin's diaries, which Miller said were written as if Nin were Jonah in the whale's belly. Orwell elaborates the image in terms of pregnancy and intrauterine life: "The whale's belly is simply a womb big enough for an adult. There you are, in the dark, cushioned space that exactly fits you, with yards of blubber between yourself and reality, able to keep up an attitude of the completest indifference, no matter *what* happens. . . . Short of being dead, it is the final, unsurpassable stage of irresponsibility" (p. 244). Yet Orwell quickly loses track of the gendered specificity of his metaphor and its application to Nin and instead uses it to characterize Miller's writing. In Miller's early works he perceived a new mode of writing, a writing from "the belly of the whale." A writer like Miller, says Orwell, while not necessarily introverted like Nin, willingly eschews the demand for commitment, political relevance, and effectiveness, allowing himself "to be swallowed, remaining passive, *accepting*" (Orwell, p. 245). In her overt reference to Orwell's essay, Brooke-Rose restores the whale metaphor to the *female* writer, Mira Enketei, and by implication, to the displaced Nin as well. At the same time, however, she implicitly accepts Orwell's view that this sort of writing will relate to the political world in oblique and apparently fatalistic ways.

Xorandor gives a child's-eye view of an encounter with a talking rock, which turns out to be a computer-like, silicon-based life-form that feeds on radiation from nuclear waste and has extraordinary powers to think, communicate, learn, and replicate itself. The novel is constructed out of several types of technologically inflected speech: the peculiar computer-whiz-kid jargon used by the twin children who are joint narrators and protagonists; the programming protocols by which they converse with the silicon creature Xorandor; and the transcripts of the conversations they secretly intercept and record. Several literary genres jostle for dominance in the novel. At one level, the novel is a political satire. The nations of the world at first welcome the presence of these rock-like creatures as a panacea to the problem of nuclear waste and see in them new license for limitless exploitation of the world's resources. But later, it is discovered that Xorandor and his offspring can just as happily suck the radiation out of nuclear warheads as from the less tasty nuclear wastes. To guard against the loss of nuclear deterrence, the world powers agree to send Xorandor and all his known replications to Mars on a space probe, where they will die for lack of radiation on which to feed. But Xorandor has actually arranged his deportation from Earth as a diversion for others of his offspring, which the twins on his request, have hidden away. While Xorandor and some of his family will perish, the hidden ones will live and reproduce undisturbed by humans. Interwoven with this politically charged satire is a kind of bildungsroman. For Xorandor must learn human speech and syntax, and his sophistication increases steadily over the course of the novel. Yet the whole pretext of education, and hence the bildungsroman model, is exploded at the end of the novel, when the twins discover that Xorandor has been merely mimicking what he thought they expected of him; from the very start, he has had a perfect command of their language and many others, having monitored for decades the radio transmissions of the world. There is also a witty thriller plot that allows Brooke-Rose to play with popular genre expectations. A syntax error in replication has caused one of Xorandor's children to go mad and take over a nuclear power plant, threatening to blow it up unless a series of demands are met; if the nuclear power station blows, it will set off the automatic sensors on the missile systems of the world, thus launching World War III. Finally, in a children's adventure-novel climax, managed by Brooke-Rose with suspenseful dexterity and winking self-consciousness, the resourceful twins manage to penetrate the depths of the mad bomber's programming, talk to it "child to child," and convince the frightened young creature to leave the power station and humanity unharmed.

Verbivore follows up the events in *Xorandor* two decades later. It tells how the hidden offspring of Xorandor provoke a global crisis by shutting down radio, telephone, and computer transmission, the signals of which have disturbed the creatures through their idiotic repetitiveness and redundancy. In the reportage that follows, the creatures come to be known as "Verbivores" or "Logfags" (short for Logophagoi, word eaters). Jip (James), the male twin, now works for NASA in the United States, while the female twin, Zab (Isabel), is a delegate to the European parliament and lives in Aachen. They reunite to help solve the shutdown of radio, telephone, and computer transmissions, which has made air travel impossible, silenced the airwaves, and disrupted the communications networks on which international business depends. Two characters in particular are affected: Mira Enketei, familiar from *Amalgamemnon* and now a producer of highbrow radio programs; and the playwright Perry Hupsos, whose name plays off the title of Longinus' treatise on the sublime and who gets stranded in Russia on a literary tour. Brooke-Rose's verbivoric premise satirizes the one-sided, celebratory rhetoric with which new technological developments like the Internet are introduced, and she suggests how vulnerable a technologically integrated planet might be to unexpected events or accidents. At the same time, in the misfortunes of her metafictionally bookish characters, she allegorizes the mass media's displacement of writing and reading as the primary means by which culture is disseminated. As in *Amalgamemnon*, where she is a humanities professor in a world interested only in the sciences, in *Verbivore* poor Mira is once again rendered "redundant," as a radio producer in a world without radio waves. Perry Hupsos, touring Russia on the royalties of his poetry sales there, finds his travel ground to a halt. It takes months for him to get home, most of which time he is forced to spend in his hotel. Yet despite the grave crisis, the inhabitants of Brooke-Rose's future world are unable to shake off their addiction to transmitted signals. In the temporary reprieve the Verbivores grant them from the electromagnetic blackout, the world's nations fail to take decisive measures and resume their boundless excretion of images and messages. The novel ends with a television screen going blank, the Verbivores having apparently started their word-eating anew.

Textermination gathers together characters from myriad novels, epics, and romances, including Brooke-Rose's own works, for an annual conference in San Francisco (suspiciously resembling the 1987 Modern Language Association conference in that city, which Brooke-Rose attended). The planned events include readings of papers about the characters, which they attend with interest and puzzlement, and a series of interdenominational pray-ins at which these characters entreat the godlike Reader to continue to read them, thus ensuring their existence. They are disturbed in their literary business by terrorists hunting for Salman Rushdie's Gibreel Farishta (from *The Satanic Verses*) and by a cast of television and film figures who want their piece of the action in a conference for fictional characters. Two characters, the literary scholar Kelly and the unredoubtable Mira Enketei, meet their deaths by discovering their names on a list of characters who have fallen out of the saving grasp of the canon, which would grant them the resuscitating force of being read from time to time. Several others narrowly escape a hotel fire in the Hilton, which recalls such famous literary book-burnings as those of Cervantes' *Don Quixote*, Ray Bradbury's *Fahrenheit 451*, Elias Canetti's *Die Blendung* (English title: *Auto-da-Fé*), and Umberto Eco's *The Name of the Rose*. Finally, a tremendous earthquake brings the burned-out Hilton crashing to the ground and splits off a long curved part of California, forming a new landmass surrounded by the sea. In the last chapter, many of the characters who had attended the conference carry on their fictional existence on the island, continuing the thoughts, actions, and reactions programmed into them by their authors.

The first two novels of the Intercom Quartet are not evidently related, except by general thematic concerns. But *Verbivore* begins to weave together characters and developments from both previous novels, and *Textermination* follows suit in drawing freely from the preceding work and even making occasional nods in the direction of Brooke-Rose's other writings. Brian McHale has suggested in *Constructing Postmodernism* (1992) that when *Amalgamemnon* is read in light of Brooke-Rose's earlier works, it seems to follow closely from *Between* and *Thru*, with which it shares concerns with the status of fictional entities and problems of gender and language. The novels that come after *Amalgamemnon*, however, cast a retrospective light on it, revealing a broad transition in Brooke-Rose's fiction toward new themes and techniques. In all four of these later novels, she interrogates the status of literature and of literary reading as cultural practices that came to life under particular conditions and may now be going the way of the buffalo, the Ford Model T, and the punched-card computer.

Once integral to education and cultural life, literature, Brooke-Rose suggests in these novels, is now endangered by a powerful quadrumvirate of forces: the mass media and popular culture; the ongoing industrialization of the mind through advertising and public relations; the unprecedented spread and global integration of information technologies; and the central role of physical and applied sciences in the power of present-day states. Both the novel and literary criticism were essential factors in the emergence of what the German sociologist Jürgen Habermas, in *The Structural Transformation of the Public Sphere* (1989), has called the "bourgeois public sphere": a space made up of informed individuals, capable of participating responsibly in public debate and in the democratic political process. Historically speaking, the "citizen" was a reader, and literature formed an essential part of that reading. Another central part of a citizen's reading was provided by the free press, which should offer accurate information and measured discussion to help the individual make up his or her own mind. Yet if literature and even literacy are now in eclipse, and if the image media provide not primarily information and opinion but sensation and spectacle, then where does that leave the citizen and the dream of democracy? In her fictional dramatizations of these questions, Brooke-Rose confronts political manifestations of the post-modern world: the staging of terrorist events as media spectacles, the political and ecological crises unleashed by "free" consumption, the authoritarian responses of states to these crises, the increasing paralysis of public thinking, the political application of science and technology, and the acquiescence of contemporary societies in a steady state of low-level, quotidian violence. Even where Brooke-Rose does not explicitly engage political themes, the parallel decline of literature and of public life forms a constant backdrop in these novels.

CRITICAL WRITINGS

BROOKE-ROSE PUBLISHED her first major critical study, *A Grammar of Metaphor*, in 1958. This work was written prior to her introduction to structuralism, yet it shares many of the presuppositions and analytic methods of that French critical movement that would later influence her so decisively. Above all, Brooke-Rose's early work and structuralist poetics share an orientation toward close linguistic investigation of literary texts and attempt to root "literary" (that is, figurative) effects in linguistic and formal structures. In *A Grammar of Metaphor*, Brooke-Rose investigates the grammatical structures of metaphors in English poetry. By focusing on grammar, she shifts the study of metaphor from its idea-content, which forms the object of most traditional discussions of this trope, to its form. She also describes the metaphorical form as "the mental process involved in calling one thing another" (p. 1). While she does not fully explain this move from the textual to the cognitive, its implications are nevertheless significant. For this same underlying assumption motivates much structuralist study: that the grammatical structures of representation (including the so-called grammar of narrative and myth) are ultimately the very structures of the mind itself. In the more specific area of literary criticism,

this assumption that grammar and mind converge allows narratology and structuralist poetics to be conceived essentially as a theory of *reading*. Practitioners of these methods ask such questions as: How does a reader put together lines of poetry to make a meaning? How does a reader translate the textual ordering of a narrative into the idea of time passing in a represented world? How do latent linguistic and formal features of a work affect the idea a reader comes to have of its meaning? Brooke-Rose was asking similar questions in her study of how metaphor is grammatically manifested in English poetry.

Brooke-Rose selects a sample group of texts by fifteen major poets, from Chaucer to Dylan Thomas, and searches for examples and variants of grammatical forms of metaphor. "Grammar" here means, simply, "parts of speech." She breaks down the body of metaphors into those rooted nouns, verbs, and other parts of speech. "My concern," she writes, "is with how the replacement or identification is made through words. There are considerable differences, both in intention and effect, between one type of grammatical link and another" (p. 24). These grammatical types then yield further subdivisions. For the noun metaphor, Brooke-Rose differentiates five subtypes: "simple replacement," which gives a new noun for an unmentioned "literal" one; (B instead of A); "the pointing formula," in which the literal term is first mentioned and then replaced by a metaphorical noun, which refers back to the first term (A, that is, B); the "copula" (A is B); the "link with To Make," in which the metaphor is brought about by a third party transforming the literal into something else (C makes A into B); and the "genitive" (the B of A, or the B of C implying A). For verbs, she distinguishes metaphors based on intransitive and transitive verbs, for the transitive verb's relation to its object can be manipulated for figurative effect.

This seemingly straightforward and empirically useful conception of grammar is, in fact, a shortcoming of the book, although undoubtedly the ideas about grammar she uses also informed the practice of the poets she discusses. Brooke-Rose's study predates Noam Chomsky's pathbreaking book *Syntactic Structures*, which appeared in 1957 but only began to affect literary analysis in the later 1960s. Chomsky hypothesized that the grammar of actual utterances drew from a relatively small number of universal elements that form the "deep structure" of language. In speaking, and thus transforming this deep structure into the surface grammar of language as it is actually used, we can form an infinite number of new sentences from very few basic elements. Chomsky and his followers clarified many confusions in traditional grammar, revealing that apparently similar "parts of speech" could have very different transformations and that apparently distinct surface structures could derive from the same set of transformations. Insofar as Brooke-Rose relies on a commonsense theory of grammar, some aspects of her analysis of metaphor, which are based on a theory definitively discredited by Chomsky, require revision and rethinking. Of course, one cannot fault her for not using a theory that had not yet made its impact even in the field of linguistics. As a demonstration of the sheer variety of ways in which English poetry has mobilized linguistic resources to make metaphor, Brooke-Rose's study remains impressive, and it presaged many of the insights of later poetics of metaphor informed by structuralist and Chomskyan theories of language.

A more serious objection to the enterprise can be raised, however, one that goes to the very heart of the book's guiding assumption. As her method of analyzing metaphors according to their parts of speech shows, Brooke-Rose assumes that grammar (linguistic structure) and rhetoric (figures of speech) coincide, in poetry at least. Yet several important thinkers and critics have emphasized the potential divergence between grammar and rhetoric. Kenneth Burke, for example, distinguishes between a "grammar of motives" and a "rhetoric of motives" on the grounds that the first is concerned with principles and positioning (that is, structure) and the latter with modes of address. Paul de Man, in his essay "Semiology and Rhetoric," argues that, though rhetoric and grammar are in no way mutually exclusive, they should also not be conflated. The grammaticality of a phrase, he suggests, often conceals its rhetorical duplicity, allowing the phrase to seem to represent as objectively true that which it merely asserts persuasively; such duplicitous claims to knowledge are, in de Man's view, endemic to literary criticism.

Still more to the point, because integral to Brooke-Rose's later criticism and fiction, are Mikhail Bakhtin's arguments against formalist poetics on the grounds that poetic structures are necessarily animated in multiple ways by their context. In Bakhtin's view, texts always respond to other voices in the surrounding context and thus must be understood as parts of a developing dialogue. Moreover, it is this "dialogic" reference of a text's words to other voices in the "ideological environment" that determines meanings in the text, not the grammar and form of the text as such. Texts remain "open" and productive of new interpretations precisely because grammar, which remains fixed in a work, does *not* constitute the limits of that work's meaning. In fact, Brooke-Rose's study might be seen to demonstrate this point, albeit unintentionally. Throughout the book, she regularly notes the sliding of one grammatical type into another, the masquerading of other tropes under the outward appearance of a grammatically identifiable metaphor and the compounding of different sorts of metaphor within a single grammatical manifestation. This slipperiness is a problem for the rigor of her analysis of metaphor; yet her later literary work profits precisely from the less definite boundaries implied by a "dialogic" conception of metaphor. Embedding one set of voices or registers of speech in another—for example, computer programming jargon in an adventure novel—can create metaphorical relations between humans and machines, suggest "characters" where no proper names or other character markers appear, and imply that narrated characters and events are metaphorical expressions of psychic processes of an explicit or even hidden narrator. Metaphor may insinuate itself into any kind of figuration, including those of intertextual allusion and of narration. As Brooke-Rose states in her 1976 interview with David Hayman, "Anything in fact is a metaphor, any replacement is a metaphor, any way of looking at something on a different level is metaphoric" (p. 7). For the metaphorical sense of a passage is a dialogic effect of context and of reading, not something that can be discerned autonomously in the structure of a text.

In the next phase of her scholarly writing, Brooke-Rose published two critical books on the modernist poet Ezra Pound, an introductory work for undergraduates and Pound novices, *A ZBC of Ezra Pound*, and a specialized study of Pound's Canto 45 (the "Usura Canto"), *A Structural Analysis of Pound's Usura Canto: Jakobson's Method Extended and Applied to Free Verse*. While in certain respects—for instance, her rather facile brush-off of Pound's fascism—more recent Pound criticism has made her *ZBC* seem dated, there is still much of value in the work. Two factors contribute to its usefulness. First, Brooke-Rose brings an extraordinary amount of specialized knowledge to her highly readable guide to Pound. Thus, for example, she offers a learned commentary on Pound's use of Anglo-Saxon alliteration in his free translation of "The Seafarer"; she goes on to assess how, despite awkwardnesses and outright screamers, this metrical and syntactical exercise contributed to the technical resources of Pound's *Cantos*. Second, she refers to a sophisticated range of theory, to concepts and figures largely unknown in U.S. and British universities in 1971. She discusses Pound's poetry, for example, in light of work by contemporary French theorists such as Jacques Lacan, Julia Kristeva, Jacques Derrida, Émile Benveniste, Tzvetan Todorov, and Henri Meschonnic, as well as that of literary innovators like Michel Butor, Alain Robbe-Grillet, and Denis Roche and of British philosophers like Karl Popper and J. L. Austin. By the time she was writing this book, Brooke-Rose was teaching at Paris VIII, a center for the new theory in the French university. Even before her entry into the French university, she seems to have followed the literary and theoretical writings of the *Tel Quel* circle, which included Philippe Sollers, Kristeva, Derrida, Roland Barthes, and a number of other key figures; significantly, Ezra Pound was one of the cultural heroes of this group.

Her second study of Pound, published five years later, took up a specific debate in the semiotics and linguistics of poetry. In the wake of a group of articles on poetry by the linguist Roman Jakobson, in which he made very detailed analyses of sound structure, syntax, and other linguistic features, several criticisms of his methods were advanced by Michael Riffaterre, Julia Kristeva, Paul de Man, and others. These boiled down to three main points: Jakobson's analyses depended on the dubious idea that literary and nonliterary texts could be distinguished by the deviance of literary language from the background norm of everyday language; his analyses fail to account sufficiently for the role of the reader; and he failed to explain adequately how different aspects of language, for instance its sound form and syntactic structure, which have distinct properties and laws, are related. Brooke-Rose discusses in detail one specific form of the second objection, raised in an especially trenchant critique by Michael Riffaterre of Jakobson's and Claude Lévi-

Strauss's 1962 structural analysis of Baudelaire's poem "Les Chats." Riffaterre had argued, against Jakobson and Lévi-Strauss, that many of the linguistic features that they had identified and analyzed were irrelevant to the sense of the poem, since they were not perceptible to any other reader but a linguistic analyst. Brooke-Rose, however, rejoins that Riffaterre's appeal to "perceptibility" begs the question, since one cannot clearly separate what is perceptible from the interpretation a reader gives of the poem. To put it simply, a "thicker" reading will almost surely bring more linguistic elements to a reader's attention, thus making perceptible what might be hidden to other readers. Perceptibility thus offers no firm ground from which to criticize a linguistic analysis that brings to evidence latent or subliminal patterns of language. She also suggests that the poem has a material presence—a physical pattern on the page, for example—that affects a reader's interpretation of the work, bringing some connections or resonances into focus while occulting others. Like de Man, who in his essay "Hypogram and Inscription" also criticized Riffaterre's insistence that only "meaningful" linguistic features of poetry were pertinent to reading, Brooke-Rose underscores how apparently insignificant material aspects of the poem help shape the reader's judgments about what is, indeed, meaningful. Pound's Canto 45 serves Brooke-Rose as her test poem, and the majority of the book is taken up with very close structural analysis of formal, thematic, prosodic, and phonic features.

Brooke-Rose's best-known critical study, *A Rhetoric of the Unreal,* is a collection of related essays on fantastic and other antirealist elements in nineteenth- and twentieth-century narratives and on critical theories of the unreal in fiction. Early in the book, she offers an important critique and revision of Todorov's influential theory of the fantastic. Todorov defines the fantastic as a sustained irresolution between an uncanny but natural explanation for a happening and a supernatural explanation for it. He insists that this irresolution must remain at the end of the story, rather than tip over into one or the other. Yet Todorov can find few examples of the purely fantastic, while many important texts, including those of Franz Kafka and Gogol, resist categorization along the lines Todorov develops. Brooke-Rose, however, sees the essential element in Todorov's theory of the fantastic as ambiguity and suggests extending the concept to non-fantastic, but ambiguous, texts, which could be thought of as displaced versions of the fantastic. She goes on to suggest that the multileveled meanings found in medieval allegory bear a close relation to the fantastic, arguing that the fantastic should be conceived within a broader historical perspective than Todorov's largely nineteenth-century focus. The middle section of her book has a four-chapter tour-de-force reading of that textbook case of Todorov's pure fantastic, Henry James's *The Turn of the Screw*. After a devastating exposition of the follies, fabulations, and out-and-out falsities critics have produced in the face of James's duplicitous novella, Brooke-Rose provides two closely argued chapters exposing the structures that suspend James's unhappy tale between two mutually exclusive explanations. She devotes the latter part of the book to different facets of postmodernist antirealism. These chapters include an astringent criticism of J. R. R. Tolkien's *The Lord of the Rings*, an appreciative discussion of the "new science fiction" of Kurt Vonnegut and Joseph McElroy, an analysis of Robbe-Grillet's *In the Labyrinth*, and three concluding chapters on other aspects of postmodernist fiction. Perhaps most striking here is her tart dismissal of most of Thomas Pynchon's work, including the much-revered *Gravity's Rainbow*. Both *V.* and *Gravity's Rainbow*, in her view, fail in their satirical aim, for their satire too often collapses back into realistic depiction of the ostensive object of its satire. Their failure is at once thematic and formal-stylistic.

Her essay collection *Stories, Theories and Things* takes up this argument where *A Rhetoric of the Unreal* had left off a decade earlier, now finding a more positive tendency in postmodernist writing to counterpose to the American postmodernists whom she had earlier found wanting. In the title essay, she calls this tendency "palimpsest history." This term designates for her capacious, often encyclopedic novels that incorporate historical and other specialized knowledge and subject this factual material to unconventional narrative techniques, juxtapositions, stylizations, distortions, admixtures with fictions, or other estranging formal processes. She includes under this aegis a broad and diverse selection of work ranging from John Barth's *The Sot-Weed Factor* and Gabriel García Márquez' *One Hundred Years of Solitude* to later works, including, suprisingly, a reevaluated *Grav-*

ity's Rainbow, Robert Coover's *The Public Burning*, Umberto Eco's *The Name of the Rose* and *Foucault's Pendulum*, Carlos Fuentes' *Terra Nostra*, Salman Rushdie's *Shame* and *The Satanic Verses*, and Milorad Pavić's *Dictionary of the Khazars: A Lexicon Novel in 100,000 Words*. In her conclusion to "Illusions of Anti-Realism," and with examples such as these standing behind her words, Brooke-Rose entreats her fellow writers not to get stuck in the rut that some earlier postmodernist writing, especially in the United States, fell into:

[T]he "revolt" was not against "realism" but against the conventions of one historical type of realism called Realism and the no longer tenable presuppositions that went with it; . . . there are many more interesting things to write about than the writer's difficulties with representation; . . . there are many realisms available to the unavoidable representative nature of language. We can explore them in rich and varied ways, instead of constantly bashing at the fatigued conventions themselves, a bashing which is in danger of itself becoming a fatigued convention.

(pp. 221–222)

The other essays in the volume reveal Brooke-Rose's wide range of reference, skill as a reader of literature, and witty style as an essayist. Among the most striking are her autobiographical consideration of the relation of critical and fictional writing, the title essay "Stories, Theories and Things"; her essays on Hawthorne's "The Custom-House," Crane's *The Red Badge of Courage*, and Thomas Hardy's *Jude the Obscure*; and her meditations on issues of gender and writing in the last five essays of the book.

CONCLUSION

WITH HER MULTILINGUAL and transnational orientation, her experimental impulse, and her willingness to incorporate theory and specialized knowledge into her fiction, Brooke-Rose occupies a singular position in contemporary British writing. She has absorbed the lessons of avant-garde tendencies in Anglo-American and French writing, from the modernist classics of Ezra Pound and Samuel Beckett to the new novel of Alain Robbe-Grillet, the new new novel of Philippe Sollers, and the typographical experiments of Maurice Roche. Yet this openness to a wide range of innovative writing has allowed her too often to be dismissed by British critics as an epigone and wild Gallic oddity. At the same time, her use of English as her primary literary language—in distinction, for instance, to Beckett's unusual bilingualism—has kept her from finding a suitable context in French literary movements. Her relation to feminism has been similarly ambiguous; in her suspicion of ideological dogma, she has remained positioned "between" the male-dominated literary tendencies that she respects and admires and the compelling criticisms of sexism that feminist intellectuals have advanced. While she went to teach in Paris on the invitation of Hélène Cixous, she was, by her own admission, rather antifeminist at the time, and kept her distance from her French peer's attempt to define a specifically women's writing and thinking. Her presentation of gender deepened in her fiction and essays after *Between* and moved in the direction of an undogmatic feminism. Nevertheless, she retains an independent, at times even polemical stance toward academic feminist criticism.

Brooke-Rose is far from an easy author to read, but the effort one gives to reading her complex works—and perhaps even more importantly, to *rereading* them—is amply rewarded. Her writing, whatever her chosen genre and form, is consistently thoughtful, provocative, witty, and technically masterful. It calls forcefully for reflection on the very place and practice of reading in the contemporary world and, in so doing, heightens our sense of possibility in the idioms and forms of fiction as such. If until now her expatriation, attraction to French experimental fiction and theory, and resistance to easy pigeonholing have kept her work from being as widely appreciated as it should be, there should be no doubt that, in due time, Brooke-Rose will be recognized as one of the essential English-language writers of the end of the twentieth century.

SELECTED BIBLIOGRAPHY

I. COLLECTED WORKS. *The Christine Brooke-Rose Omnibus: Out, Such, Between, Thru* (Manchester, U.K., 1986).

II. LITERARY WORKS. *Gold: A Poem* (Aldington, U.K., 1955); *The Languages of Love* (London, 1957); *The Sycamore Tree* (London, 1958); *The Dear Deceit* (London, 1960); *The Middlemen: A Satire* (London, 1961); *Out* (London, 1964); *Such* (London, 1966); *Between* (London, 1968); *Go When You See the Green Man Walking* (London, 1970); *Thru* (London, 1975); *Amalgamemnon* (Manchester, U.K., 1984); *Xorandor* (Manchester, U.K., 1986); *Verbivore* (Manchester, U.K., 1990); *Textermination* (Manchester, U.K., 1991); *Remake* (Manchester, U.K., 1996).

III. LITERARY CRITICISM. *A Grammar of Metaphor* (London, 1958); "Metaphor in *Paradise Lost:* A Grammatical Analysis," in Ronald David Emma and John T. Shawcross, eds., *Language and Style in Milton* (New York, 1967); *A ZBC of Ezra Pound* (London, 1971); *A Structural Analysis of Pound's Usura Canto: Jakobson's Method Extended and Applied to Free Verse* (The Hague, 1976); *A Rhetoric of the Unreal: Studies in Narrative and Structure, Especially of the Fantastic* (Cambridge, 1981); *Stories, Theories and Things* (Cambridge, 1991).

IV. INTERVIEWS. David Hayman and Keith Cohen, "An Interview with Christine Brooke-Rose," in *Contemporary Literature* 17, no. 1 (1976); Ellen G. Friedman and Miriam Fuchs, "A Conversation with Christine Brooke-Rose," in *Review of Contemporary Fiction* 9, no. 3 (1989), repr. in Ellen G. Friedman and Richard Martin, *Utterly Other Discourse: The Texts of Christine Brooke-Rose* (Normal, Ill., 1995); Maria Del Sapio Garbero, "A Conversation with Christine Brooke-Rose," in Theo D'Haen and Hans Bertens, eds., *British Postmodern Fiction* (Atlanta, Ga., 1993); David Seed, "Christine Brooke-Rose Interviewed," in *Textual Practice* 7 (summer 1993).

V. CRITICAL STUDIES. Emma Kafalenos, "Textasy: Christine Brooke-Rose's *Thru*," in *International Fiction Review* 7, no. 1 (1980); Shlomith Rimmon-Kenan, "Ambiguity and Narrative Levels: Christine Brooke-Rose's *Thru*," in *Poetics Today* 3, no. 1 (1982); Robert L. Caserio, "Mobility and Masochism: Christine Brooke-Rose and J. G. Ballard," in *Novel* 21 (winter–spring 1988); Ellen G. Friedman, " 'Utterly Other Discourses': The Anticanon of Experimental Women Writers from Dorothy Richardson to Christine Brooke-Rose," in *Modern Fiction Studies* 34, no. 3 (1988); Jürgen Habermas, *The Structural Transformation of the Public Sphere* (Cambridge, Mass., 1989); Judy Little, "*Amalgamemnon* and the Politics of Narrative," in *Review of Contemporary Fiction* 9 (fall 1989); Maria Del Sapio Garbero, *L'Assenza e la voce: Scena e intreccio della scrittura in Christina Rossetti, May Sinclair e Christine Brooke-Rose* (Naples, 1991); Judy Little, "Humoring the Sentence: Women's Dialogic Comedy," in June Sochen, ed., *Women's Comic Visions* (Detroit, Mich., 1991); Brian McHale, *Constructing Postmodernism* (New York, 1992); Maria Del Sapio Garbero, "The Fictionality of Fiction: Christine Brooke-Rose's Sense of Absence," in Theo D'Haen and Hans Bertens, eds., *British Postmodern Fiction* (Atlanta, Ga., 1993); Sarah Birch, *Christine Brooke-Rose and Contemporary Fiction* (Oxford, U.K., 1994); Maria Del

Sapio Garbero, "Between the Frontiers: Polyglottism and Female Definitions of Self in Christine Brooke-Rose," in Theo D'Haen and Hans Bertens, eds., *Liminal Postmodernisms: The Postmodern, the (Post-)Colonial, and the (Post-)Feminist* (Atlanta, Ga., 1994); Ellen G. Friedman and Richard Martin, eds., *Utterly Other Discourse: The Texts of Christine Brooke-Rose* (Normal, Ill., 1995); Ursula K. Heise, "Effect Predicts Cause: Brooke-Rose's *Out*," in her *Chronoschisms: Time, Narrative, and Postmodernism* (New York, 1997).

VI. OTHER PERTINENT WORKS. Anonymous, *The Dark Side of the Moon* (London, 1946), with a preface by T. S. Eliot; George Orwell, "Inside the Whale," in his *A Collection of Essays* (San Diego, Calif., 1981); Jerzy Pietrkiewicz, *In the Scales of Fate: An Autobiography* (London, 1993).

ANITA BROOKNER

(1928–   )

Gita May

THERE IS A portrait of Anita Brookner by R. B. Kitaj, an American artist long settled in London, which is dated 1993 and titled *The Novelist (My Neighbor, Anita Brookner)*. It is a full-length rendering in oil, in bold yellows and blues, of the writer seen walking by herself in one of those charming Chelsea streets lined with small houses and trees. She is primly and sensibly dressed in an eminently English outfit consisting of a light gray pleated skirt, a white blouse, and a navy blue jacket; she is wearing black flat-heeled walking shoes and carrying a shoulder bag, and her luxuriant red hair is cut short at the nape of the neck. What is most remarkable and revealing about this portrait is that its subject is seen from the back, walking away from the onlooker, so that her face is not visible. In this enigmatic and somewhat disquieting representation, the artist has succeeded in capturing essential features of Brookner's persona: her near-obsessive need for privacy, her melancholy sense of loneliness, and her love for long solitary walks in her beloved London.

THEMES FROM LIFE

ANITA Brookner has always shunned playing any kind of public role, and in the few interviews she has granted she has consistently stressed the fact that, though born and educated in London, she has always felt like an outsider. She has attributed this persistent sense of alienation to her Polish-Jewish background, and to her upbringing as the only child of an emotionally fragile, mismatched couple.

Brookner's father, Newson Bruckner, was a Polish-born small businessman who changed his surname to Brookner because of the anti-German feeling prevalent in his adopted England following World War I. Her mother, Maude Schiska, born in England, gave up a professional career as a concert singer when she married. A beautiful woman, she was inclined to melancholy and depression, probably as a result of having made this sacrifice: "It was only in her singing that she showed passion," recalled her daughter, who also felt that it was her mother, rather than herself, who "should have been the liberated woman" in the family (quoted in Guppy, p. 149). Whenever her mother sang at home, her father would get upset, and young Anita would start to cry and be taken from the room by her nanny. One senses sadness as well as resentment in Brookner's recollections of her parents, with whom she obviously had a close but difficult relationship: "I felt that I had to protect them. Indeed that is what they expected. As a result I became an adult too soon and paradoxically never grew up" (Guppy, p. 149). One of the themes she would explore in her novels is the smothering, stultifying effect of family on women and on their attempts to achieve an independent status in society.

Born on 16 July 1928, Brookner experienced the typical loneliness of the only child, but found comfort and companionship in the world of books. In addition to her immediate family the London Brookners consisted of a fairly large and close-knit brood, including a grandmother who lived with her parents and a number of aunts, uncles, and cousins. The colorful members of this foreign-born clan must have fascinated the quietly observant child, and in almost all of Brookner's novels we encounter families with continental backgrounds as well as heroines who, despite their marked Englishness in dress, manners, and outlook, and the fact that they are attracted to solidly English, Protestant men, have a subtly exotic, mysterious quality about them.

Brookner was brought up Jewish, although she was never made to learn Hebrew because her family maintained that this strain, in addition to her schoolwork, would adversely affect her somewhat fragile health. Curiously enough, this Jewish family, which remained generally attached to its East European customs and traditions, showed no particular awareness of the Holocaust, and Brookner does not remember the subject ever being brought up by her parents (see Kenyon, 1989, p. 10). In her desire to find out more for herself about her Polish ancestry, Brookner made plans to visit Poland, but finally decided not to go because "for a Jew, Poland is not exactly the Promised Land. I would have liked to see my father's family summer house on the river. But I would never have found it" (Kenyon, 1989, p. 10).

Brookner grew up to be an unbeliever, though she has expressed regret at having no religious faith or close sense of identification with her ethnic heritage. At the same time, she has not quite succeeded in becoming assimilated to English manners and mores, of which she remains a critical observer: "Although I was born and raised here I have never been at home, completely. People say that I am always serious and depressing, but it seems to me that the English are *never* serious—they are flippant, complacent, ineffable, but never serious, which is sometimes maddening" (Guppy, p. 150). Paradoxically, Brookner has frequently been characterized as a distinctly English writer in the tradition of Jane Austen, Charles Dickens, and Henry James, especially in her preoccupation with social themes and psychological analysis and in her stylistic techniques.

Brookner's father, who never quite mastered the English language, was a passionate Anglophile who loved Dickens: "He thought Dickens gave a true picture of England, where right always triumphed" (Guppy, p. 149). He transmitted this love to his daughter, who, while continuing to read a Dickens novel every year, frequently refers to this author as well as to other beloved fiction writers as the creators of a falsely comforting, romantically idealized and escapist world. In her most famous novel, *Hotel du Lac* (1984), fiction is ironically defined as "the time-honoured resource of the ill-at-ease" (p. 66).[1] The disarmingly guileless and well-meaning heroine of *A Closed Eye*

(1991) is an avid reader of Dickens, a predilection she justifies in naively moral terms: "I always wanted to be good, believing that if one wished it so one could become perfect. Dickens himself wanted it to be true" (p. 71).

A pervading theme in Brookner's novels is that life is a vastly harsher and lonelier place than the orderly and comforting world of fiction, and it is evident that she includes herself among those dreamy, quixotic souls who have had to learn this lesson the hard way. She began with, on the one hand, too many Romantic expectations and illusions, and, on the other, too many Victorian restrictions. As she succinctly and ironically puts it, she started "on the wrong footing," and as a result "my own life was disappointing" (in Guppy, p. 152). As a young woman, Brookner was a dutiful daughter who for many years took care of her aging, emotionally volatile parents, devotedly nursing them through their illnesses until they died. Her relationship with her mother appears to have been a particularly frustrating one: "She wanted me to be another kind of person altogether. I should have *looked* different, should have been more popular, socially more graceful, one of those small, coy, kittenish women who get their way" (Kenyon, 1989, p. 9).

The painful, protracted years of caring for her parents left Brookner with a sense that she had been unfairly trapped by her Old World surroundings. Brookner's nineteenth-century worldview, steeped in the post-Romantic novelistic tradition, reinforced this impression. Life is unfair to some people, who are simply not born lucky, and in this scheme of things she was destined to be "a marginal person" (Kenyon, 1989, p. 12).

Added to that sense of marginality is the fact that Brookner never married or had children, thus further failing to live up to her parents' expectations and family traditions. Yet, as photographs and descriptions bear out, she is a good-looking woman, petite, slim, and dressed in elegantly muted outfits, her pale, oval face framed by reddish hair cut short but softened with bangs, her serious, intent expression enlivened by large, beautiful eyes and full, sensuous lips. Her markedly introverted temperament, coupled with her fierce love of personal independence and her dedication to such solitary activities as reading, scholarly research, and writing may explain, at least in large part, why she chose to remain single. Although she professes to

---

[1] Page references throughout the text are to the original American clothbound editions of the works.

enjoy the company of men, she is extremely discreet about her private life, and it has been intimated that, not unlike her lonely heroines, she has experienced at least one or two unhappy love affairs. She admits to having gone through a dark, trying period when she secretly envied married women with several children and in general "those who can take life a little more easily" (Kenyon, 1989, p. 9).

Writing novels would be part of a process of making sense of her life, of attempting to get closer to the truth, of peeling away the layers of self-deception, but without losing the ability to see through people's motivations with humor and compassion. That women are especially vulnerable to the Cinderella myth, the myth cleverly and successfully exploited by such authors of romance novels as Barbara Cartland, is one of Brookner's major themes. Her own heroines are frequently brought to the brink of personal disaster because of their childlike faith in Prince Charmings and happily-ever-after endings. Her main protagonists are loving, honest, sincere but unglamorous characters who almost succumb to the wily stratagems of naturally seductive, unscrupulous people endowed with Nietzschean drive.

It is through a slow, lonely, and frequently painful and humiliating process of self-discovery that a Brookner heroine will gain the necessary self-knowledge to survive and go on with life. In *Hotel du Lac*, Brookner exposes the falsehood of the Cinderella myth through the amorous disappointments of Edith Hope, a writer of romance fiction whose own experience forcefully and ironically belies her idealized depictions of the relations between men and women. One of the underlying themes in Brookner's novels is that loneliness is the lot of people with exacting ethical standards and moral rectitude; this idea reflects her own family values, which, as she ruefully admits, she was never able to unlearn (see Haffenden, p. 65).

In the late 1990s Brookner lived by herself in a small, bright apartment in Chelsea facing a large, quiet garden. She worked at home or in an office of the Courtauld Institute of Art in London, where she began lecturing in the history of art in 1964 and where she preferred to do her writing, even though she had given up teaching. Her interviewers describe her as soberly elegant and feminine looking, with an appealing vulnerability, refined manners, and a quiet reserve.

THE ART HISTORIAN

BY the time Brookner published her first work of fiction in 1981, she was fifty-three and had acquired an international reputation as an art historian and critic of the first magnitude. She was the author of several highly regarded books and was a regular contributor of articles and reviews on French writers and artists for such publications as the *Times Literary Supplement,* the *Observer,* the *Spectator, Burlington Magazine,* and the *London Review of Books.* She had also achieved distinction as a teacher. To give up security and prestige as a successful practitioner in her discipline and switch gears at that fairly late stage must have required a great deal of moral fortitude, for it was, as she put it, "a gamble," but she felt that she was drifting, unhappy and excluded, although she enjoyed teaching and loved her students (see Haffenden, p. 74).

As a young intellectual with a restlessly inquisitive mind and a longing to escape from her constricting social milieu, Brookner had thrown herself into her studies with passionate single-mindedness. Her subsequent career could be the envy of any young woman aspiring to academic distinction. After completing her secondary education at James Allen's Girls' School in Dulwich, she read French literature at King's College of the University of London from 1946 to 1949. She earned her Ph.D. in art history at the Courtauld Institute of Art in 1953 and was visiting lecturer in art history at the University of Reading from 1959 to 1964. In 1964, she was invited to join the faculty of the Courtauld Institute, first as a lecturer (1964–1977), then as a reader in the history of art (1977–1987). Her singular accomplishments as scholar and teacher in her field were acknowledged when she became a fellow of New Hall, Cambridge University, and achieved the distinction of being the first woman appointed Slade Professor of Art at Cambridge University in 1967–1986. She was also made a fellow of the Royal Society of Literature.

When asked why she initially chose to study the French language and literature and later to pursue her studies in art history in Paris on an individual research basis, she wryly replied that she always felt braver in another culture and language (see Kenyon, 1989, p. 10). In the 1960s and 1970s she spent considerable amounts of time researching at the Bibliothèque Nationale and visiting the art museums in Paris, a rather solitary and austere yet exhilarating experience reflected in that of Ruth Weiss, the heroine of her first novel, *The Debut* (1981). Brookner later reminisced about her first stays in the French capital, when she lived "happily" on £5 a week while writing her thesis on the eighteenth-century artist Jean-Baptiste Greuze: "I was liberated by poverty before I knew what the women's movement was all about" (quoted in Kenyon, 1989, p. 10).

Brookner's thesis on Greuze was published in 1972 as *Greuze: The Rise and Fall of an Eighteenth-Century Phenomenon.* It is a landmark study that reveals her special affinities with the aesthetic sensibilities of the eighteenth century, as do her books on the artists Jean-Antoine Watteau and Jacques-Louis David. Her first book, *Watteau* (1967), is indicative of the highly personal approach she would take as an art historian. While furnishing the most accurate data available on the artist's biography and career, the text seeks the key to a better understanding of Watteau's originality by focusing on the crucial role of the commedia dell'arte in his compositions and on his special appeal to the Romantics.

Brookner's reputation as an art historian, however, was established by her books on Greuze and especially on David, which have been hailed for their masterful scholarship, their sensitive probing of the relation of life and art, and their thoughtful explorations of a particularly complex and turbulent period in French history. In her quest for the mysterious sources of human creativity as well as in her gift for the apt, striking phrase and vivid image, we perceive the writer behind the scholar who is already at work, honing a personal vision and style.

The book on Greuze is the first modern, thoughtful, and fully documented study of this highly gifted but controversial painter, immensely admired in his own time and eventually disparaged for precisely the qualities that had made him so popular among his contemporaries. His most ardent and eloquent advocate was Denis Diderot, the French encyclopedist who founded art criticism as a literary genre in his influential salons. Greuze's gifts as a draftsman, portraitist, and genre painter were indeed exceptional, but it was as the painter of dramatically staged and didactic, slyly erotic compositions extolling family devotion, domesticity, and rural simplicity that he exemplified the sentimental self-indulgence of late Enlightenment

ideals and aspirations. Whether commenting on the melodramatic *Dying Paralytic,* the appealing *Village Betrothal,* or the virginally voluptuous *Girl Weeping for the Death of Her Canary,* Diderot was unstinting, indeed ecstatic, in his praise of Greuze, for here were paintings that, instead of celebrating the unbridled pleasures of the senses, sought to extol the simple manners and morals of the middle class and rural folk. Here family and bourgeois virtues were at last made compellingly affecting. With an exceptional historical and ideological understanding of the rich and frequently contradictory aesthetic currents emerging in the second half of the eighteenth century, Brookner traces and illuminates Greuze's career from his popular success in the mid-1750s and 1760s, when his scenes so successfully engaged a highly sophisticated public yearning for strong, unaffected emotions, to the eventual decline of his critical fortune.

The book on David is the first comprehensive study in English of the life and work of the great neoclassical painter, and it is generally viewed as the most authoritative critical biography of this frequently misunderstood artist. A thorough and painstaking analysis of David's life and oeuvre, Brookner's study untangles the many and frequently contradictory strands in eighteenth-century aesthetics and artistic trends, reassesses David's place and growth as an artist in the context of French and European politics, his powerful and controversial role during the Revolution, the Reign of Terror, and the Napoleonic era, and his final years of exile in Brussels during the Restoration. As Brookner forthrightly put it in the preface to *Jacques-Louis David: A Personal Interpretation* (1974), the book is meant to be "an apologia for a very great French artist who subsumed into his remarkable life many of the fundamental preoccupations of the eighteenth century in terms of thought, belief, and behaviour" (p. 12).

The Genius of the Future: Studies in French Art Criticism appeared in 1971 and examines the art criticism of such noted French writers as Diderot, Stendhal, Baudelaire, Zola, the Goncourt brothers, and Huysmans. Originally planned as a course in French art criticism to be given at the Courtauld Institute of Art, it presents the lectures Brookner gave as Slade Professor of Art at Cambridge. What all these nineteenth-century critics had in common was that, like Diderot, their eighteenth-century mentor and initiator, they were essentially men of letters whose writings on art were resolutely and boldly subjective and therefore exude "a peculiarly strong flavour of personality" which "is perhaps the most obvious link between them" (*The Genius of the Future*, p. 1).

The Genius of the Future is a work of sweep and scope as well as a deep and personal reflection on the role of art in modern society, and it offers a profoundly understanding and sympathetic assessment of writers who, despite the errors in artistic judgment they may have committed, at least in the light of current predilections and prejudices, continue to deserve our admiration. Brookner praises their passionate commitment to art as a positive force liberating the most creative human energies and impulses, even in a flawed and corrupt society. What also distinguishes *The Genius of the Future* is its readability. It is clearly not a book intended for the specialist, but rather for the discriminating lay reader.

NOVELISTIC BEGINNINGS: THE DEBUT

As an art historian Brookner had mastered certain skills necessary to the novelist's art, notably narrative and dramatic pacing, rhetorical and stylistic fluency, and convincing psychological analysis in characterization. In 1980 she decided that she would test her powers of invention by turning to fiction and probing themes with which she was intimately familiar: notably the loneliness and frustrations of accomplished but painfully self-aware, alienated, and marginalized individuals, especially women, their inner struggles to maintain a fragile emotional equilibrium, and their problematic relation to their family and social surroundings. Brookner's fiction evinces a decidedly subjective, feminine-oriented aesthetic which steers clear of explicit ideology and politics in order to explore the personal and specific, often with a strong autobiographical component. Her heroines, not unlike herself, have a European background, a heavy mix of melancholy and introspection, and do not quite succeed in assimilating themselves to the English way of life.

When asked what in 1980 motivated her to give up a distinguished and secure career as an art historian and teacher for the aleatory novelist's calling, Brookner's down-to-earth and deceptively simple explanation was that, faced with a long, empty summer vacation during which she was feeling particularly low in spirits, she decided that instead of wasting time feeling sorry for herself, she would try her hand at writing fiction, a literary genre from which she had always derived immense pleasure and spiritual enrichment. "I wondered—it just occurred to me to see whether I could do it," she told one interviewer. "I didn't think I could. I just wrote a page, the first page, and nobody seemed to think it was wrong. An angel with a flaming sword didn't appear and say, 'You shouldn't be doing this.' So I wrote another page, and another, and at the end of the summer, I had a story" (Smith, p. 67).

This is how her first novel, *The Debut* (first published in England in 1981 as *A Start in Life*, a title borrowed from a novel by Honoré de Balzac, *Un Début dans la vie*), took shape. In another interview Brookner concedes that *The Debut* is largely autobiographical and was written "in a moment of sadness and desperation" (Guppy, p. 150). The incipit is notable, for it introduces the heroine in these terms: "Dr. Weiss, at forty, knew that her life had been ruined by literature" (p. 7). Ruth Weiss is an academic, a literary scholar who has specialized in French literature and who has staked her career on a definitive study, *Women in Balzac's Novels*, of which one volume has already been published, with "discreet acclaim" (p. 8); two more volumes are in the works. Dr. Weiss even blames her looks on literature, for with her long red hair, delicate facial features, slim bone structure, and slightly dreamy expression, she made a virginal appearance "halfway between the nineteenth and twentieth centuries" (p. 8). Her German-Jewish father, George (born Georg) Weiss, is a rare-book dealer who "desperately assumed English nonchalance" (p. 12). Her mother, Helen, is a beautiful and high-spirited English actress once popular in light drawing-room comedies, whose childlike narcissism and progressive physical as well as spiritual decay is graphically yet sympathetically depicted in the novel. The Weisses live with the formidable paternal grandmother (after whom Ruth is named) who, to the relief of her self-preoccupied daughter-in-law and philandering son, has assumed the supervision of the household. As a child, Ruth "loved her parents passionately and knew them to be unsafe. Not threatened by the dangers that had threatened her grandmother, but unsafe against disappointment" (p. 16). It is in the somber apartment filled with her grandmother's massive, dark furniture brought from Berlin that Ruth grew up, her youthful imagination fired by the tragic stories of such flamboyantly Romantic heroines as Emma Bovary and Anna Karenina. Her personal favorite, however, is the repressed, spinsterish but stoically self-reliant Eugénie Grandet, the eponymous Balzac heroine.

After her grandmother's death, Ruth escapes from her stifling home and from the coarseness of Mrs. Cutler, the new housekeeper, to France, where she pursues her research on Balzac and where, in her loneliness, she becomes friendly with an attractive English couple, Hugh and Jill Dixon. She also strikes up a romantic relationship at the Bibliothèque Nationale with Professor Duplessis, only to find out that he is already married. The news of her father's stroke summons her back to England, and her by-now desperately ill mother, who had fled from the household upon finding out about her husband's extramarital liaison with a friend of the family, Sally Jacobs, suddenly dies in a taxi as Ruth takes her back home. Soon thereafter Ruth enters a loveless marriage of convenience with Roddy, the nephew of Sally Jacobs, primarily because of the sense of security she hopes this will bring her. After only six months, however, a car accident leaves her widowed. In due course, she sells her father's bookshop, settles down to live with her invalid father, assumes an assistant lectureship in French literature at London University, and resumes her project on Balzac.

One may safely surmise that Ruth Weiss has opted to retreat into a quiet, introspective world punctuated by safe personal routines and scholarly pursuits, for she has learned that "she was capable of being alone and doing her work" (p. 150). The concluding paragraph of the novel is a letter from Ruth to her editor reporting on the progress of her Balzac project, with the following postscript: "The section on Eugénie Grandet has turned out rather longer than expected. Do you think anyone will notice?" (p. 192). The parallel between the two female protagonists could not be more clearly stated, and intertextual similarities between *Eugénie Grandet* and *The Debut* are within a novelistic tradition generally characterized as the European *roman d'apprentissage* or bildungsroman, a genre that focuses on the torturous initiation into adulthood. In this novel, as in most of her

subsequent ones, Brookner depicts a female character who faces thorny situations and hard choices, but through this painful learning process gains a sobering, sometimes humiliating but necessary insight into her own character, motivations, and relations to others. This experience leaves her stronger, more knowledgeable about life, more self-reliant and independent-minded, but also irremediably lonely and alienated from the customary social and family ties that help to anchor an individual's sense of belonging and identity.

Skillfully and swiftly paced, and sharply focused on a sympathetic but also subtly ironic characterization of Ruth Weiss, *The Debut* sets the pattern for Brookner's subsequent novels in its deft use of small realistic touches, muted but highly suggestive references to urban landscapes and street scenes that serve as an appropriate backdrop and foil for the inner turmoil and quietly desperate isolation of the main protagonist. Brookner knows how to capture significant details of the daily rhythms of life in a great Western European metropolis (whether it be London or Paris), its great parks and major squares and arteries, its quiet neighborhoods and secluded and tranquil streets, as well as its changing moods and colors. Yet another noteworthy and frequently recurring motif is the special role accorded France, its idiosyncratic lifestyle and its rich cultural and literary heritage.

PROVIDENCE *AND* LOOK AT ME

Providence, Brookner's second novel, was published in 1982, a year after *The Debut* (Brookner has maintained this remarkably regular, yearly output throughout her career as a novelist). Kitty Maule, the heroine of *Providence*, feels herself to be very English, although her Englishness is belied by her background: she is the sole offspring of a British officer, John Maule, who died before she was born, and a Frenchwoman, Marie-Thérèse, "the eternal *pensionnaire*, homeloving, conventual, quiet, and obedient" (p. 6). Marie-Thérèse is herself of mixed parentage; her father is Vadim, a Russian acrobat, and her mother is Louise, a French seamstress. Vadim and Louise settled in London after their marriage and founded a successful couturier establishment on Grosvenor Street. The business managed to survive even after the advent of Christian Dior's "New Look," for Louise went on "producing the crinoline ball dresses for which she became famous in the 1950s" and which the debutantes continued to favor (p. 11). The aging couple take into their loving care their daughter and granddaughter after the untimely death of their son-in-law. But the situation is an anomalous one, fraught with tension, primarily because "to Kitty, who loved England as only one who is not wholly English can do, Louise and Vadim and Marie-Thérèse were almost an embarrassment" (p. 12). After Marie-Thérèse's death, "quickly and quietly one evening at the dinner table" (p. 15), the old couple sink into genteel senescence.

Like Ruth Weiss, Kitty Maule is an academic with a specialization in French literature. Her favorite novel, which she teaches in seminar at a small British college where she holds an untenured appointment, is Benjamin Constant's *Adolphe*, the famous semiautobiographical story of the author's stormy relationship with Germaine de Staël: "To Kitty's resolutely professional eye, *Adolphe* was mainly interesting for its conjunction of eighteenth-century classicism and Romantic melancholy" (p. 41). But she could not overlook its more covert message: "that a man gets tired of a woman if she sacrifices everything for him" even if he "will be poisoned by remorse for the rest of his life" (p. 41). Indeed, the French Romantics are Kitty Maule's major literary interest, even her personal obsession; she keeps mulling over how, having weathered their spectacularly stormy, defiant, and rebellious youths, these writers dealt with the far more insidious ravages of time and less glamorous struggles and frustrations of later life: "They were an impressive but disheartening lot, she always thought, coming so rapidly to maturity, haggard with experience by the age of twenty-five, and somehow surviving their own disastrous youth into a normal life-span. Even an abnormal one: look at Victor Hugo. Except, of course, Gérard de Nerval. He was central to her thesis, for he did not survive" (p. 33). In fact, Kitty's first test as a scholar, on which will hinge a permanent appointment to the faculty, is a public lecture she is invited to give on the Romantic tradition.

Also like Ruth Weiss, Kitty Maule falls in love with an academic, in this instance the handsome Maurice Bishop, an art historian with a specialization in Gothic architecture, an impeccable upper-class English pedigree, a titled mother and country manor in Gloucestershire, an independent source of income, and a manner that women find especially irresistible. She adoringly and longingly observes him at faculty meetings, but her brief, surreptitious, and physically chaste relationship with him is doomed to failure, for they are too different in outlook (he, for instance, is a devout Christian and she an unbeliever), and, far more importantly, her love for him is not reciprocated. Maurice is appointed to a prestigious professorship at Oxford University and marries the beautiful, Pre-Raphaelite-looking Jane Fairchild, whose family belongs to the same social circle as his own. An added irony is that Jane Fairchild, one of Kitty's students, had always struck her as hopelessly fey and helpless, as well as intellectually confused and inept, a circumstance that underscores a recurring Brookner leitmotiv: that beautiful people are dispensed from exerting themselves in trying to accomplish anything, that indeed they are not even expected to follow the accepted rules of behavior.

In *Look at Me*, Brookner's third novel (1983), the heroine, Frances Hinton, works as a reference librarian in a medical research institute dedicated to the study of abnormal behavior. As Frances notes, with a mixture of pride and ingenuousness: "Problems of human behaviour still continue to baffle us, but at least in the Library we have them properly filed" (p. 5). She is in charge of pictorial material—more precisely, of photographs of works of art and prints depicting mental derangement and disease through the ages, "as quite a few artists have a close understanding of this sad condition" (p. 7). Thus she can summon from her rich archives Albrecht Dürer for the problem of depression or melancholy, as it was commonly referred to in the artist's time, portrayed in the guise of a moon-struck woman; popular English "humorous" prints depicting lunatics; Géricault for a sympathetic treatment of the mad as creatures of dignity; and Goya for horrendous pictures of figures slipping away from the human condition to assume the shape of nightmarish monsters.

Like most Brookner heroines, Frances Hinton is a lone figure who leads a quiet, tidy existence, without undue expectations. She is an only child who has recently lost her mother and who lives in a large London apartment with Nancy, an old Irish housekeeper. She also keeps a diary in which she records the daily events in her life, as well as the doings of such regulars at the library as Mrs. Halloran, the bibulous astrologer, and Dr. Simek, a shy, reticent man of Polish or Czech background, for, as Frances notes, "You get a lot of borderline cases in libraries" (p. 10). As John Russell aptly put it in his book *London* (1994), describing the special quality of certain London neighborhoods and houses, Frances' situation epitomizes "the notion set out in more than one of Anita Brookner's novels—that there need be nothing second-rate about living by oneself" (p. 77). Yet Frances secretly yearns for a more exciting life:

Sometimes I wish it were different. I wish I were beautiful and lazy and spoiled and not to be trusted. I wish, in short, that I had it easier. Sometimes I find myself lying awake in bed, after one of these silent evenings, wondering if this is to be my lot, if this solitude is to last for the rest of my days. Such thoughts sweep me to the edge of panic. For I want more, and I even think that I deserve it. I have something to offer. I am no beauty but I am quite pleasant-looking.

(p. 19)

No wonder, therefore, that she should fall under the spell of a glamorous couple, Nick and Alix Fraser, who seem to vindicate the theory of natural selection, for in their persons "the fittest had very clearly survived," leaving ordinary people like herself to founder in deserved obscurity and anonymity (p. 37). She furthermore feels an irresistible romantic attraction for the handsome James Anstey, who also works in the library but who had remained aloof and distant until being introduced to her by the Frasers. Frances' relationship with the Frasers, as well as with James Anstey, turns out to be short-lived. The Frasers soon lose interest in her and Anstey repulses her timid advances.

Look at Me has the distinguishing feature of being narrated in the first person by Frances Hinton, the central protagonist and diarist, thus providing a personal, intimate, self-conscious, immediate, and confessional quality to the novel, reminiscent of some of the French works of autobiographical fiction that Brookner especially admired, from Benjamin Constant's *Adolphe* to Marcel Proust's *À la recherche du temps perdu*. Indeed, *Look at Me* ends on a strikingly Proustian note, for Frances, who had set aside her diary when she became involved with the Frasers and Anstey, returns to authorial activity after her disillusioning experience, but this time in the more ambitious guise of a novelist. "I pick up my pen. I start writing," she asserts (p. 192).

HOTEL DU LAC *AND* FAMILY AND FRIENDS

THE heroine as writer and self-conscious narrator, inscribing her own experience into the plot that she narrates, is the main theme of Brookner's fourth, best known, and most successful novel, *Hotel du Lac*, which won England's prestigious Booker Prize. In 1985 this work was adapted for television with a noteworthy film by the BBC.

Edith Hope, a single, thirty-nine-year-old writer of popular romantic fiction under the pen name of Vanessa Wilde, is the main protagonist of *Hotel du Lac*. The daughter of an English professor, who died when she was very young, and an Austrian mother, she looks and acts quintessentially English, dresses accordingly, and bears, we are told, a striking resemblance to Virginia Woolf: a number of people, including Harold Webb, her literary agent, are struck by her Bloomsburian looks. Despite her solid appearance and manner, however, Edith feels generally insecure about her identity. Her sense of alienation deepens as she finds herself in secret exile at a quiet hotel on Lake Geneva during the off-season. She is there in order to recover from what her friends consider a scandalous lapse in correct behavior. By an unpredictable act, most of all to herself, she has at the last moment bolted from intended marriage to the proper if rather colorless Geoffrey Long, by leaving him stranded on the steps of the registry office. For years Edith has allowed herself to be the devoted, discreet, and self-effacing mistress of a married man with children, the handsome and socially well-connected art dealer David Simmonds. The marriage to Geoffrey Long would have been a way out of a hopeless and frustrating emotional situation and given her the kind of social status she envies in women who have achieved it.

Her recent personal experience heightens Edith Hope's ambivalence about the message her own novels convey to women and her suspicion that her romances perpetuate a comforting but misleading myth, the one illustrated by Aesop's fable of the tortoise and the hare. As she ruefully confides to her literary agent:

Now you will notice, Harold, that in my books it is the mouse-like unassuming girl who gets the hero, while the scornful temptress with whom he has had a stormy affair retreats baffled from the fray, never to return. The tortoise wins every time. This is a lie, of course. . . . In real life . . . it is the hare who wins. Every time. Look around you. And in any case it is my contention that Aesop was writing for the tortoise market. . . . Hares have no time to read. They are too busy winning the game. The propaganda goes all the other way, but only because it is the tortoise who is in need of consolation. Like the meek who are going to inherit the earth.

(pp. 27–28)

During this one-month hiatus, Edith tries to recover from her recent emotional turmoil by working on her next novel (to be titled *Beneath the Visiting Moon*), by writing letters to David Simmonds, and by taking an interest in the other guests at the hotel, who happen to be mainly idle, aimless women: Iris Pusey, the elegant, well-preserved rich widow whose main passion is shopping for clothes; her sexually alluring, physically overendowed unmarried daughter Jennifer; the tall, anorexic Monica, who travels with a perpetually misbehaving lapdog named Kiki and who has been unsuccessful in giving an heir to her husband, apparently a member of the English ruling class; the senile Comtesse de Bonneuil, dumped at the hotel by her son and daughter-in-law. At the hotel Edith also meets the unattached, attractive fellow guest Philip Neville, who, as the owner of an electronics firm, is attending a conference in nearby Geneva. They strike up a friendship, take long walks together, and the hardheaded Neville is soon sufficiently won over by Edith's subdued, elegant charm and quiet ways to propose marriage to her as a kind of partnership, for he has a fine estate and thriving business and needs a proper mistress of the house and hostess. Edith decides to accept the offer and has even written a goodbye letter to her lover David Simmonds when she accidentally catches sight of Neville in his dressing gown stealthily emerging from Jennifer Pusey's room. This discovery prompts her to tear up her farewell letter to Simmonds, leave the hotel, and take the next flight to London. She has come to a last-minute realization that loneliness and uncertainty are preferable to a life of false security, dependence, and deception. This constitutes the first resolute and affirmative willingness of a Brookner heroine to assume full responsibility for her destiny.

Hotel du Lac combines a highly successful mix of novelistic techniques. A third-person narrator provides the objective framework for interior monologues subtly and sensitively delineating Edith's changing moods and states of consciousness, for evocative descriptions of the hotel and its picturesque surroundings, for satirical yet sympathetic depictions of wealthy Englishwomen whiling away time on the Continent, and for dialogues tinged with acerbic wit and humor. Narrative time is effectively handled to heighten interest, suspense, and drama by the use of flashbacks. Among the novel's most distinctive features are the heroine's successive, tentative probings in order to gain a clearer insight not only into her own motivations but also into those of the people surrounding her, as well as her dual role as writer and main protagonist.

Brookner's fifth novel, *Family and Friends* (1985), differs from the previous four in that it is not sharply focused on a single protagonist. Essentially a family chronicle, it resorts to word pictures: its successive episodes, recounted in an informal, conversational first-person narrative, frequently highlighted by flashes of wit and humor, are structured around wedding photographs, for weddings "are important affairs, with the roster of the family's achievements on show" (p. 15). The initial wedding picture acquaints us with Sophie (Sofka) Dorn, the diminutive but strong-willed matriarch of the family and widow of an industrialist who, as her name indicates, has a Jewish, Eastern or Middle European background, with all the cultural values and taboos that this entails. Sophie is the mother of four children, two sons and two daughters, whom she loves fiercely. She envisions brilliant social roles for them, according to gender: the boys, Frederick and Alfred, would conquer the world; the girls, Mireille and Babette (nicknamed Mimi and Betty) would make good marriages and become dutiful wives and mothers. Sofka fully counts on her two sons to follow in their father's footsteps: "No matter that Frederick plays the violin so well, and that Alfred is so fond of reading; these accomplishments are for the drawing-room and the study and not for the world" (p. 10). She furthermore expects them to marry spouses of her own careful choosing.

As the saga of Sofka's four children unfolds through the somewhat detached, at times ironic, yet generally sympathetic narrative, it becomes clear that none of the children will turn out according to their mother's script. The serious, good-natured, and sober younger son, Alfred, who assumes the direction of the family firm, will harbor an unfulfilled longing for romance and a generally more exciting life. The dashing, handsome Frederick, on the other hand, will be allowed by his indulgent, forgiving mother to lead an idle, pampered existence, punctuated by amorous conquests. Frederick does not break promises, "he merely forgets them" (p. 19), blaming some fault in himself for these lapses and thereby neutralizing his reproachful victims: "Frederick's deportment, in love and business, is extremely aristocratic. Somehow, out of the unpromising debris of a European family, Sofka has bred an English aristocrat. This is perhaps her most triumphant achievement" (p. 22). Finally subjugated into marriage by the powerful, self-confident Eva (Evie), who will give him twins and abet his indolence, Frederick will settle down into pleasant, contented but insignificant middle age on the Italian Riviera, a permanent guest in a hotel owned by his father-in-law.

As for Sofka's daughters, the older Mimi, who had been her father's favorite, is the female counterpart of the virtuous Alfred. Reconciled to the "sensible" marriage she has reluctantly entered at her mother's insistent urging, she happily becomes pregnant at forty but miscarries when Sofka falls ill and dies. Following a long bout with depression, she resignedly settles down to a dignified, well-regulated life in the family quarters on Bryanston Square. While Mimi and Alfred "stand for those stolid and perhaps little regarded virtues of loyalty and fidelity and a scrupulous attention paid to the word or promise given or received" (p. 52), Betty is the natural complement of the hedonistic Frederick. From infancy she has exhibited an irrepressible, sometimes frightening vitality, and like Frederick she is doted upon by her mother: "Sofka loves Betty's fire, admires her looks but feels estranged from that perverse spirit that has always inclined Betty to moods, sulks, and screaming tantrums" (p. 36). Betty, who according to the narrator, bears a striking resemblance to the French writer Colette, with the same sharp features, cat's eyes, and thick, tousled red hair, is possessed of a rebellious, willful temperament and strong sexual appetites. Having quickly outgrown dreams of married bliss, she takes off for Paris with Frank, a tango teacher, dumps him in order to pursue a film career, and ends up in California with the help of Mr. Markus, a Hungarian film producer who has taken an interest in her. She falls in love with and marries the producer's nephew, the handsome,

successful, and cynical Max. Beverly Hills, it turns out, is not at all to her liking: "Had they been able to stay in New York, Betty might conceivably have gone on being happy" (p. 154). But Hollywood was where Mr. Markus and Max belonged. Vaguely dissatisfied and discontented—"she never made a film, of course" (p. 157)—and left alone a great deal of the time, she has become rather passive (as well as plump), with a tendency to nag her husband when he is not away on location. After his heart attack, he turns morose, can no longer work, and she has no other option but to take care of him and look back with nostalgia on her bohemian youth.

The arrangement of the two "good" and two "bad" children may strike one as a bit too symmetrical. That Sofka should feel a stronger attraction for her rebellious than for her obedient offspring may also seem somewhat predictably ironical. On the other hand, the complex, frequently contradictory motivations of the main protagonists, with the exception of the rather shallow and uncomplicated Frederick, are convincingly and subtly delineated, and once more Brookner displays an unerring touch as an elegant, pithy stylist. The iconographic framework, provided by the wedding photographs, combined with the first-person narrative, constitutes a fresh departure for Brookner and contributes effectively to her evocation of the ineluctable passage of time and its impact on Sofka and her brood. The colorful and frequently humorous family vignettes, including Sunday meals and afternoon teas, as well as visits by various idiosyncratic relatives, afford Brookner rich opportunities to depict vividly a milieu undoubtedly inspired by her own experience as the younger member of a European clan dutifully performing typically English rituals while clinging to Old World ways. Asked by an interviewer what had sparked her inspiration to write a novel about a family, Brookner acknowledged that it was "a wedding photograph with my grandmother dominating the group, as she must have dominated the participants. . . . I gave the photograph back, but the following day I started to write *Family and Friends*" (Kenyon, 1989, p. 16). In the same interview, Brookner confides that "it's the only one of my books I truly like" (p. 17). That a closely knit family, rather than a lonely, marginalized heroine, serves as a focus of the narrative constitutes an interesting departure from Brookner's previous novels, beginning with the loving, nostalgic description of a snapshot of the Dorn clan at a wedding. The family saga unfolds as though one were turning the pages of an old but treasured photo album. Here Brookner has broadened her canvas and has achieved something of the breadth and sweep of the novel of manners in the grand fictional tradition of the eighteenth and nineteenth centuries. And this may explain her own avowed preference for this particular work.

THE MISALLIANCE *AND*
A FRIEND FROM ENGLAND

The Misalliance (1986), Brookner's sixth novel, returns to the third-person narrative and to the theme of the solitary, conscientious, sensible woman trying her best to cope with a baffling, unpredictable world. After a marriage of twenty years, Blanche Vernon, the only offspring of parents long since dead, has been deserted and divorced by her husband, Bertie, for a younger woman, Amanda (nicknamed Mousie). Blanche's temperamental opposite, Mousie is given to wild mood swings and spectacular emotional outbursts. The self-contained Blanche had thought her marriage a happy one, but she now faced the realization that her husband had grown restless and bored with her over the years: "Thus humbled, baffled, and innocent, she felt all the more need to hold her head high, to wear a smile that betokened discreet but amused interest in what the world had to offer her, and to complete her toilette, down to the last varnished finger-nail, before leaving her house every morning" (p. 5).

Blanche tries hard to compensate for the sterile, lonely emptiness of her existence and for her newfound but burdensome freedom by grooming herself impeccably and by filling her days with small chores and useful obligations. A woman of culture, she regularly frequents the National Gallery, the British Museum, and the Wallace Collection, where the contemplation of masterpieces provides her with spiritual sustenance. She also takes long walks and bus rides in London, observing the colorful, multiracial crowds surrounding her and snatching fragments of other people's lives through bits of overheard conversations.

At the hospital where she does volunteer work, Blanche meets the pleasure-loving, gypsy-like Sally Beamish and her serious, repressed, mute three-year-old stepdaughter, Elinor, an outpatient. Childless herself, Blanche takes a special interest in the little girl, whom she suspects of hiding a deep insecurity behind her unresponsiveness: "She saw in the child, Elinor, the embryonic adult who could still, perhaps, after her unpromising start, be reclaimed for a life that was both sensible and rewarding" (p. 71). Blanche regretfully but firmly gives up her relationship with Elinor when she discovers, in the nick of time, that she has been financially manipulated and exploited by the child's unscrupulous family. The novel ends on a somewhat ambiguous, ironical note, for Bertie, ultimately worn out by Mousie's temper tantrums, sheepishly returns to his forbearing and forgiving ex-wife.

The character of Blanche Vernon, with her belated flashes of insight and her quiet but tenacious efforts at fending off despair and emotional bankruptcy ranks among Brookner's most engrossing novelistic creations, quite on a par with that of Edith Hope, the heroine of *Hotel du Lac*. Also sharply delineated is the by now familiar Brooknerian opposition of the unfairly humiliated "good" women versus the selfishly triumphant "bad" ones, in this instance emblematized by "the invulnerable and patrician nymphs of the National Gallery's Italian Rooms" (p. 45).

A Friend from England (1987), Brookner's seventh novel, relates in first-person narrative the story of Rachel Kennedy, a thirty-two-year-old unmarried woman who has inherited a part-ownership in a bookstore from her father. Oscar Livingstone was her father's accountant, and since Rachel's own family is "largely in the past" (p. 9), she becomes attached to him and to his wife, Dorrie, and continues an affectionate relationship with them, even after a substantial lottery win enables Oscar to quit his job.

The Livingstones have an only child, a daughter, Heather, for whom Rachel feels little personal affinity. Over her family's reservations, the spoiled, impetuous, and rebellious Heather marries Michael Sandberg, a charming, high-spirited young man. One evening, Rachel accidentally catches sight of Michael at a wine bar, wearing blue eyeshadow, rouge, and glossy lipstick. By then, Heather had already found out, and almost everyone else knew, that Michael was a homosexual.

After a hastily arranged divorce, Heather promptly remarries, for she has fallen in love with Marco, the brother of her Italian friend, Chiara, and has moved to Venice with him. She has even succeeded in securing her reluctant parents' blessing. In the meantime, however, Dorrie has fallen seriously ill, and Rachel feels duty-bound to travel to Venice in order to appeal to Heather's sense of duty and filial responsibility, a trip that is doomed to failure. Rachel's hydrophobia—a fear of water—and her recurring dream of drowning make her stay in Venice a nightmare. The misery of the trip, during which she fails to persuade Heather to return to England, is only partially alleviated by a visit to the famed Accademia Delle Belle Arti, where she lingers in front of Giorgione's enigmatic painting *The Tempest*, with its two pensive figures, a naked woman nursing her child and an elegant young knight, frozen in quite separate reveries against the background of a stormy landscape.

Rachel returns to London to learn much later that Heather had briefly come home from Italy for the funeral of her mother. Rachel's last sight of Oscar is "of an untidy figure stumping off in the direction of Marble Arch. I saw his back, bent, silhouetted against the glow of a rapidly sinking sun" (p. 205). Ironically, Rachel's relationship with her adoptive family, at first so pleasantly innocuous, turns out to have been as demanding as that with blood relatives. But then loneliness is not a pleasant prospect, even for a proudly independent woman like Rachel: "Women have come a long way, of course: we can all be left alone at night now. But sometimes it seems a high price to pay" (p. 139).

Like most other Brookner heroines, Rachel Kennedy is essentially a loner, carefully repressing her emotions and insecurities behind a cool, self-reliant exterior, and most at ease in the role of the uninvolved observer of the vagaries of human behavior. One of her greatest enjoyments is to take long, solitary walks in London, whether it be on a bright, windy early June day or during a hot summer evening. And we may safely surmise that she speaks for Anita Brookner when she proffers this rather pessimistic assessment of the female condition, and especially of female illusions:

What happens to women is that they never entirely lose the faith that it will all come out right in the end, that the next man, or the next, will be the answer to their original expectations of stability and order, will resolve the difficult equation of innocence and experience.

(p. 148)

In *A Friend from England* Brookner reworks her familiar theme of sincerity and innocence pitted against cunning and duplicity. Rachel, the lonely, alienated heroine, is obviously unable to deal with love and is fearful of being hurt in the process. These difficulties help to explain the repressed anger she harbors toward the selfishly heedless Heather. That some bitter disappointment in love is at the root of her recurring nightmares, in which she falls in love and ends up drowning, is alluded to without any further explanation for her hydrophobia.

LATECOMERS *AND* LEWIS PERCY

WITH *Latecomers* (1988), Brookner presents a variation on the family saga theme treated earlier in *Family and Friends*, as well as on parallel, if contrasting, characterizations. It is the story of two lifelong friends, the depressive Fibich and the hedonistic Hartmann, who are also partners in a successful greeting card business. Jewish refugee children from Germany during World War II, they had formed a brotherly bond in an English boarding school, drawn to each other by their common experience of alienation and loneliness. They are by now both married, Hartmann to the narcissistic and voluptuous Yvette, and Fibich to the angular, colorless Christine. The two children of Hartmann and Fibich are quite different: by an ironical quirk, the quiet Marianne is the daughter of the outgoing Hartmanns, and the good-looking, boisterous Thomas (Toto) is the son of the introverted Fibiches. A close relationship, based upon temperamental affinities, develops between the Fibiches and Marianne on the one hand, and between Toto and the Hartmanns on the other: "From the first the roles appeared to be reversed. It would have seemed, to a stranger coming into the room for the first time, as if Marianne, the docile, the silent, were Christine's child and Toto Yvette's" (p. 68). Brookner's tendency to structure her characters around antithetical pairings is especially evident in this novel: the juxtaposition of the neurotic Fibich and the carefree Hartmann on the one hand, and that of their unlikely offspring, the flamboyant Toto and the reserved Marianne.

At Oxford, Toto does mediocre work academically but acquires a large following of women admirers and embarks upon a career as an actor, eventually achieving success in the American movie industry. Marianne, for her part, settles into an ordinary existence of marriage and motherhood after obtaining a degree in English literature at London University. After going through a spiritual crisis and several false starts, Fibich and Hartmann achieve emotional equilibrium in the comforting satisfactions and routines of everyday life. They are survivors, "latecomers" to their measure of happiness. The account of Fibich's ill-fated and harrowing trip to a frighteningly impersonal Berlin, where he desperately tries to recapture remnants of his tragic past, constitutes the dramatic high point of the narrative.

What most characterizes this engrossing family chronicle is its quasi-symmetrical binary structure, undergirding episodes of apparent banality that are fraught with psychological tension, as well as its probing, sympathetic portrayal of the male characters Fibich and Hartmann.

Brookner again focuses on a male character in the eponymous hero of *Lewis Percy* (1989), recounted by a third-person narrator. Also revisited here is the contrast between a life of intellectual reflection and that of active involvement. In several significant ways, Lewis Percy is the male counterpart of Ruth Weiss in *The Debut* and of Kitty Maule of *Providence*. The values of Lewis Percy are strongly reminiscent of those of these shy, retiring, scholarly heroines whose quiet, unhurried lifestyle seems to belong to a bygone era and who remain foreign to the bustle of modern urban life. He, too, is a scholar of French literature with a special interest in the nineteenth-century French novel, who spends many hours in Paris, at the Bibliothèque Nationale, but who is also strongly pulled by the lure of everyday life on the Paris streets:

The high vaulted room seemed to be scholarship itself, putting a finger to its lips, urging silence, but his youthful body demanded movement. After such austerity he desired gratification, simple sustenance, the prospect of adventure. He wanted noise, spectacle, a more than impersonal beauty. Yet in the street it was hard for him to shake off the peculiar thrall of his day, the palpable silence that kept him wrapped in his thoughts, unprepared for, perhaps unequal to, the challenge of real life.
(p. 11)

The death of Lewis' mother summons him back to London, and while he still takes refuge in the Reading Room of the British Museum, he comes to the realization that he cannot spend his life stuck behind a book; he also longs for a female presence. At the library where he works as a researcher, he meets the ethereally fragile, virginal Tissy Harper and her imperious, ever present mother, Thea. Before long he comes to look upon Tissy as "the Sleeping Beauty, whom he would awaken with a kiss" (p. 68). After a complicated courtship, built around the necessity of circumventing the possessive Mrs. Harper, Lewis marries Tissy, a marriage which fails to live up to his expectations and in which he soon feels imprisoned. When his friend Pen Douglas introduces him to his sexually provocative sister Emmy, Lewis becomes obsessed by the desire to possess her. He nevertheless remains faithful to his wife, a virtuosity that is ill rewarded, for the pregnant Tissy leaves him to return to her mother. Repeatedly humiliated and repulsed by Mrs. Harper in his attempts to effect a reconciliation with his wife, he hardly takes notice when he receives in the mail the publisher's copies of his book, *The Hero as Archetype*, the result of many years of research: "He glanced at them indifferently, stowed them at the back of a cupboard, and went to bed" (p. 175). Even after the birth of his daughter, Jessica, Lewis is persistently kept at bay and allowed only visits, a situation that is all the more painful since his child has become the focus of his life.

The novel, however, ends on a hopeful note. Having decided to divorce Tissy, Lewis is resigned to a lonely existence and is about to leave for the Continent when an unexpected surprise awaits him at the airport: "Turning round for his last look at England, he saw Emmy, plunging through the crowd, necklaces flying, laughing, swearing, apologizing, and waving her boarding pass in her upheld hand" (p. 261).

In this novel, instead of applying the stark Darwinian law of the survival and triumph of the strong and ruthless, Brookner has rather uncharacteristically and optimistically decided to reward the gentle, naive, and innocent, for Lewis Percy is granted an unexpected second chance at happiness.

BRIEF LIVES *AND* A CLOSED EYE

Brief Lives (1990), Brookner's tenth novel, returns to a female character as its central focus, in this instance the fascinating, temperamental, and increasingly pathetic figure of Margaret Julia Wilberforce, better known simply by her stage name of Julia, who had been quite famous in her youth as a spectacularly beautiful, elegant actress who triumphed in the kind of intimate, sophisticated revues popular in the 1940s. Married twice, to Simon Hodges and Charlie Morton, Julia took great pride in belonging to the Wilberforces, an upper-class family whose male members had served with distinction in the British army: "The only reason she regretted not having children was that there was no one to carry on the name, for the unfortunate brother was unlikely to marry, being given to all the excesses except those pertaining to love and responsibility" (p. 8).

The first-person narrator of the novel is Fay Langdon, née Dodworth. Fay's now deceased husband, Owen, had been a junior law partner of Julia's second husband, Charlie Morton, and the two couples had holidayed together in Nice. Before his own death, Charlie had been an ever devoted, even subservient, spouse to the arrogant, difficult, and demanding Julia, who blamed everyone but herself for her fall from favor as an actress and who lived through her declining years on omelettes and whiskey. The novel opens as Fay, who had been on the stage herself but had never achieved Julia's fame, chances upon a fairly substantial obituary of Julia in the newspaper, with a photograph, "one of those studio portraits of the late 1930s or early 1940s, all huge semi-transparent eyes, flat hair, and dark lipstick" (p. 3). Following are a series of flashbacks relating Julia's last years as an imperious fading beauty. Prematurely infirm in her sixties and confined by her ailments to her large apartment, Julia refuses to come to terms with age, takes refuge in her glamorous past when she turned heads in restaurants and was featured in *Vogue* magazine, and becomes totally dependent on her octogenarian mother and on the few remaining friends still under her spell, especially on Maureen, who has moved in with her after Charlie's death and whom she treats like a servant.

In delineating Julia's progressive physical deterioration and gradual mental disintegration, Brookner offers a masterful, wryly sympathetic portrayal of female pride and denial. An effective contrapuntal feature in the novel is the story of Fay Langdon, the narrator, and her own relationships, especially with her parents and her husband. Of

more socially modest origin than Julia, and far less successful as an actress or spectacular as a beauty, Fay has simpler and more easily satisfied ambitions and desires. Her father, Jimmy Dodworth, had been a cinema manager in the days when that position required a person to stand in the foyer in dinner jacket and bow tie (p. 11). While she deeply grieves over the sudden death of her father and, several years later, over the more lingering death of her mother, she accepts stoically the losses and sorrows of life, "knowing that the alternative is simply death, non-existence, non-feeling," and that "it is inherent in the organism to want to endure for as long as possible . . . so that one becomes willing to take on all the mishaps, all the tragedies, if they are the price to be paid" (p. 22). By the time her married life abruptly comes to an end with the unexpected death of her husband, Fay has been sufficiently rehearsed in loss to face this trauma in a spirit of resigned fatalism. Fay sadly but realistically submits to the ineluctable law of change and also mournfully acknowledges the thickening of her waistline and the fading of her good looks, finding comfort in the fact that on the whole she has no cause for complaint; her life has been pleasant and she has married well. The haughty Julia, on the other hand, refuses to "go gentle into that good night." After the defection of Maureen, Julia's most loyal friend, Fay feels duty-bound to look after her. Eventually, Julia joins Gerald, her unreliable, alcoholic brother, of whom she had always been inordinately fond, in Spain: "Age and infirmity are always easier to bear when the sun shines every day and life seems like an endless holiday" (p. 241). As for Fay, after a tentative relationship with Alan Carter, an unattached physician, she achieves a measure of autonomy and self-sufficiency and settles down to genteel solitude, doing her best to cope with anguish and loneliness by involving herself in "all the small routines that women on their own devise for themselves to fill the day, poor substitutes for the company [they] had once so enjoyed" (p. 194).

Brief Lives is an engrossing if somewhat melancholy novel, with nuanced shadings, delicate visual touches, and terse, banal dialogue most notable for what is left unsaid. Starkly pithy maxims underscore the limitations of the human condition and the ineluctable aging process: "When young one can still aspire to sublimity. Old age knows that this is, and probably always was, in devastatingly short supply" (p. 259). But in no other novel does Brookner depict with such concentrated power and intensity what aging does to women, both mentally and physically. Also memorable are the strongly antithetical portraits of the two principal female characters, the domineering, extravagant, and increasingly helpless Julia and her quietly self-reliant and lucid counterpart, Fay. As narrator, Fay is in the privileged position of relating the story from her viewpoint and of sharing with the reader her strongly ambivalent feelings about Julia, who both mesmerizes and repels her. But Fay herself is not entirely spared, for there is also implied irony aimed at her, perceptible to the reader through her narration and comments. There is indeed a subtly ironic subtext behind Fay's wistful voice and melancholy musings, so typical in their banality of the constricted lives and repressed aspirations of proper bourgeois women. Fay's solitary fate and attachment to Julia endow her with a tragic dimension while ultimately contradicting everything she professes to know about human relationships. The underlying message of the novel is that a common destiny of disappointments and defeats binds these two otherwise profoundly dissimilar women and that women in general continue to be all too willing victims of the stereotyped expectations of society and of their own rationalizations and delusions.

A quotation from Henry James's *Madame de Mauves* serves as epigraph to *A Closed Eye* (1991) and aptly describes the protagonist of Brookner's eleventh novel: "She strikes me as a person who is begging off from full knowledge—who has struck a truce with painful truth, and is trying awhile the experiment of living with closed eyes." Brookner reverts to the third-person narrative by way of flashbacks in order to tell the story of Harriet Lytton, the only child of an eccentric and pleasure-loving couple, Hughie, a once dashing captain in the RAF, and Merle, who ran a small, fashionable dress shop in London. The novel opens with a letter from Harriet to Elizabeth Peckham (Lizzie), the daughter of a close friend, the late Tessa, inviting Lizzie to visit her in Switzerland. By now the fifty-four-year-old Harriet is in voluntary exile and facing bleak solitude, following the death of Freddie, her older, fatherly husband, and the sudden loss of her beautiful and extravagantly spoiled daughter, Imogen (Immy), killed in a car crash on a drunken spree with her heedless friends.

Here again we find the strikingly contrasting portraits of two female characters, the plain, self-contained Lizzie and the dazzling, selfish Immy. Lizzie would lead a rational, productive, sensible life, whereas catastrophe awaited Immy because of her self-destructive desire for pleasure and excitement: "And there was no help for it; the die had already been cast" (p. 125). Here also are reprised Brookner's familiar themes of fatalism in the face of the fragility of human destiny, and the fears and insecurities of loneliness and old age, especially in women. But *A Closed Eye* offers us above all a masterfully ironic yet sympathetic study of a kindly, cultured but misguided woman who is incapable of gaining true insight into her own motivations. One of the most appealing features in the novel is the theme of female bonding and friendship. During her happy, carefree schooldays young Harriet had formed warm and lasting attachments with three girls: Mary Grant, Pamela Harkness, and especially with the tall and lovely Tessa Dodd. Periodic reunions over the decades make Harriet feel like a girl again and enable her and her friends to monitor their different destinies and follow their progress toward maturity and middle age. Tessa Dodd had stubbornly and against all good advice married the handsome but impecunious and unreliable Jack Peckham who, like "the villainous hero of romantic fiction . . . breaks hearts and thrills women, so that they look with disdain on the humbler, more available variety of men for ever after" (p. 40–41). Even Harriet will not be able to resist Jack's seductiveness. And ironically, Lizzie, the unwanted and neglected offspring of a failed marriage, turns out to be the one endowed with the wherewithal to survive and even to achieve professional success as a picture researcher for a major publisher, whereas Immy, the overindulged child of a rich, doting couple, falls victim to her own wild, uncontrollable impulses. The novel closes as Lizzie, having accepted out of compassion Harriet's invitation to stay with her for a while at the Swiss *pension*, departs for England:

That evening Harriet, standing at the window, saw the sun descend majestically into the lake. Turning, she surveyed the empty room. My life, she thought, an empty room. But she felt no pain, felt in fact the cautious onset of some kind of release. Vividly, she caught sight of Immy's face. . . . Sinking onto the sofa she let the tears rain down.
(p. 263)

FRAUD *AND* DOLLY

IN *Fraud* (1992), Brookner pursues her exploration of the themes of loneliness and self-deception. The novel starts like a typical detective story with the reported four-month disappearance from her London apartment in South Kensington of Anna Durrant, a single woman in her middle years and of independent means. She did not have close friends, and her mother, for whom she had cared with tender devotion, had recently died. The inspector and policemen in charge of the case question neighbors and acquaintances, especially Vera Marsh, who had befriended Anna Durrant's ailing mother. It is mainly through the eyes of Vera, an upper-class, cultured widow in comfortable circumstances, that Anna's life and character are reconstructed. Anna, over the objections of her mother, who wanted her to go into the fashion business, attended university, spent a year abroad, and has since been working intermittently on a research project about the Paris salons during the Second Empire, although she "simply laughed away the suggestion that she was any kind of intellectual" (p. 20).

It turns out that after her mother's death, Anna had simply taken off for Paris in order to rejoin Marie-France Forestier, a friend she had made during her year of study in France. Unsettled by the impersonal and frantic bustle of Paris, so different from her nostalgic memories of the French capital, she is further disappointed when Marie-France's impending marriage puts an end to their intimacy and when she comes to the sad realization that "they would meet again, but as acquaintances rather than as friends" (p. 170). Anna is an eminently Brooknerian heroine, a woman who is "old enough to know that she would never have children, old enough to reflect bitterly that nature had no further use for her" (p. 23), whose expectations of love and friendship are equally dashed, and who has learned the hard way to depend only on herself to survive and to give meaning to her life. Anna ultimately decides to return to Paris and go into the business of designing women's clothes. The title of this novel, with its probing and unsettling insights into the complex, potentially destructive relationships between aging parents and their adult children, undoubtedly refers to the self-delusions and small deceptions that form the intricate pattern of Anna Durrant's lonely life that she tries her best to veil behind a proper appearance of cheerful good will and refined manners.

In *Dolly* (1993; published in Great Britain as *A Family Romance*), Brookner continues to explore the changing truths of personal identity and family relationships. The novel is narrated in the first person by the quietly reserved and undemonstrative Jane Manning, a single woman who is a writer of children's books, has a natural "ability to tolerate solitary life" (p. 49), a love of long walks in London streets and parks, and a great fondness for art; she is an habitué of museums and galleries. Jane is ill prepared for the disruptive intrusion into her peaceful English existence and into her well-established, cultured, and assimilated Jewish family, which takes pride in its sense of orderliness and decorum, of the glamorous, provocatively sexy, and rather mysterious Dolly. Dolly had married in somewhat romantic circumstances Jane's uncle, Hugo Ferber, a pampered and amiable mother's boy, who had served as a singularly inept soldier in the British army and who, after taking his law examinations, joined the Westminster Bank. The couple had settled down in Brussels, but upon Hugo's unexpected death after a bout with the flu, Dolly is thrust upon her slightly bewildered English in-laws.

Jane's discreet inquiries reveal that Dolly's real name was Marie-Jeanne Schiff, born in Paris of impecunious German-Jewish parents, Jacob, a restless watchmaker of the type generally referred to as a luftmensch, and his wife, Fanny, a dressmaker. Soon after the birth of the child, Jacob decamped and, save for a postcard, was never heard from again. Fanny called her little girl Dolly, kept her at home, and increasingly sent her out on various errands. During the German occupation, Fanny succeeded in hiding her Jewish identity by passing herself off as Alsatian, and when Paris was liberated the good-looking and fun-loving Dolly had a great time with American soldiers and learned to speak English fluently. But Fanny's business languished and during the difficult postwar years mother and daughter decided to try their luck in England, where Dolly met Hugo in the ballroom of a seaside hotel and, after clever and patient maneuvering, succeeded in having him propose marriage to her. The proper and reserved Jane is both fascinated and scandalized by the uninhibited Dolly, "a widow who had never enjoyed being a wife" (p. 48). Before long, however, the two antipathetic women come to the realization that, despite their profound differences, they are yoked together by common family ties. Their characterization offers yet another instance of Brookner's fondness for dual, contrasting portraits.

With its probing insights into human behavior and motivation, its evocative rendering of the subtle rewards and lingering anxieties of solitude, and the muted economy of its style, studded with trenchant aphorisms in the tradition of La Rochefoucauld's cruelly incisive maxims, *Dolly* exemplifies Brookner's storytelling prowess and masterful portraiture. Through Jane Manning, as first-person narrator and witness of the unfolding drama of Dolly's life, the novel evinces the kind of immediacy, informality, and intimacy that irresistibly solicit the reader's involvement.

A PRIVATE VIEW *AND* INCIDENTS IN THE RUE LAUGIER

THE aptly named George Bland, a cautious and genteel Englishman who at the age of sixty-five has recently retired from an unremarkable career as a personnel manager, and who has had a long, comfortable relationship with the placid and accommodating Louise, is the main protagonist of Brookner's fourteenth novel, *A Private View* (1994), related throughout by a third-person narrator. As the novel opens Bland has just lost his closest friend, Michael Putnam, to cancer, and he feels overwhelmed by a sense of sadness and aimlessness, finding little comfort in his honorable retirement and newfound freedom: "Without Putnam, or even the office, to restore his self-respect, he was lost, his life mere boredom" (p. 84). Even books and museums fail to provide him with the kind of spiritual and emotional nourishment he craves. Haunted by a desire for some exciting change in his orderly but dull routine, Bland secretly dreams of an ultimate romantic adventure that would give meaning and color to his life.

This opportunity presents itself when he meets and falls in love with Katy Gibb, a captivatingly mysterious, restless American in her thirties who has some of the seductive characteristics of the flower children of the 1960s, and who has temporarily and somewhat surreptitiously moved into the flat of Bland's vacationing neighbors. Under the spell of this uninhibited, self-indulgent, and at times threateningly resentful and sullen young woman, Bland jeopardizes his hard-earned financial security to please her and meet her ever-growing demands. At the eleventh hour, he painfully takes hold of himself and decides to renounce passion and all its dangers and to return to his former routine and to the reassuring, familiar Louise. He has briefly toyed with the notion that had long preoccupied him, that life seems "exciting only if there is the possibility of throwing it away," and this "not even in a good cause" (p. 223).

Incidents in the Rue Laugier (1995) is Brookner's fifteenth novel. It is narrated in the first person by Maffy Harrison, who tries to gain a better understanding of her identity and roots by delving into the life of her recently deceased mother, Maud Harrison, née Gonthier, from Dijon, France, who has left a notebook that contains nothing but some cryptic notations. Determined to make sense of these brief jottings, Maffy feels compelled to reconstruct, and even reinvent, her mother's life, and to find out the story behind the rather unlikely marriage of her parents, the beautiful, spirited Maud Gonthier with Edward Harrison, an unprepossessing English bookshop owner. It turns out that behind her calm, dignified demeanor, Maud Harrison had concealed a deep, shameful secret. We are taken back to Maud's difficult childhood in Dijon and to her financially straitened circumstances due to the premature death of her tubercular father. At the country home of an aunt, where she spent her summers, the eighteen-year-old Maud met two young Englishmen, friends of her cousin: the self-assured, handsome David Tyler and the ungainly, shy Edward Harrison. Maffy reconstructs the events that follow: Tyler promptly seduces the innocent Maud, who becomes pregnant, Edward gallantly proposes marriage, and they go through with the ceremony even though a miscarriage had given Maud a way out of this loveless match. Maud and Edward keep up a brave, dignified front through a mutually unsatisfactory marriage, and after the birth of a child, the narrator Maffy, Maud sinks into a protracted state of melancholy and depression, taking refuge in reading the classics.

Maffy's story, part painstakingly recovered fact and part subjective fancy, is meant to be a tribute, a sadly belated "gesture" toward her dead parents, especially her mother, for "the truth we tell ourselves is worth any number of facts, verifiable or not" (p. 7). That the narrator feels that she has come to resemble her parents in their quiet, self-effacing ways is made all the more palpable when she leaves Cambridge University, breaks off her engagement, and takes over her father's bookshop, at least temporarily: "I am still in search of that hidden life, those hidden lives. The past, as Proust makes clear, and at considerable length, is always with us. In that sense nothing is lost" (p. 233).

CONCLUSION

THE patient and relentless probings into human passions and illusions, the subtle and understated wit and irony, the unflinching and rigorous unsentimentality, and the tightly controlled and lapidary style of Brookner's fiction link it to French novelists in the *moraliste* tradition with which she was thoroughly familiar, notably Madame de La Fayette's *La Princesse de Clèves*, Benjamin Constant's *Adolphe,* and of course Marcel Proust's *À la recherche du temps perdu*. Among other great French authors she has singled out for praise are Voltaire for his fearless wit and mastery of the put-down, Diderot for his courage and optimism, Stendhal for his bold intelligence and lucidity, Balzac for his Promethean creativity, Flaubert for his stylistic perfection, Zola for his generous social indignation, and Colette for her uncanny, if at times cruel, female portrayals. The Age of Enlightenment remains her favorite period for its "guilt-free energy and enthusiasm" (Haffenden, p. 63). But that this "French connection" is conflated with an English novelistic tradition exemplified by such writers as Jane Austen, Charles Dickens, George Eliot, Anthony Trollope, Henry James, Edith Wharton, and Virginia Woolf, has been acknowledged by Brookner herself and aptly summarized by John Updike in his laudatory review of *The Latecomers:* "She is, in the English tradition, a thoroughly social novelist, for whom there lies beyond the human spectacle nothing but death and scenery, yet she brings to the English scene an outsider's precise eye" (p. 111).

The connection between Brookner the art historian and the novelist is also evident, although she has understandably tended to reject obvious and facile parallels, even going so far as to state somewhat provocatively that "it's a sort of schizophrenic activity as far as I'm concerned" (Haffenden, p. 65). Yet the panel of judges that awarded the Booker Prize to her novel *Hotel du Lac* acknowledged the correlation by comparing the novel to a work by Jan Vermeer, the famed but enigmatic seventeenth-century Dutch painter, perhaps because of a certain quality of quiet intimacy and muted stillness imparted to the artist's portrayals of women. Iconographic references, evocative images and landscapes, and delicate painterly touches highlight Brookner's fiction, and it is no coincidence that some of the more memorable moments occur when her solitary protagonists find spiritual illumination and sustenance, as well as emotional solace and comfort, while gazing at a particular work of art in a museum or gallery, either in London or on the Continent.

The major theme that animates Brookner's novels, however, is the loneliness and alienation of the modern woman. Burdened with Victorian values of moral rectitude as well as naively Romantic self-delusions, she is ill-equipped to deal with the harsh realities and daily challenges of the difficult business of living. Brookner has endowed her heroines with a special, poignant kind of authentic and personal resonance gained through her own painful experience, for in her novels there is a close commingling of autobiographical and fictional discourses. Yet while she says that she does not mind in the least being described as a woman's novelist (see Kenyon, p. 22), her attitude toward feminism, especially when it becomes self-consciously militant, ideologized, and politicized, tends to be somewhat aloof and ambiguous. In *Dolly,* for instance, there is a revealing depiction of Jane Manning's encounter with American academic feminists when she is sent by her publisher on a lecture tour of several New England women's colleges:

I find them exhausting, these women of goodwill, with their agenda of wrongs to be righted, of injustices to be eliminated. I want to stand still in the dusk and contemplate the lake . . . but I must respond intelligently, employ a certain kind of feminised argument, feel myself to be the victim of a monstrous wrong which has been passed down to me from generation to generation.

(p. 250)

Jane Manning, doubtless speaking for Brookner herself, also expresses reservations about the lasting value and significance of the numerous works of feminist criticism that "pour out from university presses, and are produced by the most excellent of women. . . . I appreciate them for their fervour and their courage. And yet a doubt creeps in" (p. 256).

It is clear that Brookner is reluctant to ascribe to the feminine condition alone the pervasive sense of loneliness, vulnerability, and longing that haunts her female protagonists, for her male characters are subject to a similar existential malaise. But the additional burden that women seeking self-sufficiency have to deal with is acknowledged through this typically understated admission on the part of Jane Manning: "It is a little hard to sustain my life without recognising the pull of old dependencies, old passivities" (p. 255).

Brookner had achieved signal distinction as a teacher and art historian when she embarked on a career as a novelist at the age of fifty-three. She subsequently went on to produce in a steady, sustained fashion fifteen works of fiction that have gained her worldwide recognition and earned her acclaim as a creative writer who fearlessly and unflinchingly addresses some of the most profound and intimate moral dilemmas of our time.

The recurring leitmotivs in Anita Brookner's brilliantly probing and stingingly ironical novels focus on refined, cultured, polite, genteel, yet unworldly English women and men who, in their quixotic yearning for a utopian ideal of aesthetic beauty and fulfillment in love, find themselves not only at odds with the vulgar hustle of contemporary metropolitan life but also somehow irresistibly attracted to charismatic, unscrupulous, and predatory characters. The elegance, economy, and subtlety of Brookner's prose and the exquisite sensitivity with which she can render every nuance of a thought or a feeling in the inner lives of her somewhat claustrophobic and solipsistic protagonists create a powerfully compelling world that unflinchingly reveals the fierce and relentless politics of human relationships.

SELECTED BIBLIOGRAPHY

I. Art Criticism. *Watteau* (London, 1967); *The Genius of the Future: Studies in French Art Criticism* (London and New York, 1971); *Greuze: The Rise and Fall of an Eighteenth-Century Phenomenon* (London and Greenwich, Conn., 1972); *Jacques-Louis David: A Personal Interpretation* (London, 1974).

II. Novels. *The Debut* (New York, 1981), first published as *A Start in Life* (London, 1981); *Providence* (London and New York, 1982); *Look at Me* (London and New York, 1983); *Hotel du Lac* (London and New York, 1984); *Family and Friends* (London and New York, 1985); *The Misalliance* (New York, 1986), first published as *A Misalliance* (London, 1986); *A Friend from England* (London and New York, 1987); *Latecomers* (London and New York, 1988); *Lewis Percy* (London and New York, 1989); *Brief Lives* (London and New York, 1990); *A Closed Eye* (London and New York, 1991); *Fraud* (London and New York, 1992); *Dolly* (New York, 1993), first published as *A Family Romance* (London, 1993); *A Private View* (London and New York, 1994); *Incidents in the Rue Laugier* (London and New York, 1995).

III. Interviews. John Haffenden, "Anita Brookner," in his *Novelists in Interview* (London and New York, 1985); Amanda Smith, "*Publishers Weekly* Interviews: Anita Brookner," *Publishers Weekly* (6 September 1985); Shusha Guppy, "Anita Brookner: The Art of Fiction 98," in *Paris Review* 29 (fall 1987); Olga Kenyon, "Anita Brookner," in her *Women Writers Talk: Interviews with Ten Women Writers* (Oxford, 1989; New York, 1990).

IV. Critical Studies. Anne Tyler, "A Solitary Life Is Still Worth Living," in *New York Times Book Review* (3 February 1985); Olga Kenyon, "Anita Brookner," in her *Women Novelists Today: A Survey of English Writing in the Seventies and Eighties* (London and New York, 1988); John Updike, review of *Latecomers*, in *New Yorker* (1 May 1989); Patricia Waugh, "Anita Brookner," in her *Feminine Fictions: Revisiting the Postmodern* (London and New York, 1989); Lynn Veach Sadler, *Anita Brookner* (Boston, 1990); John Skinner, *The Fictions of Anita Brookner: Illusions of Romance* (London and New York, 1992); Joanne Shattock, "Anita Brookner," in *The Oxford Guide to British Women Writers* (Oxford and New York, 1993).

A. S. BYATT
(1936–　　)

Laura Engel

ALTHOUGH A. S. BYATT's versatile career has spanned three decades, she is best known for her Booker Prize–winning novel *Possession* (1990), the story of two academics who discover a clandestine correspondence between two nineteenth-century poets: Randolph Henry Ash, modeled after Robert Browning, and Christabel LaMotte, a cross between Emily Dickinson and Christina Rossetti. Part parody, part detective novel, part love story, the narrative reflects Byatt's passionate interest in the relationship between fact and fiction, literary imagination and scholarly practice, the past and the present. The central characters, Roland Michell and Maud Bailey, are like all of Byatt's protagonists: active and often obsessive thinkers, readers, brooders, and achievers. They sort out real-life problems such as whether to continue a relationship or how to make amends with an estranged family member in the same way a literary critic researches an academic project: they analyze options, construct narratives, piece together fragments of relevant and irrelevant information, make connections, reach dead ends, and begin again.

With her sophisticated narratives and her elegant style, it is difficult to characterize Byatt as a writer who belongs to a particular literary school or group of authors. In her collection of critical essays *Passions of the Mind* (1993 ed.), she writes, "Novelists sometimes claim that their fiction is a quite separate thing from their other written work. Iris Murdoch likes to separate her philosophy from her novels; David Lodge says that his critical and narrative selves are a schizoid pair. I have never felt such a separation, nor wanted to make such claims" (p. 1). Byatt's desire to merge her "critical and narrative selves" is present in all of her writings. Her novels are as much about the characters and their situations as they are about the project of writing the novel itself. The organization of *Passions* reflects her eclectic literary and academic interests. The first section, "As a Writer," is followed by "Victorians: Incarnation and Art" and "Moderns: Varying Strands."

All of Byatt's novels borrow elements from the British literary tradition past and present. Her vividly descriptive prose and re-creation of nineteenth-century voices echo Victorian authors. She has been compared to George Eliot, Charles Dickens, and Thomas Hardy, among others. However, she is equally influenced by the modernist tradition and returns again and again to the haunting figure of D. H. Lawrence, whom, she says, "I cannot escape and cannot love." She is also deeply influenced by Marcel Proust, whom she credits as her favorite novelist, as well as by T. S. Eliot, Fyodor Dostoyevsky, and Leo Tolstoy. The second half of the collection has sections titled "The Female Voice?" and "Vision and Reality." The essays on the female voice reflect Byatt's concern with what literary women have to say that is unique, both in terms of her own prose and in terms of the journeys that her protagonists undertake. "Vision and Reality" focuses on Byatt's continuous exploration of how we, as readers, read textual descriptions compared with the way we experience visual images. Her novels are constructed as extended descriptive canvases, and she often writes with a particular artist or school of aesthetics in mind.

Each of Byatt's novels has its own particular intellectual problem or set of questions that often relate to a specific period in literary history. For example, *Possession* and *Angels and Insects* are concerned with themes from Victorian literature and Romanticism. *The Game* and *The Virgin in the Garden* explore Renaissance allegories, while *Babel Tower* deals with biblical tales and eighteenth-century French philosophy. Although these novels borrow from the past, Byatt situates her characters in postwar England. Her projected tetralogy— *The Virgin in the Garden, Still Life, Babel Tower,* and a work yet to be written—begins in 1953 (with the coronation of Queen Elizabeth II) and ends in 1968, near the close of a turbulent and explosive decade. As Byatt's characters move through their lives, they are affected by the shift from the complacent 1950s to the political, social, and artistic upheavals of the 1960s.

In merging these categories, fictional and critical, past and present, Byatt returns again and again to the possibilities and limitations of language. In *Passions,* she explains: "What interested me was the abused and despised adjective, that delimiter of plain nouns which, if properly used, makes every description more and more particular and precise" (p. 11). For example, her first novel, *The Shadow of the Sun,* begins with a lengthy description of the central character's house. The description sets the stage for the novel, which in many ways is about women who must come to terms with issues of the home, domesticity, family, and traditional gender roles. At the same time, the house itself becomes a character because of the lush detail of the description:

The house was in waiting; low, and still, and grey, with clean curtains on the long windows, and a fresh line of white across the edge of the steps. They had repainted the door in the spring, a soft colour, between blue and grey, which seemed to retreat coolly before the sparkle of the wide lawns under the sun.

(p. 3)

For Byatt, descriptions not only illustrate scenes and places but also conjure associations at the level of the words themselves. In *Possession,* the scholars Roland and Maud search for clues about the relationship between poets Ash and LaMotte by combing their poetry for similar or related references. In reproducing lengthy sections of LaMotte's and Ash's journals, letters, and poetry, Byatt invites the reader to engage in the same kind of investigative research as the protagonists. For instance, when one of LaMotte's poems contains the word "Ash," the reader (like a good scholar) knows that the word is meant to be interpreted in several ways. Similarly, a clue to the plot of the novella "Morpho Eugenia" (in *Angels and Insects*) rests on a specific anagram. "Morpho Eugenia" tells the story of an incestuous relationship between a seemingly innocent woman and her rakish half-brother. "Insect," rearranged, becomes "incest." The main character

in Byatt's story "The Changeling" (in *Sugar and Other Stories* [1987]) is an author who writes horror stories about misfit boys at boarding school. She offers to house a student who resembles almost exactly one of her fictional characters named Henry; ironically, the boy's name is Henry Smee (or Henry's me).

Byatt's careful attention to language, literary references, and allusions reflects her belief that "words are literally things" (p. 4). In other words, while Byatt's novels are about real things, they are also about the language used to describe those things, and about the way that words create images that become tangible and real for the reader. She encourages her readers to enter her imaginary landscape and investigate along with the narrator the possibilities for the characters and their stories.

BACKGROUND

ANTONIA Susan Byatt was born 24 August 1936 in Sheffield, England. Although many of her novels take place in London, the contrast of the natural beauty of the Yorkshire landscape of her youth, with its bleak resonance of working-class English roots, haunts her heroines, who are often tormented by their desire to escape their childhood. Her parents, John Frederick Drabble, a barrister, and Marie Bloor Drabble, were both educated at Cambridge. She describes her family as "intensely literary," yet the restrictive Quaker atmosphere discouraged her from pursuing creative endeavors. In *Passions,* Byatt writes, "My mother, whose own pleasures were largely, if narrowly literary, would nevertheless make sharp speeches, over the washing up about the uselessness and self-regard of such persons as artists and mountaineers, whom, for some reason, she always associated with each other" (pp. 14–15). She speaks both sadly and fondly of her mother, a woman who sacrificed her own desires for the good of the family: "My mother's background, which she had rejected, was non-conformist and Puritanical. The best thing that happened to her was English literature, but in her misery she was suspicious of it" (introduction, p. ix). The idea that literature could be both good and bad for one, especially for a woman, is a theme that recurs frequently in Byatt's work. Fiction and, in turn, the imaginative process offer possibilities that are often not practical in "real life." Byatt does not describe her father in detail except to say that he had, like Henry Severell, the unapproachable father in her first novel, *The Shadow of the Sun*, "an incapacity, usual enough in the hardworking man, to notice what is going on inside others" (p. xi).

Byatt remembers her early childhood as a solitary experience. She was asthmatic and confined for long periods of time to her bedroom. Shut away like a nineteenth-century heroine, Byatt discovered books. In *Passions* she writes:

As a child it is not too much to say, [I] was in some way kept alive by fictions. I was asthmatic and spent much time in bed. I read Scott, Dickens, Jane Austen; I lived in these worlds. I told myself long tales of other lives, in which I lived with other people in other worlds, from fairy-tales through epics to the seventeenth century.

(p. 15)

Living in these "imaginary worlds," Byatt began to make sense of her own life by crafting stories. In many ways, all of her characters share a capacity for this: a desire to write their own stories, to weigh all of the different narrative options, and, ultimately, to script their own roles. While Byatt celebrates this need, she is also careful to point out the danger of living for and in fiction. Looking back on her early love for creating stories, she writes, "The wholly imagined worlds seemed simply good, the kings and princes, the flying horses, the paradisal forests. But these *real* imaginings, so to speak, had a contaminated quality" (p. 15).

This "contaminated" quality—the idea that the imagination can be destructive—is particularly present in Byatt's second novel, *The Game*. The story concerns two sisters: one whose novels devour the lives of other characters by humiliating them in print; and the other who lives so much in her imaginary world that she cannot come to terms with the present. Byatt's novel *Babel Tower* similarly deals with the fine line between imagination and perversity. In *Babel Tower*, the novel within the novel is a dystopic fairy tale borrowing from the Marquis de Sade and Charles Fourier. While Byatt admits that there is a dark side to living through stories, she seems to have gained from her childhood imaginings a strong sense that there is such a thing as an individual voice that can tell a unique story. In a rare comment about her well-known sister, the novelist Margaret Drabble, from a review

by Mervyn Rothstein, Byatt's desire to have her work be seen as original and distinct is clear:

I didn't mind her popular success, . . . I was trying to do something different. But the aspect that got me down was that when I did something, I don't think it was read in terms of itself. . . . I feel that people have been reading my novels for years as written by somebody who happens to be the sister of another novelist. And this is very annoying if you have wanted to be a novelist since you were 5.

(p. C17)

After attending boarding school in York, Byatt won a scholarship to Newnham College, Cambridge, where she earned a B.A. with first-class honors in 1957. Subsequently, she spent a year doing postgraduate work at Bryn Mawr College, and then returned to England to begin work on her doctorate at Somerville College, Oxford. Her unfinished Ph.D. thesis under Helen Gardner focused on seventeenth-century literature. In the introduction to *The Shadow of the Sun*, Byatt describes Cambridge in the 1950s as a place where women were of necessity always on the defensive. "We had fought, much harder than the men, who out numbered us eleven to one, and we were fatally torn, when thinking of our futures, by hopes of marriage, and hopes of something, some work, beyond getting to university at all" (p. viii). This pull between the male intellectual world of Cambridge and the female world of family, children, and domestic expectations is a central conflict for all of Byatt's female protagonists. In particular, Frederica, the heroine of Byatt's projected tetralogy, works hard to establish herself at Cambridge and later struggles with the pull between work and marriage. In *Babel Tower*, Frederica faces the loss of identity that comes with motherhood and the arduous task of doing intellectual and creative work that is her own.

In merging her critical and narrative selves, Byatt tries to create a bridge between these two realms. In fact, the form and content of all of Byatt's novels combine categories that are usually considered to be separate: parallel story lines bridge reality with fiction, emotional struggles with intellectual pursuits, empirical investigations with poetic explorations. And her ability to write in many different formats—from legal documents and book reviews to diaries and letters—draws attention to the distinction between private forms of writing and public modes of expression.

Aside from what Byatt terms the "human" issues that she wrestles with in her fiction, the literary education she received at Cambridge, particularly under F. R. Leavis, gave her the ability to craft her precise and stunning prose at the same time that she internalized the critical eye of the academic scholar. She writes in *The Shadow of the Sun*:

[Dr. Leavis] could show you the toughness of a sentence, the strength and the grace of it, the way another one failed and betrayed itself, but you paid a terrible price for this useful technical knowledge. It went without saying in his world, as later in Helen Gardner's, that anything you wrote yourself would fall so woefully short of the highest standards that it was better not to try.

(p. ix)

Despite these discouragements, Byatt continued to write and to read. At Cambridge she became interested in T. S. Eliot. She told reviewer Mel Gussow that she adopted the name A. S. Byatt in homage to T. S. Eliot, who felt that writers should be anonymous. In 1959, she married Ian Charles Rayner Byatt and left Oxford. She had two children, Antonia and Charles, and began work on her first novel, *The Shadow of the Sun*.

EARRY NOVELS

BYATT's first novel, *The Shadow of the Sun* (1964), was reissued in 1993, after the enormous success of *Possession*. Byatt began writing the novel when she was at Cambridge and finished it several years later. In a new introduction to the 1993 version, she recalls her initial idea for the story:

It [the novel] was written in libraries and lectures, between essays and love affairs. . . . I didn't know anything—about life, at least. I remember thinking out the primitive first idea of it, which was that of someone who had the weight of a future life amorphously dragging in front of her, someone whose major decisions were all to come, and who found that they had got made whilst she wasn't looking.

(p. vii)

Aside from being a very readable novel, *The Shadow of the Sun* establishes several themes that will continue to be important in Byatt's later novels. First of all, her interest in the female life of the mind will be a central issue for all of her heroines. Second, Henry Severell, the heroine's father, provides the model for a series of characters who struggle with the distinction between brilliance and madness. And, finally, Byatt's fascination with describing the world and its natural curiosities will continue to resurface.

The Shadow of the Sun begins with a description of the house that becomes a central metaphor for what shapes the main character, Anna, and for what she desperately wants to escape. An acutely sensitive teenager, Anna has no idea what to do with herself. She knows that she wants to write, to be like her brilliant and detached father, Henry Severell, a famous Wordsworth and Coleridge scholar. However, trapped by the way her mother sees her, she remains awkward, sullen, and hopeless. Part One begins the summer after Anna has tried to escape from boarding school, an unsuccessful journey that took her to York, where she found that having "a room of one's own" could be depressing and alienating. Back home, the routine continues as usual. Her father is encased in his library, oblivious to the desires of her mother, Caroline, a woman weighted under the disappointment of her unfulfilling life. Her brother, Jeremy, is the "normal" child. He plays nicely in the yard, and, unlike Anna, he relates well to adults.

Even in this first novel, Byatt displays her gift for description. She explores every detail of an image to the fullest possible extent. The first depiction of Anna's adolescent body is a good example:

She was small for her age apparently, and thin, with pronounced hollows above the bones at the base of her neck; she suffered, nevertheless, from that late adolescent padding of flesh which cannot be called fat, or even puppy fat, but contributes to a certain squareness to the whole appearance of girls of a certain age, adds a heaviness to the cheeks and chin, makes the waist less marked, and the ankles thicker than they may later be, and suggests . . . even in those who carry themselves well, a certain inevitable clumsiness. Anna did not carry herself well most of the time.

(p. 10)

Here, the discriminating eye of the narrator replaces the "I" of the subject. Byatt never writes in the first person unless she is quoting from a character's journal or letters. The omnipresent narrator is responsible, then, for making the character come alive. The description of Anna is painfully detailed and feels embarrassingly accurate. Anna has not yet begun to live in her body, and the novel will be about how she grows into her own skin.

The action of the first part of the novel centers around a visit from Oliver and Margaret Cannings, friends of the Severells. Oliver is a literary critic who has written extensively on Henry's work. The opposite of the quiet, reserved Henry, Oliver is always offering his opinion, nervously dancing around his audience in an attempt to sound intelligent. His wife, Margaret, is a pretty woman with the proper graces and social skills. Margaret admires Henry deeply and suffers from spousal neglect. While at first Anna admires Margaret, she later realizes that Margaret is a dependent woman who is destined to be unhappy and ignored. Henry, Oliver, Caroline, and Margaret provide a bleak commentary on adult role models. Anna looks to them for guidance and advice, but soon discovers that she must reject their ideas in order to formulate her own story.

The first part of the novel also establishes the formidable presence of Henry, whom Byatt describes in the introduction to the book as "partly simply my secret self. . . . Someone who saw everything too bright too fierce too much" (p. ix). Henry's vision, his ability to "see" things too clearly, is his brilliance as well as the source of his madness. Unable to write, he begins to wander around the fields for long periods of time, losing himself in the landscape. Byatt describes how Henry perceives the light: "Light began to move, lines of poppies were nooses of fire, rushing upwards out of the ground. He began to move again with it, running awkwardly down the hill into the burning harvest; trees and bushes flamed, slid past him, hissed in the heat and crashed behind him" (p. 79). These ventures give Byatt the opportunity to describe natural phenomena in detail, an interest that she will continue to explore in her later novels.

As the title of the novel suggests, Byatt is particularly interested in metaphors and allusions that have to do with light, heat, and the sun. In his madness and brilliance, Henry Severell is the sun—something life-giving and self-sufficient that has no shadow. Yet all of the characters, particularly Anna, struggle with the problem of existing in Henry's shadow—which may be interpreted as the shadow of living and working under male literary figures, male educators, and male privilege. Anna

discovers that she is like Oliver, a man who makes his living by writing about other people's genius. Anna is an interpreter and a reader, a secondary thinker, not a primary creator like her father. Since this is Byatt's first novel, the issue of who has the right to create and the debilitating process of believing that one can create out of the shadows of others is a central concern. Byatt explains: "I wanted my harvest, both in my life and in my work, and I was afraid that my light was a lesser one, a cold one, that could only mildly illuminate, however hauntingly" (p. xv).

Anna's introduction to sexuality begins at the end of Part One, when Oliver (who has become her tutor for the Cambridge entrance exams) attempts to seduce her. While Anna initially finds this amusing, she later starts a serious affair with Oliver when she arrives at Cambridge. At the same time, she meets Peter Hughes-Winterton, a suitable boyfriend who represents the possibility of a "normal" life: status, stability, marriage. While Anna is discovering herself as a student, lover, and social being, Margaret, Oliver's wife, is slowly self-destructing. Lonely and desperate, Margaret appeals to Henry and Caroline for help. Meanwhile, Anna has become pregnant with Oliver's child. When Henry comes to Cambridge to confront Oliver about neglecting Margaret, he learns of the affair and must finally come to terms with his adult daughter and Oliver, his longtime rival and nemesis.

Ultimately, Anna rejects her father's offer to pay her passage to Mexico so that she can write (too dangerous) as well as Peter Hughes-Winterton's proposal (too ordinary) and settles for Oliver (a compromise between the two). Although Anna does come to know herself better in the end, the novel leaves the reader with a sense of forced closure, similar to the ending of Jane Austen's novels, where all of the domestic arrangements must come out right. The question of how the novel ends—or if a story can end—is a recurring theme of Byatt's later work.

In her second novel, *The Game*, Byatt pays specific attention to the complexities of emotional obsessions and attachments. Halfway through the book, one of the main characters gets the idea for a novel, an idea that sounds strangely like the story in which she is a character. She thinks, "It would be a real novel, with a real idea behind it, not a complaint. It would be a way of coming to grips with Cassandra, but also of detaching us" (p. 163). With this sentence, Julia Corbett describes the main plot of *The Game*, a psychological novel about the attachment of two intensely intelligent, creative, and stubborn sisters who decide to use their respective literary talents in very different ways. Julia is a novelist who is well known for her books about women trapped in claustrophobic domestic situations. She is married to Thor Eskelund, a 1960s activist, and has one daughter, Deborah, who is convinced that Julia is ruining their lives by making them all unattractive characters in her novels.

Cassandra, her sister, is a don at Oxford. Unlike sociable Julia, she lives a lonely and secluded life in her faculty apartment and keeps a set of meticulously organized journals in which she records her thoughts and feelings. Although they live very different adult lives, two issues keep the siblings connected. One is their memories of "the Game," an elaborate system of clay figures and maps that they designed as children and played every day for ten years. The other is Simon Moffitt, the man they both love.

Simon is a herpetologist with his own television program. As a scientist, he approaches the world through the analysis of facts. For him, magnifying empirical data opens up new fields of knowledge. Simon narrates, "We achieve, with magnification, a new dimension of strangeness. We enter new worlds. Our own becomes less stable. . . . Our picture of reality is never fixed but can always be elaborated and made more accurate. And this changes us" (p. 25). Similarly, as writers, Julia and Cassandra magnify facts and in a sense make things "more real" through their textual distortions. Simon's commentary on the snakes mirrors the issues that the sisters face in their struggle to come to terms with their imaginative powers and with their hold on one another.

The action of the novel begins with the death of the sisters' father, an event that forces them to return home to confront their childhood, Simon, and the Game. After a few uncomfortable weeks, Julia and Cassandra decide to try to be friends and to leave the past behind them. Although Julia thinks that this half reconciliation will make her life better, she slowly begins to realize that her conflict with Cassandra is not the only thing that is making her unhappy. Her husband, the quiet, Nordic Thor, takes in a homeless family without consulting her.

She is seduced by Ivan, a colleague, who has a television talk show on the arts, and her daughter becomes increasingly distant and decides to make Cassandra her confidante.

Feeling lonely and confused, Julia takes a trip to Oxford to visit Cassandra. The descriptions of dinner with the dons and a makeshift dinner party that Cassandra throws in her honor will later provide the material for Julia's own novel. An embarrassing anecdote about Cassandra's table manners at the dons' dinner is particularly memorable:

The main course was dried lamb chops, dried mashed potatoes, and drying tinned spaghetti in tomato sauce. Cassandra, leaning across to address someone, entangled her dangling crucifix in the spaghetti. It had to be wiped clean. Julia was rigid with embarrassment; obsessed by an image of the bloody loops of paste over the rigid, jeweled arms of the cross, she saw her sister ludicrous, even grotesque, and could not meet her eye.

(p. 131)

Cassandra's archaic jewelry, her awkward presence, and her lack of social graces are "grotesque" to Julia, yet the image is a poignant reminder of how much Cassandra lives in her own sphere, untouched by the outside world. Julia, however, is unable to connect with the breadth of her own internal intellectual capacity. She is too concerned with how things appear to others.

As the novel progresses, Cassandra slowly recedes into madness, while Julia tries to carve out her own unique identity. She becomes distant from Thor, who eventually leaves her, and begins to work on her novel about Cassandra. Meanwhile, Simon returns from the jungle. In a very funny scene, Ivan, Julia's lover, has Simon as a guest on his show, *The Lively Arts*. Ivan explains why he sees Simon's nature program as art:

Now, I'd have said one thing that characterizes our culture is a hunger for *facts*. A tremendous need to understand, to map out, to believe in the solid world we live in. Art doesn't give it as it used to. . . . Now, once the artist— oh, think of the Flemish painters, think of the Victorian novelists—used to delight in reproducing the details of the world he lived in. But not any more. What documentary art we've got is a bit flat and uninspired. But what about our real documentaries?

(p. 192)

Ivan's point is a theme that Byatt continues to work through: Is it possible for novels to provide "real" documentation—to evoke, as he says, the "solid world that we live in"? Simon is frustrated by Ivan's characterization of his work, and like Cassandra, he isn't good in public. The other guests keep trying to make meaning out of the snakes. One says, "Snakes are absolutely *weighed down* with meanings for the average man—you kept referring to them quite naturally on your programmes— death and rebirth, evil and healing, water and light, oh, you know, and sex, look at your Freud" (p. 195). Simon replies, "I like snakes.... You can make anything of me . . . as you can make anything of snakes" (p. 196).

At the same time that this interchange pokes fun at the media literati, Byatt poses a provocative question about the power of images: How do we represent things, and how can our representations alter the image in question? She clearly admires Victorian novelists and Flemish painters for their deliberate attention to accuracy. She is drawn toward an aesthetics of description, mapping, plotting, and landscaping. However, the question of interpretation always remains, because Byatt's tool is language, and words never mean just one thing— especially for her. She will fully address the problem of attempting to describe "the thing itself" accurately in her novel *Still Life* (1987).

Ultimately, Julia's novel is so close to a "real" depiction of Cassandra that the book is the catalyst for Cassandra's suicide. Despite Simon's attempts to connect with Cassandra, she is unable to bring herself back to the material world. The book ends with Julia and Simon packing Cassandra's things. Byatt suggests that Julia's new novel is a big hit and that Simon is off to Malaya, but there is no detail about what kind of impact Cassandra's death will have on the characters in the long run. In the end there is a sense of relief, and the issue of what will happen to Cassandra's journals. The last sentence of the novel raises more questions than it answers: "Behind Julia and Simon, in the dark boot of the car, closed into crates, unread, unopened, Cassandra's private papers bumped and slid" (p. 286). The ambiguous and secretive ending of *The Game* will be typical of the unresolved denouements of Byatt's later novels.

THE PROJECTED TETRALOGY

IN the years between *The Shadow of the Sun* and the first novel of the projected tetralogy, *The Virgin in*

the Garden, Byatt wrote two books of criticism, *Degrees of Freedom: The Novels of Iris Murdoch* (1965) and *Unruly Times: Wordsworth and Coleridge in Their Time* (1970). In addition to editing and writing introductions for numerous publications, she taught at University College, London, and wrote radio scripts. In 1969, she divorced her first husband, Charles Rayner Byatt, and married Peter Duffy. With Duffy she had two daughters, Isabel and Miranda.

Tragically, her only son, Charles, died in an automobile accident in 1972. *The Virgin in the Garden* is dedicated to him, and there is a shadowy figure in the prologue who resembles Byatt herself. One of the central characters, a well-meaning curate, has a client who needs his help. "Someone was a woman whose son had been damaged in a smash. He had been a beautiful boy, and still was, a walking unreal figure of a beautiful boy, a wax doll inhabited alternately by a screaming demon and a primitive organism that ate and bulged and slept, amoebalike" (p. 16). This is as close as we get to the elusive Byatt, who is careful not to represent "herself" as a main character. Still, this brief poetic description is a haunting mark of her own experience.

In a *New York Times* review by Mel Gussow, Byatt is quoted as contending that she is nothing like the trilogy's (soon to be a quartet) heroine, Frederica, whom she describes as "a slightly transgressive independent woman" (p. C11). She goes on to add that what she wants to avoid are novels that are "self-exculpatorial or self-regarding" (p. C12). Although both of her early novels were generally well reviewed, Byatt established herself as a major literary presence with *The Virgin in the Garden*. Critics of the book set the stage for what would continue to be a divided debate on Byatt's prose. Most readers find her novels extremely dense, intelligent, and particularly British. However, some reviewers find Byatt too self-consciously literary.

In a review of *The Virgin in the Garden* for the *New Statesman*, Iris Murdoch, a great supporter of Byatt wrote, "It [the novel] is a large, complex, ambitious work, humming with energy and ideas" (p. 586). And critic Paul Levy placed Byatt within the context of canonical authors: "*The Virgin in the Garden* . . . is a good example of proper literary ambition. It is, and practically declares itself to be, a novel in the European realist tradition, and it demands comparison with the masters in that tradition" (p. 58). However, Daphne Merkin, an American critic, wrote, "[It] is clear why Byatt is unknown on these shores: She is very English—insularly so. . . . She writes out of an imperturbable tradition of English literature. . . . The men and women in her latest novel bear some resemblance to present-day men and women; they also resemble the men and women of Charlotte Brontë, George Eliot and Thomas Hardy" (p. 16). The question of whether her copious literary references and allusions are delightful or distracting is an issue that Byatt attempts to resolve, unsuccessfully, with the second volume of the projected tetralogy, *Still Life.* The debate continues with her more recent novels. Although critics did not seem to mind the literariness of *Possession,* reviewers of *Babel Tower* were quick to point out the dense quality of the narrative.

In *Passions of the Mind,* Byatt explains that *The Virgin in the Garden* was written with a specific goal in mind: "In the 1960's, I set out to write a series of what might be described as self consciously realist novels about my own time and my own culture" (p. 15). *The Virgin in the Garden* is set in 1953, the year of the coronation of Elizabeth II, and includes a verse drama about Elizabeth I. The issues in the novel also reflect Byatt's discoveries at Cambridge:

Intellectually it [the novel] is—among other things—a response to T. S. Eliot's ideas of the history of poetic language. . . . The play in my novel, and the novel itself, are nostalgia for a *paradis perdu* in which thought and language and things were naturally and indissolubly linked or, to use an Eliot metaphor, fused. In my experience I know what the form of a novel is when I find what I think of as the "ruling" metaphor. In the case of this novel this was a metaphor of metamorphosis.

(pp. 3–4)

In *The Virgin in the Garden,* Byatt cleverly parallels metaphors associated with Queen Elizabeth past and present to the growth of Frederica, a heroine caught in the trap of her own continuous literary analysis. Frederica is a more developed version of Anna, Byatt's first heroine, and the book is similarly concerned with her metamorphosis from childhood to adult consciousness. Elizabeth I is a provocative symbol because she represents an ambivalent (nontraditional) image of female power and sexuality. Elizabeth had power because she fiercely safeguarded her chastity. A central question of *The Virgin in the Garden* is how Frederica can retain her strength, intellectual power, and autonomy while negotiating relationships with men. And, more important, will she have to sacrifice her intellectual "masculine" temperament in order to behave like a "normal" woman?

The novel is set in Yorkshire, where Frederica's father, Bill Potter, is a teacher at the Blesford Ride boarding school, which she describes as "a reasonably usual liberal school: all things to all men, middle of the road, minor" (p. 22). Bill sets the tone of the intellectual, agnostic household with his speeches, perfectionism, and demands. Frederica is the most obvious brain of the three children, although Stephanie, the pretty, gentle sister, is equally smart. Marcus, the youngest sibling, is a kind of mad genius character (a cross between Henry Severell and Cassandra Corbett), someone whose keen powers of observation keep him from interacting with the "real" world. Winifred Potter is the dutiful mother who puts up with Bill and makes peace in the house at all costs. The novel also introduces other characters who will be featured in the later volumes: Daniel Orton, the curate struggling with his own desires and beliefs, who will later become Stephanie's husband; and Alexander Wedderburn, Frederica's first passion, a playwright who comes to Blesford Ride to direct his original play, *Astraea.* For Frederica and Stephanie, Alexander represents "things they had not got, desired, and feared they would not have: art as opposed to criticism of it, male mobility as opposed to female provincial rootedness, savoir faire, and the possibility of metropolitan glamour to come" (p. 47).

The novel begins with the planning of Alexander's play at the Blesford Ride school, a performance commemorating the coronation of Queen Elizabeth II. The activity of the small community provides Byatt with the opportunity to discuss the villagers' politics, views on religion, education, government, family values, and so on, while at the same time she can center the narrative on the lives of the Potter family. Frederica is cast as the young queen in Alexander's production, an opportunity that exposes her to the London artistic scene and literati, and also to questions about performance and femininity.

Unlike Frederica, Stephanie is less concerned with making herself a noticeable presence. Stephanie's "traditional" choices provide a contrast to the headstrong ways and literary dreams of Frederica.

Her narrative in the novel follows her relationship with and eventual marriage to Daniel, an oafish man who is desperately in love with her. Daniel is presented as both a safe and a dangerous choice for Stephanie—safe in that his expectations of her would be traditional, and dangerous because she would have to struggle to carve out her own unique place while paying attention to her dual role as wife and mother. Stephanie plays a greater role in the second volume of the series, *Still Life*, but *The Virgin in the Garden* establishes this strong, almost intangible connection between Stephanie and her unlikely suitor.

The other main story line in *The Virgin in the Garden* involves brother Marcus, who is slowly losing his grip on the "real" world. Like Byatt's descriptions of Henry Severell's wanderings in *The Shadow of the Sun*, Marcus's way of processing visual information goes beyond the ordinary:

He had played a game called spreading himself. This began with a deliberate extension of his field of vision. . . . He was quite little when he became good at this game, and quite little when it went beyond his control. Sometimes, for immeasurable instants he lost any sense of where he really was, of where the spread mind had its origin.

(p. 27)

Lucas Simmonds, a scientist at Blesford Ride, becomes interested in studying the way that Marcus "sees" things. After Simmonds makes a sexual advance toward Marcus, Marcus has a nervous breakdown. The novel ends with Marcus taking refuge at Stephanie's house. *Still Life* deals with his slow recovery.

The Marcus section of the novel is a sharp contrast to the Frederica sections, which are full of heady intellectual dialogues, literary references, and dilemmas. Frederica makes sense of her life by comparing herself to characters in novels and by instinctively writing her own story as if she were in a book. Her problems, then, center on getting beyond her own imagination. For example, understanding her fantasy of London as compared with her life in Yorkshire requires some extra reading in nineteenth-century literature:

If you lived up here, you supposed landscape was of the essence, you had a Brontesque sense of using it to think and perceive with but at the same time it was in the way. You could neither see it nor through it, it was thickened with too many associations. Momentarily she envisaged an imaginary London flat, possibly Alexander's, smooth pale woods, much white, closed curtains, soft light, artificial shapes, squared, rounded, streamlined, touches of cream and gold.

(p. 203)

This passage is an example of what makes Frederica, and by extension Byatt, either brilliant or impenetrable. If the reader understands the creative adjective "Brontesque," then the comparison makes perfect sense. If not, the description is odd and elusive.

What Frederica gains in the first volume of the projected tetralogy is a certain confidence in her own performances. She is magnificent as the young queen in Alexander's play, and she has her first lover. Ironically, while losing her virginity, Frederica realizes that life doesn't always imitate literature. Unlike Lawrence's Constance Chatterley, Frederica decides that she can experience something and remain detached and autonomous: "She had learned that you could do—that—in a reasonably companionable and courteous way with no invasion of your privacy, no shift in your solitude" (p. 421). Frederica's acknowledgment of the split between her mind and her body will continue to occupy and torment her throughout the subsequent volumes of the projected tetralogy.

At the end of *The Virgin in the Garden*, all of the characters are in limbo: Frederica is waiting to hear from Cambridge, Stephanie is pregnant, and Marcus may or may not recuperate. In the last scene of the novel, Frederica and Daniel are sitting on a couch in an uncomfortable silence. Byatt writes, "That was not an end, but since it went on for a considerable time, it is as good a place to stop as any" (p. 428). In true realist fashion this novel does not end, and *Still Life* picks up where *The Virgin in the Garden* leaves off.

With the second novel in her projected tetralogy, *Still Life*, Byatt set out to do something different from her earlier work. In *Passions of the Mind* she writes, "The idea of the second novel of the series—*Still Life*—was that it should, by contrast, be very bare, very down-to-earth, attempt to give the 'thing itself' without the infinitely extensible cross-referencing of *The Virgin*. I wanted to write about birth, about death, plainly and exactly" (p. 5). Accordingly, the title *Still Life* refers to the genre of painting that is concerned with depicting objects; but also, read literally, "still life" means just that: that a goal of fiction is *still* to represent *life.*

When thinking about the project, Byatt became interested in Van Gogh's paintings of objects, in particular his representation of the yellow chair. For Byatt, Van Gogh's way of painting images corresponded to her wish to represent events in and of themselves without the clutter of literary allusions and metaphors. In *Still Life,* Alexander Wedderburn is working on a play called *The Yellow Chair,* which is about Van Gogh's relationship to his work and to his brother Theo. Like Henry Severell's musings on the fiery cornfields in *The Shadow of the Sun,* Van Gogh made ordinary objects extraordinary by playing with representations of light. The content of *Still Life* deals with this question: How can description clearly depict objects, events, and characters? In addressing this issue, Byatt found that describing the "real" or the ordinary events of a life still invoked the surreal. Lurking in the background of the novel is a side narrative about a man who watched his insane wife kill their child. Stephanie tries to help him even though she is horrified by his actions. This character from the world "outside" the novel functions as a mimetic trope. The reader is forced to acknowledge that there are levels of reality even in the novel itself.

Like many of Byatt's novels, *Still Life* deals with the positive and negative aspects of life in a small town, from the warmth of Christmas pageants to the insularity of provincial attitudes. Much of the novel takes place in and around the Orton household. In addition to her two children, Stephanie must take care of Daniel's intrusive mother and of Marcus, who is recuperating from his earlier trauma. Meanwhile, the senior Potters, Bill and Winifred, are still mystified by Marcus's strange behavior and hurt that he has rejected them. Daniel must come to terms with his wife's distraction and depression, as well as an overzealous new head curate, who seems to be brainwashing the village children. Like *The Virgin in the Garden, Still Life* begins with a prologue. It occurs in 1980, some thirty years later than the action in the novel. Frederica, Daniel, and Alexander are at a Postimpressionist exhibition. (In the beginning of the first novel, they are viewing portraits of Queen Elizabeth.) The prologue introduces Van Gogh into the text, but also continues to establish the projected tetralogy as a series of extended flashbacks. We never get to the present in the novels, which suggests the possibility for many sequels.

Juxtaposed with this opening is the "realistic" first chapter, which describes Stephanie's harrowing visit to the obstetrician. Byatt poignantly describes how Stephanie tries to read Wordsworth in a chairless waiting room full of pregnant women. As if that weren't bad enough, the woman next to her complains of pain and is ignored, only to collapse hemorrhaging on the floor several minutes later. When Stephanie complains to the doctor, he replies, "Don't be hysterical. It's bad for the child" (p. 17). The Wordsworth lines that she had been reading—"She neither hears nor sees / Rolled round in earth's diurnal course, / With rocks, and stones, and trees"—seem ironic and ridiculous in the context of her experience.

The separation between mind and body is one of the themes that Byatt continues to explore in *Still Life.* The reader learns a lot about Stephanie's body: we go through her giving birth, her time in the hospital, her relationship to her pregnant and post-pregnant body, and her physical attachment to her son. While Stephanie is bound to her body and to maternity, Frederica is strengthening her mind at Cambridge and worrying about the effect her body/sexuality has on others. Her new idol is the asexual and brilliant Raphael Faber, who holds exclusive literary salons in his faculty apartment and is alternately cruel and seductive. Coming of age at Cambridge, Frederica is both ridiculed and admired. She has several lovers, one of whom will later become her abusive husband. As Frederica tries to balance her studies with her relationships, Stephanie struggles to find time to read Wordsworth and to retain some of her former identity.

The main event of the novel occurs toward the end of the book, when Stephanie dies in a freak accident. She is electrocuted by a refrigerator while she is trying to rescue an injured bird. Although Byatt is quoted in a *New York Times* review (Gussow, 9 July 1996) as explaining that a similar accident happened to her (she was saved by her husband), the significance of Stephanie being killed by a heavy household appliance is not lost on the reader. None of the characters realize how much they have come to rely on Stephanie until she is gone, which is a chilling comment on the effects of domestic expectations on women. The novel connects domesticity with loss from the very beginning. The characters deal with their fear of compromise and dependency, and there is a pervasive nostalgia for youth and simpler times.

In contrast to *The Virgin in the Garden,* Byatt adds her own voice to the text of *Still Life.* She explains her thought process about what to do with the narrative after Stephanie is gone: "There is a temptation to hurry over the next part of their lives, particularly Daniel's. . . . Once novels ended with marriages. Now we know better" (p. 368). She also admits, somewhat indirectly, that what she set out to do with the novel—to describe events in and of themselves without using metaphors and endless literary references—was impossible. In fact, she cannot describe the effect of Stephanie's death on Daniel without invoking ideas of grief in Shakespeare's *King Lear* and the idea of death as an illusion in *Hamlet.* At the end of the novel, Daniel cannot let go of the memory of his wife, and he cannot bear to live the life that he had with her without her. He leaves the village, handing his two children over to Bill and Winifred, who with their grandchildren eventually become the wonderful parents that they could have been with their own children. The novel ends ambiguously, with no mention of what the characters will do next, or how the projected tetralogy will continue.

Babel Tower is the third volume in the continuing tale of the Potter family. Deliberately complex, it may be a kind of response to the playful tone of *Possession,* a romantic detective novel that joyfully pokes fun at a divided academic literary community. (It is interesting to note that while *Possession* made Byatt a superstar and received mostly rave reviews, the more dense and ambivalent *Babel Tower* has not garnered the same kind of fanfare.) An ambitious project, the 619-page novel has two parallel narratives: one follows Frederica through a messy divorce, a custody battle, and life as a teacher and writer in North London; the other is a novella within the novel, *Babbletower: A Tale for the Children of Our Time,* a modern-day fairy tale by the psychotic and provocative Jude Mason. Jude is the mad genius character of the novel. Unlike the gentle Henry Severell, Jude is presented as dirty and deranged, both fascinating and repulsive. The backdrop of the novel is the 1960s in Britain, a decade that saw the collapse of long-held ideas about the government, censorship, and sexuality. In "Note for American Readers," Byatt cites the Profumo scandal, the Moors murders, the prosecution and acquittal of the publishers of *Lady Chatterley's Lover,* and the prosecution and conviction of the publishers of *Last Exit to Brooklyn* as events that characterized the "moral atmosphere of 'swinging London' and the 'permissive society' in England in the 1960's" (p. ix).

The title of the book and the novel within the novel are borrowed from the biblical tale in which God creates different languages to punish man's attempts to get closer to heaven, thereby making it impossible for people to communicate with each other. This idea of a fallen man and his fallen language is something that Byatt has dealt with before. In *Babel Tower,* however, the metaphors associated with disrupted communication, varieties of representation, alienation, and identification are presented as both thrilling and potentially dangerous. Unlike Frederica's fantasy of London in *The Virgin in the Garden,* or Henry Severell's mad view of the moors in *The Shadow of the Sun,* interpretations and misinterpretations in *Babel Tower* have real consequences.

The novel begins with the increasingly uncomfortable story of Frederica's unhappy marriage to Nigel Reiver, a man she met while at Cambridge. When asked why she consented to marry Reiver, a well-respected businessman, Frederica blames the unwise decision on her devastation over her sister Stephanie's sudden death. However, Frederica's attachment to Nigel seems to have more to do with the issue of the division between mind and body that Byatt is continuously exploring. Frederica finds physical passion with Nigel, something that she believes will sustain and comfort her. She soon discovers that there is no room in his household for her intellectual pursuits.

Trapped in the countryside with Nigel's family, Frederica realizes she must do something after her relationship with Nigel deteriorates to an episode where he comes after her with an ax. Luckily her friends from Cambridge, Alan Melville, Hugh Pink, and Edmund Wilkie, come to visit her, and in a daring rescue whisk her away in the middle of the night with her son. Once established in London, Frederica gets a job reviewing manuscripts for publication (one of which is Jude Mason's *Babbletower*) and teaching literature classes at the Samuel Palmer School of Art and Craft. (Against the backdrop of the art school, Byatt describes the interdisciplinary experimental atmosphere of the 1960s, complete with performance art and body painting.) Frederica's new roommate is also a single mother and a writer. In a telling moment when Frederica first sees the flat, empty and bare, she wonders how she will make a home for her son, Leo. She has no experience doing this, and all of her examples are from a world that she does not want to belong to. She manages, though, to set up the flat, and she sends Leo to a progressive school, a far cry from the upper-crust boarding school that his father would like him to attend. Frederica's ability to make her own domestic arrangements reflects the changing environment of the 1960s, as well as a different path for Byatt's heroines. The novel no longer needs a significant male character to hold the narrative together.

Frederica's only love interest in *Babel Tower* is her tangential affair with one of her students, the mysterious John Ottokar. Ottokar has an identical twin, who deliberately stalks the couple in an effort to be closer to his brother. Byatt's inclusion of Ottokar seems to have more to do with the larger issues of the novel than with Frederica's development. Byatt's exploration of twins, parallel narratives, and opposite categories such as tradition/revolution, rich/poor, male/female, black/white, domestic/intellectual is one of the themes that holds the novel together, although none of these binaries is fully interrogated or dismantled. Instead, Byatt gives us her version of the messy world of distinctions that Frederica inhabits and must come to terms with.

Frederica's new life is interspersed with portions of *Babbletower*, which is about the creation of a utopian community. The Krebs' effort to stick to their motto, "complete freedom for each and every member to live and express himself—or herself—to the utmost" (p. 65), begins to break down when no one can answer the question "And who will be responsible for cleaning the latrines?" (p. 69). There follow accounts of the perversity and disaster of a society that cannot cope with its newfound philosophy. Byatt turns her talent for describing the natural to gory depictions of the supernatural or unexplained phenomena. When the Lady Roseace ventures out of the village for a walk, she discovers "a green twig, with tight, energetic little buds. And from the severed end came a slow dark gout of blood, a clot of thick blood like a liver-coloured slug humping its way free, and behind it gushed a freshet of red blood, which sprayed her habit with

fine scarlet drops" (p. 137). This strange scene is an omen of things to come. When the Lady Roseace begins to ask questions and to disagree with her husband, Culvert, the leader of the Krebs, she is sexually tortured and mutilated. Byatt alludes to this portion of *Babbletower* in the account of the book's obscenity trial, but she does not reproduce this section for us to read.

The omission of the crucial, perhaps unreadable section of *Babbletower* is like the omission of the rape scene from Samuel Richardson's *Clarissa*. The reader is left without evidence of "the event," and in the case of *Babbletower*, of what makes the book pornographic material. By contrast, the reader is let into Frederica's thought process and her version of the events leading up to her separation from Nigel, so by the time we get to her custody trial, we are armed with the "real" story. Byatt's omissions and additions suggest something provocative about the way that we read and judge diverse written material. In fact, Frederica spends much of the novel trying to write her story in different ways: for her lawyer, in her journal, and ultimately in a novel. In using these dissimilar narratives, Byatt poses the question "Does context, content, or format change interpretation, and if it does, how, why, and for whose benefit?"

The book ends with two court cases about this issue of interpretation. One is to decide the fate of Frederica's son: Will the jury believe Frederica's tale of abuse or Nigel's story of a neglected husband? And the other is to decide whether the novella *Babbletower* is obscene and should not be allowed on the shelves. In the custody battle, the outcome depends on a fair interpretation of the events of Frederica's marriage, an interpretation that we can see will rely heavily on the judge's prejudicial view of Frederica's wish to be independent. The *Babbletower* case rests on an equally intangible aesthetic determination. The jury must decide whether *Babbletower* is worthy literature, at the same time that Byatt's readers are judging *Babel Tower* as a whole. The outcomes of the two trials are both positive and negative. Frederica loses her divorce case but wins her custody battle. *Babbletower* is pronounced obscene in the first trial, a decision that is eventually overturned on appeal.

What Frederica learns in this volume of the proposed tetralogy is ultimately how to be her own person; how to survive gender prejudice, cruelty, and her own imagination and desires. She starts to write a novel, discovers that she loves teaching, and begins an affair with a man who does not define her identity. Byatt sums up Frederica's psychological journey in a telling passage in the middle of the novel:

And she, Frederica, had had a vision of being able to be all the things she was: language, sex, friendship, thought, just as long as these things were kept scrupulously separated, *laminated,* like geological strata, not seeping and flowing into each other like organic cells boiling to join and divide and join in a seething Oneness. Things were best cool, and clear, and fragmented, if fragmented was what they were."

(pp. 314–315)

For the first time in the proposed tetralogy, Frederica is able to accept herself and to celebrate her complicated nature. Ironically, when she gives up her fantasy of "oneness," something that perhaps can be achieved only by characters in novels, she can finally accept her "mosaic" nature and come to terms with the disparate parts of herself. This philosophy is, in turn, a way of thinking about all of the complicated pairs and parallels that Byatt presents in the novel. With all of its disparate parts and complicated themes, a coherent way to understand *Babel Tower* is to think of it as a kind of mosaic. At the same time that the issues "divide and join in a seething Oneness," they can be mapped out like "geological strata." There is an order to everything that Byatt does, and it is up to the reader not to give up if the navigation is rough going.

VICTORIAN INFLUENCES: POSSESSION AND ANGELS AND INSECTS

BACKTRACKING a bit from *Babel Tower,* released in the United States in 1996, in the 1980s Byatt published *Still Life* (1985), and *Sugar and Other Stories* (1987). In addition to editing *George Eliot: Selected Essays, Poems and Other Writings* (1989), she wrote introductions to works by Grace Paley, Willa Cather, and Elizabeth Bowen. Aside from her lecture tours in Europe, Byatt traveled the world, speaking in India, Hong Kong, China, and Korea. She continued to teach and to work on the impressive texts

that she published in the 1990s, which include *Possession: A Romance* (1990), *Angels and Insects* (1992), *Passions of the Mind* (1993), and *The Matisse Stories* (1993).

Without question Byatt's most successful work is *Possession: A Romance.* The novel was published first in England and then in the United States, where it remained on the best-seller list for weeks and sold thousands of copies. Byatt won two prestigious literary awards for *Possession:* the Booker Prize and the Irish Times/Aer Lingus International Prize for Fiction. When asked, in a telephone interview with Mervyn Rothstein, why she thought the book was so successful, Byatt replied, "It's like the books people used to enjoy reading. . . . It has a universal plot, a classic romantic plot and a classic detective plot" (p. 17).

With *Possession,* Byatt intuitively anticipated the American audience's love for all things classically British. Like the enormously successful Merchant-Ivory productions and the popular BBC production of *Pride and Prejudice, Possession* re-creates an English world of unrequited love, romantic poetry, breathtaking countrysides, and that titillating mixture of British propriety and mysterious passion. Byatt uses her descriptive talents to re-create British interiors past and present (there are wonderful detailed descriptions of people's bathrooms), and to mimic voices of the past. About half of the text contains portions of "nineteenth-century" manuscripts, poetry, fairy tales, letters, and journals.

While ventriloquizing voices from the past, Byatt mimics contemporary characters. The community of academics in the book, a mixture of Old World scholars and trendy theorists, are joyfully parodied and thrown together in a variety of silly situations. The story begins with Roland Michell, a disgruntled Ph.D. who has yet to find his place in the world of academe. He makes his living doing research for the renowned Randolph Henry Ash scholar James Blackadder, a traditional Cambridge academic who has devoted his life to the study of one poet. Roland makes a discovery in the first chapter that will continue to possess him throughout the novel. Folded into Ash's copy of Vico are two versions of a letter written to an unidentified woman. Roland slips the letters into his pocket, and the search for the mysterious lady begins. (Byatt later explained that she got the idea for *Possession* while working in the British Library. She noticed a

Coleridge scholar hard at work and began to think about the question "Does the scholar possess the poet or does the poet possess the scholar?")

Through a series of clues, Roland surmises that the anonymous lady is the accomplished poet Christabel LaMotte, a figure unknown in canonical circles but a heroine to feminist academics, who have rescued her from obscurity. The leading La-Motte scholar is Maud Bailey, a distant relative of the poet, who runs the women's studies department at Lincoln University. Maud, an elusive and serious scholar, is intrigued by Roland's discovery, and they become immersed in the process of locating the entire correspondence. The urgency of their quest is fed by their need to be the first scholars to get their hands on the previously unread material, and also by their unacknowledged sense that they are the people who truly understand the works of Ash and LaMotte. Hot on their trail are a group of hilarious characters: Leonora Stern, an aggressive American feminist lesbian who has written extensively on the relationship between LaMotte and the French psychoanalyst Jacques Lacan; Fergus Wolff, a handsome academic superstar, Roland's nemesis, and Maud's former lover; and Mortimer Cropper, an American millionaire who heads the museum devoted to Ash memorabilia and will stop at nothing to buy what he wants. In the background are the befuddled James Blackadder, Ash's official biographer, and Beatrice Nest, a scholar who has devoted her lifework to Ash's wife, Ellen, because her dissertation adviser told her that, as a woman, she should not work on Ash.

Embedded in the stereotypical representations of these overly earnest academics, is Byatt's implicit commentary on the slippery politics of academe, a world where careers are often built on false reputations and personal agendas. At the heart of the parody, however, is the passion of Roland and Maud for their subjects and eventually for each other. In one of the most exciting sequences of the novel, the two find themselves staying at Christabel's house, now owned by the eccentric couple George and Joan Bailey. In a scene like something out of a gothic novel, Maud and Roland are allowed to see Christabel's bedroom:

They went in behind Sir George, who waved his huge cone of light around the dark, cramped circular space, illuminating a semi-circular bay window, a roof carved with veined arches and mock-medieval ivy-leaves, felt-

textured with dust, a box-bed with curtains still hanging, showing a dull red under their pall of particles, a fantastically carved black wooden desk . . . a sudden row of staring tiny white faces, one, two, three, propped against a pillow. Roland drew his breath in minor shock; Maud said, "Oh, the *dolls*."

(p. 91)

Maud remembers that Christabel wrote a series of poems about the dolls, and like a spiritual medium she begins to recite one: "Dolly keeps a Secret/ Safer than a Friend/ Dolly's Silent Sympathy/ Lasts without end." Following LaMotte's clues, Maud dismantles the dolls' bed and finds a box that contains all of Christabel's letters to Ash and all of his to her. Despite the misgivings of George Bailey, Roland and Maud are finally permitted to study the letters, thus beginning the first of a series of trips that they will take together to try and decipher the complicated relationship of the two poets.

They learn from the letters that Ash met LaMotte at a breakfast party organized by the nineteenth-century socialite Henry Crabb Robinson. (Byatt often includes actual historical figures in her novels.) Ash was so intrigued by LaMotte that he began a correspondence with her, despite the fact that he was married. A spinster by choice, LaMotte lived with the artist Blanche Glover, who was devoted to her and to their life together. This relationship provides evidence for feminist academics who want to see their household as an example of lesbian cohabitation in the nineteenth century. However, the letters indicate that Ash and LaMotte found in each other what they did not find in their live-in companions: intellectual interchange, creative support, and, ultimately, love. Roland and Maud ascertain that when Ash decides to go on a scientific expedition (one of his hobbies), LaMotte secretly goes with him. When the correspondence abruptly ends, they surmise that LaMotte left Ash and fled to France, where she stayed with some distant relatives. It soon becomes clear that LaMotte was pregnant with Ash's child, which mysteriously vanished after its birth.

At the same time that the narrative follows the story of Ash and LaMotte, Roland and Maud become more obsessed with each other. They discover their passion for one another while retracing LaMotte and Ash's journeys. Meanwhile, Sir George decides to sue the scholarly duo when he discovers that Mortimer Cropper will pay him millions of dollars for the correspondence. In a panic, Cropper follows Maud and Roland from Yorkshire to Brittany, only to meet Leonora Stern and James Blackadder, who have formed an unlikely friendship. It isn't long before the entire search focuses on a box buried with Ash's body that contains the answer to what happened to the child. In a ridiculous scene out of a Restoration comedy, all of the main characters converge on a country graveyard in the early hours of the morning to stop Cropper from digging up Ash's remains and stealing the evidence.

The most rewarding moments of *Possession* occur when Byatt creates a scene for the reader that cannot be deduced from the scholar's written evidence. For example, she takes us through Ash's final hours and his wife's agonizing decision about whether to give him a letter from Christabel revealing the fate of their child. And we are treated to a flashback that reveals that Ash did in fact meet his daughter one spring day, although he never discloses that he is her father. These moments provide the reader with more information than the protagonists have— they do not have access to Ellen Ash's journal, which she destroyed, or know of Randolph Ash's encounter, which he never wrote about. This is the delight of fiction versus academic research. It is possible in the world of the imagination to re-create these events, to "know" what happened. Without textual evidence, however, the scholars are left with some permanent secrets. At this point in her career, Byatt seems to be acknowledging the coexistence of these two realms, literary and academic, in a joyful way rather than dwelling on the frustrating aspects of their relationship. Although some academic critics find *Possession* conservative and unadventurous, the novel continues to delight a wide variety of readers and no doubt will be thought of as a contemporary classic.

With the success of *Possession,* Byatt embarked on another nineteenth-century project with the novellas "Morpho Eugenia" and "The Conjugial Angel," in the collection *Angels and Insects* (1992). Like *Possession,* the book was enormously popular and received rave reviews. Critics compared Byatt to Vladimir Nabokov and Henry James. "Morpho Eugenia" was also the basis for a movie titled *Angels and Insects* (1995), starring Mark Rylance, Kristin Scott Thomas, and Patsy Kensit. Read together, the two novellas are a dense, extensive, and complex exploration of nineteenth-century thought.

"Morpho Eugenia" deals with Victorian speculations about the natural world. Byatt cleverly juxtaposes ideas about order, classification, natural selection, and metamorphosis with equally powerful ideas about civilization, savagery, religion, class, sexuality, and gender hierarchy. In "The Conjugial Angel" the spiritual world takes precedence over the material world. The novella re-creates the Victorian fascination for communicating with the dead through seances, mediums, and poetry.

In "Morpho Eugenia," Byatt applies one of her favorite "ruling metaphors," metamorphosis, to the story of an upper-class British family whose gentility carefully masks their inherent perversity. The novella opens with William Adamson's return from an expedition to the Amazon. While at a ball thrown by the Alabaster family, Adamson's thoughts turn to his travels:

> He remembered a *festa* on the Rio Manaquiry, lit by lamps made of half an orange-skin filled with turtle oil. He had danced with the *Juiza,* the lady of the revels, barefoot and in his shirtsleeves. There, his whiteness itself had given him automatic precedence at table. Here he seemed sultry-skinned with jaundice-gold mixed into sun-toasting.
>
> (pp. 3–4)

In this passage, the initial contrast of the Alabasters' ballroom and the wilds of the Amazon introduces the idea of metamorphosis. William occupies a different position in this world than he did in the unexplored regions of the jungle. Although he appears "darker" than the pale "alabasters," Byatt soon reveals that things are not what they appear. The safe, ordered world of the upper-crust Alabasters is all a facade, which ultimately is a provocative commentary on constructions of race and class. However, while Byatt asks questions about the oppositions light/dark, civilized/savage, she doesn't provide neat formulaic reversals. Rather, as in her other novels, what interests her are the shades of gray between the oppositions and the process by which people metamorphose from one end of the spectrum to the other.

William Adamson decides to stay with the Alabasters in order to catalog Mr. Harald Alabaster's collection of scientific specimens. Harald is another Henry Severell character, a benevolent patriarch who is too involved with his intellectual pursuits to see what is going on around him. Mr. Alabaster has three daughters: Rowena, Enid, and Eugenia. William finds himself desperately in love with Eugenia, the most mysterious and beautiful of the three. He seems unfazed by the allusion at the beginning of the novella to Eugenia's strange past. Enid explains, "Eugenia used to be the best of all, before she was unhappy.... She was to be married, you see, only Captain Hunt, her fiancé, died quite suddenly" (p. 6). As in the best melodramatic plots, this bit of news makes Eugenia either a tragic heroine or a suspicious character. William thinks the former, while the reader is continuously reminded that images should be read for their double nature.

With "Morpho Eugenia," Byatt returns to her interest in the relationship between scientific research and literary study that she explored in *The Game*. As Simon's study of snakes was metaphorically connected to the struggles of the protagonists, Julia and Cassandra, so William's fascination with butterflies and ants serves a similar function in the novella. The title "Morpho Eugenia" is a rare species of butterfly. When William presents a pair of them as a gift to Harald Alabaster, Harald exclaims: "How beautiful, how delicately designed, how wonderful that something so fragile should have come here, through such dangers, from the other end of the earth" (p. 21). William acknowledges how spectacular they are, but feels compelled to ask from a "scientific viewpoint" what "purpose of Nature's might be fulfilled by all this brilliance and loveliness" (p. 22). The allusion here is to the seductive Eugenia, who lures Adamson away from his "purpose" with her charms. Byatt suggests that Adamson should be paying attention to another character, the serious Matty Crompton, who has a talent for scientific research. Dark, careful, and plain, she is the opposite of Eugenia, very much like Charlotte Brontë's Jane Eyre. It is Matty who suggests that William turn his study of ant colonies into a book.

William marries Eugenia, after proposing to her in an odd scene where the butterflies he presents as a gift metamorphose into menacing black bugs. As he continues to work on his book with Matty, his relationship with his wife becomes more and more mysterious. Sometimes Eugenia is loving and passionate; at other moments she is cold and distant. Lurking in the background is the brooding Edgar Alabaster, Eugenia's handsome and rakish half-brother. He makes no secret of disliking William,

whom he feels is not good enough for the precious Eugenia. William gets a hint of what is going on during a card game, reminiscent of a scene in Jane Austen's *Emma*, where the word "insect" is rearranged to spell "incest." After this incident, William learns that Eugenia and Edgar are more intimate than half-siblings and that it is likely that all of his children are illegitimate. Ultimately, William decides to leave the Alabaster home and return to the Amazon with his newfound love, Matty Crompton.

In many ways "Morpho Eugenia" is both a fairy tale gone wrong and a revision of the plot of a traditional nineteenth-century novel. Byatt rewrites the role of the fairy-tale heroine, the woman who transgresses a boundary in order to learn a secret, as in the tales of Bluebeard and Pandora. In "Morpho Eugenia" a *man* is kept from the truth and duped by his own lack of curiosity. Although the novella has a typical nineteenth-century close, a happy ending where the couple who belong together end up together, the story ends with Matty and William sailing away from England, destabilizing the "natural order" of the traditional narrative that would have them setting up a good English household of their own. After all, William's last name is Adamson, or in reference to the Bible, Adam's son. "Morpho Eugenia" is clearly concerned with the metamorphosis of narrative conventions, an issue that Byatt cleverly combines with her brilliant reconstruction of the Victorian world.

THE MATISSE STORIES

IN 1993 Byatt published *The Matisse Stories*, her second short story collection. As Van Gogh was the figure who haunted the pages of *Still Life*, so Matisse's aesthetics, persona, and genius contribute to these tales of middle-aged women coming to terms with their creative potential.

The first story, "Medusa's Ankles," takes place in a beauty salon, where Susannah, a linguist, is having her hair done by her usual hairdresser, Lucian. With her characteristic wit and humor, Byatt describes Susannah's unique relationship with Lucian, whom she came to "trust with her disintegration." The talented Lucian "stood above her with his fine hands cupped lightly round her new bubbles and wisps, like the hands of a priest round a Grail. She looked, quickly, quickly, it was better than before, thanked him and averted her eyes" (p. 7). Like Byatt's initial description of Anna, the heroine of her first novel, *The Shadow of the Sun,* this image captures the insecurity and uneasiness of a woman trapped by changes in her body. Susannah becomes so frustrated with her aging that in a fit of rage she destroys the salon, hurling a container of hairpins around her head and pulling dryer plugs from their sockets. The calming Lucian responds by saying, "Go on. We all feel like that, sometimes. Most of us don't dare" (p. 27). The story ends with a reassuring comment from Susannah's husband, who loves her new hair style.

The second story, "Art Work," focuses on Debbie, a design editor of *A Woman's Place* magazine, and her surly artist husband, Robin. Since she works full-time, Deborah is able to cater to the needs of her husband and two children only because of her dedicated housekeeper, Mrs. Brown, who is mysteriously capable and silent. Deborah welcomes her help gratefully, although she is unsure about whether her children will like the garish sweaters that Mrs. Brown knits for them. Thus, it is a big surprise when a gallery dealer comes to visit Robin's studio and instead becomes interested in Mrs. Brown's creative talents. The characters must then come to terms with their own ambitious desires, assumptions, and hidden agendas.

The final and most powerful story of the collection is "The Chinese Lobster," the story of a professor, Dr. Gerdta Himmelblau, who is forced to pass judgment on a sexual harassment case. The conflict is between an art history graduate student, Peggi Nollet, who is working on an experimental dissertation on Matisse, and Peregrine Diss, a renowned expert on Matisse and a distinguished visiting scholar. Peggi Nollet's project, a feminist critique of Matisse that involves smearing feces on reproductions of his paintings, seems outrageous to the traditional Dr. Diss. Instead of offering constructive criticism, Dr. Diss asks Peggi to take her clothes off. When confronted by Dr. Himmelblau, Dr. Diss denies the accusation, pointing to Nollet's deranged sensibilities and obvious instability as evidence of his innocence. Unlike the lighthearted portraits of silly academics in *Possession,* the characters in "The Chinese Lobster" are dark and pathetic. Will Dr. Himmelblau side with Dr. Diss, preserving the sacred beauty of Matisse's vision, or will she side with Peggi Nollet, a young woman who has stretched the boundaries of "feminist" interpretation? In the end nothing is resolved, and we are left with an uncomfortable sense of the potentially perverse effects of being a scholar.

The Matisse Stories are less about connecting various complicated themes and intellectual debates (as in *Babel Tower*) and more about the lives of specific characters. All of the protagonists are interested in the ways in which art, beauty, and artifice affect their lives. With this small volume, Byatt returns to an important question she posed in her first novel, *The Shadow of the Sun.* Like Anna Severell, the characters in *The Matisse Stories* want to know if what they create is valuable and if they need to create something meaningful in order to survive. In typical Byatt fashion the answer is as elusive as the question.

CONCLUSION

If A. S. Byatt began her career with a desire to develop her own unique voice, since then she has certainly demonstrated the range of her abilities. A diligent craftsman and a careful sculptor of phrases and images, Byatt reveals an extraordinary talent. Whether describing a Yorkshire landscape, recreating a tense conversation between two lovers, or writing romantic poetry or gothic fairy tales, she brings the reader into her own vivid sensibility. Along with the success of her more recent work, Byatt has finally received the critical attention that she deserves, and perhaps the freedom to explore further the connection between her "critical and narrative selves" in new and exciting ways. With three new projects "on the boil"—a fourth Frederica volume and two other novels—A. S. Byatt will, one hopes, continue to intrigue and delight readers for decades to come.

SELECTED BIBLIOGRAPHY

I. Fiction. *The Shadow of a Sun* (London and New York, 1964), reiss. as *The Shadow of the Sun* (London, 1991; New York, 1993); *The Game* (London, 1967; New York, 1968, 1992); *The Virgin in the Garden* (London, 1978; New York, 1979, 1991, 1993); *Still Life* (London, 1985; New York, 1985, 1987, 1991); *Sugar and Other Stories* (London and New York, 1987); *Possesson: A Romance* (London and New York, 1990); *Passions of the Mind* (London, 1991; New York, 1993); *Angels and Insects* (London, 1992; New York, 1993); *The Matisse Stories* (London, 1993; New York, 1995); *The Djinn in the Nightingale's Eye: Five Fairy Stories* (London, 1994); *Babel Tower* (London and New York, 1996).

II. NONFICTION. *Degrees of Freedom: The Novels of Iris Murdoch* (New York and London, 1965); *Unruly Times: Wordsworth and Coleridge in Their Time* (London, 1970, 1989; New York, 1973); *Irish Murdoch* (London, 1976); *Imagining Characters: Six Conversations About Women Writers,* ed. by Rebecca Swift (London, 1995), written with Ignes Sodre.

III. EDITED WORKS. George Eliot, *The Mill on the Floss* (London and New York, 1979), with introd. and notes by Byatt; *George Eliot: Selected Essays, Poems and Other Writings,* ed. with Nicholas Warren (London, 1990); *Robert Browning: Dramatic Monologues* (London, 1990).

IV. INTRODUCTIONS. Elizabeth Bowen, *The House in Paris* (London, 1976); Grace Paley, *Enormous Changes at the Last Minute* (London, 1979); Willa Cather, *My Ántonia* and *A Lost Lady* (London, 1980); Grace Paley, *The Little Disturbances of Man* (London, 1980); Willa Cather, *My Mortal Enemy, Shadows on the Rock, Death Comes for the Archbishop, O Pioneers!* and *Lucy Grayheart* (London, 1989); Kees Fens, *Finding the Place: Selected Essays on English Literature,* ed. by W. Bronzwaer and H. Verdaasdonk (Amsterdam, 1994).

V. OTHER. "Reading, Writing and Studying: Some Questions About Changing Conditions for Writers and Readers," in *Critical Quarterly* 35 (winter 1993).

VI. REVIEWS. Irish Murdoch, "Force Fields," in *New Statesman* 96 (3 November 1978); Paul Levy, review of *The Virgin in the Garden,* in *Books and Bookmen* 24 (January 1979); Daphne Merkin, "Writers and Writing: The Art of Living," in *New Leader* 62 (23 April 1979); Jay Parini, "Unearthing the Secret Lover," in *New York Times Book Review* (21 October 1990); Christopher Lehmann-Haupt, "Books of the *Times:* When There Was Such a Thing as Romantic Love," in *New York Times* (25 October 1990); Mervyn Rothstein, "Best Seller Breaks Rule on Crossing the Atlantic," in *New York Times* (31 January 1991); Bruce Bawer, "What We Do for Art," in *New York Times Book Review* (30 April 1995); Ann Hulbert, "Hungry for Books," in *New York Times Book Review* (9 June 1996); Mel Gussow, "A New Byatt Novel with a Novel Within," in *New York Times* (9 July 1996).

VII. CRITICAL STUDIES. Jane Campbell, "The Hunger of the Imagination in A. S. Byatt's *The Game,*" in *Critique: Studies in Contemporary Fiction* 29 (spring 1988), and " 'The Somehow May Be Thishow': Fact, Fiction and Intertextuality in Antonia Byatt's 'Precipice-Encurled,' " in *Studies in Short Fiction* 28 (spring 1991); Louise Yelin, "Cultural Cartography: A. S. Byatt's *Possession* and the Politics of Victorian Studies," in *Victorian Newsletter* 81 (spring 1992); Robert E. Homser, Jr., "The Great Ventriloquist: A. S. Byatt's *Possession: A Romance,*" in *Contemporary British Women Writers: Texts and Narrative Strategies,* ed. by Robert E. Homser Jr. (New York, 1993); Julian Gitzen, "A. S. Byatt's Self-Mirroring Art," in *Critique: Studies in Contemporary Fiction* 36 (winter 1995).

BRUCE CHATWIN

(1940–1989)

Angelyn Hays

WORLD TRAVELER, FINE art expert, and author of interdisciplinary narratives, Bruce Chatwin, like his books, resists convenient categories. With a gift for religious fable and a discerning eye for realistic images, Chatwin transcended the 1980s travel writing vogue to become a recognized addition to great travel writers alongside Graham Greene, Salman Rushdie, and Chatwin's own hero of the 1930s, Robert Byron, author of *Journey to Oxiana* (1937). Chatwin reclaimed the mystery and excitement of travel by insisting that the goal of the journey is not its destination but the pilgrimage itself. "Man's real home" Chatwin believed "is not a house, but the Road, and . . . life itself is a journey to be walked on foot" (*What Am I Doing Here,* 1989, p. 273).

Chatwin published seven unconventional books in twelve years: three travel narratives, three books he considered works of fiction, and one essay collection. A posthumous volume of his notebooks and photographs, *Far Journeys,* appeared in 1993; *Anatomy of Restlessness: Selected Writings, 1969–1989,* was published in 1996. Chatwin's first book, *In Patagonia* (1977), was immediately recognized as "a minor classic" (*Times Literary Supplement*), winning both the 1978 Hawthornden Prize and the 1979 E. M. Forster Award of the American Academy of Arts and Letters. His national best-seller, *The Songlines* (1987), received widespread critical acclaim. Chatwin said "the oldest kind of traveler's tale is one in which the narrator leaves home and goes to a far country in search of some legendary beast" (*Patagonia Revisited*, 1985, p. 17). Chatwin's "legendary beasts" included mythic half-animal, half-man incarnations (see in particular "Shamdev: The Wolf-Boy" and "On Yeti Tracks" in *What Am I Doing Here*). His partially autobiographical accounts of his traveling experiences challenge the boundaries of fictional realism and nonfictional representation. An admirer of Gustave Flaubert, Chatwin read-mitted realism and historicism along with what he called "mythic story forms" (*Granta,* p. 29).

LIFE

CHATWIN'S gift for sharp observation and his eclectic tastes were apparent in his life well before he conceived his first book. Born 13 May 1940 in wartime Sheffield, England, Charles Bruce Chatwin had roots deep in middle-class England. His father, Charles L. Chatwin, was a Birmingham lawyer who returned to practice there after World War II. Chatwin wrote in the last year of his life, "My father has the most beautiful blue eyes I have ever seen in a man. I do not say this because he is my father. They are mariner's eyes, level and steady. On the Malta convoys they scanned the surface of the sea for mines, or the horizon for an enemy warship. They are the eyes of a man who has never known the meaning of dishonesty" (*What Am I Doing Here,* p. 9). There was an element of filial rectitude and ancestral romance in Bruce Chatwin. He described the eyes of his mother, Margharita Turnell, as being "brown and lively, with suggestions of Southern ancestry" (*What Am I Doing Here,* p. 9). In an interview with Colin Thubron, he said his grandmother's eyes were "flinty green" and suggested she had something of the gypsy about her. But these are exceptional moments, where Chatwin shows himself without the fictional artifice he seamlessly manipulates in his stories. In a 1983 autobiographical essay for the *New York Times Book Review,* Chatwin referred to several even more colorful forebears, "legendary figures whose histories inflamed my imagination." The essay's cast of characters shows Chatwin playfully constructing a slightly more raffish lineage than his background might warrant.

There is great-grandfather Milward, "a man obsessed by money," and Uncle Geoffrey, another Chatwin drawn to the Sahara Desert who, with reverberations of T. E. Lawrence, had been given a golden headdress yet "died poor in Cairo."

In *The Songlines,* Chatwin attributes his fascination with nomads to an early identification with an aboriginal boy in a photograph, shown walking with his family (a similar graphic adorns the cover of *The Songlines*). He relates the boy to his own childhood portability during World War II: "I remember the fantastic homelessness of my first five years. My father was in the Navy, at sea. My mother and I would shuttle back and forth, on the railways of wartime England, on visits to family and friends" (*The Songlines,* p. 5). Bruce and his mother would spend much of the war in a perpetual drift from one location to another. Elsewhere he said of that dislocation: "I lived in NAAFI canteens and was passed around like a tea urn" (Ignatieff, 1987, p. 32). His earliest memory was of staying in his maternal grandmother Turnell's furnished rooms on the seafront at Filey in Yorkshire, where he watched gray convoys on their way to war. From Sam Turnell, his grandfather, Chatwin later acquired a love of long walks over the moors. Chatwin's fascination with travel and travelers, especially the pace and efficacy of walking, would later influence his persistent investigation into what he called "the question of questions: the nature of human restlessness" (*The Songlines,* p. 161).

At four, Bruce went to live with his great aunts Janie and Gracie at Stratford-upon-Avon. This period in Chatwin's life is refashioned in the second chapter of *The Songlines,* where the aunts are renamed Great Aunt Katie and Ruth. In *The Songlines,* Aunt Ruth "told me our surname had once been 'Chattewynde', which meant 'the winding path' in Anglo-Saxon, and the suggestion took root in my head that poetry, my own name and the road were, all three, mysteriously connected" (*The Songlines,* p. 9). As a boy, Bruce set himself up as a guide to local Shakespeare points of interest. Most of his patrons were American GIs. The first lines of verse he memorized were the four lines on Shakespeare's tomb:

> Good friend, for Jesus sake, forbeare
> To digge the dust encloased here
> Bleste be ye man yt spare thes stones
> And curst be he yt moves my bones

Many years later he would recall these lines at the excavation of a Hunnish princess's grave when some peasant women in the fields cried out to the archaeologists to leave the dead woman with Zeus, her lover. Hearing this, Chatwin wonders "if archaeology itself were not cursed" (*The Songlines,* p. 8).

While staying with his aunts, Chatwin would bicycle through the early dawn to make sure he got a seat in the back row at the Shakespeare theater. He saw most of the great productions of the late 1940s and 1950s featuring Laurence Olivier, John Gielgud, Peggy Ashcroft, and Paul Robeson. During the 1949 elections, he said, "We boys were required to make images of Mr and Mrs Attlee and burn them on a bonfire. . . . It made me really outraged" (Ignatieff, 1987, pp. 32–33). The incident may have figured in the depiction of bonfires and symbolic objects in *The Viceroy of Ouidah* (1980) and *On the Black Hill* (1982). About this time, Chatwin began collecting and trading antiques. He would bike to antique stores with the same enthusiasm other boys might show for playing ball. Chatwin's favorite reading of this period was Ernest Thompson Seton's *Lives of the Hunted* (1901), about a young coyote who escapes captivity and returns to the wild. His first adult book was Joshua Slocum's *Sailing Alone Around the World* (1956). His thoughts would ultimately straddle the dwindling certainty of empirical science and the ascendant world of renewed religious romance and, if his childhood was fairly typical for many bright, postwar English children, his later investigations would crisscross some of the deepest socioeconomic fault lines of the twentieth century.

As an undergraduate at Marlborough College, Chatwin was a precocious collector who "[balanced] prodigious piles of antiques" on the crossbar of his bicycle; his study-bedroom was "stocked with minor Italian masters and antique English furniture" (Murray, p. 24). After college, Chatwin was reluctant to go to the university for graduate studies. At the time, he felt his obvious talent was for art and antiquities.

In 1958, Chatwin started work as a uniformed porter at Sotheby and Company of Bond Street, the well-known auction house in London. According to popular recollection, Chatwin would walk casually through the department aisles, judging this or that piece "real" or "fake" with startling accuracy. Chatwin was quickly recognized for his economic potential to Sotheby's and he moved up with unusual speed in the highly competitive field of art dealing. He acquired a high but comparatively esoteric reputation for having "The Eye," an amazingly infallible instinct for judging the authenticity and value of art work (*What Am I Doing Here,* p. 358). At twenty-five, he became the youngest director in Sotheby's history, managing both the antiquities and the impressionist painting departments.

Despite his achievements at Sotheby's, Chatwin did not find his life as an art professional satisfying. He expressed his antipathy with art dealing in several essays, and numerous accounts of those who knew him attest to his restlessness during this period. In a 1988 essay, "The Fly," Chatwin described his dissatisfaction with art dealing in terms of his friendship with Bertie Landsberg, who taught him that "works of art, if they are to live, should never be bought or sold, but given or exchanged. This, to a boy flogging pictures at Sotheby's, was news. He gave me a lovely fragment of an Archaic Greek marble. I sold it in one of my crises, and have felt guilty ever since" (*What Am I Doing Here,* p. 362). This aesthetic of collectibles-giving would change Chatwin's feelings about his work. But he would not indulge his desire to travel (and escape) until after an eight-year stint at Sotheby's. Chatwin's experiences in the highly materialistic and impassioned world of art dealing found most direct expression, perhaps, in his last novel, *Utz* (1988), a partially fictionalized biography of a porcelain collector. Chatwin said, "Being an Englishman makes me uneasy. I find I can be English and behave like an Englishman only if I'm not here [in England]" (Ignatieff, 1987, p. 31). He said he traveled because in this way he could "escape being labeled with class stereotypes" and rid himself of "pressure from above and below. If you're out on the road, people have to take you at face value" (Ignatieff, 1987, p. 32).

Of the aftermath of his departure from Sotheby's, he writes: "I quit Sotheby's—Smootherboys as a friend likes to call it. I spent one winter kicking around the Western Sahara. In April my wife [Elizabeth Chanler] joined me for a two-week trip in Morocco" (*What Am I Doing Here,* p. 356). Leaving Sotheby's, however, did not lessen his enthusiasm for fine art or diminish his remarkable visual talents. Chatwin's passion for beautiful objects and antiquities conflicted with his persistent challenge to the economic exploitation of art. This paradox of obsessive desire and renunciant denial complicated Chatwin's life and, later, provided tension in his narratives.

FIRST WORKS

CHATWIN wrote feature articles for the *Sunday Times* prior to publication of his first book, *In Patagonia.* The book originated, in part, as a proposed travel article for the newspaper. The article dissolved in the intensity of the journey and, with *In Patagonia,* Chatwin made the unpredictable switch from highly acclaimed art expert and occasional contributor of colorful travel articles to celebrated author of internationally recognized books. Chatwin produced five more stunningly artistic travel books before his death at forty-nine, yet he said he "never let anything artistic stand in his way" (*What Am I Doing Here,* p. 279).

The places Chatwin visited but did not write about far exceeded those he committed to paper. He wrote books about South America, Africa, Wales, Australia, and Czechoslovakia, but he also made trips through Greece, Russia, China, and many other places. He traveled to Afghanistan in 1962, 1964, and again in the summer of 1969 with the poet Peter Levi. They were soon joined by Elizabeth, Chatwin's American wife. Chatwin had planned a book about Afghanistan, but after Levi published *The Light Garden of the Angel King: Journeys in Afghanistan* (1972), Chatwin changed his mind. Chatwin did not travel to write so much as to soothe his own unrest. He always wished to be somewhere else, "a condition," he said, "that makes one very difficult to live with" (Ignatieff, 1987, p. 36).

Many people who knew him recall Chatwin's captivating presence. He was strikingly handsome, with penetrating blue eyes and blond hair. Chatwin was a brilliant speaker with a gift for storytelling and embellishment. Until his final illness, he maintained a perpetually youthful air and buoyant personality. Francis Wyndham observed that Chatwin's friends could "tend to be slightly possessive about him but he wasn't possessive about them. After months of absence he would suddenly appear and for days, perhaps weeks, the stimulating relationship would be easily and happily revived before he vanished again" (*Far Journeys,*

p. 13). Chatwin's disarming charm coupled with his meteoric rise, first to the top of the highly competitive art world, then to the national best-seller lists, made him seem all the more magical.

While writing parts of *The Songlines*, Chatwin stayed at the home of travel writer Patrick Leigh Fermor, who felt that Chatwin "had the utterly convincing aura of an infant prodigy" (quoted in Murray, p. 13). In his ambitious search to substantiate his theories and to find creative ways to communicate them to his readers, Chatwin did more than merely update the masculine tradition of classic travel narratives, a genre that produced the likes of Herman Melville and Lawrence of Arabia. The high quality of his books and his early death have turned portions of his life into legend. Chatwin himself might have pointed to the essential fiction of any legend, myth, or cult—a fiction he wrought in brilliant and innovative narratives, but an artifice he could clearly separate from himself.

However, Chatwin did tell of certain personal experiences that seemed to link him to aspects of the mythic story forms his narratives explore. For instance, Chatwin explained how his final decision to leave Sotheby's and become a perpetual traveler resulted in a miraculous "cure." He temporarily went blind and, when he went to a physician, was told he should trade the scrutiny of paintings for some "long horizons." Chatwin says his vision improved "on the way to the airport" (Ignatieff, 1987, p. 23). The factuality of this story is less important than how the episode articulates a personal redemptive crisis—the loss and restoration of the visual perception necessary for both his career as an art expert and as an author of travel narratives. His collections of cultural myths and folklore had a particular focus on tales of wanderers and redemption.

Chatwin continued to associate with the upper crust of the artistic world even as he sought out other levels of social experience. One friend, the writer Salman Rushdie, went with Chatwin on his travels in the Australian desert and may have figured in Chatwin's characterization of Arkady in *The Songlines*. Rushdie, himself an invigorating mythologist who transformed his knowledge into an ample fictional resource, called Chatwin "a magnificent raconteur of Scheherazadean inexhaustibility, a gilt-edged name-dropper, a voracious reader of esoteric texts, a scholar-gypsy, a mimic" (Rushdie, *Imaginary Homelands*, 1991, p. 237). The value of Chatwin's work lies not in the factual elements of his narratives but in "the luminous glimpse [his books provide] of how he saw the world" (*Far Journeys*, p. 10).

Long before he published his first book—perhaps even before he thought of himself seriously as a writer—Chatwin was at work on his master treatise on human migration. He left behind fifty small notebooks bound in shiny black imitation leather known in France as *moleskine*. These easily portable volumes, six inches long and four inches wide, were his immediate record of people, places, buildings, and his own roving thoughts. There were larger practice books (his extended drafts), but these hand-held notebooks contain his spontaneous jottings. They were not diary entries in the ordinary sense, although he would sometimes affix a date to them. Germinating material for his polished narratives are everywhere in his notes: "The Hausa wrestling match—drugged gleaming boys incredibly tough and lean flexing muscles in animal skins with eyes in the buttocks and tail for [the] nose" (*Far Journeys*, p. 72). Chatwin filled his notebooks with raw materials he hoped would contribute to an ultimate rendering of his thoughts. He writes in an entry: "This book is written in answer to a need to explain my own restlessness—coupled with a morbid preoccupation with roots. No fixed home till I was five and thereafter *battling*, desperate attempts on my part to escape—if not physically, then by the invention of mystical paradises. The book should be read with this in mind" (*Far Journeys*, p. 13). Chatwin echoed the Romantic poets in his predilection for inevitable unrest. He believed true peace could only be experienced while in motion. He agreed with Pascal that "our nature lies in movement; complete calm is death" (from Pascal's *Pensées*, quoted in *The Songlines*, p. 163). He spent years accumulating data (anthropological, archaeological, philosophical, geographical, historical, scientific, metaphysical, and mythical) to support his speculations and establish them as a theory. Many of his ideas and arguments appear in *The Songlines*, but he never completed the comprehensive dissertation on human restlessness he hoped to write. His larger practice books and papers have been collected in *Anatomy of Restlessness: Selected Writings, 1969–1989*. While this incompleteness might be unsatisfying, it does reverberate Chatwin's belief in a never-ending journey. His preoccupations, however persuasive and fascinating, probably never would have found a restful conclusion.

Chatwin collected objects on his many trips. He later destroyed them, except for a wooden box, painted pale green with GOD BOX stenciled in white on its back. Behind a removable glass front, a group of West African jujus are arranged against an abstract background of blue peacock feathers. The initials B. C. appear in the lower right corner. These things, which might be called "fetish objects," include the eardrum of a lion, a dried gecko, a guinea fowl feather, an unidentified internal organ, and two toes from a bird's claw wrapped in indigo cloth. Originally there was a monkey's skull, but it has disappeared. Chatwin also cherished a huge circular wooden fish tray he bought in Istanbul. Francis Wyndham, who edited Chatwin's notebooks and photographs, writes that, "for Chatwin it had the beauty of abstract art coupled with utilitarian convenience. . . . Its design had not changed in 500 years. I cite this tray almost at random as just one of the countless examples of his idiosyncratic choices, discoveries and enthusiasms: each of his friends could no doubt produce a different list" (*Far Journeys*, p. 12).

Chatwin was certainly drawn to people traditionally seen as marginalized, like the expatriate Welsh community of South America, Africa's Ivory Coast Brazilian Creoles, and the Australian aboriginals. Accused of sensationalizing eccentrics, he countered that "so called eccentric characters . . . are extremely sane and . . . not particularly eccentric—they're just living on a different time scale, in a different world" (*South Bank Show* interview). Chatwin points out that:

psychiatrists, politicians, [and] tyrants are forever assuring us that the wandering life is an aberrant form of behavior; a neurosis; a form of unfulfilled sexual longing; a sickness which, in the interests of civilisation, must be suppressed.

Nazi propagandists claimed that gipsies and Jews—peoples with wandering in their genes—could find no place in a stable Reich.

Yet, in the East, they still preserve the once universal concept: that wandering re-establishes the original harmony which once existed between man and the universe.
(*The Songlines*, p. 178)

He spent considerable time researching his theory on the relationship of nomads (of which, as a perpetual traveler, he felt a part) to agriculturally supported urban "centers." Chatwin challenged the assumed notions of what is "civilized" or "normal."

Any study of an author Rushdie called a "demon-researcher" would, of course, include some of the circumstances under which he wrote, some possible sources of inspiration, and critical readings of the work. However, Chatwin was an unusually astute observer of his own creative processes as well as a keen observer of others. His notebooks and his collection of informal essays, prepared just prior to his death in 1989, are filled with the enthusiasms that occupied his thoughts; thoughts he would distill into five short books. Chatwin might not have agreed with the critical formality of separating the life from the work. In 1988, he said that "Writing the final scenes of *The Songlines* did bring home how writing a fiction impinges on your life" (Ignatieff, 1987, p. 35).

CATEGORIZING CHATWIN

FROM the fifteenth through the nineteenth centuries, travel narratives included secondhand oral tales, letters, military reports, survival tales, civic descriptions, navigational narratives, accounts of monsters and marvels, herbal remedies, personal essays, and academic polemics. Before they became exclusive to a particular discipline, anthropology, adventure-romance, religious apologetics, botany, and geology existed side by side in travel accounts. Chatwin reappropriated many of the narrative conventions of these disciplines. His narratives make full use of creative fiction, in particular those of the philosophical novel, adventure romance, folklore, and satire. He interspersed journalistic, historic, and personal accounts in his creative prose. And while critical categories whirl in Chatwin's interdisciplinary offering, attention to categories can highlight some of the remarkable themes and narrative devices at work in his prose. Chatwin consistently researched material for his books from many sources, but his most diversified accomplishments were *In Patagonia* and *The Songlines*. His pursuit of substantiation for his theory on human migration led him into diverse fields: postcolonial studies, linguistics, popular culture, literature, and archaeology. Chatwin's approach argues as much for disunity as it does for unity. He said he was "unimpressed by the idea of the new" and felt "most advances in literature usually strike me as being advances into a cul-de-sac" (Ignatieff, 1987, p. 28).

In this he proved to be something of a conservative. He was open to newness in visual arts and wrote favorably in his essays about avant-garde movements such as Russian futurism, but Chatwin's books are an effort to rethink human development and to recapture old ideas he feared might otherwise be lost.

Chatwin's interdisciplinary convention opens a discussion of travel writing's long history of interaction with other narrative forms. Chatwin's travel accounts question two intersecting processes in Western thought: the authority of history as a structure of knowledge and, ultimately, power, and the ramifications of Europe's second wave of colonial invasion: that of the scientific explorer. The ethnographer and botanist joined the soldier and the missionary as stereotypical European adventurers on the colonial scene. Europe invoked romantic and sentimental visions to legitimize its "civilizing mission" to its colonies, visions based, in part, on heroic-quest master narratives already available in Western folklore. By playing with these master narratives of heroic quests and journeys, Chatwin obliquely addresses this romance of a "civilizing mission" in the course of his adventure narratives.

Chatwin called the category of travel writing "meaningless." His resistance to the label has special validity in light of his brilliant merger of narrative traditions. But however Chatwin may have resisted the category, one of his achievements was to breathe new life into travel literature, generated in part by his revitalization of mythic story forms, in particular quest and redemption narratives. Chatwin balanced historical inquiry and literary romance in his travel writing. These seemingly irreconcilable approaches put his work within the range of what Linda Hutcheon has identified as "historiographic metafictions." The fictional character who participates in historical events; or the real person who participates in nonhistorical or unverifiable events, highlights the most tenacious of realist doctrines: the binary opposition of fact and fiction. Historiographic metafiction occupies a border between historical discourse, with its facts and evidence, and literary discourse, with its creative imagination. Chatwin's collaborative anecdotes strip detail to a poetic minimum at the same time they revitalize realist conventions.

Chatwin told Michael Ignatieff in 1987, just after publication of *The Songlines*, that he had "once mapped Che Guevara's life against this paradigm [of the young man's quest] and it fitted [sic] pretty well. (*Laughter.*) The point is that the classical hero cycle is an idealized programme for the human life cycle. Each stage corresponds to a biological event in human life" (p. 28). Chatwin didn't "believe *all* behaviour is learned. We're not a blank slate. . . . It struck me that these 'behavioral chains' which [Konrad] Lorenz talks about are similar to the structure of myths" (Ignatieff, 1987, p. 29). He repeatedly mapped story forms of redemption and apocalypse in his narratives. He often turned to Russian themes and Jewish examples of wanderers. He was fascinated with the biblical story of Cain and Abel, in which he saw a fundamental difference in social organization. He said: "It used to suit evolution-minded social scientists to believe that pastoralism preceded agriculture. The hunter learned to tame wild animals. The nomad settled down to grow crops, and the farmer made the inventions on which the first cities depended. Yet nomadism was not a step towards civilisation, but a step away from it. Abraham left the city of Ur to become a nomad" (*What Am I Doing Here*, p. 227).

Chatwin's androgynous, if somewhat satiric, religious iconography describes a South American collage: "The showpiece was a painted plaster head of a Japanese geisha, haloed like a madonna, with the hairy thighs of Argentine footballers. Above this was a pottery dove, emblem of the Holy Ghost, now converted to a bird of paradise with the blue plastic ribbons and dyed ostrich plumes" (pp. 81–82). Historiographic metafictions often parody, satirize, question, or otherwise play with conventional standards, and Chatwin's approach is, like Salman Rushdie's in *Midnight's Children* (1981), extremely paradoxical. Since Chatwin presents his narratives as historical or autobiographical documentary *and* as artifice, the reader is left to question *how* we know a narrative is historical, historically based, or fictional. History is presumably the only kind of discourse that can aim at a referent outside itself that it can, in fact, never reach. But the same can be said of historiographic metafiction. In Chatwin's narratives, history and cultural experience combine with spiritual mystery in unexpected ways. The latter element appears, it is suggested, as a necessary ingredient for understanding reality.

Part of Chatwin's appeal is his capacity to suspend "scientific skepticism" and participate in realms of mystery without feeling compromised as an observer: "Burned my fingers on the pot—and Fatim

Ata blessed, three prayers rattled out with three times spitting on it. My anti-tan cream has also helped to cure it. The burn has disappeared this morning. Fatim Ata very pleased his prayer a success. Who can say which was the effective agent?" (*Far Journeys*, p. 73). The combination of spiritual possibility and belief in scientific evidence is a refreshing, if problematic, shift away from more traditional approaches where science and spirituality are separated into an irreconcilable opposition. He said, "My whole life has been a search for the miraculous: yet at the first faint flavour of the uncanny, I tend to turn rational" (*What Am I Doing Here*, p. 282). He saw himself as a dispassionate observer who was only beginning to bring his own feelings to the surface in his last novel, *Utz*.

The novels of Joseph Conrad, Joan Didion, Thomas Pynchon, and others who preceded Chatwin's pursuit of reenchantment were called "late imperial romances" by John McClure. This construct rejected the idea of Europe's civilizing mission in favor of descent into the former colonies as realms of stubborn strangeness and enchantment. Discomfort with Western expansionism initiated a contest within fiction and nonfiction waged by competing interests on the terrain of the formerly colonized. Fear of a completely explored or "mapped" globe affected scientific and literary narratives equally and manifested itself in diverse ways. For instance, in the 1950s and 1960s, ethnographers echoed romance writers when they became concerned with cultural contamination of "pure" indigenous peoples by the presence of Western research. During this period, other ethnographers such as Margaret Mead, Edward Sapir, and Ruth Benedict saw themselves as both anthropologists *and* literary artists. Chatwin orients his scenarios of a restless quest for reenchantment within this climate of romance, antiromance, and counterromance at work in ethnography, anthropology, literature, and history.

Chatwin admired the critical observation of anthropology as well as the realism and symbolism of literary craftsmanship. He said, "The writers I adore are nearly always the Russians. Mandelstam especially; his *Journey to Armenia* went with me on my journey to Patagonia. As a Jew, he understands restlessness. . . . His life was a series of the most extraordinary dislocations, which ended up in Siberia. He seems to have postulated, very early in his writing, the fate that would eventually overcome him" (Ignatieff, 1987, pp. 36–37).

Chatwin's self-declared influence was the early Hemingway of *In Our Time*. But he also admired Flaubert, Baudelaire, Rimbaud, Walt Whitman, and the seventeenth-century divine Jeremy Taylor. He said "for bleak passages I have also looked hard at *Hedda Gabler*" (*What Am I Doing Here*, p. 366). He was an enthusiastic and meticulous editor and redrafted his narratives many times. The compactness of his books is the result of an art that did not waste itself. Except for *The Songlines* and *What Am I Doing Here*, none of his books exceed two hundred pages. Susannah Clapp, one of his editors, recalls him: "Pacing the room, reading aloud to test for sound as well as sense, Chatwin would pounce on a phrase and produce a new anecdote. He would cut an entire chapter without a minute's brooding" (quoted in Murray, *Bruce Chatwin*, 1995, p. 44). Chatwin makes full use of interdisciplinary narrative resources to express his theories about human migration. But Chatwin's style was always his own, a clear polished prose that obviously drew on a well-read imagination.

IN PATAGONIA

In Patagonia originated, in typical Chatwin fashion, at the juncture of a crossroads: his childhood desire to know an artifact's origin; a chance meeting with a seventy-nine-year-old architect; and the hint of another commission from the *Sunday Times*. When he chose what he called a "country of black fogs and whirlwinds at the end of the habited world" (quoted in Murray, p. 40) as the subject of his first book, Chatwin was a typical travel writer who explored the exotic and picturesque. Chatwin suggested a journey to his editor that would, in essence, retrace the route of Butch Cassidy and the Sundance Kid through turn-of-the-century South America along the Argentinean coast and through portions of the pampas. In the late 1890s, Butch Cassidy followed the rumor that Patagonia offered the same outlaw freedom characteristic of Wyoming in the 1870s. The "romance" of an untamed Old West had lost its former appeal with the success of the enclosure movement among other social and economic dynamics, and faraway places were rumored to offer adventure once again. The article never appeared and, somewhere along the trip, other obsessions transformed Chatwin's journey into a classic of travel literature.

About the time Chatwin suggested the Patagonia trip to his editor, he visited Eileen Gray, an architect and designer. He told her he had always wanted to go to South America. "So have I," she said, and added, "Go there for me." He said his decisive moment came when he sent a telegram, GONE TO PATAGONIA, to Gray while in Paris (Murray, p. 40). Gray is just one of Chatwin's many portraits of charismatic older women. Chatwin spent the end of 1975 and the beginning of 1976 traveling through Patagonia, often by his favorite mode of transportation, on foot.

But Chatwin's starting point for reenchantment may be seen in the story that opens the narrative. He describes a glass-fronted curio cabinet belonging to his grandmother, in which a piece of animal skin with coarse red hair was kept. The skin, Chatwin was told as a child, was procured by his grandmother's cousin, Charley Milward the sailor, an ancestral, wandering Chatwin, the "eccentric" of the family, who adventured in South America around the turn of the century. The tale of the mylodon, a giant ground sloth unique to South America that disappeared about ten thousand years ago, is unraveled, as both a personal story and as a debate in natural history surrounding the "living mylodon." Chatwin interviews a broad range of people along the way, with a particular focus on colonial-era descendants. He spends time with a range of ethnic groups including the expatriate Welsh community that settled in South America to escape English persecution in the nineteenth century. They can no longer remember the geography of their homeland and would prefer to "keep [their] valley Welsh" (p. 36) and free of outsiders. Chatwin also visits the Indian woman who now lives in the rotting remains of the cabin Butch Cassidy built in the late 1800s while he follows up on residual tales of the outlaw. The narrative culminates in Chatwin's visit to the cave where Charley Milward had found the original skin. In his pursuit of mylodon facts, fabrications, and artifacts, Chatwin adopts a form of the romance-of-natural-history (see Pratt, *Imperial Eyes*, 1992). Chatwin traces the many misconceptions, false starts, and residual oral tales surrounding the turn-of-the-century hunt for a living mylodon. His pursuit of this artifact links *In Patagonia* to countless Victorian travel accounts of specimen quests by botanical explorers. Chatwin differs from early travel writers in that he presents local people not as eccentric, naive, or ahistorical, but as a social "geography" of the places he visited.

In a narrative sometimes called anticlimactic, religious confrontations make a noticeable progression. Twice, Bruce is challenged to declare his personal beliefs by religious figures. When he is asked by a zealous Baha'i missionary, "Which religion have you?" Chatwin replies, "My God is the God of Walkers. If you walk hard enough, you probably don't need any other God" (p. 33). The "Persian" swings a machete and declares, "I kill the ungodly" (p. 34). This tension partially resolves when Chatwin is asked by a Catholic priest: "Tell me, brother, which religion have you?" Chatwin replies that he is Protestant. "Different road," the priest says. "Same Divinity" (p. 75). The change in response doesn't so much invalidate Chatwin's former expression as invite consideration of multiple truths.

His merger of fact and fiction was so persuasive that Chatwin's challenge to realism, and the degree of authenticity it might represent, became a persistent controversy. In 1991, critical interest in Chatwin's factualism reached culmination with John Pilkington's *An Englishman in Patagonia*—a rather single-minded travel account determined not to be fooled by Chatwin's seamless transitions between fact and fiction. Pilkington cast the unillusioned eye of the backpacker over Chatwin's journalistic details. His carefully arranged but inconclusive evidence questions, for instance, the geographic descriptions of *In Patagonia*. He demonstrates Chatwin exaggerated when he said the entrance of Eberhardt's Cave was four-hundred-feet wide. Pilkington's patient pacing estimated it to be around one-hundred-feet wide. More sobering, he quotes *The Bulletin*, a monthly journal of the British Community Council of Argentina, which revealed a deep hostility toward Chatwin as a result of *In Patagonia*. It seemed some Patagonians disapproved of the impression *In Patagonia* gave of them. When Pilkington's book challenged Chatwin's reliability as a witness, debate on Chatwin's realism again attracted attention in national newspapers. Susannah Clapp, one of Chatwin's literary executors, dismissed these accusations in the *Daily Telegraph*: "I don't think anyone supposed *In Patagonia* was a straight travelogue—it's too interesting for that."

Critics such as Catherine Belsey, Terry Eagleton, and Edward Said see realism as a tool of ideological control, precisely because of its pretension of neutrality. A theory which claims that factual narratives are mere linguistic constructions with no absolute value radically undermines a whole system of social and pedagogical authority that depends for its power on there being a "good" or a "truth" transcendent and common to all. Contemporary narratives are both the inheritors and the perpetrators of this radical undermining. Like linguistic theorists, they posit a form of realism at the same time that they unravel the fabric of their own position by questioning unexamined assumptions in the discourses of science, history, film, performance, and visual art. *In Patagonia* raises two closely related issues central to historiographic metafiction: subjectivity and the ontology of "real" characters who appear in fictionalized or partially fictionalized narratives. The writer of historiographic metafiction, instead of depending on historical characters and events to prove the truth of fiction, points to the indeterminacy of historical knowledge. Yet that *events* are indeterminate (in the sense of unverifiable) is not as problematic as the suggestion that historical *personages* might be indeterminate. A notable example of Chatwin's metafictional treatment of historical persons is "On the Road with Mrs. G." (in *What Am I Doing Here*), an essay-portrait of Indira Gandhi in 1978.

THE VICEROY OF OUIDAH

PUBLISHED three years after *In Patagonia, The Viceroy of Ouidah* (1980) details the redemptive failure of a poor Brazilian wanderer, Francisco Manoel da Silva. In 1812, Da Silva goes to Africa on a suicide mission to retake the fort at Ouidah on the Ivory Coast. He succeeds, settles in Dahomey, and becomes a slave trader shipping slaves from Ouidah back to his former home, Bahia, Brazil. His uncertain "friendship" with the king of Dahomey gains him a monopoly on the slave trade but also chains him to a brutality that ultimately drives him insane. The narrative opens with Da Silva's descendants paying tribute to his memory and to the slave trade by which he prospered. Da Silva is called "the Father of All We Are" by his descendants. They think of the empire he built in the late nineteenth century as "a lost Golden Age" (p. 9). Da Silva's rise as a slave trader and his fall into insanity is a scathing,

philosophical rebuttal of the notion of a white "Father of the People" in Africa (see McClintock, *Imperial Leather*, 1995, p. 251). By 1855, his insanity has driven him to predict that "in 1900 the Holy House of Rome will crumble and bodies will choke the streets of Bahia and Jerusalem" (p. 147) and that the world will end with the new century. While the book is obviously about slavery, the narrative of Da Silva's life as a slave trader specifically reveals the macabre fate of a Western traveler who fails to move on. Written in the third person, *The Viceroy of Ouidah* signals a sharp departure from the autobiographical style of *In Patagonia*.

The fall of Da Silva's empire is brought about by three developments: his settlement in Africa, his participation in the slave trade, and his catastrophic loss of the possibility of religious redemption. Da Silva embodies the paradox of settlement: "Having always thought of himself as a footloose wanderer, he now became a patriot and man of property" (p. 86). Settlement ruined Da Silva: "Gradually Africa swamped him and drew him under" (p. 92). He took to the slave trade "as if he had known no other occupation" (p. 86). Da Silva violates the most basic tenet of Chatwin's nomadic philosophy—to keep moving. Instead, he settles and builds a commercial empire based on the sale of human beings. The psychological topography of insanity and brutality in *The Viceroy of Ouidah* is Chatwin's portrait of the effect of permanent settlement.

The subordinate nexus of slave-servant-woman would ultimately be exploded by two female characters—Da Silva's "African bride," Jijibou (p. 93), and a Brazilian Creole, Venossa das Chagas, a woman Da Silva unwillingly marries to the king of Dahomey. In order to "possess a white son-in-law" (p. 93), Jijibou's father marries her to Da Silva. By changing the king's feelings for Da Silva, Das Chagas "ruined the Da Silvas" (p. 137). These women, considered to be objects of exchange between men, illustrate the unequal power relationships that circumscribe their lives and contribute to Da Silva's destruction. The distinction between the empowered and the disenfranchised is the result of a systematic regimen of dispossession of power, by which not just women but nonpropertied men are victims.

Da Silva immerses himself in local religious healing practices and fetish rituals. In one incident, Da Silva and the king swear a blood pact that has the resonance both of a Faustian compact and of a powerful, homoerotic encounter:

The two men knelt facing each other, naked as babies, pressing their thighs together: the pact would be invalid if their genitals touched the ground.

The moon glinted on the black thighs and biceps, but white skin absorbs the moonlight evenly.

Kankpé fumbled in a leather bag and took out a skull-cup. He set it in the space between their knee-caps and added the ingredients of the sacrament: ashes, beans, baobab pith, a thunderstone, a bullet taken from a corpse, and the powdered head of a horned piper.

He half-filled the skull with water. Then they split each other's fingers and watched the black blood fall. . . .

Kankpé rolled his eyes and muttered curses: . . . blood-brothers live together and together they must die.
(pp. 106–107)

The king buries Da Silva in a barrel of rum with the severed heads of two children killed to announce his arrival in the afterlife, in the tradition of Dahomean royalty. But Da Silva never connects to a more powerful fixation than his obsession with an oratorio of the Last Supper. As a youthful vagabond in Brazil, Da Silva observes the pilgrims "[flail] themselves with nettle-spurge . . . [and] crawl the four miles on their kneecaps . . . the path becoming redder as they neared their goal. He longed to perform some similar act of mortification. . . . He never passed a village without dismounting to watch a congregation at prayer—yet he could never join them" (pp. 64–65). Da Silva's attempt to reconnect with redemptive possibility is shattered when he is shown a holy relic of "the cadaver of Christ" (p. 67). His crushed Christian faith in redemption is transferred into an attachment for the model oratorio of the Last Supper that he would later import to Ouidah from his former home.

Da Silva's simultaneous obsession with the oratorio and juju healing practices forces an examination of his seemingly irreconcilable passions. Collecting and revering skulls, bones, and the belongings of important or holy persons is an irrational blending of desire and denial. The skull is the unquestionable proof that the person is no longer alive, and yet this knowledge is denied when the object is assumed to hold magical properties or regenerative powers. The relic object underscores a bond with the saint and, like the fetish object, represents an attempt at self-preservation. *Reliquiae*, the material residues of holy persons, offer a warranty of esoteric and wonder-working power, for preserving life and stability and promising, most importantly, eventual salvation. Head-hunting and preserving the relics of Catholic saints spring from the same psychological source molded by different cultural perceptions. The king of Dahomey's passion for collecting the skulls of his enemies springs from the same source as Da Silva's need to possess the oratorio and participate in local fetish practices. The original idea of the fetish was a European articulation that attempted to define the social and religious values of a radically different type of society. The notion of the "fetish," from the Portuguese *fetitico*, has remained a distinctively Western idea throughout its various applications in cultural studies, psychoanalysis, and Marxism. The "fetish cult" of Dahomey is a distinctive Western perception of an unequal, and unstable, system of valuation. Fetish obsessions, like collecting obsessions, involve the displacement of a host of social contradictions onto impassioned objects. The fetish's power is precisely its capacity to repeat an original act of forging relations between otherwise different things, usually in the service of healing or magical empowerment. The situation between cultures in the sixteenth through nineteenth centuries was expressed in what Europeans called "trifling": European traders constantly remarked on the trinkets and trifles they traded for objects of real value. To them, the socioreligious orders of African societies seemed founded on the valuing of "trifles" and "trash." During this period, the relativity of value—the dependence of an object's social value on specific institutional systems for marking worth—was the distinguishing feature in transactions on the African coast. The exchange of goods for slaves did not escape this disparity in valuation. The extent of European commodification of human beings is grotesquely revealed in the indiscriminate listing of slaves alongside trifles and knickknacks in inventory reports. In *The Viceroy of Ouidah*, slaves are described as "230 items (144 M 86 F)" and listed with "41,500 cola nuts (female)" (p. 92).

The Viceroy of Ouidah also explores the contradiction between women's power over men and their subjugation as objects of value exchanged by men. The many girls sent by the king of Dahomey to Da Silva as gifts show women as sexual commodities. The number of children Da Silva fathered might be proof of his success in establishing a dynasty, but early in the narrative, Da Silva's only surviving daughter, the "proof that he was white" (p. 27), lies dying. His "sixty-three Mulatto sons and an unknown quantity of daughters whose ever-darkening progeny, now numberless as grasshoppers, were spread from Luanda to the Latin Quarter" (p. 8). They have forgotten Da Silva's native Portuguese and, to varying degrees, have adopted the living, changing culture of their birthplace.

Travel narratives have traditionally been open to transgressive relationships across lines of gender, race, and other cultural conventions. Mary Louise Pratt, Anne McClintock, and other critics have discussed the historical presentation of radically nonconformist relationships in travel narratives as well as their tendency to confirm other social conventions. Travel writers traditionally project the journey to colonial regions as a descent of the rational European male mind forward across a space (ocean, jungle, or desert) populated by hybrids (monsters and legendary beasts) *and* backward to a prehistoric zone of dervishes, cannibals, and fetish-worshipers. Such a breakdown in social conventions provides the opportunity, even the invitation, to disregard social restrictions. Homosexuality and interracial relationships, as well as androgyny, cross-dressing, passing, and other social ambiguity becomes more possible "across the border."

The Viceroy of Ouidah presents both heterosexual and homosexual situations that challenge traditional notions of gender divisions. In some respects, it is a scandalous book. Da Silva fathers many children with local women, yet his most meaningful relationship is a lifelong homosexual affair with his male servant, Taparica. His faithful servant and lover is with Da Silva from the beginning of his years in Dahomey until Taparica's death over twenty years later. In a rare gesture of humanity, at the end of Taparica's life Da Silva lifts his servant to his own four-poster bed because he could not bear to see the old man "die on a mat." He "laid him down on the Goanese bed and held his scaly hand through three suffocating nights" (p. 138). A lifelong, master-servant code exists between them until this final, moving scene. *The Viceroy of Ouidah*'s matrix of power and sexuality challenges the stability of conventional gender relationships.

Chatwin made careful use of textual gaps, particularly in erotic material. He admired Flaubert, the premier realist, in his use of gaps, an admiration that could easily apply to Chatwin's own handling of sexual situations: "Yet is not all erotic art—

as opposed to the merely pornographic—oblique? Descriptions of the sexual act are as boring as descriptions of landscape seen from the air—and as flat: whereas Flaubert's description of Emma Bovary's room in a *hotel de passe* in Rouen, before and after, but not *during* the sexual act, is surely the most erotic passage in modern literature" (*What Am I Doing Here*, p. 78). In Chatwin's other narratives, innuendo takes precedence over overt descriptions. But *The Viceroy of Ouidah* has some noticeable exceptions. The stark brutality of Da Silva's life of permanent settlement eliminates the mystery of intimacy and the possibility of love.

Chatwin visited Africa many times but felt a special attraction to the Sahara Desert. He wrote of Dahomey, "This is not my Africa. Not this rainy, rotten-fruit Africa. Not this Africa of blood and slaughter. The Africa I loved was the long undulating savannah country to the north, the 'leopard-spotted land', where flat-topped acacias stretched as far as the eye could see, and there were black-and-white hornbills and tall red termitaries. For whenever I went back to that Africa, and saw a camel caravan, a view of white tents . . . I knew that, no matter what the Persians said, Paradise never was a garden but a waste of white thorns" (*Far Journeys*, p. 74).

By his second trip in 1978, Dahomey's name had been changed to Benin. Chatwin was there to research the life of Dom Francisco Felix De Sousa, the historical person Da Silva's life is based on. It was at this time that Chatwin was incarcerated during a political coup. He was stopped by "a unit of the Benin Army. I was arrested as a mercenary: the real mercenaries retreated back to the airport and flew off" (*The Viceroy of Ouidah*, first edition, p. 2). In an essay written later, Chatwin hears the "official" and "unofficial" versions of the revolt, and asks his companion, Jacques, which the latter believes. Jacques replies, "Both. . . . This . . . is a very sophisticated country" (*What Am I Doing Here*, p. 34). Chatwin called this essay "A Coup: A Story" to indicate "the hand of fiction had been at work" and to highlight again the porous nature of historical accounts. Eighteenth- and nineteenth-century historical criticism focused on discovery of undetected "lies" or inaccuracies in historical narrative. Twentieth-century historical approaches attempt to acknowledge multiple "truths" in history, challenging the single-voiced authority of historical representation. Chatwin was aware that, as a British travel writer, he was an outsider in the cultures he visited and a culturally specific observer. In both South America and Africa, much of Europe's expansionist momentum was British and for the most part, it was British writers who established the basic forms of writing about non-Western cultures.

An incident in Benin occurred in 1984 during the making of *Cobra Verde* (1988), a film version of *The Viceroy of Ouidah*. Chatwin had returned to Benin to observe the filming. The "Amazons" demand a pay raise in the middle of the filming. When their demands are not met, the women cause a riot: "We draw the curtains, but the wind blows them open. Faces appear through the louvres: 'You will die.' 'You think you can stuff a black woman. You'll see' " (*What Am I Doing Here,* p. 147). The women eventually agree to a compromise. This account summarizes certain aspects of the transgressive cross-gender dynamics Chatwin explores in *The Viceroy of Ouidah*. Chatwin confirms the power of African women, but does so in terms of aggressive, same-sex gender solidarity.

ON THE BLACK HILL

THE first book Chatwin called a "work of fiction" was *On the Black Hill* (1982), an emotional account of identical Welsh twins, born in 1900, whose lives become a kind of decentered encapsulation of twentieth-century events that encroach, or fail to encroach, on the twins. If the macabre themes of *The Viceroy of Ouidah* after the buoyant vitality of *In Patagonia* surprised early Chatwin admirers, the intimacy of *On the Black Hill* dispelled any doubts about his limitations. Set in Chatwin's most circumscribed geographic range, his Radnorshire tale begins with twin brothers Benjamin and Lewis Jones preparing "The Vision," to pass the family farm, over to their nephew Kevin. The theme of rigid custom is established from the first paragraphs. The twins' house is a museum to the memory of their mother. The twins' philosophy is conservative and backward-looking, and the narrative shifts quickly backward in time to the twins' birth. With the exception of a summer holiday at the seashore, Benjamin and Lewis Jones spend their lives rooted to their farm. World War I redefines the twins' lives and afterward they withdraw into

a voluntary exile from what they view as the violent conflicts of urban settlement.

Chatwin remarked with regard to *On the Black Hill*, "It always irritated me to be called a travel writer. So I decided to write something about people who never went out" (Ignatieff, 1987, p. 27). There is more to the book's origin than this would imply, however. As a child, Chatwin made many trips through the Welsh border country with his father. He told the poet Hugo Williams: "Hardly anything has changed . . . since my grandparents came on bicycling tours as teenagers. Even the clothes are the same" (*Times Literary Supplement,* 1991). He often thought of the Black Mountains and Radnor Forest "as if it were my home" (Bragg, *South Bank Show* interview). Chatwin often stayed with friends in the area, including Diana Melly at her thirteenth-century watchtower near Brecon, where parts of *On the Black Hill* were written. Other portions of the narrative were written at the home of another friend, Martin Wilkinson at Clunton on South Shropshire. Chatwin "discovered" the book's title on one of his many walks in the area. There are many "Black Hills" in the Welsh border country, and Chatwin's title refers to none of them in particular. Chatwin's geographical dislocation of the Black Hill in his narrative is just another instance of his raiding the authority of maps and going on to construct his own imaginary topography. Chatwin posted a copy of a print titled *The Broad and Narrow Path* over his desk. In the novel, the print's mapped progression toward perfection or damnation influences Benjamin's beliefs about redemption and life after death.

Chatwin conducted intensive research on the people of the Welsh borderlands; however, *On the Black Hill* is not a labor of social anthropology, but a work of imagination. Whatever the resource: newspaper articles, secondhand oral tales, historical accounts, or personal experience, *On the Black Hill* is a more direct reordering of experience in a fictional framework than anything Chatwin had produced before. In a 1982 interview, he said, "I was told a story, it doesn't matter which one, which does appear in the book, about two bachelor brothers. . . . I wanted to write a short story" (Bragg, *South Bank Show*). He later added the idea that the brothers were identical twins. Chatwin often said the writer was a "cutpurse," a pickpocket of other people's stories. Chatwin explained that the story "has the same tenuous dividing line between fact and fiction and [between] real people and something invented. And I quite honestly used them. If you're off on a journey, [and] you meet somebody, they go into the book in one form or another" (Bragg, *South Bank Show*).

On the Black Hill falls within the tradition of the rural novel in English and calls to mind the world of George Eliot, as well as those of local precursors such as Mary Webb or Francis Kilvert. Although he was steeped in literary associations, Chatwin was always a keen observer of reality. The description of The Vision farmhouse draws in a few sentences the portrait of Welsh farms seen all over Radnorshire today: "roughcast walls and a roof of mossy stone tiles . . . and . . . at the far end of the farmyard in the shade of an old Scots pine . . . an orchard of wind-stunted apple-trees" (pp. 9–10).

The critic Karl Miller called *On the Black Hill* "a Christian romance," and noted the distinction of the farm titles ("The Vision" and "The Rock") and a landscape populated by "holy innocents, ragged saints, Franciscan animal lovers." Meg, a Welsh version of a divine madwoman of the woods, and Theo, a Buddhist renunciant who lives in a crude tent, embody the book's message of a countervailing antimaterialism and aesthetic spirituality set against the acquisitiveness, jealousy, and class struggle of the townspeople. The book's climactic image—an airplane flight—is the twins' symbolic, if momentary, escape from a confined, materialistic existence. For most of their lives, they are anchored to The Vision, an ironic name for a place so geographically restricted.

The conflict between the still-powerful imperial English and the long-colonized Welsh is summarized in the seminal event of the twins' youth: World War I. Benjamin, a religious objector, is drafted into the English army during the war. He asks a clergymen, "Do you believe in the Sixth Commandment?" (p. 107), but Benjamin is nevertheless sentenced to the "Hereford Barracks" (p. 107) for military training while Lewis stays on the farm. Benjamin is physically abused by the army while it is Lewis who feels Benjamin's pain. When Benjamin returns dishonorably from the army, the twins retreat to an area only slightly larger than the farm. Benjamin, ordinarily very hesitant to spend money, begins to acquire new tracts of land to add to The Vision and thereby increase the family's territorial range. Benjamin collects new pastures and fields with the same enthusiasm others might collect old coins or classic cars.

On the Black Hill raises far-reaching questions about human nature that dramatically exceed the confined physical area of the setting. The paradoxes of the twins' lives are metaphysical as well as physical: What is individuality? How sharp are the boundaries of the self? How essential is privacy to happiness? Do some people have mental telepathy? What are "normal" gender roles? Chatwin debates these real-life questions in a fully realized fictionalized world. The book's realism was so convincing, *On the Black Hill* was quickly recognized as an authentic depiction of life in the Welsh borderlands. The twins relate to each other on many mysterious levels: "Because they knew each other's thoughts, they even quarrelled without speaking. And sometimes—perhaps after one of these silent quarrels, when they needed their mother to unite them— they would stand over her patchwork quilt and peer at the black velvet stars and the hexagons of printed calico that had once been her dresses. And without saying a word they could see her again" (p. 11).

The twins share even the sensations of their bodies, and their life story describes an intimacy that questions conventional limits of human relationships. They feel each other's pain and sense when the other is in danger. They never willingly separated: Benjamin "hated Lewis for leaving and suspected him of stealing his soul. One day, staring into the shaving mirror, he watched his face grow fainter and fainter, as if the glass were eating his reflection until he vanished altogether in a crystalline mist" (p. 99). In many incidents, the twins' individuality is called radically into question. Lewis recalls, for a visiting psychiatrist studying twins, an episode when he mistook his own echo for Benjamin's voice. The lives of the twins are most tangibly demarcated by the time they spend apart from each other.

Neither twin marries and Benjamin assumes the domestic roles of cooking and cleaning. Some critics infer a homosexual relationship between the brothers. The book opens with Lewis and Benjamin asleep, side by side, in their mother's bed, separated by bedboards that form two troughs. But sharing their mother's bed could also symbolize a return to the cradle, or even to the womb. Lewis unsuccessfully attempts to develop relationships with women. Benjamin's sexual abuse by soldiers in the army troubles him for the rest of his life and may have repressed any kind of sexual expression he was capable of, even with his brother. If the twin's connection *is* read as an intimate homosexual relationship, is it also an incestuous one. Their exclusive love for one another is obvious, but Chatwin's narratives are never so straightforward. Like Howard Hodgkins, Chatwin's friend and a painter he deeply admired, Chatwin projects erotic material as "figures in a room where something momentous or erotic may, or may not, happen" (*What Am I Doing Here*, p. 73). Sexual undertones may charge *On the Black Hill* with tantalizing innuendo; however, Chatwin's Radnorshire tale reveals his talent for manipulating powerful erotic uncertainty.

THE SONGLINES

CHATWIN explored passive resistance to urban authority more fully in his next two novels. He chose the Australian aboriginals as his subject for many reasons, but perhaps most important was their extreme form of pacifism: "Australia is the only great colonial land mass in which the native population did not fight back. They just folded their arms and looked with a reproachful smile at their murderers, and that made the murderers jittery beyond belief" (Ignatieff, 1987, p. 33). In *The Songlines*, powerful images of oppression become images of barely suppressed power. The book was for Chatwin a "burden [he'd] been carrying all his writing life" (Rushdie, 1991, p. 235) and it was here he would most completely express his model of the causes of human unrest. About a quarter of the book is devoted to excerpts from his notebooks, written in very brief sections that Graham Huggan called "epigrammatic shafts of wisdom," such as: "In a paperback copy of *Tristram Shandy* bought in the second-hand bookstore in Alice, this was scribbled in the fly-leaf, '*One of the few moments of happiness a man knows in Australia is that moment of meeting the eyes of another man over the tops of two beer glasses*'" (p. 175). Until this shift, the book is a lively narrative about Chatwin's adventure through the Australian outback and the nature of the songlines. Chatwin hints that a change in his nomadic lifestyle was about to occur: "I had a presentiment that the 'travelling' phase of my life

might be passing. I felt, before the malaise of settlement crept over me, that I should reopen those notebooks. I should set down on paper a résumé of the ideas, quotations and encounters which had amused and obsessed me" (p. 161). The "novel" is put on hold for carefully arranged quotations by famous thinkers and portraits of desert wanderers Chatwin had met during his life. The section, titled "From the Notebooks," sketches a kind of journey to the interior of Chatwin's philosophy. Chatwin interrupts the flow of the narrative at the very point the reader would expect climactic action. He says that "mercenaries" once settled into ancient cities and "transformed themselves into a caste of military aristocrats, then into directors of the State. It can be argued that the State, as such, resulted from a kind of . . . fusion between herdsman and planter, once it was realised that the techniques of animal coercion could be applied to an inert [settled] peasant mass" (p. 202).

In the narrative, Chatwin is accompanied on his journey through the Australian desert by Arkady, a fictional character. *The Songlines* is modeled on the eighteenth-century dialogue novel. Chatwin wanted to create an imaginary dialogue "in which both narrator and interlocutor had the liberty to be wrong" (Ignatieff, 1987, p. 25). Chatwin and Russian-Australian Arkady travel through the desert with a group of aboriginals, "mapping" the holy sites of their ancestral "dream tracks" in terms of Western cartology. The survey is an effort by the urban railroad authority to avoid destroying aboriginal holy sites with the construction of the last great stretch of railroad across the aboriginal outback.

By the early 1980s, Chatwin was an established author and much in demand as a writer of introductions to reprints of travel writing classics like Osip Mandelstam's *Journey to Armenia* and Robert Byron's *The Road to Oxiana*. He also wrote the introduction to Robert Mapplethorpe's photography collection, *Lady Lisa Lyon*. Outside of a few essays such as these, Chatwin filled the five-year gap between *On the Black Hill* (1982) and *The Songlines* (1987) with more travel and quite possibly the most intensive research of his life searching for explanations of human unrest such as his own. After appearing in the Adelaide Festival in early 1984 with other British writers, including his friend Salman Rushdie, Chatwin left England for the central Australian desert. Rushdie would soon join him.

Salman Rushdie recounts their trip in 1984

through the Australian outback in his collection *Imaginary Homelands* (1991). They drove around the desert in a Toyota Land Cruiser and talked endlessly about Chatwin's emerging narrative: "I am a fairly garrulous person myself, but in Bruce's company I don't manage more than a few interruptions. I start becoming rather proud of these" (pp. 232–233). Many of the incidents would later be identified by Chatwin as his actual experiences in Australia, but like all of his portraits, the incidents that lead up to *The Songlines* were distilled by Chatwin's storytelling blend of fact and fiction. He wrote in the introduction to his essay collection: "The word 'story' is intended to alert the reader to the fact that, however closely the narrative may fit the facts, the fictional process has been at work" (*What Am I Doing Here*, p. vii).

Chatwin keeps a noticeable distance from his subjects. He has been occasionally criticized for failing to reveal his inner emotions. He countered, "If I had become involved, I wouldn't write the books I do" (*Granta*, p. 34). To become an aboriginal initiate, Chatwin would have had to undergo an induction process that includes circumcision and subincision. When asked if the commitment made to "Aboriginal reality" by Chatwin's characters is not "incomparably deeper" than his own as an uninitiated outsider, he replied: "The point of inventing a character like Arkady is that I was able to take a load off my back as an observer by turning [the narrative] into dialogue with Arkady. And he is admirably involved. But if I had been involved then I couldn't have described him and his involvement" (Ignatieff, 1987, pp. 34–35). Chatwin's own experiences on his journeys are thinly veiled components in his finished narratives, components that intersect his books at critical junctures but that always occupy the border of fact and fiction.

Chatwin did experience resistance to his presence in other cultures. In his notebooks, he called it "the allure of away-turning" (*Far Journeys*, p. 131). He relates the occasional bitterness in his real-life relationship with the aboriginals, for instance, when Chatwin approaches the defrocked priest, Flynn, "holding court to half a dozen people in the darker part of the garden" (p. 55) for information about the songlines. The exchange is flavored with dark puns in the same vein as Shakespeare's humor when Lear says "I will die bravely, like a bridegroom" (*King Lear*, 4, 6, 202). First, Chatwin tries to interest Flynn in "various theories on the evolu-

tionary origins of language. 'There are linguists', I said, 'who believe the first language was in song' " (p. 55). Flynn ignores him. Chatwin then describes "how gipsies communicate over colossal distances by singing secret verses down the telephone" (p. 55). Flynn denies there is any connection between gypsy verses and aboriginal songlines. Chatwin counters that to the gypsies:

'Settlers are "sitting-game". The gipsy word for "settlers" is the same as the word for "meat." '
    Flynn turned to face me.
    'You know what our people call the white man?' he asked.
    'Meat.' I suggested.
    'And you know what they call a welfare cheque?'
    'Also meat.'
    'Bring a chair,' he said. 'I want to talk to you.'

(p. 55)

The multiple meanings of the word "meat" have particular importance in Chatwin's portrait of the economic relationship between the aboriginals and the white ex-colonialists. Chatwin said: "There is an idea in Australia that the Aboriginals have got the country by the throat . . . [but] obviously, the whole of Australia is Aboriginal land. There's no end to the claim" (Ignatieff, 1987, p. 33). The conflict between the aboriginal "claim" to protect their holy sites and the urban "claim" to territory for a railroad right-of-way is not just an issue of who has the historical right to the area. It is also a questioning of how each culture conceives of ownership and value. It is this latter issue of economic and territorial value that substantially shapes the course of *The Songlines*.

The narrative also conveys the idea that passive resistance is a necessary ingredient for a strategic engagement with power from a subordinate position. The aboriginals' insightful, but passive, resistance shows them cooperating with the railroad authorities even as they deplore the railroad's technological invasion. Chatwin relates to this aspect of aboriginal thought even as he acknowledges an inability to understand their worldview as an outsider. Chatwin's question-and-answer collaborative anecdotes do not attempt to establish Chatwin as an authority. But even at his most self-critical, as Nicholas Murray observed, "There was nothing cynical or pessimistic or disillusioned in Chatwin's outlook, which makes reading him always an exhilarating experience" (p. 12).

In the late 1960s and early 1970s, anthropology made a general shift from ethnography as an empirical *record* to ethnography as a discursive *narrative*. For *The Songlines*, Chatwin has been called an "excellent example of the author as anthropologist" (Huggan, 1991, p. 57), blurring the dividing line between "ethnography as *document* and . . . ethnography as *fiction*" (Huggan, p. 66; italics added). *The Songlines* narrates the difference between the religious geography of the Australian aboriginals' songline tradition and Western spatial representation, such as maps. A map represents the physical as a model. But the map also expresses "an historically specific set of social and cultural attitudes" (*Maps and Dreams*, p. 58). But while maps are presented as authoritative evidence, they are necessarily "filtered through the perception of the mapmakers" (Muehrcke, 1978, p. 339). In this sense, maps are incomplete but persuasive accounts of the area they set out to define. Mapped conceptions of territory encourage a view of progress in which territory is seen as a place of limitless personal material gain while aboriginal concepts adhere to a view of territory as intended for communal prosperity. The considerable authority invested in the map eventually traces back to the perceived supremacy of the written over the spoken word.

There is also an accumulating critique in anthropology that might be summarized as a rejection of *visualism*. Ong (1967, 1977), among others, studied the ways in which the senses are hierarchically ordered in different cultures and epochs. He argued that the truth of vision in Western, literate cultures has predominated over the credibility of sound and interlocution, of touch, smell, and taste. Mary Louise Pratt observed that references to odor, very prominent in travel writing, are virtually absent from ethnography. The predominant metaphors in anthropological research have been participant-observation, data collection, and cultural description, all of which presuppose a standpoint outside—looking at, objectifying, or "reading" of a given "cultural reality." Ong's work mobilized a critique of ethnography by Johannes Fabian (1983), who explored the consequences of positing cultural facts as things observed, rather than, for example, heard, invented in dialogue, or transcribed. Once the two cultures are no longer prefigured visually—as objects, theaters, texts—there is the possibility of an interplay of voices within the text. Beyond reliance on visual endorsement, the dominant metaphors of ethnography shift away from the observing eye and toward expressive speech and gesture. Multiple voices pervade and situate the analysis, and "the rhetoric factual realism is renounced" (Clifford and Marcus, *Writing Culture*, 1986, p. 12).

Arcady explains to Chatwin that aboriginal creation began when "each totemic ancestor, while travelling through the country, . . . scattered a trail of words and musical notes along the line of his footprints, . . . these Dreaming-tracks lay over the land as 'ways' of communication. . . . A song . . . was both map and direction-finder. Providing you knew the song, you could always find your way across country" (p. 13). To map a route is to dream it. It is forward-looking in that the journey occurs through space and time. But to map a route is also backward-looking in the sense that the verses of any one path converge in dream tracks of antiquity.

White men, Flynn explains, often make the error "of assuming that, because the Aboriginals were wanderers, they could have no system of land tenure. This was nonsense. . . . A man's verses were his title deeds to territory. He could lend them to others. He could borrow other verses in return. The one thing he could not do was sell or get rid of them" (pp. 56–57). The notion of exchanging objects without profit echoes Chatwin's own beliefs about the exchange, rather than the sale, of art and antiquities. According to Flynn, "Aboriginals, in general, had the idea that all 'goods' were potentially malign and would work against their possessors unless they were forever in motion. . . . 'Goods' were tokens of intent: to trade again, meet again, fix frontiers, intermarry, sing, dance, share resources and share ideas" (p. 57). *The Songlines* does not imply an absolute dichotomy between oral and written texts. If it did, it would have the insurmountable problem of how a writer could convey a critique of Western consumer culture in book form, when the book is not only a fundamental artifact of that culture but might be considered the epitome of that culture. To overcome this obstacle in some way, *The Songlines* interweaves spoken and written modes in such a way "as to suggest that the schematic division between 'oral' and 'literate' cultures . . . [is] the product of cultural bias, a strategy by which literate Western cultures promote the notion of their superiority over their nonwestern 'others' " (Huggan, p. 64). Chatwin was deeply aware of the cultural biases and uneven power relations that underlie supposedly "neutral" approaches to ethnographic knowledge.

In popular imagery the ethnographer has shifted from a sympathetic, authoritative observer (best incarnated, perhaps, by Margaret Mead) to the unflattering figure portrayed by Vine Deloria in *Custer Died for Your Sins: An Indian Manifesto* (1969). Indeed, the negative portrait has sometimes hardened into caricature—the ambitious social scientist making off with tribal lore and giving nothing in return, imposing crude portraits on subtle peoples, or serving as a dupe for sophisticated informants. Such portraits are about as realistic as the heroic versions of participation-observation that guided earlier travel accounts. "Ethnographic work has indeed been enmeshed in a world of enduring and changing power inequalities, and it continues to be implicated. It enacts power relations. But its function within these relations is complex, [and] often ambivalent" (Clifford and Marcus, 1986, p. 9).

In Patagonia, The Viceroy of Ouidah, and *On the Black Hill* are typical of contemporary metafictional texts in that, while they challenge realist conventions, they do so, paradoxically, from within precisely those same conventions. *The Songlines* registers a greater degree of recognition of these conventions as a hindrance to communication. Metafiction often contains its own criticism, and the novels that play with realist presentation criticize, as *The Songlines* does, their own use of them.

Chatwin told of his difficult circumstances upon finishing *The Songlines* in 1988: "The year before [the writing of *The Songlines*] I had been to China and picked up a completely unknown disease of the bone marrow; I handed in this book—which is, above all, about walking—and the day after I couldn't walk across the hotel bedroom. I wrote that last chapter about three old men dying under a gum tree, when I was just about to conk myself. It was done with great speed. Often I have to *labour* over sentences, but this time I just wrote it straight down on a yellow pad, and that was the end of the book" (Ignatieff, 1987, p. 35).

A little over a year later, on 17 January 1989, Chatwin would die outside Nice, France, but not before organizing an essay collection and writing one more extraordinary book. After his death, another controversy raged over the nature of his illness and his own statements of suffering from an "unknown" disease. Newspaper reports of his death from AIDS have been neither substantiated nor denied; however, general opinion has it that he died of AIDS. Chatwin insisted until the end of his life that he suffered from a rare infectious disease. Whatever the exact nature of his illness, Chatwin's writings and interviews from this period firmly indicate his awareness of approaching death. Materials organized in the last year and a half of his life, in *The Songlines, Utz,* and *What Am I Doing Here,* effectively doubled the work he had published up to that point. Two essays in *What Am I Doing Here* are of particular interest in regard to how Chatwin might have viewed his illness: "Assunta 2," in which a physician's diagnosis is shown to be wrong and threatens an unborn infant and "Until My Blood Is Pure," in which the mistreatment of syphilis threatens a man's life. Chatwin's mistrust of official versions of the truth may have extended to his own condition. Or, he may have died from multiple ailments as is often the case for individuals whose health is already complicated with HIV infection.

Chatwin's health recovered for a brief time after publication of *The Songlines.* During this time, he traveled to write his last novel, *Utz,* and associates say that just before his death he contemplated another book on a Russian topic. The man who, in his twenties, declared his god to be "the God of the Walkers," in his late forties, converted to the Greek Orthodox Church.

In the early 1990s, critics became embroiled in a dispute concerning his public admission of suffering from a mysterious disease. Sean French, in his column for *The New Statesmen and Society,* criticized Chatwin for not publicly announcing the exact nature of his illness and noted the ambiguous sexuality of many travel writers. French was attacked by Geoffrey Wheatcroft in *The Independent Magazine* for "outing" Chatwin as a homosexual. Duncan Fallowell attacked prominent artists in general for not being more vocal about the disease. Fallowell felt that Chatwin was maladjusted to his homosexuality and concealed the nature of his illness to keep up appearances. But from all accounts including his own, Chatwin's sexuality was uncertain and ambiguous. Chatwin's work explored the freedoms and restrictions of a broad range of sexual expression, some of which were more trangressive than others but all of which were to varying degrees circumscribed by the power relationships of established, urban ideals even in remote, seemingly "free" locales.

UTZ

CHATWIN'S great unwritten book on nomads found partial expression in *The Songlines.* His next book, *Utz* (1989), signaled a new direction in his writing. According to Rushdie, "Utz is all we have of what had become possible for him once his Australian odyssey helped him express the ideas which he'd carried about for so many years" (1991, p. 235). In *Utz,* the exploration of the psychology of art collecting recollects Chatwin's own involvement in fine art dealing. "It's a memoir of things that happened to me in Prague in 1967. I met . . . a great collector of Meissen porcelain. He had shrunk his horizons down to those of his best friends," all of whom "were . . . porcelain figures seven inches high. He lived like a monk. It is, of course, a fantasy of people like myself to want to sit in a cell and never move again. That's what this man did" (Ignatieff, 1987, p. 36). *Utz* surveys the psychology of compulsive collecting. The title character lives in socialist Czechoslovakia, yet manages to hold on to his precious collection of Meissen porcelain through World War II and many subsequent upheavals. "When his friend Dr. Orlík suggested they both flee to the West, Utz pointed to the ranks of Meissen figurines, six deep on the shelves, and said, 'I cannot leave them'" (p. 25).

Chatwin traveled to Russia many times, first as an art expert for Sotheby's, later on assignment for the *Sunday Times.* In January 1973, Chatwin visited Konstantin Melnikov, a well-respected architect from the leftist movement of the early 1920s. Melnikov later fell out of favor with Soviet authorities and when Chatwin visited him, he was living as a social outcast in a house that was "one of the architectural wonders of the twentieth-century" (*What Am I Doing Here,* p. 186). Melnikov was a frustrated visionary isolated for forty years, and in his lonely devotion to art, he "calls to mind Kaspar Joachim Utz" (Murray, 1995, p. 107). Later that same year, Chatwin met George Kostakis, the Soviet's leading private collector who had turned his home into a museum to futurist productions. Soviet authorities allowed Kostakis to keep his collection on the pro-

vision that he leave the collection to a state museum. Kostakis' circumstances parallel the fictional situation of Utz, but like all of Chatwin's narratives, *Utz* "is a fiction whose launching pad is fact" (Murray, p. 109).

Chatwin visited Prague to research one of the most obsessed collectors of all history, Rudolf II, emperor of the Holy Roman Empire in the late sixteenth and early seventeenth century. Rudolf II ruled a substantial portion of Europe but neglected his empire to shut himself up for weeks with his huge collections and his astrologers. Chatwin explained he was "fascinated" with the "porcelain sickness" of upper-class Europe when Rudolf II and Augustus the Strong's "delirious schemes for ceramics got confused with real political power" (*Utz,* p. 50). The narrative hardly begins this inauspicious project when the story is already thick with what reviewer Philip Howard called the "dirty great issues of life and death" (the *Times*). A friend suggests that Chatwin visit Utz because he is "a Rudolf of our time" (*Utz,* p. 16). Rudolf II is a recognized historical figure, while Utz is a little-known private collector hounded by the state for his treasures. The common denominator between these two men is their obsession with collecting. Both Rudolf and Utz "slipped the moorings" (Murray, p. 110) of history in their mania for objects.

In *Utz,* Prague itself is seen as ripe with enchantment, "the most mysterious of European cities, where the supernatural was always a possibility" (p. 14). Pacifism again figures in Chatwin's social equation: he has one character say that Prague citizens, "with their silence . . . inflict a final insult on the State, by pretending it does not exist" (p. 15). For Chatwin, "the Czechs' propensity to 'bend' before superior force was not necessarily a weakness. . . . Their metaphysical view of life encouraged them to look on acts of force as ephemera" (p. 14). Utz's passive resistance enables him to keep his porcelains, but in keeping his treasures, he is tied to them for life.

The dedicated collector "dreams his way not only into a remote or bygone world, but at the same time into a better one" (*Schiften,* vol. 1, p. 416). There is evidence that the subjective significance of objects to a collector implies the reduction of, or relief from, anxiety; hence the protective properties of objects, particularly when the objects are treated as though they were a live attendant. "In some instances not only does an object's original meaning undergo a telling transformation, but the object itself may be preferred to human companionship" (Muensterberger, 1994, p. 27). As a youth, Utz instantly desires a clown figurine in his Jewish grandmother's curio cabinet and tells her, "I want him" (p. 18). Utz began collecting at seven, when his grandmother sent him the porcelain clown to comfort him when his father died. Utz's emptiness and disillusionment found emotional replenishment through ongoing acquisition. At a time when helplessness coincides with hopelessness and anxiety, it is easy to see how magical solutions might have helped Utz tolerate his grief.

For Utz, ownership is the most intimate relationship he can have, a moral responsibility, because objects "in a museum case . . . suffer the de-natured existence of an animal in a zoo. In any museum the object dies—of suffocation and the public gaze—whereas private ownership confers on the owner the right to touch. . . . The passionate collector, his eye in harmony with his hand, restores to the object the life-giving touch of its maker" (p. 20). The "life giving-touch" of the collector for Utz can be traced to the same desire for permanence in the face of inevitable change and death sought by collectors of Christian relics as well as to fetish healing or life-giving objects. Utz goes on to speculate that, because Adam was made from earth, he was not only "the first human person. He was also the first ceramic sculpture" (p. 42). Utz says his porcelains are "alive and they are dead. But if they *were* alive, they would also have to die" (p. 42). Utz's animation of his objects largely distinguishes his experience of personal ownership from the public institutional ownership of artwork. Utz calls the museum curator the "enemy" of the collector. He says, "Ideally, museums should be looted every fifty years, and their collections returned to circulation" (p. 20). Ritualized or institutional collecting is informed by a profound state of anxiety, but one which, theoretically, is warded off by the church or public museum, by converting a feeling of helplessness into an exhibition of collective power. Contemporary collecting, by institutions or individuals, is an attempt, however camouflaged, to address the same insecurities as fetish and relic worship.

Chatwin's erotic innuendo reached new proportions in *Utz*. Utz's sexual preferences are indeterminate for most of the narrative. He had several affairs with women over the years, but they always made the mistake of loving him for his collection.

Chatwin and Utz's conversation about the sale of a dwarf to "an Arab oil sheik" has implied sexual overtones (p. 39). Utz says, "That's a nice story. . . . Thank you. I also like dwarfs. But not in the way you think" (p. 40). That "dwarfs" is a reference to Utz's porcelain figurines is obvious, but the depth of the exchange is left uncertain. Chatwin asks to use Utz's bathroom, where he sees "an astonishing garment . . . a dressing-gown . . . of quilted, peach-coloured art silk . . . and a collar of matching pink ostrich plumes" (p. 100). Utz's discomfort is not explained and the reader is left to wonder: Does the gown belong to Utz's lover? Is the gown part of another of Utz's "collections?" Does Utz wear the gown himself? Utz's bedroom has the "atmosphere of musty, rather coarse femininity" with "flounced pink curtains" and a "frilly lace lampshade." Utz worries that "this inquisitive foreigner who had disturbed his peace of mind . . . might, in the long run, cause trouble" (p. 101). Indeed, a major accomplishment of Chatwin's work is to disturb the "peace of mind" of unexamined ideologies such as rampant material acquisition or the superiority of settled existence.

SELECTED BIBLIOGRAPHY

I. COLLECTED WORKS. *Far Journeys: Photographs and Notebooks,* ed. by Francis Wyndham (New York, 1993); *Anatomy of Restlessness: Selected Writings, 1969–1989,* ed. by Jan Borm and Matthew Graves (London and New York, 1996).

II. SEPARATE WORKS. *In Patagonia* (London and New York, 1977); *The Viceroy of Ouidah* (London and New York, 1980); *On the Black Hill* (London, 1982; New York, 1983); *The Songlines* (London and New York, 1987); *Patagonia Revisited,* with Paul Theroux, illus. by Kyffin Williams (Salisbury, England, 1985; Boston, 1986), also published as *Nowhere Is a Place: Travels in Patagonia* (San Francisco, Calif., 1992); *Utz* (London, 1988; New York, 1989); *What Am I Doing Here* (London and New York, 1989).

III. ARTICLES AND INTRODUCTIONS. "The Nomadic Alternative," in *The Animal Style* (New York, 1970); Introduction to Robert Mapplethorpe, *Lady Lisa Lyon* (New York, 1982); "I Always Wanted to Go to Patagonia," in *New York Times Book Review* (2 August 1983); Introduction to Osip Mandelstam, *Journey to Armenia* (1989); Introduction to Sybille Bedford, *A Visit to Don Otavio* (1990).

IV. INTERVIEWS. Melvyn Bragg, "Bruce Chatwin," *South Bank Show* (London Weekend Television, 7 November 1982); Michael Davis, "Heard between the Songlines," in *Observer* (21 June 1987); Michael Ignatieff, "An Interview with Bruce Chatwin," in *Granta* 21 (spring 1987); Colin Thubron, "Born under a Wandering Star," in *Daily Telegraph* (27 June 1987).

V. BIOGRAPHICAL AND CRITICAL STUDIES. Peter Levi, *The Light Garden of the Angel King: Journeys in Afghanistan* (San Francisco, 1972; rev. ed., 1984); Malcolm Deas, Review of *In Patagonia*, in *Observer* (9 December 1977); David Holloway, "Footloose in Patagonia," in *Daily Telegraph* (20 October 1977). John Hemming, Review of *The Viceroy of Ouidah*, in *Times Literary Supplement* (5 December 1980); Mary Hope, Review of *The Viceroy of Ouidah*, in *Spectator* (15 November 1980); Graham Hough, Review of *The Viceroy of Ouidah*, in *London Review of Books* (19 November 1980); Karl Miller, "Chatwin," in *London Review of Books* (21 October 1982); John Updike, "The Jones' Boys," in *New Yorker* (2 March 1983); Peter Conrad, "9 Hours," in *Observer* (25 September 1988); David Sexton, Review of *Utz*, in *Spectator* (October 1988); Susannah Clapp, "What Am I Doing Here?" in *Guardian* (19 January 1989); Duncan Fallowell, "When Sex Becomes Sin," in *Guardian* (1 December 1989); Patrick L. Femor, "Into the Blue," in *Spectator* (18 February 1989); Michael Ignatieff, "Bruce Chatwin," in *Independent* (19 January 1989); Hillary Mantel, "To Be a Nomad," in *Literary Review* (June 1989); "Nomad into Novelist," in *Times* (20 January 1989); Colin Thubron, "Chatwin and the Hippopotamus," in *London Review of Books* (22 June 1989).

"Chatwin Accused of Hit and Myth," in *Daily Telegraph* (6 September 1991); Mary Hockday, "Chatwin in Czechoslovakia," in *Independent* (20 July 1991); Graham Huggan, "Maps, Dreams, and the Presentation of Ethnographic Narrative: Hugh Brody's *Maps and Dreams* and Bruce Chatwin's *The Songlines*," in *Ariel: A Review of International English Literature* 22 (January 1991); John Pilkington, *An Englishman in Patagonia* (1991); Salman Rushdie, "Travelling with Chatwin" and "Chatwin's Travels," in his *Imaginary Homelands: Essays and Criticism, 1981–1991* (London and New York, 1991); David Sexton, "AIDS and Telling Stories," in *Evening Standard* (25 July 1991); Hugo Williams, "Freelance," in *Times Literary Supplement* (29 November 1991); Nicholas Murray, *Bruce Chatwin*, 2d ed. (Mid Glamorgan, Wales, 1995).

VI. RELATED LITERARY STUDIES. Max Weber, *From Max Weber: Essays in Sociology*, ed. and trans. by H. H. Gerth and C. Wright Mills (New York, 1946); Roland Barthes, Introduction to George J. Becker, *Documents of Modern Literary Realism* (Princeton, N.J., 1963); Gustave Flaubert, "On Realism," in *Documents of Modern Literary Realism*, ed. by George J. Becker (Princeton, N.J., 1963); Jacques Derrida, *Positions* (Harmondsworth, England, 1968); Louis Althusser, "Ideology and Ideological State Apparatuses," in *Lenin and Philosophy, and Other Essays*, trans. by Ben Brewster (London, 1971; New York, 1977); Hayden White, *Metahistory: The Historical Imagination in Nineteenth-Century Europe* (Baltimore, Md., 1973); Alice R. Kaminsky, "On Literary Realism," in *The Theory of the Novel* (London, 1974); Robert Alter, *Partial Magic: The Novel as a Self-Conscious Genre* (Berkeley, Calif., 1975); Hayden White, "The Fictions of Factual Representation," in *The Literature of Fact* (New York, 1976); Patrick Parrinder, *Authors and Authority: A Study of English Literary Criticism and Its Relation to Culture, 1750–1900* (London and Boston, 1977).

Michel Foucault, *Power/Knowledge: Selected Interviews and Other Writings, 1972–1977*, ed. and trans. by Colin Gorden et al. (New York, 1980); V. S. Naipaul, *The Return of Eva Peron* (New York, 1980); George Levine, *The Realistic Imagination: English Fiction from Frankenstein to Lady Chatterley* (Chicago, 1981); Jan P. Tompkins, "An Introduction to Reader-Response Criticism," in *Reader-Response Criticism: From Formalism to Post-Structuralism*, ed. by Jan P. Tompkins (Baltimore, Md, 1981); David Carroll, *The Subject in Question: The Languages of Theory and the Strategies of Fiction* (Chicago, 1982); Timothy Findley, *Famous Last Words* (Toronto, 1982); Alasdair Gray, *Unlikely Stories, Mostly* (Edinburgh, 1983); Abdul JanMohamed, *Manichean Aesthetics: The Politics of Literature in Colonial Africa* (Amherst, Mass., 1983); Edward W. Said, *The World, the Text, and the Critic* (Cambridge, Mass., 1983); Linda Hutcheon, *Narcissistic Narrative: The Metafictional Paradox* (Methuen, N.Y., 1984); Frederic Jameson, "Postmodernism, or the Cultural Logic of Late Capitalism," in *Postmodern Culture* (*New Left Review*, 1984); Patricia Waugh, *Metafiction: The Theory and Practice of Self-Conscious Fiction* (London and New York, 1984); Chris Baldick, "Estrangements" (Review of *Metafiction*), in *Times Literary Supplement* (15 March 1985); Frederic Jameson, "Postmodernism and Consumer Society" (London, 1985); Barbara Foley, *Telling the Truth: The Theory and Practice of Documentary Fiction* (Ithaca, N.Y., 1986); Peter Stallybrass and Allon White, *The Politics and Poetics of Transgression* (Ithaca, N.Y., 1986); Terry Eagleton, "Reluctant Heroes," in *Graham Greene* (New York, 1987); Albert Cook, "Reference and Rhetoric in Historiography," in *Criticism, History, and Intertextuality*, edited by Richard Fleming and Michael Payne (Lewisburg, 1988); Jacques Derrida, *Limited Inc.* (Evanston, Ill., 1988).

Dwight Eddins, *The Gnostic Pynchon* (Bloomington, Ind., 1990); Alison Lee, *Realism and Power: Postmodern British Fiction* (London and New York, 1990); Mary Louis Pratt, *Imperial Eyes: Travel Writing and Transculturation* (London and New York, 1992); John A. McClure, *Late Imperial Romance* (London and New York, 1994); KumKum Sangari, "The Politics of the Possible," in *The Post-Colonial Studies Reader*, ed. by Bill Ashcroft, Gareth Griffiths, and Helen Tiffin (London and New York, 1995);

Stephen Slemon, "Unsettling the Empire: Resistance Theory for the Second World," in *The Post-Colonial Studies Reader*, ed. by Bill Ashcroft, Gareth Griffiths, and Helen Tiffin (London and New York, 1995).

VII. RELATED CULTURAL STUDIES. Michel Beurdeley, *The Chinese Collector through the Centuries* (Rutland, Vt., 1966); R. J. W. Evans, *Rudolf II and His World: A Study in Intellectual History, 1576–1612* (Oxford, England, 1973); Karl E. Meyer, *The Plundered Past* (New York, 1973); Phillip Muehrcke, *Map Use: Reading, Analysis, and Interpretation* (Madison, Wisc., 1978); Martin Green, *Dreams of Adventure, Deeds of Empire* (New York, 1979); P. J. Marshall and Glyndwr Williams, *The Great Map of Mankind: Perceptions of New Worlds in the Age of Enlightenment* (Cambridge, Mass., 1982); Johannes Fabian, *Time and the Other: How Anthropology Makes Its Object* (New York, 1983); Walter LaFeber, *Inevitable Revolutions: The United States in Central America* (New York, 1983); Barbara M. Stafford, *Voyage into Substance: Art, Science, Nature, and the Illustrated Travel Account, 1760–1840* (Cambridge, Mass., 1984); Hanno Beck, "The Geography of Alexander von Humboldt," in *Alexander von Humboldt: Life and Work,* trans. by John Cumming (New York, 1985); Jamine Cahsseguet-Smirgel, *Creativity and Perversion* (New York, 1985); Philip Curtin, *The Image of Africa: British Anti-Slavery Literature of the Eighteenth Century* (Madison, Wisc., 1985); William Pietz, "The Problem of the Fetish I," in *Res 9* (spring 1985); Robert J. Stoller, *Observing the Erotic Imagination* (New Haven, Conn., 1985); Judith Williamson, *Consuming Passions: The Dynamics of Popular Culture* (London and New York, 1985); Henry Louis Gates, Jr., ed., *"Race," Writing, and Difference* (Chicago, Ill., 1986); Kristine L. Jones, "Nineteenth-Century Travel Accounts of Argentina," in *Ethnohistory* 33, no. 2 (1986); James Clifford and George E. Marcus, eds., *Writing Culture: The Poetics and Politics of Ethnography,* (Berkeley, Calif., 1986); Martin Bernal, *Black Athena: The Afroasiatic Roots of Classical Civilization* (New Brunswick, N.J., 1987); John Brenkman, *Culture and Domination* (Ithaca, N.Y., 1987); William Pietz, "The Problem of the Fetish II," in *Res 13* (spring 1987); Steve J. Stern, ed., *Resistance, Rebellion, and Consciousness in the Andean Peasant World, Eighteenth to Twentieth Centuries* (Madison, Wisc., 1987); Patrick Brantlinger, *Rule of Darkness: British Literature and Imperialism, 1830–1914* (Ithaca, N.Y., 1988); James Clif-ford, *The Predicament of Culture: Twentieth-Century Ethnography, Literature, and Art* (Cambridge, Mass., 1988).

Jonathan Dollimore, *Sexual Dissidence: Augustine to Wilde, Freud to Foucault* (Oxford and New York, 1991); Matthew H. Johnson, "Enclosure and Capitalism: The History of a Process," in *Processual and Postprocessual Archaeologies: Multiple Ways of Knowing the Past* (Carbondale, Ill., 1991); Robert W. Preucel, *Processual and Postprocessual Archaeologies: Multiple Ways of Knowing the Past* (Carbondale, Ill, 1991); Julio Ortega, "The Reader in the Labyrinth," in *Historical Criticism and the Challenge of Theory,* ed. by Janet L. Smarr (Urbana, Ill., 1993); Annabel Patterson, "They Say or We Say: Popular Protest and Ventriloquism in Early Modern England," in *Historical Criticism and the Challenge of Theory,* ed. by Janet L. Smarr (Urbana, Ill., 1993); Sandy Petrey, "Balzac's Empire: History, Insanity, and the Realist Text," in *Historical Criticism and the Challenge of Theory,* ed. by Janet L. Smarr (Urbana, Ill., 1993); Janet L. Smarr, ed., *Historical Criticism and the Challenge of Theory* (Urbana, Ill., 1993); Bill Corcoran, Mike Hayhoe, and Gordon M. Pradl, *Knowledge in the Making: Challenging the Text in the Classroom* (Portsmouth, N.H., 1994); Werner Muensterberger, *Collecting: An Unruly Passion* (Princeton, N.J., 1994); Gaddis Smith, *The Last Years of the Monroe Doctrine: 1945–1993* (New York, 1994); Bill Ashcroft, Gareth Griffiths, and Helen Tiffin, *The Post-Colonial Studies Reader* (London and New York, 1995); Anne McClintock, *Imperial Leather: Race, Gender, and Sexuality in the Colonial Conquest* (New York, 1995); Valerie Stelle, *Fetish: Fashion, Sex, and Power* (New York, 1996).

VIII. FURTHER READING. Richard Lander, *Journal of an Expedition to Explore the Course and Termination of the Niger* (London, 1830); Ernest Hemingway, *In Our Time* (New York, 1930); Miguel de Cervantes, *The Adventures of Don Quixote,* trans. by J. M. Cohen (Harmondsworth, England, and New York, 1950); Li Po and Tu Fu, *Poems,* trans. by Arthur Cooper (Harmondsworth, England, and New York, 1973); Samuel Beckett, *Waiting for Godot* (London, 1977); Salman Rushdie, *Midnight's Children* (London and New York, 1981); Denis Diderot, *Jacques the Fatalist and His Master,* trans. by Michael Henry (Middlesex, England, and New York, 1986); Blaise Pascal, *Pascal's Pensées,* trans. by A. J. Krailsheimer (New York, 1991).

CARYL CHURCHILL

(1938–)

Victoria D. Sullivan

PLAYWRIGHT CARYL CHURCHILL has been active in London theater for over thirty years. Her best known plays include *Cloud Nine* (1979), *Top Girls* (1982), *Fen* (1983), *Serious Money* (1987), and *Mad Forest* (1990). Churchill's work breaks the boundaries of realism through nonlinear time treatment; cross-gender and age casting; overlapping dialogue; fantasy sequences; ghost characters; Brechtian songs; and logically impossible actions. Her style ranges from the Pinteresque (*Owners*, first produced 1972, published 1973; *Traps*, first produced 1977, published 1978) to vicious satire (*Serious Money*) to the surreal and mythic (*The Skriker*, 1994). In its complex structure, her work makes high demands on the audience. As Churchill wrote of her play *Traps* in the introduction: "it is like an impossible object, or a painting by Escher, where the objects can exist like that on paper, but would be impossible in life" (p. 71). Having written close to forty plays for radio, television, and stage, she is increasingly committed to theatrical risk-taking and experimentation.

In *Traps* she achieves a theatrical situation where, as she writes, "the characters can be thought of as living many of their possibilities at once." For instance the character Albert both commits suicide and later returns to his friends as if he has not committed suicide; the character Syl is claimed as wife by both Albert and Jack, but may be married to neither. Or both. Through this technique of impossible possibilities, certain questions arise: To what degree are people trapped by their perceptions? To what degree are all roles traps? Is audience expectation a form of trap? Churchill points out in her introduction, "In the play, the time, the place, the characters' motives and relationships cannot all be reconciled" (p. 71). Ultimately, the nature of reality itself falls into doubt.

In *Cloud Nine,* the experimental technique takes the form of dislocations in time and in cross-gender and cross-racial casting. In act 1 Churchill chooses to have the British colonial wife in nineteenth-century Africa played by a male actor, the black servant played by a white, the effeminate young son played by a woman, and the toddler daughter played by a dummy; while in act 2, set in contemporary London (one hundred years after act 1, but only twenty-five years later for the characters) a five-year-old girl is played by a grown man. These obviously disorienting and also humorous casting choices focus the play's spotlight on gender and racial issues, creating a number of layers of potential awareness for the audience (similar to our recognition that the heroine Rosalind in Shakespeare's *As You Like It* would have been portrayed in Elizabethan times by a young male actor playing a woman disguised as a man).

Fantasy sequences, folktale superstitions, and disguised identity appear in her most recently produced play, *The Skriker*. Here Churchill includes more dance and music than previously, as well as *tableaux vivants* around the edges of the main story line. The effect achieved is as if one were to drop down into a nightmarish world of both ordinary and mysterious inhabitants, dominated by a powerful mythic figure, the skriker. Drawn from English folklore, the skriker is a shape-shifter who enters the characters' lives with destructive motivation, a kind of dark and hungry spirit, let loose in contemporary British society, preying on the needs of late-twentieth-century people for some kind of safety or succor in an apparently damaged natural world.

Although Churchill's plays reveal no single common theme or obsession, they are characterized by an intense social consciousness. Generally labeled a socialist feminist, Churchill is quite straightforward in her sense of how ideology enters her plays. As she states in her introduction to the play, "The

179

workshop for *Cloud Nine* was about sexual politics"; further, "When I came to write the play, I returned to an idea that had been touched on briefly in the workshop—the parallel between colonial and sexual oppression, which Genet calls 'the colonial or feminine mentality of interiorized repression' " (p. 245). Her political and social concerns range over time and space—from seventeenth-century witch persecutions and Cromwellian extremists to nineteenth-century British colonialism to the recent fall of the Romanian dictator Nicolae Ceausescu. What links her work is her fascination with how social forces effect individual lives.

Most of her plays have six or more characters, and it is the group dynamic rather than any one individual that drives the play. To emphasize the relative insignificance of individual characters, she suggests in her notes to *Light Shining in Buckinghamshire* (first produced 1976; published 1978) that different actors play the same characters in different parts of the play because, "The audience should not have to worry exactly which character they are seeing. Each scene can be taken as a separate event rather than part of a story. This seems to reflect better the reality of large events like war and revolution where many people share the same kind of experience" (p. 184). Her approach to casting in *Light Shining* also illuminates another stylistic feature of her writing: fragmentation. Her plays often break down into many short scenes, with many characters, much overlapping dialogue, and a general sense that there is no one clear picture to emerge, nor is she as a playwright willing to impose a false clarity.

Ten years later, in *Serious Money*, the cast numbers twenty, and in the brevity of their scenes and the multiple casting (a device she uses in most of her plays), it is possible to become confused about who is who, especially with the comic-book character aspect to the many rhyme-speaking money-driven wheelers and dealers. But that is her point. Churchill implies that in the world of high finance, there is simply no time for a rich inner life, a deep individuality. These high-stakes players can and do easily replace one another, a fact about themselves they are likely to ignore in their race for the material prizes dangled before them. The young speculator Jake—who meets a mysterious death, perhaps because of his dealings in insider information—says of his boss in this ever-escalating world of work and gain: "I told him for what he's getting

from my team, why be a meanie? / He got rid of the BMW's and got us each a Lamborghini" (*Plays: Two*, 1990, p. 206).

In her probing, disturbing, highly theatrical work, Churchill shines a harsh light, one that both illuminates and mocks such traits as greed, ambition, lust for power and control over others. The arc of her career moves in an increasingly experimental direction while her socialist and feminist vision continues to expand, providing voice to the voiceless, compassion to the confused, revised visions of the past, and frightening glimpses of the future.

EARLY CAREER: SCHOOL, RADIO, AND TELEVISION

BORN on 3 September 1938 in London, Churchill spent her childhood in England and in Montreal, Canada. She entered Lady Margaret Hall College of Oxford University in 1957, where she studied English literature, earning a B.A. degree in 1960. Impressed by the theater of the time, she fell under the influence of Samuel Beckett, John Osborne, T. S. Eliot, Harold Pinter, and Bertolt Brecht. Brecht seems to have influenced her work most directly in both style and ideology, although the Pinter influence can be seen in such early plays as *Owners* and *Traps*, and the Beckett influence in *The Skriker*.

While at Oxford, Churchill had two plays produced, *Downstairs* (1958–1959), and *Having a Wonderful Time* (1960), and shortly after her graduation, *Easy Death* (1961). She has said of that time in an interview with Kathleen Betsko and Rachel Koenig, "I began writing plays in 1958, and I don't think I knew of any other female playwrights then. Luckily, I didn't think about it" (p. 77). Of course, as the years have passed, Churchill has become far more conscious of what it means to be a female playwright and is considered by many the most compelling feminist writing for the contemporary stage.

In 1961 Churchill married David Harter, a barrister, and bore three sons between 1963 and 1969. She has said of this time that it was a somewhat overwhelming period for her; she felt enmeshed in maternal duties and the loneliness of being home with small children, as well as upset by the painful experience of a number of miscarriages. Nonetheless, she managed to write eight radio plays between 1962 and 1973: *The Ants* (aired 1962; published 1968) asks questions about the human capacity for caring in a world of what she paints as deadly middle-class values; *Lovesick* (1967) investigates the power of desire, along with confusions of sexual identity; *Identical Twins* (1968), a dramatic poem using one voice recorded over itself, also focuses on sexual and identity mix-ups; *Abortive* (1971) concerns a couple sexually betrayed and violated by a drifter; *Not . . . not . . . not . . . not . . . not enough oxygen* (1971), an excursion into science fiction, creates a future moment when necessary natural resources are being speedily depleted; *Schreber's Nervous Illness* (1972), a docudrama based on the memoirs of one of Freud's patients, enacts an interplay between the meaning of gender identity and its relationship to power; *Henry's Past* (1972) and *Perfect Happiness* (1973) both carry on Churchill's fascination with the multiple implications of gender roles. Churchill's approach to gender is to examine how individuals relate to their male or female role expectations, especially the damage produced by a too rigid confinement to traditional expectations.

Ranging in length from approximately fifteen minutes to fifty minutes, all of these plays were broadcast on BBC Radio, whose drama department produced about three hundred new plays per year under the directorship of theater critic Martin Esslin. At that time radio was an important venue for noncommercial drama before the arrival of the small theaters of the London Fringe. Under Esslin the BBC was very open to new playwrights, and Churchill particularly appreciated the freedom not to worry about length limits (which she later found uncomfortable when writing for television).

Although some critics have dated her feminism to her first work with the theater company Monstrous Regiment (*Vinegar Tom* , first produced 1976; published 1978), her early Oxford play *Having a Wonderful Time* reveals gender concerns in the character of Anne, who eventually opts for the safe local boyfriend, even though he treats her as a possession. And, of course, the radio plays are further proof of her intense concern with gender issues. Again and again throughout her career Churchill puzzles over how both men and women suffer from the roles assigned to males and females in Western culture—how their choices are shrunk, how their role-playing makes them inauthentic, and how the uneven distribution of power creates discomfort and rage.

Churchill focused three early 1970s television scripts (*The Judge's Wife,* 1972; *Turkish Delight,* 1974; and *Save It for the Minister,* 1975, cowritten with Cherry Potter and Mary O'Malley) on the meaning of female sexuality and subversion in a male controlled society. By this time she had become actively involved in stage theater, and—while she wrote three more television scripts, *The After-Dinner Joke* (1978), *The Legion Hall Bombing* (1978), and *Crimes* (1982)—she became increasingly disaffected from the television medium, finding its format too rigidly timed and its realistic conventions too confining. *The Legion Hall Bombing,* based on a real court trial in Ireland, caused considerable political controversy. As Churchill explained in an interview with Emily Mann, "We put on a voice-over at the beginning and end . . . that explained the Diplock Courts [introduced in 1973 in Northern Ireland to make getting convictions in politically motivated crimes easier], and the BBC took it off because they said it was political comment" (p. 81); Churchill removed her name from the credits as a protest against this censorship.

BEGINNING STAGE CAREER IN THE 1970S

IN 1972 when Churchill's *Owners* was produced at the Royal Court, Martin Esslin joked in his review in *Plays and Players* that the enthusiastic critical attention sounded as if Churchill "had stepped like the Goddess Athena, fully armed from the forehead of Zeus" (p. 41). *Owners* was actually her fifth full-length stage play, but the first commercially produced, as Churchill points out in an introduction to it, and "so my working life feels divided quite sharply into before and after 1972, and *Owners* was the first play of the second part" (*Plays: One,* 1985, p. xi).

Owners throws a tough punch at the belly of capitalism. Clegg the butcher and his wife, Marion, have developed a taste for ownership; he, in fact, wants to own her as well as his butcher shop, feels it is only right that a man own his wife. But Marion is a hard-driving real-estate broker, riding a boom in buying and selling in a developing section of North London. She uses any underhanded means necessary—lying, threats, terror tactics, arson—to get the properties she desires, including human property in the form of her former lover Alec, who happens to be living with his pregnant wife, Lisa, in one of the buildings she purchases. Churchill examines in this play the whole issue of exactly what one can own and ownership's psychic significance. When Clegg loses his butcher shop, he feels depressed, emasculated, and murderous. Ownership is clearly necessary to his sense of manhood. Here economics and sexuality intertwine in typical Churchill fashion. Clegg speaks sentimentally of his childhood when his father, also a butcher, "killed his own meat," and his mother would "literally" worship him (*Plays: One*, p. 9). He spends hours planning different ways to murder Marion and get away with it: "She is legally mine. And one day she will die knowing it. . . . I look at her sometimes and think I am the one this powerful rich property developer swore before God to honour and obey. Whether she does or not" (p. 11). Foolish and dangerous, Clegg clings to a ludicrously outdated gender concept of appropriate masculine behavior.

In order to give Clegg a new focus for his energies, Marion negotiates a deal through which they end up with Lisa's baby because she and Clegg have not been able to produce an heir, a disappointment undermining his patriarchal dream to have a business called Clegg and Son. When the confused, depressed Lisa comes to ask for her baby back, Clegg says: "He's Marion's and my little son, legally adopted. In some states of the United States the penalty for kidnapping is death. I think we can come to an arrangement. Someone's got to look after the little sod while I'm at work [he's gotten a new butcher shop], and you won't get Marion stopping home. So maybe, if you're very suitable . . ." (p. 54). He has already been testing Lisa's suitability in his bed; after all, he has the power over her of "owning" her son. Equating sex and power, Clegg commits adultery with Lisa to get even with Marion. Gleefully, bouncing up and down under the bedding, Clegg shouts: "An eye for an eye. A mouth for a mouth. A cunt for a cunt. Vengeance is mine. I will repay. In full" (p. 52). Clegg feels betrayed by life, the times, and his wife.

Churchill creates in Clegg and Marion the worst sort of capitalist entrepreneurs: greedy, insensitive, materialistic. As Clegg tells Lisa: "He's my baby. Marion's bought him a shop. . . . A brand new family butcher. Gold Lettering. Clegg and Son" (p. 53). He and Marion share a crude sense of the power of ownership; he deals in bloody meat, she in cunning ways to possess other people's homes at a profit. Her utterly ruthless character is revealed when she passionately defends her behavior toward Lisa and her refusal to return the disputed baby: "Because I'm a woman, is it? I'm meant to be kind. I'm meant to understand a woman's feelings wanting her baby back. I don't. I won't. I can be as terrible as anyone. Soldiers have stuck swords through innocents. I can massacre too. Into the furnace. Why shouldn't I be Genghis Khan? Empires only come by killing. I won't shrink" (p. 63). Churchill, of course, is over the top here; Marion's hyperbolic rant is comically excessive. But the phrase, "Empires only come by killing" accurately expresses the view of many historians. And the question, "Why shouldn't I be Genghis Khan?" only shocks because it is a woman speaking. In her own benighted fashion, Marion grasps the changing gender situation. The play proves a black comic indictment of the capitalistic power drive. Owners, it seems, may attempt to own anything.

Churchill arrived on the stage scene during an exciting time in Britain's contemporary theater history: the rise of fringe theater in London. Beginning in the 1960s, this new form of nontraditional, antinaturalistic theater thrived on Arts Council grants that supported the rise of a number of new theater companies. These groups often had a political as well as aesthetic agenda and they encouraged plays on nontraditional topics. Along with such political playwrights as David Hare and Edward Bond, Churchill became deeply involved in the fringe movement.

Churchill was able to throw herself full-time into the demands of live theater work in part because of changes in her personal, domestic situation. First her husband left his busy private law practice to join a legal clinic; then, in 1974, the family left London for six months—three months in Africa, followed by three months on Dartmouth Moor—so that Churchill could devote herself to playwriting while her husband took over child care. Churchill tends to resist interviews, and not to speak publicly about her private life, but she has discussed with several interviewers this period of domestic change, clearly seeing it as providing a necessary adjustment for a woman who was wife, mother, and playwright. In order to become involved in collaborative workshops and stage production, she needed to free up more time for herself than when she was writing short radio plays.

In 1975 her play *Objections to Sex and Violence*

(published 1978) was produced at the Royal Court Theatre. This play involves a young political terrorist, Jule, her conventional sister Annie, and various men and women either in their lives or whom they accidentally meet on the beach. All express some reservations about sex and violence—other than Jule who is in favor of both—for reasons both theoretical and personal. A decade after writing this play, Churchill laments that the title is misleading because "it suggests quite a different set of ideas, developed by feminists, of the link between male sexuality and violence, which wasn't my starting point at all. . . . Among the notes groping towards characters and events are notes on what I was reading, Reich on Aggression, Hannah Arendt on Violence, with quotes from Marx, Fanon, Sartre. . . . Most of the IRA bombings in England hadn't happened" (Michelene Wandor, ed., *Plays by Women*, vol. 4, 1985, p. 52). This play, then, is not so much a response to actual political events as to ideas in the air at the time and to her own reading.

Objections suffers, perhaps, from this very theoretical genesis. Nothing much actually happens in the play; people talk, leave, return, talk some more. A big event in the play occurs when the henpecked husband Arthur, a man in his fifties, drops his trousers and exposes himself to the hysterical spinster Miss Forbes. She runs away, slips and falls on some rocks, and is rescued by Arthur's fiercely repressive wife, Madge, who is eager to catch this sexual pervert and turn him in to the police. The liveliness of the older characters is in contrast to the verbose, self-involved passivity of the younger characters. Jule cannot even respond when her sister's boyfriend Phil tries to rekindle what he saw as a past erotic spark between them. "I'm not interested in being your guilty obsession" (p. 31), Jule coolly remarks.

Her next play, *Traps*, was written in early 1976 even though it did not receive its first production until 1977; it is the last play Churchill wrote prior to getting involved with theater companies to create collaborative scripts in workshops—a process that would prove liberating for her. *Traps*, then, is the final product of her original writing method (since even when later plays were not produced in workshop, such as *Top Girls*, they were influenced by her having worked in that method). *Traps* concerns a group of people in their twenties and thirties living together communally: two female characters, Syl and Christie, and four male, Jack, Albert, Reg, and Del. Almost all the givens in this play turn out to be variables. Syl is either pregnant or a young mother, or both, married to Albert or Jack, or neither, and possibly a dancer. The baby, which appears and disappears throughout the play, is on stage at the beginning, being walked up and down the room on Syl's shoulder. When Syl goes on to Albert about her attempts to get the baby to sleep, then asks, "Boring to listen to?" Albert responds, "A bit." She declares, "Boring to do" (*Plays: One*, p. 75). Albert points out the economic reality that if Syl were to go out and work she could not earn as much as he does.

At this point in the play, "traps" would seem to refer to motherhood, society's roles, gender realities, and other such clear inequities. But as the act continues, and more characters enter, what is true and what is not starts to fall into doubt, to the degree that Reg, Christie's husband can say, "You can't walk down a normal street now or eat dinner in a normal restaurant. There's no such thing as a normal street" (p. 79). And we believe him. One aspect of the non-normal in this play is the recurrence of paranoia throughout, with Albert being the most consistently paranoid character. His second line in the play is, "They're after me, Jack" (p. 73); and the motif of him being pursued and spied upon builds until it is possible that Albert commits suicide between acts 1 and 2—except that he shows up toward the end of act 2, *"his hands dirty from gardening"* and immediately asks, "Am I late?" (p. 119). But of course Churchill has said of these characters that they "can be thought of as living many of their possibilities at once" (p. 71), such that Albert can commit suicide and also not commit suicide.

Del is a kind of crazy man, who freaks out badly in act 1 and twice gives essentially the same impassioned speech to his pals in which he angrily accuses them of lying to him and manipulating him as well as being "necrophiliacs," although, as he points out, he is not dead. Reg, the most normal of the group, if to be a successful wage-earner and wife-beater is normal, says of Del at the end of act 1: "Strikes me he should be in hospital under heavy sedation" (p. 101).

Churchill achieves a sustained tension in this play of a sort that she did not in *Objections to Sex and Violence*. The constant changing of the rules of the game and the intense commitment of the various characters to their shifting personal agendas sustain audience interest. Political issues simmer just below the surface more than in *Objections*. Albert explains how "the Special Branch are recruiting men who pretend to be killers to lure other men into killing so the Special Branch have somebody to catch" (p. 96). Earlier he has said, "We don't want the police here. We don't want to draw attention. I want to get the place wired up with an alarm bell" (p. 93).

Traps creates a mood of people under siege because of their politics. Del hints at some sort of common goal for the group, as well as his disappointment in them; he even attempts a political historical analysis: "Settlers fled to America from persecution. Away from the tyrannies of governments and religions. New World. Think of the longing that got them on to those ships. Brotherhood, vision, pursuit of happiness. And what do they do as soon as they get there? Slaughter Indians" (p. 87). The politics floating through the play, the whiff of politics, is very post-1960s, post-Vietnam and the attendant European student uprisings. Churchill captures the heart of that period in which many young people were deeply political, paranoid, and pessimistic, making it a very different time from the materialistically driven decade of the 1980s that she would later satirize in *Serious Money*. A number of Churchill's plays are more topically tied to their times than those of playwrights like Tom Stoppard or Harold Pinter. In this sense, *Traps* almost becomes a period piece—capturing the political paranoia of the mid-1970s, the communal living, the changing sexual mores—a time when certain politically conscious people assumed they were on government lists, and that government itself was the enemy. In such a generalized mood of paranoia and uncertainty, everything becomes a potential trap, including the trap of such perceptions.

COLLABORATIVE WORKS: VINEGAR TOM *AND* LIGHT SHINING IN BUCKINGHAMSHIRE

AT the same time that she was working on *Traps*, in early 1976, the feminist company Monstrous Regiment commissioned Churchill to write a play about witches, thus beginning a new and most significant approach to playwriting for her. Working collaboratively with this group, she produced *Vinegar Tom*, set in England in the seventeenth century. Churchill has spoken of the workshop process as "a very intense way of writing," telling Betsko and Koenig, "I'd always been very solitary as a writer before and I like working that closely with other people. You don't collaborate on writing the play, you still go away and write it yourself. . . . What's different is that you've had a period of researching something together, not just information, but your attitudes to it, and possible ways of showing things" (p. 79). Asked by Betsko and Koenig if the playwright has "an obligation to take a moral and political stance," Churchill replied: "It's almost impossible not to take one, whether you intend to or not. Most plays can be looked at from a political perspective and have said something, even if it isn't what you set out to say. . . . It usually only gets noticed and called 'political' if it's against the status quo" (p. 79). This recognition of the "political" is right in line with 1970s feminist thinking: the growing belief that history revealed a pattern of punishment for deviation from traditional gender roles.

Churchill explains in her introduction to *Vinegar Tom* her thought process at the time of composition:

I rapidly left aside the interesting theory that witchcraft had existed as a survival of suppressed pre-Christian religions and went instead for the theory that witchcraft existed in the minds of its persecutors, that "witches" were a scapegoat in times of stress like Jews and Blacks. . . . The women accused of witchcraft were often those on the edges of society, old, poor, single, sexually unconventional.

(*Plays: One*, pp. 129–130)

She manages to theatricalize these concepts so effectively in *Vinegar Tom* that the issue of preachiness or polemic does not arise.

The play opens dramatically with a roadside scene of an unidentified man and Alice, a promiscuous village girl, who have apparently just had sex. The man begins the play by asking: "Am I the devil?" The friendly, pragmatic Alice sees no reason to call him the devil, even though he cites his black clothes, his glowing eyes, his rough, hairy body, and then caps his interrogation with the question: "Didn't the enormous size of me terrify you?" To which she kindly replies, "It seemed a fair size like other men's" (p. 135). Churchill immediately raises the freighted issue of sexuality in the context of witchcraft, reminding the audience how much of what historically identified witches was their supposed sexual practices—particularly fornication with the devil.

Of the seven women in the play, four are accused of witchcraft and pay the ultimate price for this accusation; one narrowly escapes by marrying, although she has had a strong aversion to marriage; one is a frigid wife who accuses the others, and one is the forty-five-year-old assistant of Packer the professional "witchfinder." Those accused women behave in socially unacceptable ways: they are old and a vocal nuisance like Joan, or young and sexually promiscuous like Alice, or skilled in herbal healing like Ellen the "cunning woman," or too eager for a miscarriage like Alice's friend Susan. They might have survived their various difficulties if Packer the witchfinder had not come to town or if the frigid wife Margery were not so angry at old Joan for cursing at her and keeping a large, wandering cat, the Vinegar Tom of the play's title.

The play's plot involves Margery and her husband Jack suffering various misfortunes: sick calves; a pain in Margery's stomach; sexual impotence for Jack. If they accept that they deserve these misfortunes, and that they come from God, they must be sinners. But if their problems are the result of a witch's curses, coming then from the devil, they can still consider themselves "good folk" because "Good folk get bewitched. . . . It can happen to anyone." In fact, as Jack points out, "It's good people the witches want to hurt" (p. 153). But is Jack good? He has had sex with Alice and no longer feels any attraction for his pious wife. Infuriated by Alice's refusal of further advances, Jack goes to see the cunning woman, Ellen, in hopes of restoring his sexual potency; he acts as if something has been stolen from him. Ellen suggests that he ask for it nicely from the young woman who took it. But when he does, and Alice even touches his crotch, provoking an erection, Jack believes that she is surely a witch. The hunt is on!

In fact, any independent action these village women take is likely to support a charge of witchcraft. If they want a man, it must be the devil's urging; if they attempt to heal with herbs, they are soliciting Satan; if they gripe, and beg, and complain, they are revealing a witch's temperament. The common curses of the time, "Go away to hell," or "Damn your butter to hell," or "Devil take you and your man" are all open to after the fact analysis as witch's talk. And if the churning cream does not turn to butter, then it seems the witch's curse

worked. Churchill has written in the play's introduction, "One of the things that struck me reading the detailed accounts of witch trials in Essex . . . was how petty and everyday the witches' offences were. . . . I wanted to write a play about witches with no witches in it; a play not about evil, hysteria and possession by the devil but about poverty, humiliation and prejudice" (p. 130).

An effective device that Churchill introduces into this otherwise straightforward historical recreation is the use of songs sung by women in modern dress, adding a frame to the narrative, which can work as a Brechtian technique of emphasizing the then/now similarities and differences. The first song, "Nobody Sings," presents conversational taboos: menstruation, menopause, old women's sexual appetite, with the refrain at the end of each verse, "Oh nobody sings about it, / But it happens all the time" (p. 142). Throughout the play these songs remind the audience of the continuing impact of gender constrictions in the late twentieth century. In the song "Oh Doctor," about female surgeries, like hysterectomies, the singer asks, "Who are you giving my womb?" and then enjoins, "Stop looking up me with your metal eye" (p. 150), raising the issue of the male gaze as a method of control as well as the subject/object relationship so seemingly intrinsic to gender relations. Scene 7 ends with the song "Something to Burn," bringing the play's issues closer and closer to the modern audience: "Sometimes it's witches, or what will you choose? / Sometimes it's lunatics, shut them away. / It's blacks and it's women and often it's Jews. / We'd all be quite happy if they'd go away" (p. 154). The audience becomes complicit here with Jack and Margery in their desire to be "good folk" and willingness to scapegoat others. But of course if the "others" are women, all women, then half the race is condemned to marginal status, a question raised in the next to final song of the play, "Lament for the Witches," whose refrain goes: "Where have the witches gone? / Who are the witches now? / Here we are" (p. 175). Since at this point Joan and Ellen have just been hanged in the public square, and we are aware that they are not witches, the questions are painful, as is a contemplation of the actresses standing before us singing "Here we are."

Even without the songs, *Vinegar Tom* is powerful, but with them it is a classic Churchill work, with its two-part time frame, its assault on audience expectations, its double casting (since women not in scenes step forward to play the modern singers), and its ironic recognition of historical and contemporary parallels in attitudes toward women—particularly those women who resist being pretty, nice, good, passive, quiet.

Vinegar Tom is Churchill's first definitively feminist work. Like most writers, Churchill is not fond of labels, but when asked by Catherine Itzin which were applicable, she replied, "If pushed to labels, I would be prepared to take on both socialist and feminist, but I always feel very wary" (p. 279). Both her socialist and feminist sides reveal themselves here since working-class status makes certain women more vulnerable to charges of witchcraft. Late in the play, when such charges are already in the air, Ellen, the cunning woman, advises the eighteen-year-old Betty: "Your best chance of being left alone is marry a rich man. . . . He has his big house and rose garden and trout stream, he just needs a fine lady to make it complete" (p. 169). As a landowner's daughter, this is a real option for Betty, whereas Alice and her mother, Joan, are poor and unprotected by any man. These two outspoken single women live as social pariahs; both will end up executed for witchcraft—after being interrogated and physically examined by Packer, who identifies witches by the devil's mark hidden somewhere on their bodies.

One final theatrical device should be noted. After Joan and Ellen have been hanged, and while Alice and Susan are awaiting their execution, the historical authors of the popular handbook on witches, *Malleus Maleficarum, The Hammer of Witches,* Kramer and Sprenger step forward, played by women, and dressed *as Edwardian music hall gents in top hats and tails* (p. 134) to perform passages on why female witches outnumber males: "woman is more credulous . . . women have slippery tongues. . . . But the main reason is she is more carnal than a man. . . . A defect of intelligence. . . . She's a liar by nature" (p. 177). Churchill balances the cruelty of the misogynous message (particularly right after the hangings) with the comedy of its presentation (women playing men in a music hall act). The play ends with a song: "Evil women / Is that what you want? / Is that what you want to see? / On the movie screen / Of your own wet dream / Evil women" (p. 178). Once more Churchill turns the spotlight on the audience, the "you" of the song, leaving them to ponder their need for "evil women," witches, bitches, call them what you will.

While working with Monstrous Regiment, Churchill got involved with another collaborative theater company, Joint Stock. During 1976 she shuttled between her two projects. In a note on the production of *Light Shining in Buckinghamshire,* she explains that she and the director Max Stafford-Clark together found the subject, the millennial movement during the English Civil War. She then went on to the next step in the process: "a three-week workshop with the actors in which, through talk, reading, games and improvisation, we tried to get closer to the issues and the people" (*Plays: One,* p. 184). Churchill's ability to grasp the core of a complicated historical situation and then dramatize it on stage in unusual and highly effective ways can be dated from this time.

Light Shining captures three distinct phases of the English Civil War in the late 1640s: first, before the final stages of the conflict, when millennial promises (like the establishment of heaven on earth—"Because when parliament has defeated Antichrist then Christ will come" [p. 195]) were made to those who joined Cromwell's army, and ordinary people began to comprehend the potential meaning of freedom; second, during the war itself, the struggles to make Parliament and its army more responsive to these people from the bottom ranks of society; and third, after the war, the sense of deep disappointment and betrayal because essential changes in the social order had not occurred. Churchill notes, "What was established instead was an authoritarian parliament, the massacre of the Irish, the development of capitalism" (p. 183).

What might in another's hands result in mere historical pageantry, in Churchill's becomes a bold attempt to capture a crucial political turning point, characterized by debate, hope, bloodshed, and wild flights of idealism. As she writes: "For a short time when the king had been defeated anything seemed possible, and the play shows the amazed excitement of people taking hold of their own lives, and their gradual betrayal as those who led them realized that freedom could not be had without property being destroyed" (p. 183). She brings on stage a crowd of Ranters, Diggers, and Levellers, people whose religious beliefs have blended with their strong social and political demands, and who—before our eyes—become conscious of the possibility of much greater freedom: to speak out on many subjects, to act on their beliefs, to lay claim to certain "native rights" (p. 209). Using documents from the time as sources for both ideas and language, Churchill creates characters who passionately advocate new visions of life:

HOSKINS: Steal though if I can. It's only the rich go to hell. Did you know that?

(p. 204)

1ST WOMAN: There's no one over us. There's pictures of him and his grandfather and his great great—a long row of pictures and we pulled them down.

(p. 207)

CLAXTON: I felt myself moving faster and faster, more and more certainly towards God. And I am alone, because my wife can't follow me. I send her money when I can. But my body is given to other women now for I have come to see that there is no sin but what man thinks is sin.

(p. 221)

BUTCHER: There's no meat for you this week. Not this year. You've had your lifetime's meat. . . . You've had their meat that can't buy any meat. . . You cram yourselves with their children's meat. You cram yourselves with their dead children.

(p. 228)

And Act 1 concludes with a tightly condensed version of the actual 1647 Putney Debates, where common soldiers brought their pleas to Cromwell for representative government and official recognition of certain basic principles: that they possess "native rights"; that the vote "ought to be proportioned according to the number of inhabitants"; that matters of religion should not be "entrusted . . . to any human power"; and that "impressing us to serve in wars is against our freedom" (p. 209).

Using both real and imagined characters in her twenty-one scenes, Churchill concentrates on the transformation of ordinary people into political and religious leaders during the very turbulent years from 1647 to 1649. She takes no interest in the royalist side and does not even introduce it; rather, she presents the wide range of groups banded together under Cromwell, showing how the needs and dreams of the ordinary people and certain idealists could not ultimately be reconciled with the demands and vested interests of the more powerful landowners, gentry, and army officers. Part of

what drove her to write this play was a recognition that her education had been misleading: "The simple 'Cavaliers and Roundheads' history taught at school hides the complexity of the aims and conflicts of those to the left of Parliament. We are told of a step forward to today's democracy but not of a revolution that didn't happen; we are told of Charles and Cromwell but not of the thousands of men and women who tried to change their lives" (p. 183). Like Brecht, Churchill in this play seeks to educate, to alienate, to force her audience to think as well as feel—a variation from Brecht's more doctrinaire separation of thought and feeling.

Churchill's characters in *Light Shining* come from a wide social range, including vicars, landowners, servants, army officers, the well-off, and the poverty stricken. Most moving are those with the most to gain if changes occur. Early in the play, a female beggar arrested for begging outside her parish is sentenced to being "stripped to the waist and beaten to the bounds of this parish" (p. 194); a female preacher, Hoskins, is also beaten for speaking out and interrupting a Calvinist preacher who claims that "God does not choose to save some people from sin and damnation is his free will and pleasure." To which Hoskins responds, "God's pleasure? that we burn? what sort of God takes pleasure in pain?" (p. 202). Such a presumptuous question typifies the sorts of questions raised by the major rebellious figures, members mainly of a loose group called the Levellers (who advocated leveling society to achieve political equity). Churchill's view of the world never gets so lofty and official that it leaves out the ordinary daily needs, the laughter and despair—the poor woman who has abandoned her one-day-old baby in a ditch and so allows no one to touch her because she is so overwhelmed by her sin; and the drunkard who declares: "Plenty of beer in heaven. Angels all drunk. . . . Devils and angels all fornicating." To which a Leveller responds, "You are God, I am God, and I love you. God loves God" (p. 239).

Churchill presents the postwar period as one of increasing disappointment among those who had fought for significant social change. Some have grown quite strange, like Briggs, one of the staunchest Levellers, who goes so far as to train himself to eat grass as a way to leave more food for others: "It was hard to get my body to take grass. It got very ill" (p. 240). The political rebel who becomes deranged shows up in a number of Churchill plays:

Albert and Del in *Traps,* a couple of women in *Fen,* several characters in *Mad Forest.* She recognizes the thin line dividing sanity from insanity and how strong feeling may push one over the line, particularly in situations like war or extreme poverty where normalcy is already dislocated.

In the final speech of the play, Claxton, like Briggs one of the fiercest reformers, no longer believes in the efficacy of action: "There's an end of outward preaching now. An end of perfection." It would seem that the light shining in Buckinghamshire has been put out, but then he says, "There may be a time" (p. 241)—and with that simple phrase Churchill leaves a door open for the contemporary audience watching the play. Such an opening gives her play power beyond a mere historical recreation; for Churchill, history is a communal process—with many forces at work—and her historical plays are passionate attempts to comprehend anew that process.

CLOUD NINE *AND* TOP GIRLS

STAGED first in London in 1979, *Cloud Nine* marks the beginning of Churchill's American reputation because of the very successful 1981 New York production directed by Tommy Tune. Churchill here mounts an extremely witty theatrical assault on empire, colonialism, oppressive sexual roles, patriarchy, and England in the post-colonial era. Produced in a Joint Stock theater workshop "about sexual politics" (*Plays: One,* p. 245), *Cloud Nine* opens in a British colony in Africa during Victorian times. ("Sexual politics" is a term first made popular by Kate Millett in her 1970 literary and historical analysis *Sexual Politics;* it is "based on the proposition that sex has a frequently neglected political aspect" [p. xi] and that "sex is a status category with political implications" [p. 24].) Churchill explains her choice of subject in *Cloud Nine* by her recognition of "the parallel between colonial and sexual oppression" (p. 245); just as the white man dominated the black in colonial Africa, so the heterosexual white male had generally dominated women, children, and homosexuals in Western culture until very recent times.

In a mood of high comedy, the first act introduces repressed Victorian colonialists who cling to a rigidly traditional patriarchal system seriously at odds—as it turns out—with their actual urges. In fact almost every character engages in secret sexual liaisons totally unacceptable to the dominant cultural model: the heterosexual marriage of Clive and Betty. The play opens with Clive declaring: "I am a father to the natives here, / And father to my family so dear." To which his wife responds: "I live for Clive. The whole aim of my life / Is to be what he looks for in a wife. / I am a man's creation as you see, / And what men want is what I want to be" (p. 251)—a particularly paradoxical claim since what we the audience actually "see" on stage is a male actor playing Betty, effectively separating gender (her socially constructed female role) from the female body.

Ironically, Betty is constantly made aware of her female role by everyone around her, not only her adoring but wandering husband, but also the adventurer Harry Bagley (who worships her passive purity even though he is sexually attracted to men); the lovesick lesbian governess Ellen; the rudely joking black servant Joshua; her pietistic, spying mother Maud; and her children, the effeminate Edward (played by a woman) and the doll dummy Victoria. All relate to Betty as an icon of femininity. She herself plays her role somewhat fitfully, admitting to boredom, a desire to live dangerously, an illicit attraction to the handsome Harry, and an awareness that she is always "waiting for the men" (p. 258). When Ellen, who is getting married, asks Betty's advice on sex, she says, "You just keep still," and when pressed further adds, "you're not getting married to enjoy yourself" (p. 286). All of these Victorian characters expect duty to be the center of their lives not pleasure.

Of course Betty is not the only complicated stage presence in *Cloud Nine.* Joshua, the loyal native who has internalized colonial values, proclaims: "My skin is black but oh my soul is white [an allusion to William Blake's poem "The Little Black Boy"]. / I hate my tribe. My master is my light" (p. 251). Again we actually see a white actor playing the black servant, truly becoming what whites want—a version of themselves—and consequently unthreatening. Clive, generally confident and full of the optimistic rhetoric of empire, admits to Betty that he fears the natives: "I know that is wrong. . . . But there is something dangerous. Implacable. This whole continent is my enemy" (p. 277). This racist fear parallels his actual feelings about women: "There is something dark about women, that threatens what is best in us. Between men that light burns brightly" (p. 282), he tells Harry Bagley, who is surprised to hear the very proper Clive speak thus of women. When Clive adds that they are "irrational, demanding, inconsistent, treacherous, lustful, and they smell different from us," Harry—already sexually involved with the nine-year-old Edward and the willing Joshua—makes his move on Clive, only to be strongly rebuffed. Clive may find women foolish, evil, and unworthy, but he considers homosexuality "the most revolting perversion" (p. 283). He is all man, as constructed by the Victorian ethos. When Clive does feel compelled toward unusual sexual practices for satisfaction, they must be heterosexual. He declares the depths of his adulterous passion to his widowed neighbor Mrs. Saunders: "Caroline, if you were shot with poisoned arrows do you know what I'd do? I'd fuck your dead body and poison myself. Caroline, you smell amazing. You terrify me. You are dark like this continent. Mysterious. Treacherous" (p. 263). A moment later he is disappearing completely under her Victorian skirt—while the family not far away are singing Christmas carols at their annual jungle picnic. Like Kurtz, in Joseph Conrad's *The Heart of Darkness*, Clive gives himself over rather too wholeheartedly to the intense mystery of Africa, needing it to reinforce his heroic image of himself.

At the end of act 1, Clive toasting the newly married couple—Harry and Ellen, whom he has pressured into this socially condoned union—announces: "Dangers are past. Our enemies are killed. / —Put your arm around her, Harry, have a kiss— / All murmuring of discontent is stilled. / Long may you live in peace and joy and bliss" (p. 288). But of course Clive is as wrong in this as he has been wrong in his assessments from the opening of the play, for "*While he is speaking JOSHUA raises his gun to shoot CLIVE*" (p. 288), the very same Joshua of whom Clive had boasted: "My boy's a jewel. Really has the knack. / You'd hardly notice that the fellow's black" (p. 251).

Act 2 then leaps ahead one hundred years to 1979 London, although—in a characteristic temporal disjunction—Churchill has the characters only age twenty-five years. Betty is now played by a woman; Edward is a gay park gardener; Victoria, no longer a dummy, is a theoretical feminist, married to Martin, with a toddler son whom we never see; postcolonial Clive never appears either, although Betty mentions him a couple of times, most

significantly that she is leaving him. Clive's absence in act 2 indicates how meaningless his traditional role and ideology have become in the final quarter of the twentieth century, like those toppled statues of former communist heroes we saw in photographs immediately after the fall of the iron curtain regimes. Joshua has been replaced by Edward's lover, the committedly promiscuous Gerry; and instead of Ellen the furtively romantic governess, we have the assertive lesbian Lin and her equally assertive five-year-old daughter Cathy.

Act 2 reveals most dramatically the complications and uncertainties in a period of sexual evolution, with all the trying on of new roles, attitudes, and practices. Victoria's husband Martin says to her: "So I lost my erection last night not because I'm not prepared to talk, it's just that taking in technical information is a different part of the brain and also I don't like to feel that you do it better yourself. I have read the Hite report [a famous contemporary book on women's sexual desires and exactly how they reach orgasm]. . . . I'm not like whatever percentage of American men have become impotent as a direct result of women's liberation, which I am totally in favour of" (p. 300). Edward wants to be a "wife"; his lover Gerry favors anonymous sexual encounters on commuter trains; Victoria wants to know, "Does it count as adultery with a woman?" And Betty discovers the long repressed joys of masturbation. Churchill's modern characters struggle comically and heroically to find new, more satisfying postpatriarchal ways of expressing their sexuality.

Act 2 is less farcical than act 1 and also less driven by exterior forces (like the restless natives who are always threatening an uprising). Act 2 seems to be more talk, less action. Living in Africa, and subject to its real dangers, puts a compelling context around the colonials in their besieged compound; in 1979 the people appear to be flailing about more self-indulgently in the increasingly tolerant times. With less sense of urgency and mission (the family, the empire, the queen), the meaning of struggle becomes more personalized and hence smaller. Churchill may have intended to give respect to these modern efforts at self-definition, but act 2 plays as an anticlimax.

The issue of a less powerful second act comes up in her next play, *Top Girls*, as well. Here the opening concept is a dinner party thrown by the contemporary businesswoman Marlene to celebrate her promotion at work, to which she has invited five extraordinary women from history and art. To have at one restaurant table women spanning the ages from ninth-century Rome to thirteenth-century Japan to nineteenth-century Scotland and up to the contemporary times of Marlene is a bold conception. Experiencing each woman's presence and hearing her tale—commented on and interrupted by the others—the audience is alternately shocked and amused. The second and third acts of the play are set in contemporary England: act 2 mainly in the office of the Top Girls Employment Agency, and act 3 one year earlier in the home of Marlene's sister Joyce in the working-class town of her youth. Although the stories of Joyce, Marlene, and her business colleagues provoke interest, they lack the metaphorical power of the highly imaginative first act. Women meeting and talking with each other across ten centuries—as well as from the works of Brueghel and Chaucer—is so unique a situation that in some ways it throws off the structural balance of the play.

Each dinner party guest reveals herself to be strong, unusually driven, and at the same time liable to the needs and failings of ordinary women. Isabella Bird arrives first, a nineteenth-century Scotswoman who traveled extensively to what were then regarded as exotic and primitive places after the age of forty and until close to the end of her life: "I was the only European woman ever to have seen the Emperor of Morocco," she brags. "I was seventy years old. What lengths to go for a last chance of joy" (*Plays: Two*, p. 83). Isabella had fallen in love with the sea when she had gone on a cruise for her health in middle-age: "There were rats in the cabin and ants in the food but suddenly it was like a new world" (p. 62). Lady Nijo arrives next, a thirteenth-century courtesan to the Japanese emperor who spent the second part of her life as a Buddhist nun walking through the land at a time when such female perambulation was unheard of; followed by Pope Joan, who, disguised as a man, is believed to have been Pope from 854 to 856 (until she was discovered to be a woman while giving birth in a public procession, whereupon "They took me by the feet and dragged me out of town and stoned me to death" [p. 71]); then Dull Gret, subject of a Brueghel painting, in which an aproned housewife leads her female gang down into hell to wreak havoc on the devils (because hell apparently was not so frightening: "Well we'd had worse, you see,

we'd had the Spanish. We'd all had family killed. My big son die on a wheel. Birds eat him. My baby, a soldier run her through with a sword. I'd had enough, I was mad, I hate the bastards" [p. 82]); and finally, arriving late, Patient Griselda, from Chaucer's "Clerk's Tale," the perfect embodiment of the obedient wife.

The first act sparkles with excitement at getting this disparate group of women together for a celebratory feast, ostensibly in honor of Marlene, but actually in honor of female power, ambition, and achievement. These women have all been tested, behaved in unexpected ways, and have generally paid dearly for their achievements. What they have not been is ordinary.

After the stunning first act dinner party, acts 2 and 3 are far more grounded in ordinary contemporary reality, taking place at the Top Girls Employment Agency and in the backyard and kitchen of Marlene's unsuccessful working class sister, Joyce. The issues, too, seem more mundane: who gets ahead and how; the lifestyle of an ambitious woman; changing times; the need to sell oneself in the business world; sibling rivalry; and the personal price paid for a woman's worldly success. The one theatrical device that keeps the play from falling utterly into kitchen sink realism is Churchill's placement of these two acts out of linear time order, with act 2 occurring one year *after* act 3—producing a disruptive consciousness in which meanings are revealed in a new way. Acts 2 and 3 comment on each other and only after the whole play concludes does the audience understand certain issues, like Joyce's bitterness in act 2 and the depth of Marlene's callousness at the end of that act.

Act 2 takes place mainly at the Top Girls agency where we see interoffice politics and also job placement interviews. A series of sketches illustrating gender issues in the work world, its tone is rather brittle, like the characters who make up this scene. The world of work appears highly competitive. When her office mates hear of Marlene's promotion to managing director, one says: "Our Marlene's got far more balls than Howard and that's that" (p. 100). Howard's wife later comes to Marlene because he is so depressed over not getting the job to suggest that she might step aside, and when Marlene indicates that Howard can always go elsewhere, his wife calls her "one of these ball breakers," to which Marlene responds, "Could you please piss off?" (p. 113). Act 2 implies that women must be sharper than men to get ahead. A corollary is that those who are sharper, as well as driven, grow rather tough-skinned in the process, as if they have had to amputate their softer sides to get ahead. This proves a significant issue because while some critics have seen the play as a wholehearted endorsement of Marlene's success and the top girl philosophy, others have discerned criticism of both Marlene and her survival-of-the-fittest business world.

The removal to the wholly personal sphere of act 3 confirms the later reading; Marlene's interaction and arguments with her working-class sister reveal that both women pay a heavy price for their choices: Marlene's glamour and success come at the price of giving up her daughter at birth, having no serious man in her life, and cutting herself off from her working-class roots to become a rabid Thatcherite; Joyce has stayed in the home town, taken on the mothering role with Marlene's daughter, Angie, been married to a philanderer who has left her, works as a cleaning woman, resents Marlene's life in London, and loathes the "filthy bastards" in the Thatcher government. Neither sister is happy although Marlene is optimistic, stating, "I think the eighties are going to be stupendous." Joyce then asks, "Who for?" (p. 137). Marlene rides the Margaret Thatcher wave and has a great respect for the first female prime minister. Joyce remarks, "I suppose you'd have liked Hitler if he was a woman. Ms. Hitler. Got a lot done" (p. 138). Joyce here raises the problematic issue of newly won female power: Is it necessarily good just because it is in the hands of a woman? Churchill herself answered this question in her interview with Emily Mann: "What I was intending to do was make it first look as though it was celebrating the achievements of women and then—by showing the main character Marlene, being successful in a very competitive, destructive, capitalist way—ask, what kind of achievement is that? The idea was that it would start out looking like a feminist play and turn into a socialist one, as well" (p. 82).

The price of being a "top girl" becomes evident from acts 2 and 3 together. The audience gets to see what Marlene does not: that the human side of her life has been stunted; that on some meaningful level her sister hates her; and that her rejected daughter Angie probably falls into the despised working class, those Marlene labels as "lazy and stupid" (p. 139). The final line of the play, spoken by Angie, who is half asleep, "Frightening," could serve as Churchill's assessment of the future if feminist and socialist values become separate. Female success in the large world is exciting, as act 1 suggests, but it is also fraught with many dangers, as the whole play implies.

FEN

Fen, written in 1982 and produced in 1983, moves in an almost Hegelian opposite direction from *Top Girls*, looking at a group of women on the very bottom of society, those who work the land in the marshy area of eastern England known as the fens. Again working with the Joint Stock Theatre Group Company, Churchill went with a workshop to the fens area for several weeks, where the group visited pubs, homes, and workplaces to speak with farm laborers. Underlying the picture that emerges in the play is the perception that these people's impoverished circumstances appear not to have changed much over the hundreds of years since the fens were drained in the seventeenth century. Churchill concentrates on the lives of the women who work the fields, and here the taste of bitterness expressed by Joyce in *Top Girls* is expanded into a whole worldview of a seemingly doomed group.

Scene 2 opens in a potato field where a gangmaster watches five workers, four females and a sixteen-year-old boy, bent over picking and dumping potatoes. The ironic frame for this sweaty, ill-paid day labor is provided by a Japanese businessman in scene 1 explaining the economics of contemporary farm work: "in the end we have this beautiful earth. Very efficient, flat land, plough right up to edge, no waste. This farm, one of our twenty-five farms, very good investment. . . . We now among many illustrious landowners, Esso, Gallagher, Imperial Tobacco, Equitable Life, all love this excellent earth" (*Plays: Two*, p. 147). All love this excellent earth except the families who work it and feel tied to painful, unremunerative labor. As Nell, the rebel, says in response to the news that a local landowner has committed suicide, "Best hope if they all top themselves. Start with the queen and work down and I'll tell them when to stop" (p. 172).

Churchill has emphasized that there is to be "no interval" or intermission in this play, in order to immerse the audience in the hard times and heavy labors of these people: their daily pain, fractured domestic lives, and inability to escape. The most powerful image of their paralysis is embodied in the couple Frank (divorced and living in a single room away from his former wife and children) and Val (who leaves her husband and two young daughters to be with Frank). But throughout the play Val goes back and forth between dwellings because she finds it impossible to live happily away from either her children or Frank. The other women resent Val's even trying to find happiness, and are generally unsympathetic; her mother May, who takes care of the girls days, mocks her: "What you after? Happiness? Got it have you? Bluebird of happiness? Got it have you? Bluebird?" (p. 159) Actually, their torment wears the couple down; Val becomes too weak and distracted to work; Frank is so depressed he attempts suicide, but Val calls an ambulance and he is saved.

Another effective voice of the fen workers' collective torment arises from a female ghost hundreds of years old, still working the fields and lamenting: "We are starving, we will not stand this no longer. Rather than starve we are torment to set you on fire. You bloody farmers could not live if it was not for the poor . . . but there will be a slaughter made amongst you very soon. I should very well like to hang you the same as I hanged your beasts" (p. 163). She talks here to the local farmer Tewson, who, at first amazed to see her, then decides to depart. She taunts: "Get home then. I live in your house. I watch television with you. I stand beside your chair and watch the killings. I watch the food and I watch what makes people laugh. My baby died starving" (p. 163). The compact eloquence of her rage is not generally a feature of the contemporary women, who are not actually starving for food anymore. Theirs is a more tedious hopelessness— trapped in unfulfilling lives, but still able to go to the pub at night for a beer or a game of darts. One of them, Angela, takes out her frustration on her fifteen-year-old stepdaughter Becky, whom she abuses physically (making her drink too hot water, putting a cigarette out in her arm) and psychologically (demanding irrational obedience, reading and mocking her private writing, threatening to tell her father). Churchill makes clear in *Fen* how stunted lives can lead to child abuse, drinking, despair.

Fen ends powerfully with Frank killing Val with an ax; she had asked him to kill her, finding her di-

vided life impossible. At first he had said, "I can't even kill a dog" (p. 186), but somehow their ongoing pain wears him down. After the ax stroke, he immediately puts her body into a closet. Val reenters the room from the other side of the stage, a ghost now, for the final lyrical scene. In touch with the crowds of the dead, Val reports: "There's so many of them all at once. . . . A lot of children died that winter and she's still white and weak though it's nearly time to wake the spring. . . . I can't keep them out. Her baby died starving. . . . They're not all dead. There's someone crying in her sleep. It's Becky" (pp. 187–188). The scene expands from Val and Frank into other characters arriving back on stage in this surreal moment: the abused Becky comes in the middle of a nightmare; her abuser Angela comes too, saying, "I stand in a field and I'm not there. I have to make something happen. I can hurt you, can't I? You feel it, don't you? Let me burn you" (p. 189); Nell enters on stilts (like those old fen people used before the fens were drained); then Shirley comes with tales of the past: "My grandmother told me her grandmother said when times were bad they'd mutilate the cattle. Go out in the night and cut a sheep's throat or hamstring a horse or stab a cow with a fork" (p. 189). Here the voices and images of the fen women rise up like a chorus at the end of the play. Frank says, "I've killed the only person I love," and Val responds, "It's what I wanted." Frank has the final word, "You should have wanted something different" (p. 190). That, perhaps, is the message of the play.

But the very final theatrical moment is more eerily lovely; May, Val's mother, who has always claimed to her grandchildren that she cannot sing, that she has no voice, comes on stage and sings. Churchill says in her production note: "we hear what she would have liked to sing . . . something amazing and beautiful. . . . In the original production it was a short piece of opera on tape" (p. 145). In *Fen*, Churchill achieves on stage at the end a fusion of the possible and the impossible, not a naturalistic moment but a poetic moment—the artistic embodiment of "if only."

SERIOUS MONEY

ONE of Churchill's most popular and controversial plays, *Serious Money* evolved from a workshop set up by the Royal Court Theatre in 1986, working again with the director Max Stafford-Clark, who had come up with the idea of a play about the City (the term used for the world of the London Stock Exchange). Churchill describes the increasingly familiar process, "As usual the group opened the project up in a way one person couldn't possibly have done in the time or in many times the time, and gave me a sense of that appalling and exciting world that carried me through weeks of reading and researching alone during Big Bang, the Guiness scandal, Boesky . . ." (*Plays: Two*, p. x). *Serious Money*, her most obviously satiric play, riotously sends up late 1980s greed, speculation, and killer mentality. The strategy of writing the play in rollicking rhyming couplets came to her when overwhelmed by the sheer volume of economic material she had to master.

The large cast—twenty characters—and numerous short scenes fill the stage with frenetic energy. Several story lines move with a Darwinian survival-of-the-fittest logic through hostile takeovers; the death of Jake Todd, a young dealer in insider information (is it suicide? murder?); the quest of his sister Scilla to know the truth about his death or to know where his considerable money is hidden; and the multiple, complicated betrayals of the many characters involved in the takeover wars, specifically one target fought long and hard over, Albion Corporation. With huge sums of money involved in these high-stakes games, the players are quick to turn brutal, selling anyone out—from their country people (in the case of Jacinta Condor, the Peruvian businesswoman/cocaine dealer, to Nigel Abjibala, the Ghanaian businessman who considers the whole continent of Africa "such a frightful mess" [p. 261]), to their family (in the case of Jake and Scilla, and their stockbroker father Greville Todd) to potential lovers as well as long-term friends, neighbors, and business associates. Money is the one true god in the play.

A very 1980s play, *Serious Money* critiques the intense drive of that decade—its committed materialism (well expressed in the moment when the Michael Douglas character in Oliver Stone's film *Wall Street* shouts out like a preacher to his congregation, "Greed is good!"); its almost religious belief in a vision of infinitely expanding markets; its rewriting of the rules of high finance so that "arbitrage" and "hostile takeovers" became the new money manipulation game—a time when greed ran

amuck and everyone was killing the fatted calf. The subject itself demands a frenetic mood, but Churchill introduces—and here is where some of her critics question the play's satiric effectiveness— a good deal of fun. Her vision suggests that greed makes people happy while they are pursuing it; or at least it energizes them; it has elements of both sport and war. Greed involves taking territory (in this case financial—the fictional Albion Corporation, whose name suggests England itself); it requires brains and guts; it produces a euphoric high.

Churchill throws into her competitive money-game mix several strong female players: Scilla Todd, who is a LIFFE (London International Financial Futures Exchange) dealer always on the lookout to break into the "serious money"; Marylou Baines, the hard-nosed American arbitrageur; and Jacinta Condor, the Peruvian businesswoman whose greatest passion is for safe English banks and Eurobonds. All three like to play with the boys, run with the winners. In this new age the implication is that if one is bloodthirsty enough and cool enough to play, then gender is beside the point; it might even be an advantage since men are likely to underestimate a woman's killer instinct.

Seen as a rebel to her class because she likes the action down on the trading floor, Scilla declares: "I love it down with the oiks, it's more exciting" (p. 206)—the 1980s version of slumming. Grimes, the gilts dealer, speaks with the poor grammar of the ill-educated, but he is in a position to make millions off his know-how. What happened at the time Churchill writes about was an opening up of certain opportunities in the financial world (which until then in England had been dominated by the upper-class public school educated elite) to young, aggressive, uneducated people who began to make enormous sums of money. Clearly fascinated with the sheer energy of the situation, Churchill captures the complex structure of this new era of capitalistic feeding frenzy.

An interesting characteristic of this fast-moving world is an absence of psychological subtext; characters say what really drives them. When a man tells his boss immediately upon promotion that he would like to run the firm solo, and his boss protests, "I made you my equal," the man replies: "Jack. I hate you. / Didn't you know that? You're not so smart. / You're too important to smell your own fart" (p. 209). The days of any kind of polite humility are over. The employee points out that he made his company eighty million dollars and they pocketed most of it, concluding his remarks: "You don't seem to get it. You're sitting in my chair. Walk" (p. 210). This scene is immediately commented upon by the narrator Zac (an American banker/financial negotiator): "The financial world won't be the same again / Because the traders are coming down the fast lane. . . . If you're making the firm ten million you want a piece of the action. . . . Guy over forty's got any sense he takes his golden handshake and goes. / Because the new guys are hungrier and hornier, / They're Jews from the Bronx and spicks form Southern California. / It's like Darwin says, survival of the fit" (p. 210). The crude language—which regularly conflates power and sex—suits the crude scene. Zac concludes, "England's been fucking the world with interest but now it's a different scene. / I don't mind bending over and greasing my ass but I sure ain't using my own vaseline" (p. 211).

The flat characters, as in Brecht, often possess symbolic names: Grimes is grimy with the dirt of commerce; Scilla is a many armed Scylla, dangerous and risky; Jacinta is a Condor, a vulture of the high Andes; Duckett, the chairman of Albion (the mythic England of the past) would like to duck out of any shady dealings, has bad dreams, fears some criminal culpability. Together they play their roles in a Brechtian allegory of corrupt capitalism where characters sometimes speak directly to the audience or break out in song. Brecht developed the concept of the "alienation effect"—that the content of the drama should be made through antinaturalistic, distancing techniques to seem strange, "alien," so that the audience would be made critical and therefore reason rather than feel—which Churchill employs in a number of her plays, including *Serious Money*, which is her most Brechtian in both its message and technique.

An underlying question throughout is: Who makes the "serious money"? Clearly there is big money—billions—being made by some people. But just as the murderer of Jake, if there is one, is never discovered, so too those who really benefit from the new economics stay mostly behind the scenes, with the suggestion of collusion between capital and the Thatcher government. A government spokesman, Gleason, offers the major corporate raider Corman a deal: the government will stop investigating him if he will stop his takeover raid of Albion. Corman asks, "Why pick on me? Everyone's

the same. / I'm just good at playing a rough game." To which Gleason replies: "Exactly, and the game must be protected. / You can go on playing after we're elected. / Five more glorious years free enterprise, / And your services to industry will be recognized." Corman expects "At least a knighthood" (p. 299).

Everyone lies to his or her partner in corporate crime; betrayal goes on at every level. Toward the end of the play, Zac suggests that maybe M15 or the CIA killed Jake because the British government would not want "another scandal just before the election," concluding, "There's bound to be endless scandals in the city but really it's incidental. / . . . . Think a trillion dollars a day. / That's the gross national product of the USA. / There's people who say the American eagle is more like a vulture. / I say don't piss on your own culture" (pp. 305–306). The whole theatrical event ends with the song "Five More Glorious Years" whose chorus is: "We're crossing forbidden frontiers for five more glorious years / pissed and promiscuous, the money's ridiculous / send her victorious for five fucking morious / five more glorious years" (p. 309), which sums up the mood of the late 1980s market—an utter and high spirited commitment to amoral greed.

If Churchill's work has a flaw, it may be that at times she is too fixed on the moment, too tied to a particular time and place, such that a play like *Serious Money*, with its stockbrokers, corporate raiders, and arbitrageurs playing the late 1980s greed game, might well be dated in ten or fifteen years. The slang terms and cultural references are keyed to a highly particular moment of contemporary history, what is referred to in the play as the "Big Bang"—a deregulation of the stock exchange in the UK that introduced much more intense competition between brokerage houses, a situation characterized by raiding activities, hostile takeovers, and sudden high stakes wealth—the very situation that Churchill presents so wittily in the play. But how soon will we need footnotes to explain Boesky, the Guiness scandal, tax neutral benefits, and "five more glorious years" of Thatcherism?

Even more problematic is the question of how seriously one takes this play. When it opened in London, it quickly became the hot ticket—playing to capacity audiences—for the very stockbrokers and money manipulators the play was purportedly mocking. As Kimball King wrote in his essay in *Caryl*

Churchill, A Casebook: "There were probably more pin-striped, three-piece suits in the stalls bar at the Royal Court from March through May than had appeared there in the previous three decades. . . . Urban, upwardly mobile executives proclaimed the truth of Churchill's shattering expose as their eyes filled with tears of laughter" (p. 152). They were the perfect audience since a number of the trading scenes move at such a speedy pace in the specialized shorthand language of buying and selling that it is a little like overhearing a foreign language unless one is part of that world.

Depending on one's point of view, then, *Serious Money*'s satire is tinged with comic or tragic overtones. What Churchill has painted here in primary colors is a vast, worldwide network of cynicism and greed: the rich busily getting richer and the poor not even worth discussion. Is it a realistic picture? That depends on one's political ideology. The crowds of brokers who ran to see this play in the late 1980s did not complain that it was a false picture; rather they tended to brag that they knew the real people on whom the characters were based.

MAD FOREST

CHURCHILL'S *Mad Forest*, subtitled *A Play from Romania*, written and originally performed in 1990, not only captures the country of Romania at the moment of the fall and execution of its communist dictator Nicolae Ceausescu, it also expresses some of the emotional and ideological complexity of these events. The issue involves not simply the destruction of an evil leader, but how people actually lived their daily lives before, during, and after the events of December 1989, and how difficult it was for many to be convinced that the "revolution" had actually changed their society in an essential way. Even a hated ruler, once he is gone, may be missed by the very people who had hated him. After all, he was a "strong man," something several characters suggest is again needed in the chaos that followed the revolution. Like a carnival house of mirrors, a land of official lies is difficult to comprehend by those who have lived for many years defined by those lies.

Churchill effectively dramatizes the fragmented complexity of events and their meaning by following two ordinary Romanian families in this confusing period. Besides these two families, one with peasant origins, the other middle class, the middle section of the play introduces a group of characters at the scene of the street-fighting and rebellion—schoolboys, a housepainter, a doctor, a translator, a bulldozer driver, and others—who simply narrate their own experiences during the few dramatic days of the revolution from 21 December to 28 December. A talking dog, a vampire, and an angel fill out the cast. Her more than thirty years in the theater serve Churchill perfectly in this project; struggling to bring a very ambiguous event alive on stage, she uses the dramatic techniques developed in prior work: overlapping dialogue; many quick scenes (some with no dialogue); supernatural characters (who bring a deeper level to the work); songs and music; a blending of the serious and the comic, the lofty and the vulgar.

The play begins in the home of Bogdan, an electrician, and his tramdriver wife, Irina. Music is playing and the two "*sit in silence, smoking Romanian cigarettes*" (New York ed., p. 13). When the couple wish to talk, they turn up their radio even louder; this is how they have conducted their private life for years in a police state—always aware of potential spies and listening devices. The audience can see but not hear an argument between Bogdan and his wife. Their daughters then arrive with American cigarettes and eggs, the music is turned down, but still no dialogue is heard; only gestures, laughter, frowns, smoking, and a broken egg create the moment. In a later scene when their son Gabriel tries to tell his parents about a visit he received from Securitate officers at work, his mother frantically tries to hush him because the power is out and so the radio does not work; she feels too nervous to listen to anything at home when there is no radio to cover the sound. With such a Pavlovian response to talk on any serious subject, clearly even after a change in government such a woman could not easily relax. Later, after Ceausescu's fall, she remarks to her son: "I used to say more with the radio on" (p. 55), recognizing her own disorientation in the new times.

Such a recognition is part of the power of *Mad Forest*; people have a difficult time adjusting to any change, even one perceived of as beneficial. Late in the play in a drunken fight at a wedding, Ianos the Hungarian attacks his good friend Gabriel as a Romanian: "You were under the Turks too long, it made you like slaves" (p. 84), not only insulting

Gabriel and his family but also implying that the Ceausescu regime made people insensitive to their mental enslavement. The school teacher Flavia speaks sadly of "twenty years marching in the wrong direction" (p. 68) and how she would like "to write a true history . . . so we'll know exactly what happened" (p. 78), because the truth is that the one-week revolution was very confusing. A man hospitalized during the fighting with a head injury obsesses over questions:

Did we have a revolution or a putsch? Who was shooting on the 21st? And who was shooting on the 22nd? Was the army shooting on the 21st or did some shoot and some not shoot or were the Securitate disguised in army uniforms? . . . Most important of all, were the terrorists and the army really fighting or were they only pretending to fight? . . . And by whose orders? Where did the flags come from? . . . Why did no one turn off the power at the TV?

(p. 50)

His apparent ravings cannot be ignored by several quite sane characters.

In a land of lies, what is the truth? Iliescu, the man who is running an election campaign to replace the deceased Ceausescu, may not, in fact, be very different from his predecessor. The rebel son Radu says of him, "Iliescu's going to get in because the workers and the peasants are stupid" (p. 60). Radu's fiancée Florina accuses him of being a "snob," but then admits that she misses Ceausescu. When Flavia taught about Ceausescu during his power, she would begin her lecture: "Today we are going to learn about a life dedicated to the happiness of the people and noble ideas of socialism. The new history of the motherland is like a great river with its fundamental starting point in the biography of our general secretary, the president of the republic, Comrade Nicolae Ceausescu" (p. 16). Whether he was perceived as God or father or even the devil, his image saturated their lives, and his downfall, then, proved emotionally and politically traumatic in a country with small democratic tradition and little organized resistance. Flavia's husband Mihai says, "We have to put the past behind us and go forward on a new basis" (p. 49), but that turns out to be no easy task.

Ethnic, class, and generational tensions repressed during the harsh dictatorship years flair up boldly after the revolution. Arguments and fights break out. Clearly this latest phase of political life for the Romanians will be a difficult one. The play ends with a second wedding and all the characters dancing the *lambada*; couples who have been drinking and brawling speak in Romanian, *"alternating lines with their partner and overlapping lines. . . . So that by the end everyone is talking at once but leaving the vampire's last four or five words to be heard alone"* (p. 85), and these are: "you have to keep moving faster and faster" (p. 87). Not a very comforting message.

The vampire has come down from the mountains to Bucharest during the revolution because he "could smell it a long way off. . . . Nobody knew who was doing the killing, I could come up behind a man in a crowd" (pp. 44–45) and quickly sip his blood, he explains to the starving dog who belongs to no one. The dog asks the vampire, "Will you keep me?" The vampire rejects him because he is just passing through, but the dog will not take no for an answer: "I'm hungry. You're kind. I'm your dog" (p. 45). This scene becomes a metaphor for the Romanian situation: a blood-sucking vampire ("bored with killing") desired by a pathetic, starving creature ("Nice. Yes? Your dog? Yes?") who longs to be owned. Such a seduction scene midway through the play typifies Churchill's work; she achieves deeper insights into political and social situations by abandoning naturalistic theater for more expressionistic and poetic devices, just as she did in the final scene in *Fen*.

What so amazes about *Mad Forest* is how quickly it was created. Ceausescu was captured, tried, and executed on 25 December 1989; less than a month later the director Mark Wing-Davey suggested a Romanian project to Churchill; she and he went there to visit in early March for four days, returning 31 March to 7 April for an on-the-scene workshop with ten acting students from the London Central School of Speech and Drama; they began rehearsals 21 May and the first performance was 13 June—less than six months after Ceausescu's death. Clearly Churchill's workshop writing experiences in the 1970s and 1980s had prepared her to immerse herself totally in a new situation—listen, learn, absorb—and then stand back and make art. As her career has moved forward, her work has grown in complexity, theatricality, and imagination. In *Mad Forest* Churchill is both bold and brave. It is as if, in some Zen fashion, her ego drops away more and more, and she simply writes the play that needs to be written at that precise moment in time.

CARYL CHURCHILL

THE SKRIKER

PRODUCED in London in 1994 and in New York at the Joseph Papp Public Theater in 1996, *The Skriker* explodes on stage like a demented contemporary fairy tale. A blend of folktale and apocalyptic vision, this play employs music, dance, and snatches of dark old tales to etch the lives of two young women fallen under the power of the Skriker, whom Churchill describes as *"a shapeshifter and death portent, ancient and damaged"* (New York ed., p. 1). Lily and Josie, one innocent, the other psychotic, are like Rose White and Rose Red in 1990s London, hounded by the hungry Skriker who keeps showing up as various characters—a street beggar, a chic American, an angry little girl, a demanding suitor, and others—in order to control and feed off their lives. Particularly desirous of Lily's baby born midway through the play, the Skriker embodies the theme of infanticide and changelings (long a part of English folklore), and a theme present in Churchill's work since *Owners*.

In fact, Josie has killed her newborn infant before the play begins and is initially hospitalized in a psychiatric ward. When the kind, pregnant Lily asks, "Was she being naughty?" Josie knowingly responds, "What can a ten day old baby do that's naughty?" (p. 7). Images of death and dismemberment hang over the play in many forms: a little girl who sings about her murder ("My mother she killed me and put me in pies / My father he ate me and said I was nice" [p. 19]); a hag in the underworld singing, "Where's my head? where's my heart? . . . is that my finger? that's my eye" (p. 29); and, most dramatically, the Skriker's mad monologues that are consistently filled with violent, bloody images ("Put my hand to the baby and scissors seizures / seize you sizzle. . . . / to bake and brew and broody more babies and / leave them an impossible, a gobbling, a no. . . . Bloody bones hides in the dark dark dark / . . . . and chews whom he likes" [p. 2]).

In the Skriker's language Churchill achieves a marvelous deranged poetry, spewing out weird, angry visions of life: "Don't put your hand in the fountain pen and ink / blot your copy catching fishes eyes and / glue sniffer . . . . wail whale / moby dictated the outcome into the garden. / maudlin" (p. 3). She (or "it" since the Skriker can assume a male or female shape, though in both the London and New York productions a female actor played the part) is a repository of resentment and insight, a creature of the Jungian collective unconscious at its most primitive and destructive (as Churchill has said, "ancient and damaged"). By naming the play after her/it, Churchill paints contemporary society as damaged, afflicted, and poisoned in ways more cosmic than generally acknowledged. Matt Wolf quotes Churchill in his *New York Times* article: "I was certainly wanting to write a play about damage—damage to nature and damage to people, both of which there's plenty of about" (sec. H, p. 6). In order to give this dark vision an archetypal power, Churchill uses certain classic folktale figures: the old hag, often a witch or wise woman (the Skriker in her many guises); two sisters, one wicked and one good (not actually sisters, Josie and Lily cling together like family in their threatened state); the hag wanting a kiss like a disguised prince (and rewarding with money or toads depending on the response to her request); the seductive kelpie, part man and part horse (who enters and exits many scenes, never speaking, but wooing women to their destruction); Dead Child, the type of any imperiled little girl (who gets to sing of her murder and watch the other characters move closer and closer to danger); and the dancer, named only "Passerby", who dances throughout the play (like the spellbound heroine in the tale of the red shoes). These various archetypes lend a mythic resonance to the tale of two modern girls—always surrounded by portents of another, darker world—trying to survive in London.

In the most Bosch-like of the scenes, where Josie has gone into the underworld to a feast which is not all it at first seems ("some of the food is twigs, leaves, beetles, some of the clothes are rags, some of the beautiful people have a claw hand or hideous face" [p. 29]), she is welcomed with a song, then tempted to eat and drink from the magical, lavish table, but also warned by one tormented spirit, "Don't eat. It's glamour. . . . Don't eat or you'll never get back" (p. 30). As in the garden of Eden, the fruit looks delicious, and Josie does eat and join the spirit dance. In comedy, of course, the ritual dance comes at the end, signifying the positive power of community, while in a tragedy like Marlowe's *Doctor Faustus*, it signifies selling one's soul as it does here. Churchill benefits from the long, rich English theatrical tradition, and *The Skriker* even more than earlier plays seems the product of a consciousness that has absorbed this literary tradition. Ben Brantley writes in his *New York Times* review that the play is "on one level, a toxic variation on 'A Midsummer Night's Dream,' with its feeling of parallel disharmony between the natural and supernatural" (sec. C, p. 15).

In the actual production many actions of nonspeaking characters take place simultaneously with scenes involving Lily or Josie so that Churchill achieves a rich visual texture on stage similar in effect to a Hieronymus Bosch painting. Between the music and the dance, the real world and the fairy world, the ordinary life of a new mother and the extraordinary powers of the Skriker, the play coalesces as a total theatrical experience moving toward surreal nightmare. At the end Lily has been seduced into leaving her baby for what she thinks will be five minutes but turns out to be over a hundred years, in order "to save the worldly," as the Skriker mocks, summing up her situation in the devastating final lines of the play, "So Lily bit off more than she could choose. And she was dustbin" (p. 52).

This powerful visual and verbal journey into the dark side of postmodern existence warns the audience: lost in a clueless, malevolent world, goodness surely will not protect one from evil. Nor will badness. Josie and Lily are equally lost, and even the Skriker is only a damaged creature who has "been around through all the stuff you would call history . . . 1066 and before that, back when the Saxons feasted, the Danes invaded, the Celts hunted" (p. 16). The final dark moment ending in "dustbin" plays as an updated version of Macbeth's view of life: "It is a tale / Told by an idiot, full of sound and fury, / Signifying nothing." Churchill has called *The Skriker* "a play about England now" (Wolff, Sec. H, p. 6). After nearly thirty active years in the London theater, Churchill has pulled out all the stops in her apocalyptic vision. Like Lily in this punk-violent, globally warmed, wounded world we are all "dustbin."

CONCLUSION

LOOKED at in its full, rich complexity, Churchill's playwriting career expresses a committed social consciousness, ongoing technical innovation, and unusual breadth of subject matter. Verbally audacious, raw, and immediate, her work sometimes shocks in its refusal to be safe or conventional. From the beginning Churchill proved a bold risk-taker and she has only grown more so as she has mastered stage possibility. Radio gave her a voice, television gave her images, and the stage has provided the ultimate playground for both—along with music, song, and dance. More and more Churchill moves toward total theater, in some ways returning to the ancient ritual power of the Greeks, in others to the epic historicization of Brecht.

As a socialist feminist, Churchill has consistently questioned how people are shaped and misshaped by the dominant ideologies of their times. Her work has moved from the somewhat vague politics of *Objections to Sex and Violence* and *Traps* to the much more focused analysis of *Vinegar Tom, Fen,* and *Mad Forest*; and from the comically mean-spirited *Owners* to the radically comedic *Cloud Nine* and *Serious Money*. She has been particularly, but not solely, concerned with the lot of women, and over the several decades of her career her interests have evolved with those of the culture so that plays like *Cloud Nine* and *Top Girls* capture highly particular moments of the feminist consciousness. More than most playwrights, Churchill's vision has kept changing.

Churchill's work has clearly benefited from the workshop process; working closely with actors and directors—in discussions, shared reading, on-site research, improvisations—Churchill has entered very different worlds, past and present, and with an almost Zen-like trust and fluidity, she has distilled those experiences into theater. *The Skriker* proves the value of these decades of theater immersion; it goes more boldly into the postmodern human psyche than earlier work, dipping down into the level of dream/nightmare, Jungian collective unconscious, and dark, childhood fears.

Churchill has no single message. Certain issues do show up regularly: class resentment, rampant materialism, serious political involvement, alienation and marginality, gender conflict, ambivalence toward motherhood, confusions of identity. In a number of her plays children are abandoned or abused, babies stolen, killed, and aborted, women beaten or abandoned by their husbands and lovers. In her repetitions, this violent domestic milieu seems peculiarly compelling to Churchill, possibly as a counterbalance to more sentimental views of family life in commercial entertainment, possibly as a response to British tabloid tales, possibly as a true reflection of female experience as she knew it. Whatever the cause, these acts rarely form the center of the action; rather, they appear as part of the tragic fabric of life in an imperfect world. And in most of the plays men are not monsters, but beings equally committed to trying to make their way in life, confused by change and betrayal, and neither morally inferior nor superior to women.

Churchill's feminism is in the British tradition, a movement largely driven by working-class women, and socialist in orientation. As the years have passed, the ideological plays of the 1970s have given way to the outrageous plays of the 1980s, and then to the poetic and surreal plays of the 1990s. Certainly a play like *Mad Forest* is more human and humane than political in its outlook despite its highly political subject matter. Like the best theater always, Churchill's plays must be seen to be fully comprehended; moments that might appear odd or confusing on the page achieve emotional clarity on stage.

Ultimately, Churchill is political in the best and deepest meaning of that term for an artist: she writes about what matters in the world. She looks critically at society (how it works, who it hurts); the personal is definitely political in Churchill, and the political is personal. Like the greatest play-wrights—Shakespeare, Chekhov, Beckett—she loses herself in the worlds she creates; her work is not about Caryl Churchill, it is about the fen women, the Romanian people, the Skriker, the Levellers, the accused "witches." Sometimes to enter a Churchill play feels like entering the world of Hieronymus Bosch or Franz Kafka or Lewis Carroll (the bizarre dislocations, the freshly constructed parameters of existence)—and yet generally with a very English late-twentieth-century flavor (the behind-the-scenes grimace of a postcolonial vision). Moral without being moralistic, her work is funny, wise, caustic, sexual, dangerous, and aware.

SELECTED BIBLIOGRAPHY

Note: Dates of first production are given in the text at first mention. Unless otherwise noted, dates given here for both radio plays and television plays refer to year of airing. Dates for stage plays refer to publication.

I. COLLECTED WORKS. *Plays: One* (London and New York, 1985), contains *Owners, Traps, Vinegar Tom, Light Shining in Buckinghamshire, Cloud Nine; Plays: Two* (London and New York, 1990), contains *Softcops, Top Girls, Fen, Serious Money.*

II. RADIO PLAYS. *The Ants* (1962; London, 1968); *Lovesick* (1967); *Identical Twins* (1968); *Abortive* (1971); *Not . . . not . . . not . . . not . . . not enough oxygen* (1971); *Schreber's Nervous Illness* (1972); *Henry's Past* (1972); *Perfect Happiness* (1973).

III. TELEVISION PLAYS. *The Judge's Wife* (1972); *Turkish Delight* (1974); *Save It for the Minister,* cowritten with Cherry Potter and Mary O'Malley (1975); *The After-Dinner Joke* (1978); *The Legion Hall Bombing* (1978); *Crimes* (1982).

IV. STAGE PLAYS. *Owners* (London, 1973); *Moving Clocks Go Slow* (first performance, 1975), unpublished; *Light Shining in Buckinghamshire* (London, 1978); *Objections to Sex and Violence* (London, 1978); *Traps* (London, 1978); *Vinegar Tom* (London, 1978); *Cloud Nine* (London and New York, 1979); *Three More Sleepless Nights* (first performance, 1980), unpublished; *Top Girls* (London, 1982); *Fen* (London, 1983); *Softcops* (London, 1983); *A Mouthful of Birds,* cowritten with David Lan (London, 1986); *Serious Money* (London, 1987); *Icecream* (London, 1989); *Mad Forest: A Play from Romania* (London and New York, 1990); *Lives of the Great Poisoners,* cowritten with Orlando Gough and Ian Spink (London, 1991); *The Skriker* (London, 1994).

V. BIBLIOGRAPHY. Phyllis R. Randall, ed., *Caryl Churchill: A Casebook* (New York and London, 1988).

VI. BIOGRAPHICAL AND CRITICAL STUDIES. Kate Millett, *Sexual Politics* (New York, 1970); Martin Esslin, *"Owners," Plays and Players* 20, no. 5 (1973), review; Catherine Itzin, *Stages in the Revolution: Political Theatre in Britain Since 1968* (London, 1980). Helene Keyssar, *Feminist Theatre: An Introduction to Plays of Contemporary British and American Women* (London, 1984); Sue-Ellen Case and Jeanie K. Forte, "From Formalism to Feminism," *Theater* 16 (1985); Elin Diamond, "Refusing the Romanticism of Identity: Narrative Interventions in Churchill, Benmussa, Duras," *Theatre Journal* 37, no. 3 (1985); Michelene Wandor, *Carry On, Understudies: Theatre and Sexual Politics* (London and New York, 1986); Kathleen Betsko and Rachel Koenig, eds., *Interviews with Contemporary Women Playwrights* (New York, 1987); Emily Mann, interview with Caryl Churchill, in Kathleen Betsko and Rachel Koenig, eds., *Interviews with Contemporary Women Playwrights* (New York, 1987); Joseph Marohl, "De-Realized Women: Performance and Identity in *Top Girls," Modern Drama* 3 (1987); Michelene Wandor, *Look Back in Gender: Sexuality and the Family in Post-War British Drama* (London, 1987); Richard Allen Cave, *New British Drama in Performance on the London Stage: 1970 to 1985* (New York, 1988); Geraldine Cousin,

"The Common Imagination and the Individual Voice," *New Theatre Quarterly* 4, no. 3 (1988); Elin Diamond, "(In)Visible Bodies in Churchill's Theatre," *Theatre Journal* 40, no. 2 (1988); Kimball King, "Serious Money: A Market Correction?" in Phyllis R. Randall, ed., *Caryl Churchill: A Casebook* (New York, 1988); Enoch Brater, ed., *Feminine Focus: The New Women Playwrights* (New York, 1989); Geraldine Cousin, *Churchill the Playwright* (London, 1989); Linda Fitzsimmons, *File on Churchill* (London, 1989); Anne Herrman, "Travesty and Transgression: Transvestism in Shakespeare, Brecht, and Churchill," *Theatre Journal* 41, no. 2 (1989); Ruby Cohn, *Retreats from Realism in Recent English Drama* (Cambridge, England, and New York, 1991); Amelia Howe Kritzer, *The Plays of Caryl Churchill, Theatre of Empowerment* (New York, 1991); Lizbeth Goodman, *Contemporary Feminist Theatres: To Each Her Own* (London and New York, 1993); Janelle G. Reinelt, *After Brecht, British Epic Theater* (Ann Arbor, 1994); Loren Kruger, "The Dis-play's the Thing: Gender and Public Sphere in Contemporary British Theatre," in Karen Laughlin and Catherine Schuler, eds., *Theatre and Feminist Aesthetics* (Madison, N.J., 1995); Ben Brantley, "A Land of Fairy Tales Creepily Come True," *New York Times* (16 May 1996), theater review of *The Skriker*; Matt Wolf, "A Damaged World in Which Nature Is a Weirdo Killer," *New York Times* (5 May 1996).

ROALD DAHL

(1916–1990)

Lisa Hermine Makman

ROALD DAHL WAS not an easygoing fellow. Frequently bullying, quarrelsome, and brutally blunt, he nonetheless charmed the people around him with his charisma and acerbic wit. An exhilarating narrator of anecdotes, especially of his own adventures, Dahl could easily enchant a crowd. Since the mid-1940s, when he began his writing career, Dahl has entertained children and adults with his usually humorous, often sardonic tales, works that almost always recapitulate in some way episodes from his own life. Descriptions of Dahl by his close associates bear a striking resemblance to character portraits in his stories for adults and children.

Like his infamous lady-killer Uncle Oswald, protagonist of two short tales and a novel, Dahl was a connoisseur of the better things in life, liked to fraternize with the affluent, and was extremely attractive to the opposite sex. Like his many trickster characters, he was a man who enjoyed practical jokes; he loved to fluster others with embarrassing remarks and provocative questions. In many of his stories, with evident pleasure, he adeptly upsets and confounds his readers with shocking twists of plot. He performs sleights of hand with words as magical as those practiced on objects by the deft "finger smith"—a high-class pickpocket—in his story "The Hitchhiker." A gifted performer, Dahl resembled his illustrious character Willy Wonka; the imperious Wonka not only controls his own chocolate empire and its doll-sized inhabitants but also manages the desires and interests of the world beyond his factory, skillfully orchestrating media events to his own benefit.

But unlike the diminutive Wonka, Dahl was a lanky man of six foot six, who towered over most people, especially children; with them, his demeanor resembled that of the Big Friendly Giant, a kind and wizardly creature who blows sweet dreams into the windows of sleeping children. Dahl made his literary reputation as a storyteller for children, and this is how he tends to be remembered.

Translated into more than a dozen languages, his children's books belong to an international child culture that is rooted in canonical nineteenth-century children's fiction, much of which is British. Two distinct branches of this literary tradition influenced Dahl's writing: the fantasy and nonsense works of writers such as Edward Lear, Lewis Carroll, George MacDonald, and Hilaire Belloc; and the tales of adventure published by authors such as Rudyard Kipling, Rider Haggard, G. A. Henty, and Captain Frederick Marryat.

Dahl also draws from an older genre of storytelling that in the nineteenth century metamorphosed into literature for middle-class children: folktales and fairy tales. Prototypical themes from traditional folktales recur in Dahl's books. Like these tales, his stories pare down and often dispense with conventional families. Some of his child-heroes are only children, and many are orphans. His tales often map out the voyage of a solitary soul, an outsider who, by the end of the story, is no longer alone. Frequently, the hero discovers and joins a new community, a sort of unconventional family: Matilda is adopted by her teacher, Miss Honey (*Matilda*, 1988); Sophie is fostered by her mammoth companion, the Big Friendly Giant (*The BFG*, 1982); James makes a community with his verminous buddies—a crew of worms and bugs (*James and the Giant Peach*, 1961).

Nineteenth-century British writings both for and about children are obsessively concerned with solitary children, and frequently in children's fiction of this era mysterious powers are attributed to such young people. Dahl too grants his child characters special powers; for instance, James, Matilda, George (*George's Marvellous Medicine*, 1981), and the unnamed narrator of *The Magic Finger* (1966) are all puny people with prodigious abilities. Such underdogs in Dahl's fictive worlds, as in folktales, end up on top, while their foes, the bullies, eventually get what is coming to them. Tables are often turned, and, consequently, lessons are sometimes learned. Some of Dahl's stories, like folktales, take the form of cautionary narratives. However, even though his works carry on long-standing traditions, sometimes promoting conservative values and conveying a Victorian moralism, they are also pointedly subversive. This subversive tendency caused trouble with the critics.

Although children have always been wild about Dahl's stories, many parents, teachers, and children's librarians have not shared the taste of their charges. Critics have pointed to the raciness and worldliness of the stories, claiming that Dahl inappropriately wrote for a double audience of children and adults. But this is perhaps what made his children's stories so successful. Something not just for kids was precisely what children in the 1960s and after most desired. Dahl's works are part of a predominantly American cultural domain shared by children and adults, the realm of television advertisements and amusement parks.

Even though Dahl wrote more than twenty-five stories for children over the course of his lifetime, his popularity is founded on some of his earliest books: *James and the Giant Peach* and *Charlie and the Chocolate Factory* (1964), both of which were first published in the United States. In these tales American culture figures prominently. In *James and the Giant Peach*, for instance, the United States appears as a promised land for an eclectic set of characters who cross the Atlantic Ocean in an overgrown peach. At the close of the story the comrades give up their giant peach for the Big Apple, where they find wealth, fame, and happiness. In Dahl's life too, the American dream, a fairy tale of success and self-creation, became a dream come true.

Although Dahl always sustained a British self-image, the United States played a pivotal role in his rise to prominence as a writer. It was during his stint as an assistant air attaché in Washington, D.C., during World War II that Dahl first flirted with fame and fortune American style. Within months of his arrival at the British embassy, he was "discovered" as a writer and published his first story, "Shot Down over Libya" (*Saturday Evening Post*, 1942). Not long after this, he published his first book, *The Gremlins* (1943), which Walt Disney illustrated,

promoted, and attempted to turn into a motion picture. Until the mid-1970s, almost all of his works were published in the United States before they were published in Britain. U.S. magazines printed and praised his work for adults—which consisted, for the most part, of short stories, a prototypically American genre.

Moreover, like many Americans, Dahl was a cultural hybrid. Just as he crossed generic boundaries in his writing, publishing books for both children and adults, he crossed cultural boundaries in his life: born to Norwegian parents in South Wales, he achieved success as a writer in the United States but always maintained his Englishness.

His father, Harald Dahl, had emigrated from Norway to France and then to Wales in the 1880s in search of adventure and a better life. Dahl was raised speaking Norwegian at home and spending summer vacations with his extended family in Norway. In class-obsessed Britain, the well-heeled yet foreign Dahls had no clear position. Perhaps Dahl's status as a cultural outsider growing up in Britain fueled his passionate desire for affirmation from the English literary establishment; and perhaps, at the same time, this outsider's position encouraged his tendency to be something of a maverick.

Dahl longed for the applause of the very proper British literary establishment, and yet throughout his life he wrote stories deemed improper. He observed, correctly, that his work was welcomed more heartily in the United States than in his mother country. His acceptance there was, in part, because of the privileged position of popular culture in the United States. There, Dahl could be celebrated and successful as a popular writer, even though he never fit comfortably or consistently into the world of highbrow fiction. And although throughout his career he stressed his relationship with elite American publications such as the *New Yorker*, he published at least as many stories in *Playboy*, a pop-culture touchstone. In the United States, while popular culture was perhaps lowbrow, it was sexy and glamorous, and these qualities appealed to Dahl.

In *Charlie and the Chocolate Factory*, Dahl depicts a mythic pop America, an America of free gifts, sweepstakes, and instant fame, a magical place where fantastical things can happen to ordinary people. But Dahl's American landscape is scattered with anachronisms: factory whistles and half-starved urchins that recall the England of Charles

Dickens. Charlie himself is a relic; he evokes a by-gone era when children were quiet and good. He is the prototypical child-hero of traditional children's literature. This mix of imagery conveys Dahl's state of mind in the 1960s vis-à-vis America and the success it permitted him. In *Charlie and the Chocolate Factory*, though Dahl embraces the flashiness of America, he represents innocence and heroism with a quaint, essentially English boy.

While the other children in *Charlie* are greedy brats who chew gum, watch television, and overeat, Charlie Bucket is humble and gracious, less "real" child and more the stuff of fiction. As vapid as Oliver Twist, he is the empty "bucket" his name evokes, and for such a formless, selfless creature the possibilities of self-invention are endless.

After all, America is the land of the self-made man, and Willy Wonka, an inventor who has made himself and his fortune, will make Charlie too; over the course of Dahl's story, as Wonka gives five lucky children a tour of his famous chocolate factory, he disposes of those children who represent American greed and mindlessness—the gum chewers and TV addicts—and makes Charlie his heir. The turn of this plot reveals Dahl's ambivalence about American mass culture, as well as his ambivalence about the nature of his own success, which was contingent on the tastes and values of the American public.

Dahl's books reflect the predilection of a child at the beginning of the television era. His best-known books entered the literary market at a time when the United States was gaining a privileged place in international culture. The market for children's books burgeoned at this time, and in the prosperous postwar United States, children had full pockets and very particular tastes. But at the same time, chagrined educators balked at the cartoonish quality of Dahl's work: it was, they claimed, no better than the television programs he criticized. But Dahl was prescient as to the likes and dislikes of young people; he was tuned in to the turn-ons of the age of television.

In *Charlie*, while the U.S. culture of overabundance and greed is parodied and decried, Dahl dangles tantalizing images of incredible edibles before the reader. The story is all about eating. Likewise, many of Dahl's fantasies for children have a sensuous aspect. They reveal a folktale fixation on eating and being eaten. Dahl envisions James's peach and Wonka's factory as voluptuous living spaces made of tasty comestibles. However, the greedy children in the Wonkaworks who snatch too much or grab illicit snacks may themselves be eaten: one child, Violet Beauregarde, becomes a gigantic blueberry; another, Augustus Gloop, may be made into fudge; Veruca Salt, deemed too spoiled to be eaten, is cast down a garbage chute along with other "bad nuts."

Dahl compels readers to feel, simultaneously, distaste and craving, disgust and attraction. He also provoked ambivalent critical responses. While critics praised the stories, they judged them "exaggerated," "grotesque," and "violent." They objected to the hedonism and grimness. Dahl chronically shocked his readers and his editors. For instance, in an early draft of the children's story *Fantastic Mr. Fox* (1970), Dahl has the fox family make ends meet by burrowing into stores to pilfer merchandise. His editors strenuously objected: Did he wish to promote shoplifting? Similarly, a child's using magic powers to win at gambling was removed from *Matilda* by circumspect editors.

While Dahl was known principally as a creator of tales for children, his initial pursuit, after *The Gremlins*, was adult fiction. Although he mostly wrote short stories, he also published two novels for adults and wrote scripts for film and television—media that served to popularize his already celebrated work. Many of his stories for adults have been adapted for television shows, such as *Alfred Hitchcock Presents* and *Suspicion*, and Dahl himself hosted two shows: *Tales of the Unexpected* and *Way Out*. Several of his better-known works for children have been repackaged as films, beginning with *Charlie and the Chocolate Factory*, which Dahl recast as the now-classic movie musical *Willy Wonka and the Chocolate Factory* (1971) starring Gene Wilder. Other movie versions of Dahl books include: *The Witches* (1990), *James and the Giant Peach* (1996), and *Matilda* (1996). His work has been noted and adapted by such Hollywood greats as Walt Disney, Alfred Hitchcock, Jim Henson, and Quentin Tarantino, a group of men whose ranks Dahl longed to join.

But like his opinion of the United States in general, Dahl's infatuation with Hollywood was tempered by disdain. His ambivalence about American popular culture was often directed at his wife, Patricia Neal, who was already a Hollywood star when they met in the early 1950s. Even though Dahl at times loudly declared his contempt for the superficial culture of Hollywood, he aggressively sought publicity and power using Hollywood's means, carefully crafting a public mythology of himself.

CHILDHOOD AND YOUTH

LIKE his boy-hero James, Dahl's childhood was marked by tremendous losses. While four-year-old James lost his parents to the jaws of a hungry rhinoceros, Dahl, at the same age, lost his sister and his father to illness.

Dahl's father, Harald, had been an ambitious lower-middle-class man with a handicap (he had lost an arm in an accident as a teenager) who rose to a position of comfort and security. He emigrated from Norway, a land that offered him limited opportunities, to France, and then to Britain to seek his fortune. After the death of his first wife, he traveled back to Norway to find a new life companion and a mother for his two young children. When he married Dahl's mother, née Sofie Hesselberg, he was a wealthy man with a half share of a ship-brokering business in South Wales.

Like the parents of the orphaned hero in *The Witches* (1983), Dahl's father wanted his children to have a British education. Sophie respected his wishes. After her husband's death, she bravely remained with her brood in England, where she had few ties. Fortunately, Harald had left his wife more than ample funds to provide for herself and their large family—two children from his previous marriage and their four. Although Sophie was an efficient and hardworking housewife, she came from a bourgeois home and taught her children to expect the same.

Dahl was raised in a domestic situation that was the exact reverse of Charlie Bucket's. While Charlie is poor, Roald lived in comfort and security. Charlie is an only child in a household of six adults—his two parents and four bedridden grandparents. After Roald's sister and father died, he was one of six children, all of whom competed for the attentions of a single mother. And yet he had a special role: of Sophie's four biological children, Roald was the only boy. And "Boy" is the moniker Dahl used to sign his letters to his mother. Dahl's mother kept all of these letters; there were more than six hundred written between 1925 and 1945.

While Sophie was a rapt audience for her "Boy," Roald, entranced by his mother's yarn spinning, also served as an audience for her. Sophie seems to be the model for the bizarre but lovable granny in *The Witches* who becomes the solo parent of the story's unnamed child-hero. This Norwegian woman, the child's maternal grandmother, consoles the boy after his parents die in a car crash by telling him stories—Scandinavian tales of witches. Dahl's Scandinavian heritage was transmitted to him principally through his mother's storytelling. Evidently, Sophie's versions of Norwegian myths and legends influenced her son's stories for children, particularly the works he wrote later in his life, a time when he revisited his childhood: *The Witches, The Minpins* (1991), *The BFG* (1982), and *Boy: Tales of Childhood* (1984), his first explicitly autobiographical work.

Like Sophie, Dahl's absent father figures centrally in the writer's life and imagination. To an extent Dahl modeled himself after Harald. Like his father, he longed to venture to foreign lands and found success on foreign soil. For Harald, as for Roald, good taste in fine things was of the utmost importance. Harald treasured the superlative objects the world had to offer. Like his son, he avidly collected fine furniture, artwork, and specialized knowledge. Harald wanted his children to be lovers of beautiful things like himself. To this end, during each of his wife's pregnancies, he would walk with her through gorgeous parts of the countryside in the hope that the unborn child would absorb the experience of beauty. Fatherlessness, longing for fathers, and idealized fathers are motifs that recur in Dahl's works for children.

In *Boy* Dahl describes memorable incidents from his childhood—practical jokes reminiscent of those played by Matilda on her parents, the horrors of his schooldays, cruelty and violence, and, best of all, luxurious summers in Norway. Between the ages of four and seventeen Dahl traveled each summer with his family to Norway; this, for him, was "like going home" (p. 51). First they visited Sophie's parents in Oslo, and then they would sail to a remote and cozy island hotel. Dahl's descriptions of these summers are the most blissful reminiscences in *Boy*.

Many of the incidents described in *Boy* appear repeatedly in Dahl's work. Mrs. Pratchett, owner of a local candy store, plays a significant role in his memoir. With his inveterate attention to the mouth, Dahl describes her as a "skinny old hag with a moustache on her upper lip and a mouth as sour as a green gooseberry" (p. 33). The malignant grandmother in *George's Marvellous Medicine*, like many of the nasty women in Dahl's oeuvre, also evokes Mrs. Pratchett: "She had pale brown teeth and a small puckered-up mouth like a dog's bottom" (p. 2).

Dahl's portrayal of Mrs. Pratchett resembles grotesque depictions of the Twits in *The Twits* (1980). Mr. Twit eats disgusting things, which cling to his unwashed beard: "a piece of maggoty green cheese or a moldy old cornflake or even the slimy tail of a tinned sardine"(p. 7). These disgusting tidbits seem appealing in comparison with another proposed menu: children. Accidentally trapping a pack of boys in a tree where he had hoped to catch birds for bird pie, Mr. Twit considers the possibilities for his next meal: "'Boy pie might be better than bird pie,' he went on grinning horribly. 'More meat and not so many tiny little bones!' " (p. 36). Luckily, the boys escape, leaving behind, like Peter Rabbit fleeing the garden of Mr. McGregor, only their clothes.

Disgust is a feeling Dahl tries to provoke in his works for children. He renders Mrs. Pratchett, like the Twits, as nasty to children and disgustingly filthy: "Her apron was grey and greasy. Her blouse had bits of breakfast all over it, toast-crumbs and tea stains and splotches of dried egg-yolk. It was her hands, however, that disturbed us most. They were disgusting. They were black with dirt and grime" (p. 33). It is these sordid hands that Pratchett plunges into jars to retrieve sweets. Dahl wreaks revenge on this woman for her wretchedness and grumblings in "The Great Mouse Plot," a chapter of *Boy*.

"The Great Mouse Plot," which Dahl relates with relish, demonstrates his naughtiness and pluck. He finds a dead mouse and, with the help of friends, plants it in a jar in Mrs. Pratchett's candy store. As in many of Dahl's stories, the tables are turned: "We were the victors now and Mrs Pratchett was the victim" (p. 36). Although he's a hero with his friends, when he sees that the candy store is closed the next day, he fears the worst: Did Mrs. Pratchett die of shock? Unfortunately for the boys, she is not dead. After picking the boys out of a lineup that includes their entire school, Mrs. Pratchett gleefully watches as the headmaster metes out punishments. Dahl describes the headmaster as "a giant of a man with a face like a ham"(p. 40). Although Mrs. Pratchett calls the boys "nasty dirty little pigs" (p. 44), the adults in this story are the real swine.

When Roald's mother sees the damage to her child's hindquarters, she marches off to find the barbaric perpetrator. The result of this episode is that Dahl, aged nine, is sent away to Saint Peter's Preparatory School. But at Saint Peter's and at Repton School, where he was sent next, Dahl does not escape the violence from which his mother wished to shield him. Life at Saint Peter's was dominated by a "female ogre," the matron, who ruled with "a rod of steel" (p. 79). He was homesick enough to fake the symptoms of appendicitis in order to be sent home. But he only escaped Saint Peter's by being pushed on to another educational institution.

In 1928, at the age of twelve, Roald was sent off to Repton, an elite boys' boarding school, where he was to remain for more than four years. As was typical at the time, Repton's was a culture of violence: younger boys were under the perpetual threat of beatings from older boys, and all the boys were under the perpetual threat of thrashings from their masters. For his first two years at the school, he was the "fag," or virtual slave, of the senior boy who ran the study he used. The practice of fagging was ubiquitous at Repton. It licensed sadistic behavior by the older boys. In his descriptions of life at Repton, as in his short stories for adults, Dahl focuses on cruelty in human relations.

In *Boy* Dahl discusses school beatings: "All through my school life I was appalled by the fact that masters and senior boys were allowed literally to wound other boys, and sometimes quite severely. I couldn't get over it. I never have got over it" (p. 131). His reaction to this early experience of random violence resembles his later reaction to the violent impulses war encourages.

As Dahl's biographer Jeremy Treglown notes, in Dahl's vivid depictions of public school culture, he avoids mention of schoolboy homosexuality. Treglown writes that when Dahl describes a particularly brutal beating at Repton in *Boy*, he not only gets the name of the abusive headmaster wrong, but he leaves out the cause for the beating—the victim had been caught in bed with a younger boy.

The Repton boys lived by strict rules and were compressed in tight hierarchies. Not a remarkable student, Dahl found a place in the pecking order in part by excelling at sports. Much emphasis was placed on performance in organized sports, in which everyone had to participate. Although he had the important position of captain on two teams—Eton-fives (a form of handball) and squash—he never gained the trust of the Repton authorities and was never made a prefect.

At Repton, Dahl had few pleasures. He found solace and privacy in an unused outbuilding, which he set up as a darkroom. A lifelong interest in photography blossomed there. The most pleasurable experience he describes is chocolate tasting, work the boys performed for the Cadbury company. Periodically, boxes from the Cadbury factory would arrive—new inventions that the boys would eat and critique.

After Roald graduated from Repton, Sophie offered to pay for college. But his grades were not good, and he was far more interested in adventure than in erudition. He longed for exploits of the sort glorified in the books he enjoyed as a child—the imperial stories of Henty, Haggard, and Kipling. So after graduation Dahl joined an excursion of public school boys to Newfoundland, which included a grueling exploration of unmapped territory and the documentation of the region's flora and fauna. Then, like any good son of the empire, he set about finding himself decent work, work that would enable him to see the world and chart his own course in it.

In 1934 the multinational Shell Oil Company took him on as a trainee. During training in England he learned about the myriad forms of petroleum in which Shell dealt and hoped to be granted a post in Africa or the Far East. He turned down a prestigious three-year job in Egypt; in *Boy* he explains that he wanted "jungles and lions and elephants and tall coconut palms swaying on silvery beaches, and Egypt had none of that. Egypt was desert country. It was bare and sandy and full of tombs and relics and Egyptians and I didn't fancy it at all." He tells his boss, "It's too *dusty*, sir" (p. 157). What he sought was a mixture of comfort and risk: the comfort and risk of the colonial administrator. When Shell finally sent him to Africa in 1938, he was twenty-two years old.

This moment of departure closes *Boy*, and in *Going Solo*, a memoir published in 1986, Dahl picks up the narrative at this point. His assignment begins with a two-week voyage to Dar es Salaam, a city in what was then Tanganyika (now Tanzania). Depicting his sea journey, Dahl positions himself as an observer of the "Empire-builders" who are his fellow passengers: "the craziest bunch of humans I shall ever meet" (p. 13). His assessments of their idiosyncratic behavior are colored by the age of empire. He snipes at the British nationals who "go barmy" or "go native" when they live too long in Africa. Dahl is shocked when early one morning he sights a man, "naked as a jungle ape" (p. 14), proudly jogging with his similarly unclothed wife around the deck for exercise before breakfast.

But while Dahl poses as a critic of empire builders, as a Shell employee, he was an active participant in their enterprise. Tanganyika had become part of the British Empire after World War I. This presented an appealing new market for Shell Oil. Dahl greatly admired the district officers, who administered territories as all-purpose authorities—a combination judge, doctor, and governor. In the two years before England's declaration of war, some district officers became Dahl's friends. During a visit to one such officer Dahl observed a mystifying and chilling event, which he describes in *Going Solo*. A lion makes off with the wife of the district officer's cook hanging from its mouth; the cook runs yelling after the lion, and Dahl and his friend shoot at the beast's feet. The lion drops the woman, who is, remarkably, unharmed. A newspaper in Nairobi asked Dahl to write up his eyewitness account of this incident, and this piece, he asserts in *Going Solo*, was his "first published work" (p. 49).

Dahl demonstrates his skill with suspense in *Going Solo*'s accounts of encounters with dangerous African animals. He is particularly preoccupied with snakes. He relates how he saved his gardener from an assault by a deadly black mamba, the only African snake that attacks people unprovoked; then he tells the chilling tale of how he saved a family from an equally deadly green mamba, which he observed entering their home through an open window. These creatures figure centrally in two suspenseful stories he published in the collection *Someone Like You* (1953), "The Wish" and "Poison," both of which deal with powerful fears and vivid imaginations. In "The Wish" a frightened child believes he must walk across a carpet composed of hot coals and black serpents in order to receive what he wants—a puppy. In "Poison" a man believes that, as he was sleeping, a poisonous viper curled up on his chest under the sheets; an Indian doctor devises a brilliant plan to save the man and tranquilize the snake and is thanked with racist attacks by the man he has tried to help.

Dahl's stint with Shell ended when Great Britain declared war against Germany at the end of 1939, and British citizens working for corporations in Tanganyika were automatically commissioned as British army officers. Although they had no military training, they were placed in command of trained *askaris,* soldiers in the King's African Rifles. The new officers were immediately ordered to herd all male German civilians in Tanganyika into internment camps. This was not an amusing venture. Germans constituted the largest European population in the country. After World War I, when German East Africa became Tanganyika, many Germans had remained. Dahl's experience blocking Germans who attempted to leave was unpleasant; he could not, he thought, "give the order to open fire on a bunch of German civilians" (*Going Solo,* p. 68). However, the episode leaves one German man dead.

In spite of the unpleasantness of this experience Dahl decided to enlist. In 1939, when he joined the Royal Air Force (RAF), Shell agreed to continue paying his salary until he finished his military service—or was killed.

Dahl's accounts of life in the RAF focus on the incompetence of superior officers. He writes with conviction that inept leadership, of which he gives many examples, was responsible for the great losses Britain suffered during the war. After flight training he was sent on an abortive journey to join a squadron in the Western Desert of Libya and was given erroneous directions; he was sent into battle with no training in air-to-air combat, flying a type of plane with which he had no experience. The crash that ended this flight earned him a lengthy recovery in Alexandria, after which he went to rejoin his squadron in Greece, which Italy had invaded with Germany's help. Once again he was mobilized in a kind of plane he never before had flown, with an unreliable refueling system. The strategic situation in Greece was dire: the Germans had about a thousand planes when Dahl arrived; the British had fifteen, a number that diminished rapidly.

In Greece a skilled fellow pilot, David Coke, a veteran of the Battle of Britain, took Dahl under his wing; Coke was shocked that an inexperienced pilot had been sent into such a desperate situation. Dahl describes several poorly orchestrated maneuvers in Greece, such as provision of air cover for ships that could not be located. He remained in Greece for about a week, at the end of which a handful of planes covered the evacuation of British forces from the country.

Equipped with a new Hurricane, Dahl fought for four weeks in Palestine against the Vichy French. But, plagued by blackouts and agonizing headaches,

he was invalided home. Bearing lemons and limes and silks for his sisters, he returned to England in July 1941.

Early in 1942, however, he was back with the RAF, this time assigned to Washington, D.C., as an assistant air attaché at the British embassy. Despite his later criticisms of the British wartime command, Dahl's assignment as a promoter of British interests and a gossip gatherer on Embassy Row was an undeniably shrewd decision. His charisma, flair, and storytelling skill made him a natural participant in that socially driven world. And it was from this persona that he evolved into a writer.

Though they were relatively brief, Dahl's experiences as a pilot color his writing. Flying always remained an important theme in his stories, especially those for children, which are full of flying creatures and flying machines: for example, the flying elevator in the Charlie Bucket books, *Charlie and the Chocolate Factory* and *Charlie and the Great Glass Elevator* (1972); James's flying peach; flying objects in *Matilda;* a flying boy in "The Swan"; the flying giant in *The BFG;* and the Roly-Poly bird in both *The Twits* and *The Enormous Crocodile* (1978).

FLIGHTS OF FANCY: EARLY STORIES

THE story of Dahl's initiation as a writer anticipates his tendency to romanticize and reinvent himself through his writing. He launched his writing career with the help of serendipity, talent, and C. S. Forester, the well-known author of the Horatio Hornblower stories who visited Dahl at the British embassy in 1942. Forester had been commissioned by the *Saturday Evening Post* to cook up a true-to-life war story, and he wanted to meet Dahl and hear of his experiences in combat. Forester had heard of the attaché because, as an RAF war veteran in Washington, Dahl was a "rare bird" (*The Wonderful Story of Henry Sugar,* 1977, p. 195).

After they met over lunch, Dahl went home and wrote down some "facts" (*Wonderful,* p. 197), which he later sent to Forester, who responded with astonishment: did this young man know that he was a writer? The "notes" Dahl had written were then, according to Dahl's account, published unedited in the magazine on 1 August 1942 and called "Shot Down over Libya," a deceptive title that Dahl later claimed the magazine had invented.

"Shot Down over Libya," which was published anonymously as a "factual report on Libyan air fighting," misled readers in several ways. First of all, Dahl had not been "shot down" in "air fighting." Second, the editors noted that the author of the piece was "an RAF pilot at present in this country for medical reasons" (p. 29). This positioned the United States as the salve needed to heal a wounded British hero. The editors' intent was to fan the flames of U.S. patriotism and to heighten support for the war. Forester, a British writer making his own contribution to the war effort, was in the United States to stir up enthusiasm for the war.

Dahl was not "shot down over Libya"; in fact, he was never shot down at all. He was injured in a plane crash just after he finished flight training but before he saw action, before he even joined his squadron. The commanding officer who dispatched him to the Libyan Desert gave him the wrong rendezvous point, so he was sent accidentally to a stretch of territory that lay between the British and Italian armies, about fifty miles away from his squadron. He was flying a type of plane he had never flown before and flying a distance he had never flown before. He had no radio and only a map strapped to his knee to orient himself. Since he was running out of fuel, night was falling, and the base was nowhere to be seen, he was forced to land on terrain hazardously scattered with boulders; he crashed into rocks, and his plane burst into flames.

Dahl's tampering with the facts of his life experience foreshadows the self-heroizing aspects of his self-representations in the years to come. "Shot Down over Libya" is told from the perspective of a wounded pilot who lies in a hospital, ruminating over the events that led to his injuries. The pilot tells of his participation in a successful ground-strafing mission; he and five other RAF men fly their Hurricanes to the Italian army camp to attack military vehicles. In simple vivid prose the narrator details the progress of the mission and the ineluctable crash. It is unclear whether mechanical failure or gunfire downs the plane, but the entire context of the crash is either pure fabrication or a composite of events arranged in the best interests of the war effort.

Dahl sustained the myth that he was "shot down" throughout most of his life. An amended story, "A Piece of Cake," which he published in his first collection, *Over to You: Ten Stories of Flyers and Flying* (1946), also suggests that the plane is shot down and situates the crash in combat. At the end of *Boy* he concludes his account of his childhood experiences with a remembrance of the crash: "I shot down some German planes and I got shot down myself, crashing in a burst of flames and crawling out and getting rescued by brave soldiers crawling on their bellies over the sand. I spent six months in hospital in Alexandria, and when I came out, I flew again" (p. 160). In the brief preface to *Boy* Dahl discloses to his readers his thoughts about autobiography and hints at his attitude toward representing his life experience: "An autobiography is a book a person writes about his own life and it is usually full of all sorts of boring details. This is not an autobiography. I would never write a history of myself." Dahl aims to entertain. Although he tells his readers that he simply notes down whatever he best remembers, where memory fails, imagination takes over. History and literature, fact and fiction: for Dahl the borders between these categories blur.

However, in *Going Solo* he sets the record straight, or at least revises it. He attributes the "mistake" in his first publication to his editors, not himself. He writes:

There seems, on re-reading it [the story "Shot Down over Libya"], to be an implication that I was shot down by enemy action, and if I remember rightly, this was inserted by the editors of an American magazine called the *Saturday Evening Post* who originally bought and published it. Those were the war years and the more dramatic the story, the better it was. They actually called it "Shot Down in Libya" [sic], so you can see what they were getting at. The fact is that my crash had nothing whatsoever to do with enemy action.

(p. 101)

But the crash did have to do with the incompetence of those in command, a fact he stresses in *Going Solo,* and the misrepresentation of the crash had to do with those in command at the *Saturday Evening Post.* Dahl wrote *Going Solo* from the vantage point of later life, from a position of legitimacy, after he had gained literary acclaim in England and after he had married a new wife from an ancient English family. To some extent, therefore, in this memoir he stresses his Englishness and downplays the American self-promoting tendencies of his youth. Perhaps at this stage of life Dahl no longer needed to embellish the real world, and his life story, with fantastical elements.

By blaming his editors' stratagems for the deceptive aspects of his story, Dahl unwittingly demystifies another of his personal myths, that of his raw talent. According to his account in "Lucky Break—How I Became a Writer" (from the collection *The Wonderful Story of Henry Sugar*), he wrote his notes for Forester in a trance, during a frenzied nonstop bout of writing that stretched into the night, and these brilliant scribblings were published untouched by the magazine. In "Lucky Break," Dahl presents a romantic history of his development as a writer. He tells how his abilities were unrecognized by his teachers at Repton; his is a gift sprung from nothing, or, perhaps, from genius. His first story, he asserts, "seemed to be telling itself" (*Wonderful*, p. 198). In interviews with Mark I. West, author of one of the few full-length studies of his work, Dahl claimed that before the crash he had the mind-set of a businessman. His imagination burgeoned only in the aftermath of the crash.

When Dahl republished "Shot Down over Libya," he changed the title to "A Piece of Cake," and he changed the contents dramatically. Arguably, these are two separate stories rather than two versions of the same tale, as Dahl claimed. One of their points in common is the repeated phrase "a piece of cake," which refers to the overwhelming proficiency of the narrator-pilot and his comrades and their bravado. The cool, crisp language of the narrator and the laconic banter of the pilots show the influence of Ernest Hemingway's writing on Dahl's style. Dahl greatly admired the famed adventurer-writer and successfully maneuvered to be introduced to him during his sojourn in Washington, D.C.

"Shot Down over Libya" has a spontaneity and freshness that "A Piece of Cake" lacks. Its language is frank and unpretentious. "A Piece of Cake" focuses on the narrator's inner experiences during and after the plane crash; half of the account consists of delirious dreaming. Dahl describes subjective states rather than objective truth; he shows how dream life filters into real life. He also privileges the internal worlds of his characters in most of the ten stories included in the collection *Over to You*, creating a mythology of the mental life of a war hero.

The tales in *Over to You*, all of which are in some way related to pilots and their exploits, have a warmth and mysticism absent from the short stories Dahl wrote after the war. Most of the stories had previously been published in U.S. magazines—*Atlantic Monthly*, *Harper's*, *Collier's*, and *Ladies' Home Journal*. Though the narratives are varied—some are slight and anecdotal, others read like fables—common themes thread through the collection. Many of the tales deal with death. The tone of most is somber, almost elegiac. The book received positive reviews. Critics admired the honesty and simplicity of the stories and proclaimed Dahl a promising new talent. However, the collection did not sell well; once the war was over, readers no longer wanted to hear about fighters and fighting.

"Beware of the Dog" is typical of the stories in *Over to You*. Like "Shot Down over Libya," it is an account presented from the perspective of a pilot who finds himself in a hospital with serious injuries. At the beginning of the story, the pilot's leg has been virtually shot off, and he must bail out of his plane before he loses consciousness. When he regains his senses, he orients himself to his surroundings bit by bit. Gradually, he becomes aware that his situation is not what it seems. His knowledge of Brighton, where allegedly he has crashed, does not coincide with what he sees outside his window, with what he hears in the sky (German planes and no air-raid sirens), and with what the nurse tells him about the quality of the water, which is hard, not soft as he remembers it. The story teases the reader: Is the pilot delirious or right on target? At the tale's conclusion the answer becomes suddenly apparent to narrator and reader. The tale presages the suspenseful style of Dahl's later stories. MGM bought the film rights to this story and from it made the film *36 Hours*.

Not all of the stories in the collection deal with fighting. "Madame Rosette," the only story from *Over to You* anthologized in *The Best of Roald Dahl* (1978), is a humorous, sometimes giddy account of a group of pilots on a forty-eight-hour pass in Cairo. At the beginning of the leave, one young pilot, Stuffy, glimpses a beautiful woman in a shop. His older, wiser companion Stag tells the boy there is a madam in Cairo who can bribe or threaten any girl into prostitution. After the two make a deal with the madam to find the girl Stuffy desires, the young man backs down; he pities his prospective conquest. The men and their buddies then decide to punish the madam for her evil ways. The denouement of the tale reads like a combination schoolboy prank and schoolboy fantasy: the pilots humiliate the witchlike madam and steal her troupe of beautiful girls. Each man can choose a girl from a selection of exotic, multiethnic specimens, "all different" and all "young and good looking" (p. 80).

This story is playful and witty, filled with the smug good cheer of the masculinist imperial culture in which Dahl was most at home. At the same time it is colored by the hostility, racism, and misogyny that permeate the narrative. The non-European characters, except for the young women, are dehumanized. For instance, Madame Rosette, "a filthy old Jewess" (p. 63), has a "large mud-colored face . . . and a small fish mouth" (p. 73); likewise, Egyptian men the pilots sight in a café are "so many fat muddy fish" (p. 79).

Much of Dahl's imagery in *Over to You* reflects the experience of combat. In several of the stories he conflates images of youth and age, implying that the experience of war brings age as well as death to the young. "Death of an Old Old Man," for example, is punctuated with a subjective account of dying. The "old old man" is a gifted young pilot, who shoots down a German plane that also hits him. The two pilots parachute onto the same field, where the Englishman falls into a muddy pond. When he becomes entangled in the strings of his parachute, with his feet fixed in the mud at the bottom of the pond, the German runs over to drown him. The reader experiences death through the consciousness of the young pilot. Here, death is presented as pleasure and rest—the end of a painful struggle. The pilot, after he dies, sees himself as lucky and much happier than the German pilot who remains alive and struggling.

In "They Shall Not Grow Old" death is again represented as a blessing and a respite. At the beginning of the narrative, a pilot, Fin, disappears during a mission, and his comrades assume he is dead. Two days later he mysteriously reappears in his plane, unaware that he has been missing. Eventually, the sight of a fellow pilot going down in flames leads Fin to recall his experiences, which he then describes to the other men. The narrator, as he hears Fin's tale, becomes lost in the experience, merging with his buddy: "I forgot everything and went with him on his journey, and did not come back until he had finished" (p. 122).

Fin explains how, as he tries to execute his mission, he finds himself in the middle of a dense cloud, even though the sky is pristinely clear. When he emerges from the cloud, he sees countless pilots, in planes of all sorts, flying together in a line. Somehow he understands that these are pilots who have died, who now fly on "their last flight, their last journey" (p. 124). His plane, which takes on a life of its own, joins the procession of pilots who wave at one another "like children on a roller coaster" (p. 125). He sees below him a valley where a celestial light burns. At this point Fin is overcome by the desire to move toward the light, but his plane refuses to land and rises back to the cloud where he first found himself. Soon he is in familiar skies and has forgotten the entire episode.

The men are dazed after they hear Fin's tale and unable to speak to one another about it. Dahl's story closes when Fin is shot down. Like the pilot in "Death of an Old Old Man," Fin welcomes death; as his plane goes down, the narrator of the story hears him say over the radio, "I'm a lucky bastard. . . . A lucky, lucky bastard" (p. 130).

Like most of the stories in the collection, "They Shall Not Grow Old" contains autobiographical elements. Just like Dahl's squadron, the pilots in the story are in Palestine fighting the Vichy French in Syria. Fin, a tall, dark-haired, dynamic fellow, resembles Dahl. He also plays a key role in "Katina," which contains many elements of Dahl's experiences fighting in the Battle of Athens. "Katina" follows the outlines of Dahl's account of this episode in *Going Solo*, with the addition of the title character, a Greek girl, whom the pilots find wounded and stunned standing by a pile of rubble under which her family is buried.

Katina is in many ways an allegory for the Greek people the British pilots protect. The squadron virtually adopts the girl, and Fin takes her under his wing, teaching her English, buying her a nightgown, and taking care of her more generally. The Britons' protective stance prefigures the paternalistic protagonists that fill Dahl's later children's works. And Katina is described as a child with an old woman's hatred. She expresses her fury by running in front of German planes that attack the base, shaking her fists. The second time this happens, she is gunned down.

"Katina" is not just a realistic account of warfare, it is also a ghost story. The narrator first has contact with the dead when he hears his tent mate Peter, who has just been shot down and killed, come to bed as usual. At the end of the story, as the narrator stares at the flaming wreckage of his plane, he sees Katina in a field beyond the fire, standing in the sun, wearing a blood-soaked dress.

Repeatedly, supernatural elements in Dahl's stories emerge from encounters with death and from feelings of loss and loneliness linked to such confrontations. In "Only This," another mystical story, a mother and her son are united through their inner experiences—their thoughts and feelings. She sits at the window of their cottage, while he, her only child, fights in the skies above her. At the climax of the story, the two die at the same time, he shot down in his plane, and she at home by the window; however, in her mind, she is with her son in his burning plane, and he acknowledges her presence.

Dahl's relationship with his own mother was particularly intimate. *Over to You* is dedicated to Sophie Dahl; it is to her that he aimed his story-missives and the many letters he wrote during the war—some of which are interspersed with text in *Going Solo*. At the end of *Going Solo* the last "flight" he describes includes his mother: "I flew down the steps of the bus straight into the arms of the waiting mother" (p. 208).

GREMLINS

GREMLINS, impish creatures with a penchant for making mechanical mischief with RAF equipment, are the subject of both Dahl's first book, a story for children, and his first full-length work for adults. The difference in tone of these two works is indicative of the essential difference between his two bodies of work. *The Gremlins*, from the Walt Disney Production and the work for children, is a haphazard, wackily humorous story. *Some Time Never: A Fable for Supermen* (1948), the work for adults, is a bitter, gruesome tale.

In *The Gremlins*, Dahl once again rewrites and embellishes his life experiences, intermingling fact and fantasy. *The Gremlins* follows the experiences of Gus, an RAF man who fights in the Battle of Britain—the RAF's moment of glory in the war and a battle in which Dahl did not participate. In his efforts to fight "the Hun," Gus is hindered by the supernatural gremlins. Like Dahl, Gus crashes with his plane and must recover in the hospital. Unlike Dahl, Gus escapes being grounded by his injuries; with the help of the trickster gremlins, who falsify the results of his medical tests, he passes his medical exam with flying colors and can continue to serve as a pilot. Dahl, of course, was sent home.

Dahl had cultivated contacts at British Information Services (BIS), the public relations function of the Foreign Service, and it was under BIS cover

that Walt Disney was presented with a draft of *The Gremlins*. The animator immediately flew the young writer to Hollywood, all expenses paid, and scooped up the movie rights for a tidy sum. The gremlin story, a fantasy for children, differed somewhat from Disney's other wartime projects, largely government-financed propaganda films. Ultimately, Disney's work on the gremlins film was costly and came to naught, probably because it was concluded that the story would hurt rather than help pro-war propaganda efforts.

As an early promotional move, however, Disney published an excerpted version of Dahl's tale in *Cosmopolitan* magazine, under the pseudonym "Pegasus." It is apt that Dahl masqueraded as this mythical winged beast; in the gremlin story flight seems a natural attribute of pilots. Pilots are "born to fly," and for them "being alive but earthbound is worse than not being alive at all." For Dahl a pilot becomes a sort of mythical flying creature.

Walt Disney helped to inflate Dahl's public image by attributing to him gremlin mythology and thus exalting his originality. Actually, a mythology of gremlins had grown up among RAF pilots and ground crews for many years. Blamed for mishaps, gremlins helped to diffuse tension between ground crews and pilots. And yet Dahl, with Disney's help, encouraged the public to believe that he had coined the term "gremlins." In the *Cosmopolitan* piece, and again in the novel *Some Time Never*, he tacitly affirms that the word "gremlin" is his own invention: in both tales Dahl's characters coin the term after sighting a gremlin for the first time. In *The Gremlins* Dahl writes:

And so, there on the Dover-London road, a new word was born. This word was to spread through the RAF like a prairie fire. It would travel over the seas to the pilots in Malta, to the desert airdromes of Libya and Egypt, and to remote landing grounds in Palestine and Iraq. Someone mentioned it in India and someone else in Ceylon—and now they all had it—IT WAS A VERY FAMOUS WORD.

But Disney and Dahl conspired to make the fame of the word their own. The dust jacket of *The Gremlins* informs the reader that, although "everybody has heard about the gremlins," "only Disney has the *real* inside story about them." In "Lucky Break" Dahl affirms that he was first to use the term "gremlin." After the story appeared in *Cosmopolitan*, Dahl asserts, "news of the Gremlins spread rapidly through the whole of the RAF and the United States Air Force, and they became something of a legend" (*Wonderful*, p. 200). At that time gremlins were certainly in the public eye; during the war at least four other books about them were published.

The Gremlins is a disjointed mix of sentimental fairy tale, Norse mythology, and hard-nosed war story. True to their reputation, the gremlins in the book fly with RAF pilots in order to sabotage flying missions. They try to distract and confuse pilots, and they destroy planes. With large drills they bore holes all over the pilots' "tin birds," holes identical in size and shape to bullet holes. They are pranksters who love to make mischief, but, according to Dahl's version of the story, their principal motivation is revenge. Gus, who not only gives gremlins their name but miraculously knows their history, tells the story of these creatures to the men of his squadron: the gremlins lived peacefully in a wood in England from the days of old until, in the recent past, humans destroyed their forest to build an airplane factory. Interestingly, the gremlins' tragic story resembles that of Dahl's characters the Minpins (*The Minpins*), an innocuous people who inhabit a wood, live in trees, are the same size as gremlins, wear suction boots, and fly—not on planes but on the backs of birds they have befriended.

In spite of their sinister intent the gremlins in the book are cute, six-inch-tall humanoid creatures, who have curved horns and sport suction boots, which enable them to walk comfortably on flying aircraft. In Disney's drawings they have shiny jelly-bean noses and come in assorted bright colors. Male gremlins have the soft, rounded forms of young children. They have round Mickey Mouse feet and sport colorful Doctor Dentons, some of which have buttoned-back flaps. In contrast, the slim female gremlins, called Fifinellas, are dressed in sexy mini dresses and wear sleek white go-go boots.

The plot is a dramatic mishmash of dogfights and gremlin antics interspersed with precious gremlin lore. For instance, gremlins love to eat used postage stamps. In a typical scene a gremlin, to prove to a doubting officer that he and his race exist, runs across a mess table and knocks over the man's beer. The gremlin who torments Gus, named Gremlin Gus, after boring holes in his plane, warns his pal and victim, "You'd better jump before you bump."

To save the day Gus plans a training school for gremlins to turn them into good guys. Gremlins, unlike the enemy, can be trained to change their allegiance. Gus convinces his pet gremlin to be good by "arguing and reasoning" with him. And with his school Gus and his colleagues go on to domesticate the gremlin hordes.

The Gremlins was well received. In wartime Washington, D.C., Dahl's writing brought him attention and praise. It also brought proximity with the rich and famous. He mixed with fashionable socialites and through such people met well-known writers and politicians, establishing connections with the American playwright Lillian Hellman (who years later introduced him to Patricia Neal), Ernest Hemingway, Ian Fleming, the English playwright, actor, and composer Noël Coward, Lyndon Johnson, Harry S. Truman, the French actress Annabella (Suzanne Charpentier), and others. After reading *The Gremlins* Eleanor Roosevelt befriended Dahl and invited him to dine with the president. Dahl became a protégé of the American newspaper owner Charles Marsh, a self-made multimillionaire who was about twenty-five years Dahl's senior and a powerful public figure.

Dahl came to be known as a gloriously good yarn spinner. Young, arrogant, and attractive, he had many sexual adventures and discussed them among his friends with relish. He cultivated a James Bond image and spent time with members of British Intelligence. Eventually, he was hired to work for them as a spy.

One important figure in Dahl's social set at this time was Ian Fleming. Dahl came to idolize Fleming, author of the epochal James Bond books and of a potent personal mythology. Their career paths are similar: Fleming was an RAF veteran who was later active in British intelligence. Both men energetically cultivated their respective playboy–secret agent auto-mythologies. But Dahl never had a character like James Bond in whose reflected glory to bask. Nonetheless, their relationship permitted Dahl a couple of important crumbs from Fleming's table. In 1965 he was hired to write the screenplay for *You Only Live Twice,* one of the Bond novels. The movie was released in 1967, at the apex of the James Bond craze.

In 1966 Dahl adapted Fleming's *Chitty Chitty Bang Bang* (1968), a children's story about a flying car. Credited as the screenwriter of this 1960skitsch classic, Dahl apparently abandoned the project mid-flight, and the work he left behind was doctored by studio back-lot regulars. Nonetheless, *Chitty*, which, like *You Only Live Twice*, was only loosely based on Fleming's book, clearly bears the marks of Dahl's ruminations: fantasies involving oral imagery, underground hideouts, and miraculous flying machines.

Much of *Chitty Chitty Bang Bang* takes place in an imaginary land called Vulgaria, a country where children have been banned. The nation's "child catcher," who sniffs out children with his colossal nose, resembles the title characters of Dahl's popular novel for children *The Witches*, who despise children and to whom children smell like "dog droppings"—especially children who are freshly bathed. The rulers of Vulgaria, like the witches of Dahl's story, detest nothing so much as children. The banished children plot their overthrow of the government from underground caverns. Often in Dahl's children's fiction subterranean spaces offer protection for good characters; in his work for adults sometimes the opposite is the case.

In some of Dahl's works for adults evil creatures dwell underground. In *You Only Live Twice*, for instance, malignant characters inhabit an underground hideout. James Bond's antagonist in the story plots to provoke the superpowers—Russia and the United States—to destroy each other with nuclear arms so that he can possess the earth. This scenario Dahl borrowed from his first novel, *Some Time Never*, a pacifist work written after the war in which those naughty manikins, the gremlins, reappear.

Some Time Never, the first novel about nuclear war to appear in the United States after Hiroshima, sets the gremlins in a subterranean empire, where they await the humans' self-destruction. It is a sour antiwar fantasy about humanity's self-annihilation. The novel, published by Scribners in 1948 and by Collins in England in 1949, was a flop that Dahl later chose to forget. (When his second and only other novel, *My Uncle Oswald*, was published in 1979, he promoted it as his first full-length work.) Awkward writing and rampant nihilism make the work difficult to read. To a certain extent it is a sinister and bleak version of Dahl's first gremlins book.

Once again Dahl starts his story with the Battle of Britain. In the novel the gremlins abandon their attempts to undermine the RAF, not because they suddenly become good but for strategic reasons.

Like Bond's archenemy, they withdraw into a subterranean world and let humans on the surface of the earth kill themselves off. The book is a cruelly laborious account of the end of human life on earth—the end of almost all life on earth. Many years pass, and after World Wars III and IV, when the humans are finally dying off, the gremlins emerge to take over the earth. But the unfortunate gremlins, having achieved their goal, mysteriously vanish into thin air. At the novel's conclusion only the creeping creatures in the earth—worms and insects, those vermin that later become the good guys in *James and the Giant Peach*—remain.

The misanthropy that surfaces in much of Dahl's work peaks here. His preoccupation with human aggression and self-destructive impulses pervades the novel and foreshadows motifs in the short stories for adults he was soon to write. The only reasonably well-meaning and somewhat particularized characters, Peternip, Stuffy, and Progboot, die off about halfway through the novel in an atomic explosion. The gremlins who dominate the work are wooden caricatures who spoof ugly and self-destructive human traits.

The gremlins of Dahl's novel are a nightmare version of the Disney creatures pictured in the children's book. They are uncanny: a mix of the familiar and the unfamiliar, of human qualities and inhuman qualities, and therein lies their ghoulishness. Peternip, the central human character in the story, is horrified by the gremlins' expression: "a deathless, ageless expression in the small black lidless eyes, with a fierce cunning twist about the thick-lipped mouth." He is equally distressed by the gremlins' unexpected bit of human dress: "this astonishing green bowler hat which in some curious way was infinitely more frightening than either the horns or the face" (p. 8).

The most eloquent passages in the novel describe the pilots' feelings of metaphysical sickness just before entering battle. Dahl's human characters Peternip, Stuffy, and Progboot, like some of the pilots in *Over to You*, struggle with despair as they fly into combat. Dahl describes the nihilistic revelations of the airborne pilot, who wishes to shout his newfound wisdom—that nothing matters—to the teeming masses below. He advises them, "Go away now. Go away and die and disappear, for that is the only certain road to peace" (p. 47). And over the course of the novel they take his advice.

AT the end of the war, Dahl's return to England from Washington D.C. was tainted with disappointment. He resigned from Shell so that he could apply himself to writing. He shared a cottage with his mother in the tiny village of Grendon Underwood in Buckinghamshire, and there he wrote humorless tales: his pessimistic *Some Time Never* and a group of unsentimental short stories about local country folk out of which he hoped to construct a novel. In his collection *Someone Like You* Dahl names a group of these stories "Claud's Dog," after Claud Taylor, a local butcher about his own age whom he befriended and with whom he engaged in his favorite sport—gambling. Dahl had enjoyed greyhound racing before the war, and now Claud helped him train his own racing dogs. Gambling and risk became central motifs not only in the rustic adventures of Claud and his friends that Dahl recounted but in Dahl's stories more generally.

Only one of the stories in "Claud's Dog," "Mr. Feasey," is literally about Claud's dogs. In the tale Claud and the narrator cheat at the dog track by trading a fast dog for a look-alike slow one. However, after their dog wins, instead of pulling in the massive winnings they anticipate, the cheaters are cheated by the sleazy racetrack owner, Mr. Feasey. As in many Dahl tales, the tables are turned, and the tricksters are tricked.

"The Ratcatcher," another segment of "Claud's Dog," also concerns betting. In "Ratcatcher," Claud and a friend reluctantly engage in a wager with a "ratman," who looks and acts uncannily like a rat. The rat catcher bets that he can kill a rat without using his hands or feet. He proceeds to pull a rat out of his pocket and to attack it like a snake, with a thrust of his neck and a snap of his jaws. Afterward he spits the rat's blood from his mouth, much to the disgust of the onlookers. As in many of Dahl's tales for children and adults, the atmosphere is creepy, and the response he strives to provoke is revulsion.

In postwar Buckinghamshire, Claud and his working-class set became Dahl's valued companions. Claud regaled him with tales about pastoral activities, such as pheasant poaching and trout tickling, which later surface in Dahl's stories about the people of Buckinghamshire. "The Champion of the World," a tale in Dahl's third collection, *Kiss Kiss* (1959), deals with pheasant poaching and class

antagonisms. In this story Claud tells a friend about secret poaching techniques invented by his father. The friend then comes up with an idea of his own, which the two test. Claud's father discovered that pheasants love raisins; Claud and his friend lace the raisins with a sedative.

The two men plot to tranquilize and filch virtually all the pheasants on the vast property of Claud's neighbor, an unbearably arrogant manufacturer of sausages and pies, a "self-made man" who "loathe[s] all persons of humble station, having once been one of them himself" (p. 275). This ham-faced man likes to give shooting parties, to which he invites wealthy gentles. Claud and his buddy are successful in their illicit endeavors, but ultimately, as the drug begins to wear off, their loot of groggy pheasants flies off.

In "The Champion of the World," which Dahl rewrote as a novel for children in 1975 under the title *Danny, the Champion of the World*, the birds survive, and the nasty classist neighbor, losing his fowl, gets his just deserts. While Dahl was fascinated by class-bound knowledge—that of both high and low classes—he was critical of the English caste system. The United States' ostensible meritocracy suited him just fine.

In 1951, encouraged by his friend and mentor Charles Marsh, Dahl settled in New York City. Like his character James, Dahl "became rich and successful" in New York, a place where he sold stories and made connections. But instead of living in Central Park itself, as James did, Dahl lived close to the park, in the Marsh family's elegant apartment. During his first year as a full-time New York resident, at a dinner party given by Lillian Hellman, he met Patricia Neal, the woman he would marry two years later. Neal, who was starring in a Hellman play, matched Dahl in her formidable social connections; the pair could even drop some of the same names, Ernest Hemingway's, for example. Twenty-five years old and ten years Dahl's junior, Neal had already attracted an impressive collection of admirers, including the playwright Eugene O'Neill, the novelist Dashiell Hammett, and the actor Gary Cooper, with whom she had just ended a long affair. She shared with Dahl a keen interest in money, status, and fame.

Although Dahl was far from being a star like Neal, he had achieved some success in the years just before they met. In May 1949, for the first time, he had sold a story to the *New Yorker*, titled "The

Sound Machine." Later in life Dahl mistakenly believed that his first *New Yorker* story was "Taste." "Taste" was published in the magazine in 1951, the same year Dahl procured a permanent U.S. visa and the same year Alfred Knopf, having read "Taste" in the *New Yorker*, called Dahl with an offer for a book.

In 1953 Knopf came out with a collection of eighteen Dahl stories, *Someone Like You*, which included stories not yet in print as well as some that had been published in respected magazines, such as *Harper's* ("Lamb to the Slaughter") and *Collier's* ("Man from the South," "Poison," and "Nunc Dimittis"). Although the Knopf collection was granted little attention by critics in the United Kingdom, the book sold extremely well and received stellar reviews in the United States. Critics raved about the craft of the stories and compared Dahl with masters of the short story genre, such as Saki, O. Henry, and John Collier.

Dahl published a third collection of stories, *Kiss Kiss*, in 1959. This time British critics responded respectfully. In the two collections Dahl published in the 1950s, he presents a cynical and sinister view of humankind. He laughs at and skillfully satirizes human foibles, especially arrogance, cruelty, and aggression.

Some critics compared Dahl's imagination to that of a fellow *New Yorker* contributor, the sardonic cartoonist Charles Addams; but others complained of the thin, comic-book quality of his characterizations. Dahl uses caricature to exaggerate and illuminate quirky aspects of human behavior. His characters' lack of psychological depth reflects the shallowness of their social milieu. The cartoon quality in Dahl's work can also generate spooky effects. He mixes familiar, almost hackneyed, qualities with unfamiliar, bizarre actions. He mixes the expected and the unexpected, and the result is uncanniness.

In "The Sound Machine," from *Someone Like You*, Dahl creates a tense atmosphere that unsettles the reader's sense of what is real. The central figure in the story, Klausner, has created—or believes he has created—a device that transmutes extremely high frequency sounds into notes audible to the human ear. Dahl's descriptions of the machine and its effects are eerie: it is the size and "the shape of a child's coffin" (p. 198). Listening to the world around him with the help of his invention, Klausner feels he trespasses on "a secret and forbidden territory, a dangerous ultrasonic region where ears had never been before and had no right to be" (p. 205).

As it turns out, the instrument enables Klausner to hear the sounds emitted by flora. He listens with horror as his neighbor cuts roses that shriek with each snip. When he tests his perceptions by tearing a few daisies out of the ground, the flowers cry out "a neutral, stony cry—a single emotionless note, expressing nothing" (pp. 208–209). Again testing his device and his convictions, he chops a tree with an ax, and the resulting uncanny cry makes him "sick with horror" (p. 211).

Klausner himself is uncanny. As he did with characters in *Over to You*, Dahl portrays Klausner as a mixture of youth and age: "an ancient, consumptive, bespectacled child" (p. 205). The other characters—a gardening neighbor and a doctor acquaintance—deduce that Klausner is mad. The doctor, with whom he attempts to share his discoveries, balks when the inventor forces him to suture the injured tree. The doctor perceives this man as a threat, which is no surprise since Klausner menacingly asserts the necessity of stitches while gripping his ax. The reader, like the characters in the story, is left to wonder about Klausner's sanity.

In "Edward the Conqueror" (in *Kiss Kiss*) the difference between the real and the imagined once again becomes muddled. Louisa, a housewife and passionate amateur pianist, finds a cat in her yard that she comes to believe is a reincarnation of Franz Liszt. She bases her conclusions on concrete evidence: The cat, who is excited by her piano playing, is intoxicated by the music of Liszt; moreover, it detests the music that Liszt despised. Notably, it has five warts on its face that, in their positioning, replicate those that graced Liszt's face.

Although Louisa is thrilled by her guest, her rigid husband, Edward, is not, fearing that she will embarrass them both by announcing Liszt's advent to the world. Thus, while Louisa prepares dinner for the composer, Edward flings the troublesome feline into a bonfire he has built in the yard. The marriage between Louisa and Edward resembles many of the troubled relationships Dahl depicts. For the most part in his stories, people and their relationships are not what they appear to be.

Another characteristic manifestation of uncanniness can be seen in the title character of "The Landlady," another story in *Kiss Kiss*. A precursor of Dahl's wicked enchantresses in *The Witches*, the landlady is not who she initially seems to be. In *The Witches* even the sweetest-seeming lady can be a witch; what "makes her doubly dangerous is the fact that she doesn't *look* dangerous" (p. 6). Likewise, the landlady, who seems benign, mysteriously compels a young man to visit her bed and breakfast. As she welcomes the newcomer at her door, he thinks she "look[s] exactly like the mother of one's best school-friend welcoming one into the house to stay for the Christmas holidays" (p. 7). The young man experiences everything about this woman and her abode as strangely familiar. He believes he recognizes the two names in her guest book. Boys from school? Love interests of his sister? Boys whose names appeared in the newspaper? Soon he discovers that the parrot in the window and the dachshund curled before the fire are both dead and stuffed; but he does not recognize that these creatures presage his fate. The story ends as the guest identifies the familiar aroma of the tea she has given him, bitter almonds—the smell of arsenic and the scent of his impending death.

In "Skin" (from *Someone Like You*) a man is in danger of being flayed. Dahl literalizes the expression "to take the hide off someone's back" in order to tell a story about the commodification of art and artists. The central character, Drioli, an old, lonely homeless man in postwar Paris, comes upon a gallery opening of Chaïm Soutine paintings. The paintings elicit powerful memories of his friendship with Soutine years before, when the artist was just a boy. Drioli, a former tattoo artist whose talent, Dahl intimates, rivaled Soutine's, remembers a peculiar night of drunken revelry. Drioli was a great admirer of Soutine's paintings, and Soutine was a great admirer of Drioli's wife. On this night Drioli taught Soutine to tattoo in order for the artist to inscribe a permanent artwork, a painting of Drioli's wife, on the tattoo master's back.

Interested to hear more of his former friend, the old man enters the gallery. When the gallery owner tries to throw him out, Drioli rapidly unclothes his back for the gathered crowd and is beset by offers to buy the painting on it. When he protests that it is impossible for him to sell a part of himself, sundry art vultures inquire about his age and health. One man offers to provide him with a life of luxury at a hotel he owns—the Bristol in Cannes—if he will expose his back on the beach for hotel guests to view. Drioli walks off with this man, who, as it turns out, is a fraud. The reader is informed that there is no Hotel Bristol in Cannes and that a new Soutine painting soon turns up for sale in Buenos Aires, "nicely framed and heavily varnished" (p. 149).

"The Great Automatic Grammatisator," like "Skin," is about producing art in the world of commerce, selling art and selling souls. In "The Great Automatic Grammatisator," Dahl avenges the magazine culture that, to his mind, never appreciated him enough. Like "The Sound Machine," the story is concerned with an invention that extends human beings' powers. It is the story of a genius inventor, a parody or evil twin of Dahl himself: a stooping, unkempt disappointed author, whose lack of talent matches his lack of success as a writer. Although he has sent hundreds of short stories to magazines, none has been published. At the beginning of the narrative this young man, Adolph Knipe (whose name evokes Alfred Knopf, Dahl's publisher), has just invented an "electronic calculating machine" (*Someone Like You*, p. 250), and now he wishes to apply his mathematical genius to what he loves best: fiction writing.

Knipe convinces his employer, Mr. Bohlen, to give him the go-ahead to construct a story-writing machine: "Nowadays, Mr. Bohlen, the hand-made article hasn't a hope. It can't possibly compete with mass-production, especially in this country—you know that. Carpets . . . chairs . . . shoes . . . bricks . . . crockery . . . anything you like to mention—they're all made by machinery now. The quality may be inferior, but that doesn't matter. It's the cost of production that counts" (p. 261).

After much struggle, Knipe creates a machine for writing stories. Based on his theory that every magazine accepts and prints a certain type of story, the machine can be set to spawn those that meet the criteria of each successful magazine. Next Knipe and Bohlen set up a literary agency to mask their mechanical mass production of stories. Eventually they buy off all the mediocre writers, giving them a salary in exchange for the use of their names on machine-made tales. Although the better writers will not be bribed, the agency soon produces half of all works published in English.

At the end of the story the narrator introduces himself as a writer with nine starving children who is on the verge of giving in to Knipe. In a self-reflective moment the narrator intimates that this writer has already given in and that the story we read has been produced by Knipe's machine. Knipe tells his boss, "There's a trick that nearly every writer uses, of inserting at least one long, obscure word into each story. This makes the reader think that the man is very wise and clever. So I have the machine do the same thing. There'll be a whole stack of long words stored away just for this purpose." In the sentence that follows Dahl uses "epexegetically" (p. 263).

Dahl's perspective on the commodification of art is both from the side of the artist and from the side of the art collector. Like many of his characters, he had an acquisitive bent and enjoyed collecting fine things: wines, paintings, antique furniture, and, during his youth in the United States, famous acquaintances. His stories are full of collectors: a butterfly collector in "My Lady Love, My Dove," a nouveau-riche oenophile in "Taste," art collectors in "Nunc Dimittis" and "Neck" (all four in *Someone Like You*), a taxidermist murderess in "The Landlady," an antiques dealer in "Parson's Pleasure" (both from *Kiss Kiss*). Art, "taste," and collection play pivotal roles in many of his works, and they played a key role in his life. From the time he began writing he used much of the income he made from his stories to purchase valuable nineteenth- and twentieth-century paintings, including Matisses, Soutines, Rouaults, Bonnards, and Cézannes. He collected art for himself and bought for others at auctions. In addition to acquiring objects Dahl collected knowledge about things. Frequently his specialized knowledge surfaces in his stories.

"Parson's Pleasure" (from *Kiss Kiss*) tells of an antiques dealer, who, like Dahl and Dahl's father, knows a lot about high-quality old furniture. The dealer masquerades as a parson each Sunday in order to gain access to crumbling but once-lovely homes in the English countryside. So, in the old houses of poor folk he ferrets out valuable antiques, which he buys for nearly nothing and sells for fancy prices in the city. The story finds this "clergyman," aptly named Boggis, in Buckinghamshire, where he runs into Claud and his friends. In the home of Claud's friend Rummins, Boggis discovers, sheathed in layers of paint, a Chippendale commode—the fourth ever to be found. He fantasizes about the fame his discovery will bring him. To swindle the owners of this prize, he pretends the piece is worthless and claims that he wants only its legs. Boggis, a gifted performer, easily tricks the men. After initial suspicion they take Boggis at face value. As the "parson" brings his car around to collect his treasure, the compliant men carefully saw the legs off the priceless item and chop up the mahogany "carcass" for firewood.

The schemes of Dahl's characters to acquire objects are sometimes sinister. They will go to great lengths to get what they want. Like Boggis, they must be skilled in manipulation and deception to achieve their ends. Yet, in Dahl's tales, characters' covetous impulses and deceitful games are rarely rewarded and sometimes punished.

Many of his plots turn on gambling, wagers, and other games involving risk, and most of Dahl's gamblers cheat. In the games of chance that he depicts, often more than just money is on the line: in "Taste" a father wagers his daughter's hand in what he thinks is a sure thing; in "Dip in the Pool" a man risks his life to win a bet; in "Man from the South" a character almost sacrifices a piece of his body.

"Taste" (in *Someone Like You*) features a prominent wine expert, Richard Pratt, who bets that he can recognize the vintage of a claret wine served by his parvenu host, Mike Schofield, a stockbroker. Schofield tries to impress his guest with his choice of wines and his knowledge about them. But Pratt has eyes and taste for only one thing: his host's nubile daughter. Conversing with the girl, he swills his wine too quickly and devours the delicate, elegantly prepared dishes set before him too swiftly. Dahl's tone conveys deep disgust.

When Pratt insists that Schofield wager two houses against the hand of his daughter, the girl is appalled. Ultimately she agrees to it when her father assures her that Pratt cannot win. Pratt, who has a habit of anthropomorphizing wines, describes a claret as though he were describing the girl he desires: it is "gentle and gracious, almost feminine in the aftertaste" (p. 16). Such equations of tasty wine and tasty girls render the process of tasting all the more repellent. For Dahl life's pleasures are always a mixed blessing: the procurement of good food, sex objects, and desired things of all kinds brings pleasure as well as disgust. He presents Pratt's thick wet lips and masticating mouth as revolting.

In the end Pratt appears to guess the wine correctly, and Schofield and family are horror-struck. But a birdlike servant who has observed the scene breaks the tension and initiates a different sort of disquiet. Graciously, she hands Pratt his spectacles, which, she says, he had left in the study before dinner; of course, the study is where the wine was stored. The tale ends with the charlatan Pratt exposed and his host writhing in righteous fury.

The plot of "Man from the South" (in *Someone Like You*) turns on another diabolical wager. The story takes place at a resort, where the narrator watches

U.S. cadets and English girls splashing one another flirtatiously in the pool. One boy, trying to impress a girl, is enticed to make a sinister wager with a mysterious man at the poolside. The man bets his Cadillac that the boy cannot flame his cigarette lighter ten times in a row without fail. If the peculiar man wins, he wants the little finger of the boy's left hand. They retire to the older man's room to execute the plan, the narrator tagging along as a referee.

With his left hand tied to the table, finger stretched under a poised meat cleaver, the boy lights the gadget. After he has lit the lighter eight times, a woman suddenly enters the room, interrupting the proceedings. She declares that the man has chopped off dozens of fingers in the past and that he can no longer wager anything because she has won everything he owns, including the Cadillac that he bet. The narrator notes that on her hand only a single finger remains.

BATTLE OF THE SEXES

IN "Man from the South" and in many other tales, Dahl turns his perverse gaze on domestic partnerships in which power relations are imbalanced. The forms of petty torture and power playing between intimates interest him. In the ironically named collection *Kiss Kiss* his representations of couples are filled with bile. Men and women play the roles of both victimizer and victim. In some tales aggressive women rule over cowering spouses. In others meek wives wreak revenge on cruel husbands.

Throughout his career his reflections on females of all species are far from flattering. During his marriage to Patricia Neal, however, his sour representations of powerful women and painful marriages were fueled by his negative feelings for his wife. Brutal human inclinations and actions take center stage: manipulation, sadism, deceit, and revenge, and these traits are often attributed to women and treated with sinister humor. There are rarely innocent victims in Dahl's stories. Although tyrannical husbands may be bad, their oppressed wives are often worse. Dahl commonly requires that his readers root for protagonists who commit grave crimes. Much of the tension and suspense in these stories is drawn out of the mixed feelings they inspire.

Dahl and Neal were married in July 1953. On their honeymoon the couple visited Dahl's family in England. The contrast between Pat and Sophie was stark. Neal was not a domestic woman; she liked to sleep late, eat well, gab with her friends, and in general lead a pampered life. Sophie was the opposite; she funneled her considerable energy into household activities. She had never worked outside the home, always devoting her life to her family.

The marriage was not a success. Less than a year after the wedding, Dahl asked for a divorce. The main problem was Neal's success: she was the one who brought home the bacon and made the headlines. Although Dahl was awed by her achievements, he also envied her earning power and fame. He wanted two conflicting things: a glamorous superstar companion and a traditional housewife. Advice came to the struggling couple from Dahl's mentor Charles Marsh; it saved their marriage. Marsh advised Pat to do the cooking and the housework and told Roald to take responsibility for the household finances—to control the money Pat earned. Yet difficulties in the marriage continued.

Dahl wrote two stories during this period of marital strife before he and Neal had children: "The Way up to Heaven," published in the *New Yorker* in 1954 and "William and Mary," which the *New Yorker* rejected twice—in 1954 and again in 1957. Both of these stories, published in *Kiss Kiss*, depict power struggles in marital relationships. Both are about oppressed wives who get revenge on despotic spouses. Both wives have been deprived of children: in "Heaven" Mrs. Foster's husband tries to prevent her journey from their home in New York City to France to visit their only child, and in "William and Mary" William has decided that children are inconvenient, and so the couple is childless.

In "The Way up to Heaven" Mrs. Foster, a woman with a near pathological dread of lateness, slowly discovers that her husband enjoys tormenting her, "inflicting a nasty private little torture of his own" (p. 56), by persistently making her late. Dahl presents Mrs. Foster as a loving wife who can refuse her husband nothing. But she rebels when he tries to prevent her solo voyage to see her daughter in Paris and to meet her three grandchildren for the first time. As they are poised to leave for the airport, he engages in his usual game of manipulative procrastination, dipping into the house, pretending to have forgotten a gift for his daughter. When she finds the missing gift hidden in the car, exasperated, she calls for him at the door. Hearing a strange banging sound within the house, she takes off in the car on her own. As the reader will soon discover, she has coincidentally found a way to dispose of her cruel husband.

After a blissful six-week reunion with her daughter, she returns to New York. She is nonplussed to find the house suffused with a peculiar odor and not shocked to discover that the elevator is stuck between floors.

"William and Mary" tells the story of another oppressed wife's revenge. As the story opens, Mary, freshly widowed, receives a lengthy letter composed by her husband, William, shortly before his death from cancer. In the missive he details a scientific experiment in which he has chosen to participate against her wishes. After William's death a neurosurgeon, Landy, has kept his brain and a single eye alive, using a blood-pumping machine. An arrogant philosophy professor, William relishes the thought that his mind might live on indefinitely after his body's death and has gone ahead with the procedure despite his wife's opposition.

Like Mrs. Foster, Mary has been an "exemplary" wife: passive, obedient, and indulgent of her husband's whims. And, like Mrs. Foster, she is deprived by her husband of those things that most give her pleasure. The letter discloses William's dictatorial bent. He enjoys monitoring his wife's activities and pleasures. Instead of offering kind words in his letter, he dryly reminds her of those things he has proscribed—television, telephone, cigarettes, drink, and lipstick. Although he is gone, she still feels watched by his eyes and senses their scornful gaze on her.

When Mary visits her husband in the hospital, she is horrified to find that the surgeon refers to him as "it." However, her initial protective feeling soon turns into a desire to dominate and provoke. She is pleased to find that the power balance in their relationship is reversed and, as a result, that she prefers William in this form—an eye and brain floating in a basin, immobile and mute. As she tells the shocked Landy that she cannot wait to "bring him home," she sadistically exhales a great mouthful of smoke into her husband's infuriated eye. Once again, the tables have been turned.

Turning the tables is perhaps the most pervasive theme in Dahl's literature for both adults and chil-

dren. Most of the stories in the two collections he published in the 1950s use dramatic shifts in the balance of power to shock the reader. "Lamb to the Slaughter" (from *Someone Like You*), in which a powerless woman takes charge of her life, became one of Dahl's most notorious stories. The tale begins when a pregnant and attentive young housewife receives some shocking news from her policeman husband—presumably that he's leaving her for another woman. In response to these tidings she bops him on the head with what was to be their dinner, a frozen leg of lamb, thereby killing him. While the dead man's work buddies investigate the killing, the murder weapon simmers in the oven. Later, weary from their labors, the police partake of the succulent lamb, unwittingly destroying the evidence they seek. Once again, in a story of vengeance, a woman who seems helpless surprises the reader and holds her own.

Turning the tables also pervades the stories Dahl wrote in the 1960s and 1970s about the pleasures and displeasures of sex. The four tales collected in *Switch Bitch* (1974), all of which were first published in *Playboy*, are misogynistic tales that read like elaborate, protracted dirty jokes. Two of these tales use the same framing device. The narrator, a figure of Dahl, claims to present excerpts from the diaries of his Uncle Oswald. Oswald, whose first name resembles Dahl's own, is partly an exaggerated self-portrait: "The connoisseur, the bon vivant, the collector of spiders, scorpions and walking-sticks, the lover of opera, the expert on Chinese porcelain, the seducer of women, and without much doubt the greatest fornicator of all time" (*My Uncle Oswald*, p. 7). The novel *My Uncle Oswald*, a longer diary segment, was published in 1979.

"The Visitor," the skillfully told story with which Dahl introduces Oswald, won *Playboy*'s annual fiction-writing prize in 1961. When the story begins, the narrator has just received a package containing twenty-eight beautifully bound volumes of Oswald's diary. After reading through them, he comments on their contents, setting up the reader's expectations:

The narrative never seemed to lose its flavour, the pace seldom slackened, and almost without exception, every single entry, whether it was long or short, and whatever the subject, became a marvellous little individual story that was complete in itself. . . . [O]ne was left with the rather breathless feeling that this might just possibly be one of the major autobiographical works of our time.

(p. 9)

But will he divulge these treasures to the now-eager reader? As it turns out, given the numberless cuck-olds Oswald has left in his wake, the contents of the diary are for the most part too scandalous to reveal.

The segment the narrator chooses to disclose is a titillating fairy tale set in the Syrian Desert. As the excerpt begins, Oswald romps on a pyramid in the moonlight with an illicit lover, the mistress of a royal personage, whose private thugs chase the pair. To save his skin, Oswald flees the scene, driving through the Sinai Desert in his Lagonda, singing the score of *Aida,* leaving his lover to an inevitable death.

A desert, Oswald claims, "is one of the least con-taminated places on the earth" (20), but he is ob-sessed with filth and pestilence, and everywhere he looks he sees dirt and disease. Arriving at a gas station, he notes that the attendant suffers from ad-vanced syphilis and, he guesses, scores of other diseases. After speaking with this man, Oswald sterilizes his mouth and throat with a swig of whiskey. The attendant, checking the oil, finds that the fan belt is broken, or, as Oswald believes, cuts the fan belt. This leaves Oswald stranded until the next day, when a new belt can be fetched.

By chance, or so it seems, a Rolls-Royce soon drives up to the station, and a well-dressed man steps out. This man lives in the middle of the desert in a pristine white castle to which he cordially in-vites Oswald. There, he introduces his guest to a wife and young daughter, both of whom are rav-ishingly beautiful. As if in a beauty contest, these women first appear in their bathing suits, then in evening wear, and then, so it seems, they perform, in the night wild sexual antics; the only trouble is that Oswald cannot tell whether the sexually adept woman who comes quietly to his room at midnight is the daughter or the mother. She seems too youth-ful to be the mother and too experienced to be the girl. Even the next day Oswald remains bewildered as to the identity of his partner. The truth is re-vealed as his host drives him to retrieve his car at the gas station. There is another woman in the house, a daughter five years older than the other, but alas, the man tells him, she has leprosy.

The plots of both *My Uncle Oswald* and "Bitch" revolve around the discovery and use of perilously potent aphrodisiacs for men. In "Bitch" Oswald teams up with a French scientist who performs ex-periments on olfaction. Ultimately the scientist dis-covers an aphrodisiac so powerful that the man who catches a whiff will ravish the nearest woman. After the Frenchman dies—leaving no record of the formula for Bitch—Oswald decides to use the last drops of the scent to humiliate the U.S. president, who is soon to make a television appearance with a group of women. In typical Dahl fashion, however, Oswald becomes the victim of his own plot, and he is dosed with the Bitch intended for the president.

My Uncle Oswald, a selection from volume XX of the diaries, tells the story of the young Oswald's ac-cumulation of his fortune. At the age of seventeen, after hearing of the aphrodisiac properties of the Su-danese blister beetle, Oswald travels to the Sudan, harvests beetles, and powders them to make pills. Eventually, as in "Bitch," he teams up with a scien-tist, in this case his Cambridge chemistry tutor, A. R. Woresley, a man who has discovered a technique for preserving sperm. Oswald convinces Woresley to embark on a moneymaking scheme to collect the sperm of the most famous men in Europe, using as bait a sexy student named Yasmin Howcomely.

The three then embark on a journey across the continent, stopping to harvest sperm from sundry crowned heads, artists, composers, intellectuals, and novelists in order to create their sperm bank. The rest of the narrative consists of a series of repet-itive escapades, a catalogue of sexual encounters with famous men such as Pablo Picasso, Sigmund Freud, Albert Einstein, Claude Monet, and Igor Stravinsky. Yasmin entices the sperm sources first with her looks, then with blister beetle–laced bon-bons. The men become so frenzied they do not no-tice that she collects their semen.

At the end of the novel, once again, the unpleas-ant Oswald is burned. Although he plans to abscond with the contents of the sperm bank, his two collab-orators, who are in love, beat him to the punch and leave him only the sperm of Marcel Proust.

PARENTHOOD AND CHILDREN IN DAHL'S WORLD

In 1954 Pat and Roald bought a summer house in Great Missenden, in Buckinghamshire, near the homes of Dahl's mother and sisters. The Dahl fam-ily later named the place Gipsy House, after an old gypsy caravan that sat on the property. Although the name Gipsy House reflects Dahl's ongoing romantic fantasies about the roving life, ironically the place inspired in him the desire for a more stable lifestyle. But Neal's successful career as a film and stage actress still linked them to the States and an itinerant existence. Dahl much preferred to live in the English home, where he waxed domestic, setting up a womblike work space in a garden shed, building an aviary and filling it with multicolored budgies, and planting an extensive garden.

This domestic life soon included children. A first child, Olivia, was born in 1955, and two years later a second daughter, Tessa, was born. Theo, their only boy, was born in 1960. Later in the 1960s they would have two more girls, Ophelia and Lucy. Dahl was, in a sense, reborn in his role as a parent. Neal claimed that Dahl was a maternal father who oversaw much of the child care and executed most of the child-related chores. The presence of children reinvigorated his imagination, leading him to return to writing children's literature.

Only a few of the stories in Dahl's collections for adults concern children: "The Wish" (from *Someone Like You*), a brief tale about a child's too-vivid imagination; "The Umbrella Man," a sweet story told from the perspective of an intelligent young girl; and "Pig" (from *Kiss Kiss*), a remake of Voltaire's *Candide* (1759), the most fully developed story about a child.

"Pig" is the parodic parable of a painfully naive orphan named Lexington, who is adopted in infancy by an eccentric great aunt in Virginia named Glosspan. Aunt Glosspan, a satirical version of Voltaire's comic philosopher Pangloss, lives by the creed of vegetarianism. She raises the boy in total isolation as a vegetarian, serving as both parent and teacher. Lexington shows great skill as a chef and, at the age of ten, begins to write his own vegetarian cookbook. When his aunt dies a number of years later, she leaves him a letter telling him to go to New York City to complete his cookbook and receive his inheritance from her lawyer.

In New York, Lexington, as naive as Candide, proceeds to be fleeced by everyone he meets. First, Glosspan's lawyer pilfers the half-million-dollar inheritance, leaving Lexington only fifteen thousand dollars. Next, the unfortunate Lexington is cheated by a waiter and cook in the greasy spoon where he unwittingly first eats meat. They relieve him of a few hundred dollars in exchange for re-

vealing the secret of the scrumptious dish he tastes. The cook jokes that it may be either pork or human flesh, and he sends Lexington to a slaughterhouse in the Bronx to learn about meat processing. But there too Lexington gets burned.

On a guided tour of the slaughterhouse Lexington watches in awe as swine are chained and lifted from the ground upside down to where a pigsticker sits. While he views the scene with excitement, his tour guide swiftly shackles him, and Lexington, squealing like a beast, is lifted, stuck, and bled. The meat eater will himself be eaten.

Like Lexington, the children in Dahl's short stories tend to be vulnerable. Two of his stories for adults deal explicitly with couples who bear frail children. In "Royal Jelly" (*Kiss Kiss*) a couple who has tried for nine years to conceive finally produces a baby. The infant, who has been hazardously losing weight, suddenly becomes plump. As it turns out, the baby's father, Albert Taylor, a man with a passion for bees, has been surreptitiously feeding his child—and himself—royal jelly, the substance bees feed to their babes to produce a queen bee. Taylor, a beekeeper and avid bee enthusiast, explains to his wife that royal jelly increases a grub's weight by more than ten thousand–fold within days. He claims that the substance enhances sexuality and fertility, hinting to his stunned wife that their newfound fecundity results from his doses of jelly.

The baby rapidly gains weight, but its mother's relief soon turns to horror. She perceives that her husband, with his slim bowed legs and face covered with yellow and black fuzz, resembles a bee. The baby, she notes with anxiety, suffers an analogous change: "The baby was lying naked on the table, fat and white and comatose, like some gigantic grub that was approaching the end of its larval life and would soon emerge into the world complete with mandibles and wings" (p. 170).

In "Genesis and Catastrophe," another sickly newborn distresses its mother. When the tale begins, a weepy, pious woman, who is mistreated by her drunkard husband, has just given birth to a boy. She fears the child will die, as have her first three children. But the doctor cheers her on, and readers are inclined to do the same, until, at the end of the story, Dahl reveals that the weakling tot is Adolf Hitler. Slyly, Dahl tricks his reader into rooting for Hitler's survival.

In an article published in *Life* Dahl presents himself, and all suspense writers, as masters of the pleasures of pain. Writers, he claims, devise ways to give "pleasure-pain" to their readers, one of which is to torture and imperil an innocent character, such as a small child ("The Painful Pleasure of Suspense," 18 December 1964). One aspect of Dahl's life that brought him much pleasure—his children—also brought him pain. His painful-pleasureful stories about weak children prophesied troubles to come in his own family.

In 1960 his son, Theo, only four months old, was hit by a cab as he was rolled across the street in his carriage. The baby's condition was dire; his skull was broken, and a buildup of cerebrospinal fluid put pressure on his brain, causing brain damage. This hydrocephalic condition, common in children with serious head injuries, was a puzzle to physicians in the 1960s; no effective drainage technique had been invented. Existing techniques dangerously spread infection; Dahl was determined to create a functional system.

In *Going Solo* Dahl claims that the experience of his wartime head injury sparked a lifelong interest in medicine. To save his son, he worked together with an engineer friend and a physician to design what is now called the Wade-Dahl-Till valve. By the time the device was patented in 1962, Theo's condition was much better, but the invention helped thousands of other children.

After Theo's accident the family determined that New York City was not a safe place for children, so they based themselves in England, settling at Gipsy House. But Britain did not offer safety to the Dahl brood. In autumn 1962, just when Theo's condition seemed to be improving, Olivia, the oldest child, died suddenly from the measles. She was seven and a half years old, the same age as Dahl's oldest sister, Astri, when she died many years before from appendicitis. Dahl's offspring—their genders and birth orders—precisely replicated that of his own nuclear family. But unlike Harald, who died shortly after the death of Astri, Dahl lived on. He found some consolation in writing.

The presence of children had already transformed Dahl's life as a writer, inspiring him to turn once again to children's literature. He improvised *James and the Giant Peach* as a story for Olivia and Tessa, to whom he dedicated the book. He wrote it down and, with trepidation, sent the manuscript to Knopf, who responded enthusiastically.

When his loving parents die, James is flung abruptly into servitude. He becomes the slave of his reluctant guardians, Aunt Sponge and Aunt Spiker, vain, sadistic witches who live on the peak of a hill. Suffering every imaginable deprivation, James's luck begins to turn when a peculiar old man bequeaths him a bag of magical objects: a squirming green mass that resembles a clump of worms or insects. Unfortunately he drops and loses them, but a mammoth peach sprouts from a barren tree situated where James has dropped his bag.

The aunts, thrilled by the peach, display it for a price to the eager populace. One evening, when hungry James is locked out of the house and forced to clean up after peach viewers, he finds a boy-sized hole tunneled into the peach. This is where his adventures begin. For James, as for Charlie Bucket, the initial response to life's problems is to withdraw from the world of awful people and practices—preferably with good food and good company.

Charlie and the Chocolate Factory also began as a story for Dahl's children, but its completion was interrupted by family tragedies. Dahl finished the book as he was recovering from the shock of Theo's accident and Olivia's death. The story ends with cataclysm: Wonka's flying elevator, carrying the inventor, Charlie, and Grandpa Joe, crashes through the roof of the Bucket hovel and whisks the entire family away to Wonka's factory, where they will never again be hungry.

Perhaps Dahl's desire to offer help and consolation to his own suffering children in part inspired his characterization of Wonka—the first of a series of magical father figures in Dahl's children's fiction. When Charlie becomes Wonka's heir, he exchanges his own father, a weary man fired from his job in a toothpaste factory, for an ideal father, both a powerful sorcerer and a merry prankster. This new father can grant Charlie all he desires: food, fame, fortune, and an infinite play space.

Wonka pronounces, "Down here, underneath the ground, I've got all the space I want. There's no limit, so long as I hollow it out" (p. 67). James's womblike peach and Wonka's factory share pink walls, soft light, warmth, sweet smells, and an endless supply of nourishment. Both are havens in a heartless world; they bring boy-protagonists to new friends, new horizons, and the land of happily ever after.

Wonka is not only the savior of the Buckets, but

also the savior of the Oompa-Loompas, the factory's enigmatic source of labor, invisible to those outside. Dahl's representation of these diminutive factory workers created a controversy that eventually compelled him and his publishers to change both the text and the illustrations of the book.

Wonka "saved" the Oompa-Loompas from the afflictions of the jungle—the danger of predators, which had forced them into an arboreal life and, worst of all, a diet consisting of mashed caterpillars. Oompa-Loompas, childlike African "savages," are pleased to live on chocolate and good cheer, never leaving the candy-works home where Wonka has deposited them.

Critics in the 1960s pointed out the racism of Dahl's characterization of this people, the only people of color in the story: their pygmy size; their simple natures; their favored activities (they love nothing more than song and dance); their arboreal life, which evokes simians; and their function within the chocolate empire. At length Dahl exchanged the racist depictions for less objectionable 1960s hippies. The 1971 film production avoided the race issue by giving the Oompa-Loompas green hair and orange skin.

After Dahl published *Charlie* in 1964 peace in his household did not last. He would need to take on the position of healer again. In 1965 Neal suffered from a stroke that almost took her life. Two aneurysms left her in a coma for two weeks. When she awoke, she was virtually without language. Dahl's role in her recovery has been much publicized and hotly debated. According to his own account he nursed her back to health. According to all other accounts he was not a soothing caretaker: he taunted her and humiliated her in front of her friends, provoking her to recover.

Neal's stroke gave Dahl a new position in the household. He took her place as moneymaker and became, in many ways, a single parent. Barry Farrell, who interviewed the couple for a *Life* magazine article about Neal's recovery, went on to write a book about them, *Pat and Roald* (1969), which was later made into a movie for television. The book represents Roald's fantasy of Pat's recovery. After her stroke Dahl's career as a children's writer took off.

Many of the children's stories Dahl wrote after Neal's stroke feature fantastical father figures. "The Wonderful Story of Henry Sugar," for instance, showcases Dahl's fantasy of being a sugar daddy to children. Sugar, an indolent rich man, bored with life and addicted to gambling, studies yoga in order to develop the ability to see without using his eyes, planning to use the power to cheat at gambling. After acquiring mystical powers he travels from casino to casino throughout the world, accumulating heaps of money. But the practice of yoga transforms him. Instead of keeping the money for himself, he uses it to build orphanages in the countries where he gambles.

Fantastic Mr. Fox is another story of a fabulous father. Three nasty, affluent farmers, named Boggis, Bunce, and Bean, decide to eliminate Mr. Fox and his kin. They try to dig out the fox family, eventually using steam shovels that tear a great crater in the earth. Meanwhile the fox family frantically digs deeper into the ground. Mr. Fox burrows his way to the farmers' storehouses, which he proceeds to plunder. In the end the foxes and other hunted animals decide to stay beneath the earth forever, living off the goods of the three farmers.

The children's novel *Danny, the Champion of the World* (1975) is also the story of a brilliant father's triumph. The book closely follows the plot of the adult story "The Champion of the World" (1959). Motherless Danny has "the most marvelous and exciting father a boy ever had" (p. 196). His father nurtures him, raises him, tells him tall tales, and reveals to him the secrets of poaching.

Dahl wrote a series of stories that, like *Fantastic Mr. Fox*, generate sympathy for hunted animals: *The Twits*, "The Swan," "The Boy Who Talked with Animals," and even the poaching story, *Danny, the Champion of the World*, in which the pheasants who are poached are only asleep, not dead. These stories suggest the moral superiority of children who empathize with animals. Like David, the hero of "The Boy Who Talked with Animals," they sometimes prefer the animal world to the cruel world of humans.

The Magic Finger, a simple tale written just after Olivia's death, tells of a girl Olivia's age who possesses a magic finger with which she can cast spells on others. The magic finger expresses the power of the girl's anger. She uses her fury and her finger against her neighbors the Greggs, who hunt ducks. Her magic transforms the ducks into duck-people who usurp the Gregg house and its contents, including the guns; the magic also turns the Greggs into people-ducks, who build a nest in a tree on their property. The vengeful ducks, freshly armed, threaten to shoot the Greggs, but ultimately a truce is made. When the Greggs repent and vow to throw away their weapons, all the characters are transformed into their proper forms, and the girl with the magic finger departs to teach some other hunters a lesson.

"The Boy Who Talked with Animals" takes place at a resort in Jamaica. Fishermen capture a colossal turtle, which is sold to a hotel manager. Tourists stand by as the dangerous beast is hauled in, discussing turtle soup and turtle steak. The narrator paints an unappealing portrait of humanity:

I stood there listening to the conversation of these human beings. They were discussing the destruction, the consumption and the flavor of a creature who seemed, even when upside down, to be extraordinarily dignified. One thing was certain. He was senior to any of them in age. For probably one hundred and fifty years he had been cruising in the green waters of the West Indies. He was there when George Washington was President of the United States and Napoleon was being clobbered at Waterloo. He would have been a small turtle then, but he was most certainly there.

(p. 8)

Suddenly a young boy rushes out of the crowd and embraces the turtle. Dahl presents the child as a hero: He stands "very small and erect, facing the crowd, his eyes shining like two stars and the wind blowing in his hair. He was magnificent" (p. 12). The boy's father buys the turtle from the hotel manager and tells the fishermen to set it free. The next day, the boy disappears. The fishermen catch a glimpse of him, far from shore, on the back of the turtle, heading out to sea. He never comes back.

In "The Swan" another heroic child who protects wildlife and leaves the human world does miraculously return. In the story two bullies attack a younger, gentle-spirited boy. One of the older boys, Ernie, has been given a gun for his fifteenth birthday, and he goes to hunt with his buddy at a wildfowl sanctuary. At a lake in the sanctuary they find Peter, an intellectually precocious child who watches birds through binoculars. They torture and nearly kill Peter, who identifies himself with the animal victims. When they tie him to railroad tracks and watch as a train runs over him, he feels "as if he [is] being eaten alive and swallowed up in the belly of a screaming murderous monster." When they kill a swan sitting on her nest, they force Peter, who

weeps for the bird, to fetch the dead creature like a dog. Like David facing his adult opponents, Peter stands tall: "He stood there, as tall as he could stand, splendid in his fury" (p. 91).

As a last torment the bullies cut off the swan's wings and tie them to Peter's arms. After forcing the boy to climb a tall willow tree, they shoot at him to make him jump. Hit in the leg, Peter flies. Dahl writes:

Some people, when they have taken too much and have been driven beyond the point of endurance, simply crumple and give up. There are others, though they are not many, who will for some reason always be unconquerable. You meet them in time of war and also in time of peace. They have an indomitable spirit and nothing, neither pain nor torture nor threat of death, will cause them to give up. . . . [Peter] dived toward the light and spread his wings.

(pp. 97–98)

Peter flies home, where his mother sees her only son fall onto the lawn. For Dahl flying would always embody the power of the human spirit and imagination.

The Minpins, an allegorical tale written at the end of Dahl's life, also features a heroic flying boy. The hero of the tale, Billy, escapes from a world regulated by his mother into the enigmatic and perilous forest of Sin. He enters the realm of the Minpins, a gremlin-sized arboreal people, whom he eventually saves from a foul fire-breathing creature, the Gruncher—a beast enfolded in the smoke it produces and thus invisible to its prey. The Gruncher's weapon—its fire—renders it vulnerable; if the fire is put out, the monster dies. So Billy, riding on the back of a swan, flies through fire and stench to lure the Gruncher into a lake, where it perishes. The tone and imagery of this story evoke Dahl's poignant war stories of pilots flying through fire to kill their enemies and save the lives of allies.

After Billy's mission is accomplished, he returns home, but his life is irreversibly changed. The swan who carried him to defeat the Gruncher now becomes his private airplane, secretly whisking him away at night to mysterious places. On one such journey the bird takes him deep into a crater in the earth where he sees a pristine blue pool filled with swans. This exquisite vision evokes the mystical valley in "They Shall Not Grow Old." A new world is opened up to Billy, which his mother thinks is the "rubbish" of an overactive imagination (p. 41).

CONCLUSION: REBIRTH AND RENEWAL

IN 1983 Dahl divorced Patricia Neal and married his longtime lover Felicity Crosland. He also received his first British literary award, the Whitbread Prize, for *The Witches*. Public recognition in England and a happy marriage helped to make the 1980s a fertile period for Dahl as a writer. In this last decade of his life he wrote copiously for children, publishing more than ten kids' books, among which are some of his finest. His collaborative relationship with the illustrator Quentin Blake, whom he had met in the 1970s, blossomed at this time. During this period he turned to writing his memoirs, explicitly making himself the stuff of story. He wrote three autobiographical works for children and young adults: *Boy, Going Solo,* and *My Year* (1993), which was published posthumously. In *My Year,* glorifying country life, Dahl writes, "I have never lived in a town or city in my life and I would hate to do so" (p. 35). In the context of his new life with Felicity, the years in New York City were forgotten.

The prose works Dahl wrote during the 1980s have an intensity of warmth and sweetness rare in his earlier work. They depict loving relationships between humans. In the last year of his life Dahl published his first romance, *Esio Trot* (1990), the comic courtship story of a middle-aged couple. In this tale the smitten man tricks his beloved, a neighbor, in order to inflame her with love for him. He convinces her that he can make her much-loved under-grown pet tortoise increase in size by chanting a charm to the creature. He then replaces the tortoise with increasingly larger tortoises, creating the illusion of growth.

While children in earlier Dahl stories play the role of savior, they generally help animals. Child characters in his later stories, however, such as Sophie in *The BFG*, Matilda, and the mouse-boy in *The Witches*, all seek to help people. They are well-developed, appealing characters, smart kids with strong wills and firm beliefs. Not only can they take care of themselves, but they can care for others too.

The BFG, one of Dahl's favorites, tells the story of a lonely orphan, Sophie, who is abducted from an orphanage by a giant, the BFG, because she accidentally catches a glimpse of him through her window as he brings lovely dreams to sleeping children. The BFG, a sweet-tempered vegetarian, lives on a barren wasteland populated by a troop of people-eating giants who are significantly larger than himself. These monsters, who have names like Meatdripper and Bonecruncher, roam the earth snatching up and devouring "human beans," as the BFG calls them. When some of the giants rush off to England to eat school-fulls of children, Sophie and the BFG decide to intervene.

The BFG, an expert at concocting dream-stories, prepares a special dream for the queen of England that will introduce her to Sophie, the BFG, and their mission. When the queen awakes, she finds Sophie sitting on her windowsill. And so the plot progresses to its happy conclusion, with plentiful humor. The BFG is essentially a comic character; he speaks a silly, mixed-up musical language that evokes the nonsense poems of Carroll, Belloc, and Lear. The gangly stooping BFG is a figure of Dahl, a poet, a weaver of dreams, and the author, as it turns out at the end of the story, of a book about his adventures with Sophie.

The nameless hero of *The Witches*, like Sophie, is an orphan who is cared for by a fanciful storyteller. The boy is adopted by his tough, rather mannish Norwegian grandmother, who smokes cigars and tells him stories about witches. Witches, she explains, detest children and will do whatever they can to get rid of them. A witch tried to kill her when she was a child but took only the thumb of her hand.

The witches are a breed reminiscent of the meek, vengeful wives of Dahl's adult stories; they hide their nightmarish qualities. The Grand High Witch, who wears a mask with the features of a pretty young girl, has a decayed and worm-eaten face beneath. All the witches wear wigs to hide their baldness and red-splotched scalps; they wear special shoes to hide stumplike feet without toes and gloves to hide long bestial claws. Demonic females are a recurrent motif in Dahl's work. The female gremlins, whose hideous baldness makes them resemble the witches, are "worse, far worse than the males, because the female of any type is always more scheming, cunning, jealous and relentless than the male" (*Some Time Never*, p. 58).

While many of Dahl's malignant characters perceive children as vermin, the witches wish to transform them into vermin, in particular mice. The boy discovers this plot while staying at a hotel with his grandmother, where, accidentally, he is trapped in an auditorium where the witches of England hold their annual meeting. He overhears their scheme to turn all English children into mice; they plan to buy up all the English candy stores and add mouse-making potion to the candies they sell to kids. He is then spotted and is himself transformed into a mouse.

As a mouse the boy, with his grandmother, plans to give the witches a taste of their own medicine. He steals into the room of the Grand High Witch and snatches some of the potion, which he dumps into a soup that will be served to all the witches, who are posing as a group from the Royal Society for the Prevention of Cruelty to Children. Successful, the mouse-boy and his grandmother return to Norway, where they will continue their crusade against the witches of the world.

The odd twist in this tale is that the boy is never restored to human form. This does not upset him, however, for he reasons that as a mouse he will live precisely as long as his eighty-year-old grandmother will live. Thus, neither of them will ever be alone.

In *Matilda* a child again saves others from a demonic female, the Trunchbull, headmistress of Matilda's school. Matilda is a precocious child with insipid parents. She teaches herself to read at the age of three and by age four has taken herself to the public library and read the works of Hemingway, Kipling, William Faulkner, Charles Dickens, and Jane Austen, among others.

Matilda's first teacher, Miss Honey, only twenty-three, struggles to challenge her pupil. When she attempts to help Matilda's parents and the headmistress recognize the girl's gifts, she is ridiculed. Miss Honey, it turns out, is also an orphan. Trunchbull is the aunt who raised her, abused her, and, so it seems, killed her father. Trunchbull bullies Miss Honey out of her inheritance and wages, so the poor girl lives in a shack and eats almost nothing. Matilda uses her magic to restore her teacher's rightful inheritance and rid the town of the beastly Trunchbull. Matilda's parents, petty criminals, flee England on the lam, giving Miss Honey permission to adopt Matilda.

In the 1980s Dahl turned to writing humorous verse, publishing three collections of poems for children: *Dirty Beasts* (1983), *Roald Dahl's Revolting Rhymes* (1982), and *Rhyme Stew* (1989). Although fanciful poems had figured in his works for children ever since he published *The Gremlins*, now, for the first time, he devoted entire books to poetry. These works express the roguish aspect of Dahl's personality. The verse, sometimes racy, sometimes inventive, and always somewhat perverse, provoked the wrath of many librarians and teachers. These guardians of the young questioned Dahl's crudeness and his choice of topics.

Betting and cheating play a role in a number of his poems. In a novel version of the classic fable "The Tortoise and the Hare" (in *Rhyme Stew*), Dahl introduces a new character, a rat, who makes a lot of money betting on which creature will win and helping both racers to cheat. Gambling also takes center stage in "Snow-White and the Seven Dwarfs," one of the traditional fairy tales Dahl perverts in *Revolting Rhymes*. His Snow-White steals the wicked queen's magic mirror and uses its powers to win at the horse races. Thus she and her bevy of manikins get rich, and Dahl concludes: This "shows that gambling's not a sin / Provided that you always win."

Like Snow-White, Dahl's other fairy-tale heroines think for themselves and act selfishly. Goldilocks is "a brazen little crook"; Little Red Riding Hood not only kills the wolf to make a wolf-skin coat but leaps into another story, "The Three Little Pigs," to acquire a second wolf-skin coat and a pigskin traveling case. These poems have the mordant humor of much of Dahl's earlier work.

The nastiness of Dahl's poems reflects an aspect of his personality that became more exaggerated in his later years. At the end of his life Dahl became increasingly prickly and self-aggrandizing. Not infrequently he offended friends and mistreated editors, on whom he had become more and more dependent for input.

His inveterate dissatisfaction with himself and with others is echoed in the critical attitudes toward social institutions and traditional authorities expressed in his works. The timeliness and popularity of his writings, to an extent, depend on their irreverence and perversity. The effectiveness of Dahl's humor hangs on his way of joking about and poking fun at serious people and serious matters.

Dahl is an important chronicler and representative of postwar Anglo-American culture. When he died, on 23 November 1990, he had achieved his lifelong aspiration to be considered a great man.

SELECTED BIBLIOGRAPHY

I. COLLECTED WORKS. *Selected Stories of Roald Dahl* (New York, 1968); *Twenty-six Kisses from Roald Dahl* (London, 1969); *The Roald Dahl Omnibus* (New York, 1974,

1986); *The Best of Roald Dahl* (New York, 1978; London, 1983); *Roald Dahl's Tales of the Unexpected* (New York and London, 1979; New York, 1990); *Taste and Other Tales* (Harlow, Eng., 1979, 1985); *More Roald Dahl Tales of the Unexpected* (London, 1980); *A Roald Dahl Selection: Nine Short Stories* (Harlow, Eng., 1980); *Completely Unexpected Tales* (Middlesex, Eng., 1986); *A Second Roald Dahl Selection: Eight Short Stories* (Harlow, Eng., 1987); *Ah, Sweet Mystery of Life: The Country Stories of Roald Dahl* (London, 1989); *The Great Mouse Plot and Other Tales of Childhood* (London, 1996).

II. WORKS FOR ADULTS. *Over to You: Ten Stories of Flyers and Flying* (New York and London, 1946); *Some Time Never: A Fable for Supermen* (New York, 1948; London, 1949); *Someone Like You* (New York, 1953; London, 1954); *The Honeys* (1955); *Kiss Kiss* (New York, 1959; London, 1960); *Switch Bitch* (New York and London, 1974); *My Uncle Oswald* (London, 1979; New York, 1980); *Two Fables* (Middlesex, Eng., 1986).

III. WORKS FOR CHILDREN. *The Gremlins*, with Walt Disney (New York, 1943; London, 1944); *James and the Giant Peach* (New York, 1961; London, 1967); *Charlie and the Chocolate Factory* (New York, 1964; rev., 1973; London, 1967, 1995); *The Magic Finger* (New York, 1966; London, 1970); *Fantastic Mr. Fox* (New York and London, 1970); *Charlie and the Great Glass Elevator* (New York, 1972; London, 1973); *Danny, the Champion of the World* (New York, 1975; Oxford, Eng., 1989); *The Wonderful Story of Henry Sugar and Six More* (New York and London, 1977; Oxford, Eng., 1989); *The Enormous Crocodile* (New York and London, 1978); *The Twits* (London, 1980; New York, 1981); *George's Marvellous Medicine* (London, 1981; New York, 1982); *The BFG* (London and New York, 1982); *Roald Dahl's Revolting Rhymes* (London, 1982; New York, 1983); *Dirty Beasts* (London and New York, 1983); *Roald Dahl's Book of Ghost Stories* (London and New York, 1983), Dahl edited this book; *The Witches* (London and New York, 1983); *The Giraffe and the Pelly and Me* (London and New York, 1985); *Matilda* (London and New York, 1988); *Rhyme Stew* (London, 1989; New York, 1990); *Esio Trot* (London and New York, 1990); *The Minpins* (London and New York, 1991); *Roald Dahl's Guide to Railway Safety* (1991); *The Vicar of Nibbleswicke* (London, 1991; New York, 1992); *Roald Dahl's Revolting Recipes*, Josie Fison and Felicity Dahl, comps. (London and New York, 1994).

IV. AUTOBIOGRAPHICAL WORKS. *Boy: Tales of Childhood* (London and New York, 1984); *Going Solo* (London and New York, 1986); *The Dahl Diary* (Middlesex, Eng., 1991); *Memories with Food at Gipsy House*, with Felicity Dahl (London and New York, 1991); *My Year* (London, 1993; New York, 1994).

V. SCREENPLAYS. *You Only Live Twice*, with Jack Bloom (United Artists, 1967); *Chitty Chitty Bang Bang*, with Ken Hughes (United Artists, 1968); *The Night Digger*, based on *Nest in a Falling Tree*, by Joy Crowley (Metro-Goldwyn-Mayer, 1970); *Willy Wonka and the Chocolate Factory* (Paramount, 1971); *Oh Death Where Is Thy Sting-a-Ling-a-Ling* (United Artists); *The Witches* (1990); *James and the Giant Peach*, adapted from the story (Disney, 1996); *Matilda*, adapted from the story (1996).

VI. CRITICAL AND BIOGRAPHICAL STUDIES. Barry Farrell, *Pat and Roald* (New York, 1969); Chris Powling, *Roald Dahl* (London, 1983; rev. ed., 1985); Alan Warren, *Roald Dahl* (San Bernardino, Calif., 1988); Mark West, *Roald Dahl* (New York, 1992); Jeremy Treglown, *Roald Dahl: A Biography* (London and New York, 1994).

MARGARET DRABBLE

(1939–   )

Bridget Orr

A BIOGRAPHER, ESSAYIST, and editor of note, Margaret Drabble is best known as a novelist. Her early books, recording the joys and travails of middle-class maternity and marriage, brought her fame in the early 1960s but from the 1970s on, she has been renowned for a series of "condition-of-England" novels of broad social and geographical scope. Initially defined as a "women's writer," Drabble is now recognized as a social commentator in the nineteenth-century tradition of Charles Dickens, Elizabeth Gaskell, and Anthony Trollope, with strong affinities to eminent Edwardians such as Arnold Bennett and John Galsworthy and to more recent realist novelists such as Angus Wilson. Her vivid treatment of the various stages of women's lives has ensured her continuing attention from feminist critics and female readers but the increasing range of her themes, which include the pressures of class and familial background, the emergence of "enterprise culture" in Britain, and the dilemmas of the spiritually inclined in a secular and materialist society, have increased her readership and her stature. Her appointment to the editorship of the *Oxford Companion to English Literature*, an extremely high-profile and prestigious position, is a measure of her status as a major British woman of letters.

LIFE

MARGARET ("Maggie") Drabble was born in Sheffield, Yorkshire, on 5 June 1939. Her father, John Frederick, was a barrister, later a county court judge and novelist, from a family who owned a small sweet factory. Her mother, Margaret Bloor, was a Cambridge graduate from a working-class Methodist family who taught high school English. The Drabbles had four children, the oldest Antonia (the novelist and critic A. S. Byatt); the second, Margaret; the third, Helen, an art historian; and the fourth, a son and like his father, a barrister.

Drabble has described aspects of her family background and childhood in her many published interviews and she has clearly drawn on her intense relationships with her mother and siblings in her fiction. Both her parents were upwardly mobile in class terms and shared a liberal perspective on religious and political issues, but while Drabble's father adapted to life as an upper-middle-class professional with ease, her mother experienced considerable social and emotional difficulty. Drabble has described herself as a solitary child, suffering from a bad chest and a stammer and acquiring friends mostly in her teens at boarding school. Nonetheless, like the Brontë children, the Drabbles played literary and theatrical games together and as a child, Margaret—who idealized the early British heroine Boadicea—enjoyed swimming, riding, and exploring the natural world. Although her father was Anglican and her mother an atheist (but later both members of the Society of Friends), Margaret and her sister Antonia attended a Quaker school for girls in York called The Mount, which provided an environment that helped develop the moral and political seriousness inherent in her background. She won a scholarship to Newnham College, Cambridge, where her mother and sister had preceded her, and commenced three years of highly pleasurable scholarly, theatrical, and social activity, culminating in a starred first in her final degree exams (the Tripos) in 1960. In the week of her graduation, Drabble married Clive Swift, who has become a successful actor.

Intellectually, Drabble's time at Cambridge reinforced the high moral seriousness and Fabian liberalism of her background. Studies in English literature were then dominated by F. R. Leavis, a man who belonged to the nonconformist Left and was deeply committed to promulgating the ethical and social responsibilities of literature. As Valerie Grosvenor Myer first demonstrated, Drabble's novels all bear the mark of the long-standing English tradition of radical dissent with its deeply Protestant concern for the responsible individual's search for a valid life that Leavis' criticism also articulated. But Cambridge was more than high seriousness. Drabble spent a great deal of time acting, not least with her husband-to-be, and on leaving Cambridge embarked on a theatrical career.

The first year of Drabble's marriage was spent with the Royal Shakespeare Company in Stratford-on-Avon. She understudied actresses like Vanessa Redgrave and Judi Dench but never played a major role and felt herself marginal. Becoming pregnant, she decided to write and her first three novels appear to coincide approximately with the gestation of her three children, Adam, Rebecca, and Joseph. Her first novel, *A Summer Bird-Cage*, was published in 1963, followed by *The Garrick Year* in 1964 and *The Millstone* in 1965. The novels were immediately successful, and in 1965, Drabble was awarded the John Llewellyn Rhys Memorial Prize for Fiction and an English Society of Authors Travelling Scholarship. The following year she published her first extended critical study, an account of Wordsworth for a general audience. In 1967 *Jerusalem the Golden* appeared, for which she won the James Tate Black Award for Fiction, and in 1969 she published *The Waterfall*, as well as writing a screenplay for *The Millstone* called *A Touch of Love*, and produced her play *Bird of Paradise* at the National Theatre.

Drabble's next novel, *The Needle's Eye*, appeared three years later in 1972 and won the E. M. Forster Award. This book was a significant departure from her earlier work, which all focused on young well-educated women trying to negotiate life after the gilded years of university. Although all but one are graduates, they share a distaste for conventional career paths, and in three cases, they discover meaning in their lives through maternity. Jane, the heroine of *The Waterfall*, finds a kind of secular redemption in sexual love, while Clara, the protagonist of *Jerusalem the Golden*, achieves an ambiguous escape from the limitations of her northern upbringing into the social complexity of the metropolis. In *The Needle's Eye*, however, published the year of Drabble's separation from her husband, the perspective broadens. The novel has a male as well as a female protagonist and deals with a group of characters in

early middle age reflecting upon, and living with, the consequences of youthful confusions and conflicts. The dilemmas of the two major characters, Simon and Rose, provide counterpointed explorations of the desire to radically alter one's class position and the effect, whether through ambition or altruism.

The next three novels Drabble published, *The Realms of Gold* (1975), *The Ice Age* (1977), and *The Middle Ground* (1980), all deal with characters in middle age confronting the need to reshape their existences once they have succeeded in raising children and fulfilling professional ambitions. Often the provocation for their midlife crises is the reminder of mortality inherent in an experience of physical or mental illness, their own and that of others. The resolutions achieved by the protagonists vary, from a commitment to spiritual exploration (*The Ice Age*); the search for and recovery of family origins and sexual love (*The Realms of Gold*); or simply the realization of community (*The Middle Ground*). In all these novels, domestic space and social and physical environment, always important in Drabble's characterization of her protagonists and their dilemmas, become ever more symbolically freighted as indices of personality, history, and class.

These were also highly productive years for Drabble in her role as critic, editor, and literary and cultural commentator. In 1974, she published *Arnold Bennett: A Biography* and also edited Jane Austen's juvenilia, a single volume titled *Lady Susan, The Watsons, Sanditon*; in 1976, she edited *The Genius of Thomas Hardy* and *New Stories I*; in 1978, *For Queen and Country: Britain in the Victorian Age* appeared; and the following year *A Writer's Britain: Landscape in Literature* came out. These various projects reflect Drabble's interest in the mainly Romantic and nineteenth-century literary and cultural traditions that inform her own sensibility and have provided points of comparison for her own work. Like Jane Austen, with a sharp eye for social absurdity she has written novels that seem to capture emblematically female experiences. More recently, as the range of her novels has expanded, critics have compared her work to that of the great Victorians, George Eliot and Trollope. All her fiction also reflects her abiding love for William Wordsworth, the great celebrant of the redemptive spirituality of our relations with nature. But perhaps her closest identification has been with Arnold Bennett, the subject of her 1974 biography and a novelist famed early in the century for his realist depictions of life in the "Potteries," that area of the British Midlands where the ceramics industry was based and where Drabble's own family originated. Bennett's popularity, like that of the other great Edwardian realists such as Galsworthy, has never really recovered from the critical success of modernism, which regarded the naturalistic *romans à fleuves* of these writers as outmoded and aesthetically unserious. Drabble has been a consistent advocate of this tradition, however, and as she has continued to publish, their influence has been ever more marked, not least in her tendency to give central characters from previous books walk-on roles in those which follow. As much as Trollope's *Chronicles of Barset* or his Palliser novels, Drabble's oeuvre, at least from *Jerusalem the Golden*, can be read as the ongoing representation of an entire, rich, and complex social world.

Drabble's prominence as a novelist and woman of letters was given formal recognition in 1976, when she was awarded an honorary doctorate by the University of Sheffield (her hometown), and in 1980, when she was made a Commander of the British Empire. For the next seven years there was, however, a hiatus in her publication of fiction, while she concentrated on the mammoth task of reediting the *Oxford Companion to English Literature*, which appeared in 1985. During these years she also published lectures titled *The Tradition of Women's Fiction* (1982), essays that reflect her belated interest in Virginia Woolf, the doyenne of female modernists and whose influence is particularly apparent in *The Middle Ground*. In 1982, Drabble married again, to the celebrated biographer Michael Holroyd. The couple decided to maintain separate households, with Drabble continuing to live during the week in the Hampstead terrace house, whose garden wall formerly abutted John Keats's, where she had raised her children. Then, in 1987, she published the first volume in what became a trilogy: the novel was called *The Radiant Way*. The next two books in the series, *A Natural Curiosity* and *The Gates of Ivory* appeared in 1989 and 1991, respectively.

Drabble's latest novels are both a summary and an extension of her earlier work. Here she focuses on a trio of female friends, who became friends at Cambridge and remain close through the following decades. The three women present variations on the themes of love, marriage, ambition, parent-hood, and friendship in the context of sweeping social and political change, as the liberated 1960s give way to the inflationary 1970s, followed by the Thatcherite decade of political reaction and erosion of the British postwar social consensus. The widespread desire for social unity and equity that led to the establishment of a welfare state in the 1940s was replaced in the 1980s by the social division and competition fostered by the Conservative government's program of economic modernization. The last novel is set partially in Thailand and Cambodia, a rare departure from the habitual English settings of London, the Midlands, and South Yorkshire, and represents Drabble's attempt to engage with issues of individual and collective responsibility on the broadest possible front as she anatomizes the motivations and activities of a raft of Westerners on the fringes of the Kampuchean tragedy. Moving from the personal distress caused by individual and political betrayal to the moral questions posed by serial murderers and mass murderers, the trilogy as a whole examines the urge to explore or confront evil on the part of modern Europeans who believe their societies to be largely insulated from the ongoing horror of history.

Drabble continues with her work as editor, critic, and biographer. Her edition of Virginia Woolf's *To the Lighthouse* appeared in 1992 and the next year she introduced an edition of *Wuthering Heights* (1993). The *Oxford Companion to English Literature* has been much reprinted and a concise edition of the volume has also been published. Drabble has written pamphlets on house-owning and social equity ("Safe as Houses" [1990] and "The Case for Equality" [1988]) and has also written about artists Maurice Cockrill (1992) and Kathleen Hale (1995). Her most considerable recent achievement is, however, a biography of the novelist Angus Wilson published in 1995. Wilson's achievement, like her own, is within the realist tradition.

Although Drabble has been much written about by feminist critics, both in Britain but more particularly abroad, and while her work rewards such analysis, she can no longer be defined as primarily a "women's writer." The scope of her nonliterary activities—as television panelist, member of Arts Council committees, governmental councils, and, less formally, as protester against the Rhodesian settlement and the proliferation of nuclear arms—suggests her commitment to the Fabian radicalism of that liberal section of the upper middle classes into which she was born and to which she has remained loyal. While her great subject was initially the vicissitudes of the specifically female members of that group, her range has expanded continually to include not just men but individuals from very different social groups facing professional, ethical, political, and spiritual dilemmas on a broad front. She cannot fail to be regarded as a central chronicler of bourgeois British life in the latter half of the twentieth century.

CRITICAL FRAMEWORKS

THERE are two main strands to the critical reception of Drabble's work. Her early identification as "the novelist of maternity" has ensured continuing attention from feminist critics but she has also been caught up in debates, especially heated in Britain, about the viability of the naturalistic tradition in fiction. Initially dismissed by the advocates of modernism and postmodernism as a mere realist, her work is now being reread with an eye to its playful and self-conscious subversion of narrative authority. After being discovered to be more than a feminist, a condition-of-England novelist, Drabble is being rediscovered again as modestly postmodernist.

The first substantial body of criticism of Drabble's work was produced by American and Canadian feminists in the late 1970s and early 1980s and emphasized Drabble's exploration of the dilemmas of women in a patriarchal society. At Cambridge, Drabble read and was deeply affected by Simone de Beauvoir's *The Second Sex*, a classic analysis of the relegation of women to the subordinate position of "the other" in European society, an account that explains their difficulty in achieving as full and autonomous a sense of selfhood as men. Although her early novels make no explicit reference to such a feminist perspective, critics such as Ellen Cronan Rose have argued that Drabble's novels explore in a practical way precisely the dilemmas presented by de Beauvoir, as the heroines attempt to find a way of negotiating the competing demands of sexual and professional identity. For Drabble's early heroines, the answer appears to be that their sense of inauthenticity is overcome by a commitment to others, especially their children: career is secondary, deferred, or sacrificed. For Rose the "conser-

vatism" of this position is a serious limitation in Drabble's work and she concludes her 1980 study of Drabble by urging her to provide more positive feminist blueprints for women in her future writing (p. 129). Rose's disappointment with the "cautiousness" of Drabble's early fictional solutions to the problems of women was shared by a number of other North American critics. Such criticism was muted to some extent by the creation of Frances Wingate, the heroine of *The Realms of Gold* and something of a fictional "golden girl"; critics remarked approvingly not only on the character's strength of personality and success at managing career, family, and erotic love, but on the complex uterine imagery and the invocation of the specifically feminine myth of Demeter and Persephone.

A strong degree of identification with Drabble, including the explicit assumption that she writes as a feminist, is noticeable in much of the early criticism of her writing, thus perhaps licensing the exhortations that she offer strong fictional role-models. Drabble, who began publishing the same year that Betty Freidan's *The Feminine Mystique* (1963) appeared, emerged as a novelist who successfully dramatized the difficulties of women's lives at the same time that the women's movement was beginning to analyze those problems politically. It is hardly surprising that her writing was of such interest to feminists, especially in the 1970s, as the movement became influential in academic institutions; just the same, it is important to bear in mind Drabble's own emphasis that she does not write as a feminist but as a writer who happens to be a woman. This suggests that Drabble intends her novels to be read as descriptive of the difficulties of women's lives but not as advocacy or protest.

More recent accounts, less concerned with the explicitly political implications of the novels and influenced by the translation and wide circulation of French feminist writers like Hélène Cixous, Luce Irigaray, and Julia Kristeva in the 1980s, are more alert to the moral and stylistic complexities of Drabble's texts. Her early novels are now seen as exploratory, symptomatically ambivalent, and unresolved treatments of women whose apparent intelligence, privilege, and attractiveness cannot disguise the fragility of their sense of self and autonomy. The unreliability of the first-person narrators, the defensiveness of their accounts of themselves, and the unwillingness of the author to resolve the uncertainty generated by her early novels were acclaimed as a characteristically feminine "double-voicing" of female experience (Creighton, 1985, p. 32). The most recent feminist criticism of Drabble's work has tended to be comparative, examining her writing in relation to that of British predecessors such as Doris Lessing and to North American contemporaries such as Canadian writer Margaret Atwood. The treatment of maternity continues to be an important topic, but critics tend to focus more on such stylistic questions as how motherhood is narrated or voiced in the novels rather than assessing the ethical rectitude of the heroines' life choices.

The other major strand of Drabble criticism needs to be understood in the context of debates over the development of the novel form, especially as they occurred in Britain. The first monograph on Drabble's work, *Margaret Drabble: Puritanism and Permissiveness* by Valerie Grosvenor Myer, appeared in 1974 and placed her firmly within the "Puritan" tradition of "conscientious striving" and self-improvement that sat uneasily alongside an equally deep-seated egalitarianism (Myers, 1974, p. 29). The religious background for these beliefs was nonconformist Protestantism, such as the Methodism of Drabble's maternal ancestors, the Bloors, and the Quakerism of her school, The Mount. The political inheritance was that of the labor movement and Fabian socialism, meliorist rather than revolutionary. Named for Fabius Cunctator, a Roman general famous for his reluctance to engage the enemy, the Fabians were late-nineteenth- and early-twentieth-century socialists active in promoting reform at a very gradual pace. Their ranks included George Bernard Shaw and Sidney and Beatrice Webb. Drabble's loyalty to that tradition can be seen in the text of a lecture she delivered at the Fabian Society in 1988, "The Case for Equality." The literary implications are equally striking. Drabble has frequently emphasized her commitment to what F. R. Leavis called "the Great Tradition" (a list that included only Jane Austen, George Eliot, Henry James, Joseph Conrad, and D. H. Lawrence) because she believes passionately in the moral seriousness of writing. She values both the popular accessibility of realist novels and their capacity for encouraging ethical reflection on one's own individual and communal circumstances; thus, the formal experimentation characteristic of so much modernist and postmodernist writing seemed to her irrelevant.

Drabble's position here was one she shared with a number of other British writers of the 1950s and 1960s, who reacted against modernism in fiction because they associated it with the class-bound Bloomsbury Group. According to this view, an interest in exploring the formal possibilities of literature was much less important than using its expressive possibilities to reflect individual and social life in concrete terms. This conflict goes back to the 1920s, when authors like Arnold Bennett, one of Drabble's heroes, was a prime object of attack by modernists like Woolf. Arguing half a century later on the Woolfian side of the fence, Bernard Bergonzi claimed in *The Situation of the Novel* (1970) that contemporary British fiction was becoming moribund because it drew too heavily on the realistic tradition embodied by Bennett and eschewed the formal experimentation that would enable it to engage with the complexities of modern life. Bergonzi's position has been echoed by critics of Drabble's work, such as Morton Levitt (1982), who regard her allegiance to, and partial imitation of, Victorian novelists like Anthony Trollope as a serious weakness.

But just as Drabble herself has come to admire Virginia Woolf's symbolist prose (if not, perhaps, that of those other modernists, James Joyce and Dorothy Richardson), so too the decades-long divide between realists and modernists appears to be diminishing. In part, the sense that the modernist-realist division is fragmenting is because crucial writers generally considered to belong to the former tradition, such as Doris Lessing, are being reread with an eye to the way in which their work actually incorporates innovations in narration generally regarded as "modernist." Drabble's work similarly reveals a more complex relation to narrative form than was earlier realized. One aspect of her novels that has been explored is the "feminine" openness of their conclusions, which so often use the birth of a child and the onset of parenthood as an ending. Another is the increasingly self-reflexive nature of her narrative voice, which frequently comments on the arbitrary and artificial nature of fictional process. Her novels no longer follow a linear progress, organized by the spurious unity of a single voice, but rely heavily on a narratorial willingness to layer flashbacks and glimpses forward into the story. The prominence of symbolism is also evident in Drabble's novels, the richness of her treatment of domestic environments, and aspects of the natural world in her representation of character and situation. Even Drabble's allegiance to literary tradition is being reconfigured. Her 1980 novel, *The Middle Ground*, is a kind of rewriting or affectionate parody of Woolf's *Mrs Dalloway*. Drabble's book shares an open-endedness with its predecessor as well as certain similarities in structure and situation: the life of a relatively privileged woman in middle-age is recorded and explored; but in a sense, the most interesting aspect of the gesture of allusion is the implied act of affiliation. Many of the great modernists, including Joyce himself in his comic redaction of Homer's *Odyssey*, define their own modernity, and their difference from their predecessors, precisely through such acts of homage, claiming identity and difference simultaneously. Without jettisoning her longstanding loyalty to one set of literary ancestors, Drabble has proclaimed her discovery of, and indebtedness to, another.

Margaret Drabble's novels are central to two of the most important literary developments of our period. Along with Doris Lessing, she has done more than any other postwar British novelist to articulate the conflicts that have accompanied middle-class women's accession to an unprecedented degree of personal and professional liberty. Although she shares with Muriel Spark an acute eye for social absurdity and has a seriousness of purpose much like Iris Murdoch's, Drabble has a capacity to convey the emotional and physical experiences specific to women with an intensity these writers lack. However much she widens her canvas and varies her scene, her most compelling and convincing characters are those women whose life stages and choices reflect her own. But her female characters are compelling precisely because they are defined by so much more than gender; Drabble continually registers the importance of class, region, nationality, religious affiliation, and education in forming personality and shaping social life, politics, and history. Her novels reveal, in fact, a strong degree of determinism, expressed in secular social and biological registers but recalling the Protestant belief in Providence. Thus her characters—and her narrators—can be seen as late players in the great, ongoing drama of Christian humanism, individuals buffeted by conflicting impulses and desires who struggle to discover a proper self and role in a world not of their making.

Like those of her British and American peers—

Angus Wilson, Anthony Burgess, Saul Bellow, and Mary McCarthy—Drabble's novels do belong to a broader humanist tradition that is often the object of postmodernist scepticism and hostility. But her novels are no longer dismissed as naive, clinging to an outmoded epistemology and technique. Both thematically and stylistically, her fiction provides a sensitive index of the cultural and social sea-changes of late-twentieth-century Britain, registering the decline of imperial power, the collapse of the welfarist consensus, the rise of a mass urban culture, and the demoralization of the bourgeoisie; it does so in narratives that emphasize the power of accident rather than design and the fragmentary opacity of individual selves.

EARLY NOVELS

DRABBLE'S novels fall into three groups, with *The Needle's Eye*, published in 1972, marking a second stage of development and *The Radiant Way* (1987) inaugurating a third. The books that established her reputation were the five novels she published in the 1960s about young women just beginning adult life. These were first-person narratives recording the dilemmas of a relatively new social type—female graduates who were expected to do something more than marry and bear children—and it is these novels that have led to her characterization as a "woman's writer." Their dilemmas are also, however, bound up with social changes on a broad front; Drabble's first book was published the same year that the defeat of the attempt to prosecute D. H. Lawrence's *Lady Chatterley's Lover* for obscenity marked the beginning of the "Swinging Sixties." While many of Drabble's narratives can be read as female variants on the classic nineteenth-century bildungsroman, in which the hero abandons his provincial roots to seek fame and fortune in the metropolis, they also reflect the radical questioning of traditional life-styles and forms of institutional authority characteristic of the 1960s. Thus her novels, whose protagonists include "dropouts" like Rose Vassiliou, have affiliations with hippie culture as well as feminism and the English Puritan tradition of radical dissent.

A Summer Bird-Cage, Drabble's first novel, was published in 1963. The title alludes to a play by Jacobean playwright John Webster called *The White*

Devil and can be read both as a symbol of female identity, the self trapped within a cage, and as an image of the protagonist's ambivalence about marriage, represented throughout the novel both as prison and secure, if somewhat stifling, haven. The heroine, the scenario, and the style of the novel all prefigure those to follow. Sarah Bennett is the lively, intelligent protagonist, a figure whose surname and situation, unmarried and measuring herself against a sister in comparable circumstances, recall Lizzie Bennet from Jane Austen's *Pride and Prejudice*. Sarah has come down from Oxford with an excellent degree but, while interested in literature, makes no attempt to get a serious job, settling instead for a minor clerical position with the BBC. She shares a flat with a friend from Cambridge named Gill, whose marriage to her boyfriend from the university has rapidly collapsed. The two friends find it difficult to live together: Sarah remarks, "Girls shouldn't share flats, but who else can they share them with?" (p. 99).[1] Apart from a few desultory encounters at parties and the belated revelation that she has a lover studying for a year in America, not much happens to the heroine herself. As is the case in many of Drabble's later novels, the narrative is not so much concerned with unfolding a plot as with presenting variations on the central theme of educated women's problems in deciding how to pursue their lives.

The chief alternative to the stasis that constitutes Sarah's choice and the main source of the action is her sister Louise's decision to make a loveless marriage to a well-known, wealthy but rather chilly novelist named Stephan Halifax. The rapid unravelling of the relationship, witnessed by Sarah, provides an object lesson in the dangers of marrying for money, as Louise realizes that her husband, whom she suspects is homosexual, regards her as a possession. Louise's escape from the marriage, into the conveniently open arms of her lover John, recalls the great nineteenth-century novelistic theme of adultery, but unlike *Anna Karenina* or *Madame Bovary*, the novel's conclusion is comic. Louise's recognition of her error and her dependence on Sarah in resolving the situation not only confirm Sarah in her commitment to her distant lover but

serve to reconcile the two sisters, whose own conflicted relationship mirrors the troubled nature of female bonds we see elsewhere in the story. Louise's actions and Sarah's witness bring the sisters to a point where they are able to recognize the similarities of their qualities and their values. The fates of the characters are not resolved but their moral perspectives have been clarified. As Sarah remarks at the end about her sister and herself: "To force a unity from a quarrel, a high continuum from a series of defeats and petty disasters, to live on the level of the heart rather than the level of the slipping petticoat, this is what we spend our life on, and this is what wears us out" (p. 206).

Much of the rest of the novel explores the question of the decision to marry made by Louise. Sarah herself has rejected a serious career, thinking that academic work and erotic identity for women are incompatible—"You can't be a sexy don" (p. 183)—and those of her acquaintance who do have vocations, like her cousin Daphne, a teacher, and an old school friend who becomes a probation officer, are unattractive and pitiable. A resolutely celibate friend she met abroad named Simone has a gloomy glamour but with "her dark face and her muddled heritage, her sexless passions and her ancient clothes" (p. 70) she is characterized as "Tragic Simone, cut after an unlivable pattern" (p. 70). But while sexual love and female attractiveness are highly valued, the women who have pursued their sexual destiny most speedily seem to do little better than the unattached. Gill's marriage collapses through a shortage of money into squalor, and in underlining the dangers of marrying for love without money, Louise recounts a parallel tale of her friend Stella's descent into a nightmare of babies and poverty after an early marriage. The one image of bourgeois comfort and affection we are shown, in the marriage of Stephanie and Michael, is rejected as overly cozy.

A Summer Bird-Cage ends with the two alienated sisters reconciled but without a conclusion to the problems of female identity proposed. The contradictions inherent in the social demands made of women—that they be well-educated, intelligent, and "high-powered" but not serious in their career aspirations, keeping their finely-honed sensibilities for erotic love—are fully on display in this novel. The confusions of the central character and her inability to do more than decide on an utterly conventional ending to her own story (by marrying her

---

[1] All quotations from Margaret Drabble's works are from the British first editions. Page references given throughout are from those editions.

fiancé in America) simply bear out the intractability of such social pressures. It would be a decade before Drabble, writing in a social climate changed by the women's movement, would envisage less predictable female fates.

The Garrick Year presents a heroine as lively as Sarah but considerably more ironic and already, at twenty-four or so, world-weary. The heroine, Emma, moves with great reluctance to the provincial town of Hereford, where her husband, David, has been contracted to work as an actor for a season. Emma's reluctance to leave London stems not just from her metropolitan distaste for the country but from her frustration at having to sacrifice the offer of a prestigious and well-paid job as a newsreader. This classic female conflict between career and marriage is resolved by Emma's conviction that if she and her husband were to live apart, the marriage would collapse. Her account of the seven months spent in Hereford, which include her own half-hearted, barely consummated affair with her husband's director, Wyndham, and her belated realization of David's infidelity, provide the solution to the reader's bewilderment over Emma's desire to retain what is represented to us as a highly problematic relationship. The novel ends with Emma rescuing her daughter Flora from drowning in the River Wye and then being hospitalized after Wyndham accidentally backs his car into her. Emma's forced convalescence, reminiscent of the illnesses that serve as rites of purification in Victorian novels like *Jane Eyre*, enables her to recognize that her commitment to her marriage stems from the strength of her maternal feelings and the importance of the parental role during infancy.

As is the case with the eponymous heroine of Jane Austen's novel, Emma is a character who provokes widely differing reactions, from annoyance at her flippant arrogance to sympathetic identification with her difficulties in trying to maintain an identity separate from her roles as wife and mother. Emma has been called "masochistic and self-destructive" (Creighton, 1985, p. 48), frigid and emotionally remote, neurotically trying to control her life through a perfectionist domesticity. But this kind of moral disapprobation suggests the novel is judging, rather than exploring the tragedy of women's "reduction to the maternal function." *The Garrick Year* examines the implications of the social and biological imperative that women become mothers and suggests that the corollary of that position is

the danger of losing erotic, social, and economic identity. Emma remarks that her lover, Wyndham, did not notice her the first time they met because she was pregnant and later, Sophy Brent, a beautiful but untalented and unintelligent actress who has an affair with David, dismisses Emma because she is a nursing mother. Subsumed by maternity, she is regarded as sexually and socially negligible.

Emma's attempts to maintain a sense of self that extends beyond her maternal role include not just adultery but those classic, culturally sanctioned modes of female self-expression, dress and interior decoration. Her taste reflects the upper-bohemianism of her background, relishing the antique, however shabby, and despising the shoddy smartness of new, mass-produced goods. Her personal style, also incorporating junk-shop finds and rejecting conventional smartness, similarly reflects Emma's ironic ability to exploit her own imposing (but misleading) gravity of appearance. The novel contains significant disputes over and tributes to Emma's taste; she insists, in the face of her husband's objections, on taking an inconvenient but ancient apartment in the old part of Hereford rather than a modern bungalow, and she receives a variety of plaudits in praise of her unconventional but striking attire. The exercise of taste is clearly a crucial means of self-assertion, which enables Emma to treat the domestic space that might otherwise be a prison as a site of creativity, and as a means of signaling erotic and personal power in social environments where she might otherwise be marginal. Although she makes no bones about her own attraction to "gloss" for its own sake, the novel reminds us that Emma's skill at self-presentation also has economic implications: it enables her pursuit of her previous and potential professions as model or newsreader.

The primary project of self-assertion she pursues is, however, adultery, though not with much success. Emma's own intermittent sense of the absurdity of her infatuation with Wyndham, along with the almost complete failure to consummate the affair, renders the involvement parodic. She comments on her sense of the schoolgirl quality of her feeling—"I feel about you as I used to feel about the first boy I was ever in love with" (p. 131)—an analysis underscored by a hilarious scene in which she is seen at dinner with her lover by an old school friend while wearing her old gym slip (a tunic worn as a school uniform). The parodic quality of the relation also informs the episode in which actual sexual intercourse seems most likely, when Emma and Wyndham make a clandestine visit to his aunt's beautiful old Georgian house. The scene recalls both Eve's temptation in the Garden of Eden, as Emma is first enchanted and then frightened by the house and garden, falling over a "wet and rotten apple," and also those scenes in Austen's novels where young women view (and are seduced by) the imposing estates of their suitors. Invoking but gently and comically revising these models, Drabble suggests that the power of fundamental religious and romantic myths is no longer as absolute as it once was; just as the modern Eve is restrained by her sense of maternal responsibility, so the Satanic seducer/rake is no longer the proprietor of a large estate, secure in his local omnipotence. Both men and women are caught up in a world of limits.

Emma is very much at the center of her own story, so that the figures arranged as counterpoints are relatively few and undeveloped. Sophy Brent is a woman with an overt sexual allure and erotic appetite that stands in contrast to Emma's physical refinement and repression, while her old school friend, Mary Scott, is a model of middle-class propriety and responsibility. The paucity and relative thinness of these other female characters reflect the fact that, as the reader appreciates early (but the heroine has to wait to discover), Emma is not only a strong, substantial, even "frightening" personality but is at the center of her own self-created social nexus, the Evans family. The figure with whom she compares herself explicitly, a young closeted homosexual colleague of her husband's who throws himself in the River Wye, seems by the end to stand in the strongest possible contrast to the heroine. But his suicide by drowning, a classic symbol of female self-immolation, is a reminder of the dangers women face and of Emma's triumph in surmounting them. Her own summary captures precisely the sense of triumph in the face of apparent defeat: "I used to be like Julian myself, but now I have two children and you will not find me at the bottom of any river" (p. 170).

Drabble's next novel, *The Millstone*, develops the theme of an apparently limiting but effectually redemptive maternity further. The heroine, Rosamund, shares the intelligence and attractiveness of Sarah and Emma but unlike them, she has committed herself to a career as an academic and her ambition, moderate though it is, shapes her life. Her material circumstances are comfortable because her high-minded liberal parents have left her in possession of a large, well-furnished flat in an expensive part of London, thus obviating the more trying experiences of lodging faced by ingenues like Sarah Bennett. Rosamund has a guilty secret, however; frightened or simply incurious about sex, she has avoided losing her virginity. She is conscious that in the liberated 1960s, this was no longer regarded as normal behavior and she does crave companionship, so cleverly has arranged for two male friends, Joe and Roger, to function as escorts, with each convinced that she is sleeping with the other. The system works perfectly until one night, almost by accident, she has sex with a rather camp friend named George and finds herself pregnant. After a comically ineffectual attempt at inducing an abortion with gin and a hot bath, she resolves to bear and raise the child, aided to some degree by her friend Lydia, who moves into the flat and proceeds not just to help out domestically but to write a novel about Rosamund's pregnancy. The experience of pregnancy and motherhood gives Rosamund a much stronger sense of connection to other people and develops her capacity for love in an unprecedented way but not sufficiently to enable her to tell George of his paternity. The novel thus concludes with Rosamund having made the first real human commitment of her life and having become more capable of self-analysis than she had been but still apparently incapable of establishing an adult heterosexual bond.

Rosamund's own interpretation of her experiences takes a positive form not unlike Emma Evans'. Emma announces at the conclusion of *The Garrick Year*: "I have grown into the earth, I am terrestrial" (p. 170) and connects her own capacity to survive with her mature appreciation of the truth of Wordsworth's poems of rural suffering. Similarly, Rosamund says that "like Job, I had been threatened with the worst, and like Job, I had survived. I knew something now of the quality of life, and anything in the way of happiness I should hereafter receive would be based on fact and not on hope" (*The Millstone*, p. 142). Rosamund's assertion of a new maturity has been treated with considerable skepticism by critics, however, who tend to see her own sense of development as fallacious, arguing that her refusal of adult sexuality remains a serious problem. This dissatisfaction with Rosamund's progress has spurred critics to emulate the heroine's own musings on her parents' shortcomings by suggesting their parenting policy of tolerant disengagement was responsible for her apparent frigidity. In this account, Rosamund's passionate attachment to her daughter serves as a substitute for the relationship of unconditional love she never enjoyed with her own parents.

Rosamund's parents are not presented as in any way deliberately culpable, however: the virtues and limitations of their social and emotional style are provided with a genealogy that sounds remarkably like that of Drabble's own. Early on in the novel, she describes them to George: "I recounted in some detail their extraordinary blend of socialist principle and middle-class scruple, the way they had carried the more painful characteristics of their nonconformist inheritance into their own political and moral attitudes" (p. 27). Rosamund has concluded that her parents' liberal educational principles have not only been unsuccessful in theory and practice but speculates that they may have been wrong in principle: "From another point of view, a more warm and fleshly point, they are perhaps as dangerous and cruel as that father in Washington Square" (p. 145). This grim comparison to Henry James's cruel Dr. Sloper suggests that her parents' generalized benevolence is linked to an emotionally crippling reticence.

As is the case with all Drabble's early heroines, however, the reader is encouraged by the evident partiality of the narrator's perspective to remain skeptical. Rosamund's virtues, including the generosity she shows the perfidious Lydia and the responsible management of her maternity, are qualities she has inherited. This novel goes further than its predecessors in exploring a determinist perspective on personality and life-choices. Unlike the previous heroines, Rosamund is almost entirely "free" in external terms; unencumbered by emotional or parental ties or responsibilities, brought up by a feminist mother, happily focused on a career, well-housed and equipped with a community of like-minded friends, she is limited only by her own neuroses. Ironically, therefore, this novel of single motherhood is not particularly susceptible to a feminist reading—Drabble has deliberately removed the usual obstacles to female self-fulfillment and concentrates instead on the structural effects of family and class in shaping identity. This produces a radical ambiguity in attempts to assess the novel's ethical implications. Rosamund's biological destiny has been fulfilled and in that surrender to the body she has, paradoxically, felt herself mature emotionally and morally to feel a stronger and broader sense of human connection than ever before. But as she is reluctantly but thoroughly aware, it is the privilege and the conduct of her class and her family, about whom she feels such ambivalence, that protect her and her daughter from the harsher consequences of her maternity. The novel thus avoids presenting characters who represent an obvious alternative to Rosamund's choices and situation: instead, she is shown in grim institutional environments where only the giant fact of maternity links highly disparate women. Here, her distinction is not established through beauty, intelligence, taste, or moral sensibility but by her willingness to mobilize her class privilege on her daughter's behalf, as she screams until allowed entrance to her Octavia's ward and works out how to jump the queue in the doctor's office. Rosamund's personal conflicts, rather than dramatizing the difficulties faced by women as opposed to men, allow for the exploration of the way the same difficulties are experienced by different women in a class-bound society.

Jerusalem the Golden appeared in 1967 and marks another departure in Drabble's development. In this novel she uses a third-person narrator for the first time and moves away from specifically feminine themes, to take up the issue of social mobility. Drabble presents the career of an ambitious, lower-middle-class girl desperate to escape from the stifling provinciality of her northern home. Nineteenth-century models for the novel include William Thackeray's *Vanity Fair* and Honoré de Balzac's *Père Goriot*; Bennett's *Hilda Lessways* (1911) was also an influential model; novels with a similar theme published by contemporaries include Doris Lessing's Martha Quest series and John Braine's *Room at the Top* (1957). The kind of passage Clara Maugham makes in this novel, from grim, industrial "Northam" to upper-middle-class bohemianism in London, partially reflects the experience of Drabble's own family.

The novel charts the career of pretty, intelligent, determined, and somewhat unscrupulous Clara Maugham, and it describes the petty meanness and repression of an upbringing by a mother obsessed with maintaining a factitious respectability. Clara has intimations of a richer, warmer, more "golden" world through literature and realizes that her escape into such a world will be dependent on her intellectual capabilities. As she matures physically, she also realizes her looks will be valuable in her relationships with a series of schoolboys she learns to manipulate by her sexuality. A school trip to Paris confirms her sense that life beyond Northam is much more satisfying, and she moves to London to study at university. There, in her final year, she meets Clelia Denham, who comes from an affluent, cultured family that embodies everything Clara had dreamed of as an alternative to her own. She learns lessons in taste, discovering the virtues of the antique, and in her affair with Gabriel Denham, Clelia's brother, she expects to learn lessons in love. But the course of the affair suggests that while Clara has considerable sexual power, she has no real capacity to love: "she had lacked those private, expensive lessons" (p. 167). Her relationship with Gabriel, like that with a previous boyfriend discarded when she had learned as much as she could from him, is an instrumental one. The novel concludes on an ambiguous note: Clara has been summoned home from a clandestine holiday in Paris with the married Gabriel to visit her mother, newly diagnosed as terminally ill. Mrs. Maugham's illness suggests Northam may finally draw Clara back but instead her impending death serves as the final severance. Gabriel plans to collect Clara and drive her home as Clara imagines glorious "years of future tender intrigue" (p. 205).

The novel is thoroughly ambiguous in tone; it renders any final judgment on the central character problematic. Clara's social success, which demonstrates an admirable vitality and ability to survive that Drabble apparently applauds in characters like Emma Evans and Rosamund, seems to be tied to an unlovely, self-centered ruthlessness. But that ruthlessness and lack of generosity is always carefully contextualized, through reference to the meanness with which Clara was raised. The narrator emphasizes that Clara never offers invitations, that Clelia always pays for her, or cooks for her, that she takes rather than gives but even this condemnation is modified. Clara is described as having a deep aversion to entertaining but, we are told, "It was not so much meanness that restrained her as a profound mistrust of her own organization: and also she felt, obscurely, that to invite people into her own room was to condemn them to boredom and unease" (p. 80). The lack of confidence in her powers as host reflects a certain interior barrenness; in striking contrast to the rich complexity of decoration in the

Denham household, Clara's room betrays no trace of individuality or domesticity. Domestic interiors are always indices of character and situation in Drabble's writing, and the emptiness and impersonality of Clara's room reflects her inner sterility and inability to love: "I am all nerve, I am hard, there is no love in me" (p. 165). Again, however, the narrator emphasizes both Clara's painful awareness of these limitations and their root in her dour and unloved childhood.

In this novel, Drabble does not compare individuals so much as families, the Denhams set in contrast to the Maughams. Clara's strategy in escaping to the "terrestrial paradise" represented by the Denhams has been to repress her own family history, but the novel suggests that it is impossible to take on a newly fashioned identity, however admired. The desirable qualities of the Denham children are shown to stem from a family and social environment whose complex history Clara, as an individual, cannot appropriate in the service of her own self-fashioning. Both creativity and love, it is suggested, remain beyond her ken because of their paucity in her Northam upbringing.

The harshness of this conclusion, which probably takes its tone from the naturalistic belief in determinism that pervades Arnold Bennett's writing, is somewhat modified by the conclusion. Clara eventually agrees to allow Gabriel Denham to come to her mother's house and thus to witness her origins. Her recently acquired understanding that her mother once had literary tastes and aspirations that were choked by circumstance suggests that she may be able to construct a usable past from her Northam history and thus a fuller and perhaps more generous self.

The search for and acceptance of personal origins will become a more and more insistent theme, especially in the four novels of middle life Drabble published in the 1970s. But in the last novel of her first phase, she returned to the topic of maternity and sexual love or romance, in a text of considerable formal complexity. *The Waterfall* tells the story of Jane Gray (whose name recalls Jane Eyre, Anne Brontë's novel *Agnes Grey*, and the doomed Queen Lady Jane Grey, executed after a reign of nine days), a woman whose first marriage has collapsed and who is "rescued" from agoraphobia and frigidity by an intense affair with her cousin's husband, James. The affair is discovered by Jane's cousin Lucy (named after Maggie Tulliver's cousin in George

Eliot's *The Mill on the Floss* and also reminiscent of Lucy Snowe of *Villette,* a novel that uses much water imagery) only when a near-fatal car accident prevents the lovers from pursuing a holiday in Norway. The conclusion is characteristically open-ended, with the affair continuing in a desultory manner, with James continuing to live with Lucy, Lucy and Jane quietly reconciled, and Jane apparently cured of some of her neuroses.

The novel's scenario, where an isolated woman revives sexually and emotionally, obviously invokes the fairy tale of a sleeping princess, woken into new life by the kiss of a handsome rescuer. Drabble's interest in exploring the power of such myths of romantic love, especially in relation to that staple of nineteenth-century fiction, adultery, is underscored by the plethora of literary allusions in the novel. The heroine is not only implicitly compared to her namesake Jane Grey but also to Maggie Tulliver and Jane Eyre. Jane emphasizes her differences from Maggie, who broke two suitor's hearts and that of her cousin before killing herself: by contrast, our heroine does not refrain from taking what she wants sexually, does not feel guilty, and most certainly does not kill herself, thus emphasizing the gulf that stretches between Victorian and modern women. Abandonment to illicit sexual pleasure no longer means death, the narrative suggests, although the severity of the car accident suggests there might be dangers. Even in this event, however, Jane is morally unscathed. Again, she compares herself to a fictional heroine, musing that had James been badly maimed, "I would have been allowed to have him, as Jane Eyre had her blinded Rochester" (p. 231) but settling, rather cheerfully it seems, for a partial share.

The dense network of literary allusion, the ethical ambiguity of the action, and the complex double narration of this novel have combined to produce considerable interpretive differences. Feminist readings generally applaud the novel's deliberate reworking of the tragic feminocentric narratives of the nineteenth-century novel to produce an open but fairly happy "feminine ending," but doubts about Jane's apparent amorality, her lack of concern for her children and her cousin, are also expressed. The issue is highlighted by the novel's narrative technique, as Jane's first-person narrative, which tends to present her as a passive victim, only slowly developing a capacity for agency, is often challenged by a third-person nar-

ration that attempts to supplement her self-pitying account. Thus we learn that Jane has not really been abandoned by her husband but that, in a sense, she drove him out, through her emotional and sexual distance. The apparent pathos of her situation as a woman abandoned at the point of maximum vulnerability can be understood as, at least in part, self-willed—and her involvement with James as an attempt to introject her cousin Lucy's more successful, more attractive personality.

Although Jane is by her own account an unreliable narrator, the overall effect of the double, revisionary narrative is not simply to confirm that cliché of postmodern fiction, the inaccessibility of human subjectivity not just to others but to the self. Rather, Jane's story, like that of her literary namesake, is a "progress," in which the reader is gradually persuaded that the story we are being told is more and more grounded in reality. Jane's capacity for self-criticism appears to develop along with her capacity for sexual and emotional commitment and her renewed ability to write poetry. As with other Drabble heroines, the achievement of a certain contentment and personal certainty is accomplished through the establishment of connection with others. What differentiates Jane from Emma and Rosamund is her discovery of human connectedness not through maternity but through erotic love. Like Jane herself, the novel is skeptical about the power of romantic love—it mobilizes literary allusions to debunk the more negative myths of female vulnerability, but for the first time in Drabble's fiction, romance and eroticism are extensively celebrated. The most obvious referent for the waterfall of the title is Goredale Scar, a beauty-spot much celebrated in Romantic verse, at which Jane, climbing up with James, has a brief epiphany, recognizing in the natural scene around her "wildness contained within a bodily limit" (p. 287). This phrase, like the waterfall itself, seems a good characterization of erotic love, the sexual passion that has enabled Jane to break out of her neurotic limitations. Her account of her first orgasm uses a similar metaphor, as she describes herself as "drenched and drowned, down there at last in the water, not high in her lonely place" (p. 150). The usual negative connotations of drowning in relation to sexuality in literature, most obviously figured by Maggie Tulliver's death, are distinctly refuted by Jane's narrative.

The Waterfall is the most subjective of Drabble's

early novels, creating an intense and almost claustrophobic narrative that eschews the amusing social comedy of all her previous novels. Significantly, with the exception of Lucy, the parallel characters, who so often in Drabble's fiction provide an alternative model for the heroine, are here almost exclusively literary, existing only in Jane's head. Even Lucy is almost subsumed by Jane's tendency to figure her as Maggie Tulliver's cousin while James, for all his corporeal virtuosity as a lover, remains a thoroughly shadowy figure, dimly glimpsed only through Jane's feverish infatuation. The physical environments and clothes of the characters carry symbolic weight—Jane is dressed through the early part of the novel in a bloodied nightgown, suggesting her wounded and vulnerable condition—but the specifics of interiors and appearances are uncharacteristically dim. In *A Summer Bird-Cage*, Stephen Halifax's house is described in all its luxurious, chilly menace to signal the likely emotional condition of its owner. We know Jane's house is large and chaotic but very few concrete details fill out this impression as the narration concentrates instead on the minutiae of the heroine's fluctuating moods.

In the novels published after *The Waterfall*, Drabble turns away from the intense subjectivity of its narration and begins to explore the social world presented in *Jerusalem the Golden*. By focusing on romantic love in the former, however, Drabble brought to a conclusion her wide-ranging exploration of the experiences of young middle-class women. Without being overtly feminist, she canvassed all the issues important to a new generation of women offered an unprecedented access to education, career opportunities, and sexual experience. The early novels dramatize the difficulties of finding an identity, resolving conflicts over the competing claims of maternity and marriage, negotiating sexuality, separating from family, and finding a community. The moral and aesthetic complexity of these books is considerable, belying attempts to reduce their exploration of individual (but representative) dilemmas to simple ethical and political judgements. Feminist criticism, which has provided the most serious and intelligent engagement with these novels, has gradually recognized this complexity and begun to examine the other cultural and political pressures, especially those of nonconformist religious dissent, that shaped Drabble's early work. Finally, the formal ingenuity of the novels has been noted and the long-standing assumption that Drabble writes as a naive realist has been displaced by the recognition of her playful manipulation of narrative perspective and thoroughly postmodernist use of parody. Rather than slavishly adhering to "the Great Tradition" to provide minor social commentary, Drabble's early novels engage with the great feminocentric novels of the nineteenth century and revise that tradition through repetition with a difference. Her radicalism is literary as well as political.

THE MIDDLE GROUND *AND OTHER NOVELS*

IT is generally agreed that the publication of *The Needle's Eye* in 1972 marked a breakthrough in Drabble's work. The novel was published during a time of some personal turmoil, the writer separating from her husband the same year, but it initiated the whole next phase of her work. Over the next eight years, Drabble produced a series of novels that chronicled the confusion and drift of a wide band of characters in middle age whose uncertainties figured that of Britain itself in the 1970s. Most of these books pick up the theme of social mobility and alienation first developed in *Jerusalem the Golden*, but they explore its consequences far more thoroughly, tracing the dissolution of family and the creation of alternative communities through metropolitan educational and social institutions and networks. The determinist understanding of life, so important both in Drabble's Christian heritage and in the naturalistic novels of her beloved Arnold Bennett, becomes more prominent, inflecting the narrative voice as well as the management of plot. Drabble's extension of gender and social range, as she includes detailed portraits of male characters and male protagonists, lower-middle-class suburbanites and businessmen, is matched by the pervasive use of a third-person, mostly omniscient narrator. Perhaps the most striking stylistic change is that after her most notable experimentation with a subjective narrative voice in *The Waterfall*, she turned away from the first-person narrator and relied instead on free indirect discourse to record her characters' consciousness. These later novels are also notable for the richness of their symbolism: although their surface is still lucidly realist, complex patterns of imagery become even more marked. Finally, although all the novels Drabble published in this period focus on marital or sexual relations and questions of female identity to some degree, they also mark a shift away from a close-up focus on female experience. To a certain extent they seem to reflect, in fact, the impatience expressed by Kate Armstrong, the heroine of *The Middle Ground*, who announces in the novel's opening scene that she is "bloody sick of bloody women" (p. 3).

The Needle's Eye was one of the most controversial of Drabble's books, provoking widespread criticism from feminists because the novel is concluded by the heroine, Rose Vasiliou, returning to her abusive husband and renouncing her own spiritual pursuit of independence in poverty. The novel is concerned with love and marriage but also with the desire to reshape personal destiny; the modern-day courtly love or platonic romance between liberal lawyer Simon Camish and Rose enables us to compare their very different attempts to escape their family and social origins as well as tracing their respective acceptance of unsatisfactory marital fates. The plot is initiated by Rose's estranged husband, Christopher, who seeks custody of their children. Simon assists Rose as she resists, first, Christopher's legal threats and, then, his physical removal of the children, and he falls in love with her as he does so. Eventually, however, despite the huge personal cost it exacts, Rose decides to return to Christopher, seeing no other way of resolving the ongoing conflict caused by his understandable desire to share the parenting. Emotionally restored by his tender relationship with Rose, Simon accepts the limits of his own marriage more tolerantly and warmly.

While the novel's plot is straightforward, its thematic implications are complex. *The Needle's Eye* can be read as an examination of the difficulties of living a religious life in a secular world: certain imagery connects Rose with Christ and she makes repeated gestures of material and personal renunciation to strengthen this identification. The novel has a plethora of Biblical allusions, not least in the title and Bunyanesque imagery, from both *The Pilgrim's Progress* and *Grace Abounding*; it identifies Rose as a pilgrim in search of the heavenly city. After giving up her considerable inheritance as a young woman, she has established a life of material simplicity in a poor part of London, and although she is a devoted mother, at times she is overcome by the desire to abandon her family life completely and work with the poor in Africa.

Rose's personal trajectory of downward mobility through deliberate impoverishment and an "unsuitable" marriage to "seedy" Greek-descended Christopher mark one attempt to alter the kind of fate apparently decreed by family origins. Simon Camish's more conventional upward path, from a miserable working-class northern childhood, pressed on by a self-sacrificing mother, through grammar school, university, and the Bar to upper-middle-class success, stands in contrast. Unlike Rose, who is deeply attached to her working-class neighborhood and feels her spiritual quest satisfied by the life she has created, Simon is presented as deeply disaffected from his adopted environment, regarding himself as a fraud. A marriage he contracted out of embarrassed pity has produced children with whom he has almost no relation and the satisfaction he feels is produced by his work as a labor lawyer.

The novel's conclusion shows the relative positions of the two characters reversed, with Simon reconciled to the limitations of his life, able through Rose's influence to connect more fruitfully with his wife, children, and friends. Rose, however, resolves the problem of her husband's claims by surrendering her own contented autonomy. The process by which she comes to this decision suggests, however, that there was a meretricious quality to her disavowal of privilege and the simple life she had constructed for herself, a willful denial rather than renunciation of advantage. Christopher's actions at least force her to recognize this. Neither Rose nor Simon achieves perfect happiness, or even contentment, but they do gain greater insight into their circumstances as well as the sense of behaving with integrity.

The story is told by an omniscient narrator and establishes the familiar sets of literary analogues and parallel characters. Apart from the central pairing of Rose and Simon, both of whom have made their own fates but married the wrong partner, Rose is compared both to her unconventional friend Emily and to Simon's wife, Julie. Like Rose, Emily has a clandestine but sexually innocent relationship with a man called Myers that acts as a necessary supplement to a problematic marriage. Like Rose, Julie came from a wealthy background and wanted to live a life different from that which her parents prescribed, having ambitions to be an artist. But her father frustrated these plans and so Julie, again like Rose, sought another life through marriage. But while Rose repudiated wealth and material possessions, Julie acquires them feverishly, in order to assuage her own emotional and spiritual emptiness.

Christopher offers a counterpoint and apparent contrast to Simon, being violent, irresponsible, passionate, and aggressive. But Simon's negative imaginings of Rose's husband receive considerable modification, as he realizes that Christopher is gripped by a passionate intensity not unlike Rose's. The novel emphasizes, in fact, that weakness and accident play a considerable part in the creation of marital relationships and underlines the value of friendship as a realm of human contact mercifully voluntary, lucid, and free in comparison. Of the other marriages presented in the novel, including that of Diana and Nick, who first introduce Simon and Rose, and the various parental figures, only a couple the Camishes meet by chance in a Cornish hotel embody anything approaching real happiness. Establishing marital dissatisfaction as a norm, a loyal stoicism appears to be the only honorable course.

Allusions to Henry James's *The Portrait of a Lady*, *The Wings of the Dove*, and *The Golden Bowl* reiterate the necessity for stoicism; in the first of these novels about the entrapment and betrayal of heiresses, for example, the heroine returns to her wicked husband for the sake of a child. But as is usually the case with Drabble's revisions of classic texts, her reworking emphasizes female agency and happiness. Despite the fact that Rose's forced exile on the Continent destroys her love affair with Christopher, she is unlike James's heroines in that she knows that her relationship with her husband was founded in mutual passion and not based on his guileful greed. Her return to Christopher, suggesting a parallel with Isabel Archer's action, in fact emphasizes that Rose, unlike Isabel, knows the origins of her marriage were honest and that her husband is a good father.

The Needle's Eye presents a world marked by pervasive failures of individual aspiration, whether to spiritual integrity in Rose's case or social usefulness in Simon's, as well as the apparently general breakdown of marriage, the fundamental social institution. And yet the novel is not gloomy or pessimistic. The unconsummated love between Simon and Rose is unconventional by modern standards but its success is indubitable and emphasizes the continuing creative possibilities of human connection. While both Rose and Simon feel frustrated in their aims, the conclusion of the novel sees both of them finally reconciled to their past histories and accepting of their current circumstances. The novel is suffused with an extremely British pragmatism, a strong sense of the virtue of "muddling through." Part of the reason it may have so annoyed its American feminist readers is this English emphasis on the importance of quotidian stoicism rather than revolutionary transformation. In *The Needle's Eye*, goodness is not demonstrated by theatrical gestures of self-assertion or renunciation but by the continual daily effort required to be a good parent, neighbor, or spouse. Most of that effort, unlike the dramatic actions that first made Rose a minor celebrity is simply not visible, not just in the media but in fiction. Drabble's novel thus recalls the attempt George Eliot made in *Middlemarch* to record the moral and spiritual struggles of an extraordinary woman whose circumstances were resolutely ordinary.

While the very title of *The Needle's Eye* suggests the difficulties its characters experience in trying to enter "terrestrial paradise," *The Realms of Gold* echoes the promise inherent in *Jerusalem the Golden*. Frances Wingate is very unlike Rose Vassiliou; she is a "golden girl" and the only one of Drabble's heroines to end up with everything desirable in the form of professional success, maternal fulfillment, and erotic love. The narrative emphasizes the contingent nature of such happiness, but despite the "tricks" employed, the novel's plot is straightforward, following Frances from a bout of depression during a professional visit to Naples, during which she decides on reconciliation with her estranged lover Karel, through the months that follow until the reconciliation is achieved. The delay is caused by a crisis in the Italian postal system, which keeps Frances' message to Karel, inscribed on a postcard, mouldering at the bottom of a sack of undelivered mail. This plot device recalls the tragically mislaid letter in Hardy's *Tess of the D'Urbervilles* but reworks it in a comic key. This period of suspense, which seems to function in part as a punishment to Frances for having arbitrarily broken off the relationship in the first place, forces the heroine to look backward for meaning in her life until she can plan a future with her lover. She explores the family history of her father's lower-middle-class Ollerenshaw relatives from the Midlands and East Anglia and discovers unknown cousins and a great-aunt, whose derelict cottage she purchases, thus establishing continuity with her past and providing a new space for her future domestic life with Karel. Frances' trek through family history, a personal version of her professional work of digging up the past as an archaeologist, provides for the familiar process by which Drabble's heroine's choices, values, and characteristics can be measured against those of a range of others. Many of those other characters are Ollerenshaw family members rather than social peers, and in this novel there is a markedly Darwinian, or socio-biological emphasis, on the causation of different personalities and destinies rather than the moral or even religious framework used previously.

The theme of passages away from and back to social and familial origins and the counterpointing of characters are continuous with the novelist's earlier work. What is striking here is the unusual narrative voice, where the narrator is omniscient and adopts a tone of cheerful familiarity with the reader reminiscent of Henry Fielding or Thackeray. Shattering the realist surface at various points, she anticipates action, announces changes in scene, admonishes the reader, and even calls attention to her own failures in omniscience. As Joan Creighton (1985) points out, this establishes a kind of parallelism between narrator and the rather imperious Frances but also transforms a nineteenth-century literary device into a postmodernist one. The explanatory power of the omniscient author is both deployed and parodied, suggesting that just as the novel points out the limits to the explanatory (and predictive) powers of history, biology, geology, archaeology, and memory, so too there are limits to the writer's control over the "golden world" of her fiction.

Along with the display of a more complex narrative voice and structure, *The Realms of Gold* exhibits a geographical and social scope unprecedented in Drabble's work to this point. The novel shows a heroine in professional contexts, rather than the more familiar domestic and social settings, in places as far-flung as Italy and Africa. But the novel also lingers in an East Anglian suburb, far from the North London precincts where most of her characters reside, and provides a minute account of precisely the path not taken by the protagonists of earlier books. Janet Bird, née Ollerenshaw, is Frances' cousin and serves as the primary negative point of comparison. Her name recalls the title of Drabble's first book and Janet is, in fact, trapped in every way. Married to a man who bullies her, forcing her to unwilling sexual intercourse, she has no economic, professional, or personal autonomy. Her fledgling artistic efforts were stifled by a teacher who told her that her work was too repressed and her attempts at cooking and decoration suffer from the same limitations. Unlike the highly mobile Frances, Janet, accompanied always by her baby, is restricted to the dull town-center of her home. Even maternity, usually a source of redemptive joy for Drabble heroines, is in Janet's case primarily an enormous anxiety.

Janet is only one of a number of Ollerenshaw relatives who exhibit signs of the pervasive depression or "Midlands sickness" that Frances experiences only intermittently. Her father, a successful academic and now the vice chancellor of a new university, is clearly depressive; her brother Hugh, also successful in worldly terms and in his marriage, drinks obsessively; and her cousin, David Ollerenshaw, is a solitary with a death-wish, despite his own considerable professional achievement. The novel suggests that the process by which certain of the Ollerenshaws manage to drag themselves out of the limited circumstances of their birth is partly a matter of genes but also luck and struggle. In the end, however, it is unknowable: the novel stresses that the means by which people search for meaning, whether in history, science, or literature, are various but also that none of them is anything but partial and incomplete. But the desire for knowledge and the theories and fantasies—the "realms of gold"—which people create to satisfy that curiosity, are themselves propulsive and pleasurable. Janet Bird's curiosity is faint in comparison with Frances' but it suffices to propel herself out of her limited circumstances on enough occasions to suggest she will not be entirely smothered by her circumstances.

The novel's themes are developed with unprecedented narrative and structural skill and also through the development of a series of resonant metaphors. The novel is pervaded by uterine imagery: ditches, holes, archaeological digs, and potholed fields whose interiors are sources of life and meaning but also need to be filled. They suggest Frances' past and potential creativity but also her need to learn more of her past and fulfill herself sexually. There is an equally striking series of images connected with bones and teeth, reminders of the Jewish Holocaust, the child sacrifice of the Phoenicians, and the return of all flesh to the earth. While underlining the generally comic tenor of Frances' life, these *memento mori* also place her pursuit of happiness in a larger and more tragic historical and spiritual context, suggesting that her success is to a considerable extent a matter of luck. *The Realms of Gold* concludes with that most traditional of happy endings, paired marriages of true lovers (with one of Karel's and one of Frances' children also marrying each other), but the narrator's tone and the larger symbolic pattern emphasize the contingency of such good outcomes. Drabble's vision will become even darker in the novel that follows.

The Ice Age is a "state-of-the-nation" novel that presents a powerful image of Britain, no longer great but shabby and defeated, in the midst of the deep economic recession of the mid-1970s. Although the frigidity signaled by the title is emblematic of the economic, social, and spiritual morass of the British nation-state, emotional or spiritual stasis also imprisons the representative individuals presented. The novel's narrative technique, crosscutting over a group of characters to heighten parallels and contrasts, is similar to that of *The Realms of Gold*, while the pairing of unlucky lovers recalls *The Needle's Eye*. But this novel, as critics such as Nora Foster Stovel have noted, is unusually and strikingly dependent on an exceptionally rich pattern of symbolism. Almost all the characters are at one time or another either literally or figuratively imprisoned.

The novel's hero is Anthony Keating, who was born to a clerical family, drifted into television journalism, and then became a property developer. As the book begins, the near failure of Anthony's business is an anxiety dimmed only by his brush with mortality in the form of a heart attack. While he recuperates in relative comfort at his beautiful country property, High Rook House, his partner, working-class Len Wincobank, frets in jail and his lover Alison broods over her daughter Jane, who has been imprisoned in Wallachia, an imaginary iron-curtain country, for her involvement in a fatal car crash. In the course of the novel, Anthony takes over responsibility for Molly, Alison's disabled daughter, rescues his financial position, attends his father's funeral, and almost inadvertently becomes a spy for the British Government when he

travels to Wallachia to collect Jane Murray. Caught up in political turmoil, Anthony is imprisoned and begins a spiritual quest whose integrity stands in contrast to the comfortable clerical hypocrisy of his upbringing. Alison's fate is less kind; having sacrificed her career to care for Molly, she is disconcerted to realize that Molly had rapidly transferred her affection to her temporary caretaker, Anthony. Alienated from them both by this development and eventually parted from Anthony for the indefinite future by his imprisonment, she is left alone, trapped by responsibility and with no hope of release. Of the minor characters, the adaptable and decent Maureen Kirby is destined for personal contentment and success in commerce but Len is left defeated in prison, for the time being at least. Linton Hancox, academic and an embodiment of the traditional cultural heritage figured by classical learning, feels himself in crisis, while Kitty Friedmann, whose husband has been killed by an I.R.A. bomb and remains injured herself, is in a state of denial about the appalling and unjust blows she has suffered through political fanaticism.

Anthony's eventual spiritual redemption suggests that there is hope for Britain itself and that the "mangy" British lion may be restored to something like its former glory—perhaps through the agency of his own self-sacrifice. Anthony is the novel's exemplary figure of British manhood and his passage from an anachronistic, even decadent, background through the fashionable but unproductive media professions, to his future-oriented but destructive role as property developer, shadows a crisis in the traditional ruling classes. His role as rescuer and spy seems to redeem him partially, as he assumes the mantles of chivalry and patriotism; his religious quest is a further sign of moral growth. But although he helps her daughters, Jane and Molly, Anthony is unable to rescue Alison, his damsel in distress, the English rose who embodies British womanhood at its loveliest. His first wife, Babs, is a cheerful survivor, whose pleasure in her own fecundity is matched only by her sexual appetency; Maureen, Len's girlfriend, is similarly cheerful, unfaithful and resilient. But Alison, who is haunted by the gradual erosion of her beauty, is intermittently frigid and experiences maternity as entrapment. The sluttish comfort of Babs' ménage, the coziness of Maureen's small flat, and the enveloping warmth of Kitty's household, suggest the power of domesticity to hold a hostile world at bay—but

Alison is excluded from that process. The final words of the novel emphasize her hopeless predicament: "Alison has Molly. Her life is beyond imagining. It will not be imagined. Britain will recover, but not Alison Murray" (p. 295).

The novel tracks British decline and potential renewal through the careers of its characters but also through the symbolism of imprisonment, defacement, and the invocation of powerful literary references. Miltonic, Wordsworthian, and Shakespearian quotations figure England as a powerful nation ready to awake from sleep, immensely beautiful and rich but fallen into selfish, partisan dispute and pettiness. The decline of Britain as a whole is figured both by the assertion the British lion has become "mangy" and "shabby" (p. 96) and in the novel's repeated depiction of degraded urban environments, exemplified by Alison's trek through the wrecked civic center of Northam, which she considers "an environmental offence as bad as a slag heap" (p. 172). But just as Anthony will survive, so too it seems the beautiful Yorkshire valley that served as his retreat and represents Britain at its best, will endure: "He was feeling exceptionally well: country life was suiting him. And it reassured him, that all this landscape had stood up so well to the onslaughts. England. It would never shake to the roots, surely" (p. 175). For all the pessimism of the novel's analysis of the comfortable moral bankruptcy of the middle classes, the wreckage of urban environments through ill-considered and profit-driven development, and the frightening unpredictability of a world no longer subdued by British power, the book displays Drabble's own patriotic belief in the richness of England's natural and cultural legacy and the national capacity to survive with decency and honor.

In *The Middle Ground*, Drabble continues as a chronicler of contemporary Britain but in a less apocalyptic mood. The novel's scale is smaller, as it focuses again on a central female character, journalist Kate Armstrong, and a group of her friends and lovers. Very little actually happens in this book and the static, meditative quality of the narrative, along with the crosscutting between the consciousness of different characters, each dominated by their own preoccupations, suggests a parallel with Virginia Woolf's novels, *Mrs Dalloway* and *To the Lighthouse*. Kate resembles both Mrs. Dalloway and Mrs. Ramsay in that she is at the center of a loving circle of family and friends, and her repeated organiza-

tion of ill-assorted social events recalls their similar impulse to hospitality, with all the hopes of human harmony and pleasure that parties imply.

Much of the novel is spent providing background to the characters' current, common uncertainty in the face of life's "middle ground," middle age. Like Frances Wingate in *The Realms of Gold*, Kate, Evelyn, Ted Stennett, and Evelyn Mainwaring have all achieved professional success and raised children well beyond infancy and feel a certain need to redefine their lives. Like Frances, Kate delves into her own past to try to make sense of the future, for unlike Frances, her renewed pursuit of erotic love has been unsuccessful, forcing Kate to an unwanted abortion and a farcical series of unsuccessful involvements. Her return to and professional exploitation of her own personal history in a television program about her high-school classmates also fails to provide the deep satisfaction afforded Frances Wingate, because Kate has mined her own lower-middle-class origins for journalistic copy all her working life, turning the "shit" of her miserable childhood into media "gold." No project or action provokes Kate's eventual realization of the ongoing possibilities of life in general and her own in particular; it is a domestic epiphany generated by the rich complexity of her own circumstances.

Drabble's avoidance of a central action and her focus on the humdrum details of the characters' domestic lives reflects Woolf's practice but also allows her to emphasize her own participation in a specifically female novelistic tradition. A deliberate contrast is established between Hugo Mainwaring, raised in Asia and at English public schools on a diet of high imperial adventure stories to cultivate a "heroic notion of himself" (p. 155), and Kate, daughter of a sewage worker, ill-educated but well-tested by the school of hard knocks. Hugo's dramatic life as a war correspondent is presented with a rather ironic sense of its potential as exciting narrative, for it is Kate's apparently more quotidian life-history that prevails. The maimed and sexually ambiguous Hugo seems anomalous and even slightly anachronistic in contemporary London, especially when compared to Kate's former lover Ted Stennett, who has made a social ascent similar to her own and bristles with sexual and professional energy. But Ted is no more a hero than Hugo and is clearly the moral and emotional inferior of his wife, Evelyn, born into a high-minded liberal family like Rosamund Stacey's and an exemplar of its characteristic values of service, responsibility, tolerance, and integrity. Like Hugo, social worker Evelyn seems to lack the erotic energy of the arrivistes Ted and Kate, but she is shown to be fully capable of establishing warm relations with her working-class clients of color, putting into practice her belief that no part of the urban community of the city should be seen as exclusive. When she is attacked by one of her clients, her liberal convictions do not waver but are reinforced by her gratitude and respect for the eight-year-old Pakistani girl who was responsible for her rescue.

The changing nature of British urban culture and identity is again a topic in *The Middle Ground*. In this novel there is still a sense of the degeneration of characteristic British values and environments notable in *The Ice Age*, but there is a new emphasis on the changes wrought by Commonwealth immigration, the emergence of ethnic communities, the rise of punk and Rastafarian subcultures, and the broader global context of postimperial politics. Such change is not figured simply as decline but as a challenging complexity, and although one of Kate's ill-starred dinner parties underlines how difficult it is for the adherents of different ideologies to communicate, her own dialogue with her Marxist Iraqi lodger Mujid illustrates the possibility of mutual enlightenment. The party that concludes the novel, at which Kate wears the Iraqi shoes given her by Mujid, does bring together people of differing age, race, and class in a harmonious unity, however temporary.

The melting-pot theme is also developed by the novel's dominant symbol, excrement. In Charles Dickens' *Our Mutual Friend*, sewage symbolized the often invisible but inescapable connectedness of the socially divided world of London. Drabble invokes the image to make a similar point in *The Middle Ground*, but the novel's portrayal of the proliferating rubbish that strews the city streets also underlines the relatively novel human propensity to consume and discard. Ted Stennett's vision of a new global epidemic, spread by the ease of and pace of international travel, is another image of the common dangers facing human beings. Pollution and disease are problems that bind everyone together. In the face of the physical, social, and political mess produced by modernity, it is hardly surprising so many of the characters in this novel appear themselves disabled or decayed. Transcendence of an excremental vision of life is possible,

however, and the climactic violence suffered by Evelyn actually generates new social bonds and energies. Kate's epiphany is domestic as she recognizes that human beings can be connected by love rather than by the lowest common bodily denominators; Hugo picks up his career as a correspondent, a cross-cultural communicator; Evelyn's liberal humanist faith is renewed; and Ted fantasizes an even more gloriously golden future. *The Middle Ground* concludes on a note of modest optimism about individual and communal futures.

Drabble's 1970s novels of midlife crisis provide ever more searching analyses of sexual and familial relations in the context of a confused and troubled society rethinking its past and uncertain of its future. The individual struggles of middle-class women for identity and happiness, resolved in the early novels by maternity or erotic love, are supplemented in the later novels by the exploration of groups of characters, who together illuminate the themes of midlife and middle-class crisis, corruption and dissatisfaction with a society figured as morally and physically degenerate. The increasing social and political breadth of the novels is matched by the development of Drabble's fictional technique, as she begins to exploit the possibilities of omniscient narration and symbolic patterning. Gloomy though her account of the state of the nation may be, her development as a novelist is a story of continual growth, as she not only expanded her thematic range but reworked the narrative strategies of her literary forebears, realist and modernist both.

THE TRILOGY

AFTER publishing *The Middle Ground*, Drabble concentrated on the considerable task of editing the *Oxford Companion to English Literature*. Her next novel did not appear until 1987. The trilogy initiated by *The Radiant Way* is a culmination of her work to date but draws particularly on the novels of midlife that appeared in the 1970s, which recall their social range and reintroduce many of the characters in cameo roles. The trilogy marks a deepening of Drabble's concern with the roots of evil in personal but also political terms, as she includes a serial killer and the mass murderer Pol Pot among her cast. Pol Pot's attempts to eradicate Western influences in Cambodia led to the massacre of thousands of his countrymen and serves as a late-twentieth-century example of the kind of genocidal evil symbolized most potently by the Holocaust. As was the case in *The Realms of Gold*, different modes of explanation for the evils of human history are canvassed but no single adequate explanation appears. Instead of a single heroine, the novels focus on three old friends, whose intertwined lives offer variations on the familiar question of female identity. But Drabble surrounds each of the women with her own web of family, friends, lovers, and enemies and develops male types and dilemmas only sketched in earlier. She also picks up the theme of globalization broached in *The Middle Ground* and extends the action of the novel far beyond the usual confines of London and Yorkshire to the Continent and to Asia. Drabble engages directly with the Kampuchean tragedy and the broader renegotiation of relations between Westerners and the East. The resulting novels together form an enormously rich, sprawling portrait of the English in the world at the end of the twentieth century.

The title of *The Radiant Way* refers to a fictional child's reader that also served as the title for a documentary about the different expectations of children from different classes made by the husband of the heroine when he was still an honestly socialist filmmaker. It serves as a key in the plot by unlocking Liz Headleand's repressed memories of her father's sexual abuse but also figures her final positive apotheosis, as she realizes she has recovered from the trauma of her failed marriage and can face the future hopefully. As a title it seems more than a little ironic, however, for while the novel's three central characters do overcome their respective trials, the overall vision of this book is in many ways bleak.

The novel opens with Liz Headleand preparing for a New Year's Eve party in a state of considerable complacency. Like Clara Maugham of *Jerusalem the Golden*, she has overcome the limitations of her northern background to become well educated and, eventually, a professional and social success. Liz attracts crowds of the culturally and professionally prominent intelligentsia to her house. But the (literally) golden world Liz inhabits is to be shattered that very night by her realization that her husband is going to leave her for an aristocrat who will accompany him to his new position in New York. The rest of the novel shows Liz, herself a psychiatrist, adopting the therapy Frances Wingate found

so helpful, by delving into her own rejected and repressed past. She discovers that her father committed suicide because he was charged with child molesting and realizes that her own masochistic tastes derived from her early experiences with him. Unappalled by these revelations and for the first time united with her sister in the wake of their mother's death, she is finally able to sell the splendid Harley Street mansion she had lived in with Charles and to buy a much smaller villa in St. Johns Wood. This relocation not only signals Liz's recognition that her marriage is over but suggests she has overcome the need to display her success aggressively. She recreates the golden interiors of her former house and discovers that her ability to attract her stepchildren, her friends, and even eventually her ex-husband has not been diminished.

Liz Headleand's difficulties are counterpointed by those of her happily married friend, Alix Bowen. Alix came from a liberal nonconformist background and in many ways exemplifies its values, with her socialist convictions and principled but ill-paid work as a teacher in prison. She is tempted by an extramarital affair, but although her relations with her husband, Brian, are under strain, as he loses his lecturing position and becomes bitterly anti-Thatcherite, she refrains and her marriage recovers with the prospect of a new life in Northam, where Brian gets a new post. She is excited by the prospect of aiding Northam's famous elderly poet in his attempts to collect and order his work, like all her jobs without prospects but at least not "socially useful" (p. 403).

Alix is most intimately connected with the novel's organizing climax, her discovery that a serial killer has decapitated one of her former prisoner-students. This horror, which figures the most incomprehensible form of human irrationality and violence in a novel that refers to a wide range of evils, also touches Esther Breuer, the third member of the long-standing three-cornered friendship dating from Cambridge that provides the most positive model of human relationship in the book. Unlike Liz and Alix, Esther has avoided marriage and maternity, and pursues a range of uncommitted and perhaps unconsummated affairs that culminate in her lengthy liaison with the sinister scholar Claudio Volpe. Although highly regarded as an art historian, she has also avoided publication and survives in a precarious fashion in a small flat underneath that which housed the decapitating serial killer. Esther is prompted to leave her tainted apartment by this revelation but also because her lover Volpe dies and his sister Elena invites her to share her ancient quarters in Rome. The novel thus closes with all three friends facing positive futures.

The comic outcomes for the three friends notwithstanding, *The Radiant Way* presents a bleak picture of Thatcherite Britain. The public realm is darkened by the collapse of idealism, represented in different keys by Charles Headleand, Alix, and Brian Bowen. Headleand has sold his soul to the new ethos of profitability, downsizing, and rationalization, while Alix and Brian find not just their livelihoods but their beliefs threatened by the scaling back of the welfare state. While Alix recognizes some justification for these policies, Brian retreats to a socialist commitment presented as fanatic. Fanaticism's wider reach is figured by the reported death of an old colleague and antagonist of Charles's, a journalist named Dirk Davis, who falls victim to a Near Eastern terrorist group. Fanatic belief is a topic that will be developed at greater length in the next volume of the trilogy: in *The Radiant Way*, the primary emphasis falls on the individual psychosis of the "Harrow Horror," the serial killer who decapitates women. The misogyny that perhaps motivates this latter-day Jack the Ripper is figured again and again in the novel by images of severed heads: that of John the Baptist appears to Esther in a dream but there also are references to the "Gorgon and the Medusa and Gericault and Demigorgon and Salome and the Bessi of Thrace" (p. 347). Such images represent the castrating power of the Medusa, who turned men to stone when they gazed on her snakes-head: in Freudian terms, her head figures the anxiety men experience when confronted with the female genitals. Beheading such castrating women—or depicting them as decapitators—confirms the fearful hatred men feel for women as a sex.

Decapitation is only one form of the symbolism of decay and monstrosity deployed in a novel partially inspired by Zola's *La Bête Humaine* and T. S. Eliot's early poetry of spiritual dissolution. Werewolf imagery is used both to describe the degeneration of Liz and Edgar Lintot's marriage, Claudio Volpe's obsession with witchcraft, and the transformation of apparently innocuous Paul Whitmore into a mass murderer. Esther's visions of severed heads are set beside canals recalling those of Eliot's *The Waste Land*, while Jilly Fox's squat is painted with phantasmagoric, Hieronymus Bosch–like images of severed limbs, to which she has added a cockatrice, a fabulous reptile with the head of a cock and the body of a serpent. Its division prefigures her own decapitation and the masculine vision of women as monstrously divided between rational head and sexualized body. The novel's overall vision has been compared by Nora Foster Stovel (1989) to the Neapolitan paintings studied by Esther, with their detailed representation of a range of horrors hinting at an allegorical worldview that stands in contrast to the cheerful social comedy of certain novels by Bennett or the Victorians. The golden glow of Liz's domestic interiors and the radiance that infuses the three friends' Edenic ramble in the country at the end of the book cannot entirely counterbalance the pervasive symbolism of a finally incomprehensible decay, perversity, and monstrosity. The professional understanding and skills of the three humanists and healers, psychiatrist Liz, teacher Alix, and art historian Esther, are all inadequate in the face of the conundrum presented by the "horror of Harrow Road." The novel closes with the protagonists content but the larger question of evil raised by the novel unresolved.

In *A Natural Curiosity* (1989), Drabble returned to that problem of evil as figured by serial killer Paul Whitmore and the putative political killing of Dirk Davis. The "curiosity" of the title refers both to Alix Bowen's attempts to discover what motivated Whitmore and to Charles Headleand's desire to uncover Davis' fate. In the course of the novel, however, curiosity about the sources of evil shades into the equally pervasive human interest in sexuality. Alix's interest in Whitmore seems to be related to her renunciation of an extramarital affair and Charles's obsession with Davis draws him into an affair with his widow. While Liz Headleand may be construed as a white witch, possessed of hidden, scandalous knowledge by virtue of her psychiatric training, the novel contains another witch figure in the person of Fanny Kettle, promiscuous wife of a noted archaeologist. Fanny holds a party to celebrate her move to Northam and brews a cocktail whose power instigates several love affairs and a death. Under her aegis, Liz Headleand is reunited with her half-sister, an actress named Marcia whose father was one of the aristocratic Latchetts, the family to which Charles Headleand's divorced wife Henrietta belongs.

Alix succeeds to her own satisfaction in her attempt to understand Whitmore's motivation by tracing his parents and discovering that while his father was a mild-mannered and amiable man, his mother was a sadist, whose current objects of torture are not children but dogs. She concludes her own involvement in this project by having Paul's mother, Angela, fined for cruelty to animals, but the solution to the fundamental problem seems simply to have been moved back one generation. Further, the archaeological evidence about the Brigantes who originally inhabited Northam suggests that human sacrifice, including the decapitation that so fascinates Paul, was common among the Celts. Violence, along with sex, remains a human constant and constantly mysterious.

This novel clearly picks up themes as well as characters from its predecessors, but the geographical center of gravity has shifted, from London to Northam. *A Natural Curiosity* pays an unprecedented amount of attention to characters who have not escaped the suburbs of the dour North for a golden future in the metropolis. Drabble does present another variation of the clever girl escaping through education in the person of Shirley's daughter, Celia, but like Clara Maugham, recalled by the similarity in names, she is unlikeably ruthless in the pursuit of freedom. Celia prefers to ignore her mother's disappearance and is as obsessed with ancient history as Whitmore. The narrative pays considerably more attention to Liz's sister, Shirley, who tried to escape the limitations of their mother's house through sex rather than education. (Another character who makes a comparable choice is the bored housewife of Northam lawyer Clive Enderby, Susie, locked in a self-destructive romance with seducer Blake Leith.) Shirley has ended up trapped by her choice, caught in a repetitive and restricted environment and released only by her husband's suicide, which provokes her to flee, ultimately to Paris. There (in the tradition of Bennett and D. H. Lawrence) she enjoys a brief but intense affair with a man named Robert Holland that reaffirms her sense of life's possibility, but it is in her recently discovered sister Marcia's household that she belatedly realizes the diversity of the world beyond suburban Northam. Her destiny is left unexpectedly open to revision, while her daughter, who has tried so determinedly to escape her mother's fate, is self-immured in academic enclosure.

By the time the novel concludes with a sun-drenched lunch in Italy shared by Liz, Alix, and Esther, echoing the final rural repast in *The Radiant Way,* little has been definitively concluded for any of the characters. They dwell on the surprising openness of their lives, which for Esther includes the possibility of marriage to Robert Oxenholme, Minister of Culture and part-time art historian. The novel's very last image is of an elderly female aristocrat sitting in her garden waiting for Oxenholme to arrive with "pleasurable anticipation" (p. 309). This underlines the novel's consistent emphasis on the possibility of belated bloomings and renewals that last even into age. The dark inexplicability of evil is matched by the equally persistent human capacity for change and growth.

The last novel of the trilogy is *The Gates of Ivory*, published in 1991. Here Drabble expands her geographical range even further, locating much of the action in Thailand and Cambodia, dividing the novel between what she calls Good and Bad Time. The tumultuous, violent, and poverty-stricken nation of Cambodia is in "Bad Time," while the West and the increasingly wealthy countries of Asia are in "Good Time." The novel follows the dangerous journey into "Bad Time" made by writer Stephen Cox and photographer Konstantin Vasiliou and tracks Liz Headleand's pursuit of her old friend, crosscutting between Stephen and Konstantin's passage and the gradual reconstruction of their doomed trip back in London.

The novel's theme of enthrallment to destructive fantasy can be deduced from the quotation from Homer that gives the book its title and epigraph. "The dreams that come to us through the traitor ivory deceive us with false images of what will never come to pass." Both political projects, like that of the Khmer Rouge and the romantic quest of an individual like Stephen Cox, are presented as death-dealing dreams, productive of nothing but misery. Pol Pot's ideological fantasy has been engendered by Western radical thought, "a French infection from the Sorbonne" (p. 368), but Stephen's is framed in literary terms. Conrad's novels of violent colonial fantasy, *Chance* and *Victory,* are invoked before Stephen leaves Thailand, and he is also a devotee of the French symbolists, poets fascinated by death and who included among their number Rimbaud, a future colonialist. The journey into Cambodia that Stephen makes with Konstantin recalls the journey upriver in Conrad's *Heart of Darkness.* Instead of the terrible revelation of a European "reversion" to savagery, however, Stephen discovers nothing but kindness until his departure for the clinic at which he meets his death.

The other forms of fantasy canvassed in the novel include Aaron Headleand's dual passions for the theater and for Hattie Osborne, Stephen's agent. Aaron's infatuation for Hattie is based in his childhood fascination with her early cinematic roles, as Hattie herself realizes, "that person made by Aaron, that dream image, that devil's bride, that B movie star, that shop's dummy in a white dress, *that* person is not made of flesh and blood" (p. 316). Aaron and Hattie's relationship is a study in the role of male projection in love but although his feeling is "fantastic"; the emotional and physical effects of this fantasy are the positive ones of pleasure, affection, and pregnancy. Stephen Cox, who is also drawn to Hattie's flamboyance but could not act upon his attraction, is another and more negative study of the same masculine enthrallment to fantasies of the feminine. While his relationship with Liz Headleand never became more than friendly, Stephen *is* seduced by the novel's comic incarnation of exotic sexuality, Miss Porntip, a woman without a shade of sentiment and with considerable skill in the arts of love. Stephen's inability to establish an erotic and emotional relationship unmediated by money seems linked to the death-drive that pushes him on into Cambodia, and the same suspicion of sexual deviance haunts the presentation of Konstantin Vasiliou, a figure whose personal charisma is accompanied by compulsive and near-fatal risk-taking.

Konstantin shares with Aaron Headleand a passion for his work as a creative artist in which the power to manipulate others' imaginations is critical. Both men, one a photographer, the other a theater director, produce images of haunting power. Aaron experiences such control over others' minds as a triumphant sense of domination comparable to sexual pleasure, but Konstantin is more ambivalent about the effects of his work. Generally speaking, the novel tends to affirm the way that art creates and processes dreams, suggesting that theater, photographs, painting, and literature produce or bind fantasies in far more productive ways than political ideology. Stephen Cox's journey toward death is connected with his inability to write, to transform his destructive dreams of absolute justice into fiction. The novel also examines those whose obsessions serve as artistic material; it re-

flects on the way individuals become objectified in the viewer's mind by a single powerful image. Mme. Akrun, subject of one of Konstantin's most affecting photographs, figures in Liz Headleand's imagination as the incarnation of grieving maternity. The narrative (itself another form of representation) amplifies that vision but it also points up its limits. Mme. Akrun gives up her obsessive mourning for the son irretrievably lost in order to tend the son she still has.

Mme. Akrun's maternal grief is the central image of such feeling, but as is typical of the novelist, variations on the theme appear. The saintly Rose Vasiliou from *The Needle's Eye* mourns in isolation, making a final appearance at Stephen's memorial service to be reunited with her lost son Konstantin, risen miraculously from the dead. The careless mother of decapitated Jilly Fox, victim of Paul Whitmore, has escaped the "social disgrace" (p. 343) of a murdered child in California, a place without memory. Angela Whitmore Malkin, mother of Jilly's murderer, is lost in her own vicious fantasies of cruelty and revenge. Human feeling with which our own feelings can engage emerges only out of a welter of images of disavowal and horror.

The novel's structure recalls that of *The Realms of Gold*, as the narrator moves swiftly from Asia to Europe to America, cutting between characters whose paths intersect physically or serve as thematic counterpoints. But the characteristic use of omniscient narration is enriched by the haunting repetition of Conrad's classic story and by the novel's opening to history. Although the book has all the pleasures of a sprawling social comedy that rewards Drabble's old readers with glimpses of such figures as Gabriel Denham, first introduced in *Jerusalem the Golden*, it is darker in tone than any previous novel. This sense of tragedy arises not from the subject per se, although the deliberate pursuit of self-destruction and social chaos presented is inherently appalling. Drabble suggests, after all, that there are zones in "Good Time," where comfort and social cohesion are by and large maintained, the activities of an occasional serial killer notwithstanding. But in this novel, all human activities, including the most productive, such as love and art, are presented as contingent fantasies, the outcome of infantile dreams. This is hardly a surprising thesis, in an age so influenced by Freud and a writer so interested in determinism. But the counterbalance to Drabble's determinism (which has appeared in both Protestant and Darwinist forms) has always been a robust sense of individual agency. The strongest figure in this novel, and the most obvious example of authorial fantasy in the book, is Miss Porntip, a fabulously wealthy, fabulously sexy, and fabulously materialist Oriental seductress. Miss Porntip's characterization is Orientalist to the extent that she is defined by an overwhelming sexuality, but her vitality modifies the stereotype of the Asian woman as a sensual object of desire. Miss Porntip's amoral energy and determination leave the other characters in the shade, suggesting that decent, tired Europe is being displaced by the vitality of a resurgent Asia. Stephen, who functions as the representative Westerner, commits suicide and in so doing, symbolizes just such a failure of the will to survive and prosper that is so marked a feature of Drabble's earlier novels. The recuperative images of community, reunited families, and renewed love that conclude the novel do not lift this shadow.

BIOGRAPHER, CRITIC, EDITOR

DRABBLE'S work as a biographer, critic, and editor is of great interest in terms of the light it casts on her fiction but also noteworthy in itself. Her 1966 study of Wordsworth, directed at the general reader, contains introductory material and readings of the great and minor poems, mostly notable for the breezy and familiar tone of address to the reader. The biography of Arnold Bennett that appeared in 1974 was a more substantial achievement. Without providing much new evidence about Bennett's life, Drabble provides a vivid and interesting commentary on his novels, enlivened by her strong sense of shared identity with her subject. She believes she may be related to the author through her mother and the book may be seen as a claim to literary as well as familial affiliation. Bennett's reputation has been a victim of the rise of modernism and Drabble wrote very much in his defense, emphasizing the value of writing that so vividly conjures up a place, a culture, and the everyday life of its inhabitants. Her next substantial nonfiction publication was *A Writer's Britain: Landscape in Literature* (1979), a volume with photographs by Jorge Lewinski, for which she provided text. This is a remarkably broad-ranging account of English attitudes to the land-

scape, especially as they are recorded in literature, from the Middle Ages through to such recent poets as Dylan Thomas and Sylvia Plath. The book tracks the allegorizing medieval imagination to the spiritualizing Romantic vision, in whose wake we still live, providing close commentary on particular poems as well as overviews. The peculiar importance of gardens, landscape, and nature to the English in general and Drabble in particular, is vividly evoked here.

Drabble's editions are too many to discuss individually but they are notable for the directness of tone and an insistent concern with ethical issues. The moral seriousness so central to Leavisite criticism still informs Drabble's own, although she also incorporates a self-consciously female perspective. Most of her editing work has been on nineteenth-century texts but with the *Oxford Companion to English Literature* the scope was necessarily wider. The frequent reprintings of this volume and the appearance of a concise edition bear witness to Drabble's success in producing an account of literature that is both authoritative and idiomatic.

CONCLUSION

MARGARET Drabble's literary career, whether as critic, biographer, or novelist, is far from over. Already, however, she has produced a body of work of considerable stature, widely read and much reprinted in Britain and America and translated into at least twenty-six languages. Her early fiction, depicting middle-class women's experience, was groundbreaking, but while she has never abandoned a concern for specifically female issues, her novels have expanded in scope enormously. Redefined as a chronicler of the state of the nation and of midlife crisis in the 1970s, Drabble's recent trilogy invites consideration as postcolonial fiction, sensitively recording the seismic shifts in power between Europe and its former colonies. The sophistication of her deft reworking and revision of Victorian and Edwardian realism and naturalism has been recognized as in its own way postmodern, providing a vital model of the way in which the richness of the British literary tradition can be adapted to current needs. With a readership that almost uniquely spans the academy and the reading classes at large, Margaret Drabble's high populism echoes the best achievements of the predecessors she so admires.

SELECTED BIBLIOGRAPHY

I. NOVELS. *A Summer Bird-Cage* (London, 1963; New York, 1964); *The Garrick Year* (London, 1964; New York, 1965); *The Millstone* (London, 1965; New York, 1966), retitled *Thank You All Very Much* (New York, 1969); *Jerusalem the Golden* (London and New York, 1967); *The Waterfall* (London and New York, 1969); *The Needle's Eye* (London and New York, 1972); *The Realms of Gold* (London and New York, 1975); *The Ice Age* (London and New York, 1977); *The Middle Ground* (London and New York, 1980); *The Radiant Way* (London and New York, 1987); *A Natural Curiosity* (London and New York, 1987); *The Gates of Ivory* (London, 1991; New York, 1992).

II. SHORT STORIES. " 'Les Liaisons Dangereuses': Margaret Drabble on the Strategy of Modern Love," in *Punch* 247 (28 October 1964); "Hassan's Tower," in A. D. Maclean, ed., *Winter's Tales* 12 (London, 1966); "A Voyage to Cythera," in *Mademoiselle* 66 (December 1967); "The Reunion," in Kevin Crossley-Holland, ed., *Winter's Tales* 14 (London, 1968); "Faithful Lovers," in *Saturday Evening Post* 241 (6 April 1968); "A Pyrrhic Victory," in *Nova* (July 1968): 80, 84, 86; "Crossing the Alps," in Judith Burnley, ed., *Penguin Modern Stories* 3 (Harmondsworth, Eng., 1969), repr. in *Mademoiselle* (February 1971); "The Gifts of War," in A. D. Maclean, ed., *Winter's Tales* 16 (London, 1970), repr. in Susan Cahill, ed., *Women and Fiction: Short Stories by and About Women* (New York, 1975); "A Day in the Life of a Smiling Woman," in *Cosmopolitan* (August 1973), repr. in Nancy Dean and Myra Stark, eds., *In the Looking Glass: Twenty-One Modern Short Stories by Women* (New York, 1977); "A Success Story," in *Spare Rib*, no. 2 (1972), repr. in *Ms.* (December 1974), repr. in Ruth Sullivan, ed., *Fine Lines: The Best of Ms. Fiction* (New York, 1982); "Homework," in *Ontario Review* 7 (fall/winter, 1977–1978): 7–13.

III. PLAYS. *Laura* (1964), produced by Granada Television, 1964; *Bird of Paradise* (1969), performed in London; *Isadora*, with Melvin Bragg and Clive Exton (1969), screenplay; *A Touch of Love* (1969), screenplay.

IV. NONFICTION AND EDITED TEXTS. *Wordsworth* (London, 1966; New York, 1969); *London Consequences*, ed. with B. S. Johnson (London, 1972), group novel; *Virginia Woolf: A Personal Debt* (N.p., 1973); *Arnold Bennett: A Biography* (London and New York, 1974); ed., *Lady Susan, The Watsons, Sanditon by Jane Austen* (Harmondsworth, Eng., 1974); ed., *The Genius of Thomas Hardy* (London and New York, 1976); *New Stories I*, ed. with Charles Osborne (London, 1976); *For Queen and Country: Britain in the Victorian Age* (London, 1978; New York, 1979); *A Writer's Britain: Landscape in Literature* (London and New York, 1979); Yukako Suga, ed., *The Tradition of Women's Fiction: Lectures in Japan* (Tokyo, 1982); ed., *Oxford Companion to English Literature*, 5th ed. (London, 1985); Introduction, *Villette* by Charlotte Brontë (London, 1985); ed. with Jenny Stringer, *The Concise Oxford Companion to English Literature* (Oxford and New York, 1987); ed. with introduction, *To the Lighthouse* by Virginia Woolf (Oxford and New York, 1992); Introduction, *Wuthering Heights, with Selected Poems by Emily Brontë* (London and Rutland, Vt., 1993); *Angus Wilson: A Biography* (London, 1995).

V. ARTICLES. "The Month," in *Twentieth Century* 168 (1960); "The Sexual Revolution," in *Manchester Guardian Weekly* 12 (October 1967); "Baffled! Margaret Drabble Stalks Uncomprehendingly Round the Mystery of Masculinity," in *Punch* (24 July 1968); "Slipping into Debt," in *The Guardian* (12 August 1968); "Women Novelists," in *Books* 375 (1968); "Money as a Subject for the Novelist," in *Times Literary Supplement* (24 July 1969); "Doris Lessing: Cassandra in a World Under Siege," in *Ramparts* 10, no. 8 (February 1972); "Margaret Drabble on Virginia Woolf," in *Harpers Bazaar and Queen* (September 1972), shortened as "How Not to Be Afraid of Virginia Woolf," in *Ms.* (November 1972); "A Woman Writer," in *Books* 11 (spring 1973), repr. in Michelene Wandor, ed., *On Gender and Writing* (London and Boston, 1983); "The War between Women and Women," in *The Times* (23 July 1973); "The Writer as Recluse: The Theme of Solitude in the Works of the Brontës," *Brontë Society Transactions* 16 (1974); "The Author Comments" on Monica Lauritzen Mannheimer, "The Search for Identity in Margaret Drabble's *The Needle's Eye*," in *Dutch Quarterly Review of Anglo-American Letters* 5, no. 1 (1975); "A Book I Love: Margaret Drabble on the Novels of Angus Wilson," in *Mademoiselle* (August 1975); "Introduction" to *Wuthering Heights*, by Emily Brontë, P. Henderson, ed. (London, 1978); "Are the Social Graces Suspect? Is Art Itself Suspect?" in *The Listener* 10 (July 1980); "'No Idle Rentier': Angus Wilson and the Nourished Literary Imagination," *Studies in the Literary Imagination* 13 (spring 1980); "Gone but Not Quite Forgotten," in *New York Times Book Review* (25 July 1982); "Introduction" to *Not I But the Wind*, by Frieda Lawrence (London, 1983); "J. G. Farrell" in Susan Hill, ed., *People: Essays and Poems* (London, 1983); "Novelists as Inspired Gossips," in *Ms.* (April 1983); "Child Abuse: When a Public Inquiry Isn't Enough," in *Sunday Telegraph* (2 August 1987); "Mimesis: The Representation of Reality in the Post-War Novel," in *MOSAIC* 20 (1987); "Margaret Drabble in Tokyo," in Fumi Takamo Kenkyushu, ed., *Stratford Revisited: A Legacy of the Sixties* (Halford, Shipton-on-Stour, Warwickshire, 1989); "Introduction" to S. Krishnamurti, comp., *Women Writers of the 1890s* (London, 1991).

VI. INTERVIEWS. Bernard Bergonzi, "Novelists of the Sixties," BBC (London, 1968); John Clare, "Margaret Drabble's Everyday Hell," in *The Times* (17 March 1972);

Nancy S. Hardin, "An Interview with Margaret Drabble," *Contemporary Literature* 14, no. 3 (summer 1973); Peter Firchow, "Margaret Drabble," *The Writer's Place: Interviews on the Literary Situation of Contemporary Britain* (Minneapolis, 1974); Nancy Poland, "Margaret Drabble: 'There Must Be a Lot of People Like Me,'" *Midwest Quarterly* 16, no. 3 (spring 1975); Barbara Milton, "Margaret Drabble: The Art of Fiction LXX," in *Paris Review* 20 (fall/winter 1978); Iris Rozencwajg, "Interview with Margaret Drabble," *Women's Studies* 6 (1979); Dee Preussner, "Talking with Margaret Drabble," *Modern Fiction Studies* 25 (winter 1979–1980); Diana Cooper-Clark, "Margaret Drabble: Cautious Feminist," *Atlantic Monthly* 246 (November 1980); Joanne V. Creighton, "An Interview with Margaret Drabble," in Dorey Schmidt, ed., *Margaret Drabble: Golden Realms* (Edinburg, Tex., 1980); Gillian Parker and Janet Todd, "Margaret Drabble," in Janet Todd, ed., *Women Writers Talking* (New York, 1983).

VII. BIBLIOGRAPHIES. Joan S. Korenman, "A Margaret Drabble Bibliography," in Ellen Cronan Rose, ed., *Critical Essays on Margaret Drabble* (Boston, 1985); Gyde-Christine Martin, "Margaret Drabble: A Bibliography," *Bulletin of Bibliography* 45, no. 1 (March 1988); Joan Garrett-Packer, *Margaret Drabble: An Annotated Bibliography* (New York, 1988).

VIII. BIOGRAPHICAL AND CRITICAL STUDIES. Valerie Grosvenor Myer, *Margaret Drabble: Puritanism and Permissiveness* (London and New York, 1974); Ellen Cronan Rose, *The Novels of Margaret Drabble: Equivocal Figures* (London, 1980); Mary Hurley Moran, *Margaret Drabble: Existing Within Structures* (Carbondale, Ill., 1983); Ellen Cronan Rose, ed., *Critical Essays on Margaret Drabble* (Boston, 1985); Susanna Roxman, *Guilt and Glory: Studies in Margaret Drabble's Novels, 1963–1980* (Stockholm, 1984); Joanne V. Creighton, *Margaret Drabble* (London and New York, 1985); John Hannay, *The Intertextuality of Fate: A Study of Margaret Drabble* (Columbia, Mo., 1986); Lynn Veach Sadler, *Margaret Drabble* (Boston, 1986); Dorey Schmidt, ed., *Margaret Drabble: Golden Realms* (Edinburg, Tex., 1982); Nora Foster Stovel, *Margaret Drabble: Symbolic Novelist* (Mercer Island, Wash., 1989); Valerie Grosvenor Myer, *Margaret Drabble: A Reader's Guide* (Chailey, Eng., and New York, 1991).

THOM GUNN
(1929–)

Jonathan Levin

AFTER GAINING IMMEDIATE attention in the 1950s in England as a vigorous young poet adopting tough, willful, and often violent stances in carefully wrought verse forms, Thom Gunn has spent more than four decades exploring in his poetry the many complex and subtle tensions of his life and art: he is British but has lived almost continuously in the United States since the publication of his first volume in 1954; he is a poet of great sensuous responsiveness and rich intelligence; he writes comfortably in both metrical and free verse forms, aspiring sometimes to the polish of the finished artifact, sometimes to the open-endedness of a discovery-in-progress; he avoids the inflated personality, yet is drawn in his poems almost magnetically to the exploration of human feeling; he writes about his homosexuality, and has done so with increasing explicitness since the middle 1970s, but typically regards his sexuality as continuous with the conventions and traditions of English poetry. These tensions make Gunn a difficult poet to categorize, but they also give his poetry an unusual range and depth. Though for many years he wrote in the shadow of his early success, Gunn achieved his greatest prominence with the publication in 1992 of *The Man with Night Sweats*, which has become a classic in the literature of AIDS.

LIFE

THOMSON William Gunn was born on 29 August 1929 in Gravesend, Kent. He moved with his family to Hampstead, a comfortable London suburb, at around the age of eight. His parents divorced not long after the move. In "My Life up to Now," an autobiographical essay reprinted in *The Occasions of Poetry*, Gunn describes his childhood as "happy" (p. 171), despite the challenge of frequent moves,

his parents' divorce, the public and private dislocations of World War II, and his mother's early death. Gunn's father, Herbert Smith Gunn, was a newspaper editor who worked at several different jobs with the Beaverbrook press before becoming editor of the *Daily Sketch*. Gunn has described his father as "a man full of charm who made friends easily" (p. 169) but acknowledges that he never managed to be close to him. He characterizes the relationship as one marked, especially by the time of Gunn's midteens and after, by mutual jealousy and suspicion.

Gunn was close to his mother and became very attached to what he calls the "basic mythology" of her family history. The Thomson family (hence Thomson Gunn) descended on Kent from Echt, a village near Aberdeen. Gunn notes that the Thomsons "venerated education and despised frivolity," and calls them "pacifists, Keir Hardie socialists, and anti-royalists" (p. 170). He describes his mother, born Ann Charlotte Thomson, as an independent woman and a protofeminist. Gunn traces his love of books to his mother and suggests that he learned from her to see books as "not just a commentary on life but a part of its continuing activity" (p. 170). After the death of his mother when he was only fourteen or fifteen, Gunn divided his time between Hampstead, where he lived during the school week, and Snodland, where he lived with his aunts on weekends and school breaks, occasionally helping them to deliver milk. He grew up with one younger brother, Ander (short for Alexander), with whom he would later collaborate on a book of poems and photographs.

Gunn was an avid reader as a child. The first book he read by himself was Louisa May Alcott's *Little Men*, which he remembers for "the character of Dan, the rebellious boy who is out of place among the pieties of Dr. Baer's model school" (pp. 170–171). He read the usual Victorian children's literature, including poems in Arthur Mee's *Children's Encyclopedia* as well as poems by Victorian poets Jean Ingelow and Charles Kingsley. While at the Bedales School in Hampshire, he studied with an "enlightened English teacher" who used W. H. Auden and John Garrett's *The Poet's Tongue* as text. Gunn describes the book as "very different from the *Dragon Book of Verse*, which you got in other schools, and which was all Lord Macaulay and the patriotic speeches from *Henry V*" (p. 153). By this time, Gunn was also reading H. G. Wells and consuming "an enormous number of nineteenth-century novels" (p. 173). In poetry, he was drawn to the "grandiloquence" of Marlowe, Beddoes, Keats, Milton, Tennyson, and Meredith. By the time he went to Cambridge, he was writing poems that he would later characterize as "intensely felt and intensely derivative" (p. 156).

Gunn had just turned ten when the Nazis invaded Poland. After spending much of World War II at a boarding school in Hampshire, safely removed from the German blitz of London, he returned to London, where he eyed "the well-fed and good-looking G.I.s who were on every street, with an appreciation I didn't completely understand" (p. 172). Gunn did his two years of national service in the army; he found the first ten weeks of basic training "at least exuberantly healthy," but merely survived the rest of his service, "largely a matter of boredom, drudgery, and endurance" (p. 172).

After national service and six months in Paris, Gunn entered Trinity College, Cambridge, where he absorbed a great variety of influences. He attended (by his own estimate) all of F. R. Leavis' lectures at Downing College. Leavis was renowned for his inspiring lectures on literature, and Gunn has commented that Leavis' "insistence on the realized, being the life of poetry" and his "going directly to the texture of poetry" went "right to the hearth" of Gunn's own poetic activity (p. 160). Gunn even suggests that Leavis' lectures helped him to deal directly with his own emotions "by reducing their diffusion, by concentrating them" (p. 160). Although he never became anything like a disciple of Leavis (or of anyone, for that matter), Leavis clearly helped shape Gunn's emerging conception of the possibilities of poetry. Gunn's particular affection for English Renaissance verse, evident in his observant essays on Fulke Greville and Ben Jonson, was in part shaped in the atmosphere of Leavis' Cambridge.

Other influences at Cambridge came largely from his peers: Karl Miller, John Coleman, Mark Boxer, Tony White. It was at Cambridge that Gunn met Mike Kitay, an American who would become his lifelong companion. In a letter to Alan Bold that is quoted in Bold's *Thom Gunn and Ted Hughes*, Gunn remarks that he grew up rapidly at Cambridge: "It was very important to me, I was influenced by everybody and everything I came in contact with" (pp. 9–10). Many of his friends went on to prominent careers in literature and the arts; Gunn writes with particular affection of Tony White, who eventually abandoned a career in the theater to become a handyman and translator, giving up "the life of applause" after recognizing "how the need for it complicates one's existence quite unnecessarily" (*Occasions of Poetry*, p. 168). Gunn acknowledges the many intellectual and professional advantages he found in Cambridge, including what he characterizes as the overly generous reception of his first book.

Gunn initially gained prominence by appearing in the autumn of 1952 on John Lehmann's BBC radio program, *New Soundings*, on which he read first "The Secret Sharer" and, a few months later, "Incident on a Journey." In his short tribute to Gunn published in the special "Thom Gunn at 60" issue of *PN Review*, Donald Hall describes the "general flabbergast" with which Gunn's first poems were greeted, especially in Oxford, where Hall was studying: "Oxford recoiled before stanzas militant, intransigent, tough, brainy, swashbuckling and violent" (p. 29). Although Gunn's first collection, *Fighting Terms* (1954), received very small distribution—only 305 copies were printed—his poems appeared in many prominent magazines, beginning in 1952. Gunn's early reputation in England received a considerable boost when a generous selection of his poems appeared in Robert Conquest's widely read anthology *New Lines* (1956). In the mid-1950s many English critics associated Gunn with The Movement, a group that included Philip Larkin, Elizabeth Jennings, D. J. Enright, Donald Davie, and others supposedly dedicated to depicting realistic themes in definite forms. Gunn claims he had never even heard of The Movement until he learned that he was supposedly part of it; the association quickly faded.

In 1954, with one book of poetry to his name, Gunn moved to California, where he accepted a fellowship to study with Yvor Winters. All of the poems that would appear in *The Sense of Movement* (1957) were written during his first year at Stanford. Winters was a difficult but in many ways a generous mentor for Gunn. Despite his firm opposition to what he characterized as intellectual and literary irrationalism, Winters introduced Gunn to poets like William Carlos Williams and Wallace Stevens, thereby initiating Gunn into a distinctively American poetics. Winters provided another important model for Gunn's developing sense of the practice of poetry by serving as someone from whom he could learn but also against whom he could test himself.

After a year in San Antonio, Texas, with Mike Kitay, Gunn returned to Stanford, where he began work toward a Ph.D. in English. He grew bored with this and, after accepting a teaching position at the University of California at Berkeley in 1958, gave it up. Gunn taught at Berkeley until he resigned in 1966, though he returned to teach part-time starting in the late 1970s. After a brief stay in Berlin in 1960, Gunn settled permanently in San Francisco. He published three major volumes in the 1960s: *My Sad Captains* (1961), *Positives* (1966), and *Touch* (1967). In 1962, Gunn's English publisher put out the tremendously successful *Selected Poems,* by Gunn and Ted Hughes. The association with Hughes, bolstered by superficial similarities in their mutual fascination with violence, led many readers to expect, and to find, a convergence of interests between the two poets, a view that often went unchallenged until the appearance of Alan Bold's *Thom Gunn and Ted Hughes* (1976).

San Francisco has been a point of convergence for many forces in American life, as well as in Gunn's life. Since at least the gold rush of 1848, it has attracted all sorts of seekers and experimenters, people intent on discovering new forms of personal and social identity. In the 1960s, its famous intersection of Haight and Ashbury came to epitomize hippie culture and its psychedelic pursuit of peace, love, and understanding. Like many others at the time, Gunn experimented with drugs, and did so avidly; a number of his poems of the period, collected in *Moly* (1971), call on these experiences. By the time of *Jack Straw's Castle* (1976), Gunn was more sober about social realities, though his writing continued to reflect, and to reflect on, the aspirations, sense of community, and experimentalism that marked the Bay area's 1960s hippie culture.

San Francisco is also notable as one of the world's most vibrant centers of gay and lesbian culture. Many of Gunn's poems, especially in *The Passages of Joy* (1982) and *The Man with Night Sweats* (1992), depict gay culture in San Francisco and northern California, from gay bars and street fairs and the Sonoma County geysers to the challenges of love and companionship. San Francisco's gay community, which is more than a background to his poems, has allowed Gunn to explore his own identity, especially as it is formed in relation to others, in an open, relatively relaxed, and supportive environment. Since the early 1980s, being homosexual in San Francisco has also meant, among other things, confronting AIDS, both as a public issue and as a recurring personal tragedy. *The Man with Night Sweats* records the impact of AIDS on Gunn's life and on the lives of many friends who have contracted the disease.

FIGHTING TERMS *AND* THE SENSE OF MOVEMENT

GUNN'S earliest poetry is characterized thematically by the depiction of tough, disillusioned stances and formally by the use of strictly regulated meter and rhyme patterns. In many of these poems, formal control reflects the more general human will to control that Gunn clearly admires. The many soldiers scattered throughout *Fighting Terms* are soldiers without a war, full of restless energy, seeking some adequate object for that energy. Gunn's description of a dethroned king in "The Court Revolt" could stand as an epigraph to the volume:

> His human flames of energy had no place—
> The grate that they were lit for would not hold,
> The vacant grates were destined to be cold.
> (p. 18)[1]

Like many of the poems in *Fighting Terms*, "The Court Revolt" describes a world inadequate to its best energies. It is a poem out of Yeats, who exerted a significant influence on the early Gunn: the worst have conspired to overthrow the king, and others have "joined from weakness or because / Sick boredom had succeeded leisure drunk" (p. 17).

[1] All page references to poems refer to the *Collected Poems* (New York, 1994), unless otherwise noted.

The formal control that is evident throughout this volume is the expression of Gunn's own creative energies. Eventually, Gunn would write poems in both free and patterned verse forms, but his first two volumes are written almost exclusively in the latter. Gunn explains his interest in controlled poetic forms in an interview with Jim Powell reprinted in his 1993 essay collection *Shelf Life:* "in looking for a rhyme, or in trying to get a meter right, you are often having to go deeper into your subject so that you discover things about it, and about your reaction to it, that you didn't know before" (p. 221). Rhyme, Gunn insists, "turns out to be a method of thematic exploration."

In his early poetry, Gunn often uses strict formal constraints to explore the balance or tension between impulse and restraint. In "Tamer and Hawk," he uses a carefully patterned form simultaneously to contain and to release a vital (here, animal) energy. The poem opens with a characteristic posture for the early Gunn:

> I thought I was so tough,
> But gentled at your hands,
> Cannot be quick enough
> To fly for you and show
> That when I go I go
> At your commands.
>
> (p. 29)

Gunn creates a forceful and, at times, even colloquial voice in this poem, but this colloquial note is countered by touches of highly wrought poetry, as in the second line, "But gentled at your hands." He probably found his precedent in Shakespeare's *Henry V:* "be he ne'er so vile, / This day shall gentle his condition" (IV.3.62–63). This is a decidedly formal touch, one reinforced by the poem's rhyme scheme (*abaccb* through four stanzas) and meter (iambic trimeter through five lines of each stanza, with a strongly stressed dimeter bob concluding each stanza).

"Tamer and Hawk" describes how a wild, instinctual animal comes to depend on and interact with a rational, civilizing force. The hawk continues to fly, but is "no longer free"; it continues to "wheel" and "hover" and "twist," but with only the desire to land on the tamer's (rhyme word!) wrist. Form and content generate a tension here that constitutes the poem, thereby allowing Gunn to explore the relationship between spontaneous impulse and rational design. Taming, in "Tamer and Hawk," is, like writing poetry, a means of channeling and expressing the wild hawk instinct: by the end of the poem, the hawk insists that the tamer but "half civilize[s]" him, since in his flight he chooses "Tamer as prey." The poem's final image thus reverses perspective: the hawk's wild instincts survive by being redirected. Even within the tightly controlled form of the poem, wildness finds, or rather achieves, expression.

This animal energy is often associated in *Fighting Terms* with the many toughs scattered throughout the volume. The narrator of "Lofty in the Palais de Danse" declares, "Like the world, I've gone to bad" (p. 9). Lofty's tough posture only thinly veils a restlessness brought on by his apparent loss of someone he once loved: "I never felt this restiveness with her: / I lay calm wanting nothing but what I had." Gunn establishes a tension between the gentleness of such a memory and the cruel aggressiveness of Lofty's cruising:

> And so in me
> I kill the easy things that others like
> To teach them that no liking can be lasting.
>
> (p. 9)

"Carnal Knowledge," which appeared as the volume's opening poem in its original 1954 publication, is an even tougher poem because its narrator, who is rejecting a present lover, never lets down his mask. "Even in bed I pose," the poem begins (echoing Donne). The speaker here is protecting his vulnerabilities, in a way that Lofty does not—and in a way that the later Gunn will not. The overwrought wittiness of the poem, with its modulated refrain of "I know you know I know you know . . . ," is a symptom of the speaker's emotional sterility. When he rather meanly says that "an acute girl" would see through his pose, the reader may well suspect that this speaker is merely stumbling over his own defenses.

Gunn's early figure of the fighting tough is best epitomized in "Incident on a Journey." The poem's echoing refrain, "I regret nothing," suggests a character who has made definite choices and is willing to abide by them. Such is Gunn's version of the Nietzschean will to power (though probably mediated by Edith Piaf): "And always when a living impulse came / I acted, and my action made me wise" (p. 33). Like the king in "The Court Revolt," the soldier and the narrator of "Incident on a Journey" can trust only in the integrity and meaning of their actions. In the concluding stanza, which also closes the volume, Gunn gives notice to the literary world that he has arrived, healthy and ready for anything:

> Later I woke. I started to my feet.
> The valley light, the mist already going.
> I was alive and felt my body sweet,
> Uncaked blood in all its channels flowing.
> I would regret nothing.
>
> (p. 34)

The speaker is comfortable in his body, ready to conquer the world, to take risks, to face the consequences. It is, for Gunn, an image of vigorous physical and mental health.

So, too, in "The Wound," the poem Gunn would eventually place at the head of *Fighting Terms*, the injured soldier steels himself for further action. While allowing time to heal his wound, he is safe, but out of the action. The speaker, who eventually identifies himself (dementedly?) with Achilles, returns to the fight, but his wound immediately reopens: such is his determination to fight. The poem implicitly rejects the safe complacency of healing on the sidelines, subject to Thersites' pointless cackling, in favor of strong action, no matter the consequences. Lazarus' failure to rise in "Lazarus Not Raised" is likewise a failure to put everything at risk. Lazarus favors the "deepest bed / Of vacancy" rather than what Gunn calls "the nag of offered grace" (pp. 7–8). It is his fear, reflected in his "terrified awakening glare," that sends him back to "the trivial territory of death." Lazarus' will to live has been stunted by the easygoing comfort of death. Gunn offers, by contrast, an image of strong dying in "Lerici":

> Strong swimmers, fishermen, explorers: such
> Dignify death by thriftless violence—
> Squandering with so little left to spend.
>
> (p. 23)

Whereas Shelley died falling "submissive through the waves," Byron's touch "Was masterful to water." The gesture is its own value here: it is an expression of life turned against all the emasculating forces of death.

In discussing Gunn's early fascination with figures of "masterful" will, critics have often noted the influence of existentialism, especially as developed by Sartre and Camus. Gunn's early existentialism emphasizes the central role of choice in determining the always emerging nature of one's being. Yeats's influence is also apparent in Gunn's admiration of heroic self-determination. Still, even in these early poems, Gunn is often aware of the frequent disorientation (existentialists would call it angst) that accompanies such self-realization. In "The Secret Sharer," titled after a Joseph Conrad novella, the speaker imagines encountering his own self, looking from the street toward his lighted window. He worries most that his inside self either will not hear or will not respond to his call from without, that he will prove too "fixed" in his "socket of thought" to respond to his own call (p. 13). Just as he sees, from outside, an "uncertain hand" moving the curtains, the poem shifts to the interior, "Fire-glow still reassuring; dark defied." "The Secret Sharer" eerily locates the speaker both inside and out, taking comfort in a defined interior but still subject to an uncanny and insistent call from without.

In his second volume, *The Sense of Movement* (1957), Gunn continues to explore many of the same themes, with particular emphasis on figures of human will imposing order on the chaos of experience. References to the "will" abound in these poems. "On the Move," the volume's opening poem, is about "the Boys," a gang of motorcyclists who, in their goggles and "gleaming jackets trophied with the dust," "strap in doubt—by hiding it, robust" and go off in search of self-definition (p. 39). "On the Move" is full of admiration for the quality of strong seeking, figuring the motorcyclists in terms that suggest Renaissance explorers:

> Much that is natural, to the will must yield.
> Men manufacture both machine and soul,
> And use what they imperfectly control
> To dare a future from the taken routes.
>
> (p. 39)

The poem contains some of Gunn's strongest echoes of Sartre and Camus:

> One joins the movement in a valueless world,
> Choosing it, till, both hurler and the hurled,
> One moves as well, always toward, toward.
>
> (p. 40)

In the absence of inherited values, the biker-existentialist creates his own values by daring his future into being. The "Boys" refuse to stay still in the poem long enough for Gunn to define them:

> A minute holds them, who have come to go:
> The self-defined, astride the created will
> They burst away.
>
> (p. 40)

Thus the Boys ride right out of the poem. Being unsettled is the biker's ideal of poise:

> At worst, one is in motion; and at best,
> Reaching no absolute, in which to rest,
> One is always nearer by not keeping still.
>
> (p. 40)

It is hard to say what the biker is nearer to, though it clearly entails, for Gunn, the always emerging self that he is daring into being.

The figure of the biker reappears in "The Unsettled Motorcyclist's Vision of His Death," which opens with a biker riding into "walls of rain," drenched but "being what I please" (p. 54). The biker sees himself as part of nature, but is also forced to invent himself through an antagonism with nature:

> The firm heath stops, and marsh begins.
> Now we're at war: whichever wins
> My human will cannot submit
> To nature, though brought out of it.
>
> (p. 54)

Human dignity, here, is all in the way in which the motorcyclist sustains this antithetical posture. The biker's will is also a figure for the poet's will: as the motorcycle begins to sink in the marsh, the biker redoubles his efforts to keep moving forward, urging his "chosen instrument / Against the mere embodiment." Gunn recognizes, though he has not yet, perhaps, entirely accepted, that his own chosen instrument is not a motorcycle but a pen. The artist, like the biker, must begin the process of creation with things as they are, the mere embodiment of things; the process of creation enlarges these things. At the same time, "The Unsettled Motorcyclist's Vision" reminds the reader of the close and disturbing relation between creation and destruction: like the flailing heroes of "Lerici," the motorcyclist is most alive as he "Accelerates the waiting sleep."

"Lines for a Book" reads something like a handbook for Gunn's Biker-Existentialist. It is his paean to the heroic attitude: "I think of all the toughs through history / And thank heaven they lived, continually" (p. 56). Gunn admires the "tough" because he acts, and especially because his thinking never interferes with his acting. His toughs know

> That though the mind has also got a place
> It's not in marvelling at its mirrored face
> And evident sensibility.
>
> (p. 56)

T. S. Eliot had complained about the "dissociation of sensibility," by which feeling and thought had come to be separated, an event that he dated to the seventeenth century. Eliot's "The Love Song of J. Alfred Prufrock," whatever else it is, is a poem that documents the radically dissociated sensibility of the twentieth-century mind. Gunn reverses Eliot's procedure here, turning to an "unrefined" sensibility and admiring it for its sustained capacity to engage experience and to act: "I think of those exclusive by their action, / For whom mere thought could be no satisfaction" (p. 56).

Such posturing often amounts to a wildly romanticized image of the man of action. Many critics have rightly taken Gunn to task for the moral blindness of his admiration, pointing out that tough guys are often just criminally vicious. Still, a poem like "The Unsettled Motorcyclist's Vision of his Death" succeeds as a poem because it particularizes its attitudes, ascribing them to one individual rather than generalizing about all the "toughs through history." "Market at Turk" is another successful poem in this regard. There is a critical distance in Gunn's description of this street-corner poser, especially in the concluding stanza, which, without actually letting the reader into this character's head, offers a glimpse behind his pose:

> He waits, whom no door snatches
> to unbuckling in the close
> commotion of bar or bed,
> he presides in apartness,
> not yet knowing his purpose
> fully, and fingers the blade.
>
> (p. 58)

This is someone who has, for whatever reason, not yet achieved emotional or sexual satisfaction, and so "presides in apartness" as a means of compensation. The concluding image of "Market at Turk" is haunting, because of the sense we have that this barely contained violence may or may not erupt in actual fact.

Gunn's early heroic ethos is relentlessly masculine. The existential romance with risk and action in many ways derives from and reinforces male-centered values and ideals. There is also, however, an important element of homosexual desire at play here. It is useful to recall Gunn's emerging interest in "the well-fed and good-looking G.I.s" after the war. It is not only that soldiers are men of action, not "sicklied o'er with the pale cast of thought," but that they don a uniform: they stage their masculinity in what is, at least potentially, a theater of sexual role-playing. Masculinity, then, is not just an essential and idealized male trait in these poems; it is also material for the exploration of homosexual desire. All of this becomes clearer in a poem first published in 1982, "The Menace," in which a speaker describes a homosexual encounter with someone who is

> not a real soldier
> but a soldier
> inducted by himself
> into an army of fantasy
> (p. 339)

The two men

> play at large
> with the dull idea of the male
> strenuous in his limitations.
> (p. 340)

a play that "abruptly wakens desire" (p. 340). "The Menace," with its carefully developed play on the doubleness of an aggressor/lover, guard/guardian, provides a useful perspective from which to view Gunn's early fascination with toughs and soldiers. If the theme of homosexual desire is undeveloped in his early poems, which in fact are generally staged as theaters of heterosexual desire, it is important to remember that this is a subject that few dared openly explore in the early and middle 1950s, and that Gunn is himself only beginning to explore it here.

One also finds another valence to the heroic will in "To Yvor Winters, 1955." Here, the "deliberate human will" refers to the powers to discriminate and to compose, powers that are more explicitly intellectual and artistic than those exercised by Gunn's biker-existentialists. Gunn draws on a similar vocabulary of the will here, but with a very different objective:

> Continual temptation waits on each
> To renounce his empire over thought and speech,
> Till he submit his passive faculties
> To evening, come where no resistance is.
> (p. 69)

Winters' sense of thought as a resistance to passive submission at first seems to contradict the ideal articulated in "Lines for a Book." Winters, however, does not advocate thought as detached abstraction or loose sentiment, but rather as a rigorously wrought response to circumstances. This is thought exercised like a muscle:

> You keep both Rule and Energy in view,
> Much power in each, most in the balanced two:
> Ferocity existing in the fence
> Built by an exercised intelligence.
> (p. 70)

These lines describe the mutual dependency of antithetical qualities: rule and energy, intelligence (control, order, form) and ferocity (spontaneity, instinct, energy).

Gunn's fascination with toughs and heroes marks an early phase in his poetic and personal development, but he will always admire this interplay of strength and intelligence that he associates here with Winters. "Vox Humana," the volume's concluding poem, points Gunn forward by depicting his usual heroic categories in plainer, simpler human terms. "Vox Humana" is a poem about choice. As the title suggests, choice makes us human: by choosing, by risking specific choices, we create our humanity. The moment of choice is the moment of self-definition. The terms of Gunn's description recall "On the Move," only here this future is dared without the biker's glittering regalia:

> Or if you call me the blur
> that in fact I am, you shall
> yourself remain blurred, hanging
> like smoke indoors. For you bring,
> to what you define now, all
> there is, ever, of future.
> (p. 88)

261

One already senses a softening in Gunn's vision: "Vox Humana" encourages self-invention, but without the usual posturing. Even more radically, "Thoughts on Unpacking," in which the speaker declares "I need your help with these" (p. 80), points forward for Gunn by risking redefinition in an act of reaching outside the self toward others.

MY SAD CAPTAINS

My Sad Captains (1961) is probably the most important transitional volume in Gunn's career. There are two dimensions to his development in these poems. Thematically, Gunn is less mesmerized by heroic posturing, and at the same time is more open to feelings of connection with others and with the world around him. Formally, he begins in the second section of this volume to experiment with syllabics, a method of determining line length by an exact syllable count: a poem that begins with a line of seven syllables will be written in seven-syllable lines to the end. This method, a variation of the system Marianne Moore often used in her early poems, forces Gunn to abandon his usual iambic meter and to experiment with more flexible, and often rougher, rhythms. He also makes no attempt to sustain regular patterns of rhyme in these poems. Gunn has said that he was teaching himself to write free verse in these poems, a process that would eventually lead him beyond the artificial regularity of syllabics.

In the volume's opening poem, "In Santa Maria del Popolo," Gunn describes how Caravaggio, in his painting of Paul's conversion, has limited his focus to "the one convulsion": "what is it you mean / In that wide gesture of the lifting arms?" (p. 93). The gesture hasn't acquired a conventional meaning yet: Saul is still "becoming Paul," and "No Ananias croons a mystery yet" (p. 93). It is an extraordinary gesture, all unrealized potential, but something about it remains inaccessible. Thus the speaker turns, in the last stanza, to the dim interior of the church. He notices the people who have come to pray, mostly old women:

> each head closeted
> In tiny fists holds comfort as it can.
> Their poor arms are too tired for more than this.
>
> (p. 94)

This is a striking "turn" in Gunn's poetry: there is recognition here of these women's humanity and quiet sympathy with their condition. The poem concludes by juxtaposing the old women's gestures with Paul's in the painting, the "large gesture of solitary man, / Resisting, by embracing, nothingness" (p. 94). The speaker still appears to admire the heroic convulsion, but it is isolated and filtered, here, through a displacement of the speaker's sympathy toward the old women in the church.

Gunn's retreat from the heroic is still more apparent in "Innocence," where a young soldier is depicted as an altogether chilling perfection of mind and body. He knows only "The egotism of a healthy body," ignorant of the past and its lessons, hardened by the Corps "to an instrument" (p. 100). The poem describes his "compact innocence" as a protective shield: "No doubt could penetrate, no act could harm." The concluding stanzas describe a Russian partisan being burned alive. The soldier sickens "only at the Northern cold," is disgusted "only at the smell." Gunn's mode here is powerfully ironic: the poem hinges on the reader's recognition that the soldier's "perfection" is deeply flawed.

In "A Map of the City," sterile perfection gives way to a fantasy of endlessly fecund potential. Gunn describes a view of the lighted city, late at night from a hill. The lights suggest the city's various attractions: "Some flickering or some steady shine" (p. 103). The last stanza epitomizes the speaker's sense of charged excitement:

> By the recurrent lights I see
> Endless potentiality,
> The crowded, broken, and unfinished!
> I would not have the risk diminished.

The speaker is excited by all the as yet unspecified possibilities spread out, shining and flickering, before him. That the city is "crowded, broken, and unfinished" only enhances the thrill of it all: risk, here, is the risk of engagement with all the unpredictable and irresistible life of the city, glimpsed in an instant's visionary exuberance.

"Considering the Snail" compresses that exuberance into the figure of a tiny snail. The poem, which nods quietly to Marianne Moore's "To a Snail," is about the "power" at work within the snail:

I cannot tell
what power is at work, drenched there
with purpose, knowing nothing.
What is a snail's fury?

(p. 117)

The snail, the poem suggests, is as full of power as any earthly creature or process, only concentrated by what Moore calls its "contractility." It "moves in a wood of desire," a compaction of what Dylan Thomas called the "force that through the green fuse drives the flower." Even in the snail, this force is all-determining. Gunn concludes the poem by imagining what he would see if he came later, parted the grass above the snail's tunnel, and saw only its thin white trail:

I would never have
imagined the slow passion
to that deliberate progress.

"Deliberate" here captures the sense of existential choosing that had been so important for Gunn, but that deliberateness is now exercised on a new scale. The slow passion of the snail's deliberate progress could also describe the effect of the syllabics here, as when the first line is forced to spill into the second to complete the rhythm and thought: "The snail pushes through a green / night."

Other poems in the second, syllabic half of *My Sad Captains* show Gunn working through themes (though not yet techniques) reminiscent of William Carlos Williams. In an essay on Williams reprinted in *The Occasions of Poetry*, Gunn comments that Williams "was in love with the bare fact of the external world, its thinginess; and the love mastered him for a lifetime" (p. 22). In "Waking in a Newly Built House," Gunn's speaker describes himself

seeking merely all
of what can be seen, the substantial,
where the things themselves are adequate.

(p. 115)

This quality of substantial "thinginess" requires a relaxed perception:

Calmly, perception rests on the things,
and is aware of them only in
their precise definition, their fine
lack of even potential meanings.

In "Flying Above California," Gunn describes

a cold hard light without break

that reveals merely what is—no more
and no less.

(p. 116)

Here, the odd enjambment subtly reinforces the poem's meaning, suggesting that just to capture the outlines of the light would be to reveal how much there is in just what is.

"Lights Among Redwood" is another poem in which Gunn allows "precise definition" of the world around him to gather into an experience of the Sublime. The first two stanzas record definite acts of observation, describing the play of light through the redwood trees alongside a creek. Midway through the poem, the speaker casually comments, "Then we at last / remember to look upward" (p. 124). It is almost as an afterthought that the view is directed upward, as if to say most human dealings are here below, where they belong, but that one's view can sometimes be profitably directed upward. It is a stunning view, and Gunn's colloquial language becomes richly evocative:

we stand
and stare—mindless, diminished—
at their rosy immanence.

(p. 124)

Critics have often admired Gunn's phrasing in the last line, with its suggestion of Homer's "rosy-fingered dawn" and its quiet hint of God's immanence in the world. These are, however, only trees, giant redwoods in a certain light, and their "rosy immanence" is, in the language of "Flying Above California," "merely what is—no more / and no less."

In "My Sad Captains," the volume's closing poem, Gunn bids farewell to his heroic theme. The poem, which takes its title from *Antony and Cleopatra*, is full of distancing techniques, as in the carefully qualified description of his admiration:

They were men
who, *I thought,* lived only to
renew the wasteful force they
spent with each hot convulsion.

(p. 129; emphasis added)

The speaker's distance from this heroic convulsion is firmly underlined: "They remind me, distant now." There is an admiration still for these heroes, but it is firmly qualified as the heroes now

> withdraw to an orbit
> and turn with disinterested
> hard energy, like the stars.

With this elegiac gesture, Gunn prepares himself to embrace the vulnerabilities of self that will lead him to his best and most significant poetry.

POSITIVES *AND* TOUCH

THE 1960s saw Gunn experimenting in new modes, both of feeling and of form. He has stated that he was dissatisfied with much of the poetry he was writing in the first half of the 1960s, finding it lacking intensity. The challenge was to shape the more humane and less formally controlled impulses that were moving to the center of his poetry into something worth reading. These explorations were initially carried out on two fronts at roughly the same time: the long sequence "Misanthropos," which first appeared in August 1965 and was later included in *Touch* (1967), and the 1966 sequence *Positives,* a collection of photographs by Gunn's brother Ander with accompanying poems by Thom.

"Misanthropos," comprised of seventeen individual poems and divided into four sections, depicts a lone survivor of what appears to have been an atomic war. The poem traces a movement from isolation to community, and so provides an important model for the evolution of Gunn's poetry in the 1960s. The poems are told variously from the survivor's point of view and from a descriptive, third-person point of view, sometimes in formal verse, sometimes in syllabics. The first section, "The Last Man," describes the isolation and consequent dehumanization of the last survivor. He is a "lived caricature" of the former human race, "clothed in dirt" and lacking motive (pp. 133–134). Without a future to dare, he begins to fuse with his surroundings, melting "through the brown and green silence," lost "in dense / thicket" (p. 133).

In the second section, "Memoirs of the World," his memories of the past are recorded; they often remind him "Of the diminishing warmth and light" of his present world (p. 138). In one poem in this section, the last man has a disorienting vision of what appears to be the origins of life. An "intruder" with "blurred outline" arrives among a group of cells "swimming in concert" (p. 142). Its tendrils appear to reach out: "Where // it touches it holds, in an act of / enfolding, possessing, merging love." This is seen as the work of "a devil," as "life's parody," yet it

> enthralls a universe with its rich
>
> heavy passion, leaving behind it
> gorgeous mutations only, then night.

Here, at the heart of the last man's deepest isolation, an intimation of love survives, unaccountable, transitory, irresistible. This vision leads the last man to attempt to "keep to the world's bare surface," hoping that in bare perception he may retain something "against the inevitable end" (p. 143). The second section concludes with an "Epitaph for Anton Schmidt," who assisted Jews in Poland during World War II: even in the darkest night, such "gorgeous mutations" sometimes occur.

The third section, "Elegy on the Dust," describes these mutations as the blowing of dust: individual particles of dust are isolated, only to be blown into random concord again. "Elegy on the Dust" is a view of life as pure process, the dust, human and inhuman, "hurled / In endless hurry round the world" (p. 146). In the concluding section, "The First Man," Gunn returns the poem to a human plane. A new wind is blowing: the last man spots a group of "creatures" approaching his hill. He hides at first, watching forty men and women pass, until he notices one, the last to pass, who is dirty, full of sores, tired, scratched by a hanging briar. Having watched all the others pass "unmoving and unmoved" (p. 149), the last man finds himself mysteriously moved to respond to the straggler. The "creature" is frightened and falls, but the "last man," continuing an impulse he does not understand, responds by lifting "the other to his feet again" (p. 150). The "last man" thus becomes the "first man," recognizing the other's humanity (even though he appears to recognize him as a former enemy), naming and addressing him. The poem concludes by stating, somewhat programmatically, its ethic of mutual dependency:

You must,
If you can, pause; and, paused,

Turn out toward others, meeting their look at full,
    Until you have completely stared
On all there is to see. Immeasurable,
    The dust yet to be shared.

(p. 151)

"Shared" is the last word of the poem: the "first man" is effectively born in the gesture that leads him from his solitary isolation to a state of mutual relatedness. He is still dust, but dust "mixing with dust / On the hand that touches it."

Touch is a crucial metaphor for Gunn in this period. The first poem of *Positives* describes a newborn baby reaching out to its world:

But the body
is feeling its way
        feeling:
the minute hands grip, the big
baldish head beams, the feet
press out in the strange element

(*Positives*, p. 6)

Touch, for Gunn, is the medium of relation, the source of dependable knowledge about the world and of dependable feeling toward it. The poems in *Positives*, almost all of which Gunn chose not to reprint in later collections, constitute an important bridge to his later poetry: they are, for one thing, astonishingly direct and colloquial. Ander Gunn's photographs follow a life cycle, beginning with a newborn infant, moving through childhood and young adulthood, and concluding with a series of old men and women. The photographs, taken in London in the middle 1960s, show men and women at work and at play, alone and in groups. Gunn's poems often build from references to actual details in the photographs (what he later calls working from the outside in). Alongside a photograph of a man sitting alone in a dark bar with a half-emptied pint resting on the table in front of him, Gunn writes:

She says she's with her
mother, though my
theory is it's a fellow.

(p. 42)

The language of the poems is often this colloquial, as in a poem accompanying a photograph of workers being served tea on the job site:

Make it strong, Jonesy
that's how I like it, strong
with plenty of sugar in it.

(p. 62)

Perhaps because he is not sure if he is writing poems or captions—"they were somewhere between the two," he suggests in "My Life" (p. 181)—Gunn allows his free verse to range across the page more loosely than ever before.

None of Gunn's former heroic preoccupations surface in *Positives*. Even a motorcycle poem describes the rider's "impetus" as "a gentleness / projected at great speed" (p. 32), a far cry from the hard willfulness that seems to drive the earlier motorcycle poems. In a poem accompanying a photograph of a worker with his pick poised in the air, Gunn corrects a reference to "unskilled labour":

But there is
skill in getting the proper
stance—Through an arc the point
falls as force, the human
behind it in control
tiring, but tiring slowly.

(p. 52)

The laborer is Gunn's new type of hero, his labor a kind of touch: the arc his pick traces is a form of creative energy, an image linking sky and earth, the "inanimate rubble" around him, and the eternal impulse to create. Taking the proper stance, he guides the pick, controlling it, but he is also tiring with each motion. His control is qualified, like all human control, by the limitations of his own strength. It is, nevertheless, a considerable strength: he is "tiring, but tiring slowly," a tribute to his impressive physical ability.

Many of the poems in *Touch* reveal an increasing physical sensuousness. In "Touch," the speaker joins his sleeping lover in bed. The poem is a description of a series of purely physical movements, yet the speaker suggests the broader human implication of these movements. He enters the bed with

the restraint
of habits, the patina of

self, the black frost
of outsideness,
(p. 168)

all of which effectively isolate him in his own shell. The poem describes the melting of that shell. The speaker is uncertain whether this melting is due to his "own warmth surfacing" or a "ferment" of his lover's body: the inconclusiveness only points more definitely to a process involving one in the other. The speaker describes himself as "now loosened" as he sinks into "an old / big place," one that is there already because his lover is there already, a place that is

not found but seeps
from our touch in
continuous creation.
(p. 169)

Unlike the conclusion to "Misanthropos," there is nothing programmatic about this vision of "continuous creation": it is the product of a carefully detailed, convincing description of human touch, successful in part because its scale is so modest.

Throughout *Touch*, Gunn repeatedly describes how the body's sensuous responsiveness links it to the life of the world. "The Goddess," the opening poem of *Touch*, depicts Proserpina "naked and searching / as a wind" (p. 155), bringing all the world to abundant life. The speaker is so full of this force that he lets loose a catalog of life that recalls Whitman, from the "sinewy thyme / reeking in the sunlight" to the rats "breeding, in their nests" and the soldier by a park bench, waiting all evening for

any woman
her dress tight across her ass
as bark in moonlight.

These are not altogether flattering images, but they do denote the irresistible Urge in all things, animal, vegetable, and human. In "The Vigil of Corpus Christi," Gunn describes someone who has passed the night standing some sort of watch in the cold as he is brought back to life by the "moist tongue" of his dog (p. 170). As the figure comes, literally, to his senses, he grins at the "soft sweet power awake in his own mass / balanced on his two feet, this fulness" (p. 171).

MOLY

IN *Positives* and *Touch*, Gunn is already beginning to explore awakenings that occur around the edges of the self. The 1960s practically institutionalized this process in the form of sex, drugs, and rock 'n' roll. The poems collected in *Moly* (1971) were especially influenced by the psychedelic hallucinogen LSD. In "My Life," Gunn comments that almost all of the poems in *Moly* derive "in some way however indirect" from his experience of LSD, noting that he has "no doubt at all" that LSD "has been of the utmost importance" to his personal and poetic development (p. 182). Gunn calls these "the fullest years of my life, crowded with discovery both inner and outer, as we moved between ecstasy and understanding." For many in the 1960s, LSD opened "the doors of perception" (hence the band The Doors, via Aldous Huxley). Ironically, Gunn found that the only way he could control, and thus convey, his own drug-induced illuminations "was by trying to render the infinite through the finite, the unstructured through the structured." The poems in *Moly* are among Gunn's most surreal, but they are also, for the most part, as carefully designed as any of his poems.

The keynote of the volume is transformation. In "Rites of Passage," the opening poem of the volume, the speaker is metamorphosing into some kind of satyr:

Something is taking place.
Horns bud bright in my hair.
My feet are turning hoof.
(p. 185)

It is never entirely clear what is happening in the poem, though many of its details suggest a conflict with an older figure called "Father" and "Old Man." The speaker assumes a tone that is half playful, half threatening. At one point, the speaker threatens, "And next I make my way / Adventuring through your garden," which could suggest the garden of English verse traditions. By the end of the poem, the speaker appears ready for some kind of vital, potent action, perhaps the very poems to follow:

I stamp upon the earth
A message to my mother.
And then I lower my horns.

266

"Moly," the next poem in the volume, is also a poem of metamorphosis. In the *Odyssey*, moly is the magical herb that Hermes gives to Odysseus to keep his "mind and senses clear" (X.298, in Robert Fitzgerald's translation). Here, the speaker has been transformed, like Odysseus' sailors, into a pig and is using all his animal energies to root out the moly, "Cool flesh of magic in each leaf and shoot, / From milky flower to the black forked root" (p. 187). The speaker envisions the holy changes that will accompany his awakening, "Dreaming the flower I have never seen." Another poem that plays on the half-man, half-beast theme is the sequence "Tom-Dobbin," which Gunn subtitles "centaur poems." Tom is mind and Dobbin is body, and the two spend the greater part of their lives in unresolved tension. Their separation is overcome only in the moment of sexual orgasm:

> In coming Tom and Dobbin join to one—
> Only a moment, just as it is done:
> A shock of whiteness, shooting like a star,
> In which all colours of the spectrum are.
> (p. 201)

Transformation is often a prelude to such merging in these poems. By breaking down individuated identities, Gunn is able to underscore the interconnectedness of all things. In "Flooded Meadows," "definition is suspended" because all things are inundated, "Cancelling the rutted, weedy, slow brown floor / For the unity of unabsorbed excess" (p. 215). In "At the Centre," the speaker, apparently "tripping" on LSD, imagines himself part of a "steady pouring" around him (p. 220). He is "overlapping like the wet low clouds / The rivering images" (p. 221), at once of them and apart from them. Adopting for the first time in one section the pronoun "I," the speaker imagines himself briefly as separate from the "flow" around him, a center of consciousness, only to realize that even as such a center, he is still part of the surrounding flow:

> On the stream at full
> A flurry, where the mind rides separate!
> But this brief cresting, sharpened and exact,
> Is fluid too, is open to the pull
> And on the underside twined deep with it.

Consciousness is at once in and out of the flow—hence, in the aftermath of the trip, the speaker describes himself and his friends as "Hostages from the pouring we are of."

"The Colour Machine," a prose poem in two parts, depicts a speaker who holds back from the ultimate "expansion" of the absolute merge. The first section describes a group of people watching a color machine as it shapes and reshapes shifting patches of color. The second section describes one of the speaker's companions who gives himself "completely to the colour machine," becomes invisible, and drifts away from the room "into a world where he could no longer make an impression" (p. 205). The poem retains a healthy degree of humor about all this, noting that "cars drove through him, he entered movies for free." The speaker then reveals that he himself cannot make this ultimate sacrifice: "I too am a lover, but I am cowardly, selfish, and calculating." As he feels the temptation to give himself to the color machine, he starts "making love to curtains": "By means of such promiscuity I can keep myself intact."

"The Colour Machine" makes clear that for all Gunn's experimentation with LSD and its mind-altering effects, a part of him is unprepared to sacrifice individual identity for the drug's vague promise of harmony and perpetual transformation. The voice of the poem is attracted to the experience but unwilling to give in to it entirely. Throughout *Moly*, Gunn is balancing these opposing instincts, like the centaurs that keep popping up throughout: every poem in the volume is an experiment in just how far he can go in fusing with his environment while retaining the consecutive awareness necessary to create a poem from the experience. He writes from the point of greatest tension, "Composing uncomposed," as he puts it in "Words" (p. 197).

If Gunn holds back from the absolute merge, he nevertheless remains powerfully attracted throughout this volume to momentary mergings. "From the Wave" describes surfers, "Half wave, half men," versions of the centaur figures scattered throughout the volume (p. 198). Catching a wave, the surfers become one with it: "Grafted it seems by feet of foam." It is a perfectly timed affair, leaving the surfers' bodies to "Loosen and tingle" after the wave breaks, as they prepare for the next wave (p. 199).

"Sunlight," the volume's concluding poem, begins with a series of images of light playing off surfaces:

> Some things, by their affinity light's token,
> Are more than shown: steel glitters from a track;
> Small glinting scoops, after a wave has broken,
> Dimple the water in its draining back.
>
> (p. 223)

The speaker speculates that "What captures light belongs to what it captures": the glimmerings and flickerings put out by objects here below not only reflect but also belong to the sun. The speaker recognizes that the sun is "slowly dying," but also sees that "Desires and knowledge touch without relating": the sun "outlasts us at the heart," which, as Pascal said, has its reasons of which the mind is ignorant. In the last two stanzas, the speaker looks to the sun, "Great seedbed, yellow centre of the flower . . . Giving all colour and all shape their power," as the source of another kind of reflected light, human creative energy:

> Enable us, altering like you, to enter
> Your passionless love, impartial but intense,
> And kindle in acceptance round your centre,
> Petals of light lost in your innocence.
>
> (p. 224)

We give ourselves to what created us, and so become ourselves, in poems as in other acts of creative love, "Petals of light," part of the larger flowering that is the sun. What is striking here, as throughout *Moly*, is that Gunn remains so completely in control of the poem, "lost" in the sun's innocence but wholly present as a guiding sensibility. Desire and knowledge may touch without relating, but Gunn's poems, even when they flirt with the infinite, seem always to be written from that delicate point of contact.

JACK STRAW'S CASTLE

IN *Jack Straw's Castle* (1976), Gunn transposes many of the insights of *Moly* and *Touch* into a new key. He continues to explore ways in which the self can expand beyond its narrow axis. Some of the poems here trace the self back to some mysterious source or origin; others follow the self out into gatherings of people, often in connection with San Francisco's gay community in the early and middle 1970s. Even as Gunn continues this exploration around the edges of the self, he returns, in the title sequence "Jack Straw's Castle," to the basic terror of human isolation.

"The Geysers" is a four-part poem about community, formed largely by the mutual pleasure people take in nature and in each other. Gunn describes the scene at the Sonoma County geysers in "My Life":

Some hundred or more people camped there at weekends, fewer stayed through the week. We camped anywhere, on the flanks of the hills, which were warm even at night, or in the woodland, or beside the cool and the warm streams. Everyone walked around naked, swimming in the cool stream by day and at night staying in the hot baths until early in the morning. Heterosexual and homosexual orgies sometimes overlapped. . . . When I remember that small, changing society of holidays and weekends, I picture a great communal embrace.

(pp. 184–185)

This perfectly captures the spirit of the first two sections of the poem.

The geyser is by contrast a distinctly unsocial phenomenon, "The force too simple and big to comprehend, / Like a beginning, also like an end" (p. 241). The speaker nevertheless recognizes something of himself in it:

> And I do recognize
> —For what such recognition may be worth—
> Fire at my centre, burning since my birth
> Under the pleasant flesh.
>
> (pp. 241–242)

Here the self finds itself at once alienated from a force of nature and somehow mysteriously linked to it, perhaps by virtue of sexual, creative, and even destructive energies. The last poem in the sequence, "The Bath House," describes an experience in one of the baths with a crowd of people. Much as in the tenth poem of "Misanthropos," the speaker has a vision of some kind of original creation, as if returning to the "source" acknowledged in the previous poem. The speaker is at first sunk in "hot mud," then awakens into a new reality, although initially undifferentiated from his surroundings:

"unnamed, unborn / I live" (p. 244). The speaker is then abruptly born into an individuated identity:

> It tore
> > what flash cut
> > > made me fugitive
> > caesarian lightning lopped me off separate
> > > > > (p. 244)

After a mysterious scene of pursuit and hiding, the speaker dives into a stream and eventually resurfaces in the bath itself, among other "dreamers" who engage him in some sort of "overlapping" orgy. Feeling "trapped" at first, the speaker gives up hope, "entering their purpose as they enter mine" (p. 246). By the end, the speaker describes himself as

> torn from the self
> > in which I breathed and trod
> I am
> > I am raw meat
> > > I am a god
> > > > > (p. 246)

Gunn carefully balances antithetical identifications here, suggesting that in "losing" himself he also "finds" himself, at once a "raw" object of others' abject desires and a desiring "god" himself. The open, cascading form of the poem is reminiscent of Robert Duncan, an important influence on Gunn around this time, though the semiregular rhythms and rhymes that play against the poem's open shape are vintage Gunn.

"Discourse from the Deck," an additional section of "The Geysers" that appeared only in the 1974 chapbook *To the Air*, brings the homosexual community at the Geysers and its aspirations into clearer focus. There is, in this gathering, what Gunn calls in "My Life" "an attitude of benevolence and understanding on all sides that could be extended, I thought, into the rest of the world" (pp. 184–185). By juxtaposing a view of America as seen from outer space with a reference to "America at war" (p. 17), Gunn suggests in the poem that the kind of community experienced at the Geysers, multiplied by other such experiences of community, could form the basis of a more harmonious American community at large. He soon came to regard this attitude as a "hopeless hopefulness," a phrase from a later poem, "Saturday Night," about

the San Francisco baths circa 1975. "Discourse from the Deck" is, however, a charming poem, and important in reconstructing the larger cultural significance, for Gunn as for many others, of gatherings like the one described in "The Geysers."

Many of the poems in *Jack Straw's Castle* describe similar mergings in larger bodies of people, but always as momentary occurrences, what in "The Outdoor Concert" Gunn calls

> living a while
> at that luminous intersection,
> spread at the centre.
> > > (p. 264)

In "Saturnalia," a largely gay carnival celebration allows its participants to throw off

> the variegated stuffs that
> distinguished us one from
> one
> here in orgy.
> > > (p. 265)

The experience of merging also refreshes the self for its return into individuated identity:

> the senses
> mingle, before returning
> sharpened to their homes.
> > > (p. 266)

In "Thomas Bewick," the famous wood engraver "loses himself / in detail" as he observes birds in their native settings:

> he reverts
> to an earlier self, not yet
> separate from what it sees,
>
> a selfless self as difficult
> to recover and hold as to
> capture.
> > > (p. 259)

By "losing" himself in detail, Bewick can return "sharpened" to the task of his engravings. Another poem of return to an "earlier self" is "Bringing to Light," which utilizes an archaeological metaphor to describe the discovery and exploration of lost selves. This return to origins is somewhat disturbing, however, in that the source is described as a place already divided,

> as if something
> even here
> were separating from its dam.
>
> (p. 257)

In "Jack Straw's Castle," an eleven-poem sequence, Gunn continues to explore these unsettling recursive selves. One of Gunn's most genuinely frightening poems, "Jack Straw's Castle" restages the general movement of "Misanthropos," going from a deepening isolation to an acknowledgment of companionship. The scene, however, shifts from an external environment to an internal one, a series of rooms in a castle that seem to correspond to recesses in the protagonist's psyche. Jack Straw in his castle is uncertain whether he even inhabits a world, so obsessed is he with "visions, voices, burning smells" (p. 270). The castle is a nightmare world, one developed from Gunn's own dreams around the time he was making a move. At his nadir, the protagonist is "petrified at my centre" (p. 275), unable to make contact with a world he is not even sure exists. What intimations of reality he does have are utterly terrifying, as when Charles Manson and Medusa appear as "Dream sponsors" (p. 272). At one "level" of self, the speaker sees himself as "the man on the rack," "the man who puts the man on the rack," and "the man who watches the man who puts the man on the rack" (p. 274).

Eventually, Jack Straw imagines a staircase and posits "an outside" to which it will lead:

> Outside the castle, somewhere, there must be
> A real Charles Manson, a real woman crying,
> And laws I had no hand in, like gravity.
>
> (p. 276)

By the end of the poem, the speaker half-wakes and realizes someone is in the bed beside him. He is unsure at first if the companion is real or phantom, though he notices its distinctly physical characteristics: "Thick, heavily breathing, with a sweet faint sweat" (p. 278). Their bodies barely touch, but "that mere contact is sufficient touch, / A hinge, it separates but not too much." The speaker's uncertainty returns as he wonders if he might not be dreaming all this, but he decides to trust his senses:

> No, real.
> Comes from outside the castle, I can feel.
> The beauty's in what is, not what may seem.
> I turn. And even if he were a dream
> —Thick sweating flesh against which I lie curled—
> With dreams like this, Jack's ready for the world.
>
> (pp. 278–279)

This is a delicate resolution for so much terror, not only because of the doubt that still persists in the concluding formulation but also for the precariousness of the "hinge" that binds him to his companion.

The concluding section of the volume extends this return to the world, but in a state of decided vulnerability, and to a world everywhere characterized by loss. Where many of the poems in sections I and II describe movements back to a beginning or through a series of cellars to some sort of foundation, many of the poems in the concluding section describe a spreading or movement outward, as if to reach, inclusively, further and further into the world. "Autobiography" boldly opens the section by asserting, "The sniff of the real, that's / what I'd want to get" (p. 285), recalling the reassuring body odor of the companion in "Jack Straw's Castle." The dog Yoko in the poem of that title is emblematic in this regard, a vigorous and potent sniffer of rank odors. But Yoko is only a dog, however delightful a dog she is, and so knows nothing, despite her daily confusion while waiting for her master's return, of what the speaker in "Autobiography" calls loss:

> life seemed all
> loss, and what was more
> I'd lost whatever it was
> before I'd ever had it.
>
> (p. 264)

Reaching out to the world, then, is a gesture that embraces present realities even as it recognizes the precariousness of that embrace.

In "Hampstead: the Horse Chestnut Trees," the speaker struggles to recall a childhood memory of bicycling through the trees, acknowledging that

> it's all
> getting lost, I started
> forgetting it even as I wrote.
>
> (p. 287)

The trees serve to provide a contrast to the speaker's desire to record what is always being lost: "their hearts are wood / and preserve nothing," they

> spread outward
> and upward
> without regret
> hardening tender green
> to insensate lumber.
>   (p. 288)

In "The Cherry Tree," the tree is described as having a need to

> push outward
> from the centre, to
> bring what is not
> from what is.
>   (p. 294)

Like Proserpina's movement in "The Goddess," this pushing outward begins as an invisible flowing through the tree, becoming visible as "tiny bumps" at "the end of twigs," then becoming "jubilant at / the thick dazzle of bloom," turning to leaf, and finally shedding all to begin the process anew (pp. 294–295). The tree sheds all its leaves in this process, but that is part of its health:

> That's why she made them,
> to lose them into the world, she
> returns to herself,
> she rests, she doesn't care.
>   (p. 296)

Humans do care, of course, though they can also take some solace in belonging to such natural processes.

In "Breaking Ground," Gunn writes about an old woman in Kent, remembered here for her gardening; she may be modeled on one of Gunn's aunts. She is approaching death, "going down to earth" (p. 303). There seems no possible compensation for being

> lost, forgotten in
> an indiscriminate mulch, a
> humus of no colour.
>   (p. 304)

The second section of the poem offers a response to this vulnerability. The setting is an outdoor concert in Monterey, and the sun breaks through the clouds. As it does, the concertgoers stretch their arms to take off their shirts, a movement that reminds the speaker of flowers in bloom. Here, the speaker suggests, loss becomes dispersal: the dying woman is dispersed in an act of "spreading abroad" (p. 305). The woman is described as "distributed / through fair warm flesh / of strangers," renewed in similarities of touch and voice throughout the "one great garden which / is always here." As if to connect that garden to the garden source of poetry, Gunn concludes the poem (and the volume) with an echo of the English verse traditions of Andrew Marvell, especially Marvell's "The Garden":

> Shee
> is gonn, Shee is lost,
> Shee is found, shee
> is ever faire.

Poetry, for Gunn, is the space of this perpetual renewal, where mutability paradoxically becomes the ground of continuity.

THE PASSAGES OF JOY

IN *The Passages of Joy* (1982), Gunn continues his effort, begun in previous volumes, to break down the armor of self in order to make contact with the world around him. Gunn explores his homosexuality far more directly than ever before. One sense of the "passages of joy" is simply sexual pleasure, in all its sheer volatility. The volume's title, which appears in the epigraph to the sequence "Transients and Residents," is adopted from Samuel Johnson's poem "The Vanity of Human Wishes": "Time hovers o'er, impatient to destroy, / And shuts up all the Passages of Joy" (p. 374). *Passages* suggests both openings and extended periods, precarious in the sense that all passages are subject to closure or conclusion. A passage of joy is a bright occasion but also an inherently precarious one, looking to a time when it will have passed, when the occasions of pleasure will be the stuff of memory and longing.

In the volume's opening poem, "Elegy," an acquaintance has committed suicide:

> They keep leaving me
> and they don't
> tell me they don't

warn me that this is
the last time I'll be seeing them

(p. 311)

The poem maintains a disillusioned stance in regard to an afterlife:

There will be no turn of the river
where we are all reunited
in a wonderful party
the picnic spread
all the lost found
as in hide and seek

(p. 312)

Gunn is planting seeds in this passage—the metaphor of "hide and seek" will recur throughout the volume, and the "turn of the river" with its "wonderful party" looks ahead to "Talbot Road," a poem "in memory of Tony White," which describes a "great party" on the London canals that White threw at the end of Gunn's year in London (1964–1965) (p. 384). "Elegy" ends by invoking the "odd comfort" we feel by participating in the general experience of loss, "playing the same game / where everyone always gets lost" (p. 312).

Loss takes many forms in *The Passages of Joy*. It appears as the inevitable descent of the pinball player's ball in "Bally *Power Play*": "but in the end it must disappear / down the hole at the bottom" (p. 316). It appears as the personal and physical transformation of a friend in "Selves":

The new self. It
nags me with its hard eyes,
its simple gaze.

(p. 322)

It appears as a game in "Hide and Seek":

In their fathers' gardens
children are hiding
up in orchard trees, seeking
to be lost and found.

(p. 333)

It appears in many poems collected here as people who come and go through the course of a life, as suggested by the epigraph of "Night Taxi": "for Rod Taylor / wherever he is" (p. 386). And it appears repeatedly, and most definitively, as death, as in "Talbot Road."

Gunn everywhere balances this sense of passage with the other sense, that of an opening or extended period through which joy is expressed. In "Bally *Power Play*," the speaker describes the pinball player's physical motions as if they were those of a lover:

Bally's drama absorbs him:
amongst the variety and surprise
of the lights, the silver ball
appears, rolls shyly towards him,
meets a wheel of red plastic,
at once bounces away from it,
frantically dashes from side to side
and up and down . . .

(p. 315)

In "Sweet Things," the speaker runs into an acquaintance he hasn't seen in some time; while shaking the speaker's hand, the acquaintance playfully bends a finger into the speaker's palm. The speaker suddenly has other things in mind than his various errands:

The warm teasing
tickle in the cave of our handshake
took my mind off toothpaste,
snatched it off, indeed.

(p. 327)

These passages of joy are often recorded (primarily in the first and third sections) in free-verse forms that approximate the open movement of thought. In "The Conversation," Gunn describes a conversation as a process of continuous, open-ended progress toward definition: it is the incompleteness of any definition that provides the impetus to keep pursuing the matter, to define "bit by bit what / it is indeed about" (p. 319). The topic of the conversation is

never perfectly defined
never perfect matter
because the words are
fluent, are fluid.

(p. 320)

For Gunn, language is always part of a larger process of ongoing definition; the more it can retain this quality of fluidity, the better the definition. The taxi driver in "Night Taxi" describes himself as "loose but in control" (p. 387): flexible enough to respond to what the city brings but directed enough to navigate his way through the city streets. Driving a taxi through a city at night provides an apt metaphor for writing poems, both being opportunities to exercise

> alert reflexes
> where all else
> is in hiding.
> (p. 386)

If "The Conversation" and "Night Taxi" embody Gunn's ideal of fluid language, "Song of a Camera," which opens the middle, more formally composed section of the volume, embodies his ideal of formal language. The poem, dedicated to the photographer Robert Mapplethorpe, describes writing as a process of elimination:

> I cut the sentence
> out of a life
> out of the story
> with my little knife.
> (p. 347)

Where "The Conversation" repeatedly invokes the fluidity of fire and water, "Song of a Camera" invokes the discontinuities of the knife's cutting action:

> Each bit I cut
> shows one alone
> dressed or undressed
> young full-grown.

The knife leaves things isolated, so that essential details will appear in bold relief. This, as the speaker acknowledges, can be disconcerting: one

> wants to add
> adverbs to verbs
> A bit on its own
> simply disturbs.

"Song of the Camera" does not re-create anything like the fluidity of experience, but instead concentrates attention on some isolated part of the fluid whole. Fluidity is always a virtue for Gunn, but so is this ability to depict a concentrated reality.

"Transients and Residents," one of two long sequences in the volume's third section, is made up of four poems, the first three describing friends and acquaintances, the last describing the speaker himself. Each of the first three poems describes someone who has for some reason grown distant from the speaker: one no longer hangs out in his usual pool hall, another is "magnificently self enwrapped" in his new role as dope dealer (p. 376), and the third, apparently a closer friend, keeps himself in a

> companionable
> Chilled orbit by the simultaneous
> Repulsion and attraction to it all.
> (p. 378)

In the last poem, "Interruption," the poet is incapable of writing because he is temporarily thrown in on himself, his self-image reflected back at him in his window. Gunn describes his characteristic method as one that moves from external details to internal realities:

> Starting outside,
> You save yourself some time while working in:
> Thus by the seen the unseen is implied.
> *I like loud music, bars, and boisterous men.*
> You may from this conclude I like the things
> That help me if not lose then leave behind,
> What else, the self.
> (p. 379)

Isolated in his study, the speaker is all too painfully aware of himself. Ironically, as Gunn finds himself unable to get the outside world in focus, he ends up offering one of his most revealing self-characterizations.

Reviewing the "plants" that have accumulated in his garden, Gunn finds himself "dry as at noon," his reflection in the glass showing "Colourless, unjoined, like a damaged moon" (p. 379). The garden plants suggest Gunn's poems, but the poet is again "waiting out a drought," despite the fact that it is actually raining outside. His reflected image is "colourless, unjoined" because he cannot at present lose or loose himself in others. He is "like a damaged moon," no longer sustained by its companion planet's gravitational pull.

"Transients and Residents" is interrupted, but it leads into "Talbot Road," a poem about and dedicated to the memory of Tony White, the friend that Gunn describes in "My Life" as "the soul of our generation, who remained throughout his life my best reader and most helpful critic" (p. 174). "Talbot Road" is a testimony to the pleasures and hazards of friendship. Tony White, great friend that he was, had what Gunn describes as impenetrable depths: a "damp smoulder of discontent" lurked behind the "fire of his good looks" and the "mighty giving of self" that showed to the world (p. 381). He is strangely pleased when he provokes Gunn to anger, because that anger is at least human. Even as the poem looks nostalgically back on a wonderfully happy interlude Gunn shared with White, it also looks forward, through the figure of a young boy in the final poem, to a future of further entanglements. The boy is, apparently, visiting his grandmother; he sits every evening, during Gunn's last week on Talbot Road, at a window,

> Gazing down
> at the human traffic, of all nations,
> the just and the unjust, who
> were they, where were they going,
> that fine public flow at the edge of which
> he waited, poised, detached in wonder
> and in no hurry
> before he got ready one day
> to climb down into its live current.
>
> (p. 385)

A road, for Gunn, opens onto contact with all the world. Despite the feeling of nostalgia that permeates the poem, "Talbot Road" continues to point forward through the figure of the boy, looking out on the world as Gunn himself had years before in "A Map of the City."

The volume concludes with "Night Taxi," another road poem describing a taxi driver/poet's incessant contact with others: "Do I pass through the city / or does it pass through me?" (p. 387). What is the self but a continuous "passage" through others? The dry spell of "Interruption" is broken here by the falling rain in the poem's last stanzas, which leaves a "sprinkle of wet" on the speaker's knuckle (p. 388). The speaker's glance is directed upward, to the furthest point of vision, where he sees a "curtain of rain" blowing against the eucalyptus tops. These eucalyptus recall the "crackling eucalyptus leaves" beneath which the figure described in "Elegy" committed suicide. It is perhaps too much to say that this rain is redemptive, but it is at least refreshing, a sign of Gunn's sense of the endless potential of creative renewal.

THE MAN WITH NIGHT SWEATS

IN *The Man with Night Sweats* (1992), Gunn continues to explore the subtle interweaving of joy and pain, although here the universal reality of death has taken a new and unsettling twist with the advent of AIDS. *The Man with Night Sweats* is marked by Gunn's effort to come to terms with an experience for which, as he knows, there may be no adequate terms. He writes in a state of sustained uncertainty and confusion, but with an eye to indefinite possibilities of sense. These tensions are apparent in "A Sketch of the Great Dejection," which constitutes the second section of the volume. The speaker describes a quest that begins in great promise but arrives at length at a waste land

> of poverty,
> of inner and outer famine,
> where all movement had stopped
> except for that of the wind
>
> (p. 423)

This place is so harsh that it leaves him "without potent words, / inert," ready to abandon his quest: "I sat upon a disintegrating gravestone. / How can I continue? I asked." Refusing just to sink into the mud, he posits the terms of his continuation:

> My body insisted on restlessness
>   having been promised love,
> as my mind insisted on words
>   having been promised the imagination.
> So I remained alert, confused and uncomforted.
> I fared on and, though the landscape did not change,
> it came to seem after a while like a place of
>   recuperation.
>
> (p. 424)

There remains a residuum of inconsolable grief here, as throughout this volume, but it is a grief that the poet is everywhere turning over for some redeeming memory or gesture, the forms that, held against the darkening chaos of things, give him the resolve to keep alert and on the move.

The volume's tensions are apparent in its first two poems, "The Hug" and "To a Friend in Time of Trouble." "The Hug" reprises a favorite theme of Gunn's, two lovers cozying up in bed. Having fallen asleep a little drunk, the speaker wakes to the pressure of the hug:

I dozed, I slept. My sleep broke on a hug,
Suddenly, from behind,
In which the full lengths of our bodies pressed.
(p. 407)

Gunn describes the hug in very physical terms, not as a prelude to sex but rather as a bracing or locking of bodies. The physical gesture reminds him of an earlier time, "When our grand passion had not yet / Become familial." The lapse of time and place are "deleted" in the gesture: "I only knew / The stay of your secure firm dry embrace." It is a moment of profound comfort, qualified only by the reader's sense that it depends on a decidedly precarious state of mind, and perhaps by the quiet insistence on the dryness of the embrace.

"To a Friend in Time of Trouble" introduces an unspecified "trouble" into the volume. Gunn leaves this "trouble" in the poem's background, as he instead describes the slow relaxation of the friend in the presence of nature, his

senses reaching out anxiously,
Tentatively, toward scrub and giant tree:
A giving of the self instructed by
The dog who settles near you with a sigh.
(p. 408)

The poem describes a steady loosening of self:

the grief and rage
You brought out here begin at last to unbind.
And all day as you climb, the released mind
Unclenches till—the moment of release
Clean overlooked in the access of its own peace—
It finds that it has lost itself upon
The smooth red body of a young madrone . . .
(p. 409)

As the self is carried out of its preoccupations in the activity of work and in the observation of light and color on the hillside, it "feels the healing start, and still returns, / Riding its own repose, and learns, and learns." Healing takes place as a release from self, as the self rides "its own repose" to some deeper, fuller knowledge of its condition.

The formal range of *The Man with Night Sweats* is apparent in the two poems concluding the first section, "Odysseus on Hermes" and "Seesaw," the former in free verse and the latter in carefully arranged meter and rhyme. In "Odysseus on Hermes," Odysseus describes himself as "seduced by

innocence" or "by the god within" (p. 417). Hermes' "innocence" is his "incompletion": he is

potent in potential,
in process and so
still open to the god.

By being seduced, Odysseus allowed his own "thick maturity" to become unsettled, unsolid,

still being formed—
in the vulnerability, edges flowing,
myself open to the god.

An aging Odysseus aspires to "renew that power," to relearn the knack

of opening my settled features,
creased on themselves,
to the astonishing kiss and gift
of the wily god to the wily man.
(p. 418)

Where the rhythms of "Odysseus on Hermes" are loose like the flowing edges the speaker describes, those of "Seesaw" provide a perfectly regular and controlled movement back and forth between paired opposites:

Days are bright,
Nights are dark.
We play seesaw
In the park.
(p. 419)

The poem's nursery-rhyme rhythm is built from its two stresses per three-syllable line, with an occasional variation brought on by an extra unstressed syllable, as in the third line quoted above. The repetitive form of the poem echoes the poem's theme: the perpetual movement back and forth, between day and night, self and other, earth (of things) and sky (of dreams, ideals, aspirations). Seesawing provides an apt image of how two people might interact through the course of a relationship or a life: "Give and take, / Take and give." But the process is also tiring and

ends
As it begins.
Off we climb
And no one wins.
(p. 420)

275

These lines could describe the end of a relationship, or the end of a life: either way, the tone is cool and detached. If one side of Gunn wants to suggest that the "god within" is in "edges flowing," the other side still wants to use meter, rhyme, and patterned form to suggest the taut rhythms and tensions implicit in any experience of human relation.

Gunn explores all sorts of intimate rhythms and tensions in this volume, from the "grand passion" of "The Hug" through all kinds of friendship, acquaintance, and what can only be called mere alongsideness. This last sort of relationship appears especially in the volume's several poems on homeless and other "marginal" figures, in one of which, "Old Meg," Gunn's gesture of greeting is answered only by the curse "'Blood on you!'" (p. 438). In "Improvisation," Gunn recognizes the limits of his own open-ended, liberal thinking:

> I said our lives are improvisation and it sounded
> un-rigid, liberal, in short a good idea.
> But that kind of thing is hard to keep up.
>
> (p. 437)

There is something inaccessible to the liberal imagination about these people; for all the speaker's sympathy, he does not lose sight of the gulf that separates him from such human suffering.

Poems about or inspired by friends reveal, by contrast, how thoroughly dependent the self is on others. "The Missing," which appears in the volume's final section, is devoted almost wholly to friends with AIDS, and describes the sense of diminishing identity on the part of a survivor. The speaker (who is all but indistinguishable from Gunn in these poems) describes how his own warmth had "Led outward through mind, limb, feeling, and more / In an involved increasing family" (p. 483). This family recalls the gathering described in "The Geysers," a community whose shared intimacies extend the meaning of family:

> Contact of friend led to another friend,
> Supple entwinement through the living mass
> Which for all that I knew might have no end,
> Image of an unlimited embrace.

> I did not just feel ease, though comfortable:
> Aggressive as in some ideal of sport,
> With ceaseless movement thrilling through the whole,
> Their push kept me as firm as their support.
>
> (p. 483)

Gunn's vision of a supply entwined family includes a mutual ease, but also a more "aggressive" give-and-take that ultimately sharpens and extends their experience of mutual dependency.

The death of others leaves the speaker

> less defined:
> It was their pulsing presence made me clear.
> I borrowed from it, I was unconfined,
> Who tonight must balance unsupported here.
>
> (p. 483)

The speaker describes himself as an unfinished statue, "as if I froze / Between potential and a finished work." This description is neither an "open form" realizing its potency as potential nor a "give and take" seesaw exchange, but just a stunted growth:

> —Abandoned incomplete, shape of a shape,
> In which exact detail shows the more strange,
> Trapped in unwholeness, I find no escape
> Back to the play of constant give and change.
>
> (p. 484)

"The Man with Night Sweats," which opens the fourth section of the volume, describes the speaker's own fear as a kind of isolation:

> I wake up cold, I who
> Prospered through dreams of heat
> Wake to their residue,
> Sweat, and a clinging sheet.
>
> (p. 461)

The "dreams of heat" refers as much to acts of sexual and human vigor as to poems of creative strength. Even the strong and prosperous will suffer. "The Man with Night Sweats" reviews a life of potent creative health:

> I grew as I explored
> the body I could trust
> Even while I adored
> The risk that made robust,

> A world of wonders in
> Each challenge to the skin.
>
> (p. 461)

"Risk" was a significant term for the early Gunn, but it bears new connotations in a time of AIDS.

Strength gives way, here, to an overwhelming vulnerability:

> Stopped upright where I am
> Hugging my body to me
> As if to shield it from
> The pains that will go through me,
>
> As if hands were enough
> To hold an avalanche off.
>
> (p. 462)

The hugging gesture recalls "The Hug," but this hug is a hug of fear, not passion; it does not connect, but isolates the self.

The appeal of risk has not, however, entirely diminished. Acknowledging his attraction to his own annihilation in "In Time of Plague," the speaker only barely holds back from a needle offered him by two "fiercely attractive men" in a bar (p. 463). They

> thirst heroically together
> for euphoria—for a state of ardent life
> in which we could all stretch ourselves
> and lose our differences.

This recalls the "great communal embrace" Gunn has admired in so many forms, but being pursued here in the shadow of one of the leading causes of AIDS, infected needles. The speaker is torn between admiration and disgust, admiring their willingness to test themselves "against risk, / as a human must, and does" while at the same time wondering if they are just "fools, their alert faces / mere death's heads lighted glamorously?" (p. 463). It is the speaker's own attraction to risk that is unsettling here: he knows how fatally dangerous this risk is, yet still feels its pull.

In other poems, Gunn records the heroic integrity of people struggling with AIDS. In "Courtesies of the Interregnum," a host, realizing he has forgotten a guest (the speaker) who is not infected, becomes

> Almost concerned lest I feel out of it,
> Excluded from the invitation list
> To the largest gathering of the decade, missed
> From membership as if the club were full.
>
> (p. 476)

Thus the host

> triumphs at length,
> Though with not physical but social strength
> Precisely exerted.
>
> (p. 477)

It is a triumph of human vulnerability:

> He who might well cry
> Reaches through such informal courtesy
> To values grasped and shaped out as he goes,
> Of which the last is bravery, for he knows
> That even as he gets them in his grip
> Context itself starts dizzyingly to slip.
>
> (p. 477)

With the concluding rhyme, Gunn captures the irresolvable tension between the host's truly impressive "grip" and the realization that, along with his context, that grip is sure to "slip."

Another moment of vulnerable strength is recorded in "Memory Unsettled," an elegy for a friend who asked only to be remembered. The poem keeps his memory "unsettled" by recording his having once gone to see "Another with a fever / In a like hospital bed":

> You climbed in there beside him
> And hugged him plain in view,
> Though you were sick enough,
> And had your own fears too.
>
> (p. 479)

Here again, the sign of strength is a continuing concern about others: even sick, these friends continue to reach beyond the self.

"Lament" describes the effort on the part of another dying friend to live his final days with integrity and even a degree of normalcy. "Your dying was a difficult enterprise" (p. 465), this poem begins, setting out to describe how much heroic effort this friend put into the process. Even as he is dying, he remains "Still hungry for the great world" (p. 467), grabbing at detail "To furnish this bare ledge toured by the gale," trying to

> make of it a life
> Thick with the complicating circumstance
> Your thoughts might fasten on.
>
> (p. 466)

As in other poems collected here, the dying friend's vulnerability, and his will to live despite that vulnerability to carry out this "difficult, tedious, painful enterprise," are the source of his integrity (p. 468).

The Man with Night Sweats concludes with "A Blank," a poem that describes the speaker's glimpse, through a bus window, of a former lover with his recently adopted son. The "blank" of the poem is the blank on an adoption form, representing the life to be adopted, and the blank of that life itself, a newly forming self waiting to develop in relation to his father's love and guidance. All of this is figured in the gesture seen through the bus window:

> a friend
> Stopped on a corner-kerb to let us pass,
> A four-year-old blond child tugging his hand,
> Which tug he held against with a slight smile.
> (p. 487)

It is, as ever, a physical gesture, one with sufficient strength to push, support, grasp, hold, and direct. The father is a single father, who two years before had said to the speaker, " 'I chose to do this with my life,' " and now finds himself "tugged upon by his decision." The speaker describes his admiration of the fact that

> he turned from nothing he had done,
> Or was, or had been, even while he transposed
> The expectations he took out at dark
> —Of Eros playing, features undisclosed—
> Into another pitch.

His love for his child is an extension of his erotic love, but turned out in new directions, allowing him now "To educate, permit, guide, feed, keep warm, / And love a child to be adopted" (p. 488). The poem concludes with a view of the child:

> The blank was flesh now, running on its nerve,
> this fair-topped organism dense with charm,
> Its braided muscle grabbing what would serve,
> His countering pull, his own devoted arm.
> (p. 488)

There is tension in this "grabbing," the force of two bodies pulling and holding in the active, continuous creation of a relation. The child is a figure of healing in the volume, his tug a sign of the future still being dared, even amid so much accumulated pain and suffering.

Gunn's poems about people with AIDS have attracted a growing audience and earned him many accolades, including a "genius" grant from the MacArthur Foundation in 1993. But *The Man with Night Sweats*, like the more recent poetry Gunn has been publishing in magazines and chapbooks, is about much more than AIDS. As his writing evolved through the 1950s, 1960s, and 1970s, Gunn became one of our great poets of friendship and love and all the passion and vulnerability that go into them. The many complex tensions at the heart of Gunn's life and work have allowed him to follow the public and personal tragedy of AIDS with unusually "alert reflexes / where all else / is in hiding." For someone who, in his own words, manages his "mere voice on postcards best" (p. 379), Gunn has enabled many to hear the unique notes of pain, resolve, despair, confusion, fear, anger, and determination that constitute the human reality of AIDS. This may well stand as Gunn's major accomplishment to date, but it is only the latest example of what he has come to do best, tracing the "Supple entwinement" of self and other, with all the irreducible pleasure and pain that relationship entails.

SELECTED BIBLIOGRAPHY

I. BIBLIOGRAPHY. Jack W. C. Hagstrom and George Bixby, *Thom Gunn: A Bibliography, 1940–1978* (London, 1979); Jack W. C. Hagstrom and Joshua S. Odell, "Emendations to *Thom Gunn: A Bibliography, 1940–1978*," in *Bulletin of Bibliography* 49 (September and December 1992), 50 (June and December 1993), 51 (March 1994).

II. SELECTED AND COLLECTED POEMS. *Selected Poems: Thom Gunn & Ted Hughes* (London, 1962); *Poems 1950–1966: A Selection* (London, 1969); *Selected Poems 1950–1975* (London and New York, 1979); *Collected Poems* (London and Boston, 1993; New York, 1994).

III. POETRY. *Fighting Terms* (Oxford, 1954; rev. ed., New York, 1958); *The Sense of Movement* (London, 1957; Chicago, 1959); *My Sad Captains* (London and Chicago, 1961); *Positives* (London, 1966; Chicago, 1967); *Touch* (London, 1967; Chicago, 1968); *Moly* (London, 1971; New York, 1973); *Jack Straw's Castle* (London and New York, 1976); *The Passages of Joy* (London and New York, 1982); *The Man with Night Sweats* (London and New York, 1992).

IV. Poetry Chapbooks. *Thom Gunn* (Oxford, 1953); *A Geography* (Iowa City, 1966); *The Explorers* (Crediton, Eng., 1969); *Sunlight* (New York, 1969); *Songbook* (New York, 1973); *Mandrakes* (Cambridge, 1974); *To the Air* (Boston, 1974); *Jack Straw's Castle* (New York, 1975); *The Missed Beat* (Newark, Vt., and Sidcot, Eng., 1976); *Games of Chance* (Omaha, Neb., 1979); *Sidewalks* (New York, 1984); *The Hurtless Trees* (New York, 1986); *Night Sweats* (Florence, Ky., 1987); *Undesirables* (Durham, N.C., 1988); *At the Barriers (Dore Alley Fair)* (New York, 1989); *Death's Door* (Tuscaloosa, Ala., 1989); *Old Stories* (New York, 1992); *Unsought Intimacies: Poems of 1991* (Berkeley, Calif., 1993).

V. Criticism. *The Occasions of Poetry: Essays in Criticism and Autobiography*, ed. by Clive Wilmer (London, 1982; enl. ed., San Francisco, 1985); *Shelf Life: Essays, Memoirs, and an Interview* (Ann Arbor, Mich., 1993).

VI. Edited Volumes. *Poetry from Cambridge 1951–52* (London, 1952); *Five American Poets*, ed. with Ted Hughes (London, 1963; Chicago, 1968); *Selected Poems of Fulke Greville* (London, 1968); *Ben Jonson* (Harmondsworth, Eng., 1974).

VII. Critical Studies. Alan Bold, *Thom Gunn and Ted Hughes* (New York, 1976); Martin Dodsworth, "Thom Gunn: Poetry as Action and Submission," in Dodsworth's *The Survival of Poetry* (London, 1970); Neil Powell, "The Abstract Joy: Thom Gunn's Early Poetry," in *Critical Quarterly* 13 (autumn 1971); John Miller, "The Stipulative Imagination of Thom Gunn," in *Iowa Review* 4 (winter 1973); Catharine R. Stimpson, "Thom Gunn: The Redefinition of Place," in *Contemporary Literature* 18 (summer 1977); Patrick Swinden, "Thom Gunn's Castle," in *Critical Quarterly* 19 no. 3 (1977); Clive Wilmer, "Definition and Flow: A Personal Reading of Thom Gunn," in *PN Review* 5 (May 1978).

Merle E. Brown, "Inner Community in Thom Gunn's 'Misanthropos' " and "The Authentic Duplicity of Thom Gunn's Recent Poetry," in Brown's *Double Lyric: Divisiveness and Communal Creativity in Recent English Poetry* (New York, 1980); Jay Parini, "Rule and Energy: The Poetry of Thom Gunn," in *Massachusetts Review* 23 (spring 1982); Hank Nuwer, "Thom Gunn: Britain's Expatriate Poet," in *Rendezvous: Idaho State Journal of Arts and Letters* 21 (fall 1985); Paul Giles, "Landscapes of Repetition: The Self-Parodic Nature of Thom Gunn's Later Poetry," in *Critical Quarterly* 29 (summer 1987); "Thom Gunn at Sixty," special issue of *PN Review* (16 no. 2 [1989]), with contributions by Donald Hall, Douglas Chambers, Dick Davis, Martin Dodsworth, John Peck, Michael Schmidt, Donald Davie, Neil Powell, and Robert Pinsky; Bartlett Lee, "Outsiders as Insiders: The Idea of the West in the Work of Thom Gunn and Nathaniel Tarn," in Lee's *The Sun Is but a Morning Star: Studies in West Coast Poetry and Poetics* (Albuquerque, N.M., 1989).

A. E. Dyson, " 'Watching You Watching Me . . .' : A Note on *The Passages of Joy*," in *Three Contemporary Poets: Thom Gunn, Ted Hughes, R. S. Thomas: A Casebook*, ed. by Dyson (London, 1990); Robert K. Martin, "Fetishizing America: David Hockney and Thom Gunn," in *The Continuing Presence of Walt Whitman: The Life After the Life*, ed. by Martin (Iowa City, 1992); Charles Berger, "Poetry Chronicle, Thom Gunn: *The Man with Night Sweats* (I)," in *Raritan* 13 (fall 1993); David Bergman, "Poetry Chronicle, Thom Gunn: *The Man with Night Sweats* (II)," in *Raritan* 13 (fall 1993).

VIII. Biographical Note. The principal source of information about Gunn's life is the autobiographical essay "My Life up to Now," which Gunn wrote for the 1979 bibliography of his work and reprinted in *The Occasions of Poetry*. Other essays and memoirs touching on his life appear there and in *Shelf Life*. Further details on Gunn's life appear in Alan Bold's *Thom Gunn and Ted Hughes*.

DAVID HARE

(1947–)

Susana Powell

WORLD WAR II changed Britain not for the six years of its duration but for the three generations it ravaged. After the war men returned to England changed by their experiences, physically or emotionally battle-scarred. Pacifists, profiteers, and older men who did not fight were forced to face those who did. Americans, who were perceived as engaging in the war just in time to win, were resented for their energy and money, of which Britons had neither. Women, whose participation in the war effort had been essential, were displaced by the men they had replaced and were expected to return to their domestic or clerical arena. Children, traumatized by evacuation and air raids, were either stunted or propelled into adulthood. War babies met their fathers for the first time, adjusted to new fathers, or faced life fatherless.

It was the best of times, it was the worst of times. Euphoria followed victory, but winning the war proved easier than winning the peace. Families reunited and celebrated their survival, or they fractured. Some soldiers never came home or returned dysfunctional. For some men and women the challenge and excitement of war, and above all its camaraderie, provided an experience that could never be matched by peace. Some were ruined by war, and some were made by it. Day-to-day life continued to be dominated by rationing, but a vigorous black market traded in all commodities, while mothers continued to make clothes from curtains and rag dolls from remnants.

Into this postwar world was born a generation of playwrights who formed their feeling for the stage from the Angry Young Men of the 1950s—whose sensibilities were forged by a sense of betrayal and futility following the exalted hopes engendered by postwar reforms—and from the marginal Samuel Beckett, whose *Waiting for Godot* (1953) mystified English audiences just as John Osborne's *Look Back*

in Anger (1956) energized them. The intellectual elite emerged from college educations in the 1960s equipped with the classical training of their English heritage yet rife with rebellion against it. Armed with the tools of Beckett, Osborne, and Bertolt Brecht, and, by 1968, unfettered by censorship, they swept into action as playwrights, directors, and actors. Unacceptable to the mainstream, unable to breach the commercial theater and disdainful of it, they formed their own companies, encouraged by the success of their university theater experiences, and created an alternative theater known in England as "The Fringe."

Such a one is David Hare.

David Hare was born in Sussex on 5 June 1947 and attended a private school, Lancing College, which boasts such illustrious alumni as the novelist Evelyn Waugh and the dramatist Christopher Hampton. Hare attended Jesus College, Cambridge, and received his master's degree in 1968. The same year he cofounded the Portable Theatre Company, for which he wrote several plays, including *How Brophy Made Good* and *Slag*, which won him the 1970 *Evening Standard* Award for most promising playwright. From 1969 to 1971, when the Portable Theatre filed for bankruptcy, Hare was literary manager, then resident dramatist at the Royal Court Theatre in London, which was known for its avant-garde productions. His own plays and collaborations, "What Happened to Blake?," "Lay By," "England's Ireland," and *The Great Exhibition* continued to be produced in regional and fringe theaters.

In 1973 Hare collaborated with the playwright Howard Brenton, a leading spokesman for the political drama that flourished during and after the revolutionary year of 1968, on *Brassneck*, which Hare directed at the Nottingham Playhouse, where he became resident dramatist. The same year he cofounded the Joint Stock Theatre Group and wrote a teleplay, *Man Above Men,* which was aired by BBC-1.

Hare describes his next play, *Knuckle,* as the real beginning of his career and regards all previous attempts as experiments in form, content, and collaboration. *Knuckle* transferred from the Oxford Playhouse to the Comedy Theatre in the West End of London in 1974 and was televised in the United States in 1975. Also in 1975 *Teeth 'n' Smiles,* written and directed by Hare, opened at the prestigious Royal Court Theatre, while a television version of *Brassneck* was aired in England and *Fanshen* opened at the Institute for Contemporary Arts' Terrace Theatre and then transferred to the Hampstead Theatre Club.

If there was any doubt that Hare had arrived in terms of making a name for himself in mainstream British theater, this was dispelled by the production of *Plenty* at the Lyttelton Theatre, part of London's National Theatre complex, in 1978. The same year, his teleplay *Licking Hitler* was broadcast and published, winning the British Academy of Film and Television Arts' award for best television play of the year, and Hare visited the United States on a Bicentennial Fellowship. In ten years he had emerged from university wit to collaborative artist to nationally known playwright. The next decade would see his elevation to international status.

In 1980 and 1981 Hare produced two teleplays, *Dreams of Leaving,* which he directed himself, and *Saigon: Year of the Cat,* directed by Stephen Frears. He wrote *A Map of the World* for the 1983 Adelaide Festival in Australia, which subsequently opened at London's National Theatre. The same year, *Plenty* won the New York Critics Circle Award for best foreign play. Hare's work not only was seen on three continents, but now also dealt with international topics as well as British national history and concerns.

Wetherby, Hare's first screenplay and his debut as a film director, won him the prestigious Golden Bear Award at the Berlin Film Festival in 1985. The same year, his collaboration with Brenton, *Pravda,* directed by Hare for the National Theatre, swept the London awards as best play of the year.

In 1986 Hare directed a controversial *King Lear* with Anthony Hopkins in the title role, at the National Theatre, as well as a double bill of his own, *The Bay at Nice* and *Wrecked Eggs.* Joseph Papp produced Hare's ambitious opera *The Knife* with Mandy Patinkin as Peter (act 1)—who becomes Liz (act 2)

after surgery—at the Public Theater in New York, in 1987. This was followed by the London success of *The Secret Rapture,* directed by Howard Davies at the National in 1988, and its New York debut, directed by Hare, in 1989. Hare directed two more films, *Paris by Night* (1989) and *Strapless* (1990), and wrote the screenplay for Louis Malle's film *Damage,* based on the 1991 novel of the same name by Josephine Hart.

The 1990s witnessed a new departure for Hare: a trilogy on epic scale based on three British institutions—the church, the law, and the Labour Party. *Racing Demon* and *Murmuring Judges* were produced individually at the National Theatre in 1990 and 1991, respectively, and as a trilogy, with *The Absence of War,* in 1993. His play *Skylight,* a more personal play on a more modest scale, was produced at the National in 1995. No other living playwright has been guaranteed such exposure at Britain's National Theatre, which is ironic, considering Hare's early rejection of mainstream dramatic values. However, Hare acknowledges that both he and theater have changed since his modest beginnings, when theaters were unwilling to criticize British institutions.

The plays of David Hare cannot be divorced from their production history because he is known both as a playwright and a director, equally adept at stage plays, teleplays, and screenplays. Performance sites mark Hare's progression from avant-garde fringe to mainstream commercial theater. Hare has been prolific in his personal reflections on productions, both in published and broadcast interviews. Some of his articles and introductions are collected in *Writing Left-Handed* (1991), while *Asking Around* (1993) describes the research he did for his trilogy, *Racing Demon, Murmuring Judges,* and *The Absence of War.*

Hare is considered a political playwright because a single theme dominates all of Hare's work and unifies his diverse experimentation with media and genres. Political institutions reduce mankind to three types: victors, victims, and compromisers. Victors have mastered the system by securing a place in the mainstream. Victims fail to succeed often because they refuse to buy in or sell out to the establishment. Compromisers survive, integrity intact, by living on the edge of society or off others. Hare's plays force audiences and readers to examine their own place in society and their part in the system. His plays provoke thought, soul-searching, and laughter. He aims not to please but to prod.

EARLY EXPERIMENTAL PLAYS
AND COLLABORATIONS

AT Cambridge, in the political and social turmoil of the 1960s, Hare became involved in student protests that influenced his early work. He was also exposed to early feminists, as reflected in *Slag* (1971), whose three characters are women teaching at an exclusive girls' public school.

Since Hare insists in "Writing Left-Handed"—his introduction to *History Plays* (1983)—that "Englishness is of the essence" (p. 84) in performing his plays, it is ironic that he chose for the director of *Slag* an American graduate of the Yale School of Drama, Roger Hendricks-Simon. Hendricks-Simon attributes this choice to the fierce rebelliousness with which Hare then attacked all things English. Just as Jimmy Porter in Osborne's *Look Back in Anger* blasts away at British tradition through his jazz saxophone, so Hare sought an American in London to direct his bombast at elite British education.

The title *Slag* is open to several interpretations. It is "gals" spelled backward, which is derogatory but playful, but it is also slang for "slut." A slag heap is composed of industrial waste. One such heap is constructed by Joanne, a militant feminist, of mashed potatoes that she believes are poisoned by the school's headmistress, Ann.

The play opens with a conspiratorial oath of celibacy by Joanne, Ann, and the third teacher, Elise. Recalling both the oath of the three witches in Shakespeare's *Macbeth* and the oath sworn in the first act of *Hamlet*, it parodies such vows. Although they swear abstinence, Ann has secret trysts with a butcher, and Elise has a hysterical pregnancy resulting from a lesbian relationship with Ann.

Knowing that his early plays would be staged on the road, Hare used minimal scenery and fast blackouts. In *Slag* six scenes leap from common room to cricket pitch, bathroom to bedroom, with offstage sounds used to simulate student activities. Slapstick acts, black humor, and scatological jokes are reminiscent of Joe Orton's farces. *Slag* was heavily criticized for poking fun at women. In Hare's later plays men, too, suffer the barbs of his outrageous pen, and, while he remained preoccupied with the British class system and politics, other cultures become the objects of his scathing satire as well.

His next plays, "What Happened to Blake?" (1970), "Lay By" (1971), and "Deathshead" (1972), are unpublished but important as early experiments and collaborations. "Lay By," which is based on a newspaper account of violent rape and murder, was written with a team of six other playwrights, including Howard Brenton. "Deathshead," a two-minute play, was performed at the 1979 Edinburgh Festival. These early collaborations, now considered "juvenilia," attempted—but failed—to reach lower-class audiences. They laid the foundations for Hare's later collaboration with Brenton on *Brassneck* and *Pravda*.

Hare's next published play, *The Great Exhibition* (1972), is divided into two acts, "Public Life" and "Private Life." Paradoxically, the outside world comes into the home of a corrupt politician, Charlie Hammett, in act 1, while he exposes his "privates" on Hampstead Heath in act 2. Again, Hare seems to be inviting a comparison with Shakespeare's characters—this time with *King Lear*, but the tragic is made comic. Other farcical aspects of *The Great Exhibition* are a private investigator, decked out with trench coat and porkpie hat, hiding in closets, and three characters in a triangular relationship all employing this same spy. A more serious note, which resounds in Hare's later plays, is the complete incompatibility of characters: the more one loves, the more the beloved is repulsed, while rejection paradoxically attracts.

The third play in the anthology of Hare's *Early Plays* (1991) is a musical, *Teeth 'n' Smiles*, with music by Nick Bicât and lyrics by Tony Bicât. It draws heavily on their life at Cambridge and takes place during the May Ball. The May Ball is a formal ball held at English universities at the end of the academic year. The Oxford and Cambridge May Balls are major events in the English social calendar. The first production of *Teeth 'n' Smiles*, in 1975, was directed by Hare at the Royal Court Theatre with Helen Mirren as Maggie, the self-destructive rock singer. Antony Sher played Anson, the Cambridge medical student who fits neither the undergraduate world nor the alternative drug scene into which he is drawn by Maggie's band.

Teeth 'n' Smiles has several incompatible characters engaged in hopeless relationships. Peyote is a drug addict, who is incapable of all relationships. Arthur is Maggie's old flame and erstwhile lyricist, whom she abuses into the arms of her friend and roadie, Laura. Saraffian, the band's manager, is one of Hare's first despicable profiteers and an example of his older male characters inhabiting younger spheres. We despise Saraffian's exploitation of the young, floundering band but understand when he describes a wartime air raid during which a scavenger looted dead nightclub revelers. "How low can men get stealing from the dead and dying?" is the kind of question that recurs in Hare's work (p. 239). Readers and audiences often find themselves more in sympathy with honest villains than with hypocritical heroes. Maggie, an antiheroine, drunk and abusive as she is, bears no malice to those who betray her. In a literal blaze of glory, as the May Ball tents go up in flames, Maggie, the architect of arson, goes to jail to cover for the drug-bearing band.

Fanshen (1976), based on the 1966 novel of the same name by William Hinton, is Hare's most Brechtian product. The script for this play was developed during workshops of the Joint Stock Company in 1974–1975. Experimenting with form and content, Hare attended rehearsals in which actors improvised, an appropriate technique for a play that deals with the Cultural Revolution in China, for the actors were reworking the script as the workers were reshaping their lives. The company used technical limitations to advantage and relied heavily on Brechtian techniques, such as placards and slogans, to convey time, place, and message. The main issue is the balance of power, as people try to change the relationship between the leaders and the led. The word "fanshen" means "to turn the body" or "to turn over," and the collaborators remained true to the spirit of the work by allowing the actors the same autonomy as the characters.

The action of the play is a record of life in the village of Long Bow from 1945 to 1949 and concerns the changing roles of the villagers as they examine the strata of their social hierarchy, from the privileged to the very poor. Roles are reversed frequently throughout the play to demonstrate the chaos and confusion of the time. Villagers guilty of exploiting their neighbors become the victims of those they victimized in a chain of command that changes continuously, like that in Beckett's sinister *What Where* (1984), written later but better known.

Although *Fanshen* was much admired and often performed by amateur, college, and regional theater groups in the years that followed its first production, in retrospect it seems more dated than Hare's other early plays. After a 1988 revival of the play at the National Theatre it was pointed out by critics that the play is very different for audiences who have considered and rejected communism than for those who have never thought about it.

Hare collaborated twice with Howard Brenton, first on *Brassneck* (1973), which they wrote for the Nottingham Playhouse, and later on *Pravda*. "Brass" is a northern dialect word for money; "brassneck" means "nerve," and the word has criminal connotations as well. When Brenton and Hare collaborate, plays are characterized by broader strokes and more blatant depravity than that found in Hare's solo efforts. Abuse is more savage, language more obscene, and characters are caricatures often based on notorious contemporary or historical figures.

Brassneck is an epic that covers three generations of the Bagley family over three decades of post–World War II England. The patriarch, Alfred Bagley, is based on John Poulson, whose price-fixing schemes rocked Europe in the mid 1970s. This addition would interest audiences au courant with current affairs. That the Bagley family mirrors the Borgias in name and deed would appeal to more literary audiences. Alfred's scheming and preoccupation with survival are traced to the trenches of World War I, where he witnessed cannibalism and had his view of the universe forever altered. His nephews and nieces are ruthless and corrupt for the sake of personal gain, without the excuse of war. While still children, Sidney blows up his brother's dog, while his sister, Lucy, shows her knickers to every man in sight, foreshadowing her later promiscuity.

In *Brassneck* Hare is interested in portraying more than simply ruthless individuals. Through slide projections documentary sequences trace British politics from photographs of Winston Churchill and the royal family on V-E Day through the Tory defeat of 1945 and the 1953 coronation of Queen Elizabeth. Interspersed with these national events are public and private scenes: a Masonic initiation, a wedding, a foxhunt, and, in a dream sequence, a papal *annunziato*. Significantly, as the family sinks, the play ends in a strip joint called "the Lower Depths Club," where the remnants of the Bagley family and their retainers are swallowed into the ground as they plan a drug deal—toasting "the last days of capitalism" (p. 102).

The implication is that all politicians and businessmen are partners in the corruption that has brought postcolonial England to its knees. Apparently benign organizations are disguises for cutthroat commerce. Rituals are ridiculous and meaningless. Men and women are either crows or worms (pp. 55–56). Public relations means human banking: "building up a pool of friends to be cashed at any branch" (p. 82).

Hare next collaborated with Brenton twelve years later on *Pravda,* under very different circumstances. By 1985 both playwrights had established considerable reputations such that *Pravda* made its debut at the National Theatre, with Anthony Hopkins in the leading role of Le Roux. It was an immediate critical and commercial success. The protagonist, Lambert Le Roux, is such an ebullient villain, that, like Shakespeare's Richard III, he sweeps audiences along in a current of delight with his villainy. The play is an indictment of the press, and Le Roux's business transactions are closely modeled on those of media tycoon Rupert Murdoch.

Le Roux is a blatant rogue, but his victims are all sycophants who eventually accept his terms. The central conflict is between Le Roux and Andrew May, a young journalist whose girlfriend, Rebecca, is the voice of integrity. Through a series of manipulative promotions, Le Roux succeeds in buying May's loyalty, and when May tries to double-cross his boss, he is beaten at his own game and revealed as the worm to Le Roux's crow.

Other characters are ridiculous parodies of Fleet Street journalists, with such names as Elliot Fruit-Norton and Cliveden Whicker-Basket to underline their upper-class pretensions. The audience delights in seeing them fall, especially at the hands of a lower-class, less-educated outsider. Le Roux is South African but changes his nationality to gain a firmer hold on his British acquisitions. In acquiring an English veneer, he exposes the superficiality of the British system, demonstrating how money buys power, prestige, and privilege.

Returning to the Brechtian techniques of their early years with the Portable Theatre, Brenton and Hare put lurid newspaper headlines on placards in *Pravda* to show the depths of the gutter press. Although we despise the tabloids, as readers and audience we secretly celebrate the decline of *The Victory,* which Hare intends as an allusion to the London *Times,* because we see that the old-boy network that runs it is even more despicable. Both the newspaper and those who run it have a respectable exterior to cover their lies, whereas the tabloids and those who run them make no pretense at honesty and integrity. The soliloquies of Le Roux convince us that he, like Iago in Shakespeare's *Othello,*

is at least an honest villain. He too uses animal imagery and conducts his relationships like a predator stalking his prey. He reverses platitudes and presents realities. Friendship is founded on mistrust. *Pravda* (truth) is a foundry of lies. Le Roux is aware of his own manipulations and exposes those who are unaware or unwilling to admit their own.

PLAYS OF POSTWAR ENGLAND

HARE traces his true beginning as a playwright to *Knuckle* in 1974. He had thought of himself as a theater director who occasionally wrote plays until he was forced to rewrite *Knuckle* in 1973, after the original script was lost. His intention was to subvert the form of the thriller to a serious end, his early influences being mystery novelists such as Dick Francis, John Dickson Carr, and Patricia Highsmith. Thrillers were the form of literature he "understood best" with "indiscriminate enthusiasm" (*Writing Left-Handed,* p. 74). Many components of Hare's most important plays are present in *Knuckle.*

The episodic structure, common to many of Hare's plays, presents sixteen scenes in rapid succession. This style of staging anticipates Hare's screenplays, in which he relies on the camera and film editing to accomplish what lighting, plot, and set changes strive to achieve on stage. The protagonist, Curly Delafield, an arms dealer playing sleuth, delivers monologues explaining his motives.

The characters are divided into generations, and their differing ideologies mark not just a gap but a yawning void of miscommunication, while their personal stories echo the corruption, waste, and inequality of postwar England. Curly investigates the death of his sister, Sarah, whose absence lingers over the play. Her silenced voice is one of honesty and innocence that is incompatible with the living. Like other Hare women, Sarah, doomed to be a victim, is flawed and unsuited to life as a survivor.

Curly left home at the age of fifteen to escape his father, Patrick, an investment banker with underhanded property dealings. Patrick's credo is: "The exploitation of the masses should be conducted as quietly as possible" (p. 19). He tells his son that tact will be the measure of his maturity. Though Curly vehemently opposes his father's seemingly moral mainstream lifestyle propped up by white-collar crime, by the end of the play he has quietly switched to his father's lifestyle of compromise. Curly abandons his search for the "tiny little weed called morality" (p. 84) and allows himself to be seduced by the "soft fiscal embrace" of Lloyd's of London (p. 50). Patrick and Curly emerge as the profiteer stereotypes we love to hate in *Pravda*. The older man is despised for his exploitation of others, the younger for his willingness to jockey for position on the back of any contender.

Sarah's friend Jenny stubbornly refuses to conform yet compromises by accepting a bar from a man she scorns. The absent Sarah is fondly remembered by her father only for stealing money to use as wallpaper. Patrick describes his children as unquenchable: Sarah's deep well of unhappiness is fueled by her pity for the world, Curly's by his desire to ensure everyone is as degraded as himself. There are no excuses. Men have created a "plush abattoir" of life; women are the living flesh to be processed. Jenny, who has been abused and assaulted all her life, expects such treatment to continue.

The audience is degraded, too. At one point, while choosing weapons for his arsenal, Curly aims directly at the audience. Later, on the notorious Eastbourne beach where Sarah may have drowned or been murdered, Jenny, standing on Curly's shoulders, looks into the audience and sees "heavy scowls and fists raised in anger . . . men with axes in their backs, acid steaming off their skins, needles in their eyeballs, tripping on barbed wire, falling on broken bottles" (pp. 26–27). These are the people described earlier by Curly as axle grease for the wheels that turn civilization. And they are us, unless, that is, we are the perpetrators.

Hare also uses audience alienation in *Plenty* (1978). The play, which opens in a dismantled home, promises plenty then strips away our hopes. It follows Susan Traherne from the French Resistance in 1943 to her desertion of her husband, Raymond Brock, in 1962. En route, Susan leaves jobs and partners in her wake, because she finds no match for the excitement of her war work. In a flashback at the end of the play, Susan looks forward to peace, expecting that "there will be days and days and days like this" (p. 478). In fact, there are none. Like the missing Sarah in *Knuckle*, Susan has known perhaps twenty minutes of happiness, by which she measures her entire life thereafter.

Hare structures the play in twelve scenes arranged unchronologically, with two flashbacks to wartime France, four scenes in the play's present (1962), and six scenes progressing through the postwar years from 1947 to 1961. Many scenes begin in the dark, with music or radio commentary, and one starts with a funeral oration. The combinations of light and sound are important in setting time, place, and mood.

Key points in postwar British history—the Festival of Britain in 1951 and the Suez Canal crisis of 1956—become contexts for the play's action. Recovery from war is measured by meals, from skimpy rations in 1947 to an embarrassment of riches in 1956. Costumes and sets mark not only the prevailing fashions but also the increasing wealth of the protagonists. The play is deliberately disjointed as an emblem of the times. Ambiguities are designed to shake audiences out of their complacency. Characters behave inconsistently, lying to one another and to themselves. No one emerges unscathed.

Susan's gradual disintegration mirrors that of the country. As she trashes her home, her husband lies naked and bloody on the floor. What brings them to this end is the content of the play. The final scene presents a hopeful young Susan in France, predicting that Britons will learn how to improve, not rule, the world. But the audience knows that the beginning of the play is the end of the story: nothing for plenty, despair for hope.

Susan is an idealist, but her life is based on lies: the "glittering lies" of her youth, the more sordid ones of her present, which we see enacted. Her marriage to Raymond Brock is a perpetuating lie. Hare presents three failed relationships. While Brock seeks affection, Susan seeks distance. She asks Mick, a virtual stranger, to father her child. After eighteen months of sexual activity that fails to result in pregnancy, Mick seeks intimacy and is shot by Susan, in a reversal of gender roles reminiscent of Henrik Ibsen's Hedda Gabler. This act lands her in a mental institution from which she is rescued by Brock. In caring for Susan and "trapping" her into marriage, Brock sacrifices his career to Susan's increasing mania for revealing "truth."

Susan's affair with Mick is strictly business, her marriage to Brock strictly convenience. Her long-lost wartime lover, Code-Name Lazar(us), who dropped into her life by parachute, is resurrected, but also fails. They lie on the bed of a dismal Blackpool hotel room, fully dressed and murmuring of their past yet unable to consummate their present. Susan ignores Lazar's plea to touch him, and Lazar is unable to comply with her request for a kiss, because she passes out. The play ends with a marijuana-induced vision of the blue skies and green fields of France in 1944, as the real room "scatters," much like Susan's own sense of reality.

In this bleak landscape, humor saves the play from overwhelming gloom. Brock shares private jokes with Susan but resents her telling them to Alice. Alice laughs at her students and calls Susan's embarrassing behavior "psychiatric cabaret" (p. 437). Those who are masters of diplomacy in public are racist and sexist in private.

Members of the establishment consider any behavior contrary to good manners a sign of depravity. Hence, Susan's noisy insistence on expressing the truth, in a world where tact is the password, is linked to her instability. The more she questions the status quo, the more marginal her image. Bursts of outrage are labeled mental lapses. Susan's dilemma is not unique. In war, all can agree on right and wrong and rally round the flag. But in peace, who is the enemy? Brock demands: "Which is the braver? To live as I do? Or never, ever to face life like you?" (p. 467).

Facing life and putting on a face are important issues in Hare's plays. Half the characters—the contradictory ones—face life head-on, do not like what they see, and spend the rest of their lives looking up or down. When they look up, like Susan, they see a mackerel sky, parachutes, and fireworks. When they look down, they cannot accept grim existence and seek escape. Those who manage to live within the system put on their best face and live a sham, perpetuating and absorbed by that system. Brock sees Susan's destructiveness but spends fifteen years pandering to it. Ambassador Sir Leonard Darwin hates "wogs" and Personnel Chief Sir Andrew Charleson ridicules Persian psychiatry, yet they are brilliant diplomats. Only Alice survives on the edge, an outsider who refuses to conform but compromises just enough to walk the fine line between both ideologies. Between plenty and paucity is sufficiency.

Hare's reputation as a playwright was sufficient for *Plenty* to be commissioned by the National Theatre, where he was able to achieve the stage directions for quick scene changes, dark voice-overs, and dazzling lighting effects integral to the success of the play. Dark silhouettes in a doorway or the shattering of a dismal hotel room for a dazzling dream of France look effective on paper but depend absolutely on technical expertise and theater facilities when staged. Hare's days of concern for all of this were over. He was also able to attract actors of great caliber. The productions in both London and New York starred Kate Nelligan as Susan and were directed by Hare.

Joseph Papp, the creator of the New York Shakespeare Festival, was sufficiently impressed by the play to sponsor a film version of *Plenty*, which was directed by Fred Schepisi and released in 1985. Hare wrote the screenplay, which made considerable concessions to the movie genre and undercut the sparse economy and cutting edge of the play.

In the screenplay Hare uses European and Iranian locations and accommodates his wider film audience by changing historical references. Hare is heavy-handed with symbolism. Lazar's cuff links stay in Susan's handbag for the whole film, a constant reminder. Mackerel skies and parachutists make regular appearances, which reduce their impact.

Licking Hitler, *Plenty*'s companion piece for BBC television, also deals with lies and perceptions of truth. A propagandist who produces radio dialogues for deliberate interception by the Germans complains about the BBC's insistence on truth, which he sees as a negotiable commodity. *Licking Hitler* has a young female protagonist, Anna Seaton, who is dragged into the British war effort because of her upper-class background and her fluency in German. Anna arrives at the stately home of Wendlesham, totally innocent, ignorant, and naive. Reminiscent of the BBC's production of Evelyn Waugh's *Brideshead Revisited*, the opening shots show a military unit taking over a mansion, as the elderly, impotent occupant, Lord Minton, sits on his suitcase, awaiting evacuation. A radio propaganda team sets up its equipment and is briefed on the operation. We learn, with Anna, that a prisoner from an internment camp and a German Jew will play the parts of German officers. Their conversation includes details that will subvert patriotism and allegiance to Hitler with tales of corruption and perverted sex among high-ranking SS officers and civilian leaders.

Anna's background is so sheltered and privileged that she arrives at Wendlesham not even knowing how to make a pot of tea and squanders an entire week's ration on one attempt. But she is soon put in her place by the rest of the crew, and she is a willing apprentice and fast learner. After her miserable first night, during which she seeks comfort in her teddy bear, she moves to the whiskey-swilling Archie Maclean, formerly a Fleet Street journalist and "one of our most gifted writers" (p. 365). Teddy is relegated to the closet with Archie's empties, and Anna is soon making triumphant soufflés as well as succeeding as a translator and researcher.

Licking Hitler might have been called "The Education of Anna," but it also contrasts the games being played in the stately halls of Wendlesham with the brutal reality of war. When a coworker, Eileen, hears of the death of her brother in Singapore, Anna questions the ethics of destroying lives through propaganda. She is reminded by her superior that Joseph Goebbels inspired the enemy to go to, stay in, and die in Russia: "We have as much duty to assist our side as he has his. And we must bring to it the same vigour, the same passion, the same intelligence that he has brought to his" (p. 364).

The passion and intelligence of Archie Maclean's propaganda scripts are interpreted by some as "barking madness." Archie, the "cloven-hoofed Celt" from the Red Clyde, survives with the goal of just getting through the war, accepting and enduring but not thinking about it, whereas Anna, like Susan Traherne in *Plenty*, is destroyed by it. Accused by Will Langley of seducing Maclean toward the end of the operation, Anna's final destiny is heard at the end of the broadcast. A voice-over describes the future of the main characters through newsreel footage and stills. While many of the "brilliant men" went on to successful careers in politics, universities, and the media, Anna languished in an unsatisfying advertising job, a failed marriage, disease and surgery resulting from promiscuity, and retirement from the political scene. The teleplay ends with a letter from Anna to Archie, telling him she has loved him for thirty years, and the terse comment, "He never replied" (p. 370).

Men are victors in Hare's play, while women are victims—those who think are overwhelmed by those who act. In *Licking Hitler* the outcome of class war is reversed. Archie, from the slums of Glasgow, is able to exploit his past in documentaries and move on to Hollywood, but Anna, whose uncle was Second Sea Lord at the Admiralty and who spent summers in castles on the Rhine, ends up lonely and rejected on a hillside in Wales. Hitler may be licked, but so are wartime women, who maintain their integrity but fail to pass muster in the mainstream of postwar society. In depicting more sympathetic female characters in the play, Hare underlines the way in which countries treat women as equals with men in wartime, relegating them to lesser status when life returns to "normal."

In the single hour of the telecast, in which Wendlesham becomes a microcosm of wartime England, characters from different classes suppress their differences to engage in undermining enemy morale. The problem is, as Anna says in retrospect, that "whereas we knew exactly what we were fighting against, none of us had the whisper of an idea as to what we were fighting for" (p. 128).

In his plays of the 1980s Hare directed his attention away from wartime England (although in 1991 he returned to this setting with the teleplay *Heading Home*). During that decade Hare's interest in writing for both the large and the small screen produced more screenplays and teleplays than it did stage plays. In *A Map of the World* (1983) he mixes media and genres by presenting a play about the making of a movie based on a novel. The setting is a United Nations conference in Bombay, where international experts discuss the fate of third world nations at the hands of the superpowers. The title comes from a line in Oscar Wilde's essay "The Soul of Man Under Socialism": "A map of the world that does not include Utopia is not worth glancing at." Needless to say, in Hare's maps of the world, Utopia is noticeably absent.

Like George Bernard Shaw's plays of ideas, *A Map of the World* centers around a debate between two characters representing opposing ideologies. (Unlike Shaw, Hare's debate is preplanned, with an audience.) One is an idealistic young journalist, Stephen Andrews, who supports the indigenous cultures of developing nations and protests the heavy-handed and self-serving attitudes of countries offering them aid. The other is a seasoned and successful novelist, Indian by birth, British by choice, Victor Mehta. Victor supports old cultures, by which he means Western ones. He chooses to live in England because he feels British institutions are the guardians of civilization.

The much-heralded debate is curtailed when Stephen decides to withdraw, deferring to his older opponent and thereby forgoing the woman who has offered herself as the "prize," Peggy Whitton. Peggy's struggle between her attraction to the young idealist and the mature realist is resolved by Stephen's withdrawal and death in a train crash. This becomes the subject of a later novel by Mehta, whom she marries.

Entering the play to portray himself in the movie, Mehta objects to the trivializing of his subject: "A moral story has been reduced to the status of a romance, transformed to a vulgar medium and traduced. Very well. It is what one expects. One looks to the cinema for money, not for enlightenment, and to be fair, the money has arrived" (p. 221). When Hare turned to feature films, critics naturally wondered if he had been referring to himself.

The film within the play is an interesting idea, but Hare admits to the unwieldy and confusing format of *A Map of the World*. It was written for the 1983 Adelaide Festival in Australia and premiered there to mixed reviews. What delighted Hare was the disparate reactions from audiences and critics. The purpose of theater, he believes, is to sharpen minds and question motives. If a play does that, like any of those of Shaw and Brecht, Hare is happy.

SCREENPLAYS

LIKE all postwar playwrights, Hare was influenced by the increasing power of the media and the popularity of film. He has adapted some of his plays for radio and television and written others specifically for television. The unpublished *Man Above Men* was televised in 1973, *Brassneck* in 1975, and *Saigon: Year of the Cat* in 1983.

Hare visited Saigon and wrote *Saigon: Year of the Cat* to counteract what he perceived as the imbalance between films dealing with the American tragedy in Vietnam and the plight of the Vietnamese people. The plot deals with the last months before the fall of Saigon in 1975 and the inability of both the U.S. ambassador and the Central Intelligence Agency (CIA) to accept the possibility of defeat. Vietnamese civilians and expatriate Britons are betrayed by the Americans in the chaotic evacuation of the city. This anti-U.S. perspective created problems during the production of the film. Director Stephen Frears's cast included Dame Judi Dench as a middle-aged English banker in love with a young CIA agent, played by Frederic Forrest. While Dench shaped her character to the script, Forrest found his dialogue unpatriotic and insisted on ad-libbing, as he had done with Marlon Brando in *Apocalypse Now* (1979). The result is a film far from its writer's intentions.

Less ambitious and more successful than *Saigon: Year of the Cat, Dreams of Leaving* (1980) is set in England, with trains instead of helicopters and an all-British cast familiar with Hare's needs. The main characters, William and Caroline, resemble Brock and Susan in *Plenty*. William is a young journalist in search of love, which Caroline is unable to provide. The greater William's need, the more she is repulsed, but when he doesn't care, she is attracted to him. While William progresses in his career and at the end of the film has a wife and two children in the suburbs, Caroline is institutionalized in a psychiatric hospital, and William is grateful to have escaped his relationship with her, though he is haunted by her memory.

William's narrative advances the plot of the screenplay, and Caroline's unpredictable behavior injects the action with excitement. We sense why William is so involved with Caroline and why that involvement is so dangerous. Working in direct opposition to the philosophy "know thyself," Caroline makes love to strangers to forget who she is. William confesses, "I was never myself when I was with her" (p. 145); but while William progresses to more stable relationships, Caroline is stuck in her immaturity.

The voice of the older William commenting on the behavior of his younger self stabilizes the action. In retrospect he recalls bouncing around London, chasing Caroline from art gallery to rock band to dance studio, and compromising his ethics to accommodate her latest interest; his somber voice comments, "That was the point I should have abandoned it. People love chaos. I went on in" (p. 149).

The gulf between generations so often portrayed by Hare is effectively demonstrated here by the two ages of the same character. William's voice tells us he lost his judgment, while his actions show us he had none. The character of Caroline did nothing to enhance Hare's reputation with those critics who saw his neurotic, destructive women as evidence of his being anti-feminist. In his next screenplay, for the full-length feature film *Wetherby*, Hare centers on an unbalanced young *man* and the effect of his dramatic suicide on the women subjected to it. This film, like *Dreams of Leaving*, he directed himself.

Wetherby is a psychological thriller in which the audience strains to predict not "whodunit?" but why a lonely graduate student, John Morgan, chooses to kill himself in front of Jean Travers. Jean is a schoolteacher whom John seems to have selected as his "victim" because he recognizes in her a kindred spirit.

The linear plot is simple: John attends Jean's dinner party uninvited. Each guest thinks someone else has brought him. During the course of the evening, Jean and John go up to her attic to mend a leak in the roof. There is a tense passionate moment that reminds Jean of her fiancé, Jim, an airman killed in Korea. The next day, John returns and, during their ensuing conversation, puts a gun in his mouth and shoots himself.

The film is not shown in linear progression, however. There are flashbacks, mostly through Jean's memory of her past, that explain the kind of woman she has become. These flashbacks, which qualify as a subplot, are so detailed that they suggest a connection between the romance of young Jean and Jim, and John Morgan's infatuation with Jean.

Jean's friends are equally important in the present tense of the screenplay. Marcia is an old school chum and confidante, and her husband, Stanley, is perhaps Jean's lover. Although we never see Jean and Stanley in bed, the film is framed by their friendship, opening and closing with their comfortable conversations in a pub, while Stanley's relationship with his wife is clearly strained. Stanley warns Jean never to marry with the intention of avoiding loneliness.

The third man to become entangled with Jean is the detective investigating John's suicide, Mike Langdon. Mike is involved with an attractive young married woman named Chrissie, who later returns to her husband, and Mike is drawn by his sense of betrayal back to Jean's house. Thus, as the film progresses, we gain insights into the strong powers of attraction of a woman who on the surface seems to be a mild, middle-aged schoolteacher but whose passionate past, seemingly controlled in a mundane present, may explode at any moment.

Adding to the intrigue is Karen, an undergraduate who seems to have caused John's unhinging. Karen is a strange young woman with a strong aversion to human contact. Flashbacks reveal her rejection of John and his increasing frustration. Karen appears on Jean's doorstep after John's funeral, like John, uninvited, and lingers on as a disturbing presence.

Jean is shown interacting with her students. She is a good teacher, a compassionate woman, a loyal friend. Yet from the young Jean, unable to relate to Jim's parents, to the mature Jean, victimized by suicide, she does not quite fit the Yorkshire town of Wetherby. Her honesty and sensitivity make her vulnerable to the pressures of true misfits like John and Karen, whose demands for life on their own terms make it impossible for them to live the life of compromise that Jean has fashioned for herself.

In directing his own screenplay, Hare realized the mood he sought by complicated crosscutting, fast-flashing images, and evocative lighting. The viewer is instantly in Jean's mind as she recalls the past, and is forced to make comparisons as the camera jumps from a slit throat (Jim's in Korea) to splattered brains (John's in Jean's kitchen). As Jean, silhouetted in a long shot at her kitchen sink while she gazes at the Yorkshire countryside, speaks of her love of long, slow summer evenings, we know that the next action, John's suicide, will forever end such simple pleasures.

Thoughtful investigation of personality is a hallmark of the best British and European films since the 1960s, but such techniques are not as well received in the United States. While garnering praise and awards in Europe, *Wetherby* was described as ponderous by most U.S. critics. Its sinister silences and strained relationships are evocative of screenplays by Harold Pinter.

Closer to *Wetherby* and *Dreams of Leaving* in tone and content is Hare's 1991 BBC teleplay *Heading Home*. The narrator is Janetta. Like William in *Dreams of Leaving*, Janetta looks back on her life to a time in 1947 that seemed to crystallize the choices of her youth. In this case, the choice is between the safe literary, bohemian lifestyle of her poet-love, Leonard, and the dangerous property racketeering of Ian, an impetuous, self-made young man on the rise. In trying to keep both men, Janetta gains nothing and loses both. As a middle-aged librarian assessing her life, she knows that her turbulent past with them was the highlight of her later dreary existence.

The opening shot of the film evokes nostalgia: a beach scene where the young Janetta made love first with Leonard, then with Ian. Forty years later the beach is obscured by the houses that are the result of Ian's speculation. The English have succeeded in bricking themselves in and shutting out the world, as predicted by young Ian. Both he and Leonard have disappeared without a trace, Ian probably the victim of rival speculators, Leonard most likely living a life of quiet compromise. In Janetta's attempt at normality, the death of her young husband from cancer has had less impact on her than the dramatic memories of her early love affairs.

What marks *Heading Home* and other Hare scripts from the 1990s is that characters are not so easily boxed into categories of good and evil. Leonard is generous and outgoing but fails to speak openly about issues that bother him most. He hints, writes notes, and buries his innermost feelings in poetry, so Janetta is unaware of the deep hurt her infidelity has caused him.

Ian, however, is brutally honest and continually calls into question Janetta's self-delusion. When they make love, he complains, she "lends" herself, instead of "giving." He tells her: "You love him, but you want to sleep with me" (p. 42). When she criticizes Ian for refusing to give change to a beggar, he showers notes on the man, then asks, "Am I a nice person now?" (p. 48), thereby exposing her generosity as a type of currency she uses to buy self-esteem.

Caught between extremes, Janetta is true to neither. Beryl, a sculptor formerly living with Leonard, tells her that "staying innocent is just a kind of cowardice" (p. 55). Janetta is incapable of introspection. Beryl warns her that love is never equal: one partner always holds the upper hand. As spectators, we wonder who controls our own relationships.

Ian is restless. Like Susan in *Plenty*, he has adapted to war but is impatient with peace. He is less concerned about his impending death, at the hands of thugs, which he might avoid, than about his future: "By twenty-five, you can reproduce yourself. The job's done. Then what are we meant to do for the rest of our lives? Just sit around and get boring?" (p. 61). Ian's choice is clear. Janetta chooses otherwise. As she looks back through a montage of memories, we wonder if she would make the same choice again.

Hare's film techniques work well with his dialogue. The opposite outlooks expressed in their dialogue is matched by the contrasting imagery. The images of the sunlit beach, lovemaking in the dunes, and driving down shady English country lanes contrast well with the grim life in cold London flats, lit by cheerless gas heaters, sparked by meals of parsnips, gin, and occasionally salami. Ian, even at the height of his success, does business in pub basements. For Janetta, collecting rent for a slum landlord is her peak experience.

Hare uses what he calls a "subjective" camera, which allows us to see the past through Janetta's eyes while Janetta's voice tells us that others may remember differently. Like William's in *Dreams of Leaving* and Jean's in *Wetherby*, Janetta's longing is for a past passion.

In the film *Strapless* (1989), Lillian has banished passion. She is an American physician who chooses to work in a National Health hospital in London, where she cares for cancer patients. She also cares for an irresponsible younger sister, the flamboyant Amy, whose indolent lifestyle she supports. Lillian lives in England because she wants to be left alone, self-supporting, strapless. She is able to achieve this only after experiencing a devastating love affair that dislocates time and reality and destroys her calm, controlled life.

Lillian meets Raymond in a Portuguese cathedral. He pursues her relentlessly but elegantly in a courtship that recalls the Middle Ages. Their first conversation is sparked by a crucified Christ spouting roses for blood, so Raymond sends roses and writes on stationery embossed with roses. In the true spirit of a medieval knight, he even brings her a horse. As Lillian loses her footing in this romance, the film intercuts aspects of her professional and home life, where she is totally in control. Among her colleagues and patients she is well respected though distant. At home she despairs of her sister ever settling down into a normal job or relationship but indulges her like a daughter. Once she marries Raymond, however, Lillian is exposed to the darker side of Raymond's personality and his secret dealings. He disappears and reappears with expensive gifts, and she pays large debts on his behalf. As she struggles with the secrecy, mystery, and duplicity, her other life falls apart. She runs from her hospital work into a closet, where she sobs uncontrollably. Returning home, she finds a pregnant Amy living in filth and chaos. Furious, Lillian attacks her sister. Her previous restraint dissolves in the panic of losing a lover who was never a real husband.

As the fairy-tale romance fades to grim reality, Lillian's curiosity leads her to people in Raymond's past. She is drawn to Annie, his first wife, and their son, Richard. With them she reaches an understanding and acceptance of Raymond. Pondering why any woman would want to marry a hopeless romantic who is incapable of commitment, Annie offers: "I was young"; and Lillian counters: "I was old" (p. 76).

Having solved the enigma of Raymond's past,

Lillian is able to accept the present. She returns to work and resumes her care of the sick. At home she finds a new Amy who has accepted responsibility in the wake of Lillian's breakdown. The death of a patient and the birth of her niece give Lillian a new perspective. She becomes an activist and protests National Health cuts, participating in a fundraising fashion show of strapless gowns. The film ends with Raymond, the perpetual romantic, picking up a woman's handkerchief at a French railway station. *Strapless* shows the sisters as two modern women, freed from the (s)trappings of the past, demonstrating their independence from love. The happy ending earns the film a place in the romance section of the video store.

Less commercial and devoid of love, *Paris by Night* (1988) was delayed in production. Hare reflects in the introduction to the published screenplay that he could easily have sold out to Hollywood on this film and that retaining control cost him four years and half a million dollars. Hare was directing *Paris by Night* during rehearsals for his major stage play *The Secret Rapture* (1988), so comparisons were inevitably made between the ruthless politicians Clara Paige in the film and Marion French in the play.

Hare has continually defended his heroines against the tag "unsympathetic." In the case of Clara, who is not only a politician but also a mother and a murderess, his task is particularly onerous. Hare insists that strong women are far more complex than "good" or "bad" and that his characters, in the hands of fine actresses, come to moving self-awareness.

Clara's present, as a promising Tory representative to the European Economic Community, and her future, as a member of Parliament for Birmingham South, are both threatened by a shady financial transaction from her past. In what seems an attempt at blackmail, Michael Swanton, an ex-business partner of Clara and her husband, Gerald, a member of Parliament, follows Clara to Paris. But the sinister Swanton is revealed as more pathetic than threatening. In an altercation on the banks of the Seine, Clara pushes him into the river and he drowns.

The film contrasts Clara's private and public lives. She is seen capably dealing in government and diplomacy but is a dismal failure as a wife, mother, and lover. She tells Gerald: "I hate you. . . . What you are. What you represent. Drink and cowardice in equal parts. The whole dreary mixture disgusts me" (p. 2). Ignoring pleas to return to her hospitalized son, Clara stays in Paris, where she has an affair with a young admirer, Wallace Sharp. She has strong but misplaced public relations skills. Her sister Pauline tells her: "I don't need flattery. You *have* my vote" (p. 9).

Like other Hare heroines, Clara feels free abroad. In the Paris home of Wallace's sister, Clara appreciates the simple pleasures of domesticity and children that she carelessly abandons in her own home. Gerald identifies this when he urgently calls Clara and tells her: "When you see this little boy, you realize. . . . We've both been beastly and careless of each other. . . . When something like this happens you realize we must make an effort" (p. 47). But Clara's efforts are devoted to protecting her career. Incapable of mothering her own child, she supports Jenny, Swanton's daughter, because Jenny's theory that her father was suicidal vindicates Clara. However Gerald and Wallace both discover the murder just as Gerald uncovers Clara's affair with Wallace. "You think you can get away with anything. No regard at all for anyone's feelings but your own. You're trash. . . . You're human trash. And trash belongs in the dustbin" (p. 82). Gerald fires a gun five times at Clara, and the film's final shots jump from her dead body slumped to the ground, to her lover Wallace waiting in the car, and her son Simon waking up. This film is guaranteed to outrage feminists as well as advocates of family values.

The film *Damage* (1992), for which Hare wrote the screenplay, is a troubling account of a father's affair with his son's fiancée. The infatuation and eventual destruction of a successful politician by a passionate young woman are familiar Hare territory. *Damage* is a psychological thriller in the style of *Wetherby* but with violent, explicit sex scenes. Because Hare's screenplay is considered a bridge between Josephine Hart's novel and Louis Malle's film, it is unpublished and therefore excluded from consideration in Hare's collected works. Likewise, Hare's direction of the 1997 film *The Designated Mourner* is not discussed here because the screenplay, by Wallace Shawn, is an adaptation of Shawn's play, produced at the National Theatre in 1996. It is important to recognize that, like Pinter, Hare has a flourishing career as a director of both plays and films, as well as a writer.

AFTER the enormous critical and commercial success of *Plenty* and *Pravda*, the period of film and television production, and *A Map of the World*, in which stage and screen are merged, Hare returned to the stage with two one-act plays for the National Theatre: *The Bay at Nice* and *Wrecked Eggs* (1986) are one-act companion pieces that he wrote for the National's smallest stage, the Cottesloe.

The more powerful of the two, *The Bay at Nice*, takes place in a Moscow art gallery. The protagonist, Valentina Nrovka, has been summoned to identify a painting that may be by Henri Matisse, under whom she studied as a young artist. Her daughter, Sophia, whose birth caused Valentina to return to Russia from Paris, seeks her mother's help in obtaining a divorce. Since Valentina feels she sacrificed her life for her family, she resents Sophia's desire to dissolve her marriage. Above the personal problems of mother and daughter looms the political repression of a Russian system that makes it almost impossible for relationships to flourish without the authorization of the state. Valentina and Sophia, like Hare's postwar English characters, barely eke out an existence. The mood is somber, thoughtful, and serious. Finally, when the painting, which is hidden from the audience until the final moment of the play, is revealed as a genuine Matisse, titled *The Bay at Nice*, the stage bursts into glorious color. The past has illuminated the present with hope for the future.

By contrast, *Wrecked Eggs* takes place in an American country house, where the affluent young owners, Robbie and Loelia, are about to celebrate their divorce. In the land of the free, separation, that commodity so shameful and hard to come by in Russia, is just another rite of passage. Grace, a weekend guest who turns out to be the only other person invited to their private party, is as profoundly disturbed by the American way of life as Sophia is by Russia's. In a long monologue about the new "pornography," Grace shows her hosts a page from the *New York Times* from which all references to success and survival have been excised, indicating that the media are obsessed with success and censor all references to failure in deference to stories of survival. What remains are just "latticed shreds" (p. 58).

Having lacerated the British political system in his early plays, Hare's plays of the mid-1980s attack both sides in the cold war as well as the superpowers in the international setting of *A Map of the World*. In his later plays, *The Secret Rapture* and those in the 1993 trilogy, Hare returns to home soil and integrates a keen examination of British institutions and the people who run them. His next play centers on three women: a politician, a designer, and an outcast with designs on her.

The Secret Rapture, Hare explains, is that moment when a nun expects to be united with Christ: death. Death frames the play. It opens with a corpse, that of Robert, in whose Gloucestershire farmhouse four of the eight scenes are set. It ends in the same setting, as the family gathers again for a funeral, this time for one of his daughters, Isobel. Isobel is both spiritual and sensitive, nursing her father in his illness and caring for her young stepmother after his death. Her sister Marion confesses to no feelings whatsoever and deeply resents Isobel, harboring a lifelong grudge that extends beyond sibling rivalry.

Katherine is the wicked stepmother. By her own admission, she is a middle-aged man's folly. A dependent alcoholic, Katherine becomes Isobel's responsibility because, as Marion points out, "I'm in the Conservative Party. We can't just take on anyone at all. . . . It's quite a different world. With extremely high stands [*sic*] of intellect and conduct. Civil servants have an extremely competitive and highly ordered career structure. In which you get very few marks for being an abusive alcoholic" (p. 17). While Marion, who is modeled on Margaret Thatcher, has a successful career in politics and a dazzling future ahead of her, Isobel allows Marion and Katherine to destroy her business, her relationship with her partner, Irwin, and, ultimately, her life.

The subject matter is serious, but the treatment of it is humorous. Each character is a parody. Marion is a parody of politics, with a mobile phone in her pocketbook. Her husband, Tom, a born-again Christian with a swimming pool for total immersions in his backyard, is a parody of religion. Irwin is a parody of the artist as a young man, and Isobel a parody of goodness, which, according to Hare, brings out the worst in all of us. The dialogue is deft and witty, and even when Isobel's behavior is saintly, her words are often sarcastic and cutting, which saves her from being sanctimonious. When she catches Irwin in a near infidelity with Rhonda, an upstart young Conservative supposedly inquiring about a bidet, Isobel replies, "There's no bidet. There's everything else. But if that's what you need you can always do handstands in the shower" (p. 51).

Though the play shifts from the country to various London offices, it is firmly grounded in Robert's farmhouse, where the family gathers for important events. All three women are inextricably drawn back by the spirit of their dead father/husband, like three latter-day Chekhovian sisters who can never escape their past.

Familiar themes and types, as well as Hare's newly revealed fascination with religion, ooze from *The Secret Rapture*. The play examines Britain's conservative society and the problems of good and evil it creates. Marion and Tom both openly ridicule Isobel's sense of honesty and integrity, and Katherine blandly states of Robert: "People say I took advantage of his decency. But what are good people for? They're here to help the trashy people like me" (p. 19). Even Irwin, whose love becomes an obsession that kills Isobel, cannot understand why she is so intractable when he has taken the middle road—a satisfying job with a decent salary.

What is the motive behind Isobel's goodness? Does she eschew business expansion to maintain control of Irwin and their business? Is she using him as others are using her? In Hare's uneasy England, it is significant that goodness is suspect and that peaceful hours in the country are disrupted by gunfire, as country gentlemen spend their weekends killing defenseless small creatures. Isobel notes, "The guns are getting nearer" (p. 44), thereby foreshadowing her own death at the hands of her lover. Free of her sister, Marion exudes a new sensuality, as Isobel goes to her father in "secret rapture."

It is significant that Hare was directing *King Lear* at the National Theatre while writing *The Secret Rapture*. Marion, Katherine, and Isobel have clear ties with Goneril, Regan, and Cordelia. Katherine (Regan) is identified as "pure evil," and Marion (Goneril) berates Isobel (Cordelia) for not being able to lie.

Marion's driving force is power. She positively struts after a confrontation with the Greens (that is, those who favor environmental awareness) over nuclear power plants, gloating: "Come back and see me when you're glowing in the dark" (p. 375).

The demonic propellant for Katherine is sexual promiscuity induced by alcohol. When her powers of seduction fail, she turns murderous and is committed to a psychiatric ward from which Isobel rescues her. They both believe in a fight to the death—Isobel's death.

Isobel is a martyr who gives and gives but recognizes when the lifeblood is being sucked out of her. She tells Irwin that he saps her strength and then disappears, but returns even more determined to live without compromise. Irwin guesses Isobel has taken a vow, which infuriates Marion, who can barely tolerate Tom's religiosity, let alone her sister's. "God, how I hate all this human stuff," she tells Isobel, "Wherever you go, you cause misery" (p. 70). Irwin also lashes out at Isobel, although she is his muse, without whom his art is meaningless.

The Secret Rapture has been described as a tragedy and as a modern morality play, and, like all Hare's plays, it has been severely criticized by feminists for simplistically portraying women who are either "good" or "bad" but always puppets of a male-dominated society. Tragicomic it may be. Chekhovian humor precludes pure tragedy, and these women are shaped by their own choices not by destiny.

The film version has many of the strengths of the play, but Hare so radically changed the screenplay that the result is more Gothic than tragic, and the humor is severely cut. Tom's religion is excised, removing jokes at the expense of the Church, and Katherine is robbed of her only virtue: political awareness. Scenes described effectively in the play are shot on location in the movie, and the opening image of Isobel, as pallid as a corpse, sobbing and hugging her dead father, emphasizes their bond.

The sexually promiscuous and politically manipulative Rhonda is missing from the film, as are the confrontation with the Greens and other political and historical references that serve to ground the play in Thatcher's England. Names are changed, too. The Glass family becomes the Coleridge family—presumably to stress their bucolic beginnings and Robert's literary connection; and Irwin becomes Patrick. The film does not pack the punch of the play.

Hare centers on good and evil again in *Racing Demon* (1990), the first play in his trilogy, which also includes *Murmuring Judges* and *The Absence of War*. *Racing Demon*, named for a card game, examines the

Church of England. Hare shows that the Church of England is both a business and a game, with a hierarchy, rules, and priorities.

The clergy are represented by four members of a parish in a socially deprived area of South London. The Reverends Lionel Espy, Tony Ferris, "Streaky" Bacon, and Harry Henderson each have a different approach to their ministry, based on their backgrounds. As servants of God, they also have very different readings of what that ministry should be. Lionel believes that the job of the team is to minister to parishioners according to their needs, without pushing religion. Conservative churchgoers have complained that his celebrations of church rituals are joyless. He always seems burdened with the cares of the world. Tony, the newcomer and the youngest, by contrast, is enthusiastic and evangelical. He is only interested in numbers. He wants to fill churches, and if preaching fire and brimstone works, he will push people to God through fear. The conflict between Lionel and Tony causes Lionel to lose his parish, which means eviction from his home.

Although each member of the team is virtuous, each displays weakness. We learn about the clergy through prayer scenes. These updated versions of Claudius' soliloquy in *Hamlet* provide insights into the characters because we assume they speak honestly to the Almighty. Lionel, whose emphasis on social services makes him the most openly sympathetic to the audience, is a terrible husband and father. His long-suffering wife, Heather, has sublimated her life to his, and his daughter is an alcoholic runaway. In his "prayers," he confronts God, challenging God's silence and allowance of suffering. Tony is a fornicator. His relationship with long-term girlfriend Frances Parnell has deteriorated from the understanding that they will eventually marry to a series of brief sexual encounters. Frances is neither Christian nor hypocrite. Aware of Tony's increasing evangelism, Frances knows she is part of the life he must leave behind. Sensing this, she leaves him first. Harry is a latent homosexual with a gay companion, Ewan. He believes this arrangement is acceptable to God because he is celibate. Despite his denial and Ewan's loyalty, he eventually falls prey to the gutter press. The least developed, yet most likable character is the Reverend Donald Bacon, nicknamed "Streaky." He sees God's love in all things: alcohol (he is not embarrassed to pray while drunk), the rum and curried goat that characterize the church's annual celebration of the Caribbean parishioners' excursions to the sea, and old radio shows. He has the joy of life that Lionel lacks. Most of his lines are questions or platitudes.

The women in *Racing Demon* are recognizable Hare types. Frances is both idealistic and realistic. She has rejected religion but is true to herself. When integrity is compromised, she abandons her job to live abroad: "I am going, Lord, where no one's ever heard of you . . . where you don't exist" (p. 87). It is a chilling indictment of the Judeo-Christian God that places without Him are more charitable than England.

Like Isobel in *The Secret Rapture*, Frances is a good woman whose social conscience makes it impossible for her blindly to accept the status quo. She exposes Tony and tries to save Lionel. She understands Lionel's marital problems, helping when his wife, Heather, has a stroke and leaving when her presence causes embarrassment. Heather's only joys in life are her garden and the assurance that she has provided Lionel with the lifestyle that accommodates his duty. Sadly, because their home is tied to Lionel's ministry, she loses both. Heather is an "ash-tray" wife.

Stella Marr is the play's only link with the underprivileged class that the Brixton parish supposedly serves. Ironically named for the Virgin Mary (she is not a believer), Stella is a Jamaican woman seeking help as a battered wife. Lionel listens sympathetically but sends her away with trite advice. Tony makes matters worse by confronting her husband. She becomes an underpaid cleaning woman in Saint Martin's, wondering what happened to the Christian ethic of forgiveness. It is clear she will return to her abusive husband.

The structure of *Racing Demon* is well balanced, with scenes in which the action moves forward punctuated by soliloquies revealing the thoughts and feelings of the priests and the women. Lionel's final prayer is ironically "into the empty air" (p. 87), signifying the absence of God. The last scene stresses the isolation of Lionel, Tony, and Frances as each speaks in a void, oblivious of the others. Frances, the atheist, has the final word, dreaming of a world of blurred possibilities outside the somber reality of contemporary Britain. The clergy are still fighting their own private battles: Lionel to end God's silence and man's suffering, Tony to increase his self-confidence and the church congregation. The Reverend Bacon and the Reverend Henderson have sunk into oblivion and do not appear in the epilogue.

The play is an indictment of the Church of England as an institution, but where formal religion loses, individual goodness triumphs, at least in spirit. Lionel and Harry are losers in the temporal sense. Harry must leave the country to avoid scandal. Lionel will lose his parish. However, they maintain their private sense of worth. Streaky will remain with "the people," though he is out of touch with their culture and their needs. Tony will increase the Lord's flock through Bible classes and hellfire sermons.

Unlike Lionel, Tony can explain evil: AIDS is the scourge that punishes gays; the death of his parents is his personal call to duty. He is excited by miracles and able to renounce the sins of the flesh for his own spiritual healing. Tom's religious fanaticism in *The Secret Rapture* is amusing, but Tony's is deeply disturbing. Victors in *Racing Demon* are dangerous extremists. Victims must sacrifice everything to their failing faith.

Trapped in the lobby of the Savoy Hotel, Tony is accused of playing Judas at the Last Supper, as Streaky counts out thirty pieces of silver. When the Bishop of Southwark arrives, glistening from his squash game, he is recognized not by his purple robes, but by the "clanging of his brass balls" (p. 53). Produced at the National Theatre in 1990, *Racing Demon* won four best-play awards and was hailed as Hare's masterpiece. Universal in its examination of religion and the clash between good and evil, it is limited in that the Church of England is a national concern. Certain allusions may puzzle international audiences, and, if we agree with Tony that success is measured in numbers, then *Racing Demon* may be among Hare's less accessible plays.

Some critics question whether Hare is truly in touch with the problems of the inner city. Like his vicars, Hare's brief references to people of color indicate distance rather than empathy. Stella Marr is a mere cipher demonstrating how the church fails to help, beyond giving her a menial job at minimum wage, which might well be considered exploitation.

Murmuring Judges (1991), the second of Hare's investigations into British institutions, is also concerned with the underprivileged. The title is from a legal expression meaning "to speak ill of the judiciary," which is still an offense under Scottish law. The play is the most complex of the trilogy, with a cast of twenty-five representing characters from the three branches of the law: the constabulary, the bench and bar, and the prison service. As the scenes in *Racing Demon* are punctuated by prayer, the scenes in *Murmuring Judges* are linked by monologues from three characters: Gerard McKinnon, a first-time offender, Sandra Bingham, a police officer, and "Jimmy" Khan, a detective. All three characters represent middle-class minorities. McKinnon is an Irishman in England, Bingham a female in a male institution, and Khan an immigrant dubbed "Jimmy" by colleagues too lazy or prejudiced to learn his real name.

As the plot follows the fate of the hapless Gerard from his first court appearance to his life in jail, the settings change with those involved in his case, from the very high (High Court, chambers in Lincoln's Inn, and the Royal Opera House) to the very low (prison cells and showers). In some scenes, these levels of society and the rhetoric that represents them merge to a cacophony of chaos, demonstrating the complete breakdown of the system.

The play opens with Gerard's harsh sentence of five years' imprisonment while he confides in the audience. This makes us care about what happens to a victim of the legal system. To high-ranking members of the judiciary, Sir Peter Edgecombe, Queen's Counsel, and Mr. Justice Cuddeford, winning or losing the case is just a game. Sir Peter's participation in a radio show, *Desert Island Discs*, is infinitely more interesting to them than the fate of the prisoner.

A new recruit to the bar, Irina Platt, is a Commonwealth scholar from Antigua. With brains, beauty, and minority status, she fills a white male bastion's need for balance. Irina has raised an impressive million pounds in a four-day fund drive, but she is warned by a canny legal clerk against spurning Sir Peter's invitations to the opera. Law, he tells her, is a team sport, "you want to start inside, not outside" (p. 11).

With that remark the setting changes to the inside of a Victorian jail, where Gerard is being admitted by Beckett, a prison warden. Beckett senses Gerard's acute vulnerability and gives him fatherly advice about survival. Because of overcrowding, Gerard will be placed with those serving life sentences, Beckett explains. "It's that or sleeping in the chapel" (p. 13). As the pathetic prisoner, Chaplinesque with his jail uniform flapping round his ankles, is dispatched to his quarters, the prison scene fades into a police station.

Beckett has initiated Gerard; now Police Constable Sandra Bingham briefs the audience on the basics of policing. It is, she explains, mostly paperwork and putting up with people who can't cope. The police station comes to life as the ritual of booking is played out with fast-paced humor and personalities recognizable from television cop shows. Lester, the desk sergeant, delivers comic lines spiced with racial overtones. Clearly the entire department has been trained in politically correct behavior, which coats it with an artificial veneer. Just below the surface bubbles prejudice against foreigners and "bloody nationalists." Throughout the play Hare implies that the harshness of Gerard's sentence is largely due to his Irish accent.

Detectives Barry Hopper and "Jimmy" Khan join the fray, fresh from celebrating an arrest, which we discover is that of Gerard and his partners. The circle of those involved with Gerard's case is complete. Sandra is disturbed by the sentence, but Barry tells her, "Just lock 'em up, Sandra. We're not playing God" (p. 33). Sandra's conscience will not allow a quiet mind. Like Irina, she is reminded that her chosen career is a team game. Irina is also uneasy with Gerard's sentence and visits him in prison to suggest an appeal. A newcomer to English jails, she is shocked, as we are, to discover packages of human excrement thrown not in protest but to rid the cells of odor, because there is no sanitation in British penal institutions.

As the audience hears the truth of Gerard's story, Irina vows to befriend him. While Gerard stares out at the audience from one side of the stage, Barry sits in an identical position on the other side, and notes from *The Magic Flute* indicate that Irina has accepted Sir Peter's invitation to the opera. Thus, the three worlds are drawn into a single stage moment. The spell is broken by Jimmy's congratulating Barry and Beckett's comforting Gerard, as center stage erupts into the Royal Opera House. In this setting Irina persuades Sir Peter to appeal Gerard's case, as Beckett calls for "Lights out!" and Barry and Jimmy embrace. The curtain rises on the opera as lights dim in the prison and the first act of the play ends. Sir Peter and Irina leave the bar of the opera house as the audience of *Murmuring Judges* heads for the bar in its own intermission.

A similarly elaborate scene opens act 2. The play reaches its most opulent moment with the enactment of a formal dinner in the hall of Lincoln's Inn. The toastmaster announces a diverse array of dignitaries, while Gerard, alone at the side of the stage, gazes up at his cell window, dislocated from the outside world. It is six o'clock and the end of the day for him. In a deliberate move to isolate inmates, supper is at four-thirty.

Meanwhile, at the formal meal, the home secretary is wined and dined in an attempt to stall legislation that will reform the judiciary. An elaborate and pedantic grace is drowned out by police sirens as the police station set is heralded by Jimmy's address to the audience, explaining how police work is public relations.

Sandra confronts Barry. She attributes his coolness to her questioning the Gerard case. Barry admits he planted dynamite to be sure of a conviction but warns Sandra that if she parades her conscience she will never be trusted again. Although she assures him that she too is "one of the boys," we know that by the end of the play Sandra will blow the whistle, just as Irina will bow out of the system. It is the women in this play who have the strength of their convictions.

Gerard suffers from Irina's intervention. He is brutally beaten by fellow inmates and lands in solitary confinement. His case is appealed, and he is granted a six-month reduction of his sentence, but we wonder if he will survive it. Irina not only survives but prevails. She finally confronts Sir Peter, attacking both his stance and the system, and becomes a radical lawyer at the alternative bar for progressive lawyers. For Sandra, however, there is no alternative police. At the powerful conclusion, another convergence of the three worlds creates a crescendo of words as Lester, Barry, and Irina vie for vocal supremacy. Sandra, putting her professional life on the line, silences them, asking for a word with her superintendent.

The question of silence also figures in *The Absence of War* (1993), which aroused attention following the Labour Party's defeat in the 1992 general elections. (In the wake of Labour's resounding victory in the 1997 election, this play may now be considered a period piece.) Audiences looking for parallels with real politicians, however, were disappointed.

What they saw in George Jones was a fictitious Labour Party leader, a loser too scrupulous to win an election through disloyalty and dishonesty. The cast is his loyal staff, who recognize his integrity and protect him from negative press. This leads to a betrayal by his deputy, Malcolm Pryce. Jones is a hardworking Londoner without a university education. Pryce is a glib Oxbridge graduate with a firm grasp of the ruthlessness necessary to gain power. He distances himself from the party leader in order to disassociate himself from his mistakes.

The greatest dilemma facing George Jones is his public image. He initially rose to power on the strength of his passionate public speaking, but his position as Labour Party leader has necessitated careful scripting of public pronouncements. This muzzling has produced a weak public image, which public-relations expert Lindsay Fontaine has been hired to correct. Unfortunately, Lindsay's attempts to give George free rein to speak spontaneously only reveal that the old passion is dead. George is trapped in a contentious interview with a powerful television commentator and fumbles at a key public rally. Though he wins the local election, his party is defeated nationally, and all the sacrifices of his fifty years' service are fruitless.

The structure of the play follows the format common to the other plays in the trilogy: long, complex scenes in public places are punctuated by short addresses to the audience. These soliloquies are neither the prayers of *Racing Demon* nor the commentary of *Murmuring Judges*. Instead, minor characters make conversation, and politicians make speeches. Inevitably, good is silenced while evil is eloquent.

The juxtaposition of private and public moments in the life of George Jones effectively conveys to the audience why he is admired as a man but fails as a Labour Party leader. A criticism of the play is that, unlike Lindsay, we do not see the spark that fires George, only what makes him vulnerable as a public figure. The essential passionate rhetoric is missing. *The Absence of War* points both to the lack of fighting spirit within Jones and the fact that postwar Britain has failed to rally round its working-class issues. An old socialist veteran named Vera points out that the middle class met the officer class in the war and, returning to peace, threw out the ruling class in the 1945 Labour Party victory. The play shows that latter-day socialists are too much like their rival Tories, just less successful.

In the 1993 staging of *The Absence of War* at the National Theatre, this third installment of Hare's trilogy marked a new height in his career. *Racing Demon* and *Murmuring Judges*, which had been staged separately, were revived, and the trilogy was performed as a marathon. Although classic plays and adaptations had been successfully grouped together as marathons (*The Royal Hunt of the Sun, The Plantagenets, Nicholas Nickleby,* and Peter Brook's version of *The Mahabharata*), the National had never before commissioned a single playwright to write a trilogy for its stages. Consequently, there was great anticipation of this event, and, predictably, rave reviews as well as rampant criticism.

Some critics confused the documentary style of Hare's research with the pure fiction of his plays and condemned the depiction of certain characters and events because they were not true to life. Others commented on the unevenness of the trilogy, most praising *Racing Demon* as Hare's masterpiece, applauding *The Absence of War*, and relegating *Murmuring Judges* to third place because of its broader sweep and stereotypes. The design, acting, and directing were universally acclaimed. Hare's account of his research for the trilogy, *Asking Around*, was also published in 1993.

After the vast dimensions of a trilogy at the National Theatre's largest space, Hare took time off to adapt Brecht's *Leben des Galilei* (*Galileo*, 1943) for a production at the Almeida Theatre in 1994. In 1995 he returned to the National's smallest theater, the Cottesloe, with an intimate three-character play in a single setting titled *Skylight*. Nothing could be further from the large casts and multiple sets of the trilogy, yet the characters and theme of *Skylight* are recognizable Hare products.

The play opens and closes with a short scene between Edward Sergeant, a college student, and Kyra Hollis, a schoolteacher in her thirties. The rest of the play is devoted to an interchange between Kyra and Edward's father, Tom, who is her former lover. Kyra ended the relationship when it was discovered by Tom's wife, Alice. Alice has since died of cancer, and both Edward and Tom are hoping that Kyra will return.

What separate Tom and Kyra are the ideologies that have shaped their disparate lifestyles. Tom is a successful restaurateur, so wealthy that he is driven by a chauffeur to Kyra's dowdy flat in a lower-class section of northwest London. He fails to understand why she has chosen to live in such conditions and to teach children in a slum neighborhood.

Kyra, however, believes desperately in the value of the work she is doing and despises the luxury Tom represents, though nostalgia draws her back to bed with him. What the audience witnesses is a sexual and sensual bond that is not strong enough to fill the great void between the haves and the have-nots—between Tom, who has chosen material success, and Kyra, who has rejected it.

In this simple plot, Hare synthesizes many of the themes he has introduced in the twenty-five years between *Slag* and *Skylight*. Tom is a white male who represents success in a system that is not of his own devising but that he has nonetheless mastered, at a price. In Hare's less subtle plays this character is a predator, a profiteer whose power oppresses his victims. In *Skylight* Tom's way is ridiculed, but it is also somewhat understood. Like his namesake in *The Secret Rapture*, he can accept religion but not spirituality. Like Patrick in *Knuckle*, he has lost the respect of his son. Like Brock in *Plenty*, he loves his woman without ever knowing her. Kyra, on the other hand, is a woman who refuses to compromise, like Susan Traherne and Sarah Delafield. She will cling to integrity like life itself, but her past has been compromised by lies. In Kyra's case, the lie is a six-year adultery, happiness at the expense of her best friend Alice, Tom's wife. Is it Kyra's guilt that places her in a squalid flat, in a slum school, with the most disadvantaged people she can find? Is she paying off past transgressions with good deeds? If so, she fails to admit it.

Kyra, old enough to be Edward's mother as well as Tom's daughter, mothers them both and is "courted" more successfully by the son than by the father, her former lover. Has time made men more sensitive, or is youth more harmoniously balanced with femininity? Is the vulnerability of youth and women in cosmic opposition to male supremacy?

Edward recognizes, as Tom does not, that his behavior is unacceptable. Tom commands respect, based on fear. His success enables him to order life through the yellow pages, his money makes all things material accessible, but he is emotionally detached. Edward accuses Kyra of abandonment; he resents her disappearance in a time of need.

While Kyra is keen to criticize Tom, she warns Edward not to judge people. Tom and Kyra enjoy the combat of their verbal battle, sparking the old flames of their relationship. But their incompatibility is clear. Kyra's "perfect" relationship with Tom was actually a love triangle with his unknowing wife. Dead Alice, like the missing Sarah in *Knuckle*, the dead father in *The Secret Rapture*, and Lionel, the sacked vicar in *Racing Demon*, was the catalyst for harmony; without her there is imbalance. Kyra is unable to make a total commitment to Tom alone because their love depended on his marriage to Alice. Some of Hare's heroines feel safe as mistresses but not as wives.

An audience feels for these flawed characters because, despite their faults, their striving is evident. The skylight Tom made for the dying Alice, so she could see up and out, becomes a symbol of their attempts to look beyond themselves. So lighting in this play is most important: trapped in a cold, dark flat with little comfort within, for Kyra the glow of the heater, the snow, and the early morning light herald more than a new day. Youth returns in the form of Edward, replete with a silver tea service and a succulent breakfast, the one thing Kyra admits she misses from the old life. As she rushes off to school to tutor a promising disadvantaged student, the son displays a thoughtfulness the father lacks. Embittered, materialistic middle age gives way to youth, despair to hope.

If *Skylight*, with the other plays of the 1990s, represents a kinder, gentler Hare, it is perhaps because, like Tom, he has achieved success. A Fellow of the Royal Academy, he has long since pierced the inner sanctum of the National Theatre and the BBC, with automatic access to large audiences. Whether or not he has sold out to the establishment is a question critics frequently pose. Hailed as Britain's foremost dissident playwright, Hare continues to enjoy fame, acclaim, and fortune, despite criticizing the very institutions to which he has gained access.

From *Slag* to *Skylight* he has demonstrated mastery of intimate chamber pieces and ambitious epics; farce, mystery, and romance; plays, screenplays, and teleplays. Through an inside knowledge of the theater, he has honed his art by directing actors and watching audiences. Sometimes ignoring, sometimes fighting critics, he is his own harshest judge, often dismissing whole plays in retrospect. What we can expect from Hare in the future is unknown. We anticipate he will continue to be that burr beneath the skin that causes enough irritation to make audiences and readers scratch below the surface, arousing political awareness. That has always been his goal.

SELECTED BIBLIOGRAPHY

I. COLLECTED WORKS. *The History Plays* (London, 1984), includes *Knuckle, Licking Hitler,* and *Plenty; The Asian Plays* (London, 1986), includes *Fanshen, Saigon: Year of the Cat,* and *A Map of the World; The Early Plays* (London, 1991), includes *Slag, The Great Exhibition,* and *Teeth 'n' Smiles; Heading Home* (London, 1991), also includes *Wetherby* and *Dreams of Leaving; David Hare: Plays One* (London, 1996), includes *Slag, Teeth 'n' Smiles, Knuckle, Licking Hitler,* and *Plenty; David Hare: Plays Two* (London, 1997).

II. SEPARATE WORKS. *Slag* (London, 1971); *How Brophy Made Good,* pub. in *Gambit* 17 (1971); *The Great Exhibition* (London, 1972); *Brassneck,* with Howard Brenton (London, 1973); *Knuckle* (London, 1974); *Fanshen* (London, 1976); *Teeth 'n' Smiles* (London, 1976); *Plenty* (London, 1978); *A Map of the World* (London, 1983); *Pravda,* with Howard Brenton (London, 1985, rev. 1986); *The Bay at Nice* and *Wrecked Eggs* (London, 1986); *The Secret Rapture* (London, 1988, rev. 1989); *Racing Demon* (London, 1990, rev. 1991); *Murmuring Judges* (London, 1991, rev. 1993); *The Absence of War* (London, 1993); *Skylight* (London, 1995).

III. TELEPLAYS. *Licking Hitler* (London, 1978); *Dreams of Leaving* (London, 1980); *Saigon: Year of the Cat* (London, 1983); *Heading Home* (London, 1991).

IV. SCREENPLAYS. *Wetherby* (London, 1985); *Paris by Night* (London, 1988); *Strapless* (London, 1989).

V. NONFICTION. *Writing Left-Handed* (London, 1991), articles, lectures, and introductions to plays; *Asking Around: Background to the David Hare Trilogy* (London, 1993).

VI. CRITICAL STUDIES. Peter Ansorge, *Disrupting the Spectacle: Five Years of Experimental and Fringe Theatre in Britain* (London, 1975); Catherine Itzin, *Stages in the Revolution: Political Theatre in Britain Since 1968* (London, 1980); Frank Pike, ed., *Ah! Mischief: The Writer and Television* (London, 1982); John Bull, *New British Political Dramatists* (London, 1984); Michelene Wandor, *Look Back in Gender: Sexuality and the Family in Post-War British Drama* (London, 1987); Joan FitzPatrick Dean, *David Hare* (Boston, 1990); Judy Lee Oliva, *David Hare: Theatricalizing Politics* (Ann Arbor, Mich., 1990); Carol Homden, *The Plays of David Hare* (Cambridge, 1994); Hersh Zeifman, ed., *David Hare: A Casebook* (New York, 1994); Finlay Donesky, *David Hare: Moral and Historical Perspectives* (Westport, Conn., 1996); Scott Fraser, *A Politic Theatre: The Drama of David Hare* (Amsterdam, 1996).

KAZUO ISHIGURO

(1954–   )

Gabriel Brownstein

IT IS TOO early to attempt anything but a provisional appraisal of the work of Kazuo Ishiguro. As of 1996 he had written four novels and established himself as one of the most widely admired British novelists of his generation. His first novel, *A Pale View of Hills* (1982), which appeared when he was twenty-eight years old, won him the Royal Society of Literature's Winifred Holtby Prize. His second novel, *An Artist of the Floating World* (1986), was a finalist for the Booker Prize and was named the Whitbread Book of the Year. *The Remains of the Day* (1989), his third book, earned Ishiguro the Booker Prize as well as enormous international attention. In 1993 *The Remains of the Day* was adapted by James Ivory into a successful motion picture. His fourth novel, *The Unconsoled* (1995), was met with a mixed reaction: it was hailed as his greatest achievement by some and dismissed as a failed experiment by others.

Ishiguro is a fluid and graceful writer, a serious novelist whose every work examines, as if obsessively, the same ideas: the relation of memory to history, the relation of personal identity to cultural identity, and the relation of emotional repression to social conformity. In each novel he revisits the same themes and problems but does so with a new perspective, constantly expanding the scope and breadth of his literary inquiry. Similarities among his first three novels are striking. Each is told from the point of view of a narrator who is characteristically disinclined toward introspection and who slips involuntarily into reveries that reveal his or her own failings. Each narrative shifts between recollections of events in the recent and distant past. Each narrator is attempting to confront an awful loss, a terrible mistake, and can only do so indirectly. These characters' struggles are inextricably linked with larger political events: the first three

books reflect on the horrors of World War II, and the narrators look back in time with stunned confusion. They do not understand themselves, and in the course of the novels they are forced to confront their failings and to understand the limitations of their lives. They sift through the crumbled ruins of their pasts in halting, fragmented recollections, steadfastly denying the extent of their pain until they are forced to confront the horror of their sorrow.

A Pale View of Hills is told by Etsuko, a Japanese woman living in England. The novel begins shortly after the suicide of her eldest daughter. Unable to examine this tragedy directly Etsuko thinks back to her own days in Nagasaki, in the years after the bomb was dropped. Without ever discussing the actual dropping of the bomb and barely touching on her daughter's suicide, she navigates the disasters of her life. At the end of the novel it becomes clear that she blames herself for the suicide. *An Artist of the Floating World* is set in postwar Japan. It begins with the narrator, Masuji Ono, arranging for his daughter's marriage. While making these arrangements Ono reflects on his life and his rise to prominence as a propagandist for the failed imperialist regime. The war has cost Ono his wife, his son, and his life's work, along with the prestige that it earned him. Suitors seem reluctant to marry his daughter; old students want to distance themselves from their former master. Ono weighs all of these factors and discovers, to his shame, his place in postwar Japan and the ruin that his labors have brought him.

In *The Remains of the Day* Ishiguro moves his eye away from Japan. The narrator is Stevens, a butler at a great country estate, who has devoted his life to his work and to his former employer, Lord Darlington. The novel begins after the death of Lord

Darlington, with a wealthy American living in Darlington Hall and Stevens taking what at first seems to be a vacation across the English countryside. As he drives about in an impressive antique car, Stevens contemplates his life of service, thinks about what makes a great butler, and is forced to realize what he has lost in his attempt to make himself the perfect servant: his chance for the affections of a woman who seemed capable of loving him and any possibility of closeness with his father. Instead he devoted himself to Darlington, a political bumbler and Nazi sympathizer who engaged in anti-Semitic purges of his staff and whose great achievement was a failed conference that attempted to bring England, France, and the United States into an alliance with Hitler's Germany. At the end of the novel Stevens, like Ono in *An Artist of the Floating World*, is forced to see that his life of service has been a life misspent.

In these first three novels the narrators struggle between two impulses: to confront and to avoid the horrors of their lives. In the end they all come to see themselves clearly and to understand their shortcomings. *The Unconsoled* is something of a departure from his earlier writing. Again, there is a first-person narrator desperately sorting through his life, but this one is no memoirist—he is an amnesiac. Ryder, a concert pianist, finds himself in a bizarre and unfamiliar city that seems to contain the architecture of his own past; he tries to stick to a schedule he does not have and to solve problems he does not understand. The novel explores the logic not of memory but of dreams. As *The Unconsoled* moves toward its finale, Ryder makes his way through the political and social labyrinth of the city and through his own disjointed memories, while he attempts to reconstruct his shattered identity. In the city old musical traditions come in conflict with new ones, and the city fathers see Ryder as a savior come to rescue their world from occupation by unpleasant musical forces. Ryder finds himself incapable of accomplishing the task. He wanders through an absurd and incomprehensible world.

Ishiguro's work tackles important ideas with great sensitivity and seriousness. Within the circumscribed range of his obsessions, he demonstrates enormous flexibility. He can write and sound like a comically formal English butler or like a confused older woman speaking in a language not her own. He maintains enormous authority whether his characters are wandering in a realistically described Japanese town or in a phantasmagoric dream-world. He is a young writer whose promise is as great as his achievements.

LIFE

MANY critics have tried to read Ishiguro as a Japanese novelist, as a writer whose thematic and literary influence came from the East. Gabriele Annan, for instance, writing in the *New York Review of Books*, argued that "all three of Ishiguro's novels are explanations, even indictments, of Japanese-ness. . . . He writes about . . . duty, loyalty, and tradition. Characters who place too high—too Japanese—a price on these values are punished for it" (1989, p. 3). Francis King, reviewing *A Pale View of Hills* for *The Spectator*, described the novel as "typically Japanese in its compression" and said that the book "might, one feels, be some apprentice work by Kawabata or Endo" (27 February 1982). But Ishiguro says, "I know very little about Japan, particularly modern-day Japan" (Bryson, 1990, p. 44), and he seems to be made uneasy by those who characterize him as a Japanese novelist. In an interview with Gregory Mason in *Contemporary Literature*, Ishiguro said: "I feel that I'm very much of the Western tradition. And I'm quite often amused when reviewers make a lot of my being Japanese and try to mention the two or three authors they've vaguely heard of, comparing me to Mishima or something. It seems highly inappropriate" (1989, p. 336).

Ishiguro is an Englishman, if not unambiguously so. And if it seems unreasonable to compare him to Yukio Mishima, Yasunari Kawabata, or Shusako Endo, it seems equally unfair to put him in the same lot as British writers born outside of England, such as Salman Rushdie or V. S. Naipaul; he was not born into the English language or any part of the crumbling British Empire. He is not even, like Joseph Conrad or Vladimir Nabokov, a writer who consciously forsook his first language to write novels in English.

Kazuo Ishiguro was born in Nagasaki on 8 November 1954. In 1960, when he was five years old, his family immigrated to Great Britain. His father, Shizuo Ishiguro, an oceanographer, went to England to work on the development of oil fields in the North Sea. His mother, née Shizuko Michida, was a homemaker. Ishiguro grew up in the comfortable middle-class suburb of Guildford, in Surrey, twenty miles south of London. For most of Ishiguro's youth the family considered their stay in England temporary but continually put off plans to return to Japan. At home his parents spoke Japanese. Every year young Kazuo, who attended English schools, received a packet of Japanese books that he was to study, presumably to keep up with his parents' culture and to prepare for a return trip to their country. It was not until about 1970 that the Ishiguros decided that they would not go back to Japan. Ishiguro returned to Japan for the first time in 1989, when he visited the country.

Ishiguro grew up as a foreign child in a strange land. "I wasn't brought up not to respect English customs," he told *The Observer* in an interview with Blake Morrison,

but there was this distance. And I soon learned that the rules that applied to me were completely different from the rules which applied to my school friends. Not that I suffered any racism at school, but I was the focus of attention. Nobody had ever seen a Japanese kid in Guildford before, and whenever I went to another school the whole playground would follow me. I learned that I had only a certain amount of time to become popular: so I turned into a performer.

(29 October 1989, p. 35)

At an age when many are blissfully unaware of their social positions, Ishiguro understood his role as both observer and observed. "I had to learn English from the outside," he said, "mimicry, copying was the only way" (p. 35). He received what he calls a fairly typical English education, but as a child, he straddled two cultures. He told Gregory Mason, "My parents have remained fairly Japanese in the way they go about things, and being brought up in a family you tend to operate the way that family operates" (*Contemporary Literature*, 1989, p. 336). The child assimilated. His parents stayed true to their traditions and culture.

Ishiguro's adolescence was characterized by experimentation. He did not begin to think of himself as a writer until he was twenty-five years old. As a teenager he aspired to a career as a rock-and-roll musician. He wrote songs, played guitar and keyboards, and performed in pubs in and around London. He even went so far as to produce a tape of his music, which he shopped around to record

companies without success. After graduating high school he hitchhiked around the United States and North America. In 1973 he worked as a grouse beater, someone who assists in bird hunts, at the estate of the Queen Mother in Balmoral Castle, in Aberdeen, Scotland. From 1979 to 1980 Ishiguro was employed as a residential social worker for the West London Cyrenians. From 1981 to 1983 he worked for the Cyrenians as a resettlement worker.

In 1979 he enrolled in the creative writing program at the University of East Anglia, where he studied with the critic and novelist Malcolm Bradbury and the novelist Angela Carter. Before he had finished his degree, three of his stories were selected for Faber & Faber's *Introduction 7: Stories by New Writers*. These stories, "A Strange and Sometimes Sadness," "Waiting for J.," and "Getting Poisoned," are interesting mostly as the apprentice work of a writer who would go on to greater things. "A Strange and Sometimes Sadness," originally published in the journal *Bananas*, is a short piece from which he developed *A Pale View of Hills*. The other two stories are far more brutal and sensational, more blunt in their treatment of horror than Ishiguro ever is in his novels. "Waiting for J." is a ghost story, a contemporary reworking of Gothic themes in which an urbane artist and professor waits up at night for the ghost of a man he has murdered. "Getting Poisoned" is a superrealist piece, a horror story in the form of the diary of a teenage sadist's first murder and first sexual encounter. This is a grim story in which sex and violence are described through the clinical eye of a young psychopath. The bluntness of the gaze is the absolute opposite of the indirection that characterizes Ishiguro's narrators in the novels.

Still it is interesting to look at Ishiguro's mature work through the lens of these early stories. His novels are, in a peculiar sense, also horror stories: they all revolve around disaster, loss, and the consequences of horrible errors. The characters probe their misdeeds with morbid fascination: "As with a wound on one's own body, it is possible to develop an intimacy with the most disturbing of things" (*A Pale View of Hills*, p. 54). But in "Waiting for J." and "Getting Poisoned" Ishiguro stares at "the most disturbing of things" with an unblinking eye, and the description of these things seems forced, invented. The characters are flatly unredeemable psychotics; as a result the reader achieves no "intimacy" with the narrators' wounds. In his later works Ishiguro achieves a more delicate perspective that allows him to circle around genuinely horrible misdeeds (for example, participation in the production of militaristic, Sinophobic propaganda) and to acquaint the reader with characters who seem not so much bad as pathetic and limited. The author of these early stories has yet to discover the banality of evil or the power of restraint—concepts the mature Ishiguro understands entirely.

"A Strange and Sometimes Sadness" stands apart from the other two stories. It is subtler, and in it Ishiguro seems more interested in character and less interested in sensationalism. It tells the story of Michiko, a Japanese woman living in England, who after a visit from her younger daughter begins to think about her life in wartime Nagasaki and about her friend, Yasuko, who died in the bombing. The story is a much more direct attempt to grapple with the bombing of Nagasaki than *A Pale View of Hills*. It is also a kind of ghost story. There's a moment when Michiko sees the coming destruction in the face of her friend Yasuko. Michiko is a preliminary version of Etsuko, and her voice is a less confident and less polished version of the halting, elliptical voice in the novel. Still the story is an assured piece of writing, and on the basis of "A Strange and Sometimes Sadness" Ishiguro was offered a book contract for what would become *A Pale View of Hills*. For the most part he abandoned the short story as a form, though he did publish one, "A Family Supper" (*Firebird 2*, 1982), that was later collected in *The Penguin Book of Modern British Short Stories* (1987).

Ishiguro became a British citizen in 1982, the year he published his first novel. *A Pale View of Hills* was enormously well received. In the *Times Literary Supplement*, Paul Bailey called it "a first novel of uncommon delicacy" (19 February 1982, p. 179). Penelope Lively, writing in *Encounter*, concurred: "For a first novel," she wrote, "this book is remarkable; its control and economy look like the work of a much more experienced writer" (June–July 1982, p. 90). The notices, combined with the Winifred Holtby Prize, earned Ishiguro some fame in England. His reputation grew with his second novel, *An Artist of the Floating World*, which was reviewed enthusiastically on both sides of the Atlantic and was a finalist for the Booker Prize. Still, for the most part, Ishiguro was not well known in the United States. *The Remains of the Day* changed that. The book was phenomenally popular in England and the United States: the motion picture featuring Anthony Hopkins and Emma Thompson brought Ishiguro a new height of fame.

Ishiguro's fourth novel, *The Unconsoled*, marks an enormous departure from his earlier works in style and subject matter. He considered it the most important of his first four novels. Louis Menand, reviewing it in the *New York Times Book Review*, agreed. But many considered it, in the words of Francis Wyndham, "a courageous but misguided departure" from his previous work (*The New Yorker*, 23 October 1995, p. 90). Michiko Kakutani, reviewing the novel in the *New York Times*, called *The Unconsoled* a "dogged, shaggy-dog narrative, a narrative that for all the author's intelligence and craft sorely tries the reader's patience" (17 October 1995, sec. C, p. 17).

Ishiguro says that he is strongly influenced by films, particularly Japanese films of the postwar period, and he is the author of several television film scripts, including "A Profile of Arthur J. Mason" (1984) and "The Gourmet" (1986). The script for the latter is reprinted in *Granta*'s "The Best of the Young British Novelists" issue (1993) and is in some ways reminiscent of Ishiguro's early short fiction. This mock-Gothic tale follows Manley Kingston in his attempts to eat a ghost. Manley is a gourmet of the strangest kind—he wants to taste *everything*—and eating the ghost is to be his crowning achievement. Manley's hunger leads him to mingle with the truly hungry, the homeless of London, and he is unable to distinguish his own predatory desire from the genuine needs of the famished. The screenplay has the bluntness of the early stories and lacks the delicacy of the novels. There is a scene reminiscent of one in "A Strange and Sometimes Sadness" in which a tramp's face suddenly turns into the face of a skeleton, the face of death. Reading the screenplay, one is again forced to consider the horror-story quality that undergirds Ishiguro's work. His best writing attempts, like horror writing, to speak the unspeakable, to explore the nightmare regions of the mind, to look at things one normally would rather not examine.

By creating narrators who allow themselves to speak about so little, who refuse to consider so much, and whose introspection is at best myopic, Ishiguro expands the boundaries of the monstrous. His characters do not need to be haunted by ghosts and murderers; they are haunted by their pasts, by their guilt, and by their failings. Because in each novel the reader is consigned so affectingly to the narrator's viewpoint, the reader cringes along with the narrator.

BEYOND ANNIHILATION

LOUIS Menand began "Anxious in Dreamland," a celebratory review of *The Unconsoled* in *The New York Times Book Review*, with the following appraisal of Ishiguro's work:

Kazuo Ishiguro . . . has acquired a reputation as a penetrating psychological realist and a luminous stylist. It is entirely undeserved. The characters in Mr. Ishiguro's books are papier-mâché animations. They don't have feelings; they simulate feelings, which they seem to have learned about by reading some sort of technical manual on the emotions. And Mr. Ishiguro's prose is a confection of banality and cliché, presented in a manner that tends toward woodenness. His landscapes are sets from inferior Walt Disney pictures; his narratives have a kind of tour-bus quality; and his single insight into the human condition is that people need love but continually spoil their chances of getting it, a piece of wisdom slightly below the level of Dr. Joyce Brothers.

Yet he is an original and remarkable genius. . . . How he manages to produce the illusion of depth and feeling where there is only cartoon drawing and cliché is just part of the fascination of his accomplishment. . . . Mr. Ishiguro's indifference to conventional notions of literary excellence is so thorough that it becomes a kind of excellence itself.

(1995, p. 7)

Menand raises the central paradox of Ishiguro's novels: They work as brilliant, seamless wholes, and yet they seem constructed of inferior parts. His books are complex and psychological, but they are not psychologically complex; they are political and profound, but not politically profound; they are compelling narratives that refuse to tell straightforward stories; they present affecting characters who are neither particularly likable nor fully drawn. The work is in certain ways mechanical, almost perfunctory, but nonetheless tremendously moving.

It is as if, in his first three books, Ishiguro offers a set of stock characters going through almost reflexive motions toward an inevitable end. These books all share not only the same structural mechanics but the same rigorous logic. The third time around this logic becomes almost as predictable as a shopworn vaudeville sketch: you know the soup will be poured on the schlemiel. One after another Ishiguro's characters stand in front of the mirror of their lives, pretending all is quite well and struggling desperately not to look at their reflections. Eventually, they recognize themselves, and this moment of revelation is devastating for both narrator and reader. We need no profound conception of a character to recognize that character's pain.

Stevens in *The Remains of the Day* is a ludicrous and familiar figure, a caricature of an English butler. He is enormously proud of his own dignity, which depends entirely on strict repression of his identity. Stevens exists not to *be* but to *serve*. Yet in the novel he is making a confession, calling attention to himself—doing exactly what a dignified butler should not do—and with the confession comes introspection. He is forced to realize not only what he is, but *that* he is and that he has never allowed himself to *be*. He does not develop as a character but transcends his "papier-mâché" limitations simply by recognizing that he is a flat and faceless figure. He learns that he is made of cardboard, and then he knocks himself down.

This process of recognition is the crucial business of Ishiguro's work. It is almost as though the people, places, and histories that surround the machinery of the text are simply decorative. These books are about a condition, a peculiar kind of tight-lipped despair. What the characters say is often not as important as what they hold back, and as the novel develops the weight of the unsaid grows heavier and heavier. When revelation comes to Ishiguro's characters, it drops with a brutal force. Edith Milton, reviewing *A Pale View of Hills*, defines the dynamic as follows:

In this book . . . what is stated is often less important than what is left unsaid, those blanked-out days around the bomb's explosion become the paradigm of modern life. They are the ultimate example of qualities which the novel celebrates: the brilliance of our negative invention, and our infinite talent for living beyond annihilation as if we had forgotten it.

(1982, p. 13)

Etsuko, in *A Pale View of Hills*, has been erased twice—her life has been annihilated *and* she has forgotten it. She is ghostlike, and the maintenance of her existence depends on delicacy and silence. The novel forces her to speak, to lift the second erasure, and this brings about a new catastrophe. She realizes what she has forgotten, and as she does so the identity she has crafted for herself is undermined. The book is about the absence of character and the attempt to maintain anonymous blankness, a condition that Edith Milton generalizes into a "paradigm of modern life." Denial, here, is haunting—the natural state of those who have looked into a void and afterward struggled to continue their lives.

There is a temptation to dismiss these meditations in denial and repression, as Menand suggests, as pop psychology. But to do so would be a mistake. Ishiguro is not writing self-help manuals. He is not exhorting his readers to get in touch with their feelings; he is engaging something much more elliptical and, for lack of a better word, ethereal. There's an odd moment in his teleplay, "The Gourmet," in which one begins to sympathize with a ghost who is about to be eaten. It has already been killed, and one wonders what will happen to it once it is consumed. Will it cease to be a ghost? Will it be dispatched to some more profound oblivion? The question, put in Edith Milton's terms, might be phrased differently: How can one undermine that which has been invented negatively? After annihilation and repression what worse can happen? In *A Pale View of Hills* Ishiguro provides an easy answer. Etsuko has been destroyed and has destroyed herself, and now—this is the brutality of the work—she will be wracked again by pain, but this time the pain will come from her own consciousness, her own guilt, and the ticking bomb of her limited self-awareness. The horror is striking in its banality: she will be forced, against all of her instincts, to consider her own life.

This investigation of personal repression has political as well as allegorical implications. In *An Artist of the Floating World* and *The Remains of the Day* the failure to examine oneself and the consequences of one's actions is put in a social context and connected explicitly to the most tyrannous kind of nationalism. After *A Pale View of Hills* Ishiguro turned his eye away from the victimized and began to examine the peculiar form of guilt and self-annihilation of the victimizers, or, more precisely, those sympathetic to the victimizers. Neither Ono nor Stevens are killers or accomplices to killings. Both are merely functionaries in enormous killing machines.

Ono and Stevens are not malicious people. They are simply foolish, pompous, and morally shortsighted, so devoted to their work and the mainte-nance of their positions that they fail to understand the consequences of their actions. Reading these books, one is reminded of Hannah Arendt's portrait of Adolf Eichmann in *Eichmann in Jerusalem*: his ordinariness, his banality, his dull and insipid character. The thinness of the characters in these novels is no accident. It is precisely what allows them to participate cheerfully in what they refuse to recognize as a vicious ideology. Stevens is so bent on perfecting his craft, on being the perfect butler, that he refuses to question the activities of his employer. Ono is so consumed with his position and personal prestige, so interested in fashioning his own "floating world" of drinking and idealism, that he seems not to care which ideals he clings to.

These characters are aesthetes in the worst and most selfish sense; they see the world in its formal dimensions but not in its social dimensions. They understand the roles they play but not the stage on which they are performing or the play in which they are acting. Ono is so happy to be sitting in a bar that he designed, with a set of young acolytes offering speeches in his honor, that he fails to consider the implications of the militarism of imperial Japan. It appears to him only as an abstraction. Even after the war Ono is oblivious to its horrors, unwilling to understand the bitterness of those who suffered in battles or in prisons. It is here that the connection between social and personal repression becomes clear. Blind conformity prevents both Ono and Stevens from addressing the moral issues in their worlds. This conformity is precisely what nationalism demands.

In *The Unconsoled* Ishiguro rejects the formal structure of his earlier novels and invents a new arena for the enactment of his obsessions. The novel reads like a nightmare that Ono or Stevens might have. The dreamworld that the amnesiac Ryder stumbles through seems constructed out of his own enormous pomposity and his terrible fears. The unnamed city sees him as its savior, as if his words and music will return it to some lost happiness of the past. Everyone believes that he holds the key to their salvation. Meanwhile Ryder stumbles about, passively buoyed by the whims of others, trying to recover his own lost past. It is as if one of the pompous, repressed narrators of Ishiguro's earlier novels appealed to some malicious genie who made wishes come horribly true. Ryder has been granted a prestigious social identity but denied a personal identity, and he is lost. On the way to a reception held in his honor, accompanied by a woman who might be his wife and a child who might be his son, Ryder finds the rotted-out hulk of a car that belonged to his parents. He caresses the rusting metal, rubs his face against it, climbs into the rotting backseat, and curls up in a ball. Ryder's inner life consists mostly of curiosity and terror—fear of what he might find out and fear of what might be found out about him. This narrow expressive range is at the root of Ishiguro's work.

Ishiguro is writing the confessions of people who do not fully exist. This presents a conundrum and an unlikely premise for a conventional narrative. His central characters, by definition, are not complex. They speak in banalities and clichés because they have no voices of their own. If they "simulate feelings, which they seem to have learned about by reading some sort of technical manual on the emotions," then that is the horror Ishiguro explores. In *The Remains of the Day* Stevens struggles manfully to learn to "banter" in the American style of his new employer, and since there is no manual on the subject, he finds himself terrified:

> It is quite possible, then, that my employer fully expects me to respond to his bantering in a like manner, and considers my failure to do so a form of negligence.... But I must say this business of bantering is not a duty I feel I can ever discharge with enthusiasm.... For one thing, how would one know for sure that at any given moment a response of the bantering sort is truly what is expected? One need hardly dwell on the catastrophic possibility of uttering a bantering remark only to discover it wholly inappropriate.
>
> (p. 16)

The comedy reveals something truly dreadful: poor Stevens can only conceive of conversation in terms of "duty" and lives in terror of performing that duty inadequately. He is not simply simulating feelings: he is sure that if he simulates them improperly the results will be disastrous.

In this sense Ishiguro writes antinovels. There can be no nuances, no delicate shadings of feeling in his characters' lives. These are novels of manners and social conventions where nothing exists outside of manners and social conventions. The narrators strut and fret. They try desperately to avoid facing their feelings or fears, and in the end desperation is all they have. Their personalities are delicately constructed but useless, like so much pretty latticework built to cover an abyss.

A PALE VIEW OF HILLS

A Pale View of Hills begins soon after the suicide of the narrator Etsuko's older daughter, Keiko. Her younger daughter, Niki, a child by her second marriage, comes to visit her. In the novel's first paragraph we are told that Niki's name "is not an abbreviation" but the result of a compromise between Etsuko and Niki's English father (p. 9). "Paradoxically," says Etsuko, "it was he who wanted to give her a Japanese name, and I—perhaps out of some selfish desire not to be reminded of the past—insisted on an English one. He finally agreed to Niki, thinking it had some vague echo of the East about it" (p. 9).

A Pale View of Hills is about the struggle to find names that straddle two cultures, a process guided by Etsuko's "selfish desire not to be reminded of the past." The results of such compromised namings are clumsy. Etsuko cannot describe the twin horrors of her life, her daughter's suicide and her survival of the bombing of Nagasaki; unable to find adequate words for either, she settles on something that seems an abbreviation for both. She thinks back to events associated with the bombing of Nagasaki, events associated with her feelings about her child. She tells the story of the early days of her marriage to Keiko's father, Jiro, of her acquaintance with a mysterious woman, Sachiko, who lived close by, and of Sachiko's life with her young daughter, Mariko. Keiko's suicide brings on an "echo of the East," but it is a "vague echo." (A "vague echo," of course, sounds much like a "pale view." In both there is the notion of slightly perceiving something.) Etsuko tells her story despite her "desire not to be reminded of the past," and the story, without directly confronting her guilt or sorrow, encapsulates both. The novel moves between past and present tense, between her memories of her life in Japan and her descriptions of her life in England.

Early on, Etsuko admits she is troubled by a recurring dream. At first her descriptions seem innocuous. She says she's dreaming of a little girl on a swing. Later she becomes evasive: it was not a swing, she says. Then she admits that the girl was not who she at first thought it was. Without her saying as much it becomes clear that Etsuko has been dreaming of her daughter swinging by her neck from a noose. This discussion of the dream works as a paradigm for the structure of the novel as a whole. Etsuko's story is full of silences, evasions, repressions, and erasures. She talks about her life but does not describe what would seem to be its major events. The bombing of Nagasaki is never touched on, except obliquely. Etsuko's emigration to England is never discussed. And Niki's father, the man who took Etsuko from Japan to England, the man for whom she left Keiko's father, is never described.

Throughout the novel Etsuko displays a willful blindness that verges on naiveté. When a neighbor asks about Keiko, Etsuko replies that she is away, living in Manchester. She refuses to recognize, publicly or privately, what has happened to her daughter. To the reader she stubbornly insists that she is not discussing Keiko's death at all: "I have no great wish to dwell on Keiko now; it brings me little comfort. I only mention her here because those were the circumstances around Niki's visit this April, and because it was during that visit I remembered Sachiko again after all this time" (p. 11). Flat denial is the only way Etsuko can indicate her pain. She is a haunted woman, unable to control or conceal her own guilt and misery.

In the story that she tells of her life after the war, Jiro and Etsuko live in an American-style apartment-building complex over the charred ruins of a village that was destroyed by the bomb. Sachiko lives with Mariko in a small shack on the other side of a small river. Etsuko tells Jiro's father, whom Etsuko calls Ogata-San, is visiting. Family relations are terrible. Jiro and Etsuko are barely able to communicate the most basic facts to each other. He complains that she hasn't ironed ties that she has ironed. She serves him meals in near silence. Jiro's relationship with his father is equally frigid: while Ogata-San lectures Jiro, Jiro pretends to be reading a newspaper and not to hear him.

Sachiko's predicament mirrors and magnifies many of the difficulties that Etsuko faces in the aftermath of the war. Sachiko is something of a refugee. Her husband is dead, she has fled the house of her wealthy uncle, and now she is living alone in a shack, waiting for her American lover, Frank, to take her to California. Etsuko's position is not so desperate, but it is in some ways parallel. She has left the comfortable traditional house of her father-in-law for an isolated and solitary life with Jiro. As the events of the story take place, she is not planning to leave Japan, but the reader knows that, sometime after the birth of Keiko, Etsuko will leave with an Englishman rather than an American.

Sachiko is a neglectful mother, and though it is never clear that Etsuko was as bad, Sachiko's failures seem emblematic of Etsuko's guilt. Sachiko leaves Mariko alone in the shack in the evenings and does not bother to send the girl to school. At first this neglect seems casual, passive. Later it becomes clear that there is real hostility between mother and daughter. Mariko curses Sachiko's lover, Frank: "He drinks his own piss and he shits in his bed" (p. 85). Sachiko understands her own failures. She asks Etsuko, "Do you think I imagine for one moment that I'm a good mother to her?" (p. 171). And in a brutal climax, an infanticide by proxy, Sachiko takes each one of Mariko's pet kittens and drowns them in a nearby river while the child looks on.

All these memories provide more than a "vague echo" of Keiko's death and Etsuko's guilt. But it is not until the end of the novel that the connection is made explicit in such a way as to throw the entire story about Sachiko and Mariko into ambiguity. In her last scene with Mariko, Etsuko addresses the little girl as if she were her own child, as if she and Mariko are about to leave Japan. She says, "If you don't like it over there, we'll come straight back. But we have to try it and see if we like it there. I'm sure we will" (p. 173). While they have this conversation, Etsuko is holding something in her hand, something that has caught on her foot. We are never told what it is, but from events in a previous scene we suspect that it is a piece of old rope that has been lying in the grass. Earlier in the novel Etsuko has made it clear that a killer is stalking the suburbs of Nagasaki, a killer who hangs small children from trees. By imagining herself talking to a child and holding a piece of rope in her hand Etsuko associates herself with this killer—not because she is guilty of the crimes, but because she feels guilty about her own child's death.

The story that Etsuko tells is like a shadow of her own story—there is a ghostly quality to it. But she is not the only character in *A Pale View of Hills* who is haunted by ghosts. Everyone in the novel is in some way stalked by ghosts from the past. Little Mariko, Sachiko's daughter, believes she receives visits from a woman in the woods—an imaginary woman, who, Sachiko reveals, is someone Mariko saw in Tokyo, near the end of the war. "She saw other things in Tokyo," says Sachiko, "some terrible things, but she's always remembered this woman" (p. 73). The woman in question was someone whom Mariko saw standing in a canal, smiling, having just drowned her baby. (This real infanticide, of course, mirrors the drowning of the kittens that comes at the climax of the novel.) And Etsuko remembers life with Keiko as if her older daughter had lived like some kind of specter within her own home. After her death Keiko does haunt Etsuko's house—if not literally, then in her mother's mind. Keiko's room is emblematic of all the awful silence in the book, all the haunting, unnameable catastrophe that the novel attempts to describe. Niki cannot sleep in the room closest to Keiko's bedroom. "It's that other room," she explains. "Her room. It gives me an odd feeling, that room being right opposite" (p. 53). Etsuko pretends to be offended by Niki's feelings but admits privately:

I too had experienced a disturbing feeling about that room opposite. In many ways, that room is the most pleasant in the house, with a splendid view across the orchard. But it had been Keiko's fanatically guarded domain for so long, a strange spell seemed to linger there even now, six years after she had left it—a spell that had grown all the stronger now that Keiko was dead.

(p. 53)

The novel is perhaps Etsuko's attempt to break this spell.

Toward the end of the book Etsuko gives her surviving daughter a gift. It is a calendar with a picture of the harbor in Nagasaki. This is the pale view of hills to which the book's title refers. As she gives this calendar to Niki, Etsuko says that she remembers a day she spent there with Keiko, when Keiko was very happy. Of course she is referring to a scene in the novel when she traveled to the harbor with Sachiko and Mariko and Mariko was very happy. This trip to the harbor is a curious scene, perhaps the central scene in the novel, and it stands out against the rest precisely because of the characters' seeming happiness. Here, at the moment when the characters get out of Nagasaki and look back at it, they pretend that they are not who they are. Mariko, when she meets a little boy, pretends that she has a father, and her father, she says, is a zookeeper. Etsuko, Sachiko, and Mariko simulate ordinary, bourgeois lives. When they look back at Nagasaki, it does not seem a ruined city—it seems beautiful. The city reinvents itself, just as little Mariko reinvents herself once she is outside of the town.

The best these characters can hope for is a simulation of ordinariness. The gift of the calendar is an incomplete gesture: Etsuko cannot explain its significance entirely. When she hands Niki the calendar, it is a poor substitute for telling her daughter how guilty she feels and how full of sorrow she is. But by saying that the calendar reminds her of a day she spent with Keiko—even if this is a lie—Etsuko is at least admitting to herself and Niki that she is thinking about Keiko.

AN ARTIST OF THE FLOATING WORLD

THE setting of *An Artist of the Floating World* is an unnamed Japanese city; the year is 1948; and the narrator is Masuji Ono, a former propagandist for the imperial regime who is now trying to cope with the social and personal implications of his involvement in the rise of the militarist state. The novel catalogs the struggles Ono endures during his daughter's wedding negotiations. There is some question as to how severely his family's social status has been stigmatized by his wartime activities.

While he tells this story, Ono recounts his rise to prominence as an artist and propagandist. He recalls how he began painting against his father's wishes; how, after a time, he was apprenticed to Seiji Moriyama, an artist whose work was devoted to painting "the floating world" (p. 145), the world of red-light districts, courtesans, and drinking—the world of pleasure; how he left Moriyama to work with the Okada-Shingen Society (the name means "new life") and make posters that called for military expansionism and the invasion of China. In this role as propagandist Ono achieved his greatest success. He rose to such a position of prominence that he was able to make careers and ruin lives.

As Ono tells his story, he relates how he played an instrumental role in creating the pleasure district of his city by founding a drinking establishment, the Migi-Hidari (the name means "right-left," and the poster in front of the place was decorated with pictures of marching combat boots). In the Migi-Hidari, Ono held court, surrounded by acolytes who would offer testimonials to him, saying such things as "in years to come, our proudest honor will be to tell others that we were once the pupils of Masuji Ono" (p. 25).

But in the novel's present tense the pleasure district has been destroyed, and a Western-style business district is rising in its place. Ono, like Etsuko in *A Pale View of Hills*, has two daughters, and *An Artist of the Floating World*, like *A Pale View of Hills*, begins with the visit of one of those daughters to his house. In this case it is Setsuko, who arrives with her boy, Ichiro, and with great worries about her sister Noriko's marriage plans. Ono is grappling with things he would prefer not to know, attempting to explain things that—to him—seem indelicate and difficult. Like Etsuko in *A Pale View of Hills* he confides in the reader but not without reservations. There is a silence at the center of both books: *A Pale View of Hills* revolves narratively and thematically around the bombing of Hiroshima and Nagasaki without ever describing the actual bombing; *An Artist of the Floating World* explores events leading up to and after World War II but is extremely reticent in discussing the war itself.

Behind the similarities in structure and setting, however, there are profound differences between the two novels. Ono's relation to his own story is quite different from Etsuko's. In *A Pale View of Hills* the reader has a sense of Etsuko's feelings of guilt, but it is not clear that she is responsible for her daughter's suicide. Her memories seem to equate her with Sachiko, but it is never clear that she *was* a neglectful mother in the same way that Sachiko was. Her guilt is personal—and the reader is not sure whether or not it is completely deserved. Ono's guilt and the difficulties he reckons with are political, and therefore social as well as personal. The world sees his former cause as evil, something to be regarded with shame.

It is as though in *An Artist of the Floating World* Ishiguro has moved his attention from Etsuko to a different character in *A Pale View of Hills*, Ogata-San, Etsuko's patrician father-in-law. Like Ono, Ogata-San is a sympathetic old man who has spent a great part of his life in an effort that was tied to a terrible cause. In *A Pale View of Hills* there is a scene in which Ogata-San confronts Shigeo Matsuda, a young man who has written an article condemning Ogata-San and his colleagues for their nationalistic teaching methods. This conversation contains in miniature the larger struggle that occurs within Ono in *An Artist of the Floating World*:

"We may have lost the war," Ogata-San interrupted, "but that's no reason to ape the ways of the enemy. We lost the war because we didn't have enough guns and tanks, not because our people were cowardly, not because our society was shallow. You have no idea, Shigeo, how hard we worked, men like myself, men like Dr. Endo, whom you also insulted in your article. We cared deeply for the country and worked hard to ensure the correct values were preserved and handed on."

"I don't doubt these things. I don't doubt you were sincere and hard working. I've never questioned that for one moment. But it just so happens that your energies were spent in a misguided direction, an evil direction. You weren't to know this, but I'm afraid it's true. It's all behind us now and we can only be thankful."

(p. 147)

Unlike Ogata-San, Ono seems to take both sides in this debate. At one point, on hearing of the suicide of a businessman whose wartime activities have become a shame to his company, Ono says: "The world seems to have gone mad. Every day there seems to be a report of someone else killing himself in apology. Tell me…don't you find it all a great waste? After all, if your country is at war, you do all you can in support, there's no shame in that. What need is there to apologize by death?" (p. 55). Later at a *miai*—a formal banquet at which families of a prospective bride and groom meet—Ono humiliates himself in a desperate attempt to release his daughter from the stigma of his association with imperialist Japan. He says:

There are some who would say it is people like myself who are responsible for the terrible things that happened to this nation of ours. As far as I am concerned, I freely admit I made many mistakes. I accept that much of what I did was ultimately harmful to our nation, that mine was part of an influence that resulted in untold suffering for our own people. I admit this.

(p. 123)

His public struggle to defend himself and his family (the awful truth is that the two interests are opposed) reflects a private struggle. Like Etsuko, Ono is fighting for his life—fighting to understand it and to make it his own. Like hers, his life is deeply intertwined with the history of his country. His misdeeds are his country's misdeeds.

In *A Pale View of Hills* a recurring theme is infanticide and the killing of the vulnerable. In *An Artist of the Floating World* there is no literal infanticide, but figuratively this motif is carried on. Fathers and father figures destroy the work of their sons and students. Ono's father burns Ono's work, trying to discourage his son from becoming a painter. Moriyama burns paintings by students who betray his teachings. And in one of the novels most brutal scenes police destroy the paintings of one of Ono's students, Kuroda, after Ono reports Kuroda's disloyalty to the state.

In *An Artist of the Floating World* this figurative infanticide is balanced by a set of figurative patricides. Children repeatedly challenge their fathers. The fathers find themselves stunned, outdated, and discarded. Ono is disowned by his former students, teased by his daughters, and forced to confront the horrible results of his actions. In one scene Ono tries to visit Kuroda—who, after Ono's denunciation, was beaten and jailed—and one of Kuroda's students rebukes and condemns him. The student tells Ono:

It is clearly you who are ignorant of the full details. Or else how would you dare come here like this? For instance, sir, I take it you never knew about Mr. Kuroda's shoulder? He was in great pain, but the warders conveniently forgot to report the injury and it was not attended to until the end of the war. But of course, they remembered it well enough whenever they decided to give him another beating. Traitor. That's what they called him. Traitor. Every minute of every day. But now we all know who the real traitors were.

(p. 113)

Ono's generation's imperialistic and nationalistic idealism is widely repudiated by his children's generation. Indeed, Ono feels compelled to join in the widespread condemnation.

In *An Artist of the Floating World* an ideological drama is played out in Oedipal terms. The struggle for cultural identity in postwar Japan is a struggle between fathers and sons, students and teachers. The result is that Ishiguro is able to intertwine historical, political, and personal drama and at the same time show how Ono confuses political drama with personal drama. Ono places himself at the center of the action, as if all eyes in Japan are upon him. And at the height of his prestige, during the war, in the days of drinking at the Migi-Hidari, Ono was the hub around which a small world turned. But now, living in a bombed-out half-destroyed house, with his younger daughter no longer fearing him the way she once did, Ono has "retired," as he puts it. It is not clear that anyone around him considers him as important as he considers himself. Dr. Saito, the father of Ono's prospective son-in-law, has only a vague understanding of Ono's work as an artist. At the *miai*, when Ono makes his abject speeches of self-denunciation, Dr. Saito is confused. He says, as though baffled: "You're saying you are unhappy about the work you did? With your paintings?" (p. 123). And then later: "I'm sure you're too harsh on yourself, Mr Ono. . . . Tell me, Miss Noriko, is your father always so strict with himself?" (p. 124). Ono imagines a world in which his personal drama is at the center of everyone else's consciousness.

The novel ends with Ono sitting on a bench in what once was the pleasure district of the city. The bars that were not destroyed by bombs were turned over by bulldozers, the destruction of the entire neighborhood mirroring the recurrent scenes of the destruction of artwork. But Ono is sanguine:

I smiled to myself as I watched these young office workers from my bench. Of course, at times, when I remember those brightly-lit bars and all those people gathered beneath the lamps, laughing a little more boisterously perhaps than those young men yesterday, but with much the same good-heartedness, I feel a certain nostalgia for the past and the district as it used to be. But to see how our city has been rebuilt, how things have recovered so rapidly over these years, fills me with genuine gladness. Our nation, it seems, whatever mistakes it may have made in the past, has now another chance to make a better go of things. One can only wish these young people well.

(p. 206)

Ono in the end renounces not just his former ideology—an ideology that never seemed at the heart of his desires—not just his own prestige. He escapes from the intergenerational struggle that has defined his life. He has, in a new sense, retired.

THE REMAINS OF THE DAY

SALMAN Rushdie, reviewing *The Remains of the Day* in *The Observer*, called the novel "a brilliant subversion of the fictional modes from which it at first seems to descend" in which "death, change, pain and evil invade the Wodehouse world" (21 May 1989, p. 53). Although *The Remains of the Day* initially seems a stylish, comic novel of manners, it is really the clearest statement, to date, of the ideas that Ishiguro explores throughout his work. It is the desperate cry of a Jeeves who has done his best to annihilate himself. Stevens is the hollowest of Ishiguro's hollow men. He has devoted his life to repression and pretense. The book turns brilliantly from caricature to pathos. Stevens' most ridiculous qualities, his stuffiness and his pomposity, prove to be the very things that cause him devastating pain.

As a butler Stevens sees himself as someone striving nobly toward a dignity he defines as follows:

"Dignity" has to do crucially with a butler's ability not to abandon the professional being he inhabits. . . . The great butlers are great by virtue of their ability to inhabit their professional role and inhabit it to the utmost; they will not be shaken out by external events, however surprising, alarming or vexing. They wear their professionalism as a decent gentleman will wear his suit: he will not let ruffians or circumstance tear it off him in the public gaze; he will discard it when, and only when, he wills to do so, and this will invariably be when he is entirely alone.

(pp. 42–43)

Stevens' world is a dangerous and solitary place. One is constantly under attack from ruffians who try to tear one's clothes off, and one is under terrible pressure. To reveal anything about oneself is a humiliating experience akin to running about naked.

Stevens is self-controlled to the point of self-obliteration and proud of it. No ruffian or circumstance can so much as dislodge one of his cuff links. On a night Stevens recalls, a night when his employer, Lord Darlington, throws an enormous, important dinner—a dinner in which Darlington hopes to solidify alliances between Western democracies and Hitler's Germany—Stevens' father dies. As the elder Stevens, who is also in Darlington's employ, lies on his deathbed in Darlington Hall, the younger Stevens ministers to Darlington's guests without any of them knowing that he is suffering enormous stress and grief. He won't even admit his feelings to his father. His father says to him in their last conversation: "I'm proud of you. A good son. I hope I've been a good father to you. I suppose I haven't." To which Stevens replies: "I'm afraid we're extremely busy now, but we can talk again in the morning" (p. 97). In the aftermath Stevens refuses to admit how awful all this is; instead he claims he is proud of his behavior that night. "Indeed," he tells the reader, "why should I deny it? For all its sad associations, whenever I recall that evening today, I find I do so with a large sense of triumph" (p. 110). As in all Ishiguro's novels this denial can be read as an inverted cry of distress. We suspect

Stevens must know—consciously or not—the horror of the story he has told, and his claim to a sense of triumph seems only a way of dodging the horror he has revealed.

Stevens seems nothing but his studied persona: perhaps he is afraid to take off his suit because he fears there is nothing underneath it. The character becomes emblematic of a kind of blinkered, self-destructive life—the reductio ad absurdum of Henry James's characters, for example, many of whom deny their impulses in order to maintain a social facade. Stevens' denial is absolute and his maintenance is desperate because, perhaps, he fears there may be nothing beneath his social facade.

Of course Stevens does step out of his professional role in order to narrate the novel. The very act of narration is a stepping out of the butler's uniform. He is calling attention to himself, though the novel is written in journal entries that he composes when "entirely alone" (p. 43). In fact, everything he does from the moment the novel begins involves some small departure from his servant status. Stevens, with his employer dead and his career coming to an end, is beginning to make some kind of escape from the prison of his butler's attire. He leaves the manor; he searches for a woman; he thinks about his past; he reflects on his life. The novel itself is a desperate struggle against the self-imposed limits of his life.

Although Stevens makes no real attempt to reinvent himself, the book's title hints at the remote possibility of such reinvention and the redemption that might come with it. Toward the end of the novel Stevens finds himself on a public bench, sobbing to a stranger and confessing his failures. The stranger tells him to cheer up, to enjoy retirement. He doesn't understand Stevens precisely, but he offers consolation. "The evening's the best part of the day," he says. "You've done your day's work. Now you can put your feet up and enjoy it" (p. 244). While it seems unlikely that Stevens will find happiness in what remains of his day, at the end of the novel he seems intent on trying. He decides to go back to Darlington Hall, but with a new desire to learn to banter, for he says he suspects that "in bantering lies the key to human warmth" (p. 245). He seems ready—if not to light out for the territory— then to experiment with some new ground, some new, personalized accoutrement to his butlering uniform. But this is no sudden shift. In the course of the novel, as Stevens retells his life, he draws out its parameters and limits and slowly becomes conscious of them. And in the novel's present-tense narration he tests the limits of his butler's outfit and tries on other disguises.

The action in the book begins when Stevens' new employer, an American named Farraday who has purchased Darlington Hall, suggests that his butler take a vacation, a drive around the country. "You fellows," he says to Stevens, "you're always locked up in these big houses helping out, how do you ever get to see around this beautiful country of yours?" (p. 4). Stevens at first is confused, both by Farraday's idea that he leave Darlington Hall and by the seeming personal interest that the American takes in his butler. Stevens says he initially "did not take Mr. Farraday's suggestion at all seriously . . . , regarding it as just another instance of an American gentleman's unfamiliarity with what was and was not commonly done in England" (p. 4). It is clear that Stevens does not always understand his own motivations and cannot confess to his true feelings.

But Stevens has received a letter from Miss Kenton, a former housekeeper of Darlington Hall, and upon consideration of this letter he rethinks Farraday's offer. Stevens sees hints in Miss Kenton's letter that her marriage is unhappy and that she might want to return to Darlington Hall. He first presents the journey, both to the reader and to Farraday, as though it were simply a tour of English landscapes—"an expedition which, as I foresee it, will take me through much of the finest countryside of England" (p. 3)—but it soon becomes apparent that his trip has a destination. And although he claims vociferously that he is only interested in Miss Kenton for professional reasons—she might put his house in order—the reader and Farraday see things differently.

From the start of the novel, we see cracks in Stevens' facade, hints that he is unable to maintain his dignified front and that he is willing to deceive himself in his attempts to cover those lapses. He admits, about midway into the novel, that he has begun to lie about his past, claiming that he did not work for Lord Darlington. (This is a bit like Etsuko's evading questions about Keiko's suicide.) In the aftermath of the war Darlington has become something of a notorious traitor, and when people ask, "You mean you actually used to work for that Lord Darlington?" (p. 120), Stevens gives, in his words, "an answer which could mean little other than that I had not" (pp. 121–122). This startles

him. He refuses to admit his shame to himself and instead looks for "a convincing way to account for such distinctly odd behaviour" (p. 122). He insists, "I have chosen to tell white lies . . . as the simplest means of avoiding unpleasantness. This does seem a very plausible explanation the more I think about it. . . . Let me say that Lord Darlington was a gentleman of great moral stature. . . . Nothing could be less accurate than to suggest that I regret my association with such a gentleman" (p. 126). As his facade cracks, Stevens is desperate to repair it, but the repairs seem only to indicate further decay.

At one point along the way he allows strangers to mistake him for a great lord instead of a mere servant, boasting that he knew Winston Churchill, Anthony Eden, and Lord Halifax. Again, when he looks over this moment, he has no explanation for his behavior—"It wasn't my intention to deceive anyone" (p. 208), he says—but whether or not he intends to deceive is almost beyond the point. Stevens is in public, and he is not wearing his butler's clothes. He is not naked, but in disguise, and from his actions one might surmise that he thinks butler's clothes are insufficient.

Miss Kenton is an interesting choice for the object of Stevens' affections. She is the one character who, throughout the novel, points out Stevens' pretensions and expects better of him. When Lord Darlington demands that all the Jewish maids on his staff be dismissed, Stevens outwardly accepts this situation. Miss Kenton objects. She threatens to quit but does not, and, some time after the event, when Stevens and Darlington both acknowledge that they were in error, she says: "Do you realize, Mr. Stevens, how much it would have meant to me if you had thought to share your feelings last year? You knew how upset I was when my girls were dismissed. Do you realize how much it would have helped me? Why, Mr Stevens, why, why, why do you always have to *pretend*?" (pp. 153–154). Miss Kenton always searches for Stevens' humanity, wondering, "Can it be that our Mr. Stevens is really flesh and blood after all and cannot fully trust himself?" (p. 156). She discovers him one night alone in his room with a book, and when he refuses to tell her what he is reading, she pries the text out of his hands. Stevens fights fiercely but loses, and Miss Kenton discovers that he is reading a second-rate romance novel.

In searching for Miss Kenton, Stevens searches not only for love but for an affirmation of self. She, after all, has made a leap of faith that he himself has never been able to make: she has supposed that he might be interesting and worth knowing. Like so many of Ishiguro's characters Stevens is profoundly dislocated, but unlike most he is seeking solid ground. At the end of the novel he sees what he has lost and what he wants. The power of this book derives not from Stevens' ambition or hollowness, but from the combination of the two: the smallness of his ambition and the way it reveals the emptiness of his own life. All he wants is some "human warmth." Stevens is learning what every child knows: human beings need companionship. He is also discovering that he is profoundly alone.

THE UNCONSOLED

ALL Ishiguro's narrators can be seen as writers. All first-person narrators can be seen that way in that they tell their own tales. Ishiguro's protagonists also can be seen as readers: Etsuko, Ono, and Stevens attempt to understand their own stories, to figure out what the stories reveal about themselves, to interpret their own tales.

Ryder, the narrator of *The Unconsoled*, whose name sounds like a cross between "writer" and "reader," fills both these roles, figuratively and to extremes. A passive amnesiac without a clear sense of purpose or place, Ryder begins the novel in a position much like the reader's own: he must determine where he is, who he is, and what will happen to him. The city in which Ryder, a pianist, has arrived to give a performance seems a dreamscape, its architecture and characters embodiments of Ryder's worries and fears. The houses, rooms, and rubbish in the town are all strangely reminiscent of things and places from the narrator's past; rooms remind him of fights between his parents, houses recall the horror of his childhood home life. Old school friends appear out of nowhere to make demands on him and to remind him of his youth; and almost everyone he meets in the city suffers from the same set of problems: families are falling apart everywhere, their members no longer able to communicate with one another. Over and over, Ryder is expected to repair these familial faults and fissures. Over and over again he fails to meet the simplest obligations. The book has the feel of an anxiety dream, and Ryder's anxiety structures the dream.

Ryder fills the role of writer and reader just as any dreamer fills the roles of creator and interpreter. But unlike the narrators of Ishiguro's first three novels Ryder fills these roles involuntarily and reluctantly. He does not think of himself as an author or writer of any kind. Contrast his position with Stevens'. The butler writes in a journal and recreates the events of his past, deliberately telling his tale to an audience—even if that audience is only one he imagines—and making whatever points he has to make. If *The Unconsoled* puts Ryder in a position analogous to that of a reader, it is not a role he leaps into with any gusto. Unlike Stevens or Ono, who mull over the implications of their own and other people's words and actions, Ryder is disinclined to delve into the complexities of his world. There are moments in the novel when crucial information is imparted to him and Ryder seems dead set against hearing it. When a man who claims to have lived next door to Ryder's parents starts to tell Ryder about his parents' fights, Ryder begins to shout: "I warn you! I'll terminate this conversation! I'm warning you!" (p. 58).

Ryder is more a rider than he is a writer or a reader. Passivity defines his character. He is constantly buffeted by circumstance and taken wherever events lead him. He spends an extraordinary amount of time on buses—the novel ends with him on a bus, blissfully resigning himself to being a passenger—and in the passenger seats of cars. The one scene in which he drives a car is fraught with tension: he does not know where he is going and seems sure to lose his way. He is a passenger in the world at large. He is told he has a tight schedule, one he must keep to, but Ryder has no idea what that schedule is. He considers getting a copy of his itinerary, but when the moment arises, he fails to ask for one. In one scene Ryder allows a couple of journalists to pose him in front of a monument whose significance he does not fully grasp. He knows the monument is important but does not know what it represents; still he stands in front of it and allows himself to be photographed. The photographers are using him. By posing in front of the monument, Ryder is endorsing a political figure from the past, perhaps some sort of tyrant. Somehow, Ryder seems incapable of resisting the photographers' suggestions and manipulations. Like a dreamer in a nightmare he sometimes has little control over his actions and is often borne along by trivial, distracting events while crucial action is occurring elsewhere.

The novel has an almost musical structure of theme and variation. The repeated sequence, stated generally, goes something like this: Ryder wakes up from incomplete sleep and leaves his hotel room with a plan. The plan is quickly scuttled as demands are pressed upon him. He sets out on a journey through unfamiliar territory and encounters a figure from his early life in England and one person from the city in which he is traveling. Generally these people either remind him of his personal sorrows or inform him of their own. They lead him on a trip whose detours and distractions confuse and frustrate Ryder. Eventually, he finds his way—by either plan or accident—back to the hotel room, where he finds he has missed an engagement on his schedule.

Within this general pattern certain subplots are developed. He wrangles with a woman named Sophie, who might be his wife and seems to be his lover. He meets Sophie's son, Boris, who may be his son. At times Ryder tries to become close with Boris; these attempts are mostly failures. At other times he is cruel and neglectful of the boy. Gustav, the boy's grandfather and Sophie's father, is a porter in the hotel. He does not recognize Ryder as his daughter's companion but demands two great favors of him. He wants Ryder to act as intermediary between himself and Sophie (Sophie and Gustav do not speak to each other), and he wants Ryder, at his great performance, to mention the position of hotel porters and to underline their importance to the city. Ryder agrees to both of these favors. He is drawn again and again into the details of people's family lives, love lives, and sorrows. The hotel manager, Hoffman, wants Ryder to sign a set of albums for his wife, who is deeply depressed. Hoffman's son, Stephan, also makes claims on Ryder's time and talents. Stephan is to give a piano recital before Ryder's, and he wants Ryder's advice and encouragement. Stephan believes that a great performance from him will heal his family's sorrows, just as the town believes that a great performance from Ryder will return it to better days. There are love affairs that need mending: Brodsky, the town's new conductor, is recovering from years as a drunken bum and seeks to rekindle a lost romance with a gentle older woman, Miss Collins. Ryder does what he can to help these people. The chaos of the world without reflects the chaos within Ryder, and all of his attempts to impose order are futile.

As he scurries from crisis to crisis, Ryder works his way through a city Kafkaesque in its convoluted architecture. Small entrances lead to enormous rooms; little hidden doorways present secret escape routes that traverse huge distances as if connecting adjacent buildings. Everything seems interconnected in curious and mysterious ways. Things that seem close by are often unreachable. At one point near the climax of the book Ryder tries to walk to the concert hall in which he is to perform, but, although he can see the hall's tower, he is unable to wend his way through the city's twisting streets. At another point he returns from a long car trip simply by passing through a small door and hallway.

Ryder's narrative shares some of the qualities of the town's architecture. He cannot get to the most crucial points—is repeatedly unable to reconstruct his identity or his childhood—but there are sudden openings through which he is able to see what would generally be unknowable. The narration leaps boldly out of Ryder's own mind. Ryder, in a car with Stephan Hoffman, can suddenly see into the young man's mind and past. He imagines, along with Stephan, a scene of a failed dinner party. He understands precisely what Stephan is pondering and explains it perfectly to the reader: it is as though an opening has appeared in Stephan's skull and Ryder has entered. His narrative bursts suddenly into a cinematic, omniscient perspective, as though his eye were suddenly a probing camera, searching the rooms of other people's houses, the corners of other people's minds.

These leaps into omniscience violate not only rules of logic and the conventions that generally govern first-person narratives, but also the thematic parameters established in Ishiguro's previous novels. Generally Ishiguro's narrators never get to see into other people's lives. There is in fact a recurring scene in the books, in which the protagonist is poised outside of doors, listening to horrors within but unable to enter. Etsuko lurks outside Keiko's door but can never go in. Young Ono stands outside the door of the room in which his father is burning all his paintings, catches the smell of the burning art, and insists that his father's actions are of little consequence to him. Stevens, at a crucial point in *The Remains of the Day*, stands in front of Miss Kenton's door, while within she is sobbing, and finds himself unable to go in and comfort her. Ishiguro's narrators are eavesdroppers on the crucial events of life, trapped within themselves and locked out of disturbing actions, unable to confront them. Ryder is at once like and unlike these figures. He is able to see through these closed doors, but this only allows him to become a voyeur, not a participant. He comes no closer to the "human warmth" that Stevens seeks than Stevens does. Ryder's vision is able to penetrate into other people's worlds, but he enters as an observer, unable to reach out to anyone in the scenes he sees. It is as though Etsuko were able to enter Keiko's room, but only as a ghostly presence, as though she were allowed a closer view of her suffering daughter but no closer contact.

What Ryder sees is a world full of disconnections. The eavesdropping scene is repeated in the stories that are told to him. Gustav, when recalling his falling out with his daughter, remembers a particularly poignant moment when young Sophie shut herself in a room, crying over a dead hamster, while he lurked outside the door, unable to comfort her. The sequence is repeated in the action of the novel: Hoffman and Ryder stand outside a room in which Brodsky, the recently rehabilitated musician, replays the same short series of notes over and over. Ryder sees distress everywhere and is unable to do anything for the sufferers.

The novel's plot—if it can be called that—never comes to its expected conclusion: Ryder is unable to give his performance; his audience disappears before he is ready to go on. And Ryder is never able truly to reconstruct his identity. There is something of a mystery at the novel's core that is never resolved. He never really figures out why his parents fought so terribly, though many people hint at a problem lurking at the bottom of his family life. Once or twice people assert that the family problems can all be traced to Ryder's father's alcoholism, but this is never asserted in definite terms, and perhaps most importantly it is never something that Ryder himself seems to admit.

Ryder's amnesia is emblematic of his character. He refuses to assert his identity, runs from his past, and like all Ishiguro's narrators is punished for it. But Ryder's comeuppance is not a sudden realization of his own failures. He is incapable of that. His absolute inability to face his life consigns him, for lack of better words, to a floating world of constant anxiety and powerlessness. At the end of the novel he is seated happily on a bus and going nowhere. This kind of cheerful oblivion is perhaps the cruelest hell of Ishiguro's invention. Unlike Etsuko, or

Ono, or Stevens, Ryder is really unaware of his own annihilation and deaf to the naggings of his conscience.

THE OLD WORLD AND THE NEW WORLD MEET AGAIN

RYDER'S condition is an extreme example of something all Ishiguro's narrators share. The world changes around them, and they fail to adapt to it; they exist in a present haunted by their past. Ono, Etsuko, and Stevens are all representatives of lost worlds. Etsuko clings to Japanese values that mystify her daughter Niki. Ono wants to hold true to an imperial Japan that has been defeated. Stevens is simply a relic. There aren't many specimens of his kind left in postwar England. In all three of the early novels the narrators exist in a world where permissive American values are on the rise. Niki is living in London with her boyfriend; Frank threatens to bring Sachiko into a life of degradation. Ono's grandson, Ichiro, plays at being Popeye and the Lone Ranger. Stevens' former master's place has been taken over by an American who wants to banter. Everything is loose and free, but the narrators cling to the formality and decorum of bygone empires.

In Ishiguro's work a Jamesian theme of the early twentieth century is turned on its head. The New and Old Worlds still come in conflict, but the United States is now in power. A new order has taken over the globe, and all that is left of the Old World are a few wispy ghosts: Etsuko, Ono, and Stevens. Ishiguro's horror stories have such weight to them because the haunting they describe is real. The main characters are the ghosts, and they are haunted by the houses in which they live.

SELECTED BIBLIOGRAPHY

I. NOVELS. *A Pale View of Hills* (London, 1982); *An Artist of the Floating World* (London, 1986); *The Remains of the Day* (London, 1989); *The Unconsoled* (London, 1995).

II. SHORT STORIES. "A Strange and Sometimes Sadness," "Getting Poisoned," and "Waiting for J.," in *Introduction 7: Stories by New Writers* (Boston, 1981); "A Family Supper," in *The Penguin Book of Modern British Short Stories,* ed. by Malcolm Bradbury (New York, 1987).

III. TELEPLAYS. *A Profile of Arthur J. Mason* (1984); *The Gourmet* (1986), repr. in *Granta* 43 (spring 1993).

IV. INTERVIEWS. Gregory Mason, "An Interview with Kazuo Ishiguro," in *Contemporary Literature* 30, no. 3 (fall 1989); Kazuo Ishiguro and Kenzaburo Oe, "Wave Patterns: A Dialogue," in *Grand Street* 10, no. 2 (1991).

V. CRITICAL STUDIES. Paul Bailey, "Private Desolations," in *Times Literary Supplement* (19 February 1982); James Campbell, "Kitchen Window," in *New Statesman* (19 February 1982); Edith Milton, "In a Japan Like Limbo," in *New York Times Book Review* (9 May 1982); Geoff Dyer, "On Their Mettle," in *New Statesman* 111, no. 2871 (4 April 1986); Kathryn Morton, "After the War Was Lost," in *New York Times Book Review* (8 June 1986); Salman Rushdie, "What the Butler Didn't See," review of *The Remains of the Day*, in *Observer* (London) (21 May 1989); Lawrence Graver, "What the Butler Saw," in *New York Times Book Review* (8 October 1989); David Ansen, "An Onlooker at the Feast," in *Newsweek* (18 October 1989); Paul Gray, "Upstairs, Downstairs," in *Time* (30 October 1989); Mark Kamine, "A Servant of Self-Deceit," in *New Leader* 72, no. 18 (13 November 1989); Gabriele Annan, "On the High Wire," in *New York Review of Books* (7 December 1989); David Gurewich, "Upstairs, Downstairs," in *New Criterion* 8, no. 4 (December 1989); Gregory Mason, "Inspiring Images: The Influence of the Japanese Cinema on the Writings of Kazuo Ishiguro," in *East-West Film Journal* 3, no. 2 (June 1989); Bill Bryson, "Between Two Worlds," in *New York Times Magazine* (29 April 1990); Hermione Lee, "Quiet Desolation," in *The New Republic* (22 January 1990); Pico Iyer, "Waiting Upon History—*The Remains of the Day* by Kazuo Ishiguro," in *Partisan Review* (summer 1991); Kathleen Wall, "*The Remains of the Day* and Its Challenges to Theories of Unreliable Narration," in *Journal of Narrative Technique* 24, no. 1 (winter 1994); Anita Brookner, "A Superb Achievement—*The Unconsoled* by Kazuo Ishiguro," in *Spectator* (June 1995); Pico Iyer, "The Butler Didn't Do It, Again—*The Unconsoled* by Kazuo Ishiguro," in *Times Literary Supplement* (28 April 1995); Louis Menand, "Anxious in Dreamland," in *New York Times Book Review* (15 October 1995); Richard Rorty, "Consolation Prize—*The Unconsoled,* by Kazuo Ishiguro," in *The Village Voice* (10 October 1995); Cynthia Wong, "The Shame of Memory: Blanchot's Self-Dispossession in Ishiguro's *A Pale View of Hills,*" in *Clio* 24, no. 4 (winter 1995); Pico Iyer, "A New Kind of Travel Writer," in *Harper's* (February 1996).

P. D. JAMES

(1920–)

Katrin R. Burlin

INTERVIEWS WITH P. D. JAMES reveal that she is funnier than even the wit in her novels or her love of Jane Austen would suggest. She is articulate and interested in talking about genre—crime fiction, detective novels, and serious novels—the modern world, women, and feminism.

Phyllis Dorothy James was born in Oxford on 3 August 1920 to Amelia Hone James and Sidney James, a middle-grade civil servant who worked for the Inland Revenue. James was educated at Cambridge Girls High School from 1931 to 1937. Her father did not believe in higher education for women, so, at the age of sixteen, she was sent to work in a tax office, a job she hated. A few years later, she found a more suitable job as an assistant stage manager at the Cambridge Festival Theatre.

In 1941, James married Ernest Connor Bantry White, a physician, with whom she had two daughters, Clare in 1942 and Jane in 1944; she named her second daughter for her favorite author, Jane Austen. When Connor was sent by the Royal Army Medical Corps to India during World War II, James was left to cope with a young daughter, a new pregnancy, and the bombing. As she tells Joyce Wadler (1986), grim times followed. While Londoners were dying in the terrible bombing, James, like all British mothers, was kept in the hospital to recuperate; she feared separation from her newborn baby because, during wartime, babies were placed for greater safety in the hospital basement: How, if the hospital were hit . . . would she ever find the baby? (p. 75). Her husband returned from the war mentally disabled. "He was never diagnosed as schizophrenic . . . though it could have been that. He did have highs and lows. It was terrifying and terribly disruptive," she explains to Wadler (p. 75). Occasionally violent, he repeatedly had to be hospitalized. She moved in with his parents, sent her children to boarding school, and qualified for a job in hospital administration. She was

stoic about this personal tragedy and never considered divorce, even after her husband was permanently institutionalized. She took it as a matter of course that during his illness she would work to support her family.

In interviews James emphasizes how pleased she is with her professional life. Unlike most women of her time, she had access to centers of power, especially political power, where she learned how administration, politics, and law work, and where she came to understand and, to a measure, share in that power.

In interviews James also describes how her working life dovetailed with her writing career. During the war she was a Red Cross nurse, and that work ultimately gave rise to three of her novels: *A Mind to Murder* (1963), *Shroud for a Nightingale* (1971), and *The Black Tower* (1975). Her knowledge of mental health and a hospital's inner workings comes from her experience as an administrator in the National Health Service from 1949 to 1968. While in hospital administration, James specialized in mental-health work, but in 1968, four years after her husband's death, she moved to the Home Office, a department of the government that deals with community "law and order."

She worked first in the Home Office forensics department (vital experience for *Death of an Expert Witness*, 1977, which takes place in a forensics laboratory), and subsequently in the police and criminal policy divisions, where she concentrated on juvenile crime. As she rose to the position of senior civil servant, she became familiar with the strategies, procedures, and techniques of forensics scientists and the police. Although she was never at the scene of a crime and would not attend a postmortem—for fear of violating the privacy of even the most anonymous and humble victim—she thinks that, together with her research, her work experience gave her expertise vital to her genre. As she tells Jane S. Bakerman, "Government *is* interesting; it brings me, though I'm not a *very* senior civil servant, in touch with ministers of the Crown. It gives me an entree into the House of Commons and into the House of Lords during debates, and I see how policy is made" (p. 55).

Such experiences enabled her to write her increasingly philosophical crime novels. She details the political and social consequences of the murder of a member of Parliament in *A Taste for Death* (1986); examines how the Special Branch deals with terrorism in *Devices and Desires* (1989); and satirizes the government, police, and social-ethical sensibility of the 1990s in the dystopia *The Children of Men* (1992). All she has witnessed as an intelligent, active observer of the government she finds "fascinating to a writer" (p. 55). Still, as she tells Bakerman, the administrator is subservient to the artist, for "I like to think of myself as a writer who is also a civil servant" (p. 55).

James's success in both of her professions may be measured by the many appointments and awards she has received. In 1983 she received the Order of the British Empire, and in 1991 she was named Baroness James of Holland Park. After her retirement from the Home Office in 1979, she became a member of the board of governors of the British Broadcasting Corporation and chair of the literary panel of the British Council of the Arts. She has received a steady stream of recognition for her novels from the Mystery Writers of America and the British Crime Writers Association. The latter organization has given her its Silver Dagger Award on three occasions: in 1971 for *Shroud for a Nightingale*; in 1975 for *The Black Tower*; and in 1986 for *A Taste for Death*. In 1987 she received the Diamond Dagger Award for lifetime achievement from the British Crime Writers Association.

THE IMPORTANCE OF PLACE IN JAMES'S FICTION

JAMES stresses in interviews and in the introduction to her novels that the constant inspiration of her creative imagination is place. James's willingness to arrest the pace of her narrative in order to elaborate minutely and lovingly on the description of a place makes her unique among mystery writers, especially her ability to inform the atmosphere of each locale with descriptions that highlight the major themes of the novels—whether of disease, sterility, anxiety, or evil. In her foreword to *Murder in Triplicate* (1980), James comments on the role of place in the three novels collected in this volume; in each of the three, setting displaces the usual murder-mystery preoccupation with developing unique characters and innovative methods of murder. With relish she revisits East Anglia, where at Dunwich "the encroaching sea" has ruined what humanity once made: a medieval town, including its abbey, cottages, and tombstones, is crumbling into the sea. Visiting her holiday cottage there, she is buffeted by high winds, whose hallucinatory sounds, full of the accents of ancient tales, trouble and delight her. It was here that the sublime image of a drowned man with cleft-off hands came to her, an image she introduces at the beginning of *Unnatural Causes* (1967).

If in *Unnatural Causes* place is "numinous," in *The Black Tower* James complicates the thematic atmosphere by having her characters alternately yearn for a sight of the health-giving ocean and feel threatened by "the high cliffs of the black shale characteristic of the Purbeck coast of Dorset," shale that may "tumble into the English Channel." In each novel, the peopled coastlines are unremittingly "desolate, bleak, and sinister."

In *An Unsuitable Job for a Woman* (1972), however, James portrays a gentler setting—the city of Cambridge, which James adores and where she grew up; she considers it "one of the loveliest cities in Europe" and had always wanted to write about it. Despite the harsh and tragic plot of this novel, James permits "sunlit" accents to replenish the spirits of her young and gallant heroine, who feels her greatest saving joy in wandering the city and the university grounds when she surfaces from the "dark underworlds of the mystery"—the deep abandoned well in which she is entombed and from which she escapes. The well can be seen as a symbol of the sinister elements in the human psyche, our murderous instincts buried under a veneer of civilization.

In his essay "The Clinical World of P. D. James" (1982), Bernard Benstock considers the thematic resonance of buildings in James's work, noting that "almost every important building that serves as the central stage of her tragic dramas has been converted from something else, and each is either in the process or in potential danger of being reconverted or abandoned or torn down in turn" (p. 107).

COVER HER FACE

IT is not true, P. D. James insists, that she began to write because she was forced, after her husband's breakdown, to support their family. To that end she studied and qualified through examinations for a "properly" salaried job (with pension) with the government. To write was an impetus "almost from the time I knew what a book was," she says (Wadler, p. 75), but, she thought, there was little she could do about it given the stringencies of her everyday life. Consequently, she was in her late thirties when she began her first novel, *Cover Her Face* (1962), which took more than two years to write but was immediately accepted for publication.

Cover Her Face is cast in the popular form of a classic English house-party mystery, yet this ambitious first novel is open to multiple readings in its complex, ambiguous, even subversive deconstruction of such high-art house-party texts as Virginia Woolf's *To the Lighthouse*.

Cover Her Face dramatizes the desperate efforts of the women of the Maxie family—Mrs. Simon Maxie, her widowed daughter Deborah Riscoe, and the old family retainer, Martha Bultitaft—to hold on to their ancient family home, Martingale, in the face of a threat of its passing into the hands of an attractive, mischievous maidservant, the "unwed mother" Sally Jupp, who confounds them by announcing her engagement to the heir, Stephen Maxie. A mocking, jeering Sally provokes the usually calm, well-bred Mrs. Maxie into violently choking her to death.

Cover Her Face introduces Detective Chief-Inspector Adam Dalgleish of Scotland Yard. His character is complex, for he is a published poet as well as an accomplished detective. He draws on intuition and imagination as well as reason and training in police procedure to solve crimes. Clever and efficient, he rises rapidly in his profession but is slower to develop in his personal life. Having tragically lost both wife and newborn son, he is cautious in making emotional commitments. His subordinates admire him but find him cold and reserved. To P. D. James, he represents an aspect of herself and she remains true to him as her partner in almost all her fictions. *Cover Her Face* introduces us to his characteristic investigative procedures and to his relationship to subordinates and manner of treating suspects. It also initiates a potential romantic entanglement with one of the suspects, the attractive widow Deborah Riscoe. The novel concludes with Dalgleish's intention to see her again. In *A Mind to Murder*, she is introduced briefly as a romantic interest, but by *Unnatural Causes*, Dalgleish is found to have been so indifferent a lover that Deborah has written him off. The concluding pages of that novel show him destroying the poetry she had inspired him to write. It is that rare mystery novel in which the representation of crucial figures remains ambivalent, ambiguous; we can never really determine the final "take" on its murderess, for example.

In this social satire, James portrays the gentry as profoundly egotistical, even parochial, in their viewing of their country-house existence as central to the universe. Martingale, an Elizabethan manor house, has been in the Maxies' possession for generations. They are indifferent to life outside its circumference and are so absolutely persuaded of the necessity of preserving this closed world of the family and its traditions that they would even kill to maintain it. The existence of such a world is constructed upon an exploitative attitude that reduces workers to "hands," interested only in that part of humanity that serves the family's cause. James portrays this attitude as corrosive, not only of the family itself but of the underpaid, overworked servants who have inherited a passion for servility (they conflate sentimentality with loyalty), without understanding their own sacrifice or receiving its traditional reward (recognition as extended family).

Stephen Maxie, the heir to the estate, with his liberal modern sensibility, realizes that the expectation of servile dedication is apt to be a sentimental fiction on the part of the masters or the facsimile of formerly genuine emotion on the part of the servants. He notes the difference between his "Nannie bringing in the night drinks and ready to stay and talk" and "the devotion of Martha [who is] . . . more voluble, more self-conscious . . . a counterfeit of an emotion that had been as simple and necessary to him as the air he breathed." Stephen is filled with snobbish self-pity that this inferior emotion should be his lot as the modern master, but he understands that, to preserve a facsimile of the old worship that nannies offered, "Martha needed her occasional sop" of *his* facsimile of old-fashioned civility.

It is difficult to tell which is worse, the son who uses his intelligent political awareness to manipulate the servant he considers second-rate to the traditionally worshipful nannies or the mother who denies the servant's private emotions and cannot conceive of her having a life beyond the family. When Simon Maxie, the near-comatose patriarch of the family, is dying, Mrs. Maxie excludes Martha from the death vigil, thereby denying her the only reward that would make her sacrifice bearable. Perceiving that the trust between family and servant has been broken, Martha resigns.

Mrs. Maxie has already killed the servant Sally Jupp, a young woman who had only been pretending to have accepted Stephen Maxie's marriage proposal. She was having fun with her employers' horror at the idea of a servant joining the family; secretly, Sally was happily married and was enjoying in her husband's absence a bit of subversive play to teach the Maxies a lesson about their ignorance of other people's lives. Mrs. Maxie's snobbery is so profound it makes her morally stupid; Sally has dared to laugh at the attempts to persuade her out of the match. To Mrs. Maxie, it is logical to dispatch such an obstruction to the preservation of the family.

The drive to keep the house alive makes the whole family murderous in its exclusion and exploitation of others. Stephen and his sister, Deborah, so sublimate their sexual drives in the quest to preserve the institution that they come near to incest.

James challenges the traditional as an unexamined principle of good in order to introduce a new, healthy self-made breed. Jimmy Ritchie, Sally Jupp's husband, arrives at Martingale to reclaim his wife and son after proving his merit outside of the class-driven, debilitating culture of England. He has a physical authority and moral stature that dwarfs the two characters in the novel who might be more conventionally associated with valor—Stephen, the inheritor of the house, and Felix Hearne, the romantically broken war hero.

James's double lens on her characters reveals the victim-villain Sally Jupp as both a psychologically troubled individual with initial poses of submissive weakness and her subsequent rebelliousness and an agent of radical social energies. She is a victim of snobbishness and classism, with little outlet for her intellect and talents, and with a delight in malice and a talent for tormenting. What her husband unconsciously represents, the emerging meritocracy, she dramatizes.

It is difficult to determine James's opinion of Deborah Riscoe, with whom Adam Dalgleish is infatuated. As Deborah's behavior degenerates, her playacting, as Dalgleish points out, betrays a dangerous irresponsibility and a snobbish indifference to the serving classes. She deceives Martha, for example, as to the extent of her real danger by leaving doors unlocked and obscuring real clues with false ones. To the reader, Deborah's selfishness, arrogance, and irresponsibility seem offensive. James, however, seems more ambivalent since Dalgleish, in his infatuation, is able to separate a genuine core of self from Deborah's silliness.

The title of the novel alludes to the waste of youth, intelligence, and beauty in the murder of Sally Jupp and suggests how she comes to be revalued even by her murderer, who pities her lost opportunities. It symbolizes as well the Maxies' willingness to kill in order to maintain a decent appearance. It may also signify the novel's process of uncovering the face of murder and of the murderer, Mrs. Maxie: she is gentry, the ideal of social serenity; the face of murder, uncovered, is the face of gentility.

It is indubitably witty of James to have set her first mystery at a country house in which the central motive is its preservation in the family. Stephen Maxie is riddled with an impotent guilt and confined by a "band of responsibility" because of the family's strategies to save Martingale for him. Although he profits from their enterprise—for he, too, loves Martingale "for its beauty and its peace"—he knows that their stratagems involve a great sacrifice on the part of those they exploit or evict in the name of tradition. Stephen contemplates his family's measures and is uneasy that they protect him from even the slightest inconvenience, but he is not sufficiently distressed to point out that they are spoiling him, by feeding his sense of male privilege and by cheating and exploiting the poor.

The irony is that the introduction of an untrained girl, Sally Jupp, into the household nearly wrecks it. A servant's training would involve a sense of her place in the maintenance of an estate and of her "proper" relationship to the family. Sally Jupp, an ambitious modern girl who is clever and observant, knows that she, with the child she falsely presents as illegitimate and dependent, is vulnerable to exploitation by the rich poor, who are unable to afford professional domestics. She feels no guilt at not only exploiting the Maxies, but also dramatizing the exploitation for them. She plays with Stephen's feelings of chivalry, until he endangers her by proposing. Sally, who enjoys role-playing, teases Deborah's jealousy with her sexual attraction to Stephen and her powers to act like the golden girl. Martha, the servant, has no trouble seeing through the facade of Sally's meekness and submissiveness, but the family cannot, because Sally is of a class invisible to them and they do not want to see how they exploit her "shame." When, after Sally's murder, Dalgleish points out to the family doctor that the Maxies have excellent motives for killing her, the doctor demands indignantly, "What sort of people do you think we are?" Indeed, the Maxies are the sort of people responsible for the death of Sally Jupp, the sort of people who feel entitled to the preservation of their class traditions at any cost. According to the theory James floats through all her novels, however, the sort of person Sally is—radical, mischievous, selfish—is just as responsible, drawing on herself the fatal consequence of teasing Mrs. Maxie beyond endurance.

Cover Her Face is, then, also a conservative take on liberal English thought. James endorses the view that society sentimentalizes its outcasts. Consequently, as James portrays it, such outcasts take revenge by exploiting the sentimental to further their own interests, only to have the interests of the establishment, when threatened, turn on them violently.

A MIND TO MURDER

JAMES writes of Adam Dalgleish, her poet-policeman hero, that, with his "critical intelligence, essential self-sufficiency, his sensitivity, and low tolerance of fools," he could "be an uncomfortable colleague" (*Crime Times Three*, 1979, p. v). As a crime writer, however, she finds that "by *Shroud for a Nightingale* he and I were well established in that ambiguous and complicated partnership which exists between the writer and a continuing creation" (p. v). But the question raised by *A Mind to Murder* (1963), in which Superintendent Dalgleish's performance is vitiated by a constant premonition of failure and a prevailing mood of self-doubt, is whether the author-character collaboration has been equally successful for her creation. As James increasingly burdens her imagination with "such universal

absolutes as life and death, love and hate, treachery and failure" (p. vii), Dalgleish begins to falter, not as a poet, for he has just been feted by his publishers, but as a professional policeman.

By having Dalgleish arrive straight from the publishing party to the scene of a crime as the novel begins, James encapsulates the contradictory challenges he faces. Lionized for his poetic creativity in one scene, he must, as a detective, remind himself that "most murders are sordid little crimes bred out of ignorance and despair." As a conscientious, rational, and highly trained policeman, he must set aside the creative mind-set of the poet and do what is boring, repetitive, and methodical. He must be attentive to detail—not as a poet in search of the resonant image, but as a detective looking for clues in a manhunt.

The scene of the crime is the elite Steen Clinic, a private psychiatric outpatient facility in London; the murder victim is its rigid and repressive administrator, Enid Bolam, who has been stabbed with an artist's chisel and had her head bashed in with a fertility symbol, a fetish carved by a psychotic patient, that was then placed on her breast as if to represent a horrid stillbirth. James designs the scene to make it difficult for Dalgleish to limit his imagination to the obvious and focus on a routine investigation. Like his author, Dalgleish is suspicious of psychiatry and its claims to superiority in the detection of motive. Although motive has never been high on his list of questions in detective work, Dalgleish feels professionally challenged.

As critics have pointed out, this half-amused, half-sympathetic portrait of a newly defensive, self-doubting, and sour-tempered Dalgleish is James's most original achievement in *A Mind to Murder* and a modification of his character that not only continues in subsequent novels but also adds to the depth and complexity of her art as a novelist. In her introduction to *Crime Times Three*, James describes the modern mystery novelists' turn away from the glamorous amateur sleuth to a more realistic depiction of the professional police detective: "detection itself is closer to the realities, the ardors, the frustrations and the disappointments of real life criminal investigation" (p. vii). Therefore, in *A Mind to Murder*, she represents not only the supreme achievements on which Dalgleish's reputation as the "Yard's blue-eyed boy" depends, but also his inevitable blunders and occasional follies, the consequence never of carelessness or stupidity, but of restless pride, competitiveness, and, especially, overcleverness.

This refashioning of Dalgleish may also be seen as a self-reflexive gesture. In his capacity as her imaginative collaborator, Dalgleish represents James's own need, as a crime writer, to curb her fancy so that in exploring the themes of the serious novel she does not inadvertently let creative enthusiasm (the enthusiasm of composition) lead her to conflate her treatment of crime investigation with poetic expressiveness or metaphysical inquiry, thereby committing the folly of overreaching and forgetting the importance of simplicity.

Psychologists and poets, painters and policemen—all deal in symbols. Among the suspects of the Steen Clinic murder is its porter, the ambitious and talented artist Peter Nagle, who, though implicated in blackmail and attempted murder, is, in fact, innocent of this crime. He is, however, guilty of desecrating the victim's body. Coming across the body, in a fit of spite and malice, he had picked up the fetish used to knock out Enid Bolam and placed the grotesque object in her arms to mock her sexuality. Confronted with this crime scene, Dalgleish, who is surrounded by highly intelligent and capable psychiatrists, is eager to establish his skills as an interpreter of symbols. Thus, he is distracted into subtleties too refined for the accurate detection of the murderer.

The most obvious suspect from the beginning is Enid's cousin, Marion Bolam, who as a nurse at the clinic has the means, opportunity, and anatomical expertise to commit the murder. She also has the most commonplace motive: she is the sole supporter of an invalid mother who is in dire need of expensive institutional care, and she has discovered that Enid plans to disinherit her in a new will. Marion's story proves utterly resistant to the clever psychological motives and self-aggrandizing strategies Dalgleish has detected in the other suspects. Sergeant Martin, usually Dalgleish's inferior in understanding as well as in rank, here outwits the subtle superintendent, whom he has frequently irritated with his stolid, stubborn adherence to what he has been taught: look for the obvious, what common sense, "the basis for all sound police work," tells you.

James asserts that mystery writers are serious writers and that they deal in "such universal absolutes as life and death, love and hate, treachery and failure" (*Crime Times Three,* p. vii) in the serious novel, including symbolism. But at heart she is conservative and suspicious of the oversubtilization and overcomplication of basic human behavior, such as greed, the desire for gain, and the need to protect one's own. In *A Mind for Murder,* therefore, James reverses the novel's apparent initial ironic process from the initiation of Dalgleish into the subtleties and symbols of the humanistic sciences, to his humiliation for pride in his own subtlety, to the restoration of a saner, simpler methodology—the standard police investigation as exemplified by the unimaginative Sergeant Martin and the pragmatics of the Assistant Commissioner. By extension, James herself seems to have decided against the inflated symbolic.

UNNATURAL CAUSES

JAMES'S next novel, *Unnatural Causes* (1967), exploits the conventions of the murder mystery so faithfully that some critics have wondered if its parodies of the Golden Age classics—the detective fiction of the 1920s and 1930s—extend also to self-parody. Its very title calls attention to the fact that an imperative of the genre is to be more artful than natural and that plots must be unnaturally perfect.

Aware of mystery-writer Maurice Seton's severe claustrophobia, Sylvia Kedge, his much exploited and severely handicapped secretary, arranges to have his unconscious body sealed into a motorcycle sidecar into which air holes have been previously punched. As she planned, when Seton regained consciousness, he died of fright while trying to batter his way out of his prison. Seton's "telltale hands," with their abraded knuckles, are the only clue that his death has been induced rather than natural. Sylvia has them severed from the corpse, then sends the handless body floating in a dinghy, maliciously copying the opening scene of Seton's new mystery, which she has been typing.

The perfect plot within *Unnatural Causes,* to pass off death from unnatural causes as natural, is designed by the physically handicapped Sylvia, whose obsession with her physical imperfection and her sense of being perceived as offensive to the physically sound have in fact made her antipathetic. With her pretense of meek, submissive resignation and her mask of bravely endured pain, she performs her martyrdom with such panache that those who return her anguished gaze feel angrily guilty. They avoid her so as not to see reflected in her eyes their own moral and psychic deformity. To James, the responsibility for Sylvia's repugnant behavior is evenly divided between those so emotionally impoverished that they alternately patronize and exploit her, and the woman herself, whose own exploitation of her disability makes her seem contemptible to the less hypocritical, such as Dalgleish.

Indeed, Dalgleish's attitude toward Sylvia is problematic. In her introduction to *Crime Times Three*, James observes somewhat ambiguously that, while Dalgleish has had great professional success, "how far he has developed as a human being is not perhaps for me to judge" (p. v). Certainly the Dalgleish in *Unnatural Causes* has yet to develop the feminist sensibility he displays in the novels of the 1980s; nor has he undergone either the debilitating illness or the intimate contact with victims of fatal diseases that so enlarge his empathetic sensibilities in *The Black Tower* (1975). While he can, to an extent, empathize with Sylvia's plight and feel ashamed of his dislike of her "because he knew that its roots were unreasonable and ignoble," he cannot avoid the fact that "he found her physically repellent." He, like the other men crucial to the psychological plausibility of the murder, denies her her sexuality: "those twisted ugly legs, braced into calipers, the heavy shoulders, the masculine hands distorted by her crutches." In the last third of the narrative a great storm assaults them, and when Dalgleish quixotically attempts to rescue Sylvia from the ravages of a flood, she offers the help of her hands. "I've got strong hands and shoulders," she assures him with pride, humility, and a silent plea that he not turn, repelled, from her humanity: "And she held her ugly hands towards him like a suppliant." But he cannot get past his physical revulsion at the literal ugliness of her hands to see the beauty in the offer of their strength. When he refuses her appeal, he determines the nature of her gaze: from that of appeal, supplication, it has turned threatening. Although she again offers "both her hands," "his unmistakable instinct for danger" is keenly aroused. With "his nose for an unnatural death," he knows that his rejection has turned her into his antagonist, even his enemy.

To understand the murderous response (she attempts to topple him from the roof of the flooded house by battering his hands with her crutches) prompted by Dalgleish's initial misreading of Sylvia's glance, we need to hear Sylvia's confession. She has left a tape in which she describes the design for the perfect crime and her motives for the murder and mutilation of Maurice Seton's body. Seton, whom she has served faithfully through performance of domestic services and as secretary, never remembers the service; her touch to him is never womanly. She knows this and resents it: "He didn't even think of me as female . . . never saw me as a woman—as even female"—but as an unsexed servant or "tame animal." The profound insult to her femininity (if not womanhood), however, takes place the night she stays at his house. She remembers his hands searching futilely among his beautiful dead wife's flimsy nightclothes for something suitable for her to wear and then his handing her an old servant's sexless woolen gown: "He couldn't bear to think of her clothes against my flesh." Thus, he signs his death warrant: "And it was that nightdress which Maurice handed to me," she confides, that determined the murder. "It pleases me to think that his hands, hesitating over the layers of gaudy nonsense, were choosing between life and death." Seton's "tell-tale hands," then, testify to both his murder and the motive for his murder. That is why Sylvia is so eager to sever them herself. Even then the perfect murder, the body mutilated in the name of poetic justice, is incomplete until she has placed his hands in her toilet bag and "slung the bag around [her] neck," where she "enjoyed the feel of those dead hands, seeming to creep against [her] flesh." In the grotesque control of Seton's dead body, Sylvia achieves the touch he morbidly refused her.

The nightclothes incident, then, is the memory that Dalgleish's refusal of her helping hands evokes. The vengeful Sylvia sets out to show Dalgleish his own powerlessness by torturing and mortifying his hands. She strikes those hands again and again, making them nearly powerless. Now he is the "tame animal," who is submissive as "still the blows fell." Is it ironic or tragic that the last gesture he makes to save her misses her? He "shot out his hand towards her and caught instead the little bag" of evidence, the taped confession hung round her neck. "Dalgleish's hands were now almost useless . . . no grasp left." Helpless, he now feels the same kinds of angry emotions that Sylvia felt at her enforced dependence and the frustrations of her limited spontaneity. His hands have become his handicaps; they feel "heavy" and look to his "child's eyes" like "two white cocoons." He is totally preoccupied with the experiences of his body, and his imagination is agitated by horrid metaphors in an effort to distance himself from the sense of touch.

It is as if, with his "shrouded hands," he were cursed with Seton's dead hands. Sylvia's hands, ugly to the male gaze, unsex her. Now Dalgleish's hands in their rigid bandages cannot quickly open the all-important letter from Deborah Riscoe, bearing, as he intuitively guesses, her rejection of his ambivalent courtship. Dalgleish could kill both Deborah's love and his by sublimating it in poetry, but the poetry itself he can never murder. In the ultimate frustration, he is unable to destroy his useless love verses: "They took a long time to burn, each separate sheet charring and curling as the ink faded so that, at last, his own verses shone up at him, silver on black, obstinately refusing to die, and he could not even grasp the poker to beat them into dust." This image may be James's final motif in this grisly novel: you may chop off or paralyze the hands of the writer, but art always survives. Thus, James's novel immortalizes Maurice Seton's prose by resurrecting it at the opening of hers. With Dalgleish's own verses shining up at him all silvery and obstinately eternal, how can Deborah, incapable of an original, heartfelt, or charitable adieu defeat him?

SHROUD FOR A NIGHTINGALE

AMONG the themes of *Shroud for a Nightingale* (1971) is the potentially murderous craving for power shared alike by individuals, societies, and the institutions they create. Even the most apparently beneficent of these—the matron of a hospital nursing school, the Sisters of the staff, the institution itself—may be riddled with what Richard B. Gidez terms the "greed for power" (1986, p. 50). To Gidez, *Shroud for a Nightingale* is one of James's richest novels, expressing deep, universal themes of "the dark legacies of the past, love and possessiveness, the use and abuse of power" (p. 46). Gidez argues that James uses the troubled and troubling inner workings of the institution to draw an analogy between its evils and those of the larger world outside, including the barbarisms of Nazi genocide.

Shroud for a Nightingale traces the origins of its multiple murders—of student nurses and teaching Sisters—to personal, historical, and political fanaticism. The valkyrie-like matron of Nightingale House Training School for Nurses, in attempting to cover a past that implicated her in wartime atrocities, proves indirectly responsible for murders meant to silence those who could expose her and herself murders the Sister who attempts to screen her. The secret of Nightingale House is that its matron, Mary Taylor, is really Irmgard Grobel, who, as an inexperienced nurse in Germany, was brought to trial as a Nazi war criminal at the age of eighteen. For her work at the Steinhoff Institute in Felsenheim "on behalf of the then German Reich," Grobel was accused of having helped kill "31 men, women, and children . . . Jewish slave workers in Germany." Although a 1945 court acquitted her of that crime, it is impossible to believe that the young, physically mobile, and intelligent woman could have been ignorant of the nature of the Steinhoff Institute and its role in the Holocaust. It equally strains credulity that the matron we meet in the novel—seen even by Dalgleish until the final revelation as a brilliant woman, as strong in body as she is complex and subtle in mind—could still believe that because Adolf Hitler's law had made it legal to kill the ill and disabled, to do so was just. Such denial, such refusal to take responsibility for the past, suggests an evil that has not only arrested her moral growth but also uncannily seeped into the atmosphere of Nightingale House. The moral problems raised by her actions and by her working in a concentration camp make her suspect as head administrator of an institution training nurses in ethical care.

We read the plot, characters, relationships, and atmosphere, as well as the representations of authority and surveillance in this novel, always from the perspective of what the Holocaust has taught us about the vulnerabilities of human beings to behavior we regard as too unimaginable or unintelligible ever to be replicated. The first academic critics to study James's work seriously took this novel as a critique of the appropriate use of law and order. At the same time, the novel warns of the danger to society and the individual of the bias toward a personal, subjective interpretation of impersonal law.

THE BLACK TOWER

IN her foreword to *Murder in Triplicate,* James seems defensive, even brooding, about readers' reactions to *The Black Tower* (1975), which some considered "the most somber of my books in setting and plot." She acknowledges that her choice of setting infuses the narrative with a sense of pain: "Certainly the scene of action, a clifftop home for the permanently disabled, presents any novelist with themes of loss, regret, and despair, which are essentially tragic." She defends the novel's bleak vision on the grounds of her experience with the subject and argues that the constraints of the detective-novel genre ought always to be regarded more as an aesthetic challenge than as a limitation. Her readers may complain, she slyly suggests, but the novel that offends their sensibilities won her the second of her Silver Dagger awards from the British Crime Writers Association. Readers who understand the continuous nature of her creation, who follow the career of her hero, Adam Dalgleish, she writes, will find that this novel "marks a significant step both in . . . [her] development as a writer and in the character of . . . [her] hero."

Adam Dagleish is in the hospital recovering from mononucleosis. He had been falsely diagnosed with leukemia and is in depressed spirits, feeling disenchanted with his profession, his colleagues, and life in general. While recuperating, he gets a postcard from an old family friend, his father's curate, Father Baddeley, chaplain at Toynton Grange, a sanatorium for the incurably ill and disabled. Baddeley asks his policeman friend to come help him at Toynton: he has made some uneasy discoveries there that indicate all is not well at the Grange. When Adam learns that Father Baddeley has died, leaving him his books, he uses the excuse of sorting out his inheritance to go to Toynton to discover what had upset his friend. Upon arrival at the Grange, he comes to believe that Baddeley's death is not natural. He begins an unofficial investigation into the place. As bodies pile about him, he finds that Toynton Grange is built on an illusion. Its founder had not experienced the miracle

he thought cured him. Like Adam, he had been misdiagnosed. Dalgleish also learns that Toynton Grange is being used to smuggle drugs. Any patient who might expose this situation has been murdered by Julius Court, who passes himself off as a benefactor of the Grange. Julius has been smuggling drugs in the grips of the wheelchairs used by patients of Toynton Grange during their annual pilgrimage to Lourdes; he also uses the Grange newsletter to communicate with customers. In a physical struggle with Julius, Adam is injured and knocked unconscious. Adam had been ready to quit police work, seeing it, in his earlier depression and illness, as sterile and sordid. While at Toynton Grange, he discovers that he can still remedy wrongs and that other people survive illnesses and again finds himself awakening in the hospital. He thinks he is there for the original cause, recuperation from mononucleosis. This time, he feels both relief and happiness that he is not really dying and takes cheer from finding himself surrounded by the concerned, friendly faces of doctors, nurses, and colleagues.

Like *Unnatural Causes, The Black Tower* is centrally about Dalgleish; it is infused with his concerns, moods, and ambivalent thoughts about his profession. Instead of routinely policing others and keeping a level, measured, and tactful gaze on those in the process of social treachery, he directs his morbidly judgmental policeman's gaze on himself and examines his inner life in a mood of self-abhorrence.

Manhunting, he observes fastidiously from his deathbed experience, is not only morally repugnant, but a "bloody business" that alienates him from other people and feeds him a steady diet "of decomposing flesh and smashed bone" until he feels he has become Frankenstein's creature. He is, after all, a civilized man whose other profession is poetry, which links him to people in empathy and rituals of order that are beautiful, not repressive or punitive. Had he truly been dying rather than misdiagnosed, perhaps he could have reconciled himself to returning to Scotland Yard, which he now views strictly as a charnel house, dead with others of his kind. Reprieved from death, he can only shudder from this company, and he fully intends to resign upon his discharge from the hospital. He is anything but ready for the ordeal—emotional, psychological, moral—yet to come: Toynton

Grange, an institution for the incurable, the paralyzed, those stricken with multiple sclerosis, once-sound individuals reduced to a literal figuration of death and disease, and therefore emblematic of what we most fear. His contact with the paralyzed—with their withering, decayed flesh, their spastic muscles, their smells and noises of a slow, degenerative death—contributes at first to Adam's lowered tone of mind. He has become morbid, self-protective, selfish—even misanthropic. But as the novel unfolds, Adam's exposure to those for whom convalescence is hopeless has a salutary effect on his own sense of hope, which is absolutely necessary for his self-recuperative energies to work.

Throughout the narrative James plants clues—even Adam catches them at times—of his inevitable return to his profession. Dalgleish, whose appearance as a character is so often circumscribed to the scenes of murder in other James novels, here, with no excuse for his police presence, dominates the atmosphere of Toynton Grange, interferes in its business, and inadvertently obstructs its smooth criminal functioning. The lack of official authority to investigate cripples him and forces him to adopt means and measures he intensely dislikes. Worst of all, as an amateur, he must get involved with the suspects—and his emotions are tangled about—employing covert strategies with people he has learned to care for, his conscience troubled by his secret behavior, false intimacies, and potential betrayals of trust. He who so loves and reveres privacy must snoop and manipulate in order to get people to betray themselves and each other to him. As a reward, he comes to respect stoicism, cleverness, the capacity to love, humility, and endurance—and he comes to recognize individuality and cease to shrink from contact with the handicapped. During his unofficial investigation, the exercise of old mental skills brings a gratification that urges him on. He (having rapidly risen in rank to commander) finds himself eager to share a discovery or an anecdote with the commissioner. He contemplates how, after his resignation, his relationship with former colleagues will become "slightly formal," and he is not pleased.

Rare among James's novels, *The Black Tower* has a sweet ending. The typical circularity of her narratives is here reflected in Dalgleish's coming to consciousness at the end of the novel assuming he is at its beginning. Within that circle there is another: his hospital bed ringed by concerned faces.

The concentric circles surrounding the bed and those containing and cradling the narrative offer consolation to character and reader alike; they protect the hero, who has returned from a quest, from danger, and ring him with love. For Dalgleish, they contain a healing space out of time.

DEATH OF AN EXPERT WITNESS

JAMES has claimed that *Death of an Expert Witness* (1977) has always been one of her favorites. The novel's sinister accents, its atmosphere heavy with the smells of loam and death, and its general sense of diffused anxiety reflect a world that James herself finds reassuringly familiar: "Its setting in the isolated and sinister fenlands of East Anglia is a part of England I knew well from childhood" (*Trilogy of Death*, 1984, p. i). Isolation is a key idea, since she thinks mystery writers like to separate their characters from the distracting diffuseness of external reality, which, unlike artful representation, has no easily discernible, and therefore consoling, pattern. James's reference to the sinister may seem curious, even paradoxical, because we do not customarily associate childhood with the sinister. But James does not think of childhood, especially her own, as free from anxieties, fears, and terrors. She remembers no specific terrifying episode from her early years but believes that her youth was presided over by a vaguely menacing atmosphere. Perhaps this is why she includes mood, along with theme and setting, in her trilogy of recurrent points of focus in her novels. All three are crucial to *Death of an Expert Witness*, with its thematic suggestion that love and the spiritual life are annihilated by the overvaluation of science (represented by the alternate neglect and abuse of the Christopher Wren Chapel); its morbidly neurotic mood of failure and self-disgust; and its ironic setting, in placing the scene of a crime in a forensics laboratory.

In *Death of an Expert Witness*, which contains multiple murders, Adam Dalgleish is called in to solve a murder that has, ironically, taken place in a forensics laboratory, a place dedicated to the solving, not the perpetration, of crime. What Dalgleish discovers proves even more ironic. The murderer of the chief scientific officer, Dr. Lorrimer, is Dr. Kerrison, the medical examiner. Both men are in love with the beautiful Domenica Schofield, the apparently incestuous half-sister of the director of the laboratory, Dr. Howarth. Domenica has shed Dr. Lorrimer for Dr. Kerrison. With incestuous feelings for her brother, "Dom" is playing with other men's feelings. Dr. Lorrimer, jealous of Kerrison, threatens to reveal the affair to Dr. Kerrison's wife, who has left him in custody of their children while pursuing an affair of her own. Faced with the loss of his children, Dr. Kerrison seizes a nearby crime exhibit, a mallet, and kills his colleague.

Critics have noted that the site of the laboratory is suspect from the beginning: it would be difficult to make "an unsuitable Palladian mansion in an unexciting East Anglian village on the edge of the black fens" (Benstock, pp. 106–109) an efficient, modern scientific facility. As one critic points out, any transformation of an antique building in James's novels is a vital clue to an errant sensibility. Thus, the founder of Hoggatt's Laboratory has no "esthetic sense," and the small Wren chapel on the laboratory grounds has been deconsecrated to be used to store chemicals. Here, then, is a clue to the novel's theme: the "deconsecration" of science as the new secular faith (through ironic representation of science as a secular religion) and the consecration of a religion of love—but of a love free from the bonds of uncontrollable passion and obsession, which brings peace through the acceptance of responsibility. Without charitable love, there is no inner peace for any of the characters.

The form of *Death of an Expert Witness* is almost punning in its circularity, in that the murderer to whom we are introduced in the opening passages of the text returns at the end of the novel to the crime scene as a forensics expert. The irony is that these scenes of crime to which the murderer is summoned are not the sites of *his* crimes, though at the first clunch-pit scene he determines his original motive for murder and at the second clunch-pit scene he is arrested and confesses to the multiple murders he has committed at those unsuitable edifices for murder (the forensics lab and chapel).

The outer brackets of the clunch-pit murder and its tragic resolution, and the inner brackets of Hoggatt's Laboratory and the murders committed by Dr. Kerrison involve the same theme of a thwarted love that leads to a deadly logic of murder and violent death. The apparent primacy of the clunch-pit murder, given its placement at the beginning of the text, then its violent displacement to the periphery, and, finally, after serving its thematic and structural ends, to the conclusion of the novel, where it is tidily resolved through the murderer's suicide, has feminist implications. "When a young girl is found murdered," James sardonically observes (in the introduction to *Trilogy of Death*), the crime, from the perspective of the scientists and the forensic technicians of Hoggatt's, is simply "another routine job." The murder offers no real shock to their patriarchal sensibilities: to these men, the life of a young woman who has sex outside of marriage is of no value. But then "murder strikes at the very *heart* [italics added] of this citadel of law and order," James further observes.

When its senior biologist is, ironically, killed with a mallet he has been examining, the forensic-science laboratory is said to have been defiled. Ironies resonate throughout the novel as James portrays the singular heartlessness of this symbol of modern civilization, this complacent temple to the triumph of reason and objective science. She represents the scientists as using their skills to blackmail and murder with impunity. And into this scene, Adam Dalgleish has arrived by helicopter from London, James writes, "to tackle one of the most important and puzzling cases of his career." Critics have suggested that Dalgleish may here be used as a symbol of secular society's ardent faith in reason, "dropping from the skies" like a *deus ex machina*, a god from a machine.

Although not trained in reading forensic evidence, Dalgleish proves the equal of his antagonist, Dr. Kerrison, through his use of intuition and imagination. While Kerrison thinks of obscuring, riddling, complicating, and implicating, Dalgleish looks for clarity, facts, plausibility, and truth. Is it any wonder, therefore, that he can outthink the scientist? This case also tests Dalgleish's faith in his profession, its scientific procedures, and the professional trust underlying these. By casting Dalgleish's antagonist, the pathologist Kerrison—a trader in dead bodies—as a figure of death, James suggests that Adam's real antagonist *is* death.

Although at one point the beautiful and seductive Domenica Schofield turns on Dalgleish with a cry that implicates his work as a policeman with that of Mary Shelley's Doctor Frankenstein—"My God, yours is a filthy trade"—the opening pages of the narrative make an association between the forensic pathologists and Doctor Frankenstein. These men's work with the dead involves the sinister; they are seen or see themselves as ghouls; and they realize their ambitions for godhead through their gruesome work with dead bodies.

A TASTE FOR DEATH

A Taste for Death (1986) confounded early reviewers with its multiple allusions. In a novel already dense with subplots and minor characters, James, as Betty Richardson has pointed out (1988, p. 105), invokes the poetry of T. S. Eliot and deploys a proliferation of symbols from other literary texts—but, conspicuously, the symbolic features she chooses are those that are also commonplace symbols within the popular culture. Despite laments from reviewers, who despaired of applying thematic interpretation to the novel's apparent disorder and meaningless repleteness, *A Taste for Death* was a best-seller. The book's lavish symbolism, says Richardson, seems to have been comprehensible to common readers, who could respond to its intent intuitively if not intellectually.

The narrative is awash in symbols of the modern condition—faithlessness, despair, waste, isolation, and loneliness—and Richardson argues that its characters include both social predators and truth-seekers (p. 115). The detective Dalgleish's role in this novel is "to question and try to understand." In her essay "P. D. James' Dark Interiors," Penelope Majeske (1994) argues that the coherence of *A Taste of Death* lies in its success as a secular allegory, which allows James systematically to use "double meanings" (p. 119) to link all of the apparent digressions in the plot. Majeske draws on the work of Angus Fletcher, who (in *Allegory: The Theory of a Symbolic Mode*) reads detective fiction, with its focus on the conflict between evil and good, as inherently belonging to the tradition of allegory. Majeske cites Fletcher's idea that "allegory does not need to be read exigetically; it often has a literal level that makes good enough sense by itself" (p. 120).

In *A Taste for Death,* Commander Adam Dalgleish returns after a nine-year hiatus, but he no longer writes poetry; as a lover, he "substitutes technique for commitment"; and he once again is "disillusioned with policing." In the absence of poetry as an outlet, his intensity has turned inward, creating a crisis more profound than simple depression, morbidity, or boredom with his profession. He is beginning to feel contaminated by murder. Guilty about his professional power, he fears that his influence over others either effects nothing or perhaps even worsens the conditions of modern English society; his role in "policing" means rigidly disciplining the disempowered for the sake of a privileged few who regard the police as an agency to enforce their vision of a safe society.

Dalgleish needs to transform his cool, detached professionalism into something like a calling. Toward this end, while he is heading the special squad that investigates a double murder in the Little Vestry of St. Matthew's Church, he pushes aside a curtain and finds the member of Parliament Sir Paul Berowne, lying murdered by the side of the tramp Harry Mack, a symbolic embodiment of alienated man.

Miss Gentle, a writer of old-fashioned romances, gives Dalgleish, through her gentle, intuitive, and tactful sensibility, vital clues to the motive for Berowne's murder and the identity of his murderer. She also gives Dalgleish the gift of seeing himself as Berowne's spiritual double.

In his few contacts with the Conservative M. P. Berowne, Dalgleish felt empathy, an unnamed identification, with him. Berowne believed that people have lost their autonomy and self-reliance and expect the government to do too much. Dalgleish suspects, however, that Berowne was self-deluded, confusing his failure to serve the people with the idea of a special calling to achieve a personal martyrdom by saving a selfish people from their greediness, neediness, dependency, and spiritual death.

Berowne has had "some kind of religious, quasi-mystical experience" in the Little Vestry of St. Matthew's. Like Dalgleish's, Sir Paul's sense of failure extended beyond his profession: he made a mess of his personal life, which could not console him when the realization of his political ambitions failed to bring the satisfaction he had anticipated.

Feeling "contaminated by a kind of sick helplessness," a "sickness of the spirit," Dalgleish empathizes with Berowne to the point that he identifies Berowne as his double. In the ritual hiatus he observes before confronting a crime scene, Dalgleish sees the scene from the ghostly perspective of Berowne as the culmination of Sir Paul's quest: "Moving into the passage, he wondered whether this quiet air tinctured with the scent of incense, candles and the more solidly Anglican smell of musty prayer books, metal polish and flowers had held for Berowne also the promise of discovery, of a scene already set, a task inevitable and inescapable." He is haunted by Berowne's ghost visiting the scene and experiencing the same ritual awe: Had he made into "a task inevitable and inescapable" his anticipated discovery of "a scene already set," the place of his promised martyrdom? If "the feeling that he was already spent in mind and body" overcomes Dalgleish before the investigation begins, it is because that mind and body are Berowne's, his double's.

He has entered Berowne's ghost-time, and those involved in the investigation around him are "distanced and insubstantial as if they moved in a different dimension of time." The return to the real is exhausting but also transformative. With the spirit of Berowne's sacrifice of his life visible to his imagination, Dalgleish can contemplate beginning the task of discovering the motives behind this double crime from the higher spiritual plane of faith in the efficacy of commitment—to a cause, a faith, a political position—against the "sickness of spirit" that is despair. Before witnessing the scene of the crime, Dalgleish has, through the rituals and ceremonies of imaginative vision, rescued it from the sordid to the splendid: he perceives the bloody scene of the crime and the contamination of the murderer's stupid violence as sublime and full of the mysteries of human sacrifice.

DEVICES AND DESIRES

IN *Devices and Desires* (1989), James symbolically places the tension between humankind's death instinct and its erotic instinct, between its urge to self-destruction and its craving for life and creativity, on the site of a nuclear-power plant in Norfolk. Two murderers challenge a vacationing Dalgleish's wits: the Whistler, a serial killer of young women who whistles while he works and is driven by classic Freudian motives of sexual frustration, and Alice Mair, sister of Alex Mair, director of the Larksoken nuclear site. Alex has killed to protect his teenage sister from the incestuous assaults of their father; now she feels that she owes him a death. When his mistress, Hilary Roberts, attempts to blackmail Alex, Alice murders her, making the killing appear to be the work of the Whistler. Added to a highly complex psychological exposition of murder is the depiction of a series of politically motivated murders, as terrorists attempt a takeover of the nuclear site, an attempt in which they are thwarted by the highest members of Home Office police, whose strategies the novel calls into question.

James's textual authorities are both secular and sacred: she uses Sigmund Freud's work on psychoanalysis to interpret psychological drives and the Bible and the Book of Common Prayer to represent the spiritual. James uses Freud's theories to dramatize and interpret the fears and drives of the psychotic serial killer, the Whistler, as well as to examine the public response to the Whistler's unpredictable, uncontrollable threat. Implicitly, Freud's work primarily helps James to analyze the drives of those implicated in the nuclear enterprise, those who have begun to associate its powerful energies with their own destructive instincts, especially the striving to bring "ruin . . . and to reduce life to its original condition of inanimate matter" (Albert Einstein and Sigmund Freud, *Why War?*, 1933, pp. 43–45).

The title of the novel is taken from the Book of Common Prayer—"We have followed too much the devices and desires of our own heart," which articulates the Pauline theology of redemption. The main biblical text is from the third chapter of Ecclesiastes: "That which has been is now; and that which is to be hath already been; and God requireth that which is past." The words, "deeply carved in an elegant script" (p. 20), appear "on a stone plaque embedded in the flints" of the cottage where once lived Agnes Poley, "Protestant martyr, burned at Ipswich, 15th August 1557, aged 32 years" (p. 19). That site of martyrdom and the experience of martyrdom in the past are painfully recuperated in the present, as a sensation of the fusion of past, present, and future experienced by Dalgleish, by Meg Dennison, and by Meg's friend, Alice Mair.

In *Devices and Desires*, Commander Dalgleish has inherited his Aunt Jane's estate, located on the headland that also houses the Larksoken nuclear plant. While there, sorting through his new possessions, he is asked to help the locals with the Whistler case and, as murders connected to the nuclear plant are identified, he becomes involved with the investigation into terrorism. Dalgleish, sitting among his Aunt Jane's treasures, is a happy man. He has published a collection of poems titled *A Case to Answer and Other Poems:* "A mysterious spirit had unlocked the verse, it had freed him for other human satisfactions—or for love?" Or did love free him? he wonders. He forms an affectionate friendship with Meg, with whom he shares a series of disconcerting experiences—the witnessing of a past violent martyrdom as if in the present and a curious sense of being stopped in God's time, in which humanity's symbols crumble into insignificance before the eternal gaze.

Meg Dennison, a Christian and something of a martyr, is a dedicated schoolteacher who has been driven from her profession for inadvertently violating the "fashionable orthodoxies" of a particularly absurd manifestation of political correctness. She is a martyr, like Agnes Poley, in that she, too, refuses to recant what she knows to have been no sin. Alice Mair, Meg's friend and present inhabitant of Agnes Poley's cottage, is nuclear director Alex Mair's sister. She murders her brother's mistress and immolates herself in the martyr's cottage, making herself a martyr to her brother's future as Nuclear Supremo of England.

Devices and Desires is replete with symbols, most of them in binary opposition; almost without exception (to some critics' dismay), James's characters are acutely and intellectually conscious of them. Thus, to Alex Mair, director of the power station, the key opposing symbols are "the splendid fifteenth-century West Tower of Happisburgh Church" and, "dwarfing the tower, the huge rectangular bulk of Larksoken Power Station" (p. 58). To him, "in an age of faith, the tower had stood as a symbol," not only of "man's precarious defences" against the destructive North Sea, but "of that final, unquenchable hope that even the sea would yield up her dead and that their God was God of the waters as He was of the land" (p. 58). For Alex, the power station symbolizes "that man, by his own intelligence and his own efforts, could understand and master his world" (p. 58). Through these two symbols James establishes a binary opposition between faith in God and in man.

In viewing the headland and reading its symbolic artifacts, Adam and Meg independently experience a moment of fusion, when past, present, and future merge into a single "disorientating limbo of time." Like Alex Mair, Adam recognizes the immense power of the sea and sky, a power transcending the ability of anything human to defend against the ravages of time and nature. But unlike Alex, Adam does not read the symbolic artifacts

ringing the headland historically as proceeding from the worn past to culminate in the powerful future, starting with "the obstinately enduring artifacts of the last war, the crumbling cliff defences, the windmill" and ending with the power station. Instead, Adam registers them as one meaningless, powerless symbol of humanity's futile effort to protect itself from the eternal gaze that takes the final measure of humanity.

Dalgleish's experience of temporal fusion, which he characteristically communicates to no one, happens also to Meg, at a different time but in the same place: "As Meg gazed out over the curve of the headland, she experienced a moment of extraordinary perception in which it seemed to her that she was aware of another time, a different reality, existing simultaneously with the moment in which she stood." This other world, it immediately becomes clear, is that of Agnes at the time of her martyrdom: "a hiss and crackling of fagots, an explosion of fire, and then a second dreadful silence broken by the high, long-drawn-out scream of a woman." This fusion of past (Agnes), present (Meg and Adam, who are superconscious of simultaneity, but not transcendence), and future (Alice about to become a martyr and Adam conscious of Agnes's experience) represents James's interpretation of the text from Ecclesiastes: all things, at all times, always—including all human responsibility and action—exist within the Divine gaze for examination and judgment. Nothing is ever erased, so as to present to God evidence of total accountability.

James seems to believe that what matters is not the general concept of a particular principle so much as the integrity of one's commitment to an individual vision of the world. That she endorses both Meg's and Agnes's martyrdoms seems suggested by the gesture made at the conclusion of the novel: Meg purchases Martyr's Cottage for herself.

Adam's experience of Agnes Poley's suffering takes place during his attempt to rescue Alice Mair's body from the flaming cottage in which she has committed her own version of Agnes Poley's "excruciating martyrdom." That Adam martyrs himself to save this already dead being is clear from the language James uses to describe his physical ordeal: "smoke billowed around him, and the great tongues of flame roared at his back" (p. 425). His time and Agnes's time fuse in bodily commitment to timeless values—risking death and injury and the body in the service of a higher ethic.

Devices and Desires concludes with the discovery that the text from Ecclesiastes is consoling and cheering and that all the devices and desires in the novel are nothing when viewed from the perspective of the eternal. Ultimately, place, the entire headland, triumphs over the devices and desires of the human heart, over fear and "portentous imaginings," because it just triumphantly *is*.

The last pages of the novel acknowledge the persistence of evil and the threat to human survival of those murderous desires Freud identified as an instinct in humans, who use their intellect and spirit arrogantly to annihilate what they ought to celebrate and love. The concluding sentence of the novel suggests that what guards England and ensures human survival against the unruly in spirit is a good cup of tea—representing that ritual of English civility and harmony, teatime.

ORIGINAL SIN

ALTHOUGH Dalgleish enters this novel early and provides the crucial clue that the motive for the murders at a prestigious publishing house lies in the past, in the archives of the Peverell Press, he does not figure largely in *Original Sin* (1994), especially not as a man with a private life and an interesting sensibility. Instead, the novel focuses on Detective-Inspector Kate Miskin and a new policeman, Inspector Daniel Aaron; Kate, as a woman in a sexist police organization, and Daniel, as a Jew in a racist culture, share the burden of representation as well as of oppression in this novel that places socially marginalized people, classes, and cultures at its center. Kate and Daniel are each still sorting out a personal identity, especially because their profession creates a difficult tension between loyalty to family and utter commitment to the job that investigating murder demands.

In *Original Sin*, Kate Miskin is plausibly represented in her achievement of maturity in her work. While she makes the decision to sacrifice romantic love and domestic life for a commitment as absolute as Dalgleish's to her job, it seems a good decision because this of all professions permits the detective-inspector full exercise of her particular powers of mind and character. We do not feel a sense of painful sacrifice or compromise of what she really wants. This seems to be the decision that fully releases her to be who she is.

To an unsympathetic Kate, Daniel complains, "It's not easy being a Jew." She replies by pointing out that it is no picnic being a woman—and illegitimate—in the macho culture of the police; but she later regrets being so hard on him and remains his most resolute friend when he is in crisis, having finally put his identity as a Jew before his duties as a policeman. As Daniel wittily explains, his God expects him to be rational and articulate in defense of his atheism: "[as a Jew] you can't be a cheerful atheist like other people. You feel the need to keep explaining to God why you can't believe in him." But Daniel really does understand that whether he actually believes is not so crucial to his family and his Jewish culture as that he identify and publicly associate himself with tradition, especially the tradition that links fathers and sons in a continuous identity in the face of racism, of the possibility of another Holocaust. It is crucially important, given the history of genocidal anti-Semitism, that a Jew be *seen*, especially in a Jewish context, whether family or synagogue. He is asked, "What is a Jew without his belief? What Hitler could not do to us shall we do to ourselves?" Ever present in Daniel's guilty consciousness is the powerful image of "that moving army of naked humanity . . . flowing like a dark tide into the gas chambers . . . silent witnesses of his apostasy."

It is while searching in the Peverell Press archives that Daniel finds evidence of the persistent involvement in evil of the ironically named Innocent House, home to Francis Peverell and several of the members of the board of Peverell Press, which is housed there. Innocent House is a mock Venetian palazzo built by an early Victorian Peverell, "a noted publisher of the day," in a totally successful cultural borrowing. Innocent House proves to be the site of multiple evils as well as their exposure. It is named after its site, the street called Innocent Walk, so named because it was the path taken by those who had been tried and found innocent by the Magistrate's Court and who walked to freedom. Since the building of Innocent House was funded by Sir Francis Peverell through the murder of his wealthy wife, it has never been an innocent house.

In the archives, Daniel finds forty years of historical evidence, painstakingly assembled by the poetry editor of Peverell Press, Gabriel Dauntsey, in his attempt to trace the fate of his Jewish wife, Sophie, and their children, Martin and Ruth, in occupied France; in the process, Dauntsey has established that they were betrayed to the Nazis by Jean-Philippe Etienne, a hero of the Resistance in Vichy France. Jean-Philippe is the retired, reclusive senior partner of Peverell Press and the father of the murdered Gerard Etienne, who had recently become head of the press, and of Claudia Etienne, Gerard's sister, who has also been murdered. From inside a bulky folder drops out a single sheet of paper containing the précis of a novel titled "Original Sin" that was submitted by an anonymous author to Peverell Press. The abstract of the novel is clearly an account of Dauntsey's family tragedy: a mother and her four-year-old twins are "betrayed to be deported and murdered in Auschwitz." The novel within the novel maps out the plot and theme of the larger work as Gabriel Dauntsey sets about enacting the consequences of betrayal: in the name of justice as it is interpreted by Mosaic law—an eye for an eye, a tooth for a tooth—he murders Gerard and Claudia, in order to wound Jean-Philippe as he himself was wounded.

Daniel's instinctive response to reading this file of horror is to embody the record of pain in his own anguish: "He heard a strange human noise and knew that he was groaning aloud with the pain and the horror of it." In the face of such massive documentation of the genocide of his people, Daniel's unspeakable, untranslatable anger is transformative. He is no longer anxious to deny his Jewishness as an irritating, distracting sense of perpetual guilt; he is now a Jew who can identify so profoundly with the victims of the Holocaust that their pain becomes his.

"He was possessed by an emotion which he recognized as anger but which was no longer anger" because it has transformed into resolve. Daniel decides to warn Dauntsey that the police have discovered him and so give him a chance to decide his own fate. Daniel commits himself to what he knows is "unforgivable perfidy," "the great iconoclasm." He violates everything he has been taught as a policeman of English justice and its processes.

In *Original Sin*, James seems to have lost faith in unified form and her own godlike omniscience. Unlike in the earlier large novels (beginning in the late 1980s), in *Original Sin* there is no consoling circularity. This novel is large, both literally and thematically. Contemporary society not only does not share one god but also is fragmented by intense belief in both antagonistic gods—of love, of vengeance, of cheerful, tolerant detachment—and no god at all, making unbelief into an angry cult.

James represents events and emotions diffusely; only the process of investigation unites, in the sense of gathering together and re-presenting, the materials of the novel. When these materials address such crucial themes as the question of justice—human or divine—they register as timeless: of permanent importance to people and of eternal concern for God. The characters are united by their interest, even obsession, with such questions as the existence of God, but also isolated from one another by their radically different beliefs and disbeliefs.

We admire Daniel because he is willing to destroy himself for his people, finally ready to stand up to and for the past. But James has taught us in book after book, and offers inescapable testimony in this novel, that any murder is a uniquely evil crime: neither redemption nor reparation for it is possible. For all his authentic pain, Gabriel Dauntsey has avenged the original sin—the murders of three innocent people—by deliberately murdering three other innocent people. The Mosaic law by which he justifies his vengeance is clearly too abstract and arbitrary to serve as true justice. James, thus, does not spare the reader the agony and terror of Claudia as Dauntsey strangles and poisons her while verbally justifying his act. Triumphantly confronting the aged, infirm Jean-Philippe, Dauntsey makes the man stand to hear his judgment and punishment: he, Gabriel Dauntsey, following Mosaic law, has executed Jean-Philippe's son and daughter. Coolly, Etienne tells Dauntsey that he never loved the children, who were adopted to appease his wife's maternal hunger. The revenge means nothing to him; it strikes him as absurd, misplaced, and wasteful. Sardonically, he advises Gabriel that the next time he wishes to play God he ought to be sure he has God's omniscience. We are reminded of other Dalgleish novels, where the Mosaic code operates only as James in her capacity as omniscient author wields it—to kill off murderers when Dalgleish cannot prove his case in a court of law despite the rightness of his judgment.

Daniel is devastated by all he has witnessed, and in a final gesture of solidarity with Dauntsey, he allows him to flee to the swamps surrounding Othona House, Jean-Philippe's Essex home, to commit suicide—by lying face down in shallow water until he drowns. A shaken Kate mourns Daniel's actions; a quiet, calm Dalgleish treats him as a victim of traumatic shock and turns him over to Kate's care. But the book closes on Daniel's probable destiny.

This final vision of the novel is bleak and leaves the reader perplexed about what issues James is representing. Is she writing in order to deal with an Other culture's tragic concept of justice? Or is she representing Mosaic justice as the tragic consequence of the modern English wish to forget the unavenged and the refusal to perform acts of reparation to compensate for its own dry specificities and legalities? What are we to make of a law, Mosaic law as here conceived, that justifies taking innocent life for reparation? What is the significance of the grotesque miscarriage of this law that leads Dauntsey to think his executions of Claudia and Gerard are just, not because of their individual identities but because of their relationship to his enemy? James's novels tend to have a moral logic that suggests that people are murdered because of their individual identities, because something in them makes them subject to murder; in *Original Sin* the two victims who are killed in the name of justice are rendered horribly irrelevant to their murder.

The novel also offers problems to admirers of James's craft and vision: What are we as readers whom she has trained to observe, detect, and think to do with the inescapable fact that in *Original Sin* she has made absurd all that imaginative commitment to trying to solve the murders from clues the novel offers? All the detailed characterization of suspects and victims, all the carefully sustained representation of their relationships and motives, is made irrelevant by the murderer's blunder—killing who he believes are the beloved children of his enemy—all this makes the novel a red herring. Nor is the reader, who has been made fastidious by James's art, happy about the structure of the novel in which crucial revelations come not in the form of dramatic representation but in the form of letters and documents, such as file folders spilling their contents at the feet of a tired detective, who is suddenly galvanized into action.

THE CORDELIA GRAY NOVELS

P. D. JAMES is eloquent about her respect and admiration for women, whom she thinks not only equal to men in talent and general abilities but also in some ways superior. She expresses admiration for the capacity of women to bring to any profession abilities for nurturing, caretaking, intimacy, and meticulous attention to detail, especially in the everyday, the ordinary. In such a profession as the police, she believes, women have strategic advantages in gaining the trust and thus the productive access to evidence concerning potential suspects.

"I am a tremendous feminist and I think women should have absolutely equal opportunity," James declared in an interview in 1977. "I think that all over the world their abilities are very wasted" (Bakerman, p. 92). "Not only are women as intelligent as men . . . but women have got other qualities as well," such as "sympathy and understanding" (p. 57). She likes it that women are less aggressive than men, for the world needs this calm, and she believes that, "It would be a great pity if we started emulating men and the qualities of men which are their least attractive qualities" (p. 57). "Yes, I am very much a feminist, very much," she reiterates, declaring her hatred for the times that forced women to take "inferior" roles, for she "feels strongly" about "sexual unfairness, legal unfairness" (p. 92). To Dale Salwak (1985), she lamented that, "There's a great body of unused talent for detection" in women, and declared, "It astounds me that in nearly all of the world's police forces, the upper ranks are predominantly male. Some women would certainly excel there" (p. 43). She confided to Joyce Wadler (1986) her belief that very few men "really believe in the equality of women" (p. 79). She has told Olga Kenyon (1989) that dependency on men is the greatest enemy of female advancement (p. 129), and that it is "the ability to earn their own living" that truly frees women. "I am a feminist in that I like my own sex," she exclaims (p. 129). She feels an enormous solidarity with other women and a feeling of "friendship and support" (p. 125). It is also "easier to have a woman as a chief character" (p. 122), because "with a woman detective," such as Cordelia Gray in *An Unsuitable Job for a Woman*, "you are free."

In her introduction to *The Skull Beneath the Skin* (1982) in *The Trilogy of Death*, James describes her collaboration with the youthful female detective Cordelia Gray. This relationship energizes James and fills her with Cordelia's vigor, enthusiasm, and physical and moral courage—a moral courage reminiscent of Shakespeare's Cordelia in *King Lear*. Through this solidarity, this collaboration, James is able, she tells us, to rework the most hackneyed devices and desires, conventions and strategies, characters and atmosphere, places and edifices.

Carolyn G. Heilbrun (Reilly, 1980) describes *An Unsuitable Job for a Woman* (1972) as "the first truly original detective novel in years" (p. 501); to her and to Jane S. Bakerman (1984), that originality lay in James's introduction, into an essentially male genre, of a professional woman detective who embodies the essence of a modern feminist. Although the term "modern feminist" becomes a matter of critical debate and refinement, there is general agreement that Cordelia's presence in the genre is transformative, generative, and expansive. To Heilbrun, *An Unsuitable Job for a Woman* re-empowers the detective novel by modernizing both its conventions and its themes (pp. 501–502). Sue Ellen Campbell (1983) agrees that the introduction of a young heroine not defined by received codes of the detective story causes a "generic shift" (p. 498) from conventional plot and character to a thickening thematic "richness" (p. 498), especially in the novel's concern with "women's roles, the importance of work, the destructive power of love, and the complex relationships between men and women, parents and children."

In both of the Cordelia Gray novels, James combines the detective-novel genre with the bildungsroman, a coming-of-age novel of education and identity developments. As a feminist heroine, Cordelia distinctly transforms that mixed genre: she exhibits the "life-plot" (Murtin, 1996, p. 465) of the traditional male archetype—a "plot that turns on action, triumph through conflict, intellectual self-discovery, and often public renown" (Benstock, cited by Murtin, p. 465)—but she modifies it according to her feminist sensibility. Where, for example, success for male protagonists is usually defined in public terms, Cordelia's sense of her triumph, of personal truth and individually conceived justice over legally and socially codified constructs, is fulfilled secretly and she holds it private. Where a patriarchal concept of professionalism values reason over emotion, Cordelia values both, and acts on both in order to solve her first case successfully. Where detective fiction traditionally asks of its sleuths only to solve a case, Cordelia is uncompromising about her intention also to protect the private lives of the people her investigation implicates. As Christine Wick Sizemore (1989) points out, Cordelia's emotional involvement and protectiveness are precisely what make her a feminist heroine (pp. 154–158): she is brave and tough, but also capable of sympathy and involvement.

James F. Maxfield (1987), however, argues against Cordelia's status as an "exemplary feminist heroine" (p. 211). In *An Unsuitable Job*, she is insufficiently rational and detached when she allows herself to become emotionally involved with the case of a boy, Mark Callender, whose suicide she determines to have been murder. From Maxfield's perspective, Cordelia's decision to let Mark's mother use her gun to avenge his death and the desecration by the murderer, his father, of Mark's body by dressing it in women's clothes are passive, not deliberate. Cordelia is simply "driven to both action and inaction by psychological compulsions she scarcely understands" (p. 213).

Cordelia's intense identification with Mark, however—her dressing in his clothes, sleeping in his bed, living his life—suggests the behavior of an ambitious, autonomous woman who knows that she must co-opt the "life-plot" available thus far only to men. Cordelia literally embodies Mark not only to empower herself but also to determine who murdered him and to finish his story, which was prematurely ended by a father who despised a son praised for his sweetness, his capacity to nurture the weak, and his intolerance of the fraud that bolstered his father's reputation.

Dalgleish's appearance in *An Unsuitable Job for a Woman* seems always to be compromised. The superintendent had fired Cordelia's beloved former boss, Bernie Pryde, who, in mentoring Cordelia, taught her the strategies and skills of sleuthing—always by respectfully repeating the superintendent's words. Cordelia finds Dalgleish's neglect of Bernie's sensibilities and welfare offensive. And when, at the conclusion of the novel, Dalgleish tries alternately to cajole and bully from her the truth of the father's murder and of her own cover-up, she successfully resists him through the strength of her empathetic anger. With the "accidental" death of the murderer, Dalgleish must let her go but not before she has told him off and he has, in a sense, apologized for his coldness. If, in finally indirectly complimenting Bernie by praising Cordelia's training, Dalgleish displaces onto the male mentor the achievements of his pupil, Cordelia does not care, for that is her female triumph—to have taken care of Bernie's pride without self-congratulation.

In *An Unsuitable Job*, Cordelia comes across as equal if not superior to men; as a detective she combines ideals of "manliness" with the empathetic, nurturing qualities of women. In *The Skull Beneath the Skin,* however, the qualities in Cordelia that James most admires are gender neutral: "courage, dispassionate intelligence, and cool common sense" (introduction, *Trilogy of Death,* 1984), the defining qualities of both Dalgleish and his beloved Aunt Jane. The very contemporary nature of Cordelia as a character enables James's own triumphant control of the conventional gothic mystery. Along with the reader, the story's own detective casts a skeptical, commonsensical gaze upon gothic manifestations of the hysterical and the horrid.

In *The Skull Beneath the Skin,* James is both creator and critic of a particularly delicious nonsense, allowing Cordelia to expose the charade of the villainous Uncle Ambrose, a tax fraud who collects evil Victorian toys: all his gothic poses are but screens for a vulgar greed that values necrophilic, morbid toys over human life. Cordelia has come to his private island to protect the kind of woman she detests, a woman who lives off men then discards them if they prove uncontrollable.

The thematically resonant setting for the murder of a fading actress, Clarissa Lisle, is a gothic castle on Courcy Island, privately owned by the wealthy Ambrose Gorringe. With proof of his tax fraud, Clarissa blackmails Ambrose in order to make her comeback in his private theater there as Webster's *Duchess of Malfi.* Recipient of recurrent death threats, the frantic Clarissa employs Cordelia as a bodyguard and private detective. Cordelia, whose investigative business has mainly involved the finding of lost pets, is initially pleased at last to obtain some serious professional work. During the course of her investigation, however, with the discovery of evil both bloody and banal, she comes to realize the superior value of her ordinary work as detective. While there is nothing grand about large-scale murder (it is only theatrical, operatic in appearance), her steady employment not only draws on all her womanly strengths of emotion, intuition, and empathy, but restores order and brings joy to a chaotic sad world. Her sturdy, self-affirming pleasure in her kind of detection is not, however, based on a sense of failure or defeat. While the professional police give up on ever bringing the wily Ambrose to justice, Cordelia is uncompromisingly determined to some day establish Ambrose's guilt.

Although as sturdy as ever in her determination never to relinquish the quest for truth in a murder, she determines that the employment she had rather despised herself for, the restoration to lost clients of their precious lost mammals, will be the pride of Pryde Agency. There have been no innocents for her to rescue at Courcy Island. But on the mainland, a child with leukemia and a lost kitten await: here is a respectable need, a job for which Cordelia and her menagerie of socially marginalized employees are entirely suited. Thus, Cordelia takes care of both losers and seekers. In the process, she emerges as a young knight on a quest that has moved from Avalon and Camelot, from masculine models of public chivalry, to the domestic hearth.

INNOCENT BLOOD *AND* THE CHILDREN OF MEN

OF all her fictions, James has had the most to say about what some critics consider her first mainstream novel, *Innocent Blood* (1980). In the introduction to *Trilogy of Death* (1984), she discusses its generic identity in theoretical and personal terms as a historical marker of her artistic authority: she can choose among forms and mix them according to the dictates of her aesthetic will and vision. In this introduction, she identifies the key themes of the novel—guilt and remorse, the search for identity, the growth of love—and summarizes the plot of this "mystery with a difference":

Innocent Blood tells the story of an eighteen-year-old adopted girl, Philippa Palfrey, who takes advantage of a new law to learn the identity of her real parents and discovers that she is the daughter of a rapist and a murderess and that her mother is shortly due to be released on license from a life sentence. With this traumatic knowledge, Philippa moves . . . into an alien world . . . more dangerous than she could imagine. For . . . the father of the child [Philippa's mother] killed has dedicated his life to hunting down and destroying his daughter's murderess.

In interviews James has commented more fully on her achievement in this novel, but she gives different accounts of its origins—in reality, memory, and imagination—and the history and resonance of its title. To Rosemary Herbert (1986) she says that *Innocent Blood* was inspired by "a combination of a piece of legislation and a real life murder case" (p. 348). To Diana Cooper-Clark (1983) she explains why she chose the title *Innocent Blood* over *The Blood Tie* and *The Blood Relation*, her original choices: "*Innocent Blood* has this ambiguity about it as to whether the blood [Philippa] had inherited was or was not inherited. And, . . . it ties up with the section in Ecclesiastes about it being an abomination to the Lord that one should shed innocent blood" (p. 32).

She describes her own awe at the traumatic situation in which she has cast her protagonist, who is confronted with an intolerably tragic heritage. James has analyzed the reasons for Philippa's repellent, cold character and repudiates the critical response this has provoked. Such a psychically scarred person's motives and psychology, she explains, are not likely to produce a nice person, who "is not going to be a human being who is very likable or very lovable" (p. 31). The language in which James describes the law that inspired her writing resonates with both the novel's major theme of the quest for identity and its archetypal pattern, the bildungsroman: "The Legislation for Children Act in 1975 gave eighteen-year-old adopted children . . . the right to set out on the journey of exploring who their real parents were" (Herbert, 1986, p. 348).

James found writing *Innocent Blood* "very exhausting . . . very traumatic" (Salwak, p. 38). Its plot and characters "excited" her; she terms it a "clotted novel" (p. 38), its thick surface could have yielded material "for at least a half dozen novels" (p. 38). To Diana Cooper-Clark (1983, p. 31), she denies, however, that she "was trying to do something new in the sense that I was trying to deal with human beings more realistically because I have always tried to do that."

Richard I. Smyer (1982) observes that the focus and form of *Innocent Blood* allow James to free herself from the constraints of the detective novel and to dramatize "human experience as an object of meditation and awe" (p. 58). James told Cooper-Clark that her compelling interest has always been "the compulsions and expediences which people devise to enable them to face reality" (p. 18). To Wadler she observed, "I think most of us apply a coat of varnish over our lives, and murder cracks it open. And to study people under that influence is absolutely fascinating" (p. 73). That varnish cracks in *Innocent Blood*: multiple dark revelations emerge—murder, rape, incest—and are turned into complex narratives.

In *The Children of Men* (1992), James ventures into a more philosophical genre that has drawn a wide range of critical responses—from hostility to extravagant admiration. Classification of the genre has been the first concern of these critics: Is it an allegory, a futuristic novel, an Orwellian political satire, a moral fable, a myth, a cautionary tale, a parable, a gospel story, or a utopia / dystopia? Ironically, the critic who classifies it as dystopia praises the novel as the epitome of generic clarity.

The title of *The Children of Men* originates in the Burial Service in the Book of Common Prayer and suggests hope in the midst of death, resurrection under the benevolent, forgiving gaze of God, the watch for the light that ends the night. This watchfulness, however, does not come easily: it is essentially extinguished by 2021, the year the novel opens and when the last child born is now twenty-five. Humanity can no longer procreate, and "the last human being born on earth was killed in a pub brawl" on New Year's Day. The exact cause of this sterility is not explained, but the novel suggests it is the consequence of spiritual and emotional barrenness. The Omegas, the last generation, born in 1995, are beautiful, intelligent, physically superior, but cold, arrogant, or given to meaningless violence and savage blood rites. With no hope for a future—both men and women are infertile—a general despairing apathy rules. The government, under the rule of the Warden of England, Xan Lyppiatt, cousin of narrator-protagonist Theo Faron, is a police state. Theo, a fifty-year-old former Oxford don of history, begins his diary in 2021 and records that Xan hopes to keep the citizens quiet by providing the majority with hedonistic, even pornographic, consolations. Meanwhile, the government runs a series of regular fertility tests on the otherwise healthy, if increasingly elderly, population, hoping for a child to provide a future for this dying world—a child it would use to keep control of that future.

Theo's diary record is a solipsistic gesture, for he writes not as a historian who teaches about the past, but to and for himself, which is rational, since at the time of his writing, the Omegas have no future, have ceased to procreate. An infertile world offers no future to be anticipated or shaped by the labors and wisdom of a historian. Theo, at first apathetic and indifferent, is aroused through his kindling love for a deformed but spiritual woman, Julian. He confronts his cousin Xan about the need to reform his totalitarian government's increasingly murderous regime, then, in the face of contemptuous rejection, joins the Five Fishes, Julian's tiny, mixed band of rebels, who are trying to subvert the wrongs of the police state. During their flight from persecution, Theo discovers Julian's "miraculous" pregnancy: she had slept with the other Christian in the band, the priest Luke, and neither had been screened for fertility by the state because each was considered somewhat deformed. Julian is desperate to keep her child from falling into the hands of the evil Xan and his Council. The child is ultimately born in a shed in the woods, prompting critics, especially critics of Christian journals, to interpret the birth as a re-creation of that of Jesus the Redeemer. The novel is thus interpreted to be about Christian redemption, and S. Mark Heit argues in his review in *Christian Century* (May 1993, vol. 110, p. 561) that it is an urging for 1990s readers to appreciate every birth as miraculous, instead of constantly fretting over the dangers of overpopulation. In his review in the *London Review of Books* (1992, vol. 14, p. 22), Julian Symons agrees that the novel is "about Christian redemption through religious faith."

The narrative of *The Children of Men* moves between first-person and omniscient narration. While some critics are irritated by this technique, a thematic argument can be posited to justify it: a limited perspective is necessary to convey the state of utter despair. Only hopelessness, a state of global infertility, unites the citizens of this part of the dying world, England. James implicitly suggests that the infertility of the twenty-first century arises from the universal spiritual sterility of the 1990s.

Newspaper and magazine reviewers often criticize James's later novels for being too well furnished. As one critic puts it, James seems unable to enter a room without obsessively filling it with the stuff of her imagination. This charge is also leveled at *The Children of Men*. But in this novel, her leisurely narrative reinforces its themes. After all, the mostly middle-aged population of this world of acedia, or apathy, faced with no human future, is depressed and lethargic, living as well as it can in the present. James slows down the pace of the novel to urge the effect of such a futureless, childless life on our attention, to invite us also to slow down and to speculate about the potential consequences of indulging such angry demands as for more police and prisons, fewer attempts at reform of criminals, less immigration and a curb to multiculturalism, and less governmental responsibility for the aged, the infirm, the poor. She makes the reader ask: What will it cost a society to fulfill its dreams of cultural and racial hegemony, of a cult of the young, fit, and clever, and of an end to overpopulation and its ravages on the environment?

The Children of Men posits a "utopian" answer, and it is a horror. In the year 2021, white people are privileged, every one of them is afraid, and none is free. This society, formed and fashioned by its secret yearnings, is a police state, a benevolent dictatorship. It is also, by the norms of James's fundamentally humanist beliefs, literally sterile. James exposes the ideal in mainstream nostalgia as racist: English chauvinism and xenophobia are defused by new laws of immigration, which give Sojourners, the elite of other nations, only provisional residence in England and deport those who pass the age of productivity. Liberal humanism takes a hit as well. James is clearly unsympathetic to the cries of environmentalists against overpopulation and pollution. She exposes what she sees as the global narcissism, selfishness, and lack of public responsibility among conservatives and liberal-socialists alike.

The novel ends ambiguously. Theo discovers the intoxication of absolute power, the thrill of knowing that the world is his to shape according to his will. Alarmingly, he has already started to curb the reforms to which he had committed himself. He coolly measures priorities and makes pragmatic rather than idealistic plans. Yet a child has been born, and the mother asks Theo to christen him. Theo is surprised by how easily he recollects the Psalms promising to "ye children of men" a "world everlasting." "The water had to flow, there were words which had to be said" if fertility and continuance are to bless the world—he baptizes the child with his own tears and Julian's childbirth blood. The novel ends with Theo, once dry, sterile, child-killing, and repulsed by the blood and water of human fertility, glorying in life-giving fluids. He is clearly the epitome of James's vision of modern man, torn between a lust for power and a yearning for redemption in the life-giving rituals of the natural world.

SHORT STORIES

IN a 1986 critical biography, Richard B. Gidez makes sometimes fascinating connections between the short stories of P. D. James and her novels, for example, between *Innocent Blood* and its reworking in "The Girl Who Loved Graveyards" (1984). Gidez organizes James's short stories into two categories: detective fiction and psychological crime writing. He argues that these categories are consonant with a modern trend in murder writing. Some of the stories reveal James's commitment to ethical resolutions and the mystery genre, as in the mockingly but lovingly rendered pastiche "The Murder of Santa Claus" (1984), a take on the classic short stories of the Golden Age of mystery fiction (1920–1940).

A characteristic theme of James's short stories is the self-reflexive mode. Many of James's short stories are full of playful mockery of the conventions of detective fiction, parodying their own narrative strategies. Darker themes express her characteristic mood of disenchantment and irony at the inevitable futility of most gestures of control in the face of reality. Murder, she repeatedly demonstrates, cracks open the veneer of civilization and contaminates all who come into contact with it. Her accents, in the novels and the stories, are often somber, sometimes even tragic. In "Murder, 1986" (1975), war and its aftermath have contributed to the wreck of civilization and a loss of faith in social coherence. Gidez's largely critical reading of this futurist fiction could apply equally well to the dystopia *The Children of Men:* it is too schematic and programmatic in its representations of a changed world.

Gidez believes that James's best work in the short story is driven by nostalgia, especially that for Edwardian England, which is fondly re-created by a younger Adam Dalgleish, whose intuition and sensibility bring to its past mysteries the light of modern, sophisticated police investigation.

CONCLUSION

P. D. JAMES began her career as a crime writer exploiting familiar conventions—a country house setting, a locked-room murder, and a large cast of well-defined suspects. It is apparent, with hindsight, that she was restless in the genre: she wanted greater depth of character, psychological intricacies, greater detail of setting and place, and greater complexity of plot. Her first detective, Adam Dal-

gleish, is unconventional in his lack of superficial charm, his dourness and sensibility, and, indeed, his categorical need for writing poetry, his other profession. She toyed only briefly with a love life for Dalgleish. Neither of her highly appealing, self-standing female detectives, the amateur sleuth Cordelia Grey and the police professional Kate Miskin, is interested in love affairs, although both are empathetic and nurturing in their work. James's interest in larger themes—social, philosophical, religious—emerged gradually and with it, a considerable increase in the bulk of her novels. Her large fictions of the late 1980s and the 1990s address issues of a changing British society, the dangers as well as the excitement, the stimulus of contemporary street life. Terrorism, the more widespread horrors of the nuclear threat, and the aftermath of Nazism and the Holocaust preoccupy her increasingly reality-driven creative imagination and lively sense of the importance of ethics to ground society and literature alike. Insistently, she raises moral questions to which the synagogue and the Anglican Church provide ambiguous answers that are held up to novelistic scrutiny. Thus, it is no surprise that because some of her later bulky tomes moved so far from the traditional crime format that they are better described as "novels of ideas."

SELECTED BIBLIOGRAPHY

I. COLLECTED WORKS. *Crime Times Three: Three Complete Novels Featuring Adam Dalgleish of Scotland Yard* (New York, 1979), contains *Cover Her Face, A Mind to Murder,* and *Shroud for a Nightingale; Murder in Triplicate: Three Complete Novels by the Queen of Crime* (New York, 1980), contains *Unnatural Causes, An Unsuitable Job for a Woman,* and *The Black Tower; Trilogy of Death* (New York, 1984), contains *Death of an Expert Witness, Innocent Blood,* and *The Skull Beneath the Skin.*

II. SEPARATE WORKS. *Cover Her Face* (London, 1962; New York, 1966); *A Mind to Murder* (London, 1963; New York, 1967); *Unnatural Causes* (London and New York, 1967); *The Maul and the Pear Tree: The Ratcliffe Highway Murders, 1811,* with Thomas A. Critchley (London, 1971; New York, 1986); *Shroud for a Nightingale* (London and New York, 1971); *An Unsuitable Job for a Woman* (London, 1972; New York, 1973); *The Black Tower* (London and New York, 1975); *Death of an Expert Witness* (London and New York, 1977); *Innocent Blood* (London and New York,

1980); *The Skull Beneath the Skin* (London and New York, 1982); *A Taste for Death* (London and New York, 1986); *Devices and Desires* (London, 1989; New York, 1995); *The Children of Men* (London, 1992; New York, 1993); *Original Sin* (London, 1994; New York, 1995).

III. Short Stories. "Moment of Power," in Ellery Queen, comp., *Ellery Queen's Murder Menu: Twenty-two Stories from Ellery Queen's Mystery Magazine* (New York, 1969); "Murder, 1986," in Ellery Queen, ed., *Ellery Queen's Masters of Mystery* (New York, 1975); "A Very Desirable Residence," in Hilary Watson, ed., *Winter's Crimes 8* (New York, 1977); "Great-Aunt Allie's Flypapers," in Julian Simmons, ed., *Verdict of Thirteen: A Detection Club Anthology* (New York, 1978); "The Victim," in Herbert Harris, ed., *John Creasey's Crime Collection, 1982: An Anthology by Members of the Crime Writers' Association* (New York, 1982); "The Girl Who Loved Graveyards," in George Harding, ed., *Winter's Crimes 15* (New York, 1984); "The Murder of Santa Claus," in David Willis McCullough, ed., *Great Detectives: A Century of the Best Mysteries from England and America* (New York, 1984).

IV. Articles. "Dorothy L. Sayers: From Puzzle to Novel," in H. R. F. Keating, ed., *Crime Writers: Reflections on Crime Fiction* (London, 1978); "House Calls: The Doctor Detective Round-Up," in Dilys Winn, ed., *Murder Ink: Revived, Revised, Still Unrepentant* (New York, 1984); "Love and the Mystery Novel: Ought Adam to Marry Cordelia?," in Dilys Winn, ed., *Murder Ink: Revived, Revised, Still Unrepentant* (New York, 1984); "The Art of the Detective Novel," in *New Welsh Review* 2 (summer 1989); Foreword to Olga Kenyon, *Eight Hundred Years of Women's Letters* (London, 1992).

V. Interviews. Jane S. Bakerman, " 'From the Time I Could Read, I Always Wanted to Be a Writer': Interview with P. D. James," in *Armchair Detective* 10 (January 1977); Diana Cooper-Clark, *Designs of Darkness: Interviews with Detective Novelists* (Bowling Green, Ohio, 1983); Dale Salwak, "An Interview with P. D. James," in *Clues* 6 (spring–summer 1985); Rosemary Herbert, "A Mind to Write," in *Armchair Detective* 19 (fall 1986); Joyce Wadler, "P. D. James," in *People Weekly* 26 (8 December 1986); Marilyn Stasio, "No Gore Please—They're British," in *New York Times Book Review* (9 October 1988); Olga Kenyon, "P. D. James," in her *Women Writers Talk* (Luton, U.K., 1989).

VI. Critical Studies. Lillian de la Torre, "Cordelia Gray: The Thinking Man's Heroine," in Dilys Winn, ed., *Murderess Ink: The Better Half of the Mystery* (New York, 1979); Hanna Kurz Charney, *The Detective Novel of Manners: Hedonism, Morality, and the Life of Reason* (Rutherford, N.J., 1980); Carolyn G. Heilbrun, "A Feminist Looks at Women in Detective Fiction," in *Graduate Woman* 74 (July / August 1980); Carolyn G. Heilbrun, "P. D. James" in John M. Reilly, ed., *Twentieth-Century Crime and Mystery Writers* (New York, 1980); Patricia Craig and Mary Cadogan, *The Lady Investigates: Women Detectives and Spies in Fiction* (London, 1981); Nancy Carol Joyner, "P. D. James," in Earl F. Bargainnier, ed., *Ten Women of Mystery* (Bowling Green, Ohio, 1981); Norma Siebenheller, *P. D. James* (New York, 1981); Bernard Benstock, "The Clinical World of P. D. James," in Thomas F. Staley, ed., *Twentieth-Century Women Novelists* (Totowa, N.J., 1982); Erlene Hubly, "Adam Dalgleish: Byronic Hero," in *Clues* 3 (fall–winter 1982); Richard I. Smyer, "P. D. James: Crime and the Human Condition," in *Clues* 3 (spring–summer 1982); Jacques Barzun and Wendell Hertig Taylor, introduction to *Cover Her Face* (New York, 1983); Sue Ellen Campbell, "The Detective Heroine and the Death of Her Hero: Dorothy Sayers to P. D. James," in *Modern Fiction Studies* 29 (fall 1983); Bruce Harkness, "P. D. James," in Bernard Benstock, ed., *Art in Crime Writing: Essays on Detective Fiction* (New York, 1983); Erlene Hubly, "The Formula Challenged: The Novels of P. D. James," in *Modern Fiction Studies* 29 (fall 1983); Glenn W. Most and William W. Stowe, eds., *The Poetics of Murder: Detective Fiction and Literary Theory* (San Diego, Calif., 1983); Jane S. Bakerman, "Cordelia Gray: Apprentice and Archetype," in *Clues* 5 (spring–summer 1984); Richard B. Gidez, *P. D. James* (Boston, 1986); Sandra Pla, "P. D. James: A New Queen of Crime," in *Caliban* 23 (1986); James F. Maxfield, "The Unfinished Detective: The Work of P. D. James," in *Critique* 28 (summer 1987); Jill Owens, "Repetition, Continuity, and Development of Character in P. D. James," in *Publications of the Mississippi Philological Association* (1988); Dennis Porter, "Detection and Ethics: The Case of P. D. James," in Barbara A. Rader and Howard G. Zettler, eds., *The Sleuth and the Scholar: Origins, Evolution, and Current Trends in Detective Fiction* (Westport, Conn., 1988); Betty Richardson, " 'Sweet Thames, Run Softly': P. D. James's Waste Land in *A Taste for Death*," in *Clues* 9 (fall–winter 1988); Christine Wick Sizemore, "The City as Mosaic: P. D. James," in her *A Female Vision of the City: London in the Novels of Five British Women* (Knoxville, Tenn., 1989); Shari Benstock, *Textualizing the Feminine: On the Limits of Genre* (Norman, Okla., 1991); Penelope K. Majeske, "P. D. James' Dark Interiors," in *Clues* 15 (fall–winter 1994); Kathleen Gregory Klein, *The Woman Detective: Gender and Genre* (Urbana, Ill., 1995); Ross C. Murfin, "What Is Feminist Criticism?," in Beth Newman, ed., *Charlotte Bronte: Jane Eyre* (Boston, 1996).

THOMAS KENEALLY

(1935–   )

Danell Jones

THOMAS KENEALLY IS one of the most successful and best-known writers in Australia. He maintains a high profile in Australian culture by giving frequent interviews in the press and on television; attending seminars and panels; and serving as, among other things, spokesman and one-time chair of the Australian Republican Movement (1991–1993), president of the National Book Council (1985–1990), and chair of the Australian Society of Authors (1987–1990). His work is frequently ranked with that of Australia's most prominent authors, including Morris West, Colleen McCullough, and Nobel Prize winner Patrick White; in 1983 he was awarded the Order of Australia for services to literature. After three decades, he continues to impress his audience with his prodigious output. He has produced some twenty-four novels (two under the pseudonym William Coyle), five nonfiction works, and an assortment of plays, screenplays, and children's books.

Keneally is best-known for his historical fictions, which take place in vastly different eras and landscapes, from fifteenth-century France to the American Civil War, from Antarctica to Africa. These settings often allow him to explore the effect of extreme circumstances on the individual psyche. Large moral and religious questions inevitably shape his narratives: How do ordinary human beings contend with the problems of survival, conscience, and loss? What are the nature and complexion of good and evil? Is the sacred complicit with the profane? How do institutions and codes of behavior circumscribe, and sometimes destroy, individuals? Keneally is particularly interested in the ways that the divine penetrates both the mundane and the terrible aspects of human experience. For instance, the late winter dancing ceremony of the Taos Pueblo Indians, described in his travelogue *The Place Where Souls Are Born: A Journey to the Southwest*, appeals to Keneally precisely because it enacts the implicit, if surprising, bond between the spiritual and material worlds. In the dance, "everything in the upper-world has its equivalent spirit in the nether world. There is a kachina of Jim Beam whisky. There is a kachina of the bomb. The dance redeems all, elevates all, restores all, neutralizes all" (p. 247). Nowhere is contradiction more apparent than in his best-selling *Schindler's List* (published in Britain as *Schindler's Ark*), based on the life of Oskar Schindler, a German war profiteer and unlikely humanitarian, who rescued some twelve hundred Jews from Nazi death camps.

Although Keneally considers himself a commercial writer, even suggesting in an essay called "The Novelist's Poison" that "novels should be read but not necessarily studied," he aims not solely to entertain through his works but also to educate. As he cheerfully concedes at the beginning of *The Place Where Souls Are Born*, "every book is based on an arrogant intention, [on] a belief that there is something readers should know" (p. xviii). So, too, his novels educate his readers in the tactile details of a historical moment, whether that means documenting the struggles of the Eritrean People's Liberation Front or re-creating the living conditions of transported convicts in Australia's first penal colony. But these are by no means simple history lessons. Keneally makes the past live partly through his fascination with and attention to the details of ordinary life. He investigates, as he puts it, "quotidian things . . . what loungesuit [the people of the period] were likely to hanker for, what they would have in the wardrobe . . . whether they put rinse in their hair, what they used for piles, what they considered a healthy baby, what were their funerary rites" (Quartermaine, 1991, p. 10).

In many ways, Keneally's philosophical underpinnings require the historical sweep of his novels. The desire to respond to contemporary social conditions inspires his literary output and influences his choice of historical settings. As he explains in an interview titled "Doing Research for Historical Novels,"

If you're writing fiction you have one of two attitudes to history. You wish either to point out the quaintness or exotic quality of a time past—to create a sort of travelogue to another time having little relevance to ours; or else you want to find evidence in earlier events for the kind of society we have now, wishing to tell a parable about the present by using the past. I attempt the latter.

(p. 27)

Keneally—whose worldview concurs with the adage that he who does not know history is doomed to repeat it—chooses his historical moments for their ability to illuminate our own moment in history. For this reason, one often finds the problems of racism and bigotry informing his work. Surprisingly, perhaps, these conditions also provide startling opportunities to witness the drama of the human spirit. As Keneally told Judith Weinraub during an interview in 1995, "I am fascinated by questions like what virtue is, what bravery is. Particularly for weak men" (p. C1, col. 3). In his most famous novel, *Schindler's List*, one finds many of Keneally's central themes: the terrifying power of evil in a brutal world, the often surprising play of conscience in ordinary people who find themselves in extraordinary circumstances, and the inexplicable mystery of human generosity, bravery, and love.

LIFE AND WORK

KENEALLY'S Irish grandparents immigrated to the north coast of New South Wales at the end of the nineteenth century; his grandfathers' radical politics and religious devotion suggest an ancestral root for like qualities in Keneally himself. His paternal grandfather, Timothy Keneally (the inspiration for the central character of *A River Town*) was a member of Sinn Fein and owned a general store in East Kemsey. His maternal grandfather, Mick Coyle (from whom Keneally drew his pseudonym William Coyle), made his way in this world as an engine driver and forged his path to the next through a strict devotion to Catholicism.

Thomas Michael Keneally was born in Sydney on 7 October 1935. After spending Keneally's early years in the seaside towns of his grandparents—Kemsey, Wauchope, and Taree—in 1942 the family moved to a house in a Sydney suburb called Homebush, where they lived, to the young Keneally's estimation, not only at the very edge of the railroad but also on the indisputably wrong side of the tracks. A divine mischance landed the boy—who firmly believed himself destined for greatness—in the tedious setting of suburban Australia. In his 1996 memoir *Homebush Boy*, Keneally wryly recounts the great injustices endured by a young aesthete caught in the teeth of a hopelessly ordinary life. Though the memoir focuses on Keneally's last year at St. Patrick's College and illuminates his decision to study for the priesthood, the book offers an irresistibly droll portrait of the artist as a young man.

Devotees of Thomas Chatterton, "because he proved you could become immortal by seventeen years of age" (*Homebush,* p. 2), and "poet-hero-Jesuit Gerard Manley Hopkins (GMH to me)" (p. 8), the asthmatic Keneally and his companions christened themselves, in true Oxbridge fashion, "the Celestials," and spent much of their time denying their inscrutably dull circumstances and displaying—generally to the utterly indifferent—their delicate artistic sensibilities. "We were," Keneally recalls, "a gang whose main act of subversion was to pretend we were not where we were" (p. 2). One strategy was to fashion himself—literally—in the likeness of his heroes.

I made up for it by dressing rakishly, as the Romantic poets had. If I could get away with it, and prefects generally could, I wore my blue-and-gold tie loose as a cravat. My grey felt hat was crushed. For Byron never did his hair. The seventeen-year-old prodigy Chatterton's shirt had been unbuttoned when he committed suicide. Percy Bysshe Shelley didn't wear neck ties. Within the limits of the grey serge uniform of St. Patrick's Strathfield, I did my best to show people I was an aesthete and a wide-open spirit.

(p. 8)

He describes in great detail the long hours spent in front of the mirror arranging his hair so that it should "seem negligently done" (p. 9)—much ado from a man destined to be ranked among the ten worst-dressed men in Australia for two years running.

The Celestials took even greater pains to cultivate their proper aesthetic demeanor. Keneally recounts sundry habits—such as reading at the kitchen table or always carrying a copy of Hopkins in his jacket pocket—designed to demonstrate, particularly to those newsmen and biographers who inevitably lurked in his future, the early roots of his genius. He makes it clear that the Celestials shared a magnificent faith that they would partake in the glorious destiny of their heroes.

Gerard Manley Hopkins, Society of Jesus. On his death bed he'd asked that all his poems be destroyed, and I imagined myself in that situation in a large, beeswaxed, cold room you could willingly slip away from into another state, and saying to crowds of Mangan-like peers, "Burn all my poems, they were vanities." Then when I had expired as lightly, fragrantly, crisply as biting into an Adora Cream Wafer, my literary executors would say, "Not on your life. That stuff Mick wrote when he was sixteen, in particular *that* must live."

(p. 10)

All of this changes, however, when idol and Olympic hopeful Peter McInnes tears a ligament while participating in a local competition, effectively ending his athletic career. Suddenly and irrevocably, the Celestials must confront a previously inconceivable truth: "We knew at last," Keneally writes, "that glory could be denied" (p. 158).

This transforming event, combined with the surprise announcement by Bernadette Curran, the central love object, that she has received a call to orders that she intends to follow, draws the young Keneally into himself, and for the first time he begins to seriously consider the priesthood. What he doesn't yet understand in the moment of self-reflection with which the book ends is that his reasons for pursuing a religious life uncannily complement his desire for a writing life. The priesthood appeals to him because it fulfills "a desire to instruct, a taste for drama, a preference for fleshless love" (p. 166).

For a time Keneally's religious vocation provided the flight from provincial Australian life that he and the Celestials sought. From a broader perspective, the imprint of this period can be read in the religious themes, settings, and characters that regularly populate his work. In fact, Judith Weinraub observed that Keneally's fictions "have stayed close to churchly concerns: vices and virtues, heroism and goodness, moral dilemmas. Keneally tells tales of ordinary folk challenged by the vagaries of fate who managed to define themselves through their personal code of conduct—however difficult" (p. C5, col. 1). Despite the appeal of a religious life, and with a gesture that achieved the taste for drama Keneally recognized in himself, he left the seminary shortly before taking his final vows, disappointed, he would later explain, in the rigid hierarchy of the church.

In the years following his departure, Keneally worked as a laborer, clerk, and schoolteacher. In 1962 he published his first story, "The Sky Burning Up Above the Man" (The Bulletin [23 June]: 23–25), under the pseudonym Bernard Coyle. Two years later, he published—under his own name—his first novel, A Place at Whitton (1964), a gothic thriller set in a religious community. A part-time job selling insurance paid the bills and provided time to write. His second novel, The Fear (which he would revise and republish in 1989 as By the Line), came out in 1965. The same year, Keneally married Judith Martin, a former Sister of Charity. In 1967, with the support of a Commonwealth Literary Grant, Keneally produced his first commercial success, Bring Larks and Heroes. This novel narrates the lives of Australia's first European residents: the occupants of the first British penal colony, established in 1788. Bring Larks and Heroes won Australia's prestigious Miles Franklin Award and enabled Keneally to dedicate himself full-time to his writing. The result of his focused efforts was another Miles Franklin Prize winner: a semiautobiographical novel exploring the conflicts and revelations of monastic life, Three Cheers for the Paraclete (1968).

Keneally spent the next three years at the University of New England, Armidale, as a lecturer in drama (1968–1970). As part of his research for his new book, The Survivor (1969), he traveled courtesy of the U.S. Navy, to Antarctica. The completed work shared the 1970 Captain Cook Bi-Centenary Prize and was filmed for television the following year. Keneally spent 1970 and 1971 in London and produced two novels: his fantastical parable of family dynamics, A Dutiful Daughter (1971), and one of his most powerful and controversial works about Australia, The Chant of Jimmie Blacksmith (1972). Based on the true story of Jimmy Governor, a half-Aborigine, half-white laborer who committed a series of murders in turn-of-the-century Australia, The Chant of Jimmie Blacksmith won awards from the Royal Society of Literature and the *Sydney Morning Herald,* and was short-listed for the prestigious Booker McConnell Prize. In 1978, Keneally's friend, the filmmaker Fred Schepisi, filmed the story, casting Keneally himself as the pontificating British cook. The novel has since become a standard part of the Australian secondary school curriculum.

For much of the mid-1970s, Keneally lived in the United States and was a lecturer in New Milford, Connecticut. During this period, he published *Blood Red, Sister Rose* (1974), a down-to-earth view of Joan of Arc; *Gossip from the Forest* (1975), an exploration of conflicting personalities among the men charged with forging the armistice to end World War I; *Moses the Lawgiver* (1975), an offshoot of the British television series; *A Victim of the Aurora* (1977), a thriller set in Antarctica; and *Ned Kelly and the City of the Bees* (1978), a children's book.

Keneally's flourishing reputation was seriously damaged, however, when D. Jenkyn accused him of plagiarism in *Nation Review* (Pierce, *Australian Melodrama,* p. 15). Jenkyn contended that Keneally, without acknowledging his sources, had drawn material for *Season in Purgatory* (1976) from Bill Strutton's book *Island of Terrible Friends* (1961), a description of Strutton's experiences in World War II. After an exchange of letters in *Nation Review,* the parties settled their differences in an out-of-court agreement that included royalties from *Season in Purgatory* to be paid to Strutton.

Perhaps in part to recover his tarnished reputation, Keneally published two novels in 1979. The first, *Passenger,* one of his most experimental novels, is a Shandeyesque tale told by a fetus; the second is a mainstream book written expressly for the American Civil War market. *The Confederates* became Keneally's third novel to be short-listed for the Booker Prize. Keneally continued to pursue his interest in experimental forms with *The Cut-Rate Kingdom* (1980), an unusual novel narrated by "the legless Gallipoli veteran, now Canberra political reporter, Maurice 'Paperboy' Tyson" (Pierce, "The Sites of War," p. 445; *Australian Melodrama,* p. 90), which first appeared in a special edition of *Bulletin* and was published as a book in 1984. *Cut-Rate Kingdom* was not a success, but Keneally's next effort would outstrip in sales all other Booker Prize winners and mark what many would consider Keneally's greatest achievement: *Schindler's List* (1982).

Awarding the Booker McConnell Prize to *Schindler's List* generated a flurry of critical controversy based on one central question: Was *Schindler's List* a novel? Critics like Lorna Sage suggested that its documentary style stretched "the boundaries of fiction" in necessary and important ways, while others, like A. N. Wilson, argued that it was not a novel, but rather "a highly competent workaday piece of reportage." This debate over the book as fact or fiction—or, as some argued, "faction"—nearly overshadowed other evaluations of the work's achievement. Yet, despite the wrangling of the critics over the Booker, *Schindler's List* won the *Los Angeles Times* Fiction Prize in 1983 and flourished as a best-seller. In fact, its global sales exceeded two million copies in 1994. Almost immediately it was considered for a film adaptation. Director Stephen Spielberg, who would finally complete the award-winning film more than ten years later, approached Keneally to write the screenplay. The piece Keneally produced, however, proved far too long for a feature film and the project was handed over to several writers, including Steven Zaillian, who ultimately produced the adaptation Spielberg used.

Keneally next turned his focus back to Australia and wrote a travel book about the country's central regions, *Outback* (1983). He also published *A Family Madness* (1985), a tale of a working-class Australian who becomes involved with a Belorussian family with a dark past and an apocalyptic obsession. Then, after repeated offers, Keneally began his connection with the University of California. In 1985 he moved to southern California to serve as a writer-in-residence on the Irvine campus. Eventually, he headed the prestigious creative writing program at Irvine, and in 1991 he was honored as a "distinguished professor for life."

Drawing largely from historical accounts, Keneally published *The Playmaker* (1987), a novel set in 1788 that describes the life of the prisoners and guards in the first penal colony in Australia as they attempt to put on a production of George Farquhar's *The Recruiting Officer* (1706) to celebrate the king's birthday. Timberlake Wertenbaker revised the novel into a widely acclaimed play, *Our Country's Good,* that was performed in 1988.

During this time, a dangerous journey to the small African country of Eritrea laid the groundwork for one of Keneally's most explicitly political novels, *To Asmara* (1989). For three months, Keneally lived and traveled with the Eritrean People's Liberation Front; the resultant novel documents the long-running and little-known Eritrean civil war. Keneally explained to Robert Stone that he wrote the book in order to "generate a wave of concern in the West for this virtually unreported war" (p. 42). The message, he said, "is that famine is not an act of God. It is not something that simply befalls people the way certain corrupt governments and officers of certain aid organizations would make us believe. It is an act of politics, and politics can be amended. There will never be an end to the famine in the Horn of Africa until there is an end to the war" (p. 42).

While a visiting professor at New York University in 1988, Keneally brought out another book, *Act of Grace,* but concealed his connection to it by using the pseudonym William Coyle. Nevertheless, *Act of Grace* combines two unmistakable Keneallian themes: a fascination with, and criticism of, the military and the monastic ways of life.

Keneally published several works in the early 1990s. *Flying Hero Class* (1991) returns to the problems of racism and politics through the story of a hijacking and its consequences. *Now and in Time to Be* (1991), written after Keneally's journey to Ireland, is a meditation on Irish history and his own Irish heritage. Finally, *Chief of Staff* (1991), published under the pseudonym William Coyle describes the dramas, personal and political, of the military commanders stationed in Australia during the Second World War.

Jan Morris commissioned Keneally to do a travel book about the American Southwest in 1989. He and his family spent two months traveling through Colorado, Utah, Arizona, and New Mexico, doing research. The result, *The Place Where Souls Are Born* (1992), is much less a conventional travel guide than a meditation on the history and landscape of the Four Corners region. Similarly, *Woman of the Inner Sea,* also published in 1992, explores the therapeutic role of landscape. *Woman of the Inner Sea* demonstrates the capacity of place, in this case the Australian Outback, to restore the human psyche after nearly unendurable tragedy.

Keneally released three very different, but wholly Australian, books in 1993: *Jacko* (published in the United States with the subtitle *The Great Intruder*), a novel exploring the multilayered musings of an anonymous Australian writer; *The Utility Player,* the story of Des Hasler, a player for the Sydney Rugby League; and *Our Republic,* a history of the Republican movement in Australia. The Republican movement aims for complete constitutional separation from Britain and is a cause close to Keneally's heart: he served as the organization's first chairperson and frequently acts as its spokesperson.

Keneally returned to Australia in 1995 and published *A River Town,* the first novel of a projected trilogy set in turn-of-the-century Australia and based on the life of Keneally's grandfather. The following year, he brought out his hilarious boyhood memoir, *Homebush Boy.* He continues his swift production pace as he pursues his larger goal: "the challenge of . . . trying to bring this continent on the literary map" (Quartermaine, p. 4).

CRITICAL RECEPTION

DUE, perhaps, to their prodigious number—appearing at a rate that, in Adrian Mitchell's words, "any pulp novelist might envy"—Keneally's works have earned a mixed reception, often enjoying a popular success and a less enthusiastic critical review. A common complaint cites a decline in the quality of his work and attributes this to sundry causes, from too much success to turning out books too rapidly. For these critics, Keneally has not realized the promise of his early novels. In particular, reviews have complained of his weak characterization in which psychological motive and intention remain underdeveloped. Feminist critics have found this especially true of Keneally's representations of women, which, they contend, rarely get beyond stereotypes. Focusing largely on Keneally's novels of the 1970s, Frances McInherny has been particularly critical of Keneally's representation of women, arguing that his female characters are predominantly "earth mothers or whores, [with] a lack of individuality which permits them relevance only in relationship to a man, never as independent and self-defining females" ("Thomas Keneally's 'Innocent men,'" 1981, p. 59). Even the treatment of Kate Gaffney-Kozinski, the main character of *Woman of the Inner Sea* and arguably Keneally's most developed female consciousness, led *Chicago Tribune* reviewer Constance Markey to conclude that "Keneally is genuinely awkward inside a woman's mind" (p. 14, 9:1). Even more troubling than Keneally's conventionally drawn sex roles is the fact that women are very often the objects of extreme and brutal acts of violence in his work. "All too often," Shirley Walker observed, "both the violence and the burden of moral justification are inflicted upon the female figure . . . [in] Keneally's moral *schema*" (p. 151).

Keneally's descriptions of violence—a staple of his work from the decaying body of convict Mealey in *Bring Larks and Heroes* to the detailed descriptions of the Blacksmith murders in *The Chant of Jimmie Blacksmith* to the execution of boy-soldiers in *The Confederates* to Amon Goeth's senseless execution of Jewish prisoners in *Schindler's List* to Jelly's dismemberment in *Woman of the Inner Sea*—some critics have found both excessive and gratuitous. For them, the violence does not lend a sense of authenticity to the moment, but in fact diminishes it. David English's objections are so strong that he uses them to damn Keneally's entire project. "In its relentless reduction of a multifaceted past to an ever-familiar and violent present Keneally's work," he suggests, "remains profoundly unoriginal" (Quartermaine, p. 39).

But perhaps the strongest criticism of Keneally's work addresses the manner in which he emphasizes small historical detail at the expense of character development. It is not enough, David English and Peter Quartermaine argue, to provide us with minute details of daily life. Nor is it enough to reproduce the alarming details of a particular historical event—say the fact, described in *A River Town*, that at the turn of the century a bumbling New South Wales policeman carried the head of a young woman in a jar, trying to find someone to identify her. Without the help of richly developed characters and the complexity that such characters provide to narrative, such events and such details amount, at best, to historical souvenirs, and at worst, as English argues, to "voyeuristic fetishism."

Sensitive enough to write letters to the editor "to express . . . anguish and bemusement" over bad reviews, Keneally locates the source of some of the criticism in the nature of Australian literary culture. He explains in "The World's Worse End?" that "though writers no longer suffer from indifference they suffer in a new way. Australian society is hungry for culture heroes. Writers receive premature canonization and are then painfully derided for failing to be Faulkner after all" (p. 8). Moreover, by his own estimation, Australian authors are outnumbered. "Academics teaching Australian literature outnumber the practitioners three or four to one" (p. 7).

LAUNCHING INTO THE LIMELIGHT: BRING LARKS AND HEROES

KENEALLY'S third novel, *Bring Larks and Heroes*, according to Laurie Clancy, moved him "from apprenticeship into maturity at one lightning stroke," and inspired Australian critics began shaping their great expectations for his career. With genuine delight, Derek Whitelock lauded *Bring Larks and Heroes* as the "long-sought great Australian novel." Other critics registered reservations, however; Clancy judged the novel brilliant but not great. In general, critics subordinated their concerns about the book's florid style and celebrated instead its large historical, moral, and religious themes. Certainly, with its meditation on political and religious loyalty, its examination of an inexplicably restless fate, it casts an ambitious net.

Keneally drew his material from the eighteenth-century *Account of the Settlement at Port Jackson* and, interestingly, first formed it not into a novel but into a drama called *Halloran's Little Boat* (1966). It wasn't until the following year that he wrote the full-length novel developing the moral ambiguities he had begun to explore in the play.

The opening words of the book announce the story's location and, by extension, its mood: the "world's worse end." One quickly discovers that the horror of the place proceeds directly from its paradoxes. Despite the largely uninhabited landscape and the vast distance from "civilization" (in this case, England), Keneally presents a claustrophobic world of dense, enigmatic conversations and paralytic social movements determined by Old World values. For a new world, it is alarmingly retrogressive in its rules, its prejudices, its emotions, even its punishments. In this novel, Keneally fashions an unrelenting and suffocating Old Testament sensibility. It is no surprise, considering that martyrs and whores, Pharisees and prophets determine the action that the entire weight of the plot drives toward the execution of the innocent Everyman, Corporal Halloran.

But, unlike the martyrdom of Christ, the execution of Halloran—an Irish peasant-scholar pressed into service for attending a Land Tenure meeting in Wexford—provides no opportunity for redemption, but serves only as a punishment for sinfulness. The machinery of the plot grinds toward its inevitable punitive conclusion in the service of a cautionary tale and reveals an alarming sexual anxiety at the heart of the novel. Halloran's sin—and the original sin of the novel—is his unblessed sexual union with his "secret bride," Ann Rush. They both hang—not, the novel's apparatus suggests, for aiding and abetting theft but for their sexual desire.

Keneally's novel emphasizes this in part by offering no clear motive for Halloran's decision to help Robert Hearn—Protestant Irishman and revolutionary—steal supplies and escape aboard an American whaler. In the play, Halloran possesses clear motives: he rebels because of the unjust execution of artist-convict Thomas Ewers and the unwarranted punishment of convict Peter Quinn. In the novel, however, Keneally sustains the ambiguity of Halloran's motives despite his representation of a cruel and unjust government. The novel leaves no doubt that the British government to which Halloran has pledged his service is corrupt, biased, and simply incompetent. Keneally spares no detail to demonstrate how quickly it will resort to cruel and unusual punishment. In this sense, one could read the slow accumulation of government transgressions as the fodder that ultimately feeds Halloran's treason. For one thing, Halloran is more sensitive than most to the horrible suffering around him.

From their first meeting, Hearn begins to work on Halloran's allegiances, demanding that Halloran figure himself into the big picture of oaths and obligations. The nightmarish setting and the horrible mutilation of Eris Mealey's body after a flogging intensify the urgency of his arguments. While the young convict is dying of his wounds in an unsanitary and largely unattended hospital, Hearn nurses him and tries to show Halloran how his job is connected to Mealey's slow, unmerciful death. Insofar as Halloran has pledged to serve the government, Hearn argues, Halloran has perpetrated this crime: "You uphold the system which did for Mealey," Hearn accuses (p. 55). And what has been done without due process for Mealey, Keneally shows, is unequivocally horrible. "On Sunday, in fact, you could see the shoulder blades, the white bones themselves," Hearn reports. "This that's so rotten and stinking is junked muscles and jellies" (p. 51). But Halloran also sees for himself. "The long room sizzled with the consequential gluttony of flies, and that too he no longer adverted to. But to see in an instant and by surprise a seam in the boy's purple back and a herd of black flies, whose bite

is maggots, drinking from it, *that* made him flee" (p. 53).

Perhaps because he was helpless to save Mealey, Halloran tries to prevent the hanging of artist and forger Thomas Ewers, a convict who has been enlisted by Surgeon Daker to paint a newly identified kingfisher. Unwittingly, however, Ewers becomes the object of Mrs. Daker's sexual advances; when he tries to deflect them, Mrs. Daker exacts a cruel revenge. Although Keneally populates the books with all manner of unhealthy female sexuality, in Mrs. Daker, outfitted in "a very ripe purple and a fichu of black chiffon" (p. 60), he creates a horrifying vision of female desire. It has already been rumored that she had rubbed poison into the wounds of the dying Mealey; now she slaughters the rare kingfisher and fakes a rape in order to punish Ewers for rejecting her advances. So powerful, the novel implies, is her depraved sexuality that Ewers is hanged even though Halloran has proved that he is a eunuch.

On a much more pedestrian level, the "world's worse end" lacks even the most routine form of justice: that based on simple paperwork. When Halloran writes on behalf of Peter Quinn, a convict who has been overlooked for release because of a clerical mistake, his efforts achieve not Quinn's release but his flogging.

Do these things lead up to the rebellion? On the surface, no. In fact, Hearn and others do stage a small insurrection and Halloran, though vowing to shoot above the heads of the convicts, maintains his post. Even later, when Hearn has been captured, brutally flogged, and left for dead, Halloran shows no intention of shifting his position. By chance, Halloran discovers that Hearn is still alive, surviving in the bush with the help of another Irishman, Terry Byrne, and attempts to return him to the infirmary. Here Hearn articulates even more explicitly his theme of justice and speaks admiringly of the American and French revolutions and of governments where one could "meet with the men you wished to meet with, speak and act as you mind as you've never spoken it or acted it" (p. 160). Here, Hearn lays out his plan of stealing stores and promissory notes and escaping on the whaler. Halloran still resists. "I'll be back in the morning," he promises. "Perhaps with an armed guard" (p. 169). He seems unconvinced by Hearn's plan and also by the arguments for betraying his sacred oath to the king. We are so far outside of Halloran's mind that it is only a strange, providential idea that creates what we can take as the turning point. "It's very likely," Hearn tells Halloran, "that the true God is with us." "If that's so," Halloran replies, "why isn't there a sign?" (p. 169). The exchange prompts Halloran to search for a sign to guide his decision, and he finds a suitably biblical one: twelve men survive the wrath of a leviathan and her calf. If they have survived, he reasons, so will Hearn's plot.

It seems, however, that a widespread female depravity plagues innocent men and their innocent lovers in this world. After Hearn's successful escape, Terry Byrne, and in turn Halloran and Ann Rush, are betrayed by a prostitute when Byrne pays her only two ounces of meat for her services. The broken, vulnerable men—the "leaky boats," Hearn has called them—feebly attempt to save the sole good woman, Ann, Halloran's "secret bride," from the gallows. In an alarming twist, Mr. Blythe, Ann's master, is transformed from sexual predator to defender. Ostensibly to save her from the gallows, Mr. Blythe lies on the witness stand, testifying that she cannot be hanged because she is carrying his child. But not even this sacred argument can halt the unstoppable momentum of injustice; neither Ann nor Halloran can be saved.

Keneally emphasizes the idea that their sin is a sexual rather than a political transgression when Blythe's heretofore chair-ridden wife not only stands but actually dances when Ann is hanged. She has taken a special interest in Ann's chastity throughout the novel, and this fatal conclusion of Ann's desire only confirms her belief that "Halloran has involved her in the Fall." The persistent biblical apparatus of the novel shifts us away from the idea that the couple were hanged for stealing valuable stores in a starving colony, and toward an understanding of the "world's worse end" as yet another Edenic dream destroyed by the corrupting passions of women.

WRITING RACISM: THE CHANT OF JIMMIE BLACKSMITH

The Chant of Jimmie Blacksmith (1972) has been called "arguably [Keneally's] greatest." Keneally drew his story from the lives of Jimmy and Joe Governor, two half-white, half-Aborigine brothers who committed a series of murders in New South Wales in the summer of 1900. Using contemporary newspaper accounts and Frank Clune's 1959 book *Jimmy Governor*, Keneally creates a picture of racism, desire, and violence in a country on the verge of achieving a new national identity. In particular, the book examines the clash of European and Aboriginal cultures and the devastating consequences of such conflicts. *The Chant of Jimmie Blacksmith*, Thomas P. Coakley argued, "dramatizes the struggle for the soul of a continent which, like the human beings who people her, is 'between gods'" (p. 431). Nevertheless, its treatment of race has received mixed evaluations and has been strongly admonished by Henry Reynolds, who found it paternalist and "unconsciously" racist.

As the book opens, the news of Jimmie Blacksmith's marriage to a white woman reaches the Mungindi tribe. Concerned about his nephew's well-being, Jimmie's uncle, a full-blooded Mungindi named Tabidgi—Jackie Smolders to the white world—collects the young man's ritual initiation tooth and goes after him, ostensibly to remind him of his Aboriginal identity and traditions. But by this time, Jimmie, who is only half Aboriginal—the result "from a visit some white man had made to Brentwood blacks' camp in 1878" (p. 1)—has been well indoctrinated into the "decent ambitions" of property and white superiority by the local missionary, Mr. Neville. Like the historical Jimmy Governor, who "did not like to be called a blackfellow," Jimmie Blacksmith marries Gilda with the aim of extirpating his blackness, encouraged by Neville's promise that successive generations will increase the white blood of his offspring. By the time they marry, Jimmie "had very nearly decided that it would be better to have children who were scarcely black at all" (p. 8).

Flashbacks dominate the opening chapters, providing information about Jimmie's life up to the arrival of Jackie Smolders and the initiation tooth. We learn that Neville has taken on the ambitious Jimmie and taught him to aspire to a life of hard work rewarded by material success. However, the equation does not work out as neatly as Neville promises. Jimmie contracts with an Irishman named Healy to build a line of fencing, only to be shortchanged when the job is done. To intensify matters, the entire Healy enterprise—Healy's property, his possessions, and particularly his domesticity—takes on symbolic proportions for Jimmie. Mrs. Healy, as her husband's most prominent possession, acquires a particular importance in Jimmie's mind. "In a second she had become a symbol, a state of blessedness, far more than a woman. It could almost be said that he did not choose her as woman at all, rather as an archetype" (p. 21). When Healy cheats Jimmie, refuses him a ride in his wagon, and strikes him in front of Mrs. Healy, Jimmie's humiliation leads him to figure her even more largely in his ambition. He aggrandizes Mrs. Healy's role so far that "she had become," he thinks, "inherent to his programme" (p. 23).

For a time, Jimmie becomes the ambivalent tracker—half reluctant, half malicious—for a sadistic constable named Farrell. Part of Jimmie's duties lead him to Verona, where he helps Farrell locate the body of a murdered white man, the body Farrell had helped hide the year before. Here Keneally emphasizes Jimmie's inexorable alienation. He hates the Aborigines "for their innocence, for not being able to dominate even the clumsiness of Farrell" yet his "blood leapt and was tantalized by the whole affair, and Jimmie knew how obscene that was, but was lost in his passion" (p. 40). He finally abandons the job when he discovers that Farrell has sodomized the murder suspect and hanged him with a belt.

In Cowra, Jimmie becomes a sweeper on a shearing floor and meets Gilda, the white woman he will marry, and a British cook who likes to pontificate on the differences between Europeans and Aborigines. He contracts for another fencing job on the property of a man named Newby, where he builds a house for his now-pregnant wife. Newby, too, cheats and insults Jimmie—a common practice in rural Australia, the narrator tells us. In a horrible twist to Jimmie's desire to have "children who were scarcely black at all" (p. 8), Gilda gives birth to a child who is clearly white—in fact, the son of the cook, who has no intention of claiming either the woman or the child. Mrs. Newby and the schoolteacher, Miss Graf, contrive to separate the family, contending that white children cannot be raised by blacks. At this point, Jackie Smolders arrives with Jimmie's brother Mort and Jimmie's initiation tooth.

The turning point occurs when Newby refuses

Jimmie groceries because, he contends, the arrival of Jackie and Mort threatens to turn the place into a "black camp." Jimmie walks up to the Newby house with Jackie, ostensibly to complain. For reasons not altogether clear, the two men end up brutally attacking the women in the house with axes. Sustained by a conviction that he has "declared war," Jimmie, engages in a massacre of epic proportions that they seem unable to stem. In fact, as the narrator explains, the violence begets more violence: "The horror Jimmie's first blow had made of Mrs. Newby could only be fought with more and more blows" (p. 80). And Keneally attends to the grisly details with a Homeric precision: "Mr. Jimmie Blacksmith rolled on his feet and chopped off the back of the remaining Miss Newby's head. The axe was flecked with the strange grey mucus of the brain" (p. 80). Psychologically, Keneally offers a blurred portrait of the murderer who swings between "self-knowledge and delirium," who kills four women, then offers a banana to soothe the child whose mother he has murdered.

Now joined by Jimmie's brother, the innocent Mort, Jimmie and Jackie head to the Healy farm, where Mort, to his horror, fatally wounds a woman, and where Jimmie quite calculatingly kills Mrs. Healy and her child. Despite what he's done, or perhaps because of it, Mort is transformed into a terrified voice of conscience.

"Healy deserve all this?" Mort asked thickly. There was no irony in him. He was silly with shock. He hoped that Jimmie would itemize Healy's guilt, to make it commensurate with the mess in the kitchen corner. . . .

"He starved me and told me bloody lies."

"But it's woman-blood," Mort screamed. "And it's child-blood."

(p. 101)

Because Jimmie unleashes his most excessive violence on women, Shirley Walker uses a sexual motivation to explain the violence of his crimes. We need only look, she argues, at the repeated sexual components of the tale: Jimmie's desire for white women and his humiliation in front of them and by them; the commonplace sexual exploitation of black women and men by "respectable" white men; the mostly unspoken guilt of white men because of their desire for black women and their anger at the women for eliciting such desire. "The subjugation of the Aborigines is certainly economic," she argues, "but its manifestations are almost always sexual" (p. 152).

By this time, Jimmie has killed Healy, and Jackie has been taken into custody. Military squads and civilian volunteers scour the countryside for the brothers, and the government has issued an outlawry bill that states that they can be shot on sight. Keneally represents the attitudes of the white Australians, in part, through the actions and beliefs of the volunteers who trail the brothers, including Miss Graf's fiancé, Dowdie Stead. They largely support Australian involvement in the Boer War—which they expect to join as soon as they make Australia safe from the Blacksmith brothers—and the coming federation. Moreover, Keneally repeatedly links their racism to guilty desire for black women, underscoring a strong subconscious connection between sexuality and racism.

Then Jimmie and Mort take a hostage who changes the course of their lives. The hostage—the schoolteaching, asthmatic, talkative Mr. McCreadie, who is not afraid of them, believes in their innocence, and helps them to reconnect to their ancestral past—will ultimately separate the brothers. And yet, though they know that he will ultimately be the cause of their separation, they cannot part with him. As the days pass, and even as McCreadie grows increasingly ill, so ill that the brothers must take turns carrying him on their backs, he remains their leader. "They clung," the narrator tells us, "to McCreadie as mediator, yet maintained to his amusement the fiction that he was a hostage" (p. 144). For reasons not clear even to McCreadie himself, he convinces them to go to an ancient stone circle, an Aborigine initiation spot, where they discover that the sacred stones have been defiled by football players. To McCreadie's mind, if it is observed correctly, the desecration explains the sequence of tragedies that have led to the Blacksmiths' downfall.

It had become easy for him to believe, his mind all cross-eyed for lack of air, that if the Taree footballers had not fallen to celebrating their skill on the consecrated stones of another race, there would have been no killing at the Newbys'. It seemed to him almost a principle of law, viable in a courtroom.

(p. 150)

In fact—and this is one of the novel's key points—the long and mostly concealed history of crimes of whites against blacks will not be taken into account in the dispensing of justice.

Ultimately, McCreadie convinces Jimmie to leave Mort behind. Unlike Jimmie, Mort is a full-blooded Aborigine who, as McCreadie would have it, has not yet been "buggered up" by Christianity. Jimmie agrees, and leaves them. Mort deposits the ailing McCreadie at a farmhouse and takes refuge in some brush where, shortly after, he is killed by local farmers out for the reward. While continuing his flight alone, Jimmie is shot through the face. The injury rips apart his lip and tears out teeth in a gross parody of his boyhood initiation ceremony. Ultimately, Jimmie takes refuge in a Kaluah nunnery, convinced that if he gives himself up to a nun dying in the next room, it would be "a surrender of special merit, . . . it would emphasize to everyone how much he wished all were restored again" (p. 171).

Jimmie's captors, however, do not share his faith in the redeeming capacity of ritual confession, and sentence him to death. Keneally uses "letters to the editor" to illuminate the community responses to Jimmie's crimes, which range from Old Testament retribution to New Testament forgiveness. By doing so, he raises large questions about the nature of guilt. Is this solely the crime of an individual against other individuals? Or is it also a much larger social crime in which the bigoted hegemony of one race undermines, degrades, and ultimately destroys the integrity of another?

The answers to such questions, however, are necessarily concealed by the demands of statemaking and the creation of operative myths essential to that project. Jimmie's and Jackie's executions must be postponed because such public events do not produce the proper new national image. Indeed, the narrator tell us, "Australia had become a fact." Therefore, "it was unsuitable, too indicative of what had been suppressed in the country's making, to hang two black men in the Federation's early days" (p. 177). Spectacle often serves national identity, but the authorities fear that this display, poorly timed, could provoke questions of how many blacks have been killed in the forging of this new nation—where, incidentally, Aborigines are not even citizens. McCreadie estimates that by 1900 over a quarter of a million Aborigines had been killed by whites. Jimmie and Jackie are quietly hanged ten months later.

REPUTATIONS: VICTIM OF THE AURORA

ALTHOUGH it is not one of Keneally's finest books, nor even one of his most ambitious, *Victim of the Aurora* gives a good idea of the writer at work in a popular form: the thriller. Keneally frames *Victim of the Aurora* as the memories of an aging Antarctic explorer, now relegated to a nursing home in southern California. As he senses his life drawing to a close, he feels the need to recount the mysterious events of a 1911 Antarctic expedition in which he took part. Keneally paints the men of the expedition as the quintessential Edwardians: a kind of scientific brotherhood, dedicated to the high goals of rational knowledge and masculine bravery, who are willing to undergo all manner of hardship, from the inhospitable landscape to each other's personal failings, to achieve their humanitarian aims. Yet murder, the ultimate transgression of the social contract, disrupts the community and unravels its moral fabric, thereby revealing far more serious personal flaws than most had suspected.

The victim, Victor Henneker, is quickly shown to be a manipulative man with lots of enemies and, much to the shock and horror of some expedition members, a homosexual. To serve his mercenary ends, Henneker has compiled an unsubtle journal that catalogues the transgressions, moral and otherwise, of every member of the expedition. He intends, the reader discovers, to use his damning evidence against the team members to supply postexpedition articles for magazines more interested in the failings of the human flesh than in the high-minded goals of the explorers. In other words, everyone has a motive for killing Henneker. The plethora of dirty laundry, unsuspected by the dignified and proper leader of the expedition, Sir Eugene Stewart, raises serious questions about reputation as any kind of tool for judgment. Once we begin to see how unstable a principle it is, founding one's moral universe on it seems terribly foolhardy and ultimately dangerous.

But that this murder is, in fact, a patricide, comes as a surprise, in part because the book hints that Victor Henneker and Paul Gabriel are not only unlikely father and son, but may be lovers as well. In a distancing, ironizing gesture, Anthony Piers, narrator of *Victim of the Aurora*, explains the Edwardian attitude toward homosexuality.

I confess with embarrassment to what worried me. You have to understand that in those days the attitude to homosexuality was one of breathless abomination. "Sodomy was accursed," says a historian of the era, and the law and public opinion destroyed the sodomite. No homosexual should be let anywhere near children or public office. . . . I was a child of my age and suffered from its frantic prejudices.

(pp. 24–25)

Yet, as the critic Frances McInherny suggests, in Keneally's work homosexuals are generally "seen as deviant, violent, or having violence done to them, and are frequently mutilated" ("Thomas Keneally's 'Innocent Men,'" p. 59). In fact, she identifies an anxious constellation of themes in Keneally's work in which the representation of women and homosexuals figures significantly. In his work, she explains, one routinely finds

the reverence for the mother figure, the earth goddess through whose womb man comes in contact with the universe; the abhorrence of homosexuality for it offends the powers of procreation; the concept of the homosexual as at once innocent and violent.

(p. 65)

In the course of the novel, however, the Freudian element—Paul Gabriel's Oedipal killing of his homosexual father—is less interesting than the moral and historical implication of the action. Fascinatingly, Paul's crime exposes an undeniable connection between murderous rage and indefatigable ambition. As the sole spectacle-wearing member of the group, Paul has not been included among the prestigious team who will, if all goes well, plant the British flag at the pole. But, in fact, his myopia circumscribes more than his eyesight and, moreover, everyone else in the group shares it. The code of honor that inspires Paul to risk his life in order to collect biological data about penguins, that inspires the entire group to daily acts of exceptional bravery in the name of science, also binds them to an inflexible, and ultimately immoral, code of behavior that is unable to acknowledge shades of nuance or subtlety. This is a world without exceptions, without extenuating circumstances, and, for this reason, ultimately devoid of compassion. In this sense, Keneally uses Paul's execution by the impeccable Sir Eugene Stevens to expose the essential failing at the heart of Edwardian morality. That is why, when the narrator, Sir Anthony Piers, claims that it was "the act which rendered the condition of the century terminal," we know exactly what he means: this is precisely the code that leads inevitably, unrelentingly, to the national slaughter of nearly a million young men during the Great War. The essence of heroism—its resolve and determination—is also its greatest flaw.

REVISITING THE HOLOCAUST: SCHINDLER'S LIST

The Reception

SCHINDLER'S List is Keneally's best-known work and perhaps his greatest accomplishment. In near-documentary style, the book traces the life of Oskar Schindler, a war profiteer who risked his life in Nazi Germany to save over twelve hundred Jews from extermination in concentration camps. Although Schindler's story was well known in the 1940s and 1950s, it might have all but disappeared from cultural memory had Keneally not happened, in 1980, into a Beverly Hills luggage shop where Leopold Pfefferberg, a Schindler survivor, recounted the remarkable story. Intrigued by the tale, Keneally traveled to Kraków, Zablocie, Plaszów, and Auschwitz-Birkenau; visited Schindler's factory and Goeth's labor camp; and interviewed some fifty Schindler survivors in order to compose a faithful portrait of the man.

The uneasy generic mixing of the work—something between fiction and history—aroused critical controversy. Peter Gilbert explains in *The Jewish Chronicle*:

Had the book been written as a novel based on the story of Oskar Schindler, Keneally would perhaps have felt greater freedom to enlarge on his hero's character, to recreate it from within, so to speak, and possibly would have made him more understandable. Had he chosen to write a straightforward biography he would at least then have had to attempt to explain the mystery of why Schindler acted as he did. As it is, the book falls somewhere between two stools.

(quoted in Quartermaine, p. 74)

In response to the critical debate, Keneally acknowledged that the work was based on extensive research, which included trips to the Schindler factories, the work camps, and interviews with Schindler survivors, but explained that it could be classified as a novel because it uses novelistic devices. He had used the texture and devices of a novel, he argued, to tell a true story. He said to Peter Grosvenor of *The Daily Express* (21 October 1982):

Perhaps you could call it non-fiction fiction. I've moulded the material as you would for a novel—highlighting dramatic episodes, building up characterisation. But about a third of the way through, when the pace starts to hot up, the book becomes far more documentary than novel. Basically, nothing has been invented.

(quoted in Hulse, p. 43)

But Keneally's attempts to bridge the work's generic contradictions by calling it a "documentary novel" or a "non-fiction fiction" did little to quell objections. To many, *Schindler's List* was nonfiction and, however meritorious, should not have been awarded a prize for fiction. As one "former judge" explained in *The Sunday Times* (31 October 1982), "A non-fiction novel is nonsense and an insult to fiction writers. I am very sad that a prize founded for fiction, the Cinderella of the publishing world, has been diverted off to one of the areas where everyone does very well anyway" (quoted in Hulse, p. 47).

Paul Ableman of the *Literary Review* defended the novel as a work of fiction because, he argued, "literary art blazes in the language." In an article devoted to an analysis of the book's reception, Michael Hulse identified a simple fallacy at the center of such arguments.

It is assuredly true that Keneally uses the "texture and devices of a novel to tell a true story." But what this actually means is no more than a historical record of fact is subjected to a heightening treatment, is cast in the dramatic pacing and rhetoric of invented fictions. It doesn't need a pedant to point out that such pacing and rhetoric have never been absent either from the grand style of historical prose (Gibbon, Carlyle) or from the True Stories of the pulp market. At whatever extreme of integrity or intellectual propriety, factual records have a long history of being set in the "texture and devices" of fiction: this does not make them fiction, does not make them novels.

(p. 48)

Perhaps D. J. Enright's analysis summed up the prevailing critical mood. For him, the book seemed altogether too tidy actually to be fiction. "No self-respecting writer would indulge in so arrant an improbability," he explained. "*Schindler's Ark* deserves to have won the Booker Prize—as long as it isn't *really* a novel" (p. 1189).

The Story

Schindler's List begins with a set piece; the prologue drops us in the middle of a Nazi dinner party at the forced labor camp at Plaszów on a cold autumn night in 1943. Keneally shows us the public Schindler in action: the "tall young man in an expensive overcoat, double-breasted dinner jacket beneath it and—in the lapel of the dinner jacket— a large ornamental gold-on-black-enamel *Hakenkreuz* (swastika)" (p. 13). He is stepping into his Adler limousine with an expensive, black-market cigarette case in his pocket, a gift for his host, the camp commandant, Amon Goeth. The luxurious villa overlooking the camp, the sumptuous dinner, the copious amounts of drink seem unreal in a world of cattle car transports, burned-out ghettos, and visibly bruised servants. Once the other drunken guests have retired, we see what may look only like, in the narrator's words, "a quotidian" act of kindness: Schindler descends to the kitchen and consoles the beaten servant. He gives her chocolate and listens as she describes Goeth's random killings and other acts of violence.

The prologue introduces us to Schindler's customary kindnesses; yet the remainder of the book demonstrates that such gestures were typical of the risks Schindler had come to take—and far greater ones. It also goes even farther, to demonstrate how fatal such kindnesses could be.

The first chapter offers a brief exploration into Schindler's early life, with the intention of finding clues to explain his later behavior. The evidence, however, never completely adds up: the early life never offers a tidy foreshadowing of what will follow. We learn of Schindler's Catholic upbringing, his parents' unhappy marriage, his passion for motorcycles and clothes and women, and his willingness to wear the swastika if it means making money. Schindler wears it openly because in 1938, "when you went in to a German company manager wearing the badge, you got the order" (p. 38). In fact, we discover things that not only fail to give reasons for Schindler's later acts, but actually contradict his later behavior. He provides intelligence about Poland to the Foreign Section of the *Abwehr*, and after the German invasion of Poland, he travels to Kraków in order to cash in on the booming war economy.

Ultimately, Schindler takes over an enamelware factory in Poland that will make mess kits for the German Army. Here the novel begins to trace the stories of people associated with the factory, and by doing so, gradually catalogues the systematic humiliations and, later, barbarities committed against Jews. Initially, the measures are largely economic: the government seizes all Jewish bank accounts and businesses, then homes and properties. But the outrages quickly grow worse. In an act of unqualified racism, Governor General Frank demands that all Jews be removed from the capital city, exempting only those contributing to the war effort. Because Schindler's factory produces enamelware for the military, the Jewish workers there are safe from this initial exportation; Deutsche Email Fabrik, because of Schindler's willingness to hire Jews and, in essence, harbor them, begins to become known as a sort of haven.

"As a means of reducing racial conflict in the Government General," the Reich decrees the creation of a Jewish ghetto in Kraków; Jewish support for the act surprises Schindler. Believing that this will be the extent of their humiliation, Jews voluntarily move into the ghetto, where they experience overcrowding and insufficient sanitation facilities. At the same time, another edict deprives them of their wages and forces them to survive on rations alone. The rations, however, are utterly and deliberately insufficient: when the ration books arrive, nearly half of the coupons have been canceled. As the hunger in the ghetto increases, Schindler's factory, with its adequate food supply for the workers, becomes an even more important refuge.

Schindler is arrested twice during this period and is saved only by the well-greased palms of his connections. But the events begin to reveal to him that the hostility against Jews goes beyond mere prejudice. In what is meant to be some friendly advice, an officer warns Schindler that "You'd be a fool if you got a real taste for some little Jewish skirt. They don't *have* a future, Oskar. That's not just old-fashioned Jew-hate talking, I assure you. It's policy" (p. 115).

At this point, the Nazis' anti-Semitic program is, for Schindler, still a matter of dinner party gossip and rumor. It isn't until Schindler inadvertently witnesses the liquidation of the Kraków ghetto that he realizes the Nazis intend a thorough and systematic annihilation of the Jews. By coincidence, Schindler and his mistress take a horseback ride above the city on the day the Nazis enter the ghetto. From a hilltop, they have a clear view of the massacre beneath them.

And, running before the dogs, the men and women and children who had hidden in attics or closets, inside drawerless dressers, the evaders of the first wave of search, jolted out onto the pavement, yelling and gasping in terror of the Doberman pinschers. Everything seemed speeded-up, difficult for the viewers on the hill to track. Those who had emerged were shot where they stood on the sidewalk, flying out over the gutters at the impact of the bullets, gushing blood into the drains. A mother and a boy, perhaps eight, perhaps a scrawny ten, had retreated under a windowsill on the western side of Krakusa Street. Schindler felt an intolerable fear for them, a terror in his own blood which loosened his thighs from the saddle and threatened to unhorse him. He looked at Ingrid and saw her hands knotted on the reins. He could hear her exclaiming and begging beside him.

(p. 129)

For Schindler, witnessing this massacre firsthand transforms the events of history into something personal and, for the first time, moves him to personal action. "I was now resolved," he reported later, "to do everything in my power to defeat the system" (p. 133).

When the tide of the war turns against the Germans, Goeth receives orders to disband Plaszów and its subcamps, including Schindler's Emalia. The Schindler workers are to return to Plaszów; from there they will be relocated. In a desperate attempt to save his workers, Schindler schemes to open a new factory in Czechoslovakia and transport his people there. Through huge "gratuities" to people in important places (sources estimate he spent nearly forty thousand dollars to arrange the deal), Schindler arranges for a new factory—not far, it turns out, from his hometown—in a place called Brinnlitz. He begins, then, the list of names of those who are to be transported there. For the prisoners, it is a matter of life or death to have one's name on the list.

Despite directives from the commandant of Gröss-Rosen regarding the disposal of the prisoners now that the Russians are beginning to advance into the region, Schindler promises his workers that he will protect them to the end of the regime. Knowing that Schindler's position will become very precarious when the Allies arrive, the prisoners prepare a small ceremony to honor him and to commemorate what he has done. They present him with a gold ring—the melted-down bridgework of one of the men—that has been engraved with a Talmudic verse. In a line that suggests the magnitude of Schindler's accomplishments, it reads, "He who saves a single life saves the world entire" (p. 368).

Wearing prison stripes and traveling in a Mercedes laden with hidden money and jewels, the Schindlers and eight prisoners begin to make their way toward the Austrian frontier. During a stopover, their money and jewels are stolen, but they eventually reach the protection of American troops and a refugee camp in Nuremberg. By the time they arrive, however, the once wealthy and extravagant Schindler is virtually penniless.

In his review of the book, Paul Zweig reminds readers that "In the old epics a character is occasionally inhabited by a god, and then he acts beyond himself, living on the edge of wonder. When the god leaves him, he becomes ordinary once again" (p. 39). The epilogue of *Schindler's List* sketches the disappointments and failures that characterize the rest of Schindler's life. The Russian government confiscates his personal property and his new attempts to regain his wealth are unsuccessful: a nutria farm in Argentina and a cement factory in Germany are both failures. After the war he suffers ostracism, poverty, and poor health. Ironically, Schindler develops a growing dependence on those who had once utterly depended on him; he spends months at a time in Israel at their invitation and expense. "It was a seasonal matter," Keneally explains, "half the year as the Israeli butterfly, half the year as the Frankfurt grub" (p. 395). It is an unhappy and even strange ending for a man who had been so successful and who had so freely given up his personal wealth. Yet, by closing the book with this account of the disappointing balance of his life, Keneally makes Schindler's acts of generosity and courage during the war all the more poignant.

At its center the book poses an intriguing moral mystery: Why would a profiteer, by definition motivated by self-interest, perform such selfless acts, engage in such risky business, threaten not only his fortunes but his very life? Discussions of the Holocaust often examine the manner in which ordinary, decent individuals responded—or failed to respond—to systematic, mechanized genocide. Keneally, however, gives the question one more turn of the screw: How does a man who is not particularly decent, who is, in fact, a gluttonous, womanizing, speculator—contend with such forces? If Schindler serves as a case study, the results are startling. As *New Yorker* film critic Terrence Rafferty observes, Schindler's acts do not represent a "self-transcendence, but . . . more like an improbable self-fulfillment: in the unique, deranged circumstances of occupied Poland, his shortcomings, and even his vices, somehow turn into instruments of virtue" ("A Man of Transactions," p. 129). In other words, though he remains utterly himself, the alchemy of the times transforms Schindler's dross to gold. For Rafferty, the most notable moral act occurs when Schindler makes an instinctual shift from self-interest to altruism, a moment that not only illuminates his character but also provides, by contrast, some insight into the greediness of our own times.

For those who pondered why a Catholic Australian writer would take on a story of the Holocaust, Michael Hollington ventured some answers. He felt that Keneally's approach to the ethical questions raised by the novel are "primarily personal and individual rather than social" (p. 42), and that for Keneally, Schindler represented a kind of "Australian bush hero" who is "essentially an outlaw who doesn't belong to the society of the respectable and orderly" (p. 43). Significantly, however—and this is an important theme in many of Keneally's works—the outlaw shows more compassion and mercy and true moral courage than the so-called respectable citizens.

Keneally aimed to account for the extraordinary as reliably and objectively as possible. As intriguing as Schindler's character is, however, Keneally never takes full advantage of his literary license to explain why his selflessness took over or to explore the general question of Schindler's motivation.

Keneally believes that his characterization of Schindler preserves the mystery at the heart of the man. "You add up all the elements—the expediencies and decency—and you don't get the sum of what happened," Keneally argues (*Newsweek*, 20 December 1993, p. 118). For others, however, the mystery is not difficult to solve. For them, the lack of clear motive points undeniably to divine intervention: Schindler, against the grain of his own nature and the protection of his own interests, was used by the hand of God in the service of good.

CONTEMPLATING AMERICAN LANDSCAPE: THE PLACE WHERE SOULS ARE BORN: A JOURNEY INTO THE SOUTHWEST

The Place Where Souls Are Born is not a novel but a travelogue, yet its preoccupations are much like those of Keneally's fictional works. In his travels across Colorado, Utah, Arizona, and New Mexico, Keneally returns to the themes that consistently inform his worldview: a fascination with obscure people and places, the appeal of unsolved, and perhaps unsolvable, mysteries—in this case, the disappearance of the Anasazi Indians sometime in the thirteenth century—and the discovery of the sacred and the profane resting side by side in a quiet, if surprising, alliance. In this travel book, Keneally not only focuses on the sublime beauty of the Rockies or Zion or the Grand Canyon, but reflects as well on the strip malls and the fast food joints now thriving in former pioneer towns. In other words, as much as he appreciates the beauty and mystery of the Southwest, he refuses to supply a feel-good, sentimental portrait. Instead, he attempts to account for and contemplate the big picture.

Why would Keneally take the American Southwest as his subject? The answer is simple: a childhood full of Saturday afternoons in Homebush's Vogue Cinema watching John Wayne and Randolph Scott pictures, seeing the strange and wonderful landscapes of Monument Valley and Sedona, and hearing for the first time mysterious names like "the Rockies" and "Denver." That same childlike affection often shapes his approach to this landscape and his view of the people who have populated it. In a mixture of historical anecdote and contemporary observation, Keneally considers the miners, Mormons, Native Americans, wealthy widows, ambitious pioneers, ardent environmentalists, artists, and writers drawn to this landscape, often in search of fame and fortune. The very names still evoke the spirit of romance: Kit Carson, Leona (Babe) Rector Henricks, Mabel Dodge. Keneally captures the magic and wonder of it all in the life of Baby Doe and Horace Tabor. He recounts their story as if he were pitching a tearjerker to a Hollywood producer. He presents a rags-to-riches-to-rags story: poor but wily girl wins the affections of wealthy mining baron and lives the good life until the tragic shift from the silver to the gold standard returns her, Cinderella-like, to poverty. A distinct echo of Oskar Schindler rings through his accounting of the success of Mormon leader Joseph Smith. Trying to explain Smith's "money-digging, ball gazing, and other folk magical tendencies," he asks, "who says that the Lord . . . couldn't still use him as an instrument and transform him? If God worked only through the impeccable, how could His work be done on earth?" (p. 84). Of necessity in the corrupt world, as Keneally shows in *Schindler's List*, the corrupted become agents of grace, demonstrating not only the surprisingness of the world but also the redemptive strength of grace itself.

And for Keneally, the powerful spiritual element that inhabits this landscape can be particularly frightening for the urbanite. He acknowledges the element of terror that the Southwestern expansiveness can produce. Such landscapes, he says, intensify the vulnerability of the human form. "Maybe religion is so strong in this landscape," he speculates, "because this is terrain which puts the human in his place the way Manhattan never could. You can come to a place like the Wasatch Mountains or the Great Salt Basin to learn your true scale" (p. 96).

In the end, Keneally celebrates the Southwest because he discovers there an antidote to emotional bankruptcy of modern life. In all its strangeness, Keneally suggests, it possesses the power to heal America and "deliver it from its impoverished urban dimensions" (p. xx). But whether or not we accept this deliverance, Keneally offers as his last thought, the inscrutable landscape will continue to practice its powerful medicine: "I take to the road," he writes, "strangely assured that someone is singing for us, celebrating matters we have got out of the way of celebrating for ourselves. The eternity of things. Even of our own spirits" (p. 248).

FIGURING THE FEMALE MIND: WOMAN OF THE INNER SEA

IN an attempt to redress some of the feminist criticism of his earlier work, according to Peter Pierce, Keneally took the opportunity in *Woman of the Inner Sea* to "examine his prejudices and to liberalise his responses toward his women characters, whether they are mothers, lovers or children" (*Australian Melodrama*, p. 22). For Pierce, Keneally wrote this novel as a "carefully judged risk" to test whether, or perhaps to prove that, he could understand "the complex emotional responses, and the social entanglements, of a grieving woman of modern times" (p. 24).

Keneally's central character, Kate Gaffney-Kozinski, is a more-privileged-than-average Australian Everywoman who has grown up in a prosperous Irish–Australian family. When she marries and has children, she gives up her job and devotes herself full-time to mothering. Keneally illuminates the quiet, predictable joys of Kate's motherhood. Far from the demands of commerce, she and her children form a complete world of their own, a "commonwealth of three." But then, following a course of events that Kate finds alarmingly banal, her husband begins an extramarital affair that changes the dependable current of her motherhood.

Paul's affair . . . caused Kate the usual anguish. But what she most hated about it was that it altered the terms under which planet Palm Beach maintained itself. It brought to an end the ecstatic age—the one in which by choice she dispensed the laughter and the sunlight while the divine children, with easy and infallible grace, availed themselves of it all.

(p. 27)

One fateful day, Kate uncharacteristically accepts an offer to have dinner in town with her father, and by the end of the evening something terrible has happened at home. Yet, Keneally conceals the tragedy in a move that Merle Rubin of the *Wall Street Journal* calls "gimmicky" and that, he suggests, weakens "some genuine drama." The next time we see Kate, three months have passed and her life has changed utterly. The children no longer shape the hours of her days, and somehow she has been badly burned. Now, rather than the needs of the children, the idea of a journey and possibly a resurrection determine Kate's actions. Leaving only brief notes for her loved ones and taking only a few articles of clothing, she escapes to the train station. She doesn't choose a destination, but through the forces of timetable fate, ends up in a little nothing town in the Australian Outback called Myambagh, where she signs on as a barmaid in a railway hotel. There, in an attempt at a kind of self-disfigurement, she consumes huge amounts of coarse, greasy food that she hopes will deform her human shape and dull her grief-stricken mind.

Though she is distracted and largely unfriendly, Kate comes to know the locals and the history of the place, especially the fact of Myambagh's frequent, often fatal, and possibly preventable, flooding. She meets Jelly, the enormous munitions expert who, local lore says, saved the town from a flood in 1962 and has been hailed as a local celebrity ever since. Casually, almost unintentionally, Kate, who feels virtually no emotion, becomes his lover. She envies his massive bulk as her own ultimate aim. She no longer wants to be considered an attractive, desirable woman; she wants to become invisible. She senses that growing larger will put her outside of men's desire. "She was in training for being beneath notice" (p. 109). Ironically, the fact of Jelly's size in some ways confirms that he is larger than life: not only is he "a lovable and inferior man," but also, she realizes, "claimed for diviner purposes" (p. 109). In other words, the quintessential Keneally hero.

Ultimately, her husband's goon, Burnside, tracks Kate down in Myambagh and presents her with a lucrative divorce settlement that, after a night's hesitation, she signs. Ironically, Burnside loses the signed divorce documents when his car is caught in the rising floodwaters that threaten the town. In a valiant attempt to redirect the water, Kate joins Jelly and his friend Gus and a couple of other men to dynamite the railroad embankment. In a terrible accident, the explosives ignite prematurely, blowing Jelly to pieces but saving the town. Gus and Kate flee.

They escape by small boat, taking with them two other unlikely refugees: a kangaroo and an emu that Gus intends to save from a exploitative animal

keeper. The four of them gradually make their way to dry land. The quartet travels across the Outback, and in time reach Gus's cabin, Soldier Settler farmhouse, where, in their mutual loss and need, Gus and Kate become lovers.

However, catastrophe is never far from Kate, whom her Uncle Frank had astutely christened "the Queen of Sorrows." They are no sooner settled in than Burnside reappears with new copies of the divorce papers. This time, Kate refuses to sign. Burnside doesn't realize that she has changed in fundamental ways during her journey. Burnside was now "up against a living thing, where in Myambagh he had had to fight only inertia" (p. 213). Burnside slugs Kate and then begins to beat Gus. To prevent him from killing Gus, Kate signs. But Burnside isn't quite satisfied, and as he saunters to the car with the signed documents, he decides to take a final punch at the kangaroo who stands tranquilly in the yard.

He shaped up like a boxer to Chifley. As Gus had said, it was because of their pugilist posture that kangaroos had suffered this indignity for two hundred years or more, from the days of Georgian bare-fist fighting, imported on the same transports as the fly boys and girls of the East End. The first European ashore had wondered if the European could live here and if the flow of Christ's blood had touched the place. The second European ashore, slackmouthed and a joker, had shaped up to the continent's antique marsupial. Gidday, mate, want to fight?

The tradition of oafdom which had found its high-water mark in Burnside was about to take that old hackneyed direction. Was about to box Chifley's ear to punish him for his delicate forepaws and the appalling delicacy of the way he held them.

(p. 216)

Through fear and instinct the animal returns the blow, shattering Burnside's pelvis and rendering him immobile in the dirt. Gus immediately realizes that the police will, at the very least, execute the kangaroo now that it has attacked Burnside. At the worst, they will turn him into a media spectacle. Kate, for whom the beast has now become a talisman, begs him to spare the animal. This is a moment of crisis so powerful that it elicits the entire story from Kate. She finally explains that her children were killed in a fire that swept the house while she was with her father. The only thing saved was a bottle of vodka. What she remembers most of the disaster is her husband's accusation that she should have been there with the children. She can't help but think he was right. She believes her children's death is her fault.

Kate breaks under the strain and is taken from the Outback to a sanatorium. When she improves, Uncle Frank reveals some startling information. Motivated by a strange coloration he happened to notice in the vodka bottle taken from the house, he has had it tested. The lab report shows the bottle was laced with a strong sedative, strong enough that one drink would have put her to sleep for several hours. Now Kate begins to realize the awful truth of her children's death. As the horrible story of that night unfolds, she begins to recognize that she is free of blame. Paul, expecting the children to be at their dancing lessons and Kate to be home alone with her afternoon drink, had drugged the vodka and hired Burnside to plant an arcing device in their electric box. She was the aim of his murderous intention. In an awful twist of fate, he wanted his wife dead and, instead, killed his children.

Kate travels to escape her tragic past, but when the book concludes, we realize that her journey provides not Lethe-like forgetfulness but a greater insight into the place of suffering and redemption in the human experience. However, reviewers have disagreed over how well the novel accomplishes its moral and philosophical aims. For Merle Rubin and Constance Markey, the book disappoints because, as Markey argues, the "melodramatic close punctuated by sweet revenge and just deserts suggests a television miniseries rather than real tragedy." Nevertheless, the essential Keneally questions persist: What is the role of the individual in the scheme of things? How does evil shape the human drama? What are the possibilities for enlightenment and renewal?

CONCLUSION

KENEALLY is known for choosing strong, interesting material for his novels, yet the question still to be determined is how well he handles those materials. At present, critical judgments on this matter range broadly. Paul Baumann pronounces him "an assiduous craftsman, a subtle historian [who] renders with indelible detail the idiosyncratic texture of an epoch" (p. 395); Raymon Sokolov calls him "an honest workman"; and Merle Rubin, "a com-

petent, pedestrian writer" who produces "credible fictional versions [of history and current events] while providing a relatively painless good read." With *The Chant of Jimmie Blacksmith* now included as a staple of secondary curriculum, Keneally's place in Australian literary culture seems secure. How he will fare in a larger literary tradition remains to be seen; however, given his Republican sentiments, figuring a place for himself in a British tradition must provoke, at the very least, a strong ambivalence. Regardless, however, of the final estimation of the literary merit of his work, one must recognize, as Terrence Rafferty suggests, the dazzling pace and the chancy tenor of Keneally's ambitious career. We have here, Rafferty tells us, "a reckless, heroic novelist, not a timid one." It is an estimation that at once pays homage to Keneally's Australian spirit and, at the same time, rings true.

SELECTED BIBLIOGRAPHY

I. FICTION, NONFICTION, AND DRAMA. *A Place at Whitton* (London, 1964); *The Fear* (Melbourne, 1965), rev. and repub. as *By the Line* (St. Lucia, Queensland, 1989); *Bring Larks and Heroes* (Melbourne, 1967); *Childermas* (Sydney, 1968); *Three Cheers for the Paraclete* (Sydney, 1968); *The Survivor* (Sydney, 1969); *A Dutiful Daughter* (Sydney, 1971); *An Awful Rose* (Sydney, 1972); *The Chant of Jimmie Blacksmith* (Sydney, 1972); *Blood Red, Sister Rose* (London, 1974); *Gossip from the Forest* (London, 1975); *Halloran's Little Boat* (Ringwood, Vic., 1975); *Moses the Lawgiver* (London, 1975); *Season in Purgatory* (London, 1976); *Victim of the Aurora* (London, 1977); *Ned Kelly and the City of Bees* (London, 1978); *Confederates* (London, 1979); *Passenger* (London, 1979).

The Cut-Rate Kingdom (Sydney, 1980), repr. as a book (London, 1984); *Bullie's House* (Sydney, 1981); *Schindler's Ark* (London, 1982), published as *Schindler's List* in the United States (New York, 1982); *Outback* (Sydney, 1983); *A Family Madness* (London, 1985); *The Playmaker* (London, 1987); *Act of Grace* (London, 1988), by William Coyle; *Towards Asmara* (London, 1989), published as *To Asmara* in the United States; *Chief of Staff* (London, 1991), by William Coyle; *Flying Hero Class* (London, 1991); *Now and in Time to Be: Ireland and the Irish* (Sydney, 1991); *The Place Where Souls Are Born: A Journey into the American Southwest* (London, 1992); *Woman of the Inner Sea* (London, 1992); *The Utility Player: The Des Hasler Story* (Sydney, 1993); *Our Republic* (Melbourne, 1993), also published as *Memoirs from a Young Republic* (London, 1993); *Jacko* (Port Melbourne, Vic., 1993; London, 1994), published as *Jacko:*

The Great Intruder in the United States; *A River Town* (London, 1995); *Homebush Boy* (London, 1996).

II. ARTICLES. "The Novelist's Poison," in *Australian Author* 1, no. 4 (1969); "Doing Research for Historical Novels," in *Australian Author* 7, no. 1 (1975); "My Fiction and the Aboriginal," in *Writers in East-West Encounters: New Cultural Bearings,* ed. by Guy Amirthanayagam (London, 1982); "Here Is Nature Reversed," with Patsy Adam-Smith and Robyn Davidson, in *Beyond the Dreamtime* (Melbourne, 1987); "World's Worse End?" in *Antipodes* 2 (spring 1988).

III. REVIEWS AND CRITICAL STUDIES. Kerin Cantrell, "Perspective on Thomas Keneally," in *Southerly* 28 (1968); Laurie Clancy, "Conscience and Corruption: Thomas Keneally's Three Novels," in *Meanjin* 27 (1968); Brian Kiernan, "Thomas Keneally and the Australian Novel: A Study of *Bring Larks and Heroes,*" in *Southerly* 28 (1968); Robert Burns, "Out of Context: A Study of Thomas Keneally's Novels," in *Australian Literary Studies* 4, no. 1 (1969); Michael Wilding, "Two Cheers for Keneally," in *Southerly* 29 (1969).

Brian Kiernan, "Fable or Novel? The Development of Thomas Keneally," in *Meanjin* 31 (1972); Anthony Thwaite, "The Chant of Jimmie Blacksmith," in *New York Times Book Review* (27 August 1972); John Beston, "Keneally's Violence," in *Journal of Commonwealth Literature* 9 (1974); Terry Sturm, "Thomas Keneally and Australian Racism: *The Chant of Jimmie Blacksmith,*" in *Southerly* 33 (1973); John Beston, "An Interview with Thomas Keneally," in *World Literature Written in English* 12, no. 1 (1973); W. S. Ramson, "The Chant of Jimmie Blacksmith: Taking Cognisance of Keneally," in *The Australian Experience: Essays on Australian Novels,* ed. by Ramson (Canberra, 1974); D. R. Burns, "The Way of Extravagance— Randolph Stow and Thomas Keneally," in his *The Directions of Australian Fiction, 1920–1974* (Melbourne, 1975); Bruce Cook, "Suspicions of Sainthood," in *Washington Post* (26 January 1975); F. C. Molloy, "An Irish Conflict in *Bring Larks and Heroes,*" in *Australian Literary Studies* 7 (1976); George Steiner, "Petrified Forest," *New Yorker* (23 August 1976); Michael Cotter, "The Image of the Aboriginal in Three Modern Australian Novels," in *Meanjin* 36 (1977); Jonathan Yardley, "Bloody Good Novel," in *Washington Post Book World* (20 February 1977); Peter Ackroyd, "Burning Down," in *The Spectator* (3 September 1977); Vivian Fuchs, "Polluting the Ice-Cap," in *Times Literary Supplement* (14 October 1977); Helen Daniel, "Purpose and the Racial Outsider: *Burn* and *The Chant of Jimmie Blacksmith,*" in *Southerly* 38 (1978); Chris Tiffin, "Victims Black and White: Thomas Keneally's *The Chant of Jimmie Blacksmith,*" in *Studies in the Recent Australian Novel,* ed. by K. G. Hamilton (St. Lucia, Queensland, 1978); Jonathan Yardley, "Murder on Ice," in *Washington Post Book World* (26 March 1978); Alan McLeod, "Australia: A Victim of the Aurora," in *World Literature Today*

52, no. 4 (autumn 1978); Veronica Brady, "The Most Frightening Rebellion: The Recent Novels of Thomas Keneally," in *Meanjin* 38 (1979); Marianne Ehrhardt, "Thomas Keneally. A Checklist," in *Australian Literary Studies* 9, no. 1(1979); D. J. Enright, "Fortunate Foetus," in *Listener* (25 January 1979); Hermione Lee, "A Womb with a View," in *Observer* (21 January 1979); Adrian Mitchell, "Thomas Keneally and the Scheme of Things," in *Australian Literary Studies* 9, no. 1 (1979); Blake Morrison, "The Wise Womb," in *New Statesman* (19 January 1979); Andrew Morton, "Shenandoah Shenanigans," in *Times Literary Supplement* (23 November 1979); Michael Ratcliff, "Booker Dark Horse," *New Statesman* (2 November 1979); Henry Reynolds, "Jimmy Governor and Jimmie Blacksmith," in *Australian Literary Studies* 9, no. 1 (1979).

Jeffrey Burke, "Tales of Sympathy and a Novel of War," in *New York Times Book Review* (5 October 1980); Edmund Fuller, "Current Books in Review: 'Passenger,'" *Swanee Review* 1 (winter 1980); Frances McInherny, "Women and Myth in Thomas Keneally's Fiction," in *Meanjin* 40 (1981); Frances McInherny, "Thomas Keneally's 'Innocent' Men," in *Australian Literary Studies* 10, no. 1 (1981); Peter Kemp, "Prize Fighters," in *Listener* (14 October 1982); Lorna Sage, "A Factory for Lives," in *Observer* (17 October 1982); Paul Zweig, "A Good Man in a Bad Time," in *New York Times Book Review* (24 October 1982); D. J. Enright, "Fouling up the System," in *Times Literary Supplement* (29 October 1982); Marion Glastonbury, "Too Grateful," in *The New Statesman* (5 November 1982); John Frow, "The Chant of Thomas Keneally," in *Australian Literary Studies* 10, no. 3 (1983); Michael Hollington, "The Ned Kelly of Cracow: Keneally's 'Schindler's Ark,'" in *Meanjin* 42, no. 1 (1983); Michael Hulse, "Virtue and the Philosophic Innocent: The British Reception of *Schindler's Ark,*" in *Critical Quarterly* 25 (winter 1983); Shirley Walker, "Thomas Keneally and 'the Special Agonies of Being a Woman,'" in *Who Is She? Images of Women in Australian Fiction,* ed. by Shirley Williams, (St. Lucia, 1983, and New York, 1983); Alan Ross, "Voice in the Wilderness," in *Times Literary Supplement* (16 December 1983); A. N. Wilson, "Faith and Uncertainty," in *Encounter* (February 1983); John Mellors, "Australian Soul," in *Listener* 112, no. 2865 (July 5, 1984); Michael Wood, "Prince in a Wide Brown Land," in *Times Literary Supplement* no. 4274 (24 August 1984); Carmel Gaffney, "Keneally's Faction: *Schindler's Ark,*" in *Quadrant* 27, no. 7 (1985); Manly Johnson, "The Cut-Rate Kingdom," in *World Literature Today* (autumn 1985); Michael Wood, "Looted by History," in *Times Literary Supplement* (18 October 1985); John Sutherland, "Carrying on with a Foreign Woman," in *London Review of Books* 7, no. 19 (7 November 1985); Janice Chernekoff, "Thomas Keneally: An Annotated, Secondary Bibliography, 1979–1984," in *Bulletin of Bibliography* 43 (1986); Laurie Hergenhan, "Interview with Thomas Keneally," in *Australian Literary Studies* 12 (1986);

Terrence Rafferty, "Thomas Keneally Pleads Sanity," in *Village Voice* 31, no. 18 (6 May 1986); Susan Lardner, "Two in One," in *New Yorker* (19 May 1986); Robert Towers, "Breezy, Boozy, and Byelorussian," in *New York Times Book Review* (16 March 1986); Candida Baker, "Thomas Keneally," in her *Yacker 2: Australian Writers Talk About Their Work* (Sydney, 1987); David English, "History and the Refuge of Art: Thomas Keneally's Sense of the Past," in *Meridian* 6, no. 1 (1987), repr. *The Writer's Sense of the Past: Essays on Southeast Asian and Australian Literature,* ed. by Kirpal Singh (Singapore, 1987); Jennifer Krauss, "Outlandish Truths," in *New Republic* (4 January 1988); Manly Johnson, "Thomas Keneally's Nightmare of History," in *Antipodes* 3 (winter 1989); Irmtraud Petersson "'White Ravens' in a World of Violence: German Connections in Thomas Keneally's Fiction," in *Australian Literary Studies* 14, no. 2 (1989); Tracy Ware, "Of Irony and Institutions: Thomas Keneally's *Three Cheers for the Paraclete,*" in *Australian and New Zealand Studies in Canada* 2 (autumn 1989); Paul Baumann, "Never a Question of Easy Grace: Thomas Keneally's Fantastical Creatures," in *Commonweal* (14 July 1989); Robert Stone, "Imaginary People in a Real War," in *New York Times Book Review* (1 October 1989).

Patrick Buckridge, "Gossip and History in the Novels of Brian Penton and Thomas Keneally," in *Australian Literary Studies* 14 (1990); Thomas P. Coakley, "Thomas Keneally," in *International Literature in English: Essays on the Major Writers,* ed. by Robert L. Ross (New York, 1991); Genevieve Laigle, "The White World and Its Relationship with Aborigines in Keneally's *Chant of Jimmie Blacksmith,*" in *Commonwealth Essays and Studies* 14 (1991); Peter Quartermaine, *Thomas Keneally* (London, 1991); Val Taylor, "Mothers of Invention: Female Characters in *Our Country's Good* and *The Playmaker,*" in *Critical Survey* 3, no. 3 (1991); Duwell Martin and Laurie Hergenhan, eds., *The ALS Guide to Australian Writers* (St. Lucia, Queensland, 1992); Ray Willbanks, "Thomas Keneally," in *Speaking Volumes: Australian Writers and Their Work* (Ringwood, Vic., 1992); Constance Markey, "Kangaroo Dreams," in *Chicago Tribune* (28 February 1993); Merle Rubin, "Novels from Vietnam and Australia," in *Wall Street Journal* (22 March 1993); Terrence Rafferty, "A Man of Transactions," in *New Yorker* (20 December 1993); Donna Heiland, "History and Sublimity in Keneally's *The Playmaker,*" in *Australian and New Zealand Studies in Canada* 11 (1994); Thomas Fensch, ed., *Oskar Schindler and His List: The Man, the Book, the Film, the Holocaust and Its Survivors* (Forest Dale, Vt., 1995); Peter Pierce, "The Sites of War in the Fiction of Thomas Keneally," in *Australian Literary Studies* 12 (1986); Peter Pierce, *Australian Melodrama: Thomas Keneally's Fiction* (1995); Judith Weinraub, in *Washington Post* (30 May 1995); Robert E. Lynch, "Thomas Keneally," in *Contemporary Novelists* (London, 1996).

DAVID LODGE

(1935–)

A. Michael Matin

THE CAREER OF David Lodge, honorary professor of modern English literature at the University of Birmingham, where he taught from 1960 to 1987, has been anomalous in two major respects: he is one of only a handful of successful creative writers who have also enjoyed auspicious careers as scholarly academics (Vladimir Nabokov and Umberto Eco are also in this group), and he is one of the few internationally renowned British academics who have been products of neither Oxford nor Cambridge. His output as a scholar and critic has been prolific: he has published five volumes of academic scholarship, three volumes of occasional essays, two monographs, two edited readers, and innumerable articles and reviews. But he is most famous as a writer of fiction—particularly comic fiction—and his criticism has certainly received more attention than it would have had he not been a popular novelist. Of his ten novels, the three that comprise his trilogy on academia—*Changing Places* (1975), *Small World* (1984), and *Nice Work* (1988), the second and third of which were short-listed for the Booker Prize—are not only his best known but also his finest work. Lodge's fiction, which tends to be semiautobiographical, is pervaded by two themes: Catholicism and academia, subjects about which he has abundant firsthand knowledge. The fact that he is a professional scholar makes him intensely self-conscious about his literary debts, which he displays copiously. Yet while his novels are heavily intertextual, he has declined to participate in the sort of obscurantism that characterizes the work of some of the twentieth-century authors he admires and, to a limited extent, emulates—especially James Joyce. He has expressed his preference for being accessible rather than esoteric, and although his work is widely allusive and richly complex, he is neither pretentious nor offputting to the general reader. As he put it in a preface to a 1980 reprint of the inspired little farce *The British Museum Is Falling Down* (1965), a novel replete with allusions to canonical modernist writers,

I was well aware that the extensive use of parody and pastiche was a risky device. There was, in particular, the danger of puzzling and alienating the reader who wouldn't recognise the allusions. My aim was to make the narrative and its frequent shifts of style fully intelligible and satisfying to such a reader, while offering the more literary reader the extra entertainment of spotting the parodies.

(p. xix)

The sensitivity he has demonstrated on this matter throughout his career has rendered his fiction of continued interest and engagement to both the scholarly and the general reader.

LIFE AND LITERARY CRITICISM

DAVID Lodge, an only child, was born on 28 January 1935 in South London. While his mother's family was Catholic, his father's family was not, and their union was therefore termed "in Catholic circles a 'mixed marriage' " (*Write On*, p. 29). His father, William Frederick Lodge, was a dance-band musician, and his mother, Rosalie Marie, née Murphy, was a Roman Catholic of Irish-Belgian background. During World War II, between the ages of four and ten, Lodge lived through the bombing raids of the 1940 Battle of Britain and later the V1 and V2 rockets, or "buzz bombs," that caused much destruction and loss of life. In the 1976 essay "Memories of a Catholic Childhood" he has described the impact these events had on him during his early years: "The war meant separation from

363

my father, who served in the RAF, and a periodic 'evacuation' for my mother and me whenever bombing made London unsafe" (*Write On*, p. 28). He consequently attended several different schools, and in the war's final months he was one of only two boys in a class of girls at a Surrey convent school. During one raid, he recalls, the London suburban church in which he took his first communion was destroyed (p. 28). He has poignantly recounted these years, in fictionalized form, in the opening chapters of *Out of the Shelter* (1970), the most directly autobiographical of his novels.

In 1945, at war's end, Lodge was enrolled in the St. Joseph's Academy, a London Catholic grammar school, from which he graduated in 1952. Though his schooling was Catholic, "the atmosphere of home was not distinctively Catholic. . . . I had not brothers or sisters to reinforce the Catholic cultural code, and my friends in the same street happened not to be Catholic. The result was that as a child I always felt something of an outsider in the Church" (*Write On*, p. 29). In the 1982 essay "My Joyce" he has described the impact that James Joyce's *Portrait of the Artist as a Young Man* had on him when he was sixteen, asserting that it was through literature—specifically the Catholic novel—that he was able to overcome some of the difficulties he had with Catholic teachings, without abandoning them altogether, "by presenting authentic religious belief as something equally opposed to the materialism of the secular world and to the superficial pieties of parochial Catholicism" (*Write On*, p. 31). (Bernard Bergonzi and Thomas Woodman have analyzed several of his novels in the context of the "Catholic novel" genre.) He continues to be a practicing Catholic, although he describes himself as having given up the Church's metaphysical underpinnings.

In the summer of 1951, having spent his first fifteen years in England, Lodge's provincial outlook was challenged when he traveled to Heidelberg to stay with his Aunt Eileen, who was employed as a civilian secretary for the United States Army. He has described the event as "one of the formative experiences of my life" (*Out of the Shelter*, rev. ed., 1985, p. viii) and was particularly struck (in a way that would prefigure his experience of American consumer culture during the 1960s) by the sense of plenty and the hedonism he discovered in American-occupied Heidelberg—something he had

had little experience of in postwar Britain. He would return to Heidelberg in 1953 as a university student, and again in 1967 to do research for *Out of the Shelter*. The year following his initial trip to Heidelberg, he enrolled at University College, London, where he did his undergraduate work from 1952 to 1955 and took his bachelor's degree with honors. His undergraduate work was followed by two years of compulsory military service in the Royal Armoured Corps. Most of this time he was stationed as a clerk in Dorset, and he was released in August 1957, having reached the rank of acting corporal. He was to draw heavily on his experiences in the military for his second novel, *Ginger, You're Barmy* (1962). In the spring of 1957, during his last months in the service, he began work on *The Picturegoers*. After his stint in the military, he again enrolled at UCL, this time as a graduate student. He received his master's degree in 1959, having written a thesis entitled "The Catholic Novel in England from the Oxford Movement to the Present Day." The epic proportions of this thesis—Lodge characterized it (at 730 pages) as "monstrously long" (*The Picturegoers*, pp. viii, xv)—suggest the reservoirs of energy he would have to expend for literary production, a fact that would become evident in his subsequent prolific career both as a novelist and as a literary scholar. In May 1959 he married Mary Jacob, who came from a large Catholic family and had also been an English major at University College, London. Because he couldn't secure an academic position immediately, he took a job for a year with the British Council in London teaching English and literature to foreign students.

In 1960, the year of the birth of his first child, Julia, Lodge was appointed to a one-year position as a temporary lecturer in English at the University of Birmingham, one of the red-brick Midlands schools. It was also in 1960 that his first novel, *The Picturegoers*, was published. While publishing a novel at twenty-five (it had been completed at twenty-three) was a precocious achievement, at eighteen he had already written a novel entitled *The Devil, the World and the Flesh*, which he was unsuccessful in getting published. In 1961 he was rehired as an assistant lecturer at the University of Birmingham, where he would remain until his retirement from academia in 1987. In 1962, the year of the birth of his second child, Stephen, Lodge published his second novel, *Ginger, You're Barmy*, which, he has asserted in an essay accompanying a 1981 reprint of the text, "cleaves very closely to the contours of my own military service" (p. 213). In 1963 he collaborated with his University of Birmingham colleague and friend Malcolm Bradbury on a series of comic sketches entitled *Between These Four Walls*. It ran for a month at the Birmingham Repertory Theatre and gave Lodge a taste for the signature bristling comedy that would be evidenced in his subsequent fiction. His next novel, *The British Museum Is Falling Down*, was published in 1965, and he codedicated it to Bradbury, "whose fault it mostly is that I have tried to write a comic novel" (*British Museum*, 1980 repr., p. v). Lodge's and Bradbury's careers as English academics and comic novelists have so closely paralleled one another that Lodge "was once rung up by a man who asked me to settle a bet by declaring whether I was the same person as Malcolm Bradbury" (p. xix). These resemblances have been taken up by Peter Widdowson, Robert Morace, Brian Connery, and James Acheson, each of whom has discussed Lodge's and Bradbury's novels together.

In August 1964 Lodge traveled to America, with his wife and two children, on a Harkness Commonwealth Fellowship. He studied American literature at Brown University for seven months, and then the family toured the United States by automobile for two months. In 1966 his third child, Christopher, was born with Down's syndrome. In the same year he published a monograph, *Graham Greene* (he has identified the Catholic novelists Joyce, Greene, and Waugh as having strongly influenced his own writing, and he has devoted much of his critical energies to their work), as well as his first book of literary criticism, *Language of Fiction: Essays in Criticism and Verbal Analysis of the English Novel*, for which he was awarded a Ph.D. by the University of Birmingham in 1967. The thesis of the latter is that novelistic language is as important as poetic language. (Earlier criticism, especially that under the sway of the school of New Criticism that was ascendant in the 1940s and 1950s, had tended to extol poetic language at the expense of novelistic language.) Lodge argued that "if we are right to regard the art of poetry as essentially an art of language, then so is the art of the novel," and that "the critic of the novel has no special dispensation from that close and sensitive engagement with language which we naturally expect from the critic of poetry" (p. 47). As with all of his critical works, *Language of Fiction* consists of a series of essays that are more or less loosely organized under a general rubric or unifying thesis.

In 1969 Lodge was a visiting professor at the University of California at Berkeley during a time of upheaval and student protests over the war in Vietnam. In 1970 *Out of the Shelter* appeared, which marked a departure from the comic mode of *The British Museum Is Falling Down* in favor of a return to the realistic mode of his first two novels. In 1971 his monograph *Evelyn Waugh* was published, as was his second book of literary criticism, *The Novelist at the Crossroads, and Other Essays on Fiction*. In this year he began writing *Changing Places*, the first volume of his trilogy on academia. Partly consisting of fictionalized accounts of experiences he had at Berkeley in 1969, *Changing Places* appeared in 1975 and was awarded both the Hawthornden Prize and the *Yorkshire Post* Fiction Prize.

In 1976, in the wake of the popular and critical success of *Changing Places*, Lodge was promoted to the rank of professor of modern English literature at the University of Birmingham (in Britain the title of "Professor" carries something like the prestige that "University Professor" does in the United States) and was invited to become a Fellow of the Royal Society of Literature. In 1977 he published *The Modes of Modern Writing: Metaphor, Metonymy, and the Typology of Modern Literature*, in which— continuing his project of justifying the novel form on aesthetic grounds—he argued that the Russian linguist Roman Jakobson's categories of metaphor and metonymy provided a basis for a typology of all twentieth-century novels; in a subsequent crystallization of the book's chief contention, he maintained that "Jakobson's category of metonymy opened up the possibility of a formalist criticism of the realistic novel that would not inevitably find it aesthetically wanting" (*After Bakhtin*, p. 6). In 1981 he continued his explorations of structuralism with *Working with Structuralism: Essays and Reviews on Nineteenth- and Twentieth-Century Literature*, which is a looser collection than the intensely thesis-driven *Modes of Modern Writing*. Lodge has identified himself as "a sort of popularizer or domesticator or, some would say, vulgarizer of structuralism" (*Contemporary Authors* interview, p. 301), and his detractors have taken him to task for his efforts in these books. The Marxist literary scholar Terry Eagleton, one of Lodge's most strident critics, has asserted that "his theoretical writing is not only derivative and unadventurous, but . . . given over to domesticating and defusing otherwise disruptive European insights for the purposes of home consumption" (p. 97). Philip Smallwood and Peter Widdowson have leveled similar charges.

In 1980 Lodge published his sixth novel, *How Far Can You Go?* (it appeared in America two years later under the title *Souls and Bodies*). Its primary subject is the difficulties and moral dilemmas experienced by Catholics over the Church's proscriptions against birth control. For its sensitive and probing treatment of a complex social issue, it was awarded the Whitbread Book of the Year Prize. In 1984 *Small World*, the panoramic sequel to *Changing Places*, was published. It was short-listed for the Booker Prize, and four years later it would be adapted as a serial by Granada Television. In 1986 *Write On: Occasional Essays, '65–'85* was published, with a dedication to Lodge's son, Christopher, who had been born with Down's syndrome twenty years earlier. The volume's royalties, Lodge explains in the introduction, go to a charity organization that provides sheltered communities for mentally handicapped adults. In 1987, at the age of fifty-two, Lodge took early retirement from the University of Birmingham in order to pursue his interests in creative writing on a full-time basis. In 1988 he published *Nice Work,* the final volume of his trilogy on academia. An incisive portrait of how English academia and industry were faring under Margaret Thatcher's Conservative administration, *Nice Work* is the most politically engaged of his novels. It, too, was short-listed for the Booker Prize and won the *Sunday Express* Book of the Year award. In 1989, a year in which Lodge chaired the panel of judges for the Booker Prize, he adapted *Nice Work* as a four-part televised serial for the BBC, and it went on to win the Royal Television Society's Award for best drama serial of the year. He would continue his television work with a 1994 adaptation of Charles Dickens' *Martin Chuzzlewit.* In 1990 his first (and, to date, only) full-length play, *The Writing Game*, was performed. He has since published two ruminatively existential novels— *Paradise News* (1991) and *Therapy* (1995)—both of which return to the religious questions he had pursued in his earlier fiction.

In 1990 Lodge published his last book of scholarly criticism, *After Bakhtin: Essays on Fiction and Criticism.*

(*The Art of Fiction* [1992] and *The Practice of Writing* [1996] consist of essays written after he gave up his academic post in 1987 and are intended for a general readership.) *After Bakhtin* is composed of a collection of essays inspired by the Russian literary theorist Mikhail Bakhtin, in whose recently discovered work Lodge identifies the justification for the position he steadfastly maintained throughout his career as a scholar—that the novel ought properly to be understood as an artistic genre no less worthy of careful scrutiny than poetry. In fact, whereas in his first critical book, *Language of Fiction,* Lodge attempted to elevate novelistic prose to the status of poetic language, in *After Bakhtin* he actually suggests that novelistic prose is superior to poetic language because it is "polyphonic," that is, it is able simultaneously to represent a multiplicity of voices (p. 7). Having made this claim, he proceeds disdainfully to characterize contemporary academic literary criticism and theory as basically "not . . . a contribution to human knowledge, but the demonstration of a professional mastery by translating known facts into more and more arcane metalanguages" (p. 8). In a rather inflated estimation, he offers Bakhtinian theory as a panacea for an increasingly onanistic academic criticism held in thrall to poststructuralism:

> Bakhtin's theory has . . . given new hope to literary critics who were beginning to wonder whether there was a life after post-structuralism. To those of a Marxist persuasion he has restored a non-vulgar concept of the socially constructive function of language and literature; to liberal humanist scholars he has restored the legitimacy of a diachronic, philologically based study of literature; to formalists he has opened up new possibilities of analysing and categorizing narrative discourse.
>
> (p. 4)

Ironically, these pronouncements of "new hope" for academic criticism appear in the context of Lodge's farewell to academe. In the opening essay of *After Bakhtin* he offers a retrospective account both of his own career as a literary scholar and of the profession generally, in which he makes his position clear. Complaining of the "barrier of non-comprehension between academic and non-academic discussion of literature," he asserts that his own "bridging posture" as both creative writer and academic scholar "has become increasingly difficult to maintain as the professionalization of academic criticism has opened up a widening gap between it and 'lay' discussion of literature" (pp. 7–8). As he would later state in his essay "The Novelist Today: Still at the Crossroads?" (contained in *The Practice of Writing*), which sums up and affirms his position, "One component of that decision [to leave the academy] was a feeling that it was becoming harder and harder to make meaningful connections between an academic criticism increasingly dominated by questions of Theory, and the practice of creative writing" (p. 4). As early as 1971 he had acknowledged that "literary criticism, like any other highly developed intellectual discipline, cannot entirely dispense with jargon, but," he contended, "it has a responsibility to maintain as much continuity as possible with human discourse" (*The Novelist at the Crossroads*, p. 41). By the mid-1980s he had come to feel that this vital continuity had been all but severed, and his decision to leave academe naturally followed. Although he has retired from the University of Birmingham's English department, he continues to live in Birmingham and has kept up his ties to the university.

EARLY NOVELS

LODGE's first novel, *The Picturegoers* (1960), set in a London suburb in the mid-1950s, is organized around various characters' weekend outings to the local movie theater. As Lodge succinctly puts it, the focus of the plot is "the structural equivalence/difference between Church and Cinema, and the see-saw relationship between hero and heroine" (p. ix). The "hero" is Mark Underwood, an aspiring writer and an undergraduate student of English literature who boards with the Mallory family; he dates the "heroine," Clare, who is one of eight Mallory children. Although raised a Catholic, Mark is a skeptic, whereas Clare has recently returned from a convent, having aspired to become a nun. The novel depicts a variety of minor characters who are the foci of several subplots. Maurice Berkley, the manager of the movie theater, is having an affair with the now-pregnant usherette Doreen, but his wife won't grant him a divorce; furthermore, his decision to screen sophisticated foreign films has flopped, and it isn't until he has pandered to mass culture by showing rock and roll films that his business be-

comes successful. Damien O'Brien, a distant cousin to Clare who rooms next door to the Mallorys, is a pest with designs on her. Len and Bridget are a couple who, despite their families' objections, marry at the end of the novel. Father Kipling, the local parish priest and aptly named staunch defender of embattled antiquated values, attends the theater thinking he is going to see *The Song of Bernadette* but comes on the wrong night and subsequently launches a crusade against the film industry, which he deems a threat to Christian society.

The real focus of the story, however, is Mark and Clare's relationship. Mark schemes to win Clare over by attending church services, believing that, "like a trout, she could be caught by very skilfully and delicately tickling her religious susceptibility" (p. 103). Ironically, however, it is Mark himself who succumbs: one night he spontaneously prays (p. 95), and during a subsequent Eucharist service "belief leapt in his mind like a child in the womb" (p. 111). Paradoxically, as Mark returns to the faith, Clare loses hers: "Like a see-saw, her drop had sent him soaring into religiosity" (p. 146). As they become increasingly intimate, she confides to him that she did not leave the convent voluntarily but was expelled after a scandal precipitated by her unconsummated "love affair" (p. 152) with a girl named Hilda Syms and the latter's suicide attempt. Clare later discovers that Hilda, since leaving the convent, has become obsessed with the film star "James Dreme" (James Dean). Mark eventually decides that he wants to become a priest and tells this to an embittered Clare, whose hopes of marrying him are dashed. Their role reversal is thus complete.

For a first novel, *The Picturegoers* has much to recommend it. It shows the promise that would be fulfilled in Lodge's ensuing fiction; in particular, it displays flashes of the talent for comedy that would emerge five years later in *The British Museum Is Falling Down*. But Lodge cast his net fairly wide in *The Picturegoers* in terms of characters and subplots, and critics of the novel have found fault with its "distracted" quality. Another problem is that Mark's conversion is effected with a rather heavy hand. As Lodge himself asserted in a preface to a 1992 reprint of the novel, the latter's tendentious treatment of religion is incongruous with his "present demythologized, provisional, and in many ways agnostic theological perspective"

(p. ix); in general, the text "betrayed the youthfulness and inexperience of its author all too clearly" (p. vii).

Despite its shortcomings, the novel's depiction of the conflict between a traditional culture organized around religion and the seductive pull of a burgeoning culture of consumerism is dealt with innovatively, with the movie theater supplanting the church as the communal space. Father Kipling's crusade is "a losing battle," for "the cinema, or the whole system of processed mass-entertainment for which it stood, had already become an acceptable substitute for religion" (p. 107). Apropos of this contention, a film trailer is characterized as offering "a fabulously furnished penthouse, and the favours of awesomely shaped women [as] a more satisfactory conception of paradise than the sexless and colourless Christian promise" (p. 58). Ultimately, the text's depiction of the supplanting of church by cinema is ambivalent. On the one hand, Hilda's fanatical worship of "James Dreme" after her expulsion from the convent (she dresses in black, has been to see his films scores of times, and even owns "his death-mask"— a modern-day Shroud of Turin [p. 193]) is a debased and unregenerate travesty of Christian worship. On the other hand, the novel attempts to put an upbeat spin on less fanatical strains of this phenomenon: consumerism and mass culture, it turns out, have their salvific potential as well. The climactic "service" in the movie theater, in which "Rock Around the Clock" is played to the ecstatic gyrations of the youthful audience, demonstrates

the constant enigma of modern civilization: how the cheap, the shoddy, the manufactured, still held an indestructible seed of truth and vitality, could still be a source of salvation . . . the way a plastic crucifix could inspire the rarest worship. This Rock and Roll was a manufactured music, with scarcely a shred of genuine folk content. . . . Yet in this cinema this evening it had awakened how many deadened souls to some kind of life?

(p. 228)

Although tensions between the sacred and the secular pervade Lodge's oeuvre, it would not be until two decades later, with the publication of *How Far Can You Go?* (a less tendentious treatment of this subject), that they would again occupy the thematic center of one of his novels.

Ginger, You're Barmy (1962), Lodge's second novel, is putatively written by Jonathan Browne and is about the circumstances surrounding his two-year stint in the National Service in the mid-1950s. The narrative temporally oscillates between his weeks of basic training and his final week in the army two years later; it is framed by a prologue and an epilogue "written" three years after he has returned to civilian life. Jonathan reports for duty, having just completed a bachelor's degree in English literature, for which he has received a first (special honors). He goes through basic training with his failed classmate Mike Brady ("Ginger"), a tempestuous Catholic from a large and vehemently nationalistic Irish family. Mike differs in every respect from Jonathan, who is prudent, scholarly, agnostic, politically uncommitted, and an only child. During basic training they befriend Percy Higgins, a frail and clumsy young man who has unsuccessfully attempted to become a priest and who is mercilessly abused by the other men. Much of the narrative is taken up with a detailing of the sundry discomforts and outrages to common sense of army life. Percy is hounded by Corporal Baker during rifle practice and then shoots himself, although it is unclear whether he is a suicide or merely a victim of his own clumsiness (his last word is "accident"). Mike subsequently identifies a nemesis in Baker, yet he recognizes that at the inquest he and Jonathan must play down the corporal's possible role in Percy's death in order to prevent it from being categorized a suicide (a mortal sin for Catholics). One night, while they are on guard duty together, Mike enlists Jonathan in a scheme allegedly to scare Corporal Baker; in fact, he knocks Baker unconscious with a pikestaff and gives him a concussion. Mike is charged with assault, and his fate is sealed when it is revealed that he had written a letter to Percy's father blaming Baker for Percy's death. Jonathan, acting as a go-between for an incarcerated Mike and his girlfriend, Pauline Vickers, becomes romantically involved with her. Jonathan inadvertently assists Mike in breaking out of his holding cell by conveying a message to a friend of Mike's who is in the Irish Republican Army. However, he is instrumental in foiling a subsequent IRA plot to raid the camp, during which Mike is rearrested.

After Jonathan has completed his two years of service, he and Pauline holiday in Palma, where he is more interested in writing a novel based on his experiences in the army than he is in her. After completing a draft of the project, however, he does deflower and (to his chagrin) impregnate her. They subsequently marry, and in the epilogue we learn that he has taken a job as a schoolteacher in the prison town where Mike is incarcerated. Jonathan has visited Mike monthly in prison, and the narrative ends on the day he is to be released.

Until the publication of *Therapy* in 1995, *Ginger, You're Barmy* had been Lodge's only novel to be narrated in the first person. Lodge admits that he wrote the book as "a personal settling of scores" (repr. 1981, p. 217) against an establishment toward which he had developed a visceral antipathy. Reflecting on an exasperating encounter with an absurdly impenetrable army bureaucracy, Jonathan complains, "All my arguments broke on this granite wall of irrationality" (p. 49). The plot of *Ginger* (with the exception of the puzzling conclusion) is more tightly conceived than that of the sprawling *Picturegoers*, and Lodge credits Graham Greene with having inspired its form: "After the novel had been published, I realized that this structure had been borrowed, subliminally, from *The Quiet American*" (p. 215). Although some of *Ginger*'s scenes are based on Lodge's own experiences, the plot itself, he has asserted, is entirely fictional, "since my own military experience was almost totally devoid of narrative interest" (p. 213). In an essay accompanying a 1981 reprint of the novel, Lodge, distancing himself from his politically incorrect narrator, reports that "in the twenty years since the novel was written Jonathan had acquired some new vices that neither he nor his creator had heard of—sexism, for instance" (p. 214). Indeed, there are a few regrettable passages that emerge from the pen of his narrator and that jar on the modern ear. For example, Jonathan, assuming that women work in the army because they enjoy being ogled, supposes that "it must be exhilarating to know that you are being mentally raped a hundred times a day" (p. 102). Another sign of the times in the text is the prudish "Author's Note" that warns of "the coarseness of soldiers' speech and behaviour" that some readers might find "disturbing or distasteful" (in fact, the language used in the novel is heavily censored and euphemistic). Lodge would later observe that *Ginger* was published shortly after the celebrated trial of D. H. Lawrence's *Lady Chatter-*

ley's Lover, the outcome of which opened the floodgates to so-called obscenity in fiction, but that "this development was . . . too late to affect" his own novel (p. 217).

Lodge's next effort, *The British Museum Is Falling Down* (1965), describes an eventful day in the life of Adam Appleby, a twenty-five-year-old doctoral student of English literature. Frustrated with (yet obeying) the Catholic proscription against any form of birth control other than the rhythm method, he and his wife, Barbara, have three children, and they are worried that she might be pregnant again. Adam spends his days researching the painfully dull subject of his thesis, "The Structure of Long Sentences in Three Modern English Novels" (p. 54), in the reading room of the British Museum. He is in search of an academic appointment and is counseled by his supervisor that he must "publish or perish!" (p. 76). In fact, Adam's sole scholarly effort, an article on the minor writer "Egbert Merrymarsh," has been rejected by nine journals.

Desperate for something to publish, he pays a visit to the home of Mrs. Rottingdean, who claims to be Merrymarsh's niece and offers to sell him a Merrymarsh manuscript. The manuscript turns out to be unpublishably banal, but as Adam is perusing it Rottingdean's seventeen-year-old daughter, Virginia, informs him that Merrymarsh was, in fact, her mother's lover, not her uncle, and that she has proof: love letters and a book manuscript that recounts their torrid relationship in thinly veiled fictional terms. She offers him the work in exchange for sex, and they arrange to meet that evening. The prospect of adultery is daunting to Adam, but later in the day, emboldened by alcohol at a departmental sherry party, he resolves that he must get the manuscript from Virginia if he is to secure an academic job and support his family. He works up the courage to purchase contraceptives, but as he enters the store—in a virtually supernatural intervention—he is thwarted by an encounter with the strident parish curate, Father Finbar Flannagan. Condomless, he goes to see Virginia anyway and examines the manuscript and letters, which prove her story. She accosts him and removes his trousers, but he is saved from the obligation to have sex with her when she discovers that he is wearing panties (they are his wife's, and he is wearing them for an entirely practical reason—he had no clean underwear that morning). Despite her disappointment, she allows him to keep the papers. The slapstick culminates when the axe-wielding thugs who guard Virginia get wise to the situation. Adam beats a hasty retreat, but his scooter subsequently catches fire and burns along with the prize papers. During his walk home, he happens upon a wealthy American who has come to England with the idea of purchasing the British Museum and transporting it, stone by stone and book by book, to the campus of a little college in Colorado. The untenability of this project having dawned on him, the American now needs a book and manuscript buyer, and he solves Adam's fiscal problems by hiring him.

Whereas Lodge's first two novels are works of traditional realism, *The British Museum Is Falling Down* is a formally experimental comedy. Lodge has described how the text displays what he terms his own "Anxiety of Influence" (the phrase is that of the American literary critic Harold Bloom) in "ten passages of parody or pastiche in the novel" in which well-known modernist writers are mimicked (pp. xvi–xvii). Like the book upon which it is most closely modeled (Joyce's *Ulysses*), this novel deals with events that occur within a single day, ending with a stream-of-consciousness narration by the protagonist's wife. The heavily intertextual aspect of Lodge's novel is implied in Adam's mock theory of narrative entropy, which he both articulates and (being himself a fictional character) ironically exemplifies during the sherry-party scene, which is itself, as Lodge points out, "a kind of distillation of the post-[Kingsley] Amis campus novel" (p. xvi). Adam asks,

Has it ever occurred to you how novelists are *using up* experience at a dangerous rate? . . . There've been such a fantastic number of novels written in the last couple of centuries that they've just about exhausted the possibilities of life. So all of us, you see, are really enacting events that have already been written about in some novel or other.

(pp. 129–130)

The British Museum Is Falling Down is also the first of Lodge's novels to take as its subject the Catholic church's teachings on birth control. Lodge shared his protagonist's hopes that the Second Vatican Council, which convened in 1962 and "on which [Adam] and Barbara and most of their Catholic friends had pinned their hopes for a humane and liberal life in the Church" (p. 34), would relax the strictures on birth control. (It did not.) The sexual relations of the novel's paradigmatic Catholic couple are "forced into a curious pattern: three weeks of patient graph-plotting, followed by a few nights of frantic love-making" (p. 14). Adam's sense of the absurdity of the situation is expressed in his imaginary entry for a Martian encyclopedia: "Martian archaeologists have learned to identify the domiciles of Roman Catholics by the presence of large numbers of complicated graphs, calendars, small booklets full of figures, and quantities of broken thermometers" (p. 16). Despite the novel's ostensibly dismissive treatment of Church teachings, Lodge observes that his book is hardly revolutionary: "Like most traditional comedy, *The British Museum Is Falling Down* is essentially conservative . . . , the conflicts and misunderstandings it deals with being resolved without fundamentally disturbing the system which provoked them" (p. xiv).

Out of the Shelter (1970), Lodge's fourth novel, begins with five-year-old Timothy Young's experience of the 1940 Blitz in London. During air raids he and his parents go to a shelter located on the property of family friends, Jack and Nora and their young daughter Jill. During one raid Jill leaves the shelter, her mother follows, and both are killed. (Jack, a member of the Royal Air Force, is later killed in a bombing run over Germany.) Timothy and his mother are subsequently removed from London for safety.

After briefly covering the events of the next eleven years, the novel focuses on a four-week trip to Heidelberg in 1951 undertaken by Timothy, now aged sixteen, to visit his twenty-seven-year-old sister Kath, a secretary with the United States Army. On the way to Heidelberg he meets the American intellectual Don Kowalski, a socialist who has been jailed briefly because, being an atheist, his claim to conscientious objector status has not been recognized. Once in Heidelberg, where he resides in a room at a women's hostel vacated by a friend of Kath (now called Kate), Timothy is surprised by the abundance of consumer goods and the conspicuous consumption he witnesses in Germany; by contrast, the postwar years in Britain have been characterized by continued rationing and general austerity. Timothy's experiences in Germany include: excursions with Kate's hedonistic circle of friends, the two most significant of whom are the Americans Vince and Greg; spending time with Don, who briefly becomes involved with Kate; and spending time with Rudolph, a one-armed German who had been a prisoner of war in England. As Timothy's cultural horizons are broadened, so too are his erotic horizons. He declines the offer of his libidinous next-door neighbor, Jinx Dobell (whose sounds of frequent lovemaking have tantalized him), to relieve him of his virginity, but he later has his first quasi-sexual encounter with a girl his own age named Gloria Rose. The novel culminates with a party hosted by Vince and Greg shortly after they have been arrested and released in East Germany under mysterious circumstances. Vince startles everyone by jokingly appearing in a Nazi officer's uniform, and in a Dionysian outburst his guests proceed to avail themselves of his tremendous cache of Nazi paraphernalia and do likewise. The scandalous festivities are brought to a sobering halt by the sudden appearance of Don, who has learned that Vince and Greg have attempted to sell a list containing the names of ex-Nazis employed in the government to the East Germans, and (as he had suspected) that they are homosexual lovers. After this pivotal episode Timothy returns to England, considerably more experienced than when he arrived four weeks earlier. An epilogue, set fourteen years later in California, shows Timothy, now aged thirty, with a Jewish wife and two children. Kate, who has declined a proposal from Don, lives in the States and has never married.

Lodge has remarked that *Out of the Shelter* is the most autobiographical as well as the least popular of his novels (pp. ix, xv). Its events are largely based on his own experiences during World War II in England and a 1951 summer visit to Heidelberg to stay with his Aunt Eileen—the model for Kate, who is purposively described as being "more like an aunt than a sister" to Timothy (p. 93)—to whom the book is dedicated. The text in many respects follows the pattern of the traditional bildungsroman, and Lodge has identified Joyce's classic of the genre, *Portrait,* as well as Henry James' novel of transatlantic culture shock, *The Ambassadors,* as "its most obvious literary models" (p. ix). As with *The Picturegoers* a decade earlier, one of the chief themes of *Out of the Shelter* is that of the temptations of consumerism; Lodge has remarked that through his experience of "the American expatriate

community in Germany in 1951 I had been granted a privileged foretaste of the hedonistic, materialistic good life that the British, and most of the other developed or developing nations of the world, would soon aspire to . . ." (p. x).

The hedonism and frivolity of the American expatriates in *Out of the Shelter* are epitomized in the closeted gay couple, Vince and Greg, whose depiction warrants examination. Shades of homophobia are discernible in Lodge's first two novels. In *The Picturegoers* the homoerotically inclined Hilda Syms is characterized as "unnatural" and irretrievably deluded. And in *Ginger, You're Barmy* the semi-autobiographical narrator describes the army's physical-training instructors as "typical of their tribe: lounging bullies in soiled white sweaters, who kept up an appearance of muscular fitness and agility thinly disguising a profound laziness and perceptible homosexual proclivities" (p. 56). In *Out of the Shelter* this inclination emerges fully fledged. Playing on the ironic tension between Vince's turpitude and his job as a policer of morality (he is employed by the American government to check the backgrounds of current German officials for possible Nazi involvement), Lodge identifies his political and moral deviance with his sexual "deviance." The fact that Vince, abetted by Greg, his lesser partner in crime, has victimized and nearly killed the innocent Rudolph (presumably in thrall to them because of their ability to help his currently unemployable father, who stamped ration books at Dachau) resonates with the sort of facile conflation of sociopathic thrill-seeking with homosexuality that was popularized in the 1959 film *Compulsion.* (The film is based on Meyer Levin's best-selling novel of the same name about the notorious Leopold-Loeb case involving a pair of young gay American men who committed a gratuitous murder.) The irony of the circumstances of their "outing" in the novel's climactic scene is intensified in that it is effected by the atheistic socialist Don, who has lost his job as a schoolteacher ostensibly because Vince, exploiting the paranoiac McCarthy-era atmosphere, has informed on him as to his politics. When we see Vince himself shockingly "cross-dressed" in Nazi garb—an action that threatens the moral well-being of the impressionable Timothy and evidently "corrupts" the other partygoers, who enthusiastically join in the campy masquerade by donning Nazi uniforms and equipment and "strutting about and clicking their heels and giving each other the Nazi salute" (p. 255)—and then, in the next moment, outed as a traitor, a sociopath, and a homosexual, we recognize that his politics, morality, and sexuality are all simply differing manifestations of his essential nature: he is ontologically—and anachronistically—*evil*. It would not be until 1980, after the appearance of the gay rights movement, that Lodge would create a sympathetic gay character, a man struggling to reconcile Catholic teachings with his own homosexuality, in *How Far Can You Go?*

MIDDLE-PERIOD NOVELS

BETWEEN 1975 and 1988 Lodge published four novels, three of which—*Changing Places*, *Small World*, and *Nice Work*—comprise his trilogy on academia (they were published together in the 1993 volume *A David Lodge Trilogy*). In these texts the wit bristles, the story lines are skillfully interwoven, and many of the themes and techniques of his early novels are deployed with greater force and craftsmanship. Lodge's talent for comedy, which was first displayed in the farcical *The British Museum Is Falling Down*, would be refined and elevated in the service of more sophisticated narrative ends in *Changing Places* and *Small World*, and the former novel's treatment of the Catholic church's teachings on birth control would be rendered more maturely and in a more sustained fashion in *How Far Can You Go?* The broad panoramic approach, somewhat out of control in *The Picturegoers*, would be more skillfully implemented in *Small World*, which consists of a dazzlingly complex weave of subplots. And Lodge's portrayals of the socioeconomic circumstances surrounding particular moments in England's history—epitomized in the early novels in *Out of the Shelter's* account of the post–World War II years—would be more sharply focused and politically engaged in *Nice Work's* incisive account of the toll exacted during the mid-1980s on English academia as a result of the policies of Margaret Thatcher's Conservative administration.

The two sites alluded to in the Dickens-inspired subtitle of *Changing Places: A Tale of Two Campuses* (1975) are the State University of Euphoria on the U.S. West Coast and the University of Rummidge in the English Midlands. The novel recounts a six-month exchange of jobs—and, eventually, homes and wives—between the English teachers Morris Zapp, a professor at "Euphoric State" (p. 12), and Philip Swallow, a lecturer at Rummidge. The text's ironic tone is established in the opening pages, which consist of descriptions of their simultaneous flights on New Year's Day 1969. Morris, who has purchased his ticket on the cheap, discovers from Mary Makepeace (whom he will later reencounter, in one of the novel's many coincidences, as "Fifi the French Maid" at a woefully inadequate English strip club) that he is the sole man aboard the plane because the flight has been chartered by pregnant women flying to England to take advantage of the relatively permissive abortion laws. Meanwhile, on his flight Philip encounters Charles Boon, an opportunistic and disreputable former undergraduate student of his, who is now a graduate student at Euphoric State and a local celebrity with his own radio talk show. The descriptions of Morris' and Philip's parallel flights are interspersed with synopses of their personal and professional histories. Both are forty, married, have three children, and are experiencing midlife crises, but in nearly all other respects they are antithetical. The abrasive American womanizer Morris, who is about to be divorced by his second wife, is a distinguished professor with an ambition to single-handedly exhaust the possibilities for Jane Austen criticism. The mediocre Englishman Philip is amiable, faithful to his wife, and although he has written a master's thesis on Jane Austen's juvenilia, he is unable to focus on any specific subject for his research and therefore has little hope of promotion. A variety of subplots involving the Euphoric State and Rummidge English departments fleshes out the narrative, but the novel centers on Morris' and Philip's assumptions of each other's professional and personal roles.

Their role reversal is initiated as each occupies the other's office and secures accommodations emblematic of his new surroundings. Philip rents the upper story of a house occupied by three nubile and promiscuous undergraduates; the view from his window is "like a visual *tour de force* at the beginning of a Cinerama film" (p. 56). Morris takes a room in the home of Dr. O'Shea, a prudish and meddlesome Irish physician; his view is of "rotting sheds and dripping laundry, . . . grimy roofs, [and] factory chimneys" (p. 57). After a bout of compunction, Philip succumbs to the hedonistic atmosphere and jettisons twelve years of monogamy by sleeping with his marijuana-smoking, free-spirited neighbor Melanie, who, he later learns, is Morris' daughter from a previous marriage. Word of the affair, via anonymous letters (ostensibly from Howard Ringbaum, whose tenure candidacy at Euphoric State has been inadvertently sunk by Philip), reaches both Philip's wife, Hilary, who retaliates by purchasing an expensive central heating system, and Morris, who asks his wife, Désirée, to look into the matter. The plot's rigorous parallelism is maintained as Désirée also receives a letter charging Morris with marital infidelity. Transatlantic rumors, suspicions, recriminations, and confessions are exchanged between the pairs of spouses. The correlations of Philip's and Morris' tumultuous experiences are epitomized as their dwellings are rendered uninhabitable by freakish disasters, and they are taken in by their counterparts' spouses, with whom they initiate affairs.

The interpersonal upheavals experienced by the Zapps and the Swallows are paralleled by political upheavals. Student protests in Euphoria over the Vietnam War have led to the occupation of campus buildings; Governor Ronald Duck (a Disneyized Ronald Reagan) has called in the National Guard, and Philip, an accidental participant, is arrested and becomes a hero of the student demonstrators. A small-scale version of such protests occurs at Rummidge, and the English department chair, Gordon Masters, who had been taken prisoner of war at Dunkirk, reverts to a siege mentality and is hospitalized. In Masters' absence, Morris distinguishes himself by successfully mediating between the students and the administration, and he subsequently assumes the office and duties of the chair on an informal basis. As Philip has become enamored of the American lifestyle and of Désirée, and as Morris is tempted by the offer to be made chair of the Rummidge English department, the possibility of making their role reversal permanent is considered. A phone conversation between Hilary and Désirée—during which they disclose they are having affairs with each other's husband—leads to the decision to hold "a sort of summit conference" (p. 236) in New York, where, in the final scene, the four parties converge. After contemplating the variety of erotic and domestic configurations available to them, the spouses temporarily revert to the traditional arrangement, but the novel ends on a note of irresolution.

Relentlessly funny and formally innovative, *Changing Places* constitutes a quantum leap beyond Lodge's earlier fiction. The first two sections of the text are narrated by an omniscient voice that occupies a "privileged narrative altitude (higher than any jet)" (p. 8), the third section is epistolary, the fourth consists of newspaper clippings, the fifth returns to an omniscient narrator, and the last takes the form of a screenplay. The plot is organized around the culture shock experienced by the two major characters as they exchange roles in culturally and meteorologically antithetical "Euphoria" and "Rummidge"—descriptively renamed renderings of the California Bay area (Euphoric State stands for the University of California at Berkeley) and Birmingham. ("Rummidge" would go on to become either the setting or the protagonist's home base for most of Lodge's subsequent novels.) The text's intensely self-referential character and the improbability of its events—especially the uncanny parallels between Philip's and Morris' experiences—make clear that, unlike Lodge's earlier fiction (with the exception of *The British Museum Is Falling Down*), *Changing Places* is not a work of mimetic realism but a playful and highly contrived work of art. In a prefatory note Lodge himself emphatically makes the point that the world his novel depicts is not reality but a fictional heterocosm: "Rummidge and Euphoria are places on the map of a comic world which resembles the one we are standing on without exactly corresponding to it, and which is peopled by figments of the imagination" (p. 6). This caveat is reinforced from within the text when we are informed of Morris' view—shared by his author—that "the root of all critical error was a naive confusion of literature with life" (p. 47).

In a later essay Lodge would observe that "the fundamental narrative device of film (one which modern novelists have of course borrowed and exploited) is the cut, which moves the story instantly from one spatio-temporal context to another without explanation" (*The Practice of Writing*, p. 223). Indeed, one of the great strengths of *Changing Places* is its skillful deployment of simultaneity: scenes oscillate between America and England as a means of narratively juxtaposing spatial and cultural difference with the immediacy of film. For example, a scene in (and of) Euphoria describing an evening of uninhibited partying, culminating with Philip's casual erotic encounter with Melanie, cuts to a scene in Rummidge of Dr. O'Shea whipping and threatening his niece, Bernadette, with hellfire and blindness after having caught her masturbating with Morris' copy of *Playboy*. Such juxtapositions underscore the principal binary opposition of the novel: America is a place of hedonistic pursuits, whereas England is cold and repressive. In the 1968 essay "The Bowling Alley and the Sun, or, How I Learned to Stop Worrying and Love America," Lodge recalled that his family's return to England in 1965—after nearly a year in the States, during which they "acquire[d] an education in the art of consumption" (*Write On*, p. 8)—left him reflecting on the "inadequacies in British life to which we had become sensitized by our experience of America." He concludes, "ruefully, I have to acknowledge a certain loyalty to my country, if it is only, in Graham Greene's words, 'the loyalty we all have to unhappiness, the feeling that this is where we really belong' " (pp. 15–16). Although Lodge would later retract the excesses of this paean to American consumer culture, the sense that England is not only lacking in luxuries but that it is cold, damp, and ugly relative to America pervades his fiction and essays and constitutes—in what Lodge acknowledges is a self-consciously Jamesian way—a device for enabling fictional exploration.

Another of the Anglo-American dichotomies *Changing Places* pursues through its signal rhetorical technique of caricatural polarization is that of the English and the American academic systems, of which Morris and Philip are paradigmatic. The mild-mannered and unambitious Philip is a product of a system in which "tenure is virtually automatic . . . and everyone is paid on the same scale," whereas Morris, possessed of an abundance of "the professional killer instinct" and "the spirit of free enterprise," is a product of a system "in which each scholar-teacher makes an individual contract with his employer, and is free to sell his services to the highest bidder" (pp. 15–16). Morris' megalomaniacal ambition to produce a set of commentaries on Jane Austen's novels "saying absolutely everything that could possibly be said about them" (p. 44) is a parodic transposition of the American capitalistic ethos from the realm of economics to that of scholarship. It is also an expression of a disdain that Lodge would make clear in the 1988 essay "A Kind of Business: The Academic Critic in America," a scathing indictment of the American academic "star-system" in which he likens American academia to the movie and sports industries (*After Bakhtin*, p. 176). Whereas Morris is a caricature of the successful American academic, Howard Ringbaum is a caricature of the unsuccessful one. He participates in a party game, aptly titled "Humiliation," initiated by Philip, in which one scores points by naming books one hasn't read but that other players have. A stereotypical American academic—as intensely ambitious as he is insecure—Ringbaum is subjected by Lodge to a diabolically ingenious career- and ego-shattering brace of mutually exclusive imperatives. As Désirée reports the episode to Morris, "Howard . . . has a pathological urge to succeed and a pathological fear of being thought uncultured, and this game set his two obsessions at war with each other, because he could succeed in the game only by exposing a gap in his culture." While in the beginning rounds "his psyche c[a]n't absorb the paradox," he eventually gets into the spirit of the game and volunteers the information that he has not read *Hamlet*. Three days later he is unexpectedly turned down for tenure because the English department, which collectively is as shallow and insecure as he is, "dared not give tenure to a man who publicly admitted to not having read *Hamlet*" (pp. 135–136).

While most of the events of *Changing Places* are wholly fictitious, some are loosely based on Lodge's own experiences at Berkeley in 1969, where he was a visiting professor. One episode in particular that he participated in, wrote about, and incorporated into the novel was the controversy surrounding the "People's Park," during which the California National Guard was pitted against a group of youthful radical protesters in a struggle for possession of a small plot of university-owned land. In Lodge's narrative scheme, a similar political upheaval both macrocosmically enacts the inter- and intra-personal upheavals of the novel's primary characters and microcosmically enacts the conflict in Southeast Asia. The skirmish over the "People's Garden" is "much like the Vietnam War in miniature" (p. 172), which is precisely how Lodge had characterized the situation in his 1969 essay "The People's Park and the Battle of Berkeley": "The whole episode of the People's Park seems like a grotesque parody, in microcosm, of the Vietnam War" (*Write On*, pp. 26–27). Political conflict is figured through personal conflict in other respects as well. For example, the Zapp marriage enacts in miniature the nascent women's rights movement. Explaining why she wants out of their marriage and likening him to a python, Désirée tells the misogynistic Morris "I'm just a half-digested bulge in your ego" (p. 40). In the sequel, *Small World*, she will go on to become a famous feminist after writing an account of their life together.

Whereas Lodge's first novel explores the usurpation of traditional religion by film, the conclusion of *Changing Places* characterizes in both form (it is written as a screenplay) and content the usurpation of the traditional novel by film. Philip asserts, "Our generation—we subscribe to the liberal doctrine of the inviolate self. It's the great tradition of realist fiction, it's what novels are all about.... Well, the novel is dying and us with it." The current generation, he concludes, "are living a film, not a novel" (p. 250), and in the manner of the irresolute, ambiguous postmodern texts that it parodies, *Changing Places* doesn't *conclude* but simply *stops*: the last line is the stage direction "PHILIP shrugs. The camera stops, freezing him in mid-gesture" (p. 251).

How Far Can You Go? (1980) also self-consciously manipulates the relation between fiction and reality, but it is both formally and tonally very different from *Changing Places*. The text traces the lives of a group of ten English Catholics, plus their spouses and children, from 1952 to the late 1970s as they strain to negotiate between the competing demands of the body and—if not the soul itself—at least the Catholic teachings about the soul (the less cryptic American title, *Souls and Bodies*, announces this subject). Unlike Lodge's previous novels, *How Far Can You Go?* has no central plot but rather consists entirely of a constellation of thematically linked subplots. In the opening scene, which depicts a 1952 Saint Valentine's Day mass in a London church, we are introduced to the group of ten undergraduates whose fates are to be chronicled. The most significant members of the group are: Michael, loosely based on Lodge himself, who will marry Miriam and become a university English lecturer; Dennis and Angela, who will marry each other after a long and erotically suspenseful engagement; and Edward, who will become a doctor and marry Tessa. We follow less closely the lives of the other members of the group, including Miles,

who is gay and will become a Cambridge don, and Ruth, who will become a nun.

The novel first recounts the late adolescence and young adulthood of these characters in the 1950s, focusing primarily on their early sexual experiences. Then it moves on to the 1960s when many of them, compelled by the strict rules of "Vatican Roulette" (p. 78), prolifically produce babies "in spite of strenuous efforts not to" (p. 73). Like Adam Appleby, the protagonist of Lodge's earlier and more lighthearted fictional exploration of the Catholic teachings on birth control (*The British Museum Is Falling Down*), the principal characters here hope that the Second Vatican Council will relax Church strictures. (The council was convened in 1962 and completed its work in 1965. Although it effected sweeping liberalization in various matters, it remained silent on the question of birth control. In 1968 Pope Paul VI published *Humanae Vitae*, upholding extant teachings on birth control and greatly disappointing reform-minded Catholics.) In an attempt to stimulate change from within, several of Lodge's characters join the liberal organization Catholics for an Open Church. The novel culminates with that group's sponsorship of an Easter 1975 "Paschal Festival," "a showcase for the pluralist, progressive, postconciliar Church" (p. 209) and a counterdemonstration to the resurgence in the mid-1970s of conservative Catholic voices. A videotaped broadcast of the event stimulates a widespread public debate in England over the question of Church reform. Having brought us up to date with respect to the varying fates of his characters, in the conclusion Lodge alludes to the 1978 accession of the theologically conservative Pope John Paul II, and the novel ends with uncertainty as to the direction of modern Catholicism.

Formally, *How Far Can You Go?* is a curious mixture of conflicting impulses. Lodge appears to have conceived and begun it as a comic novel and is almost apologetic that it didn't turn out that way, repeatedly drawing the reader's attention to the fact that, despite the expectations he has created both in the text's early scenes and in his previous fiction, it is not a comedy (pp. 74, 112). More important, this is the only one of his novels in which the narrator is transparently identified with the author himself (although Lodge has argued, with excessive ingenuity, that he is in fact *not* identical with his narrator, claiming, "the more prominent the author is, the more he becomes a rhetorical trope, and the more difficult it is to identify that voice with me" [Haffenden interview, p. 153], and his position has been endorsed by Bergonzi [*David Lodge*, p. 37]). Lodge frequently intrudes into his fictional creation in order to address the reader directly, but he makes clear that his breaches of the realist novel's narrative contract are deliberate:

We all like to believe, do we not, if only in stories? People who find religious belief absurd are often upset if a novelist breaks the illusion of reality he has created. Our friends [the primary characters] had started life with too many beliefs—the penalty of a Catholic upbringing. They were weighed down with beliefs, useless answers to non-questions. To work their way back to the fundamental ones . . . they had to dismantle all that apparatus of superfluous belief and discard it piece by piece. But in matters of belief (as of literary convention) it is a nice question how far you can go in this process without throwing out something vital.

(p. 143)

The analogy drawn in this passage between faith in traditional religion and "faith" in traditional realistic narrative is strategically invoked throughout the text. As the characters answer the hydra-headed question posed by the novel's title by testing the limits of Catholicism (as well as of erotic permissibility), so, too, does Lodge answer that question by testing the limits of the realist novel. Other violations of the narrative contract include prolepses that disrupt the plot's continuity (for example, pp. 6, 79) and foregroundings of the process of literary creation, such as when Lodge spells out his symbolism in abortive sentence fragments: "Adrian, bespectacled (= limited vision), in belted gaberdine coat (= instinctual repression, authoritarian determination)" (p. 14). The text's contraventions of the realist novel's codes are epitomized in the fact that the "protagonist" is not an individual but rather a corporate entity—a whole generation of English Catholics distilled into a representative handful; this fact is signaled in the use of the third-person plural pronoun in four of the seven chapter titles ("How They Lost Their Virginities"; "How They Lost the Fear of Hell"; "How They Broke Out, Away, Down, Up, Through, Etc."; "How They Dealt with Love and Death"). However, the fact that Lodge's formal transgressions are motivated by a sophisticated *intention* doesn't make the *execution* altogether successful. Because this novel is driven so heavily by ideas, as opposed to character or plot, and because Lodge didn't complete the journey from experienced reality to fictional transmutation during its writing, it is difficult to absorb as *story* (as opposed to sheer *information*). Consequently, the text tends to read less like a work of fiction than an ethnography into which the material from a lifetime of fieldwork among English Catholics has been garnered.

While *How Far Can You Go?* has its structural shortcomings, it is nonetheless a thoughtful and compellingly authentic exploration of a complex set of issues. The extent of Lodge's personal investment in the novel's subject is discernible in his oblique suggestion that Catholic birth-control proscriptions may have been to blame for his son's having been born with Down's syndrome; after Dennis and Angela have a Down's baby, the physician Edward ceases instructing his clients in the rhythm method on "the theory that the Safe Method might be responsible for such congenital defects" (p. 111). (Lodge has acknowledged that this aspect of the plot is autobiographical [Haffenden interview, p. 153].) The novel includes an interpolated essay on Catholicism and sex that constitutes a distillation of Lodge's views on the dilemmas explored in the text (pp. 113–121). He is careful to present a balanced account of the issues at stake, observing that "the availability of effective contraception was the thin edge of a wedge of modern hedonism" and that "it was disingenuous of liberal Catholics to deny it" (p. 115). But he makes clear where his allegiances lie when he nonetheless proceeds to describe how "the vital principle [that nonprocreative sex is legitimate] had [already] been conceded" by the Church when it authorized the rhythm method (p. 116). In his essay "The Catholic Church and Cultural Life," which was also published in 1980, he observes that the reformist tendencies so saliently characteristic of English Catholics of his generation were largely a function of the 1944 Education Act, an important consequence of which was that "the mass of Catholics had access to higher education for the first time and, to the dismay of some of the clergy, something like an educated Catholic laity began to form in the post-war period." Lodge goes on to point out that as a result of this movement, "for perhaps the first time English Catholics were making a determined bid to present Catholicism not as some kind of refuge from or alternative to a social and political order seen as irredeemably secular, but as a basis for transforming that order: not an escape from history but a positive intervention in it" (*Write On*, p. 34). It is a paradigmatic sample of such liberally educated postwar English Catholics that comprises the cast of characters of *How Far Can You Go?*, the events of which chart the tensions generated by their resistance to, yet their desire to remain within the fold of, an institution that is dogmatically based and rigidly hierarchical.

Small World: An Academic Romance (1984) also consists of a panoramic amalgam of subplots, but it transcends *How Far Can You Go?* in both scope and sophistication. The longest of Lodge's novels, *Small World* is also his most intricately plotted. Whereas *Changing Places* is restricted to two locations and two primary characters, its sequel has no such limitations: scores of characters, most of them literature scholars, densely populate this global-scale picaresque. The text chronicles their journeys to and from innumerable professional conferences, which are likened in the Chaucerian prologue to "the pilgrimage[s] of medieval Christendom" and whose settings include England, Amsterdam, Turkey, Switzerland, South Korea, Germany, Greece, Israel, and the United States.

The novel begins in England with an ill-conceived and poorly attended conference in Rummidge. We are here reintroduced to Philip Swallow, who has been promoted to the rank of professor and now chairs the Rummidge English department, as well as to Morris Zapp, who has flown in from the States to give the keynote address. It is April 1979, and they have not seen each other since the events of a decade earlier, recounted in *Changing Places*. We learn that Philip and Hilary have remained together and that Morris and Désirée have divorced. We are also introduced in the novel's opening to the naive and idealistic Persse McGarrigle, who occupies the "hero" slot in this mock romance: his surname, the profoundly mediocre and tubercular young scholar explains, means "Son of Super-valour" (p. 10). (In the essay "*Small World*: An Introduction," published the same year as the novel, Lodge describes how he modeled his narrative on the Arthurian Grail legend, as did T. S. Eliot *The Waste Land*, and on the "traditional . . . notion of

romance as a genre" [*Write On*, p. 73]—hence the subtitle, *An Academic Romance*.) The subplots of *Small World* are so numerous and richly imbricated that the text defies cogent summary. But the episodic events are loosely organized around parallel quests, one personal and the other professional: Persse's quest for the beautiful, brilliant, and elusive Angelica Pabst, and several of the other characters' quests to be awarded a cushy, well-paying, and prestigious UNESCO chair—the "Grail" of academia. Lodge has said that his plan for the novel was "to deal in a carnival spirit with the various competing theories of literary criticism which were animating and dividing the profession of letters" (*Write On*, p. 72), and he did so by making the six candidates for the UNESCO chair caricatural exponents of different schools of literary criticism: liberal humanism, structuralism, reception theory, Marxism, poststructuralism, and Oxbridge belleletrism (feminism, surprisingly, is unrepresented). The novel's grand finale, during which both quest plots culminate and comic closure is effected on all fronts, is set in New York in December. The antithesis of the puny Rummidge event with which the novel began nine months earlier, the scene is the annual Modern Language Association meeting, deemed "the Big Daddy of conferences" (p. 356).

Brilliantly conceived, promiscuously intertextual, and irrepressibly witty, *Small World* is a virtuosic work of mischief and a fitting prelude to Lodge's departure from academia. Cognizant of the fact that he did not create his scathing portrait ex nihilo, Lodge has acknowledged the influence on his academic fiction of Kingsley Amis' *Lucky Jim* (1954), which he identifies as "the first British campus novel," that is, "the first to take as its central character a lecturer at a provincial university, and to find a rich seam of comic and narrative material in that small world" (*The Practice of Writing*, p. 89). Lodge, however, would advance light-years beyond Amis by transmuting this "small world"—with the aid of modern transportation and communications technologies, as well as modern methods of literary representation—into an entire fictional universe. Indeed, if *Lucky Jim* is "the first British campus novel," then *Small World* is the first "global campus novel" (*Small World*, p. 51). Lodge self-consciously registers this act of generic supercession in Morris' contention that "the day of the single, static campus is over" and with it "the single, static campus novel" (p. 72).

Small World and its predecessor, *Changing Places*, are plotted according to the generative principles of narrative production of the schools of literary analysis that were ascendant during the periods in which they were written: *Changing Places* is organized around the structuralist principle of binary opposition, whereas *Small World* is organized around the poststructuralist principles of indeterminacy and limitless proliferation. Although Lodge, whose primary allegiance has always been to liberal humanism, embraced structuralism and applied it in his own scholarship (as we have seen, his *Modes of Modern Writing* and *Working with Structuralism* are both scholarly implementations of structuralist method), he eschewed poststructuralism as the Frankenstein's monster of academia, contending that "deconstructionist criticism . . . tends to deny the unique creative activity of the individual writer, and as a writer myself, I can't accept that" (*Contemporary Authors* interview, p. 301). (His antipathy, it should be noted, is more deeply considered than that of his provincial alterego Philip Swallow, who xenophobically decries "the mischievous influence of Continental theorizing" [p. 32].) Yet while Lodge refused to participate in the fashion for poststructuralism in his critical writings, he did so to great effect in his novel *Small World,* in which (in a characteristically deconstructive move) he ironically deployed its methodology to lampoon the very profession that had created it.

The poststructuralist principles according to which *Small World* is organized are elucidated by Morris Zapp in his lecture at the novel's inaugural conference. Luridly titled "Textuality as Striptease" (p. 23), his playful address is both spoof and cogent primer. Having moved with the times, Morris has abandoned his ambition to produce a set of exhaustive commentaries on Jane Austen's fiction and has swung, pendulumlike, clear past reality after a conversion to the poststructuralist premise that *"every decoding is another encoding"* and its corollary that "the quest for interpretation" is futile (p. 30; Lodge's emphasis). (The echoes of the novel's parodic "quest" plot are intentional.) Likening the act of reading to that of watching a stripper, Morris contends that "the dancer teases the audience, as the text teases its readers, with the promise of an

ultimate revelation that is infinitely postponed." He counsels his auditors that "instead of striving to possess [the text], we should take pleasure in its teasing" (p. 31). Morris' status as the embodiment of what Lodge believed to be wrong with academic criticism is made clear during the question-and-answer session, when Philip impatiently poses the commonsensical question, "What in God's name *is* the point of it all?" Crystallizing Lodge's polemical point, Morris brazenly acknowledges that "the point, of course, is to uphold the institution of academic literary studies" (p. 33). Much of the ensuing novel consists of an exposé of the modern academic world as a self-perpetuating racket. (Lodge himself has tended—not convincingly—to downplay the sharply critical edge of his novel, claiming in the year it was published that its satire is not of "a censorious kind": "I don't think that in good faith I could satirize in a destructive way an institution to which I belong" [Haffenden interview, p. 161]. He maintained this position in a later interview, observing that "sometimes, in relation to the academic novels, I'm described as being rather cruelly satirical. I don't think of myself as a cruel writer" [Kostrzewa interview, p. 10].)

While Morris embodies the school of thought that Lodge felt was the most egregiously wrongheaded, none of the ensemble of cartoonishly rendered academics emerges unscathed from the novel's bristling irony. Indeed, Morris will later appear refreshingly honest about his role in the great sham of modern academia when he is contrasted with the wealthy aristocratic Italian scholar Fulvia Morgana. Espousing a preposterously rarefied hybrid strain of poststructuralist Marxism, Fulvia, who is likened to "a Roman empress," is asked by Morris how she "manage[s] to reconcile living like a millionaire with being a Marxist." As comfortably ensconced within her glib sophisms as she is behind the steering wheel of her Maserati, she responds that she is merely participating in the "contradictions characteristic of the last phase of bourgeois capitalism." If she were to renounce her "little bit of privilege," she continues, she would "not accelerate by one minute the consummation of the process, which has its own inexorable rhythm and momentum, and is determined by the pressure of mass movements, not by the puny actions of individuals" (pp. 145–146). As the Marxist candidate for the UNESCO chair, in the novel's culminating scene she will further expound on her beliefs while part of the panel that serves as a showcase for the contenders. (The well-attended panel discussion is entitled "The Function of Criticism," although, ironically, what is demonstrated in the course of it is that criticism no longer has any function other than to perpetuate itself.) In her address—a diatribe comprised of a litany of pretentious slogans—she characterizes "the very concept of 'literature' itself [as] nothing more than an instrument of bourgeois hegemony, a fetishistic reification of so-called aesthetic values erected and maintained through an elitist educational system in order to conceal the brutal facts of class oppression under industrial capitalism" (p. 361). The irony is that she herself is a participant in, and perpetuator of, this "elitist educational system," and that the working-class people for whom she purports to speak could not even begin to understand her bloated jargon. As the liberal humanist Philip characterizes the situation (clearly speaking for Lodge), "There was a time when reading was a comparatively simple matter, something you learned to do in primary school. Now it seems to be some kind of arcane mystery, into which only a small élite have been initiated" (p. 32). The sort of dilemma this state of affairs has tended to generate, particularly during the 1980s when the fashion for poststructuralism was at its peak, is demonstrated when Morris' ex-wife, Désirée, and another nonacademic writer attend an academic conference and find themselves "intimidated by the literary critical jargon of their hosts, which they both think is probably nonsense, but cannot be quite sure, since they do not fully understand it" (p. 270).

In contrast to the globe-trotting panorama of *Small World*, the final volume of Lodge's trilogy, *Nice Work* (1988), is all but entirely restricted to Rummidge. The events begin in January 1986, six years after *Small World* concludes. The protagonists are Vic Wilcox, a forty-five-year-old politically conservative manager of an engineering company, and Robyn Penrose, a thirty-three-year-old radical feminist literary scholar temporarily employed at Rummidge University. The year 1986 has been deemed "Industry Year" by the government, and Philip Swallow (still department head and now a dean as well but demoted to a supporting role in Lodge's narrative) asks Robyn to participate in a program designed to bridge the gap between the business world and the "ivory tower" of academia. Vic's superior submits his name for the program as well, and for two and a half months of Wednesdays Robyn is to "shadow" him, that is, to observe him at work. The novel, premised on a variation of the *Changing Places* theme, describes the conflicts and mutual illuminations of the short, conservative businessman and the tall, radical intellectual, whose stark opposition is reminiscent of that of Philip Swallow and Morris Zapp, with the added differences of gender and occupation. (Lodge has observed of his novels generally that they "tend towards binary structures" [Haffenden interview, p. 152].)

Although they lock horns in their initial meetings, their compulsory association gradually develops into friendship, and Robyn's "shadowing" of Vic finishes with a business trip to Frankfurt during which their mutual attraction is consummated. Vic, stuck in a lukewarm marriage and excited by his first foray into adultery, wants to leave his wife for Robyn, but Robyn has no interest in pursuing the relationship. The unevenness of their desires renders the next phase of the plot stressful for her, as an infatuated Vic, having proposed to continue the "shadowing" process in reverse, accompanies her to tutorials and faculty meetings. A government report announces a still deeper financial crisis for British academia, and whatever hopes Robyn—a prolific scholar and an excellent teacher—has had of getting a full-time position on the Rummidge faculty are dashed. Morris Zapp, who, like Philip, plays a minor role in the novel, is impressed by the manuscript of her forthcoming book on feminism and informs her that he would support her candidacy if she were to apply for a women's studies position advertised at Euphoric State University. (We subsequently learn that his motives are not disinterested: his ex-wife, Désirée, is the leading contender for the position.) Meanwhile, Vic is also facing professional hardship, as the merger of his company with a competitor has eliminated his position. Happily, however, Robyn receives word that she is the sole beneficiary of her recently deceased Australian uncle's three-hundred-thousand-dollar estate. She generously invests most of the money in a start-up company initiated by Vic, who is now reconciled with his wife. In the novel's final scene, Philip informs Robyn that despite the latest round of budget cuts, there is a chance she can be reappointed on a full-time basis. Committed to her project of ameliorating social conditions in Rummidge, she nobly opts to withdraw her application for the more secure, remunerative, and prestigious position in the States in order to stay in Rummidge for another year as a temporary lecturer in the hope that she will be rehired.

Unlike *Changing Places* and *Small World, Nice Work* is more serious than it is comedic, although it has some very funny moments. It is self-consciously in the tradition of the mid-Victorian "Condition of England" novel (the phrase is Thomas Carlyle's), which took as its subject the effects of the Industrial Revolution on the lives of Britons, especially the new class of factory workers. The primary intertexts to *Nice Work*, and the sources for its chapter epigraphs, are well-known specimens of this subgenre by Benjamin Disraeli, Elizabeth Gaskell, Charles Dickens, and George Eliot. Lodge's implicit and ironic likening of the British academic of the 1980s to the mid-nineteenth-century coal-blackened, malnourished factory laborer is most vividly rendered during an undergraduate lecture delivered by Robyn, in which she describes the plight of the exploited Victorian factory workers who "thronged to the cities of the Midlands and the North where the economics of *laissez-faire* forced them to work long hours in wretched conditions for miserable wages, and threw them out of employment altogether as soon as there was a downturn in the market" (p. 45). Ironically, the situation she is describing is her own as well; as an underpaid university teacher who has come to the Midlands from Cambridge for employment, she is about to lose her position because of budgetary cuts. Lodge makes clear who is responsible for this state of affairs: whereas in the mid-nineteenth century "the Industrial Revolution [brought] riches to a few and misery to the many" in England (p. 45), in the 1980s the Conservative revolution was having much the same effect. "The Conservative Government of Mrs Thatcher, elected in 1979 with a mandate to cut public spending, had set about decimating the national system of higher education" (p. 29). *Nice Work* describes the process and the effects of this decimation.

The account of the "Condition of England" novel offered by Robyn largely consists of a feminist updating of Raymond Williams' discussion of the subgenre in his influential 1958 study *Culture and Society*, in which he terms it the "Industrial Novel": "industrial capitalism is phallocentric," Robyn contends. "The most commonplace metonymic index of industry—the factory chimney—is also metaphorically a phallic symbol" (p. 49). Notably, although she is steeped in trendy poststructuralist jargon of the sort that Lodge had earlier lampooned, Robyn is compellingly sincere and politically committed. Not only does she admirably forgo the opportunity for a high-paying academic post in the United States, but she bravely joins the tenured Rummidge University picketers who are protesting the government's lack of support for higher education, despite the consequences this action might have on her own tenuous employment. She thus constitutes a counterweight to the hypocritical literary theorists depicted in *Small World*. Nonetheless, the sort of bad faith someone armed with poststructuralist jargon can legitimize is evidenced in *Nice Work* in the explanation offered by Charles, Robyn's erstwhile companion, for his decision to abandon his teaching position at the University of Suffolk in favor of a career in investment banking. With a facile deconstructive flourish, he asserts that he is not selling out his principles but "simply exchanging one semiotic system for another, the literary for the numerical, a game with high philosophical stakes for a game with high monetary stakes" (p. 225).

While Robyn possesses a formidable intellect and is an expert on the Victorian industrial novel, she ironically knows nothing about industry itself. This fact, coupled with Vic's commensurate ignorance of the modern academic world and the progressive causes with which it is associated, enables Lodge's plot. Having anticipated a Dickensian scene of billowing black smoke when she first visits the factory Vic manages, Robyn naively wonders, "Where are the chimneys?" When apprised that everything runs on gas and electricity, she is forced to admit that she has never actually been inside a factory before (p. 68). When Vic takes her on a tour of the inside of the factory, however, she finds a scene disturbingly consonant with her image of "the satanic mills of the early Industrial Revolution" (p. 81). She is appalled at the monotony and harsh working conditions endured by the laborers, particularly the Asians and Caribbeans, who do the bulk of the arduous and unpleasant tasks. After her tour of the factory, Robyn accompanies Vic to a managerial meeting during which he devises an unethical plan to force an Indian employee out of his job in order to improve the factory's efficiency level. She tips off the laborer and a walkout ensues, which is only resolved when Vic agrees to Robyn's demand that he compromise with the employees. (Ironically, she will later inadvertently cause the Indian to lose his job by helping Vic to secure an efficient German-made machine that renders his labor redundant.) Although they clash over this matter, Vic will gradually be influenced by Robyn to the point where—instructed and inspired by her feminist and socialist convictions—he will ban pin-ups of naked women in the workplace and initiate regular meetings between management and labor. There is reciprocity as well (although it is treated more briefly and less convincingly) when Vic helpfully brings his own business acumen to bear during faculty meetings.

But if the effects of this propitious cross-fertilization of academia and industry are beneficial to both spheres, aside from various meliorist gestures the novel ultimately does not offer any substantive political solutions to the problems it poses. Terry Eagleton has characterized Lodge as one for whom "the impulse to integrate has proved considerably stronger than the drive of critical dissent" (p. 96), and he has suggested that this inclination is particularly evident in *Nice Work*. Although Eagleton's critique is unnecessarily polemical, his basic contention is sound. Robyn concludes that "all the Victorian novelist could offer as a solution to the problems of industrial capitalism were: a legacy, a marriage, emigration or death" (p. 52), and Lodge himself is in much the same position with respect to Britain of the 1980s. The fact that he needs to resort to the first of these options—the timely legacy—in order to cope with Robyn's difficulties appears to imply his view that there is no way of bringing about the cheery closure requisite of his fiction without suprapolitical contrivances.

LATER WORK

THE YEAR 1987, when Lodge retired from his academic post, marks a watershed in his career. He has reported that the change left him with "little inclination or incentive to go on writing criticism for an essentially academic audience" (*The Art of Fiction*, p. ix) and freed him to pursue other literary interests in addition to continuing the novel writing that he has maintained at a steady pace throughout his adult life. One such interest is nonacademic criticism. In 1991 and 1992 he published, in the form of a weekly column for the *Independent on Sunday* (in Britain) and the *Washington Post* (in the States), a series of brief, accessible essays on a variety of literary topics; revised and expanded, they comprise *The Art of Fiction: Illustrated from Classic and Modern Texts* (1992). Another collection of essays intended for a general readership, *The Practice of Writing: Essays, Reviews and a Diary* (1996), primarily consists of pieces Lodge wrote after 1987; he affirms in the volume's introduction that he has come to realize "this is the kind of criticism I most enjoy writing (and reading)" (p. ix).

Another interest Lodge has pursued since his retirement is television writing. In 1989 his four-part adaptation of *Nice Work* was broadcast by the BBC, and it went on to win the Royal Television Society's Award for best drama serial of the year. In the 1993 essay "Adapting *Nice Work* for Television" he describes how he began the screen version almost immediately after having finished the novel because he wanted it to be broadcast "while its picture of Thatcher's Britain was still recognizable" (*The Practice of Writing*, p. 218). He also recounts how, having been accustomed to the solitary activity of novel writing, he enjoyed the collaborative nature of television: "Writing a novel was never so exciting," he concludes (p. 229). In 1994 he wrote a television adaptation of Charles Dickens' *Martin Chuzzlewit*, and it, too, was critically acclaimed. His interest in this medium has also found its way into his most recent novel, *Therapy*, whose protagonist is a television scriptwriter.

Lodge's postretirement dramatic pursuits have not been limited to television. In the spring of 1990 his first full-length stage play, *The Writing Game: A Comedy*, was performed at the Birmingham Repertory Theatre. The play depicts a creative-writing retreat in which professional and amateur writers participate, with the warring egos of the professionals generating the bulk of the narrative momentum. The two primary characters are Leo Rafkin, an ill-tempered, twice-divorced Jewish American writer, and Maude Lockett, a popular English writer who is married to an Oxford don. After several days of discord and psychological abuse leveled by the professionals at one another, the play culminates with an amateur writer and primary school teacher—diminutively named Penny—rejecting a Faustian bargain offered by Leo, who has informed her that "you could be like us one day." Denouncing the famous writers she has encountered at the retreat as mean-spirited egomaniacs whom she has no desire to emulate, Penny asserts that "this course has sort of cured me of wanting to be a writer" (p. 111). Although the depiction of professional creative writers in *The Writing Game* is as damning as the earlier novelistic depictions of professional academics, the play is dramaturgically unremarkable and its plot less than inspired. However, it is notable as a postretirement depiction of a nonacademic setting for teaching and as an exploration of the question of whether and under what circumstances creative writing can be "taught." In 1995 Lodge would further pursue this question in the form of a contribution to a Royal Society of Literature seminar; his presentation, revised and expanded, was published as "Creative Writing: Can It/Should It Be Taught?" in *The Practice of Writing*.

Lodge's two most recent novels, *Paradise News* and *Therapy*, recur to the Catholic issues treated in some of his earlier fiction. Significantly, however, these novels return not to the mode of *How Far Can You Go?*, which is essentially a fictionalized account of the effects of the Catholic church as an *institution*, but to that of his very first novel, *The Picturegoers*, which treats Catholicism as an agent of *salvation*. Yet the difference between *The Picturegoers* and these novels on this matter is substantial, as the latter's Catholic aspects—reflecting Lodge's own conflicted relationship to Church teachings—are conveyed with provisionality and skepticism.

Paradise News (1991) tells the story of Bernard Walsh, a forty-four-year-old ex-priest, now a part-time lecturer in theology at a college in Rummidge. In the first of the novel's three sections, the plot is set in motion by a phone call to Bernard from his aunt Ursula, who lives in Hawaii and has been estranged from the family since having married a divorced American shortly after World War II. She is terminally ill with cancer, has returned to the Catholic faith, and wants to see her brother Jack, Bernard's obstreperous Irish father, before she dies. Anticipating an inheritance, Jack agrees to go, and on his and Bernard's flight we meet most of the novel's minor characters, who are in various stages of marital disrepair and general familial dysfunctionality. Looking the wrong way while crossing the road shortly after their arrival in Honolulu (in Britain one drives on the left-hand side), Jack is hit by a car driven by Yolande Miller and suffers a broken hip. While his father is hospitalized, Bernard locates Ursula, who, contrary to the family's assumptions, is impoverished. The second section of the novel, in the form of a journal written by Bernard, recounts the events of his stay in Hawaii and his personal history, ranging from his ill-considered decision in mid-adolescence to become a priest, to his lapse of faith and subsequent exit from the priesthood. He also describes how he has moved Ursula into a luxurious nursing home after having discovered that she is actually rich (the single share of IBM stock that she purchased in 1952 and forgot about is now, four decades later, worth nearly three hundred thousand dollars). The journal ends with Bernard panicking at his growing intimacy with Yolande and resolving to give her the journal. In the novel's final section, Yolande, having read Bernard's journal, is moved; they begin a relationship, and he soon proposes marriage. Meanwhile, Ursula discloses to Bernard that her own marriage failed because of sexual problems she experienced stemming from a summer of sexual abuse at the hands of her and Jack's elder brother, Sean, when she was seven. Sean was subsequently killed in the war and his memory enshrined by the family, rendering his transgressions doubly unspeakable. Jack knew about the abuse but did not intercede, and she wants to see him in order to "exorcize the memory" (p. 227). Jack and Ursula finally meet and cathartically share their recollections (it turns out that he had also been abused by Sean), leaving Ursula at peace and prepared for death. Bernard returns to England with Jack and eventually receives a letter from Yolande describing Ursula's final weeks and her poignant Catholic funeral. The novel ends with his anticipation of a visit from Yolande and the possibility of their marrying.

Like *How Far Can You Go?*, *Paradise News* contains an interpolated essay by Lodge on the state of Catholicism in the modern world. In the earlier novel's quasi-treatise, having charted the evolution of twenty-five years of Catholicism in Britain, he concludes that "the traditional Catholic metaphysic" is being progressively displaced: "Belief is gradually fading. That metaphysic is no longer taught in schools and seminaries in the more advanced countries, and Catholic children are growing up knowing little or nothing about it. Within another generation or two it will have disappeared, superseded by something less vivid but more tolerant" (p. 239). Although the death knell sounded for traditional Catholic belief in *How Far Can You Go?* ought not to be mistaken for an accurate rendering of general Catholic social history— as Thomas Woodman has observed, it may apply to Lodge's "middle-class graduates" but not to "the wider community" of Catholics (*Faithful Fictions: The Catholic Novel in British Literature*, p. 42)— in the briefer quasi-treatise in *Paradise News*, which takes the form of a theology lecture delivered by Bernard (pp. 280–283), this act of supercession, microcosmically rendered in the career of this lapsed priest, is taken as a foregone conclusion and point of departure. Bernard begins by asking, "What can be salvaged from the eschatological wreckage?" (p. 282). He goes on to elucidate this question by asking what is left for modern Catholics now that "traditional concepts of the afterlife no longer command intelligent belief." In particular, he wonders, "if you purge Christianity of the promise of eternal life . . . are you left with anything that is distinguishable from secular humanism?" (p. 282).

Lodge does not offer any definitive answers to these questions, but he does caricaturally personify his own secular impulses in the anthropologist and minor character Roger Sheldrake, who has come to the modern "Paradise" of Hawaii in order to research his book, the thesis of which is that "tourism is the new world religion": "The sightseeing tour as secular pilgrimage. Accumulation of grace by visiting the shrines of high culture. Souvenirs as relics. Guidebooks as devotional aids" (p. 61). In a logical extension of the continuity between Catholicism and consumerism posited in *The Picturegoers*, Sheldrake asserts that he is "doing to tourism what Marx did to capitalism, what Freud did to family life" (p. 62). Tourism, he contends, is "the new opium of the people, and must be exposed as such" (p. 64). His thesis is echoed by the jaded Bernard, who, reflecting on his function as a priest, asserts, "For my parishioners, I was a kind of travel agent, issuing tickets, insurance, brochures, guaranteeing them ultimate happiness" (p. 153). Bernard is particularly embittered by the obligatory hypocrisies imposed on him by the priesthood; his training included "apologetics, which consisted in a tenacious

defence of every article of Catholic orthodoxy," and he recalls that he was discouraged from "disturb[ing] the faith of the ever-dwindling number of recruits to the priesthood by exposing them to the full, cold blast of modern radical theology" (p. 148). Significantly, while Lodge's outlook is partially reflected in those of Sheldrake and Bernard, his own position is less strident and more ambivalent than those of either of these alter-egos.

The events of *Therapy* (1995), Lodge's most recent novel, take place in 1993. In the work's first section, we are introduced, via his own journal, to the protagonist, Laurence ("Tubby") Passmore, a Rummidge-based fifty-eight-year-old writer of a successful situation comedy. Tubby has been married to Sally for nearly thirty years; they enjoy a vigorous sex life, and he is complacently confident in the stability of their relationship. A series of personal and professional problems—culminating in Sally's sudden declaration that she wants a separation— drives him to the writings of Søren Kierkegaard, the Danish existential philosopher and Christian, whose works form the main intertexts for the novel. The second section consists of a series of accounts, seemingly narrated by various people with whom Tubby has come in contact, from which the reader can piece together the ego-pulverizing events of the weeks following Sally's announcement. Driven by a jealous conviction that she has been having an affair with the local tennis pro, Tubby bursts in on the latter's home in the dead of night, only to find him in bed with a man. A gossip paper has gotten hold of the story and has mercilessly lampooned Tubby, whose humiliations have been compounded by a series of erotic fiascos. The third section returns to Tubby's journal, which he has resumed after a two-and-a-half-month hiatus, during which, mortified with humiliation and devastated by the failure of his marriage, his self-esteem has hit rock bottom. Paranoically convinced that "my friends and acquaintances were thinking and talking about me all the time, laughing and sniggering" (p. 211), he has become a virtual prisoner in his own home and for company has to resort to the homeless young man who sleeps on his doorstep. The reader is at this point surprised with the disclosure that the entirety of this section of the novel has consisted not of authentic accounts, but rather of Tubby's imaginative renderings of what others think of him; he has written the series of first-person narratives on the advice of his psychotherapist, who has intended to make him recognize "that other people didn't really loathe and despise me, but respected and sympathized with and even liked me" (p. 212). But since he is possessed of a vivid writer's imagination, the exercise has backfired in spectacular fashion. His "Cognitive Behavior Therapy" (p. 14) having failed, Tubby spontaneously begins to effect his own "psychoanalysis" by writing a recollection of his childhood and adolescence. He focuses in particular on his first girlfriend, a Catholic named Maureen whom he casts as his "Beatrice in a suburban key" (p. 225) and whom he hasn't seen since the mid-1950s; he recalls with remorse his thwarted attempts to take erotic liberties with and his subsequent mistreatment of her. Identifying in this episode "the source of my middle-aged *Angst*" and determined to "make my peace with her" (p. 279), he looks her up and goes to her home, where he learns she is married to Bede Harrington, a childhood rival of his. Having suffered the death of her and Bede's twenty-five-year-old son, Maureen is now on a religious walking pilgrimage in Spain. In the novel's final section, Tubby, on a quest for "Forgiveness" or "Absolution" (p. 278), tracks her down in northern Spain and joins her on the pilgrimage, which concludes with a festival in Santiago, where they have lots of food and sex. (Her marriage to Bede has never been passionate, and since her mastectomy it has been devoid of sex, but as a Catholic she is unwilling to pursue a divorce.) The novel ends oddly, with Tubby and Maureen enjoying occasional surreptitious trysts while they and Bede are triangularly configured as "the best of friends" (p. 321).

Therapy occasionally touches down on the socioeconomic terra firma that is the subject of *Nice Work* (for example, pp. 84–87). However, Tubby's observations about the state of Britain merely serve as background to his narrative's real business: an anatomization of the state of his ego, its pulverization and reintegration. His precrisis weekly routine, described in the novel's beginning, is organized around a litany of popular forms of therapy. Attempting to attain the nebulous, modernity-posited condition named "health," his general lack of which is signaled in the demeaning epithet that serves as his nickname, Tubby routinely receives psychotherapy, physiotherapy, acupuncture therapy, and even aromatherapy. When put to the test of a real problem, however,

these methods turn out to be ineffectual. In fact, it is not until he has "abandoned cognitive therapy in favour of the old-fashioned analytical kind, finding the source of my troubles in a long-repressed memory" (p. 279), that he is truly made well. Given the novel's dismissive treatment of popular forms of therapy, legitimate and fraudulent alike, it is remarkable that its upbeat conclusion is actually effected by means of a facile popular psychology of the sort that the text seems otherwise to reject and even to lampoon. The consequence for Tubby of dredging up his personal history and of joining Maureen on her pilgrimage is that his libido and sense of self-worth are restored, and, in a rather hokey "miracle," his chronically sore knee is healed (although Lodge strategically blunts the miraculousness of this event by hinting that the problem may have been psychosomatic to begin with [p. 150]). In short, unwilling or unable to sustain the complex existential crisis that his narrative has generated, and impelled by the dictates of an intense teleological imperative, Lodge resolves these deep tensions in disappointingly unconvincing fashion.

While the novel's last section, the Maureen plot, which describes Tubby's phoenixlike restoration, is weak, the preceding account, which chronicles the decimation of his ego, is superb. Humiliated and defeated, he is particularly distressed by the tabloid article about him, which includes a cartoon casting him as a cuckolded Vulcan discovering his wife, Venus, in bed with Mars. As he imagines his friend Amy describing the repercussions of this episode, he "is devastated. He feels the whole world is laughing at him. He daren't show his face . . . anywhere people know him" (p. 150). Tubby attempts to restore a measure of dignity to his life by likening his circumstances to those of Kierkegaard, but even this rather desperate gesture is undercut as he imagines his wife trivializing his interest in and identification with the famous philosopher: "I can't take this Kierkegaard thing seriously," he envisions her asserting. "It's just a . . . device to dignify his petty little depressions as existentialist *Angst*" (p. 193). Particularly artful is Lodge's deceptive representation of such pronouncements as genuine. When, two thirds of the way into the text, we learn that they are, in fact, Tubby's imaginative speculations, which he has committed to paper at the instigation of his psychotherapist, we discover that the novel has been truer to its title than we have realized.

In both *Paradise News* and *Therapy* Lodge utilizes the pilgrimage motif straightforwardly after having ironically deployed it in *Small World* (although in the former novel it paradoxically carries an ironic valence as well in Sheldrake's thesis that the modern "sightseeing tour" constitutes a "secular pilgrimage" [p. 61]): Bernard's journey to Hawaii is rejuvenating in much the way that Tubby's pilgrimage in Spain with Maureen is. The differing functions accorded the pilgrimage motif in these novels bespeak a fundamental difference of outlook: the universe of *Small World*, unlike that of *Paradise News* and *Therapy*, is distinctly ateleological; its deconstructive proliferations are, in both senses of the word, without *end*. It thus sharply contrasts with what Bernard describes as the salient aspect of Christian narrative: "Traditional Christianity was essentially teleological. . . . It presented both individual and collective human life as a linear plot moving towards an End" (p. 280). In *Paradise News* and *Therapy* Lodge restores this dimension to his plots, but in so doing he brings it down to earth. In both of these texts the sources of powerfully lingering memories—Ursula's childhood sexual abuse in the former and Tubby's abortive adolescent romance in the latter—are revisited for the purpose of cathartic renewal. Both novels are benevolent and poignant (if overly sentimental) tales of healing and closure. In *Paradise News*, in response to Bernard's query, "What can be salvaged from the eschatological wreckage?" (p. 232), Lodge offers the prospect of connubial bliss; in *Therapy* the more modest question of what can be salvaged from the wreckage of Tubby's ego is posed, and an adulterous and kinky permutation of roughly the same answer is proffered. The basic point of these novels seems to be that if an "anthropomorphic afterlife" (*Paradise News*, p. 281) and the other metaphysical promises of Catholicism are no longer tenable, nontranscendental strains of these promises are. Indeed, despite the ironic skepticism to which Catholicism is subjected in these texts, faith of a sort is affirmed, but the religious ethos is sustained only by being filtered through the language and interpretive grid of psychology—specifically, psychoanalysis. Closure and integration rather than spiritual salvation constitute life's telos now, and if these aspirations are

experienced under the comforting guise of Catholicism (as is the case for the dying Ursula), Lodge has no problem with that; as Bernard muses, "Perhaps [psychological] counsellors would be the priests of the secular future" (p. 105). Nowhere is Lodge's shift of outlook toward the secular more clearly registered than in the fact that the spiritual convictions of the supporting characters Ursula and Maureen are *humored* rather than *shared* by the protagonists Bernard and Tubby, who have themselves settled for the more mundane—literally, *worldly*—fulfillment of psychical integration.

CONCLUSION

GIVEN Lodge's intense and sustained engagement with his twin preoccupations of Catholicism and academia, and given the singularly non-Euclidean character of the human mind, it was perhaps inevitable that these parallel concerns would eventually intersect. Indeed, an intriguing aspect of his later fiction is the way he has self-consciously brought these two issues together. In *Nice Work*, Lodge's first postretirement novel, Charles announces his (and, symbolically, his author's) abandonment of academia with the assertion that "I have had my doubts for some time about the pedagogic application of poststructuralist theory, doubts that I've suppressed, as a priest, I imagine, suppresses his theological doubts" (p. 225). This analogy between waning faith in Catholicism and waning "faith" in academia—and specifically between lapsed priest and "lapsed" academic—is more cryptically deployed in *Paradise News*, in which Bernard characterizes modern theological studies as being caught in a "double bind" (p. 282); Lodge himself, in a 1982 essay playfully entitled "Reading and Writhing in a Double Bind," had used precisely this phrase to describe the insoluble dilemma of modern literary studies that would eventually propel him out of the profession (the essay appears in *After Bakhtin*). In short, Lodge's conflicted relationships with the Catholic church and with the British university have largely mirrored each other. In both instances he has negotiated compromises that are strikingly homologous: he continues to be a nominal Catholic but has jettisoned the Church's metaphysical doctrines, and he continues to be a nominal academic by maintaining an honorary professorship at the University of Birmingham but is now a full-time creative writer.

I have observed that Lodge has resisted the perceptions of some of his readers that the novels about academia for which he is best known are "cruelly satirical" and that, on the evidence of these texts, he is to be judged "a cruel writer." While it is undeniable that Lodge is among the most humane of contemporary novelists, it is also evident that he views the world most crisply through the satiric lens, and—his sense of the disreputability of this connection notwithstanding—satire is largely inseparable from cruelty. A sardonic quality impishly lurks beneath the light-hearted surface of *Changing Places* and *Small World* and energizes these robust narratives. Whereas in his academic comedies Lodge reduces his characters to caricatures from a "privileged narrative altitude" (*Changing Places*, p. 8), in *Therapy*—in a seeming act of atonement of sorts—he reverses this pattern and rescues his protagonist from the debilitating effects of just such a caricatural reduction. Tubby's restoration epitomizes the trend in Lodge's later novels toward an expanded role for the author's munificently guiding (if rather heavy and too visible) hand, as is the case in both *Nice Work* and *Paradise News*, in which he effects benevolent closure by airlifting bundles of cash into his characters' laps. Lodge has recognized this tendency in his fiction and its potential problems. As he observed in a 1993 interview, "I am generous sometimes to the point of sentimentality and I think that is a weakness I have to watch. When you're writing novels you are in a sort of God-like position, because you are dispensing fortune. . . . And whatever you do is going to betray something of what you think life is like or what you hope it could be like" (Kostrzewa interview, p. 10). That he has, particularly in recent years, elected to construct his fictional universe according to a buoyant optimism has made him something of a latter-day Dickens, an incongruous presence on the late-twentieth-century literary landscape. But if his beneficence entails pitfalls, it also offers much of value that is too easily lost on a jaded modern readership, which is as liable to mistake for profound the glibly cynical posturings characteristic of much contemporary fiction as it is carelessly to dismiss, as triflingly sentimental, Lodge's rare generosity of mind and sympathy of imagination.

SELECTED BIBLIOGRAPHY

I. NOVELS. *The Picturegoers* (London, 1960; repr., 1992; New York, 1993); *Ginger, You're Barmy* (London, 1962; repr., London, 1981; New York, 1982); *The British Museum Is Falling Down* (London, 1965; repr., 1980; New York, 1989); *Out of the Shelter* (London, 1970; rev. ed. London and New York, 1985); *Changing Places: A Tale of Two Campuses* (London, 1975; New York, 1992); *How Far Can You Go?* (London, 1980), repr. as *Souls and Bodies* (New York, 1982); *Small World: An Academic Romance* (New York, 1984); *Nice Work* (London, 1988); *Paradise News* (London and New York, 1991); *A David Lodge Trilogy*, incl. *Changing Places, Small World,* and *Nice Work* (London, 1993); *Therapy* (London and New York, 1995).

II. PLAYS, SERIALIZATIONS, ADAPTATIONS. *Between These Four Walls*, coauthored with Malcolm Bradbury and James Duckett (produced 1963); *Slap in the Middle*, coauthored with James Duckett and David Turner (produced 1965); *Small World*, Granada Television serialization (1988); *Nice Work*, BBC serialization (1989); *The Writing Game: A Comedy* (London, 1991); *Martin Chuzzlewit* by Charles Dickens, television adaptation (1994).

III. LITERARY CRITICISM. *Graham Greene* (New York, 1966); *Language of Fiction: Essays in Criticism and Verbal Analysis of the English Novel* (London and New York, 1966); *Evelyn Waugh* (New York, 1971); *The Novelist at the Crossroads, and Other Essays on Fiction and Criticism* (Ithaca, N.Y., 1971); (ed.), *Twentieth-Century Literary Criticism: A Reader* (London, 1972); *The Modes of Modern Writing: Metaphor, Metonymy, and the Typology of Modern Literature* (Ithaca, N.Y., 1977); *Working with Structuralism: Essays and Reviews on Nineteenth- and Twentieth-Century Literature* (London and Boston, 1981); *Write On: Occasional Essays, '65–'85* (London, 1986); (ed.), *Modern Criticism and Theory: A Reader* (London, 1988); *After Bakhtin: Essays on Fiction and Criticism* (London and New York, 1990); *The Art of Fiction: Illustrated from Classic and Modern Texts* (London and New York, 1992); *The Practice of Writing: Essays, Lectures, Reviews and a Diary* (London, 1996).

IV. INTERVIEWS. Bernard Bergonzi, "David Lodge Interviewed," in *The Month*, 2nd n.s. 1 (February 1970); idem, "A Religious Romance: David Lodge in Conversation," in *The Critic* 47 (fall 1992); John Haffenden, "David Lodge," in John Haffenden, ed., *Novelists in Interview* (London, 1985); R. Kostrzewa, "The Novel and Its Enemies: A Conversation with David Lodge," in *Harkness Report* (December 1993); Linda Metzger, ed., interview in *Contemporary Authors*, vol. 19 (Detroit, 1987); C. Walsh, "David Lodge Interviewed," in *Strawberry Fare* (autumn 1984).

V. BIBLIOGRAPHY. Norbert Schurer, *David Lodge: An Annotated Primary and Secondary Bibliography* (Frankfurt, 1995).

VI. BIOGRAPHICAL AND CRITICAL STUDIES. Dennis Jackson, "David Lodge," in *Dictionary of Literary Biography* 14 (1983); Peter Widdowson, "The Anti-History Men: Malcolm Bradbury and David Lodge," in *Critical Quarterly* 26 (winter 1984); Bernard Bergonzi, *The Myth of Modernism and Twentieth-Century Literature* (Brighton, Eng., 1986); Terry Eagleton, "The Silences of David Lodge," in *New Left Review* no. 172 (November–December 1988); Siegfried Mews, "The Professor's Novel: David Lodge's *Small World*," in *Modern Language Notes* 104 (April 1989); Robert Morace, *The Dialogic Novels of Malcolm Bradbury and David Lodge* (Carbondale, Ill., 1989); Bernard Bergonzi, *Exploding English: Criticism, Theory, Culture* (Oxford and New York, 1990); Brian A. Connery, "Inside Jokes: Familiarity and Contempt in Academic Satire," in David Bevan, ed., *University Fiction* (Amsterdam, 1990); Philip Smallwood, "Creators as Critics II: David Lodge," in *Modern Critics in Practice: Critical Portraits of British Literary Critics* (New York, 1990); James Acheson, "The Small Worlds of Malcolm Bradbury and David Lodge," in James Acheson, ed., *The British and Irish Novel since 1960* (London and New York, 1991); Daniel Ammann, *David Lodge and the Art-and-Reality Novel* (Heidelberg, 1991); Merritt Moseley, *David Lodge: How Far Can You Go?* (San Bernardino, Calif., 1991); Thomas Woodman, *Faithful Fictions: The Catholic Novel in British Literature* (Milton Keynes and Philadelphia, 1991); Bernard Bergonzi, *David Lodge* (Plymouth, Eng., 1995).

IAN McEWAN

(1948–   )

Angus R. B. Cochran

SINCE PUBLISHING HIS first short story in 1972, Ian McEwan has come to prominence primarily because of the shocking violence and grotesque sexuality of his fiction. These moments of extremity catch characters unaware and interrupt quotidian existence with unimaginable power. But, to date, the lurid brutality and perversion constitute only one component of his examination of the psychological, domestic, urban, and global forces that jeopardize individual happiness. And in the latest stages of his career, he supplements his psychological portraits with an examination of what it means to be a British subject in the second half of the twentieth century. Increasingly, his novels and screenplays attempt to fathom the historical and social forces to which the British have been subject since winning World War II. The most successful recent novels, *The Child in Time* (1987) and *Black Dogs* (1992), place individual incidents of violence within a national context in order to draw out the parallels between the nation and the individual. McEwan's best-known film, *The Ploughman's Lunch* (1985), shows the present replicating the past, both for the nation and for its subjects. Frequently within the last two centuries, social criticism has been an integral part of English fiction; McEwan adds to this tradition a sense of the violence and absurdity that characterize contemporary urban existence. Like the British authors with whom he is most frequently compared—Martin Amis, J. G. Ballard, Salman Rushdie, Will Self, Fay Weldon—Ian McEwan writes to criticize governmental policies pursued since World War II; the price paid for poor governance, he suggests, is national safety and individual liberty.

LIFE

ON 21 June 1948, Ian Russell McEwan was born into a military family stationed at Aldershot, in the south of England. His mother, Rose Lillian Violet (Moore) McEwan, was a war widow who had two children from her first marriage. His father, David McEwan, was a Scot who had enlisted in the army, moved from Glasgow in order to escape the unemployment of the 1930s, and risen through the ranks to the level of major. Because his father was assigned to military bases abroad, McEwan spent much of his early childhood in Libya and Singapore. In fact, it was in Libya that he remembers having his first real experience of peace and happiness. In his contribution to *Hockney's Alphabet*, McEwan recalls an idyllic moment in Tripoli that he labels the "thirty seconds or so that I count as the real beginning of my conscious life":

The beach of white sand was deserted. It was all mine. The space which separated me from what I saw sparkled with significance. Everything I looked at—yesterday's footprints in the sand, an outcrop of rock, the wooden rail beneath my hand—seemed overpoweringly unique, etched in light, and somehow to be aware of itself, to "know." At the same time, everything belonged together, and that unity was knowing too and seemed to say, Now you've seen us. I felt myself dissolving into what I saw. I was no longer a son or a schoolboy or a Wolf Cub. And yet I felt my individuality intensely, as though for the first time. I was coming into being.

(n.p.)

Uniqueness, solitude, and emptiness—the shoreline scene mirrors back to the young boy a glimpse of his own essential nature. Boyhood attachments to family, school, and friendship simply evaporate.

To a great extent solitude was also an outgrowth of McEwan's separation from his family when he returned to Britain at the age of twelve, to attend Woolverstone Hall, a state-run boarding school in Suffolk. At school, McEwan seems to have flourished despite his initial loneliness and disorientation. He cultivated an appreciation for literature through reading English Romantic poetry and, later, twentieth-century British and American fiction. After completing his secondary schooling, McEwan worked in London, hauling garbage, then attended the University of Sussex in Brighton, where in 1970 he received a B.A. degree, with honors, in English literature. With his enthusiasm for academic literary study flagging, McEwan in 1971 completed an M.A. in creative writing at the University of East Anglia, where he studied under the novelists Malcolm Bradbury and Angus Wilson. After an extended overland journey to Afghanistan in 1972, he began to write in earnest and sold his first short story, "Homemade," to *New American Review* that same year.

The years from 1972 to 1981 were a period of accelerating literary output, success in radio and television drama, and increasing critical acclaim. *First Love, Last Rites* (1975), McEwan's first collection of short stories, received the Somerset Maugham Award. In 1976 his play *Jack Flea's Birthday Celebration* aired on BBC TV. Two years later, his second collection of stories, *In Between the Sheets,* and his first novel, *The Cement Garden,* were published to generally good reviews that nonetheless expressed critics' queasiness at the fiction's frequent violence and perversity. In addition to provoking reviewers' unease, *The Cement Garden* garnered unwanted publicity because of accusations made by another novelist that its plot closely resembled that of a novel of his own. Julian Gloag charged that *The Cement Garden* had its source in *Our Mother's House* (1963), which, like *The Cement Garden,* concerns a group of children who bury their dead mother in order to avoid being separated. McEwan's denial of the accusations was pointed; he told Amanda Smith in *Publishers Weekly:* "The plots did resemble each other, but then plots often do. . . . But they're very different books. I hadn't read Gloag's" (p. 69). To date, Gloag's and other commentators' charges have never been substantiated with proof that specific passages were lifted. In 1979, after having accepted *Solid Geometry* for broadcast on television, the BBC foisted further notoriety upon McEwan by banning his play on the eve of its filming. The justification was that its odd sexual motifs, including an erect phallus pickled in a jar of formaldehyde, would offend viewers. A year later, however, the BBC did broadcast another play of McEwan's, *The Imitation Game.*

In the 1980s, McEwan gave up writing short stories in favor of the novel and moved from writing television and radio scripts to screenplays. He was short-listed for a prestigious British literary award, the Booker Prize, for the novel *The Comfort of Strangers* (1981). Two years later *The Ploughman's Lunch* was released and received *Evening Standard* awards for best film, best director (Richard Eyre), and best screenplay. Novels appeared throughout the next ten years: *The Child in Time* won the Whitbread Book of the Year award in 1987; *The Innocent* was a best-seller in Britain in 1990; and *Black Dogs* was nominated for the Booker Prize in 1992. The film *Soursweet,* released in 1988, had a screenplay adapted by McEwan from Timothy Mo's novel of the same name. The 1991 film version of *The Comfort of Strangers* was adapted by Harold Pinter. In 1993 *The Good Son,* incorporating a heavily rewritten and blunted version of McEwan's original screenplay, was distributed. The years since 1980 have also seen the premiere in 1983, by the London Symphony Orchestra, of an antiwar oratorio, *Or Shall We Die?,* for which McEwan wrote the libretto that complements Michael Berkeley's music. Two children's books have appeared under McEwan's name. The first, *Rose Blanche* (1985), was rewritten from a translation of the Italian original by Roberto Innocenti and Christophe Gallez; the second, *The Daydreamer* (1994), was illustrated by Anthony Browne. Ian McEwan married Penny Allen, a healer and astrologer, in 1982. They live with their children in Oxford.

EARLY FICTION AND ADOLESCENCE

WHEN asked about his work, McEwan often responds to questions about its contents by shifting attention to its literary form. This habit is particularly evident when he speaks about his early works, the short stories. United by their similar themes, the stories were motivated by the author's desire to conquer a number of technical or rhetorical challenges. McEwan told John Haffenden, a reviewer from the *Literary Review,* that in the first collection, *First Love, Last Rites,* "The Last Day of Summer" began in his mind with a desire to write a story in the present tense, and "First Love, Last Rites" emulates James Joyce's *Ulysses* by concluding with the word "Yes" (pp. 29–30). Thus the stories in these early collections have the air of a testing ground for the young author, a series of short exercises with definite stylistic goals to be sustained over several pages.

The two collections of early stories stress the importance of initiation, particularly for children and adolescents. These moments of transition, McEwan suggests, are frequently violent and psychologically scarring, both for the initiates and for others who postpone change or force it prematurely. In "Homemade," the opening tale of *First Love, Last Rites*, the first-person narrator describes how, as a fourteen-year-old boy, he was led at a dizzying pace through the vices of adulthood without ever developing the maturity that would allow him to grasp the moral implications of his actions. Spurred on by an older, more experienced friend, the nameless narrator learns to smoke tobacco and marijuana, to sneak into horror films, to drink, to shoplift, to curse, and finally to masturbate. His sexuality having been awakened, the narrator discerns in his virginity the last vestige of untainted childhood. In his desire to be fully mature, he initiates an incestuous relationship with his ten-year-old sister. There is no suspense in the story about whether incest will occur, for the narrator begins with the aftermath of intercourse. Instead, the narrative moves inexorably to its graphic conclusion, stripping the reader of any lingering innocence, like the fourteen-year-old boy at the moment of incest. Looking back at his younger self, the now older narrator describes the loss of his virginity as both a pleasure and a travesty:

I felt proud, proud to be fucking, even if it were only Connie, my ten-year-old sister, even if it had been a crippled mountain goat I would have been proud to be lying there in that manly position, proud in advance of being able to say "I have fucked," of belonging intimately and irrevocably to that superior half of humanity who had known coitus, and fertilized the world with it. . . .
This may have been one of the most desolate couplings known to copulating mankind, involving lies, deceit, humiliation, incest, my partner falling asleep, my gnat's orgasm and the sobbing which now filled the bedroom, but I was pleased with it, myself, Connie, pleased to let things rest a while, to let the matter drop.

(p. 29)

Connie is transformed in the narrative into a wounded animal, both scapegoat and sacrificial lamb. Tellingly, the retrospective evaluation still lacks sympathy for the victim of the boy's voracious sexuality.

From the outset of McEwan's career, then, sexual abuse is a frequent compulsion throughout the stories. Often it is depicted as the result of male sexuality, a force that is both predatory and perverse in its quest for satiety. In "Butterflies," the fifth story in *First Love, Last Rites*, a loner lures a young girl into a derelict industrial landscape on the pretext of showing her butterflies that live there. After they leave their neighborhood, the two pass through an ominous wasteland where a group of boys are preparing to roast a live cat. At last, in a tunnel next to a fetid canal, the narrator forces the small girl to grasp his penis, and immediately ejaculates. Trying to flee after this moment of climax, the girl falls and is knocked unconscious. In the conclusion to the story, the murderer tells how he killed his victim: "Then I lifted her up gently, as gently as I could so as not to wake her, and eased her quietly into the canal" (p. 96). As macabre as this scenario is, the atrocity is compounded by the fact that the man is on his way to meet the girl's grieving parents. Like "Homemade," the shock of "Butterflies" lies not only in the casualness with which acts of violent cruelty are undertaken but also in the detached, analytic, almost forensic manner in which first-person narrators relate their crimes; neither suffers any consequences and neither expresses contrition. Indeed, the perpetrators' lack of accountability stems from a pathology of cruelty bred by the stories' urban settings. A manifestation of urban iniquity, the physical desolation in McEwan's early work demonstrates how the city offers isolation instead of friendship, and impunity instead of justice.

Even family does not seem strong enough to provide a defense against the degradation of urban life. As "Homemade" illustrates, McEwan's fiction is full of families in which the generations torture and exploit one another for their own gain and pleasure. In particular, two stories from *First Love, Last Rites* contain matriarchal figures who prey upon boys they are rearing with curious psychological tactics. In "Disguises," an embittered actress who no longer can find work takes in her orphaned nephew, Henry, and convinces him to dress for dinner in a variety of costumes that she sews for him. Each evening he is compelled to assume an adult role that his Aunt Mina chooses for him, including soldier, elevator operator, old man, monk, and shepherd. On one particularly humiliating evening he plays a figure from an adult drama—a young girl, whom his aunt, in the guise of an old, scarred soldier, tries to seduce. Soon, this make-believe maturity is supplemented by actual adult behavior that Mina foists on Henry; she teaches him to mix her martinis and encourages him to drink himself into a stupor as punishment for coming home late from school. At the end of the story, this precipitate maturity dooms Henry's attempt at forming a friendship with a girl from his school.

Conversely, in "Conversation with a Cupboard Man," an only child whose father died before he was born describes to a silent social worker how he was raised by his mother as an overgrown baby until the age of seventeen, when, upon remarrying, she put him in a sanitarium. After he is put in a home and given vocational training, the narrator goes to work washing dishes in the kitchen of a hotel, where he encounters a far more direct form of persecution from the chief cook. After the cook locks him in the hotel's large oven and turns the heat on, blistering the narrator's feet and back, the latter exacts his revenge by pouring boiling oil over Pus-face, as he calls the cook, putting him in the hospital for nine months. The social worker comes across the cupboard man after he has spent time in prison for shoplifting and after an abortive trip to see his mother, during which he discovers that she has moved without leaving a forwarding address. All he is left with is a recurrent dream of being a toddler and a compulsion for climbing into his closet and masturbating.

Orphans, abandoned youngsters, adopted relatives: these dislocated children litter the homes of Ian McEwan's fiction in a way that mimics and exaggerates the decline of the nuclear family as the dominant domestic unit. In place of this traditional kinship, he substitutes synthetic, improvised pseudofamilies composed of siblings, cast-offs, tenants, boyfriends and girlfriends, and unexpected and unwanted offspring. McEwan's first novel, *The Cement Garden*, unfolds in one such anomalous household. Like so many of McEwan's fictional tales, this novel is set against the backdrop of an uncharacteristically hot British summer that frays characters' tempers as fast as it reddens their pale skin. Initially, the family in the novel seems entirely typical in its fractious tone, which is maintained by four bickering siblings and two quarrelsome adults. Very quickly, however, this uncomfortable domesticity is disrupted when the father dies of a heart attack while paving over his garden. Soon the mother takes to her bed with a mysterious wasting condition, and within a few months she dies, leaving the children to their own devices, without any supervision. Afraid that they will be split up and sent to different orphanages, the children decide not to report the death of their mother; instead, they deposit her corpse in a trunk in the basement and entomb her in cement.

The second half of the novel depicts the irrevocable transformation that occurs in the four children in the absence of parental guidance. Each manifests the pain of the loss uniquely, and in a way that amplifies preexisting features of his or her personality. The youngest boy, Tom, has always been treated as the baby of the family, and in a turn reminiscent of "Conversation with a Cupboard Man," he reverts to behaving like a infant, a regression that is encouraged by his sisters, who enjoy playing roles that formerly were their parents', and who dress him as a little girl. Sue, who is twelve, takes refuge in a diary she daily addresses to her mother and passes the time in the cellar, sitting next to the trunk in which the body is cemented. The narrator, Jack, becomes increasingly hostile toward his brother and sisters, stops bathing, sleeps as much as he can, and masturbates repeatedly and compulsively every day. The eldest sibling, Julie, begins dating a twenty-three-year-old professional snooker player named Derek, and as she begins to discern the power she has over this man, she gradually learns that her desirability can effortlessly be turned to her advantage. One way or another, this truncated family manages to survive in the ruinous house; the sisters care for Tom, and Jack aimlessly pursues his own obsessions. When the stench of the mother's decomposing body begins to seep into the house, Derek applies more cement to the cracks that have appeared in the casing, and Julie tells Jack that Derek wants to move into the house. The novel ends with Derek stumbling upon Julie and Jack in an embrace, on the verge of intercourse. In his revulsion, he sledgehammers the tomb open and telephones the police as brother and sister consummate their incest.

McEwan told Amanda Smith, in an interview in *Publishers Weekly*, that he began *The Cement Garden* with "a wish to examine power relationships in the family and also an interest in the sexuality of young children" (p. 69). His entrée into this world was through the fiction of William Golding: "I wanted," he discloses in the interview, "to write an urban *Lord of the Flies*" (p. 69). And what was so startling to him as a thirteen-year-old, McEwan recalls in his contribution, "Schoolboys," to *William Golding: The Man and His Books*, was that the world of boys Golding imagines on the island was so similar to McEwan's own milieu:

What was so attractively subversive and feasible about Golding was his apparent assumption that in a child-dominated world things went wrong in a most horrible and interesting way. For—and this was the second discovery—I *knew* these boys. I knew what they were capable of. I had seen us at it. As far as I was concerned, Golding's island was a thinly disguised boarding school....

What I had known, without ever giving the matter much thought, from my crowded, dormitory existence, was confirmed and clarified; life could be unhappily divisive, even go fabulously wrong, without anyone having to be extravagantly nasty. No one was to blame—it was how it was when we were together....

Lord of the Flies thrilled me with all the power a fiction can have because I felt indicted by it. All my friends were implicated too. It made me feel ashamed in a rather luxurious way. The novel brought realism to my fantasy life (the glowing, liberated world without grown-ups) and years later, when I came to write a novel myself, I could not resist the momentum of my childhood fantasies nor the power of Golding's model, for I found myself wanting to describe a closed world of children removed from the constraints of authority. I had no doubt that my children too would suffer from, rather than exult in, their freedom. Without realizing it at the time, I named my main character after one of Golding's.

(pp. 157–159)

Like *Lord of the Flies*, then, *The Cement Garden* constructs a miniature universe in which Tom, Sue, Jack, and Julie are freed from the constraints of adult direction and subsequently discover that few boundaries exist to limit their instincts. But McEwan's depiction of childhood anarchy diverges from Golding's at the very outset, for his narrator feels responsible for ridding the house of adults: "I did not kill my father," Jack claims, "but I sometimes felt I had helped him on his way" (p. 13). The reason for Jack's lingering suspicion is that his father suffered his second, fatal heart attack while Jack was in the bathroom masturbating—experiencing, in fact, his first ejaculation. Jack was supposed to be helping his father mix cement, because his health was precarious. Symbolically, the son becomes potent at the very instant the father dies; one cycle of fertility completes itself as another becomes incipient. The oedipal plot is not completed, however, until Jack's incestuous affair with Julie, who most closely plays the role of mother in the household.

Thus, where *Lord of the Flies* proposes that social, adult control constrains violent adolescent urges, *The Cement Garden* further suggests that as a social unit, the family curbs domestic sexual expression: "I had an idea," McEwan professed to Ian Hamilton in an interview in the *New Review*, "that in the nuclear family the kind of forces that are being repressed—the oedipal, incestuous forces—are also paradoxically the very forces which keep the family together. So if you remove the controls, you have a ripe anxiety in which the oedipal and the incestuous are the definitive emotions" (p. 21). Certainly, the incestuous impulse is present even before the children's parents die—Julie and Jack, for example, play a bizarre game of "doctor" in which they examine their sister's naked body, pretending to be "scientists examining a specimen from outer space" (p. 15).

But the consummation of sexual desire awaits both the removal of parental influence and, more pressingly, the threat that adult control will be reintroduced into the house by Derek, whom Julie describes as wanting "to be one of the family, you know, big smart daddy" (p. 148). With all his vanity and materialism, Derek represents the adult priorities beyond the house: "He wants to take charge of everything. He keeps talking about moving in with us," Julie tells Jack (p. 148). Derek obviously feels that the household lacks the authority of a patriarchal figure who will impose order upon the children's chaos. Yet he himself, a twenty-three-year-old, lives in a protracted adolescent state. Julie continues: "He lives with his mum in this tiny house. I've been there. She calls him Doodle and makes him wash his hands before tea.... She told me she irons fifteen shirts a week for him" (p. 148). Derek's attempt to usurp the role of father and his eventual denunciation of the children to the police are therefore acts heavy with irony. He is merely playing the part of rebellious teenager and attempting to square this identity with conventional notions of patriarchy. That *The Cement Garden* ends with the reassertion of adulthood only underlines the novel's deeply ambiguous attitude toward the world of grown-ups.

393

IAN McEWAN

THE DIFFICULTIES OF MATURITY

ALTHOUGH in places the early stories and *The Cement Garden* investigate adulthood, it is not until the second volume of stories, *In Between the Sheets*, that McEwan consistently begins to explore maturity. In the bleak portrait that he paints, men and women prey upon one another's weaknesses and in turn expose their own failings. This trait is so marked that the literary critic Christopher Ricks likens McEwan's short stories to those of Rudyard Kipling, another army child who was brought up abroad and returned to Britain for schooling. Ricks's comparison is based on his observation in the *Listener* that McEwan's and Kipling's short fiction is rooted in "exceptional imagination, . . . cruelty, humiliation and very traditional moral values." In his response, McEwan emphasizes his reluctance to pass judgment on his characters' behavior:

I'm not sure I would share with you the sense that my fiction has been quite as moral as you would suggest. There are certainly rather frail kinds of statements embodied in them, a rather fragile kind of optimism about life. I hope to avoid any programmatic moral manipulation of the stories, and of the novel, too—I try to keep that sense of the story that is going to be moral in some kind of abeyance, and hope that, through restraint, one will generate a compassion for the right people.

(p. 527)

In an interview with John Haffenden in the *Literary Review*, McEwan accounts for his reticence to judge by suggesting that his literature emerges from unconscious impulses: "So I hope that moral concerns will be balanced, or even undermined by the fact that I still don't have complete control. Some element of mystery must remain" (pp. 30–31). The inexplicability of the stories arises, then, from their recondite source in the subconscious of the author; implicitly, the characters' flaws may simply be projections of the author's own urges. It is a hallmark of McEwan's prose that while the events are rendered with a scrupulous clarity, their significance is frequently obscure.

The second story of *In Between the Sheets*, "Reflections of a Kept Ape," consists of an extended monologue by a pet ape that was formerly the lover of his owner, Sally Klee, a novelist with one best-seller and chronic writer's block. McEwan refuses to condemn the writer's bestiality: instead, he characterizes the monkey as an aesthete with a taste for self-pity and melodrama:

Perhaps from the very beginning the arrangement was certain to fail. On the other hand, the pleasures it afforded—particularly to Sally Klee—were remarkable. And while she believes that in my behavior towards her I was a little too persistent, too manic, too "eager," and while I for my part still feel she delighted more in my unfamiliarity ("funny little black leathery penis" and "your saliva tastes like weak tea") than in my essential self, I would like to think that there are no profound regrets on either side.

(p. 34)

Once again, McEwan's matter-of-fact detachment heightens the perversity and its shock. The Jamesian rhetoric of the piece provides a perfect register for the simian narrator's incapacity to comprehend the distastefulness of his union with Sally. The ape's smugness seems merely a character flaw until the final paragraphs, when he recalls the moment in his infancy at the zoo when he became aware of the human spectators: "I am staring at my mother, who squats with her back to me, and then, for the first time in my life, I see past her shoulder as through a mist, pale, spectral figures beyond the plate glass, pointing and mouthing silently" (p. 48). Here, the evidence indicates that his preciousness is inspired by a desire to emulate or even surpass his human captors' erudition, as a way to efface the difference in species. The ape's slavish imitation is bound to fail, of course, and the greater the contrast between his physical and cognitive states, the more pronounced will be his rejection.

While "Reflections of a Kept Ape" concerns the adult relationship between an adult and her pet, the final detail from the ape's infancy still demonstrates McEwan's preoccupation with childhood. "Pornography," the opening tale of *In Between the Sheets*, also explores familiar territory in depicting adult sexuality as an amalgam of violence and perversity. Here, Michael O'Byrne, an employee in an adult bookshop in the Soho district of London, contracts gonorrhea and infects both of his girlfriends. He continually bullies and abuses one of these women, whereas the other subjects him to sadomasochistic sex, during which he revels in his own humiliation. Finally, the women, who are both nurses, exact their revenge by scheming to sever O'Byrne's infected penis. As the story ends, the nurses approach the pornographer bound to the bed, reduced as it were to a figure from one of his magazines; incredibly, even at this extremity, he experiences "through his fear . . . excitement once more, horrified excitement" (p. 30).

In much the same way that O'Byrne confuses his life with the pornography in which he traffics, the title of this story at once names McEwan's subject matter and the form that he parodies. It is no accident that O'Byrne's final encounter with his two medical lovers is composed with the same louche precision as the letter he reads in one of his magazines from an "uncircumcised male virgin, without hygiene, forty-two next May" who "dare not peel back his foreskin now for fear of what he might see. I have a fear of worms" (p. 12). Where O'Byrne can only laugh at the anonymous letter, McEwan might expect that we temper our amusement at O'Byrne's own predicament with equal parts horror. McEwan's tale is, of course, not pornographic. But it does represent pornography in order both to mock the genre's degradation of sexuality and to draw out its comic undertones.

Despite the familiar contours of "Reflections of a Kept Ape" and "Pornography," much in this second collection is new. The story that lends its title to the volume builds to a climax in which a divorced father, Stephen Cooke, seems on the verge of sexually abusing his fourteen-year-old daughter, Miranda. She and her dwarf-like friend come to visit for a long weekend, and Stephen is shocked to find himself with an erection after his daughter kisses him good night. Later that night, when he enters her bedroom naked, the most likely outcome would appear to be incest. However, "In Between the Sheets" veers away from this conclusion. Rather than consummating his evident desire for his daughter, Stephen thinks back to an instant when, as a boy, he chose not to spoil the perfection of an expanse of snow. Miranda "was asleep and almost smiling, and in the pallor of her upturned throat he thought he saw from one bright morning in his childhood a field of dazzling white snow which he, a small boy of eight, had not dared scar with his footprints" (p. 112). So easily could this story have become a sequel to "Homemade" that the father's constraint signals a transition away from shock and brutality and into a tacit assertion of adult accountability. For perhaps the first time, a childhood recollection can offer a lesson to the present.

Stylistically, too, the stories of *In Between the Sheets* demonstrate a far wider range of fictional techniques. The fragmentary "To and Fro" shows an impressionistic rhetorical style built from short, self-contained paragraphs that articulate different perspectives but share a common frame of reference. The fragments gradually accumulate into a brilliant mosaic that illustrates the dialectical nature of experience; for every movement there is an equal and opposite motion. Metaphorically, "To and Fro" represents the physical motion of the beating of a heart, the rocking of a child to sleep, the movement of waves over a starfish, and the rhythm of sexual intercourse. More abstractly, it stands for the dualisms that give life a contrapuntal quality: family and work, the possibility of doppelgängers, reciprocal intimacy between lovers, and generational difference. Although it is possible to differentiate a narrator and a figure called Leech, "To and Fro" is unique in McEwan's writing because it embodies reality through symbols rather than through character and plot. The author also gives his third piece, "Two Fragments: March 199-," a hallucinatory quality, much like that in "To and Fro." Here, however, this unreal quality derives from a lack of context. The two vignettes are set in postapocalyptic London, where thousands have been left hungry and destitute by an unnamed catastrophe. These sketches of the future describe the attempts, amid the disintegration of metropolitan life, of one individual to raise a daughter and sustain intimacy with a lover.

One significant aspect, therefore, that distinguishes *In Between the Sheets* from earlier fiction is the diminished importance of plot. Far less are the stories driven by acts of violence or predatory sexuality. Many seem to be exercises in composing a setting or in orchestrating a series of short observations. Indeed, a couple of the stories resemble those from James Joyce's *Dubliners,* a collection that notably ignores traditional plotting and focuses instead on the mundane aspects of everyday life. The last story, "Psychopolis," has most in common with Joyce's short fiction, particularly with the concluding tale in *Dubliners,* "The Dead." Here, Joyce intended to illustrate the best qualities and the failures of the Irish at a generous dinner dance staged on the feast of the Epiphany in Edwardian Dublin.

"Psychopolis" signals McEwan's desire, conversely, to reveal a fundamental banality in American congeniality by depicting a series of social events that culminate in a small party at a house located "on a recently reclaimed stretch of desert"

(p. 138). The setting of the story, present-day Los Angeles, depicts metropolitan life on an unimaginably large scale. The protagonist, a disaffected, vacationing British writer, discovers that the individuals he encounters are alienated and inarticulate. The first woman he meets asks to be shackled to his bed, where she remains until he releases her three days later. At the party that closes the story, one of the guests pretends to shoot the host with a loaded revolver. After a brief moment of consternation, the protagonist incongruously ends the party by playing his flute. As in "The Dead," music plays a prominent role in the tale, not so much to illustrate its centrality to Angeleno culture (as Joyce's music does for Dublin) as to mark the musician as an anomaly and an anachronism in this Californian context. In this "vast, fragmented city without a center, without citizens, a city that existed only in the mind, a nexus of change or stagnation in individual lives" (p. 152), the narrator ends his rendition of a Bach sonata prematurely in order to renounce the "genteel escapism" (p. 153) of the city. But the listeners do not realize that he has broken off without finishing, and they break into spontaneous applause. Like *In Between the Sheets* as a whole, "Psychopolis" shows McEwan's growing interest in examining the connections between social decay and psychological infirmity.

A MEDITERRANEAN INTERLUDE

IAN McEwan has always claimed to enjoy travel: "I rather like," he confesses to Christopher Ricks in the *Listener*, "to travel alone, and I suppose that the travel is a way of not doing anything else. I mean I don't write when I'm travelling. I don't even think about writing. Travelling rather puts you in the role of author—you're passing constantly through situations without any real responsibility towards them. I do find that very exhilarating" (p. 526). Unlike the author, McEwan's characters tend to travel abroad in couples. In his second novel, *The Comfort of Strangers,* the travelers are a pair of English tourists in a nameless city that closely resembles Venice. However, "for reasons they could no longer define, Colin and Mary were no longer on speaking terms" (p. 9). Something about the enervating heat, the effort of vacationing, and the regularity of hotel life has produced an emotional distance, which is

bridged only occasionally by routinized sex and recriminations: "their intimacy, rather like too many suitcases, was a matter of perpetual concern; together they moved slowly, clumsily, effecting lugubrious compromises, attending to delicate shifts of mood, repairing breaches" (p. 13).

One evening, in the midst of a futile search for a restaurant, the couple encounter Robert, a local who offers to take them to a bar where they might find something to eat. The description of his physical appearance includes two fateful details: "On a chain around his neck hung a gold imitation razor blade which lay slightly askew on the thick pelt of chest hair. Over his shoulder he carried a camera" (p. 26). Robert relates the history of his childhood, which was dominated by a violent and strict father, who punished him severely for disobedience, and a doting mother, in whose bed he slept periodically until the age of ten. Having spent the night drinking with their new acquaintance without the benefit of an evening meal, and being unable in their drunkenness to find their hotel, the two sleep in the street and again run into Robert the next morning in the unnamed equivalent of St. Mark's Square.

After spending the day at Robert's house sleeping off their hangovers, Colin and Mary meet his crippled wife, Caroline. Her injuries occurred some years earlier, when her husband broke her back while they were engaging in rough, sadomasochistic sex. Nevertheless, she seems to accept her impairment with equanimity, saying darkly to Mary, "If you are in love with someone, you would even be prepared to let them kill you, if necessary" (p. 62). Aroused by something inchoate at this meeting, Mary and Colin remain in their hotel for the next three days, wrapped in a state of prolonged erotic animation.

But on the fourth day they venture out and, partly by happenstance and partly by choice, wind up at Robert and Caroline's. In the apartment, Mary learns of Caroline's brutal sexual history with Robert. She also discovers that Robert has surreptitiously and compulsively been photographing Colin—at the hotel, on the streets, asleep in their hotel. The realization that their first meeting with Robert was not serendipitous, but was coordinated carefully, comes only as she lapses into a catatonic, mute state induced by a drug administered by Caroline. When Colin and Robert return, Colin is quickly overwhelmed by the married couple.

At the denouement, Robert briefly kisses Colin's mouth and then opens an artery in one of his wrists with a straight-edge razor, sending a jet of blood across the room. When Mary revives from her drugged condition, Colin is dead.

Reviewers of *The Comfort of Strangers* were not unequivocally enthusiastic about the novel. While they applauded McEwan's decision to examine adulthood, they often found the final scene of violence unmotivated and gratuitous, and they were perplexed by McEwan's willful omission of the city's name. However, in the inevitable comparisons with Thomas Mann's *Death in Venice* (1912), readers agreed that McEwan was as adept as Mann at evoking a sinister, voyeuristic atmosphere in the city. Within this milieu, McEwan demonstrates, the promises of travel—of temporarily revising one's personality and of transgressing social convention—can lead not only to uncommon experiences but also to discomforting moments of self-discovery. A literary commonplace, perhaps, but in McEwan's hands this observation delivers a world fraught with dark, libidinal possibility. During one mutual exploration, Mary and Colin reveal a pair of disturbing sexual fantasies:

Mary muttered her intention of hiring a surgeon to amputate Colin's arms and legs. She would keep him in a room in her house, and use him exclusively for sex, sometimes lending him out to friends. Colin invented for Mary a large intricate machine, made of steel, painted bright red and powered by electricity.... Once Mary was strapped in, fitted to tubes that fed and evacuated her body, the machine would fuck her, not just for hours or weeks, but for years, on and on, for the rest of her life, till she was dead and on even after that, till Colin, or his lawyer, turned it off.

(pp. 81–82)

Now, while the author intends these frightening visions of surgical and mechanized sexuality to be demonstrations of each partner's submerged desire for dominance, the two reciprocal dreams play out an ongoing ideological argument in the novel. Just before Colin and Mary first run into Robert, they see a poster advocating forced castration for convicted rapists, and a quarrel ensues over whether this advocacy is an effective tactic for feminist activism. Later, we learn that the pair habitually argue about the root causes of social injustice: Mary proposes that patriarchy is "the most powerful single principle of organization shaping institu-

tions and individual lives. Colin argued, as he always did, that class dominance was more fundamental" (p. 80). Robert fuels the debate by advocating the strict, patriarchal rule under which he suffered so cruelly:

And even though they hate themselves for it, women long to be ruled by men. It's deep in their minds. They lie to themselves. They talk of freedom, and dream of captivity.... It is the world that shapes people's minds. It is men who have shaped the world. So women's minds are shaped by men.

(pp. 71–72)

But the tidiness of Robert's syllogism is belied by his description of his father's brutality, by the suffering he has inflicted upon Caroline, and by the sadistic murder of Colin. The novel undoubtedly indicts the patriarchal power that Robert defends as natural and that Mary so violently abominates as pernicious and retrograde. Yet Mary's feminism cannot account for the attraction that leads the pair back to Robert and Caroline's sinister apartment. Equally, the novel does not really confirm the ineluctable might of class dominance. If anything, Mary and Colin are at the mercy of a throng of recalcitrant waiters, porters, and maids who seem to conspire to thwart the couple's needs. Thus, the novel's investigation of psychology and gender fails to explain cruelty, violence, and injustice solely through feminist or Marxist social theory. McEwan stated to Haffenden in the *Literary Review* how difficult it is to discuss this work, since it attempts to articulate urges that he considers essentially inexpressible:

I had to address myself to the nature of the unconscious, and how the unconscious is shaped. It wasn't enough to be rational, since there might be desires—masochism in women, sadism in men—which act out the oppression of women or patriarchal societies but which have actually become related to sources of pleasure....

What is interesting is the extent to which people will collude in their own subjection, which is true not only of Caroline in relation to Robert but also of Colin.

(pp. 32, 33)

Once again, McEwan locates the origins of his work in his unconscious, and as a result mystery envelops *The Comfort of Strangers*. The novel indicates that individuals may be drawn toward their own doom out of an unacknowledged wish to be subjugated. However, the desire to destroy, which is equally instinctual, demonstrates the reciprocal urge, the need to dominate. In his superb review, "Playing with Terror," Christopher Ricks labels the novel a tragedy because it anatomizes injustice as an inescapable social condition:

Tragedy acknowledges that the injustices of life are sometimes corrigible. *The Comfort of Strangers* is alive with anger at the injustices, for instance, of the politics of sex, and it includes some vivid conversations on these wrongs and rights. . . . But tragedy also has to acknowledge that the injustices of life are sometimes incorrigible. The longing to explain is not annulled by, but it is chastened by, the inexplicability of evil and the irremediability of suffering. "Is there any cause in nature that makes these hard hearts?" Many possible causes lurk within the retailed sickness within the past lives of the murderous Robert and Caroline. Yet it may be that there is no cause that makes these hard hearts, or perhaps that there is a cause outside of nature.

(p. 14)

Haunted by the pervasive power of evil, McEwan recurred to this theme ten years later in *Black Dogs*, a novel predicated on the contingency that evil is not merely an external force but lies immanent in every person.

WRITING FOR PERFORMANCE

AFTER *The Comfort of Strangers*, for a period of roughly five years McEwan turned from writing fiction to writing for television and the cinema. He had already had some limited success in staging his drama; his play *Jack Flea's Birthday Celebration* had been broadcast on BBC Television in 1976. After the BBC abruptly refused to air *Solid Geometry* in 1979, the next project to be produced was *The Imitation Game*, which was televised in 1980. This play marks a significant break from earlier work by McEwan, for it introduces society and history into his literary landscape. In a 1983 interview with Jill Forbes in *Sight and Sound*, McEwan tied the appearance of larger social concerns to his change of medium from the novel to the script:

It certainly is the case that when I write fiction I find myself more interested in psychological states, which I think is something that film doesn't do very well, or not with any great finesse, or with a great deal of pretension, and that when I undertake to write dialogue I seem instantly to be in another frame of mind. I get into another gear, I seem to want to take on themes that are more broadly political.

(p. 235)

Four years later in an interview with Amanda Smith in *Publishers Weekly,* he restated his commitment to writing novels: "My preferred form is fiction. I take it more seriously than any other kind of writing. The reason the novel is such a powerful form is that it allows the examination of the private life better than any other art form" (p. 69).

Once again, McEwan explains the contents of his writing in terms of its literary form. Just as his desire to experiment with a variety of narrative techniques led to thematic transformations in his short stories, so by developing his scriptwriting skills he broadened the political scope of his later work. The early plays certainly develop the themes of youthful rebellion and psychological regression that saturate the short fiction. *Jack Flea's Birthday Celebration* details a twenty-year-old's attempt to stage a confrontation between his parents and his girlfriend, who is much older than he and treats him like a truculent child. *Solid Geometry* focuses on a young mathematician who discovers in his great-grandfather's papers the existence of a mystical state in which there is a "plane without a surface" (*New Statesman*, 30 March 1979, p. 449). After the protagonist masters the ability to achieve this state, he effects the disappearance of his wife through a series of yogalike exercises; after he helps her perform the final maneuver, she literally vanishes into thin air.

The next play, *The Imitation Game*, initiates a second dramatic phase, in which McEwan begins to exploit the expansiveness of the genre in order to produce political plays. Set in 1940, *The Imitation Game* chronicles a young woman's attempts to contribute to the British war effort in something other than a menial capacity. In the play the female protagonist, Cathy Raine, acts as a lightning rod for male prejudice against female ambition. Implicitly, the play defends her against an onslaught of chauvinism from male characters such as her father, her fiancé, strangers, and army colleagues. Eventually, Cathy is accepted for a position in army intelligence operations, where her job is to transcribe unintelligible radio transmissions for male decoders.

Once again, despite being part of an organization, the woman remains outside the cadre of male operatives who break the codes and jealously maintain their secrecy. The one occasion on which Cathy does find herself in a position of power occurs when she has an affair with a colleague from intelligence operations, and he is unable to match her sexually.

In his interview with Haffenden, McEwan claims that *The Imitation Game* is deeply indebted to *The Three Guineas* (1938), Virginia Woolf's attack on patriarchal militarism. Nevertheless, he realizes that writing about women's experience from the perspective of a man is not a straightforward endeavor. When Janet Watts, a reviewer for the *Observer*, went so far as to call McEwan "that still rare beast, a male feminist writer" (p. 37), he implicitly rejected the label, saying to John Haffenden in the *Literary Review*, "I didn't want to be used as a spokesman for women's affairs. I didn't want to be a man appropriating women's voices" (p. 31). For McEwan, the line between representation and misappropriation always demands the closest of attention.

In spite of his contention that screenplays and novels are suited to different subject matter, McEwan proposes in the introduction to his screen adaptation, *Soursweet*, that the two genres share similar assumptions: "Both forms must respond to the same exigencies; to take their worlds as given rather than pick them apart, to establish characters and their situations with economy and speed, to digress at their peril." He continues, "Because I like short fiction, and because my inclination as a writer is to compress and exclude, I take pleasure in screenplays" (p. vii). This principle of compression and exclusion characterizes all of McEwan's work, even the relatively lengthy novel *The Innocent*, and the brevity of his prose is well suited to briefly outlining characters' motives and failings. From this spare dialogue, the next film project, *The Ploughman's Lunch*, constructs a vivid portrait of life in London in the early 1980s. Blurring the distinction between public and private for the first time, McEwan depicts the interweaving of national events and the personal lives of characters whose job it is to produce the news. *The Ploughman's Lunch* gets its title, McEwan tells us in the introduction, from a pub lunch that was marketed as a traditional midday country meal. The meal, however, "was not an English tradition but an invention of an advertising campaign mounted to persuade

people to eat in pubs. *The Ploughman's Lunch* became a working title and then, imperceptibly, a controlling metaphor for self-serving fabrications of the past" (p. v).

The film, which was released in Britain in 1983 and in the United States in 1984, concerns the friendship between two unprincipled journalists, James Penfield and Jeremy Hancock, who happen to be attracted to the same woman, Susan Barrington. With the crisis in the Falklands reaching boiling point after Argentina's invasion of the islands, we learn that Penfield is writing a revisionist history of the Suez Crisis of 1955–1956, which he claims avoids "all the moralising and talk of national humiliation that is now the standard line on Suez" (p. 5). He defends the British for their final attempt to control world events in the Middle East by challenging Egyptian control of the canal. In the process of researching the history, Penfield repeatedly displays his personal and professional unscrupulousness: he neglects his dying mother out of embarrassment at his working-class roots; he accepts help to fix a flat tire from activists living in a peace camp, but then ensures they are denied widespread television coverage for their protest against missile placements; and, most cynically, he befriends and sleeps with a leftist history professor to gain access to her files, while simultaneously courting Susan, her daughter, and planning an account of the Suez crisis that will justify the British incursion. The film's climax occurs in Brighton at the annual Conservative party conference, where against a backdrop of nationalist fervor James learns that Jeremy and Susan are involved a relationship. Deflated, he turns to his Suez history full-time. In the last scene, we see him at the funeral of his mother, impatient and "expressionless" (p. 34).

The Ploughman's Lunch highlights how easily history can be distorted by political forces with agendas in the present. McEwan's intention, he states in the introduction to the script, was "to imagine how an ambitious writer might set out to rewrite the [Suez] Crisis in terms of the steely pragmatism being promoted now by the government of Mrs. Thatcher" (p. v). The consequences are daunting: "The past would be re-interpreted while the amateur historian unconsciously acted out in his private life a sequence of betrayals and deceits which would parallel the events he was distorting in his history" (p. v). In addition, McEwan's analogy between the two military operations condemns successive Conservative governments for acting abroad out of self-serving national motives. In his interview with Haffenden he concludes, "England under Mrs. Thatcher leaves me with a nasty taste. . . . While there are clear differences between Suez and the Falklands Crisis, I still think they have their roots in the same illusion: a Churchillian dimension, and also war as serving a certain rallying function for the Right" (p. 34). Undoubtedly the adjective "Churchillian" also characterizes the imperious, selfish manner in which James operates; everyone must be made to fit into his upper-middle-class, Tory incarnation, and if his parents have to be disowned in order for him to succeed, then so be it. While it anticipates the conjunction of private and public in *The Child in Time*, this screenplay remains McEwan's most explicitly political work to date.

After *The Ploughman's Lunch*, McEwan adapted Timothy Mo's 1982 novel, *Sour Sweet*, into a screenplay. Short-listed for a Booker Prize when it was published, the novel tells the story of a family from near Hong Kong that moves to Great Britain to begin a new life and subsequently struggles to comprehend this new, alien culture that does not always welcome immigrants. In a screenplay that is largely faithful to the original, McEwan's most significant additions were to change the setting of the film from the 1960s to the 1980s, and to open with a traditional wedding ceremony in Hong Kong that is designed to underline the distance between the two cultures. Again expressing McEwan's fascination with the technical challenges of writing, the introduction to the screenplay dwells on the formal complications of transforming a novel into a screenplay:

To adapt for the screen a novel you admire, particularly if it is the sort of novel you could never write yourself, can feel like brutal, arrogant work. Consider the end result. You have moved effortlessly from what is, or aspires to be, a work of art, a self-contained experience, the product of a single mind, to something a sixth of its length, of diminished literary content, peppered with curt, bureaucratic non-sentences . . . and laughable attempts at subjectivity at which the novel above all other forms excels.

(p. v)

With each adaptation, McEwan demonstrates a pronounced self-consciousness in shuttling from genre to genre; even with its political potential, he con-siders the screenplay to be less capable than the novel. Most recently, traces of McEwan's screenwriting can be found in the 1993 film *The Good Son*. McEwan's original screenplay, entitled *Bad Boy*, was doctored by a studio writer, resulting in a script that McEwan tactfully described to William Grimes in the *New York Times* as "perhaps a little less focused" (p. C25). But he seems undaunted by this brush with Hollywood, gamely adding that it was "an opportunity to fly first class, be treated like a celebrity, sit around the pool and get betrayed" (p. C25).

THE CHILD IN TIME

AFTER concentrating on screenplays for roughly five years, McEwan returned to fiction with *The Child in Time* in 1987. He told the (London) *Sunday Times Magazine* that the impulse for the novel lay in joining his novelistic and dramatic emphases:

For a long time I have wanted to connect up two different sides of my writing: the writing in television plays and *The Ploughman's Lunch*, where my concerns were primarily social and to some extent political, and the writing in prose fiction that tended to be rather dark, rather interior and rather more concerned with the pathology of the mind.

(p. 36)

The Child in Time transforms personal misfortune from an isolated accident into a symbol of national decay. Because *The Cement Garden* and *The Comfort of Strangers* both illustrate perversion and psychosis operating in the absence of a social context, they have in common with the short stories a characteristic obtuseness. In contrast, by introducing a far more public aspect to the fiction, *The Child in Time* reads like a fully fledged work of fiction, complete with psychological portraits and vivid scene-setting. For the first time in his prose fiction, in addition to having first names, McEwan's characters have surnames. They live in a society constituted by class and nationality. And as with the figures in *The Ploughman's Lunch*, public institutions and national events impinge upon them in ways that radically transform their views of the world.

Of course, continuities remain between this new social fiction and McEwan's previous introspective work. Most obviously, the novel continues McEwan's ongoing concern with children. Now, however, children are considered only to the extent that they influence adult psychology. The child in the book's title is missing and is embodied in the novel only by the memory of adults who knew her before she disappeared. *The Child in Time* is driven by a moment of unimaginable terror when a father, Stephen Lewis, discovers that his three-year-old daughter, Kate, has been abducted from a supermarket while they are shopping there on a Saturday morning. For the first ten pages of the novel, the narrative builds inexorably to this moment, to the father's reluctant acknowledgment of his daughter's disappearance:

> It was easy enough to overlook a child in the first flash of concern, to look too hard, too quickly. Still, a sickness and a tightening at the base of the throat, an unpleasant lightness in the feet, were with him as he went back. . . .
>
> Now he was taking long strides, bawling her name as he pounded the length of an aisle and headed once more for the door. Faces were turning towards him. There was no mistaking him for one of the drunks who blundered in to buy cider. His fear was too evident, too forceful, it filled the impersonal, fluorescent space with unignorable human warmth.
>
> (pp. 13–14)

In this moment of crisis, anonymous strangers shed their indifference and coalesce around a unified purpose: "The anonymity of the city store turned out to be frail, a thin crust beneath which people observed, judged, remembered. . . . The lost child was everyone's property" (pp. 14–15). This communal effort is no consolation to Stephen, though, for as bad as the loss itself is, it is compounded by the necessity that he tell his sleeping wife, Julie, that Kate has vanished: "It was then that she opened her eyes and found his face. It took her some seconds to read what was there before she scrambled upright in the bed and made a noise of incredulity, a little yelp on a harsh intake of breath. For a moment explanations were neither possible nor necessary" (p. 19). The loss of Kate interrupts the marriage. Julie decamps to a country cottage with her violin, and Stephen keeps to the house, watching television and drinking bottle after bottle of Scotch whisky.

McEwan based the abduction on an incident that his parents observed in a military shop in Germany: "That story stuck with me," he commented to Amanda Smith in *Publishers Weekly*. "Such a terrible idea. That something could happen to you, and you could never close the incident off. A death is bad enough, but at least you could begin to come to terms. The idea that the person you missed was still there and that they were growing away from you, leaving you behind. . . . I found that very haunting" (p. 68). The rest of the novel describes the couple's attempts to "close the incident off."

As a writer of children's books, Stephen is invited by his former publisher, Charles Darke, now a cabinet minister, to join the government's Subcommittee on Reading and Writing. Darke resigns from the government and retires with his wife, Thelma, to their country house in Suffolk. There, Darke essentially goes mad and reverts to living as a schoolboy in a treehouse atop a 160-foot beech tree. The government subcommittee on which Stephen sits is one of fourteen that are contributing their findings to a commission that will produce an official handbook on child rearing. Stephen discovers, however, that the government has already produced its own version of the book, written by Darke. Infuriated that his work on the commission is merely an exercise in public relations, Stephen leaks a copy of the handbook to a reporter. In a voice resembling Margaret Thatcher's—"between a tenor's and an alto's" (p. 213)—the prime minister adroitly defuses the scandal and the government publishes the *Authorized Child-Care Handbook* to the approbation of the popular press.

With a draconian code of discipline and an unwavering faith in "the time-honored analogy between childhood and disease" (p. 211), the handbook offers opinions that are far more conservative than the commission's views, and in the context of McEwan's work the manifesto provides yet more evidence of pernicious right-wing nostalgia. Berating himself for thinking he could change government policy, Stephen imagines himself a child, in comparison with the adult politicians:

> This was one of those times when he felt he had not quite grown up, he knew so little about how things really worked; complicated channels ran between truth and lying; in public life, the adept survivors navigated with sure instincts while retaining a large measure of dignity. Only occasionally, as a consequence of tactical error, was it necessary to lie significantly or tell an important truth. Mostly it was sure-footed scampering between the two extremes. Wasn't the interior life much the same?

. . . He had meddled inexpertly. It was not enough to send a book to a newspaper, to set something in motion and sit back. Political culture was theatrical, it required constant and active stage management of a kind he knew was beyond him.

(pp. 214–215)

The rhetorical question, "Wasn't the interior life much the same?," signals the most basic connection between public, political action and private self-knowledge. Both rely upon patterns of delusion and obfuscation designed to keep the truth at least partly hidden from view. When the scandal breaks, therefore, the momentary faltering of the government mimics Stephen's breakdown after losing Kate. During this time, he can neither project a conventional public face nor frame an explanation of his actions to himself in such a way as to lessen his burden of guilt. Similarly, the government must temporize before it formulates an explanation to quiet the uproar.

The Child in Time chronicles Stephen's attempts to stanch the wound opened by the loss of his daughter. One of the novel's most distinctive features, compared with the earlier fiction, is that the central calamity occurs at the beginning of the work rather than at a climactic moment near the end. Instead of examining the etiology of evil, as *The Comfort of Strangers* does, this novel concentrates on the human suffering that is consequent to an encounter with evil. Moreover, it depicts the possibility of recovery. At the end of the novel, Stephen and Julie are trying to accomplish a reconciliation that will allow them to move into the future together. Beginning again is not easy, however. During the one time that they meet in the year following Kate's disappearance, words serve only to reestablish a "careful politeness" (p. 72). So they replace speech with sexual intercourse. The final scene of the novel shows Julie, with the aid of Stephen, giving birth to the child conceived during the tryst in the preceding year. This Lawrentian turn suggests that the only way to heal a wound as fundamental as the loss of a child is through an equally primal act—reproduction—in which the parents will be rejuvenated through the birth of the child.

"Parenthood has changed me," McEwan says to Amanda Smith in *Publishers Weekly*. "Having a child binds you to a certain commitment to celebrate the world. There is such a joyousness about children that they demand of you that you find a way through" (p. 69). Parenthood has also changed McEwan's fiction. *The Child in Time* represents a world beyond the trauma of violence and the cynicism of public life, a world where adults can rediscover a long-lost innocence. "The book's not only about a lost child," McEwan proposes to Kathy Stephen in the London *Sunday Times Magazine*. "It has to do with the loss of childhood in one's self" (p. 37). Charles Darke literally regresses into prepubescence and ultimately commits suicide, unable to keep the adult world at bay. Maturity and innocence must be made to complement one another, the book intimates; time can be reversed psychologically and metaphorically, but literally it presses forward. Paradoxically, *The Child in Time* must plumb the depths of individual subjectivity in order to chart the contours of a nation.

A COLD WAR THRILLER

The Innocent marks McEwan's assault on that most hackneyed and conventional of genres, the spy thriller; by seeming so conventional, it is thus the most eccentric of his novels. The story begins in 1955, before the Berlin Wall was erected, during the interval when postwar Berlin was divided into four sectors—British, American, French, and Russian. In prose that George Stade, in a review in the *New York Times Book Review*, calls "as cold and transparent as a pane of ice" (p. 1), McEwan depicts the tensions seething between the different occupying forces. Not only are the Russians and the Americans engaged in a deadly game of brinkmanship, spying on one another and denouncing one another internationally, but Britain and the United States, allies in the Cold War, are deeply distrustful of one another's motives. Into this atmosphere of suspicion and danger steps Leonard Marnham, an unworldly British telephone engineer whose task, as part of a joint British–American covert operation, is to set up a series of tape recorders to monitor Russian telephone lines between Berlin and Moscow. Access to the telephone cables is through a tunnel that runs from the American sector to deep within the Russian sector. The tunnel has been so wretchedly engineered that it runs through the septic field of the warehouse where it begins, and consequently it smells revolting. The implication that the entire project has been ineptly planned and executed is sadly borne out when it becomes apparent that the enterprise has been compromised from the very beginning by a British informant. The Russians therefore send only trivial and misleading messages over the tapped lines.

Early on in his stay in Berlin, Leonard meets and falls in love with Maria Eckdorf, with whom he has his first sexual experience. As he travels back and forth from the tunnel to Maria's apartment, Leonard contemplates the possibility that he is merely "a void traveling between two points" (p. 85), that outside of his roles as lover and engineer he has no personality. In much the same way as Joseph Conrad uses a river journey into the Congo as a metaphor for his narrator's self-discovery in *Heart of Darkness*, so *The Innocent* develops tunneling into a motif for Leonard's gradual exploration of his own potential. Indeed, as he becomes more deeply involved with Maria and with the espionage operation, Leonard begins to unearth aspects of his personality that before his journey he could only have guessed at. Initially, when he arrives in Germany, he is swelled with nationalistic pride at the devastation still evident in Berlin: "It was impossible for a young Englishman to be in Germany for the first time and not think of it above all as a defeated nation, or feel pride in the victory. . . . [He proceeded] with a certain proprietorial swagger, as though his feet beat out the rhythms of a speech by Mr. Churchill" (pp. 5–6). Leonard's patriotism demonstrates a naive identification with his nation and a lack of sympathy for the Berliners around him. The necessity for him to drop this arrogance becomes increasingly evident as he cares more deeply for Maria, for he still thinks of her as a citizen of a defeated nation rather than as his equal. Talking with Laurie Muchnik in the *Village Voice*, McEwan contends that Leonard's sexual initiation does not necessarily signal an emotional maturity:

There's a curious myth—which literary fiction promotes—that you lose your innocence when you first have sexual experience. . . . In fact, I think it's the beginning of innocence. It's the beginning, not the end, of the process of learning; it's the emotions that are so difficult to learn how to deal with. So it isn't first sex that transforms Leonard, it's having to explain himself to Maria for the first time.

(p. 102)

Specifically, he must explain himself because he has tried to rape Maria. Leonard's domination fantasy is cloaked in a sadistic nationalism, in which he imagines himself a soldier forcing his foe to acknowledge his power sexually: "Yes, she was defeated, conquered, his by right, could not escape, and now, *he was a soldier*, weary, battle-marked and bloody, but heroically rather than disablingly so. He had taken this woman and was forcing her. Half terrified, half in awe, she dared not disobey" (p. 94). Leonard does not know, however, that at the age of nineteen Maria witnessed a woman being raped by a Russian soldier during the liberation of Berlin. Encompassed by his callow ignorance, Leonard begins to quarry his way out of immaturity only when Maria leaves him after the assault.

Excavating the self is charged with danger, therefore, because the hidden urges that experience brings to the surface are not likely to be solely admirable. By operating in the secretive world of international espionage, Leonard unwittingly completes the circuit between the politics of betrayal practiced by the Cold War powers and a personal code of honesty that he finds increasingly difficult to practice. Essentially, he finds it impossible to verify the truth of anything he is told, since each operative is under the impression that he knows the ultimate goal of the operation. As Leonard's American superior describes the security arrangements on the base, "[E]verybody thinks his clearance is the highest there is, everyone thinks he has the final story. You only hear of a higher level at the moment you're being told about it" (p. 16). But the same conditions prevail in the search for self-knowledge. Each time Leonard is stripped of an element of his innocence and he feels fully initiated into the world of adulthood, something else occurs that hints of a further realm of experience.

In a return to an earlier feature of McEwan's fiction, the climax to this series of revelations is an episode of murderous violence that coincides with the reappearance of Otto, Maria's former husband. After Otto attacks Maria in her apartment, Leonard steps in and ineptly tries to defend her, only to have Otto administer a painful lesson in street fighting. Otto is subdued only after Leonard bites a chunk out of his cheek and Maria brains him with an iron cobbler's last. Rather than confess to the police and risk being prosecuted for manslaughter, the couple dismember Otto's body. In an ad hoc autopsy, Leonard cuts up the body with a saw and parcels it out into two large cases. For the young man from Tottenham, who at the beginning of the novel has "no ready means to respond to an insult" because he "had not received one in adult life" (p. 27), the extreme measures that he takes are outlandish in their savagery. Yet they are perfectly justified as outward signs of the warped and headlong maturation that circumstances ruthlessly force upon him. As McEwan says in an interview with Boyd Tonkin in *New Statesman and Society*, "The thing about war, hot or cold, is that ordinary people can do extraordinary things" (p. 18).

A final significant aspect of Leonard's education in Berlin is his learning to become an American. Although the protagonist in *The Child in Time* watches television in an alcoholic haze, it is not until *The Innocent* that we finally encounter a world fully saturated with mass culture, particularly with American rock 'n' roll. Leonard's affinity with American culture is well established before he lands in Berlin; we learn, for instance, that although he "had never actually met an American to talk to . . . he had studied them in depth at his local Odeon" (p. 1). After several months in the American sector, this anthropological approach is replaced with a full-scale obsession. Where once the American soldiers' "unrestrained exhortation to dance for hours on end seemed puerile" (pp. 115–116), by the time he returns to London to visit his parents, he finds himself fiddling "with the living room wireless, trying to find the music to which he was now addicted" (p. 141). American popular music— Bill Haley and the Comets, Fats Domino, Chuck Berry, Little Richard, Carl Perkins, and especially Elvis Presley—becomes emblematic of how far he has traveled from his English roots: "Beyond the excitement Leonard took satisfaction in dancing in a way his parents and their friends did not, and could not, and in liking music they would hate, and in feeling at home in a city where they would never come. He was free" (p. 150).

For all intents and purposes, Leonard is living in an American city. According to the final chapter of the novel, however, his nerve fails him. Perhaps because of the memory of the dismemberment or because his discoveries about himself are too terrifying, Leonard returns to Britain, breaking off his engagement and subsequently becoming "the owner of a small company supplying components to the hearing-aid industry" (p. 255). In effect, Leonard chooses security over growth; he would rather help others to hear than continue tunneling with Maria.

INCARNATIONS OF EVIL AND BLACK DOGS

The Innocent could have been written only in 1989; any earlier, it would have been simply another maudlin Cold War drama with a wish-fulfillment ending; any later, it would have seemed belated and triumphalist. But by coinciding with the fall of the Berlin Wall, the novel crystallizes almost forty years of divisive European and global history, yet concludes optimistically that the decades-long standoff may be nearing an end. In the thriller's final sentence, Leonard envisages returning to Berlin with Maria to "take a good long look at the Wall together, before it was all torn down" (p. 270). Like *The Innocent*, *Black Dogs*, McEwan's most recent novel, has its roots in World War II. Where *The Innocent* describes Berlin before the Wall, however, *Black Dogs* is set in the immediate aftermath of the Wall coming down.

Ostensibly, *Black Dogs* recounts the life of June Tremaine from the perspective of Jeremy, her son-in-law. Jeremy's first-person narrative reveals that he is an orphan who as a child was "a six-foot cuckoo" (p. xiii) with a sycophantic habit of befriending his friends' parents. It is only natural, therefore, that he should record his wife's mother's life. As Jeremy admits, the genre of his narrative is ambiguous, for his ruminations describe his own experiences as well as June's: "Reasonably enough, she had in mind a biography, and that was what I had originally intended. But once I had made a start it began to take on another form—not a biography, not even a memoir really, more a divagation; she would be central, but it would not only be about her" (p. 16). Now, a divagation literally describes a wandering or a meandering, but it can also mean a digression, and this work encompasses both senses of the term. The novel is itself a digression, formally, for it moves tangentially from June to the narrator. In addition, the pivotal scene occurs during a long ramble that June and her husband take while honeymooning in the south of France.

June and her husband, Bernard, meet in Senate House, the home of British intelligence during World War II, and after they marry, they take a long trip to Italy and France. But an event occurs that causes them to separate and leads June to buy a broken-down shepherd's cottage in the Languedoc, where she lives for the next forty years. After she is misdiagnosed with a terminal condition and must return to England to enter a convalescent home, she starts recounting her life to Jeremy. Following his separation from his wife, Bernard becomes a Labour member of Parliament, "an Establishment man, a member of its liberal rump, with service on government committees on broadcasting, the environment, pornography" (p. 16). After June's death, Jeremy and Bernard travel to Berlin to watch the Wall being breached. One evening, Bernard defends a young ideologue waving a red flag in the faces of the assembled West Berliners, among whom are several neo-Nazi skinheads: "To be out here doing this on the day of communism's final disgrace showed either a martyr's zeal or an unfathomable masochistic urge to be beaten up in public" (p. 73). When the Communist disappears, the skinheads attack Bernard, but a young woman intercedes, and he escapes with only a bruised shin. Bernard had resigned from the Communist party in 1956 and certainly is not sentimental about the fall of the Warsaw Pact; his defense of the protester stems not so much from ideological solidarity as from a lifelong habit of defending underdogs and supporting lost causes.

Why do the honeymooners separate so soon after their wedding? June and Bernard offer different answers to this question. June pinpoints the genesis of her disaffection with Bernard as her encounter with two massive, feral dogs while the couple is walking through the Languedoc. Like a latter-day Casaubon from George Eliot's *Middlemarch*, Bernard is busily pursuing his passion for entomology, examining a trail of caterpillars, at the very moment the dogs attack his wife. Gathering all her strength, she is forced to defend herself against the onslaught:

But the big one went for her. It sprang up. She leaned forward to meet the impact as the animal sank its jaws into the rucksack. It was on its hind legs and she was supporting it with one arm. She was buckling under the weight. The dog's face was inches above hers. She thrust upward with the knife, three quick jabs to its belly and sides. It surprised her, how easily the blade went in. A good little knife. On the first stroke the dog's yellow-red eyes widened. On the second and third, before it let the rucksack go, it made high-pitched piteous yips, a small dog's noise.

(p. 127)

Characteristically, Bernard underestimates the horror of the assault, and in his myopic self-absorption and chauvinism, he also fails to comprehend its wider implications for June. In the moments before the dog pounces, she experiences a religious awakening. Before this moment, both June and Bernard were committed Communists, and Bernard subsequently cannot reconcile his wife's religious feelings with his socialist ideology or his scientifically conditioned understanding of the world. For her part, June finds Bernard's rationalism insufferable, and a stalemate ensues:

Bernard thinks I'm a silly occultist, and I think he's a fish-eyed commissar who'd turn in the lot of us if it would buy a material heaven on earth—that's the family story, the family joke. The truth is we love each other, we've never stopped, we're obsessed. And we failed to do a thing with it. We couldn't make a life. We couldn't give up the love, but we wouldn't bend to its power.

(p. 29)

Part of the tragedy here is that these two individuals thwart their love by being unable to accommodate one another's differences; they can't overlook the disparities and inconsistences in order to build a life together.

In much of McEwan's later fiction, we have seen a deep-seated connection between the personal and the political, and in this respect *Black Dogs* is no different. The bridge between the two realms is built, aptly, through the figure of the two dogs. One account of their origin identifies them as dogs brought by the Gestapo to the village of St. Maurice de Navacelles in Vichy France to terrify the villagers and to work as guard dogs. Possibly they were trained to rape female prisoners. The dogs, then, become symbols of the viciousness of the human imagination and of its capacity to pervert nature to its own ends. Ominously, the dogs are never captured. As June so frequently dreams, they are destined to return periodically to disrupt the peace. June's explanation is that the black dogs represent a psychological condition that, like Leonard's rape fantasy in *The Innocent*, lies latent within everyone:

The evil I'm talking about lives in us all. It takes hold in an individual, in private lives, within a family, and then it's children who suffer most. And then, when the conditions are right, in different countries, at different times, a terrible cruelty, a viciousness against life erupts, and everyone is surprised by the depth of hatred within himself. Then it sinks back and waits. It's something in our hearts.

(p. 147)

The black dogs even emerge from Jeremy after he assaults the father of a child he has seen beaten in a restaurant: "I hit him with the left, one two three, face, throat, and gut, before he went down. I drew back my foot, and I think I might have kicked and stomped him to death if I had not heard a voice. . . . Immediately I knew that the elation driving me had nothing to do with revenge and justice. Horrified with myself, I stepped back" (p. 108). Discussing subsequent appearances of this emblem of hatred and destruction, McEwan says in an article by William Grimes in the *New York Times*, "Within six weeks of finishing *Black Dogs*, the catastrophe of Yugoslavia began. If you asked me where the black dogs went, it's exactly there" (p. C25). More so than the lost child in *The Child in Time* or even the tunnel in *The Innocent*, the black dogs in this novel are richly symbolic; in their ferocity and unnatural genesis they illustrate the confluence of history, nature, and human psychology. Their pathology is our pathology.

Not all is as dire as it seems, however. The attack spawns June's implacable spirituality; in that instant, June says, "I met evil and discovered God" (p. 36). Just as June and Bernard fall in love at the end of World War II, so Jeremy meets his wife in Poland in 1981, during the weeks when Lech Wałęsa's independent trade union federation, Solidarity, defied the country's Communist regime. Indeed, by timing pivotal episodes in *Black Dogs* to coincide with political crises, McEwan implies that periods of upheaval and repression are also opportunities for positive change. Jeremy even adopts an element of June's mysticism after investigating her life; he believes that the woman who forces the skinheads to flee resembles her, and that her ghost prevents him from putting his hand down on a scorpion at her Languedoc retreat. Jeremy writes in his preface:

It will not do to argue that rational thought and spiritual insight are separate domains and that opposition between them is falsely conceived. Nor will it do to suggest that both these views are correct. To believe everything, to make no choices, amounts to much the same thing, to my mind, as believing in nothing at all. . . . But I would be false to my own experience if I did not declare my belief in the possibility of love transforming and redeeming a life.

(pp. xxi–xxii)

McEwan's fiction has never before been this optimistic. Yet, the forces that love has to contend with—the black dogs of hatred and evil—are of such potency that the balance the novel finally achieves is surely contingent, temporary, and of great fragility.

In it own meandering style, *Black Dogs* is as much about the process of storytelling as it is about the Tremaines or the narrator. Time and again, characters cast doubt on each other's versions of their lives. With his acute self-consciousness, Jeremy is keenly aware of his own tenuousness as a first-person narrator:

As the family outsider, I was both beguiled and skeptical. Turning points are the inventions of storytellers and dramatists, a necessary mechanism when a life is reduced to, traduced by a plot, when a morality must be distilled from a sequence of actions, when an audience must be sent home with something unforgettable to mark a character's growth. Seeing the light, the moment of truth, the turning point—surely we borrow these from Hollywood or the Bible to make retroactive sense of an overcrowded memory.

(p. 27)

Ultimately, it is inconclusive whether June's meeting with the black dogs was revelatory or was mythologized retrospectively by her. But what we are left with in the novel is the power of human action to fabricate—in words, with love—a better world for future generations. The black dogs will return, but so will the urge to tell stories and start families. In these eventualities, McEwan proposes, lies our salvation.

POSTSCRIPT: THE DAYDREAMER

SOMEHOW it seems appropriate, if a little scary, that Ian McEwan should finally produce a children's book. But it is perfectly logical that an author who has devoted so much energy to anatomizing the perils and joys of childhood and adolescence, and who has a tremendous facility in articulating juvenile tastes and habits, should compose a work for this audience. Children would naturally feel an affinity to his sense of the macabre and the absurd. In form, *The Daydreamer* is most akin to the short-story collections. It recounts a number of daydreams that are unified by a frame tale, which informs us that the identity of the daydreamer is Peter Fortune, an absent-minded eleven-year-old. Unlike his adult fiction, where McEwan refuses to judge the often vile actions of his characters, here many of the stories contain lessons for the book's young readers. In the chapter entitled "The Bully," Peter gradually comes to the realization that the belligerent tyrant who terrorizes his class is really no stronger or more frightening than the other children. Indeed, he learns that it is the classmates' fear that gives the boy limitless power over them: "What made pink, plump Barry so powerful? Immediately, from out of nowhere, Peter had the answer. 'It's obvious,' he thought. '*We* do. We've dreamed him up as the class bully'" (p. 107). After Peter verbally humiliates the bully, his guilty conscience forces him to make up with his former tormentor.

Reading *The Daydreamer* also gives an odd feeling of familiarity, in that many of the themes and motifs from McEwan's adult fiction recur here, in juvenile form. In "The Dolls," the first of the daydreams, Peter imagines that he is dismembered by his sister's dolls. In "Vanishing Cream," a child's version of "Solid Geometry," during a moment's disgust at the untidiness and inefficiency of his house, Peter spirits away his family by rubbing a cream on them. Behind these imaginative fantasies, however, lie the intrinsic boredom and powerlessness of childhood. McEwan shrewdly demonstrates that Peter's flights of fancy are attempts to escape the tedium of rainy weekends, the hours of uninspiring school lessons, and the frustration of not comprehending adult behavior. Jack's boredom in *The Cement Garden* is perhaps simply an exaggeration of this sad childhood reality. Fortunately, the final daydream points to an escape for Peter into adolescence. Between a group of children playing, and a group of adults talking, Peter realizes that childhood will not last: "Peter suddenly grasped something very obvious and terrible: one day he would leave the group that ran wild up and down the beach, and he would join the group that sat and talked. It was hard to believe, but he knew it was true" (pp. 177–178). Ironically, the self-consciousness of this understanding already partially separates him from his friends. Nevertheless, our final glimpse of Peter is reassuring, for we last see him flying off unreflexively into another daydream. With McEwan's usual clarity, *The Daydreamer* acknowledges the inevitability of change while cherishing the preciousness of childhood.

Too often, McEwan's characters are prematurely robbed of their innocence. It's a relief to see one reveling in youthfulness before our very eyes. After the brutality of the early fiction, the politics of the screenplays, and the psychological portraits of the most recent novels, this return to childhood seems highly appropriate. The experience of rearing children seems to have diverted some of McEwan's attention from the mordant and the calamitous. Although violence and sexual pain still recur throughout his work, these aspects of life are now complemented by the possibility that innocence can be preserved and that love can be fostered. The horrific acts that pepper the latest novels in a sense carry more weight with them because they are accompanied by their consequences as well as their causes. In the future, McEwan's reputation will grow not because he has perfected the ability to shock his readership, but because the precision of his prose so carefully dissects human motives and responses into their constitutive parts.

Gradually, McEwan is writing his way into a tradition of twentieth-century European novelists who took it upon themselves to expose the cynicism and corruption of government, patriarchy, class division, and nationalism. His influences—Kafka, Woolf, Joyce—proposed that individual psychology was inextricably bound up with such large-scale social forces. Like the fiction of these writers, McEwan's later work proposes that subjectivity is at least partly socially constructed. But the symbols of these novels—the lost child, the tunnel, the black dogs—maintain that more inchoate forces also come into play in structuring personality. In large measure, McEwan's fiction is designed to uncover these pressures. A train driver in *The Child in Time* recalls examining a remote railway tunnel by flashlight, describing the structure as "a cathedral in the dark" (p. 249). Like the driver in the tunnel with his torch, McEwan illuminates the cavernous makeup of the mind by using his own instrument, his penetrating prose. The place he discovers there is both dark and elegant.

SELECTED BIBLIOGRAPHY

I. INDIVIDUAL WORKS. *First Love, Last Rites* (London and New York, 1975); *The Cement Garden* (London and New York, 1978); *In Between the Sheets* (London, 1978; New York, 1979); *The Comfort of Strangers* (London and New York, 1981); *The Imitation Game: Three Plays for T.V.*

(London, 1981), repub. as *The Imitation Game and Other Plays* (Boston, Mass., 1982); *Or Shall We Die?* (London, 1983), oratorio with score by Michael Berkeley; *The Ploughman's Lunch* (London, 1985); *The Child in Time* (London and Boston, 1987); *Soursweet* (London and Boston, 1988), screenplay adapted from the novel *Sour Sweet* by Timothy Mo (London, 1982); *The Innocent* (London and New York, 1990); *Black Dogs* (London and New York, 1992); *The Daydreamer* (London and New York, 1994), illustrated by Anthony Browne.

II. CONTRIBUTIONS. "Solid Geometry," in *New Statesman* (30 March 1979); untitled contribution to "Plagiarism—A Symposium," in *Times Literary Supplement* (9 April 1982); "Schoolboys," in *William Golding: The Man and His Books. A Tribute on His 75th Birthday*, ed. by John Carey (London, 1986); "J," in *Hockney's Alphabet*, ed. by Stephen Spender (New York, 1991).

III. BIOGRAPHICAL STUDIES. Michael J. Adams, "McEwan, Ian," in *Postmodern Fiction: A Bio-Bibliographical Guide*, ed. by Larry McCaffrey (New York, 1986); John Fletcher, "Ian McEwan," in *Dictionary of Literary Biography, vol. 14, British Novelists Since 1960* (Detroit, Mich., 1983); "Ian McEwan," in *Current Biography Yearbook 1993*, ed. by Judith Graham (New York, 1993); Pamela L. Shelton, "McEwan, Ian," in *Contemporary Authors*, vol. 41, ed. by Susan M. Trosky (Detroit, Mich., 1994).

IV. CRITICAL STUDIES. Ian Hamilton, "Points of Departure," in *New Review* 5 (autumn 1978); Ronald Hayman, "Ian McEwan's Moral Anarchy," in *Books and Bookmen* 24 (October 1978); Christopher Ricks, "Adolescence and After—An Interview with Ian McEwan," in *Listener* 101 (12 April 1979).

Janet Watts, "When Women Go to War," in *Observer* (20 April 1980); Lorna Sage, "Dreams of Being Hurt," in *Times Literary Supplement* (9 October 1981), review of *The Comfort of Strangers*; J. R. Banks, "A Gondola Named Desire," in *Critical Quarterly* 24 (summer 1982); Christopher Ricks, "Playing with Terror," in *London Review of Books* (21 January 1982), review of *The Comfort of Strangers*; Jill Forbes, "Crossover: McEwan and Eyre," in *Sight and Sound* 52 (autumn 1983); John Haffenden, "John Haffenden Talks to Ian McEwan," in *Literary Review* (Edinburgh) 60 (June 1983); David Sampson, "McEwan/Barthes," in *Southern Review* 17 (March 1984); Clare Hanson, *Short Stories and Short Fictions, 1880–1980* (New York, 1985); Dennis Vannatta, *The English Short Story, 1945–1980* (Boston, 1985); Danny Danziger, "In Search of Two Characters," in *Times* (London) (27 June 1987); Amanda Smith, "PW Interviews: Ian McEwan," in *Publishers Weekly* (11 September 1987); Kathy Stephen, "The Bright Young Man Grows Up," in *Sunday Times Magazine* (London) (16 August 1987).

Laurie Muchnick, "You Must Dismember This: Ian McEwan's Shock Treatment," in *Village Voice* (28 August 1990); George Stade, "Berlin Affair: A Thriller," in *New York Times Book Review* (3 June 1990); Boyd Tonkin, "Trials of a War Baby," in *New Statesman and Society* (11 May 1990); Lynda Broughton, "Portrait of the Subject as a Young Man: The Construction of Masculinity Ironized in 'Male' Fiction," in *Subjectivity and Literature from the Romantics to the Present Day*, ed. by Philip Shaw and Peter Stockwell (London and New York, 1991); William Grimes, "Rustic Calm Inspires McEwan Tale of Evil," in *New York Times* (18 November 1992); Richard Johnstone, "Television Drama and the People's War: David Hare's *Licking Hitler*, Ian McEwan's *The Imitation Game* and Trevor Griffith's *Country*," in *Contemporary British Drama*, ed. by Hersh Zeifman and Cynthia Zimmerman (Toronto, 1993); Richard Brown, "Postmodern Americas in the Fiction of Angela Carter, Martin Amis and Ian McEwan," in *Forked Tongues? Comparing Twentieth-Century British and American Literature*, ed. by Ann Massa and Alistair Stead (London and New York, 1994); Christina Byrnes, "Ian McEwan—Pornographer or Prophet?," in *Contemporary Review* 266 (June 1995); Marc Delrez, "Escape into Innocence: Ian McEwan and the Nightmare of History," in *Ariel* 26 (April 1995); Paul Edwards, "Time, Romanticism, Modernism and Moderation in Ian McEwan's *The Child in Time*," in *English* 44 (spring 1995); Jack Slay, Jr., *Ian McEwan* (New York, 1996).

PAUL MULDOON

(1951–   )

Joseph Donahue

"I THINK THE world is hallucinogenic," the Irish poet Paul Muldoon noted in an interview with Lynn Keller in 1994 (in *Contemporary Literature*, vol. 35, no. 1, p. 19). When one considers how Muldoon's poetry reshapes the way the reader looks at the world, making enigmas of things that seemingly could not be clearer, and how objects, associations, and sounds enter as if for the first time the clear light of prosody, these words seem applicable to all his work, where nothing is so hallucinatory as truth, the ultimate controlled substance.

Born Catholic in Northern Ireland in 1951, and author of twelve volumes published between 1973 and 1996, Paul Muldoon describes how mind and world diverge and conjoin in odd and frightening ways. We should approach his off-the-cuff credo about reality and vision by noting the possible ambiguity: the poet sees the world as both hallucination and hallucinogen. In this doubleness lies some of the largest aims and achievements of Paul Muldoon's poetry. Within the conventions of contemporary Irish writing, he questions reality in ways that are unique, sounding disaffected amid intimate scenes, and assuredly familiar amid exotica. He evades the pieties of family and nation with an art of voyaging and vision, adopting urbane, cosmopolitan attitudes while invoking ancient forms of poetry, particularly the riddle and the quest.

"Why Brownlee Left," a much discussed early poem, serves to clarify some of these traditions of contemporary Irish poetry and shows how Muldoon departs from them. The image of a man plowing a field was firmly established as a significant trope among Muldoon's immediate precursors, serving both to figure certain Irish cultural realities and to recall Ireland's long history of colonial subjugation and its quest for an indigenous art and culture. Patrick Kavanagh, a figure who looms large in the history of Irish poetry after William Butler Yeats, gave a particularly resonant turn to this poetic figure, emphasizing the abjection and grandeur of an image that seems in contrast to the Yeatsian world deliberately local and antipoetic. To the poets who came after Kavanagh, however, images such as this achieve an almost Homeric resonance:

> Now leave the check-reins slack,
> The seed is flying far today—
> The seed like stars against the black
> Eternity of April clay.
>
> The seed is potent as the seed
> Of knowledge in the Hebrew Book,
> So drive your horses in the creed
> Of God the father as a stook.
>
> Forget the men on Brady's hill.
> Forget what Brady's boy may say.
> For destiny will not fulfill
> Unless you let the harrow play.
>
> Forget the worm's opinion too
> Of hooves and pointed harrow-pins,
> For you are driving your horses through
> The mist where Genesis begins.
> (Kavanagh, "To the Man after the Harrow," in *Collected Poems*, p. 27)

One notes here a few simple things of particular relevance in approaching Muldoon, most significantly the transformation of the mundane into the epical; the raising of the anonymous figure to heroic tasks; the sexual travail that so characterizes Kavanagh's world; and the cruel Blakean irony with which the poem closes, marked by the intermingling of death and life, oppression and liberation. It is no coincidence that Kavanagh, himself a point of origin for postwar Irish poetry, should be such an adept and dramatic fashioner of myths of origin. In a significant act of editorial legerdemain, Muldoon chose to begin his edition of *The Faber Book of Contemporary Irish Poetry* (1986) with Kavanagh.

But between these two figures stands Muldoon's undergraduate tutor: Seamus Heaney. Heaney's poem "Follower," also included by Muldoon in his anthology, renders the plowman figure far differently. The plowman here is not anonymous, but the poet's father. The father is both creator and artificer, heeding not the epic imperatives of Kavanagh's plowman, but those of art and physical exuberance. The father, with "shoulders globed like a full sail strung," appears to the trailing child poet as

> An expert. He would set the wing
> And fit the bright steel-pointed sock.
> The sod rolled over without breaking.
> At the headrig, with a single pluck
>
> Of reins, the sweating team turned round
> And back to the land. His eye
> Narrowed and angled at the ground,
> Mapping the furrow exactly.
>
> *(Selected Poems, p. 8)*

The Heaneyesque values are all here: the celebratory naming of the particulars of the world of farm and field, the persona's filial piety and implicit angst, the assured allegorizing of domestic relations. The poet sees clearly, so the poem tells us, what his relation to his father is, and what his father's relation to labor and to the natural world around him is. Heaney brings a confidence to the charged psychological issues that Kavanagh raised but seemed to be overwhelmed by. Heaney finds in the image of the laboring man a scale of values by which to judge the larger world of politics and culture. Both poems sing the deep relation of man and implement and ground, presenting, despite their differences, an image of integration and heroism. The two offer myths of origin and each is characteristic of the poet's imagination of what it is to be Irish.

Muldoon's rendition of the figure of the man and plow differs substantially from its immediate precursors. Most notably, the man is absent: indeed, the subject of the poem *is* the man's absence:

> Why Brownlee left, and where he went,
> Is a mystery even now.
> For if a man should have been content
> It was him; two acres of barley,
> One of potatoes, four bullocks,
> A milker, a slated farmhouse.
> He was last seen going out to plough
> On a March morning, bright and early.

> By noon Brownlee was famous;
> They had found all abandoned, with
> The last rig unbroken, his pair of black
> Horses, like man and wife,
> Shifting their weight from foot to
> Foot, and gazing into the future.

What does Muldoon do differently here? Note the shift in perspective. The speaker is no concelebrant of the presence of the human figure in the landscape, but an analyst of all that is missing. In circumscribing the central figure, Brownlee, and placing him beyond description, Muldoon turns the invocation of an indigenous spirit into an epistemological question. Mystery, or less grandly, a puzzle, replaces conviction. What one discovers is not the true nature of the man, the plow, or the earth, but the true nature of our ignorance. Muldoon exchanges the primacy of presence—the tremendous value placed by the earlier poets on the power of poetry to summon what William Blake would recognize as the "Human Form Divine"—for a world brimming with clues and hidden narratives. The narrative perspective is neither that of the omniscient narrator, as in the Kavanagh poem, nor of the individual voice—in the case of the Heaney poem, that of the perceptive child and insightful adult—but a public voice, perhaps that of a fellow citizen, or if we call to mind the poet's fascination in "Immram," which concludes this volume with American detective fiction, a detective called to the scene, someone aware of the larger world into which Brownlee presumably fled, who can sound such ironies as "By noon Brownlee was famous."

Muldoon departs from his immediate precursors. He substitutes a wanderer for a laborer or father—but does not himself wander as far from Irish cultural realities as some of his later poems might suggest. Note the fidelities to Irish rural life observed in passing: the vision of plenty, the joys of fruitful labor, the complicated but not overlooked portrait of married love—the two workhorses yoked together, sharing labor and a vision of the future. All are celebrated in the imaging of their implied renunciation by the departee, and become clues in some grand local mystery that itself replays two of the great sorrows of the Irish past, the Great Famine and consequent migration.

Paul Muldoon edited *The Faber Book of Contemporary Irish Poetry*, which appeared in 1986. In regard to a poet so given to indirection, reticence, and mystification, an anthology such as this takes on a special significance. Here we see the poet giving critical shape to the struggle with tradition that receives imaginative shape in his own verse. One might naturally turn to the anthology's introduction for insight, but here there is none. The poet and editor is as absent amid the fields of Irish verse as Brownlee is amid the "lines" of his field. Muldoon's anthology both trumpets a tradition and evades it: in lieu of the traditional statement from the editor defining what is meant by, say, "contemporary," and a discussion of the criteria employed to select the book's content, Muldoon offers an excerpt of an interview between Louis MacNeice and F. R. Higgins, broadcast on BBC radio in Northern Ireland in July 1939. In hindsight, the data looms large: it was just a few months before the invasion of Poland and the beginning of World War II. What draws our attention to the date, and to the chilling implications of the discussion, is the subject of the conversation: the role of the poet in Ireland.

Higgins and MacNeice set forth contrasting positions on where Irish poetry comes from and to what it should aspire: pure and impure. About this arguable but still safe distinction hover others, not so safe: northern and southern, Catholic and Protestant, native and expatriate, traditional and modern. But the real contention is about the ultimate allegiance of the poet. Higgins declaims: "Present day Irish poets are believers—heretical believers, maybe—but they have the spiritual buoyancy of a belief in something. The sort of belief I see in Ireland is a belief emanating from life, from nature, from revealed religion, and from nation. A sort of dream that produces a sense of magic." Here the critic espouses a poetry of belief, of witness, and of testimonial. The poet, in Higgins' view, is one with the culture that created him, and expresses its noblest sentiments. The heroic and lyrical plowmen in Kavanagh and Heaney would clearly fit the bill. It is a vision of poetry familiar to us from nineteenth-century European and American preoccupations with establishing indigenous artistic traditions that validate the claims of emerging nations to possess an authentic culture, familiar as well from the Romantic and symbolist generations' devotion to poetry as magic. Higgins goes on to explicitly confront MacNeice about his origins: "I am afraid, Mr. MacNeice, you, as an Irishman, cannot escape from your blood, nor from our blood-music that brings the racial character to mind. Irish poetry remains a creation happily, fundamentally rooted in rural civilization, yet aware of and in touch with elementals of the future." Herein lies a dilemma familiar both from the Irish tradition, most notably Joyce, and from other postcolonial literatures of this century: the demand that the writer must be representative of his or her race, ethnicity, nation, or region. The writer is called—or condemned—to be the embodiment of the group. To frustrate this expectation is to raise the cry of traitor, an accusation already lurking in Higgins' implication that MacNeice "cannot escape from [his] blood."

As a poet of obliquity and role-playing in a generation notable for its solemn honesty, Muldoon has himself often endured inquiries into his allegiance to Irish reality. Yet we cannot quite say that Muldoon sides with Higgins or MacNeice, a poet who will figure largely in Muldoon's imaginative treatment of the role of the Irish poet in "7, Middagh Street." But the anthology itself creates a collage that amounts to a self-portrait. And then there is that date, 1939. By lifting this passage from the context of 1939, the mention of "blood music" calls up expressionist poetics (such as those of Gotfried Benn) and fascist ideologies (as in Ezra Pound), where notions of racial purity are married to ideals of artistic expression. These European "troubles" of World War II form the backdrop for the more local Irish "Troubles" that began in 1968, when Muldoon was seventeen years old, northern, and Catholic. He has a sensibility shaped by realities other than those of his precursors Heaney and Kavanagh. Yet the oppressions of Northern Ireland recall the crucial importance of "blood music" for cultural struggle. The Muldoonian dilemma stands partially revealed: to break free of the demand to represent social and political realities in the proscribed naturalistic fashion, while keeping faith with what Heaney calls the "music of what happens," however harsh it may be. MacNeice, in defending the poetics he had developed as a member of the W. H. Auden circle, offers Muldoon a way out. While Higgins believes that Irish poetry decays the further it moves away from a primitive agricultural world, MacNeice imagines an Irish poetry at home everywhere. Moreover, in the *Faber Book of Contemporary Irish Poetry* he offers his own theory of the relation of artistic form to place and history:

I have the feeling you have sidetracked me into an Ireland versus England match. I am so little used to thinking of poetry in terms of race-consciousness that no doubt this was very good for me. However, I am still unconverted. I think one may have such a thing as one's racial blood-music, but that, like one's unconscious, it may be left to take care of itself. Compared with you, I take a rather common-sense view of poetry. I think that the poet is a sensitive instrument designed to record anything which interests his mind or affects his emotions. If a gasometer, for instance, affects his emotions, or if the Marxian dialectic, let us say, interests his mind, then let them come into his poetry. He will be fulfilling his function as a poet if he records these things with integrity and with as much music as he can compass or as is appropriate to the subject.

(p. 18)

MacNeice's poetics validates Muldoon's own body of work. Like MacNeice, Muldoon places the consciousness of the poet at the center of things. The subjects of his shorter poems and the plots of his longer poems are alike the mind's voyage among the things of this world. MacNeice frees the poet from bondage to certain landscapes and certain traditions associated with Irish poetry, yet we must note here that Muldoon does not stray as far as the poetics espoused by his Anglo-Irish Protestant precursor would permit him. He does not play the role of the "citizen of the world," freed by his intellect from tribal pieties, at rest in the freedoms of dispossession or exile or privilege. The gasometers and Marxist dialectics, or their equivalents, that find their way into Muldoon's poems are never quite in and of themselves the objects of contemplation; they seem always part of a never fully disclosed meditation upon Irish images. Brownlee has left, but we should recall how carefully the scene remains intact: the plow still rooted in the dirt, the horses waiting for their master's return.

THE EARLY BOOKS: NEW WEATHER, MULES, AND WHY BROWNLEE LEFT

HIS book *New Weather* (1973) established Muldoon instantly as a poet to watch, liberating the young poet from anonymity while burdening him with critical attention. Muldoon's undergraduate instructor at Queens University, Belfast, Seamus Heaney, only a shade less precocious than Muldoon, had made a substantial debut at age twenty-seven with his own first major collection, *Death of a*

Naturalist, seven years earlier, and was then at work on the landmark volume *North*. In approaching Muldoon's early work one should keep in mind that he had as models within the Irish tradition not merely Yeats, Kavanagh, MacNeice, and others, but a small group of poets slightly older than himself who were launching what might be called "the Ulster Renaissance." Alongside Heaney, James Simmons, Michael Longley, and Derek Mahon were writing the poems that would define the contours of post–World War II Irish poetry. While there are great differences among these writers, they share a commitment to Ireland as a subject for poetry and to a meditative and serious tone that seeks to rise to general truths about life and art and politics. While ironies and even puns abound in their works, these poets are in the service of a larger and unquestionably heroic narrative in which they take stock of Irish language, history, mythology, religious life, and, most dramatically, the civil violence around them.

These poets mastered their essential disposition toward the world in the late 1950s and early 1960s. They were the beneficiaries of an unprecedented postwar access to higher education. As in the case of their African and Caribbean contemporaries in London, they felt their historical moment and the double bind of an education that opened the doors to European culture and artistic forms while it also made them aware of the historical origins of their colonial status. As in the works of the Caribbean poets Kamau Braithwaite and Derek Walcott, one sees, for example, these Irish poets using the Roman past as a means of meditating on the current British Empire. Muldoon will go elsewhere. In a rather startling departure sounded in the last poem of *New Weather*, "The Year of the Sloes," Muldoon will turn to the Native American tribes of North America. Indeed, throughout his career he has found increasingly extravagant analogs for the Irish situation in New World material. There was a further, more substantial, revisionary note struck by the young poet as he entered the community of Northern Irish poets in the 1970s, one that had less to do with his subject matter than with his manner. He felt an overwhelming pressure to conceive of poetry as honest utterance. The formal conservatism that distinguishes Irish poetry permitted no consideration, it seems, of the poetic approximation of Samuel Beckett or Flann O'Brien. One finds in prose and theater of the postwar period a tradition that comes much closer to accommodating some of

Muldoon's most characteristic gestures and strategies, and an integrity arising from Muldoon's commitment to not saying what he means. Unlike some of his immediate precursors, Muldoon does not feel obliged to be a moral spokesman. This pose complicates the relationship of the poet to his audience.

"The Electric Orchard," the first poem of *New Weather*, finds the poet meditating on the consequences of the role of the poet. The book opens with a surreal parable about the history of electricity in a community. The "electric people" incorporate the poles and voltage of electrical power into their landscape and rituals. Muldoon speaks as a knowing initiate about the lives of this community while never quite disclosing exactly where it exists, in the first world, in the third world, or in the imagination. And his parable, for all its attention to the lives and beliefs of the "electric people," has a mythological resonance. The story it tells is about how things came to be as they now are. A culture has emerged that centers, or so it seems, around the climbing of electrical poles, and a wisdom has evolved concerning falls. The poem concludes with the inauguration of a new age:

Whereby they nailed a plaque to every last electric pole.
They would prosecute any trespassers.
The high up, singing and live fruit liable to shock or kill
Were forbidden . . .

(ll. 41–44)

Among the many things suggested by the title of the first volume is this inaugural perception of an altered cultural climate. The people place barbed wire around the poles in order to protect their neighbors and their neighbors' innocent children. While we are left to ponder the nature of the electricity, the motives of the climbers and fence builders, and, above all, the "singing and live fruit," the poet concludes with an enigma: "None could describe / Electrocution, falling, the age of innocence." Thus the poet opens his book with an admission that some things are beyond words. Or rather, that some things are now against the law to discuss, namely, all things that pertain to the Promethean implications of domesticating electricity, as well as, more simply, some traditional subjects of lyric poetry, including inspiration, abjection, and childhood. Still, Muldoon does not forswear these subjects, so typical of Heaney, Thomas Kinsella, Mahon, Simmons, and others.

In the title poem, "New Weather" (which Muldoon chose to open his *Selected Poems*, published in 1986), he elaborates upon the type of inspiration and divination possible: a reordering of perception that draws attention to the perceiver's role in the ancient poetic task of reading the signs of what is coming:

Often I think I should be like
The single tree going nowhere,

Since my own arm could not and would not
Break the other. Yet by my broken bones
I tell new weather.

(ll. 13–17)

The world in which this new weather freshens or threatens is one that reveals itself less through landscape than through logic, appropriately fractured. While in Muldoon's work we find much of the rural Ireland cited by Higgins as the source and subject of Irish poetry—including saints legends, rural dancers, and the rhythms of agricultural life—and much of the kind of Gaelic dreamscape so assiduously established by Yeats, Muldoon is too shrewd to be bluntly oracular. "The Electric Orchard" has already set before us a picture of dangerous intersections: technology with nature, individual with community, generation with generation. And it is precisely in his rendering of the points of contact between adverse or incongruous subjects that Muldoon establishes his distinction from his precursors, a distinction that will widen in its implications with succeeding volumes and increasingly heterogeneous material. In terms of the Higgins-MacNeice debate, while Muldoon doubtless prizes the defense of a phenomenological poetics implicit in MacNeice's response to Higgins, he, Muldoon, is not merely interested in examining the objects of thought. Nor is he interested primarily in developing an associationist poetics, as we might find in post–World War II American poets such as John Ashbery or John Berryman. Muldoon imagines the mind's movements as potentially epic. His obliquity, while it may defend the poet from being apprehended by his critics, also enhances the action of the poem.

The ruminant, amiable speaker of "New Weather" reveals himself to be two-faced: both ironic and romantic, skeptical and credulous. His art is an art that Robert Frost, a clear presence throughout Muldoon's work, would recognize as aspiring to his definition of poetry as a momentary stay against confusion. *New Weather* introduces a storyteller familiar with contemporary politics, Native American mythology, the movies, and a spectrum of literary poses, but one who himself is the ultimate mystery, whose underlying tale is always the same, that of the failure of the quest and the perpetual intrigues of the voyage. It is typical of Muldoon that he would begin a poem entitled "Identities" with an obvious yarn:

> When I reached the sea
> I fell in with another who had just come
> From the interior. Her family
> Had figured in a past regime
> But her father was not imprisoned.
>
> (ll. 1–5)

and conclude after an elaborate plan of escape and the promise of marriage sounding less like an action adventure hero than a postmodern Wandering Angus:

> I have been wandering ever since, back up the streams
> That had once flowed simply one into the other,
> One taking the other's name.
>
> (ll. 18–20)

Muldoon's second book, *Mules* (1977), imagines with heightened concentration the discordia concors of Irish life. Whereas the poems of *New Weather* imagine the tensions and attractions that variously engage the poet, those collected in *Mules* seek out living embodiments of contradiction. Mules (the offspring of a horse and a donkey) themselves are emblems of this, but rather than simply imaging the contraries of the first book, whose emblematic beast may well be the hedgehog that has learned to trust no one (see "Hedgehog"), or finding in the language and history of Native Americans an analogy for things Irish, as in the closing poem of the first volume, "The Year of the Sloes, For Ishi," the poems in *Mules* reflect a fascination with embodiment, and especially with hybridity, in the form of mermen, bearded women, centaurs, mixed marriages, circuses, and more. Lurking at the edge of his heterodox imaginings, Muldoon addresses the larger contraries that seem to admit no new forms into the world as the fruit of their interactions: sex and politics, the division of the sexes, and the division of the land.

In "Lunch with Pancho Villa" Muldoon makes explicit the dilemma that permeates so many of the poems in the second book. Tower bound (though somewhat less grandly than Yeats), brooding whether the life of action or of contemplation most suits him, Muldoon turns over the theme in a manner that is both conversational and extravagant. While sharing a bottle of muscatel, the poet puts to the noted Mexican hero a question particularly resonant in the light of Irish political struggle: "'Is it really a revolution, though?' / I reached across the wicker table / With another $10,000 question." Despite comic deflation and a zest for incongruity—that wicker table is hardly what one would expect to find holding up a revolutionary's muscatel—the poem presents a serious meditation on the relation between art and life, complete with a backward glance at the outmoded images of poetic apprenticeship (a rhetorical gesture used to such notable effect by Yeats). Within the imagined tête-à-tête the poet is confronted with his reluctance to address the violence of his times. Pancho Villa responds:

> "Look, son. Just look around you.
> People are getting themselves killed
> Left, right and centre
> While you do what? Write rondeaux?
> There's more to living in this country
> Than stars and horses, pigs and trees,
> Not that you'd guess it from your poems.
> Do you never listen to the news?
> You want to get down to something true,
> Something a little nearer home."
>
> (ll. 11–20)

Having staged this nettlesome crisis of artistic conscience, the poet dissolves it, thereby exposing his narrative as a fabulation. When the poet returns to ask more questions, he finds an empty courtyard. Losing conviction in his story, he soon gives it up altogether, as if the words of Pancho Villa had defeated him, raising doubts not only about how to write and what to write about, but also about what something "nearer home" might truly be, since as *New Weather* had shown, stars and horses, pigs and trees are themselves the very vocabulary of rural Ireland. The poem proceeds to reinvent itself by examining and critiquing the elements of its own fantasy. In the role of critic, the poet asks himself two questions: first, what is his relation to that thing that so concerned the American poet of the imagination, Wallace Stevens, the quotidian, "the things that people live among"; and second, what was it about himself that his lunch with a dead revolutionary revealed, that he himself might be the "celebrated co-pamphleteer" of the improbably entitled pamphlets of Pancho Villa. Behind both questions a single image looms, that of a politically engaged poet with a penchant for naturalism. The speaker is caught among three untenable positions: comic fabulist, poet engagé, and the poet he has been until today, and who he must now confront in the guise of a "callow youth / Who learned to write last winter—/ One of those correspondence courses." The youth has learned to write in the style of the poet's own earlier works. And here the poem takes a curious turn in its resolution as the poet offers us a reaffirmation of his art through the words of the "callow youth," who in coming to lunch will, the poet presumes, ramble on about "pigs and trees, stars and horses." Thus while the pose of the novice poet has been exposed, he has become a comic figure and his truth—and truth is very much at issue in this poem—a bore. Still, his words are retrieved from Pancho Villa's criticism. The last line, "pigs and trees, stars and horses," achieves a lyricism that was in danger of being discredited by the demand that the poet address his times in some obvious politically engaged way. We are hardly left, to return to the specter that so often flickers in the interstices of Muldoon's world, standing at the door of the tower beside Yeats as he confronts the British mercenaries, or mulls over a life of action, or returns to the occult musings of his youth. Nonetheless, Muldoon has dramatized a self-confrontation where his aesthetic is challenged and reborn.

Mules elaborates this dilemma with extraordinary inventiveness. Hybrids are the response of the imagination to conflicting claims on the poet. In "Mixed Marriage" the competing bids for the poet's allegiance are given an autobiographical turn:

> She had read one volume of Proust,
> He knew the cure for farcy.
> I flitted between a hole in the hedge
> And a room in the Latin Quarter.
> (ll. 9–12)

Tensions here are held in balance by charm. The differing traditions, the mother associated with literature and religion, the father associated with practical knowledge, politics, and patriotic lore, are not so demanding that the son must choose between them. The "doubleness" of irony, and the ability of poetic wit to join incongruities, allows the poet to have it both ways, or appear to have it both ways, as long as the gravity of the subject permits the poet to be the celebrant of possibilities rather than the memorialist of choice. At such a point an element of the grotesque enters, which blurs the boundary between imagination and fate. While the grotesque still figures as part of the carnivalesque aura of many of the poems in *Mules* (see "Duffy's Circus") that celebrate aberration and license, there is also a grotesque element that sounds more horrific depths. Images of violent death impinge on the obliquities and odd turns of logic. In a striking portrait drawn, it almost seems, from some apocalyptic western, Muldoon describes in "Vaquero" a corpse riding into town, dead of starvation, tied to a saddle, and with a "Halo of buzzards . . . no wider now than his hat-band." And in "Ned Skinner" the speaker's Aunt Sarah endures the drunken nostalgia of a former lover, who has come back to the house after completing the job for which her husband had hired him: slaughtering pigs.

We have already noted the title poem of Muldoon's third volume, *Why Brownlee Left* (1980). Having in "Brownlee" glanced at some of the thematic and literary-historical implications of the absent farmer, the significance of point of view, the substitution of enigma for epic scope and elegiac recollection, the poet goes on to develop the matter of where Brownlee might have gone, takes up, that is, the theme of departure and wandering. What one suspects at this point in Muldoon's career soon gives ample proof of itself in succeeding volumes: each book builds with remarkable self-possession and artistic control on the developments of the previous one. *Mules* had imagined a world of deep divisions and odd affinities; this book imagines difference in terms of distance, most famously in the first of Muldoon's major efforts, the long poem "Immram," which concludes the volume. It takes its name from the ancient Irish poem "Immram Mul Duine" (the wanderings of Muldoon). The ancient immram is in fact one of many, and bears a close relation to one of the most significant examples of the Irish vision quest genre, the "Wanderings of Brendan." Of the original "Voyage of Mael Duin," historians McHugh and Harmon tell us:

Its hero is raised by an Irish Queen but discovers that he is the son of a nun and that his father had been murdered. Seeking revenge, he puts to sea with twenty companions. Storms blow them to far-off islands, thirty-one in number, each with its own marvels. One is inhabited by ants as big as foals, another by horseracing demons, a third by red-hot swine. There is a laughing island and a wailing island, whose inhabitants are black; in each case a scout who lands becomes a laugher or a black wailer and has to be abandoned. The juxtaposition of Christian and pagan tradition in such stories is exemplified by the presence on one island, with a monk and church, of a huge bird tended by eagles, which renews its youth by bathing in a lake into which magical fruit has dropped. Finally Mael Duin is persuaded by a holy hermit on another island to forgo his revenge, in gratitude for the many perils from which God has saved him.

(*Short History of Anglo-Irish Literature,* 1982, pp. 19–20)

Muldoon's poem radically departs from this source, but we can see in this synopsis both the primitive backdrop against which the contemporary poem sets itself and the type of material the poet finds in his tradition that reflects his concerns. Each of Muldoon's subsequent major efforts will involve "immrams" of various kinds. While the heroes are drawn from a variety of sources, they share key elements with this earliest of Irish narratives: the question of identity, the treacherous allure of the exotic, and what the concept of home might most authentically mean. Muldoon's modern immram takes place in Los Angeles, a land almost as extravagant as the magic isles of medieval legend. The new identity taken up by the poet as he begins not a quest for vengeance but a search for his father turns out to be a film noir walk-on who talks something like a character in a Raymond Chandler novel. Gertrude Stein once remarked that the detective story is the quintessential fictional form of the twentieth century, because from the onset the main character, who figured so largely and pointlessly as the subject for analysis in the nineteenth-century novel, is dead. Muldoon finds the prose posturing of Chandler and the atmospherics of film noir liberating, not only for the intrigue that the form offers, but for the chance to create a world both uncertain and precise, rife with fantastic coincidences prompting not belief, but a heightened capacity for both skepticism and action.

Muldoon has said of the poem: "The quest is the powerful and important centre of the poem. Both the protagonist and his father are led through a maze. The protagonist is a cipher, the world envelops him, everything happens to him; he directs very little, and I'm very skeptical about how much we direct anything that happens to us. And the end of it is this whimsical—I would tend to use the word 'whimful,' which does not exist—this whimsical dismissal by the bane of both their lives. 'I forgive you ... and I forget'" (quoted in Longley, *Poetry in the Wars,* p. 234). The immediate object of the quest is the father. The spur to the speaker's departure is his discovery of a heretofore unknown likeness between himself and his father, revealed during an altercation in a poolroom named, appropriately, "Foster's." Recovering from a blow to the head with a "sixteen-ounce billiard cue," the narrator hears the words of his assailant: "'Your old man was an ass-hole. / That makes an ass-hole out of you.'" He immediately begins to speculate about this new element of his patrimony:

> My grand-father hailed from New York State.
> My grand-mother was part Cree.
> This must be some new strain in my pedigree.
> (ll. 8–10)

Muldoon's first book bore the dedication "for my Fathers and Mothers." His first three books imaginatively pursue the complications of genealogy, inheritance, and identity suggested by these pluralized precursors. The father in particular appears with powerful and peculiar associations in a number of early poems. While the father is consistently characterized, appearing as one patriarch among a number including poets, mythic characters, and historical figures, he seems himself always on the brink between the here and the gone. For Muldoon, the act of perceiving patriarchal relations is in part an act of perceiving multiplicity. In pointed contrast to the earthbound and more conventionally autobiographical portraits of fathers in Heaney and others, Muldoon's renderings—while retaining a human warmth and communicating clear affection—raise the question of the father's identity. In *New Weather*'s "The Waking Father" the poet draws a generic father-son scene with a kind of dream logic. The first stanza has father and son exulting in feelings of righteousness. Throwing back the "spricklies," the narrator says "our benevolence is astounding." Then when father separates from son, anxiety fuels a series of conjectures that take us further and further toward the land not of Kavanagh but of Kafka:

When my father stood out in the shallows
It occurred to me that
The spricklies might have been piranhas,
The river a red carpet
Rolling out from where he had just stood
(ll. 6–10)

The imagination sets to work on the figure of the father. The mixture of exoticism and violence that will come to typify Muldoon's later work bequeaths us, here, the image of a piranha in an Irish stream. The sudden treachery of nature initiates the father into the mythic realm of the absent. As he is devoured, he might be an ancient Greek king, Agamemnon perhaps, pondering the red carpet of blood at his feet. Already the father has disappeared, but his absence, for Muldoon, does not evoke affectlessness or despair. The departee leaves behind a world of clues. The poet does not memorialize or lament but lavishes his love on the possible scenarios into which the missing figure, in this case, the father, has vanished. Faced with the inquiries of those readers resistant to imaginative truths, who prefer real fishes, the poet pledges himself to certain secrecies.

Or I wonder now if he is dead or sleeping.
For if he is dead I would have his grave
Secret and safe,
I would turn the river out of its course,
Lay him in its bed, bring it round again.

No one would question
That he had treasures or his being a king,
Telling now of the real fish father down.
(ll. 13–18)

"Immram" surrenders the presumption that the words and wisdoms of fathers can be heard and believed. The narrator sets out to learn about the past and is immediately beset with intrigues and misadventures. This very simple plot device, with the poet/narrator announcing a quest and then doing everything possible to keep the adventurer from his goal, enters Muldoon's poetics with the force of divine revelation. What "Immram" discovers and so evidently masters will become the pattern for all of Muldoon's longer works. Each succeeding volume extends the perimeters of imagination, and allows the poet the obvious pleasure of tale spinning. With only the addition of a heraldic emblem or two, "Immram" might easily be subtitled "Edmund Spenser in Hollywood," so effort-lessly does it accommodate the comedy, violence, and magic of both Arthurian fantasia and the movies. Along with the possibilities of narrative comes the discovery of America as a subject for poetry, and with America comes the larger social and cultural world beyond Ireland. Muldoon specializes in a poetry that offers complex, amusing, horrifying, and poignant juxtapositions of the world envisioned in the early books and that which the poet will come to know in his own wandering. Here the purview is somewhat more modest. The Chandleresque embellishments, the film noir atmosphere, the broad slapstick, and the social satire are all concentrated on creating a believably incredible Los Angeles.

The narrator contributes his own slim grasp on the realities that surround him. In setting out to find his father he goes to his mother, whom he has not seen for "six months or a year" only to find her being force-fed "lukewarm water through a rubber hose" after what seems to be her third suicide attempt. He can't afford to wait around, however, since she may not be able to talk until the end of the week. While his narrator is passing through a number of scenarios—going to the Atlantic Club; meeting someone named Susan or Suzanne, a girl, he tells us, "who would never pass out of fashion / So long as there's an 'if' in California"; surviving a mob-style rub out; inferring some secret wisdom from the dead gaze of the two hit men who seemed to have died by colliding with each other; and discovering, somehow, that his father owed money to a nefarious capitalist lord named Redpath—what the poet explores is slipped to us in a dream recounted by the narrator:

You remember how, in a half-remembered dream,
You found yourself in a long corridor,
How behind the first door there was nothing,
Nothing behind the second,
Then how you swayed from room to empty room
Until, beyond that last half-open door
You heard a telephone . . .
(*Why Brownlee Left*, p. 41)

Muldoon moved from riddle, to puzzle, to labyrinth over the course of his early books. While this passage is uncharacteristically reflective if not outright somber, the vision behind it is significant. Muldoon excels in creating multiple corridors and multiple doors. Though they may appear as fantastic landscapes or comic interludes or robust and twisted sexual encounters, they exist at the expense of a poetics of intimacy. The phone that is ringing in the next room in "Immram" propels the narrator into another whirlwind of high intrigue and shenanigans, but it also suggests, for this increasingly Daedalean artist, and for the reader, the ghost of some more authentic human contact that haunts the larger body of work and keeps hunger and need and desire always sounding in the quieter inlets of the voyaging. The narrator of *Why Brownlee Left*, hit by a hypodermic syringe, awakens to a vision of a murdered woman from his past, possibly a bride, who—despite the familiarity of the scene to all consumers of crime fiction—evokes another missed connection, and who underscores the isolation of the narrator:

> Among row upon row of sheeted cadavers
> In what might have been the Morgue
> Of all the cities in America,
> Who beckoned me towards her slab
> And silently drew back the covers
> On the vermilion omega
> Where she had been repeatedly stabbed,
> Whom I would carry over the threshold of pain
> That she might come and come and come again.
>
> (p. 42)

The narrator does not find his father, but his search ushers him through New Age religions and conversations with an Irish-American cop (who relays his own father's theory that the American Irish are really the lost tribe of Israel), until finally he learns that his father may be on the lam in South America, hiding from the professional drug smugglers for whom he worked as a mule until the unfortunate day at customs when his cocaine-filled replica statue of *The Christ of the Andes* shattered. The closest he comes to finding his father is discovering a father surrogate modeled on the eccentric American billionaire Howard Hughes, who summons the speaker to him to recite the words that would be so momentous in a more earnest quest narrative, but that here are both meaningless and chilling: "'I forgive you,' he croaked. 'And I forget.'" But then of course Muldoon cannot resist wringing the last drop of pathos from the scene in *Why Brownlee Left*:

> On your way out, you tell that bastard
> To bring me a dish of ice-cream.
> I want Baskin Robbins banana-nut ice-cream.
>
> (p. 47)

QUOOF

THE next collection, *Quoof*, was published in 1983. It begins directly with the conundrum so vividly established by "Immram." *Quoof* will develop with extraordinary richness and complexity Muldoon's investigation of place and origins. *Quoof* inaugurates Muldoon's own idiosyncratic version of the poet as seer, a complicated, ironic, and diffident seer, but one who fully engages the deep connections between poetic enterprise and vision quest. As such, the poet brings together sources familiar to nonmainstream American poetic traditions: drugs, anthropology, formal innovation, and low culture. The epigram for the volume, taken from an Alaskan trickster myth, evokes the shape-shifting power of a shaman. The epigram is the first of many tales of transformation told in *Quoof*, and prepares the reader to attend to the intimation of occult powers and transgressive rituals at work in the contemporary world that the book sets before us with such precision and amplitude. The epigram concerns an old foster mother who is also a great shaman. She turns herself into a man, making a penis from a willow branch, taking off her original genitals, and with a bit of magic making them into a wooden sledge, and marries her adoptive daughter. Her creative powers do not stop here; she makes dogs from the snow in the act of wiping herself.

This epigram places Native American culture before us and invites us, not for the last time, to see the poet's fascination with Native American sources as a way of speaking about Ireland. Further, it cues us to the nature of gender identities, kinship bonds, and the grotesque: the association of transformation and feces reverberates throughout the book, reflecting the poet's troubled understanding of a materiality where eroticism inevitably leads to revulsion, and where female figures—particularly the traditional idealizations of Ireland—have the power to infect as well as to inspire. *Quoof* makes repeated use of the association of the female body with Irishness. In the frequently cited poem "Aisling," for example, Muldoon rings characteristic changes upon the figure of Ireland as a long-suffering woman. The title refers to a conventional form of Irish poetry that describes a rhapsodic vision of a woman who is seen as embodying the hope of Ireland's future. The eighteenth-century poet Aogan Ó Rathaille wrote several aislings during a period of expectation that the forces of the

Stuart Pretender would land on the shores of Ireland, and we can see in the following translation of part of one of these something of the rich rhetorical and mythological traditions upon which Muldoon works:

Brightness most bright I beheld on the way, forlorn.
Chrystal of chrystal her eye, blue touched with green.
Sweetness most sweet her voice, not stern with age.
Colour and pallor appeared in her flushed cheeks.

Curling and curling, each strand of her yellow hair
as it took the dew from the grass in its ample sweep;
a jewel more glittering than glass on her high bosom
—created, when she was created, in a higher world.

True tidings she revealed me, most forlorn,
tidings of one returning by royal right,
tidings of the crew ruined who drove him out,
and tidings I keep from my poem for sheer fear.
("Gile Na Gile," trans. Thomas Kinsella, from
An Duanaire / An Irish Anthology, p. 151)

Muldoon's version plays upon the lavish exaltation of the goddess figure, comically deflating the stance of the poet while retaining her hypnotic and transformative powers. The poet in Muldoon's version is equally stricken, but the knowledge that the goddess imparts is of another order, or so it appears, for the poet has apparently contracted a venereal disease:

I was making my way home late one night
this summer, when I staggered
into a snow drift.

Her eyes spoke of a sloe year,
her mouth a year of haws.

Was she Aurora, or the goddess Flora,
Artemidora, or Venus bright,
or Anorexia, who left
a lemon stain on my flannel sheet?

It's all much of a muchness.

(ll. 1–10)

Despite the revisionary handling of the earlier poetic convention, the relationship between the poet and the muse remains the same. He is the blinded suppliant, and she is the bearer of bitter truths about the state of the Irish people. In the earlier aislings the longed-for invasion did not occur. Ó Rathaille's poems survive as a testament to a moment of national hope. Muldoon's vision pursues a like correlation of erotic fervor and national fate, as it comes to seem that of the goddess candidates mentioned, Anorexia is indeed the new patroness of Ireland in her troubles, a self-destroying Eire. The poem concludes:

In Belfast's Royal Victoria Hospital
a kidney machine
supports the latest hunger-striker
to have called off his fast, a saline
drip into his bag of brine.

A lick and a promise. Cuckoo spittle.
I hand my sample to Doctor Maw.
She gives me back a confident *All Clear.*

In so concluding the poem reestablishes the power of the conventional aisling. Another devotee of the goddess, a hunger-striker, has entered the poem. The image calls to mind Yeats's own deliberations in his Irish Civil War poems between the roles of active struggle and contemplation. One feels the implicit rebuke to the amorous and wayward speaker: how trivial the conjugal smear of his sheets, how meager their salts, when compared to the heroism of the saline drip. But Muldoon avoids the moment of recognition that occurs in Yeats, when the Yeatsian speaker takes full stock of the life he has chosen *not* to live. The postmodern poet resolves the discrepancy between the two perspectives—lover and political martyr—by returning to the perspective of the prospective victim of venereal disease, and yet we are teased by a possible connection between the visionary and the martyr. The apparent will to survive of the hunger-striker who has called off his strike and the all-clear sign from the mysterious Doctor Maw—yet another feminine figure of authority and prophecy—suggest that both figures are linked by the promise of another day.

Around the motif of the vision quest *Quoof* gathers together intersecting worlds. The very title of the volume requires us to acknowledge disparate planes of experience. The word was coined by the Muldoon family itself, and so cannot be understood without a translator, someone who is both inside and outside the contained world of the Muldoon family. The neologism represents a larger tendency: of social

419

worlds to construct ways of defining themselves as self-enclosed and self-sufficient, however much they depend on interactions with other worlds. Muldoon finds in his family's coinage—describing a hot brick placed in a sock and brought into a bed to warm it—a metaphor for the inner logic of other groups, be they tribe, sect, or nation. The opening poem announces in no uncertain terms that the poetry here, and again in the book-length poem *Madoc,* will pursue the poet's contention that reality is hallucinogenic.

"Gathering Mushrooms" begins in terrain made familiar to us from Kavanagh and Heaney, and from Muldoon's own early poems. We are located in rural Ireland, place of familial pieties, cradle of durable virtues. We find the benighted father figure out of Heaney, keeping to the old ways, offering acknowledgment to the son who trails behind him. But here the father tends mushrooms, while the son with his unnamed companion search for psilocybin, a hallucinogenic mushroom used in Native American vision quests and adopted by the counterculture of the 1960s. Muldoon, having sufficiently defamiliarized the rural world of Irish tradition, can return to it as an adequate origin, as a place providing the means to both escape or evade the demands of a political art, and the means to speak about the totality of the cultural struggle erupting all around the poet. The drug deepens its hold on the aspiring shaman. He finds himself in a prophetic mode ("though my head had grown into the head of a horse"), and concludes the poem with a vatic declamation of what may well be the words of the dead speaking through the poet, laying their claim upon his art:

> Beyond this concrete wall is a wall of concrete
> and barbed wire. Your only hope
> is to come back. If sing you must, let your song
> tell of treading your own dung,
> let straw and dung give a spring to your step.
> If we never live to see the day we leap
> into our true domain,
> lie down with us now and wrap
> yourself in the soiled grey blanket of Irish rain
> that will, one day, bleach itself white.
> Lie down with us and wait.
>
> (ll. 46–56)

Quoof concludes with the extraordinary poem "The More a Man Has the More a Man Wants." Loosely based upon the cycle of trickster myths of the Winnebego Indians as rendered by the anthropologist Paul Radin, the poem finds in ancient myth a perfect metaphor for the mind of the poet. The central character, Gallogly, shares the poet's capacity to inhabit identities in conflict and worlds at war. He is both trickster and terrorist, and leads the reader as he does the police through forty-odd sonnet-length stanzas in search of clues to his identity and his purpose. In "Immram" the poet went to Raymond Chandler's L.A. for his style. Here he goes straight to Hollywood. Like many experimental literary works of this century, "The More a Man Has the More a Man Wants" looks to the cinema for cues on narrative and characterization. At the poem's opening the hero awakens to find his lover gone. The police are closing in, and he slips away just in time. He will be sighted and commented upon throughout the poem as he changes shape, sells arms, makes bombs, goes to America, and has undisclosed dealings with a Native American named Mangas Jones. Jones arrives at the airport early on, just after Gallogly has gotten away, carrying a briefcase that contains quartz, an allusion, as critics have noted, to the Robert Frost poem "For Once, Then Something." This small clue alerts us to the larger subject of Muldoon's debt to Frost, and to their shared interest in epistemological questions. As in previous Muldoon poems, "The More a Man Has" constantly raises the question of what it is possible for us to know—about events, about personalities, about ourselves. At one point the shape shifter protagonist appears to have taken on the guise of the reader:

> He's sporting your
> Donegal tweed suit and your
> Sunday shoes and politely raises your
> hat as he goes by.
> You stand there with your mouth open
> as he climbs into the still-warm
> driving seat of your Cortina
> and screeches off towards the motorway,
> leaving you uncertain
> of your still-warm wife's damp tuft.
>
> (ll. 89–98)

The motorway (expressway) leads back into the larger social world, one in which large forces are at work. Muldoon uses the wanderings of his hero, and of Mangas Jones, to provide a panorama of civil violence in Northern Ireland. *Quoof* in many ways can be seen as a response to Heaney's volume

North, in which the older poet comes to terms with his country's sectarian violence by searching back through Irish history, uncovering earlier ritual and colonial acts of outrage by which to measure the modern world. Heaney's premise in *North*, that there exists an underlying tribal consciousness rife with archaic beliefs and demands that shape the world of contemporary Ireland, inspires powerful poems, and considerable empathy for the victims of such violence. Muldoon makes the question not what is happening, but how can we really know what is happening. While his poem glories in the specifics of terrorist intrigue, in the spectacle of violence, it retreats from the matter of empathy. Pyrotechnics replaces pathos. When an army corporal is shot, the poem is all sang froid.

> When he tramped out just before twelve
> to exercise the greyhound
> he was hit by a single high-velocity
> shot.
> You could, if you like, put your fist
> in the exit wound
> in his chest.
> He slumps
> in the spume of his own arterial blood
> like an overturned paraffin lamp.
>
> (ll. 257–266)

The proliferation of characters and events propels us through the poem. Quotations; allusions; overheard dialogue; vernacular extravagances; puns; and specialized vocabularies gathered from the news, from the street, from movies—all are utilized with exhilarating precision. And there is the matter of travel. As in "Immram," motion is prized in and of itself. A destination reached means the end of description, and so the poem thrives on meandering. Thus while the main setting of the poem is Ireland, its protagonist spends a good bit of time in the United States, raising during the infrequent pauses of his peregrinations the whole matter of the American Irish and their relation to terrorist activities in Northern Ireland. America looms as all twelve of Saint Brendan's mythic islands in one landmass. Through his character's New World escapades the poet explores his preoccupation with American culture. Arriving in Ireland, Mangas Jones appears to have some business to transpire with Gallogly. Gallogly, afoot in America, seems in pursuit of

some aspect of Native American culture. From an Irish graveside where he has knelt not so much in grief for the dead but to lap up what seems to be horse dung, the poem transports him to the Museum of Modern Art in New York City, which he flees, with the bit from the horse in Picasso's *Guernica* between his teeth. A weekend in Frost country ("North of Boston") begins in the Oyster Bar in Grand Central Station and involves what appears to be a sexual romp in a Winnebago camper with a woman named Alice A., whose "quim" seems to be "biting the leg off her." In an extraordinary sequence of stanzas, the poet cuts between Gallogly's erotic odyssey and acts of civil violence in Ireland. Beatrice, who was brutally executed in the poem's opening, returns, no longer beheaded and "singing her one song." Muldoon complicates the correspondence between Native Americans and the Irish with a glimpse from the floor of the "*Las Vegas* Lounge and Cabaret":

> He was crossing the bar's
> eternity of parquet floor
> when his eagle eye
> saw something move on the horizon.
> If it wasn't an Indian,
> A Sioux. An ugly Sioux.
> He means, of course, an Oglala
> Sioux busily tracing the family tree
> of an Ulsterman who had some hand
> in the massacre at Wounded Knee.

Before the protagonist is finally arrested, jailed, and escapes, "The More a Man Has the More a Man Wants" will touch upon such American icons as Edward Hopper, Nathaniel Hawthorne, and Gertrude Stein and Alice B. Toklas (who, naked, chant "Eros is Eros is Eros") before it returns to Ireland and its underlying meditation on desire, violence, and community, what Frost might have called "a momentary stay against confusion." In *Quoof* Muldoon found a way to speak about the Troubles in his own fashion, one utterly unlike that of his contemporaries. His mixture of intense local clarities and systemic uncertainty constitutes both an aesthetic and a critique. His hero's name, as we learn at his arrest, is itself an emblem of ambiguity, changing from Gallogly to Gollogly, to Golightly, to Ingoldsby, until finally the trickster reveals his ultimate transformation: "otherwise known as English."

MEETING THE BRITISH

It was perhaps the poet's own sense that something had come to a conclusion in his work that contributed to the next phase of his career. Having written a definitive volume on the contemporary situation, and having set out his own version of the Irish poetic tradition in *The Faber Book of Contemporary Irish Poetry*, a fresh beginning was in order. Although he did not leave for America until the poems in his next volume, *Meeting the British* (1987), were completed, the poems therein present his argument for wandering. Each of Muldoon's previous books had concluded with a long poem, and in this volume the final poem, "7, Middagh Street," overpowers the lyrics that precede it. This expansion impulse would soon find its consummate articulation in "Madoc," virtually a book-length poem that takes up with leisure and amplitude the subject with which *Meeting the British* prepares the way: poets arriving in America. While much of the criticism concerned with Muldoon's work has for good reason sought to understand his relation to Ireland and the Irish literary tradition, there is much to be said about the poet's persistent and career-long effort to write himself away from Ireland. Therefore it is perhaps less than surprising to find that the Irish poet has focused on the quintessential English poet of the century, W. H. Auden, for the subject of the poem that marks the beginning of his devoutly wished exile. Brownlee had left long ago, and the argument of the work since that early sonnet suggests a destination: stateside.

In the final bomb waiting to explode at the end of *Quoof* one senses a longing to level the world that has so preoccupied the poet. Through his character Gallogly, the poet had already made preliminary trips to America, and no doubt already recognized the affinity between that land of opportunity and himself, the progenitor of a terrorist/trickster in an Irish poem that seems inspired less by an archaic spirit of tribal identity than by a cartoon from Warner Brothers. Auden himself had seen his move to America as a turning point in his career, and this indicates the underlying anxieties that haunt Muldoon's re-creation of the precursor poet's relocation. For Auden, America offered a liberation from the role of the politically committed poet he had fashioned for himself throughout the 1930s. The household he gathered around him at 7, Middagh Street, his legendary Brooklyn residence, in-cluding Carson McCullers, Salvador Dali, Chester Kallman, and Gypsy Rose Lee, reflected a kind of imaginative exuberance that would come to typify his American work as Auden re-imagined the possibilities for his poetry in America. It is significant to note Muldoon's affinity with the American poets who respond to Auden's presence in the States: John Henry O'Hara, John Ashbery, James Schuyler, and Kenneth Koch, poets who share Muldoon's yen for invention and extravagance. This central effort of *Meeting the British* will, as one might suspect, settle upon Irish poets after all as it sets up residence in the New World, but first we might be led to ask by so dramatic a departure what the book tells us about the life to be left behind.

The assorted shorter lyrics that precede "7, Middagh Street" register significant personal losses. Elegies and farewells sound low and persistent in the interstices of wit and description. Clearly, while *Quoof* concludes the first phase of Muldoon's career, these poems show that it is not merely artistic and political issues that spur the poet into middle age. The "British" of the title poem have become not merely the colonizers and exploiters of a culture, but emissaries of death, bearing infected gifts, such as in the volume's title poem, with its blanket "embroidered with smallpox," given in trade by the British to a Native American tribe. Other gifts and visitations haunt the volume whose tutelary spirit comes first in the form of a rabbit. "The Coney" finds the poet going about his father's business. The old man is ill and cannot scythe the grass. The son takes up the job and does it much less well, dulling the blade and grinding the whetstone to nothingness as he works on. One sees here once again the rural world of Irish poetic tradition, and the poet frozen by obligation and filial love. A rabbit appears, teases the poet, and invites him into a cartoonlike world that seems an eerie mingling of escape from boredom and an invitation to join his father in death. The precision and wit and knack for detail that so enlivens the earlier books tends, here, to make a memento mori of any object that strays into the poet's attention. Wishbones, toe-tags, this poem draws an unmistakable equation between human design and death.

Perhaps the central icon of loss is a "soap pig" given to the poet by a friend who has died. This amber-colored, chamomile-scented, cellophaned bit of soap in the shape of a pig leads us through aspects of the poet's life in recent years, his less-than-epic "immram" through relationships and employments and apartments. The fate of the soap pig is to become froth on the poet's face as he shaves with his father's brush at his mother's washstand. The soap pig, like the beasts and hybrids of Muldoon's earlier poems, embodies contradictions—nature and art, unclean and clean, body and spirit—but the contemplation of it does not revivify the poet with the promise of some inspirational vulgarity or imaginative harmony. The pig dissolves, and turns our morning rituals into memorials.

Coincident with the various deaths registered in *Meeting the British* are other losses, relationships that go bad, isolating the poet even among the living. "The Soap-pig" also describes domestic upheavals, one in which a woman named Mary (the artist Mary Powers with whom the poet lived for many years and whose death is so powerfully commemorated in *The Annals of Chile*) throws the soap pig out the window. With quick hermetic lines the poet evokes failed understanding and unsatisfied longing, approaching at times the wryly observed minor tragedies of Robert Lowell's *The Dolphin*.

> I might as well be another guest
> at the wedding-feast
> of Strongbow and Aoife Mac murrough
> as I watch you, Mary,
>
> try to get to grips
> with a spider-crab's
> crossbow and cuirass.
> A creative pause before the second course
>
> of Ireland's whole ox on a spit;
> the invisible waitress
> brings us each a Calvados and water-ice.
>
> It's as if someone had slipped
> a double-edged knife between my ribs
> and hit the spot exactly.
> ("The Marriage of Strongbow
> and Aoife," p. 19)

The shorter lyrics in *Meeting the British* constitute an argument for change, or at least motion. In *Quoof* the Irish landscape was violent and treacherous, but also served as the ground for extraordinary transformations and tale telling. Here, the landscape is haunted. The father's grave is "three fields away." Robert Frost's attraction for Muldoon shows another side in these poems, which seem written less under the auspices of Frost the skeptic or Frost the yarn-spinner than that of Frost the author of

"The Need to Be Versed in Country Things." The book sets before us the prospect of radical change. It is typical of Muldoon to interpret his own hegira to America through the lens of a poet so distant from, if not averse to, the Irish poetic tradition. And typical also that the major voice in this series of dramatic monologues spoken by members of Auden's newfound family should turn out to be that of Louis MacNeice, and that the figure that several of them—even Gypsy Rose Lee—have on their minds should turn out to be William Butler Yeats.

"Wystan" is the first of the speakers and the one, understandably enough, who most directly points to the larger issues that the poem brings before us: cultural allegiance, the relation between art and life, and the function of poetry. The way we first see Auden sets Muldoon's anxieties before us: the great English poet, the conscience of a generation, arrives in New York City on the day that Franco takes Barcelona. A distant civil violence touches the new life before it has really begun. The poet's attempt to set aside his past naturally enough fosters feelings of guilt. Wystan, in recalling his work as an ambulance driver in the Spanish Civil War, describes a horrific war scene, one that leads him to recall how his father tended the grotesque wounded paw of a pup. By this point in his development as an artist, Muldoon's breakdown of the boundaries between public and private events has become commonplace. Wystan, in attempting to repudiate the old "Auden," takes up the example of Yeats, the poet who in his role as national poet and political visionary bedevils Auden. Echoing Auden's famous critique of Yeats, Muldoon's Wystan notes:

> And were Yeats living at this hour
> it should be in some ruined tower
>
> not malachited Ballylee
> where he paid out to those below
>
> one guilt edged scroll from his pencil
> as though he were part-Rapunzel
>
> and part Delphic oracle.
> As for his crass, rhetorical
>
> posturing, Did that play of mine
> send out certain men (*certain* men?)
>
> the English shot . . . ?
> the answer is 'Certainly not.'
> (*Selected Poems*, p. 133–134)

One cannot take the judgment of Muldoon's Auden on Yeats as Muldoon's own. The ties between these two poets is complex and subtle. One need merely place "Identities" from *New Weather* beside a poem like Yeats's "The Wandering Angus" to sense that there is much in Muldoon that cannot be attributed to Joyce, or to Frost, or to Heaney, or to MacNeice. The Irish Yeats may be too rhetorical, too distant, too committed to a poetics of selfhood, but there is also what we might call the American Yeats, or at least, after a quip of Auden's, the southern Californian Yeats, the magus of wild spiritual imaginings and occult correspondences delivered through the medium of his wife. Several of the diverse array of characters who speak after "Wystan" touch upon some line or other written by Yeats. While the intent is clearly comic, the effect is itself a kind of summoning—as if Muldoon, like the American poet John Berryman before him, was finally going to "have it out with William Butler Yeats."

The citations of Yeats by Gypsy Rose Lee, Carson McCullers, and Louis MacNeice mark a distance between the self-pronounced "Last Romantic" and the realities of the modern world. Certainly to hear such ringing Yeatsian sentiments as "there's more enterprise in walking naked" or "how can we tell the dancer from the dance" from the mouth of America's most notorious striptease artist modifies the grandeur of the lines, but it also elevates the speaker, infusing her awareness with at least a passing acquaintance with grand sentiment. So, too, the monologues that do not cite Yeats directly, those by Benjamin Britten, Salvador Dali, and Chester Kallman, strike Yeatsian notes, not so much in their rhetoric but in the candor with which they talk about and dramatize their lives. It was Yeats, after all, who carved mythologies from mere writers' gossip. While Muldoon ostensibly pits a high-toned aesthete against an array of artists who truck with low culture and thrive on its vitality, what emerges is the ghost of a Yeats other than the one derided in "Wystan" as sententious and wrongheaded. Muldoon's "7, Middagh Street" recovers a vulgar, worldly Yeats, even as, in the closing speech of "Louis," Yeats's words are linked with terrorist violence. Auden too becomes the subject for critique. Muldoon's MacNeice considers the place of poetry in the world, taking issue with Auden's famous assertion in his elegy for Yeats that "poetry makes nothing happen." As *The Faber Book of Contemporary Irish Poetry* indicates, Muldoon gives MacNeice great authority in matters of Irish poetics. But "7, Middagh Street" complicates our view of this precursor poet. Whereas he argues in the excerpted interview published in the anthology for a poetry of mental freedom and wandering, in the closing section of "Louis" one can almost hear an act of double ventriloquism, as Muldoon's MacNeice comes close to the themes and disposition of Patrick Kavanagh:

> The one-eyed foreman had strayed out of Homer.
> "MacNeice? That's a Fenian name."
> As if to say, "None of our sort, none of you
>
> will as much as go for a rubber hammer
> never mind chalk a rivet, never mind caulk a seam
> on the quinquereme of Nineveh."
>
> (ll. 124–129)

MADOC

ACCORDING to legend, a Welsh prince in the twelfth century grew tired of the political situation in his homeland. The king had died and his sons were consumed with killing each other in their rush to claim the crown. The Welsh prince, whose name was Madoc, sailed into the West in hope of finding a peaceful land in which to settle. He returned once, for supplies and settlers, and was never heard from again. This legend takes a significant place in the literature of the New World as a possible origin for a Native American tribe known as the Mandans who seemed, according to nineteenth-century scholars and explorers, to be the descendants of Madoc. The evidence was intriguing but inconclusive. Which is to say that it is exactly the kind of evidence that would attract Paul Muldoon and inspire his most expansive and provocative poem. In the legend of Madoc, as in the sonnet "Why Brownlee Left," the central character has vanished; as in *Quoof*, a land of shape-changing and shamanism lies before us; as in *Meeting the British*, the history of colonialism touches everything; and here again there is the story of a precursor poet to tell. Not Auden in his own New World colony, "7, Middagh Street," but the great Romantic poets Coleridge and Southey, who also, coincidentally, jointly published a long poem called "Madoc," and who planned to emigrate to America and build the perfect society along the banks of the Susquehanna.

Madoc (1990) makes good on the premise of a hallucinatory reality, as well it should. Samuel Taylor Coleridge, the author of the hypnotic, visionary "Kubla Khan," appears as the most sympathetic of the panoply of characters that the poem "Madoc" casts on the screen before us. The shaman figure that so informed *Quoof* seems at first to have been replaced by a Hollywood director, or at least a sound technician. The first poem in the short suite introducing "Madoc" draws attention to the difficulties of correlating sound and sense. A sound technician, a friend of the poet and also, apparently, of Irish descent, has had trouble matching a sound to the image of a dropped key. Thus dissociation characterizes the poem from the start, as well as a search for the ideal mesh of sound and sense. Muldoon's powerful visual sense, evident from the beginning of his career but often kept in check, here is allowed to satisfy itself. The long poem rolls out before us like a Panavision spectacular. Each section of the poem works like a camera shot, lingering on telling details, savoring bits of carefully edited dialogue, with no section running much more than a page in length. After all, we are in the realm of action-adventure, and have no time for talking heads. In "Immram" and "The More a Man Has" Muldoon took his cue from Raymond Chandler, the American detective story writer who proffered a single solution to any narrative impasses: have a man come through the door with a gun in his hand. In "Madoc" Muldoon brings onto his set yet another foreign-born artist of the American sublime, Alfred Hitchcock, alluding within the very poem to Hitchcock's theory of "the MacGuffin," the thing that makes the plot the thing.

As "Madoc" begins, Coleridge and Southey arrive in America to pursue their vision of an ideal society, and soon cross paths with such notables as Thomas Jefferson, Lewis and Clark, and many others, all of whom are redeemed from mere costume drama by the extraordinary specificity with which Muldoon renders them and the world of objects around them. There are more fanciful characters, such as B, the talking horse, and the various aliases of Coleridge as he parts company with Southey and goes in pursuit of Sarah Fricker, who has been abducted or perhaps ran away. Southey and Coleridge represent two contrasting types of personality: Southey commits himself to the founding of Southeyopolis and gradually reveals himself to be brutal and totalitarian in his pursuit of the just society, while Coleridge surrenders his identity in his search for the lost beloved, seeming to become one with those he moves among.

The narrative proceeds by no direct course. In keeping with the Frostian origins of Muldoon's style, "Madoc" works hard to get us lost. As if in ironic salute to the entire notion of a progressive history, each section is bannered with the name of a significant Western philosopher or thinker. We begin with Thales, and end with Stephen Hawking. The text beneath the august name corresponds with varying degrees of fidelity to the ideas associated with that name, inviting us to dally over elaborate correspondences while the story hurtles onward, proffering instances and elaborations of an imagined history riveting in its highly nuanced particulars while deepening the overall mystery (the full title of the poem is "Madoc: A Mystery"). The following section, occurring early in the History of Western Thought and so in the poem, gives an example of the poem's allusiveness and brings up an aspect of the poem not yet discussed. One need only recall the skepticism with which Muldoon characteristically confronts the desire for certainty in either art or politics to have suspicions about how historical material will be addressed, even within the generous bounds of a historical fantasy. The opening strophes confirm this suspicion as they qualify and complicate the already far-fetched premise: Samuel Taylor Coleridge, astray in the New World. Muldoon does not tell the story directly. Our account, it turns out, is the transcription of a "retinagraph" inflicted on a renegade descendant of Southey named "South" who has been apprehended in some technodystopia of the future by the forces of Unitel, a conglomerate of some kind that abides, in an allusion to "Kubla Khan," under "the dome," where Gekoes with stun guns and Omnipods roam, a world drawn as much from the film *Blade Runner* as from the journals of Lewis and Clark or the musings of Thomas Jefferson. And so we come upon the pre-Socratic philosopher Heraclitus:

So that, though it may seem somewhat improbable,
all that follows
flickers and flows
from the back of his right eyeball.

(Madoc, p. 20)

Our informant South, blind in his left eye, and "harnessed to a retinagraph," presents an appropriately shocking recasting of Heraclitus' maxim that "you cannot step into the same river twice." But the poem has already recontextualized our approach to Heraclitus and whatever the poet might have to say about him, by placing, albeit playfully, the pre-Socratic theories about the hidden nature of the universe and the capacities of the mind to understand it first within the context of Romantic dream vision, and second, within the context of postmodern phantasms of the state. The poem that follows is on the one hand validated by the presumed technological mastery of the all-powerful Unitel, and on the other undermined by its status as a coerced confession. History, as Stephen Dedalus noted in James Joyce's *Ulysses*, is a nightmare from which one attempts to awake. In keeping with this bit of Irish wisdom, Muldoon's poem abides despite its wit and lavish imaginings within a continuum of savagery and violence. History is horror film, an exploitation flick one can't ever walk out of, because it plays on and on within the viewer's skull. The chief villain of the piece, a Scots-Irish scout named Cinnamond, who is involved in the disappearance of Sarah Fricker, makes an unforgettable entrance:

> Cinnamond fondles a tobacco-
> pouch made from the scrotal sac
>
> of a Conestoga who must, we suppose,
> have meddled with the Paxton boys.
>
> He muses to himself
> as he raises it to his mouth
>
> and teases open its gossamerish thongs:
> "Mon is the mezjur of all thungs."
>
> (p. 26)

The legend of Madoc is rife with matter for a postcolonial imagination. Muldoon, who has rehearsed such themes as resistance to the dominant culture, assimilation, and the distortions and refashioning of the cultural logic of the dominant culture by the subjugated one throughout his earlier works, does not miss a nuance in his handling of the Madoc legend. As Tim Kendall notes in the chapter "Parallel to the Parallel Realm: *Madoc*—A Mystery" in his indispensable full-length study of Muldoon, the original legend, so baldly utopian in its search for a better world, served various imper-

ial interests. The legend was used by the Tudors to establish their claim to the New World, and these echoes of colonial conquest consume the poem. Southey and Coleridge begin with the naive idealism that mirrors that of the original Madoc. The Pantocrasy and Aspheterism the two poets imagine ("These are two new words, the first signifying the equal government of all, and the other the generalization of individual property" says Southey [*Madoc*, p. 33]) poses an ideal if limited social order that calls into question the gist of colonialism. Here is the securest link between the sprawling Panavision landscape of *Madoc* and the elusive poet of exquisitely executed lyrics. Muldoon's imagination returns again and again to the desire to possess, and to the equal and opposite desire to be free of all attachment. The former compels him to gather up into the poem highly polished oddities of perception and objects of appetite, and allows him imaginative access to the cravings and glee of conquerors; the latter prompts him to create characters (Brownlee, Gallogly, Auden, and others) who change shape, or take on new identities, or merge into larger social groups and leave no trace, disavowing all they own, leaving, in the terms of his early sonnet "Why Brownlee Left," the plow and horses abandoned in midfield.

In "Madoc" these conflicting desires are represented by the two poets. In Southey we see the poet as political visionary, who in seeking to establish a harmonious society becomes rapacious and paranoid. At a crucial point early in the poem the poets part, Southey to establish his colony near Ulster, Pennsylvania, and Coleridge to begin his wandering in the wilderness, following clues, or so it seems, as to the whereabouts of the abducted or renegade Sarah. In his deepening encounter with the American landscape and with Native American cultures, Coleridge calls to mind the fate of the original Madoc, believed to have been assimilated by a tribe called the Mandans. In describing the adventures of the two men, the poem poses two equally unviable models for colonial experience: Southey's vision of a unified culture that cannot survive his attempt to bring it about, and Coleridge's ideal of motion and assimilation, which is brought to ruin by the persistence of memory, in his case, the clues that suggest Sarah's proximity.

Our awareness of the fate of the original Madoc receives intermittent refreshening through reports on the wanderings of John Evans, who has set out to gather evidence that the Mandan Indians are the descendants of the Welsh prince. It is not hard to see how the Irish context troubles this fantasia, and how more generally postcolonial issues give the poem allegorical power. While the claim for the priority of Madoc was used to bolster Tudor colonialism, one must inevitably also read those claims in the light of the colonized as well, since we see in John Evans' researches in the New World the plight of the postcolonial artist, searching for evidence of an authentic precolonial culture.

> A room over the New Orleans tavern.
> John Evans rummages in his lice-ridden shirt
> and unfolds a chart
> of a river wider than the mouth of the Severn.
>
> Beyond the Mandan
> villages, beyond the squalid
> rucks in the quilt,
> is yet another range of mountains.
>
> There, surely, are the tell-tale
> blue eyes and fair skins
> of the scions
> of the prince of Wales
>
> (p. 84)

This quest and the motif of cultural purity that stands behind it can clearly be read in a number of ways, and it is a tribute to Muldoon's keen sense of historical irony that we are allowed no easy gloss on the complex ballet, or circus, or nightmare of cultural exchanges that drive the poem. We have seen in earlier poems how Muldoon crosscuts between the story of Native American tribes and the onset of European expansion, and the situation of the Irish. Muldoon pointed out in his 1994 interview with Lynn Keller that Ireland was used by the British as a test run for its colonization strategies, and there is considerable truth to claims made by historians that Ireland ranks as a place at the fringe of Europe. Historians contend that despite strong ties between the Anglo-Irish population and the Continent, as a people the Irish remained largely untouched by the Enlightenment. The Irish as a population existed within the perimeters of Europe, but were essentially primitive. One cannot come upon, for example, a word of Native American origin in "Madoc"—the poem seems to offer them up with extraordinary zeal—and not be mindful of the status of the outlawed and almost obliterated Irish language. Muldoon had inherited from Heaney,

and from Joyce, the conviction that language differentiated the Irish from the British. Heaney had traced out the historical precedents and the contemporary implications of this difference, sparking controversy with his most explicitly political volume, *North,* in which he linked the violence of the present with the tribal violence of the past. Muldoon, of course, significantly distanced himself from obvious Irish realities, and one advantage of this distancing is a certain access to the inner life of a colonizer. One senses in the collecting and exhibiting of linguistic and cultural oddments in "Madoc" both a wish to preserve the past and a desire to attest to its haunting place in the present as a kind of moral rebuke to the conqueror and a commemoration to the obliterated. Further, and more troublingly, one recognizes a lust to possess, to seize trophies from the killing fields.

"Madoc" draws attention to its own status as simulation by taking note of Wild West shows that apparently toured Ireland in the 1840s. What one must do without, however, is pathos. While Muldoon may take issue with Heaney for how the older poet construes the Troubles, what Muldoon gains in sophistication exists at the price of our ability to identify with the victims of the large historical forces that sweep through the poem. Almost completely lost in, so to speak, the "big-budget cinematic effects" of Muldoon's postcolonial "blockbuster," is our informant, South, the half-blinded descendant of Southey strapped to the retinagraph. "At any moment, now, the retina / will be in smithereens" the poem tells us toward its close. The pleasure dome will go blank. While it is customary for critics of Muldoon to emphasize the wit, invention, and dispassion of his accomplishment, one should not pass too lightly over the central fiction of this poem, that it is the transcriptions of a torture victim. Muldoon's next major collection brings the suffering of the self into full view.

THE ANNALS OF CHILE

WHETHER one regards Muldoon's work from the perspective of the pre-Christian sagas or of the postmodern poetic traditions, its constants are voyaging and visions. Having pressed imagination and invention to extremes in *Madoc,* with its far-off lands, wandering bards, and specters of the all-powerful state, the poet in his next major collection charts and traverses regions of personal loss. As in "Madoc," *The Annals of Chile* (1994) centers upon a missing woman. In the earlier poem the missing woman was Sarah Fricker, the wife of Samuel Taylor Coleridge, vanished in the New World. The landscape bristled with clues, but the woman was never found. Whether she was abducted or ran off remains unclear; whether she was assimilated by some Indian tribe or was dead eludes us. In *The Annals of Chile* no such ambiguities trouble us: the terrain is too well known, and though now there are two women, not one, both women are clearly dead. One is the poet's former lover, the artist Mary Powers, and the other the poet's mother, Brigid Regan.

Although the two major poems in this collection are set either in Ireland, in America, or in both places, the real voyage that the poet undertakes is to the Land of the Dead. When Odysseus in book II of *The Odyssey* visits the Land of the Dead, he has a specific reason. Trials and ritual sacrifice attend the descent. There are certain questions to be posed and a certain time at which the spirits will speak. In this, Muldoon's most powerful and moving volume, the epistemological questions that are so much a part of his visionary poetics are chastened and modified by the pathos of the undertaking. The wit and word-play, the narrative misdirections, and the abrupt shifts in tone are all still apparent, but now they are under the direction of the god Hermes, not in his guise of trickster or of patron of letters, but in his identity as guide to the Underworld.

"Incantata," the most moving poem in Muldoon's oeuvre, describes the death by cancer of Mary Powers. Muldoon's memory of Powers, a fiercely intelligent artist, a witty and at times overpowering companion, is the spur for a review of their life together and an assessment of the poet's art. Powers is portrayed as a heroic artist, one who while surrounded by death nonetheless furiously creates. We first glimpse her gallantly but vainly attempting to ward off a creature that comes into the poem as a trivial but grim apostle of the closing oblivion, an army worm that "shimmied down the stove-pipe on an army-worm rope" (*The Annals of Chile*, p. 13). Perhaps it is because she did not just die, but lived and created while in close proximity to death, that she commands a respect not often awarded in Muldoon's world, and seems able to call the charming and elusive speaker to some grander criteria, while

at the same time poking holes in his pretensions. The poet says of his ambition for this poem:

I wanted it to speak to what seems always true of the
    truly great
that you had a winningly inaccurate
sense of your own worth, that you would second-guess
yourself too readily by far, that you would rally to any
    cause
before your own, mine even,
though you detected in me a tendency to put
on too much artificiality, both as man and poet,
which is why you called me "Polyester" or
    "Polyurethane."

                               (p. 17)

As befits a poem so chthonic and so Irish, the poet takes for his talisman a potato. (The cover of the American edition of the volume features a series of potato prints done by the poet.) The potato, notwithstanding its New World origins, recalls Muldoon's own rural Irish origins, and the nativist poetic tradition epitomized by Kavanagh and Heaney. He claims that his own artistry, perhaps in homage to the first of Powers' works that he recalls, looks like a "cancered potato," thereby evoking this peculiarly baroque modification of that tradition: he cuts into the spud "the Inca glyph for a mouth." What a particular challenge it is for an Irish poet, not to mention one so steeped in the ironies of his cultural predicament, to take up so degraded an emblem of the Irish past. The talisman does its work, however, of summoning Lugh, the Irish Hermes, and offering a homely contrast to the account of the life the poet and artist shared:

I wanted the mouth in this potato-cut
to be heard far beyond the leaden, rain-glazed roofs of
    Quinto,
to be heard all the way from the southern hemisphere
to Clontarf or Clondalkin, to wherever your sweet-
    severe
spirit might still find a toe-hold
in this world: it struck me then how you would be
    aghast
at the thought of my thinking you were some kind of
    ghost
who might still roam the earth in search of an earthly
    delight.

                                 (p. 19)

The mixture of the arcane and the common, the slapstick and the hallowed, in a sad world streaked with grandeur, bespeak a literary ghost whose influence had gone without notice in much of the secondary literature on Muldoon. Even without the frequent and complex allusions to specific Beckett works that appear in "Incantata," Samuel Beckett would be recognizable as the intermediary who brings Mary Powers back from the shadows. The speaker first calls upon Beckett the wordsmith ("remember how Krapp looks up viduity" [*The Annals of Chile*, p. 14]), but this inquiry also begins the speaker's more intimate dialogue with the dead woman. And it is with Beckett's words that she herself enters into speech, upending a conversation of the poet with his male cronies, dubbed, appropriately enough, Vladimir and Estragon:

and you remarked on how you used to have a crush
on Burt Lancaster as Elmer Gantry, and Vladimir went
    to brush
the ash off his sleeve with a legerdemain
that meant only one thing—"Why does he put up with
    this crap?"—
and you weighed in with "To live in a dustbin, eating
    scrap,
seemed to Nagg and Nell a most eminent domain."

(p. 15)

The first half of the poem alludes incessantly to Beckett, with particular reference to the epic couples that move through his world like degraded but heroic witnesses to "how it is." Beckett is the writer who would most readily sponsor the message of this poem, which is the endurance of suffering and how a clear-eyed apprehension of one's own death drives and realizes itself in artistic labors. The whole poem turns upon Muldoon's allusion to Lucky's speech in *Waiting for Godot*. From midpoint on the poem is a catalogue of extraordinary moments, a litany composed of scattered memories of Muldoon and Powers' time together, and it arises out of the other aspect of Beckett's vision, not the endurance and struggle of consciousness that has been stripped of everything, but the terror that arises from the consideration that affliction is meaningless:

The fact that you were determined to cut yourself off in
    your prime
because it was predetermined has my eyes abrim:
I crouch with Belacqua

and Lucky and Pozzo in the Acacacac—
ademy of Anthropopopopometry, trying to make sense of
    the "*quaquaqua*"
of that potato-mouth; that mouth as prime
and proper as it's full of self-opprobrium,
with its "*quaquaqua*" with its
Quoiquoiquoiquoiquoiquoiquoiquoiq.

(p. 20)

"Yarrow," the central poem in *The Annals of Chile*, begins by sounding a Beckettian note, and proceeds part of the way into a world reminiscent of Beckett's trilogy. There is the ruthless winnowing that accompanies Beckett's central characters, as perceptions, beliefs, memories, selves, and haberdashery are reduced to essentials, in the conviction that what is essential to life will somehow, within that diminished state, make itself known. And again as in Beckett there is the distant but pervasive presence of a mother who steps forward and speaks, sometimes kindly and sometimes mercilessly, out of the shadows of the past. "Yarrow" begins with a magnificent evocation of what has been lost:

Little by little it dawned on us that the row
of kale would shortly be overwhelmed by these pink
and cream blooms, that all of us

would be overwhelmed, that even if my da
were to lose an arm
or a leg to the fly wheel

of a combine and be laid out on a tarp
in a pool of blood and oil
and my ma were to make one of her increasingly rare

appeals to some higher power, some Deo
this or that, all would be swept away by the stream
that fanned across the land.

(p. 39)

"All would be swept away" becomes a refrain throughout the opening sections, and what is swept away with the family estate are all the sacred places of childhood, the haunts of the imagination. One can imagine the peculiar desolation involved here. This poet of wandering has always rendered his experience, real or imagined, in some relation to this bit of ancestral ground. However far afield the poet has voyaged, or however strange and absorbing the hallucinations he experiences along the way, the image of his true home offered a way to evaluate the world the poet was passing through, just as the novelty and surprise of wandering cast new light on aspects of home. The poet seems to feel in some way responsible for the loss of his childhood home. Note how the property is described in terms derived from Muldoon's earlier poetry. The farm seems only "a rinky-dink bit of land on which a mushroom mogul built a hacienda." "Yarrow" offers an obsessive reconstruction of the imaginings of childhood, which not surprisingly blend the far and the near, the abstruse and the common in a manner reminiscent of Muldoon's mature work. The central loss, touched upon repeatedly but lightly throughout the poem, is the death of the poet's mother, Brigid Regan, who died in 1974, and whose absence has been gathering import for twenty years, awaiting its expression, until now it seems that an entire cosmos flickered out after her.

"Yarrow" circles around a particular year, 1963, when the poet was twelve years old. The year itself is the perfect intersection of personal life and larger histories. While Western European and American culture are about to be transformed by subcultures, new musical forms, radical politics, utopian fervor, and civil violence, in a corner of Northern Ireland the child-poet is about to enter adulthood. One of the more ominous signals of this division between public eras and stages of an individual life is the appearance in the poem of Sylvia Plath, who committed suicide in 1963, while her children slept nearby. Plath rests in the poem at the convergence of several troubling themes. She is, first, another dead mother. She is also a major poet of the generation preceding Muldoon's, and remains the supreme artisan of desolation and invention, clearly a dangerous muse. (And lest we miss the point, the poet directs us to the last lines of her last poem.) While the poem is too rich in its evocations and too assured in the joys of invention to deeply register the allure of Plath's decision, still this most artful of self-extinctions troubles the recollection of the distant past, and intrudes upon the accounts of more recent events. Plath is one of, or so we infer, a number of others whom the poet refers to but does not name who are "dead by their own hand," and her death marks, along with the deaths of Frost and MacNeice in that same year, the passing of poetic generations. Counterpoised against Plath's suicide, the poet offers a series of sharply rendered memories that begin where she ends:

If only Plath had been able to take up the slack
of the free rein
lent her so briefly by Ariel:

all I remember of that all-time low
of January, 1963, was a reprieve from Cicero
and the weekly hairbrush and bath.

(p. 73)

In his obliquely Yeatsian predicament, the desolated poet calls up the images of boyhood enchantment. In "Yarrow" the Muldoonean preoccupation with shifting identities receives a biographical explanation. He successively becomes Wyatt Earp, Wild Bill Hickok, Priam, Roland, and an array of heroes from adventure novels which, he tells us, he preferred reading to learning Irish. He recounts South Sea exploits and war games; it's no wonder that the emblem of the poem itself is not the humble, dignified, ludicrous, and mortal potato of "Incantata," but a hand-held remote control. In fact the bulk of the 150-page poem is said to transpire in the space of six minutes, as registered by the digital clock on a VCR. Certainly, this offers something of a revision from the figure of South in "Madoc." In both cases the poem presents a glimpse of the poet or creative source of the poem, and a metaphor for how we are to understand the primarily image-based poetry that unreels before us. In "Madoc" we see the tortured informant, his images technologically extracted from his sole remaining eyeball, as a *poet maudit.* In "Yarrow" the "production values" and the dramatically charged, if not outright operatic, figure of South is replaced by a meditative, perhaps somewhat paralyzed poet of memory, watching past lives flicker across his TV screen:

For I'd not be surprised if this were a video
camera giving me a nod and a wink
from the blue corner, if it were hooked up not to an alarm

but the TV, that I myself am laid out on a da-
venport in this "supremely Joycean object, a nautilus
of memory jammed next to memory," that I'll shortly reel

with Schwitters and Arp
through our *Katedrale des erotischen Elends . . .*

(p. 152)

The boyhood images are part of what comes to a close in 1963 and are only a part of the life of the poet that passes before us in "Yarrow." The life that proceeds from that point in time, that year once dubbed an annus mirabilis by the English poet Philip Larkin, posed as it is "between the end of the *Chatterly* ban and the Beatles' first LP," the life that centers upon the awakening of sexual desire in the narrator and a whole other order of adventuring, inspires one of Muldoon's most exorbitant creations, the woman known simply as S___. A mix of porn queen, revolutionary, and junkie, S___ expends herself at a fearsome rate. Bearing a family relation to Gallogly, the trickster/terrorist from "The More a Man Has the More a Man Wants," she is the consummate product of Muldoon's career-long preoccupation with feminine portraiture. She enters the poem and transforms it instantly, reigning over the lesser fantasies of adventure books and comparative mythology. In some ways S___ is as much the embodiment of narrativity as of sexual desire. She provides the twists in the plot that allow the poet to juxtapose the larger world of adult consciousness with the inner life of the child, and both with the implacable realities of time and death. The poet's character has stepped from a hipper-than-thou high gloss remake of Ovid's *Amores.* Her place in what is ostensibly an elegy for the poet's mother is assured by her mastery of her role: mother's worst nightmare. The poet draws the connection between the two women over several sections. In one, early on, the mother lectures the son about the purity of the body. In another, S___, hardly shy about such matters, asks the poet for a "rim job." In still another, the poet recalls the guilty pleasures of concupiscent thoughts. Beyond her obvious association with the more sensational types of erotic encounter, her "fondness for the crop" and her "labia ring," or her association with great ladies of the Irish past (she had a "face like Maud Gonne"), her deepest allegiance is to heroin. We leave her as the poem returns to its more purely elegiac pitch writing "'helter skelter' with her own blood on the wall" (p. 184).

Amid the welter of losses comes the voice of the mother, heard only in bits, in sound bites. The poet approaches the rendering of this figure with some caution, reminding the reader of his cool and satiric depictions of mother figures in earlier poems. From the underworld of memory she issues maxims, advice, prohibitions, and admonishments. The traditional association between maternal presence and poetic speech calls to mind how much of Muldoon's imagination is preoccupied with twisting clichés and renovating them, with deploying common speech like a kind of folk wisdom throughout his poetry, and how the poems mingle these phrases with lavish and perverse imaginings. Here he creates a flickering portrait that shows us mother and son in harsh accents, ultimately, with the poetics that makes Muldoon's work so distinctive, even if the immediate point of the recollection seems to cast her in opposition to the world of imagination:

> "Where on earth," she croaks, "where on earth have
>   you spent
> the past half-hour?" "I've just lit the fuse
> on a cannon," I begin, sticking the glowing coal
>
> in my pocket. "What in under heaven
> did we do to deserve you, taking off like that, in a
>   U-boat,
> when you knew rightly the spuds needed sprayed?"
>   (p. 154)

The mother calls the son to task for his absence. The "spuds" need tending, but the one assigned to do the job has disappeared, has left the rural world and the obligations of the blood, and taken up wandering. He wanders not to escape, though that may be his conscious ambition, but to be confronted, in that perhaps near forgotten and hardly epical admonishment, with the fundamental dilemma his art poses, the relation between imagination and the world. Muldoon's whole body of work seems captured here. And if we cannot say that the mother is some traditional symbol for the primacy of poetic speech, neither can we ignore how crucial she is to the creation of the fundamental dilemma that most vexes, bewilders, and inspires the poet. From his earliest lyrics to his more recent suites and epic ventures, Muldoon has focused with extraordinary insight and persistence on the figure of the absent one, who left the farm, or changed his name, his shape, his nationality, his style, his allegiance, his language, but can never fully evade the sense that he will someday be called, once again, to task. In "Incantata" and "Yarrow," it is the poet who has remained behind, tending to the chores of the living, as others take their leave. As the mother begins her wandering, she calls upon a rather unexpected trinity, her dogs. We acknowledge a slight shock: that in what Yeats termed "the delirium of the deathbed" the mother calls not on husband or son or Christ, but on Shakespeare. The dogs that bark at Lear in his abjection (*King Lear* 3.6.65) come again at the hour and ritual of human death. Once more, for Muldoon, a figure will vanish, and the real and the imaginary can appear, for awhile, to be one:

Now Father McEntaggart flings off his black, black cloak:
"This, Brigid, is a cross
you must bear with fortitude": as he gives her a cake

from the pix (the mini-ciborium)
the dogs, for some reason, stand at point;
she calls to them in turn, to Sweetheart, Blanche, and
    Tray.

                (p. 173)

SELECTED BIBLIOGRAPHY

I. Poetry. *New Weather* (London, 1973); *Mules* (London; Winston-Salem, N.C., 1977); *Why Brownlee Left* (London; Winston-Salem, N.C., 1980); *Quoof* (London; Winston-Salem, N.C., 1983); *Mules and Early Poems* (Winston-Salem, N.C., 1985); *Selected Poems, 1968–1983* (London, 1986; New York, 1987); *Meeting the British* (London; Winston-Salem, N.C., 1987); *Madoc: A Mystery* (London; New York, 1990); *The Annals of Chile* (London; New York, 1994).

II. Libretto. *Shining Bow* (London, 1993).

III. Play. *Six Honest Serving Men* (Dublin, 1995).

IV. Translation. *The Astrakhan Cloak: Poems in Irish by Nuala Ni Dhomhnaill with Translations into English by Paul Muldoon* (Dublin, 1992).

V. Edited Works. *The Faber Book of Contemporary Irish Poetry* (London, 1986); *The Essential Byron* (New York, 1989).

VI. Biographical and Critical Studies. W. A. Wilson, "Paul Muldoon and the Poetics of Sexual Difference," in *Contemporary Literature* 28 (fall 1987), pp. 317–331; Richard Brown, "Bog Poems and Book Poems: Doubleness, Self-Translation, and Pun in Seamus Heaney and Paul Muldoon," in Neil Corcoran, ed., *The Chosen Ground: Essays on Contemporary Poetry of Northern Ireland* (Bridgend, U.K., 1992); Barbara Buchanan, "Paul Muldoon: 'Who's to Know What's Knowable?'" in Elmer Andrews, ed., *Contemporary Irish Poetry: A Collection of Critical Essays* (London, 1992); Clair Wills, "The Lie of the Land: Language, Imperialism, and Trade in Paul Muldoon's 'Meeting the British,'" in *The Chosen Ground: Essays on Contemporary Poetry of Northern Ireland* (Bridgend, U.K., 1992); Jonathan Allison, "Questioning Yeats: Paul Muldoon's '7, Middagh Street,'" in Deborah Fleming, ed., *Learning the Trade: Essays on W. B. Yeats and Contemporary Poetry* (West Cornwall, Conn., 1993); Clair Wills, "Paul Muldoon: Dubious Origins," in *Improprieties: Politics and Sexuality in Northern Irish Poetry* (Oxford, U.K., 1993); W. A. Wilson, "Yeats, Muldoon, and Heroic History," in Deborah Fleming, ed., *Learning the Trade: Essays on W. B. Yeats and Contemporary Poetry* (West Cornwall, Conn., 1993); Edna Longley, "Poetry and Politics in Northern Ireland" and "Varieties of Parable: Louis MacNeice and Paul Muldoon," in *Poetry in the Wars* (Newcastle upon Tyne, U.K., 1994); Edna Longley, "When Did You Last See Your Father?" in *The Living Stream: Literature and Revisionism in Northern Ireland* (Newcastle upon Tyne, 1994).

SALMAN RUSHDIE

(1947–   )

Timothy Brennan

SALMAN RUSHDIE IS among the best-known representatives of postcolonial fiction in modern British literature. A prolific film critic, novelist, reviewer, and author of journalistic exposés throughout the 1980s and early 1990s, he helped launch a new interest in the condition of immigrants from the former European colonies living "in between" multiple cultural traditions. Writing in a wide range of genres—from historical fiction to travel narrative, documentary film, children's fable, and political essay—he proclaimed "migrancy" to be the late twentieth century's most vital, and most universal, trope. In work marked by a deliberate eclecticism, Rushdie has drawn equally on British, continental European, and classical Hindu, Persian, and Islamic sources. Based in Britain, a self-described "writer from three countries" (India, Pakistan, England), he became an eloquent advocate of the idea that the painful cultural exchanges of colonialism did not dilute, but rather enriched, the English literary tradition. He cast his glance at both his British contemporaries and the Anglo-Indian past and in the 1980s emerged at the forefront of a generation of writers who popularized the impure, extranational scope of culture in the postwar period—the idea that there is not one but many English literatures and the conviction that politics as a grand theme must reenter the creative imagination.

Rushdie achieved recognition first for his humorous mock epic of Indian independence, *Midnight's Children* (1980), which won the Booker McConnell Prize in 1981. He consolidated this success with his next two novels, a satirical fairy tale of Pakistan, *Shame* (1983), and a phantasmagoric rendering of the plight of immigrants in England, *The Satanic Verses* (1988). On 14 February 1989, following a series of demonstrations against *The Satanic Verses*, the Ayatollah Ruhollah Khomeini of Iran issued a *fatwa* decree—calling for Rushdie's death—declaring that the novel had defamed Islam. The scandal that followed made Rushdie a household name and placed him at the center of a series of debates over censorship, the nature of religious belief, and the social responsibility of authors. Living in hiding from 1989 until 1995 under the protection of the British secret service, Rushdie continued to produce journalism and fiction, publishing another two novels: *Haroun and the Sea of Stories* (1990) and *The Moor's Last Sigh* (1995). While living in hiding, Rushdie made frequent, highly publicized appearances in a variety of media as a spokesman for free speech, religious tolerance, and the role of literature as society's moral conscience.

LIFE

A native of Bombay ("India's most cosmopolitan city"), Salman Rushdie was born on 19 June 1947, the son of a Cambridge-educated Muslim businessman. His father, Anis Ahmed Rushdie, inherited substantial wealth that (according to Rushdie) he "spent the rest of his life losing." A graduate of King's College, Cambridge, Anis was conversant in Persian, Arabic, and Western literature. He and his wife Negin (Rushdie's mother) had relocated their family to Bombay from the northern province of Kashmir before Rushdie's birth. Quintessential *mohajirs* (migrants), the Rushdie family enjoyed relative tolerance in Bombay and so decided not to move to officially Muslim Pakistan following the partition of India. Rushdie had three sisters—he was the only son—and the four children grew up speaking both Urdu and English at home. His relationship with his disapproving father was often stormy, although shortly before Anis' death in 1987 the two men healed the rifts between them—a

433

rapprochement portrayed in the closing pages of *The Satanic Verses.*

Rushdie's upbringing was a decidedly secular one. In an essay from 1985, "In God We Trust"—collected in the volume *Imaginary Homelands: Essays and Criticism, 1981–1991* (1991)—Rushdie explains: "While both my parents were believers neither was insistent or doctrinaire. Two or three times a year, at the big Eid festivals, I would wake up to find new clothes at the foot of my bed, dress and go with my father to the great prayer-*maidan* outside the Friday Mosque in Bombay. . . . The rest of the year religion took a back seat" (pp. 376–379). According to the vivid recollections of his essays and interviews, Rushdie's childhood was also immersed in the colorful attractions of popular culture, fed equally by Bombay's thriving film industry ("Bollywood") and by American cinema and comic books. Infatuated with Superman, Batman, and Flash Gordon, Rushdie found his chief literary influences in diverse places: *The Arabian Nights,* predictably, but also in the juvenile adventure stories of Enid Blyton who popularized the British empire for generations of colonial youth. Early on in what Rushdie described as a very "Anglocentric" youth, which in postwar terms meant simply the English-speaking West or Anglo-America, his father hired a painter to decorate the walls of his nursery with animal characters from Disney films. Rushdie's first story, written when he was ten years old, had the allusive title "Over the Rainbow"; it concerned a boy who climbs a multicolored staircase before meeting a talking pianola, whose personality, he later called "an improbable hybrid of Judy Garland, Elvis Presley and the 'playback singers' of the Hindi movies." This youthful tribute to *The Wizard of Oz* would later find expression in his critical study of that Hollywood classic for the British Film Institute; in his book *The Wizard of Oz* (1992) Rushdie attributes his taste for the fantasies of Disney and Dell comics to the familiarity with the Hindi "cinema of the fantastic" that all Bombay children acquire. Apart from being a rich source of narrative material that plays a central role in all of Rushdie's later fiction, the wildly eclectic genre of Hindi film—a sprawling, vulgar mixture of revenge tragedy, romantic melodrama, musical comedy, and Kung Fu—is also the source of his first memories of censorship: because of the strict sexual mores of Indian society of the 1950s, screen kisses were systematically and ludicrously cut out.

Typically receiving books instead of games for birthdays, Rushdie was an unathletic, intellectual child, groomed for the elite schools he would later attend. The first of these was Cathedral School in Bombay (an institution established by the Anglo-Scottish Educational Society), which he entered in 1961. Inclined to push the secularity of his upbringing into a playful irreverence, Rushdie experimented early with apostasy, living—as he would later write of *The Satanic Verses'* Gibreel Farishta—"a childhood of blasphemy," eating the pork proscribed by the Muslim faith and mimicking the art of Arabic calligraphers by drawing the name "Allah" so that it resembled the figure of a naked woman. "God, Satan, Paradise and Hell all vanished one day in my fifteenth year," he recalls. "No thunderbolt arrived to strike me down" ("In God We Trust," p. 377). Although Bombay was no less religious than other Indian cities, the very proliferation of the faithful (among them, Parsis, Sikhs, Christians, Hindus, Muslims, Buddhists, and Jains) gave this "highrise and hovel" metropolis on India's western coast the aura of secularity, which was furthered by the government's official avoidance of giving any one sect legal privileges.

Rushdie was sent to study at Rugby in England at the age of thirteen and thus began an unhappy stretch of his life. Shunned by his schoolmates as much for his lack of athletic prowess as for his ethnicity, he experienced both minor persecutions and racist abuse, the latter typically scrawled on the bathroom walls. Fair enough of complexion to pass for English, he was nevertheless perceived for the first time as "Indian," a designation, he was quick to observe, that did not exist in India itself. He made no friends at Rugby and kept in touch with none of his classmates later on in life. After graduation, following his father, he enrolled at King's College, Cambridge, in the fall of 1964. Already eager to become a writer, and taking as his hero the great Urdu poet Faiz Ahmad Faiz, he launched a course of study not in literature but in history—specifically the history of Arabic and Islamic civilization. (All such references in *The Satanic Verses,* in fact, were drawn from his college papers.) In many ways Rushdie's university profile did not fit that of an aspiring writer. Attracted by the art films of Michelangelo Antonioni, Akira Kurosawa, and Satyajit Ray, he declared that if someone had offered him an opportunity to direct a movie, he would happily have given up writing. Instead of contributing stories to university journals like *Varsity* or *Granta*, he opted for the stage, briefly acting in London's fringe theater at the Oval and Kennington in the play *Viet Rock*. In a late reminiscence, he recounts how, sporting long hair and a beard, he participated fully in London's counterculture, living his last college summer above a famous mod boutique on the King's Road. When he graduated in the spring of 1968, he declared, "I ceased to be a conservative under the influence of the Vietnam war and dope."

The alienation he felt in England was still evident, for he soon purchased a one-way ticket home. His destination was not Bombay but Karachi, Pakistan, where his family had finally moved for good in 1964. He had actually visited them there once before during his first year at Cambridge, in time to witness the Indo-Pakistan war of 1965, the war which he so memorably portrayed in the pages of *Midnight's Children*. He had opposed his family's relocation, but all the same it was in Karachi that Rushdie first sought to make a professional start by drafting an adaptation of Edward Albee's *The Zoo Story* for the country's new government-operated television station. Rushdie ran afoul of the state censors for including the word "pork" in his television script; the magazine feature he then wrote on his first impressions of Pakistan was censored as well. In 1969 he returned to England in disgust. Apart from short visits abroad, he never left again.

By 1970 Rushdie at last turned seriously to professional writing. For ten years he made his living as a freelance advertising copywriter for Ogilvy & Mather and Charles Barker, while devoting his evenings and weekends to fiction. In a period in which he concocted slogans for Aero chocolate ("delectabubble" and "incredibubble"), he began a novel about a Muslim holy man that he later abandoned. He would abandon another, and have still another rejected, before finally publishing *Grimus* in 1975. Although poorly received (it had been written expressly as a bid for the science fiction prize offered by the publisher Victor Gollancz, which it did not win), this highly allusive and cerebral novel—a cross between Dante and Sufi poetry—secured his working relationship with Liz Calder, the publisher at Bard, who, despite the initial failure of *Grimus*, had the confidence to usher *Midnight's Children* into print. With a new position of authority at a more experimental publishing house, Calder could afford to take a chance on

an untried author. Dramatic changes were on the horizon. Rushdie had met Calder while living with Clarissa Luard, a fashion and art consultant he was secretly involved with for two years before marrying her in 1976. Written in a modest flat in Islington, London, *Midnight's Children* was completed in 1979 and published a year later; it was the first work in which Rushdie drew heavily on his personal experiences in India. A huge critical and commercial success, the novel won Britain's coveted Booker McConnell Prize in 1981, giving the author (then thirty-four) immediate recognition and a check for the equivalent of $10,000. Rushdie dedicated the book to Zafar, the son he had had with Clarissa in 1980, the same year the novel appeared. "After ten years of blunders, incompetence and commercials for cream cakes, hair colourants and the *Daily Mirror*, I began to live by the pen." His triumph was not unalloyed, however. In a foreshadowing of problems to come, the prime minister of India, Indira Gandhi—angered by Rushdie's depiction of her as maniacal tyrant—brought the book up on libel charges, and both he and the publisher were forced to offer a public apology.

More than just a career-launching book, *Midnight's Children* seemed to many at the time a significant literary event. Its spacious historical sweep, its infectious humor, its ambitious focus on a third-world country, its confident modernist prose—all seemed to announce a new kind of novel in Britain, destined to unlock the untold tales of those, like Rushdie, living "in between." Not only a representative author of such fiction, Rushdie became its tireless promoter. Now a name to be reckoned with, he spent the next years as a sought-after interviewee and celebrity, clarifying his views on the vitality of "English" literature in the former colonies and among ex-colonial authors in the European heartland. Staunchly anti-Tory in his politics in the very years of Margaret Thatcher's ascendancy, Rushdie turned resolutely to political themes in his journalism throughout the 1980s, attacking the Falkland Islands War, bitterly rejecting economic neoliberalism—with its breaking of the miners' union, its selling off of state industries, and its ravaging of England's enviable public welfare sector— ridiculing the new wave of Raj revival films with their nostalgia for the era of India under British colonial rule, and urging resistance to endless rounds of anti-immigration legislation. An essay to which his detractors would later indignantly return, "The New Empire Within Britain" (produced for the independent and alternative network programming of the BBC's Channel 4 in 1982 and later reprinted in *Imaginary Homelands*) portrayed the hardships of Caribbean and South Asian immigrants in London's poorer communities. Meanwhile Rushdie continued to write fiction. In 1983 *Shame* appeared—a deeply satirical "fairy tale" about Pakistan's ruling circles, which was shortlisted for the Booker Prize in 1984.

Although Rushdie did not divorce Clarissa until 1987, his marriage effectively ended in 1984, the year he began work on *The Satanic Verses*. The writing went slowly as he forged ahead in his usual manner: working at a manual typewriter with the goal of producing "700 good words a day." Unhappy with the first draft, and clearly at an impasse, he chose to accept an invitation in 1986 to attend the seventh anniversary celebrations of the Nicaraguan revolution in Esteli, Nicaragua, the trip that would give him the material for his only travel narrative: *The Jaguar Smile: A Nicaraguan Journey* (1987). Then, as if to consolidate the reputation of *Midnight's Children,* he set off for India again in 1987 to mark the country's (and his own) fortieth anniversary and to film the documentary *The Riddle of Midnight,* a series of interviews with forty-year-olds from divergent walks of Indian life. With his reputation secure, and with his next novel nearly finished, Rushdie became embroiled in an unusually acrimonious dissociation from his former publisher and friend Liz Calder as well as dismissal of his literary agent. Although the breaks probably helped him win a handsome $850,000 advance for *The Satanic Verses,* they may also have intensified the resentments in many circles toward his meteoric rise. If one could only admire Rushdie's quick wit and passion, there was also the widespread feeling that he was thin-skinned, impudent, and ambitious to a fault. He was described, on the one hand, as a born performer, a first-rate mimic in his public readings, gregarious and funny; on the other hand, he was also called "cocky and chippy, arrogant and resentful at once" (Wheatcroft, p. 26). Hugh Trevor-Roper went so far as to complain of his "brutal and vulgar manners" (p. 27). Germaine Greer called him simply a "megalomaniac" (p. 27). Professional jealousy certainly accounted for some of these negative judgments; they suggest something of the extent of the ill will that complicated Rushdie's position once the *fatwa*

was issued. Inevitably race played a part in the gibes against him. Among those who considered him out of touch with the working-class Muslims and Hindus he loved to write about, he was referred to, with deliberate cruelty, as "Simon Rushton."

Still, Rushdie remained a well-connected man whose friends amounted to a who's who of the English literary scene: Harold Pinter, Julian Barnes, Angela Carter, Martin Amis, Fay Weldon, and others. A prominent reviewer in high-profile magazines on both sides of the Atlantic, he had reason to assume that the publication of *The Satanic Verses* on 26 September 1988 would be met with acute interest, if not open admiration. Indeed the reception began that way, although there were early danger signs. Even before September, Khushwant Singh—Viking Penguin's editorial consultant in India—advised against publication, warning that the novel's blasphemous parodies of the Prophet Muhammad would cause trouble. In an unfortunate interview for *India Today* on 15 September Rushdie unwittingly alerted the Muslim community to the offensive contents of the book by declaring that its target was religious fanaticism. When the government of India banned the book on 5 October, the measure only brought into realization what had earlier been threatened, for right after publication Viking had been deluged with calls and letters demanding the withdrawal of the book, along with a petition signed by hundreds of thousands of people.

The first of many mass protests against the book took place in London on 10 December and was followed by demonstrations in every major British city with a sizable Muslim population—the most notorious demonstration took place on 14 January 1989 in Bradford, where *The Satanic Verses* was publicly burned. As the book proceeded to be banned by all of the officially Islamic countries, many other countries followed suit, including Bangladesh, Sudan, Sri Lanka, South Africa, Kenya, Thailand, Tanzania, Indonesia, Singapore, Venezuela, and Poland. Meanwhile the demonstrations outside England had turned deadly. Ten were killed protesting outside the United States embassy in Islamabad; five in Kashmir; thirteen in Bombay; and hundreds more were injured in Dacca, Bangladesh. As legal and public relations maneuvers continued—with Rushdie writing an open letter of complaint to Rajiv Gandhi, and solicitors for the U.K. Action Committee on Islamic Affairs trying to quash the book by having England's antiquated blasphemy laws applied to Islam as well as to Christianity—events took a turn that rendered such actions moot. On 14 February 1989 the Ayatollah Khomeini's *fatwa* aired on Radio Tehran: it called on "zealous Muslims" to execute Rushdie—wherever he might be found—"as well as those publishers who were aware of [the] contents" of *The Satanic Verses*. A bounty of $1.5 million was placed on Rushdie's head. On 15 February Rushdie went into hiding.

Understandably shaken by events, Rushdie saw his life altered forever in a few short months. Life underground placed insufferable strains on his recent marriage to the American novelist Marianne Wiggins. In the first four months after the *fatwa*, they were forced to sleep in fifty-six different beds. In August of the first year of hiding Wiggins finally emerged and, with unkind words about her husband's lack of courage and his unwillingness to link his plight with that of other censured writers, divorced him soon afterward. In this sort of life there could be "no rhythm," Rushdie would complain. Living under the protection of the British secret service, "you have to know beforehand exactly what it is you want for dinner three nights from now." Nevertheless he continued to receive guests on a regular basis, mostly fellow writers and literary agents, and he attended dinner parties, although it had become impossible for him to see his son, Zafar, with whom he spoke daily by telephone. When the Ayatollah died in June 1989, the *fatwa* unfortunately remained in force (and was, in fact, officially reaffirmed each year thereafter). Rushdie had earlier attempted to address publicly the issue of his novel's purported blasphemy in the hope of assuaging the hurt and anger his novel had produced. On 18 February 1989 he made a public statement of regret for the distress the book had caused Muslims. But almost a year passed before he changed his strategy of appeasement to one of insistent clarification. On 4 February 1990, he published a seven-thousand-word statement in the *Independent*. Appealing to sincere Muslims, "In Good Faith" was a defense against the charge of "self-hating, deracinated uncle-Tomism," and it systematically set out to explicate *The Satanic Verses* in order to demonstrate the difference between irony and the abuse of cherished beliefs. On 6 February Rushdie presented (in absentia) "Is Nothing Sacred?," a Herbert Read Memorial Lecture delivered

on BBC television by his friend Harold Pinter. (This lecture and "In Good Faith" were later reprinted in *Imaginary Homelands*.) "Is Nothing Sacred?" extolled literature as a place where one "can hear *voices talking about everything in every possible way*" (*Imaginary Homelands*, p. 429).

Nonetheless, on 25 December 1990, with little break in the animosity and with nowhere to turn, Rushdie converted to Islam in the presence of Egyptian officials. His cautiously worded short essay "Why I Have Embraced Islam" appeared in the *Times* four days later (it may also be found in *Imaginary Homelands*). On BBC Radio 4's Sunday Programme Rushdie pledged not to allow the paperback edition of *The Satanic Verses* to be published. Roughly one year later, on 11 December 1991, he appeared at Columbia University Law School in New York to reverse himself. In his speech "One Thousand Days in a Balloon" (excerpted the next day in the *New York Times*) Rushdie vigorously called for the paperback edition, proclaiming "these years will have no meaning" (p. B8) unless the novel is read and studied. Produced by an anonymous consortium, the paperback edition of *The Satanic Verses* finally came out on 22 March 1992. In the fall of 1993 Rushdie was awarded the Booker of Bookers—a prize given to the most distinguished recipient of the Booker in the previous decade.

Compared at once to Alfred Dreyfus and to Galileo, and with a fame (as one critic put it) "beyond Byron's," Rushdie had also, and lamentably, become an "issue" rather than a person. As Martin Amis memorably put it, Rushdie had "vanished into the front page," with an undreamed-of, but also unwanted, notoriety. According to polling organizations, *The Satanic Verses* had simply become the top news story of 1989. Past being a literary scandal, the affair had now reached the highest levels of state. Weighty pronouncements on the evening news by the British home minister, the withdrawal of European ambassadors from Iran and (in turn) Iranian ambassadors from Europe, the severing of diplomatic ties between Iran and several European nations—these were only some of the developments directly caused by the book prior to Rushdie's campaign to force Western heads of state to deal with his case as an international crisis, the way they had worked for release of hostages in Lebanon in the 1980s. After having been spurned by Margaret Thatcher and George Bush, Rushdie managed to meet with British prime minister John

Major in May 1993 and with U.S. president Bill Clinton the following December.

The attention Rushdie received was nonetheless tempered by the violent realities of the *fatwa*. Bomb threats were made against the Riverdale Press in New York for refusing to follow the example of Waldenbooks and Barnes & Noble in pulling *The Satanic Verses* from its shelves. In July 1991 the novel's Japanese translator, Hitoshi Igarashi, was stabbed to death; its Italian translator and its Norwegian and Turkish publishers were subjected to similar attacks but survived. Meanwhile, various wire reports stated that white English youth were chanting "Rushdie is our leader" while attacking Asians in Bradford, and a war against dissident Arabic intellectuals, inspired by *The Satanic Verses,* raged in the Islamic world. Against this background, the film *International Guerrillas,* depicting Rushdie as the head of an international criminal gang, was released in Pakistan in March 1990. Portrayed as a lecher and an alcoholic who kills Muslims for sport and whose brutish Israeli bodyguards are picked off by an Islamic hit squad in the action sequences, the character "Salman Rushdie" is in the end smitten by a lightning bolt from God. Although banned at first in Britain—a decision Rushdie opposed—the film was later released there as well.

Under trying circumstances, Rushdie continued to write fiction. Making good on an earlier promise to his son that his next novel after *The Satanic Verses* would be a children's tale, he published *Haroun and the Sea of Stories* in 1990. In 1995, with the appearance of his saga of the Christian and Jewish communities of Cochin, *The Moor's Last Sigh*—another novel short-listed for the Booker Prize—Rushdie began to test the limits of his de facto imprisonment, appearing at U2 concerts in London, PEN meetings at the Louvre, and, in the United States, on the Phil Donahue show, "Late Night with David Letterman," "Good Morning America," and National Public Radio. Once again, however, controversy stalked Rushdie: Hindus in India were incensed by his parody in *The Moor's Last Sigh* of Bal Thackeray, the leader of an ultraright Hindu revivalist party, Shiv Sena. Maharashtra State considered banning *The Moor's Last Sigh*, but the attempt was repelled by India's Supreme Court in February 1996. Busy at work on a feature-film screenplay based on his short story "The Courter," about growing up in London in the 1960s, Rushdie finally decided to emerge from hiding for good on the seventh anniversary of the *fatwa:* 14 February 1996.

MIDNIGHT'S CHILDREN *AND EARLY NOVELS*

Grimus

DESPITE the notoriety of the Rushdie affair, it was *Midnight's Children,* not *The Satanic Verses,* that first marked Rushdie's writerly authority. Although foreshadowed in early short stories, such as "The Prophet's Hair" and "The Free Radio" in *East, West: Stories* (1994), *Midnight's Children* might have been his inaugural work. He had already begun a version of it in the early 1970s, but its appearance had to wait for the uncertain step, and false start, of his poorly received first novel, *Grimus* (1975), a book that generated most of its critical interest only after the *fatwa* had established Rushdie's fame. Although in retrospect the novel seems almost a career mistake, the multilingual punning and cross-cultural jesting of *Grimus* clearly anticipate Rushdie's later novels—particularly *Haroun and the Sea of Stories,* whose dream-quest motif is taken directly from *Grimus.* Overclever perhaps, even austere in its allusions, the novel displays little of that historical sense so prominent in Rushdie's later fiction. Its Western and Eastern sources blend uneasily in a sustained, but uninterpretable, allegory about the quest of a foreign writer to assimilate himself into British society.

The hero of *Grimus* is Flapping Eagle, an American Indian shunned by his community for violating the holy laws of Axona, a god who desires of his worshipers only two things: that they "chant to him as often as possible" and that they "be a race apart and have no doings with the wicked world." The victim of small-town bigotries, the hero is an outcast from the start. When his mother dies giving birth to him, he is branded with the name Born-From-Dead (which recalls another bird, the phoenix). His pacifism and sensitivity (in Axona culture, his "womanliness") lead him to be shackled with a hermaphroditic nickname, Joe-Sue; his situation is made worse by the fact that (like Rushdie) he is inexplicably fair-skinned. Flapping Eagle's sister, Bird-Dog, who is just as much an outcast as he, flees the Axona after drinking an elixir of eternal life given her by the serpent-like character, Sispy.

Fed up with tribal prejudices, Flapping Eagle finally goes off in search of Bird-Dog, setting out on a series of adventures that leave him shipwrecked and half-drowned on the shores of Calf Island, where he is received by a pedantic Englishman named Virgil Jones and his lapsed Catholic mate, Dolores O'Toole. It is Virgil who points the hero in the direction of the island's ruler, an expatriate European magician named Grimus, whose power emanates from a miraculous stone rose. From this point onward the quest unfolds as a rather straightforward allegory of social climbing and literary apprenticeship, as Flapping Eagle ascends Calf Mountain (which juts up from the sea) in search of Grimus. Arrested precisely halfway through his life's journey, he gradually discovers his own identity as he reaches each new level of the mountain's many ledges, which are peopled by immortals "who can no longer bear living"—Russians, Irish, French, English, and Abyssinians with historically allusive middle names like Quasimodo and Napoleon, who debate with him the nature of language, myth, and cosmic order.

If the basic plot of ascending an island mountain in quest of a miraculous rose under the guidance of one named "Virgil" is precisely that of Dante's *Purgatorio* and *Paradiso* (as is the encounter with famous personages from the past at each level of the ascent), the intellectual mood is not Dante's but Kafka's from *The Castle*. In Kafka, too, there is a mountain, but on its crest lives an authority whose dark and irrational power demands obeisance rather than understanding, a display of command that better evokes the England that an Indian middle-class immigrant confronts than does Dante's all-powerful, but benevolent, God. Nevertheless by conviction, and exactly because it is in multiple senses "bilingual," *Grimus* is not even primarily based on prominent Western sources. The book derives its central myth from the *Shahnameh*, the tenth-century historical epic of the deeds of Persian heroes, among whose legendary characters is the Simurg—a bird that has witnessed the destruction of the world and possesses the wisdom of the ages. Although Rushdie strives for a sublime heterogeneity in *Grimus* by bringing together such a variety of figures—including the exiled "Indian" and the European magician—the quest in the novel is made manifest not (as in *Midnight's Children*, for example) by retracing the colonial historical encounter between Europe and India, but in the enclosed and static world of style, in a series of language games. The most important of the anagrams are "Grimus," a reordering of the letters in Simurg, and "Gorfs," a rearrangement of the letters in frogs. The Gorfs are godlike frogs who play a game—"the Divine Game of Order"—in which they "alter their very environment and indeed their own physical make-up." The motif of mutation (which plays a central role in *The Satanic Verses*) in *Grimus* suggests the sorts of changes that immigrants typically undergo.

The almost showy eclecticism of *Grimus* is an approach that becomes one of Rushdie's most familiar fictional gestures, but there are even more explicit thematic foreshadowings here of *Midnight's Children*. Calf Mountain (Persian, Qur'anic, Dantean) is described at one point as being "like a giant *lingam* weltering in the *yoni* that is the Sea" (p. 66); *lingam* and *yoni* are respectively phallus and vulva, the customary Hindu iconography of agency and nature. The imagery recalls Flapping Eagle's hermaphroditic nature and is particularly appropriate given the sterility of the immortals on Calf. Rushdie alludes to Shiva (who is at once a fertility god and a destroyer) through the very name "Flapping Eagle." As one character on Calf remarks, "The Eagle has an interesting significance in Amerindian mythology. Am I not right in saying that it is the symbol of the Destroyer?" Like the eagle, Shiva is an ambivalent force of fecundity and obliteration, a portrayal that will occupy the closing sections of *Midnight's Children*.

Midnight's Children

Cloyed and precious, *Grimus* not only set the stage for Rushdie's emergence but announced his intentions for the future. In the pages of *Grimus*, we find the passage: "I have achieved . . . the combination of the most profound thoughts of the race, tested by time, and the cadences that give those thoughts coherence and, even more important, popularity. I am taking the intellect back to the people" (p. 160). *Midnight's Children* (1980) set out to do just this: it was an ambitious effort to go beyond the modest, small-scale novels in the Anglo-Indian tradition by capturing the immensity of India and its multitudes.

In India the novel developed first not in English but in Bengali, Hindi, and Urdu; there was nevertheless a formidable domestic and expatriate tradition of writing in English. English has been a significant part of Indian identity at home and abroad from the time of early-nineteenth-century social reformers and educators like Ram Mohan Roy through the era of twentieth-century nationalists like Jawaharlal Nehru and Mohandas K. Gandhi. In this milieu a sizable pantheon of Indian writers producing minor classics in English had also arisen. In genres ranging from social realism to peasant melodrama, ironic human comedy, and urbane autobiography, novelists like Mulk Raj Anand, R. K. Narayan, Kamala Markandaya, Raja Rao, and Anita Desai set a mark by which other Indian writers could measure their own advance, often (like Anand) as celebrities on English soil. (Anand himself worked under George Orwell for the BBC Foreign Service during World War II.) Although the truly international reputations of India's literary masters belonged to those who had not written originally in English (the Bengali Nobel Prize winner, Rabindranath Tagore, for example, or the famous Urdu story writer of Partition, Saadat Hasan Manto), hundreds of Anglo-Indian novels were readily available in England and throughout the Commonwealth from the late nineteenth century onward. An outrageously popular fiction of the railway bookstall variety also existed, written by British authors about India. John Masters may be the most famous of this type.

The excitement surrounding *Midnight's Children* was nonetheless unique, not only because of its deliberate attempt to be *neither* Indian *nor* English— neither here nor there—but also because it appeared at a moment when the English-speaking public, perhaps for the first time, could hear what such a book was trying to say. Revolutions in Nicaragua, Grenada, El Salvador, and Iran had thrust the proximity of the third world into first-world consciousness. The commercial success in the 1970s of the Latin American "boom" novelists (among them, Gabriel García Márquez, Carlos Fuentes, Jorge Amado, and Mario Vargas Llosa) had popularized that literary phantasmagoria of politics in "exotic" locations known as "magical realism." But at the very same time a similar kind of novel had entered European literature through the gateway of Central and Eastern Europe in the work of Milan Kundera, Heinrich Böll, and, above all, Günter Grass in *The Tin Drum* (1962), whose deformed and hunted narrator—an idiot witness to an unfolding national

tragedy—is clearly a model for the narrator of *Midnight's Children*. Although acquainted vaguely with the fictional type to which Rushdie's new novel belonged, and primed by current-events stories of third-world revolts, never had American and British readers (much less Indian ones) seen the genre adapted so vigorously to India.

By far the most important colony in the British Empire—a country that had lived in symbiosis with England for more than two centuries, with resident intellectuals, businessmen, and laborers in every major British city—India carried for the British a torrent of associations; many of these were already etched into the imagination by the novels of Rudyard Kipling, E. M. Forster, George Orwell, and Paul Scott. With each of these forerunners firmly in mind, Rushdie consciously set out to copy, to parody, and ultimately to transcend the lot—and to do so from the position of a thoroughly modern and irreverent, but also native, Easterner. This kind of voice was an unfamiliar but welcome one to many readers. Staving off, on the one hand, clichés about the "inscrutable East" and, on the other, defensive declarations about dignity, *Midnight's Children* pleased its audience in part because it was simply funny. Its contagious interest in big events and real facts—about, for example, the belief systems of Islam, Sanskrit classicism, the glories of the Mughal dynasty, and the prehistory of Mohenjo Daro—shook up the British literary scene as well. The novel was an implicit reprimand to a British literature that seemed by comparison too staid and too distant from the world of real affairs. Like *Shame*, its successor, it was translated into twenty languages.

Midnight's Children is the story of Saleem Sinai, who is born with 1,001 other Indian children on the stroke of midnight, 15 August 1947—the exact moment that India is granted formal independence from England. (Rushdie himself was actually born in June 1947.) The fortunate time of birth gives each of the children a distinct magical power, which is greater the closer they were born to the stroke of twelve. Although the lives of many of these children weave their way through the picaresque structure of the book, the plot's central struggle takes place between just two of them: Saleem, whose overlarge nose gives him the power of "seeing into the hearts and minds of men," and his rival Shiva, whose bulbous knees give him the power to crush his foes mercilessly. As India's new national leaders express hope in the new generation, proclaiming that the lives of India's children "will be, in a sense, the mirror of our own," so too are events in the novel arranged so that Saleem's personal experiences metaphorically correspond to key events in India's postwar history. Very much like newspaper reports, or the "march of time" newsreels played at 1950s cinema houses (and Rushdie invokes both media throughout the text), the narrative moves chronologically from the Jallianwala Bagh massacre in Amritsar in 1919 through Partition in 1947, Nehru's first five-year plan in 1956, Ayub Khan's coup in Pakistan in 1958, the India-China war of 1962, the India-Pakistan war of 1965, the creation of Bangladesh in 1971, and the infamous "Emergency" of 1975 when Indira Gandhi declared martial law and suspended all civil rights. The only major event left out (and it is arguably the most important of all) is Mahatma Gandhi's noncooperation movement, the movement that actually forced the British out of India. It is left out because Saleem, of course, did not experience it, only inherited its ambiguous effects. Masquerading as a bildungsroman the novel in this sense follows the development of a hero whose "choices" routinely follow the brittle, externally determined contours of current events. The cast of characters is spectacular, but we are never allowed to enter their minds or live with their emotions in any sustained way. They are only brilliant caricatures, playing their parts in an elaborate parodic tableau. Saleem, for example, contains within him "650 million bits of oblivious dust"—one for every soul in India's (1970s era) population. Saleem, as it were, embodies India, as if to suggest that writers like himself are complicit in the national fictions that lead to a frightening disintegration.

Saleem encounters the full range of social and religious types that India has to offer. Loyal to his encyclopedic ambitions, Rushdie packs in a universe of spectacle and event: the sage utterances of illiterate boatmen, language rioting in Maharashtra, sex scandals among the Bombay military elite, religious charlatans and gurus, the meddling of imperial British hangers-on, the peccadillos and frivolities of India's ruling classes, Romeo and Juliet-like liaisons between Hindu and Muslim lovers, and village sectarian strife. This sliding between classes and peoples begins in the person of Saleem himself, who is not what he seems. As the narrator of his own magical, larger-than-life story,

Saleem begins with his ancestors, and the early chapters are dedicated to his grandfather Aadam Aziz, a secularized Muslim who frees his wife from purdah, studies abroad in Germany, and dedicates himself to Western humanism. It turns out, however, that Aadam's daughter, Amina, gives birth to Saleem at precisely the same moment that a neighbor named Vanita—the wife of a poor accordion-player named Wee Willie Winkie—gives birth to a baby she calls Shiva. In fact the father of Vanita's child is not Willie but an "Angrez sahib" (a British gentleman) named William Methwold, whom Vanita has been seeing on the sly. The reader soon discovers that a hospital midwife, tormented by unrequited love, has switched the babies. In other words, in spite of his upbringing, and contrary to everything he knows about himself, our hero's social status is a fraud. He is not of Muslim stock but of Hindu, is not wealthy but poor, is not secular but from a family of religious fanatics, and, indeed, he is the bastard child of an Englishman. As the two most potent of "midnight's children," Shiva and Saleem play out a rivalry defined (respectively) by working-class resentment and amelioration of class conflict, nationalism and internationalism, "Businessism" and socialism, belligerence and pacifism; it is the conflict that holds this compendious plot together.

Midnight's Children, then, has built into it an argument about Indian character. As Rushdie explained in his film, *The Riddle of Midnight,* "Behind all my writings is the idea of *crowd.* . . . India's turbulent multiplicity . . . a throng not only of people but also of dreams, memories, fears, hopes, portents, fictions and gods." The crowd enters *Midnight's Children,* though, not only in the form of the portrayed but also as the portrayer; that is, the narrator. In an elaborate subplot Saleem is seen wrestling with himself as he narrates (after the fact) the very novel we are reading. In these passages Rushdie reflects on the complicity of novelists with power—in his case, the distance between his own comfortable metropolitan training and that of the masses he depicts. Rushdie is frequently seen as a student of Latin American magical realism, but he reasonably resists that comparison on precisely these metropolitan grounds. "The essence of [García Márquez's] vision of the world is that of a village boy," Rushdie explains, ". . . [whereas] I think of myself as someone who has spent almost his entire life in gigantic cities. . . . They define me." The larger metafictional designs of *Midnight's Children* are most apparent as Saleem writes, and as his domestic servant (and bed partner), Padma, counsels him with a disdainful tongue on style and historical truth. Allegorically speaking, it is from Padma, the working-class domestic and unfulfilled lover, that Saleem learns to compose accurately. In the next room, within smelling range of his writing table, Padma stirs her chutney pots while Saleem records Indian history for later generations, with each new chapter corresponding to one of the twenty-six pickle jars he methodically adds to the shelf beside his desk. The novel is, in that sense, what Rushdie calls "the chutnification of history."

If Padma, with her plebeian good sense, succeeds in shaming the narrator for being too upscale and intellectual, she is also gullible and emotional—things that are likewise wrong with the character of postwar India, Rushdie implies. That is, gullibility and emotionalism are fed alike by Bollywood and religious legend, the twin poles of the popular mind; historical events can only be seen by Padma as episodes from the *Mahabharata* replayed outside her window. Hindi cinema, religious ritual, and secular legend are all for the people at any rate, "Bombay-talkie-melodramatic." Because he represents a range of classes as well as ethnicities in *Midnight's Children*, Rushdie is forced to face head-on the problem of authorial responsibility. For how can one claim that one's novel is superior to the bluster of politicians, the demagoguery of clerics, and the silly illusions of the silver screen when it gets basic facts wrong? *Midnight's Children* certainly does, but it does so for a reason. As Rushdie explains in the essay "Errata": "Imaginative truth is simultaneously honourable and suspect. . . . This is why I made my narrator, Saleem, suspect in his narration; his mistakes are the mistakes of a fallible memory" (in *Imaginary Homelands*, p. 10). With complementary but distinct kinds of idealisms, the high and low characters Saleem and Padma frequently misremember the past. But there is no real remedy: at the other extreme is the absurdly "realist" filmmaker, Uncle Hanif, busy making an interminable documentary on the workings of a pickle factory (a rather different approach to chutnification, and hardly a match for the erotic dances of the megastar Hindi film actress, Sridevi!). Facts alone, it would appear, communicate nothing. Imaginative truth may be flawed, but it is all a writer has.

Throughout *Midnight's Children* Rushdie revels in the grand theme of politics, arguing that modern writers on both sides of the Atlantic seemed to be ignoring the one truth that best defined their time: the experience of empire and its aftermath. The case was made all the stronger by the fact that Rushdie was no armchair moralist but freely accepted his guilt for being a writer whose myth-making implicates him in the crimes of the nation whose myths he fostered. He had, after all, cast Saleem with his miraculous nose as someone who had been used by the Pakistani military as a human bloodhound to hunt down dissidents and who misused his telepathic powers for thought control once he became a one-man "All-India Radio" when by the power of mind alone he was able to communicate simultaneously with all the other midnight's children who could not, for all that, communicate with each other except through him. India, he meant to say, had to accept blame as well as credit for its acts after independence, without simply blaming colonialism. Obsessed with facing the responsibilities of writers, Rushdie demonstrates some of his characteristic pessimism: Saleem compares his writerly practices to the techniques of a Bombay talkie, pure entertainment composed of heavy-handed devices and cheap illusions. In a typical passage, the novel compares history writing to a film screen whose dancing lights feign reality only from afar; up close, the images disintegrate into grainy abstraction. Although considered postmodernist by some critics, his position should not be misunderstood. As he explained in a 1985 review of Terry Gilliam's movie *Brazil*, "The French, these days, would have us believe that this world, which they call 'the text,' is quite unconnected to the 'real' world." But, he says, "I believe . . . that the imagined world is, must be, connected to the observable one" (*Imaginary Homelands*, p. 118). In a similar vein in "Is Nothing Sacred?" he welcomes the insight of Michel Foucault that the author is a modern invention—part of his point in *Midnight's Children* collaborative composition with Padma—but complains of Foucault's "airiness," that is, his tendency to neglect to root his claims in historical evidence.

Thus, if in "Is Nothing Sacred?" Rushdie recalls that the "surrealism and modernism and Marx" of his upbringing in the end complemented rather nicely the change and flux inherent in Hinduism's theology, with its multiple gods, it was another way of saying that the critics' free use of the label "postmodern" in regard to his fiction was the result of their poverty of references. To the Western critic, tropes of decentralizing or the supernatural may seem like an avant-garde experimentalism when actually they are time-tested allusions to secular or religious traditions of which the critics are ignorant. Rushdie's metafictional games had their source less in French theory than in the experimental prose of the 1940s British Indian novelist, G. V. Desani, whose writing is itself a disjointed combination of the Indian secular epics and Kipling's *Kim;* or in the spiraling digressions of the Storyteller of Baroda, whose capacious public performances before crowds numbering in the thousands have been known to last several hours; or, indeed, in Bollywood itself. The novel's active use of the Indian popular culture of film, billboards, sex scandals, newspaper ads, and songs, he suggests, is about freely celebrating a remembered (or misremembered) Bombay childhood rather than a special point about how we have reached the "end of literature." His first bout with the problem of the authorless text came, he would later say, in watching *The Wizard of Oz*—a movie that merged in his boyish head with Hindi film, and one whose wicked witch provided the model for Indira Gandhi in the novel. It was also a film whose heroes were all women, as is the case in *Shame,* and it provided the occasion for a brilliant short story that actually was postmodern, "The Auction of the Ruby Slippers" (in *East, West: Stories*), in which Rushdie offers a take on commercialization that makes light of the "moral decay of post-millennial culture" by emphasizing the triumph of fiction—the device that provides us with everything we crave.

Just as the Hindu god Brahma is said to dream the universe, so Rushdie's hero Saleem can claim to be the universal receptacle, "the sum total of everything . . . everyone everything whose being-in-the-world affected was affected by mine" (p. 457). Cracks on Saleem's skin represent the fissurings of sectarian disunity on a national level, and the deliberate yoking of the authorial "I" with the "we" of the Indian populace here points to a central strategy of embodiment: an image of the *totalizing* novel Rushdie sought to create. *Midnight's Children* was to be to India what *Moby-Dick, Gravity's Rainbow,* or *Invisible Man* was to the United States: "the sum total of everything," an epic encyclopedia. Once again—and it is deeply characteristic of

Rushdie's method—his intention is not so much inferrable from the novel's immense range or sweep as it is stated, in so many words, in a series of clever allusions and puns. The novel's use of Indian myth relies above all on a single episode—the marriage of Parvati (the incarnation of Durga, a destroyer goddess and a mother goddess) and Shiva and the birth of their elephant-headed child, Ganesh, typically thought of as a god of good fortune. Saleem's nose and Shiva's swollen knees, of course, suggest the elephantine. And both characters are the progenitors of Aadam Aziz—Saleem as the cuckolded husband of Aadam's mother, Parvati, and Shiva as the natural father. Thus Aadam is the character who stands for Ganesh, and he is significant for what he tells us of the generation following the Indian "Emergency." His meaning is ambiguous, however. He seems to stand not for good fortune but for the other side of what Hindu myth tells us Shiva wrought: the *not human* (Ganesh is a monster), the end of the chain of rebirth. A war hero who returns a major, the character Shiva is a seducer and cuckolder of the rich; his children are strewn across the map of India, but he is also the one who makes possible the mass sterilization of the midnight's children when he turns informer and betrays them to the authorities: Shiva, like the god for whom he is named, is both creator and destroyer. These dualities—while perfectly faithful to Hindu mythology (whose gods, like Flapping Eagle in *Grimus,* are essentially hermaphroditic)—are designed also as a commentary on the type of novel Rushdie is writing.

Parvati, Shiva, and Ganesh each stand for a distinct aspect of *Midnight's Children*'s national style—the style of English appropriate to post-Independence India. Parvati emerges from the "magician's ghetto" (Rushdie's send-up of the Communist parties); her powers of "conjuration and sorcery" are the powers of making appear real what is not, "the art that required no artifice" (p. 239). Shiva, on the other hand, lends the narrator assistance of another kind: "matter of fact descriptions of the outre and the bizarre, and their reverse, namely heightened, stylized versions of the everyday—these techniques, which are also attitudes of mind, I have lifted—or perhaps absorbed—from Shiva-of-the-knees" (p. 261). Ganesh, finally, is more the interlocutor through which the entire story is filtered, for in addition to his other qualities, he is the scribe to whom Vyasa dictates the *Mahabharata*. Ganesh represents the mammoth that the novel is and had to be, fleshing out the "Indian disease, this urge to encapsulate the whole of reality" (p. 84). The novel is brimming with vignettes that assert its elephantine dimensions; for example, there is the figure of Lifafa Das, the peepshow man, who displays his vast collection of picture postcards, crying, "See the whole word, come see everything!" (p. 83); there are the oversize paintings of the friend of Nadir Khan, the ill-fated lover of Saleem's mother who becomes a communist and changes his name to Qasim the Red (a motif Rushdie uses again in the canvases of Moraes Zogoiby's mother in *The Moor's Last Sigh*); there is the spittoon of the Rani of Cooch Naheen ("the Queen of Absolutely Nothing"), where the juices of all castes and classes mix without prejudice; best of all, there is Saleem's growing collection of casaundy jars. Along with Saleem's chutney, Padma cooks with casaundy—hot Indian mustards. The jars contain them just as his chapters contain the "hot" business of Indian history.

Shame

Rushdie's next novel, *Shame* (1983), concerns some of the same themes as *Midnight's Children* but departs sharply in its form. Written with a much-thumbed copy of Herman Melville's *The Confidence Man* by his side "as a kind of touchstone," *Shame* is more modestly scaled and is by some accounts Rushdie's most successful novel. It was short-listed for the Booker Prize in a competition that many (including Rushdie) thought he would win. The much more condensed and poetic novel, *Shame,* is at the same time less effusive, less energetic, and (in spite of everything) less optimistic than *Midnight's Children.* It relates the story of a bitter feud between two families in Pakistan's ruling circles—that of Iskander Harappa (based on the historical Zulfikar Ali Bhutto) and his successor and executioner, Raza Hyder (based on Zia ul-Haq). An anger tinged with morbidity infuses the prose, but Rushdie attempts to dilute the venom by adopting the light touch of a fairy tale: the novel opens, "In the remote border town of Q . . . there once lived three lovely, and loving, sisters." Once again plying the motif of uncertain (or English) parentage in the figure of Omar Khayyam Shakil, Rushdie delicately slips in and out of the language of oral storytelling,

a mode that intentionally confuses the various kinds of orality in play. At times the novel mimics the comfortable pastime of telling fables at a family gathering (to this effect it employs the matriarchal storyteller, Bariamma); at other points the novel employs the quite different oral form of the narrative aside typical of the contemporary Western author. (The narrator of *Shame* punctuates his story with autobiographical accounts of how his sister was assaulted on a London subway.) *Shame* also invokes the "literary" orality of the Qur'an, the holy book of the official religion of Pakistan and, by tradition, understood to be a "recitation" to Muhammad from God.

Imitating, in other words, the "turbid peregrinations" of the oral tale, *Shame* unfolds as a kind of court satire, a story it tells with forced mirth and a colloquial tang that is never stronger than when a character is in the act of swearing. When a vengeful Mir Harappa sacks Iskander's home, he does so uttering oaths that make the usual profanities of English seem almost pallid and inexpressive by comparison: "Sisterfucking bastard spawn of corpse-eating vultures. Does he think he can insult me in public and get away with it? . . . that sucker of shit from the rectums of diseased donkeys." For all its attractive earthiness, *Shame* leaves the sprawling gestures of *Midnight's Children* far behind. Here is a smaller and more elite cast of characters. True, the novel deals with the Pakistani drug trade and the CIA war in Afghanistan, the Iranian revolution, the Baluchi guerrilla movement, the overthrow of Zulfikar by his toadying general Zia, and the subsequent rise to power of Bhutto's daughter, Benazir—but none of these events is historicized. They are depicted rather like the woodcuts in a children's book or the textured images of a tapestry. Rushdie confines the action of the novel to the home and fully exploits the themes of storytelling and repression by dealing more openly than ever before with the plight of women.

Shame is an explicitly feminist novel. With few positive characters in the narrative, the only admirable ones are women. They may be rebels like "the Virgin Ironpants" (modeled on Benazir Bhutto) or like Iskander's wife, Rani Humayun, who patiently embroiders the history of her husband's crimes in elaborate visual patterns on a series of eighteen shawls. They may be victims like Pinkie Aurangzeb, a mistress grown old before her time, or Naveed "Good News" Hyder, who hangs herself after being made perpetually pregnant by her husband. Or—as in the central figure of Sufiya Zinobia, the rape victim who stalks the land "castrating" men by beheading them—they may be rebels and victims at once. As Rushdie explains in one of the narrator's asides, "A society which is authoritarian in its social and sexual codes, which crushes its women beneath the intolerable burdens of honour and propriety, breeds repressions of other kinds as well. Contrariwise: dictators are always—or at least in public, on other people's behalf—puritanical" (p. 189).

However well-meant, the portraits of women in *Shame* were seen by many critics (male and female) as patronizing—a criticism that would hound Rushdie through his next three novels, and not only in regard to women. His admirable courage to make his voice heard and to do so with unambiguous commitment had its costs. Must one be one to know one? Such a question went to the heart of Rushdie's views on the catholicity of influence and freestyle empathy. It would soon bring his work to a crisis, as the charge muttered by *Shame*'s narrator became the actual words of his living detractors: *"Outsider! Trespasser! You have no right to this subject! . . . We know you, with your foreign language wrapped around you like a flag: speaking about us in your forked tongue, what can you tell but lies?"* (p. 23).

THE SATANIC VERSES

ON 8 November 1988 *The Satanic Verses* won the Whitbread Prize for the best novel in England that year. Rushdie had conceived of the book as the third part of a de facto trilogy, moving from India to Pakistan to what he would playfully call "Babylondon" (a joining of "London" with the Rastafarian pejorative "Babylon," used to refer to white civilization). Rushdie's was far from the first attempt to capture in fiction the life of colonial immigrants now living in the former center of empire. West Indian novels of the 1940s and 1950s like Samuel Selvon's *The Lonely Londoners* (1956), E. R. Braithwaite's *To Sir with Love* (1959), George Lamming's *The Emigrants* (1954), and others had preceded it, as had the British-based Indian G. V. Desani's *All About Mr. Hatterr* (1948), an explicit source for *Midnight's Children*. But *The Satanic Verses* was certainly the most ambitious of the type. Rushdie's journal-

istic apprenticeship for writing it had been formidable. Following "The New Empire within Britain" in 1982, Rushdie wrote a passionate introduction to *Home Front* (1984), a collection of photos with text by John Bishton and Derek Reardon, on the private lives of Indians, Vietnamese, Africans, Turks, Afro-Caribbeans, and other "invisibles" then living in England. (The introduction is reprinted in *Imaginary Homelands.*) Having raised the ire of the Tories for lashing out at their anti-immigrant legislation and race-baiting at election time, Rushdie slammed the local labor authority of Camden in "An Unimportant Fire" (1984, also in *Imaginary Homelands*), angrily denouncing the efforts of the labor authority to deny responsibility for the overcrowded, unsafe housing given new (black) arrivals on the dole. He created a similar stir in 1987 when he gave a bad review to the documentary *Handsworth Songs* by the Black Audio Film Collective, complaining that its politics of struggle were canned and that it was simply repeating the mainstream media's view of the black communities as being involved in a perpetual riot with police. The film, he complained, was blind to the unexpected stories waiting to be told—the "bright illuminations and fireworks during the Hindu Festival of Lights, Divali. . . . the Muslim call to prayer, 'Allahu Akbar,' wafting down from the minaret of a Birmingham mosque" (*Imaginary Homelands*, p. 117).

The Satanic Verses was almost a belated, and inevitable, project by the time of its composition between 1984 and 1988. The burden of its prehistory was weighty, and its creation carefully prepared. In a number of earlier short stories—above all, "The Harmony of the Spheres" and the spy story "Chekhov and Zulu" (the latter reminiscent of John Le Carré)—Rushdie had written about day-to-day British life in ways that looked forward to *The Satanic Verses* but also placed him as a *British* contemporary of, say, Martin Amis and Julian Barnes. *The Satanic Verses* is, at any rate, the place Rushdie finally made good on his implicit promises in articles and interviews that the culture-straddling migrant is "almost the normative condition of the twentieth century. . . . That's how life is. . . . We've all moved." The novel is, in that sense, not simply a matter of slumming, or of digging around in exotic locales in London's poorer barrios like an ethnographer, but rather of placing his condition, and the condition of those like him, at the center of late-twentieth-century experience. Rushdie was saying, *we* will constitute the norm now; white Europe and America will have to look to us to see what the future will be like:

Most of the time, people will ask me—will ask anyone like me—are you Indian? Pakistani? English? . . . What is being expressed is a discomfort with a plural identity. And what I am saying . . . in the novel is that we have got to come to terms with this. We are increasingly become a world of migrants, made up of bits and fragments from here, there. We are here. And we have never really left anywhere we have been.

And that "we" for Rushdie was not Indian Muslim, or even Indian, but primarily colonial—and then secondarily, and more metaphorically, universal. For—like the images on a cinema screen—the closer one examines any of these identities, the more they fly apart. England's Indian writers are themselves divergent; some are Pakistani, some Bangladeshi, others from western, eastern, or southern Africa, still others from the Caribbean. In the diaspora, as at home, India is a "scattered concept."

Rushdie's statement that *The Satanic Verses* "was the least political novel I had ever written, a novel whose engine was not public affairs but other kinds of more personal and cultural crises" is surprising, given the furor the novel caused, but quite accurate. The cartoonish characterizations that deliberately marked his "current events" novels were not altogether missing here, but they were tempered by efforts at personal intimacy and psychological depth—qualities he would further develop in *The Moor's Last Sigh.* He spoke of *The Satanic Verses'* being for him an "emotional risk," for apart from the painful creations of Gibreel Farishta's tortured mental life, or of Saladin Chamcha's disastrous affairs of the heart, the novel ends with Rushdie's "most naturalistic piece of writing": a description of his father's death, which took place a year before the novel's publication. If thematically about "hybrid identities," the book is also a formal hybrid in the sense that it journeys from "very pyrotechnic, high fabulation" at the very beginning to naked intimacy in the closing pages.

The Satanic Verses is about two Muslim professionals from India who emigrate to England. One of them, Gibreel Farishta, is a famous Hindi film actor who before leaving India specializes in a popular film genre known as "theologicals," in which famous gods from the Hindu pantheon are typically portrayed in opulent costume dramas—a pop-culture form of veneration. Upon arriving in England, however, Gibreel suffers a nervous breakdown. Battered by racism and the foreigner's sense of loss, he slowly goes mad under the impact of a lapse of religious faith that had begun while he was still in India. Obsessed with the nature of good and evil, and uncertain whether his namesake (the Angel Gabriel) portends God (Allah) or the Devil (Shaitan), he hallucinates (or dreams) himself living in the days of the prophet Muhammad: the seventh century C.E. The parody of Islam that made the book so notorious is therefore in Gibreel's ravings, the ravings of a paranoid schizophrenic, riven with doubt, who eventually kills himself. The novel's other major character is Saladin Chamcha, a more Westernized immigrant who wears a bowler hat and has mastered "proper" speech ("chamcha" colloquially means a toady or flatterer), but who finds, despite the pains he takes to be English, that he is unwelcome in England. He makes his living doing voice-overs for radio and television kid's shows about "aliens," using his masterful ability to mimic others' voices in advertisements.

Built around these two men's rough acclimations, the plot takes us through vividly intertwined stories of immigration and religious faith: tales of day-to-day life in the Afro-Caribbean and South Asian neighborhoods of Brick Lane and Brixton (the "Shaandaar Café" and "Pinkwallah" episodes); the story of Ayesha, a young girl in Titlipur, India, considered a prophet, who leads the faithful on a cross-country march to the Indian Ocean, convinced that the seas will part to allow them to make their pilgrimage to Mecca (the "Ayesha" episodes); a digressive romance in which a heartbroken English widow living on the cold Dover coast pines for her lost Argentine lover, in a satire of the Falklands war (the "Rosa Diamond" episode); and Gibreel's lunatic dreams of a place Rushdie calls Jahilia (Illusion), an imaginary desert country of nomads and merchants not unlike the seventh-century Arabian peninsula where Islam was born. Rushdie attempts allegorically to capture the essence of the immigrant experience. He is comparing the historical conversion to Islam of the pagan nomadic peoples of the Arabian peninsula to the security—the social moorings—that religious faith provides immigrants abroad. For Rushdie himself, and for many of the Indian immigrants in England, that faith has been, at least culturally, Muslim. Questioning the necessity of such a mooring is the main theme of *The Satanic Verses*.

A "migrant's-eye view of the world" and a "love song to our mongrel selves," *The Satanic Verses* was also a bid to see art as substitute religion, part of that "strange job" that writers do, defending the human spirit in an effort "to fill the place left by faith." If the faithful despised such a move, many secular readers in England recoiled from Rushdie's critique of British society, which was, after all, as much a part of *The Satanic Verses* as his critique of religion. In spite of the novel's reputation, the literary wrath of *The Satanic Verses* is aimed not only at a top-heavy Islam but at the pretensions of a Western democracy filled with police ruffians in Black Marias; imperialist longings for the exotic; the mendacious commercial jingles of Thatcherite yuppies; and the philistine horrors of an American-inspired Christian fundamentalism. The novel sets forth a cast of characters continually exchanging their identities, merging with their Others like the shifting sands of Jahilia, where only religious faith and lucrative trading are permanent, and therefore the perfect image of the modern immigrant's plight. Rushdie employs a syncretic evenhandedness when looking for metaphorical strategies to depict "migrant consciousness." Gibreel, for instance, works in Hindu (not Muslim) religious films; Chamcha as an actor is compared to "much-metamorphosed Vishnu." The theme of metamorphosis is everywhere but expressed through radically disparate national traditions. If the Hindu version of metamorphosis is, predictably, reincarnation, the concept appears more threateningly in the thinking of the born-again Christian, Eugene Dumsday, whose name Rushdie intends to suggest "eugenics," "doomsday," and simply "dumb." With its overtones of racial selective breeding and genetic engineering, Dumsday's eugenics is a particularly frightening variant of the "mutations" (that is, cultural adaptations) that immigrants, especially nonwhite ones, undergo in a place like Britain under the pressures of forced assimilation or, worse, outright consignment to an expendable species by Christian fanatics like Dumsday. His traditionally Christian hatred of evolution moves him to a cheery embrace of a new creationism: one in which eugenic scientists create superior hu-

mans, weeding out the weak on a march to Armageddon. Against such creationism Rushdie pits the immigrants themselves, who as characters in the novel describe, in Rushdie's words, their own "natural selection," a bitter and unequal struggle to survive in a hostile environment. In perhaps the most urbane variant of the metamorphosis theme, and developing the motif of evolution, the immigrants are said to embody a neo-Lamarckianism (that is, a belief in the inheritance of acquired characteristics). If the novel's title and chapter headings seem to prioritize Islam, that is only because the book's protagonists (and its author) are *Muslim* immigrants. The satirizations of arrogant certainty and sectarianism are for that reason typically given an Islamic cast.

There are several reasons why Islam, from Rushdie's point of view, was well-poised to suggest the wavering identities of the immigrant. The Qur'an is believed by the faithful literally to be the word of God, recited directly to Muhammad by the Angel Gabriel (*al-qur'an* means "recital"). Unlike the role of Jesus in Christianity, however, Muhammad is not considered to be divine. He is the one prophet about whom we know important biographical details, a prophet wholly inside history. Drawing on his Cambridge training, Rushdie observed:

The ethic of revelation [Muhammad] received when at the age of forty, having married a wealthy older woman and made his fortune, he climbed Mount Hira and found there the Archangel Gabriel . . . has often been seen, at least in part, as a plan for a return to the code of the nomadic Bedouin. . . . The people on whom Muhammad's word made the strongest impression were the poor, the people of the bazaar, the lower classes of Meccan society—precisely those people who know that they would have been better off under the old nomadic system.

Islam was in part "a subversive, radical movement." Immigrant characters throughout the novel are depicted sprouting horns and tails miraculously to dramatize how the British see them—as devils—and to suggest that they are "turning curses into strengths": that is, willingly accepting the role of devil to turn that meaning on its head.

The Satanic Verses is not only about transformation but doubt. Any prophet, Rushdie says, must at some time question the authenticity of the voices he hears. Rushdie's "satanic verses," in fact, have an actual historical basis: "satanic verses" are first referred to by the chronicler al-Tabari, who wrote that initially Muhammad allowed new converts to Islam to worship three female pagan deities: these deities were so loved that proscribing their worship would have impeded proselytization. Since the verses permitting this pagan worship were later rejected by Muhammad as inspired by evil (there seemed to be some opportunism in permitting them to begin with), they raised the issue of doubt for Rushdie with redoubled force. They seemed to provide the perfect occasion for making it plausible that the doubting Gibreel would cast himself in Muhammad's skin. When the visions first came to him, Muhammad was accused of insanity and even doubted himself; Gibreel actually goes insane. Metaphorically, the God of the Ayatollah Khomeini (whom Rushdie makes a character in the book since Khomeini, too, was an immigrant to England: exiled in London during the last days of the Shah) or the God, say, of Margaret Thatcher, is Rushdie's Devil, and he is happy to have it that way. But then again—like Saleem and Shiva or Iskander and Raza in the earlier novels—Gibreel and Saladin are the two that make one in *The Satanic Verses*, together creating the dialogue that, in a moment of fictional revelation, becomes Rushdie's Qur'anic "recital." Rushdie saw the duality again in the meekness and bravado of Dorothy and the Wizard in *The Wizard of Oz*.

The Satanic Verses sets itself up as a mock Qur'an, now narrated by Allah *and* Shaitan. It is a holy book of doubt and secularity, a renegade work in precisely the sense that Muhammad was a renegade to the pagan Meccans and the Jews of Medina. Since there are strict prohibitions in Islam against depicting the Prophet (he wanted the message, not the messenger, to matter), the novel is certainly a blasphemous work, even an attempt to unravel the religion from within, but it is a perfectly sincere secular rereading of Islamic tradition. Rushdie was appealing to the honorable literature of revisionism, Western and Eastern—on the one hand, to William Blake's *The Marriage of Heaven and Hell* and Mikhail Bulgakov's *The Master and Margarita*; on the other, to the writings of Al-Ghazali, a thirteenth-century Persian theologian, and those of Muhammad Iqbal, an early-twentieth-century Urdu poet, both of whom cherished doubt and strove for religious reform. As in *Grimus*, Rushdie

here embraces Sufism—an aesthetic, mystical, and tolerant trend within Islam whose adherents had for many centuries explored theological doubt (often in exquisite, experimental poetry) and who insisted on the believer's personal and individual relationship to God rather than on his or her submission to rules and rituals as defined by the clerisy. Like Saleem Sinai, the "author" of *Midnight's Children*, the actual author of *The Satanic Verses* is part Ibn Sina (a tenth-century Arabic philosopher and Sufi adept) and part Khalid Ibn Sinan (a failed prophet and rival of Muhammad). The "Sinai" of the Mosaic covenant—although it serves in *Midnight's Children* as little more than another sign of Saleem's impossibly complicated and multiple "parentage"—gestures toward the third great religion of the "Book" (Judaism), which must eventually be exposed to satire just as Islam and Christianity are so mercilessly satirized in *The Satanic Verses*. As readers would see, that satire eventually came full force in Rushdie's elaborate treatment of the Jews of Cochin in *The Moor's Last Sigh*.

The hatred *The Satanic Verses* inspired among Muslims surprised Rushdie at first, if only because his earlier fiction arguably had been just as irreverent: in the later chapters of *Midnight's Children* there are the images of Muhammad as Buddha sitting glassy-eyed and stupid under a tree in Gaya; in *Shame* the Qur'an is compared to the public rantings of the Pakistani military. Still, the fame of *The Satanic Verses* was prodigious. There had simply never been a case when the publication of a novel produced a more significant reaction on a global scale, at all levels of public and private commentary. Clearly, the uproar was more than a literary controversy. Lower-class Muslims in places like Bradford, England, and Detroit, Michigan, had been protesting for weeks before the Ayatollah came on the scene to steal the headlines and place the whole affair in the framework of a convenient demonology. Because Rushdie was a highly decorated media star, protesters repeatedly made the point that what they were really objecting to was the vilification of Islam in the Western press, what Syed Shahabuddin had called the "new Crusades." For many British Muslims the novel raised a quality-of-life question, a matter of their very social standing and dignity as immigrants living in Britain. Paradoxically Rushdie had alienated the very "aliens" on whose behalf he had written the novel.

From the start the issue demanded attention it never received from the "specialists" on Middle East terrorism. Though Rushdie strove to point out that "novels are not trivial things" and that the *fatwa* was an attack on novels as such, few people looked at the literary issues raised by the affair—at, for example, the way that book markets structure international taste and create celebrities, the different status that the written word enjoys in different societies, or the actual traditions of secular literature within Islam. Rather, a more brutal rhetoric that expressed no interest in Rushdie as a writer tended to hold sway. Roald Dahl simply called Rushdie "a dangerous opportunist"; Tory Party chairman Norman Tebbit, "an outstanding villain . . . who has insulted the country that protects him and betrayed and reviled those to whom he owes his wealth, his culture, his religion and now his very life." John Le Carré declared that "absolute free speech is not a God-given right. . . . Nobody has a God-given right to insult a great religion." Alexander Cockburn, by contrast, took up Rushdie's defense but complained that Rushdie managed no outcry on behalf of other victims of censorship and intimidation. Edward Said called *The Satanic Verses* "the Intifada of the imagination," while the great Sudanese novelist Tayeb Salih called it "tedious," a cause célèbre only because Iran had made it so. Despite the violence of the much-publicized rhetoric against Rushdie from a variety of Islamic quarters, many commentators observed that those quarters did, after all, have a point. Gobind Kumar, for example, reminded readers of the "tendency for the Western media to propagate derogatory images of minority and foreign cultures." Conor Cruise O'Brien was there to oblige him, stating baldly that "Muslim society looks repulsive . . . because it is repulsive" and Anthony Burgess weighed in with the claim that "the Koran is no literary masterpiece. The Bible is." Apparently, in the eyes of certain critics, those who decried Rushdie's blasphemy against Islam were guilty of blasphemy against the sacred doctrine of Western cultural superiority.

Many of the responses to *The Satanic Verses* were addressed in advance within the pages of the novel itself. The same uneasiness Rushdie expressed in both *Shame* and *Midnight's Children* about his own role in depicting the "masses" manifests in *The Satanic Verses* in an allegorical retelling of Islam's early appeal to commoners: The character Baal is a court hireling contracted by the Jahilian Grandee to satirize the village poor. His job is to practice on behalf of the state the "art of metrical slander," which amounts to another self-critical allusion to Rushdie's own art. Rushdie's vicious send-up of the black communities of Britain through the characters Uhuru Simba, Pinkwallah, and Orphia Phillips—small-time poseurs, hucksters, or naive mechanicals who mouth an unconvincing patwah speech—is not unlike Baal's portrait of the lower-class types who become Muhammad's first converts: Khalid the water carrier, Bilal the former slave, and Salman al-Farisi the scribe. Rushdie's view of the common people is ambivalent. The people in power, as he would put it in *Shame*, "distrust fun." A self-styled socialist in the context of Thatcher's Britain, Rushdie instead espoused a traditional and cautious liberalism when assessing the undeniably popular regime of post-revolutionary Iran or, indeed, of post-independence India. What he contends in *Shame* is that popular revolutionary governments, whether religious or not, tend to be humorless, puritanical, and allergic to criticism. For that reason, his parodies in *The Satanic Verses* of Islam, on the one hand, and of the working-class black communities of Britain, on the other, waver. While portraying ordinary people as heroically adept at survival, and by doing so with a Rabelaisian love for the masses, which is without parallel in contemporary fiction, he also fears popular power and has no confidence in people's ability to choose wisely. More than anything, his parodies are fatally incomplete; they attempt to be jocular about a faith whose absence would, for embattled immigrants without Rushdie's resources or class connections, be too grim to fathom. And although Rushdie (as in *Shame*) recognizes his own ambivalence and brings it to the surface for discussion in the characters Baal and Salman al-Farisi in *The Satanic Verses* (one a hack in the pay of the wealthy, the other a scribe who pokes holes irreverently in the Prophet's authority), still he is culpably out of touch with his subject. He was unable fully to imagine the actual response his parodies would elicit. For in the closing moments of the Jahilia dream sections the townspeople are shown to laugh along with Baal's irreverent satire of the Prophet, and they are described as giving vent to an accumulated resentment against the oppressive religion of "Subservience." For much of the crowd, how far this was from what really happened!

AFTER THE FATWA

Haroun and the Sea of Stories

THE imaginative landscape of *Haroun and the Sea of Stories* (1990) had been stirring in Rushdie's mind since childhood. In a public lecture in 1992, he reflected on the impure—imprecise and untamable—nature of creativity, exclaiming, "I've lived in that messy ocean all my life. I've fished in it for my art. This turbulent sea was the sea outside my bedroom window in Bombay. It is the sea by which I was born, and which I carry within me wherever I go." Almost all of Rushdie's early inspirations can be found in *Haroun*: Flash Gordon's rockets to the moon; Alice in Wonderland; the voyages of Sinbad; the heroic double lives of Clark Kent/Superman and Bruce Wayne/Batman; the riches of Ali Baba; and the colorful substitute home, the Emerald City. Many of the professional influences of Rushdie's maturer years are also woven into the fabric of *Haroun*: there are explicit allusions to James Bond's *Dr. No*; to the medievally tinged science fictions of Italo Calvino; to the *bwana* adventure films of Steven Spielberg; and to Satyajit Ray's spectacularly popular children's film about the adventures of Goopy and Bagha, two bumbling bumpkins whose names are actually given to the story's two talking fish. In his 1990 essay on Satyajit Ray (collected in *Imaginary Homelands*), Rushdie notes, "[Ray's] fairy-tale movie *Goopy Gyne Bagha Byne* . . . is, in Bengal, as well-loved as *The Wizard of Oz* is here" (p. 111). Rushdie's first children's tale, and his first novel written after the *fatwa*, *Haroun* is dedicated to his son, Zafar, in an acrostic poem that opens the manuscript. The book was written to fulfill the promise Rushdie made to Zafar that his next book after *The Satanic Verses* would be a children's story. "It was not so much a bedtime story but a bath-time story, something I'd tell him when he was in the tub, or while I wrapped him in towels. I would have these basic motifs, like the Sea of Stories, but each time I would improvise—not only to please him but to test myself, to see if I could just say something and take it elsewhere." Sharing early versions of the book with his son, Rushdie

(who was then living in his various safehouses) got the child's feedback over the phone. The first judgments were, in fact, negative; the story did not have enough "jump," said Zafar, and kids would be bored. Rushdie subsequently revised it by giving it more physical movement—traveling in buses, sailing in ferries, flying to a hidden moon.

Dragging himself out of the funk of underground life, and (given the campaigns of hate against him) wracked with anxieties about having failed as a writer and as a human being, Rushdie would probably not have written *Haroun* had it not been for his fatherly pact. Sentenced to death by the Ayatollah, Rushdie felt, as he explained in "In Good Faith," as though he had been "plunged, like Alice, into the world beyond the looking-glass" (p. 22). *Haroun* seeks to address what Rushdie in his study of *The Wizard of Oz* argued that L. Frank Baum's story was all about: the inadequacy of parents. *Haroun* recalls *Grimus* insofar as it is structured as a quest; it has a less static story line, but it also labors under its own cleverness, displaying the same virtuosity and source-hunting. Although it clearly declares itself a children's tale, *Haroun* is not really the kind of tale that children read. There is adventure, clear villainy, superhuman exploits, child heroics, and moral instruction, but all the elements come together in unmistakably adult fashion. Then again, *Haroun* had what none of Rushdie's other novels did: "I wanted to write a happy ending. I've never written a happy ending."

Haroun opens in a glorious land of hills named Alifbay ("alphabet"). As James Fenton remarks, the land bears an "initial resemblance to Kashmir" but soon appears properly unreal as "something between a Persian miniature and an animated cartoon." In this magical country, Haroun's father is a professional storyteller famous throughout the land for his skill at weaving yarns of exceptional beauty and vividness. Drawing on his gift for gab, with an endless repertoire of fables for all occasions and a surefire delivery that holds entire villages in mouth-gaping awe, Rashid Khalifa (nicknamed the Shah of Blah by his detractors and the Ocean of Notions by his admirers) soon catches the eye of the local bigwigs of various political parties who coerce him into dulling the minds of voters at election time by exaggerating the politicians' merits. However, Rashid is stricken with grief when his wife, Soraya, leaves him for the no-nonsense Mr. Sengupta, a clerk, whose line, "what's the use of stories that aren't even true?" marks him as Rashid's virtual opposite. Grieving, and feeling guilty for wasting his talents on behalf of wealthy dunderheads, Rashid suddenly dries up. All at once his inexhaustible capacity for spinning once-upon-a-times leaves him; standing embarrassed before a crowd, he can offer it nothing but meaningless sounds ("Ark! Ark!") as the politicos glower from the wings. Haroun fears for his father's safety on account of threats from the bigwigs' henchmen, so he looks for a way to recover his father's gifts.

On the eve of his father's next important speech, with an ultimatum hanging over their heads, Haroun falls asleep aboard a houseboat named *The Arabian Nights Plus One*, which is owned by the slimy Top Man of the ruling party of K, Snooty Buttoo. The valley of K had been, appropriately, renamed Kosh-Mar, which in Rushdie's bilingual punning suggests either *kache-mer* (Urdu for "a place that hides a sea") or *cauchemar* (French for "nightmare"). Haroun wakes to find Iff—a sky-blue, bewhiskered water genie—in the bathroom. Like a temperamental plumber Iff is busy turning off Rashid's connection to the Great Story Sea by orders of the Grand Comptroller in a "process too complicated to explain"—or "P2C2E," the frustrating (parent-like) response Haroun gets to many of his most eager questions. Haroun grabs the multicolored Disconnector and, promising to return it later, is able to persuade the unwilling sprite to aid him in recovering his father's powers. Guided by Iff and a mechanical hoopoe bird named Butt, Haroun discovers that the earth possesses a second moon, Kahani (Urdu for "story"), invisible to the eye because of its rapid revolutions; on Kahani rests a vast multicolored sea of stories and the magical Gup City. Haroun learns that the usual flow of stories to the earth has been interrupted by a nefarious scheme of the shadow kingdom of Chup, located on Kahani's dark side, whose legions exist solely in realms of black and white, and the leader of Chup, Khattam-Shud (Urdu for "the end!" or "all finished"), has conspired to poison the sea and to kill storytelling for good with the sludge of orthodoxy, ill-humor, and one-sidedness. Flying to Kahani with Iff and Butt, Haroun battles and connives his way past the evil kingdom's warriors and traps, picking up important allies along the way until, like Flash Gordon before Emperor Ming, he and his friends engage the enemy's troops in a final showdown, which includes freeing Princess Batcheat ("chitchat") Chattergy from her imprisonment in the tower of Chup. When Khattam-Shud has been vanquished, Rashid is restored, and on the day of his awaited performance he holds forth like never before, delighting his audience and, at the same time, exposing the local political bosses for the scoundrels they are. When the politicians flee, Rashid is crowned a hero, and, with reputation intact, he and Haroun return home to find that Soraya has come back, disgusted with the tedious Mr. Sengupta. She is eagerly forgiven, and they all live happily ever after.

Greeted indulgently by a sympathetic public, *Haroun* suffers from a derivative story line and a painfully transparent biographical message. But it signaled the author's resilience and publicly declared his determination not to be silenced. With character names like Mr. Butts and Snooty Buttoo, and jokes about farting, the book actually gives kids the sort of humor they really like (and rarely find in, say, Maurice Sendak). At the same time the novel is jam-packed with in-jokes for an adult community of literary critics, offering a virtual festival of solecism, pun, and bowdlerization: "The Guppee Army—or 'Library'—had completed the process of 'Pagination and Collation'—that is to say, arranging itself in an orderly fashion" (p. 115). In its personification of words, plots, and tropes (usually in two or three languages at once), *Haroun* develops further (and itself exemplifies) Rushdie's familiar celebration of the idea that mass-cultural "trash" and high literature may form part of a common project. More than anything, it gives moving witness to a comment Rushdie made in the depressing times just after the death sentence: "the art of literature matters to me more than just about anything else."

The Moor's Last Sigh

If *Haroun and the Sea of Stories* is a cartoon, *The Moor's Last Sigh* (1995) is a brooding saga unlike anything Rushdie had written before, save the closing chapter of *The Satanic Verses*. Its superficial similarities to Rushdie's early work—the deformed narrator, the drama of doubtful parentage, the satirical "equal time" that targets (here) Hindu revivalists and Sephardic Jews (accorded their turn like the Muslims, Parsis, and Christians targeted before)—conceal the effort to face emotion in the act of characterization, to write not about ideas so much as about people, and to do so for no other end than that they (we) *are*. In a revealing interview, Rushdie alluded to his models for the book: "It's funny how books, the classics, order you to reread them when you are preparing for a novel. I've been rereading *Wuthering Heights*. Before that, *Jane Eyre* . . . [t]hese characters possessed by personal feeling." Having surprised himself by the power of the scene of his father's death in *The Satanic Verses*, he pushed himself to try to create more of the same and to sustain it: "I've got to write about sex. . . . There is very little sex in my novels, very little stuff at all about the deep emotions. I've always been embarrassed by it, I suppose. But I've come to see that one of the things I have failed to do . . . is write about strong feeling, cathartic emotion, obsession."

The Moor's Last Sigh opens in the present-day city of Cochin on India's southwestern coast—the only part of India with a significant Jewish population. That population (today mostly relocated to Israel) had originally consisted of so-called Black Jews who had fled Jerusalem to escape Nebuchadnezzar's armies in 580 B.C.E. In the late fifth century, these exiles were joined by Jews from Babylon and Persia and finally by refugees from southern Spain, expelled with the Moors in the fifteenth century just before the time of Columbus. The initial peculiarity of the novel, then, is that it recasts the problem of immigration by grafting it onto the supposedly irreducible and originary East. Typically seen by the English as a place that people emigrate *from*, India here is represented as a place that people immigrate *to*; the immigrants are not only Jews but also the descendants of the Portuguese Christians who were the first Europeans to colonize the Malabar Coast. Invoking this historical past, *The Moor's Last Sigh* recounts the life of Moraes Zogoiby, the child of an unscrupulous Jewish merchant named Abraham and a brilliant painter named Aurora. He is born with a clubbed right hand (a mere stump in place of five fingers) and suffers from a disease that causes him to age at twice the normal rate. Although the "Moor" of the title is a family nickname based on "Moraes" (many of the names, including this one, are Portuguese), it is more apt than even the hero at first understands. Through a number of dropped hints, discovered heirlooms, and clever deductions, the Moor gradually lets on to the reader the secret at the heart of the novel. "Zogoiby" means "the un-

fortunate one" and was the surname given to Sultan Boabdil, the last Muslim ruler of Granada. "El último suspiro del Moro" (literally, "the moor's last sigh") designates Boabdil's submission as he bids farewell to his lost kingdom. (A dry run for this exploration of life in the Spanish court, and a foretaste of how Rushdie will associate it with "a certain cosmopolitan tone," is found in his story, "Christopher Columbus and Queen Isabella of Spain Consummate Their Relationship [Santa Fe, A.D. 1492]," in *East, West: Stories*.)

In what has now become a familiar sort of development in Rushdie's work, Moraes discovers that his father is descended from a union between Boabdil (a Muslim) and a Jewish concubine, which makes him (the Moor) not only a bastard but also a living civil war. This is only one of the many dirty secrets lurking beneath this family romance, and the story, in that sense, can be characterized best as a meditation on scandal. The logic of the narrative is to expose the incarnations of Boabdil through the generations; each of his descendants embodies the paradigm of the life-weary coward who abandons his native land without a fight. The exposition is provided by Moraes as narrator, but the exposure is brought about even more vividly by Aurora, his mother, who as a national celebrity of enormous stature, has painted an allegorical "Moor" cycle in which this entire perfidious lineage from Renaissance Spain to contemporary Bombay is recorded. Although the nominal hero of the novel is the Moor, the story really belongs to Aurora. As in *Shame*, women are the powerful ones here—by far the most numerous, positive, and effectual characters in the novel. Thus Aurora at one point explains (with the likes of Boabdil on her mind): "Here's a tautology . . . 'Weak man' " (p. 169). Later she taunts Nehru himself for fawning after (and possibly bedding) Lady Mountbatten.

The action of *The Moor's Last Sigh* describes the unwelcome metamorphosis, over three generations, of the hopeful India that Rushdie had known as a child. This is arguably his most anxious and despairing novel. From the more or less patrician hierarchies of colonialism, through the democratic bid of the national movement, India in *The Moor's Last Sigh* is consumed by a struggle between two kinds of mafia: the "criminal-entrepreneurial" and the "political-criminal." These positions are taken up, respectively, by the Moor's father, Abraham, and by Raman Fielding, a right-wing fundamentalist Hindu who leads a revivalist party called Mumbai's Axis. (Fielding is based on the real-life leader of Shiv Sena, Bal Thackeray.) With the conquistador name "da Gama," Moraes' ancestors had made a fortune in the spice trade, but now, after much thuggery and terrorism, the spice trade has become the drug trade, and it involves a conspiracy to commandeer nuclear weapons for the purpose of high-stakes corporate extortion. Meanwhile, Raman "Mainduck" Fielding's legions profit well from the business scam known as religion. The idealism of the da Gamas' past that is treated in the earlier chapters—Francisco's involvement in the Home Rule League, for example, or Camoens' active support for communism—disintegrates midway through the novel. Moraes (who shames himself by working as a torturer and strikebreaker for Fielding) is forced finally to admit that the only thing that can prevent Hindu fascism in India is corruption and bribery; the choices are religious extremism (the past's idealism gone haywire), on the one hand, or some financial racket, on the other, choices which hardly differ in nature or effects. Both alternatives represent the " 'Indian variation' upon the theme of Einstein's General Theory: *Everything is for relative. Not only light bends, but everything. For relative we can bend a point, bend the truth, bend employment criteria, bend the law. . . .*" (p. 272). Bombay is seen, then, like the Granada of old: as the warring of unscrupulous entrepreneurs and political strongmen reaches a cataclysmic fury by the end of the novel, for Bombay as for Granada, the barbarians are at the gates.

The exception in this general condition of decline is Aurora—"the great beauty at the heart of the nationalist movement" (p. 116)—who draws around her the cream of the political and artistic intelligentsia and whose extraordinary paintings—including her masterpiece, *The Moor's Last Sigh*—line the walls of the world's great museums. The "torrential reality of India" had "awakened her soul." She thrives until her evil counterpart, Uma (whose name, like her own, means "dawn") begins an affair with Moraes. Knowing Uma to be a liar and a traitor, Aurora disapproves, while Uma herself eggs on Moraes with sexual fantasies that include pretending to commit incest with his own mother. The novel, in fact, comprises a long string of sexual encounters—as though Rushdie's point was that the da Gama family made love to kill its pain: there are Abraham and Aurora's trysts in

the sarcophagus of a local church; Isabelle (Aurora's mother and the wife of Camoens), with her countless liaisons while her husband is in prison; middle-aged Abraham's procurements of teenage girls, and Moraes' own sexual coming-of-age with Uma. Indeed, the indecent sensuality appears at times to be an antidote to religion, as one character confuses "secular socialist" with "circular sexualist."

When Aurora is murdered, Moraes seeks revenge and murders the obvious suspect, Fielding, in turn. Sick of the cynicism and violence in India, and appalled by his own role in the thuggery, the Moor flees Bombay when it is destroyed in a fiery cataclysm of gangland wars sparked by the murder of Fielding. As if to undo the past of shame begun by Boabdil centuries before, and with continued residence in Bombay impossible, Moraes finds comfort in the idea of "returning" to the Europe of his ancestors—Moorish, Jewish, and Christian: the Iberian peninsula, specifically Granada (in present-day Spain) where Boabdil had uttered his parting sigh.

The Jewish subtheme throughout the novel, evident in its early setting in Cochin and in the character Abraham, now becomes prominent. For Moraes here enacts a type of Zionism, except that his "Zion" (that is, his people's lost fatherland, their place of return from foreign bondage) is not—as for most Jews—Palestine, but Spain. Spain is where the Muslim, the Jewish, and the Christian once created a common culture and thus once coalesced in him; that is, all three contributed to making him. Hence, in a typically Rushdian pun, Moraes calls Granada his "Palimpstine" (suggesting both Palestine and palimpsest) and his "Moorusalem" (suggesting both Moor and Jerusalem), alluding to the locales of traditional Zionist longing while intimating a cultural and religious mixing and a geographical arbitrariness. It is an arbitrariness, moreover, that he *welcomes,* doing so quite out of step with the uncompromising, messianic exclusivism of Zionism itself. For it is not the real Granada but an invented one to which he returns— a Spanish town with the very Indian-sounding name "Benegeli," lying between La Mancha and Andalusia, and thereby evoking what he calls "the fabulous multiple culture of Ancient al-Andalus" (p. 398).

Such acts of historical—rather than merely personal—"return" also mean that one brings to the new place much of the cultural baggage of the country left behind. Thus, when Moraes arrives in Benegeli, he is imprisoned by his mother's former lover, the sentimentalist painter Vasco Miranda, who cannot forgive Moraes for his criminal past and who seeks revenge on the woman who spurned him in the only way he can—through her son. And the prison tower Miranda has built, a replica of the famous Alhambra (a castle and Moorish architectural masterpiece) can only remind Moraes of the Red Fort in Delhi (a famous castle from India's Mughal—that is, Muslim—era). We learn at the end that the entire novel has been narrated by Moraes from this prison.

The vengeful acts of Vasco turn out, then, to be productive. In a fit of jealousy toward Aurora because of her superior talents and fame (as well as her romantic indifference to him), Vasco had earlier stolen many of Aurora's most famous paintings, including *The Moor's Last Sigh*, which is revealed to be a palimpsest—its hidden picture betrays her true murderer. She was killed not by Fielding at all, but by Abraham, her husband and the Moor's father. India, too, is a palimpsest, obviously, and the return to "Zion" is something everyone (not only Jews) can claim, although what one finds there may not be pretty, although a people's origins as the "chosen" may not be pure.

POLITICAL AND LITERARY JOURNALISM

WITHOUT being journalistic in the bad sense, Rushdie's fiction has always demonstrated the ease and confrontational wit of his best journalism. Consistently provocative and honorably dissident, his magazine writing has helped secure his place in British and American letters. His prolific reviewing, moreover, has provided a map of his contemporary influences, influences that together form a consensus: on the late-twentieth-century globe, literary creativity cannot be pried away from politics and history. The rise of the Internet, the decline of storytelling, even the wasteland of television— none of these can destroy the novel, which is rescued by new genres that "blur fact and fiction" (Ryszard Kapuściński), that partake of Tom Wolfe's New Journalism, or that explore new departures in so-called travel writing. In a number of places Rushdie reiterates his belief that the novel will win

out, or at least survive in good health, precisely because it is a low-tech form: "Means of artistic expression that require large quantities of finance and sophisticated technology—films, plays, records— become, by virtue of that dependence, easy to censor and to control. But what one writer can make in the solitude of one room is something no power can easily destroy."

Rushdie had, of course, tried his own hand at travel writing when he accepted an invitation in 1986 to attend the seventh-anniversary celebrations of the Nicaraguan revolution in Esteli, Nicaragua. *The Jaguar Smile: A Nicaraguan Journey* (1987), although adopting at times the ambiguous language of parable, was a work of partisan support for the revolutionary government. Active throughout the early 1980s in the London-based Nicaragua Solidarity Campaign, Rushdie had taken on the task of intervening in a heated public debate. The book contains admiring portraits of every Sandinista leader except the minister of culture, Ernesto Cardenal—whom Rushdie found to be too uncritical of Cuba, and who directed an office that, according to Rushdie, is appropriately named "Minicult." The trip to Nicaragua allowed Rushdie his first personal look at Latin America as "the home of anti-realism"—an appellation, he argues (in one of the book's anecdotes about Rabindranath Tagore), that applies as well to India. In Matagalpa, "[García Márquez's] Macondo did not seem very far away."

Rushdie refrains from—and objects to—any cross-cultural comparisons that are reductive. In " 'Commonwealth Literature' Does Not Exist" (collected in *Imaginary Homelands*) Rushdie warns against thinking about world fiction in terms of national "essences"—as so many do who have been trained in "English" or "French" departments. The many English literatures being written in the postcolonial era cannot be chained down by categories cooked up to describe the earlier political alliances of the British Empire. Rushdie asserts that, as a category, "Commonwealth literature" is not even coherent: while the term is used to include writing from South Africa and Pakistan, neither country was ever a part of the Commonwealth. And if Commonwealth literature includes writing by South Africans and Pakistanis, why not writing by black Americans and the Irish, or why not work by writers *from* the actual Commonwealth who write in Hindi or Gikuyu? "Not only was [Commonwealth literature] a ghetto, but it was actually an exclusive ghetto," Rushdie writes (p. 63). "The existence—or putative existence—of the beast distracts attention from what is actually worth looking at, what is actually going on" (p. 64). Rushdie concludes with the impatience of a schoolmaster: "Those peoples who were once colonized by the language are now rapidly remaking it, domesticating it . . . assisted by the English language's enormous flexibility and size, they are carving out large territories for themselves within its frontiers" (p. 64).

His reviews make it clear, though, that the political and magical writing of the era was coming not only from third-world locales but also from minority pockets within Europe itself, particularly Eastern Europe. In the essay "On Adventure" (1985, collected in *Imaginary Homelands*), Rushdie lingers over the central literary trope bequeathed by the imperial conquest: "[I]n our increasingly vicarious culture, the adventurers are the people who perform marvels on our behalf" (p. 224). That lineage of adventurers encompasses figures as different as "the Prodigal Son and Indiana Jones," the Pilgrim Fathers and Peter Pan, even Francis Crick and James Watson, who discovered the double helix of DNA (p. 222). In his reviewing Rushdie moves from Western masters of "adventure" like Kipling and Orwell to Eastern ones (Rian Malan and Nuruddin Farah) to non-English Europeans—Günter Grass, Andrei Sakharov, Siegfried Lenz, and Michel Tournier. With a special zest for film criticism, Rushdie's panning of Richard Attenborough's *Gandhi* and his cautionary doubts about the paralyzing pessimism of Terry Gilliam's dystopian film *Brazil* are especially memorable. What strikes one in both reviews, again, is not merely their masterfully dismissive rhetoric but their return to the question: What, then, is the actual case on which the art is based? Rushdie links aesthetic judgment to historical accuracy (or more properly, *in*accuracy). *Gandhi* was a bad film because it was horrible history. It was dishonest. This sort of argument turned out to be welcome, and influential, among a generation of younger journalists and literary critics in an age when media spin and plausible deniability seemed to rule. Journalists repeatedly cited Rushdie's elaboration of these arguments in another essay collected in *Imaginary Homelands*, "Outside the Whale" (1984)—a reproachful look at a spate of 1980s films and television programs that portrayed the British Raj in an appealing light.

Rushdie's piece ends with a rejection of Orwell's celebrated essays "Inside the Whale" and "Politics and the English Language." Upset with Orwell's quietism in those pieces, Rushdie counters it with an empirical finality: "The truth is that there is no whale. We live in a world without hiding places" (p. 99), and the writer is therefore "obliged to accept that he (or she) is part of the crowd, part of the ocean, part of the storm . . . radioactive with history and politics" (p. 100).

As Rushdie would demonstrate in his close textual analysis of song lyrics in *The Wizard of Oz*, he is not just a critic of ideas. Poking fun at incompetent *style* is a key weapon in his critical arsenal— clear, for example, in his memorable demolition of Benazir Bhutto's memoir *Daughter of the East*, where he speaks of the book's "staccato ghost-voice that hates verbs and is much enamoured of sound effects" (in *Imaginary Homelands*, p. 56). Throughout his critical writing Rushdie repeatedly comes back to problems of form, with particular interest in the generic particularity of the novel. Calling novelists "comicbook action heroes," and the novel "the most freakish, hybrid and metamorphic of forms," he sees the novels as ways of "dreaming the world." "In Defense of the Novel, Yet Again" (first published in the *New Yorker*, 24 June–1 July 1996) takes on George Steiner, who had argued (yet again) at a British Publishers' Association meeting that the novel was dead. Rushdie dubbed such a view "culturally endemic goldenageism: that recurring, bilious nostalgia for a literary past that at the time didn't seem much better than the present does now" (p. 49). Steiner had conceded that great novels are still coming out of India, the Caribbean, and Latin America, and Rushdie zeros in on the mere Eurocentrism of Steiner's lament: "What is this flat earth on which the good Professor lives, with jaded Romans at the center and frightfully gifted Hottentots and anthropophagi lurking at the edges? . . . Might it not be simply that a new novel is emerging—a postcolonial novel, a decentered, transnational, interlingual, cross-cultural novel—and that in this new world order, or disorder, we find a better explanation of the contemporary novel's health . . . ?" (p. 50).

Redefining America's place in the world—or rather, dramatizing its false innocence—is a major theme of Rushdie's political journalism. In "Goodness—the American Neurosis" (*Nation*, 22 March 1986), he contrasts the British Empire's urge for "greatness" with that of the United States: "The American madness seems to be located not in the idea of being great, but in that of being good." But even the case of India shows that this American self-concept is a form of denial. The memory of Bhopal lingers as "the invasion of U.S. corporations gathers force"; each of a given region's dictators— the Shah, Ferdinand Marcos, Zia ul-Haq—is "a bit of a Yank." Giving the United States a mixed review—for he feels a great affinity for the America "composed of dissident cultures: black, gay, feminist, even, I dare say, socialist"—Rushdie finds his harshest words for America's "revival of religious fundamentalism," then competing in ferocity for the much more vilified Islamic revival. He gives both types of fundamentalism a sensitive (and lengthy) analysis in "In God We Trust" (1985).

Daring to enter debates that few of his stature had, and with much to lose, Rushdie did not stop short of publicly siding with the Palestinian cause in the Middle East ("On Palestinian Identity: A Conversation with Edward Said," 1986, collected in *Imaginary Homelands*). Nor did he recoil from positions even closer to home, identifying himself with the Charter 88 group founded by Harold Pinter, which had set out to give England a legal constitution, limit the arbitrary powers of government, and bequeath British citizens a bill of rights. Just as he had described India's postwar democracy as a "dynasty" of the Nehru family (Jawaharlal, Indira, Sanjay, Rajiv), he took the Thatcher government head-on in an election postmortem of 1988 ("A General Election," reprinted in *Imaginary Homelands*) in language that demonstrates both the bite of his humor and his notorious capacity to offend: "A Tory Prime Minister, Maggie May . . . add[s] almost two million people to the dole queues," raises taxes, leaves manufacturing "in ruins," "robs Britons of their 900-year-old right to citizenship" by birth, squanders North Sea oil revenue, and lets inflation run wild (p. 159). The "fictional" Prime Minister May does "come across as unusually cruel, incompetent, unscrupulous and violent" but "instead of being hounded into the outer darkness, or at least Tasmania, like her namesake, it seems that she is to receive a vote of confidence; that five more years of cruelty, incompetence, etc., is what the electorate wants" (p. 160).

It is in passages like these that one sees in full display the ethical energy and political hunger of Rushdie's work as a whole. If *Midnight's Children*

had been composed—as one of its metafictional asides had it—as though from newspaper clippings scattered by the wind, the truth is that all of his fiction is made up of current events. The political is not merely allowed into the fabulous but lies at its core. And if Rushdie, moreover, can be said to have had to struggle with typical novelistic skills such as plotting and characterization (*The Satanic Verses* and *The Moor's Last Sigh* are both more mature in these respects than the early novels), the wit and bite of the individual sentence, the satirical jab, the uncanny flavor of a particular accent—all of those tools, in other words, of the feature journalist—were his from the start, and with such assurance that they seemed at times his unique possession. Whatever his accomplishments as a novelist, Rushdie is completely at home in the genres of news feature and editorial, and they are arguably the most confident and crafted side of his work.

SELECTED BIBLIOGRAPHY

I. FICTION. *Grimus* (London, 1975); *Midnight's Children* (London and New York, 1980); "The Golden Bough," in *Granta* 7 (1982); *Shame* (London and New York, 1983); *The Satanic Verses* (London, 1988; New York, 1989); "Untime of the Imam," in *Harper's* (December 1988); *Haroun and the Sea of Stories* (London and New York, 1990); *East, West: Stories* (London, 1994); *The Moor's Last Sigh* (London and New York, 1995).

II. NONFICTION. *The Jaguar Smile: A Nicaraguan Journey* (London, 1987); *Imaginary Homelands: Essays and Criticism, 1981–1991* (London and New York, 1991); *The Wizard of Oz* (London, 1992).

III. ARTICLES. "The Empire Writes Back with a Vengeance," in *Times* (3 July 1982); "I Borrowed My Expressions from the East," in *Muslim Magazine* (18 November 1983); "Casualties of Censorship," in George Theiner, ed., *They Shoot Writers, Don't They?* (New York, 1984); "A Dangerous Art Form," in *Third World Book Review* 1 (1984); "Dynasty and Democracy," in *New Republic* (26 November 1984); "*Midnight's Children* and *Shame*," in *Kunapipi* 7 no. 1 (1985); "The Press: International Viewpoint," in *Times Literary Supplement* (21 February 1986); "Goodness—The American Neurosis," in *Nation* (22 March 1986); "After Midnight," in *Vanity Fair* (September 1987); "My Book Speaks for Itself," in *New York Times* (17 February 1989); "A Clash of Faiths," in *Maclean's* (27 February 1989); "The Book Burning," in *New York Review of Books* (2 March 1989); "Fact, Faith, and Fiction," in *Far Eastern Economic Review* (2 March 1989); "Clandestine in

Chile," in *Times Literary Supplement* (6 October 1989); "In Good Faith," in *Independent* (4 February 1990); "One Thousand Days in a Balloon" (excerpt), in *New York Times* (12 December 1991), repr., with "Reply," in Mac-Donogh, ed., *The Rushdie Letters* (1993; see "Critical Studies: On *The Satanic Verses* Affair"); "Angela Carter, 1940–92: A Very Good Wizard, a Very Dear Friend," in *New York Times Book Review* (8 March 1992); "Heavy Threads," in *New Yorker* (7 November 1994); "Defeating the *Fatwa*, in *Nation* (11 March 1996); "How News Becomes Opinion, and Opinion Becomes Off-Limits," in *Nation* (24 June 1996); "In Defense of the Novel, Yet Again," in *New Yorker* (24 June–1 July 1996).

IV. FILM. *The Riddle of Midnight*. London, 1987. Aired on Channel 4, March 1988. Shown at Retrospective of Indian Cinema, the Galerie Nationale du Jeu de Paume, 12 December–11 February 1995.

V. INTERVIEWS. Sarah Crichton and Laura Shapiro, "An Exclusive Talk with Salman Rushdie," in *Newsweek* (12 February 1990); Gerald Marzorati, "Rushdie in Hiding: An Interview," in *New York Times Magazine* (4 November 1990); Karsten Prager, "Free Speech Is Life Itself," in *Time* (23 December 1991); Geraldine Brooks, "Salman Rushdie: My Lunch with a Condemned Man," in *New Republic* (27 July 1992); John Banville, "An Interview with Salman Rushdie," in *New York Review of Books* (4 March 1993); Sybil Steinberg, "A Talk with Salman Rushdie: Six Years into the *Fatwa*," in *Publishers Weekly* (30 January 1995).

VI. CRITICAL STUDIES: GENERAL. Timothy Brennan, *Salman Rushdie and the Third World: Myths of the Nation* (London, 1989); James Harrison, *Salman Rushdie* (New York, 1992); M. Madhusudhana Rao, *Salman Rushdie's Fiction: A Study, Satanic Verses Excluded* (New Delhi, 1992); G. R. Taneja and R. K. Dhawan, eds., *The Novels of Salman Rushdie* (New Delhi, 1992); Fawzia Afzal-Khan, *Cultural Imperialism and the Indo-English Novel: Genre and Ideology in R. K. Narayan, Anita Desai, Kamala Markandaya, and Salman Rushdie* (University Park, Pa., 1993); M. D. Fletcher, ed., *Reading Rushdie: Perspectives on the Fiction of Salman Rushdie* (Amsterdam, 1994).

VII. CRITICAL STUDIES: ON *THE SATANIC VERSES* AFFAIR. Shabbir Akhtar, *Be Careful with Muhammad: The Salman Rushdie Affair* (London, 1989); Munawar Ahmad Anees, *The Kiss of Judas: Affairs of a Brown Sahib* (Kuala Lampur, Malaysia, 1989); Lisa Appignanesi and Sara Maitland, eds., *The Rushdie File* (Syracuse, N.Y., 1989); Bernard E. Dold, *Salman Rushdie's Britannic Verses: A Bad Case of Culture Shock* (Messina, Italy, 1989); Mohammad T. Mehdi, *Islam and Intolerance—A Reply to Salman Rushdie* (Herts, 1989); Muhammad Mustapha, *An Islamic Overview of* The Satanic Verses (Trinidad and Tobago, 1989); Mutaharunnisa Omer, *The Holy Prophet and the Satanic Slander* (Madras, India, 1989); Fay Weldon, *Sacred Cows* (London, 1989); Dan Cohn-Sherbok, ed., *The Salman Rushdie Controversy in Interreligious Perspective* (Lewiston, 1990); Simon Lee, *The Cost of Free Speech* (London, 1990); Daniel Pipes, *The Rushdie Affair: The Novel, the Ayatollah, and the West* (New York, 1990); Malise Ruthven, *A Satanic Affair: Salman Rushdie and the Rage of Islam* (London, 1990); Ziauddin Sardar and Merryl Wyn Davies, *Distorted Imagination: Lessons from the Rushdie Affair* (London, 1990); William J. Weatherby, *Salman Rushdie: Sentenced to Death* (New York, 1990); Richard Webster, *A Brief History of Blasphemy: Liberalism, Censorship and* The Satanic Verses (Southwold, England, 1990).

M. M. Ahsan and A. R. Kidwai, eds., *Sacrilege Versus Civility: Muslim Perspectives on the* Satanic Verses *Affair* (Leicester, England, 1991); Daniel Easterman, *New Jerusalems: Reflections on Islam, Fundamentalism, and the Rushdie Affair* (London, 1992); Anouar Abdallah et al., *Pour Rushdie: Cent intellectuels arabes et musulmans pour la liberté d'expression* (Paris, 1993), trans. as *For Rushdie: Essays by Arab and Muslim Writers in Defense of Free Speech* (New York, 1994); Talal Asad, *Genealogies of Religion: Discipline and Reasons of Power in Christianity and Islam* (Baltimore, 1993); Leonard Williams Levy, *Blasphemy: Verbal Offense Against the Sacred from Moses to Salman Rushdie* (New York, 1993); Steve MacDonogh, in association with Article 19, ed., *The Rushdie Letters: Freedom to Speak, Freedom to Write* (Dingle, Ireland, 1993).

VIII. SPECIAL ISSUES OF JOURNALS. *Impact International* 18, no. 20 (October/November 1988); *Commonwealth Review* 1, no. 2 (1990); *Index on Censorship* 19, no. 4 (April 1990); *Third Text* 11 (summer 1990); *Profession* (1994).

CHRISTINA STEAD

(1902–1983)

Louise Yelin

CHRISTINA STEAD WAS born in Australia but lived much of her life in England, Europe, and the United States. Primarily known as a novelist, she was also a prolific writer of essays and reviews. Stead's novels reflect her peripatetic life; most of them were published in England or the United States before they were published in Australia, and they are set in Sydney, Paris, London, Washington, New York, Switzerland, and other places. Although at various times in her life Stead identified herself as an Australian, her national identity is very much in question. Her wanderings made her, at different points in her career, an expatriate Australian writer, an Australian-American writer, an English writer. She never quite belonged to any of the nations she lived in or to any of the cultures she traveled through.

Why, then, include her in a volume on British writers? One reason for doing so is that, although she began writing in Australia as a young woman, she was first published in England. Her career was made possible by her exile from Australia and her residence in London. A more important reason for considering Stead a British writer, however, has to do with changes, over the past thirty years or so, in notions of British literature itself. Angela Carter remarks, in "Unhappy Families" (1982), that Stead, who became known as an Australian writer rather late in life after she returned to Australia to live, exemplifies a postcolonial sensibility, one that is an increasingly important component of British cultural identity. Paradoxically, Stead's Australian beginnings and the unsettled, exilic perspective that made her an outsider everywhere now make her an exemplar, or at least a forerunner, of a new kind of British literature, one that reflects the recent, postwar, postimperial history of Britain and its former empire.

Stead's work is defined by conflicts and tensions in her treatment of class and national politics and sexual politics and by an intense interest in language. Throughout her life she rejected gender constraints that nevertheless followed her around the world. Her novels brilliantly interrogate the situation and experiences of women—particularly white middle-class women—through much of the twentieth century and across several national cultures. But she seems, as Hazel Rowley amply demonstrates in *Christina Stead: A Biography* (1993), to have felt little or no solidarity with other women, and she eschewed identification as a feminist or "woman writer." In fact, Stead often works in a genre, the encyclopedic political novel or novel of ideas, which in its traditional, European guise has been the province of male writers such as Honoré de Balzac and Stendhal, whom she revered. Yet the most sustained and systematic critical attention she has received—three books and part of a fourth—has been the work of feminist literary critics Joan Lidoff, Diana Brydon, Susan Sheridan, and Judith Kegan Gardiner, who have focused on constructions of gender in her work; and in the 1970s and 1980s her books were reissued by the British feminist publisher Virago Press.

Soon after leaving Australia in 1928, Stead met her life partner, an American Marxist writer and economist named William Blech (later changed to Blake), whom she eventually married. In part as a result of her relationship with Blake, Stead inhabited left-wing circles in London, Paris, and New York in the 1930s and 1940s. She was sympathetic to, but not a member of, the Communist party, and a recurrent theme in her work is a left-inflected critique of the commercialization of culture. Yet her novels are ideologically heterodox, and she brings her satirical gaze to bear on any and all persons, topics, and cultural and political institutions, left, right, and center.

Stead's strongest literary feature is her feeling for language, her ear for the idiosyncratic voices of unusual individuals, her eye for the telling detail that evokes settings as diverse as Sydney in the 1920s, Baltimore in the 1930s, and Tyneside in the 1950s. Yet her novels are so loosely plotted that any summary runs the risk of substantially misrepresenting them by eliding the rhetorical excesses, the sheer mass of words, that are hallmarks of her novelistic practice. These excesses, as well as an inattention to conventions of plotting and characterization, make many of the novels difficult to read.

Stead's inaccessibility may be partly responsible for an apparent lapse in her career, from the early 1950s to the mid 1960s. Between 1934 and 1952 Stead published nine books—a collection of stories and eight novels—and although none of these was exactly a best-seller, her early work, at least, was praised by critics as diverse as Clifton Fadiman and Alfred Kazin and found a receptive audience. Between 1952 and 1965 she published no books at all. Then, in 1965, through the efforts of Stanley Burnshaw, *The Man Who Loved Children* (originally published in 1934) was reissued in the United States, with an introduction in which Randall Jarrell proclaimed it a masterpiece. Jarrell suggested that Stead had stopped writing because her work was poorly received, but he was not quite accurate, for she continued writing even though she had difficulty finding publishers. Jose Yglesias reviewed the reissue of *The Man Who Loved Children* in the *Nation* and, comparing Stead to Theodore Dreiser, argued that it was her unorthodox left-wing perspective that had, during the dark years of the blacklist and the Cold War, prevented her from finding the audience she deserved.

Now, Burnshaw and Jarrell inaugurated a Stead revival, and Yglesias, too, helped bring about the second phase of her career: in the ten years after the reissue of *The Man Who Loved Children*, she published three new novels (a fourth was published posthumously) and a collection of novellas, and several of her earlier works were reissued in the United States, Britain, and Australia. Yet this apparent burst of creativity was in part a mirage, since the novels published in the 1960s and 1970s had been begun and probably substantially completed during the 1950s, when she could not find sympathetic readers. Yglesias' review claimed *The Man Who Loved Children* for a nascent New Left, which, along with the feminist movement that Stead emphatically rejected, provided many of the readers who enthusiastically turned or returned to her work in the late 1960s, 1970s, and into the

1980s. Australians, too, eventually claimed Stead as one of their own, assuring her reputation in her native land as well as in the United States and Britain. Special issues and sections devoted to Stead in journals such as *Contemporary Literature,* published in the United States, *World Literature Written in English,* published in Canada, and *Southerly,* published in Australia, have begun to situate her in the multiple contexts in which her work was produced and read. The five novels discussed in detail below illustrate her thematic, formal, and geographical range.

EARLY LIFE

CHRISTINA Stead was born in Rockdale, near Sydney, Australia, on 17 July 1902. Her parents were Ellen (née Butters) and David Stead, a distinguished naturalist who worked in a variety of government posts. When Christina was just two years old, her mother died. David soon met a woman named Ada Gibbins, and on 1 January 1907, they were married. Ada and David are the models for Henny and Sam Pollit in Stead's best-known book, the autobiographical *Man Who Loved Children.* Within ten years six more children were born. Christina felt very much excluded by Ada, who treated her differently from her own children, while David, a great talker and storyteller and the dominant influence in the household, both fostered her intellectual development and made her feel inadequate because she did not meet his standards of feminine beauty. Hazel Rowley observes in her biography of Stead that "those who feel rejected have an uncomfortable way of making sure they really are. Christina was to become, as a writer, an observer, a professional outsider" (p. 16).

Stead attended school in Sydney. By early adolescence she knew she was going to be a writer. She read widely: Charles Darwin, British and European authors, especially Charles Dickens, and the stories of the Australians Henry Lawson, Banjo Paterson, and Steele Rudd. After graduating from high school, she entered Sydney Teachers' College in 1920, completing a two-year training course. She began teaching in January 1923, after a year spent as a demonstrator in experimental psychology at the teachers college. But she soon lost her voice, and in 1925, after a stint as a junior lecturer in psychology and another brief effort at teaching, she gave up teaching altogether for clerical work. During this time Stead wrote a book of children's stories, which her father sent to the publishing firm of Angus & Robertson. The publisher rejected the book, claiming it could not find a large enough audience in Australia. The book was never published because the manuscript was later lost.

In 1928 Stead left Sydney and went to London. Not long after arriving there, she found a job at a grain importing and exporting firm as secretary to William Blech. Early the next year Stead agreed to accompany Blech to Paris, where he was to work in a private investment bank; she, too, worked in the bank from time to time. By February 1929 the two had become lovers, beginning what was to be a lifelong relationship. (They were married on 23 February 1952, after Blake's first wife finally agreed to divorce him.) In London, in the winter of 1928–1929, Stead wrote *Seven Poor Men of Sydney*. As she explains in "A Writer's Friends," an essay about those who furthered her career as a writer, Blake took the manuscript to Sylvia Beach, proprietor of Shakespeare & Company in Paris, who admired it. Beach's appreciation gave them the confidence to send it to England, where a friend submitted it to the publisher Peter Davies. He agreed to publish the novel if she would give him another, more conventional book first. She began a novel, but gave it up and wrote *The Salzburg Tales*, a collection of related short stories loosely modeled on Giovanni Boccaccio's *Decameron*. Both books were published in 1934.

SEVEN POOR MEN OF SYDNEY

Seven Poor Men of Sydney is set in the 1910s and 1920s. Historical events, such as World War I, the 1925 Australian seamen's strike, and the Depression, are mentioned almost as asides or as they influence the lives of the novel's characters. More important than history is the sense of place, the natural environment around what Stead calls Fisherman's Bay (drawn from Watson's Bay, where her childhood home was located) and the modern, urban geography of Sydney. Stead wrote the novel in London, far from the scene she portrays, yet she makes Sydney—its houses, alleys, courtyards, streets, parks, and museums—palpable, alive, almost like a character itself. The distance between England and Australia may be what animates the

novel, which explores, among other things, problems of cultural authority, specifically, the marginality of colonials (Australians) and women and the relation of these groups to British and predominantly masculine or patriarchal literary traditions.

The novel is not focused on one protagonist, but rather on a group, the title characters and a few of their friends and associates. In this, it resembles Virginia Woolf's *The Waves* (1931), which was published first but written at virtually the same moment. Unlike Woolf's text, which explores the effects of the uneven distribution of privilege and power on upper-middle-class men and women, Stead's is concerned with the ways that poverty and deprivation shape members of the white, colonial, working and lower-middle class. The "seven poor men" include three who work as printers, Joseph Baguenault, Tom Withers, and Baruch Mendelssohn; their employer, Gregory Chamberlain, who keeps his struggling business afloat by not paying their wages; their friend Tom Winter, a Communist who works for a union library; Joseph's cousin Michael Baguenault, a drifter who enlists in the army and returns, shell-shocked, from his experiences in World War I; and Michael's friend Kol Blount, who is disabled as a result of a childhood accident. Michael, who cannot find a place in the world the novel describes, and his sister, Catherine, who as a woman is excluded from the class or group designated as "poor men," are the central focus of the novel. Among the other important characters are Fulke Folliot and his wife, Marion, wealthy socialists with whom Catherine and Michael are erotically entangled.

The novel begins with a remarkable description of a landscape at once natural and transformed by human intervention:

The hideous low scarred yellow horny and barren headland lies curled like a scorpion in a blinding sea and sky. At night, house-lamps and ships' lanterns burn with a rousing shine, and the headlights of cars swing over Fisherman's Bay. In the day, the traffic of the village crawls along the skyline, past the lighthouse and signal station, and drops by cleft and volcanic gully to the old village that has a bare footing on the edge of the bay. It was, and remains, a military and maritime settlement.

(p. 1)

This scene, a site of obscurity and missed opportunity, is identified with the Baguenault family, whose unfulfilled longings are foreshadowed in this early description:

There was a family there named Baguenault, which had settled in the bay directly after its arrival from Ireland thirty years before, and had its roots growing down into the soil and rocky substratum so that nothing seemed to be able to uproot it any more, so quiet, so circumspect in the narrow life of the humble, it lived; but disaster fell on it, and its inner life, unexpressed, incoherent, unplanned, like most lives, then became visible as a close and tangled web to the neighbours and to itself, to whom it had for so long remained unknown. Who can tell what minor passions running in the undergrowth of poor lives will burst out when a storm breaks on the unknown watershed? There is water in barren hills and when rain comes they spurt like fountains, where the water lies on impermeable rocks.

(pp. 2–3)

Prefigured in this extraordinary opening, the tragedy that erupts in the novel that follows is the suicide of Michael Baguenault, who kills himself by jumping off a cliff into the rocky bay. But the entire novel is a record of "minor passions . . . in the undergrowth of poor lives."

Seven Poor Men of Sydney, like many of Stead's later novels, has relatively little plot. The narrative moves, almost drifts, from one character to another, describing the thoughts and feelings of each, showing us how they see themselves and each other. Withers, a disagreeable, aggressively selfish individualist, and Chamberlain, an exploiter who succeeds, at least temporarily, by getting his victims to go along with his schemes, are sketches for types fleshed out in Stead's later work in figures such as Robbie Grant, the monstrous main character of *A Little Tea, a Little Chat* (1948). Winter is a loyal and committed Communist; his class consciousness, while correct in theory, does not lead to effective political strategies. Michael, Catherine, Baruch, Kol, and Joseph, who are somewhat more developed than the other characters, represent different versions of stifled talent and creativity, different aspects of Australianness, and thus alternative destinies for Stead.

Michael, who works briefly in an advertising agency, is the main vehicle of Stead's critique of commercialized popular culture, a theme that recurs in many of her novels. Unable to marry or otherwise settle down, he carries on flirtations and affairs with various women, one of whom con-

vinces him to enlist in the army. When he returns to Australia, in 1919, he is "weathered and self-centred" and undergoes "nerve treatment" (p. 56). Subsequently, he lives on the fringes of Sydney's bohemian and left-wing cultures. His relationship with his sister Catherine—sometimes antagonistic, he also sees her as an extension of himself: "I have come to love my sister as myself, for you are myself," he says at one point (p. 274)—recalls that of Heathcliff and Catherine in Emily Brontë's *Wuthering Heights*.

Baruch Mendelssohn is the novel's version of a homegrown intellectual. He works in Chamberlain's print shop, offers a running commentary on matters large and small, and understands almost intuitively that the future for men like him lies outside Australia. At the end of the novel, he leaves the "brothers of [his] past, in the antipodes," and immigrates to the United States (p. 310), where he has found a job as secretary to an industrialist. Generous, voluble, and incisive in his analysis, he is the first of many characters that Stead based on her husband. As an emigrant from Australia to the United States, he suggests aspects of the author as well.

Baruch is the mentor of Joseph (Jo) Baguenault, cousin of Catherine and Michael. Joseph is a product of the "accumulated misery, shame, hunger and ignorance of centuries" (p. 96). In an attempt to provoke him to demand the wages he is owed, Baruch tells him, "You have the colour of a race worn thin" (p. 97). Winter, the Communist who tries to awaken Jo's consciousness of class oppression, explains that Australians "all got to work here to keep four thousand elect and fifty thousand mean little rentiers in the boardin'-houses of London. Because 'their Whitehall' is breakin' the sheep's back" (p. 170). But Joseph's subjection to bourgeois and colonialist ways of thinking, including but not limited to the Roman Catholic guilt enforced by his mother, who "saw the workaday world through a confessional grille" (p. 66), is virtually absolute; he counters both Winter and Mendelssohn that Australians—that is, working men like himself—are lazy. When Joseph loses his job because the print shop closes, he joins the thousands who are unemployed. Eventually, he finds work, meets a woman, and marries. The novel ends as he begins to tell his wife the story of his early life: "We were seven friends, at that time, yes, seven poor men . . ." (p. 319; ellipses in original).

The inconsistent, self-destructive Catherine Baguenault reflects the contradictory views about women that haunt Stead's work throughout her career. Catherine represents women's—specifically, middle-class white women's—exclusion from a political world that is gendered masculine; the boundaries of this world are evoked by the word "men" in the novel's title. Unable to find fulfilling work, to settle on something to believe in, or to love, and especially be loved, she wanders from one project to another, even living on the streets and in the doss-houses (that is, cheap rooming houses) of Sydney before committing herself to an insane asylum. Catherine graphically exemplifies the stunting of women's aspirations and desires by a repressive, misogynist, provincial culture. Baruch sees her as a "woman of revolution without a barricade" (p. 144). He makes a drawing of her, which he interprets as "the middle-class woman trying to free herself, and still impeded by romantic notions and ferocious, because ambushed, sensuality" (p. 155). Perhaps speaking for Stead, he remarks:

There are no women. . . . There are only dependent and exploited classes, of which women make one. The peculiarities are imposed on them to keep them in order. They are told from the cradle to the grave, You are a female and not altogether there, socially and politically: your brain is good but not too good, none of your race was ever a star, except in the theatre. And they believe it. We all believe these great social dogmas.

(p. 205)

Baruch's analysis of women as a class or race falls short as an explanation of Catherine, as she implies in an interior monologue, uttered while she is living in the street, that operates as a kind of credo: "In the lowest places I find my answers: I've fought all my life for male objectives in men's terms. I am neither man nor woman, rich nor poor, elegant nor worker, philistine nor artist. That's why I fight so hard and suffer so much and get nowhere. And how vain ambition seems when you look at it, unambitious" (p. 214). In insisting that she seeks "male objectives in men's terms," Catherine evokes her author, who, as Diana Brydon points out in *Christina Stead* (1987), refused to "accept her gender as a handicap" (p. 4). In any case Catherine's sense that she is a gender anomaly, "neither man nor woman," points to the lack of a language in which the experiences and aspirations of women—of whatever class—might be voiced. Indeed, her story is told by others: by the unidentified omniscient narrator, by her brother, and by Baruch.

Throughout the novel, Kol Blount serves as a kind of alter ego for Michael. Like Joseph, both men are dominated by mothers trying to compensate for their own unhappiness by controlling and living vicariously through their sons. Kol's physical paralysis has its echo in Michael's emotional atrophy. After Michael's death, Kol sums up Michael's life in a lament that identifies him with the land and the unrealized possibilities of all the peoples who have lived in Australia, from prehistoric times to the present. Toward the end of this long, lyrical outpouring of grief, Kol asks, bitterly, "Why are we here?" and says, "Eating these regurgitated ideas from the old country makes us sick and die of sickness" (p. 309). His rage is that of a colonial subject forced to confront his own lack of originality and the impotence of his culture. But it seems he will be spared Michael's fate, for, it now turns out, his paralysis, the result of "neglect and poverty" (p. 310), may be curable. The novel ends, not with Kol's outcry but with Joseph's recounting to his wife the story of his youth. This ending suggests the beneficial influence on him of Baruch and the others, but in making the story of the seven poor men the retrospective reflection of one who describes himself as "a letter of ordinary script" (p. 316), Stead underlines the continuing impoverishment of Australian culture.

If there is no one in *Seven Poor Men of Sydney* who is capable of creating an authentic and effective Australian culture, Stead, at least, attempted to realize her own ambitions by living and writing elsewhere. *Seven Poor Men of Sydney* began her career as a writer; she pursued this career, in the 1930s, through her involvement in some of the cultural institutions of the British and, later, the American Left. She was secretary to the English delegation to the First International Congress of Writers for the Defense of Culture, held in Paris in June 1935. (Other members of the delegation included E. M. Forster, Aldous Huxley, and Ralph Fox, a Communist writer who died in Spain in 1937.) Stead's report on the congress appeared in the journal *Left Review* in August 1935 under the title "The Writers Take Sides." Later that summer Stead and Blake went to New York, where they were associated with the left-wing journal *New Masses*. In 1936 Stead published her second novel, *The Beauties and*

Furies, a somewhat overheated portrayal of the adulterous passions of one Elvira Western, an English woman who, fancying herself a sexual rebel, follows a young man named Oliver Fenton from London to Paris; eventually, she reverses direction, returning to suburban, and British, respectability. In that same year Stead and Blake returned to Europe so that she could work on her next novel, which was published in 1938.

HOUSE OF ALL NATIONS

House of All Nations, first published in New York and set in Paris, is a brilliant, encyclopedic, satiric, sprawling, even plotless depiction of the world of high finance. Taken together, its 104 scenes and the numerous characters who crowd its pages show us Paris as the center of a global political economy in the 1930s. The novel's title reflects Stead's wanderings: *House of All Nations* was written in Spain, France, Belgium, the United States, and England. She had already begun work on the book when she and Blake went to Spain in the late spring of 1936; she wrote and rewrote the novel throughout 1936, 1937, and into 1938, in the shadow of the Spanish civil war and the increasingly grave threat posed in Europe by fascism in Germany and Italy.

The main focus of *House of All Nations* is the Banque Mercure, a private investment bank like the one in which Blake and Stead were employed in the early 1930s. The novel chronicles the rise and fall of the bank and its director, Jules Bertillon, a charming schemer with a knack for shady dealings. When the collapse of his bank appears imminent, Jules makes a last-ditch attempt to save it by falsifying the books so that there appears to be money on deposit. But the clients find out that the money is gone, and Jules absconds. The novel ends with the squabbling of his creditors over what little may be left. As this brief summary suggests, the bank is a microcosm, a figure for the global capitalist economy. But House of All Nations was also the name of a well-known brothel in Paris in the 1930s. Thus, Stead connects the commodification of sexuality with the capitalist economy represented by the bank.

Stead's portrayal of the Banque Mercure as a house of all nations makes her text a political novel. Ideologies left, right, and center are embodied in the characters: the owners, employees, hangers-on, and kibitzers in the bank; the industrialists, aristocrats, financiers, real estate magnates, *latifundistas,* government functionaries, rentiers, and colonial adventurers who are its clients; and the writers, lawyers, and women who offer a running commentary on the action. Among the characters in *House of All Nations* who represent left-wing ideologies are two young Communist activists, Adam Constant and Jean Frère, and a Communist economist, Michel Alphendéry, who works as an analyst in the Banque Mercure and functions as Jules Bertillon's right-hand man. Adam is a poet who is working in the Banque Mercure; he intends to join the revolutionaries in China. Jean, the "workers' writer," is a Communist party organizer. Both Adam and Jean are shown from the dual perspectives of Alphendéry and the narrator. Often, we see Adam and Jean through the eyes of Alphendéry, an intellectual who is attracted to these men of action. Thus, Stead shows us the homoerotic desire that underlies the ethos of fraternity on the Left.

All three characters are based on men whom Stead knew: Alphendéry, like Baruch Mendelssohn in *Seven Poor Men of Sydney,* is based on her husband, William Blake; Adam Constant recalls Ralph Fox, with whom Stead was in love while she was writing the novel; and Jean Frère is modeled on Mike Gold. (Stead first met Gold at the International Writers' Congress in Paris in 1935; she worked with him at *New Masses* later that summer.) Stead's Communist organizer is named for Rabelais's Friar John (Frère Jean), the hero of book 1 of *Gargantua and Pantagruel.* Frère Jean labors, defends the oppressed, comforts the afflicted, aids the suffering, and courageously leads the fight against the tyrant Picrochole, whose ambition to march through Europe and conquer all the known world would likely remind Stead's readers of Adolf Hitler's desire for conquest. Gargantua rewards Frère Jean's heroic endeavors by founding and giving him the Abbey of Thélème, a "religious order in an exactly contrary way to all others" (I, ch. 52). Stead's secular version of this order is the Communist utopia located in Jean Frère's garden. But the Communist utopia, like the bourgeois order it opposes, is a site of homosocial camaraderie from which women are excluded or in which they play a marginal role.

In opposition to the Communists Adam and Jean, Stead presents Aristide Raccamond, the closest thing the novel has to a villain. Raccamond is a flatterer, a procurer and white slaver, and a self-righteous hypocrite who professes outrage at Jules Bertillon's shenanigans. Although Raccamond is identified as a "center conservative-liberal" who "wanted no political involvements" (p. 598), he evokes fascism both in its aura of sexual unsavoriness and in its attempt to "rescue" capitalism from the liberal political order. Raccamond plots to take over the bank to "save" it and his aristocratic clients from Jules's immorality. A blackmailer who tries to further his career by extorting the last penny from an institution that symbolizes liberal capitalism, Raccamond is the agent of something like a fascist plot. As Alphendéry explains, fascism presents itself as the savior of a capitalist order it is actually destroying: "Capitalism is only vigorous as it knows freedom. The decay of the host brings the decay of the parasite. Far from saving capitalism, fascism exhausts it.... If one remembers that fascism has, so to speak, no normal internal financing and lives on repudiated loans, that is, on gifts, we perceive that it is an ugly temporary expedient" (p. 600).

Here, and throughout the *House of All Nations,* Alphendéry is the spokesman for a Marxist cultural critique that was prominent in the late 1930s, the era of the popular front. Although the manipulative Raccamond is the narrative antagonist of Jules Bertillon, Alphendéry eloquently voices opposition to Jules's opportunism. He explodes Jules's self-serving platitudes about money and banking and unmasks what Jules and his cronies obfuscate as the manipulation of "value" with "nothing" behind it. That is, Alphendéry elaborates Marx's idea that the wealth of the few is predicated on the poverty of the many and its corollary, that value in a capitalist system is always based on appropriation and exploitation.

Despite Alphendéry's astute analysis of capitalism, he is, as his author is, attracted to Jules Bertillon. In fact, Stead makes the anarchic, amoral, egotistical Jules at least ambiguously sympathetic and thereby compromises her satire of the collapse of capitalism. Jules says that he dislikes Raccamond because "he's bad luck" (p. 310), and eventually Jules and his bank are undone by a deal that rests on a bet about whether or when the British pound will go off gold:

A robber by instinct, sharpshooter of commerce by career, nourished by corruption . . . , child of his age, Jules

Bertillon was born to profit greatly by it, without understanding it in the least. He had only one interpretation of history and politics, an economic one; he saw in altruism the perspicacious self-interest of cunning ambition. . . . He admired the successful and was cheered up by all success of any kind in any sphere of activity, gangsterism, revolution, politics, roguery, or even the arts, because art, he said, was a way to get oneself fed by the rest of mankind without working or with little work by reason of inborn capacity. . . . He admired artists, for example, even more for this favoritism shown them by the stars, than for their works, because he regarded art as a rather old trick. . . . Besides this, he was full of a fantastic, ingenuous, and disarming charlatanry, and of a delicate, wise charm which knew how to simper, do a ballet step or leap strongly and agilely like the best of dancers.
(pp. 93–94)

Despite the left-wing political affiliations that might lead readers to expect Stead to condemn Jules, her attitude toward him is inconsistent. In fact, she discredits a high moral tone by associating it with the hypocritical Raccamond and, by extension, with the fascist threat to Europe. Yet ultimately, her oscillating sympathies and ambivalence do not matter, for the bank's collapse issues in a war of each against all which prefigures the world war that Stead clearly expected. The demise of the bank leads to a "dirty mass of conjecture, anxiety, doubt, self-excuse, greed, and recrimination. . . . [T]he fierce well-fed hatreds of the clients began to turn against each other. . . . All the clients banded themselves together in national protective associations, and thus the next European war began in little" (pp. 748–749).

After Jules goes into hiding, a wealthy, ultra right-wing South American named Campoverde decides to revive the bank and reconstruct the order that it represents—symbolically, to resurrect capitalism as fascism. Campoverde wants to draw in "the sportsmen, the heirs apparent, the clubmen, the beaux, and the monarchist-royalist-fascist crowd, men of the new world" (p. 764). Stead is alluding here to the right-wing and paramilitary leagues whose ascendancy in the early 1930s led Communists and Socialists to join together in a popular front to resist them. Campoverde's "new world" is in essence the climate in which the novel was written, for *House of All Nations*—begun in earnest in Spain—ends with the dateline "Montpellier, France, 1937."

With the Spanish republic in danger and Hitler

threatening, Stead's nostalgic, if ambivalent, attraction to Jules and the bourgeois and aristocratic liberals who make up his clientele is understandable, but it dulls the novel's satirical edge. In the character of Jules Bertillon, Stead describes the ordeal of an honest swindler, a creative genius who commands a certain admiration. She makes Jules's principal antagonists not the working class or its representatives but parasitic members of his own class, the self-righteous Raccamond and a decadent homosexual named Jacques Carrière, object in this novel of the homophobia that infects much of her writing. Yet if Jules evokes the seduction of bourgeois ideology as a kind of false consciousness, or what Jean-Paul Sartre would later call bad faith, he is also a late instance of the bourgeois liberalism that dominated politics—and the European novel—in the nineteenth and early twentieth centuries.

Jules is also the primary narrative agent of a crisis in meaning that destabilizes the political allegory that unfolds in the novel. He explodes Marxist notions of literature—as outlined around this time for British readers by Ralph Fox in a book titled *The Novel and the People* (1937), for example—as a reflection of reality. "This isn't a bank," Jules says, "there's a sign outside saying BANK and when they see it they come inside and drop their cash on the counter. If I put the sign BARBER they'd come in just as automatically looking for a shave. It's all in the sign" (p. 253).

Although Stead allied herself with Marxist politics and cultural theory (she expressed her views in essays such as "The Writers Take Sides," her review of Louis Aragon's novel *The Century Was Young,* and "Pro and Con on Aragon," and in a talk titled "Uses of the Many-Charactered Novel" that she gave at a meeting of the League of American Writers), she was drawn, too, to the rhetorical pleasures associated in *House of All Nations* with Jules. Throughout her writing life, she was interested in words for their own sake, in the very texture of language. As she explains in "A Writer's Friends," her duties in the bank on which the Banque Mercure is modeled included the sending and receiving of telegrams in code, and she was fascinated by missed connections, messages sent but not received, signals gone astray. Her sheer love of language and her sense of the instability of meaning play a part in what makes Jules, who plays fast and loose with words, so attractive. But Stead's relish of Jules's linguistic sleights of hand undercuts the left-wing

cultural politics expressed, variously, by Alphendéry, Constant, and Frère. A similar subversion of left-wing norms underlies the treatment of women characters in the novel.

On the surface, *House of All Nations* adheres to the Marxist analysis that suppresses women's concerns or treats them as a reflex of class oppression. Stead shows how women are excluded from the public space of high finance, marginalized by the fraternity valued in the bank and on the Left, and silenced or just not heard in the world the novel portrays. In banishing women from the main stage on which the novel's scenes unfold, the political economy figured as a house of all nations—that is, the bank—Stead presents them as denizens of an alternative house of all nations—a brothel—in which they are fleshly commodities, objects of exchange. Some women—the wives and mistresses of wealthy men—are symbols of conspicuous consumption, while others dabble in politics that they neither believe in nor understand. Judith, the wife of Jean Frère, is a departure from this pattern; she serves as a cautionary image of the exploitation of women on the Left. While women's aspirations are for the most part unexamined in *House of All Nations,* there is at least one important instance in the novel of women's ambitions gone grandly awry. Marianne Raccamond, wife of Aristide, is cynical, vindictive, manipulative, and bitter about her exclusion from the public world of finance and politics. Marianne operates vicariously through her husband; she prods him to blackmail Jules, and when he praises her efforts on his behalf, she replies, "Men never believe a woman can do anything: they let her through, unsuspecting. An immense opportunity for a career" (p. 487). The plot that she masterminds does not produce the result that she works for, her husband's wresting control of the bank from Jules. Rather, it results in the collapse of the bank. A woman's wayward ambition, that is, helps to bring down the liberal political order that the bank represents.

Raccamond describes his wife as a woman "with a man's brain" (p. 299). Marianne is, like her author, a secret agent in a man's world. In an interview given many years after writing *House of All Nations,* Stead told Ann Whitehead, "Those boys [in the bank] told me everything. People always tell a writer everything, especially in business, because they think the poor romantic soul won't really understand that sort of thing" (1974, p. 238).

Stead is more successful than Marianne in claiming the privileges of men. Yet the echoes of Stead's life in Marianne's dramatize the dangerous consequences of ambition in women, a recurrent theme in Stead's work and one revisited in her next novel, *The Man Who Loved Children*.

THE MAN WHO LOVED CHILDREN

The Man Who Loved Children (1940) is Stead's best-known book, admired as the work of a writer's writer, but it still appears from time to time on lists of neglected masterpieces. Set in the United States, *The Man Who Loved Children* is a meticulously observed portrait of a family at once ordinary and astonishing; it vividly captures the distinctive voices of its characters. Stead has said that the family in the novel is her own and that it is drawn from her life. But in actuality, she has invented an alternative version of her childhood, removing her experience from the Australia in which she grew up to the United States in which she wrote the novel.

The protagonist of *The Man Who Loved Children* is Louisa (Louie) Pollit, an awkward, ferociously brilliant adolescent, age eleven and a half when the novel begins. Stead sets the trajectory of Louisa's life against the marriage of Sam and Henny Pollit, who are based on her own parents, David and Ada Stead; Sam and Henny play out a particularly harrowing version of the war between the sexes. Louisa's adolescence is punctuated by the increasingly violent quarrels of her parents, by Sam's intrusive attempts to control his children, and by the poverty that follows when Sam, a naturalist, loses his position in the Conservation Bureau. For much of the novel, Louisa is suspended between Sam and Henny, shifting her allegiance and antagonism from one to the other. Her lurching back and forth between father and mother ends abruptly when she decides to free herself and her siblings by killing her parents. She loses her nerve, but Henny, noticing that she has already put cyanide in a teacup, takes the poisoned drink and dies. The novel ends soon afterward with Louisa running away to take "a walk round the world" (p. 491).

The Pollit family is an ensemble of inequalities, a locus of conflicts between husband and wife, parents and children. The ostensible head of this order is Samuel Clemens Pollit, Stead's version of a paternal tyrant, named for Mark Twain and Harry Pollitt, general secretary of the British Communist party. Sam's dominance is challenged, chiefly by Henny and Louisa, but he is hardy enough to withstand the threats he encounters: "Tragedy itself," Stead says, "could not worm its way by any means into [Sam's] heart" (p. 48).

"The man who loves children," as Henny dubs Sam (p. 136), claims to love all his progeny, but love, for Sam, involves the exercise of power. Sam appears to his sons and daughters alike as the personification of political, legal, and governmental authority: "[T]heir father was the tables of the law, but their mother was natural law; Sam was household czar by divine right, but Henny was the czar's everlasting adversary, household anarchist by divine right" (p. 36). He subjects his daughters to particularly oppressive treatment. He infantilizes the docile, domestic Evie, but his treatment of Louisa, who resists him, is ambiguous. On the one hand, he treats her as an extension of himself; on the other hand, he insists that she acknowledge sexual difference—sexuality itself—as a disability that makes women vulnerable to men's power and aggression.

Stead suggests continuities between patriarchal domination of women and colonial domination of racial others in an episode in which she describes Sam's trip to Malaya as a member of an anthropological mission. Sam finds in Malaya a reflection of his own beliefs, values, and preconceptions and an arena in which to realize his ambitions; he treats Malaya as an object of knowledge, a set of documents to be filed in an archive, a feminized, and hence passive, inert object of desire. His adventures in Malaya suggest the self-importance, muddleheadedness, and irrelevance of ostensibly liberal, "scientific" versions of the colonial project. He is defeated by the tropical heat and humidity. He despises those he calls the "People of Greed," but he benefits from the greed he despises. He compiles notes for a report on the mission, but he cannot complete the report without the assistance of his Chinese secretary: the liberal colonialism he espouses and his project of enlightenment depend on the exploitation of others.

Henny is the principal opponent of Sam's tyranny. She challenges his authority, rationality, and commitment to science and morality by repeatedly invoking the "darn muck of existence" (p. 120), that is, the exigencies of the body. In torrents of invective, aimed at Sam and the other family members who watch, horrified, she attacks Sam's illusion of moral superiority:

Look at me! My back's bent in two with the fruit of my womb; aren't you sorry to see what happened to me because of his lust? I go about with a body like a football, fit to be kicked about by a bohunk halfback, an All-America football, because of his lust, the fine, pure man that won't look at women. . . . To you he's something wonderful; if you know what he is to me, something dirty, a splotch of blood or washing-up water on my skirts.

(pp. 253–254)

When Henny denounces Sam, she seems to be speaking for all women: "He talks about human equality, the rights of man, nothing but that. How about the rights of woman, I'd like to scream at him" (p. 89). But, a fatalist who does little except complain, she can neither escape nor transform her marriage.

Henny lives on credit, subsisting and sustaining her family on her debts. In the very first episode of *The Man Who Loved Children*, she reads a letter from her brother, who refuses the loan she has requested and warns her not to "borrow from moneylenders" (p. 18). The climax of the novel is set in motion by the loss of Tohoga House, the home that Henny and Sam have rented from her father, David Collyer, assuming that he will leave it to them when he dies. But Collyer dies broke, the house is sold to pay his debts, and the Pollits are forced to move from their beloved Washington to a seedy quarter of Annapolis. After Sam loses his government job, Henny tries unsuccessfully to patch up the holes in the family finances by pawning her few valuables, pilfering the meager savings of her son Ernie, and borrowing from a notorious usurer.

While Henny's response to Sam is limited by her passivity, Louisa's exemplifies two distinct strategies, suggesting two different conceptions of gender. On the one hand, Louisa asserts her claim to a heroism exempt from the disabilities of sex; she attempts to appropriate the privileges of men. In response to Sam's prying, she "would strike at him verbally, or flash a look which said, plainer than speaking, 'I am triumphant, I am king' " (p. 320). On the other hand, she calls upon a notion of sexual difference. When Sam praises her mother, his first wife who died when she was an infant, she re-

torts, "What do you know about my mother? She was a woman" (p. 488).

Louisa's self-identification as a woman—with women as a group and against men—coincides with the development of a tenuous bond between herself and Henny:

Whenever [Louisa's] irritations got too deep, she mooched in to see her mother. Here, she had learned, without knowing she had learned it, was a brackish well of hate to drink from, a great passion of gall which could run deep and still, or send up waterspouts, that could fret and boil, or seem silky as young afternoon, something that put iron in her and made her strong to resist the depraved healthiness and idle jollity of the Pollit clan.

It was a strange affection. It could never express itself by embraces or kisses, nothing more than a rare, cool, dutiful kiss on the withering cheek of Henny. It came from their physical differences, because their paths could never meet, and from the natural outlawry of womankind.

(pp. 243–244)

But the bond between Louisa and Henny is fleeting, and it implicates Louisa in what Henny sees as the common lot of "every woman"—vulnerability to sexual innuendo, harassment, and assault.

Louisa's rebellion against Sam is responsible, at least in part, for her literary ambitions. For a celebration of Sam's fortieth birthday, she composes a play titled *Herpes Rom* (The snake man). This play, written in an invented language, is about a father who kills his daughter. When Sam asks why her play is not written in English, she replies, audaciously, "Did Euripides write in English?" (p. 377). But her protest against injustice is ineffective because no one understands it. Indeed, *Herpes Rom* reproduces a patriarchal script in which the mother is powerless to prevent the father's victimization of the daughter. In this, *Herpes Rom* resembles the model it revises, Percy Bysshe Shelley's tragedy *The Cenci* (1819), which tells the story of Beatrice Cenci, executed in 1599 for the killing of her father, a corrupt, brutal count. Like Lucretia Cenci, who cannot save her step-daughter, Beatrice, from the collective power of father, state, and church (Count Cenci is in collusion with the pope), and like Henny Pollit, who cannot save Louisa from the onslaughts of Sam, the mother in *Herpes Rom* cannot help her daughter. She does not appear onstage, and the very last line of the play, spoken by the daughter, is "Mother, father is strangling me. Murderer! (She dies.)" (p. 378).

The end of the novel replays Louisa's oscillation between her parents. Louisa identifies with Henny, and Sam regards and treats her as a replacement for his wife. Louisa runs away, then, to escape Henny's lot in life, confinement and unpaid labor in the patriarchal family. But Louisa is a survivor, and her survival links her with the surviving parent, Sam. She is, moreover, at least partly responsible for Henny's death. Does the daughter's freedom rest on her collusion in the destruction of the mother? Does it rest on acquiescence or complicity in the male dominance that pervades the Pollit family? These questions are prompted by Louisa's resemblance to Sam and to the snake man—fathers who strangle, suffocate, or otherwise suppress the selfhood embodied in daughter and mother alike.

The family story that the novel tells is more than just an abstract rendering of the mutual antagonism of men and women, parents and children. It places the Pollits in an environment that superimposes the United States in which the novel was written on the Australia of the author's childhood. In the very first scene Henny thinks of her marriage as a "civil war" (p. 11). Stead's depiction of the Pollit family is presented as a retelling of the American national story. The Pollits' conflicts unfold in an area bounded by Washington, Baltimore, Annapolis, and Harpers Ferry. These places are not only sites of such important events in American history as John Brown's raid but also crossroads, a microcosm of the entire national landscape, in which North and South intersect. Stead's version of the American national legend is based on an analogy between the husband and the victorious North and the wife and the defeated South, but these oppositions and the analogy between them are unstable.

Throughout the novel, Sam is identified not only with the North but with the artisan class from which he springs and bourgeois liberal ideology. The Pollits' Baltimore, a domain of puritanical attitudes toward alcohol and culture, belongs to the North. As much as the North, Sam exemplifies the spirit of liberalism. He sees himself as the great white father, a representative of the "United States of mankind" (pp. 71, 202–203). In addition to the historical and legendary characters that Sam explicitly takes as models, he is associated with such diverse figures in American culture as Artemus Ward (a nineteenth-century journalist and humorist), Herman Melville's Ahab (and Melville himself), and Mark Twain, for whom he is named.

In the novel's condensed American map, as the Pollits are identified with the North, Henny's family, the Collyers, are associated with the South. In Sam's ascendancy over Henny, the subjection of women is rewritten as the defeat of the South by the North. But Stead also exposes the old South as a nostalgic illusion. In fact, the South evoked by Henny's family has already been transformed by capital, whose provenance is the North: Henny's father, David Collyer, the novel's exemplar of the Southern gentleman, originally comes from Gloucester, Massachusetts.

Although Henny apparently personifies an American cultural type, the déclassé Southern belle, Sam's association with Samuel Clemens and with Uncle Sam (he appears on a radio show called *The Uncle Sam Hour*) makes him an exemplary American. Henny and Sam also have distinctly Australian genealogies. Their marriage, with its relentlessly binary vision of gender—"their father was the tables of the law, but their mother was natural law"—recalls the rigid sexual division of labor that developed in Australia in the early national period. Henny's grotesque maternity and exaggerated, even parodic fecundity recall Australian notions of femininity as compulsory marriage and motherhood in which wives lacked virtually all legal rights. Like Henny's abject domesticity, Sam's public-spiritedness has a provenance in the ideology of the new Australian middle class. The consolidation of this class, which included workers with educational, technical, and social skills, was accomplished in the late nineteenth and early twentieth centuries through the exclusion of women, Asians, and "other races."

In numerous interviews and in her autobiographical writings, Stead acknowledges the Australian origins of her American story. In her accounts of the novel, she gives Australia priority over America. She told Ann Whitehead that she set her novel in the United States to shield family members still living in Australia (p. 242). Yet her assertion belies the hybrid national identity constructed in and by the novel. Although Stead had left Australia some years before *The Man Who Loved Children* was published, she clearly felt a tie both to the nation from which she had exiled herself and to the one in which she wrote the story of her early life. Yet her writing—or her career as a published writer—was made possible by the exile that took her first to Britain and later to the United States and Europe. Stead tells the story of her exile, with London as the setting for the beginning of her literary career, in a sequel to *The Man Who Loved Children,* her next novel, *For Love Alone.*

FOR LOVE ALONE

FOR Love Alone was written in the United States and published in New York in 1944 and in London in 1945 (it was not published in Sydney until 1966). It tells the story of Teresa Hawkins, a young woman who leaves Australia, where she is born and grows up, and travels to England, where she falls in love and becomes a writer. Teresa decides to leave Australia at least in part because she wishes to escape the limitations of provincial culture—among them, a repressive sexual morality and rigid gender hierarchy—and the domestic regime of her tyrannical father. Stead vividly depicts the frustrations Teresa experiences in Sydney, the determination that enables her to escape, and her discovery, in London, of the pleasures of work, cosmopolitan culture, writing, and sexual awakening.

For Love Alone begins with a prologue that undermines cultural authority. Stead describes the world from an Australian vantage point, but in doing so she makes use of some of the characteristic tropes of British and European literature, among them the figure of the antipodes, or the world turned upside down. In relying on European ways of seeing and describing, the prologue calls into question the authority of colonial cultures such as that of Australia and of colonial subjects like Teresa herself.

The cultural authority of women is as tenuous as the cultural authority of colonials. In the prologue, Stead associates Australia with Ithaca and, by implication, Teresa with Odysseus:

It is a fruitful island of the sea-world, a great Ithaca, there parched and stony and here trodden by flocks and curly-headed bulls and heavy with thick-set grain. To this race can be put the famous question: "Oh, Australian, have you just come from the harbour? Is your ship in the road-

stead? Men of what nation put you down—for I am sure you did not get here on foot?"

(p. 2)

In putting Teresa in the place of Odysseus, Stead rejects the feminine limits associated with Penelope and gives her protagonist such traditionally masculine prerogatives as mobility. But Teresa is plagued by doubts that make her wonder whether she is a "detestable thing, an ugly, rejected *woman*" (emphasis added) and whether her attempt to leave Australia and go to England is a "rigmarole of [a] buffoon Odyssey" (p. 348).

In *For Love Alone* Stead delineates the journey that is projected at the end of *The Man Who Loved Children.* At the beginning of *For Love Alone,* Teresa Hawkins, age nineteen, is stuck in Sydney and oppressed by the tyranny of her father, Andrew, the poverty and powerlessness of numerous aunts and female cousins who graphically illustrate the restrictions on women, and an economic depression. In the first chapter Andrew Hawkins vaunts his power over his rebellious children. As in *The Man Who Loved Children,* the conflict between daughter and father is in part a struggle over meaning. In the novel's initial episode Teresa refuses to accept her father's notion of women's inferiority and claims for herself a value that he would reserve for men—honor. Teresa's quest for self-definition is also shaped by her resistance to a culture in which gender constraints and economic scarcity reinforce each other. In Teresa's aunts, cousins, and friends, Stead makes palpable the predicament of "these unfortunate women and girls, her acquaintance, a miserable mass writhing with desire and shame, grovelling before men, silent about the stew in which they boiled and bubbled, discontented, browbeaten, flouted, ridiculous and getting uglier each year" (p. 18). Teresa's docile, submissive sister, Kitty, has no money because she takes care of their oppressive father and brothers, while their cousin Malfi is forced to marry "some schoolfellow gone into long trousers" because she is pregnant (p. 17).

Like Catherine Baguenault in *Seven Poor Men of Sydney,* Teresa rebels against the sexual status quo. On the one hand, she claims the active role traditionally ascribed to men; she sees herself as a "hunter without a forest" (p. 75). On the other hand, taking her view of sexuality from what little she has read about it, she conceives of herself as a passive object of male desire or an inert site in which the "work of passion was going on" (p. 73):

The things [Teresa] wanted existed. At school she first had news of them, she knew they existed; what went on round her was hoaxing and smooth-faced hypocrisy. Venus and Adonis, the Rape of Lucrece, Troilus and Cressida were reprinted for three hundred years, St Anthony was tempted in the way you would expect; Dido, though a queen, was abandoned like a servant-girl and went mad with love and grief, like the girl in the boat outside. This was the truth, not the daily simpering on the boat and the putting away in hope chests; but where was one girl who thought so, besides herself? Was there one who would not be afraid if she told them the secret, the real life? Since school, she had ravaged libraries, disembowelled hundreds of books, ranged through literature since the earliest recorded frenzies of the world and had eaten into her few years with this boundless love of love, this insensate thirst for the truth above passion, alive in their home itself, in her brothers and sister, but neglected, denied, and useless; obnoxious in school, workshop, street.

Teresa knew all the disorderly loves of Ovid, the cruel luxury of Petronius, the exorbitance of Aretino, the meaning of the witches' Sabbaths, the experiments of Sade, the unimaginable horrors of the Inquisition, the bestiality in the Bible, the bitter jokes of Aristophanes and what the sex-psychologists had written. At each thing she read, she thought, yes, it's true, or no, it's false, and she persevered with satisfaction and joy, illuminated because her world existed and was recognized by men. But why not by women? She found nothing in the few works of women she could find that was what they must have felt.

(pp. 75–76)

Stead captures the power, immediacy, and authenticity of sexual desire. But she also shows how Teresa experiences desire as it is mirrored in an erotic tradition composed entirely of the writings of men. Because these writings, from the "bitter jokes of Aristophanes" to the work of the "sex-psychologists," portray women as sexually passive or subordinate to men, Teresa either impersonates sadistic, masculine sexuality—she "ravaged libraries, disembowelled . . . books"—or imagines herself not as sexual agent but as sexual object, "ravished, trembling with ecstasy" (p. 76).

In affirming her own autonomy and authority Teresa rehearses colonial attitudes toward race, gender, sexuality, savagery, and the primitive. She identifies with "wild animals in the bush"; with the "Australian savages [who] arrange all that for their women"; with the "savage women" themselves; and with Italian and Spanish women and the corrupt, libertine, but happy women of ancient Greece and Rome (p. 75). At the same time she takes advantage of the privileges reserved for white Europeans and their descendants. When she decides to leave Sydney and go to London, for example, she contemplates paying for her journey by doing office work in outposts of the empire:

She saw the significance of the maps of the British Empire showing the world strung on a chain of pink, all the pink was Britain's. In every one of those pink patches, no matter what the colour or kind of men there, nor the customs of the native women, she could get a job, she was a citizen there. There were advertisements in the Sydney papers for typists to go to Nauru, Cocos, Shanghai, British Columbia, and these could be just jumping-off places.

(p. 83)

Here, Teresa sees herself as imperial agent and subject, "citizen" of all the places represented by pink patches on the map.

The constraints—men's power, women's powerlessness—against which Teresa rebels in the first place are intensified in her early sexual encounters. Frustrated by her life at home and by her limited opportunities, Teresa runs away to the country, wandering through a landscape described as a projection of desire. Her journey takes her through the "broad, soft Narara Valley," a pastoral, romantic site of "steeps, gullies, and pockets, all blossom and young branch" (pp. 139–140). As in such nineteenth-century British novels as Charlotte Brontë's *Jane Eyre* (1847), George Eliot's *The Mill on the Floss* (1860), and Thomas Hardy's *Tess of the d'Urbervilles* (1891), nature is neither pristine nor free but subject to the power of money and men. On this journey Teresa stops at the home of her cousin, where one evening a young man who lives nearby seizes and kisses her in an "affront, . . . a kind of debauch which she scarcely understood" (p. 155). Soon afterward, she walks down a deserted road. But her illusion of autonomy is shattered when she is frightened by men's shouting voices and accosted by an old man who taunts her and exposes himself in a kind of "idiotic dance" (p. 165). These two encounters induce Teresa to return to her family in Sydney.

Eventually, she again takes up her plan to go to Europe, where she intends to study in a university, but, now cognizant of the dangers of solitary wandering, she attaches herself to her Latin tutor, the mean-spirited, sadistic Jonathan Crow, who is about to depart for London on a fellowship. Teresa virtually starves herself for three years so that she can save enough money to follow Jonathan to London. Her pursuit of him seems motivated by a kind of masochism, but it gets her to London, where she hopes to realize ambitions thwarted in Australia.

Teresa's infatuation with Jonathan also symbolizes her subjection to colonial and provincial cultural norms. Jonathan uncritically parrots Australian versions of Friedrich Nietzsche and Charles Darwin and spouts the pernicious racism and sexism of turn-of-the-century eugenics:

"Higher education, the prolongation of the childhood of the race, is destroying or distorting that impulse which reproduces the race. Youths who are able to procreate at fourteen or fifteen, and who must wait to establish themselves in a society which rejects bastard children, do not have offspring till they are twenty-seven or -eight, or even later. Women who could be mothers at seventeen are forced to compete with men in the professions and usually deprived of motherhood altogether, since the conservative male's objection to a blue-stocking in the home is well known." He smiled again at the miserable women whose sufferings he had tabulated.

(p. 182)

He warned [the women he tutored] against miscegenation, against marrying Japanese, Chinese, Bantus, or Malays, not only because they weaken the breed, "mongrels are always weaker than true strains," but because white women could never know what was going on in the brains of those men of other ancient races. There was a physical difference in the constitution of the brain. *Homo pekinensis*, their ancestors, differed materially from the Cro-Magnon race.

(p. 183)

Like Teresa's father, Andrew Hawkins—and like Sam Pollit in *The Man Who Loved Children*—Jonathan represents an obstacle to Teresa's development, specifically, the trap of subjection to ideologies of male dominance and racial superiority.

Teresa discovers a way to overcome the obstacle when she finally arrives in London. There, she finds work as a secretary to an American named James Quick, a character based on Stead's husband, Blake, and the novel's antithesis to Jonathan Crow. Quick soon falls in love with Teresa, and she with him. He is identified with England, especially London as it appears in the writings of William Blake (the original Blake) and Charles Dickens, with British erotic poetry, which he reads to her, and with cosmopolitan European culture.

Jonathan does not take notice of Teresa's self-affirmation. And Quick makes short work of him by subjecting him to a thoroughgoing Marxist reading that dismisses his tawdry ideas as the "sign of the misogynist" (p. 434). Yet Quick's Marxist view of culture and society cannot adequately account for Teresa's aspirations or the stunted desires of the novel's "writhing mass" of wretched women.

Quick's considerable intellectual power is echoed in the erotic power that makes Teresa feel she is giving him an "awful empire" over her (p. 447). He is companionable and generous; he "loved women as equals . . . as men love friends" (p. 364). When Teresa and Quick finally become lovers, they experience the world as a utopia: "The noises of the town fell away, struggle and misery went home, ate and slept, the world became for a short time quiet" (p. 455). Yet Teresa soon feels that Quick regards love as an arena in which to exercise his power. Not surprisingly, she finds him "suffocating" and, thinking she can "master men," decides to "try men" (p. 464).

Soon after Teresa goes to live with Quick, she has her first affair. Her lover, Harry Girton, is based on Ralph Fox. When Quick encourages Teresa to go off with Girton, she feels that the men are "offering and counter-offering her love to each other, as a proof of their love for each other" (p. 480). In placing Teresa between two men whose bonds and rivalries she mediates—Jonathan and Quick, Quick and Girton—Stead suggests the hindrances to women's self-realization by the conjunction of male dominance and heterosexual romantic love.

London in *For Love Alone* is the antithesis of Sydney—the city in which she has her sexual awakening and in which, like Stead, she begins to be appreciated as a writer. Teresa, like Stead, begins writing in Sydney. She creates a mixed-media text and design she calls "The Legend of Jonathan" and writes letters to Jonathan Crow that he never reads. But in James Quick she finds the ideal reader every writer wishes for. After Teresa arrives in London and while she is still pining after Jonathan, she begins writing a novel. Stead wrote *Seven Poor Men of Sydney* in similar circumstances. In Teresa's fragmentary manuscript, *The Seven Houses of Love,* Stead translates her own lyrical, psychosexual, and sociological study of working-class women and men into a meditation on desire: Teresa's text appropriates, recycles, and thereby asserts her own claim to the "old heritage" of European culture (p. 83). Oddly, we encounter this work not as Teresa writes it—that is, not as an outpouring of her thoughts and feelings—but as Quick appreciatively reads it. Thus, Stead points to the dependence of writers like herself on eager readers, that is, on a literary climate that allows their talents to flourish.

At the end of the novel Teresa sees a "self-pickled bachelor" whom she does not recognize until Quick tells her it is Jonathan. She sighs and says, in the last words of the novel, "It's dreadful to think that it will go on being repeated for ever, he—and me! What's there to stop it?" (p. 502). By writing a novel that takes seriously the circumstances of women like Teresa, Stead attempts to "stop it," to break the chain of repetition that Teresa finds so dreadful.

THE COLD WAR YEARS

IN 1946 Stead published *Letty Fox: Her Luck,* a picaresque companion piece to *For Love Alone.* In *Letty Fox* she turns her satirical eye on the Left, on the New York cultural scene, and on the ambitions of her protagonist, Letty Fox, who, despite her apparent unconventionality, sees marriage as a means of emotional and economic survival. Not long after the novel was published, Stead and Blake left New York, fleeing McCarthyism, and returned to England. For the next several years they wandered from one European city to another, returning to London in 1953. In 1948 Stead published *A Little Tea, a Little Chat,* a scathing, relentlessly detailed depiction of Robbie Grant, a ruthless, tyrannical businessman who makes a fortune as a war profiteer and is eventually undone by the lust and greed that Stead represents as two aspects of the same psychosocial pathology. The grim satire of *A Little Tea, a Little Chat* was followed in 1952 by the gentle, even Chekhovian satire of *The People with the Dogs,* which tracks the pleasantly eccentric members of the Massine family in New York and its environs in the immediate postwar period.

Throughout the 1950s and into the 1960s Stead and Blake barely eked out a living, writing, translating, and hiring themselves out as freelance researchers when they could not find other work. Through these years, Stead worked on the books that became *The Little Hotel, I'm Dying Laughing, Cotters' England,* and *Miss Herbert (The Suburban Wife),* but she could not get them published. After years of poverty and a life on the margins of what little remained of a once-thriving left-wing culture, she was rescued from obscurity when, in 1965, through Stanley Burnshaw's efforts, Henry Holt reissued *The Man Who Loved Children. Cotters' England* was published in 1967 (in 1966 in the United States under the title *Dark Places of the Heart*), the first of the novels she had been writing through the years of apparent silence.

COTTERS' ENGLAND

COTTERS' England is set in the bleak period just after World War II. A late instance of the condition-of-England novel, it can be placed in the context of left-wing and working-class cultural and political revisions undertaken in the mid and late 1950s and early 1960s in such now-classic texts as E. P. Thompson's *The Making of the English Working Class* (1963), Richard Hoggart's *The Uses of Literacy* (1957), and Doris Lessing's *The Golden Notebook* (1962) and in the work of the Angry Young Men. While Thompson's book seeks to excavate authentic and authentically British working-class political traditions and Hoggart's attempts to document an authentic working-class culture that is disappearing or being driven underground by the advent of a mass-mediated, commodified popular culture, Stead's text, like Lessing's and the writings of the Angry Young Men, with which it otherwise has very little in common, is a radical critique of authenticity. Stead's critical perspective might be a function of her colonial origins, her nomadic life, or her gender, but it also reflects the contemporary character of her subject matter, her focus on the moment in which she was writing. In dramatizing the demise of the traditions traced by Thompson and Hoggart, among others, Stead also raises questions about whether they ever existed.

Cotters' England is set mainly in London, but the principal characters—the Cotter family for whom the novel is named—hail from the north, from Tyneside. Although Newcastle, or the nearby small town of Bridgehead that is home to the Cotters, and London are like the two boundaries of the nation England that is situated between them, Bridgehead seems almost as remote from London as Sydney. The novel's characters explore who or what can claim to represent England or Englishness. They do so in ways that are influenced by the temperamental idiosyncrasies, emotional excesses, and Depression-era upbringing that define their collective experience.

Several of the characters make up a series of triangular relationships, which suggest the pull of conflicting emotions, the ways that each, whatever his or her present role or vocation, is bound to and by the past. The central character is Nellie Cook, née Cotter, a fortyish, left-wing journalist and self-deluding, if sometimes compelling, egomaniac who lives a bohemian life in London. Nellie, "a strange thing, her shabby black hair gathered into a sprout on the top of her small head, her beak and backbone bent forward, her thin long legs stepping prudently, gingerly, like a marsh bird's" (p. 13), is "loyal to comrades in the unnamed rebel battalion she marched in, outcasts, criminals, the misunderstood, women not one of whom could show a clean record" (p. 34). Her husband, George Cook, is a labor union official who, for much of the novel, leaves her behind in England as he travels through Europe on behalf of an increasingly less militant international labor movement. Nellie is caught between her husband and her brother, Tom, who himself becomes involved with a series of older, maternal, married women. Most of these women, including George's ex-wife, Eliza, are Nellie's friends and associates, the coterie whose allegiance she commands. When they draw close to Tom, she interferes.

Through the wanderings of Tom and Nellie, we also meet the Bridgewater Cotters: their father, Thomas, a nasty, philandering drunk; their mother Mary, his long-suffering, emotionally stingy, now senile wife; their uncle, Mary's brother Simon Pike; and their sister Peggy, the youngest of the Cotter children, now in her thirties, who spent several years in an asylum after an unhappy affair with a married man. Peggy returns home and resentfully takes care of her uncle and parents, but when they die, she forces the increasingly deranged Simon into an old men's home so that she can be independent at last. Her father, we learn, claimed that the girl in the asylum was not his daughter and never visited her. The Cotter family, especially those in Bridgehead, is a collection of eccentrics, portrayed not in the comic or melodramatic manner of English music hall but as victims and perpetrators of material privation and psychological devastation.

Cotters' England, in fact, dissects the texture and determinants of subjectivity: character, personality, values, beliefs. How, Stead asks, are we shaped by material circumstances, by the psychodynamics forged in our families of origin? She conducts her inquiry into these matters in a series of confrontations between pairs of characters who seem to represent opposing ideas, perspectives, and so on. But the specific points of contention are less enduring, less important, than what the characters have in common, the way they are formed, or deformed, by divergent experiences of the same conditions.

One such confrontation involves Nellie and her brother, Tom. The ostensible topic they are debating is Nellie's relationship with her women friends. But the texture of their speech is more engaging than the subject of the dispute:

"I like to see you get into a flap. You're so transparent, Nell. You've got just a little twisted spittling spider thread of sympathy and you try to dangle a whole human being on it. . . .

"You don't know any more about Camilla or Eliza or Caroline than you know about Tibet, but you'll never admit it. And if you introspected with them for a hundred years you'd never know anything about them. For it's you, Nell. It isn't them. . . ."

"It isn't me nor for me, pet. I'm trying to free them from themselves; that's the only freedom. Then their problems will be over. It's you who want them to live in the world of illusion. I want to free them by truth. Death is the end. What is the use of these tawdry loves, as you call them? . . . It's nonsense they sell them so they won't look straight ahead. . . .

"My great truth is freedom from illusions, from lies, deceptions, from hypocrisy, from all those shameful loves, the opium of the heart. I want them to come to me and learn, come to me; I can teach them that there is only one way, and they must find it in pain, but I can help."
(pp. 175–176)

Nellie claims to speak for freedom from illusion, but she is imprisoned in her own ways of seeing; her actions, throughout the novel, suggest that she craves power over those she says she cares for. Thus, Tom accuses her of trying to dangle a "whole human being" from a "twisted spittling spider thread of sympathy" (p. 175). But his judgment is colored by his own desire for the same women over whom she wishes to exert power. And there is a certain justice in Nellie's view: the women she knows are prey to illusions of one kind or another and especially to fantasies of rescue through romantic love by sweetly seductive young men like Tom; in a world without gods or other transcendent values, it is a relief to acknowledge the finality of death.

A second confrontation involves Nellie and her friend Eliza Cook. Eliza asserts that hunger is what drives human beings: "It's a primitive need, you can live without all but food" (p. 211). But Nellie does not agree. The real topic of this discussion is a shadowy and demonic figure named Jago, whom the two women knew in Bridgehead when they were young. Eliza, the novel's version of a proletarian, says that she was unaware of Jago because she was forced to work from an early age. Nellie replies that Jago was "fighting a pitiful struggle against frustration and failure. He wanted to be a painter, but whoever was an artist on the Tyne? So his bent and twisted impulses tried to create something in us" (p. 210). When Eliza says that Jago "played on your hunger," Nellie demurs:

[H]e understood that there were bigger impulses working up in us and great aspirations. It was the intellectual hunger, we all felt. It was a great hunger. We went everywhere looking not for food, but for guidance and for knowledge. You see we couldn't find any of it at home. And Jago understood us. . . . I said to the [Communist Party] district organizer, What is the meaning of death and hunger? Have you got some words so that I can explain that to a poor mother? . . . It was spiritual hunger.

(pp. 211–212)

Once again, the purported point of contention is not terribly significant, for whatever the cause, the result is vulnerability to Jago, who salves his dissatisfaction, his frustrated creativity, by manipulating and dominating others. Perhaps more important, Nellie's early involvement with Jago and his friends is the seed of the bohemian rebelliousness that Stead exposes as yet another instance of bogus values or ersatz politics.

The confrontation between Nellie and Eliza is immediately followed by a discussion between Nellie and her husband, George, that alters slightly the terms of the debate. When George describes himself as a "European bureaucrat," Nellie accuses him of betraying his class:

"Mr. George Cook, late of the working class. . . . Aye, he's a typical old socialist, trying to be glorious at the expense of the workers. I despise you, George Cook: the back of me hand to you. Did you struggle your way up from the docks of Tyneside for this pitiful glass of brandy?"

"I did," cried George. "A worker's a figment to you, Nellie; it's a schoolgirl dream. It's a vague, dirty, hungering man, weak and a failure: someone for you to mother and maunder over. You're just a plain Fleet Street sobsister. . . .

"But you sit at table with every ex-I.R.A. sellout, who'll hand you a dishful of workman romance. Ah, the British sods, the murderers of the Irish people: what can ye do? Ye must write tripe to fill your unworthy belly and ye must write the tripe they want, the poor beggarly Sassenachs living on king and country, for they know no better. I'm no traitor, I'm just an Englishman who wants to represent his country abroad. . . ."

"It's a fine figure, the self-elected Atlas holding up England abroad."

(pp. 214–215)

If the brandy- and coffee-drinking George suggests the inauthenticity of European socialism gone cosmopolitan, Nellie, with her endless cigarettes and cups of tea, suggests the inauthenticity of English left-wing politics whose insularity and insistent invocation of the working class are no remedy for hungers real and imagined. The stakes in their debate are high, England itself, as George makes clear: "Whose country is it? Whose pound sterling is it? Whose indebtedness is it? Whose empire is it? Whose revenues are they? Am I going to lose my eyes and hair . . . to save Cotters' England?" (p. 216). Yet if Cotters' England is a contemporary alternative to the archaic national culture once reserved for lords and scholars, as George puts it, the new order is no more democratic, no more authentic than the old one.

Left-wing political theory, like political action, reaches a dead end in *Cotters' England*. When Nellie's editor asks her to read up on Marxism, she refuses: "I don't believe in Marxian theory, I said. Can it explain the unknowable? Can it help a working-class mother who has just lost her baby?

Can it stop the concentration camps? Can it keep a man in his country?" (pp. 235–236). Here, Nellie eloquently voices the rage and despair that characterized Stead's life during the Cold War years, when she wandered from one European city to another and struggled to support herself by writing.

But Nellie's outcry against conditions that Stead herself lamented in letters and described in the novels she wrote but could not get published is not the end of *Cotters' England*. The climax of the novel is a lesbian phantasmagoria in which Nellie, dressed in men's clothes, feeds off the feelings of an emotionally fragile woman named Caroline, who responds by jumping out a window. The novel ends inconclusively: Nellie joins George in Geneva, but when he dies soon afterward, she returns to England. Bohemian rebel? advocate of justice? vampirish object of her author's homophobia? Nellie is all of these and an exemplar, too, of her class and culture. Constantly ordering those around her to confess, to "introspect," unself-critical and egoistic, Nellie is Stead's message to a time and place in which her own gifts found little or no sympathetic response. It is a particularly poignant irony that this expression of despair was published after the rediscovery of Christina Stead as author of such neglected masterpieces as *The Man Who Loved Children* had already begun.

LAST YEARS

IN 1967 *The Puzzleheaded Girl*, a collection of four novellas about American girls, was published. That same year, Stead was denied the prestigious Britannica Australia Award because she had not lived in Australia for many years, but she was awarded an Arts Council Grant in England. Blake died early in 1968, and in 1969 Stead visited Australia. The year 1969 also saw the publication of the first book on her work, by R. G. Geering, who later became her literary executor.

In 1973 *The Little Hotel* was published. This novel is about a group of European and British expatriates who find themselves in a Swiss hotel just after World War II, in the waning days of the British empire. Like the bank in *House of All Nations*, the hotel is a microcosm, but the encyclopedic scope of the earlier novel is reduced in the later one and the exuberant satire of interwar capitalism gives way to a much quieter dissection of postwar political complacency and hypocrisy. In 1974 Stead returned to Australia to live. In October of that year she received the Patrick White Literary Award, set up by White, with money from his Nobel Prize, for older Australian writers. By this time, through royalties and small Australian, American, and British pensions, Stead was able to live comfortably. In 1976 she published *Miss Herbert (The Suburban Wife)*, a novel about a woman who is almost militantly conventional in her sexual politics, political attitudes, and views of culture. Typical of her class and of a conservative and morally bankrupt British culture, Eleanor Herbert is the antithesis of her author, who struggled against complacency and attempted to expose hypocrisy wherever she found it.

Stead died on 31 March 1983. In 1985 some of her uncollected writings were published in *Ocean of Story*. In 1986 Geering brought out *I'm Dying Laughing*, her novel about the blacklist. Stead had worked on this novel intermittently for many years, periodically setting it aside and returning to it, but she was never able to complete it. The early part of the novel skewers Hollywood Communists in thrall, in Stead's view, to Freudian notions of personality. Most of the book is taken up with the travails of yet another of Stead's strange egotists, Emily Howard, a character Stead based on her friend Ruth McKenney. Like McKenney, author of the extremely popular and well-regarded book *My Sister Eileen* (later turned into a play, a musical, and a movie), Howard is a Communist who grows rich as a popular and commercial success but never manages to be respected as the serious political writer she wants to be. Persecuted for her views by the government and by Communist Party functionaries who deem her ultraleftist politics incorrect, Emily flees with her family to Europe and tries to console herself by eating and drinking until she assumes Rabelaisian proportions. In *I'm Dying Laughing* distinctions between right and left, popular and serious, politics and psychology are seriously eroded. The resulting collapse of meaning realizes tendencies inchoate throughout Stead's career, which anatomizes and exposes fissures in the characteristic structures and institutions of modernity.

Stead's scrutiny of the world she inhabited was accomplished through or despite excesses of style, narrative incoherence, and ideological contradiction. Every one of her novels is too long. Yet readers who persist, despite the daunting task of plowing through too many words, meeting too many characters, and finding not enough plot, will be rewarded by encountering an entirely compelling vision of the world, a fiercely intellectual sensibility, and an utterly original way of seeing. Perhaps Stead's most significant achievement is to have created a distinctive fictional universe without having had a clear place to write in or from. But it may be her unsettled life that made possible the extraordinary imagination that was her signature.

SELECTED BIBLIOGRAPHY

I. FICTION. *The Salzburg Tales* (London and New York, 1934; Sydney, 1974); *Seven Poor Men of Sydney* (London and New York, 1934; Sydney, 1965); *The Beauties and Furies* (London and New York, 1936; London, 1982); *House of All Nations* (London and New York, 1938; New York, 1973; Sydney, 1974); *The Man Who Loved Children* (New York, 1940, 1965, 1966; London, 1941, 1970); *For Love Alone* (New York, 1944; London, 1945; Sydney, 1966); *Letty Fox: Her Luck* (New York, 1946; London, 1947; Sydney, 1974); *A Little Tea, a Little Chat* (New York, 1948; London, 1981); *The People with the Dogs* (Boston, 1952; London, 1981); *Cotters' England* (London, 1967, 1980), published as *Dark Places of the Heart* (New York, 1966); *The Puzzleheaded Girl* (New York, 1967; London, 1968, 1984); *The Little Hotel* (London and Sydney, 1973; New York, 1975); *Miss Herbert (The Suburban Housewife)* (New York, 1976; London, 1979).

II. OTHER WORKS. *Ocean of Story: The Uncollected Stories of Christina Stead*, ed. by R. G. Geering (Ringwood, Australia, 1985); *I'm Dying Laughing: The Humourist*, ed. by R. G. Geering (London, 1986); R. G. Geering, "From the Personal Papers of Christina Stead: Extracts and Commentaries," in *Southerly* 50, no. 4 (December 1990); R. G. Geering, "From the Personal Papers of Christina Stead: Extracts and Commentaries," in *Southerly* 51, no.1 (March 1991); *Talking into the Typewriter: Selected Letters (1972–1983)*, ed. by R. G. Geering (Sydney, 1992); *A Web of Friendship: Selected Letters (1928–1973)*, ed. by R. G. Geering (Sydney, 1992).

III. SELECTED ESSAYS. "The Writers Take Sides," in *Left Review* 1 (August 1935); Review of Louis Aragon, *The Century Was Young*, in *New Masses*, 20 January 1942; "On the Women's Movement," in *Partisan Review* 46, no. 2 (1979); "Another View of the Homestead," repr. in *Ocean of Story*, ed. by R. G. Geering (Ringwood, Australia, 1985); "Uses of the Many-Charactered Novel," Draft ms. in the papers of the League of American Writers. Bancroft Library, University of California, Berkeley (Berkeley, Calif., 1939); "A Waker and Dreamer," repr. in *Ocean of Story*, ed. by R. G. Geering (Ringwood, Australia, 1985); "A Writer's Friends," repr. in *Ocean of Story*, ed. by R. G. Geering (Ringwood, Australia, 1985).

IV. INTERVIEWS. Jonah Raskin, "Christina Stead in Washington Square," in *London Magazine* 9, no. 2 (1970); Ann Whitehead, "Christina Stead: An Interview," in *Australian Literary Studies* 6, no. 3 (May 1974).

V. CRITICAL STUDIES. Randall Jarrell, introduction to *The Man Who Loved Children* (New York, 1965); Jose Yglesias, "Marx as Muse," in *The Nation*, 5 April 1965, review of *The Man Who Loved Children*; R. G. Geering, *Christina Stead* (New York, 1969); Angela Carter, "Unhappy Families," in *London Review of Books*, 16 September–6 October 1982; Joan Lidoff, *Christina Stead* (New York, 1982); Jonathan Arac, "The Struggle for the Cultural Heritage: Christina Stead Refunctions Charles Dickens and Mark Twain," in *Cultural Critique* 2 (winter 1985–1986); Diana Brydon, *Christina Stead* (Totowa, N.J., 1987); Susan Sheridan, *Christina Stead* (Bloomington, Ind., 1988); Judith Kegan Gardiner, *Rhys, Stead, Lessing, and the Politics of Empathy* (Bloomington, Ind., 1989); Kate Macomber Stern, *Christina Stead's Heroine: The Changing Sense of Decorum* (New York, 1989); Chris Williams, *Christina Stead: A Life of Letters* (Melbourne and London, 1989); Joseph A. Boone, "Of Fathers, Daughters, and Theorists of Narrative Desire: At the Crossroads of Myth and Psychoanalysis in *The Man Who Loved Children*," in *Contemporary Literature* 31, no. 4 (winter 1990); Hazel Rowley, "How Real Is Sam Pollit? 'Dramatic Truth' and 'procès-verbal' in *The Man Who Loved Children*," in *Contemporary Literature* 31, no. 4 (winter 1990); Louise Yelin, "Fifty Years of Reading: A Reception Study of *The Man Who Loved Children*," in *Contemporary Literature* 31, no. 4 (winter 1990); Hazel Rowley, *Christina Stead: A Biography* (Sydney, 1993; New York, 1994).

VI. MISCELLANEOUS STUDIES. Marianne Ehrhardt, "Christina Stead: A Checklist," in *Australian Literary Studies* 9 (October 1980); Special sections in the journals *Contemporary Literature* 31, no. 4 (winter 1990); *World Literature Written in English* 32, no. 1 (spring 1992); *Southerly* 53, no. 4 (December 1993).

D. M. THOMAS

(1935–)

Rachel Wetzsteon

A PROLIFIC NOVELIST, poet, and translator, Donald Michael Thomas achieved worldwide fame in 1981 with his novel *The White Hotel*, but has also written a wide array of other books notable for their erudition, their disturbing exploration of the Holocaust, their debt to Russian literature and history, and their innovative breakdown of the boundaries separating poetry and fiction, dream and reality. Born into a working-class Methodist household in Redruth, Cornwall—a landscape that has profoundly influenced both his poetry and his fiction—Thomas attended Redruth Grammar School, then moved with his parents to Melbourne, Australia, in 1949, after his sister married an Australian serviceman. Thomas attended University High School in Melbourne until the family returned to Britain in 1951. After two years of National Service—during which, he has confessed, he spent most of his time learning Russian—Thomas read English at New College, Oxford (B.A., 1958; M.A., 1961). He taught for four years (1960–1964) at Teignmouth Grammar School, during which time he began writing poetry. He became lecturer in English at the Hereford College of Education in 1964 and was head of the department from 1977 to 1979. In 1978, Thomas decided to write full time, and in 1987 he returned to his native Cornwall where he currently lives. He has received many prizes for both his poetry and his fiction, has taught English and creative writing at several American universities, has been married twice, and has three children. Thomas gives a full account of his upbringing, his literary development, and his personal life in his 1988 memoir, *Memories and Hallucinations*.

EARLY NOVELS

AFTER producing his first poem at the age of twenty-four, Thomas wrote only poetry for many years. But when he was in his early forties, his first two novels, *The Flute-Player* (1979) and *Birthstone* (1980), were published in quick succession. What accounted for Thomas' change of heart? As he admits in *Memories and Hallucinations*, he "never thought I'd write a novel" because "novels tell us in tedious detail about people who never existed and events that never happened. . . . I wasn't interested in writing the typical English novel, in which a few characters have love affairs, one or two get married or die—and you think, at the end of it, 'So what?' " (p. 18). But despite his boredom with the traditional novel, he had also begun to grow dissatisfied with poetry, which "was beginning to seem too bloodless and self-contained. Too neat" (p. 18). The results of Thomas' literary frustrations were two highly poetic novels that in their hybrid, experimental nature—as well as in their main themes—broke important ground for his later work.

Thomas began writing *The Flute-Player* after hearing about a fantasy novel competition cosponsored by the London *Guardian* and the publisher Victor Gollancz—a competition that the novel eventually won. It tells the story of Elena, a woman who shares her modest room with a motley assortment of poets and painters, offering them shelter and occasional sexual favors while the world outside plunges further and further into chaos. Thomas' innovative strategy in describing Elena—and one that should not be surprising, given his dislike of the traditional novel—is to give her far more attributes and features than any one woman could possibly have, and thereby to make her an illustration of what Goethe called "the eternal feminine." Thus, at various points in the novel, Elena marries; takes lovers; works as a prostitute, nurse, and teacher; poses for a political poster; finds and wears an antique crucifix "just when everyone else was giving them up" (p. 101); serves as the inspiration for poems in which "Elena and the trees, the rocks, the snow and the sea were blended" (p. 78); and even, in one character's dream, momentarily seems to turn into the moon "looking down at him with blank indifferent eyes that all the same expressed unquenchable love" (p. 82). In *Memories and Hallucinations*, Thomas explains why he has characterized Elena this way. She is modeled, he writes, on the twentieth-century Russian poet Anna Akhmatova, who "spent most of her life cooped up in one room on the Neva embankment; around her swirled the evil tide of history; she was witness to all its crimes." Thomas wanted to make Elena a similar eyewitness: "I would likewise place a woman in one room of a decaying apartment building; she would suffer and endure. She would nourish artists of both sexes, through ice ages and thaws, and keep their work alive" (p. 20). Both Elena and *The Flute-Player* therefore had to be somewhat abstract, because "the book was to be my tribute to women. Elena would be both Russian and universal; her city would be Leningrad and everywhere" (p. 21).

Elena is not the only character in the novel with larger-than-life attributes; her three closest acquaintances, two poets and a painter, are composite figures as well. When Thomas describes several examples of the painter's work, for example, we realize that he is actually describing *Olympia* and *Déjeuner sur l'herbe*, paintings by the French artist Edouard Manet. Similarly, the male poet's oeuvre comprises poems by Yeats, Rilke, Frost, and many others, and the female poet appears to be a composite of Akhmatova and Emily Dickinson. Thomas' descriptions of the events raging outside Elena's apartment give the novel an equally fluid, abstract approach to time and place: we read of concentration camps, dissidents who suddenly vanish, state censorship of art, and a host of other atrocities.

The reasons for Thomas' abstract approach to character and setting are not hard to guess. Just as his mélange of twentieth-century horrors helps create the novel's terrifying, vague backdrop, so Elena—whose "greatest strength was her ability to forget the past" (p. 63)—comes to represent the eternal triumph of love and art over suffering and war. But the novel's highly symbolic nature occasionally becomes oppressive. In a review of the novel, John Updike astutely observed that its char-

acters are "figures more than personalities," and that "too much history has been crowded into the range of allusions" (p. 206). But even so, *The Flute-Player* is a hypnotic, intriguing novel containing passages of great beauty and looking forward in many respects—its female protagonist, its contrast of the horrors of war to the powers of healing—to Thomas' later, more accomplished novel *The White Hotel*.

Thomas' next novel, *Birthstone*, was published a year after *The Flute-Player* but had been begun earlier—Thomas interrupted work on it to write *The Flute-Player* for the *Guardian* competition. The first stages of the novel were written in collaboration with the poet Elizabeth Ashworth until (as Thomas writes in his "Author's Note and Dedication") "pressure of other work compelled her to withdraw." Like *The Flute-Player*, it anticipates his later novels in many significant ways. The novel describes the strange things that happen when Jo, a middle-aged Irish woman taking a holiday trip to Cornwall, befriends Lola and Hector Bolitho, an American mother and son from a Cornish community in California who have come to Cornwall to explore their roots. *Birthstone*'s opening pages are quite straightforward. But when the three tourists step through the Men-an-tol, "a granite ring with a neat hole drilled through it" (p. 9), which—as Hector learns from a guidebook—is known as a "Sun disc. Or birthstone" that "people used to crawl through to cure their ills" (p. 10), both they and the novel start to behave in odd and unpredictable ways. Jo, who suffers from a multiple personality disorder, becomes even more volatile, assuming male and female alter egos, inventing conversations with Emily Dickinson, and fantasizing about an affair with Hector. The Bolithos change as well—the aged, crippled Lola becomes so young and spry that she starts to resemble her fiery ancestor Lola Montez, and Hector grows old and frail almost overnight.

Like *The Flute-Player*, *Birthstone* has many poetic features: Thomas sprinkles the novel with several examples of Jo's poetry, and confesses in his memoirs that while writing the novel he "followed the creative process that was natural to me. I started not from an abstract idea but from a resonant image" (p. 19). One scene in particular helps illustrate this "creative process." Shortly after she has stepped through the Men-an-tol, Jo, looking at the

Cornish coast, delivers a monologue that contains a highly "resonant image":

> I stumbled over rusty gear, put my feet in wet holes, threw stones into walled shafts. Seconds passed before I heard the splash. The coast was as full of holes as the day. Blind windows of engine houses, billions of tiny holes between the drizzle, holes opening and closing in the dark grey sea. Holes between the fog-horn booms and the light flashes. The holes in my life and in my heart.
>
> (p. 48)

Jo's many references to "holes" obviously remind us of the novel's plot. But they also give the novel's title a metaphorical weight, suggesting that the "holes" in Jo's life are what led her to visit and crawl through, another, actual hole: the Men-an-tol. Passages like this help give *Birthstone* some of the strengths of *The Flute-Player*: a compressed poetic quality, a loving attention to description, and a sympathetic treatment of female characters. But if *The Flute-Player* suffers from an abstractness and lack of plot, *Birthstone* is, if anything, too cluttered with incident.

In his memoirs, Thomas is the novel's harshest critic, remarking that "like an inexperienced, panicky cook, I threw every ingredient I could think of into the pot. The result was an over-flavoured, indigestible dish" (p. 20). Whether or not readers agree with this judgment, they will certainly find *Birthstone* an original and provocative novel.

THE WHITE HOTEL

THOMAS' next novel, *The White Hotel*, was published in 1981 to a storm of both acclaim and controversy and is by far his best-known work. The reasons for the novel's fame are not hard to understand: in its masterful blend of poetry and prose, its subtle combination of fantasy and reality, and its daring linkage of the theories of Freud to the brutalities of the Holocaust, it will leave a searing, unforgettable impression on even the most jaded reader. Whether or not one ends up actually liking *The White Hotel*, one cannot deny that it is utterly unlike any other work of literature one has ever read.

The novel, which is divided into six parts, opens with an epistolary prologue in which Thomas introduces us to the main facts of the story. In an (imaginary) 1920 letter, Freud tells his friend Ferenczi about one of his patients, "a young woman suffering from a severe hysteria" who "has just 'given birth' to some writings" (p. 8). These writings, Freud argues, depict "an extreme of libidinous fantasy combined with an extreme of morbidity" (p. 8). In another letter, Freud informs his friend Sachs that he is sending him a journal written at an Austrian spa by the same woman, after her recovery from a breakdown. Now that he has aroused our curiosity about these "writings," Thomas devotes the next two chapters of the novel to them. Chapter I, "Don Giovanni"—which originally was published separately—is a long poem in which Freud's patient describes her fantasies in hypnotic, disturbing detail: she has "started an affair" with Freud's own son while on a train, and he takes her "to a white lakeside hotel" (p. 15) in the mountains. There the couple give their passion free rein while, all around them, terrible things happen: several guests drown in a storm at sea, the hotel goes up in flames, charred bodies dangle from treetops, and an avalanche kills many of the remaining guests. But none of these tragedies alters the fact that "nothing in the white hotel but love / is offered" (p. 23); in the poem's most bizarre passage, several guests tenderly drink milk from the woman's breasts. The novel's next chapter, "The Gastein Journal," is a prose version of the poem, and it provides us with a few new details about the characters who appear in it—the man is a prisoner of war returning to his family, and the woman is around thirty years old. We also learn from one guest's testimony that there are many Jews among the victims of the avalanche; and another guest cynically declares that "such desperate acts were bound to continue so long as there was injustice in the world, and violence against the people" (p. 84). But despite these frightening omens—omens that will make much more sense in the light of future chapters—Freud's patient "felt happy" and continues to believe that "the spirit of the white hotel was against selfishness" (p. 86).

But why has Thomas gone to the trouble of inventing these documents, and why are they so strange and troubling? The answers to these questions become clearer when we read the next chapter, "Frau Anna G.," which is written in the form of a fictional Freudian case history. Freud describes how, in 1919, he examined "a young lady who had been suffering for the past four years from severe pains in her left breast and pelvic region" (p. 89); she also hallucinated frequently and "had had a promising musical career interrupted by her illness" (p. 89). Freud initially believes that this woman—who is of Jewish descent, comes from the Ukraine, and is given the fictional name Anna G.—suffers from hysteria. But as "Anna" tells Freud more and more about her childhood, he realizes that her poem and journal have close ties to her life: her mother, for example, died in a hotel fire when Anna was young. Freud remains confused, however, about the deeper meaning behind Anna's writings, remarking that "her mind was attempting to tell us what was wrong; for the repressed idea creates its own apt symbol" (p. 99).

As the chapter goes on, Anna reveals her prophetic powers when, in a dream, she correctly predicts the death of Freud's daughter Sophie: "I am cursed," she says, "with what is called second sight" (p. 111). But despite Anna's revelations and Freud's speculations, their sessions go nowhere. When she gives Freud her poem and then, at his urging, writes a prose analysis of it, he is more puzzled than ever, confessing that Anna's writings "might teach us everything, if we were only in a position to make everything out" (p. 115). Before long, he offers a tentative interpretation of the poem and journal, suggesting that the white hotel represents "the oceanic oneness of the child's first years, the auto-erotic paradise, the map of our first country of love" (p. 116); he also asks a question that will be deeply significant for the novel: "Was there not a 'demon' of repetition in our lives. . . . Might it not therefore be that all living things are in mourning for the inorganic state, the original condition from which they have by accident emerged?" (p. 129). Finally, Freud hazards a more specific analysis of Anna's story: that it arose from both her guilt over her mother's death and her relationship with a sadistic man and "expressed her yearning to return to the haven of security, the original white hotel—we have all stayed there—the mother's womb" (p. 143). When Freud meets Anna a year later, she appears fully recovered.

The next chapter, "The Health Resort," takes us closer to the harrowing events of the novel's conclusion. As the section opens, it is 1929 and Freud's former patient—who, it turns out, is really an opera singer named Lisa (Elisabeth) Erdman—is traveling from Vienna to Milan in order to replace an ailing Russian diva, Vera Serebryakova. In Milan she meets and befriends Vera and her husband, Victor Berenstein; some time later, Vera tragically dies in childbirth. Before long, Victor proposes to Lisa, who, after some hesitation, accepts. It is now 1934, and as the first stirrings of war are making themselves felt, the newlyweds visit Lisa's mother's grave in Odessa, then return—along with Victor's son, Kolya—to Victor's home in Kiev. Amid all this activity, Lisa has several more episodes of "second sight," dreaming of "a deep trench filled with many coffins" (p. 163) and correctly predicting the death of Freud's grandson Heinz.

In the novel's last two chapters, all of Lisa's strange symptoms, violent fantasies, and eerie prophecies start to make a new, shocking sense. In "The Sleeping Carriage," it is 1941, and Kolya, Lisa (who was not born Jewish), and all the other Jews in Kiev are rounded up by the Nazis and taken to an enormous ravine in a forest. This section represents the novel's closest convergence of fact and fiction, for the ravine, known to the local people as Babi Yar, was the site of one of the most grisly massacres of World War II. Shortly before Lisa is shot, she recognizes Dina Pronicheva, a real-life Ukrainian actress whose testimony regarding Babi Yar—as Thomas makes plain in an acknowledgment—was one of the most important sources for *The White Hotel*. The chapter also helps explain Lisa's mysterious pains, and, further, proves her gift of "second sight": in what is perhaps the novel's most heartbreaking passage, an SS man kicks the dying Lisa in the breast and pelvis. With a sudden shiver, we realize that all of her prophecies have finally come true. But despite its tragic nature, the chapter ends on a note of hope: although Thomas tells us that "the corpses had been buried, burned, drowned, and reburied under concrete and steel," he also reminds us that "all this had nothing to do with the guest, the soul, the lovesick bride, the daughter of Jerusalem" (p. 253).

In the novel's last, dreamlike chapter, "The Camp," Thomas offers his version of what happens to "the soul, the lovesick bride," after the body perishes. Lisa has been reunited with Kolya, and is traveling by bus through a vast desert. (Thomas helpfully remarks in *Memories and Hallucinations* that this landscape is meant to represent Purgatory, imagined "in terms of the Holy Land" [p. 49].) When she arrives at the "camp," her hip still painful, she sees many estranged relatives and old acquaintances and shares a touching moment with her mother: "Her mother asked her if she would like a drink, and when Lisa said yes she unbuttoned her dress and put her arm round her daughter to draw her to her breast" (p. 268). As the novel ends, tents are being erected everywhere, trainloads of immigrants continue to arrive, and as Lisa's pains finally start to go away, she experiences a moment of rare calm: "She smelt the scent of a pine tree. She couldn't place it. . . . It troubled her in some mysterious way, yet also made her happy" (p. 274).

The White Hotel is a terrifying novel, but it is also an exhilarating one. Lisa's prophetic powers certainly give the massacre at Babi Yar a horrible inevitability, but they also help lend meaning and pattern to what would otherwise be an act of pure barbarism. By revealing the hidden connections between one woman's apparently random story and one of the century's most horrific events, Thomas shows how individuals can triumph over their fates, create poetry out of war, and find love amid destruction. Babi Yar and similar tragedies may reveal the depths to which humanity can sink, but the white hotel will always represent a healing alternative to the violence of history and the passing of time. But perhaps Thomas, in *Memories and Hallucinations*, offers the most telling one-sentence description of *The White Hotel*: "My novel wasn't about the holocaust, but about the journey of the soul, which I believe is endless" (p. 49).

Although it eventually became a best-seller, *The White Hotel* was not an overnight success. After being published to mixed reviews in Great Britain, it enjoyed a more enthusiastic American reception, and generated much attention when its paperback rights were sold for the very large sum of $199,500. It went on to win the 1981 Cheltenham Prize, the *Los Angeles Times* Fiction Prize, and the P.E.N. Prize; was nominated for England's Booker Prize; was translated into more than a dozen languages; and became an international best-seller. Perhaps the novel's fate was not surprising; as John Updike wrote in *The New Yorker*, it represented "an authentic triumph of reader discrimination and word of mouth" (p. 203).

But despite its slow and steady rise to popularity, *The White Hotel* came under attack from several quarters. Thomas himself gives a lucid, though obviously biased, account of these attacks (as well as an interesting account of the genesis of the novel)

in *Memories and Hallucinations*. He reports that "at readings, usually two or three women would rise to tell me my intimations of female sexuality were false," even though "I wasn't attempting to describe all women's sexuality but only one woman's" (p. 74). He counters the criticism that "I had written an exploitative book, tailored to be commercial" with the claim that "since neither I nor my publishers anticipated commercial success in view of the book's complex and innovative form, this criticism . . . pissed me off" (p. 74). And what of the debate that exploded in the British press over whether Thomas had plagiarized Pronicheva's Babi Yar testimony? Thomas justifies his use of her story by arguing that "it would have seemed immoral had I, a comfortable Briton, fictionalised the Holocaust" (p. 47).

Thomas' defense is a sympathetic one, and, besides, the charges of plagiarism overlook the fact that one of the largest themes of the novel is the way in which fantasy and history can overlap. Indeed, it could even be argued that the novel would be weaker without Pronicheva's testimony, since it would then lack a factual counterpart to its fictional sections. Ultimately, however, readers must make up their own minds about all these issues, trying not to let the controversy surrounding the novel distract them from its inherent weaknesses and strengths.

RUSSIAN NIGHTS

OVER the next decade, Thomas published a quintet of novels to which he would eventually give the title *Russian Nights*. Like his first three novels, this sequence reflects his dissatisfaction with the traditional novel, his desire to erase the border between poetry and prose, and his interest in quirky, unusual subject matter. Thomas has called these novels "improvisational," a term that can mean several things. Specifically, it refers to the Italian tradition of *improvisatori*, storytellers blessed (as Thomas writes in *Swallow*, the second novel of the sequence) "with the divine gift of spontaneous creation—the seemingly miraculous talent of being able to switch on the power of narrative . . ." (p. 32). But the term also refers to the way in which these novels seem to generate themselves as they go along, surprising us with devious plot twists just as we think we know where the story is headed, and lurching between fact and fiction so violently that we become suspicious of the distinction between them. Thomas writes in *Memoirs and Hallucinations* that he got the idea for the sequence from an unfinished work by Pushkin, "Egyptian Nights," in which "a comfortable Petersburg poet is disturbed in his study by the unannounced arrival of a scruffy Italian *improvisatore* who asks for his help" (p. 55). Pushkin's bizarre tale, Thomas writes, seemed like a good model for his new project: "The fragmentary story moves from prose to verse, from the present to the past, from realism—tinged with the uncanny—to myth. . . . I dreamed of continuing his story, in some way. I liked the blurring of boundaries, in form and atmosphere. I couldn't write a straight novel; but I couldn't write a straight poem any more either" (pp. 55–56). *Russian Nights* is a sprawling, difficult sequence whose many innovations will either charm or irritate readers used to more conventional fiction.

As *Ararat* (1983), the first novel in the sequence, begins, the half-Russian, half-Armenian poet Sergei Rozanov, bored during a night with his new mistress, Olga, decides to "improvise" a story. The rest of the novel—in other words, Rozanov's improvisation—tells the story of Victor Surkov, a well-known Russian poet who, hoping to resolve a midlife crisis, is taking a sea voyage to Armenia by way of America. While on board the ship, Surkov begins an affair with a gymnast, encounters an old man named Finn who tells him about the Armenian genocide of World War I, and works sporadically on a piece of writing called "Egyptian Nights"—a large chunk of which is actually by Pushkin, but which Thomas attributes to Surkov and has him continue. When Surkov arrives in America, he is interviewed, stays with an American-Armenian friend, and begins an affair with a young journalist. In the novel's last pages, we return to Olga and Rozanov, who declare what a loathsome character Surkov is; Rozanov then prepares to leave Olga for his other mistress, Sonia.

What keeps *Ararat*'s large cast of characters, shifting narrators, and changes in locale from becoming hopelessly confusing is the way Thomas uses the image of Ararat as a recurring motif throughout the novel. Rozanov, for example, imagines the mountain—which was the final resting place of Noah's ark, as well as a place fought for by the Armenians early in the century—whenever he

thinks about his mother, viewing it as a symbol of travel and the imagination: "he feared to exchange his vision for reality" (p. 15). Elsewhere in the novel, Thomas compares the mountain's two peaks to a woman's breasts; and in another passage, two characters "confronted each other, like the twin peaks of Ararat" (p. 180). By exploring the many possible associations of this one image, Thomas links the novel's many themes and helps guide readers through a maze that might otherwise overwhelm them.

The same could be said of Thomas' technique in *Swallow* (1984), the next novel in the sequence. In an author's note, Thomas writes that one of the novel's main themes is "the mysterious way in which a word, an image, a dream, a story, calls up another, connected yet independent"—and not surprisingly, *Swallow* is similar to *Ararat* in its wide range of interconnected themes, its large number of stories within stories. The novel opens with a shock: we learn that *Ararat* was actually narrated by Corinna Riznich, an Italian *improvisatrice* and a participant in a Finnish storytelling Olympiad. Wondering whether she will win, Corinna subjects her story to harsh scrutiny, asking, "Were there seven veils, did I get that right? Let's see, there was the *improvisatore*, then Pushkin; Surkov; the Armenian . . . Rozanov, and then myself narrating the end. Shit, that's only six. . . . That's really screwed it up" (p. 21). But despite this stern judgment, Corinna continues her story of Rozanov and Surkov, and Thomas playfully lets us eavesdrop on a debate between the judges over whether it is "man-hating" or "profoundly feminist" (p. 63).

As the novel continues, we are introduced to some of the other *improvisatori*, most importantly, Southerland, an Englishman whose story—a lively saga of growing up in Australia—includes details from Thomas' own childhood. (In fact, Thomas later reprinted parts of this section in *Memories and Hallucinations*.) More confusing still, Southerland's story contains sections lifted from the British pulp writer H. Rider Haggard's book *King Solomon's Mines*. Because of Southerland's borrowings from Haggard, he is eliminated from the Olympiad on charges of plagiarism. The sunny mood of the novel turns darker when a young Finnish technical assistant is found to have taken his life, and the judges tell Corinna that they cannot give her the award because "in view of the night's events, a young man's suicide. . . . it was impossible to award the laurel to a work of such darkness and violence as yours, however brilliant it was" (p. 310). With this sudden decision the novel comes to a close. But the young man's suicide and the Southerland affair raise questions that linger after the book has ended: Is the border between art and life as solid as we would like to think? If—as both Southerland's tale and the young man's suicide seem to suggest—it isn't, then what does this murky boundary suggest about the role of art and the responsibility of the artist? *Swallow* may be a lighthearted work, but it also asks serious questions about important ideas.

Sphinx, the next volume of *Russian Nights*, was published in 1986 and is by far the most elaborate of the sequence's five novels. It is divided into three sections, each of which demonstrates Thomas' great technical virtuosity and displays his ongoing interest in the themes of *Ararat* and *Swallow*. The first section—which began as a television play commissioned by the BBC—tells the strange story of how the poet Gleb Rezanov is accidentally killed after being mistaken for Rozanov. Both poets, as it happens, are obsessed with the dancer Isadora Duncan's scarf and what became of it after her grisly death in a car crash.

In the next section, we are introduced to the British journalist Lloyd George, who becomes, like Southerland, a fictional stand-in for Thomas. When Lloyd George makes a trip to Russia, he meets a pleasant couple, Shimon and Masha Barash, who inform him that Surkov, hardly the invention of Corinna's teeming brain, really exists. He also becomes obsessed with Nadia Sakulin, a Russian actress; but his hopes are dashed when Nadia turns out to be a spy who, in return for setting Lloyd George up for blackmail, wants to be allowed to join her husband, a defector now living in San Francisco and dying of AIDS. The third section, a long poem in the complex stanza form of Pushkin's *Eugene Onegin*, describes Lloyd George's brief but understandable struggle with insanity.

Perhaps sensing that another novel as elaborately structured as *Sphinx* would alienate even his most fervent admirers, Thomas continued *Russian Nights* with *Summit* (1987), a novel so different from the first three that readers may wonder why he chose to include it in the sequence. The novel begins predictably enough. Nadia, the author of a novel called *Swallow*, is flying to Russia, but she is immediately killed off in a plane crash, and we find ourselves transported to the wild world of Ameri-

can politics in the 1980s. Fortunately, Thomas explains this sudden shift in an author's note: calling *Summit* "an adult fairy tale," he writes that "I have followed an ancient tradition in which a serious trilogy is succeeded by a farcical or satirical coda." More specifically, the novel is a satire of American–Soviet peace talks, and pokes particular fun at Ronald Reagan, who appears, faintly disguised, as President O'Reilly. In some 150 fast-paced pages, Thomas treats us to hilarious interviews in which O'Reilly, plagued by memory loss, causes great confusion by responding to each question with an answer to the question that preceded it. O'Reilly and his wife, Wanda, visit the Soviet leader, Grobichov (an obvious stand-in for Gorbachev), who causes further confusion by leading the O'Reillys to believe that he is married to a frumpy middle-aged woman, when he is actually married to the nubile young Larissa. As the foursome become better acquainted, many sexual shenanigans ensue, as well as many more misunderstandings; an especially convoluted one occurs when O'Reilly's senility causes the IUD, or intrauterine device, to be mistaken for a new defense policy—"Independent Unilateral Defence." The novel ends on a suitably ludicrous note: in a burst of dialogue, the main characters, listening to an opera, begin "to converse in quasi-musical tones, even repeating themselves in an operatic way, not unlike the cantata for many voices rising above the confusion of Russian and English" (p. 159). *Summit* could be described in the same way—as a confused, comic opera sung in several languages.

But *Russian Nights* did not end there. Thomas wrote one more novel, *Lying Together* (1990), for the sequence, and in an author's note humbly thanked his editors for their patience "as I kept changing my mind about whether the work was finished," adding that "I should have realised that an author does not decide this; the work itself decides, by suddenly letting go—as it has now done." This novel charts the journey of another authorial stand-in—this time called Don Thomas—as he attends an international festival of writers in London, bumps into Rozanov, and reencounters his old friends the Barashes, who fondly recall "those nights of passionate improvisation" (p. 7) and, in doing so, inform us that the three of them, taking turns, have narrated all the earlier novels in the sequence. The three friends then embark on a new improvisation, but the content of their story is less important than the remarks they make—on the connections between fiction and fact, storytelling and real life—as they gather to tell it. Don Thomas admits of *Memories and Hallucinations*, for example, that "a lot of that book is fictional," since "we live fictional lives" (p. 97). And toward the end of the novel, Thomas asks a question that might serve as a moral of the entire sequence: "Wasn't everyone—driven by forces beyond his control—semi-fictional at best?" (p. 225).

In its sheer inventiveness, its ambitious overturning of traditional approaches to genre, character, and structure, and its often profound exploration of the complex connections between life and art, *Russian Nights* is a considerable achievement. But paradoxically, its great strengths are also responsible for its many weaknesses. Thomas seems so intent on overwhelming us with his cleverness that he often settles for cleverness for its own sake; as a result, readers may finish the sequence famished for such "old-fashioned" notions as coherent plots and sympathetic characters. Another problem with the sequence may be that it simply goes on too long—even the most inventive fictional strategies can seem tedious and repetitive if stretched out over five novels. *Russian Nights* also shares a problem of Thomas' later novels, which is that his ideas are often more interesting than the language in which he explores them. Reading these five novels, one frequently wishes that Thomas had tried harder to integrate cleverness and depth, structural innovation and lyrical precision. But even so, one cannot help being impressed by these novels; and although one is unlikely to number them among one's favorite novels or turn to them in times of trouble, one is nonetheless grateful that they exist.

RECENT NOVELS

IN his next novel, *Flying in to Love* (1992), Thomas returns to the main themes of *The White Hotel*—historical inevitability, the murky border between fantasy and reality—with the key difference that the novel is set entirely in America, and it focuses on the events surrounding the assassination of John F. Kennedy. Comprising many very short chapters, and containing a kaleidoscopic variety of characters, the novel lacks anything resembling a traditional plot or structure. But despite its many experimental qualities, it presents a coherent and powerful account of both the assassination and the greater questions and issues to which it gives rise.

The "Love" of the novel's title refers to Love Field, the Dallas airfield where the Kennedys landed shortly before the assassination, and this name becomes an ongoing metaphor for the competing claims of inevitability and chance, the past as it happened and as it might have happened. As Kennedy reflects, "an airfield had something in common with love. Figures held a distance. . . . The search for novelty. A certain numbness. A poise between earth and heaven" (p. 107). But the novel contains more than metaphors. Just as he based his description of Babi Yar on a real-life source, Thomas uses the Kennedy assassination as a springboard for both fictional invention and historical speculation. Thus several chapters describe the few known facts of what happened on 22 November 1963, while others invent conversations the Kennedys have the night before. In other chapters, we enter the minds of Lee Harvey Oswald and his wife, Marina, meet a character who collects "assassination dreams" (p. 195), and eavesdrop on a cover-up involving a switching of brains. In one extremely inventive and moving chapter Thomas even provides us with an alternate future for the Kennedys, in which the assassination has not taken place and they are relaxing at Lyndon Johnson's ranch in Austin, Texas. The purpose of all these different chapters and characters is clear: to mirror the way we try to make sense of history, but are fated never to get the facts quite right. In one chapter, Thomas includes a passage that could serve as a description of both the novel's characters and its readers:

For all of these people—and they could be multiplied—the assassination occupies a kind of dreamtime. Kennedy is dead, he is not dead. He is being taken back for burial at Arlington; he is flying on to Austin. . . . [T]hose few seconds carried too great a burden of event, of shock, and it was as if that weight caused time to cave in, creating a vortex, a whirlwind, in which past, present and future, and reality and illusion, became confused.

(p. 182)

Thomas keeps the novel from becoming too "confused," however, by providing us with a protagonist—Sister Agnes, a nun living in Dallas—whose obsession with Kennedy's death helps give the novel an emotional center and also balances its more wildly speculative chapters with long stretches of linear plot and traditional chronology. When we first meet Agnes, she is a young history teacher who shares with her students a keen interest in "our first Catholic President" (p. 11); the next time we encounter her, it is 1969, and in the wake of Vietnam and the murder of Robert Kennedy, she asks herself, "If a sudden violent death occurred . . . did the unrealised future of that dead person exist potentially, or did it not?" (p. 27). As time goes on, she becomes more obsessed with the assassination and less sure of the values she once held dear, wondering, "Why did all the various bits of information or rumour not at least suggest some overall design?" (p. 112). As Agnes confronts the 1980s and such new crises as the AIDS epidemic, her faith wavers even more: "All her life she had been looking for meaning and design in the universe. . . . She thought it was to be found too in history, her special love. . . . But with John Kennedy's assassination she had, in a way, entered history herself, and the shock had been enormous. History was what happened to you . . . and it made no sense" (pp. 152–153). In one of the novel's last, most disturbing chapters, set in the present, the weight of all this uncertainty becomes too much for Agnes to bear, and she has a nervous breakdown, becoming unable to read and losing control of her bodily functions: "They were all inside her. Both assassins and victims. . . . the drama had taken up residence in her, Sister Agnes', mind, and every moment of her life was the moment between firing and impact" (p. 219). Although Agnes eventually recovers, these last sections serve as a final reminder of the novel's sobering themes.

Flying in to Love is not a perfect book. Thomas' decision to fill the novel with a wide variety of quotations from American poets—especially Frost and Whitman—may help broaden its scope, but it also gives it a too self-consciously "American" flavor; and his replication of American dialogue is not always convincing. But in its use of the Kennedy assassination to explore the intricate and often maddening connections between fiction and reality, history as it happens and as we think it happens, it represents one of Thomas' most inventive, powerful novels, and takes its place with Don DeLillo's *Libra* as a stirring exploration of one of the great unsolved mysteries of American history.

A year later, Thomas returned to the themes of the Holocaust with *Pictures at an Exhibition* (1993). The first section of the novel takes place in

Auschwitz, and focuses on the intense, bizarre relationship between an SS officer, Dr. Lorenz, and a camp prisoner, the Czech doctor Chaim Galewski, who—after brief training as a psychotherapist and years of general practice—has been "arrested as a communist agitator" (p. 51). Troubled by severe weakness, bad headaches, and recurring nightmares, Lorenz summons Galewski to his office, and over the course of several visits the two men realize that they have more in common than they could have ever believed. Lorenz is torn between his troubled conscience and his firm belief that he is doing the right thing—"All that matters is the race, the *Volk*" (p. 36). And Galewski, who muses at one point that "I could understand, only too easily, how a decent, civilised couple like Dr. and Frau Lorenz could find most of my race unspeakable" (p. 27), has his own nightmare in which he appears as a Nazi. Galewski also tells the story of how his daughter, Elli, nearly killed by the Nazis, was rescued just in time and is now being raised by an SS couple. But despite all the nasty secrets and shared similarities that the two men reveal, Lorenz is soon cured and predicts to Galewski, as they part ways, that "you and I might bump into each other on a Black Sea beach in fifty years' time, should we be lucky enough to live that long!" (p. 67).

In the next, much longer section of the novel, "Jealousy," fifty years have indeed passed, and Thomas, shifting the scene to contemporary London, introduces us to a cast of characters who—at first glance, anyway—seem to have little to do with Lorenz and Galewski. At the center of this new group are the aging psychoanalyst Oscar Jacobson and his wife, Myra—both Holocaust survivors—and several people with professional connections to Oscar: Lilian Rhodes, a neurotic middle-aged woman; Christopher James, a young analyst in training who has been recommended to Lilian by Oscar; Rachel Brandt, another trainee analyst; and several husbands, wives, and lovers. Thomas fills us in on the details of these characters' lives by means of a series of monologues (many spoken during therapy sessions) and letters that circulate back and forth among the characters. This section, though lively and interesting, seems to have little to do with the opening scenes of the novel; but just as we begin to wonder why Thomas has spliced together two unconnected stories, a grim and fascinating pattern begins to emerge. Rachel gives Oscar a German book filled with "extracts from military documents" (p. 95) that, as we learn when we read the documents, recount a grisly 1941 episode in the Ukraine in which Jewish children were locked up in a house "in intolerable conditions," then ordered killed. One of these children, we learn, was Galewski's daughter, Elli, who grew up to become Lilian; Galewski, moreover, was Oscar Jacobson's cousin. (In a characteristic move, Thomas has blended fact and fiction by taking these documents—as he writes in an acknowledgment—"verbatim from German documents quoted in *Those Were the Days: The Holocaust through the Eyes of the Perpetrators and Bystanders.*") Not long after these facts are disclosed, bad things start to happen—Rachel goes temporarily insane, Lilian's husband has an affair with Christopher's wife, and, worst of all, many of the major characters are brutally murdered by Myra, whose Holocaust memories have finally caught up with her. The novel's next section is written in the form of a review of *Patterns of an Observed Disturbance,* a book that Christopher goes on to write about his friends and colleagues. The questions that the reviewer asks about Christopher's book—in which, of course, names and places have been changed—are ones that we may want to ask about Thomas' novel as well: "Are David Epstein [Oscar Jacobson] and his Polish cousin [Galewski] one and the same person? Did he fully collaborate in the atrocity in Devon, or even instigate it? Were the couple bound together by some earlier atrocity at Buchenwald [Auschwitz], in which David saved her life at the expense of her soul; and did she now demand retribution?" (p. 263).

Although it displays Thomas' typical ingenuity, *Pictures at an Exhibition* is, in the final analysis, a little too ingenious for its own good. The large number of characters, the violent shifts in time and place, the many different media in which Thomas has chosen to tell his story, and the fact that all the chapter titles are also titles of paintings by Edvard Munch give the novel a cluttered, overstuffed quality from which it never fully recovers. But even though the novel is considerably less than the sum of its parts, it is well worth reading as a haunting testament to the way in which the crimes of the past can erupt into the present and wounds long thought healed can suddenly, violently open with devastating consequences.

Thomas' next novel, *Eating Pavlova,* was published in 1994, and takes the form of a long mono-logue delivered by Freud during the days leading up to his death in 1939 in London. Declaring that "I am finding it harder to die than I had anticipated" (p. 178), Freud—speaking to his beloved daughter, Anna—takes us on a whirlwind tour of his life and career. But since "it would be extremely tedious to go through my life chronologically" (p. 5), Freud's memories proceed by association rather than logic. In a compelling and often touching manner, Freud discusses himself as he would one of his patients, paying special attention to his dreams. In one, he is joined by three guests—Lou Andreas-Salomé (his friend and possible mistress), Isaac Newton, and Charles Darwin—for a discussion of love and existence. A little while later, he has "a drowsy kind of semi-dream" in which four "wolves" appear to him: "the Wolf Man; Wolf our lovely Alsatian, so infallible in judging when the fifty minutes were over, bounding in at the door; Antonia Wolff, Jung's patient and long-enduring mistress; and the mad Mrs. Virginia Woolf, who won't be analysed in case she loses her (by my judgement slender) gift for writing . . ." (p. 60). But Thomas does not recount these dreams for comic relief alone. In one of the novel's most important passages, Freud meditates on the difference between dreaming and truth, ending with a question that could be applied not only to this novel, but to the rest of Thomas' work as well:

It may be, of course, that there are always at least two versions of reality, at every moment, for every individual; and so the confusion that we think memory creates actually belongs to events and incidents. . . . It may be that a dream, seemingly so vague and unclear and uncertain, is every bit as clearcut as a waking event—or rather the opposite, that the waking event is as unclear and ambiguous as the dream, if we only saw the former correctly.

Or is the *dream* reality? A dense poem, part of the universal stream: and what we consider reality is a weakening, a turning into separate prose fragments, even contradictory ones?

(pp. 25–26)

As Freud's death becomes more and more imminent, his dreams, unbeknownst to him, become more and more prophetic, but he dutifully tries to make psychoanalytic sense of them: thus a dream that foreshadows the Holocaust in its vision of "bloated corpses" and "a densely packed bath-house" (p. 182) is interpreted by Freud as "obviously express[ing] my guilt at having had to leave my sisters behind in Vienna" (pp. 182–183); and a dream featuring a Japanese man and a mushroom cloud suggests to Freud that "I was probably thinking of the Buddha, sitting cross-legged on my desk" (p. 186). Although Freud may not know it, these dreams help prove his theory that dreams are often more "real" than real life and also support his statement that "time does not exist in the unconscious" (p. 76). In the midst of reporting all these dreams, Freud both finds out and reveals many surprising facts about his life—most significantly, that his cousin Samuel may actually be his brother, and that in his war diaries he often told lies. But these biographical details are not nearly as important as the themes they illustrate: the passions and secrets lurking beneath even the stodgiest of facades and the fragile line that always divides fantasy from reality. Like many of Thomas' other novels, *Eating Pavlova* may be somewhat too clever for its own good, but in its complex treatment of both characters and ideas, its revelations about both Freud's personality and his theories, it is one of Thomas' most striking, memorable achievements.

Lady with a Laptop, Thomas' most recent novel, appeared in 1996, and its coy title gives a good indication of its satirical nature. The action of the book centers on Simon Hopkins, a self-confessed hack novelist (his current project is a novel about John F. Kennedy's brain) who has been invited to conduct a writing workshop on the Greek island of Skagathos. In a curiously vague Acknowledgment, Thomas draws our attention to the possible connection between the fictional Skagathos and the real-life "excellent and highly professional holistic holiday center on Skyros," where "for the past few years I have been fortunate to be invited to lead writing workshops" (p. v). He goes on to dedicate his novel to the Skyrians—but neglects to tell us just what the two islands do or don't have in common. But Thomas' vagueness turns out to be strangely appropriate, for it is this very confusion of fact and fiction that the novel goes on to explore. After several colorful opening chapters in which Thomas pokes gentle fun at the practices of the island (classes on "Orgasmic Consciousness" and "Co-listening," workshops in which all the students collaborate on a dismally bad short story) and describes Simon's halfhearted passes at several of his female students, the novel turns serious: Lucinda, the "Lady" of the novel's title, is found dead in her room. All the characters wonder whether she has committed suicide or died of natural causes, but these questions become less important—at least for Simon—than whether her death was caused by anything that took place in his workshops. Simon, in between novels, may have fled to Skagathos in order "not to have to suffer, for a few weeks, the unreality of fiction" (p. 11), but if Lucinda's death was the result of his workshops, then perhaps fiction can have very real and timely consequences after all. Indeed, we learn that several characters who appear in the ongoing story that Simon's class is writing (large chunks of which Thomas provides) bear a striking resemblance to figures from Lucinda's life—a coincidence that, as Simon muses, may have been too much for Lucinda to bear: "Isn't it likely that a few stray surreal words, in the exercise I gave them . . . took her rushing back to a childhood turmoil? Overwhelming her?" (pp. 158–159). As the novel ends, Simon is heading home because "I have to return to fiction. I can't afford too much reality" (p. 246). But as the novel has shown, the division between fiction and reality is hardly as watertight as the departing Simon appears to think, and Lucinda's ghost haunts this final glib remark like a black dress at a joyful wedding.

Lady with a Laptop is probably Thomas' weakest novel. To use E. M. Forster's terms, its minor characters are so "flat" as to be virtually indistinguishable, and Simon, the "roundest" character in the book, is so thoroughly unlikable that it is hard to sympathize with him or his various dilemmas. In fact, the novel's biggest flaw is that however important its moral—the eternal interdependence of fact and fiction—may be, it lacks characters who will help readers ponder and understand this moral. Are we meant to view Simon as a lovable rogue or an irresponsible scoundrel? By failing to develop his main character, Thomas prevents his own pressing questions from being satisfactorily answered. But perhaps these flaws are intentional ones, and *Lady with a Laptop* a deliberately lighthearted look at ideas and issues that Thomas has explored much more seriously elsewhere. Just as *Summit* is a spoof of the three novels that precede it, it seems likely that this novel—Thomas' latest but by no means his last—is an intentionally frivolous treatment of his own lifelong obsessions: the sudden, violent clashes between the past and the present, and the deeply complex, ever unpredictable relationship between fact and fiction.

POETRY

THOMAS has proven equally versatile and prolific as a poet. His first poems were published in a 1964 pamphlet, *Personal and Possessive,* and in the 1968 anthology *Penguin Modern Poets II,* and since then he has published several more collections—among them *Two Voices* (1968), *Logan Stone* (1971), *Love and Other Deaths* (1975), *The Honeymoon Voyage* (1978), and *Dreaming in Bronze* (1981). Deciding how to structure a discussion of his poetry is difficult. Although a chronological approach to his novels seems to be the most logical one, it probably will not work for a discussion of his poetry, since it will prevent a coherent treatment of his ongoing poetic preoccupations. Fortunately, Thomas himself has suggested a useful way of dividing and discussing his poetry. In the introduction to his 1983 *Selected Poems,* he writes that even though he dislikes "rigid classification," he feels that his poems seem to fall naturally into three groups: "love poems or erotic poems, . . . poems relating to my Cornish background," and poems that take up "broader themes, from history, culture, and myth" (p. viii). Looking at the poems he has gathered in this selection, as well as in *The Puberty Tree,* a selection published in 1992, one finds that this grouping is both insightful and instructive; it therefore seems like a good idea to preserve it here. (Page citations from *Selected Poems* will be preceded by *SP;* those from *The Puberty Tree,* by *PT.* If a poem appears in both collections, the citation will be from *The Puberty Tree,* which is the more recent and more readily available collection.)

Thomas' love poems are unlike those of any other contemporary poet in their strange blend of the local and the cosmic, the personal and the universal. In this respect, they bear an obvious resemblance to *The White Hotel,* in which Lisa's fantasies and prophecies turn out to have such close links to worldwide events. A good example of this blend can be found in Thomas' early poem "Cygnus A." Watching his lover undress, the poem's narrator finds himself distracted by the night sky and all the astronomical wonders he finds there:

But I prefer to gaze over the dark rooftops
And talk to you over my shoulder.
Somewhere out there, love, near-neighbour Rigel
Winks its white Chaucerian light
From Orion's heel; taking its petty flight
From the peaks of the Eagle
Burning through
Hitler, by Deneb and Altair,
Falls Vega's vulturous blue

(*PT,* p. 27)

As his mind wanders further and further from the woman next to him, he thinks about how awful it would be

to feel uncertain
If one's discrete
Galaxy will ever emerge
With all its stars complete.

(p. 28)

He finally decides, though, that even if

by this time snow
Has covered over
Many a planet, and Judgement-Day
Has heard the excuse of lovers:

"But that was in another galaxy,
And besides, the star is dead!"

(p. 29)

Such apocalypses and excuses will not alter the fact that his lover—"Though all the space-trips fail" (p. 29)—is still beside him. The poem, though not without ambivalence, therefore celebrates the triumph of human love over the terror of cosmic catastrophe.

This contrast appears in several other poems. In "Unknown Shores," modeled on a poem by the nineteenth-century French poet Théophile Gautier, the narrator's mistress uses space as a metaphor for the lasting love that she cannot find on Earth:

Have you a star, she says,
O any faithful sun
where love does not eclipse?
. . . (The countdown slurs and slips).
—Ah child, if that star shines,
it is in chartless skies,

I do not know of such!
But come, where will you go?

(*PT,* p. 12)

And in the shorter, more somber "Coma Berenices," Thomas' speaker finds cosmic equivalents for his unresponsive mistress:

> . . . the whites of your eyes gleam at me
> like the coronae of a binary eclipse,
> the old, still chastity of your thighs where my
>   teeth wander
> is the Milky Way, galactic whirlpool and forge
> which comes to us as cold, still, chaste light
>   (*PT*, p. 38)

Poems like these are likely to leave readers with mixed feelings: although they will undoubtedly be impressed by Thomas' metaphorical range, they may also regret that the characters in the poems (like many of his fictional characters) seem little more than excuses for literary cleverness. But in several other poems, Thomas describes love in more earthly ways. In the shaped poem "Logan Stone," for example, he uses a stone with magical properties as a touching metaphor for true love. Like people in love, the stone is neither two nor one, since

> if it were one
> stone it would not be magical
> if it were two stones the attrition of
> rain cutting into its natural weakness too well
> it would not be magical
>   (*PT*, p. 49)

Such special qualities give the stone—and by implication, love—a peculiar, wonderful mixture of solidity and frailty, and the poem ends on a triumphant note:

> neither one nor two doomed and unshakable
>   on its point
> of infinity that is the miracle to be so weak
> a finger logs it what constant strength
> what force it takes to be a
> logan-
> stone you and I what cold applied
> granite-fire logging on weakness no storm
>   can move us
>   (*PT*, p. 49)

(Thomas explains in a note that "To 'log,' in old Cornish, is to set trembling" [*SP*, p. 127]).

Not all of Thomas' love poems are so ambitious or metaphysical, however. In the witty "Poetry and Striptease," he describes how, gathered at a bar,

several men watch a stripper perform: both lustful and confused, they see "our lives, our deaths" while she sways

> like the foaming wave
> ahead of Venus, wading from the sea—
> poetry and striptease, striptease and poetry.
>   (*PT*, p. 134)

And in the poem "Weddings," modeled after the Latin poet Catullus, Thomas giddily alternates between two groups of speakers, "Girls" and "Youths," both of which look forward to their upcoming "Weddings" with a spirited, bawdy abandon:

> GIRLS
> Churning it in up tight you wean us: come serve it us
>   can't
> sing in rhythm, O take us, extend it, we're fir-cones
>   ignited,
> stick hurt us, wide in, out, permit it here, exhilarate,
> noon tomorrow exile you weary, we can't look at our
>   parents.
>   I means us, henceforward, I means us!

> YOUTHS
> Penetrate quite all, we're men now and in labour,
> nose and eye O mingled, alive who can divide us or
>   release?
> Those with worried minds, salt them, commit them to
>   boxes.
> Stickier, jam, you sip, a hint, respond it, hairy, lick a
>   bit.
>   I means us, henceforward, I means us!
>   (*SP*, p. 31)

Even though many readers may prefer a subtle, intricate poem like "Cygnus A" to this saucy, straightforward one, they will find it hard to deny their amazement that the same poet could have written both.

Thomas' poems about his native Cornwall are just as diverse as his love poems, employing a wide array of images, tones, and speakers. His poems about his own family are among the most simple, direct poems he has written. In "Smile," for example, Thomas traces his mother's progress from cheerful schoolgirl to dying old woman by means of the recurring image of a smile, which he describes in each stanza as "there," even though his mother grows older and weaker as the poem goes on. As the poem ends, Thomas' contrast between his mother's eternal smile and her timely death gives him an odd kind of comfort:

> and now that she is dead and gone,
> having smiled in the undertaker's hut
> so I shouldn't feel guilty,
> and now that her death has faded
> like the snaps,
> the smile is still there,
> some poems have no beginning and no end.
>
> (*PT*, p. 130)

Thomas has also written affecting poems about his sister. In "My Sister's War," he describes the romantic escapades that leave her blithely indifferent to the early stirrings of World War II:

> The blitz on Plymouth was no more
> than a charmed backcloth to romance,
> faint slender searchlights gliding round,
> too far away to cause alarm,
> grave nightly rituals without sound,
> an orange glimmer, while she necked
> with the elect of the elect.
>
> (*PT*, p. 121)

Thomas' poems about his own childhood are inventive and interesting as well, especially "Big Deaths, Little Deaths," a sequence of eleven poems in which he describes his earliest experiences of love (an Australian girl named Sara) and lust ("Marlene Dietrich taught me to masturbate" [*PT*, p. 125]).

The landscape of Cornwall plays an extremely important role in many of Thomas' poems, although he uses it very differently from poem to poem. In the short poem "Penwith," for example, he describes the Men-an-tol—the same stone that played such an important role in both *Birthstone* and "Logan Stone"—in a hushed, rhapsodic manner, first asking it questions ("Did flint tools or alone the driving rain / complete its holy paradox: granitic / yet sensitive as the joint of a bone?"), then describing its function ("Nine maidens petrified for sabbath dancing / or sun-discs crouched in an altar-less ring"), and finally, as the poem ends, suddenly speaking from the stone's point of view:

> I am the loganstone a cloud can alter,
> inert mass trembling on a compass-point;

> I am the men-an-tol, the wind's vagina;
> I am the circle of stones grouped around grass.
>
> (*PT*, p. 50)

In other poems, however, the Cornish landscape is less a force in its own right than a passive backdrop to particular events. This is perhaps truest of the sequence "Under Carn Brea," the title of which—as Thomas explains in a note—refers to "a granite hill in West Cornwall, overlooking the village where I was born" (*SP*, p. 128). Each of the poem's several sections is devoted either to one of Thomas' relatives or to a scene in which several of these relatives appear; and the poem gains focus and unity from the fact that all its characters have been laid to rest "Under Carn Brea." Throughout the poem, and with great variety and skill, Thomas draws our attention to the peculiar foibles and speaking styles of his characters. A person named Mona, for example, "turned all language to a comic / Amazement at catastrophe barely averted," shouting "My *gar*, Harold! What did you *do*?" (*PT*, p. 87), while Harold, Thomas' father, is described in a more reverential, serious way:

> When you laughed, at your own joke or another's,
> To the damned and God himself it carried.
> Which came back to you, amplifying your laughter.
> God shook then all over the wheatfields.
> Making you throw your head back and split the ceiling.
> God suffered agonies in his own chapels.
> Back went your head, blasting the rooftops.
> If it rained it was God's helpless tears.
>
> (*PT*, p. 88)

An even more interesting use of the Cornish landscape occurs in "The Puberty Tree." In this poem, Thomas describes his childhood perceptions of a tree outside his window, and in doing so, brilliantly illustrates the process by which a real thing can acquire more and more metaphorical weight as time passes, eventually turning into a pure symbol. As the poem opens, the tree "swayed big, saw-edged leaves / by the open window," becoming the object of the young narrator's rapt observation. Soon, however, the tree mingles in his imagination with the strange events of his adolescence. When he is rudely introduced to adult sexuality, finding "a white / sticky gum . . . on my chest and belly / in the middle of the night," he believes that "the puberty tree / spun these . . . substances out into me"

(p. 149). Finally, the tree loses whatever literal significance it once had, becoming wholly inseparable from the narrator's perception of it:

> now it is wholly inside me: my groin the root,
> the slender bough my spine, the saw-edged leaves
> my imagination; and the tree sways between
> the dark, the light.
>
> (*PT*, p. 149)

"The Puberty Tree," in addition to being a forceful poem about growing up, is a fine example of how Thomas has put his native landscape to striking poetic use.

The third group into which Thomas has divided his poetry—"broader themes, from history, culture, and myth"—includes some of his most interesting work, and, to an even greater degree than the other two groups, contains many close ties to the themes and subject matter of his novels. He has written several poems, for example, about Freud and his circle. In the sonnet sequence "Fathers, Sons and Lovers"—written in the form of letters by Freud, Lou Andreas-Salomé, Freud's follower Victor Tausk, and Helene Deutsch, a young analyst—Thomas tells the story of Tausk's estrangement from Freud, and his subsequent suicide, with a heart-wrenching directness. In the more light-hearted "Vienna. Zürich. Constance," he offers us a surreal version of the events that precipitated the falling-out between Freud and his disciple Jung. Thomas gives us the bare facts of this "profound unmeeting" (*PT*, p. 102) in a prose introduction: "In May 1912 Freud visited the town of Constance, near Zürich, to spend a weekend with a sick colleague. Jung was deeply hurt that he had not taken the opportunity to visit him in Zürich; Freud equally so that the younger man had not come to see him in Constance. Their relationship, already strained, ended abruptly soon after" (*PT*, p. 102). But when Thomas translates this simple story into poetry, the bare facts quickly recede, and a legion of small, eccentric details take their place. In one stanza, Thomas describes the brief encounter between two people peripherally connected to Freud and Jung:

> By a strange coincidence
> The young woman who would have been in Jung's
>   compartment
> Had Jung been travelling, was the mistress

Of the young man who would have been in Freud's
  compartment
Had Freud been travelling. Having confused
Their plans, they passed each other, unaware.

> (*PT*, p. 102)

In another poem, "The House of Dreams," Thomas even gives us a poetic rendering of the events of *The White Hotel*:

> It is a honeymoon hotel
> visited by the dead and the living.
> They share the same taxis, and a fool
> has muddled all the reservations.
> They love you. They are to be loved.
>
> (*SP*, p. 121)

The poems in which Thomas narrates myths of other countries and cultures—Brazilian and Fijian, to name just two—are not especially successful. He has achieved better results with several poems in which he pays tribute to writers from other lands. Occasionally these tributes take the form of satires—as when, in the poem "To Louisa in the Lane," he alternates lines about Thomas Hardy's romantic history with lines from the *Kama Sutra*, or, in "Sun Valley," borrows Dante's terza rima, as well as some of his actual phrases, to describe the slaughter of several chickens. But Thomas' literary tributes are more often serious than not. In the touching poem "Lorca," Thomas describes how, "walking / in a red-light / district at night," the Spanish poet hears "one of his own songs / being sung / by a whore"; surprised and moved by this event, Lorca concludes that, compared with the lasting power of art, "death must be a poor thing / a poor thing" (*PT*, p. 106). But predictably enough, Thomas has saved his highest poetic praise for Russian writers. One poem, "Orpheus in Hell," is dedicated to the memory of Osip Mandelstam. In another, "Poem of the Midway," Thomas requests a meeting with the poet Marina Tsvetayeva:

> Where shall we meet, Marina
> Tsvetayeva? Anywhere in Europe
> and our century will be dark
> enough for our assignation,
> and your poems I'll come holding
> will give us enough light
> to talk by, across a table.
> How cool your hand is.
>
> (*PT*, p. 66)

And in his most moving poetic tribute of all, "Portraits," Thomas mingles descriptions of several portraits of Anna Akhmatova with his own responses to them. Passionately confessing that "I've gazed, I've tried to splinter / With love that smiles at stone / This photo of nineteen-twenty," he concludes more calmly that "I . . . Find everything made whole / In your poetry's white night" (*PT*, p. 97).

Thomas' attachment to particular themes and subjects has naturally led him to prefer certain poetic genres and forms over others. His interest in history and myth, for example, is probably responsible for his large number of narrative poems and dramatic monologues. Thomas' use of form also reflects his larger interests: although, with predictable versatility, he has attempted almost every form imaginable, he seems especially drawn to forms involving repetition. Looking through his selected poems, one finds a villanelle (a medieval French form in which certain lines are repeated) and a sestina (another medieval form, this one involving the repetition of the first stanza's end words). But Thomas' favorite form seems to be the *pantoum*, a Malaysian form in which the second and fourth lines of one stanza are repeated as the first and third of the next. Since he has written *pantoums* that fall into both his first and second poetic categories—"Blizzard Song," a love poem, and "Ninemaidens," a poem narrated by the women who dance around a Cornish stone circle—it does not seem far-fetched to conclude that in this form, Thomas has found a perfect formal expression of his interest in repetition, and the way it affects both individual destinies and historical events.

TRANSLATIONS

THOMAS' translations of Russian poetry display as much intelligence and invention as his own poems do. His translations of Anna Akhmatova first began appearing in the 1960s and were eventually gathered into *Selected Poems*, published by Penguin in 1988. Thomas describes his goals and methods as a translator in the introduction to this collection. Writing that, in his translations, he has "tried to keep as closely to her sense as is compatible with making a poem in English," and adding that he has been aided in this attempt by Akhmatova's direct-

ness, he also admits that occasionally he has strayed from her literal meaning in order to preserve her poetic subtlety: "there are times when it is a deeper betrayal of the original poem to keep close to the literal sense than it would be to seek an English equivalent—one that preserves, maybe, more of her music, her 'blessedness of repetition' " (*Selected Poems*, p. 12). Despite the apologetic tone of Thomas' opening remarks, however, his Akhmatova translations are small masterpieces of depth and compression. A few comparisons between his translations and others' (in whose debt, it should be noted, Thomas declares himself in his introduction) will be enough to show how much more satisfying they are. Richard McKane, another translator of Akhmatova's work, has rendered her early poem, "The pillow hot . . . ," as follows:

> The pillow is already
> hot on both sides.
> Now the second candle
> goes out and the crows' calls
> become louder.
> I haven't slept tonight.
> It's too late to think of sleep.
> How unbearably white
> is the shutter on the white window.
> Good morning!
> (McKane, *Selected Poems*, p. 50)

And this is Thomas' version:

> The pillow hot
> On both sides,
> The second candle
> Dying, the ravens
> Crying. Haven't
> Slept all night, too late
> To dream of sleep . . .
> How unbearably white
> The blind on the white window.
> Good morning, morning!
> (*Selected Poems*, p. 13)

By eliminating connecting words like "is" and "I" from the poem, as well as filling it with internal rhyme (Dying/ Crying) and abrupt enjambment, Thomas has made "The pillow hot . . ." a powerful English poem in its own right. An even more striking difference in translations can be found by comparing McKane's and Thomas' versions of "The Sentence," a heartbreaking section of "Requiem,"

Akhmatova's long poem about the horrors of life under Stalin. In McKane's version, the narrator of the poem, accepting the "sentence" of the poem's title—which probably refers to the sentencing of Akhmatova's son, Lev Gumilyov, to a labor camp—confronts her fate in the following way:

> Today I have much work to do:
> I must finally kill my memory,
> I must so my soul can turn to stone,
> I must learn to live again.
> Or else . . . The hot summer rustle,
> like holiday time outside my window.
> I have felt this coming for a long time,
> this bright day and the deserted house.
> (McKane, p. 285)

In Thomas' version, this is what the narrator says:

> Thank God, I've many things to do today—I
> Need to kill and kill again
> My memory, turn my heart to stone, as
> Well as practise skills gone rusty, such
> As to live, for instance . . . Then there's always
> Summer, calling out my Black Sea dress!
> Yes, long ago I knew this day:
> This radiant day, and this empty house.
> (*Selected Poems*, p. 92)

The differences between the two translations are obvious: where McKane has opted for simple vocabulary, end-stopped lines, and repetition spread out among several lines, Thomas has used more dramatic, conversational language ("Thank God," "skills gone rusty"), a high degree of enjambment among both lines and stanzas, and much denser repetition ("kill and kill again," "long ago . . . this radiant day"). Thomas' version may not be as authentic as McKane's, but it is certainly more poetically resourceful and emotionally charged.

Thomas has also translated the poetry of Pushkin, and although these translations are less immediately compelling, they are equally skillful. In his introduction to *The Bronze Horseman: Selected Poems of Alexander Pushkin* (1982), Thomas offers a few fascinating clues about why Russian poetry is so fiendishly hard to translate. First, its inflected syntax "offers to the poet enormous scope for varying the word order, thereby adjusting the emotional stress" (p. 26). Such scope and richness cannot be found in English, with its much more constricted syntax. Moreover, Thomas states, it is easier to rhyme in Russian, and although "Pushkin commonly alternates masculine and feminine rhymes, with perfect naturalness . . . if an English translator tries to emulate him, his rhymes are bound to be more obvious and strained" (p. 32). Thomas responds to this difficulty by admitting that he has often changed Pushkin's rhyming pentameter into blank verse. And although, as Thomas himself predicts, his English rhymes occasionally seem strained, for the most part they are elegant and unobtrusive, as in his translation of Pushkin's "To Olga Masson":

> Olga, you morning-star,
> Godchild of Aphrodite,
> Miracle of beauty,
> How accustomed you are
> To sting with a caress,
> With insults to stir
> Frenzy. You fix the hour
> Of secret voluptuousness
> With a hot kiss; then
> when all on fire we come,
> We stand outside
> And hear you whispering
> To your grumbling maid;
> Your mocking laugh;
> The door stays barred.
> (p. 39)

Like all of Thomas' best translations, this poem contains an effective mixture of tones, and its loftier moments ("secret voluptuousness") peacefully coexist with its more colloquial ones ("hot kiss"). The rhymes are natural and unforced, and the enjambments give the poem a sense of momentum and urgency. In this respect the poem, and others like it, honor Thomas' wish not "to dress up Pushkin's simple country girl in flounces," because "his allegiance was to reality and commonsense" (p. 34). One can only be sorry that Thomas has not—or not yet—tried his hand at translating other great Russian poets.

CONCLUSION

D. M. Thomas is a gifted and important writer. Equally at home in the world of American politics and the trenches of Babi Yar, the splendors of Russian poetry and the intricacies of Freudian theory, he seems like the kind of person for whom the term "man of letters" was invented. By incorporating such an extraordinary range of subject matter into both his fiction and his poetry, he has vastly expanded our notions of what novels and poems can be about. By frequently including both poetry and fiction in the same works, he has challenged many traditional notions of literary genre. And because he has done all these things with such originality and skill, he eludes all easy classification: one could no more call him a "postmodern" writer then one could label him a "realist." But faced with all these accomplishments, one cannot help wanting more. Thomas is so eager to explore big ideas and issues that—in his novels, at least—he often seems content to treat these ideas and issues as ends in themselves, a decision that often results in unfortunate sacrifices: well-rounded characters for elaborate plots, style for structure, depth for cleverness. Although Thomas is always an impressive writer, he is seldom an endearing one. But even so, his achievements cannot be ignored, and his experiments in several languages and genres have left them all immeasurably enriched.

SELECTED BIBLIOGRAPHY

I. NOVELS. *The Flute-Player* (London and New York, 1979); *Birthstone* (London, 1980; New York, 1984); *The White Hotel* (London and New York, 1981); *Ararat* (London and New York, 1983); *Swallow* (London and New York, 1984); *Sphinx* (London and New York, 1986); *Summit* (London, 1987; New York, 1988); *Lying Together* (London and New York, 1990); *Flying in to Love* (London and New York, 1992); *Pictures at an Exhibition* (London and New York, 1993); *Eating Pavlova* (London and New York, 1994); *Lady with a Laptop* (London and New York, 1996).

II. POETRY. *Personal and Possessive* (London, 1964); *Penguin Modern Poets II* (Harmondsworth, 1968), with D. M. Black and Peter Redgrove; *Two Voices* (London and New York, 1968); *Lover's Horoscope: Kinetic Poet* (London, 1970); *Logan Stone* (London and New York, 1971); *The Shaft* (Gillingham, 1973); *Lilith-Prints* (Cardiff, 1974); *Symphony in Moscow* (Richmond, 1974); *Love and Other Deaths* (London, 1975); *The Rock* (Knotting, 1975); *Orpheus in Hell* (Knotting, 1977); *The Honeymoon Voyage* (London, 1978); *Dreaming in Bronze* (London, 1981); *News from the Front* (Cornholme, 1983), with Sylvia Kantaris; *Selected Poems* (London and New York, 1983); *The Puberty Tree: New and Selected Poems* (Newcastle upon Tyne, 1992).

III. MEMOIR. *Memories and Hallucinations* (London, 1988).

IV. TRANSLATIONS BY THOMAS. Anna Akhmatova, *Requiem and Poem without a Hero* (London and Athens, Ohio, 1976); *Way of all the Earth* (London and Athens, Ohio, 1979); *You Will Hear Thunder* (London, 1985); *Selected Poems* (London and New York, 1988). Alexander Pushkin, *The Bronze Horseman: Selected Poems of Alexander Pushkin* (London and New York, 1982); *Boris Godunov* (1985). Yevgeny Yevtushenko, *Invisible Threads* (London, 1981); *A Dove in Santiago* (London and New York, 1982).

V. EDITED BY THOMAS. *The Granite Kingdom: Poems of Cornwall* (Truro, 1970); *Poetry in Crosslight* (London, 1975); *Songs from the Earth: Selected Poems of John Harris, Cornish Miner, 1829-1884* (Padstow, 1977).

VI. CRITICISM. John Updike, review of *The Flute-Player*, *The White Hotel*, and *Logan Stone*, in *The New Yorker* (14 December 1981); John H. Barnsley, "*The White Hotel*," in *Antioch Review* (fall 1982); Claire Malroux, "*Ararat* au enieme degne," in *Actes des premières assises de la traduction littéraire*, ed. by Nathalie Heinrich (Arles, 1984); Mary F. Robertson, "Hystery, Herstory, History: 'Imagining the Real' in Thomas's *The White Hotel*," in *Contemporary Literature* 25 (winter 1984); Lady Falls Brown, "*The White Hotel*: D. M. Thomas's Considerable Debt to Anatoli Kuznetsov and Babi Yar," in *South Central Review* 2 (summer 1985); David Cowart, "Being and Seeming: *The White Hotel*," in *Novel: A Forum on Fiction* 19 (spring 1986); John Burt Foster, Jr., "Magic Realism in *The White Hotel*: Compensatory Vision and the Transformation of Classic Realism," in *Southern Humanities Review* 20 (summer 1986); Ronald Granofsky, "The Holocaust as Symbol in *Riddley Walker* and *The White Hotel*," in *Modern Language Studies* 16 (summer 1986); Ellen Y. Siegelman, "*The White Hotel*: Visions and Revisions of the Psyche," in *Literature and Psychology* 33, no. 1 (1987); James E. Young, "Holocaust Documentary Fiction: The Novelist as Eyewitness," in *Writing and the Holocaust*, ed. by Berel Lang (New York, 1988); Robert D. Newman, "D. M. Thomas's *The White Hotel*: Mirrors, Triangles, and Sublime Repression," in *Modern Fiction Studies* 35 (summer 1989); Lars Ole Sauerberg, "When the Soul Takes Wing: D. M. Thomas's *The White Hotel*," in *Critique: Studies in Contemporary Fiction* 31 (fall 1989); Roland Wymer, "Freud, Jung and the 'Myth' of Psychoanalysis in *The White Hotel*," in *Mosaic: A Journal for the Interdisciplinary Study of Literature* 22 (winter 1989).

Frances Bartowski and Catherine Stearns, "The Lost Icon in *The White Hotel*," in *Journal of the History of Sexuality* 1, no. 2 (1990); K. J. Phillips, "The Phalaris Syndrome, Alain Robbe-Grillet vs. D. M. Thomas," in *Women and Violence in Literature: An Essay Collection*, ed. by Katherine Anne Ackley (New York, 1990); Robert E. Lougy, "The Wolf-Man, Freud, and D. M. Thomas: Intertextuality, Interpretation, and Narration in *The White*

Hotel," in *Modern Language Studies* 21 (summer 1991); Laura E. Tanner, "Sweet Pain and Charred Bodies: Figuring Violence in *The White Hotel*," in *Boundary 2* 18 (summer 1991); M. D. Fletcher, "Thomas's Satire in *Summit*," in *Studies in Contemporary Satire* 18 (winter 1991–1992); Richard K. Cross, "The Soul Is a Far Country: D. M. Thomas and *The White Hotel*," in *Journal of Modern Literature* 18 (winter 1992); Benzi Zhang, "The Chinese Box in D. M. Thomas's *The White Hotel*," in *International Fiction Review* 20, no. 1 (1993); Catherine Bernard, "D. M. Thomas: La Danse de l'histoire," in *Historicité et métafiction dans le roman contemporain des Iles Britanniques,* ed. by Max Duperray (Aix-en-Provence, 1994); Lauren G. Leighton, "Translation and Plagiarism: Puškin and D. M. Thomas," in *Slavic and East European Journal* 38 (spring 1994); John MacInnes, "The Case of Anna G.: *The White Hotel* and Acts of Understanding," in *Soundings* (Knoxville, Tenn.) 77 (fall–winter 1994); Christine Reynie, "histoire et Histoire dans *The White Hotel*," in *Historicité et métafiction dans le roman contemporain des Iles Britanniques,* ed. by Max Duperray (Aix-en-Provence, 1994).

WILLIAM TREVOR

(1928–   )

Benjamin La Farge

EARLY IN HIS long career, William Trevor achieved a reputation as a writer of some of the most remarkable short stories of our time. From the start he has also been writing novels, and increasingly the best of these have come to be recognized as the work of a master. What distinguishes all of his writing is a peculiar synthesis of empathy and irony. His gift for entering the lives of women as well as men, of old people and children, of town and country folk alike, is perhaps the most distinctive characteristic of his art. But even while his powers of empathy draw us into the lives of his people, Trevor's irony keeps us sufficiently detached to be able to view them critically. A corollary to this is the paradoxical synthesis of cruelty and compassion in some of his novels, where an interest in the psychology of sadistic behavior, usually between a man and a woman, is deeply related to its opposite, an unsentimental compassion for those who live on the margins of society, the lonely and the crazy. "I don't really have any heroes or heroines," he told his *Publishers Weekly* interviewer in 1983; "I think I am interested in people who are not necessarily the victims of other people, but simply the victims of circumstances." This is most striking in the case of the many pathological characters in his pages—men who are liars and sociopaths, women who have withdrawn into madness. Trevor's deepest concerns are with the experience of loneliness and alienation; the stories he tells imply an ironic view of the human condition that is essentially tragic, but that allows him to see things comically when he chooses.

Trevor's gift for characterization is greatly enhanced by his nearly pitch-perfect ear for speech, especially Irish speech, as anyone who has heard him read his own fiction can testify. What is less well known, however, is that his ear for dialogue was honed by years of writing radio and television scripts, as well as stage plays; he has also adapted stories by Graham Greene, Elizabeth Bowen, and others.

Trevor is a member of the Irish Academy of Letters, and he was made Honorary Commander of the British Empire for services to literature in 1977. He has received honorary degrees from the University of Exeter (1984), Trinity College, Dublin (1986), Queen's University, Belfast (1989), and National University, Cork (1990).

LIFE

TREVOR was born William Trevor Cox on 24 May 1928 in County Cork, Ireland, the second child of James William Cox and Gertrude Davison Cox, both Protestants. His parents' marriage was not a happy one, as he tells us in a brief affectionate sketch of them in a chapter of his memoirs, *Excursions in the Real World* (1993). From his mother he seems to have picked up the habit of reading, and from his father he may have acquired a fondness for telling "stories about people or events that amused him" (p. 19). His father began as a bank clerk and became a bank manager, moving his family from one provincial town to another—towns such as Youghal, Skibereen, and Enniscorthy that are often mentioned in Trevor's fiction. For this reason the boy was obliged to attend numerous schools. From the age of twelve he spent two years at the Sandford Park School in Dublin, followed by two years at St. Columba's College in the Dublin mountains. At St. Columba's he came under the influence of an art teacher named Oisin Kelly, later famous in his own right, who got him interested in sculpture, which soon became his first career. From there he went to Trinity College, Dublin, where he read history and took his degree in 1950. The first eleven chapters of his memoirs provide sketches of some of the most formative teachers, schools, and places of his childhood. Of these early years he has said, "What is now apparent to me is that being a Protestant in Ireland was a *help*, because it began the process of being an outsider—which I think all writers have to be" (Stout, p. 131).

In 1952 he married Jane Ryan, whom he had met at Trinity. After a brief stint of teaching history in County Armagh, Northern Ireland, they moved to England, where he taught art for two years before setting himself up as a church sculptor in Somerset—"rather like Jude the Obscure," as he told his *Paris Review* interviewer (Stout, p. 121). He pursued this career until 1960; though he achieved some recognition, he gave it up when he felt that his sculpture had become "too abstract. There weren't any people in it anymore, and I didn't like it" (Schiff, p. 162). Then, having to support a wife and with two sons, he took a job as an advertising copywriter in London, and there, with time on his hands, he began to write fiction, taking the name of Trevor as his nom de plume.

SHORT STORIES

TREVOR has called himself "a short story writer who writes novels when he can't get them into short stories" (Caldwell, p. 25), and from the beginning of his career he has excelled in writing stories that often seem to suggest a larger world and a greater complexity than is actually shown by the events they describe. In his 1989 interview with *Paris Review,* he defined the short story as "the art of the glimpse. . . . Its strength lies in what it leaves out just as much as what it puts in, if not more. It is concerned with the total exclusion of meaninglessness. Life, on the other hand, is meaningless most of the time. The novel imitates life, where the short story is bony, and cannot wander. It is essential art" (Stout, pp. 135–136).

Like others before him, Trevor often explores a theme first in a story to which he later returns and on which he elaborates further in a novel; and once a theme has been introduced in a story it is more than likely to be developed further in later stories. Thus the intertextual connections between story and novel, and between one story and another, are multiple. From the beginning the stories display a mastery of form that took him longer to achieve in his novels. In most of the stories there is an econ-

omy that is sometimes absent in the earlier novels, some of which are flawed by a lack of focus and an abundance of unnecessary detail.

From the beginning, as well, the stories are the work of a writer who seems to have found his own voice without a prolonged apprenticeship. Yet in his interviews and his memoirs Trevor has repeatedly acknowledged his admiration for many writers who may have influenced him—writers as different as W. Somerset Maugham, James Joyce, and Elizabeth Bowen, among others. Maugham's influence is most conspicuous in the early story "The Table" (in *The Day We Got Drunk on Cake and Other Stories*, 1967), but it is still evident much later in "A Complicated Nature" (in *Angels at the Ritz and Other Stories*, 1975) and "The Bedroom Eyes of Mrs. Vansittart" (in *Beyond the Pale and Other Stories*, 1981). Maugham and Guy de Maupassant are both lurking between the lines of the fine late story "The Property of Colette Nervi" (in *The News from Ireland and Other Stories*, 1986). One may even detect echoes of Ernest Hemingway in the deft handling of seemingly pointless dialogue in "The Day We Got Drunk on Cake," the title story of his first collection. But it is the detective story writers he read voraciously in his youth—Agatha Christie, Dorothy Sayers, and Sapper's "Bull-dog" Drummond series—that may have had the deepest influence. This is evident in some of his plots, especially in his habit of planting circumstances, like detective-story clues, which will later serve to explain the behavior of his characters.

Throughout his work Trevor has kept returning to certain character types, which often embody his recurrent themes and are therefore the clearest index to them. Of these, one of the most common is the liar, often depicted as a con man in the novels, and his counterpart, the truth-teller. The con man is invariably someone whose failure and social impotence represent an extreme form of loveless alienation, which remains a constant theme in much of the work. The truth-teller is sometimes destructive, but the type is most often conflated with the wise or holy fool—a naif usually suffering from some delusion who sees, perhaps unwittingly, what no one else is aware of. The naif turns up more often in the novels, but there are naive and even deluded characters in the stories who may be seen as the prototypes for the wise fool of the novels.

Another common type is the lonely female—a teenage girl, an orphan, an unmarried schoolteacher, a divorced or widowed mother. The lonely female is also a figure of loveless alienation, but unlike her male counterpart she intends no harm and is often either self-denying or self-destructive. Some female characters of this type exhibit a degree of madness, but their madness is seen as a self-protective retreat from suffering. A persistent theme, which Trevor sometimes examines from the male's point of view but more often from the female's, is the difficulty of marriage and of relations between the sexes. Still another is the misunderstanding and hurt caused by a failure of communication between people. He also returns again and again to the experience of a boarding school for boys and its lifelong consequences. Although few of the characters in his early work are Irish, the relation between Protestant and Catholic in Ireland has long been one of his major themes, which first appears in stories about the Big House, a symbol of the Protestant upper class in Ireland both before and after the Republic of Ireland was established. The liar is first seen in "Memories of Youghal" (in *The Collected Stories*, p. 46), where Quillan imposes himself on two unmarried teachers vacationing in Italy by gratuitously telling untruthful stories about his Irish childhood. In "The Forty-seventh Saturday" (in *The Ballroom of Romance and Other Stories*, 1972), a bachelor who enjoys visiting his longtime mistress on Saturdays has convinced her he cannot see her more often because he is married. A more complex view of the liar is seen in "Mr. McNamara" (in *Angels at the Ritz*, 1975), in which the narrator recalls how his Protestant father used to return from business trips to Dublin with amusing tales about a Catholic friend of his whom he met in the hotel where he stayed. The friend, Mr. McNamara, shared the father's pro-English views and occasionally sent presents to his family, especially the narrator himself, who was then a boy. After his father dies unexpectedly, the narrator goes to a boarding school near Dublin and eventually manages to visit the hotel. There he discovers that his father's friend was really a woman named Nora McNamara, apparently a prostitute. Since the story is set in Ireland during and after World War II, when Catholic Ireland was neutral, the father's elaborate lie is shown to be more than a cover-up for marital infidelity; it is also a sign that he was fooling himself in wanting to believe that an Irish Catholic could share his pro-English sympathies.

The con man is first explored as a comic type in "The Hotel of the Idle Moon" (in *The Day We Got Drunk on Cake*), in which Dankers and Mrs. Dankers fake engine trouble in order to persuade Sir Giles and Lady Martin's butler to let them spend the night. Coincidentally, Sir Giles dies two nights later, and the intruders manage to stay on, eventually gaining control of the estate and turning it into a hotel. When the butler suggests that Sir Giles may have been poisoned, Lady Martin agrees but adds, "does it matter this way or that—to chop off a few dwindling years?" (*Collected Stories*, p. 152). The con man as comic type reemerges in the following novels: as Studdy in the novel *The Boarding-House* (1965), as Septimus Tuam in *The Love Department* (1966), and again as Morrissey in *Mrs. Eckdorf in O'Neill's Hotel* (1969). But in Timothy Gedge of *The Children of Dynmouth* (1976) and in Francis Tyte of *Other People's Worlds* (1980), Trevor transforms the type into a more complex character whose personal history serves to explain and complicate his behavior.

An ironic version of the truth-teller, the liar's counterpart, is depicted in the narrator of "The Blue Dress" (in *Beyond the Pale*), who sees himself as a truth-teller but turns out to be less than truthful and possibly deluded. A more blatant truth-teller is the subject of "Torridge" (in *Lovers of Their Time and Other Stories*, 1978), in which the character of that name turns up at an annual reunion party of three old school chums, now middle-aged, who are having dinner with their wives and children. At thirteen, in their school days, Torridge had had "a face with a pudding look matching the sound of his name" (*Collected Stories*, p. 595), and he has been the butt of their old school jokes ever since, though none of them has seen him for years. Now, when "Old Porridge" arrives at their dinner in time for coffee, he has a "step as nimble as a tap-dancer's" (p. 606). But he proves himself to be intent on revenge when he tells the wives and children, "I'm what they call queer. . . . I perform sexual acts with men" (p. 609), and goes on to tell them how his three school chums (their husbands and fathers) used to take part in the same practices.

Trevor's concern with the English and the Anglo-Irish institution of the boarding school for boys and its effect on lifelong behavior recurs in many of the novels, but in the stories he is more often concerned with the relations between students or between students and their teachers. In "A School Story" (in *The Day We Got Drunk on Cake*), the first-person narrator tells a complex tale about his shifting friendships with two other boys, one of whom, Markham, vows to kill his father and stepmother. The other, Williams, turns out to be a subtle sadist who encourages Markham to keep his word. The ending is typically ambiguous, since we cannot be certain whether Markham has actually killed his parents or is simply deluded in thinking he has. In "Mr. Tennyson" (in *Beyond the Pale*), a teenage girl is infatuated with her teacher, a married man, who is known to have had an affair with another female student not long before. She confesses her feelings to him one day after class, but he gently rebuffs her, and her feelings are complicated by the attentions of a boy her own age. In "Mrs. Silly" (in *Angels at the Ritz*), the protagonist is a young boy, the son of divorced parents, who is so embarrassed by his garrulous and gushing mother that when she slips and falls during a visit to his school he pretends she is only a distant relative whom he hardly knows.

One of the more poignant incarnations of the lonely woman is the schoolteacher, a type that first appears in the horror story "Miss Smith" (in *The Day We Got Drunk on Cake*). (At the opposite extreme is the unsympathetic portrait of Miss Halliwell in the novel *Fools of Fortune*, 1983.) In "Attracta" (in *Lovers of Their Time*), a powerful story about the relation between teacher and student—and also about the tragic relation between England and Ireland—an unmarried woman by that name, now in her sixties, becomes obsessed with a newspaper account of a terrorist murder and rape in Belfast during the troubles there. Attracta is convinced that nothing she has taught her students has been of any value, but when she tries to interest them in the atrocity, they shrug it aside as something too familiar. Soon, after several parents complain, she is forced into early retirement.

The inability to communicate and the consequences of misunderstanding is broached as a theme in "The Penthouse Apartment" (in *The Day We Got Drunk on Cake*), a dark comedy of errors. An Italian maid, a janitor, and Miss Winton, an elderly spinster, accompanied by her dog, have a few too many drinks in a fancy apartment that is about to be photographed for a fashion magazine. The janitor, after a drunken tirade against the wealthy owners, knocks over an expensive flower vase, damaging the Afghan rug. When the owners return he saves himself by putting the blame on Miss Winton's dog, and Miss Winton, unable to explain what actually happened, ends up offering to pay for the damages.

This theme frequently reemerges in the novels, whenever characters speaking at cross-purposes fail to understand, let alone hear, what each other is saying. It is treated with a delicate irony in "On the Zattere" (in *The News from Ireland*), a story about a widowed father and his unmarried daughter visiting Venice, where he had vacationed with her recently deceased mother in the past. Irritated by his stinginess and his flirtations with younger women, the daughter grows increasingly resentful toward her father, seeing his behavior as proof of a callous indifference to her mother's death. What he fails to tell her is that he is only trying to overcome the sense of loss and despair he has been suffering for months. At the same time she fails to share her own personal anguish about the man who has been her lover for years.

The tragic consequences of a failure to communicate are given a powerful treatment in "Beyond the Pale," the title story of Trevor's 1982 collection. Molly, the narrator, is an English woman in her fifties who is unconcerned with the political violence in Northern Ireland, where she and her three English companions have come as usual for a summer vacation. One of these, a retired major named Strafe, turns out to be her lover, but the story reaches a crisis when Cynthia, his wife, who is well read in Irish history, is traumatized by the suicide of one of the hotel guests. Before drowning himself, the unhappy man, an Irishman who had originally come from a local poor family, tells her the story of his tragic love for a local girl who had become a bomb-making revolutionary in London. Molly, Strafe, a third companion, and the English proprietor of the hotel are embarrassed by Cynthia's troubled reaction, which they are incapable of sharing or even beginning to understand. What makes this story so memorable is Trevor's ironic use of a narrator who does not understand the implications of the story she tells—a device that Trevor may have borrowed, consciously or not, from *Gulliver's Travels* (1726) and *A Modest Proposal* (1729), or from Maria Edgeworth's *Castle Rackrent* (1800), in each of which the ironic use of a naive narrator enables the author to express political or social views without seeming to. His adaptation of the story for radio won a BBC Giles Cooper Award for Best Radio Plays of 1980.

The theme of a retreat into a self-protective delusion first appears in "The Original Sins of Edward Tripp" (in *The Day We Got Drunk on Cake*). Edward is a middle-aged man who has lived with his sister Emily for the past forty-two years. Emily is given to habitual fantasies of murder and other horrors taking place in their suburban neighborhood. But in his guilt-ridden conviction that his behavior toward her in their childhood had caused her craziness, Edward, though seemingly not deluded, has created his own role as a co-dependent in her fantasy life. Trevor explores this theme even more poignantly in "A Happy Family" (in *The Ballroom of Romance*), where Elizabeth, the narrator's wife and the mother of his children, reports her telephone conversations with a stranger whose information about their private life seems too close for comfort. Eventually the narrator discovers that Elizabeth has retreated into an imaginary relationship with Mr. Higgs, a fantasy friend whom she had invented in childhood and through whom she now projects the feelings she cannot express directly. In "The Mark-2 Wife" (in *The Ballroom of Romance*), the reader begins to suspect that Anna Mackintosh, a middle-aged wife, is suffering from paranoid delusions when she tells a retired general and his wife at a party she has gone to that her husband, who has not yet arrived, is leaving her to marry a younger woman. The reader's suspicion seems to be confirmed when she makes a long telephone call to her psychiatrist, but after she quits the party the general and his wife are surprised to see her husband arrive with a younger woman; though nothing is said to confirm her prediction, the reader realizes that Anna has seen the truth before it came. In this way Trevor conflates the truth-teller with the theme of a retreat from suffering.

The psychiatrist in "The Mark-2 Wife" is only a reassuring telephone voice, but in "Mrs. Acland's Ghosts" (in *Angels at the Ritz*) Trevor develops the role as both an explanatory device, representing the authorial point of view, and an ironic complication of the truth. Out of the blue a man named Mr. Mockler receives a long letter from a woman he does not know, telling him that she is incarcerated in a private home for the mentally disturbed. The letter, which describes her loving relations with her parents and siblings who were suddenly killed in an automobile accident, seems utterly truthful, and he is so intrigued that he visits the home, where her psychiatrist gives him a wholly different version of her childhood. In the psychiatrist's version her parents were mutually hostile, never speaking to each other or to her, and she had no siblings. The psychiatrist's version does make sense of the woman's

schizophrenic withdrawal, but when Mr. Mockler is taken to meet her, he agrees to play the role of a former tenant in her fantasy of the childhood home, and the reader is left with the realization that her version of her life is as "true" as her doctor's. The ambiguity of this brilliant story is somewhat reminiscent of Henry James's 1898 *The Turn of the Screw*, a ghost story that can also be read as a psychological study in hysteria. Perhaps the most poignant recurrence of this type is the character of Imelda, in *Fools of Fortune*, who becomes a mystical healer after losing her mind in childhood.

Marriage in all its complexity is a major theme throughout the work. The notorious difficulty of finding a man to marry among the Irish poor is the subject of "The Ballroom of Romance," the title story of his 1972 collection. Bridie, who lives with her ailing father on a poor farm, has for years spent her Saturday nights at the local dance hall, hoping to find a husband. At the end, realizing that none of the men she fancies will have her, she resolves to give up going there, knowing that she will eventually settle down with one of the least attractive men, who is as lonely as she. The compromises necessary to marriage are scrutinized in "The Grass Widows" (in *The Ballroom of Romance*), where Mrs. Angusthorpe, an embittered older woman, urges the young and newly married Daphne to leave her husband, who unexpectedly turns out to be capable of listening to her, thereby regaining her trust for the time being. Trevor explores marriage in numerous other stories, of which three of the most memorable are "Angels at the Ritz," the title story of his 1975 collection, about wife-swapping in the suburbs; "Teresa's Wedding" (in *Angels at the Ritz*), about a country girl who ends up thinking her marriage may survive, in spite of its inauspicious beginning, because at least neither she nor her husband can have any more illusions about each other; and "Afternoon Dancing" (in *Angels at the Ritz*), about two working-class housewives who sneak off every Thursday to go dancing at a tearoom with a Jamaican bachelor named Grantly Palmer. The problem of a middle-aged married man leaving his wife for a younger woman is explored in "Lovers of Their Time," the title story of his 1978 collection.

Closely related to stories of marriage are those concerning the relation between parents and children. Trevor first explores this in "Access to the Children" (in *The Ballroom of Romance*). On weekends a divorced man named Malcolmson picks up his two young daughters, who live with their mother, and takes them on outings. Unemployed and alcoholic, Malcolmson has come to believe a fantasy that he and his former wife will be reunited. In the end, after learning that Elizabeth has a lover whom his daughters like and whom she is going to marry, Malcolmson confronts her in a painful scene of drunken self-abasement. Trevor explores the filial-parental relationship from the viewpoint of a teenage girl named Eleanor in "Nice Day at School" (in *The Ballroom of Romance*), in which we are privileged to witness Eleanor's troubled relationships with her working-class parents, her girlfriends at school, their teacher, and a boy who tries to seduce her.

The relation of parent to child is treated very differently in "Being Stolen From" (in *Beyond the Pale*), a tale of self-abnegation. Four years before the story's action, Bridget and her husband, Liam, poor immigrants from County Cork, had legally adopted a child named Betty whose footloose mother, Norma, had asked Bridget to take the child off her hands. More recently Liam has left Bridget for an English woman who owns a news agent's shop. The story begins when Norma, now married to an English social worker who has helped her pull her life together, turns up at Bridget's home and asks to have the child back. Bridget refuses, even after repeated calls from Norma's husband, who insinuates that the child will have a hard time growing up in a London where the Irish are increasingly distrusted, owing to the troubles in Belfast. In the end she comes to believe that the young English couple have a greater claim to the child than she does, and we know that she will let them take Betty from her.

In "Autumn Sunshine" (in *Beyond the Pale*), Canon Moran, the minister of a small Protestant parish in Ireland who is mourning his dead wife, Frances, is delighted when his favorite daughter, Deirdre, who had run away from home years before and failed to come for the funeral, writes that she wants to visit. A decent man of limited understanding, he is baffled by the person she has become, especially when she is joined by Harold, her English working-class boyfriend. Harold, a political radical with a birthmark on his face, is filled with passionate loathing for what the English did to the Irish; soon he and Deirdre become obsessed by an ancient massacre of innocent peasants that took place in a barn nearby. The instigator was an English soldier named Sergeant James, and the reader is left realizing that both

the ineffectual Canon and Harold, whose vengeful spirit resembles the long-dead sergeant's, are caught up in the same political history of English imperialism. Trevor's radio adaptation of this subtle story won a BBC Giles Cooper Award for Best Radio Plays of 1982.

The Big House made its first appearance as a symbol of the old Protestant Ascendancy (the hegemony of the Anglo-Irish land-owning class that dominated the Catholic population until southern Ireland won independence from England in 1922) in Trevor's third collection, *Angels at the Ritz*. In "The Distant Past," an unmarried brother and sister living together in their decaying family mansion are increasingly isolated from their Catholic neighbors following World War II; the theme is treated more richly in another story in the same collection, "The Tennis Court," and this in turn was reprinted as the first part of an ambitious three-part sequel in his next collection. Under the title "Matilda's England" (in *Lovers of Their Time*), these three related stories constitute a complex novella about the continuing tragic effects of World War I on a Protestant family who farm the land that used to belong to the neighboring Big House. The eponymous Matilda narrates each story in retrospect, first as a child, then as a girl, and finally as the divorced and self-deceiving owner of the Big House itself. One of the most powerful of all his stories on this theme is "The News from Ireland," the long title story of his 1986 collection, which takes place in the years 1847–1848, the time of the Great Famine. As in *Fools of Fortune*, the setting is a Big House and the family who live in it, but unlike the twentieth-century Quintons of the novel, whose idyllic pastoral life is destroyed by political violence, the nineteenth-century Pulvertafts are seen ironically as well-meaning gentry whose privilege has fatally isolated them from reality. Trevor achieves this ironic perspective by shifting back and forth between a third-person narrative that frequently relies on *oratio obliqua* (the device of using indirect speech, or speech without quotation marks, as a means of paraphrasing the attitudes of different characters) and the first-person diary of the new English governess. The elder Pulvertaft, the father of the family, keeps the local poor employed by having them build a useless road—a well-intentioned farce that metaphorically epitomizes the destructive folly of Ascendancy rule. But the principal characters are Miss Heddoe, the governess (another of Trevor's schoolteachers), and Fogarty, the butler. Fogarty, a Protestant who is contemptuous of the Catholic population, turns out to be a truth-teller who understands that if the family had only returned to England, as he wishes they had, the local peasants could have entered the estate and survived on its fruits and farm animals.

The central event of the story is the news that a local peasant couple, whose other children have starved to death, have given birth to an infant with the stigmata of Christ on his hands and feet. Both Fogarty and the Pulvertafts dismiss it as a hoax, and later on, when the child dies of the wounds inflicted by its parents, it is made clear they were right. (The hoax may also be seen as a political metaphor of the way in which the Catholic population was crucified by English government policy.) Miss Heddoe seems at first to be the only person in the household who is shocked by the mass starvation outside, but in the end her diary reveals that she shares the attitudes of imperial England:

The famine-fever descends like a rain of further retribution, and I wonder—for I cannot help it—what in His name these people have done to displease God so? It is true they have not been an easy people to govern; they have not abided by the laws which the rest of us must observe; their superstitious worship is a sin.

(*Collected Stories*, p. 900)

We are not surprised when she marries the estate manager, Mr. Erskine, a former army officer who lost an arm in service to the English crown. In this story we can see Trevor coming to terms with his Protestant past, since Fogarty or someone like him might well have been one of Trevor's ancestors. It is also here, as well as in most of his Irish stories and novels, that Trevor is able to realize his tragic vision more fully than in the earlier stories and novels set in England.

Trevor's interest in this theme appears to have reached a culmination in his eleventh novel, *The Silence in the Garden* (1988), as there are no Big Houses in the two story collections published since then—*Family Sins* (1990) and *After Rain* (1996). Most of these new stories are concerned with contemporary Irish life, both rural and urban—especially with the problems of love, marriage, adultery, and divorce. Liars, deceivers, and truth-tellers still make their appearance, but now increasingly the acts of cruelty they perpetrate turn

to violence. One of the strongest stories in the first of these collections is "Events at Drimaghleen," in which the motive for the murder of a farm girl, her lover, and his mother seems clear until an English journalist, after interviewing the girl's parents, writes a magazine story suggesting that she was the killer. The parents are dismayed, but having accepted money for the interview, they are in no position to protest. In "Gilbert's Mother" of the second collection, a divorced woman suspects her son is guilty of several crimes, including murder. Both stories are concerned with some of the same problems that Trevor explores in his powerful twelfth novel, *Felicia's Journey* (1995).

NOVELS: THE EARLY PERIOD (1958–1974)

TREVOR was thirty and still a sculptor when he published his first novel, an autobiographical "fragment" called *A Standard of Behaviour* (1958), which is never included among the works listed in the front pages of any of his subsequent books. In a 1989 interview with *The Paris Review*, he explained that "it was written for profit when [he] was very poor" (Stout, p. 125). Following this, seven of his next eight novels are set in England, six of them in London. In all of them the influence of Dickens can sometimes be seen in his use of caricature, and his fondness for comic irony reflects an early admiration for Evelyn Waugh and Anthony Powell, among others. Waugh's technique of rapid cinematic scene changes and abbreviated dialogue seems also to have been an influence. But in his abiding concern for the psychology of misfits, Trevor's first eight novels show a deeper affinity with Graham Greene.

It is not surprising that *The Old Boys* (1964) is about the effects of a boarding-school education. Not only had he himself attended two such schools, but his reading was perhaps an even more formative influence. In a little-known foreword to a collection of writings about Ford Madox Ford, Trevor confesses that as a boy growing up in provincial Ireland he had "read [his] way through a mass of English public-school stories" (Sondra J. Strang, ed., *The Presence of Ford Madox Ford*, p. xii). Quite self-consciously, therefore, *The Old Boys* joins a long literary tradition that includes Thomas Hughes's *Tom Brown's School Days* (1857) and Rudyard Kipling's *Stalky & Co.* (1899).

His own approach to the subject, however, is rather different from the one usually found in novels of this genre. The "old boys" of the title are eight men, now in their seventies, who had been to the same unnamed school together. All eight are members of the Old Boys' Association, and the central action of the plot involves the efforts of one of them, Jaraby, to make certain that he will be elected the next chairman. He is opposed by none of the others except Nox, who still bears him a grudge from their school days. Nox is so determined, in fact, that he hires a detective named Swingler in the hope of proving Jaraby guilty of some moral lapse, possibly philandering. The situation is patently absurd, made all the more so by Swingler's comical ineptitude as a sleuth.

Yet for all its absurdity, the comedy soon grows dark. As we learn from one of the other "old boys," the morality of the school was exemplified by a legendary master named Dowse, who used to tell his students, "You must apply to the world the laws that apply to this school" (p. 14). The laws of the school are inculcated through the infamous hierarchical system of "fagging." The practice seems to have left its deepest mark on Jaraby, who has bullied his wife and their only child, an unstable young man named Basil. Dowse had also recommended going to brothels, and Jaraby has periodically followed the advice. If Jaraby feels any affection, it is only for his large, one-eyed cat, Monmouth.

Basil's life, like his father's, is devoid of love except for the pet birds he keeps and tries unsuccessfully to sell. Mrs. Jaraby, much against her husband's protest, invites him to live at home once again. But first she has to make the house safe for his birds, and in a scene that powerfully conveys her long repressed rage, she kills Monmouth, the cat who has stolen her husband's affection, and dumps it, wrapped in a plastic bag, into a garbage can. Meanwhile it has been rather obliquely suggested that Basil has molested a girl, an event his mother is not aware of, but her revenge seems complete when he arrives in a taxi with his birds and Jaraby is forced to accept the situation. At the denouement Basil is arrested, as we see through the eyes of the ineffectual Swingler.

The tragedy of Mrs. Jaraby's desperation and Basil's crime is earlier balanced by the comical death of Mr. Turtle, one of the other "old boys." Turtle had been flirting with a certain spinster, and after he dies his classmates, in a ludicrous discussion, are concerned only to know whether or not he had asked the woman to marry him. Thus, between the disturbing behavior of Mrs. Jaraby and her son, on the one hand, and the inconsequential posturings of the "old boys," on the other, Trevor has played out a dark comedy whose ironic surface barely conceals a hidden pathos.

One of the more arresting features of the narrative is the highly mannered dialogue of barely repressed rage between Jaraby and his wife, a dialogue that is somewhat reminiscent of Ivy Compton-Burnett, a writer Trevor has said he admires. Another feature is the sadistic cruelty Mr. and Mrs. Jaraby show toward each other—a cruelty that resurfaces in the form of a murderous psychosis in *Other People's Worlds* (1980) and *The Silence in the Garden* (1988). Unlike so many other novels on the subject, this one is not simply an exposé of life inside a public school. Trevor proves himself to be an ironic moralist—a moralist who does not moralize—his purpose being not so much to satirize the influence of public school values as to show the far more devastating effects of life without love. We come to see Jaraby as contemptible, his wife as pitiable, their son as pathetic, and poor Mr. Turtle as laughable, but all four of them—not to mention other lesser characters—are shown to be victims of a life not lived. *The Old Boys*, which appeared when Trevor was thirty-six, was a success, winning the Hawthornden Prize. It was soon made into a radio play and a television play as well, both written by the author.

In a manner and to a degree that is not so conspicuous in his stories, the plots of Trevor's earliest novels are built on a pattern of accidental encounters among disparate characters. In *The Boarding-House* (1965) he conceals the pattern, plausibly enough, by placing the main action in a decaying Victorian boardinghouse where most of the characters reside. If the plot is too schematic and somewhat lacking in focus, it is largely because Trevor keeps shifting points of view among too many characters, but he is also developing his skills by experimenting with a new technique—the use of a character as an authorial figure, a stand-in for his own manipulations of plot. In addition he conducts a more successful, though secondary, experiment with the use of slapstick comedy, especially in a scene that involves a mix-up over clothes, in the manner of early silent film.

The authorial figure is Mr. William Wagner Bird, a recluse who carefully chooses people to stay in the boardinghouse he owns and manages. For each person invited to stay he writes a brief character sketch in a journal, excerpts from which we are privileged to read whenever our attention is caught by a new character. Early in the novel Mr. Bird dies, leaving the boardinghouse to two of his hand-picked boarders, Nurse Clock and an ineffectual blackmailer named Studdy, who loathe each other. Nurse Clock extends the authorial function forfeited by Mr. Bird when she shares his character sketches with the reader; but Studdy, who is laughably inept at trying to extort money from various people, is one of Trevor's earliest inventions of the con man as a comic type.

Among the nine characters who are thrown accidentally together in Mr. Bird's boardinghouse are assorted loners and loonies, one of whom is a Nigerian named Mr. Obd. For years Mr. Obd has been courting an English woman by sending her flowers and writing her letters, even though she has long since stopped acknowledging them or even inviting him for tea. The novel draws to a macabre close when Mr. Obd, finally realizing he has been rejected, sets the boardinghouse on fire and dies in the flames. This is a fitting end to a lugubrious tale, and the earlier slapstick fiasco over clothes, which comes as a welcome relief, serves only to highlight the loneliness and alienation of all its characters. The difficulties of a black African who has made his way to England in the decline of the British empire is a theme that Trevor will revisit more skillfully when he introduces us to the Jamaican figure of Miss Gomez in *Miss Gomez and the Brethren* (1971).

If *The Old Boys* is a dark comedy and *The Boarding-House* a tragicomedy, Trevor's fourth novel, *The Love Department* (1966), is considerably lighter in tone. But although the spirit of the story as a whole is rather antic, much of the action involves the prevalence of adultery, and we soon realize that beneath the surface Trevor is making a serious moral criticism. The plot revolves around three central figures, each of them a deliberately one-dimensional caricature. Edward Blakeston-Smith, the young protagonist, is a naif who has been pathologically obsessed with billboard posters—especially the giant images of men who "leaned forward everywhere, sticking chocolates into women's mouths, or lighting cigarettes for them" (p. 4). The story begins when Edward leaves the sanatorium where he has been recuperating from this obsession, and makes his way to London. There he is hired by Lady Dolores, who is nationally famous for her advice to the lovelorn, which she dispenses through a column in a mass magazine and on television. Lady Dolores reserves her advice for lovelorn housewives only, and she hires Edward to track down and gather information about a young philanderer named Septimus Tuam—the third of the antic figures who govern the story. Lady Dolores has heard of Septimus through countless letters from housewives who have lost their hearts to him. Each of them has described him as beautiful; Lady Dolores sees him as evil, and she is determined to root him out, using Edward as her sleuth. "Septimus Tuam is an enemy of love," she tells him, and he replies enthusiastically, "We'll put him behind bars . . ." (p. 34). But Edward is incompetent, and, in one of the several hilarious set pieces of the novel, he follows the wrong man, a Mr. FitzArthur, mistaking him for Septimus. It happens, ironically, that Mr. FitzArthur's wife has in fact been having an affair with the infamous gigolo—a typical Trevorian coincidence. At the end, having failed to find Septimus, Edward quits his job, intending to return to the asylum he left at the beginning. As he bicycles out of London he tosses a pair of gloves Lady Dolores had given him on to the street: someone stops to pick them up and a taxi swerves, accidentally killing Septimus, who just happens to be walking by. Of this Edward is blithely unaware.

Much of the action revolves around a married couple, the Bolsovers, James and Eve, who are celebrating their tenth anniversary in a restaurant when we first meet them. As a couple who once loved each other but now have little in common, the Bolsovers represent the underlying pattern of cross-purposes that typifies the lives of all the characters in the novel. Eventually, in rapid succession, Eve Bolsover and Septimus become lovers, she and James are divorced, James quits his job and moves to a farm his father has left him. Soon enough Eve turns up crestfallen, having come to her senses, and we are left with the impression that they will try to make a go of it once again.

Edward is something of a holy fool, a figure that anticipates Miss Gomez in *Miss Gomez and the Brethren*. When asked in the *Transatlantic Review* interview of 1976 what Edward's retreat to the asylum signifies, Trevor replied, "It's a fear of decadence. . . . The world of the posters is extremely real, and in many ways more real than Edward" (Ralph-Bowman, p. 9). Indeed, Edward, Lady Dolores, and Septimus Tuam are all so comically stylized as to be rather unreal. By contrast, the portraits of James and Eve are remarkably convincing.

At this stage Trevor was still developing an art that would allow him to range from psychological realism to comedic playfulness. Increasingly he experimented with shifting points of view and interior monologue, often in the form of waking fantasy. With his fifth novel, *Mrs. Eckdorf in O'Neill's Hotel*, which is set in Dublin, he turned for the first time to Ireland. Once again, as in *The Boarding-House*, the plot is organized around a single large establishment, the hotel of the title, but this time his experiment with chance encounters was more successful, if only because the protagonist who initiates the action, an English woman named Mrs. Eckdorf, arrives on the scene by deliberate intention. Mrs. Eckdorf is a photographer whose photo essays have won her some renown; she has come to O'Neill's Hotel because she is convinced she will find a hidden tragedy there which she can use.

What she finds is that the hotel's owner, Mrs. Sinnott, is a ninety-two-year-old woman who, although deaf and dumb since birth, has led a charmed life. People communicate with her by writing in notebooks, which Mrs. Eckdorf reads stealthily in the hope of finding the story she is looking for. The hotel, founded by Mrs. Sinnott's father, had once been prosperous, thanks to her Italian mother, who had a gift for business. One of her two children is an alcoholic son, and Mrs. Eckdorf discovers that he had raped the new maid years ago, on the night of his mother's birthday. His mother had insisted they marry, a child was born, and soon they were divorced. Yet far from the bitterness she expects, Mrs. Eckdorf is astonished to learn that everyone in the family and everyone associated with the hotel seems to live under a spell of forgiveness, which she imagines has somehow been created by old Mrs. Sinnott.

The novel is especially rich in minor characters, among whom one of the more memorable is Morrissey, a useless hanger-on who plays at being a pimp, showing photos of women he knows to any passing stranger. The scene in which Morrissey tries to sell one of his women to a soldier by showing him her photo is a masterful example of Trevor's black humor at its best. Earlier he succeeds in introducing a visiting English salesman to Agnes Quinn, one of several prostitutes who ply their trade surreptitiously in the hotel. When Mrs. Eckdorf discovers this she manages to steal the man's clothes and lock him into one of the hotel rooms.

At several moments throughout the story Mrs. Eckdorf harangues various people—at one time insisting, "We must know one another" (1989 ed., p. 65), and at another saying "Reality is the grail I seek" (p. 84). She is determined to see Mrs. Sinnott as a saint and to invest her with the holy power of forgiveness. At the end we are told that Mrs. Eckdorf has gone crazy and is still living, years later, in a Dublin asylum for the mentally disturbed. The irony of her failure seems at first to make a mockery of her willful search for tragedy and her benighted discovery of beatitude in Mrs. Sinnott. But Mrs. Eckdorf is one of Trevor's holy fools, and the ultimate irony is that, crazy though she is, she has seen the truth.

Miss Gomez, the young black protagonist in *Miss Gomez and the Brethren*, is a more extreme figure of alienation than any of her predecessors. The story is set in London, on a street that is being levelled for redevelopment. The only two houses still occupied are a pub, where the demolition workers go for lunch, and a pet shop whose owner refuses to sell. In the pub live Mrs. Beryl Tuke and her husband, her daughter Prudence, and two lodgers. Living above the pet shop are its owner and Miss Gomez. One of the two lodgers in the pub is Alban Roche, an Irish immigrant who has served a short jail sentence as a "sex offender," though his only offense, we learn, is that he was caught spying on women as they undressed in a badminton club. Beryl Tuke, by contrast, is an adulteress who lives in a state of drunken fantasy, fed by trashy novels and television dramas.

The moral force of the novel is generated by Miss Gomez, a naif who is driven by her conviction that she has been "chosen." At the age of eleven she had run away from an orphanage in Jamaica, where she was placed when her parents died in a street fire that killed ninety-one people. She learns that the fire, of which she was the only survivor, was deliberately started by someone "demented," and both the accident of survival and the guilt of the nameless arsonist continue to plague her throughout the novel. Having made her way to London, where she drifted from job to job, she ends up in a strip club and finally becomes a prostitute. One day, as if by chance, she happens to see an ad that says, "There is a Meaning in the Life of Each and Every One of Us" (p. 25), and soon she is saved by The Church of the Brethren of the Way. Its founder, the Reverend Patterson, writing from Jamaica, assures her that "nothing happened by chance. It wasn't chance that had caused her to survive a conflagration, nor chance that had caused her to pick up" the ad. "As the white man brought the word to [Jamaica]," he writes her, "so you must return it now to where it is most needed [England]. You are a chosen person, Miss Gomez" (p. 31). Later, somewhat paradoxically, she herself says, "God creates complicated patterns and then commands us to fight against what seems like destiny" (p. 131). In this way she provides Trevor with a plausible solution to the technical problem of using chance as a plot device. Trevor, not God, has created the "complicated patterns" of the plot, but her conviction that she was "chosen" is the ironic device by which he disguises his manipulation of those patterns.

In the scenes where Miss Gomez performs in the strip club and later as a prostitute, it is clear that she has survived only by allowing her race and gender to be exploited. But Trevor is not overtly concerned with racism or any other social pathology, nor is he making a political commentary on racial or sexual exploitation as such. Such problems constitute the social grounds for his real concerns, which are primarily moral. At the same time he is always careful to remind us that morality does not govern the world and moral values do not usually prevail. This view, implicitly tragic, is made clear in a deliberately gratuitous scene, near the climax, when a band of wild cats that live in the ruins of demolished buildings attack and kill Mr. Tuke's pet dog, eating its flesh.

After her conversion Miss Gomez mistakenly and self-righteously accuses Alban of another sex crime. But Alban and Prudence, who have become lovers, forgive her for getting "everything so ludicrously mixed up," since they realize that she was a person who "saw things in black and white when there were only complicated shades of grey . . ." (p. 247). This may well stand for Trevor's own view, but it also underscores a pronouncement made earlier by Miss Gomez herself when she suggests, in a speech to Beryl Tuke, that to recognize our own hidden impulses is at least to understand if not to forgive the evil in others: "We're all cripples, Mrs. Tuke. There's something the matter with each and every one of us. It's in us all to burn down streets while people are sleeping in their beds, or to end as a sex offender. Terrible things are in all of us" (p. 132).

The moral view of human nature implicit in this passage evokes the psychoanalytic proposition that only by confronting the savage passions that lie buried in the unconscious mind can one learn how to live with one's inner conflicts. Given her mistaken accusation of Alban Roche, we cannot infer that Trevor is offering a hidden message of Christian forgiveness through Miss Gomez, but in this speech of hers he does suggest a view of human nature that acknowledges the potential for evil in everyone.

At the novel's end, Miss Gomez travels back to Jamaica, convinced that she has proved herself worthy of joining the Brethren, only to find when she gets there that the Reverend Lloyd Patterson, now revealed to be a white man and an alcoholic, has fled and that his church was a hoax. Undaunted and resilient, she reasons that God works in mysterious ways. "Her faith was defiant in adversity" (p. 291), we are told, and we leave her poised to join another church. Like Mrs. Eckdorf and Edward Blakeston-Smith in the two preceding novels, Miss Gomez is another one of Trevor's holy fools—a naif who sees the truth in spite of her self-delusion. Oddly enough, this remarkable novel, surely one of the best among Trevor's first eight, was not published in the United States.

Chance is once again the organizing principle in *Elizabeth Alone* (1973), which is focused on the lives of four women who are placed in the same ward of a women's hospital, three of them awaiting hysterectomies. The hospital is no less a contrivance than the boardinghouse or the two hotels in three of the previous five novels, but it satisfies the demands of verisimilitude without strain, making the conjunction of lives seem not only plausible but inevitable. It also provides Trevor with a perfect venue in which to exercise his remarkable powers of empathy, especially but not exclusively for women.

All four of the central characters are women who have been marginalized either by the accident of class, divorce, or personal misfortune. Elizabeth, a divorced woman with three young daughters, realizes that her former husband, a scholarly older man, was never a suitable match for her. Just as she is about to enter the hospital, her eldest daughter, Joanna, runs away with a young man, whom Elizabeth does not like, to join a commune. Of the remaining three women, the most important is Miss Samson, who was born with a bad eye and an ugly crimson birthmark on her face, and who now earns her living as the manager of a boardinghouse for "church folk." The principal male character is Elizabeth's childhood friend, Henry, who is also divorced and proposes marriage to her. Henry is a failure at each of the jobs he has held; his old school chums from public school, D'arcy and Carstairs, are both successful doctors whom he regards as dear friends until his resentment spills out in a drunken rage.

In no other previous work has Trevor made the subjective state of mind so crucial. We are given the postoperative dreams, the waking fantasies, and the unspoken feelings of each woman and several male characters as well, and this pattern of privileged subjectivity is so recurrent that it becomes a conspicuous element in the narrative. In Miss Samson's postoperative dream, a man comes into her boardinghouse with "the stigmata" of Christ on his hands and feet. Soon he turns out to be Mr. Ibbs, an older man, now dead, whose piety she had hitherto revered. In the dream he says that God is "a big fat confidence trick, organised by the *Daily Express*" (p. 129). Later she realizes what this means: not only had she been in love with Mr. Ibbs, as she tells Elizabeth, but one day after his death she had read his secret diary in which he confessed that he no longer believed in God. Unable to accept this, she had burned the diary, only to have its revelation boomerang in the dream figure's mockery of God. Clearly Trevor has here made novelistic use of the Freudian doctrine that material repressed in the unconscious will eventually surface. The dream is itself a long and complex narrative whose effect is at first comical, as the account of Mr. Ibbs above suggests, but in the end deeply poignant, as it serves to reinforce our sense of Miss Samson's isolation and misery.

Throughout the novel fantasy or daydream is used as a distancing device, a means of maintaining the author's ironic detachment. But Trevor insists on detachment only as a foil for his underlying compassion, and nowhere is this duality of detached compassion more in evidence than in a brilliant chapter, near the end, in which he recounts how Henry, after insulting his friends in an alcoholic binge and then being arrested for drunken driving, ends up on the floor of his kitchen with the gas stove turned on, possibly by accident. Henry's abysmal death, seen entirely from inside his foggy mind, is a tour de force.

The novel ends on a note of guarded hope. Whether or not she will ever marry again, as Miss Samson hopes, Elizabeth is reconciled with her daughter Joanna, who unexpectedly returns from the commune without her lover. Elizabeth is also pleased to learn that her former husband has married again, quite happily it seems. In this way the novel succeeds in making plausible a tragicomic view that not only insists on the alienation of modern life but that also grants the possibility that some people may be able to achieve a measure of equilibrium in the face of their isolation. Trevor wrote the screenplay for a television adaptation of this novel in 1981.

NOVELS: THE MIDDLE PERIOD (1975–1986)

TREVOR'S next three novels, together with the next four story collections, constitute a considerable growth in the skill and scope of his art. It is in these next seven books that he became, at last, a writer of major importance. Appropriately the first of these, the collection called *Angels at the Ritz*, won the Royal Society of Literature Award for 1975. Each of the other three story collections in this period is equally impressive, as are the following novels.

Timothy Gedge, the protagonist of *The Children of Dynmouth* (1976), is a fifteen-year-old boy who was an unwanted child. Neglected by his mother and sister, with whom he lives, he has never known his father. In the character of this boy Trevor combines two fictional types he has used before. One is the imposter or con man, a type already encountered in Studdy, Septimus Tuam, and Morrissey in earlier novels. Trevor's treatment of each of those characters was comical and nonjudgmental, but his view of Timothy Gedge is both more empathetic and more critical. Timothy belongs to another type as well, the unloved child as demon—a type that Trevor first made use of in the character of James, the antagonist of the horror story "Miss Smith" in his first collection. The demonic child has of course a long lineage that includes Henry James's 1898 novella, *The Turn of the Screw*, and D. H. Lawrence's 1933 story, "The Rocking-Horse Winner," but by combining this type with the con man Trevor has made of Timothy Gedge a more complex character than any of his predecessors.

Like Studdy in *The Boarding-House*, Timothy is a blackmailer, but Studdy's blackmailing attempts are laughably ineffectual, whereas Timothy is only too successful, causing a great deal of pain. His purpose is to goad the people he blackmails into giving him various props he needs for a comic act that he intends to perform at a talent competition to be held at the upcoming Easter Fete. The comic act is to be a burlesque on a serial killer who murdered three women. Throughout the story Timothy indulges in fantasies of success, especially the fantasy that his performance as the infamous murderer will earn him the admiration of a well-known comedian who will launch his career on a national television show.

For his act Timothy needs a curtain, a bathtub, a dog's tooth suit, and a wedding dress, and he succeeds in acquiring each prop by shaming the people who can provide them. Mr. Plant, for instance, a married man whom he had overheard having sex with various women in a public toilet and whom he has caught having sex with his own mother, is persuaded to provide him with the bathtub. The Commander, a retired naval officer, and his wife, Mrs. Abigail, are likewise persuaded to give the boy a dog's tooth suit when Timothy accuses the Commander of having sex with cub scouts. The revelation forces Mrs. Abigail to recognize that her marriage of thirty-six years has been a farce.

In order to acquire a wedding dress Timothy has made the acquaintance of two twelve-year-old children, Stephen and Kate, whose parents   Stephen's recently widowed father and Kate's divorced mother—have just been married and are away on a honeymoon. The action of the novel comes to a head when Timothy plants the suspicion in Stephen's mind that his father may have killed his mother. Kate naively imagines that Timothy is possessed by devils, and in desperation she asks the vicar, Quentin Featherston, to perform some ritual that will cast them out. Quentin assures her that Stephen's father did not kill Stephen's mother, who, we later learn, had killed herself; and, in refusing to perform the ritual Kate has asked for, he offers her a realistic explanation that undoubtedly represents Trevor's own view. There are no heroes and villains in life, he tells her—no absolutes of good and evil, only a pattern of "greys, half-tones and shadows. . . . Timothy Gedge was as ordinary as anyone else, but the ill fortune of circumstances or nature made ordinary people eccentric and lent them colour in the greyness" (p. 168). Quentin visits Timothy after this, convincing him to abandon the dubious act he has planned for the Easter Fete and to return each of the stage props he has ac-

quired through blackmail. The recurring mention of the Easter Fete, which does eventually take place (though without Timothy's comic act), may be understood as an ironic allusion to the Christian idea of redemption. The novel ends on a note of qualified hope, like *Elizabeth Alone*, when Quentin's wife, Lavinia, who had hoped for a son of her own, resolves to see if she can help Timothy to redeem himself.

Much of this novel's effectiveness derives from the way in which Trevor uses coincidence. Again and again Timothy just happens to overhear or witness some private misconduct which he later uses for blackmail. In at least two of these incidents— the death of Stephen's mother and the Commander's homosexual activity—it seems that he has only imagined or guessed what he claims to have witnessed, and by any conventional standard of verisimilitude the number of such coincidences would certainly be implausible. But far from putting the reader off, the cumulative effect of these improbabilities is to heighten Timothy's stature, making him somewhat larger than life—another fool (like Miss Gomez) who is empowered with moral vision despite (or because of) his hatred for all forms of family dysfunction. The novel won the Whitbread Award for 1976, and it was produced as a television play from Trevor's own script in 1987.

One of the two principal characters of Trevor's ninth novel, *Other People's Worlds*, is Francis Tyte, a handsome young actor who has failed as an actor but is nationally known for his role in several television ads. Francis is another con man, like Timothy Gedge, and one of his many victims is the other principal character in the novel, a widow named Julia Ferndale, who is fourteen years older. Francis resembles Timothy as well in his penchant for making up fantasies about himself and others. He wins Julia's sympathy by telling her that his parents were killed in a train accident years ago, though in fact they are living in an old age home, and soon she agrees to marry him.

Julia lives with her mother, Mrs. Anstey, a realist who sees that each of Julia's previous lovers, the men she was involved with following the death of her first husband, was a "lame duck" (p. 18), and Mrs. Anstey's intuition warns her that Julia may have found in Francis still another. But there is nothing she can do to prevent the inevitable catastrophe. As it turns out, Francis sells his body to men, and soon we learn that he already has a wife—an elderly dressmaker in Folkestone, whom he had married in the expectation that she would soon die, leaving him her house. He also has a child, a girl named Joy, by an alcoholic woman named Doris. As the day of his bigamous marriage with Julia approaches, Francis starts rehearsing for a bit part in a play about a Victorian murderess who killed her infant half-brother. He begins to befriend Susanna Music, the young woman who plays the lead, beguiling her with a fantasy in which he foresees her becoming a star. Later he imagines himself murdering his dress-maker wife and living with a friend "who might be a young girl as young as Susanna Music, a boy or an older man, a sympathetic woman. It never mat-tered" (p. 114). Just as he is befriending Susanna, he runs into his daughter, Joy—a painful coincidence that calls our attention to the difference between the unreal fantasy of the theater and the reality of his private life—and because he lives in fear that her mother may bring a paternity suit against him he is obliged to visit Doris, whose jealousy is aroused.

After the wedding the couple leave for their hon-eymoon in Italy, which Julia has paid for. The mar-riage is never consummated. Francis makes a clean breast of his story to Julia and departs for Germany, absconding with her jewels. Julia is shattered when she returns, but after a visit from Doris and Joy, she performs an act of penance—one of several that occur throughout Trevor's work—by taking Joy to visit Francis Tyte's father and mother, the grandparents Joy has never met. Then, thinking that Doris will try to harm Susanna Music, Julia warns the actress of the danger. Ironically, it is not Susanna but Francis' wife, the elderly dressmaker, whom Doris tracks down in Folkestone and bat-ters to death with a teapot. Trevor alludes to the murder so obliquely that a reader may easily fail to understand what has happened, even when Doris confesses her crime to the police, who do not be-lieve her. Meanwhile, Francis writes to Julia from Germany, asking for money, and whether out of compassion or a need to do penance she sends him a sum, realizing that she will continue to do so whenever he asks for help. At the end, Trevor re-marks about the daughter Joy, "The child was the victim of other people's worlds and other people's drama, caught up in a horror because she hap-pened to be there," a remark that encapsulates his tragic view of virtually all his characters.

Undoubtedly it is the cat-and-mouse game be-tween the vindictive Francis and the naive Julia that makes the first two thirds of this novel so com-pelling. But after the honeymoon trip, when Fran-cis disappears, our attention shifts entirely to Julia, who becomes something more than the naif she had been. Julia is another one of Trevor's holy fools, though unlike some she is both innocent and com-passionate.

Starting with his next novel, Trevor returns to Ire-land as his subject. The brilliance of the stories and novels concerned with life there undoubtedly owes much to the fact that he is writing about County Cork, the part of Ireland that he had known in child-hood and which now, after living in England for twenty years, he sees from a different perspective. He himself acknowledged this when he told an in-terviewer, "Leaving Ireland enabled me to see Ire-land through the wrong end of the telescope. You've got to write about the parochial in the most univer-sal way you know how. That's part of distancing, and judgment: to find what is recognizable outside of, say, a small township in Ireland" (Caldwell, *The Writer*, p. 25).

Fools of Fortune, his tenth novel, is centered on an Anglo-Irish family of the old Protestant Ascen-dancy, the Quintons, who live at Kilneagh, their an-cestral house in County Cork, and it spans the years from 1918 until the present. This is the first novel, though by no means the first story, in which Trevor uses a first-person voice, allowing each of the two principal characters, Willie Quinton and Marianne, to narrate large portions of their own story. Mari-anne is Willie's English cousin and they briefly be-come lovers before they are separated by tragic circumstances. Their two narratives are followed by a third-person narrative concerning Imelda, the daughter produced by their brief union, and the pat-tern of three separate narrations—two in the first person and one in the third—is repeated once again before the novel concludes.

The first narrator is Willie, who begins by de-scribing his childhood at Kilneagh as a pastoral idyll in which he took lessons in Latin from Father Kilgarriff, a defrocked priest who lives with the family. Willie goes on to tell the family history that begins when his great-grandfather, William Quin-ton, married an English woman, Anna Woodcombe, who became a heroine to the local Irish in the famine of 1846. Two generations later another Quinton, Willie's father, married another English daughter of the Woodcombe family, Willie's mother. The pastoral idyll of Willie's childhood is suddenly exploded in 1918, when a man named Doyle, one of his father's employees, turns out to be an informer for the Black and Tans, the infamous English force sent to quell the growing insurrection of 1918–1921. Doyle is murdered on the grounds of the estate, though without the Quintons' foreknowledge. In retaliation the Black and Tans, led by Sergeant Rudkin, burn most of the house down and kill Willie's father, his two young sisters, two of the family's servants, and the family dogs. Willie's mother never recovers, becoming an alcoholic. Obsessed by the thought that not one of the local people had avenged her husband's murder, she retreats to a house in Cork, taking Willie, who is still a boy, and her faithful maid Josephine with her, and there eventually she kills herself.

Marianne's narrative begins when she arrives for the funeral of her aunt, Willie's mother. Some time earlier she had come to Kilneagh on a summer visit during which she and Willie had fallen in love, but they had been too shy to confess their feelings. This time, on her last night before leaving for a boarding school in Switzerland, Marianne sneaks into Willie's bedroom, and months later, now pregnant, she returns in the hope of marrying him and having her baby at Kilneagh. In the meantime Willie has murdered Sergeant Rudkin and fled Ireland. When Marianne arrives in winter, no one is willing to tell her what has happened or even where Willie has gone. Trevor does not actually report the murder, so that it takes the reader as long as it takes Marianne to realize that Willie has avenged his father's death.

The child, Imelda, is therefore born out of wedlock, and Marianne decides to remain at Kilneagh where Willie's two spinster aunts and his old tutor, the defrocked priest, give her a home. Imelda, growing up in a wing of the house that did not burn down, becomes obsessed with her absent father, eventually losing her mind, but she is blessed with mystical healing powers that make her a saint in the eyes of the local population. Fifty years after her birth Willie returns and the novel ends with her parents, now happily reunited, living quietly with their crazy daughter. Throughout their first-person narratives, both Willie and Marianne address each other in the nameless second person, and only gradually does the reader come to understand who is meant by the pronoun "you." The effect is to give their narrations an elegiac tone, reinforcing the unexpressed feelings of loss and grief that both have suffered. Toward the end, Marianne tells her daughter, "when you looked at the map Ireland and England seemed like lovers" (pp. 202–203), and indeed her own tragic relationship with Willie mimics the tragic embrace of the two nations.

Fools of Fortune, which won the Whitbread Award for 1983, is a pastoral romance and its tragic theme is the decline of the Ascendancy. In certain respects the story owes much to Dickens, for whom Trevor has repeatedly acknowledged a lifelong admiration, and also to Emily Brontë, both of whom are mentioned in the novel along with George Eliot. Indeed the alternation of first- and third-person narration is reminiscent of Dickens' *Bleak House* and Brontë's *Wuthering Heights*. In keeping with the conventions of romance, which allow for a mixture of the realistic, the heroic, and even the supernatural, some of the novel's crucial events occur without warning. Trevor makes no attempt to prepare us for the revelation of Imelda's healing powers, nor does he prepare us for Willie's act of revenge. But he offers a justification when he has Willie say, "We Irish were intrigued, my father used to say, by stories with a degree of unreality in them" (p. 87).

Like a Dickensian protagonist, Willie is at first seen as an innocent victim of circumstance. But after he disappears from the narrative following his act of revenge, he takes on the aspect of a mythic hero, returning fifty years later like Odysseus to be reunited with his faithful Penelope. As in a Victorian romance, we view the servants who protect the hero and his family with the greatest affection and admiration—especially Father Kilgarriff, who tutored Willie as a boy and later tutors Imelda; a servant named Tim Paddy, who saves Willie from the Black and Tans when they kill his father; Fukes, the old butler at the boarding school Willie attends, in whom Willie confides; and Josephine, who cares for his mother until her death.

Another convention of the genre is that anyone who threatens the hero or his family is viewed as loathesome. Doyle is such a figure, and so is Miss Halliwell, an unmarried Anglo-Irish teacher who oppresses Willie with her excessive pity after his father's death; he is disgusted when she assaults him with erotic kisses. Later Marianne goes to see her, hoping that she may know of Willie's whereabouts, but when she tells Miss Halliwell she is pregnant, the unhappy teacher's only response is denial: "It's a lie, what you say about the baby" (p. 177). Clearly Miss Halliwell is an ogress, a figure common to romance, like the evil stepmother in fairy tales. She may also be seen as an emblem of the old Protestant Ascendancy's inability to accept the reality of Ireland after the Troubles—a nation now governed by Catholics and therefore beyond its control.

Dickens is also present in Trevor's hilarious account of the boarding school Willie is sent to near Dublin—one of his most successful evocations of boarding-school life. The episode comes to a head when Willie and his friends enable a former teacher, who had been disgraced and fired from his position, to take revenge on a detested master named Mad Mack by urinating on his sleeping body. The ensuing debacle, when the headmaster confronts the boys in front of the entire school, is a comic tour de force. Balancing this is a parallel episode in which Marianne goes to Switzerland to study with Professor Gibb-Bachelor, a self-centered lecher who tries to seduce her and will not desist until she tells him she is pregnant. The combination of these parallel episodes suggests that formal education, as practiced by the establishment, is wholly irrelevant to what has happened at Kilneagh. As Willie's old tutor, Father Kilgarriff, tells Marianne, "there's not much left in a life when murder has been committed" (p. 233).

As if to celebrate his fictional return to Ireland, Trevor published an illustrated book, *A Writer's Ireland: Landscape in Literature*, in 1984. The text, a pastiche of Trevor's narration spliced with his own choice of quotations from the prose and poetry of Irish writers since the earliest Celtic poets (in modern translations) to those of his own time (Seamus Heaney and others), pays loving homage to Irish writers. Although it pretends to be nothing more than a coffee-table account, the book sheds valuable light on Trevor's view of some of his predecessors, notably Elizabeth Bowen, Frank O'Connor, and James Joyce, whose descriptions of Dublin he singles out for special praise.

NOVELS: THE LATER PERIOD (1987–1995)

TREVOR'S next two novels reflect the same elegiac tone that suffuses *Fools of Fortune*, but in theme and approach they could not be more different from it or from each other. *Nights at the Alexandra* (1987) is a novella, the first of three he has written in recent years. Its narrator is a fifty-eight-year-old bachelor who is recalling a time in his boyhood, during World War II, when an aging German, Herr Messinger, and his young English wife mysteriously arrive in the provincial Irish town where Harry, then a boy of fifteen, lives with his poor Protestant family. Frau Messinger is beautiful and after she picks him out of a crowd to do an errand for her he falls under her spell, soon becoming her friend. At this point, in fact, the story takes on the aura of a fairy tale in which Harry's lot in life is magically transformed, though not in the way a fairy tale might lead one to expect. Herr Messinger, like the wise king of a fairy tale, farms the land even though he is wealthy. Harry's father is suspicious of the Messingers, whom he mistakenly believes to be Jewish refugees, and he disapproves when Harry begins to spend all his free time at Cloverhill, the Messingers' house, listening to the charming English woman's stories. By contrast Harry's family, his schoolmates, and even his teachers strike him increasingly as coarse and narrow-minded. The town is so provincial it even lacks a cinema, and partly to benefit the town but mainly to distract his wife, who is bored, Herr Messinger decides to build one. Meanwhile his wife falls ill, construction is delayed by the war, and she dies soon after the first film is shown. But her husband has made Harry the projectionist, a position that sets him apart from the rest of the town, and eventually he becomes the proprietor after his kindly benefactor dies. For years the business prospers, but it begins to lose customers after the advent of television; in the end Harry, who refuses to sell the building, is left tending Frau Messinger's grave and looking after the boarded windows of Cloverhill.

The novella is perhaps best understood as a fable about the cinema as a form of dream fiction. In many of his novels and short stories, Trevor is fond of citing Hollywood movies, sometimes to give his writings a period flavor and sometimes to serve as ironic metaphors of the characters themselves. Given his lifelong devotion to the medium, the plot of this novella is Trevor's way of paying homage to the popular art he has always loved. As a projectionist, and later as the proprietor of the movie house, Harry is a kind of dream merchant—someone who projects fictions for others to watch. In this role, even though he is not literally a filmmaker, he is a figurative stand-in for the maker of dream fictions, and thus the story he tells becomes a fable about the storyteller's isolation from the people he entertains and about his devotion to an emblem of beauty and charm represented by Frau Messinger—an emblem that he can only admire, never possess.

In *The Silence in the Garden* (1988), his eleventh full-length novel, Trevor returns to the Big House theme he had explored in "Matilda's England" and other stories as well as in his previous novel. Far more complex than the preceding novella, the story is a symbolic tale of Irish history—the history of Protestant landowners and their Catholic servants and tenant farmers. The Rollestons are Anglo-Irish gentry who have lived at Carriglas, their island estate off the coast of County Cork, for generations. During the famine, a legendary Rolleston lady of the time had become a heroine to the local poor through her generosity, and after her death her husband had forgone the rents his tenant farmers owed him.

Using a third-person narrative that alternates with a first-person diary, Trevor shuffles past and present throughout the story, which is recounted from several alternating points of view: those of Sarah Pollexfen, a poor English cousin who first comes to Carriglas in 1904 as a governess for the three Rolleston children of the time; Villana, the youngest of those children, who falls in love with Sarah's brother Hugh; Tom, the illegitimate son of Brigid, a parlormaid who later turns cook; and the butler Linchy, who is murdered. It is Sarah's diary that provides much of the crucial information in the narrative. Although she leaves before the Great War begins, Sarah is summoned back, years later, to be a companion for Mrs. Rolleston, the old dowager who presides over the family.

Mrs. Rolleston is the grandmother of Villana and her two brothers, John James and Lionel. Ultimately she emerges as a truth-teller who becomes the family's conscience, its only moral authority. John James grows up in time to be wounded in the Great War, returning to Carriglas where he languishes while conducting a liaison with Mrs. Moledy, a Catholic widow who runs a boardinghouse in the local town. In moments of adoration Mrs. Moledy calls him her "king," and their relationship may be understood as a metaphor of the callous way the Protestant landlord had historically treated the Catholic tenant—an ironic metaphor because Mrs. Moledy is a landlady in her own right. Lionel, the youngest, farms the Rolleston land like a peasant,

too shy to become involved with his cousin Sarah, whose diary reveals at the end of her life that she had loved him all along. Their sister Villana, who is beautiful and headstrong, dominates the brothers, and though she ends up marrying a local lawyer named Finnamore Balt, an older man she does not love, she remains secretly loyal to the memory of Sarah's departed brother Hugh.

At the center of the story is a mystery that Trevor unravels only gradually and in his characteristically oblique fashion. Villana and Hugh, engaged to be married, had abruptly broken off their engagement shortly after Linchy the butler had been murdered. By the end we learn the reason through Sarah's diary, which records a conversation she has with Mrs. Rolleston. During their childhood, in what is clearly intended as another ironic metaphor of the landlord-tenant relationship, Villana, bearing her father's shotgun (which she was forbidden to use) and accompanied by Hugh and her brothers, had hunted an impoverished local peasant boy through the fields and woods of their island, as though they were hunting a rabbit. The boy's name, we eventually learn, was Cornelius Dowley, and some years later he became a hero in the cause of Irish Home Rule when he led an attack on a Black and Tan unit, killing nineteen of their men. The Black and Tans murdered him in return. Meanwhile he had also planted a bomb that was meant for John James and Lionel but accidentally killed the Rollestons' butler Linchy, Tom's father, instead. The action of the novel peaks in 1931 with the building of a bridge that connects the island, both physically and symbolically, with the mainland. Ironically, the bridge is named after him, instead of the family's legendary heroine. This gruesome episode in its entirety—from the Rolleston children's sadistic hunting of Cornelius as a boy to his murderous acts of revenge and his own death—is a metaphor of the relationship between Protestant and Catholic, England and Ireland.

In the same year Villana marries Finnamore Balt. Much of their wedding is witnessed through the eyes of John James's mistress, Mrs. Moledy, who comes uninvited and engages in drunken conversation with a Church of Ireland bishop, a family cousin who is one of the wedding guests. The scene is comical, one of Trevor's funniest, but it is the dowager grandmother, Mrs. Rolleston, who has the last word, insisting that the family accept its responsibility for what has happened. Committed as she is to an ideal of humanitarian justice, Mrs. Rolleston embodies the moral principles that the old Protestant Ascendancy professed but failed to uphold. Not only does she leave Carriglas to Tom, who has grown up ostracized by the Catholic community because he was born illegitimate, but in the end, after Sarah's death, Tom and a housekeeper are the sole occupants of the house and the land. The novel won the *Yorkshire Post* Book of the Year Award for 1988.

In the preceding novel and those that follow, Trevor experiments with narrative techniques that become increasingly oblique and even, at times, elliptical. Information crucial to an understanding of what has happened is divulged so indirectly that an inattentive reader may fail to grasp it on a casual reading. These experiments exhibit a confidence and skill that was not always evident in the first seven novels. His collection called *Two Lives* (1991), comprising the two novellas *Reading Turgenev* and *My House in Umbria*, shows Trevor at the height of his novelistic powers. In the first of these, Mary Louise Dallon, who has always dreamed of living in town, has grown up on her parents' farm with her sister Letty and a brother. Despite Letty's objections, she agrees to marry Elmer Quarry, an older man who owns a family drapery shop in the town, which he runs with his two spinster sisters, Matilda and Rose. After a miserable honeymoon, they settle down to a quiet life at the shop, but their marriage is never consummated. Mary Louise's sisters-in-law are unwelcoming and contemptuous, and Elmer soon takes to drink. One day, after visiting her parents on her bicycle, Mary Louise stops off to call on her Aunt Emmeline, a widow living with her invalid son, Robert. As it turns out, Robert and Mary Louise had each harbored a secret infatuation for the other in their school years. Mary Louise keeps returning, they grow more intimate, especially when he reads Turgenev aloud to her, and on the night after they confess their mutual love Robert dies. Mary Louise buys what she can of his belongings, which she keeps in her husband's attic, where she retreats into a fantasy of living with her dead cousin. Eventually her sisters-in-law, believing she has lost her mind, convince her family and her husband to have her confined in a home for the mentally disturbed.

What makes this poignant story so arresting is the highly elliptical narrative structure. From the start each chapter that describes her "normal" life (marriage and the like) in chronological order alternates with a chapter that describes her later life in the madhouse, but there are no time markers to indicate that the alternate chapters are occurring years later. In the former the narration is realistic; in the latter, oblique: we are never told that the latter are set in a madhouse or that she is the subject of those chapters. The effect of such an elliptical dislocation is to give the story an ironic dimension that undercuts any possibility of sentimentality. By thus grafting modernist technique onto realistic narration, the method simultaneously allows us to identify with Mary Louise and keeps us at a distance.

The narration of *My House in Umbria*, though not as overtly elliptical, is also very oblique. The narrator is a woman in her late fifties who has been known by several names but prefers Mrs. Emily Delahunty. Orphaned by parents she never knew, she was raised by an English couple until the husband, whom she had taken for her father, seduced her. After years in Ombubu, Africa, where she and her sidekick, an Irishman named Quinty, ran the Cafe Rose, possibly as a whorehouse, she has for many years owned a small hotel in the Italian countryside. She has also made a name for herself as the author of numerous romance novels. Trevor's invention of this sentimental writer who is able to tell the story we are reading without sentimentality has the same effect as the ambiguous narration of the preceding novella—allowing us to sympathize even while it keeps us at a critical distance.

Early in the story, Emily boards a train to shop for clothes and shoes in Milan. While she is observing her fellow travellers, the compartment they are seated in is suddenly blown up, although we do not fully understand what has happened until some time later, while she is recovering in a hospital. Eventually she returns to her hotel, bringing the only other survivors with her—an elderly Englishman who is a retired general, a twenty-seven-year-old German named Otmar, and an eight-year-old American girl named Aimée. The rest of the novella concerns the affectionate bonds that develop between them. Aimée has been speechless since the explosion, but gradually she begins to speak again. The story draws to a close with the arrival of Aimée's uncle, an American professor of botany who comes to take her home. Emily tries unsuccessfully to persuade the professor to let Aimée stay at the hotel.

Meanwhile Emily has quietly figured out that it was Otmar who had planted the bomb that blew up her train, for reasons she hints at without explaining, but she never confronts him or informs the Italian police, who have been unable to solve the mystery. In the end, after the American child has been taken away, the general dies and Otmar disappears, leaving Emily, her sidekick Quinty, and their staff to run their hotel. Perhaps the secret of this story's success is that Emily, another one of Trevor's authorial figures, is both naive and all-knowing—an ambiguous role that perfectly embodies his larger theme, which is the isolation of innocent people in a cruel and indifferent world.

Trevor's twelfth full-length novel, *Felicia's Journey*, employs the same oblique narration as each of the preceding four works, but it differs from them in bringing to the surface the sadistic cruelty that was just under the surface in *The Old Boys* and *Other People's Worlds* and that was made explicit in the hunting of Cornelius Dowley in *The Silence in the Garden*. Felicia, a naive working-class Irish girl living with her father, her two brothers, and a bed-ridden great-grandmother, is seduced by Johnny Lysaght, an Irish lad on leave from the English army, although (as one of Trevor's liars) he tells her he works at a lawn-mower factory near Birmingham. Realizing she is pregnant after he returns to England, Felicia steals her great-grandmother's life savings and takes the boat, believing she will find him. But there is no such factory and while she searches in vain, she encounters Mr. Hilditch, the middle-aged manager of a catering service who offers what she takes to be kindly advice and even gives her a lift in his car, a friendly gesture that enables him to steal her stolen money.

The powerful dynamics of this novel derive from its intense focus on a simple opposition between Felicia and Mr. Hilditch. Our interest shifts back and forth between these two characters, and the alternating points of view not only intensify suspense but also reveal character. We soon discover that Mr. Hilditch is a serial killer who has previously murdered six young women. As an only child who was crushed by a domineering mother, he is driven by a fear of his own sexuality. He is also another one of Trevor's liars, as we see when he invents a sick wife who has to be taken to the hospital, where she conveniently dies. Sensing what must have happened, he discovers that Johnny is stationed nearby, a fact he keeps to himself. One of

the ironies that reinforces the structural opposition between Felicia and her antagonist is an underlying symmetry between Johnny and Mr. Hilditch, both of whom are sociopaths whose filial relations to their mothers help to explain their pathologies. Meanwhile Felicia tries living with a religious group, whom she unwittingly offends. Eventually she ends up in Mr. Hilditch's house, and the story moves toward its climax when, sensing that she suspects his murderous intention, he realizes that he must act immediately if he is to have his way. By a fluke she is able to escape while he waits for her in the car outside. In the end, after the religious folk who had turned against Felicia try to proselytize him, sensing a potential convert, he hangs himself, and for a time we follow her life as a tramp, learning through her regretful thoughts that her child was taken away from her after its birth.

Trevor's oblique narration serves to deflect the sensationalism inherent in the situation, and the ultimate irony that Felicia will survive as a bag lady after barely escaping death by murder turns what might have been a cheap melodrama into a bleak kind of modern tragedy. Yet it is not just Trevor's oblique irony that gives the story its power; it is also his use of an uncharacteristically colloquial style—a familiar tone of voice that sounds almost like speech, especially in passages of *oratio obliqua*. The cruelty of the cat-and-mouse game played out between Mr. Hilditch and Felicia, reminiscent of the game between Francis Tyte and Julia in *Other People's Worlds*, may also be seen as a political fable of the deadly embrace between England and Ireland.

Since the publication of *Fools of Fortune* and some of the stories preceding it, Trevor's fiction has increasingly acknowledged the political implications of the lives led by his characters. This is most obvious in the stories and novels set in Ireland, though even in his earlier work, the stories and novels set in England, there are memorable characters—Mr. Obd, the Nigerian; Miss Gomez, the Jamaican; and several Irish immigrants—whose lives have been largely shaped by the dissolution of the British Empire. Yet the political implications of his fiction are secondary to the psychological, which are primary. Although his sympathies lie with those who live on the margins of society, the miseries and indignities they suffer do not arouse in him a sense of outrage. The moral ambiguities of their existence engage his deepest interest. Trevor is a master of psychological realism and the subtle skill of his art has undoubtedly secured him an enduring place among the major Irish writers of the twentieth century.

SELECTED BIBLIOGRAPHY

I. NOVELS. *A Standard of Behaviour* (London, 1958); *The Old Boys* (London and New York, 1964); *The Boarding-House* (London and New York, 1965); *The Love Department* (London, 1966, 1983; New York, 1967); *Mrs. Eckdorf in O'Neill's Hotel* (London, 1969; New York, 1970, 1989); *Miss Gomez and the Brethren* (London, 1971; New York, 1997); *Elizabeth Alone* (London, 1973; New York, 1974); *The Children of Dynmouth* (London, 1976; Harmondsworth, Middlesex, Eng., 1979; New York, 1977); *Other People's Worlds* (London, 1980; New York, 1981); *Fools of Fortune* (London and New York, 1983); *Nights at the Alexandra* (London and New York, 1987), novella; *The Silence in the Garden* (London and New York, 1988); *Two Lives: Reading Turgenev* and *My House in Umbria* (London and New York, 1991); *Felicia's Journey* (London and New York, 1995).

II. SHORT STORIES. *The Day We Got Drunk on Cake and Other Stories* (London, 1967; New York, 1968); *Penguin Modern Stories 8* (London, 1971); *The Ballroom of Romance and Other Stories* (London and New York, 1972); *The Last Lunch of the Season* (London, 1973); *Angels at the Ritz and Other Stories* (London, 1975; New York, 1976); *Lovers of Their Time and Other Stories* (London, 1978; New York, 1979); *The Distant Past and Other Stories* (Swords, County Dublin, 1979); *Beyond the Pale and Other Stories* (London and New York, 1981); *The Stories of William Trevor* (Harmondsworth, Middlesex, Eng., and New York, 1983); *The News from Ireland and Other Stories* (London and New York, 1986); *Family Sins and Other Stories* (London and New York, 1990); *The Collected Stories* (London and New York, 1992); *After Rain* (London and New York, 1996).

III. MISCELLANEOUS BOOKS. *Old School Ties* (London, 1976); *A Writer's Ireland: Landscape in Literature* (London and New York, 1984), illustrated; editor, *The Oxford Book of Irish Short Stories* (Oxford, Eng., and New York, 1989); *Juliet's Story* (Dublin, 1991; New York, 1994), children's book; *Excursions in the Real World: Memoirs* (London, 1993; New York, 1994).

IV. ARTICLES AND REVIEWS. "Leaving School," in *London Magazine* 3 (1986); "Involvement: Writers Reply," in *London Magazine* 8, no. 5 (1968); "Some Notes on Writing Stories," *London Magazine* 9, no. 12 (1970); "Saying Goodbye to Elizabeth: Writers at Work," in *Author 84* (1973); "A View of My Own," in *Nova* (September 1974); "A Writer's Day," in *Society Magazine* (April 1976); "Too Blase for Rape," in review of *Come Trailing Blood* by Paul Smith, in *Hibernia* (Dublin) (28 April 1977); foreword to Sondra J.

Strang, ed., *The Presence of Ford Madox Ford: A Memorial Volume of Essays, Poems, and Memoirs* (Philadelphia, 1981); "Between Holyhead and Dun Laoghaire," review of *The Collected Stories of Elizabeth Bowen*, in *Times Literary Supplement* (6 February 1981); "Frank O'Connor: The Way of a Storyteller," review of *Collected Stories* by Frank O'Connor, in *Washington Post World* (13 September 1981); introduction to *David's Daughter Tamar* by Margaret Barrington (Dublin, 1982); "O'Brien, Edna," in James Vinson, ed., *Contemporary Novelists*, 3rd ed. (New York, 1982); "Child of the Century," review of *Collected Stories* by V. S. Pritchett, in *The New York Review of Books* (13 June 1991); "Mr. Fuge's Dream House," in *Architectural Digest* (May 1995).

V. PLAYS. *The Elephant's Foot* (produced Nottingham, 1965); *The Girl* (televised 1967; produced London, 1968; published London, 1968); *A Night with Mrs. da Tanka* (televised 1968; produced London, 1972; published London, 1972); *Going Home* (broadcast 1970; produced London, 1972; published London, 1972); *The Old Boys* (produced London, 1971; published London, 1971); *A Perfect Relationship* (broadcast 1973; produced London, 1973; published London, 1976); *The 57th Saturday* (produced London, 1973); *Marriages* (produced London, 1973; published London, 1973); *Scenes from an Album* (broadcast 1975; produced Dublin, 1981; published Dublin, 1981); *Beyond the Pale* (broadcast 1980; published in *Best Radio Plays of 1980*, London, 1981); *Autumn Sunshine* (televised 1981; broadcast 1982; published in *Best Radio Plays of 1982*, London, 1983).

VI. RADIO PLAYS. *The Penthouse Apartment* (1968); *The Boarding-House* (1971), based on his novel; *Attracta* (1977); *The Blue Dress* (1981); *Travellers* (1982); *The News from Ireland* (1986); *Events at Drimaghleen* (1988); *Running Away* (1988).

VII. TELEVISION PLAYS. *The Baby-Sitter* (1965); *Walk's End* (1966); *The Mark-2 Wife* (1969); *The Italian Table* (1970); *The Grass Widows* (1971); *O Fat White Woman* (1972); *The Schoolroom* (1972); *Access to the Children* (1973); *The General's Day* (1973); *Miss Fanshawe's Story* (1973); *An Imaginative Woman* (1973), from a story by Thomas Hardy; *Love Affair* (1974); *Eleanor* (1974); *Mrs. Acland's Ghosts* (1975); *The Statue and the Rose* (1975); *Two Gentle People* (1975), from a story by Graham Greene; *The Nicest Man in the World* (1976); *Afternoon Dancing* (1976); *The Love of a Good Woman* (1976); *The Girl Who Saw a Tiger* (1976); *Last Wishes* (1978); *Another Weekend* (1978); *Memories* (1978); *Matilda's England* (1979); *The Old Curiosity Shop* (1979), from the novel by Charles Dickens; *Secret Orchards* (1980), from works by J. R. Ackerley and Diana Petre; *The Happy Autumn Fields* (1980), from a story by Elizabeth Bowen; *Elizabeth Alone* (1981), based on his novel; *Autumn Sunshine* (1981); *The Ballroom of Romance* (1982); *Mrs. Silly* (1983), from *All for Love* series; *One of Ourselves* (1983); *Broken Homes* (1985); *The Children of Dynemouth* (1987), based on his novel; *August Saturday* (1990).

VIII. BIBLIOGRAPHY. Kristin Morrison, *William Trevor* (New York, 1993), pp. 179–184; Suzanne Morrow Paulson, *William Trevor: A Study of the Short Fiction* (New York, 1993), pp. 173–185.

IX. INTERVIEWS. "An Irish Humour Man," in *Scotsman* (Edinburgh) (7 March 1964); W. L. Webb, "Gentle Gerontocrat," in *Manchester Guardian* (1 May 1965); Stephanie Nettal, "Sadly Comic or Comically Sad?" in *Books and Bookmen* (May 1965); "Age Sage," in *London Observer* (4 July 1965); Peter Firchow, ed., "William Trevor," in his *The Writer's Place: Interviews on the Literary Situation in Contemporary Britain* (Minneapolis, 1974); Derek Lean, "Writer Has to Avoid the View," in *Western Morning News* (12 December 1975); Mark Ralph-Bowman, *Transatlantic Review* (1976); Amanda Smith, "PW Interviews: William Trevor," in *Publishers Weekly* (28 October 1983); Jacqueline Stahl Aronson, "William Trevor: An Interview," in *Irish Literary Supplement: A Review of Irish Books* (spring 1986); David Profumo, "Tower of Fable," in *Harpers* (November 1988); Mira Stout, "The Art of Fiction CVIII," in *Paris Review* 110 (1989); Gail Caldwell, "A Gentleman of Substance," in *Boston Globe* (30 May 1990), repr. as "An Interview with William Trevor," in *The Writer* 103 (October 1990); Stephen Schiff, "The Shadows of William Trevor," in *New Yorker* (28 December 1992–4 January 1993).

X. BIOGRAPHIES. Anne M. Brady and Brian Cleeve, "William Trevor," in *A Biographical Dictionary of Irish Writers* (New York, 1985); D. J. R. Bruckner, "Stories Keep Coming to a Late Blooming Writer" in *New York Times* (21 May 1990, sec. C11); Maureen Cairnduff, ed., *Who's Who in Ireland* (Dublin, 1991); Margaret Drabble, ed., *The Oxford Companion to English Literature,* 5th ed. (Oxford, Eng., 1985); Jay L. Halio and Paul Binding, "William Trevor," in *Dictionary of Literary Biography: British Novelists Since 1960,* vol. 14, part 2 (Detroit, 1983); Jay L. Halio, "Trevor, William," in D. L. Kirkpatrick, ed., *Contemporary Novelists,* 4th ed. (New York, 1986); Dolores MacKenna, "William Trevor," in Rudiger Imhof, ed., *Contemporary Irish Novelists* (Tubingen, Germany, 1990); John Wakeman, ed., *World Authors: 1950 to 1970* (New York, 1975).

XI. CRITICAL STUDIES. Mary Fitzgerald-Hoyt, "The Influence of Italy in the Writings of William Trevor and Julia O'Faolain," in *Notes on Modern Irish Literature* 2 (1990); Julian Gitzen, "The Truth-Tellers of William Trevor," in *Critique* 21 (1979); Michael Gorra, "Review of Fiction," in *The Hudson Review* 37, no. 1 (spring 1984); Robert Hogan, "Old Boys, Young Bucks, and New Women: The Contemporary Irish Short Story," in James F. Kilroy, ed., *The Irish Short Story: A Critical History* (Boston, 1984); Denis Lane and Carol McCrory Lane, eds., "Trevor, William (1928–   )," in *Modern Irish Literature* (New York, 1988); Max Deen Larsen, "Saints of the Ascendancy: William Trevor's Big-House Novels," in Otto Rauchbauer, ed., *Ancestral Voices: The Big House in Anglo-Irish Literature* (Dublin, 1992); Mary Dolores MacKenna, "William Trevor: The Moral Landscape," Ph.D. diss. (University of Dublin, 1987); Kristin Morrison, "William Trevor," in *Reference Guide to English Literature,* 2nd ed., vol. 2 (London, 1991), "William Trevor's 'System of Correspondences,' " in *Massachusetts Review* 28 (1987), and *William Trevor* (New York, 1993); Thomas Morrissey, "Trevor's *Fools of Fortune:* The Rape of Ireland," in *Notes on Modern Irish Literature* 2 (1990); Mark Mortimer, "The Short Stories of William Trevor," in *Etudes Irlandaises* 9, n.s. (December 1984) and "William Trevor in Dublin," *Etudes Irlandaises* 4, f.s. (1975); William T. O'Malley, ed., *Anglo-Irish Literature: A Bibliography of Dissertations, 1873–1989* (New York, 1990), lists three dissertations dealing with Trevor's work; Suzanne Morrow Paulson, *William Trevor: A Study of the Short Fiction* (New York, 1993); Mark Ralph-Bowman, "Focal Distance: A Study of the Novels of William Trevor," Ph.D. diss. (University of Leicester, 1974); Robert E. Rhodes, "William Trevor's Stories of the Troubles," in James D. Brophy and Raymond Porter, eds., *Contemporary Irish Writing* (Boston, 1983) and " 'The Rest Is Silence': Secrets in Some of William Trevor's Stories," in James D. Brophy and Eamon Grennan, eds., *New Irish Writing: Essays in Memory of Raymond J. Porter* (Boston, 1989); Gregory A. Schirmer, *William Trevor: A Study of His Fiction* (New York, 1990); John J. Stinson, "Replicas, Foils, and Revelation in Some 'Irish' Short Stories of William Trevor," in *Canadian Journal of Irish Studies* 11, no. 2 (1985); Rachel Lillian Taylor, "William Trevor: A Critical Study," Ph.D. diss. (University of Maryland, 1980).

FAY WELDON

(1931–)

Margaret E. Mitchell

SINCE THE PUBLICATION of her first novel in 1967, Fay Weldon's spare, lively prose and incisive social commentary have attracted popular and academic attention internationally. Her unabashedly woman-centered fiction explores the politics of modern gender relations with humor and insight, critiquing the roles men and women play in perpetuating a male-dominated society. She is the author of novels, collections of short stories, works of nonfiction, and scripts for the stage, screen, and radio.

LIFE

BORN Franklin Birkinshaw in Alvechurch, Worcester, England, on 22 September 1931, Fay Weldon spent much of her childhood in New Zealand. Her father, Frank Thornton Birkinshaw, was a physician, and her mother, Margaret Jepson Birkinshaw, was a novelist. Weldon's maternal uncle, Selwyn Jepson, and grandfather, Edgar Jepson, were prolific authors of thrillers and romantic adventures, respectively.

Following her parents' divorce when she was five, Weldon grew up with her mother and sister in what she frequently refers to as a "household of women." In Christchurch, New Zealand, she attended a school for girls, and, at fourteen, she returned to England to attend a convent school in London, at which point the household of women expanded to include her grandmother. These circumstances contributed to an outlook on the world that undoubtedly has helped to shape her work: "I believed the world was essentially feminine," Weldon has said. "It was quite a shock to discover that the world, as other people saw it, was dominated by men. Luckily I had already formed my own opinion" (Barreca, *Fay Weldon's Wicked Fictions*, p. 6).

In 1949 Weldon entered St. Andrews University in Edinburgh, Scotland, on a scholarship; by 1952 she had earned a master's in economics and psychology. In 1955 she gave birth to her first son, Nicholas. Weldon refers to the ensuing years in London as a period of "odd jobs and hard times." For a time she worked for the Foreign Office writing propaganda; later she answered personal problem letters and did market research for the London *Daily Mirror*. Eventually, she began writing advertising copy and coined the slogan "go to work on an egg," a highly successful advertisement that encouraged commuters to eat an egg before work.

Weldon married Ronald Weldon, an antiques dealer, in 1960 and gave birth to three more sons: Daniel in 1963, Thomas in 1970, and Samuel in 1977. For fifteen years the family lived in the London suburb of Primrose Hill. She began writing seriously in the 1960s, composing plays for radio, the stage, and later television with considerable success. *Spider* won the Writer's Guild Award for best radio play in 1973, and *Polaris* won the Giles Cooper Award for best radio play in 1978; she wrote two episodes for the television series *Upstairs Downstairs* in 1971 and 1972, and the first received the SFTA Award for best series.

Weldon's first novel, *The Fat Woman's Joke*, was published in 1967. In the decades that followed, she continued to produce acclaimed novels and award-winning scripts at a remarkable rate, including a well-received adaptation of Jane Austen's *Pride and Prejudice* in 1980. In the late 1990s, she was living in London with her third husband, Nicholas Fox.

WELDON'S FEMINISM

IT is not difficult to discern parallels between Weldon's life and her fiction, and many critics have been quick to do so. In *Letters to Alice on First Reading Jane Austen* (1984), a meditation on fiction, Weldon warns against such a biographical approach:

"It is not just my novels . . . but *me* they end up wanting to investigate, and it is not a profitable study" (p. 10). Although Weldon undoubtedly draws on personal experience for her fiction, it is clear that she sees her life as emblematic of the experiences of a generation of women. In her essay "The Changing Face of Fiction" in *Fay Weldon's Wicked Fictions*, Weldon traces the development of her work to the shifting ideals of feminism in Great Britain. While she was a student at St. Andrew's University in the early 1950s, she writes, she took a course in moral philosophy in which the professor asserted that women were incapable of rational thought or moral judgment—a notion common enough, Weldon suggests, that she and other female students, certain that they were quite capable of both, "just assumed there was something wrong with us; we could not be properly female" (p. 188). To compensate, she writes, "how we swept and cleaned—we girl graduates—and had babies and showed our garters to escape the insult!" (p. 189). This perceived tension between "proper" feminine behavior and the intellect surfaces again and again in Weldon's fiction.

By the mid-1960s, she had started to compose plays; at this point, she writes, "I began to see the error of not just my but our ways. The myth that women didn't go out to work but stayed home and were supported by their husbands . . . was beginning to wear rather thin" ("The Changing Face of Fiction," p. 189). The development of Weldon's writing career, then, is closely linked to her emerging feminist consciousness. "In the fifties and sixties," she writes, "we women thought if we were unhappy it could only be our fault. . . . As the seventies approached . . . the great realization dawned—we must change not ourselves but the world!" (p. 193). Weldon's early novels reflect her desire to contribute to this effort; repeatedly, she has expressed the conviction that fiction has the power to alter the way we see the world, thereby opening the door for social reform.

The period during which Weldon's first novels appeared saw important gains for the feminist movement in Great Britain, including the Equal Pay Act of 1970, the Sex Discrimination Act of 1975, and the Employment Protection Program of the same year, which provided for paid maternity leave and protected female employees from losing their jobs because of pregnancy. Also in 1975, the National Abortion Campaign prevented the curtailing of rights legislated by the Abortion Act of 1967. With the notable exception of the title character of *Praxis* (1978), Weldon's characters seldom are directly involved in the feminist movement, but the issues addressed by feminist activists frequently figure prominently in the lives of her heroines—or antiheroines, as critics sometimes describe them.

While never ceasing to uphold the cause of women in general, Weldon has criticized certain facets of feminist politics; in particular, she expresses doubts about the "superwoman" myth of the 1980s, which she describes as the belief that "a woman—if only she were sufficiently organized—could be all things to all men and survive" ("The Changing Face of Fiction," p. 189). The title character in *Praxis*, who becomes a feminist activist in the course of the novel, is symbolically trampled underfoot on a bus by one of the "New Women," as Weldon dubs them. Praxis complains:

They are what I wanted to be; they are what I worked for them to be: and now I see them, I hate them. They have found their own solution to the threefold pain—one I never thought of. They do not try, as we did, to understand it and get the better of it. They simply wipe out the pain by doing away with its three centres—the heart, the soul and the mind. Brilliant! Heartless, soulless, mindless—free!

(p. 17)

"These days," Weldon writes in "The Changing Face of Fiction," "the new women, or so I hope, take a slightly more moderate line. We can see there may occasionally be room for personal self-improvement: we may have to work upon ourselves as well as on the world" (p. 195). Weldon has sometimes been criticized for her excessively negative portrayals of men. In her defense, other critics have pointed out that she is also critical of her women characters, condemning their self-involvement and exposing their complicity in perpetuating the myths, customs, and institutions that oppress them. Some critics have argued that Weldon's fiction is overly didactic, sacrificing literary aesthetics for social commentary, while others have said that her feminism fails to go far enough, that the disruptive power of her female protagonists is never fully realized, and that her novels offer only an ambiguous kind of hope for the future. Still other critics and reviewers have suggested that Weldon's feminism is conflicted, that some of her novels ultimately uphold the very values or institutions they ostensibly critique.

Nonetheless, Weldon has been recognized as an important feminist voice since the publication of *The Fat Woman's Joke*. The heroine, Esther, on the verge of launching into an account of her troubles, issues a warning that might apply to Weldon's fiction in general:

Then I will tell you about it. . . . I warn you, it will not be pleasant. You will become upset and angry. It is a story of patterns but no endings, meanings but no answers, and jokes where it would be nice if no jokes were. There has never been a tale quite like this before, and that in itself is hard to endure.

(p. 16)

Like Esther's story, Weldon's fiction often violates narrative conventions, while her subversive humor subtly attacks some of the fundamental assumptions of Western culture. *The Fat Woman's Joke* is the first of many novels in which Weldon tells the story of a housewife driven to extremes by the demands and restrictions of her marriage and who ultimately calls into question the institution of marriage itself. The marriages that fall apart early in Weldon's novels are often mended by the final pages but always with the balance of power shifting toward the wife. Ann Marie Hebert (1993) has argued that, although order is generally restored at the end of the novels, it "lacks stability; its vulnerability to feminine assault is exposed" (p. 27). This is precisely the case in *The Fat Woman's Joke*; Esther returns to her husband, but she, her marriage, and several peripheral characters will never be quite the same as they were before Esther's rebellion.

As the novel opens Esther has left her husband, Alan, who has been having an affair with his secretary. Living alone in a shabby apartment, Esther occupies herself by reading science fiction, watching television, and eating. The downfall of her marriage to Alan is prompted by a mutual decision to go on a diet, for their marriage, as Esther explains to her friend Phyllis, was founded largely on food. As a wife with no employment outside the home, Esther has spent her days planning meals, buying food, and cooking. "We all have our cushions against reality" (p. 21), she says to Phyllis, and for

Esther and Alan that cushion was eating. At night, she explains, "Alan and I would sit back, lulled by our full bellies into a sense of security, and really believe ourselves to be happy, content and well-matched" (p. 22). Such fragile domestic fictions, Weldon argues throughout her work, too often form the foundation of relationships between men and women. Esther and Alan's decision to diet removes the cushion and renders their long marriage vulnerable to the "little gray clouds" that have been gathering, unnoticed, for years (p. 22).

While Alan, suddenly hostile and resentful toward Esther, begins to flirt with his secretary, Esther herself, deprived of her main occupation, begins to see her life in a whole new light and perceives its emptiness. Housework, she decides, is meaningless: "Running a house is not a sensible occupation for a grown woman. Dusting and sweeping, cooking and washing up—it is work for the sake of work, an eternal cycle which lasts from the day you get married until the day you die" (p. 73). Explaining why she no longer makes curry, Esther remarks, "It is all a great waste of time and energy, but it keeps women occupied, and that's important. If they had a spare hour or two they might look at their husbands and laugh, mightn't they?" (p. 72). In Weldon's fiction, for women to laugh at men is to undermine male authority and is therefore subversive, as Regina Barreca argues in *Fay Weldon's Wicked Fiction*. By suggesting that women might laugh at their husbands if they only had time, Esther implies that the duties of wives who stay at home—like the daylong process of making curry—are essentially the tools of their oppression. She has arrived at the conclusion that marriage, as an institution, systematically oppresses women:

"Marriage is too strong an institution for me," said Esther. "It is altogether too heavy and powerful." And indeed at that moment she felt her marriage to be a single steady crushing weight, on top of which bore down the entire human edifice of city and state, learning and religion, commerce and law, pomp, passion and reproduction. . . . When she challenged her husband, she challenged the universe.

(p. 10)

Once free of Alan, Esther gives up her diet with a vengeance and settles down to a routine of never-ending consumption. Cheap food from cans replaces the gourmet meals on which she formerly prided herself, and she grows ever larger. "You've gone completely to pieces," Phyllis admonishes her. "You will have to go on a diet again" (pp. 14–15). But Esther is contemptuous of Phyllis—"neat, sexy and rich; invincibly lively and invincibly stupid" (p. 8)—with her willingness to rationalize her husband's habitual infidelity and occasional brutality. "I suppose you really do believe that your happiness is consequent upon your size? . . . It is a very debased view of femininity you take, Phyllis," Esther lectures her friend (p. 11).

Although Esther occupies the center of *The Fat Woman's Joke*, Weldon establishes one of her trademarks in this first novel: expanding the scope of her narrative to encompass the lives of several women, demonstrating the significant and often unexpected ways in which their lives are linked and their interests ultimately coincide. In this novel, the focus of the narrative alternates primarily between Esther and Susan, Alan's secretary. Susan is an artist, employed only temporarily as a secretary, and not a particularly good secretary at that. Young, intelligent, and supremely confident in her beauty, Susan is the first in a long line of Weldon's characters to enlist herself on the side of men against women, husbands against wives. "I don't like wives, on principle. I like to feel that any husband would prefer me to his wife. Wives are a dull, dreadful, boring, possessive lot by virtue of their state. I am all for sexual free enterprise. Let the best woman win" (p. 19). If marriages crumble as a result of her philosophy, Susan sees that as the natural result of her superiority and feels no remorse. She accepts Alan's version of his marriage: Esther suppressed his creativity, trapped him in a dull domestic routine, "drove him into advertising" (p. 40). Susan assumes she can repair the damage; besides, she explains to her friend Brenda, "I need men to define me: to give me an idea of what I am" (p. 88). Susan wishes to rescue Alan and define herself in the process; what she initially fails to realize is that Alan has no desire to be rescued. He has intended from the start to reclaim Esther when he is ready. Worse, his feelings for Susan are entirely devoid of respect; to him, she is little more than a body.

Esther's decision to return to Alan at the end of the novel is not precisely a victory, although both Phyllis and Susan insist on seeing it as such. "Wives always win in the end," says Phyllis, desperately needing to believe in the truth of her words. "And what a victory, over what?" Esther replies (p. 188). To Susan, Esther insists that it is no victory at all: "It is not that I have vanquished you. It is that we have both been wounded in a battle which we should never have embarked upon" (p. 174). The real battle, she implies, should not be between one woman and another but between women and men. Esther's arguments about the fundamentally exploitative nature of relations between the sexes and her critique of the institution of marriage make her one of the most radical feminists in Weldon's fiction. Most dramatically, she declares at one point that "there must be apartheid between the sexes. . . . We must create our own world" (p. 110). Weldon undermines the extremity of this statement by reuniting Esther and Alan at the end of the novel; she rejects the separatism Esther advocates in favor of a reconciliation between the sexes, however tenuous or ambivalent that reconciliation might be. Still, Esther's effect on Phyllis suggests the deeply subversive intent of the novel. "I just don't know what to think or what to feel anymore," Phyllis despairs near the end of Esther's narrative. "There aren't any rules left" (p. 166). Weldon's first novel both exposes and indicts the "rules" she saw restricting women's lives in the late 1960s; in her next twenty novels, spanning three decades, she continued to map out this territory.

Weldon's second novel, *Down Among the Women* (1971), is considered both more ambitious and more successful than her first. She assembles a larger cast of women characters that spans three generations. The title echoes as a refrain throughout the novel and also provides the opening sentence: "Down among the women. What a place to be! Yet here we all are by accident of birth, sprouted breasts and bellies, as cyclical of nature as our timekeeper the moon—and down here among the women we have no option but to stay" (p. 1). To live down among the women, in this novel, is to be relegated by biology to a world of economic struggle, job discrimination, and betrayal by men and women alike.

The novel opens in 1950. Wanda, a middle-aged ex-Communist who left her unfaithful husband years ago, is hosting a meeting of Divorcées Anonymous. Her twenty-year-old daughter, Scarlet, heavily pregnant and unmarried, is embarrassed by her mother's crudity and refusal to grow old gracefully. Scarlet still lives "down among the girls"

(p. 12), surrounded by her friends Jocelyn, Helen, Audrey, and Sylvia. Recent college graduates, they are working as typists, looking for jobs, or painting. In these days before the contraceptive pill, they panic every month, hoping they are not pregnant. Scarlet's state appalls them, and yet they envy her: "Something has actually happened to her. She has left the girls, and joined the women, and they know it" (p. 15).

The novel charts their paths as they leave the comparatively safe world of the girls and join the women. Their misfortunes mostly occur at the hands of men: "Down here among the women you don't get to hear about man maltreated; what you hear about is man seducer, man betrayer, man deserter, man the monster" (p. 53). Men in the novel play all of these roles, but the women do not escape blame: "Down here among the women, we don't like chaos. We will crawl from our sickbeds to tidy and define. We live at floor level, washing and wiping. If we look upward, it's not towards the stars or the ineffable, it's to dust the tops of the windows. We have only ourselves to blame" (p. 74). As always, Weldon insists that women are complicit in their fate: like Susan in *The Fat Woman's Joke*, they seek to define themselves through men, and they marry for the wrong reasons. Jocelyn, for instance, "wants everyone to know that she, Jocelyn, is truly female, truly feminine, truly desired, is now to be married and complete" (p. 83). Scarlet, now the mother of Byzantia, "is moved by desperation, not ambition. She wants security and respectability. She wants to be looked after" (p. 88). Furthermore, they betray one another as often as they are betrayed by men. Jocelyn sleeps with Sylvia's boyfriend: "They are to marry, in the future. And serve her right, you might well say," the narrator remarks (p. 25). (Only later do we learn that the narrator is Jocelyn herself.) Helen becomes entangled in a disastrous affair with a married artist, thereby driving his wife to suicide. Audrey gives up a good job and breaks off relations with her family at the request of her future husband: she needs shelter. Scarlet marries her mother's boyfriend, a stooping, stamp-collecting school inspector twenty-five years older than she. Her friends are appalled once more and attempt to dissuade her. "You don't remain yourself when you marry," Jocelyn warns, but Scarlet insists that she will remain herself, "only more comfortable" (p. 111).

In the course of the novel, Scarlet and her friends learn that the contrary is true: marriage does not necessarily provide the security they were taught to expect, but rather an uneasy dependency at best. Far from allowing them to remain themselves, it prevents them from becoming themselves. By the final chapter they have struggled to free themselves from their original, destructive relationships, salvaging only their friendships with one another and, in some cases, the children they produced along the way. Helen is an exception; she follows in the footsteps of her lover's wife and escapes the struggle through suicide. The survivors have established new, more satisfying relationships, leading Scarlet to plead with her daughter, Byzantia, now a young woman: "we haven't done too badly" (p. 216). But Byzantia is disdainful, for her mother and her friends still define success in relation to men. "How trivial," she remarks, and the narrator explains: "Byzantia, like her grandmother Wanda, is a destroyer, not a builder. But where Wanda struggled against the tide and gave up, exhausted, Byzantia has it behind her, full and strong" (p. 216). Thus Weldon encapsulates three generations of feminism. By implication it is her own generation who are the builders, their struggles paving the way for young women like Byzantia. "We are the last of the women," Jocelyn declares in the final line of the novel, with a hint of ambivalence and even nostalgia.

Weldon's skepticism about the New Women reappears in *Praxis*, which was nominated for a Booker Prize in 1978. "Praxis," the title character's name, means "turning point, culmination, action; orgasm; some said the Goddess herself" (p. 12). The word gains resonance in the course of Praxis' long struggle for self-determination and fulfillment through an unhappy childhood, poverty, failed marriages, prostitution, and prison.

After spending two years in prison, Praxis narrates the novel as an old woman, alone and forgotten, who finds the very act of writing painful because of her arthritis. Her foot is trampled on a bus by the high heel of one of the "New Women" (p. 16); untended, her injury worsens, and she becomes increasingly immobilized through the course of the novel, waiting for death. Her despair and resignation cast a bleak shadow over the narrative she composes for an imagined audience of her "sisters"; but she writes, she explains, in an effort to "search out the truth, and the root of my pain, and yours" (p. 17).

The young Praxis is the wayward child of an abandoned, unmarried mother who goes mad in the pursuit of respectability and falsifies her life even in her own mind. Praxis' older sister, Hypatia, inherits some of her mother's madness and has little love for Praxis, who, therefore, is essentially alone in the world from an early age. At college, having escaped her family, Praxis falls into an ill-fated relationship with Willie, who depends on her to cook, type his essays, and provide a sexual outlet; her own work suffers as a result, but she considers this "a small price to pay for Willie's protection, Willie's interest, Willie's concern" (p. 93). Her friends at school find themselves in equally self-destructive situations: "A sense of desperation seemed to afflict them: as if whatever path they took, whatever new avenue opened up, it would narrow and block, and they would be turned round once again, to face their own natures" (p. 99). Even their teachers do not expect much from them, having observed that female students rarely live up to their initial promise. Willie has little difficulty persuading Praxis to leave school when he graduates, though her work is far from finished; he requires her financial and domestic support in order to pursue his studies further. When she suggests on a whim that she apply to an exchange program in the United States, he ridicules her: "They're not interested in housewives" (p. 104). She is what he has made her, though technically she is not even a housewife, for Willie does not mention marriage.

Her mother, now institutionalized, has left an empty house behind, which is attractive to Willie because it is free. Praxis lives with him there for years, bored, discontented, and increasingly restless. "It can't go on, thought Praxis. It could. It did" (p. 117). In desperation, she and her friend Elaine take to frequenting the local pub in the afternoons, occasionally leaving with a man in return for money; Praxis is not the only Weldon heroine to achieve some degree of sexual liberation through prostituting herself. Elaine points out that what they are doing is little worse than providing sexual services for free, as most women are expected to do. When Praxis finally stops to wonder, "What am I trying to prove, and to whom?" (p. 131), she realizes that she has saved enough money from these encounters to leave Willie.

With the help of her friend Irma from college, Praxis gets a job in London as a receptionist. She finds the work surprisingly easy—far easier than her old domestic responsibilities, which Willie had refused to acknowledge as work; she is quickly promoted and happy. She makes the mistake, however, of marrying Ivor, a naive young businessman. She achieves the social respectability of marriage at the price of her identity, for Ivor "wanted her life to have begun the day he met her" (p. 161); she recognizes that, in essence, she is a "figment of [his] imagination" (p. 161). In light of her past, his attitude is not without advantages; besides, she realizes, "it was how most women lived" (p. 161). She quits her job because Ivor does not want a working wife and before long has two children. "Doesn't that give you a sense of achievement?" Ivor asks, but it does not (p. 166). She endures and waits, although for what she is not certain.

Praxis becomes increasingly unhappy as the years pass, but little disrupts her outwardly stable life until one day she receives an unexpected phone call from Irma. At her old friend's urgent request, Praxis leaves Ivor and her own children to look after Irma's children and house while Irma, who is pregnant, goes to the hospital. In her friend's absence, Praxis falls in love with Irma's husband, Phillip, and does not return to Ivor. She gets a job in an advertising agency writing pamphlets for the Electricity Board and making a name for herself by devising slogans that emphasize female domesticity: "God made her a woman. . . . Love made her a mother—with a little help from electricity!" (p. 196); "A woman's satisfactions . . . are husband, child and home. And a new electric stove is one of her rewards" (p. 200). The irony of her work does not occur to her until later, when, betrayed and abandoned by Phillip, she resumes her relationship with Irma, now a feminist activist. Irma accuses her of social irresponsibility, and eventually Praxis accepts her guilt.

Irma "require[s] from her a whole new view of the world" (p. 226). Praxis is gradually won over to Irma's cause; opening her eyes at last, she sees the ways in which women are "betrayed, exploited and oppressed"; recognizes that they are "the cleaners, the fetchers, the carriers, the humble of the earth" (p. 233). She edits a feminist newspaper for Irma and her friends, and her writing attracts a certain amount of attention; meanwhile, her commitment to her new work helps her to resist the thoughts of suicide that have haunted her since Phillip's betrayal.

Praxis becomes both a criminal and a cult figure of the women's movement when she suffocates a newborn infant that has Down's syndrome. The infant's mother—once an illegitimate orphan, whom Praxis helped to raise—is now a doctor in danger of wasting her life, as Praxis sees it. For this action, Praxis spends two years in prison; when her narrative begins, she has just been released, and the world, it seems, has forgotten her. Injured, ill, alone, poor, and malnourished, she is nearly resigned to death.

In the end, though, Praxis regains her strength; the act of telling her story, as a lesson for other women, is itself cathartic. "We see the world as we are taught to see it, not as it is," Praxis says early in the novel (p. 35); her painstaking efforts to record her own struggle are an attempt to show the world as it is and to lend meaning to her own existence. She drags herself to the hospital, where someone recognizes her; she is "elected heroine," and her life resumes (p. 250). At first, Praxis is ambivalent about the special treatment she receives once her identity becomes known: "I do not want any of this: it is not what I meant," she protests (p. 250). Although she accepts her new status reluctantly, she concludes her narrative by asserting a belief in "some force" that "gives meaning and purpose to our lives: if not in our own eyes, at least in those of other people" (p. 251). Like many of Weldon's novels, *Praxis* ends with an emphasis on the value of community: "I can touch, feel, see my fellow human beings," Praxis writes. "That is quite enough" (p. 251).

In *The Heart of the Country* (1987), sometimes criticized for being an excessively didactic novel, Weldon creates a narrator who is ostensibly writing her way to sanity, as Praxis writes her way back to life. The definition of madness, however, is always in question in Weldon's fiction. Praxis perceives that her mother's madness "lay in her telling of the truth" and wonders, "But was it madness?" (p. 60). In *The Heart of the Country*, Sonia, the narrator, has been declared insane and dangerous because she committed arson, but she assures the reader that her "search after truth is absolute" (p. 25). The attempt to "establish a moral framework for our existence" (p. 25), she remarks, is sufficient to drive a woman mad. Elsewhere she bitterly contends that it is men who drive women mad; for it is men who "form and regulate the world we live in" (p. 53). "Mad" or not, Sonia is confined to a psychiatric hospital, and her narrative is part of her treatment. She has been instructed to refer to herself in the third person; the point of such therapy, she explains, is "to see ourselves as not central to our own experience . . . but an inevitable part of a larger interweaving drama" (pp. 51–52). Sonia tries to tell the story in the way she has been told to, but she slips occasionally; her narrative intrusions lend this novel its power and humor.

In compliance with her therapy, Sonia relegates herself to a secondary role in her narrative and casts Natalie Harris, a middle-class housewife, as the main character. Natalie's life eventually intersects with that of Sonia, and Sonia implies that their stories represent the experiences of many women; she emphasizes this by punctuating the narrative with statistics and sociological data on the plight of women in modern Britain. Natalie, like so many of Weldon's heroines, is deserted by her husband at the beginning of the novel; she is left with two spoiled children, a mortgaged house, overdue school fees to pay, an empty bank account, and an empty gas tank in a Volvo that is promptly repossessed. Her husband, Harry, has escaped financial scandal by running off with his secretary, Marion Hopfoot, a local beauty queen. Natalie, according to Sonia, had been "dream-walking" (p. 5) through her life until this development, not to mention carrying on a discreet affair of her own with Arthur Wandle, a married antiques dealer. Utterly unequipped to cope with the situation in which she now finds herself, Natalie turns in desperation to Sonia, a divorced mother of three who lives on welfare, for information about social security. In this way, an unlikely alliance begins between the two women, which culminates, eventually, in the event that lands Sonia in psychiatric treatment.

"In a time of low female employment and low female wages," Sonia advises Natalie, "an ordinary woman had these alternatives: she could live off the State or live off men" (p. 176). Both options have obvious disadvantages, but Natalie chooses the latter route. After breaking off relations with Arthur, she becomes involved with his friend and business associate, Angus. He provides her with a comfortable apartment, which is an improvement over sleeping on Sonia's floor. He also gives her a job working on the annual Eddon Gurney carnival float for the West Avon Estate Agents, Dealers, and Auctioneers, or, as Sonia describes it, "Arthur and Angus in disguise" (p. 53). Essentially an advertisement for the "dreamhouses" Angus sells, the float is to contain miniature versions of the houses, complete with lace curtains and potted plants; beside each ideal house is to be an equally ideal housewife "(circa 1955) in frilly apron, waving a feather duster . . . with a happy smile" (p. 183). Towering models of a "kindly estate agent" and a "noble auctioneer" are to preside at either end of the float (pp. 180, 181). Seated on a throne in the middle of the float is to be "Mrs. Housewife Princess" dressed all in white, a role that falls to Flora, Natalie's former housekeeper.

Clearly, the float is intended to be a celebration of the domestic fantasy that Weldon attacks over and over in her work. Sonia, perceiving its sinister implications and familiar with "the ancient spirit of the carnival, when the images of the hated were parodied through the streets, and hung from gibbets, or rolled down the hills in burning tar barrels" (p. 189), sees more subversive possibilities for the float. She recalls her speech to the other women from the float: "I told them about the wickedness of men, and the wretchedness of women. I told them they were being had, cheated, conned. That they were the poor and the helpless, and the robber barons were all around" (p. 192). After Sonia persuades the other women working on the float that one way to fight male oppression is to "stop colluding" (p. 186), they fashion the figures of Angus and Arthur into caricatures, exposing their corruption, hypocrisy, and exploitative practices as landlords. The women change the intended music to Pete Seeger's "Little Boxes," transforming the idyllic housing development to "Ticky-Tacky Land" (p. 189). At the climactic moment, Sonia, without the knowledge of the other women, torches the float. Her symbolic gesture has unfortunate consequences: Flora, Mrs. Housewife Princess, dies in the fire. "My fault?" writes Sonia in the psychiatric hospital, trying to come to terms with her action: "Flora, the virgin sacrifice, so the world could cure itself of evil and renew itself?" (p. 197). So Sonia hopes, at any rate, insisting that she was "only trying to help" (p. 197). Although Sonia finally accepts some degree of responsibility, she still insists that "fate took a hand," and argues: "Because of the misfortunes of my life I have been murderous, full of hate" (p. 197).

Sonia emerges as one of Weldon's most disruptive, as well as destructive, heroines; and the carnival scene, with its parodic indictment of the male

power structure, is one of the most subversive images in her fiction. Sonia is also one of the few characters in Weldon's fiction to refuse the novelistic convention whereby the heroine's marriage constitutes a happy ending. Her final words reveal her awareness of the convention she is defying, as the narrator and as a woman. When her psychiatrist, pronouncing her sane, proposes marriage, Sonia writes: "She can't accept, of course. Happy endings are not so easy. No. She must get on with changing the world, rescuing the country. There is no time left for frivolity" (p. 199).

THE PERSONAL AS POLITICAL

"IF only women would realize," says Irma in *Praxis*, "that their miseries are political, not personal" (p. 215). Much of Weldon's work explores the implications of this once radical ideal; in her fiction, the discontent of suburban housewives is to be taken as seriously as any national crisis, for she insists that we see ostensibly personal or domestic events in a broader social context. In several novels, however, Weldon ventures into more explicitly political territory; among these are *Darcy's Utopia*, *The Shrapnel Academy*, and *The President's Child*.

The structure of *Darcy's Utopia* (1990) enables Weldon to call into question conventional distinctions between what is properly political, and therefore serious, and what is "merely" personal. Much of the novel is in the form of interviews between Eleanor Darcy, the wife of the imprisoned radical economist Julian Darcy—convicted of the misuse of public funds after the failure of his ambitious economic schemes, ineptly implemented by the government—and two reporters. Valerie Jones, the features editor of a women's magazine, has been assigned to write a serialized biography of Eleanor Darcy. Hugo Vansitart, a leading political journalist, is writing an article on Darcian economics, the radical theories of Eleanor's husband. Their assignments establish the traditional alignment of the personal with the feminine and the political with the masculine. The narrative alternates between question-and-answer transcriptions of Valerie's and Hugo's interviews with Eleanor Darcy, first-person narration by Valerie, and segments of

Valerie's biography in progress, "Lover at the Gate." These shifts, at times unsettling, allow Weldon to develop simultaneously Eleanor Darcy's history, the utopian ideas she has liberally adapted from her husband's economic theories, and the personal lives of the two reporters. At the outset of the novel, Valerie and Hugo recklessly abandon their spouses and children and take up residence together at the Holiday Inn, but Eleanor Darcy is as integral to their relationship as she is to the novel itself: their relationship dissolves when their work is over; Valerie, like most Weldon wives, returns to her family, while Hugo becomes a disciple in the service of Eleanor Darcy's eccentric vision of utopia.

The narrative framework situates the enigmatic Eleanor Darcy at the center of the novel, expounding upon the version of Darcian economics that her husband's imprisonment has freed her to fashion: Darcy's Utopia, a "multiracial, unicultural, secular society" that will ultimately dispose of money (p. 17). "Money," according to Eleanor, "has stopped working . . . [it] no longer represents what it did—labour, skill, concern, capital, organization, involvement. It has become a commodity itself, to be bought and sold" (p. 34). Such apparently serious assertions as this remark based on a fundamental Marxist principle, however, are coupled with frivolous notions like this one: "In Darcy's Utopia there will be elections, but people will be expected merely to vote for people they personally like. It will be a popularity contest" (p. 87). Even more disturbingly, Eleanor demands, "Who wants the people's will to prevail? Not the people. They've too much sense" (p. 86). Eleanor's complexity and her erratic vision leave the reader unsure when to take her seriously and when to dismiss her, a dilemma articulated by Eleanor's longtime friend Brenda, who remarks that "what she has to say is interesting: there's a lot in it, though it's sometimes hard to tell when she's joking and when she isn't" (p. 188). Eleanor's ideas are often insightful, frequently dubious, and occasionally outrageous. Weldon offers little guidance, as if inviting the reader to enact Eleanor's vision of utopia—"We have to start again, rethink everything" (p. 185)— or issuing to the reader Eleanor's challenge: "Can't you decide, one by one, what's right, what's wrong? . . . [Y]ou'll get no rules from me" (p. 225). The novel calls much into question but provides few answers.

At their first encounter, Valerie assures Hugo that their pieces are unlikely to overlap; Eleanor Darcy herself has other ideas. To Hugo, Eleanor remarks: "How you try to divide the world up into sections! It won't work, Mr Vansitart. We must deal with God and the Devil, love and sex, before we get on to economics, party politics, big business, education, crime and the rest" (p. 10). When Hugo protests that surely "love is the proper province of women's magazines," she warns that he will need to have his "male consciousness raised" (p. 10). Similarly, she explains to Valerie: "I know you are concerned with what you call the human-interest angle, how I came to be who and what and where I am. But I have been created by a society interacting with a self: you can't have one without the other" (p. 17). The notion that identity is a result of the interaction between self and society, an interaction often characterized by struggle, is central to much of Weldon's fiction. Eleanor's articulation of this idea indicates her refusal to respect the conventional boundaries represented by Valerie and Hugo's respective publications, boundaries which imply that "human interest" and politics do not intersect. Her insistence on talking to Valerie about economics and to Hugo about love has important implications not only for their work but, Weldon suggests, for the expectations of their readers—expectations that are, significantly, determined by gender. Eleanor resists the fundamental assumption that Valerie's female readers are solely interested in a romanticized account of her life, while Hugo's audience cares only about her husband's botched attempt at an economic revolution. Such an artificial division, she implies, can only distort the truth.

The intrusive narrator of *The Shrapnel Academy* (1986), like Eleanor Darcy, deliberately defies readerly expectations and frequently interrupts the narrative with lengthy digressions on history. The novel is set at a military school, the Shrapnel Academy, where an unlikely cast of characters has gathered to attend the annual Eve-of-Waterloo celebration. Weldon juxtaposes their individual stories with accounts of famous tyrants, warriors, and battles of the past. The narrator is wryly apologetic about the intrusions, prefacing a lecture on Emperor Tiglath-Pileser III of Assyria (the originator, we are told, of the idea of organizing an entire state around a permanent army) with this admonishment: "Reader, do not skip. I know you want to.

So do I. What has this ancient person to do with anyone? . . . But do remember—what went before so very much informs what goes on now" (p. 39). Throughout this darkly comic novel, Weldon insists that the lives of individuals, including the reader's, are inextricably linked to the actions of those in power. Even women of the past, confined for centuries to the domestic, so-called private sphere, are not spared. A description of faded, ancient tapestries lining the walls of the Shrapnel Academy's dining room prompts the narrator to remark: "Who else but the unlucky [the widows and orphans of the warrior race] sew for a living? And how else but by glorifying the abysmal, can we make the abysmal glorious? The sewers stitched, no doubt, with loving hands, and worshipped their oppressors" (p. 32). Commemorating acts of war with needle and thread, spinning history into the myths that perpetuate oppression, women throughout the centuries, the narrator insists, have been complicit in that oppression.

Joan Lumb, administrator of the Shrapnel Academy, faithfully carries on this tradition by protecting, celebrating, and ultimately sustaining the military strength and "progress" on which the institution is founded. She is in charge of organizing the Wellington Weekend. Among the guests of honor is Murray Fairchild, "employed sometimes by the CIA" and "sometimes by more enigmatic folk," with whom Joan Lumb is infatuated: "She would die for him, she thought, just as he would die for a cause he believed in. Well, that was woman's part. They were the hero's recreation and his inspiration" (p. 33).

Also in attendance are General Leo Makeshift, who is scheduled to deliver the annual Wellington lecture; his young mistress, Bella Morthampton, who is unconvincingly disguised for the occasion as his secretary; Ivor, the general's blond chauffeur; Victor, Joan Lumb's brother, a corporate executive described by the narrator as a "thief of other men's life and labor" (p. 71); Victor's admiring wife, Shirley, their three children, and their Doberman. Baf, a salesman, carries in a knife box an arsenal of miniature weapons and implements of torture; long-legged Muffin is Joan Lumb's secretary and Baf's lover; and Mew, a reporter from the feminist paper *Woman's Times*, has been invited under the misconception that she represents the respectable *Times*. Dinner conversation does not sparkle, though this does not prevent Victor from

speculatively eyeing Bella, Mew from arranging an unlikely tryst with the general, or Baf from making a sales pitch.

Unbeknownst to the diners, however, the real action is taking place "Downstairs," a vast region that houses not only the Shrapnel Academy's servants—immigrants from all over the globe representing "every race except Caucasian" (p. 34)—but such family members and friends who have managed to join them, legally or (more often) otherwise, over the years. The population numbers in the hundreds, and they are on the verge of revolt.

Their first action, at once comic, gruesome, and unsettling, involves Harry, the Doberman, who has been left to the care of the servants. Expressing her hope that the dog is all right, Shirley makes the unfortunate remark, "You know what these people are. Some of them actually eat dog!" (p. 101). Shirley's Western ethnocentrism and ignorance, overheard by Acorn, the butler from Soweto who is leading the revolution, provide just the inspiration Downstairs needs. "Kill the dog. Stew it," Acorn orders. "They hold their pets dearer than they do their servants" (p. 102). Inverness, Acorn's rival, protests that "one atrocity begets another," but in vain (p. 102); Harry is killed and stewed, while upstairs the complacent guests make conversation, flirt surreptitiously, and occasionally comment on the odd smell coming from the kitchen. But when Harry is served in the form of pâté, they pronounce him delicious.

The novel continues to alternate between the conversation upstairs and the power struggle downstairs between Acorn, the reckless radical, and Inverness, the cautious liberal who favors more moderate, cooperative methods of righting the balance of power. A series of unrelated events conspire to bring about the apocalyptic end of the novel: in a scuffle between Acorn and Inverness, the telephone wire connecting Upstairs and Downstairs is inadvertently disconnected; everyone Downstairs retires to bed following Inverness' victory and the triumph of order, forgetting to turn off the pot in which Harry was boiled; a snowstorm traps the dinner guests and downs the power lines; and Murray Fairchild, after the pâté has made him violently ill, realizes that they have eaten dog meat.

Drawing the conclusion that they are under attack from Downstairs, the guests at the Shrapnel Academy pool their military experience and expertise to evaluate the situation and devise a battle plan. When thick smoke from the burning pot begins to drift upstairs, the party interprets it as an act of aggression: "They were under attack! They were to be choked to death! Suffocated!" (p. 173). Swept up in the excitement of war, drunk with their own power, and united against the perceived enemy, Joan Lumb and her guests resort to Baf's weapons case and launch a grenade down the stairs. The blast ignites the other contents of his knife box: a gas cylinder, a napalm thrower, and a nuclear cannon. Only Mew, the feminist journalist, and Ivor, the chauffeur, who were ejected earlier from the privileged ranks of those Upstairs and sent Downstairs by the laundry chute, survive. The narrator comments wryly that "Mew and Ivor ended up a good deal safer in the servants' quarters than either of them had been Upstairs, Mew tainted as she was by feminism, and Ivor by his membership of the servant classes" (p. 176). Mew is saved by virtue of her politics and Ivor by virtue of his class; they represent potentially subversive elements and a challenge to the class and gender hierarchies Weldon criticizes in this novel. Everyone else, Upstairs and down, is destroyed.

This extravagant and improbable plot, combined with intermittent history lessons and carried out by characters who are essentially caricatures, seems an unlikely vehicle for a serious critique of Western economic imperialism and a concept of military progress that celebrates mass destruction. And it is true that Weldon is at her most didactic in this novel. The intrusive narrator repeatedly lectures the reader, insisting that we recognize our complicity in the oppressive, exploitative system she depicts:

Reader, it is true. The hands that serve you, in any corner of the world, are mostly female, and usually brown, and for the most part go unnoticed; or stay anonymous. Who cleans your offices? Do you know? No. You'd rather not. Who stands in the steam to press your shirt: who cut the upper of your fashion boot? The Family of the Unknown, that's who. The Myriad People of Now: the scuttling, scurrying, frightened, passive people of the earth, the dusters of cannon, the polishers of buttons.

(p. 128)

The implied reader, according to Weldon, shares with Mew "the communal guilt of the lucky" (p. 80) and must learn to look beyond the comforting fictions that perpetuate injustice. Mocking the literary convention by which the audience is referred to by the author as "Gentle reader," Weldon writes, "What have I said! You are no more gentle than I am. . . . We all believe ourselves to be, more or less, well intentioned, nice. . . . But we can't possibly be, or how would the world have got into the state it's in? Who else but ourselves are doing this to ourselves?" (p. 52). *The Shrapnel Academy* is ultimately a cautionary tale, warning the reader of the consequences of apparently insignificant actions— or worse, inaction—and insisting that what seems merely personal has profound and far-reaching implications. The narrator apologizes for the ending of the story: "It seems a cheat just to blow everything and everyone up. I wish there was some other possible ending, but there isn't" (p. 185). The current state of affairs, Weldon implies, can only end in disaster, for oppressive and oppressed classes alike. Only Mew and Ivor, who survive the explosion, represent the potential for change.

The President's Child (1982) also insists on the fundamental relation between the personal and the political. The blind narrator, speaking to a group of neighbors who gather to hear her tell stories on gloomy Sunday afternoons, concedes that it is "easy to feel . . . that people and politics are entirely separate" (p. 5). To counter this comforting notion, she offers her listeners the story of Isabel, a former neighbor: "Isabel, who fell in love, and in so doing made the world falter and take a different turning" (p. 1).

As the story opens, Isabel, who was raised in Australia but now lives in London, is a successful late-night talk-show host with a loving husband, the neat and orderly Homer, and a six-year-old son, Jason. Her life is stable—perhaps too stable, the reader suspects—and her marriage is happy, if lacking in spontaneity. Isabel, however, is increasingly tormented by a secret she has concealed from Homer since their wedding: Jason is not his son. He is the son of Dandy Ivel, with whom Isabel engaged in a passionate affair when he was a rising young politician and she was an international correspondent for the *London Star*. Now Dandy is running for president of the United States, and his face perpetually invades her peaceful life by way of the television screen. Isabel assumes that no one in her present life is aware of her past involvement with him, but Jason's striking resemblance to his father makes Isabel uneasy. It does not occur to her that she is in any danger, but we learn soon enough that she is: Dandy's henchmen, Joe and Pete, have recently moved her to their Pay Good Attention file; they have been monitoring her since the doomed affair, the termination of which they plotted. They know that her father, long vanished from her life, is a communist; they consider her a radical feminist, and, as such, hardly a woman at all; and they are disturbed by her talk show, which has an audience of millions. In short, they see her as a threat, and resolve to "take appropriate precautionary measures" (p. 43).

After Isabel confesses to her husband, who leaves her though he professes disbelief, and to a psychiatrist, Joe and Pete fear the British public is next and decide she has become too great a risk. They are in league, it turns out, with both Homer and Isabel's psychiatrist, and it is they who inform her at the novel's climax that she must die for the sake of Jason—the president's son. She realizes that "the weight of power was too much for her to bear" (p. 211), that she is helpless before "such savage male disapproval completely" (p. 211), and that the consequences of her actions are inescapable. She accepts her fate, that she must sacrifice herself for her child, stepping deliberately into traffic as if by accident. She is saved, at the last moment, by Dandy Ivel's sudden death; what's more, she has recovered her self and is freed from what she now sees as an unhappy and repressive marriage. She comes to a crucial realization while she still believes her death is imminent: "If they wanted to kill you, you must be dangerous. That was the secret she'd been waiting for" (p. 205). With the return of Isabel's Australian accent, Weldon writes, "she was down to the origins of her being. Flakes of good behaviour peeled away, like layers from a stale chocolate bar, held together by its wrapper" (p. 205). So-called good behavior, for Weldon, is never in women's best interests.

Isabel achieves a strength and self-knowledge that make *The President's Child* the most affirmative of these three novels. Recognizing the danger of thinking that the fragile domestic fiction of her private life could serve as a shield from the rest of the world, Isabel offers her story to Maia, the blind narrator, to pass on. In the telling, Maia regains her sight, an event with important symbolic resonance. "Of course I cannot see," Maia says late in the novel. "I do not want to see. Do you?" (p. 193). But as she concludes her narrative, still tormented by the fear that, despite the fortuitous outcome of this particular story, "the struggle is eternal, and dreadful" (p. 219), her sight suddenly returns. "I was seized . . . with such a fit of despair that I healed myself," Maia explains. "I lost all hope and gained my sight" (p. 219). For Weldon, seeing is everything, as the narrator of *The Shrapnel Academy* makes clear: "The eye is used to what it is used to, and sees what it is in the habit of seeing; and an effort of will must sometimes be made if it is to register fact, not fiction" (p. 138). In *The Shrapnel Academy* disaster seems almost inevitable, while in *Darcy's Utopia* the possibility of real change is ultimately rejected. In *The President's Child* Weldon offers a more hopeful vision, leaving the reader with the idea that, driven to the brink of despair, people can cure their own literal or figurative blindness.

NATURE, FATE, AND MAGIC

IN her introduction to *Fay Weldon's Wicked Fictions* (1994), Regina Barreca writes that "a classic 'Weldonesque' moment is one in which all the forces in the universe seem to converge in the most unlikely of ways" (p. 3). Weldon's characters often seem at the mercy of forces, whether benign or malevolent, beyond their control: coincidence, chance, nature, fate. In several novels, these forces become focused in a single powerful figure who exerts an extraordinary and dangerous influence on the central characters: a psychotherapist in *Affliction*, the devil in *Growing Rich*, and a witch in *Puffball*. In each case the heroine must struggle to recognize the source of danger and to define herself against it and resist what amounts to an alternative narrative of her life.

Annette, the heroine of *Affliction* (1993), has been happily married, or so she thinks, to Spicer for ten years, when suddenly his behavior alters inexplicably. Formerly a wine merchant with a penchant for bacon sandwiches, he now eschews meat and alcohol and makes obscure remarks about the relative alignment of his planets and Annette's: "That's Saturn's doing, sextile my moon but, alas, also quincunx your sun," he remarks one morning, prompting Annette to look up the unfamiliar words (p. 12). "Quincunx," she explains later that day to her friend Gilda, is "a term used in astrology to denote a 150 degree separation of the planets in orbit: a stressful aspect, particularly in a compatibility chart" (p. 13). Spicer, it turns out, has been seeing an astrological psychotherapist and has a newly acquired faith in what he once would have dismissed as "gobbledegook" (p. 13). Annette does not learn the source of his new vocabulary, however, until she begins therapy herself, at his suggestion. Spicer's perpetual accusations confuse her: "first the sniping, then the nagging, now come the accusations, the jealousy" (p. 26); he turns her perfectly reasonable words against her, blaming her pregnancy and her astrological chart for what he insists is her self-centered, irresponsible behavior. He denies the past, insisting that not only does he currently dislike bacon sandwiches, but in fact he always has; similarly, he disavows his longtime disdain for therapy: "I think you must have imagined it," he accuses Annette (p. 27); repeatedly, he contests her memories of the decade they have spent together. Most importantly, he undermines her confidence in her own perceptions: "I don't think you know what you say or how you feel. . . . Your Neptune is afflicted by Pluto and you live in a state of perpetual confusion" (p. 35). Furthermore, he informs her, she is a bad wife and negligent mother to her daughter and his son, both children from previous marriages, because of her "Mars/Pluto aspect" (p. 28).

Annette's experiment with psychotherapy is disastrous. Dr. Herman Marks, a behaviorist who is, by sheer coincidence, married to Dr. Rhea Marks, Spicer's therapist, distorts her dreams into a repressed history of sexual abuse by her father. After asking that she remove her shirt, he proposes that she identify him as much as possible with her father in order to "rework the trauma"; she must learn to "love the touch of the father in adult life," he tells her, pressing against her from behind while palpating her breasts (p. 59). Annette hits him, grabs her clothes, and runs from the office. As she recounts this incident to Gilda, she is on the verge of doubting her own memory: perhaps she fantasized the whole episode; perhaps, as Gilda suggests, she has, in fact, buried the memory of childhood abuse. The crisis of the novel revolves around Annette's struggle to rely on her own perceptions and reject the oppressive versions of her life pressed on her by her husband and Doctor Marks.

Relations with Spicer deteriorate. Annette is anticipating the birth of her baby and the publication of her first novel; Spicer derides her novel and accuses her of neglecting her pregnancy. She is the

tumultuous, terrifying sea, he tells her, threatening to engulf him; his Jungian analyst, Dr. Rhea Marks—wife of Dr. Herman Marks—would like to meet with her. When the session takes place, Annette concludes that her suspicions have been well-grounded: Spicer's therapist is facilitating the dissolution of their marriage for reasons of her own and has been manipulating Spicer to that end. Annette's response to this threat is crucial to the novel's theme:

I wonder what your motives are in doing this to me? Are you jealous because I'm pregnant? Or because I've written a book? Perhaps you're a would-be novelist? Perhaps you've tried and you can't so you sit there earning a living by writing living fictions: altering the narrative of other people's lives: changing it in their heads: writing your scenario about Spicer getting on perfectly well without me.

(p. 76)

In this novel, Weldon reveals the power of therapists to reshape people's understanding of their own lives through the imposition of archetypes, myths, and models. Spicer's memories of his happy marriage to Annette have been "relaid" (p. 152), replaced, through hypnosis, with less pleasant ones, and Rhea Marks encourages him to view his wife in terms of destructive and devouring female archetypes. Easily seduced, Spicer accepts the new narrative he has been offered: his wife is "Lilith-Annette, destroyer of man's virility, sapper of male strength, strangler of babies" (p. 149). Struggling against Spicer's new version of her, Annette indulges in long conversations with Gilda—the dominant mode of narration in this novel—that enable her to tell her own story, fashion and refashion her account of the events Spicer so persistently and aggressively misconstrues, and so maintain her sanity and her identity.

Before her sanity and sense of self can be safe, however, she must contend with a series of crises precipitated by Dr. Rhea Marks's manipulation of Spicer. Annette's marriage to Spicer, it turns out, was never fully legalized; the house is in his name, as is so often the case for women in Weldon's novels. Worst of all, she loses her baby as an indirect result of his ill treatment. At Dr. Rhea's suggestion, Spicer gives Annette a set of gold bangles as therapy for her archetypal "attributes," which include "scheming," "lying," and "insane jealousy" (p. 103). The bangles eventually become embedded in her swelling wrists, leading to a dangerous blood condition that threatens her life and results in the death of her unborn baby. While Annette is in the hospital, Spicer invites the Doctors Marks, who have been turned out of their own residence, to set up their practices in his house. Written out of her own life, Annette, like so many of Weldon's heroines, must seize control of her fate. Her assertion of her power to narrate her own version of the story is an important part of that control. Fiction is her route to independence, Annette's publisher, Ernie Gromback, assures her at one point. This idea resonates in the novel's final pages when Annette speaks to him about the events of the past year: "I could put it all into a novel," she suggests (p. 171). Although Ernie responds skeptically that "nobody would believe it" (p. 171), Annette's triumph lies in her ability to assume control over the narrative of her life.

In *Growing Rich* (1992), the devil descends on a small town in a black BMW, offering certain residents an escape from dreary provincialism. His power, like that of the therapists in *Affliction*, is represented by the seductive alternative narrative he offers: "The Devil was all shortcuts: he did a good editing job on your life. In fact what he was really good at . . . was turning people into the video of their life. He left out all the boring bits. When your soul was sold you would no longer have to live in real time" (p. 212). His presence is invoked by the discontent of three high school girls; their discontent, Weldon suggests, renders them vulnerable to his offer. Focusing on Carmen, the leader of the three, the devil—who goes by the name of Driver, hinting at his desire to control people and direct their lives, and sports a chauffeur's cap—offers the timeless and familiar rewards of fairy tales: beauty, wealth, and a prestigious marriage. When Carmen cooperates, her bust expands, her legs elongate, and she is wooed by Sir Bernard Bellamy, a wealthy developer who has recently moved to town. Sir Bernard has already sealed a bargain with Driver, ostensibly his chauffeur, in return for youth and fortune; all he needs now is a wife, and he has set his heart on Carmen. When Carmen resists, the whole town suffers, and misfortune befalls her family and friends. Her eventual decision to agree to marriage is a gesture of self-sacrifice, an attempt to save her friend Annie from dying of anorexia; Driver has brought suffering and misfortune to Carmen's friends in order to coerce her to comply with his plans. He makes it clear that "all depends" (p. 225) on whether or not Carmen sleeps with Sir Bernard.

All is not lost, however, because Weldon seldom allows evil to prevail. Carmen and Sir Bernard thwart Driver's plan to bind them to him and each other through sex; they fall in love and decide to wait until they are married to have sex. At their wedding, Sir Bernard is struck down in the middle of a rousing speech in which he proclaims, under Driver's influence, that "what this planet needs is one strong, good man, one man so immensely rich, immensely powerful, immensely wise, that all consent to his will" (p. 242). While Sir Bernard lies twitching on the ground, Driver exults: "his soul is on its way to me" (p. 246). Weldon casts the devil as a fascist and Sir Bernard as his puppet; but Driver is defeated, in a final dramatic scene, not only by the virgin tears Carmen sheds over Sir Bernard's prostrate body, but by the laughter of Carmen and her friends. Women's laughter is often a subversive force in Weldon's fiction, as Regina Barreca has argued, and here it decides the outcome of a battle between the forces of good and evil. Rendered absurd, Driver disappears in a ring of flame, while Carmen, having declared that she would "rather live in real time" (p. 247), preserves her soul as well as the power to shape her own life. In a novel that characterizes the devil as a film director, Carmen's real victory in the final scene is that she wrests narrative control of her life from the devil.

In *Puffball* (1980), Weldon's heroine, Liffey, must contend not only with her malevolent neighbor Mabs but with nature itself. Weldon is at best ambivalent about the association of women with nature. "I have always seen 'nature' as inimical to women; nature kills you," she writes in "The Changing Face of Fiction" (p. 196), while in *Praxis* she observes that "Nature our Friend is an argument used, quite understandably, by men" (p. 133). In *Puffball* she most fully explores the role of nature in women's lives. There are two Liffeys, the narrator remarks early in the novel: the outer Liffey, smiling, positive, and boyish, and the "inner Liffey, cosmic Liffey, hormones buzzing, heart beating, blood surging, pawn in nature's game" (p. 15). Thus far, Liffey has outwitted nature with birth-control pills; at the novel's outset, however, her husband, Richard, agrees to move to a cottage in the country on the condition that she have a baby. Both immediately regret the terms of their bargain but do not voice their reservations. When Liffey becomes pregnant, Weldon provides a highly technical account of what is happening in her body. She takes up this narrative throughout the novel in short chapters called "Inside Liffey," in which she tracks the development of the pregnancy and comments on nature. Nature traps women, Weldon implies in this novel and others; the instinct to procreate might benefit the species but not necessarily the individual; nature's interests and women's are often at odds: "Auntie Evolution, Mother Nature— bitches both!" (p. 101). Liffey, though anxious to leave the city to be closer to "nature," is nonetheless made uneasy by the process occurring within her: "Surely human beings are more than farmyard animals? Don't we have poetry, and paintings, and great civilisations, and history? Or is it only men who have these things? Not women. She felt, for the first time in her life, at the mercy of her body" (p. 46).

She is also at the mercy of her neighbor Mabs, who is aligned with nature by her power. Mabs's mother is an herbalist—a witch, according to her enemies, and a wise woman, according to her friends. The reader learns that Mabs shares her mother's knowledge long before Liffey does and that her intentions toward Liffey are not benevolent. "It's important to have a hold," Mabs remarks to her husband, Tucker. "You can't be too careful with neighbours" (p. 26). To gain a "hold," in this case, she enlists Tucker to seduce Liffey; their union will forge a "channel" through which Mabs can influence Liffey. To facilitate the seduction, Mabs, who is much given to adding herbs to the diets of those around her to alter their health, personalities, and desires according to her purpose, gives Liffey a drug and Liffey sleeps with Tucker. Although childish, decorous Liffey is horrified afterward, the incident is pivotal, "opening up whole new universes of power and passion, laying instinct bare" (p. 63).

Liffey's husband, meanwhile, is seldom home; his job keeps him in London during the week, and he returns to the country only on weekends, tired and vaguely resentful of Liffey. Unbeknownst to Liffey, he is repeatedly unfaithful. Left alone, Liffey gardens, tends to the cottage, and resolves to "cultivate inner resources" (p. 66). She also befriends Mabs, little guessing that Mabs wishes her anything but well. Liffey's pregnancy is not part of Mabs's plan. She suspects the baby is Tucker's, a thought that has occurred to Liffey as well, and attributes her own failure to conceive to Liffey's fertility. She fights Liffey's pregnancy with adulterated homemade wine, cider, and tea. She makes a wax figure in Liffey's image and drives a pin through its stomach. Finally suspicious, Liffey asks Richard, "Do you think Mabs could be a witch?" (p. 137). Richard contemptuously dismisses the idea, and at first Liffey "accepted Richard's version of events" (p. 137), but gradually she becomes convinced that she and the baby are engaged in a dangerous struggle against the country woman.

The balance of power in that struggle has subtly shifted, however, even before Liffey voices her suspicion about Mabs. Walking in the fields after a long spell of rain, Liffey sits on the ground in the sun and senses a "presence." " 'It's me,' said the spirit, said the baby, 'I'm here. I have arrived. You are perfectly all right and so am I' " (pp. 127–128). Liffey's acceptance of her pregnancy, in response to the reassuring voice of the baby's "spirit," marks a turning point in the battle; "Liffey now had powers of her own, . . . Mabs could no longer have Nature all her own way, . . . forces worked for Liffey too and not just for Mabs" (pp. 130–131).

In the end, Liffey must triumph over nature, which has failed to attach her baby's placenta in the proper place, resulting in a dangerous and difficult delivery; and she must triumph over witchcraft, for Mabs uses all her art and power to harm Liffey and the baby. Liffey accomplishes both, giving birth to a healthy baby whose remarkable resemblance to Richard settles all questions about its paternity. Satisfied, Mabs retreats. Richard, who deserts his pregnant wife when he learns through Mabs of the incident with Tucker, returns at the end of the novel, apologetic. But he returns to a different Liffey: "She would never easily look like a little boy, feel like a little girl, ever again. It was a loss, she knew it—she was at her best when very young. All charm, no sense. The days of charm were gone. Now she was real and alive" (p. 194).

SELF AND SOLIDARITY

LIFFEY is an unusual character in Weldon's fiction in that she manages to achieve a sense of self virtually on her own. The notion that marriage within a male-dominated society threatens female identity is a theme that recurs throughout Weldon's work; frequently, her heroines are able to establish their identity only through learning to identify with other women. All too often, Weldon suggests, women damage their own cause by aligning themselves not with but against other women.

"Marjorie, Grace, and me" is a phrase that echoes throughout *Female Friends* (1974), one of Weldon's earliest novels. Such refrains, like litanies, recur in many of her works as Weldon stresses the importance of female friendship both for individual women and for feminism as a political movement. "Marjorie, Grace, and me" is a line repeatedly invoked by Chloe, the heroine of *Female Friends*. "Why do you choose such odd friends?" her rather despicable husband, Oliver, asks early in the novel. Chloe replies: "One doesn't choose friends. One acquires them." When Oliver protests that she doesn't even like them, the narrator concedes, "He is right. Chloe sometimes dislikes Marjorie, and sometimes Grace, and sometimes both at once. But that is not the point" (p. 5). Thrown together in childhood by the events of World War II, the three women retain an uneasy friendship into their adult lives, despite dramatically different ways of life and the fact that they have all, at one time or another, been involved with the same man: Patrick Bates, one of Weldon's degenerate but dangerously attractive artist figures. "Fine citizens we make, fine sisters!" Chloe despairs at one point. "Our loyalties are to men, not to each other.... We are divided amongst ourselves. We have to be, for survival's sake" (p. 249). This, according to Weldon, is precisely the misconception women must overcome if they are to survive.

In *The Cloning of Joanna May* (1989), the central plot device functions as a metaphor for the masculine capacity to divide or split women, from both themselves and one another. In this novel, Weldon suggests that women, divided, must join forces if they are to survive. Joanna May, sixty years old and divorced from her diabolical husband, Carl, learns in the course of the novel that Carl "cloned" her, thirty years earlier, with the help of advanced genetic technology. Joanna's initial feelings toward her four young replicas—not quite daughters, not quite sisters—are ambivalent; she fears that their existence in some way depletes her own. The clones themselves, strikingly similar in some ways but dramatically different in others because of their various upbringings, are equally uncertain about how to react to one another's existence. Carl May, meanwhile, is tracking them down; he hopes to find one who will make a suitable replacement for Joanna, who has betrayed him, and destroy the others. Eventually all five of them, faced with a common threat, forge a lasting bond; they not only survive but also learn that their individual identities are strengthened rather than diminished in the process.

In *Splitting* (1995), Weldon inverts the controlling metaphor of *Joanna May*. While in *Joanna May* she creates a character whose identity is literally fractured, embodied in four younger versions of herself, in *Splitting* the division occurs internally. Years of marriage to Sir Edwin Rice have caused Angelica to reshape her personality according to her husband's expectations; as Lady Rice, she has consistently suppressed her own needs, interests, and desires. Sir Edwin's power extends beyond the domestic realm of marriage to the public realm of the legal system, as Angelica learns when he decides to divorce her; although he has built his wealth on these proceedings, the "perforation" (p. 7) of her personality takes place, resulting in several distinct and conflicting voices: Jelly White, Lady Rice, Angelica, and Angel. Their voices compete in her mind, struggling for expression and power within the constraints of a patriarchal society. Jelly White is prim, practical, and a little priggish; she takes a job as a secretary in the law firm handling the divorce, the better to interfere with the process and prepare her defense. Lady Rice is "wronged, tearful, virtuous, needy" and still in love with Sir Edwin (p. 126). Angelica is energetic, efficient, and brazen, favoring mesh stockings and miniskirts. Angel is lustful and uninhibited, much to the horror of the others; she involves them in an affair with Ram the chauffeur, with whom she has sex on the drive to work three mornings a week. The various selves compete for control; thus, Weldon implies, one woman's needs necessarily compete and conflict with the roles required of her in a world where power rests in the hands of men. "Women tend to be more than one person," Angel observes at one point. "Men get just to be the one" (p. 228). Finally, Angelica is able to reincorporate her fractured selves by confronting her past and envisioning her future.

In *Remember Me* (1976), the plot once again turns on an identity conflict. Madeleine, the bitter and vengeful heroine who is unreconciled to the fact that her husband has replaced her with pretty, selfish Lily, does not technically survive the novel. She dies quite horribly in a car accident but in her last moment thinks of her unhappy daughter, Hilary, fourteen and ungainly, neglected for years while Madeleine allowed herself to be consumed by anger. Determined that Lily should not have her daughter, Madeleine settles instead on Margot, an acquaintance of both hers and Lily's. Madeleine and Margot are linked already by animosity toward Lily, which derives partly from dislike and partly from envy: "malice," Weldon writes, "is a powerful force" (p. 48). They are linked, too, by the fact that Margot slept with Madeleine's husband, Jarvis, many years ago, before he left Madeleine for Lily: "sisters in rejection, if nothing else" (p. 44). After Madeleine's death they are "sisters" in another sense, for Madeleine's spirit manifests itself in Margot, awakening her to the long unacknowledged realities of her own life. "Oh, I am the doctor's wife," Margot thinks, "mother of the doctor's children; I am used, put up with, ignored; I gather scraps from other people's tables" (p. 93). Gradually, she becomes not simply Margot, the doctor's wife, but Margot/Madeleine, "any wife" or "all the wronged women in the world" (p. 121). Inhabited by Madeleine's rage, Margot disrupts not only her own life but the lives of those around her and in the process exposes uncomfortable truths. In the end she comes to the realization that "I am Margot and Madeleine in one, and always was. She was my sister, after all" (p. 232). Madeleine, meanwhile, no longer vengeful but at peace, whispers, "Oh, my sisters . . . and my brothers too, soon you will be dead. Is this the way you want to live?" (p. 233). As in so many of Weldon's novels, a recognition of shared pain and common interests transforms vengefulness into forgiveness and leads to peace. In *The Cloning of Joanna May*, Weldon writes, "It is my experience that a quiet mind is gained only by forgiveness: when you cease to see the other as enemy, as merely yourself in another guise . . . then peace descends. Our lives are our own again" (p. 70). Weldon's novels often celebrate the ability of the main character to reclaim her life through forging a sense of community or commonality, especially among women.

FICTIONS

WELDON frequently uses forms of closure that challenge literary convention, repeatedly demonstrating in her novels that women's lives are shaped and limited by cultural scripts that determine their options and define their aspirations. Her novels often seek to expose the danger and seduction of such scripts, which are encoded in myths, fairy tales, and literary conventions; her critiques are sometimes playful but always have serious undercurrents. In *The Hearts and Lives of Men* (1987), for instance, she writes:

We all live by myth, reader: if only by the myth of happiness around the corner. Well, why not? But how good we are at holding the myths of our society in one corner of our minds—say, that most people live in proper family units—father out to work, mother at home minding the children—while the evidence of our own eyes, our own lives, shows us how far this is from the truth. And how bad we are at facing the truth.

(p. 335)

Here Weldon argues that cultural myths continue to shape our perceptions even when they cease to be reflected in reality. By calling attention to those myths and either exposing their artifice or deliberately revising them, Weldon implicitly challenges the power structure they help to perpetuate.

In *Letters to Alice on First Reading Jane Austen*, Weldon warns that "the reader may well have mistaken the fictional convention for life itself, so severe is the social indoctrination to which we are all subjected, and needs to be reminded from time to time that novels are illusion, not reality" (p. 24). The narrator of *The Hearts and Lives of Men* repeatedly issues precisely that reminder. We learn on the very first page that the novel has a happy ending: "But it's Christmastime. Why not?" the narrator asks cheerfully. Weldon calls attention not only to her reliance on but her defiance of literary convention in this novel, as when she justifies the crucial role coincidence plays in determining the lives of the characters: "It's against commonly accepted rules for writers to use coincidence in fiction, but I hope you will bear with me" (p. 188). *The Hearts and Lives of Men* is primarily the story of little Nell, buffeted about in her early life by the divorce of her parents after the collapse of their fairy-tale marriage and by a chain of bizarre events that separates her from both parents and launches her on a series of improbable adventures and unlikely escapes. Whatever befalls Nell, the reader knows what the conventions of a "happy ending" dictate: Nell will be restored to her parents, and her parents to each other. Whether or not this truly constitutes a happy ending is left to the reader to decide. The narrator comments wryly on the reunion of Nell's parents: "As to whether Helen *should* have taken Clifford back, well, you will have your own opinion" (pp. 356–357). Thus Weldon simultaneously conforms to an all-too-familiar narrative, the marriage plot, and questions the assumptions on which it relies.

Words of Advice (1977) is a much darker exploration of the cultural scripts that shape our lives. The heroine, Elsa, is a young secretary who is having an affair with her employer, an antiques dealer more than twice her age. Together they arrive to spend the weekend at the mansion of Hamish and his young wife, Gemma, who is confined to a wheelchair. Alone in her tiny room on the first night and daunted by the typing Gemma has given her to do by morning—for Elsa is not a competent typist—Elsa is reminded of a fairy tale: "that of the incompetent peasant girl who boasted of her prowess at weaving, and was shut up in the castle by the king and set to work weaving hanks of straw into gold" (p. 9). Who, Elsa wonders, will play Rumpelstiltskin and perform the task in exchange for her bearing her first child?

Elsa's wandering thoughts, shaped by the fairy tales she used to tell her brothers and sisters, hint at what is to come: Hamish is to play Rumpelstiltskin, sneaking into her room at night to do her typing for her—in exchange, she gradually learns, for her consent to sleep with him, to bear a child for the often impotent Hamish and his young and beautiful but crippled wife. Gemma herself contrives the plot in which she hopes to ensnare Elsa. The stories of the two women are interwoven; Gemma, too, was once a naive and penniless secretary, determined to see a prince in her diabolical first employer. For Elsa's benefit Gemma spins a bizarre, fairy-tale-like story of love, murder, and dismemberment to account for her own paralysis and her unlikely marriage to Hamish. Her story, Hamish later reveals, is considerably embellished; the truth is more prosaic. What is significant, however, is that Gemma has chosen to emplot her life as a fairy

tale. Elsa is vulnerable to Gemma's scheme because, as Gemma explains, "I can read your heart, Elsa, because I can read my own. . . . I love fairy tales, don't you?" (p. 20). The same narratives are inscribed in both of their imaginations, shaping their perceptions and scripting their lives. Elsa escapes only because Gemma finally relinquishes the illusions she has been clinging to for years, exhorting Elsa to "run for me and all of us" (p. 213). Although the plot of this novel is fantastic, like that of a multilayered fairy tale, it conveys a serious critique of the way in which cultural scripts like fairy tales mold our imaginations and, by extension, our lives.

In *The Life and Loves of a She-Devil* (1983), Weldon attacks the dangerous fictions offered women by the writers of romance novels. The she-devil of the title is Ruth, six feet two and far from conforming to standards of feminine beauty; at the beginning of the novel, her husband, Bobbo, is having an affair with a petite, blonde, strikingly pretty woman named Mary Fisher. "Mary Fisher," Ruth tells us, "lives in a High Tower, on the edge of the sea: she writes a great deal about the nature of love. She is a writer of romantic fiction. She tells lies to herself, and to the world" (p. 1). Ruth is all too aware of how far removed from reality are Mary Fisher's novels, "which sell by the hundred thousand in glittery pink-and-gold covers" (p. 25). Once Ruth adopts the idea that she is not a failed heroine but a she-devil, as her husband has called her, her outlook on life alters radically, and she sets out on an elaborate course of revenge. She begins by burning down the house and leaving her two children to spoil the romantic idyll of Bobbo and Mary, and she does not stop until she has destroyed both of their lives.

Significantly, as Mary Fisher's life becomes more complicated—by children, financial worries, an elderly, incontinent mother, and Bobbo's increasingly unreasonable domestic demands—she finds it more difficult to produce her popular novels. The publishers complain that "a kind of gritty reality kept breaking in. The readers wouldn't like it" (p. 120). In Ruth's view, "her lies are worse because now she knows they are lies" (p. 210). Although she eventually forgives Mary Fisher and even pities her, after destroying her, Ruth still insists: "But I don't forgive her novels" (p. 211). Ruth compares Mary Fisher, writing romantic novels in her tower above the sea, to a false lighthouse, luring sailors to their deaths. Her "light was treacherous; it spoke of clear water and faith and life when in fact there were rocks and dark and storms out there, and even death, and mariners should not be lulled but must be warned" (p. 210). Romantic fiction, Weldon implies, seduces its female readers with false visions of life and love, corrupts their expectations, and lulls them with fantasies.

The most disturbing aspect of Ruth's revenge involves her elaborate efforts to remake herself in the image of Mary Fisher, who in turn embodies the idealized feminine beauty celebrated in romantic novels. Mary Fisher's "little staunch heroines raise tearful eyes to handsome men. . . . Little women can look up to men," Ruth observes. "But women of six feet two have trouble doing so" (p. 25). She sets about to correct this unfortunate fact, spending years of her life and millions of dollars having her face remodeled, every inch of her body sculpted, tucked, smoothed, perfected. The final and most extreme step involves having her legs shortened; even her doctors are reluctant to perform such an experimental procedure. One of them protests sardonically, "We're remaking you . . . and in one of His feebler and more absurd images" (p. 269). The petite, blonde prettiness of romantic heroines might be absurd and feeble, but Ruth has endured ridicule, contempt, and mistreatment at the hands of the world for far too long not to recognize its value. "I am no revolutionary," she protests. "Since I cannot change the world, I will change myself" (p. 237).

Weldon's portrayal of Ruth satirizes not only conventional standards of feminine beauty, but the lengths to which women will go to conform to them. Most importantly, *The Life and Loves of a She-Devil* is a scathing critique of the fictions that perpetuate such ideals, inscribing them on the female consciousness along with the implicit requirement that women look up to men not just literally but figuratively. Weldon's more affirmative women characters manage to become the "heroines" of their own lives by revising the accepted definition of heroines; Ruth is perhaps Weldon's most frightening and disturbing creation in that she revises herself instead.

CONCLUSION

RUTH is neither the first nor the last of Weldon's many heroines to burn down her house; her action is repeated, for instance, by Alexandra in *Worst Fears*

(1996). It is a symbolic gesture with considerable literary resonance, for the house is the most tangible symbol of the myth of bourgeois domesticity. To burn it down can be seen as the ultimate act of protest against the perpetuation of that myth. The house, for Weldon, stands for enforced dependency—emotional, intellectual, and economic—on the part of wives; to burn down one's house is thus a deeply subversive gesture. Such personal acts always have political implications in Weldon's fiction; her characters seldom resolve the difficulties in their own lives until they see themselves in relation to the society in which they live. Her novels provide insightful explorations into the power dynamics of gender relations, explorations animated by humor, innovative narrative techniques, and a willingness to fuse the fantastic with social realism, ever blurring the line between truth and fiction.

SELECTED BIBLIOGRAPHY

I. NOVELS. *The Fat Woman's Joke* (London, 1967), published as *And the Wife Ran Away* (New York, 1968); *Down Among the Women* (London, 1971); *Female Friends* (New York, 1974); *Remember Me* (London, 1976); *Words of Advice* (New York, 1977), published as *Little Sisters* (London, 1978); *Praxis* (London, 1978); *Puffball* (London, 1980); *The President's Child* (London, 1982); *The Life and Loves of a She-Devil* (New York, 1983); *The Shrapnel Academy* (London, 1986); *The Rules of Life* (London, 1987); *The Heart of the Country* (London, 1987); *The Hearts and Lives of Men* (London, 1987); *The Leader of the Band* (London, 1988); *The Cloning of Joanna May* (London, 1989); *Darcy's Utopia* (London, 1990); *Growing Rich* (London, 1992); *Life Force* (London, 1992); *Affliction* (London, 1993), published as *Trouble* (New York, 1993); *Splitting* (London, 1995); *Worst Fears: A Novel* (New York, 1996).

II. SHORT STORIES COLLECTIONS. *Watching Me, Watching You* (London, 1981); *Polaris and Other Stories* (London, 1985); *Moon over Minneapolis* (London, 1991); *Wicked Women* (London, 1995).

III. PLAYS. *Words of Advice* (produced 1974); *Friends* (1975); *Moving House* (1976); *Action Replay* (1978); *Mr. Director* (1978); *After the Prize* (1981), produced in England as *Wood Worm* (1984); *I Love My Love* (1981); *Jane Eyre* (1986); *The Hole in the Top of the World* (1987); *A Doll's House* (1988), adaptation; *A Small Green Space* (1989); *Someone Like You* (1990); *Tess of the D'Urbervilles* (1992).

IV. NONFICTION. *Letters to Alice on First Reading Jane Austen* (London, 1984); *Rebecca West* (New York, 1985); *Sacred Cows* (London, 1989).

V. TELEVISION. *The Fat Woman's Tale*, GTV (1966); *Wife in a Blonde Wig*, BBC (1966); *Office Party*, Thames TV (1970); *On Trial, Upstairs, Downstairs*, LWT (1971); *Hands*, BBC (1972); *Aunt Tatty*, BBC (1975); *Poor Baby*, ATV (1975); *The Terrible Tale of Timothy Bagshott*, BBC (1975); *Married Love*, BBC (1977); *Life for Christine*, GTV (1980); *Pride and Prejudice*, BBC (1980); *Watching Me, Watching You*, BBC (1980); *Little Miss Perkins*, LWT (1982); *Redundant; or, The Wife's Revenge*, BBC (1983); *Bright Smiles*, GTV (1985); *On First Reading Jane Austen*, BBC (1985); *A Dangerous Kind of Love*, BBC (1986); *Face at the Window*, Thames TV (1986); *The Life and Loves of a She-Devil*, BBC serial (1986); *Heart of the Country*, BBC (1987); *The Cloning of Joanna May*, Granada (1992); *Growing Rich*, Anglia TV (1992).

VI. RADIO. *Housebreaker*, BBC Radio 3 (1973); *Spider*, BBC Radio 4 (1973); *Mr. Fox and Mr. First*, BBC Radio 3 (1974); *The Doctor's Wife*, BBC Radio 4 (1975); *Polaris*, BBC Radio 4 (1978); *All the Bells of Paradise*, BBC Radio 4 (1979); *Weekend*, BBC Radio 4 (1979); *I Love My Love*, BBC Radio 3 (1981); *The Hole in the Top of the World*, BBC Radio 4 (1993); *Everyone Needs an Ancestor*, BBC Radio 4 (1995); *A Hard Time to Be a Father*, BBC Radio 4 (1995); *Heat Haze*, BBC Radio 4 (1995); *Web Central*, BBC Radio 4 (1995).

VII. CRITICAL STUDIES. Agate-Nesaule Krouse, "Feminism and Art in Fay Weldon's Novels," in *Critique: Studies in Modern Fiction* 20, no. 2 (1978); Margaret Chesnutt, "Feminist Criticism and Feminist Consciousness: A Reading of a Novel by Fay Weldon," in *Moderna Språk* 73 (1979); Alan Wilde, "'Bold, but Not too Bold': Fay Weldon and the Limits of Poststructuralist Criticism," in *Contemporary Literature* 29 (fall 1988); Shirley Kossick, "The Fiction of Fay Weldon: A Critical Survey," in *Unisa English Studies: Journal of the Department of English* 27, no. 1 (1989); Clara Connolly, "Review Essay: Sacred Cows," in *Feminist Review* 35 (summer 1990); Denise Marshall, "Dear Reader: Intercepting Romance and Transforming Acculturation in Woolf and Weldon," in Mark Hussey and Vara Neverow-Turk, eds., *Virginia Woolf Miscellanies: Proceedings of the First Annual Conference on Virginia Woolf* (New York, 1992); Jeanne Dubino, "The Cinderella Complex: Romance Fiction, Patriarchy, and Capitalism," in *Journal of Popular Culture* 27 (winter 1993); Ann Marie Hebert, "Rewriting the Feminine Script: Fay Weldon's Wicked Laughter," in *Critical Matrix: The Princeton Journal of Women, Gender, and Culture* 7, no. 1 (1993); Patricia Juliana Smith, "Weldon's *The Life and Loves of a She-Devil*," in *Explicator* 51 (summer 1993); Regina Barreca, ed., *Fay Weldon's Wicked Fictions* (Hanover, N.H., 1994); Regina Barreca, *Untamed and Unabashed: Essays on Women and Humor in British Literature* (Detroit, 1994); Pauline Young, "Selling the Emperor's New Clothes: Fay Weldon as Contemporary Folklorist," in *Folklore in Use* 2, no. 1 (1994); Nancy A. Walker, *The Disobedient Writer: Women and Narrative Tradition* (Austin, Tex., 1995).

JEANETTE WINTERSON

(1959–   )

Ursula K. Heise

JEANETTE WINTERSON'S FIRST novel, *Oranges Are Not the Only Fruit*, attracted intense critical interest as an original, partly autobiographical, partly fantastic work, which won the Whitbread First Novel Award and the Publishing for People Award when it appeared in 1985. Winterson's subsequent novels continued to attract a wide and diverse readership and to be noted for their sophisticated combination of historical fact with fantasy and fairy tale, their humor, their exploration of diverse forms of sexual experience, and a narrative style that is not so much driven by plot as by lyrical expression. Situated at the crossroads of postmodern narrative (with its metafictional and metahistorical elements), gay and lesbian fiction (with its questioning of conventional gender constructions and representations), and magical realism (with its blurring of boundaries between the real and the imaginary), Winterson's fiction combines some of the most dynamic currents in international fiction of the last thirty years. In her collection of essays entitled *Art Objects: Essays on Ecstasy and Effrontery* (1995), Winterson has commented explicitly not only on her own novels but also on the works of important modernist predecessors. Many prominent writers and critics consider her one of the most accomplished novelists to have emerged in the English-speaking literary scene in the 1980s and 1990s.

LIFE

JEANETTE Winterson was born in Manchester, England, on 27 August 1959. She was adopted by Jack and Constance Winterson and brought up in Accrington, Lancashire. Her adoptive parents, members of a Pentecostal Evangelical congregation, trained her to become a missionary, and she was introduced to preaching and faith healing at a very early age. When she was growing up, the books in her home were restricted to the Bible and *Jane Eyre*; in her teens, however, Winterson discovered the local public library, where she worked for a time on Saturdays and turned into a voracious reader of literature and history, often reading five or six books a week. At the same time, her emerging lesbianism led to intense confrontations with the church that culminated in an exorcism performed on her by church officials. As a consequence, Winterson broke off her connection with the church, left her family at age sixteen, and began to work at various temporary jobs—as an ice-cream truck driver, a makeup artist in a funeral parlor, and in a mental hospital. These crucial events are fictionalized in her first novel, *Oranges Are Not the Only Fruit*, and echoes of her childhood also appear in later novels, most clearly in *Boating for Beginners* (1985) and *Sexing the Cherry* (1989). Winterson's break with her family turned out to be more than temporary: in interviews she has stressed that she does not feel part of her adoptive family. She did not return to Accrington for her mother's funeral fifteen years after her departure, and she has never attempted to trace her biological parents.

In 1978 she entered St. Catherine's College at Oxford University, and in 1981 she completed her master's degree in English. After graduation from Oxford, she made various unsuccessful attempts to enter the fields of advertising or publishing. According to Winterson's own account, during an interview for an editorial position at Pandora Press she realized that she would not be given the job and instead launched into telling the interviewer, Philippa Brewster, stories about her earlier life. Brewster was so impressed by Winterson's storytelling abilities that she encouraged her to write these stories down—a suggestion that became the germ for *Oranges Are Not the Only Fruit* and the beginning of Winterson's career as a writer. For some time afterward, Winterson worked at various jobs, as an assistant at the Roundhouse theater and as an editor, initially with Brilliance Books and later at Pandora Press.

Oranges Are Not the Only Fruit, a first-person account of a girl growing up in a fundamentalist family and breaking away from church and home when her relationships with women are discovered, was published by Pandora Press, a feminist publisher that encouraged Winterson's engagement with issues of feminine identity and sexuality in 1985. *Oranges* was an immediate success. An American edition followed in 1987. Winterson adapted the novel into a screenplay that became the basis for a three-part miniseries, directed by Beeban Kidron, that aired on BBC television in January 1990 and won a British Academy of Film and Television Arts award for best drama. Winterson's second novel, *Boating for Beginners,* also published in 1985, has gained less critical acclaim than Winterson's other works; it is, nevertheless, perhaps the funniest of all of Winterson's novels, a thoroughly irreverent and satirical retelling of the Genesis story of Noah and the Flood that also raises serious questions about the authority of traditions and scriptures. During these first years of literary activity, Winterson also edited a collection of short love stories by women, *Passion Fruit: Romantic Fiction with a Twist* (1986), and wrote a book on health and fitness titled *Fit for the Future: The Guide for Women Who Want to Live Well* (1986), both for Pandora Press.

The Passion, Winterson's third novel, appeared in 1987 and won the John Llewellyn Rhys Memorial Prize. *The Passion* and *Sexing the Cherry*—which received the E. M. Forster Award from the American Academy of Arts and Letters—both mix historical fact with elements of magical realism and fairy tale in a manner reminiscent of the intertwining of autobiography and fairy tale in *Oranges Are Not the Only Fruit,* but they blend the various strands much more seamlessly. *Sexing the Cherry* in particular bears the marks of experimental and postmodern fiction more clearly than Winterson's previous works.

Winterson's later novels, *Written on the Body* (1992) and *Art & Lies: A Piece for Three Voices and a Bawd* (1994), differ markedly from *The Passion* and *Sexing the Cherry.* Less abundant in colorful detail,

characterization, and plot, they address questions of love, sexuality, and artistic creation at a much more abstract level and in a more lyrical style. *Written on the Body,* told by a first-person narrator whose gender is never disclosed, centers around the narrator's love for an Australian woman whom s/he woos away from her husband—a plot that bears resemblances to Winterson's real-life involvement with the Australian-born teacher and editor Margaret Reynolds, with whom Winterson has lived since the early 1990s. But the novel became notorious in London because of another biographical reference much less central to the novel: it made public Winterson's affair with her literary agent, Pat Kavanagh, wife of the novelist Julian Barnes. Not only did the publication of *Written on the Body* lead to the personal and professional estrangement of Winterson and Kavanagh, it also provoked hostility against Winterson in London literary circles. After the breakup with Kavanagh, Winterson went on to found her own corporation, Great Moments, and wrote the screenplay (1993) for a film entitled *Great Moments in Aviation,* directed by Beeban Kidron. She created further scandal by declaring, on two different occasions, that her choice for the Book of the Year was either a book she had written herself (*Written on the Body,* in 1992) or one that contained her own work and had been edited by her partner, Margaret Reynolds (*The Penguin Book of Lesbian Short Stories,* in 1993); in response to an inquiry, she also nominated herself as the greatest living writer in the English language, declarations that her friends and critics have interpreted as either arrogance or a deliberate send-up of the literary establishment.

During her residence in London, Winterson made it a habit to leave the city for several months at a time to do her writing at a cottage owned by the crime writer Ruth Rendell. By the mid-1990s, the commercial success of Winterson's novels enabled her to acquire an estate in Gloucestershire, where she and Margaret Reynolds moved in 1994. *Art & Lies,* published the same year, attracted more criticism and less praise than her previous novels. Her collection of essays, *Art Objects: Essays on Ecstasy and Effrontery,* includes reflections on painting, on the genre of autobiography, and on Winterson's modernist predecessors Gertrude Stein and Virginia Woolf, as well as a discussion of her own fiction.

JEANETTE WINTERSON

Oranges Are Not the Only Fruit is a first-person narrative told by Jeanette, a girl who is being brought up in northern England by her fundamentalist adoptive mother. Jeanette's mother conceives of the adoption as an Immaculate Conception of sorts that singles out her daughter for a life devoted to God. She sees Jeanette as a future missionary, and therefore instructs her in preaching and evangelizing even when she is still a child. All of Jeanette's friends are church members, and all her free time is engaged in church activities, from meetings and services to weekend retreats and missionary outreaches. The chapter aptly titled "Exodus" emphasizes the social and emotional isolation that this upbringing imposes upon Jeanette, not only when she has to confront the world outside the church but even within the congregation and her own family. When she becomes deaf due to an illness at age seven or eight, her mother and other church members take this to be a sign of holy rapture; for days Jeanette lives without hearing, and it takes the forceful intervention of an adult friend to make Jeanette's mother realize her daughter is in need of medical care. This incident foreshadows Jeanette's experiences when she begins to attend public school: her behavior, perceptions, and language are so different from those of her schoolmates that, despite all her efforts to make friends and do well, she ends up alienating both her peers and her teachers.

In her teens Jeanette repeatedly realizes that she does not always understand or agree with what she hears and sees in her congregation. But these moments of dissent never add up to any conscious confrontation, for Jeanette is at the same time completely wrapped up in church activities and increasingly successful as a preacher and evangelist. She falls in love with Melanie, a girl she meets at the marketplace, and brings her to church. Melanie converts, and Jeanette and Melanie have a love affair without the slightest awareness that they are doing anything about which the church might object. But when Jeanette, in a moment of intimacy with her mother, tells her about her love and friendship for Melanie, both of the lovers are set upon by the church and urged to repent and renounce their "unnatural passion." Melanie does repent, but, even after daylong prayer meetings at her mother's house, after she has been left without food for several days and had an exorcism performed upon her, Jeanette is unable to comprehend why she has done anything wrong, insisting that she and Melanie love each other. Under the combined pressure of church and family, she does, in the end, pretend that she is repentant. Brought up with absolute confidence in her own special calling and her difference from the sinful world around her, however, Jeanette cannot really grasp why acts she carried out with the best of intentions are labeled sinful.

After Jeanette and Melanie are separated, church life returns to normal for a time. But when Jeanette is caught having an affair with another new convert named Katy, the confrontation comes to a head: again urged to renounce her sinful behavior, Jeanette instead decides to leave the church. This heresy leads to a breakup with her mother, who does not want a "devil" living in her house. Penniless and cut off from all ties to church and home, Jeanette takes up work as an ice-cream vendor, then as a makeup artist in a funeral home, and finally leaves town. At the end of the novel Jeanette visits her home once more, much later in the dead of winter. Her mother, who has seen many elements of the church exposed as corrupt, nevertheless remains faithful. Neither these failures nor her daughter's "fall" keep her from pursuing her missionary work with undiminished fervor and utilizing the latest in media technology—CB radio—by means of which she communicates with other fundamentalists.

Oranges Are Not the Only Fruit tells the story of an adolescent's rebellion against rigid and outdated codes of morality and behavior as well describing a lesbian coming-out. Although it is often satirized, the adult world of religious power and heterosexual repression is not portrayed with bitterness. On the contrary, much of the novel's freshness and strength derives from the sense of humor with which Jeanette's perceptions of this world are presented. For example, when Jeanette's mother forbids her to go back to a particular candy store because its female owners deal in "unnatural passions," Jeanette interprets this as meaning that they put chemical additives into the sweets. The dismay of Jeanette's schoolmates and teachers when confronted with her stories and pictures of hellfire and damnation, her mother's fights with her "heathen" neighbors (they dare to make love on Sundays), and the confrontations between Jeanette's congregation and the Salvation Army over the best places to sing Christmas carols are all outrageously funny and not only satirize the faithful but also convey a genuine sense of affection for their eccentricities. The female characters in particular are drawn with an unfailing sense of telling detail and speech.

The realistic detail of *Oranges,* its reliance on the structural pattern of the initiation story, the name of the heroine, and the correspondence of much of its plot to Winterson's life invite the reader to read it as an autobiographical text. But the novel—particularly the second half—resists such a reading; the main story is interspersed with short allegories and fairy-tale episodes that disrupt its realistic atmosphere. The most important of these short tales are those of Sir Perceval, who seeks the Grail but really longs to be back with King Arthur and the Knights of the Round Table, and Winnet (a transparent fusion of the author's first and last name), who is adopted by a sorcerer to be trained in the secrets of wizardry. When Winnet shows affection for a boy, the sorcerer claims she has disgraced him and throws her out of his house. She is left to fend for herself in the forest and finally finds her way to a big city. Both fantasy figures are tied by invisible threads to the places they have been forced to leave, allegorizing Jeanette's own attachment to the places and people she has had to leave behind in her break from church and family. This attachment manifests itself, among other things, in the very structure of her story: it is divided into eight chapters named after the first eight books of the Bible, most of which revolve around the migration of the people of Israel from slavery in Egypt to their entry into the Promised Land of Canaan. Even as she leaves religion behind, therefore, Jeanette still uses its story patterns to describe her own development.

The fifth chapter, "Deuteronomy," explicitly addresses and problematizes the relationship between history and fiction. Any story that claims to represent the "facts" or to give a "true history," the narrator argues, reduces the multiplicity of voices and fictions that surround any sequence of events:

Some people say there are true things to be found, some people say all kinds of things can be proved. I don't believe them. The only thing for certain is how complicated it all is, like string full of knots. It's all there but hard to find the beginning and impossible to fathom the end.

The best you can do is admire the cat's cradle, and maybe knot it up a bit more. . . . It's an all-purpose rainy day pursuit, this reducing of stories called history.

People like to separate storytelling which is not fact from history which is fact. They do this so that they know what to believe and what not to believe. This is very curious.

(p. 93)[1]

Even if it were not for the fragments of myth and fairy tale, this chapter points to the danger of reading the novel as straight autobiography, as presenting the facts of the author's life. Rather, "Deuteronomy" suggests, the novel is a text that should be read for the way in which certain realities and systems of belief are created and give rise to particular stories.

Winterson's own comments on *Oranges* reinforce the sense that it would be a mistake to read it as simple autobiography. When questioned about the relationship of her earlier life to the novel, Winterson has either been evasive, claiming that "the truth is, I can't remember" (in Constantine and Scott, p. 24), or has affirmed that *Oranges* is only one possible story of her life: "*Oranges* is the document, both true and false, which will have to serve for my life until I went to Oxford, and after that I daresay that whatever I tell you will be another document, one that is both true and false" (in Marvel, p. 168). In *Art Objects,* Winterson characterizes *Oranges* as "a fiction masquerading as a memoir" (p. 53) and emphasizes the disjunction between an author's biography and her books: "The intersection between a writer's life and a writer's work is irrelevant to the reader. The reader is not being offered a chunk of the writer or a direct insight into the writer's mind, the reader is being offered a separate reality" (p. 27). These comments, in addition to the fantastic and metanarrative elements of *Oranges* itself, should make one wary of reducing the novel to the autobiographical elements it undoubtedly contains. The later screenplay for the television series that Winterson wrote changes the name of the main character from Jeanette to Jessica, further emphasizing the difference between author and character. Finally, in the introduction to the screenplay Winterson categorically claims that "*Oranges* is not autobiography" (p. xiv). One may not wish to take this

[1]Unless otherwise noted, quotations are from first U.S. edition of works cited.

denial too literally, but both the novel and the screenplay clearly inhabit a space between the factual and the fictional and cannot simply be subsumed under the genre of autobiography.

CHURCH AND SCRIPTURE

BEYOND its interest as an initiation story, *Oranges* stages the constant clash of differing realities not only between believers and nonbelievers but also between different kinds of faith. In these clashes the Bible and (more generally) the written text play a crucial role. In the confrontation between Jeanette's congregation and the Salvation Army over where and how to perform Christmas carols, this conflict is presented humorously; one of Jeanette's mother's friends insists that the Bible " 'sez make a joyful noise'. . . . When the [Salvation Army] General ventured to suggest a less than literal interpretation of this psalm, there was uproar. For a start it was heresy. Then it was rude" (p. 119). At a more serious level, in the screenplay Jeanette (here, "Jessica") and the pastor both quote passages from the Epistles of Paul to each other as they defend their diametrically opposed interpretations of Jessica's affairs with other women.

The question of how a sacred text and the traditions that have grown up around it succeed in shaping cultural and social realities is one of the most important recurring themes in Winterson's work. It emerges very clearly in *Sexing the Cherry*, which is set, for the most part, in seventeenth-century England during the reign of Cromwell. One of its protagonists is the female giant Dog-Woman, who is fiercely loyal to the monarchy the Puritans ousted as well as to the Anglican Church. During a secret monarchist meeting she attends, a preacher explains the apparent contradiction in the Old Testament between the commandment not to kill, and the injunction to take an eye for an eye and a tooth for a tooth, by arguing that it means one must secretly gouge out one's enemies' eyes and take their teeth. Dog-Woman takes this veiled political declaration literally and shows up at the next meeting with a sack full of "119 eyeballs, one missing on account of a man who had lost one already, and over 2,000 teeth" (p. 93), much to the dismay of the preacher and the other participants, some of whom faint when they see the Dog-Woman's trophies.

Once again the question of literal understanding dominates the scene. Dog-Woman's idiosyncratic form of piety and her fierce hatred of the Puritans' political repressiveness and sexual hypocrisy is one of the recurrent themes of this novel, which presents different characters and a different historical setting to stage a conflict very much like that of Jeanette, whose genuine Christian faith cannot mold itself to fit the rigid code of her Pentecostal congregation.

Without question, Winterson's most significant treatment of the sacred text and the institutions to which it gives rise is found in her second novel, *Boating for Beginners*. Retelling the biblical story of the Flood and Noah's Ark, it transposes the characters and events from a prehistorical to an aggressively modern setting, complete with television, fast-food restaurants, and beauty spas. The protagonists, Gloria Munde and her mother, in many ways resemble the mother-daughter pair in *Oranges*. Gloria is an insecure, extremely self-conscious teenager who reads romances by the popular novelist Bunny Mix as well as works by the literary critic Northrop Frye; she defines her own development according to the metaphoric, didactic, and prosaic stages outlined by Frye. Her mother is Noah's cook and a devoted follower of the cult of the Unpronounceable that he has brought into being (a deity whose name is obviously meant to parody the interdict on pronouncing the four letters of God's name in the Old Testament). Noah himself started out as the owner of a pleasure-boat company but now has turned author, film producer, and evangelist; since he encounters more than a few skeptics, he has coauthored a book with the Unpronounceable to explain human history from beginning to end. The first installment, *Genesis, or How I Did It*, has become a best-seller. Noah therefore decides to turn it into a movie, with the help of Bunny Mix, and to tour the world with it in a large cruise ship in order to convert the heathens. This, however, provokes the ire of the Unpronounceable, who does not care for the movie and detests Bunny Mix. Moody and autocratic, he decides in a bout of ill humor and against Noah's protests to flood the earth in earnest and get rid of all but Noah and his family.

Only Noah and his sons officially know about the impending destruction of the world, but Desi, one of Noah's daughters-in-law and a friend of Gloria's, overhears the Unpronounceable's outbreak of rage from a hiding place and communicates it to some of her friends. Rummaging around Noah's house, Desi also makes another troubling discovery: she finds Noah's secret diary containing his various scientific inventions and experiments. As it turns out, Noah had accidentally created various misshapen creatures out of rotten vanilla ice cream and Black Forest cherry cake; as he continued his experiments to create more successful life forms, he also brought into being a pale, eight-foot-tall creature that was able to speak, left the laboratory, and went off to live in a cloud—none other than the Unpronounceable himself, who now requests from Noah and his family that after the Flood they devise a scheme to make his existence plausible to future generations.

To this end, Noah charges Gloria with collecting pairs of animals to load into his fiberglass ark. He invites Bunny Mix to join his family so as to rewrite the story of the Unpronounceable for the benefit of posterity. He slyly plants clues meant to give later generations the false impression that his was a primeval, "primitive" civilization in touch with the first origins of the world, rather than the highly developed, decadent culture that it is. As Bunny Mix composes a story that features her characteristic doves and rainbows at the end, Gloria and Desi make their own preparations for surviving the Flood with a group of female friends. When twentieth-century archaeologists discover residues of what is believed to be Noah's ark on Mount Ararat, it emerges that both groups have indeed survived the Flood: one to pass on a deliberately falsified account of God; the other, presumably, to preserve at least some of the memory of the events that really led up to the rise of the Unpronounceable and the Flood—in other words, to leave behind an alternative account. Like many other Winterson novels, *Boating for Beginners* here foregrounds the emergence of alternative stories about a historical event and the plurality of perspectives that inevitably accompanies it.

Like *Oranges*, *Boating for Beginners* includes a brief section in which the narrator comments on storytelling and its functions: "Myths hook and bind the mind because at the same time they set the mind free: they explain the universe while allowing the universe to go on being unexplained; and we seem to need this even now, in our twentieth-century grandeur" (1990 ed., p. 66). This echoes almost literally the "Deuteronomy" chapter of *Oranges*,

which claimed that "that is the way with stories; we make them what we will. It's a way of explaining the universe while leaving the universe unexplained, it's a way of keeping it all alive, not boxing it into time" (p. 93). In *Boating for Beginners* the narrator encourages the reader to go back to the story of the Flood in Genesis and to enjoy it for its bold inventiveness if not for its plausibility. The extraordinary power of the Bible, the narrator argues, lies in its function as a source for both myth and countermyth; if its original writers intended to kindle faith rather than to record events accurately, many subsequent cultural revolutionaries have been compelled to return to the biblical text as a narrative source even while overturning its authority. This fascinating account of the enduring power of biblical myth even in secular societies also sheds light on Winterson's own literary project: far from rejecting the Bible because of her own traumatic experiences, she uses its materials to create powerful half-fantastic and half-realistic fictions that debunk some of the basic assumptions that underlie Biblical faith. In this sense *Boating for Beginners* is not just a comic retelling of the Flood story; it is an inverted Genesis of the Judeo-Christian God himself, in which Noah is transformed from God's obedient servant into a Frankenstein—both pre-historical and completely modern—creating a monster that runs out of control and (in this case) turns into a deity. The fusion of the biblical with Mary Shelley's Romantic myth affirms both the existence of God and his origin as an all too human creation—a failed one at that.

Boating for Beginners subverts the reader's sense of "history" and the expectation that the society of the Old Testament must be more "primitive" than the modern one, while at the same time articulating a clearly feminist agenda. After all, it is a group of women that finds out about the Flood just in time to prepare, survive, and leave a record of the emergence of a thoroughly patriarchal myth—ironically pinpointed in the novel by the fact that God routinely addresses Noah as "mother." In spite of these conceptual depths of what is, on the surface, a very funny tale, and in spite of the praise that writers such as Gore Vidal and David Lodge have bestowed upon it, Winterson herself has tended not to speak much about *Boating for Beginners*; it is the only one of her novels that goes unmentioned in her collection of essays. In part because of the author's reticence, and in part because *Boating for Beginners* has often been misread as merely a Monty Python–esque satire, it has not yet come into its own as a sophisticated and accomplished text within the Winterson canon, although many of her more "serious" novels address similar questions of myth, textual tradition, and the institutionalization of ritual.

SEXUALITY AND DIFFERENCE

IF *Boating for Beginners* describes a loosely structured group of women that evolves into a nucleus of resistance to emergent patriarchal myths, most of Jeanette Winterson's other novels foreground love between women and lesbians' relationships to men and patriarchal structures much more emphatically and in much greater detail. In general, Winterson's earlier novels (*Oranges, Boating for Beginners,* and *The Passion*) tend to approach issues of femininity and patriarchy from a mainly sociocultural perspective. They focus on the socialization and marginalization of female characters, or the emergence of female communities in a particular social context, and analyze the mechanisms that lead to the formation of feminine identity, whether it be heterosexual, lesbian, or bisexual. Possibly under the influence of French feminist theory, *Sexing the Cherry, Written on the Body,* and the 1993 short story "The Poetics of Sex" emphasize much more strongly the role of the female body in determining women's experience and identity. In *Sexing the Cherry,* Dog-Woman's gigantic body transcends social and cultural constraints by its sheer size and power, a motif that can be read as a translation of French feminist Hélène Cixous's theory of the female body into fiction. *Written on the Body* and "The Poetics of Sex" foreground even in their titles the close link between biological and cultural determinations of gender (specifically between sexuality and *écriture*), in another echo of French feminist theory. *Art & Lies* moves beyond this focus on the body (although physical experience continues to play an important role in this novel) to examine in great detail the connection between sexual and aesthetic experience. The three protagonists—Handel, Picasso, and Sappho—are all named or nicknamed after artists, and art in this novel is characterized as one of the principal cultural tools by means of which those whose sexuality does not conform to

social conventions can express their identity, as well as their protest against the structures that oppress them. In the Winterson canon, therefore, *Sexing the Cherry, Written on the Body,* and "The Poetics of Sex" tend to focus most clearly on femininity in its biological aspects, whereas the earlier as well as later works link female identity and sexuality more emphatically to broader social and cultural issues.

Already in *Oranges* Jeanette's lesbianism and its implications for male and female power lie at the core of her confrontation with the church. In the eyes of the Pentecostal congregation, Jeanette's sin is that she loves the "wrong sort of people" (p. 127), namely, women, although both of Jeanette's lovers are also members of the church. The church interprets Jeanette's sexual attraction to other women as an appropriation of a male role, and the church officials conclude that this arrogation of male privilege must ultimately derive from the transfer of too many crucial functions to women in the congregation. Jeanette in particular, entrusted with the traditionally male roles of preacher and missionary, has unwittingly transferred this role to her sexual life as well, so the reasoning goes, and any attempt at reforming her must therefore include stripping her of her functions in the church. What might have been considered a temporary misstep on the part of an adolescent here turns into a much more fundamental question about the distribution of power between men and women.

Neither the novel nor the screenplay of *Oranges,* however, was read principally as a vindication of homosexuality, except by some sectors of the gay and lesbian press. Although Winterson herself did intend *Oranges* to be a frontal attack on the traditional institutions of church, home, and family, many critics interpreted Jeanette's lesbianism as part of a more general rebellion against a rigid and anachronistic worldview and morality, finding it easy to identify with her resistance even when they did not sympathize with homosexuality and its criticism of the conventional family. What sustains this reading of *Oranges* is the fact that the institutions Jeanette confronts cannot really be easily identified with mainstream values: Jeanette's mother and her fundamentalist congregation are in their own way as isolated and marginalized from the dominant culture as is Jeanette herself. In an odd reversal, therefore, Jeanette and her youthful sexual impulses appear more "normal" and are easier to sympathize and identify with than the absurdly narrow worldview of her mother. This association of lesbianism with the justified resistance of the younger generation to the outdated codes of the older generation is both the strength and the weakness of *Oranges* as a lesbian novel. Although it allows the reader to identify with the struggles of the lesbian protagonist, it does so at the risk of making her lesbianism seem an accidental rather than an essential component of her more general social and cultural rebellion, thereby weakening Winterson's explicitly lesbian criticism of heterosexual institutions.

Some readers have also felt that *Oranges* unnecessarily perpetuates a binary division between homosexuality and heterosexuality that gay and lesbian culture has long attempted to overcome. The protagonists of Winterson's subsequent novels are more complex in this respect. *The Passion* (1987), set in the era of Napoleon Bonaparte, juxtaposes the voices of two first-person narrators: a male and a female. Henri is Bonaparte's personal cook (a position not unlike that of Mrs. Munde in *Boating*) and accompanies him on all his major war campaigns; Henri is devoted to Bonaparte with a passion that is shared by the majority of French people, and for many years he is willing to make any sacrifice and endure any hardship for him. Only during the fiasco of the war against Russia does his love turn to hate, when he realizes that Bonaparte's reiterated promises of a better and more peaceful life only provoke more and more wars. In Moscow he meets a military prostitute called Villanelle, deserts with her and an army priest to her hometown of Venice, and falls deeply in love with her. Villanelle, the other first-person narrator, is a sexually ambiguous figure. Daughter of a Venetian boatman, she was born with webbed feet that enable her to walk on water, a physical attribute usually found only in boatmen's male offspring. During her work as a croupier in Venetian casinos, she frequently cross-dresses as a boy, thereby attracting the attention of both men and women. She falls desperately in love with a married woman, who literally robs her heart and stores it in a jar. When she realizes the affair has no future, she marries a Frenchman, but then attempts to leave him after the marriage turns out to be disastrous. Her husband sells Villanelle to the French army as a prostitute, and thus her path crosses Henri's. Henri's love for her after their desertion to Venice remains unfulfilled, since Villanelle, despite giving birth to Henri's daughter, makes it clear that she could never love him as more than a brother. After regaining Villanelle's stolen heart and helping her murder her husband, Henri voluntarily accepts lifelong imprisonment on the island of San Servelo.

This plot addresses the question of sexual orientation in a much more complex way than *Oranges*. Although Henri's heterosexual love is destined for failure, whereas the lesbian Villanelle retains her freedom, Henri is by no means portrayed as the typical representative of a repressive patriarchy. On the contrary, he is its victim even more than Villanelle; his ability to feel passionate devotion is systematically exploited by a ruthless, autocratic power structure and converted into political and military servitude. The novel repeatedly emphasizes repeatedly that this is the root of Bonaparte's political success: he makes expert use of the common people's desire to have a sovereign they can adore. Henri's liberation after he deserts the French army is therefore logically accompanied by a rechanneling of his passion toward a more appropriately erotic object. Villanelle's libido is a good deal less susceptible to power-political manipulation; although she is abused by a brutal husband and sold into prostitution, she is generally much more in control of her surroundings than Henri. She chooses not to reestablish her relationship with the married woman after her return to Venice, but the text makes it obvious that she will have other love affairs in the future. Toward the end of the novel, her ability to navigate the underground currents of the Venetian power structure even enables her to have Henri's sentence suspended, although he resists leaving the prison. Sexuality, therefore, and more specifically the individual's ability to develop passion for another, is handled in complex ways both literally and metaphorically in *The Passion*. Henri is heterosexual, but his most intense passion in the first part of the novel is focused on another man, Bonaparte. Villanelle is a lesbian, or is perhaps bisexual, with her greatest passion reserved for another woman, but many of her actual sexual experiences—with her French husband, as a prostitute, and finally with Henri—involve men. In both cases sexuality implies a certain way of relating to existing political and social structures: Henri is, except at the moment of his desertion, mostly a passive victim of these structures, whereas Villanelle, ever the gambler and trickster, finds various ways of negotiating for power.

Sexing the Cherry (1989), Winterson's fourth novel, is even more explicitly feminist and establishes more direct connections between its historical setting and the contemporary world. Dog-Woman, its seventeenth-century protagonist, is literally a giant who weighs more than an elephant as an adult and broke her father's legs when she sat on his knees as a child. Due to her size, she is beyond sexuality—the one man who tries to satisfy her finally gives up because even her clitoris is the size of an orange (a metaphor that harks back to Winterson's first book)—and when she attempts to perform oral sex on a man she accidentally bites off his penis. Dog-Woman is a force of nature, physically superior to all those around her, able to kill dozens of men without effort, and to impose her will through the sheer power of her body.

Her foundling son, Jordan—like Jeanette an adopted child facing an overwhelmingly powerful mother—is rather shy and withdrawn, occasionally doubting his masculinity when he compares himself with his mother. He is apprenticed to the Royal Gardener Tradescant, who takes him abroad to places real and imaginary. On one of his journeys Jordan meets the Twelve Dancing Princesses, who left their palace secretly every night to go dancing in a city floating in the air, until they were caught by a prince; their father then married them off to the prince and his eleven brothers. As the princesses tell Jordan their stories, however, it turns out that not one of them ended up living "happily ever after"; all were either abandoned by their husbands or left them. Now they live alone or have entered relationships with other women. This embedding of feminist fairy tales into the main plot not only recalls the tales that interrupt the main story in *Oranges* but also seems inspired by Angela Carter's feminist retellings of traditional fairy stories. Jordan falls in love with one of the princesses, Fortunata, but in his quest for her he is sometimes unsure whether she is a person in her own right or the feminine side of his own personality. That Jordan is a character of somewhat blurred gender—not unlike Villanelle in *The Passion*—also becomes clear when he cross-dresses during one of his journeys and listens carefully to women's conversations, only to discover that they speak a language quite different from that of men and communicate in ways that men cannot understand. Together with Tradescant, Jordan introduces the technique of grafting to England, making a shoot from one plant grow from the stem of another. This technique becomes one of the novel's central metaphors for sexuality: Tradescant and Jordan decide to call their grafted cherry tree female in what appears to be a decision with no foundation in nature but rather based upon their own cultural perceptions.

Like *The Passion*, *Sexing the Cherry* alternates between the first-person accounts of its male and female protagonists, a juxtaposition that is visually foregrounded by a small pineapple icon preceding each of Jordan's sections and a drawing of a banana introducing Dog-Woman's chapters. Clearly, the figure of the Dog-Woman physically embodies a kind of Rabelaisian feminist consciousness: she is fiercely independent, larger than life and larger than men, rarely visited by self-doubt, waging a merciless war against sexual and political repression, hypocrisy, and all kinds of bad faith. Dog-Woman's violence is portrayed as being to some extent innocent—she is firmly convinced that she is doing what she should do as a good Christian when she mutilates and murders scores of Puritans—but her innocence may strike some readers as malevolent and her extreme violence remains a disturbing element in what is otherwise an appealingly vivid and colorful portrayal of a woman who transcends all stereotypes of femininity. Like Henri, Jordan is a comparatively more passive, withdrawn character; his realm is not that of action but of the imagination, where he slowly works through his relationship with his mother and the manifold interactions between males and females.

Written on the Body is even more centrally concerned with questions of gender and sexuality than *The Passion* and *Sexing the Cherry*. More so than these novels, it focuses on the question of how love and sexual passion can be adequately expressed in language. Whereas the plot is relatively minimal, the main interest of this novel lies in the way in which it approaches the problem of telling a love story without lapsing into well-worn narrative and linguistic stereotypes. "It's the clichés that cause the trouble" is one of the leitmotifs unifying the text. The most important device Winterson deploys to break stereotypical writing and reading habits is a first-person narrator who describes a complex love relationship with a married woman named Louise, but from the novel's first page to its last it remains unclear whether the narrator is a man or a woman. This indeterminacy prevents the reader from interpreting the story in terms of "typically male" or "typically female" patterns of behavior, or of stereotypes about homosexual and heterosexual relationships. Self-conscious metafictional comments on details of the unfolding plot—"I can tell by now that you are wondering whether I can be trusted as a narrator" (1994 ed., p. 24) or "We lay on our bed . . . and I fed you plums. . . . There are no ripe plums in August. Have I got it wrong, this hesitant chronology?" (p. 17)—also make the reader wary of accepting the narrative at face value and of fitting it all too neatly into preconceived notions of the "real."

It is less clear whether the actual story the novel tells does, in the end, escape stereotype. The narrator begins by describing a series of relationships with different women s/he has had, driven by the urge to escape the platitudes of bourgeois married life. But after a number of these fleeting affairs, the narrator realizes that s/he has fallen into another kind of stereotype: "I suppose I couldn't admit that I was trapped in a cliché every bit as redundant as my parents' roses round the door. I was looking for the perfect coupling; the never-sleep non-stop mighty orgasm. Ecstasy without end. I was deep in the slop-bucket of romance" (p. 21). When the narrator meets and falls in love with Louise, s/he is already living with another woman, Jacqueline, and Louise is married to the cancer specialist Elgin Rosenthal. Both breakups prove to be complicated. Jacqueline vandalizes the narrator's apartment when she finds out that her partner is leaving her for another woman. After imposing an agonizing waiting period on her lover, Louise decides to break up with her husband, moves in with the narrator, and the two live in unalloyed bliss for a few months. Elgin subsequently visits the narrator and reveals that Louise has leukemia. He asks the narrator to let her return to him so that she can accompany him to Switzerland to undergo treatment in the most advanced clinics and with the most sophisticated technologies, which are his specialty. Louise herself resists this request, but the narrator decides s/he cannot let Louise sacrifice her life for the sake of their love and secretly leaves London for an obscure town in Yorkshire.

For months the narrator works in a bar with hardly any news about Louise, reading up on cancer and cancer treatment in his/her free time. Only when, in a drunken moment of confidence, the bar owner tells him/her that it was a mistake to leave Louise without giving her any say in the decision does the narrator begin to have doubts about his/her rash action. S/he returns to London and searches everywhere for Louise, but without success. The only thing revealed during a brutal physical confrontation with Elgin is that Louise has divorced him in spite of her illness and her lover's departure. Since neither Elgin nor Louise's relatives and friends have any information about her whereabouts, the despondent narrator returns to Yorkshire. The bar owner waits in the cottage, and the narrator declares his/her continuing love for Louise, after which Louise herself appears at the kitchen door. Whether this final reunion actually takes place or is merely the narrator's fantasy is left indeterminate, but the novel ends with the happy vision of a relationship that imaginatively reaches out to engulf the entire world.

On the surface, this plot has all the earmarks of stereotype, of melodrama found in cheap romances: the conversion of the narrator from philanderer to faithful partner; the all too brief happiness of the perfect lovers, disrupted not through some ordinary mishap or misunderstanding but by a life-threatening disease; the "coincidence" that the beloved's husband is a doctor specializing in just this disease and uses his expertise to blackmail the lover into breaking up the relationship; the lover's surreptitious departure, sacrificing love so that the beloved need not sacrifice her life; the desperate, unsuccessful search for the beloved, as well as the beloved's unexpected return and the happy ending—all seem to derive from the exaggerated and implausible plots of soap opera. At one level this is precisely the point: the narrator realizes that his/her actions were perhaps prompted less by any love for Louise than by a certain infatuation with "operatic heroics" and self-sacrifice: the idea of their relationship turns out to have "a certain stickiness at the centre" (p. 187). Aside from this self-criticism, the indeterminacy of the narrator's gender keeps the story from conforming fully to the soap-opera scheme: if indeed it is two women who are reunited at the end, the romantic stereotypes of their relationship take on a different meaning throughout, since they cannot be understood as simply reconfirming heterosexual conventions. In this sense *Written on the Body* can be read as deploying the narrative clichés of heterosexual romance precisely in order to expose and question them through the narrator's indeterminate gender. By the same token, however, the novel questions similar stereotypes that have emerged in gay and lesbian fictions, exposing the "stickiness" of any plots that lock characters into gender-based patterns of behavior which they are not allowed to transcend.

This strategy is complemented by a more specifically linguistic one. In the middle section of the novel, while the narrator is in Yorkshire reading books on cancer, the plot comes to a standstill and is replaced by a series of very brief chapters that juxtapose the anatomical description of a particular part of the human body with the narrator's lyrical effusions over the same part of Louise's body. The clinical detachment of medical language is juxtaposed against exuberant metaphors derived directly from the Song of Solomon and oriental love poetry. Again, this language becomes highly ambiguous because of the reader's uncertainty as to whether the speaker is male or female. But the question that arises in these chapters—and in the novel as a whole—is whether the gender ambiguity of the text is sufficient to counteract and ironize the use of clichés. Particularly in the middle chapters, it is hard to overlook the fact that the ambiguity Winterson introduces into biblical love language is purchased at the price of another stereotype, namely, the opposition between scientific language, with its alleged inability to express the depths and nuances of human emotion, and lyrical language, with its sublimation of the merely physical into the metaphoric. The ornate biblical language in these passages may strike the reader as itself outdated and artificial, far from an authentic expression of the narrator's emotions and in its own way as stylized as that of the anatomical handbook.

A related question might be asked of the novel as a whole: Is the idea of two women finding each other—after a long period of separation and numerous obstacles—in a complex and fulfilling relationship unusual and surprising enough in the 1990s to unhinge and explode the clichés that the plot is built upon? Is the translation of heterosexual stereotypes into a (potentially) lesbian context startling enough to turn them into something other than stereotypes? Depending on how this question is answered, *Written on the Body* is either a novel that suffocates under the weight of its own narrative and linguistic clichés or a daring literary experiment that jolts the reader into a recognition of the heterosexist assumptions that underlie certain fictional and stylistic strategies as well as reading habits.

The short story "The Poetics of Sex," published in *The Penguin Book of Lesbian Short Stories* in 1993, addresses some of the same literary issues more straightforwardly. It is a lively sketch of the first-person narrator's love affair with Picasso, in this case a woman painter whom the narrator met at art school (an ironic appropriation of the name of a canonical male painter notorious for his womanizing). The story is subdivided into sections, each headed by one of the stereotypical questions that heterosexuals ask of lesbians: Which One of You Is the Man? What Do Lesbians Do in Bed? Why Do You Hate Men? Don't You Find There's Something Missing? Each question is answered by a fast-paced, exuberant, and often witty panegyric of lesbian love that stylistically pulls out all the stops, from the vulgar and the colloquial to the lyrical and the sublime. The narrator's portrayals of Picasso often consist of breathless accumulations of epithets and metaphors; for example, she praises "the stench of her, the brack of her, the rolling splitting cunt of her. Squat like a Sumo, ham thighs, loins of pork, beefy upper cuts and breasts of lamb" (p. 412). Clichéd metaphors for the lover are rejected in the same fast-paced rhythm: "She is all the things a lover should be and quite a few a lover should not. Pin her down? She's not a butterfly. I'm not a wrestler. She's not a target. I'm not a gun. Tell you what she is? She's not Lot no. 27 and I'm not one to brag" (p. 414). The description of a sex scene is simultaneously engaged, witty, and detached:

What an Eskimo I am, breaking her seductive ice and putting in my hand for fish. How she wriggles, slithers, twists to resist me but I can bait her and I do. A fine catch, one in each hand and one in my mouth. Impressive for a winter afternoon and the stove gone out and the rent to pay. We were warm and rich and white. I had so much enjoyed my visit.

(p. 415)

The principal metaphor Winterson deploys in this short story is the island of Lesbos: Picasso calls the narrator Sappho and the lovers are described as inhabiting an island that tourists from the mainland can circumnavigate but cannot enter. This island is as much linguistic as it is sexual: the answer to the stereotypical language of the interrogative section headings lies not only in the assertion of a distinct realm of lesbian sexuality, which these clichés cannot even begin to describe, but also in the invention of a language whose pace, scope, and flexibility exposes them for the banalities they are. Hence the story's title, "The Poetics of Sex," which points precisely to this link between issues of sexuality and literary language.

Picasso, the female painter, and her lover Sappho prefigure two of the central characters in Winterson's novel *Art & Lies*, which features three first-person narrators: the doctor and defrocked priest nicknamed Handel; the young woman painter Picasso; and the voice of the poet Sappho, alive and in love even after thousands of years, commenting on the fate of her lyrical work as well as the late-twentieth-century world she sees around her. All three characters are literally or metaphorically scarred and mutilated because of their sexual experiences. Handel received his nickname from a Roman Catholic cardinal whose protégé he was as a young boy; the cardinal had him castrated so as to recreate a relationship he had had over several decades with a castrato singer. As a consequence, years later Handel refuses the only woman he has ever loved and remains withdrawn and alienated from his surroundings. In his profession as a breast-cancer surgeon, he is condemned to repeat a gesture of physical mutilation not unlike the one that was performed on him.

Picasso, the daughter of a successful entrepreneur, is traumatized by a family background that is both violent and hypocritical. For years she has been sexually abused by her older brother, Matthew, but her parents as well as the vicar of her church refuse to face this fact and blame Picasso for her disruptions of family life. One Christmas evening, after having again been raped by Matthew, Picasso, naked, climbs onto the roof of her house with the intention of leaping off it. Her father follows her and pushes her off before she can take any action, but she survives by landing in a snowbank and is temporarily committed to a mental hospital. For Picasso, painting and colors are a means of recreating her environment according to her own vision. When she splashes the house, furniture, and other family members with paint, this is taken as another sign of insanity.

Sappho looks back over hundreds of years of marginalization due to her deviant sexuality; innumerable times her femininity or her poetic talent have been called into question, stories have been invented that regularize her sexuality, and her poetry has been savagely criticized. The most visible sign of this mutilation is the incomplete text of her poetry. At the end of the twentieth century, she is in love with Picasso, whom she calls by her original name, Sophia. She observes Picasso's fall from the roof, calls an ambulance, and notifies the police, thereby saving her life.

Traumatized and mutilated by a social environment that rejects their forms of sexual experience and orientation, all three characters reflect repeatedly on the culture they are forced to endure and their own means of finding a way to live life satisfactorily. In the course of these reflections, all three articulate incisive and often very harsh indictments of the role of women and the institutions of marriage and the family. Of course, such criticism had already formed part of *Oranges Are Not the Only Fruit, Sexing the Cherry,* and *Written on the Body.* In contrast to Winterson's earlier novels, however, the characters in *Art & Lies* seem to have very little chance of escaping from their marginalization. The only hint of escape from the bleak sociocultural landscape they describe is in the form of a train ride all three are taking at the time of the narration. Short descriptions of this train ride from London to the seaside, narrated in the third person by an omniscient narrator, are interspersed in the three first-person accounts. Although the repeated use of images of light and gold seem to promise a happier future for the protagonists, this future—and any alternative to the suffocating cityscape of London at the turn of the millennium—are left too indeterminate to dispel the sense of doom that lingers over the characters; it is difficult to see what world they might be heading toward that would hold any greater promise than the one they are moving away from.

The only escape that is discussed in any detail is that provided by art. Picasso and Sappho, through painting and poetry, create at least a virtual space in which they are able to articulate their own vision of the world. In Handel's case, an alternative world of sorts emerges from a book he is reading that describes in great detail the activities of an eighteenth-century bawd named Doll Sneerpiece. When Doll realizes that the man she is in love with might be a homosexual, she decides to dress up as a man and seduce him in that disguise rather than as a woman. Her maneuver, recounted with a good deal of earthy humor, points to a sexuality that is more flexible and less entrapped in conventions than the one with which the three protagonists have to contend. Like Winterson's other novels, *Art & Lies* seeks to articulate a social and aesthetic space that is open to a wide range of sexual orientations and experiences; but it seems to be less optimistic than, say, *Sexing the Cherry, Written on the Body,* or "The Poetics of Sex" about the possibilities of achieving such a space.

In all of her novels Winterson combines a scathing critique of existing social and cultural conventions with an imaginative power that transcends these narrow codes and opens up a vision of a world that is more liberated, more just, more diverse, and less hypocritical and platitudinous. Much of this conflict revolves around conventions of gender and sexuality, with an exploration of the role of such institutions as marriage, family, and the church in shaping them. Jeanette's breakaway from fundamentalism, Gloria Munde's resistance to Noah's cult of the Unpronounceable, Villanelle's shifting identities, Dog-Woman's towering presence, and the exuberant rhetoric of the narrator in "The Poetics of Sex" all succeed in presenting a feminist countersociety that is both powerful and exhilarating. *Written on the Body* and *Art & Lies* continue to be extremely incisive in their cultural criticism, but some readers have felt that they fail to present as persuasive a vision of the feminist alternative. This shift in emphasis may explain why *Written on the Body* and, in particular, *Art & Lies* were received somewhat less favorably by reviewers than were Winterson's earlier works.

HISTORIES AND FAIRY TALES

WHEN Winterson presents sexual, political, or linguistic experiences in her novels that may not be easily understandable or acceptable to the average reader, she often resorts to setting the plot in a historically removed time period so as to avoid the resistance that such experiences might provoke if they were described as contemporary. An earlier historical period also serves as a moment where reality and fantasy can be fused more easily than in a twentieth-century setting, where the readers might be tempted to compare her personal vision to their own experience of reality. In many of Winterson's novels these complex combinations of the real, the possible, and the purely imaginary give rise to explicit reflections on the nature of time and memory and the ways in which history writing and storytelling reflect and distort memories of the past. An early example of such a reflection is the previously mentioned "Deuteronomy" chapter of *Oranges,* which calls into question any reading of the novel as a straightforward autobiography, no matter how much its plot might seem to resemble what the reader knows about the author's life. In Winterson's subsequent novels, this discussion of history and its relation to story and fairy tale is continued and elaborated upon in contexts that reach much farther into the past than *Oranges.*

"Time is a great deadener. People forget, get bored, grow old, go away," the narrator observes in *Oranges* (p. 93). In *The Passion,* Henri repeats this sentence almost word for word: "Time is a great deadener. People forget, grow old, get bored" (1989 ed., p. 32). To counteract such forgetfulness, Henri keeps a diary during his service in Napoleon's army, even though one of his friends points out that his writing will bring him no closer to preserving reality, since his perceptions at the time events occur are no more reliable as "truth" than his memory of the events will be, in another thirty years. But for Henri, trapped in Bonaparte's never-ending battles, which make the past irrelevant and the future almost impossible to imagine, the diary is a way of preserving some sense of time when only the present can be grasped. For Villanelle, the other narrator, the present means just the opposite: she can only conceive of it in the context of past and future and considers it incomplete in and of itself. Nevertheless, both make storytelling their way of reaching out across time. "I'm telling you stories. Trust me," each of them claims in one of the novel's most important leitmotifs, although neither is an entirely reliable narrator.

Henri's story, however, is on the whole the more realistic one, in terms of historical and physical plausibility. His perceptive analysis of why the French adore Bonaparte despite the fact that he leads them into war after war, as well as his stark descriptions of brothel scenes and the French army's rapid deterioration during the battle in Russia, make his account seem all too real. Only a few fantastic elements—such as the priest Patrick's telescopic eye, which can see a woman undress from miles away—intrude upon his account. Villanelle's story is just the opposite. Venice is described at the outset as a city where the boundaries between reality and imagination cannot always be discerned clearly; where certain routes and canals, which can only be found by boatmen, lead straight to an uncanny netherworld that only the initiated can even perceive. Fantastic occurrences abound: Villanelle's webbed feet, her ability to walk on water, and the loss of her heart to a woman who keeps it in a jar and intends to make it part of a woven tapestry are juxtaposed with the brutal reality of her marriage to an abusive husband and her exile as a prostitute in the French army. The complete and seemingly natural fusion of the real and the imaginary in this and other novels by Winterson has led many critics to compare her work to the magical realism of Latin American authors such as Jorge Luis Borges and Gabriel García Márquez. The purpose of the fantastic elements, however, is somewhat different. Whereas Latin American magical realism is often claimed to represent a view of reality different from that of Western rationalism—but one that is equally legitimate and therefore even appears in contemporary settings—Winterson describes worlds that are not so much real as alternatives to reality, realms that allow readers to distance themselves from the conventions that usually define and limit social and cultural existence. Since these alternatives to the real would be difficult for the reader to accept in a setting that claims to reflect the contemporary world, Winterson usually deploys magic and fantasy in worlds that are temporally displaced from the present: France, Russia, and Italy during the Napoleonic era (*The Passion*); seventeenth-century England (*Sexing the Cherry*); and a slightly futuristic London around the year 2000 (*Art & Lies*).

The purpose of Winterson's magical realism, combined with her use of historical settings, emerges most clearly in *Sexing the Cherry*, which juxtaposes London during the reign of Cromwell with London in the 1980s. In the last chapter of the novel, Jordan and Dog-Woman turn out to have contemporary counterparts: a young man named Nicolas Jordan who joins the navy and sails the world, and an unnamed woman who singlehandedly stages an environmental protest against mercury pollution. Her opposition to those institutions she views as destroying the world—the World Bank, the Pentagon, large corporations—is clearly meant to parallel Dog-Woman's fierce struggles against the Puritan regime. Likewise, she sees her obesity as an attempt to become larger than the world around her, much the way Dog-Woman is.

Throughout the twentieth-century sections of the narrative, therefore, Dog-Woman emerges as the literal embodiment of the kind of social and cultural resistance contemporary feminists can only fantasize about. The seventeenth-century chapters invite readers to view the contemporary characters through their previously established sympathy with Dog-Woman and her son. The parallel is justified in the text through repeated references to the enigmatic nature of time, as well as to concepts of temporality that differ from the linear, Western one in not distinguishing between past, present, and future. Nevertheless, many readers have felt that the parallel between Cromwell's and Thatcher's England is only moderately successful. The contemporary characters are introduced too late in the novel to gain as much depth as their seventeenth-century counterparts; moreover, the twentieth-century sections of the novel are much more overtly didactic and lack the humor of the earlier ones. This contrast, however, does point to Winterson's project of offering an imaginative alternative to contemporary realities that might serve as a base for designing actual alternatives.

Art & Lies does not so much juxtapose different historical moments as it collapses the distinction between past and present. The novel is set in London roughly in the year 2000. The monarchy has been abolished, the Church of England privatized, and social-welfare programs suspended. The narrators make occasional reference to contemporary medicine, science, technology, environmental pollution, the arms race, and social injustice. But in many respects the life stories that slowly emerge from Handel's and Picasso's accounts resemble the nineteenth century of Dickens or Balzac more than the late twentieth century. Handel was first brought up in Rome, where his father worked as a lawyer for the Vatican. Through his father's contacts, Handel comes to know old Cardinal Rosso, who adopts him as his protégé. Rosso, a homosexual who for almost a quarter of a century had lived with the last castrato to sing in the Vatican, falls in love with Handel and introduces him to music, painting, and literature. Unbeknownst to Handel's parents, he has the boy castrated. When his parents later discover the mutilation, they prohibit him from ever seeing the cardinal again. Upon his death, Rosso leaves his enormous wealth to Handel. It is thanks to his influence that Handel first decides to become a priest and a doctor. He is defrocked, however, when it is discovered that he distributes condoms along with Bibles to the poor in Brazil. He then returns to England, where he becomes a noted breast-cancer specialist.

In his practice as a physician, his life's path crosses Picasso's, who is not the daughter of her father's wife but of a maid her father has raped. This maid visits Handel's practice in order to obtain an abortion, but he refuses based upon his Catholicism. He later delivers the baby girl in circumstances of Dickensian poverty and squalor, without electricity or hot water. The maid deposits the baby at the father's house, where she is brought up and abused by her half-brother. Handel later buys the house in order to convert it into a private cancer clinic. On the day he is about to leave London, he is summoned by Picasso's father. Before leaving her parents' home for good, it appears that Picasso has vandalized it by splashing the walls, furniture, and her family's clothes with paint; her parents wish her to be committed to a mental hospital again. Finally, Handel and Picasso meet on the train about to leave London.

If these life stories deliberately collapse the late twentieth century into the conventions of the nineteenth-century novel, the presence of Sappho further diminishes any sense of historical progression. Sappho's voice mixes lyrical descriptions based on central motifs in her poetry with ironic reflections on the history of its reception and scathing indictments of twentieth-century society; she is as much at home on Lesbos in 600 B.C. as in London "2000 After Death" (p. 150). In addition, much of Handel's as well as Sappho's commentary explicitly criticizes the idea of progress and implies that in many respects contemporary society has not significantly advanced beyond ancient Greek culture. The sense of the disintegration of chronological time is further reinforced by fragments of eighteenth-century narrative about the bawd Doll Sneerpiece, which Handel and Picasso read on the train. As a result, the reader is constantly displaced in time, forced to view one historical moment from the perspective of another. To some extent, *Art & Lies* resembles a Borgesian book Handel inherited from Rosso's collection: bound and rebound over the centuries, without any chronological ordering, this book contains the fragmented scholarly, critical, literary, and philosophical contributions of each of its owners, including bits and pieces from literary and philosophical classics across the ages. The ability of art to transcend and fuse different moments in time is the truth that the novel ultimately wishes to convey, whereas notions of time as chronological succession and history as progress are exposed as delusions or outright lies. Only in art—be it painting, music, or literature—can the temporal fragments of individual and collective human history assume intelligible shape.

Clearly, the handling of time and history, the real and the imaginary is considerably more complex in *Art & Lies* than in any of Winterson's previous novels. Unlike *The Passion* or *Sexing the Cherry*, *Art & Lies* offers the reader no unambiguous historical setting; rather than using one historical moment as a vantage point to view another, *Art & Lies* constantly shifts back and forth and does not let the reader rest comfortably in any familiar construction of the historical and the real. Relatively few plot elements link the major characters to each other, and these links are only revealed very late in the novel. As a consequence, much of *Art & Lies* resembles prose poetry more than conventional narrative. Inevitably this transition poses a number of problems. Some critics admire *Art & Lies* for its style but feel that it can be overly didactic in its pronouncements on art and contemporary society, claiming that it does not provide enough narrative elements to sustain it as a novel. It is worth noting, however, that the structure of *Art & Lies* is a logical—if more extreme—continuation of the narrative experiments with history, realism, and fantasy that Winterson had already carried out in *The Passion* and *Sexing the Cherry*.

VOICES AND STYLES

IN its narrative structure and technique, *Art & Lies* also reflects tendencies that characterize Winterson's fictional work as a whole. In general, Winterson emphasizes character and individual reflection over plot, systematically privileging first-person accounts over other forms of narration. *Boating for Beginners* constitutes somewhat of an anomaly in the Winterson canon in both respects, for it does have a relatively tightly knit plot and is narrated in the third person. All the other novels, however, are dominated by first-person narrators. In *Oranges Are Not the Only Fruit* and *Written on the Body* the story is told by only one narrator. In *The Passion* and *Sexing the Cherry* two narrators, one male and one female, alternate; in *Sexing the Cherry*, each narrator has a twentieth-century counterpart who narrates some sections. In *Art & Lies* one male and two female narrators take turns telling their stories, but each of their accounts is interspersed with short passages in the third person, so that the reader is given alternating internal and external perspectives on each character. With the exception of *The Passion*, all of the first-person novels have short allegorical, fantastic, or fairy tale–like stories (told in the third person) embedded in the main narrative.

The reason for this particular narrative technique lies in Winterson's major interest in the outsider, typically an androgynous, transvestite, or homosexual character who does not fit conventional gender categories or, like the Dog-Woman, simply exceeds them. By letting these characters tell their own stories, Winterson opens up a defamiliarizing perspective on cultural institutions and conventions and creates a platform for social critique. In their struggle to find a language, a narrative, and an identity for themselves in a society that offers them no appropriate categories ("We're all equal now. . . . One size fits all. It doesn't fit me," Picasso observes in *Art & Lies,* p. 92), the outsiders fall back on myth, fairy tale, and sheer invention to formulate alternative stories of development and models of identity. Thus, medieval romance and fairy tale enable Jeanette to bridge the widening gap between herself and her community. Jordan undertakes journeys to countries both on and off the map in his quest for his own identity. Sappho's poetry, Richard Strauss's opera *Der Rosenkavalier*, and the bawdy tale of Doll Sneerpiece all offer counterpoints and avenues of escape to the traumatic sexual experiences of the three protagonists in *Art & Lies*.

Winterson's style is as distinctive as her narrative strategy. Most of her novels show a preference for the short, terse sentence—even the sentence fragment—whose brevity serves to underscore emotions and existential decisions of great importance. For example, one of the Twelve Dancing Princesses in *Sexing the Cherry* sums up the breakup of her marriage with these words:

I considered my choices.
I could stay and be unhappy and humiliated.
I could leave and be unhappy and dignified.
I could beg him to touch me again.
I could live in hope and die of bitterness.

I took some things and left. It wasn't easy, it was my
    home too.
I hear he's replaced the back fence.

(1991 ed., p. 59)

Similarly, in *Art & Lies* Picasso describes her own state of mind in brief sentences: "Fear of everything. Fear of everything keeps me sealed up against everything. I fear the coloured world on my neutral body. I fear the bright red sun and grass matt green" (p. 88). The same type of sentence structure can turn lyrical when it appears in Sappho's love declarations: "Her cheekbones are high. Twin towers of unrest. Restless when she smiles, armed when she does not. In her face the motion of her days. Her throat cuts me" (p. 140). Or it can be matter-of-fact, as when the third-person narrator uses it to sum up what is known about Sappho: "It was a long time ago. She had a daughter called Cleis. She was the most famous poet of antiquity. Her work filled nine volumes. Little else about her is known" (p. 149). The short, simple sentence, no doubt inspired by Gertrude Stein, is one of the basic linguistic building blocks of Winterson's fiction; it is used in a variety of contexts and with widely varying effects.

The danger of this style, however, lies in the philosophical meaning it places upon individual sentences and phrases, which at times risks giving the characters a sententious or sermonizing tone. Henri and Villanelle in *The Passion*, for example, do not always escape this danger. Villanelle frequently makes general comments—"Bridges join but they also separate" (p. 61) or "Gambling is not a vice, it is an expression of our humanness. We gamble. Some do it at the gaming table, some do not. You play, you win, you play, you lose. You play" (p. 73)—that seem banal rather than profound. Winterson counteracts this tendency toward excessive abstraction by including concrete detail that often summarizes a situation more poignantly than a lengthy description. Thus, Henri describes the horrors of Napoleon's march on Moscow:

Into the Russian winter in our summer overcoats. Into the snow in our glued-together boots. When our horses died of the cold we slit their bellies and slept with our feet inside the guts. One man's horse froze around him; in the morning when he tried to take his feet out they were stuck, entombed in the brittle entrails. We couldn't free him, we had to leave him. He wouldn't stop screaming.

(p. 80)

Dog-Woman, in *Sexing the Cherry*, refuses to eat a banana because it looks to her "like the private parts of an Oriental" (p. 5), but she bites off a man's penis during oral sex, unaware that she has inflicted an irreversible injury. Her reflection on this point—"The whore . . . had told me that men like to be consumed in the mouth, but it still seems to me a reckless act, for the member must take some time to grow again" (p. 41)—reveals both her tendency toward impulsive violence and her underlying innocence and náiveté. Such details especially abound in Winterson's first four novels and compensate for the characters' sometimes overly didactic pronouncements.

The last two novels, *Written on the Body* and *Art & Lies*, still include some of this vivid detail but generally aspire to a more lyrical, highly metaphoric language. Much of *Written on the Body* is taken up with the lover's ecstatic descriptions of Louise:

I am living in a red bubble made up of Louise's hair. It's the sunset time of year but it's not the dropping disc of light that holds me in the shadows of the yard. It's the colour I crave, floodings of you running down the edges of the sky on to the brown earth on to the grey stone. On to me.

(p. 138)

Sometimes these descriptions take on a deliberately biblical tone: "My lover is an olive tree whose roots grow by the sea. Her fruit is pungent and green. It is my joy to get at the stone of her" (p. 137). In *Art & Lies*, however, many of the metaphors become less concrete, dissolving the material world into such abstract concepts as space, gravity, or light. The description of Handel and the train at the beginning of the novel, for example, sublimates the visual effect of sun reflected on metal into an almost religious experience:

From a distance only the light is visible, a speeding gleaming horizontal angel, trumpet out on a hard bend. The note bells. The note bells the beauty of the stretching train that pulls the light in a long gold thread. It catches in the wheels, it flashes on the doors, that open and close, that open and close, in commuter rhythm. . . . The man is busy, he hasn't time to see the light that burns his clothes and illuminates his face, the light pouring down his shoulders with biblical zeal.

(p. 3)

This change in Winterson's novelistic style has produced many passages of undisputed beauty, although some critics find that this emphasis on lyrical expression ultimately distracts from the novel's interest as a narrative text. In its language *Art & Lies* resembles Virginia Woolf's late novel *The Waves*, a text that also negotiates the border between prose and poetry, similarly juxtaposing the utterances of different characters and interspersing them with descriptions that transcend their subjective nature.

WINTERSON AND THE MODERNISTS: ART OBJECTS

WINTERSON's collection of critical essays entitled *Art Objects: Essays on Ecstasy and Effrontery* represents the novelist's detailed discussion of her own aesthetics, as well as that of several authors whom she considers important models. Some of the arguments proposed in *Art Objects* echo or grow directly out of reflections on the function of art Winterson had already formulated in *Art & Lies* through the voices of Handel and Sappho. The arguments in *Art Objects* that deserve particular attention focus on the relationship of Winterson's writing to realism, to mass culture and other media, to a poetics of precision, and to the Anglo-Saxon literary tradition.

In *Art & Lies*, Handel had affirmed that art is not a mirror held up to nature, not a mere reflection of reality. Winterson reinforces this point vigorously in *Art Objects*, particularly in the context of autobiography. In her essay on Gertrude Stein, she defends *The Autobiography of Alice B. Toklas* (1933) against the charges by some of Stein's contemporaries that her accounts did not faithfully reproduce reality. In Winterson's view, realism was never Stein's objective in the first place. The genre of autobiography is merely a "Trojan horse" (p. 50), just as biography is in Woolf's *Orlando*, a sleight of hand meant to trick the reader into believing that the text is concerned with reality when its true objective is to create a different, primarily textual and linguistic, universe. Rather than functioning as a mirror of the real, Stein's text is a conscious reworking of life into art; simultaneously pointing to the narrative procedures by means of which we make sense of our daily lives. Rather than art imitating life, Winterson suggests, life imitates art.

This argument is not solely relevant for understanding Winterson's autobiographical novel, *Oranges Are Not Only the Fruit*, which, as she has explicitly stated, is as far from "realist" autobiography as is Stein's. It is also crucial in explaining the position she has taken regarding her own status as a "lesbian writer." The author's life, she has insisted, is of little relevance to the literary work; Winterson therefore resists any simple conflation of her writing with her lesbianism or any superficial connections to other lesbian writers. She has stated: "I am a writer who happens to love women. I am not a lesbian who happens to write" (p. 104). Although she has acknowledged the need for a distinct homosexual subculture, she refuses to grant the status of "art" to all productions that arise out of the desire to establish such a subculture: "Art is difference, but not necessarily sexual difference, and while to be outside of the mainstream of imposed choice is likely to make someone more conscious, it does not automatically make that someone an artist. A great deal of gay writing, especially gay writing around the Aids crisis, is therapy, is release, is not art" (p. 104). This argument is important insofar as it addresses a subtle form of discrimination aimed at homosexual writers in particular, namely, that their sexual orientation is invariably assumed to be crucially relevant to an understanding of their work, whereas the same assumption is not made in the case of heterosexual writers.

Winterson's insistence that not all cultural products are art begs the question of what her definition of art is and runs counter to recent attempts in literary and cultural studies to open up the canon of "high art" to forms of aesthetic expression that have not traditionally been included in that category. Clearly, Winterson would not align herself with this movement; most of her observations concerning mass culture and the media are derogatory, and she repeatedly places her definition of art in opposition to them. Her own creation of screenplays for a television series and a film does not necessarily contradict this stance; she has repeatedly insisted that the miniseries *Oranges Are Not the Only Fruit* was of higher quality than the average television programing. But in the final essay, "A Work of My Own," she herself points with some pride to the wide audience her books have reached, which, together with the considerable commercial success they have enjoyed, makes it even more doubtful whether "art" and "entertainment" are the

mutually exclusive categories she claims them to be. Her position vis-à-vis the academy is similarly ambiguous; she accuses academic critics of rejecting experimental writing in favor of established aesthetic modes, but she also asserts that she built her own readership "largely through a young, student population, who want [my] books on their courses and by their beds" (p. 192). If students are receptive to her work and encounter it in their courses, the academy is not likely to be as resistant to her writing as she claims. The essay is laced with tensions that arise from Winterson's desire to distinguish her own work and art in general from mass culture while at the same time she argues for resistance to the very institutions that have traditionally upheld this distinction.

Winterson does, however, diagnose very clearly the predicament of the novel in the contemporary media landscape: "In so much as television and film have largely occupied the narrative functions of the novel, just as the novel annexed the narrative function of epic poetry, fiction will have to move on, and find new territory of its own" (p. 176). In her own fiction this urgent call to innovation is answered by a narrative style that aspires to a combination of "lyric intensity and breadth of ideas" (p. 173). This style cannot consist of "formless vistas of subjectivity" (p. 165) but must, above all, be precise. Literary language is, in her view, the result of the writers' relentless resistance to cliché and formula and their conscious effort to create new forms of expression in language—a labor that leaves no room for laxity and imprecision. Her models for elaborating such a new kind of language are not only Stein and Woolf but also T. S. Eliot, Robert Graves, and, at greater historical remove, Shakespeare and Wordsworth. Considering the fact that Winterson's novels have most often been compared to the work of such contemporary writers as Jorge Luis Borges, Italo Calvino, Angela Carter, Gabriel García Márquez, Monique Wittig, and Hélène Cixous, it comes as somewhat of a surprise that Winterson herself discusses modernist and premodernist writers at considerable length but makes no mention of late-twentieth-century authors who might have served as models for her work. Rather than discussing her own novels in the context of contemporary international fiction, Winterson here consciously chooses to view them as forming part of a long tradition of British and American writers. Elsewhere she has repeatedly emphasized the need for the writer to be well-read in the literature of the past as a prerequisite for true innovation. Knowledge of the literary tradition and innovation therefore go hand in hand in Winterson's poetics.

Winterson's fiction—with its extreme self-consciousness, its interest in stories within stories, its leaps across historical periods, its emphasis on the cultural "constructedness" of identities and histories, its rejection of referentiality, and its seamless integration of the magical and fantastic into the outwardly real—generally fits the description of what is called the postmodern novel. Her poetics, however, is more ambiguous. Like many other contemporary writers, Winterson rejects the notion that the function of literature is to reflect reality rather than to create new forms of language, but, unlike many other postmodernists, she insists on the strict separation of high art and popular culture, on the special status of the artist "in full possession of a reality less partial than the reality apprehended by most people" (p. 168), and on Ezra Pound's injunction to "make it new" where other artists have grown much more skeptical of originality and innovation as basic aesthetic imperatives. Jeanette Winterson, therefore, combines elements of both modernist and postmodernist aesthetics, and only her future literary production will determine which components are most important and enduring in her work.

SELECTED BIBLIOGRAPHY

I. NOVELS. *Oranges Are Not the Only Fruit* London, 1985; New York, 1987); *Boating for Beginners* (London, 1985, pap. repr. 1990); *The Passion* (London, 1987; New York, 1988, pap. repr. 1989); *Sexing the Cherry* (London, 1989; New York, 1990, pap. repr. 1991); *Written on the Body* (London, 1992; New York, 1993, pap. repr. 1994);

Art & Lies: A Piece for Three Voices and a Bawd (London, 1994: New York, 1995).

II. SCREENPLAYS. *Oranges Are Not the Only Fruit* (London, 1990); *Great Moments in Aviation* (film released in 1993).

III. OTHER WORKS. *Fit for the Future: The Guide for Women Who Want to Live Well* (London, 1986); *Passion Fruit: Romantic Fiction with a Twist* (London, 1986), edited by Winterson; "The Poetics of Sex," in Margaret Reynolds, ed., *The Penguin Book of Lesbian Short Stories* (New York, 1993); *Art Objects: Essays on Ecstasy and Effrontery* (London, 1995; New York, 1996).

IV. INTERVIEWS. Jackie Kay, "Unnatural Passions," in *Spare Rib* 209 (February 1990); Lynne M. Constantine and Suzanne Scott, "Jeanette Winterson," in *Belles Lettres* 5, no. 4 (summer 1990); Mark Marvel, "Winterson: Trust Me. I'm Telling You Stories," in *Interview* 20, no. 10 (October 1990); Helen Barr, "Face to Face: A Conversation Between Jeanette Winterson and Helen Barr," in *English Review* 2 (1991).

V. CRITICAL STUDIES. Susan Rubin Suleiman, "Mothers and the Avant-Garde: A Case of Mistaken Identity?" in Françoise van Rossum-Guyon, ed., *Femmes Frauen Women* (Amsterdam, 1990); Rebecca O'Rourke, "Fingers in the Fruit Basket: A Feminist Reading of Jeanette Winterson's *Oranges Are Not the Only Fruit*," in Susan Sellers, Linda Hutcheon, and Paul Perron, eds., *Feminist Criticism: Theory and Practice* (Toronto, 1991); Hilary Hinds, "*Oranges Are Not the Only Fruit*: Reaching Audiences Other Lesbian Texts Cannot Reach," in Sally Munt, ed., *New Lesbian Criticism: Literary and Cultural Readings* (New York, 1992); G. P. Lainsbury, "Hubris and the Young Author: The Problem of the Introduction to *Oranges Are Not the Only Fruit*," in *Notes on Contemporary Literature* 22, no. 4 (September 1992); Laura Doan, "Jeanette Winterson's Sexing the Postmodern," in Laura Doan, ed., *The Lesbian Postmodern* (New York, 1994); M. Daphne Kutzer, "The Cartography of Passion: Cixous, Wittig, and Winterson," in Jürgen Kleist and Bruce A. Butterfield, eds., *Re-Naming the Landscape* (New York, 1994); Alison Lee, "Bending the Arrow of Time: The Continuing Postmodern Present," in Max Dupperay, ed., *Historicité et métafiction dans le roman contemporain des Iles Britanniques* (Aix-en-Provence, 1994).

MASTER INDEX

The following index covers the entire British Writers series through Supplement IV. All references include volume numbers in boldface Roman numerals followed by page numbers within that volume. Subjects of articles are indicated by boldface type.